Nineteenth-Century Literature Criticism

Guide to Gale Literary Criticism Series

For criticism on	Consult these Gale series
Authors now living or who died after December 31, 1959	*CONTEMPORARY LITERARY CRITICISM (CLC)*
Authors who died between 1900 and 1959	*TWENTIETH-CENTURY LITERARY CRITICISM (TCLC)*
Authors who died between 1800 and 1899	*NINETEENTH-CENTURY LITERATURE CRITICISM (NCLC)*
Authors who died between 1400 and 1799	*LITERATURE CRITICISM FROM 1400 TO 1800 (LC)* *SHAKESPEAREAN CRITICISM (SC)*
Authors who died before 1400	*CLASSICAL AND MEDIEVAL LITERATURE CRITICISM (CMLC)*
Authors of books for children and young adults	*CHILDREN'S LITERATURE REVIEW (CLR)*
Dramatists	*DRAMA CRITICISM (DC)*
Poets	*POETRY CRITICISM (PC)*
Short story writers	*SHORT STORY CRITICISM (SSC)*
Black writers of the past two hundred years	*BLACK LITERATURE CRITICISM (BLC)*
Hispanic writers of the late nineteenth and twentieth centuries	*HISPANIC LITERATURE CRITICISM (HLC)*
Native North American writers and orators of the eighteenth, nineteenth, and twentieth centuries	*NATIVE NORTH AMERICAN LITERATURE (NNAL)*
Major authors from the Renaissance to the present	*WORLD LITERATURE CRITICISM, 1500 TO THE PRESENT (WLC)*

ISSN 0732-1864

Volume 75

Nineteenth-Century Literature Criticism

Excerpts from Criticism of the
Works of Novelists, Poets, Playwrights,
Short Story Writers, Philosophers, and Other
Creative Writers Who Died between 1800
and 1899, from the First Published Critical
Appraisals to Current Evaluations

Suzanne Dewsbury
Editor

The Gale Group

DETROIT • SAN FRANCISCO • LONDON • BOSTON • WOODBRIDGE, CT

STAFF

Suzanne Dewsbury, *Editor*

nna Barberi, Craig Hutchison, *Assistant Editors*
Janet Witalec, *Managing Editor*

Maria L. Franklin, *Permissions Manager*
Kimberly F. Smilay, *Permissions Specialist*
Kelly A. Quin, *Permissions Associates*
Erin Bealmear, Sandra K. Gore, *Permissions Assistant*

Victoria B. Cariappa, *Research Manager*
Patricia T. Ballard, Wendy Festerling, Tracie A. Richardson,
Corrine Stocker, Cheryl Warnock, *Research Associates*
Timothy Lehnerer, *Research Assistant*

Mary Beth Trimper, *Production Director*
Cindy Range, *Production Assistant*

Gary Leach, *Graphic Artist*
Randy Bassett, *Image Database Supervisor*
Robert Duncan, Michael Logusz, *Imaging Specialists*
Pamela A. Reed, *Imaging Coordinator*

This book is printed on acid-free paper that meets the minimum requirements of American National Standard for Information Sciences—Permanence Paper for Printed Library Materials, ANSI Z39.48-1984.

Library of Congress Catalog Card Number 84-643008
ISBN 0-7876-2877-8
ISSN 0732-1864
Printed in the United States of America

10 9 8 7 6 5 4 3 2 1

Contents

Preface vii

Acknowledgments xi

William Barnes 1801-1886 1
    English poet and philologist

Hugh Blair 1718-1800 112
    Scottish preacher, professor, rhetorician, and literary critic

Matthias Claudius 1740-1815 180
    German poet, journalist, critic, and letter writer

Timofei Nikolaevich Granovskii 1813-1855 228
    Russian historian

Sarah Josepha Hale 1788-1879 278
    American journalist, biographer, novelist, short story writer, and poet

Literary Criticism Series Cumulative Author Index 369

Literary Criticism Series Topic Index 439

NCLC Cumulative Nationality Index 449

NCLC-75 Title Index 453

Preface

Since its inception in 1981, *Nineteenth-Century Literature Criticism* has been a valuable resource for students and librarians seeking critical commentary on writers of this transitional period in world history. Designated an "Outstanding Reference Source" by the American Library Association with the publication of its first volume, *NCLC* has since been purchased by over 6,000 school, public, and university libraries. The series has covered more than 300 authors representing 29 nationalities and over 17,000 titles. No other reference source has surveyed the critical reaction to nineteenth-century authors and literature as thoroughly as *NCLC*.

Scope of the Series

NCLC is designed to introduce students and advanced readers to the authors of the nineteenth century, and to the most significant interpretations of these authors' works. The great poets, novelists, short story writers, playwrights, and philosophers of this period are frequently studied in high school and college literature courses. By organizing and reprinting commentary written on these authors, *NCLC* helps students develop valuable insight into literary history, promotes a better understanding of the texts, and sparks ideas for papers and assignments. Each entry in *NCLC* presents a comprehensive survey of an author's career or an individual work of literature and provides the user with a multiplicity of interpretations and assessments. Such variety allows students to pursue their own interests; furthermore, it fosters an awareness that literature is dynamic and responsive to many different opinions.

Every fourth volume of *NCLC* is devoted to literary topics that cannot be covered under the author approach used in the rest of the series. Such topics include literary movements, prominent themes in nineteenth-century literature, literary reaction to political and historical events, significant eras in literary history, prominent literary anniversaries, and the literatures of cultures that are often overlooked by English-speaking readers.

NCLC continues the survey of criticism of world literature begun by Gale's *Contemporary Literary Criticism (CLC)* and *Twentieth-Century Literary Criticism (TCLC),* both of which excerpt and reprint commentary on authors of the twentieth century. For additional information about *TCLC, CLC,* and Gale's other criticism series, users should consult the Guide to Gale Literary Criticism Series preceding the title page in this volume.

Coverage

Each volume of *NCLC* is carefully compiled to present:

- criticism of authors, or literary topics, representing a variety of genres and nationalities
- both major and lesser-known writers and literary works of the period
- 4-8 authors or 4-6 topics per volume
- individual entries that survey critical response to an author's work or a topic in literary history, including early criticism to reflect initial reactions, later criticism to represent any rise or decline in reputation, and current retrospective analyses.

Organization

An author entry consists of the following elements: author heading, biographical and critical introduction, list of principal works, excerpts of criticism (each preceded by a bibliographic citation and an annotation), and a bibliography of further reading.

- The **Author Heading** consists of the name under which the author most commonly wrote, followed by birth and death dates. If an author wrote consistently under a pseudonym, the pseudonym will be listed in the author heading and the real name given in parentheses on the first line of the biographical and critical introduction. Also located at the beginning of the introduction to the author entry are any name variations under which an author wrote, including transliterated forms for an author whose language uses a nonroman alphabet.

- The **Biographical and Critical Introduction** outlines the author's life and career, as well as the critical issues surrounding his or her work. References are provided to past volumes of *NCLC* in which further information about the author may be found.

- Most *NCLC* entries include a **Portrait** of the author. Many entries also contain reproductions of materials pertinent to an author's career, including manuscript pages, title pages, dust jackets, letters, and drawings, as well as photographs of important people, places, and events in an author's life.

- The list of **Principal Works** is chronological by date of first publication and identifies the genre of each work. In the case of foreign authors with both foreign-language publications and English translations, the English-language version is given in brackets. Unless otherwise indicated, dramas are dated by first performance, not first publication.

- **Criticism** in each author entry is arranged chronologically to provide a perspective on changes in critical evaluation over the years. All titles of works by the author featured in the entry are printed in boldface type to enable the user to easily locate discussion of particular works. Also for purposes of easier identification, the critic's name and the publication date of the essay are given at the beginning of each piece of criticism. Unsigned criticism is preceded by the title of the journal in which it appeared. Publication information (such as publisher names and book prices) and some parenthetical numerical references (such as page and line references to specific editions of works) have been deleted at the editors' discretion to provide smoother reading of the text. Footnotes that appear with previously published pieces of criticism are reprinted at the end of each essay or excerpt. In the case of excerpted criticism, only those footnotes that pertain to the excerpted text are included.

- A complete **Bibliographic Citation** provides original publication information for each piece of criticism.

- Critical excerpts are prefaced by **Annotations** providing the reader with a summary of the critical intent of the piece. Also included, when appropriate, is information about the critic's reputation, individual approach to literary criticism, and particular expertise in an author's works, as well as information about the relative importance of the critical excerpt. In some cases, the annotations cross-reference excerpts by critics who discuss each other's commentary.

- An annotated list of **Further Reading** appearing at the end of each entry suggests secondary sources on the author. In some cases it includes essays for which the editors could not obtain reprint rights.

Cumulative Indexes

■ Each volume of *NCLC* contains a cumulative **Author Index** listing all authors who have appeared in Gale's Literary Criticism Series, along with cross-references to such biographical series as *Contemporary Authors* and *Dictionary of Literary Biography*. Useful for locating authors within the various series, this index is particularly valuable for those authors who are identified with a certain period but who, because of their death dates, are placed in another, or for those authors whose careers span two periods. For example, Fyodor Dostoevsky is found in *NCLC*, yet Leo Tolstoy, another major nineteenth-century Russian novelist, is found in *TCLC* because he died after 1899.

■ Each *NCLC* volume includes a cumulative **Nationality Index** which lists all authors who have appeared in *NCLC*, arranged alphabetically under their respective nationalities.

■ Each new volume in Gale's Literary Criticism Series includes a cumulative **Topic Index**, which lists all literary topics treated in *NCLC, TCLC, LC 1400-1800*, and the *CLC* Yearbook.

■ Each new volume of *NCLC*, with the exception of the Topics volumes, contains a **Title Index** listing the titles of all literary works discussed in the volume. In response to numerous suggestions from librarians, Gale has also produced a **Special Paperbound Edition** of the *NCLC* title index. This annual cumulation lists all titles discussed in the series since its inception. Additional copies of the index are available on request. Librarians and patrons have welcomed this separate index: it saves shelf space, is easy to use, and is recyclable upon receipt of the following year's cumulation. Titles discussed in the Topics volume entries are not included in the *NCLC* cumulative index.

Citing *Nineteenth-Century Literature Criticism*

When writing papers, students who quote directly from any volume in Gale's Literary Criticism Series may use the following general forms to footnote reprinted criticism. The first example pertains to material drawn from periodicals, the second to material reprinted from books:

[1]Kim McQuaid, "William Apes, Pequot: An Indian Reformer in the Jackson Era," *The New England Quarterly*, 50 (December 1977), 605-25; excerpted and reprinted in *Nineteenth-Century Literature Criticism*, Vol. 73, ed. Janet Witalec (Farmington Hills, Mich.: The Gale Group, 1999), pp. 3-4.

[2]Richard Harter Fogle, *The Imagery of Keats and Shelley: A Comparative Study* (Archon Books, 1949); excerpted and reprinted in *Nineteenth-Century Literary Criticism*, Vol. 73, ed. Janet Witalec (Farmington Hills, Mich.: The Gale Group, 1999), pp. 157-69.

Suggestions Are Welcome

In response to suggestions, several features have been added to *NCLC* since the series began, including annotations to excerpted criticism, a cumulative index to authors in all Gale literary criticism series, entries devoted to criticism on a single work by a major author, more illustrations, and a title index listing all literary works discussed in the series.

Readers who wish to suggest authors, single works, or topics to appear in future volumes, or who have other suggestions, are cordially invited to write: The Editors, *Nineteenth-Century Literature Criticism*, The Gale Group, 27500 Drake Rd., Farmington Hills, MI 48331-3535; call toll-free at 1-800-347-GALE.

Acknowledgments

The editors wish to thank the copyright holders of the excerpted criticism included in this volume and the permissions managers of many book and magazine publishing companies for assisting us in securing reproduction rights. We are also grateful to the staffs of the Detroit Public Library, the Library of Congress, the University of Detroit Mercy Library, Wayne State University Purdy/Kresge Library Complex, and the University of Michigan Libraries for making their resources available to us. Following is a list of the copyright holders who have granted us permission to reproduce material in this volume of *NCLC*. Every effort has been made to trace copyright, but if omissions have been made, please let us know.

COPYRIGHTED EXCERPTS IN *NCLC*, VOLUME 75, WERE REPRODUCED FROM THE FOLLOWING PERIODICALS:

American Periodicals: A Journal of History, Criticism, and Bibliography, v. 3, 1993. Reproduced by permission.—*Canadian Slavonic Papers: Revue Canadienne des Slavistes*, v. XV, Winter, 1973. Copyright © Canadian Slavonic Papers, Canada, 1973. Reproduced by permission.—*The Eighteenth-Century: Theory and Interpretation*, v. 30, Spring, 1989 for "Clio and Ethics: Practical Morality in Enlightened Scotland" by John Dwyer. Reproduced by permission of the author.—*Legacy: A Journal of American Women Writers*, v. 14, 1997. Copyright © 1997 The Pennsylvania State University, University Park, PA. Reproduced by permission.—*The Listener*, v. LXVIII, n. 1742, August 16, 1962 for "The Poetry of William Barnes" by Philip Larkin. © British Broadcasting Corp. 1982. Reproduced in United States by permission of Farrar, Straus and Giroux, Inc. In the United Kingdom by permission of Faber & Faber Ltd.—*Modern Language Notes*, v. 102, April, 1987. Copyright © 1987. Reproduced by permission of The Johns Hopkins University Press.—*The New England Quarterly*, v. LXIII, June, 1990 for "Onward Christian Women: Sarah J. Hale's History of the World" by Nina Baym; v. LXVIII, December, 1995 for "Errand into Africa: Colonization and Nation Building in Sarah J. Hale's Liberia" by Susan M. Ryan. Copyright © 1990, 1995 by The New England Quarterly. Both reproduced by permission of the publisher and the respective authors.—*The Review of English Studies*, v. VII, January, 1931 for "Blair on Ossian" by R. W. Chapman. Reproduced by permission of Oxford University Press.—*Rhetoric Society Quarterly*, v. XVII, Summer, 1987. © Copyright 1987, Rhetoric Society of America. Reproduced by permission.—*Seminar: A Journal of Germanic Studies*, v. XVIII, February, 1982. © The Canadian Association of University Teachers of German 1982. Reproduced by permission of the publisher.—*Studies in Soviet Thought*, v. 18, August, 1978 for "T. N. Granovskii: On the Meaning of History" by Nicholas S. Racheotes. Copyright © 1978 by D. Reidel Publishing Company, Dordrecht, Holland. All rights reserved. Reproduced by permission of Kluwer Academic Publishers and the author.—*University of Toronto Quarterly*, v. 56, Winter, 1986/7. Reproduced by permission of University of Toronto Press Incorporated.—*Victorian Studies*, v, VI, June, 1963. Reproduced by permission of the Trustees of Indiana University.

COPYRIGHTED EXCERPTS IN *NCLC*, VOLUME 75, WERE REPRODUCED FROM THE FOLLOWING BOOKS:

Bardes, Barbara A. and Suzanne Gossett. From "Sarah J. Hale, Selective Promoter of Her Sex" in *A Living of Words: American Women in Print Culture*. Edited by Susan Albertine. The University

author.—Roosevelt, Priscilla Reynolds. From *Apostle of Russian Liberalism: Timofei Granovsky*. Oriental Research Partners, 1986. Reproduced by permission.—Rowland, Herbert. From *Matthias Claudius*. Twayne Publishers, 1983. Copyright © 1983 by G. K. Hall & Company. All rights reserved. Reproduced with the permission of the author.—Rowland, Herbert. From *Mattias Claudius: Language as "Infamous Funnel" and Its Imperatives*. Fairleigh Dickinson University Press, 1997. © 1997 by Associated University Presses, Inc. All rights reserved. Reproduced by permission.—Schapiro, Leonard. From *Rationalism and Nationalism in Russian Nineteenth-Century Political Thought*. Yale University Press, 1967. Copyright © 1967 by Yale University. Reproduced by permission.—Sisson, C. H. From *Art and Action*. Methuen, 1965. © 1965 by C. H. Sisson. All rights reserved. Reproduced by permission of Laurence Pollinger Ltd. for the author.—Ulman, H. Lewis. From *Things, Thoughts, Words, and Actions: The Problem of Language in Late Eighteenth-Century British Rhetorical Theory*. Southern Illinois University Press, 1994. Copyright © 1994 by the Board of Trustees, Southern Illinois University. All rights reserved. Reproduced by permission of Southern Illinois University Press.—Unwin, Rayner. From *The Rural Muse: Studies in the Peasant Poetry of England*. George Allen and Unwin Ltd., 1954. Copyright 1954 by George Allen and Unwin Ltd. Reproduced by permission of the author.

PHOTOGRAPHS AND ILLUSTRATIONS APPEARING IN *NCLC*, VOLUME 75, WERE RECEIVED FROM THE FOLLOWING SOURCES:

A title page for "Lectures on Rhetoric and Belles Lettres" by Hugh Blair, D. D. and F. R. S. Edin, New York, 1815, photograph. The Department of Rare Books and Special Collections, The University of Michigan Library. Reproduced by permission.—A title page for "Poems of Rural Life in the Dorset Dialect" by William Barnes, London, C. Kegan Paul & Co., 1879, photograph. The Department of Rare Books and Special Collections, The University of Michigan Library. Reproduced by permission.—A title page for "Polnoe Sobraine sochinenii (Complete Collection of Literary Works)" by Timofei Granovskii, 1905, photograph. The Department of Rare Books and Special Collections, The University of Michigan Library. Reproduced by permission.—Blair D. D., Hugh, engraving. Archive Photos, Inc. Reproduced by permission.—Claudius, Matthias, engraving. Archive Photos, Inc. Reproduced by permission.—Fig. 4.4, "Maternal Instruction" from Godey's Magazine and Lady's Book, edited by Sarah J. Hale, March, 1845, painted by J. C. Timbrell and engraved by J. Bannister, photograph. Division of Rare and Manuscript Collection, Carl A. Kroch Library, Cornell University. Reproduced by permission.—William Barnes, 1886, photograph of a wood engraving. The Granger Collection, New York. Reproduced by permission.

William Barnes

1801-1886

English poet and philologist.

INTRODUCTION

William Barnes is considered an outstanding regional poet, who produced highly regarded verse in the dialect of Blackmore Vale—a semi-secluded valley in the southern English county of Dorsetshire. This poetry, which preserves the speech and character of rural life in early nineteenth-century England, earned Barnes the enduring designation as "the Dorset Poet." An accomplished philologist as well as a versifier, Barnes also composed extensive linguistic, grammatical, and historical works, including several writings on Anglo-Saxon etymology which would inform his poetry. Overall, Barnes's collected poems are thought to represent a celebration of the pastoral ideals of harmony with nature and gentleness as represented by the people and language of Blackmore Vale, while his prose writing is said to offer tacit criticism of modern notions of economic, social, and scientific progress which he believed threatened to destroy the cultural traditions of the past.

Biographical Information

Barnes was born in Bagber near Sturminster Newton, the principal town in Blackmore Vale, Dorsetshire, England. His father was a relatively poor farmer, though he descended from a family of gentlemen. Barnes attended grammar school in Sturminster, and in his early teens worked for a solicitor in town. During this time he began to display varied and extensive interests: in modern and classical languages, Welsh poetry, music, mathematics, and many other subjects. In 1817, he traveled to Dorchester. There he again was employed as a solicitor's clerk and met Julia Miles, who would later become his wife. Barnes published his first book of poetry, a pamphlet of ten poems in the Queen's English entitled *Poetical Pieces,* in 1820, but failed to derive any significant notoriety from the work. At the age of twenty-two Barnes, looking for an increase in his wealth for marriage, traveled to Wiltshire where he became a schoolmaster in the town of Mere. He would continue as an educator for the next four decades. A higher salary allowed Barnes to marry Julia Miles in 1827. In 1835 he and his wife returned to Dorchester, where Barnes opened a small school. He continued to pursue his philological studies and write poetry, with many of

his verses appearing in the *Dorset County Chronicle.* Barnes then published what would become his defining collection, *Poems of Rural Life in the Dorset Dialect,* in 1844. He was encouraged to produce works in the national idiom as well, culminating in *Poems Partly of Rural Life in National English* (1846). In 1847 Barnes, now the father of seven children of whom six had survived, was ordained a deacon (later a priest) in the parish of Whitcomb. He received his degree of Bachelor of Divinity from Cambridge University in 1850. After his wife fell ill in 1852 and died, a bereaved Barnes produced several poems of love and grief that appeared in his second and third collections of dialect poetry in 1859 and 1862. During the last twenty-five years of his life Barnes retired from teaching and became the parish priest at Winterbourne Came. His literary production of this period was primarily focused on prose, particularly on philological works. In 1885 the respected Dorset novelist and poet Thomas Hardy moved near Barnes, but their friendship was brief. Barnes, by now a familiar and highly-respected figure in Dorset, died the following year.

Major Works

Barnes arranged his first poetic collection, *Poems of Rural Life in the Dorset Dialect,* seasonally, fitting the individual poems into spring, summer, fall, and winter sections, along with a fifth "miscellaneous" category. The work is largely comprised of portraits of country people and glimpses of rural life in the Blackmore Vale region of Dorset. The pieces in *Poems of Rural Life,* along with its sequels *Hwomely Rhymes. A Second Collection of Poems in the Dorset Dialect* (1859) and *Poems of Rural Life in the Dorset Dialect. Third Collection* (1862), encompass a variety of verse forms and display a considerable technical range, featuring devices used in the poetry of the medieval Welsh, Anglo-Saxons, Persians, and others. Critics observe in Barnes's eclogues, lyrics, and idylls simple, but vivid natural imagery and a pastoral sensibility. His works include several autobiographical and emotional lyrics related to his love for and loss of his wife, including "My Darling Julia" and "Wife A-Prais'd." Within his series of dialect eclogues are several which protest the neglectful treatment of Dorsetshire farmers in an age of agricultural enclosures: "The 'Lotments" and "The Common A-Took In." Another political eclogue, "The Times," an animal fable of a crow and a pig, objects both to the labor policies of the Chartists and to new agricultural laws in England, while "The Happy Daes When I Wer Young" includes a reference to the encroachment of modern science—characterized as "venom"—on the humbly faithful of Dorset. More typical of Barnes's often professed belief in universal harmony and natural beauty, his well-known poem "My Orcha'd in Linden Lea" features a content laborer wandering through a secluded orchard. The poem likewise demonstrates Barnes's eclectic technical virtuosity and demonstrates the poet's use of Welsh *cynghanedd,* a sound pattern of consonants later adopted by Gerard Manley Hopkins. Barnes's celebration of pastoral beauty and his nostalgia for the past are likewise seen in works such as "Zummer Stream," "Hallowed Pleäces," and one of his final poems "The Geäte a-Vallèn To."

Among Barnes's volumes on art, language, and society, *Philological Grammar* (1854) derives from his research and comparison of sixty languages and their essential components. *Tiw; or, A View of the Roots and Stems of the English as a Teutonic Language* (1862) locates approximately fifty principal English root words from provincial dialects. Barnes formulates his aesthetic theory primarily in the essay "Thoughts on Beauty and Art" (1861), which sets what is "beautiful in art . . . in accordance with the beautiful in nature." Barnes's prescient essay *Views of Labour and Gold* (1859) considers "the possible effect of the increase of great working-capitals and monopolies on the labourer's freedom or welfare."

Critical Reception

When considering his own work, Barnes expressed the belief that his dialect poems were not only about the people of Dorset, but also primarily intended for them. His *Poems of Rural Life* was well received locally, particularly by the *Dorset County Chronicle,* and by *The Gentleman's Magazine,* a national periodical. Despite critical approval, popular interest in his verse was lacking. Soon after his death, several of his literary acquaintances, including Coventry Patmore and fellow Dorset-native Thomas Hardy, published favorable pieces designed to increase popular awareness of Barnes's poetic accomplishments, but with limited success. By the mid-twentieth century, commentators had begun to assess Barnes's poetry more critically and to recognize the full extent of his philological research, as well as the considerable effects of these scholarly pursuits on the nature and development of his poetic output. Contemporary estimations of Barnes have continued to acknowledge the strengths of his dialect verse and to contrast these regional works with Barnes's poems in national English, which have generally been considered of inferior quality. Barnes's considerable influence on the later, more well-known poets Thomas Hardy, Gerard Manley Hopkins, and Alfred, Lord Tennyson has recently been observed. Barnes has additionally been recognized for his preservationist philosophy and for his stalwart opposition to the inclusion of Latin, Greek, and French vocabulary—rather than words of Anglo-Saxon origin—in the English language.

PRINCIPAL WORKS

Poetical Pieces (poetry) 1820
Orra, a Lapland Tale (poetry) 1822
Poems of Rural Life in the Dorset Dialect (poetry) 1844
Poems Partly of Rural Life in National English (poetry) 1846
Humilis Domus: Some Thoughts on the Abodes, Life and Social Conditions of the Poor, Especially in Dorsetshire (essay) 1849
Se Gefylsta, An Anglo-Saxon Delectus (linguistics) 1849
A Philological Grammar (linguistics) 1854
Notes on Ancient Britain and the Britons (history) 1858
Hwomely Rhymes. A Second Collection of Poems in the Dorset Dialect (poetry) 1859
Views of Labour and Gold (essay) 1859
"Thoughts on Beauty and Art" (essay) 1861
Poems of Rural Life in the Dorset Dialect. Third Collection (poetry) 1862
Tiw; or, A View of the Roots and Stems of the English as a Teutonic Language (linguistics) 1862

A Grammar and Glossary of the Dorset Dialect (linguistics) 1863

Poems of Rural Life in Common English (poetry) 1868

Early England and the Saxon-English (history and linguistics) 1869

A Selection from Unpublished Poems (poetry) 1870

An Outline of the English Speech-Craft (linguistics) 1878

An Outline of Rede-Craft (logic) 1880

Select Poems of William Barnes [edited by Thomas Hardy] (poetry) 1908

Select Poems of Rural Life in the Dorset Dialect [edited by William Miles Barnes] (poetry) 1909

Selected Poems of William Barnes [edited by Geoffrey Grigson] (poetry) 1950

The Poems of William Barnes. 2 vols. [edited by Bernard Jones] (poetry) 1962

CRITICISM

Francis Turner Palgrave (essay date 1886)

SOURCE: "William Barnes and His Poems of Rural Life in the Dorset Dialect," in *William Barnes of Dorset*, by Giles Dugdale, Cassell and Co. Ltd., 1953, pp. 245-66.

[*In the following essay, a lecture originally delivered by Palgrave in 1886 and published with brief editorial comments by Giles Dugdale in 1953, Palgrave offers his assessment of Barnes's dialect poetry and his "reasons, both why Barnes has not gained popularity, and . . . why he deserves it."*]

Professor Palgrave began by giving an outline of William Barnes' life and then continued:

I will now first try to define the general aims and characteristics of Barnes as a poet, in as few words as possible, wishing to leave his work to speak for itself; which, indeed, if we approach with hearts at once unbiassed and sensitive, is the one and only way of gaining the pleasure inherent in all true poetry. Like Theocritus, Vergil, Tasso, Spenser, and Milton, Barnes had received, or, rather, given himself a full literary education. He was an eminent example of genuine high culture. But more than any of these great forerunners in the Pastoral, he devoted his Muse to rural poetry. More, perhaps, than anyone known to me, he presents the image of the true idyllist. The Pastoral has been often, and often justly, blamed as artificial, it slips easily into affectation and unreality; it has always been difficult for the poets to keep their music from wandering out of the rustic key. From these faults I think no one has been more eminently free than Barnes. He paints rural life with a width of range, with a variety of human interests, unsurpassed by any Pastoralist

known to me; yet, at the same time, he retains himself within its limits with unerring accuracy. The idea and the execution are always in perfect accordance. No pastoral poetry is more uniformly and delightfully sincere, fresher from homely life, more untouched by literary or imitative infusion. Barnes' inventive imagination was, in fact, so fertile that he never needed to look for subjects beyond his native horizon; in all his three hundred and more songs, I hardly discover a trace of previous poetry, new or ancient.

Upon these grounds it may be claimed that Barnes was true to the idea of the Pastoral with unique fidelity. In all his work there is no allegory of his own life, as in Vergil; no intrusive "scrannel" note of theological bigotry, as in Lycidas; no bucolic disguise, as in the *Aminta* and *the Shepheard's Calender.* As he has told us himself, he had but one ultimate aim in writing throughout, which he defined much as Wordsworth defined his own object, "to add sunlight to daylight", to give pure, high, and lasting pleasure; to enlarge his own country folks' stock of healthy happiness. And this he set himself to do by a true picture of the whole Dorset life and landscape before him, drawn in the homely grace of the dialect, handed down in Blackmore Vale from the old days of Wessex.

It was truly "as a lover or a child" that Barnes felt for his own country; he would have joined Wordsworth in that passionate cry—

> *Ah! not for emerald fields alone,*
>   *With ambient streams more pure and bright*
> *Than fabled Cytherea's zone*
>   *Glittering before the Thunderer's sight,*
> *Is to my heart of hearts endeared*
> *The ground where we were born and reared.*

And, as a true philologist, he felt also the immense poetical value of our old English dialects; a value increasing daily as the literary language, by inevitable law, parts with its pictorial expressiveness.

His song never varies from the key thus chosen. As another poet has well said of him, [Coventry Patmore, *Fortnightly Review,* November, 1886.] his poems are "the faultless expression of elementary feelings and perceptions". Thoughts and words are such as would be natural or congenial to what one may call the finer mind of the labouring countryman; to the sound intelligence, the heartiness of the heart, which this true child of the soil well knew lay often beneath the rough, rural figures of farmer and cottager. It is with these that Barnes throughout identifies himself; painting them always in their plain, downright simplicity; in toil, struggle, hardship; in their games and feasts; their rough kindly humour, their frank courtships—the day and the day's work sufficient for them—and yet the horizon of the future life neither unfelt nor unacknowledged. But mere animal coarseness, sordid want, cunning and meanness triumphant, these are excluded; in this sense he idealizes the reality of life. Tragedy also rarely occurs; it would jar with the cheerful tone, the dominant aim of healthy happiness. Simplicity, beauty, humanity, are his unfailing notes, and in accordance with this, one of his oldest friends attests, "he was never heard to say an unkind word of any human creature".

Barnes, although in the points I have just noticed unlike Crabbe—that stern, remorseless painter of common life—in another way may be well compared with him. Crabbe, as a great living poet once remarked to me, has probably set before us more human characters than any poet since Shakespeare. I think we may truly say the same of the number of scenes which Barnes has found and presented in his native Dorset. His "motives", if I may use a convenient phrase, are almost endless; and although many, of course, must be drawn from closely similar materials, yet it is surprising with what skill they are always kept distinct. I now propose to give some idea of his wealth in this respect by quoting a few of his poems, and describing others, taking first general pictures of village life. The Dorset dialect is easy enough in a book, but in reading it will be better that I should put the poems into ordinary English. They lose thus, of course, not a little, but the loss is inevitable.

I begin with a song upon the village maidens of Blackmore valley, in which the poet spent his boyhood:—

"Blackmwore Maidens"

[He then read the full poem]

With what a tender lightness of touch do these lines unite the future to the present! They should be compared with the narrative of a simple country ride, **"Gwain to Brookwell"**, in which the poet, with the same natural ease, sets before us the mingled comedy and tragedy of life; each passing before us just as scenes go by when we are travelling. Then we find such other scenes as the village Sparrow feast, with the comic song of the wit of the country-side; the contrast between the bachelor and the married man; the tale of the old woman whose market-horse, unknown to her, had been a cavalry charger, and carries her, in her red cloak, into the middle of the ranks; the Gainsborough-like picture of an old-fashioned squire—

That used to ramble drough the sheädes
O' timber, or the burmèn gleädes,
An' come at evenèn up the leäze
Wi' red-eär'd dogs bezide his knees,
An' hold his gun, a-hangèn drough
His eärmpit, out above his tooe.

Barnes is so impersonal, keeps himself, with true ancient epic simplicity, so wholly out of sight, that the rural clergy hardly appear among his figures; and when the Squire, as here, is the subject, it is less his place in the present than in the past which is put before us—the poet always handling things or persons dead and gone with a tender reverence. But he is no sentimental dreamer, and the rural questions of the day are discussed with great shrewdness and comic power in a number of eclogues. Such is the dialogue on allotments, urging the great importance of their nearness to the cottages, or that on enclosing a common. In another, Tom is a "leaguer", a socialist of some sort; John argues good-humouredly against his theories, overwhelming him at last with a racy fable. When, in lighter style, he paints, till we seem to see them, the troubles and perplexities of the carters, whose waggon has stuck fast in a miry road; or we have a set of country riddles told by youth and girl; the stage-coach and the railway are contrasted; or, as the poet's last word, the little adventures of a "Lot o' Maïdens a-runnèn the Vields", lightly touched with an almost Italian comic vivacity.

In a different vein Barnes has made a perfect little piece out of the simple description of the country-folk filling their Church in silence; whilst the taking-in of small waste spaces lying by the lanes' side—still, happily, a characteristic feature of Dorset—is a natural matter for the protest of this born lover of Nature and of Childhood:—

The children wull soon have noo pleäce
Vor to plaÿ in, an' if they do grow,

They wull have a thin musheroom feäce,
Wi' their bodies, so sumple as dough.
But a man is a-meäde ov a child,
An' his limbs do grow worksome by plaÿ;
An' if the young child's little body's a-
spweil'd
Why the man's wull the sooner decaÿ.
But wealth is wo'th now mwore than health is
wo'th;
*   Let it all goo,*
If 't'ull bring but a sov'rèn or two.

Vor to breed the young fox or the heäre,
We can gi'e up whole eäcres o' ground,
But the greens be a-grudg'd, vor to rear
Our young children up healthy an' sound,
Why, there woont be a-left the next age
A green spot where their veet can goo free;
An' the goocoo wull soon be committed to
cage
Vor a trespass in zomebody's tree.
Vor 'tis lock'èn up, Thomas, an' blockèn up,
Stranger or brother,
Men mussen come nigh woone another.

I might add endless more scenes from this moving diorama of life; all with the same characteristics; all painted not only with absolute simplicity, but absolute sincerity. This poet's eye, like Keats', is always upon his object. The details are so true, so sharply rendered, that they seem purely photographic; yet if we look at them close, if we recall similar country scenes, we shall see (as in all true landscape painting), that everywhere they are modified and idealized to bring them within the range of poetical art.

Barnes' poems have also, almost without exception, a finished unity, as delicately managed as what we find in the Greek lyrics, rounded off with the perfection of an ode by Horace. It is thus, and thus only, that he reveals his close study of classical poetry, and of Petrarch—(an ancient, as it were in his own despite, precisely through that portion of his work where he was most modern)—who was one of his special favourites. And it is by this art that Barnes has given grace and life to many pieces, the subject-matter of which seems, in itself, almost too slight and familiar. They gain their effect by their perfection as wholes.

Nothing, at first sight, seems easier than such a style, as the myriad attempts which have been made in it prove. But it demands, from him who would succeed in it, absolute freedom from egotism, simple disinterestedness, perfect translucency of soul, and these gifts are far too rare to permit frequent success;—at any rate, when poetry has passed beyond the first flush and freshness of its youth.

Sincerity, simplicity, unity—these are the broad features of Barnes, regarded as an artist in words, which have been thus far before us. Let me now complete this general sketch of his style by calling attention to the peculiar attitude which the poet maintains throughout his work. I may term it an attitude of reserve; of disinterestedness; an entire absence of egotism. He himself is hardly seen in the long gallery of his creations; like Shakespeare, he is felt only as the combining and creating human spirit. As in Homer, everything is shown to us by external, sensible images, by putting the scene in immediate simplicity before us. Poetry of this kind calls forth our thoughts in place of directly suggesting thoughts to us. Hence also, although full of high purpose and meaning, Barnes hardly ever moralizes; he is too great an artist to spoil his poetry by preaching; only, perhaps, a line or two at the close carry us, with equal firmness and lucidity of touch, beyond this world into the region of the world unseen. To put it in one word, this is objective poetry, in a singularly pure and perfect form: I know of no modern writer who has mastered it with such unvarying success, and on a scale so considerable.

Every style, however, as the saying is, has "the defects of its qualities". A true criticism will never pass these over; and he should be the more careful to notice them

who is likely to fall into exaggerated praise in the endeavour to do justice to "neglected virtue". Barnes' purely objective, impersonal manner now and then tends to be bald or thin in its effect. As with Herrick, his Devon fellow-countryman of old, "rural ditties" and "oaten flute", now and then may appear primitive and pale at first hearing, to ears familiar only with the full crash and compass of the modern orchestra. There is a monotony like that of skies and seas and forests, in these "short and simple annals of the poor", however finely discriminated. Perhaps the poet's own beautiful and gracious nature, never letting him "say an unkind word of any human creature", has made light and brightness too constant in his pictures: "Hic ver adsiduum, atque alienis mensibus æstas!"

Like those of another master of the exquisite, Fra Angelico, we may sometimes miss the contrast of effective shadow. Again, to them whose taste in poetry can find no pleasure except in subtle analysis of character and emotion, in speculation upon the problems and perplexities of life, in personal revelations of feeling, introspective brooding, colour and sensuousness for their own sake—in a word, to those who are simply led captive and enslaved by the dominant fashions of the age; to all such, Barnes will seem an anachronism, an Elizabethan, like Herrick or Keats, born out of his proper century. But in Oxford I may look with confidence for a wider, healthier, more liberal taste; in the best sense of the word, for a classical judgment.

Returning now to the poems, I must briefly notice the peculiar part which landscape plays in them. This is governed everywhere by that objective character which I have just tried to define. Nature is looked at by Barnes, as by the Greeks, in her pure simplicity; as the picture which surrounds us; as the scenery and background of human life, not in the modern mode of which Wordsworth, Shelley, and others have given us splendid examples, as a living power to teach man, or sympathize almost consciously with him. But he does not, with the Greeks, treat nature as the outward manifestation of divine or half-divine existences. She appears, rather, as a sort of unconscious reflex of human life. The landscape of each season, in its turn, seems, indeed, to Barnes to be the genuine echo of our emotions; but it is an echo only; our hearts have, as it were, supplied Nature with the answer which she gives back to us. Yet this echo is so close and dear to the rural poet's mind, that the landscape is always intertwined in his verse with its dominant human interests. His descriptions are so accurate and lively in their details, that one's first word would be to call them strikingly pictorial. But if we look close we shall find that (true to the essential laws of poetry), no painter could really reproduce them. It is always some human thought or sentiment which gives the picture its unity, its effectiveness. To use his own expressive phrase, he sees and paints the landscape not only with eye-sight, but with mind-sight.

In consequence of this attitude towards Nature, this constant interfusion of the human, it is as difficult to find a specimen of pure landscape in Barnes as it is in ancient poetry. **"Jeäne"** and **"Zummer"**, quoted later on, illustrate his method. I will here insert only an extract, the last lines of which have a pathetic interest from the fact that it was in October that this bright-souled lover of Spring was called away:—

"May"

Come out o' door, 'tis Spring! 'tis Maÿ!
The trees be green, the vields be gaÿ;
The weather's warm, the winter blast,
Wi' all his train of clouds, is past;
The zun do rise while vo'k do sleep.
To teäke a higher daily sweep,
Wi' cloudless feäce a-flingèn down
His sparklèn light upon the groun'.

We'll wind up roun' the hill, an' look
All down the thickly-timber'd nook,
Out where the squier's house do show
His grey-wall'd peaks up drough the row
O' shoddy elems, where the rook
Do build her nest; an' where the brook
Do creep along the meäds, an' lie
To catch the brightness o' the sky;
An' cows, in water to theïr knees,
Do stan' a-whiskèn off the vlees.

Mother o' blossoms, and ov' all
That's feär a-vield vrom Spring till Fall,
The gookoo over white-weäv'd seas
Do come to sing in thy green trees,
An' buttervlees, in giddy flight,
Do gleäm the mwost by thy gaÿ light.
Oh! when, at last, my fleshly eyes
Shall shut upon the vields an' skies,
Mid zummer's zunny days be gone,
An' winter's clouds be comèn on:
Nor mid I draw upon the e'th
O' thy sweet air my leätest breath;
Alassen I mid want to stay
Behine' for thee, O flow'ry May!

I have noticed Barnes' sympathetic reverence for the past, for the labours of our forefathers. All that survives of the work wrought by vanished hands has a sweet pathos for him. This tone is heard whenever he touches on the old manor-houses in which Dorset is rich, whilst describing them always from the point of view which might strike intelligent country folk, whose thoughts turn naturally less to architectural picturesqueness than to the life once lived within them. Thus, in the **"Girt (great) Wold House o'**

Mossy Stwone" we have this scene from the days of Queen Anne or Queen Charlotte:—

An' there wer walks of peävement, broad
Enough to meäke a carriage-road,
Where steätely leädies woonce did use
To walk wi' hoops an' high-heel shoes,
When yonder hollow woak wer sound,
Avore the walls wer ivy-bound,
Avore the elems met above
The road between 'em, where they drove
Their coach all up or down the road
A-comèn hwome or gwain abroad.
The zummer air o' theäse green hill
'V a-heav'd in bosoms now all still,
An' all their hopes an' all their tears
Be unknown things ov other years.

Even the little stone figure of a child—some rococo Cupid, doubtless—set on a pillar in a park, becomes a living thing to the poet. In whatever weather,

You'll zee his pretty smile betwixt
His little sheäde-mark'd lips a-fix'd;
As there his little sheäpe do bide
Drought day an' night, an' time an' tide,
An' never change his size or dress,
Nor overgrow his prettiness,

Barnes has given also one general picture of the four Seasons, personified as figures who pass in turn over the face of what he calls a "year-clock";—an idea suggested, perhaps, by the elaborate piece of mediæval mechanism which was brought away from Glastonbury, and marks the hours still in Wells Cathedral. It would be injustice to mutilate by partial quotation this, which seems to me the most brilliant piece of his Nature painting. I class it with the lovely poem of Keats named "Fancy", as holding the second rank in that peculiar style, of which Milton's "Allegro" and "Penseroso" are the hitherto unrivalled masterpieces.

Scenes, however, from individual life, pictures of the cottage home with its joys and sorrows, of course fill the greater part of the collection. I begin with a song of village love-making:—

"My Love Is Good"

[Professor Palgrave next quoted this long poem in full.]

Here we note how the refrain, with its graceful system of rhyme and assonance, lifts and keeps the rustic plainness of the song at its due poetic level. Somewhat in the same key is the **"Farmer's Woldest Da'ter"**, a first-rate piece of shrewd humour and good feeling. **"Gwaïn down the steps vor Water"** paints a country maiden at a well, with the homely,

Doric, beauty of Theocritus in his "Sicilian hours". Many others I must pass over. Most of them tell of happy love; but in the **"Hope a-left behind"**, the **"Broken Heart"**, the singularly pathetic **"Love Child"**, and others, the tragic side is painted with great force, but also with a complete freedom from sentimental exaggeration. I have only space to quote

"The Broken Heart"

[Which he proceeded to do.]

A picture of married life may follow.

"Jeäne"

> We now mid hope vor better cheer,
>   My smilèn wife o' twice vive year.
> Let others frown if thou bist near
>   Wi' hope upon thy brow, Jeäne;
> For I vu'st lov'd thee when thy light
> Young sheäpe vu'st grew to woman's height;
> I lov'd thee near, an' out of zight,
>   An' I do love thee now, Jeäne.
>
> An' we've a-trod the sheenèn bleäde
> Ov eegrass in the zummer sheäde,
> An' when the leaves begun to feäde
>   Wi' zummer in the weäne, Jeäne;
> An' we've a-wander'd drough the groun'
> O' swayèn wheat a-turnèn brown,
> An' we've a-stroll'd together roun'
>   The brook an' drough the leäne, Jeäne.
>
> An' nwone but I can ever tell
> Ov all thy tears that have a-vell
> When trials meäde thy bosom swell,
>   An' nwone but thou o' mine, Jeäne;
> An' now my heart, that heav'd wi' pride
> Back then to have thee at my zide,
> Do love thee mwore as years do slide,
>   An' leäve them times behine, Jeäne.

The **"Married peäir's Love walk"**, **"Hallowed pleäces"** (a visit to a wife's old home), **"Woone smile mwore"**, **"The slantèn light o' Fall"** (a christening scene in Autumn), **"Fatherhood"**, **"Tweil (toil)"**—these titles may serve to indicate the poet's range. I quote two stanzas from the last named:—the scene is the cottager's garden.

> In wall-zide sheädes, by leafy bowers,
>   Underneath the swayèn tree,
> O' leäte, as round the bloomèn flowers,
>   Lowly humm'd the giddy bee,
> My children's small left voot did smite
> Their tiny speäde, the while the right
> Did trample on a deäisy head,
> Bezïde the flower's dousty bed,

> An' though their work wer idle then,
>   They a-smilèn, an' a-tweilèn,
> Still did work an' work ageän.
> Now their little limbs be stronger,
>   Deeper now their väice do sound;
> An' their little veet be longer,
>   An' do tread on other ground:
> An' rust is on the little bleädes
>   Ov all the broken-hafted speädes,
> An' flow'rs that wer my hope an' pride
> Ha' long agoo a-bloom'd an' died,
> But still as I did leäbor then
>   Vor love ov all them children small,
> Zoo now I'll tweil an' tweil ageän.

In these home-pictures every word tells, and there is not a word too many. They show the finest art; or, as it would be more true to say, conceal it. Children especially are drawn with a touch equally firm and tender; humorous or pathetic, as the subject may be, never falling into mere petty prettiness or sentimental commonplace. Scattered examples of similar happy painting of childhood may be found among our poetry, that of Blake, great in both fields of art, especially. But, few, I think, are the poets who, in this difficult region, can show so many successes as Barnes—so many triumphs of seemingly artless art.

My last quotation leads me to another gift in which Barnes excels—that by which, perhaps, he is best known, so far as one can correctly speak of him as known at all—his gift in pathetic delineation. Such subjects, in our own time especially, are commonly treated in what I may call a highly-coloured manner; the poet, by his epithets and his own reflections upon the situation before him, points out and emphasizes the pathos of his "motive". In the simpler style prevalent of old—the best examples of which are found in Homer—the poet relies wholly upon his clear setting forth of the situation, on the unadorned translucency with which he renders the scene. Such a picture calls, as it were, in silence to the depths of our sympathy; by its own force it pierces, in the phrase of Euripides, *to the very marrow of the soul*. The heart may reply to the pathos, but the poet does not himself supply us with the answer.

Scott has a little ballad, the "Maid of Neidpath", which is one of the most exquisite examples in literature of this style of the pathetic, and it is thus that Barnes always writes. I quote two or three specimens, the beauty of which will need little comment from me.

"The Wife A-Lost"

[Which has already been quoted in full.]

One could hardly find a better example than this of the contrast between true feeling and sentimentalism: between "Sense and Sensibility", as immortalized by Jane Austen.

"Readen ov a Headstone"

As I wer readèn ov a stwone
In Grenley church-yard all alwone,
A little maïd ran up, wi' pride
To zee me there, an' push'd a-zide
A bunch of bennets that did hide
  A verse her father, as she zäid,
  Put up above her mother's head,
    To tell how much he loved her.

The verse wer short, but very good,
I stood an' larn'd en where I stood:—
"Mid God, dear Meäry, gi'e me greäce
To vind lik' thee, a better pleäce,
Where I woonce mwore mid zee thy feäce;
  An' bring thy children up to know
  His word, that they mid come an' show
    Thy soul how much I lov'd thee."

"Where's father, then," I zaid, "my chile?"
"Dead too," she answer'd wi'd a smile;
"An' I an' brother Jim do bide
At Betty White's, o' tother zide
O' road." "Mid He, my chile," I cried,
  "That's Father to the fatherless,
  Become thy Father now, an' bless,
    An' keep, an' leäd, an' love thee."

Though she've a-lost, I thought, so much,
Still He don't let the thoughts o't touch
Her litsome heart by day or night;
An' zoo, if we could teäke it right,
Do show He'll meäke his burdens light
  To weaker souls, an' that his smile
  Is sweet upon a harmless chile,
    When they be dead that lov'd it.

The next I have chosen, leaving out reluctantly the somewhat less unknown **"Ellen Brine"**, exemplifies Barnes in his narrative vein.

"The Turnstile"

[Professor Palgrave here read **"The Turnstile"**.]

My last example **"Woak Hill"**, describes a widower leaving the home where he had lived with his wife; "house-ridden", being the Dorset equivalent for the North-country "flitting". The pathos of this is singularly refined and delicate. The thought and the feeling are of very subtle beauty, but the poet—always true to himself—has rendered them with a Doric simplicity. Note the touch, where the imagined Presence of the lost wife is painted by the single word, *light*.

"Woak Hill"

[was then read in full.]

I must touch, too briefly, on the technical side of Barnes' art in poetry; rhythm, metre, rhyme, assonances, use of refrain, and choice of words. There is nothing small or unimportant in genuine fine art. Each and every atom of these things, in a finished artist, will contribute to the power of his verse over mind and heart. But how this effect has been gained we shall hardly be conscious; the art will have hidden itself away; the means will be lost in the end. It is thus with Barnes. Pitching all his poems in the key appropriate to his own country-folk, he writes for the most part in a familiar, short, iambic metre, well known from the time of its Hellenic inventors, as the nearest to common speech. This he saves from monotony by his singularly perfect and singularly unaffected system of rhymes—rhymes never forced, yet constantly delighting us by their rural freshness. And lest they should still cloy, he has taken from our early English poetry delicate cross-rhymes, inserted in the course of his lines; or gentle assonances, such as those which may be noted in **"Ellen Brine"**.

"Woak Hill" is a beautiful example of this method; until we stop to think, the fact that, like Collins' lovely "Ode to Evening", it is written in assonances without rhyme, would not, I think, strike any reader.

Rhyming metres and stanzas, when short, as Barnes' generally are, bring one up often with a too rapid, or too strongly marked, close; the rhythm hence seems to fail in continuity, the stanza ends with an over-emphatic, with an almost jarring, chord. Barnes employs a peculiar system of refrain to avoid these defects. His refrain commonly echoes the metre, in a softer, more delicate tone, with an effect like what is termed in music the "perfect cadence". **"Ellen Brine"**, the **"Headstwone"**, **"My Love is Good"**, are instances. When, however, he has a lively, humorous theme, the burden changes into a more brilliant key, summing up and intensifying the rhythmical movement, with a chorus-like strain. The **"Coach"**, the spirited **"Praise o' Do'set"**, into which, as in duty bound, the poet's whole soul has gone—the **"Ivy"**, the **"Shy Man"**, close after this fashion.

After Barnes' pathetic verse, I give a fragment from a boldly-written song of straightforward, yet essentially modest independence;—one of those pieces in which the predominant tone is manliness and true-hearted fellowship:—

No, I'm a man, I'm vull a man,
You beat my manhood, if you can.

. . . . .

A young-cheäk'd mother's tears mid vall,
When woone a-lost, not half man-tall,
Vrom little hand, a-called vrom plaÿ,
Do leäve noo tool, but drop a taÿ,
An' die avore he's father-free
  To sheape his life by his own plan;
An' vull an angel he shall be,
  But here on e'th not vull a man,
    No; I could boast if others can,
      I'm vull a man.

Friendship, of course, is another marked topic. **"A Wold Friend"** will be found an excellent example. Manly spirit supplies the common theme of these poems. But a girl's brave heart is honoured in the humorous—

"Don't Ceäre"

[Which Professor Palgrave read.]

The piece somewhat obscurely named **"Withstanders"** is an example of Barnes' most serious manner. Here he takes the attitude of those who have to look upon the evil and injustice of this world, without the power of conquering or redressing them; who can only wait for the day when the mystery of wrong will be solved, the final triumph of the Good and Right.

"Withstanders"

[He here read the poem in full.]

In these few lines, meseems, the poet has concentrated the battle of right and wrong, the oppressor and the oppressed, with what simplicity of phrase! what manly pathos! what fineness of art! By way of contrast I will now quote one specimen of Barnes' humorous work. What I said of his pathos, applies here also; the method is the same. The scenes or persons have always humour in themselves, as pictures passing before our eyes; they are not comic through the poet's choice of humorous diction. Playful and kindly, they make us smile, as it were, by their own right.

"The Shy Man"

[was here quoted in full.]

Last, for the sake of its music, its Shakespearean charm:

"Zummer an' Winter"

When I led by zummer streams
  The pride o' Lea, as naïghbours thought her,
While the zun, wi' evenèn beams,
  Did cast our sheades athirt the water;

Winds a-blowèn,
Streams a-flowèn,
Skies a-glowen,
Tokens ov my jay zoo fleetèn,
Heighten'd it, that happy meetèn.

Then, when maïd an' man took pleäces,
  Gay in winter's Chris'mas, dances,
Showèn in their merry feäces
  Kindly smiles an' glisnèn glances;
    Stars a-winkèn,
    Day a-shrinkèn,
    Sheädes a-zinkèn,
Brought anew the happy meetèn,
That did meäke the night too fleetèn.

Why has this poet, so perfect in his art, so clear and lifelike in describing, so happy in invention of subject, so sweet and lofty in his tone, why has he never as yet reached popularity? Why, thus far, must the audience he has found be one which, looking to our English-speaking and reading millions, can be described only as Milton's "fit, though few"? He did not write for fame; and are we to say that Fame, like the spiteful goddesses of Hellenic legend, avenged herself for the slight? I think it has been so in some degree. Our modern culture, widening more than deepening, calls forth and encourages so vast a crowd of voices, that we do not generally care to listen, except to those who flatter or shout for a hearing. At times, a true poet may raise a note so resonant, or so piercing, that we are, at last, constrained to give audience. But we shut our ears to the small, still voice, though, perhaps, having in it more of the divine than louder utterances.

The quotations and criticisms, which I have now offered, may supply some reasons, both why Barnes has not gained popularity, and also, as I hope, why he deserves it.

First and foremost has been his use of dialect; and this may probably seem to many an all-sufficient reason. Yet I will venture to call it nothing better than sheer, simple, indolence. The Dorset, as Barnes prints it, differs from literary English, almost wholly, in a few obvious forms of spelling. If a real, good, country word comes in, one has but to turn to the Glossary at the end of the volume; when any genuine lover of poetry will be glad to enrich his memory with words, racy of the soil, and living memorials of old England.

To pass from words to substance. Of the poet's general style, I have already spoken, and of the limitations, which this, like every other style, involves. But here we may probably find the other main reason why he has not been popular. Working for love of his art, and for love of his fellow-countryfolk, he has never tried to fall in with the literary current of the day. In a "subjective age", as Goethe described it sixty years since,

Barnes has been obstinate in his objectivity. He is indifferent to coloured diction, to sensuous metaphor, to allusions and ornaments added for decoration's sake. Politics, religion, ethics, are only implied. He avoids all display of personal feeling, all self-conscious confession, all inward conflict, and, keeping his eye always on his object, leaves the reader to be moved or not by its simple presentation. His three hundred scenes from the drama of rural life supply, indeed, abundant material for the subtle analysis, in which our day is so fertile. But it finds no expression among them.

I hope I shall not be understood as depreciating the style now popular, by thus attempting to do justice to another. This would be to fall into that narrow one-sided taste which makes us at strife with our own pleasure. For the style of Barnes, however, may be justly claimed that, if his plain, ancient, objective manner appeals less to the sympathy of contemporaries, it has in itself certain sure signs of duration. The special thoughts, likings, struggles, problems of every age, in their very essence, are transitory. The fashion of the world changes. The decorations and colours of the day please no longer. "Qui nunc amavit, cras non amat." But if his gift be true, permanency will always be with the poet whose song is of the elementary thoughts and passions of man, the things that have been, and will be again; it will be, above all, with him who writes with his eye on his object, not on himself. And, from this view-point, I liken the general difference of the two styles, objective and subjective, to the difference between a work of sculpture and a work of painting—between marble in its colourless eternity, and the too-fleeting rainbow of the canvas.

To sum up. Contemporary critical judgment is always so thoroughly insecure that it will be best to make no attempt to assign the place, due to the poet whom England has lost, in our literature. Nor, of course, can I here enter on the alluring work of comparing him with other writers of pastoral poetry. But it will, perhaps, not be disputed that he has the quality which Mr. Arnold long since skilfully defined as *distinction;* and this, at least, will at no time want the affectionate admiration of the best judges. Barnes never wrote for fame, he never wrote for money; not having leisure for them, I suppose, as Plato said. But on our long roll I find no poet who has more persistently and single-mindedly aimed at the true end of Poetry, high and durable pleasure; who has striven more earnestly in the interest of healthy happiness. To no one does the phrase "holy simplicity", *sancta simplicitas,* apply more accurately. His song is as fresh and spontaneous as the bird's; as an old poet expresses it beautifully, it was to Barnes:

No pains, but pleasure, to do the dictates dear
Of inward living nature,—what doth move

The Nightingale to sing so sweet and clear,
The Thrush, or Lark that, mounting high
  above,
Chants her shrill notes to heedless ears of
  corn,
Heavily hanging in the dewy morn.

Sincerity, sweetness, a hand that does not seem as if it could wander from the line of beauty, an originality which exempts him from all indebtedness to preceding pastoral poets—these are among his characteristic notes. He has, in my eyes, a place so unique that I can hardly compare him with any other single writer. Perhaps Mozart has the same magical charm, the sweetness, the cry of human pathos, the unremitting and inseparable presence of beauty. Add to this that, with a seldom-equalled inventiveness in his subjects, Barnes never fails to maintain the impression of unity. True poet in a very rare sense, he keeps the balance between the Ideal and the Real with delicate and unswerving accuracy. He deserves the praise which Shakespeare, by the mouth of Polixenes, whilst defining the craft of the gardener, gives, as it were in a figure, to Poetry:—

This is an art
Which does mend nature, change it rather;
  but
The art itself is nature.

Thomas Hardy (essay date 1908)

SOURCE: Preface to *Select Poems of William Barnes,* edited by Thomas Hardy, Humphrey Milford, 1908, pp. iii-xii.

[*In the following preface to* Select Poems of William Barnes, *Hardy explores the unique character of Barnes's dialect poetry.*]

This volume of verse [***Select Poems of William Barnes***] includes, to the best of my judgement, the greater part of that which is of the highest value in the poetry of William Barnes. I have been moved to undertake the selection by a thought that has overridden some immediate objections to such an attempt,—that I chance to be (I believe) one of the few living persons having a practical acquaintance with letters who knew familiarly the Dorset dialect when it was spoken as Barnes writes it, or, perhaps, who know it as it is spoken now. Since his death, education in the west of England as elsewhere has gone on with its silent and inevitable effacements, reducing the speech of this country to uniformity, and obliterating every year many a fine old local word. The process is always the same: the word is ridiculed by the newly taught; it gets into disgrace; it is heard in holes and corners only; it dies; and, worst of all, it leaves no synonym. In the villages that one recognizes to be the scenes of these pastorals the poet's nouns, adjectives, and idioms daily cease to be understood by the younger generation, the luxury of four demonstrative pronouns, of which he was so proud, vanishes by their compression into the two of common English, and the suffix to verbs which marks continuity of action is almost everywhere shorn away.

To cull from a dead writer's whole achievement in verse portions that shall exhibit him is a task of no small difficulty, and of some temerity. There is involved, first of all, the question of right. A selector may say: These are the pieces that please me best; but he may not be entitled to hold that they are the best in themselves and for everybody. This opens the problem of equating the personality—of adjusting the idiosyncrasy of the chooser to mean pitch. If it can be done in some degree—one may doubt it—there has to be borne in mind the continually changing taste of the times. But, assuming average critical capacity in the compiler, that he represents his own time, and that he finds it no great toil to come to a conclusion on which in his view are the highest levels and the lowest of a poet's execution, the complete field of the work examined almost always contains a large intermediate tract where the accomplishment is of nearly uniform merit throughout, selection from which must be by a process of sampling rather than of gleaning; many a poem, too, of indifferent achievement in its wholeness may contain some line, couplet, or stanza of great excellence; and contrariwise, a bad or irrelevant verse may mar the good remainder; in each case the choice is puzzled, and the balance struck by a single mind can hardly escape being questioned here and there.

A word may be said on the arrangement of the poems as 'lyrical and elegiac'; 'descriptive and meditative'; 'humorous'; a classification which has been adopted with this author in the present volume for the first time. It is an old story that such divisions may be open to grave objection, in respect, at least, of the verse of the majority of poets, who write in the accepted language. For one thing, many fine poems that have lyric moments are not entirely lyrical; many largely narrative poems are not entirely narrative; many personal reflections or meditations in verse hover across the frontiers of lyricism. To this general opinion I would add that the same lines may be lyrical to one temperament and meditative to another; nay, lyrical and not lyrical to the same reader at different times, according to his mood and circumstance. Gray's *Elegy* may be instanced as a poem that has almost made itself notorious by claiming to be a lyric in particular humours, situations, and weathers, and waiving the claim in others.

One might, to be sure, as a smart impromptu, narrow down the definition of lyric to the safe boundary of poetry that has all its nouns in the vocative case, and so settle the question by the simple touchstone of the grammar-book, adducing the *Benedicite* as a shining example. But this qualification would be disconcerting in its stringency, and cause a fluttering of the leaves of many an accepted anthology.

A story which was told the writer by Mr. Barnes himself may be apposite here. When a pupil of his was announced in the *Times* as having come out at the top in the Indian Service examination-list of those days, the schoolmaster was overwhelmed with letters from anxious parents requesting him at any price to make their sons come out at the top also. He replied that he willingly would, but that it took two to do it. It depends, in truth, upon the other person, the reader, whether certain numbers shall be raised to lyric pitch or not; and if he does not bring to the page of these potentially lyric productions a lyrical quality of mind, they must be classed, for him, as non-lyrical.

However, to pass the niceties of this question by. In the exceptional instance of a poet like Barnes who writes in a dialect only, a new condition arises to influence considerations of assortment. Lovers of poetry who are but imperfectly acquainted with his vocabulary and idiom may yet be desirous of learning something of his message; and the most elementary guidance is of help to such students, for they are liable to mistake their author on the very threshold. For some reason or none, many persons suppose that when anything is penned in the tongue of the country-side, the primary intent is burlesque or ridicule, and this especially if the speech be one in which the sibilant has the rough sound, and is expressed by Z. Indeed, scores of thriving storytellers and dramatists seem to believe that by transmuting the flattest conversation into a dialect that never existed, and making the talkers say 'be' where they would really say 'is', a Falstaffian richness is at once imparted to its qualities.

But to a person to whom a dialect is native its sounds are as consonant with moods of sorrow as with moods of mirth: there is no grotesqueness in it as such. Nor was there to Barnes. To provide an alien reader with a rough clue to the taste of the kernel that may be expected under the shell of the spelling has seemed to be worth while, and to justify a division into heads that may in some cases appear arbitrary.

In respect of the other helps—the glosses and paraphrases given on each page—it may be assumed that they are but a sorry substitute for the full significance the original words bear to those who read them without translation, and know their delicate ability to express the doings, joys and jests, troubles, sorrows, needs and sicknesses of life in the rural world as elsewhere. The Dorset dialect being—or having been—a tongue, and not a corruption, it is the old question over again, that of the translation of poetry; which, to the full, is admittedly impossible. And further; gesture and facial expression figure so largely in the speech of husband-men as to be speech itself; hence in the mind's eye of those who know it in its original setting each word of theirs is accompanied by the qualifying face-play which no construing can express.

It may appear strange to some, as it did to friends in his lifetime, that a man of insight who had the spirit of poesy in him should have persisted year after year in writing in a fast-perishing language, and on themes which in some not remote time would be familiar to nobody, leaving him pathetically like

> A ghostly cricket, creaking where a house was
>   burned;

—a language with the added disadvantage by comparison with other dead tongues that no master or books would be readily available for the acquisition of its finer meanings. He himself simply said that he could not help it, no doubt feeling his idylls to be an extemporization, or impulse, without prevision or power of appraisement on his own part.

Yet it seems to the present writer that Barnes, despite this, really belonged to the literary school of such poets as Tennyson, Gray, and Collins, rather than to that of the old unpremeditating singers in dialect. Primarily spontaneous, he was academic closely after; and we find him warbling his native wood-notes with a watchful eye on the predetermined score, a far remove from the popular impression of him as the naif and rude bard who sings only because he must, and who submits the uncouth lines of his page to us without knowing how they come there. Goethe never knew better of his; nor Milton; nor, in their rhymes, Poe; nor, in their whimsical alliterations here and there, Langland and the versifiers of the fourteenth and fifteenth centuries.

In his aim at closeness of phrase to his vision he strained at times the capacities of dialect, and went wilfully outside the dramatization of peasant talk. Such a lover of the art of expression was this pen-man of a dialect that had no literature, that on some occasions he would allow art to overpower spontaneity and to cripple inspiration; though, be it remembered, he never tampered with the dialect itself. His ingenious internal rhymes, his subtle juxtaposition of kindred lippings and vowel-sounds, show a fastidiousness in word-selection that is surprising in verse which professes to represent the habitual modes of language among the western peasantry. We do not find in the dialect balladists of the seventeenth century, or in Burns (with whom he has sometimes been measured), such careful finish, such verbal dexterities, such searchings for the most cunning syllables, such satisfaction with the best phrase. Had he not begun with dialect, and seen himself recog-

nized as an adept in it before he had quite found himself as a poet, who knows that he might not have brought upon his muse the disaster that has befallen so many earnest versifiers of recent time, have become a slave to the passion for form, and have wasted all his substance in whittling at its shape.

From such, however, he was saved by the conditions of his scene, characters, and vocabulary. It may have been, indeed, that he saw this tendency in himself, and retained the dialect as a corrective to the tendency. Whether or no, by a felicitous instinct he does at times break into sudden irregularities in the midst of his subtle rhythms and measures, as if feeling rebelled against further drill. Then his self-consciousness ends, and his naturalness is saved.

But criticism is so easy, and art so hard: criticism so flimsy, and the life-seer's voice so lasting. When we consider what such appreciativeness as Arnold's could allow his prejudice to say about the highest-soaring among all our lyricists; what strange criticism Shelley himself could indulge in now and then; that the history of criticism is mainly the history of error, which has not even, as many errors have, quaintness enough to make it interesting, we may well doubt the utility of such writing on the sand. What is the use of saying, as has been said of Barnes, that compound epithets like 'the blue-hill'd worold', 'the wide-horn'd cow,' 'the grey-topp'd heights of Paladore,' are a high-handed enlargement of the ordinary ideas of the field-folk into whose mouths they are put? These things are justified by the art of every age when they can claim to be, as here, singularly precise and beautiful definitions of what is signified; which in these instances, too, apply with double force to the deeply tinged horizon, to the breed of kine, to the aspect of Shaftesbury Hill, characteristic of the Vale within which most of his revelations are enshrined.

Dialect, it may be added, offered another advantage to him as the writer, whatever difficulties it may have for strangers who try to follow it. Even if he often used the dramatic form of peasant speakers as a pretext for the expression of his own mind and experiences—which cannot be doubted—yet he did not always do this, and the assumed character of husband-man or hamleteer enabled him to elude in his verse those dreams and speculations that cannot leave alone the mystery of things,—possibly an unworthy mystery and disappointing if solved, though one that has a harrowing fascination for many poets,—and helped him to fall back on dramatic truth, by making his personages express the notions of life prevalent in their sphere.

As by the screen of dialect, so by the intense localization aforesaid, much is lost to the outsider who by looking into Barnes's pages only revives general recollections of country life. Yet many passages may shine into that reader's mind through the veil which partly hides them; and it is hoped and believed that, even in a superficial reading, something more of this poet's charm will be gathered from the present selection by persons to whom the Wessex R and Z are uncouth misfortunes, and the dying words those of an unlamented language that need leave behind it no grammar of its secrets and no key to its tomb.

E. M. Forster (essay date 1939)

SOURCE: "William Barnes," in *Two Cheers for Democracy,* Edward Arnold and Co., 1951, pp. 209-12.

[*In the following essay, originally composed in 1939, Forster praises Barnes's gentle and skillful poetry.*]

It is surprising that William Barnes has not been more widely worshipped. Perhaps there was a touch of pride in his gentleness, which led him to conceal himself from notoriety beneath the veil of the Dorset dialect. The veil is slight: anyone can lift it after half an hour's reading. Yet it seems to have served his purpose, and to have confined him to the audience whom he loved. He should have been a popular poet, for he writes of matters which move everyone and in a way which everyone can understand. There is no mysticism in him beyond the trust that we shall, through the goodness of God, be reunited to the dead whom we have loved. There is no difficult or disturbing view of society, no crankiness, no harshness of diction or thought. He is truly, sweetly, affectionately, a Yes-man, and considering how many worthless Yes-men are being boosted to-day as national assets, it is surprising that he should have been left alone, he a clergyman, he a schoolmaster, he of the soil. Propaganda has passed him by. He has been left where he wished, to his own people, and to the few outsiders who have cared to lift the veil and win an easy and a rich reward. To read him is to enter a friendly cottage where a family party is in full swing. One misses many of the allusions, one is not connected with the party by blood, yet one has no sense of intrusion. The party, like all unsophisticated gatherings, welcomes the entire human race. And when, to the jokes and the chatter, there is added the scent of the roses at the casement, and the sighing of the wind down the lane, and the memory of the past loveliness and kindness that are gone—and faith in the future loveliness and kindness that will return with the next generation—the effect is overwhelming. It is impossible to read a poem like '**Woak Hill**' without tears in one's eyes. Or rather, if one has not tears in one's eyes at the end of '**Woak Hill**' one has not read it. It is impossible to praise the author of '**Uncle and Aunt**' in the balanced language of the study. 'I shake hands with you in my heart,' wrote an old Dorsetshire ser-vant from her London basement-kitchen. Those are the words in which he has to be praised.

If, suspicious of so much amiability, we start pulling him to pieces, we discover that contrary to expectation he is a scholar. Like A. E. Housman, he knew exactly what he was doing in verse, and he knew what others had done. He sang Dorset because he had to, but not without premeditation; he was not the gifted rustic who smudged some of the effects in Burns. '**Woak Hill**' itself is composed in an elaborate Persian metre, the Pearl, and even those who discount its pathos are obliged to admire its dexterity. Other poems are written as Ghazels, others imitate or adapt recondite Bardic metres, and all of them have their words in the right places. Light words—rose-petals of words, withered leaves, red dowst o' the ridges; but they fall into their places with the assurance of marble.

> Sweet Be'mi'ster, that bist a-bound
> By green an' woody hills all round,
> Wi' hedges, reache'n up between
> A thousan' vields o'zummer green,
> Where elems' lofty heads do drow
> Their sheädes vor haÿ-meäkers below,
> An' wild hedge-flow'r's do charm the souls
> O' maïdens in their evenèn strolls.

The technical skill of 'wild hedge-flow'r's' is notable; the verse is heavily pulled up by the lightest element in its subject-matter. We pause, we put on the brake for flowers, and the scenes through which we have been sliding coalesce and are saved from too much smoothness. In the last line the natural speed of the verse is released. Forward we go again, after having been clamped by beauty. It is amazing that a writer who always puts the heart first can so keep his head. His genius worked not by a series of happy hits but by using the poetic intelligence, and it is the more amazing since his prose-intelligence was provincial. He believed, for instance, that only Anglo-Saxon words should be employed in English, and he wrote a philological grammar in which vowels become 'breath-sounds,' and consonants 'clippings.' To believe this and yet to create touching poetry in which Anglo-Saxon words are mainly employed is a unique achievement.

His life—except for the loss of his beloved wife and for an occasional trouble over his school—was a very happy one. His temperament, though profound, was equable. He was rooted where he could grow, and was never assailed by lusts or nerve-storms. He could live through the Labourers' Revolt of 1830 without its shadows falling across his verse, and he could help his neighbour, Colonel Shrapnel, with some mathematical formulae. Good Colonel Shrapnel was working out a new type of explosive. When the railway was extended to Dorchester it vexed some people, but he and his pupils found some fine geological specimens in the chalk cuttings. Even the new stove so unwisely installed at St. Peter's did not function fatally.

> The carbonic acid gas [writes his daughter] which rose from beneath the floor of the aisles had first the effect of making the little children drop down insensible, and one by one they were carried out. Next the more delicate young people succumbed, among whom were two or three of William Barnes's household. At length even the strong ones began to suffer and went out in groups, leaving the rector preaching to empty benches, very much bewildered to know what was happening, for the heavy fumes had not yet reached him in the pulpit. The streets were full of groups of suffering people, helping to support others more suffering than themselves. One young woman fell into a swoon which lasted three hours.

All this he survived. The little trials of life, like its deeper sorrows, were accepted by him bravely, and with the belief that joy must prevail. For the joy beyond death he had the authority of his Church; for joy upon earth he could point to the recurring generations of village life:

> Vor daughters ha' mornen when mothers ha'
>   night,
> An' there's beauty alive when the feäirest is
>   dead;
> As when woone sparklèn weäve do sink down
>   from the light,
> Another do come up an' catch it instead.

Yet the heart retains its preferences and joy is compatible with personal loss:

> Smile on, happy maïdens! but I shall noo
>   mwore
> Zee the maïd I do miss under evenèn's dim
>   sky,
> An' my heart is a-touch'd to see you avore
> The doors, vor to chatty an' zee vo'k goo by.

Out of the goodness of his heart, his muse commends sweetness, modesty, innocent mirth, piety, domesticated manliness. He never destroys and seldom criticises, and those who believe that no poetry can be great unless it is rebellious will condemn him as too Sunday-schoolish. But a muse can attend a Sunday school. She disobeys all rules. 'There can be no art without love,' he wrote. That too is a rule, and therefore not universally true, but it is true of his own art. He gathered up all the happiness and beauty he could see around him, he invented more, he poured it out as a continuous offering upon the countryside, and when he was told that the offering would from its nature perish he replied:

'To write in what some may deem a fast out-wearing speech-form may seem as idle as the writing of one's name in snow on a spring day. I cannot help it. It is my mother tongue, and it is to my mind the only true speech of the life that I draw.'

In his old age, as he sat by the fire in the comfortable rectory at Came, he heard the garden gate clanging behind some friends who had just left him, perhaps for ever. The sound moved him to poetry, and he called his daughter and began to dictate '**The Geäte a-vallèn to.**'

> In the zunsheen of our summers
>   Wi' the hay time now a-come
> How busy wer we out a'vield
>   Wi' vew a-left at hwome,
> When waggons rumbled out ov yard,
>   Red-wheeled wi' body blue,
> And back behind 'em loudly slamm'd
>   The geäte a-vallèn to.

When he had finished dictating he paused, and listened to the sounds clanging back through the centuries. 'Observe that word "geäte",' he said. 'That is how King Alfred would have pronounced it, and how it was called in the Saxon Chronicle, which tells us of King Edward, who was slain at Corfe's geäte.' He paused again and continued: 'Ah! if the Court had not been moved to London, then the speech of King Alfred, of which our Dorset is the remnant, would have been the Court language of to-day.'

William Barnes had not many regrets, but this was one of them.

Geoffrey Grigson (essay date 1946)

SOURCE: "William Barnes: 1800-1886," in *The Mint: A Miscellany of Literature, Art and Criticism,* edited by Geoffrey Grigson, George Routledge and Sons Ltd., 1946, pp. 72-101.

[*In the following excerpt, Grigson evaluates Barnes's collected works of poetry and speculates on the influence of his verse.*]

[William Barnes's] first book was **Poetical Pieces,** printed for him in Dorchester in 1820—ten poems in ordinary English. He was then twenty years old, and there is nothing much to mark in these conventional album verses but their neatness, and the fact that he began to write in normal English, and for many years continued to do so. **Orra: A Lapland Tale,** Dorchester-printed in 1822, is worth more. It stands to his later writing like *Gebir* to the rest of Landor, or *Midnight* to Crabbe, or *A Vision of The Mermaids* to the rest of Hopkins, and it came partly out of his reading of Joseph Acerbi's *Travels Through Sweden, Finland, and Lapland to the North Cape,* a travel book published twenty years before, and partly from eighteenth-century visions of the frozen sea. The title-page text comes from Dryden's version of the Georgics:

> There as they say perpetual night is found
> In silence brooding on th' unhappy ground.

And the subject is Orra's search for her lover, a night she spends in a frozen cave, where her boat breaks away, so that the answer (undescribed) must be death. Barnes's unending love of clear, contrasting colour is now put down for the first time:

> Her bosom seemed, beneath her long black
>   hair,
>   Like snowy hills beneath the clouds of
>   night—
> As graceful as the silvery cloud
>   That glides upon the summer air—
>
> And softly now her snowy eyelids close,
>   Weighed down by slumber, o'er bright blue
>   eyes—

There are three seedlings which develop in his later poetry. In *A Vision of the Mermaids* Hopkins's way of making a detailed jewellery out of his observation already shows itself lusciously and thick. In Barnes's *Orra,* you see already how carefully he is going to select, and how sparsely, and so how brightly, he is going to use colours for emotion.

Out of its order—because it is almost as little known—it will be as well to look inside the last of his early books in ordinary English, *Poems Partly of Rural Life,* published in 1846, in London. The sonnets, and probably many of the other poems in this book, were written much earlier—most of the sonnets in 1830 (when he also wrote sonnets in Italian). Barnes's poems never develop an emotional, or rather a psychological, subtlety. When—as often—they are exceedingly sure and moving, simple, elemental feelings are made to pull at our hearts by an intricate subtlety of rhythm and pattern. That subtlety he had not made perfect by 1830, so that the simplicity of statement stands out a bit too much. Yet I do not see why so classical and serene a poem as his fifth sonnet, **"Leaves,"** should remain obscure:

> Leaves of the summer, lovely summer's pride,
>   Sweet is the shade below your silent tree,
>   Whether in waving copses, where ye hide
>   My roamings, or in fields that let me see
>   The open sky; and whether ye may be
> Around the low-stemm'd oak, robust and
>   wide;

Or taper ash upon the mountain side;
  Or lowland elm; your shade is sweet to me.

> Whether ye wave above the early flow'rs
>   In lively green; or whether, rustling sere,
>   Ye fly on playful winds, around my feet,
> In dying autumn; lovely are your bow'rs,
>   Ye dying children of the year;
>   Holy the silence of your calm retreat.

And other poems to be remarked in this book are **"A Winter Night," "Rustic Childhood," "The Lane,"** and **"Burncombe Hollow."** Two stanzas from **"Rustic Childhood"** will show Barnes's eye for light and for objects. Many nineteenth-century poets observed exquisitely, but not many could order this observation so well as Barnes, and space it out with such an infallible effect:

> . . . Or in the grassy drove by ranks
> Of white-stemm'd ashes, or by banks
> Of narrow lanes, in-winding round
> The hedgy sides of shelving ground;
> Where low-shot light struck in to end
> Again at some cool-shaded bend,
> Where we might see through darkleav'd
>   boughs
> The evening light on green hill-brows.
>   I knew you young, and love you now,
>   O shining grass, and shady bough.
>
> Or on the hillock where I lay
> At rest on some bright holyday;
> When short noon-shadows lay below
> The thorn in blossom white as snow;
> And warm air bent the glist' ning tops
> Or bushes in the lowland copse,
> Before the blue hills swelling high
> And far against the southern sky.
>   I knew you young, and love you now,
>   O shining grass, and shady bough.

The same qualities, not yet finally intensified and refined, you can read in **"The Lane"**:

> I love the narrow lane's dark bows,
> When summer glows or winter blows;
> Or when the hedge-born primrose hides
> Its head upon the drybanksides
> By ribby-rinded maple shoots,
> Or round the dark-stemm'd hazel's roots;
> Where weather-beaten ivy winds
> Unwith'ring o'er the elm's brown rinds
> And where the ashes white bough whips
> The whistling air with coal-black tips;
> And where the grassy ground, beside
> The gravel-washing brook, lies wide . . .
> And wither'd leaves, too wet to ride
> The winds, line ev'ry ditches side . . .

I find very little forced or awkward about **"The Lane"**, and I have normalized the italic letters of the original, which Barnes put in to show how the poem was written on the alliterative principles of Old English poetry—again an anticipation by many years of Hopkins's concern with Old English. (Barnes had much else to import into the nineteenth century, out of the wide reaches of his scholarship and his curiosity.)

v

Barnes's poems in normal English up to, and after this 1846 volume, are more numerous and more accomplished than is realized, but in the Dorset dialect he certainly did come to the top of his classical perfection. Thomas Hardy has quoted from Barnes's statement that he wrote in dialect because he could not help it: 'To write in what some may deem a fast out-wearing speech form, may seem as idle as writing one's name in the snow of a spring day. I cannot help it. It is my mother tongue, and is to my mind the only true speech of the life that I draw.'[8] That always struck me as rather a puzzling statement. It is true that, having spoken in dialect as a child, for some time he probably kept a Dorset accent (as Coleridge kept something of a Devonshire accent). As a man, he could no doubt slip from English into Dorset English (he preached his sermons in Dorset); but his first promptings were to write poems in plain English, which he did until he was 34, and continued to do, at intervals, all through his life. And after 1867, for his last nineteen years, he reverted to English and wrote only one poem in dialect.[9] In other words he could perfectly well help it, and often did. Had Barnes made a statement which was obviously untrue? In his fragment of his own life he wrote a little differently: 'As to my Dorset Poems and others, I wrote them so to say, as if I could not well help it, the writing of them was not work but like the playing of music, the refreshment of the mind from care or irksomeness'.[10]

And others—that is to say, it was a general statement about all his poems, and perhaps a deliberate qualifying of his earlier statement that he could not help it—as if he felt that, if nearly true, it was not quite true enough.

Writing in dialect began as a preference, a choice which Barnes made out of his philological delvings. His daughter confirms that in her *Life* of William Barnes and says 'when he began, it was as much the spirit of the philologist as the poet which moved him'. And she quotes his statement that 'the Dorset dialect is a broad and bold shape of the English language, as the Doric was of the Greek. It is rich in humour, strong in raillery and hyperbole; and altogether as fit a vehicle of rustic feeling and thought, as the Doric is found in the *Idyllia* of Theocritus'[11]; and elsewhere, several years after his first Dorset poems were written, but several

years before the first book of them came out, he affirmed that Dorset dialect was 'purer and more regular than that which has been adopted as the national speech'.[12] So, far from being a spontaneous act, this choice of dialect was a learned perversity, which he was able to carry through, since dialect had been his first speech, without the defects of being perverse. Once he began, he found he could do it by nature. Then, no doubt, he could not help continuing.

What I mean will be clarified by thinking of Doughty, who set out to revitalize English by reviving, with an early dictionary always alongside his writing hand, the dead, unspoken English of the sixteenth century. Doughty is unreadable, Barnes is a delight. Barnes is genuine, Doughty a monster, and perverse, with all the defects of perversity.

And as a prolegomenon to the Dorset poems it is worth referring also to Hopkins's letters. Hopkins had already admired Barnes for a good many years when Coventry Patmore sent him three volumes in 1885, and he had some sharp words with Bridges (who admired Doughty) over Bridges' 'contemptuous opinion' of Barnes—'the supposed emotions of peasants'. 'I hold your contemptuous opinion an unhappy mistake: he is a perfect artist and of a most spontaneous inspiration; it is as if Dorset life and Dorset landscape had taken flesh and tongue in the man';[13] and writing earlier to Bridges, he makes a comparison, the rightness of which I will not argue about, between Barnes and Robert Burns. Burns, he says, does not translate: take away the Scotchness and something ordinary remains, but Barnes does translate, and without a great loss.[14] And that at least is true: a lack of knowledge of the euphony of Dorset dialect does not, to my ear, make it impossible to enjoy Barnes's poems clearly and intensely. There are two lines I keep among the furniture of memory, and keep in this form:

> The cuckoo over white-waved seas
> Do come to sing in thy green trees.

Barnes wrote:

> The gookoo over white-weäv'd seas
> Do come to zing in thy green trees.

The translation I make, more or less without meaning to, is much nearer Barnes's writing than, shall I say, Barnes's, or anyone else's reading of the Idyls of Theocritus was ever near to the original sound of Theocritus; and though I have no suspicion that Barnes ever wrote any of his Dorset poems first in ordinary English—in the English he habitually used in his reading, in his letters, and, I suppose, in his thoughts, the English versions that he did make of some of the Dorset poems are no less lively and authentic. The

English version of **"The Mother's Dream,"** for instance, is not less good than the Dorset original.[15]

vi

There is a remark in Llewellyn Powys's letters that Barnes never writes about the sea. That is nearly, if not quite, true of all his poems except **Orra,** and the superb image of the cuckoo. He had no taste for the sea, one of many facts which mark him off from other poets and painters and writers of his time—Darley, Tennyson, Swinburne, Patmore, Courbet, Melville, Emily Brontë, for example. And there is a deeper explanation for it than a land-locked childhood, and Barnes's intense cultivation of his inland, rural imagery. He had no use for the swell and turbulence and endless width of the sea—for its lack of form. He is not a poet for expansive mystery, or for crossing the bar, for the infinite in any way.[16] He does not feel lost, or overwhelmed, or bound to fight against a universal ocean. He accepts, and does not interrogate, the universe. And his form, and his observation, are two things I want to explain. However narrow Barnes may have been, form and observation are qualities in his verse that we can profit by. He was not a fragmentary poet, or a Samuel Palmer with eight or nine years of lyrical vision and explosion. Lyrics such as **"White an' Blue,"** with its airy vitality and youthfulness, were written when Barnes was nearly 70 years old. And often it is not easy, so much are his poems conceived or carried out as a unit, to isolate a stanza or an image for admiration. Coventry Patmore well remarked 'often there is not a single line worth remembering in what is, nevertheless, upon the whole a very memorable poem'.[17] The poems are rhythmically united, and tied together still more tightly by refrains. When I was putting together my anthology *The Romantics*—this will illustrate the unity I am talking of—I ended Barnes's poem **"The Sky A-clearèn"** at a point where I could bring out the pictorial exquisiteness of the third stanza—one of his colour-contrasts:

> The drevèn scud that auvercast
> The zummer sky is all a-past,
> An' softer âir, a-blowèn droo
> The quiv'ren boughs, da shiake the vew
> Laste râin draps off the leaves lik' dew;
>   An' piaviers now a-gettèn dry,
>   Da steam below the zunny sky
>   That's now so vast a-clearèn.

> The shiades that wer a-lost below
> The starmy cloud, agen da show
> Ther mockèn shiapes below the light;
> An' house-walls be a-lookèn white,
> An' vo'ke da stir oonce muore in zight,
>   An' busy birds upon the wing
>   Da whiver roun' the boughs an' zing,
>   To zee the sky a-clearèn.

> Below the hill's an ash; below
> The ash, white elder-flow'rs da blow;
> Below the elder is a bed
> O' robinhoods o' blushin' red;
> An' there, wi' nunches all a-spread,
>   The hây-miakers, wi' each a cup
>   O' drink, da smile to zee hold up
>   The râin, an' sky a-clearèn . . .

It was just possible to do it—to make the multilation, and let it stand—but I felt the poem, like that, seemed to bleed. Its form, like a statue with an arm broken above the elbow, foretold the rest. The rest, it is true, is touched—this is Barnes's Victorian vice—with a weak sentiment, even if the remaining stanzas are demanded by the broken pattern:

> . . . Mid blushèn maïdens wi' their zong
> Still draw their white-stemm'd reäkes among
> The long-back'd weäles an' new meäde pooks,
> By brown-stemm'd trees an' cloty brooks;
> But have noo call to spweil their looks
>   By work, that God could never meäke
>   Their weaker han's to underteäke,
>   Though skies mid be a-cleärèn.

> 'Tis wrong vor women's han's to clips
> The zull an' reap-hook, speädes an' whips;
> An men abroad, should leäve, by right,
> Their bit o' vier up at night
>   An' hang upon the hedge to dry
>   Their snow-white linen, when the sky
>   In winter is a-clearèn.

But what mutilation would be possible at all in a later poem such as **"My Love's Guardian Angel,"** where the refrain is worked up to the emotional weight of its last use?

> As in the cool-aïr'd road I come by,
>   —in the night,
> Under the moon-climb'd height o' the sky,
>   —in the night,
> There by the lime's broad lim's I did stäy,
> While in the aïr dark sheädes were at pläy
> Up on the windor-glass, that did keep
> Lew vrom the wind my true-love asleep,
>   —in the night.

> While in the grey-wall'd height o' the tow'r,
>   —in the night,
> Sounded the midnight bell wi' the hour,
>   —in the night,
> There come a bright-heaïr'd angel that shed
> Light vrom her white robe's zilvery thread,
> Wi' her vore-vinger held up to meäke
> Silence around lest sleepers mid weäke,
>   —in the night.

'Oh! then,' I whisper'd, 'do I behold
      —in the night,
Linda, my true-love, here in the cwold,
      —in the night?'
'No', she did answer, 'you do misteäke:
She is asleep, 'tis I be aweäke,
I be her angel brightly a-drest
Watchèn her slumber while she do rest,
      —in the night.'

Zee how the clear win's, brisk in the bough,
      —in the night,
While they do pass, don't smite on her brow,
      —in the night;
Zee how the cloud-sheädes naïseless do zweep
Over the house-top where she's asleep.
You, too, goo on, though times mid be near,
When you, wi' me, mid speäk to her ear
      —in the night.

vii

Barnes's Italian journals I have not been able to see, but he seldom put down any more detail about the poems he was engaged on than a laconic 'scrivendo versi' or 'versi scritti',[18] so it would not be possible from them to date either their evolution or his complicated experiments in form. *Poems of Rural Life in the Dorset Dialect,* his third book of poems, was published in 1844, when he was already in his forties. Much of the contents must be earlier than that: he had written his first dialect poem, **"The 'Lotments"**, I think, ten years before when he was recovering from an illness.[19] And here I may give the names of all his later collections. Few libraries have his poems complete. *Orra* is not in the British Museum. The recent *Cambridge Bibliography of English Literature* doubts if there is a copy, though two exist, as well as the manuscript, in the Museum at Dorchester. After the first Dorset collection of 1844 and the English poems of 1846, came in 1859 *Hwomely Rhymes;* in 1863 *Poems in the Dorset Dialect; Third Collection;* in 1868 *Poems of Rural Life in Common English;* in 1870 *A Selection from Unpublished Poems,* published by Winterbourne Monkton school; and in 1906, posthumously, *Poems in the Dorset Dialect,* printed by the *Dorset County Chronicle.* Several of his best poems are in this last rare pamphlet, which the British Museum lacks, as it lacks *Orra* and the pamphlet of 1870.

Through all these books, all these poems, he steadily keeps up his sheer skill, with much variation in form. Hardy noticed that 'on some occasions he would allow art to overpower spontaneity, and to cripple inspiration'[20]; but he allows that rarely enough, and his art is so fine and certain that he seldom seems monotonous through mannered repetition, or overworking, of suc-cessful effects. If I read Clare's poems, so deficient was Clare in this cultivated strength of Barnes, I find myself overfed with the visionary substance of poetry, which has simply been put down in the readiest, easiest and most obvious jog-trot form. Barnes was less completely *in* the world of nature than Clare. He does not achieve Clare's absolute hits,—he is not a seer—but he does not come down to Clare's dribble of absolute misses.

Form to him was fitness: he wrote several things about it, and he explored as well the origin and simplest nature of poetry. 'Matters most interesting to me are those belonging to man, in his life of body mind and soul, so in his speech, manners, laws and works.'[21] As for man, 'the natural man is unfallen man, as he was finished by the hand of God, when He saw all that He had made to be very good'.[22] And whatever fallen man may be, 'the beautiful in nature is the unmarred result of God's first creative or forming will . . . . the beautiful in art is the result of an unmistaken working in man in accordance with the beautiful in nature'.[23] He maintained 'there is no high aim but the beautiful. Follow nature: work to her truth'.[24] But 'the beautiful is also the good by reason of a fitness or harmony which it possesses'.[25] He admired 'the beauty and truth of colour and action in the Dutch school; and'—since he is anything but Dutch—'the harmony, tone, and effect of colour, even with bad drawing, and, in some cases, it may be with a want of depth, in a work of Turner'.[26] In all the beautiful things of a landscape, he discovered fitness—'fitness of water to irrigate growth, and to run for all lips to the sea; fitness of land to take and send onward the stream; fitness of strength to weight, as of the stem to the head of a tree; fitness of elasticity to force, as that of the poplar, and the bough whose very name is bending, and the bullrush and grass to the wind; fitness of protection to life, as in the armed holly and thorn, and the bush, or ditch-guarded epilobium; and a harmony of the whole with the good of man'.[27]

Harmony was a favourite word, and harmonic proportion a favourite topic, with Barnes. He wanted harmonic proportion in churches—'that too little understood and wonderfully neglected principle of harmony in form as well as in sound'[28] ought to be applied, so he maintained, to the relative heights of the tower, the nave and the chancel. He framed his pictures and bound his books in harmonic proportion. He held that poetry must keep in with the fitness of nature and must conform to the nature of speech and the natural cause of poetry among men. 'Speech was shapen of the breath-sounds of speakers, for the ear of hearers, and not from speechtokens (letters) in books',[29] and discovering what he could about the origins of poetry from books of travel and philology and his own study of European and Oriental literature, he believed that poetry did not spring from cultivation or refinement, but from elemental necessity: 'there has never been a full-shaped tongue that has sounded from the lips of generations of any tribe without the voice of song; and . . . to a bookless and unwriting people verse is rather a need than a joy'.[30] It is curious to find him down in his Dorset isolation writing that 'the measures of song . . . may themselves be measured, not only by the steps of the dramatic dance, but by the steps of a march, or by the strokes of oars, as in the Tonga songs of the kind called Towálo or paddle songs, which Mariner says are never accompanied with instrumental music, but which are short songs sung in canoes while paddling, the strokes of the paddles being coincident with the cadence of the tune'.[31]

In English poetry, his own practice was based on the Enlightenment; and no doubt he owed that salutary basis, in part, to being out of the swim, to being brought up in a countryside where the eighteenth century was still alive in the nineteenth; and to associating early with old-fashioned men for whom the Augustans were more important, still, than Wordsworth, or Keats, or Shelley. Such is the viable advantage of not always being modern, or up to date. He was little touched with an Elizabethan or a Miltonic romanticism, much as he studied the structure and prosody of Milton and the Elizabethans. Spontaneity, singing because you must, 'like the playing of music, the refreshment of the mind from care or irksomeness'—yes. But he read Dryden and Pope, and he quoted Mrs. Cooper on Waller's poetry, that Waller 'rode the Pegasus of wit with the curb of good manners'.[32] It would be interesting to know when he first read and absorbed the Earl of Mulgrave's *Essay Upon Poetry,* with its emphatic praise of Homer and its emphasis on 'exact *Propriety* of Words and Thought' in the writing of songs:

> *Expression* easie, and the *Fancy* high,
> Yet *that* not seem to *creep,* nor *this* to *fly;*
> No Words transpir'd, but in such *order* all,
> As, tho' by Care, may seem by Chance to *fall.*

Mulgrave, said Barnes, 'writes to fancy or genius

> . . . I am fain
> To check thy course, and use the needful rein.

Without *judgement,* fancy is but mad', he quoted, and went on, 'A Welsh bardic canon says: the three qualifications of poetry are endowment of *genius, judgement* from experience, and *happiness of mind. '*[33] Paraphrasing Mulgrave, he liked lines which are written 'with a skill that conceals skill', that 'keep all the strait rules of verse, yet flow as freely as if they were wholly untied'. Then, 'we cannot but feel that kind of pleasure which is afforded by the easy doing of a high feat, besides that which is afforded by good writing'.[34]

After all that, neither the complexity of his lyric dodges and formalities, nor his care (how different from much in Tennyson) to pick over his observation and select from it, and never or seldom to overcrowd, continue to be surprising, however rare they are in other men's poetry between 1830 and 1870.

To analyse Barnes's skill exactly, one would need some degree of his own knowledge of Italian, of Persian (Petrarch and Sa'di were his favourites) and of Welsh, and other languages as well. On his eighteenth-century basis of 'exact propriety of word and thought' he heightened his verse in every way he could, by setting himself tasks of every kind. There are clues to this heightening, and to his mind, in the elaborate exemplification of rhyme in his ***Philological Grammar*** (1854), a book which he 'formed from a comparison of more than sixty languages'. He sympathizes with all rhyming tasks which can be alloyed into the structure of a poem. 'A poet may impose upon himself any task,—as that he will introduce some forechosen word into every distich or line, or exclude it from his poem; or that every line shall end with a noun; or that his poem shall take a chosen form to the sight; or he may bind himself to work out any unusual fancy.' He mentions George Herbert's poems in the form of wings or an altar, reproves Addison for calling Milton's matching of words of the same root 'poor and trifling', as in

> That brought into this world a world of woe
> Which tempted our attempt.

'However poor and trifling this figure might have seemed to Addison, it is sometimes very striking, as shown in the spontaneous language of mental emotion', and he gives other examples of the root-matching, 'called by the Persians . . . derivation', from Virgil, Sophocles, Crabbe, Tennyson, Cowper, Coleridge, George Herbert, Shakespeare and other Elizabethans. Other poets of his age had taken from Elizabethans only an attitude, or fairy nothings (compare much of Darley or Hood), or insubstantial horrors. Barnes looked at the way they wrote, their word-repetitions, their collocation of two words alike in sound, unlike in meaning, their acrostics, their elaborate alliterations, and so on, which are paralleled by the elaborations and conventions of the Persian mediæval poetry he so much enjoyed. The Persian poets and the Elizabethan lyric writers (and, for that matter the English poets of the Enlightenment whom Barnes learned from first of all) concerned themselves more with virtuosity of language than with originality of ideas. Beside the Augustan uniformity of common sense and a commonly held stock of knowledge, one could place the statement of the Arab historian, Ibn Khaldún, that 'the Art of Discourse, whether in verse or prose, lies only in words, not in ideas . . . ideas are common to all, and are at the disposal of every understanding, to employ as it will, needing no art'.[35] That certainly was how Barnes thought of poetry, elaborate in art, simple in ideas, and straightforward in effect. And he transfers much of the elaboration that he discusses to his own verse—for example, from Eastern poetry the 'kind of word rhyming, or word-matching' called *adorning,* 'in which every word of a line is answered by another of the same measure and rhyme in the other line of the distich':

> As trees be bright
> Wi' bees in flight.[36]

The Persians, he says, use an ornamental punning or 'full-matching . . .' a full likeness in sound, of words which differ in meaning. He used it in **"The Wold Wall."**

> Ah! well-a-dae! O wall adieu.

He used the peculiar parallelism of Hebrew poetry—the principle of 'Tell it not in Gath, publish it not in the streets of Askalon'—in **"Melhill Feast,"** for example:

> The road she had come by then was soon
> The one of my paths that best I knew,
> By glittering gossamer and dew,
> *Evening by evening, moon by moon—*

or in the uncollected **"Troubles of the Day"**:

> As there, along the elmy hedge, I go
> By banksides white with parsley—parsley-
> bloom.

Welsh and Irish poetry were sources for him. For instance, in Irish poetry 'there is a kind of under-rhyme, or rhyme called *union,* which is the under-rhyming or rhyming of the last word or breath-sound in one line, with one in the middle of the following one'. Here it is in **"Times o' Year"**:

> Here did swäy the eltrot *flow'rs*
> When the *hours* o' night wer vew,
> An' the zun, wi' eärly *beams*
> Brighten'd *streams,* an' dried the dew . . .

But his most pronounced Celtic borrowing is the *cynghanedd,* the Welsh repetition of consonatal sounds in the two parts of a line, divided by a cæsura, which is better known in English through its use by Gerard Hopkins. The familiar instance comes as a refrain in the poem so celebrated through its musical setting, **"My Orcha'd in Linden Lea,"** in which the apple tree

> Do leän down low in Linden Lea,

where the *cynghanedd* consonants are DLNDNL/NLNDNL; but there are plenty more, such as 'In our abode in Arby Wood', or 'An' love to roost, where they can live at rest'.

Hopkins was made a bit uneasy about this particular borrowing. Barnes he wrote 'comes, like Homer and all poets of native epic, provided with epithets, images, and so on which seem to have been tested and digested for a long while in their native air and to have a *keeping* which nothing else could give; but in fact they are rather all of his own finding and first throwing off'.[37] This he thought 'very high praise' and he found his rhythms 'charming and characteristic', as they are, certainly. But his use of *cynghanedd* he did not think successful. 'To tell the truth, I think I could do that better' and he added that it was 'an artificial thing and not much in his line'.[38] I believe Hopkins was half-true, and half-wrong in not realizing how much Barnes's line was at once conscious and unconscious art—half-true, because although Barnes's most perfect poems are sometimes elaborate tasks, they are usually ones influenced by his borrowings from world prosody, but not embodying them pure and direct.

Barnes's soul was not lit by sulphur, he did not, like Melville, measure himself against fate or walk on the sea-bottom, 'left bare by faith's receding wave', or wrestle with God, or hang, as Hopkins hung, desperately, on the dreadful cliffs of the mind; he may, as Hopkins agreed with Bridges in saying, have 'lacked fire' (though that is not always so, in my judgment), but he *knew* and felt as much about the function in human life, the origins, nature, and adornment, of lyrical poetry, and its form, as any poet who has written in English. To paraphrase a valuable remark of Auden's, he disciplined himself and proved the power of his creative impluses by accepting the limitations of form. He created a system of poetry for his own use.

viii

And Barnes knew also about the interest of poetry. Form and interest, structure and selective observation—in these, in the lack of them, have been most apparent the weakness of English poetry (and painting too), in the last hundred years. Barnes, Hopkins, Hardy (though his forms, in spite of his study of Barnes, have an intricate tight roughness like a clump of brambles), Auden, though not I think Yeats, and not Eliot, in spite of their degrees of stature, have been strong where others have been weak in both of these qualities. Observation, not always well selected, and seldom well alloyed and organized in form, has been common enough. But by itself the similarity of the shape of poems on the pages of books shows at one look the monotonous lack of skill in form, and lack of concern for it, which have been so common. In the matter of interest, in selective observation, it may be that we are catching up; it may be that talented English writers of verse go on being deficient now mainly in any passion for the structure of verse (in these, in structure and interest, may I say that those admirers of each other, Miss Sitwell, who chatters like four knitting needles about vowels and consonants and the colour and physique of sound, and Mr. Stephen Spender, are still in the infant's class?). But, whatever the advance, it may be just as well to finish on Barnes's epithets, images, and substance.

I have quoted Barnes's view of nature, though not completely: man has fallen, and nature as well is not unmarred, but 'the beautiful in nature'—that is 'the unmarred result of God's first creative or forming will' and 'the beautiful in art is the unmistaken working of man' in accordance with this unmarred result, which is good also by its fitness or harmony. The fallen working to the unfallen.[39] 'Look for pleasure', Barnes wrote, 'at the line of beauty, and other curves of charming grace in the wind-blown stems of grass, and bowing barley or wheat; in the water-shaken bulrush, in the leaves of plants, and in the petals of flowers; in the outlines of birds, and even their feathers and eggs; in the flowing lines of the greyhound, the horse and cat, and other animals; in the shell of the mollusc, and in the wings and markings of insects; in the swell of the downy cheek, the rounded chin, the flowing bendings of the pole and back, and the outswelling and inwinding lines from the head to the leg of woman stepping onward in the pride of youthful grace; and tell us whether nature does not show us graceful curves enough to win us from ugliness, even in a porringer.'[40] And 'fitness' made him an enemy of veneers and shams: 'does nature make you a handsome tree or flower near your town, and slight her work in the world? or light up your water for a crowd-sought park, and not for the wanderers in the wilds? No. Nature and true art are faithful. . . . We have churches with a fine, high-wrought street end, and brick walls behind, out of man's sight (poor Pugin's eyesore!), as if the builders worked not for good, but for man; and so a low aim has wrought a low work of art. Of such a sham some writer speaks somewhat in the following strain,—for I quote from memory:

> They built the front, upon my word,
>   As fine as any abbey:
> But thinking they might cheat the Lord,
>   They made the back part shabby.'[41]

Nature must therefore be sifted for the authentic, for the beautiful in nature; and the heavy grain of this sifting, its force, is concentrated into Barnes's epithets— 'green-treed':

> As evenèn aïr, in green-treed spring,
> Do sheäke the new-sprung pa'sley bed—

or 'sweet-breath'd':

> An' sweet-breath'd children's hangèn heads
> Be laid wi' kisses, on their beds—

or 'dim-roaded' night, or 'blue-hill'd' as an epithet for the world, or 'sky-back'd', for the flight of clouds, and many more—epithets which are impressed with the force of experience. He told Palgrave that 'he had taken Homer, and him only, as his model in aiming at the one proper epithet in describing'.[42] And this sifting gives his epithets a serenity and wide truth that one misses in the particular detail of much Preraphaelite description, from Tennyson to the passionate observation of Hopkins. Read, or broadcast to an audience who have not the texts in front of them and do not know them, Dyer's eighteenth-century "Grongar Hill" and Tennyson's over-embroidered "Progress of Spring" (an early poem, it is true), and one poem is fuddling, the other comes to the audience clear through the simplicity and sparingness of its effects. Barnes's poems, are, for effects, half-way between the two; but riding his Pegasus on the rein, he would never go so far from the wide truth as Tennyson peering unfamiliarly into the inside of a horse-chestnut flower for an image:

> a but less vivid hue
> Than of that islet in the chestnut-bloom
> Flamed in his cheek—

Barnes holds the rein at some such limit as 'where the black-spotted bean-bloom is out' or 'thatch-brow'd windows'.

He keeps in with this restraint in preferring the quickly-taken truth of descriptions of states of light, states of air, and states of colour—sometimes all three in one. For instance in **"My Love's Guardian Angel,"** which I have quoted:

> As in the cool-aïr'd road I come by,
>   —in the night . . .

in

> High over head the white-rimm'd clouds went on,
> Wi' woone a-comèn up, vor woone a-gone;
> An' feäir they floated in their sky-back'd flight,
> But still they never meäde a sound to me—

or

> I'm out when snow's a-lyèn white
>   In keen-aïr'd vields that I do pass,
> An' moonbeams, vrom above, do smite
>   On ice an' sleeper's window-glass—

or in three stanzas from **"In the Spring"**:

> . . . O grey-leafy pinks o' the geärden,
>   Now bear her sweet blossoms;

Now deck wi' a rwose bud, O briar,
  Her head in the Spring.

O light-rollèn wind, blow me hither
  The vaïce ov her talkèn,
O bring vrom her veet the light doust
  She do tread in the Spring.

O zun, meäke the gil' cups all glitter
  In goold all around her,
An' meäke o' the deäisys' white flowers
  A bed in the Spring . . .

But Barnes's use of colour is often, as I have said, the setting of one colour sharp against another one, a visual antithesis, like two halves of a line in Pope balanced against each other. Long after he had begun this, he began to look deliberately for its counterpart and warrant in nature, making a list of 'the contacts of sundry pairs of colours on natural bodies', such as white and black in the bean blossom, yellow and orange in toadflax or the brimstone butterfly. 'Nature is very sparing of showy contrasts of warm and cold colours. Red and blue are very rare, and of yellow and blue the cases are but few; and black and blue are found in lepidoptera more often than white and blue are seen in our Flora and Fauna.'[43]

Blue and white, all the same, was the coupling he most often repeated, though frequently he set yellow against black:

There near the wheatrick's yellow back,
  That shone like gold before the sky,
Some rooks with wings of glossy black
  Came on down wheeling from on high
And lightly pitched upon their feet
Among the stubble of the wheat—

White sometimes against red (I have quoted one example—elder flowers against red campion):

Oh! the cherry-tree blossom'd all white
  And again with its cherries was red—

Or white against green as in the cuckoo lines or **"Zummer Thoughts in Winter Time"**:

When white sleev'd mowers' whetted bleädes
Rung sh'ill along the green-bough'd gleädes.

But blue and white began with *Orra* (and even before that in a poem in his first book of 1820):

And softly now her snowy eyelids close,
  Weighed down by slumber, o'er her bright
  blue eyes,
As bound beneath the cold and wintry snows,
  The azure wave of ocean frozen lies—

and they were observed together again and again, in his wife, in skies, in butterflies, in flowers against sky or reflected sky. Examples are in **"White an' Blue,"** where the colours are the substance of the poem, in **"The Water Crowfoot"**:

Thy beds o' snow-white buds do gleam
  So feäir upon the sky-blue stream

—in **"Zummer Stream"**:

There by the path, in grass knee-high,
Wer buttervlies in giddy flight,
All white above the deäsies white,
Or blue below the deep blue sky

—in **"Not Sing at Night"** (a poem not reprinted since its appearance in the Poet's Corner which Barnes inhabited so often in the *Dorset County Chronicle*):

Or where below the clear blue sky
The snow white linen hung to dry,

And blue and white well express the mathematics, the clear, the serene, and the harmonious in Barnes's make. Blue and white are the serenity of nature—the nature, said Barnes, which 'is the best school of art', adding 'and of schools of art among men those are best that are nature's best interpreters'.[44]

ix

We have too much of a habit now of reflecting our discontent with an author's political convictions, or his political indifference, or his inconsistency, back on to all of his work, as though the issues of the sadness of our time were immeasurably greater than ever before in the human race. We forget that there are still for each of us what we must regard as constant transcending verities, that what appears to be 'reaction' may be much more vitalizing than the thirty-shilling suit of modernity or *avantegarde,* or immediate politics, that being a trimmer need not imply a lack of inward truth, whether the trimmers are Dryden, or Turgenev, or a good many living European authors who have touches of Munich about them. Barnes may, in a very good sense, be a minor poet; but not in the sense that his writing is a mess of words occasionally lit by a sparkle of pure intuition. And I may have suggested, wrongly, if you recall the quotation from Patmore, that Barnes was indifferent to the times, or separated from them entirely. As far as not being indifferent possesses value, that was not so. The anxious bewilderment between faith and science scarcely reached him, and scarcely ripples in his poetry. I can only recall one open reference to it in his poem, **"The Happy Daes When I Wer Young."**

Vrom where wer all this venom brought
To kill our hope an' fâint our thought?

Clear Brook! they water coodden bring
Sich venom vrom thy rocky spring—

—the venom being 'what's a-ta'k'd about By many now,—that to despise The la's o' God an' man is wise'; and he affirmed in another poem

My peace is rest, my faïth is hope
An' freedom's my unbounded scope.

'That is a subject connected with politics, not with poetry', he said to his son when he reminded him of a request that he should write a Dorset recruiting poem. 'That is a subject connected with politics, not with poetry. I have never written any of my poems but one with a drift. I write pictures which I see in my mind'.[45] The one poem, the early Dorset Eclogue, **"The Times,"** with its fable of the pig and the crow, he had written against the Chartists. He felt that the Chartists would unsettle the Dorset labourer without remedying his condition; and, with his views of God, nature, man, harmony and fitness, what did disturb him, deeply, was the unfitness he saw in the social development of the nineteenth century, and in the consequent decay of freedom; the unfitness which caused him to write the curious amalgam of wisdom and simplicity he called *Views of Labour and Gold* (1859), in which he was concerned 'to show the possible effect of the increase of great working-capitals and monopolies on the labourer's freedom or welfare'. Two extracts will give its tenor:

'The kindness which is done by capital when it affords employment to people from whom, by a monopoly, it has taken their little business, is such as one might do to a cock by adorning his head with a plume made of feathers pulled out of his own tail.'

'It is more healthy to rack one's mind in effectual devices to win a skilful end, than to work as a machine without a free aim or thought; and so, as a Hindoo poet says, to be like a smith's bellows, breathing without life'.

But Barnes's social views, simply consistent with his views of the world, of life and art, are only a stroke in the drawing of a full portrait of Barnes. They are less important than the wavy, mazy, slow, river-like rhythm of his poem **"The Clote"** (clote is the yellow water-lily):

O zummer clote, when the brook's a-slidèn
So slow an' smooth down his zedgy bed,
Upon thy brode leaves so siafe a-ridèn
The water's top wi' thy yoller head,
By black-rin'd allers,
An' weedy shallers,
Thee then dost float, goolden zummer clote.

—less important than the rhythm with which he patterned his life and his impulses to describe and sing. There are poems which are slightly embarrassing, in which Barnes tails—I hesitate to describe it so—into a provincialism of sentiment; but his tailings are more innocent and slighter than the monstrous wallowing falls into the same weakness—not confined to Dorset—of some of Barnes's greatest coevals.[46] And even his weakest poems are strengthened by their pattern and dexterity. In the narrow sense, there are not art-and-society reasons for urging that Barnes should be read, urging that he should have the status given to him ungrudgingly by Patmore, Hopkins, and Thomas Hardy. He may—and I think he did—give to English writing more than has ever been suggested or allowed. Hardy he very much influenced, and Hardy's rhetoric and pattern were the first to strike the authentic note in Auden's life: 'He was both my Keats and my Carl Sandburg'[47]—the note and the Contemporary Scene. And how much effect did he have on Gerard Hopkins, who read Barnes when he was an undergraduate, complimented him by critical admiration, and put some of his poems to music? Both Hopkins and Barnes were after a revitalized language for poetry. Were Barnes's poems—to name only a little thing—the seeds of Hopkins's own concern for Welsh and for Anglo-Saxon? Is it entirely a coincidence of period and a consequence of identical aims that 'or as a short-stand-night-watch quick foreflown' and 'which at early morn with blowing-green-blithe bloom'[48] are not lines by Hopkins, but translations from Old Friesian by Barnes? Or that both invented their own critical terms rather than take them ready-made and devitalized from philologists and prosody? Or was Barnes not the instigator of much which has come down through Hardy and through Hopkins as well?

Yet these questions are only, again, the more trivial baits to reading him—to reading one of the few nineteenth-century poets who 'conceived of art, like life, as being a self-discipline rather than a self-expression'. Barnes, if he were more read, could become one of the healthy, if lesser, antidotes to the Romantic disease. He is not a rustic aberration; and it is to me one of the signs of the uninquisitive untasteful scholarship and spiritual laziness of scholars and publishers in England that there is no complete, critical edition of Barnes, and that no one has ever brushed together, for example, his fragments of translation and the many English poems not included in his three English collections.

Certainly Thomas Hardy's *Selected Poems of William Barnes* (it is still in print) did Barnes a service; but it neither served him, nor does it serve us, with our present change of need, by any means adequately.

Just as Barnes kept in Dorset during his life, so he has been kept there ever since. The point is to deliver him—

to extract him from his rather snobbishly affixed integument of mud; to exhibit his mind's cool-aired quality.

Notes

[7] 'W. Barnes left no list of his poems, and rarely talked of them . . . he seems to have written when the inspiration was upon him, and, having written, he was satisfied.' His son, Rev. W. Miles Barnes, in the introduction to *Poems in the Dorset Dialect,* 1906, p. 2.

[8] Preface to *Select Poems of William Barnes,* 1908, p. viii. For the full statement see preface to *Poems of Rural Life in the Dorset Dialect, Third Collection,* 1862, p. iii.

[9] Introduction by Rev. W. Miles Barnes, to *Poems in the Dorset Dialect,* 1906.

[10] 'Notes on the Life of William Barnes', by himself. MS. transcript in possession of the Barnes family.

[11] *Life,* p. 84.

[12] *Gentleman's Magazine,* January 1840, p. 31.

[13] *The Letters of Gerard Manley Hopkins to Robert Bridges,* ed. C. C. Abbott, 1935, p. 221. The date of the letter is Sept. 1st, 1885.

[14] *Ibid.,* p. 87, August 14th, 1879.

[15] The Dorset original of 'The Mother's Dream' is in *Poems in the Dorset Dialect,* 1906. The Rev. W. Miles Barnes explains in the introduction that many of the poems in *Poems of Rural Life in Common English* (1868) were translations from the Dorset.

[16] Tennyson—it is typical of the nineteenth century—writes of death as crossing the bar and putting out to sea. The eighteenth-century attitude is to sail calmly or contemplate storm from the quiet of the harbour, e.g. Matthew Green:

> I make (may heav'n propitious send
> Such wind and weather to the end)
> Neither becalm'd, nor over-blown,
> Life's voyage to the world unknown.

(The Spleen)

[17] 'William Barnes, the Dorsetshire Poet', *Macmillan's Magazine,* vol. vi, 1862, p. 156.

[18] *Poems in the Dorset Dialect,* 1906. Introduction, p. 3.

[19] '1834 I wrote the first of my *Poems of Rural Life in the Dorset Dialect* . . . The first Dorset Idyl was written in my room when I was uphalening from a sickness, an ailing of the liver.' MS. Scrapbook in Dorchester Museum.

[20] *Select Poems of William Barnes,* 1908. Preface, p. ix.

[21] Transcript of MS. 'Notes on the Life of William Barnes', by himself, in possession of the Barnes family.

[22] Review: 'Patmore's Poems', in *Fraser's Magazine,* July, 1863, p. 130.

[23] 'Thoughts on Beauty and Art', *Macmillan's Magazine,* vol. IV, May-Oct. 1861, p. 126.

[24] *Ibid.,* p. 126.

[25] *Ibid.,* p. 128.

[26] *Ibid.,* p. 137.

[27] *Ibid.,* p. 133.

[28] Letter on harmonic proportion as applied to churches in *Gentleman's Magazine,* December, 1843.

[29] From the 'Fore-say' in *An Outline of English Speech-Craft,* 1878.

[30] 'The Old Bardic Poetry', *Macmillan's Magazine,* vol. XVI, 1867, p. 306.

[31] 'On the Credibility of Old Song, History and Tradition', *Fraser's Magazine,* September, 1863.

[32] 'Plagiarism and Coincidence', *Macmillan's Magazine,* vol. XV, November, 1886, p. 77:

[33] *Ibid.,* p. 77.

[34] 'The Old Bardic Poetry', *Macmillan's Magazine,* vol. XVI, 1867, p. 307.

[35] Quoted by E. G. Browne: *A Literary History of Persia,* vol. II, 1906, p. 85.

[36] This and the few subsequent quotations are from Barnes's *Philological Grammar* (1854).

[37] In *Further Letters of Gerard Manley Hopkins,* ed. C. C. Abbott, 1938. Letter to Patmore, October 6th, 1886.

[38] *Ibid.*

[39] 'Thoughts on Beauty and Art', *Macmillan's Magazine,* vol. IV, 1861, p. 126.

[40] *Ibid.,* p. 128.

[41] Thoughts on Beauty and Art', *Macmillan's Magazine,* vol. IV, 1861, p. 136.

[42] *Francis Turner Palgrave,* by Gwenllian Palgrave, 1899, p. 185.

[43] 'Thoughts on Beauty and Art', *Macmillan's Magazine,* vol. IV, 1861, p. 132.

[44] 'Thoughts on Beauty and Art', *Macmillan's Magazine,* vol. IV, 1861, p. 132.

[45] *Life of William Barnes,* p. 323.

[46] There is nothing metaphysical about Barnes; and the Persian poet he appears to have liked best, Sa'dí, was also the least metaphysical, or mystical, of the great Persians, the most 'homely', and the one most abundantly translated into English between 1850 and the eighties; though he also admired Háfiz. Barnes greatly liked *The Angel in the House;* but I doubt if Patmore's *Unknown Eros* (which he read) would have spoken much to him.

[47] 'A Literary Transference', *Southern Review,* vol. VI, No. I, Summer, 1940, p. 80.

[48] *Early England and the Saxon English,* 1869, p. 173.

Rayner Unwin (essay date 1954)

SOURCE: "The Language of Speech: Relph and Barnes," in *The Rural Muse: Studies in the Peasant Poetry of England,* George Allen and Unwin Ltd., 1954, pp. 143-64.

[*In the following excerpt, Unwin investigates Barnes's philological writings and describes the "pastoral simplicity" of his dialect poetry.*]

Except as a forerunner [Josiah] Relph is of little importance compared with the greatest English dialect poet, William Barnes. It happened that Barnes was born in the first year of the nineteenth century, but the dates of his life and works are singularly irrelevant in considering his poetry. He was as isolated and independent of external influence as any poet that has ever written. The sea of faith might ebb or flow, passions might be stirred and intellects perplexed, but Barnes continued to live a tranquil and happy life in the Vale of Blackmore. Dorsetshire was his microcosm, and the intellectual isolation in which he lived unnoticed was to him a calm but complete unit of existence. Tennyson, who, after having drawn the elderly Barnes into uneasy speculations on Darwin and Pantheism, commented "he is not accustomed to strong views theologic," might have extended his statement without confining it to theology.

Barnes's retirement was not occasioned by misanthropy, but because he needed to be withdrawn in order to judge things in their simplicity and fitness. The beautiful and the good (terms that in his poetry would never be left naked in their abstraction) were to be found in nature, and through nature in art. Their virtues would be evident from the harmony and accord that were inherent in them. The craft of interpretation was a timeless one; and Barnes in his restrained artistry had much of the classicist in him, in the minute clarity of his observation something of Pre-Raphaelite brilliance, and in his ability to use the inanimate in nature as a touchstone for human feeling he held a key to Romanticism. But he would acknowledge no master except Homer, and no influences from poets in his own tongue. He was, as Patmore described him, "of no school but that of Nature."

The biography of Barnes lacks the pathos of a peasant-poet struggling for fame. Such attention as he did, belatedly, attract he did not solicit, and ambition was but one of the strong passions that had no part in his life. His father was a farmer in the Vale of Blackmore, in Dorset, and William in due course was sent to a nearby Dame's School where he received a rudimentary education, and displayed an enthusiasm for learning that made him parochially noticeable. Having left school Barnes's ability to write gained him a post in a solicitor's office, and gave him time to pursue his exceedingly eclectic bents. He studied Persian and Hindustani, explored the intricacies of Welsh poetry, and wrote a diary in Italian. His interests extended to mechanics and mathematics, in which he was something of an inventor, for he succeeded in making an instrument to describe ellipses, and with less success, an ingenious pair of swimming-shoes. He played the flute, violin, and piano, made chessmen on a lathe, and produced engravings after the manner of Bewick. These are but some of the astonishing variety of interests that Barnes displayed from an early age.

As might be expected the solicitor's office was soon exchanged for the village school. But schoolmastering in a rural district gave Barnes little opportunity to meet or converse with his peers. He himself was shy and awkward, but not, by any interpretation, naïve or ignorant. Yet in his love of the countryside and of domestic pursuits he was a voluntary exile from all contemporary intellectual contacts. Barnes married, became prematurely bald, was a humane disciplinarian (and consequently a popular schoolmaster), and settled down to live amongst a small circle of friends of intellectually low stature.

Barnes's literary activity was hardly less diverse than his other enthusiasms. During his days as a schoolmaster he wrote comedies for the local theatre (none of them is preserved), and published privately in Dorchester a small volume of verses, and ***Orra, a Lapland Tale.*** Neither of these productions is particularly memorable, although they contain the seeds of the brightness, clarity, and selectivity of colour that were to appear in his later works.

Barnes's chief occupation during his early pedagogical career was to write school-books. These ranged in subject between geography and etymology, perspective and Roman numerals, Aesop and Hindu fakirs. At first they were privately printed, but later he contributed his random thoughts to such periodicals as *The Gentleman's Magazine.* At one time Barnes even considered writing "a work of fiction," and was only deterred for lack of a plot.

Barnes possessed that rare combination, an ever-gleaning mind and a fluent pen. In his activities he was nearest, perhaps, to the complete man of the Renaissance, to whom no knowledge was worthless or unattainable in whatever field of learning it lay. Gradually, however, his interests crystallized, not towards poetry, which always remained to him "simply a refreshment of mind from cares and irksomeness," but towards philology. It was this enormous mistake in what he conceived to be his vocation that sheltered Barnes from the notice of the world for so long. When he was over sixty years of age Coventry Patmore discovered him, and announced that he "appears to consider that his *forte* lies in philology and antiquarianism, and to be endowed with a naïve ignorance of the fact that he is one of our very first poets." But before this his local reputation as a poet was well established. His verse readings were always well-attended, for his poetry was immediately comprehensible, written as it was in the dialect of his neighbourhood, and about scenes and incidents familiar to all who lived in that locality.

In 1847 Barnes was ordained deacon, and next year priest. After a short term of residence he received his degree of Bachelor of Divinity from Cambridge in his fiftieth year. But it was only a small, donative parish that he obtained, and not until twelve years later did the living at Winterbourne Came, which he had long desired, fall to him. Thereafter he never departed far or willingly from his birthplace, the Vale of Blackmore. Here he created his own Palace of Art, and as no one so inconvenient as Darwin or Bishop Colenso came to Dorset, he remained mentally unperplexed and created poetry (amongst other things) refreshing by reason of its lack of bewilderment. Barnes was never a part of the day-to-day world. Fifteen years after Thoreau had published *Walden* he replied to a letter from an American friend: "You have in one of your poems the name Walden, the name of a householder, a dairyman of this parish." Barnes's whole attitude of mind was that of a parochial antiquarianist. This attitude remained with

him, for in his old age he once exclaimed indignantly, having just heard the word "bicycle," "why don't you call it 'wheel-saddle'?"

With the poetry of his contemporaries, or even of his predecessors, Barnes was supremely unconcerned. "I do not want," he said, "to be trammelled with the thoughts and styles of other poets, and I take none as my model except the Persian and Italian authors." It is true of him, more than of any other poet, that he hammered out his own method of poetic expression alone and without guidance. How out of touch he was with contemporary opinion may be gathered from his sincere praise of Waller's wit and good manners, and the greater interest he displayed in the Tonga paddle songs, called Towolo, or the three qualifications of poetry in the Welsh bardic canon, than in the fact that poets of no mean ability were writing in his own language. Therefore, as Mr. Grigson in his recent edition of Barnes's poems has pointed out, he borrowed from the literature of Ireland the underrhyme (as in **"Times o' Year"**), from the Persians he imitated the matching of sounds in half lines—a sort of rhyming pun (as in **"The Wold Wall"**), from the Hebrew he took psalmic parallelism (as in **"Melhill Feast"**), and from the Welsh, in anticipation of Hopkins, he used a repetition of the same consonants in half-lines, split by a caesura. In short, as Mr. Grigson remarks, "he created a system of poetry for his own use."

It is difficult to know which of Barnes's diverse activities to approach first. To consider him as a poet without a knowledge of his background as a scholarly antiquarian would not do him justice. We must therefore glance at his more painstaking, though less permanent works in philology before passing to the recreation in which his true genius lay. Even in the study of antiquities and languages Barnes had the eagerness and (often misdirected) enthusiasm of the talented amateur. When a sewer was dug through his garden he triumphantly retrieved a bone hairpin and a stone stud; in a series of articles in *The Ladies' Treasury* on the art of adornment, he devoted one to the subject of tattooing. But in more serious vein Barnes produced a great quantity of philologically weighty material, which he published, at no great profit to himself (he never looked on publication as in any way an addition to his income), either in the learned periodicals or as independent books. It was the age of Max Müller, and certainly after the publication of ***Tiw: or, a View on the roots and stems of the English as a Teutonic tongue,*** Barnes could claim the doubtful reputation of being an English chip from Müller's German workshop.

The first and greatest of Barnes's learned works is his ***Philological Grammar,*** with the grandiose sub-title, "formed from a comparison of more than sixty languages." The first page contains a list of them. It includes such a diversity as Maeso-Gothic, Wendish, Damulican, Khoordish, Greenlandish, Lazistanish, Cheremissian, Lapponic, and Bisaya. The sub-title might well have been "Babel." The Grammar itself is a compendium of enormous erudition: it is in effect a world Grammar. As may be imagined it is highly complicated, yet Barnes had an orderly mind, and everything is carefully and methodically classified. In the sections on Prosody and Rhyme, probably the most pertinent to our immediate study, may be seen in the original those many poetic attributes that Barnes took from other languages to incorporate into his own poetry. But the critics fought shy of his weighty and laborious Grammar, which (in the phrase of his aggrieved daughter), "found but little favour with the general reader."

Barnes was undeterred, and his next book, *Tiw,* was if anything even more difficult to comprehend. More interesting, and closely connected with his use of dialect words was his *Grammar and Glossary of the Dorset Dialect,* later expanded as *A Glossary of the Dorset Dialect, with a Grammar of its Word Shapening and Wording.* "The Dorset has more freedom than has the more straitly bound book-speech," he claimed, and proceeded to justify his dialect as a "pure well of English undefiled." After a history of South-West English from earliest times, Barnes demonstrates the Dorset dialect by translating (with an impishness that we are to see in his poetry) the Queen's Speech from the Throne into a highly irreverent brogue. Her Majesty, for example, "do trust that theäse fruits mid be a-took, as proofs that the wealth-springs o' the land ben't aweakened."

The nature of the Grammar is again best seen by examining a small section in detail. Pronouns, for instance. "Whereas Dorset men are laughed at for what is taken as their misuse of pronouns," Barnes writes, "yet the pronouns of true Dorset, are fitted to one of the finest outplannings of speech that I have found." Here Barnes's dialectal pride, and disconcerting use of invented phrases to describe parts of speech (even more noticeable in his later works), is apparent. He continues to tell how "Full shapen things" (such as trees, tools, etc.), have a personal class of pronoun, *he,* with an accusative, *en;* whereas "unshapen quantities" of stuff have an impersonal class of pronoun, *it.* In the demonstratives, the personal class is *theäse* and *thick;* the impersonal, *this* and *that.* There are, therefore, Barnes proudly announces, four demonstratives in Dorset, but only two in English.

The "Glossary of the Dorset Dialect," which Barnes appends to his Grammar, contains some of the most memorable words and usages that any phrase-book can offer. Some are more beautiful than their original (Daffidowndilly: Daffodil), many are more pungent (Magoty: Fanciful. Slommock: A Slatternly Woman). Some of these usages are now almost common speech: (Baffle, Blether, Piggy-Back, Cubby-Hole); all of them are highly expressive. Certain phrases are peculiar to the local way of life (Sholduerens: Cider made from stolen apples carried home on the shoulders), and a majority concern the objects of common sight, often used to materialize abstractions (To owl about: To wander by night), or to incorporate local lore [Pissabed: Dandelion ("said to be very diuretic, whence its name")]. Certainly the Glossary is a list to linger over, and Barnes's free use of such words is a great part of the fascination of his poetry. Barnes cannot be said to use a plain style when such decorative words are incorporated.

In *An Outline of English Speech-Craft* Barnes once more picks up the Anglo-Saxon cudgels (he had previously published a Grammar of that language), this time in favour of ousting foreign, in favour of native, words from the language. Some of his most memorable suggestions are, Soaksome (for Bibulous), Wortlore (for Botany), and Folkdom (for Democracy). The book was a favourite of its author's, but its recommendations can scarcely be taken seriously. Barnes must have had sympathy with the boy in his own school who "scrope out the 'p' in psalm' cos he didn't spell nothen."

The last of Barnes's serious works was written in his eightieth year (though those here mentioned are of necessity selective, since his output was enormous). *An Outline of Rede-Craft* is a study in Logic, which by the extreme anglicization of its style was written in a language of its own. Thus a syllogism becomes a "Three-Stepped Redeship," a proposition a "Thought-Putting," and a dilemma a "Two-Horned Redeship."

It is strange when one turns from Barnes the Philologist, contorted in semantic pedantries, to find Barnes the Poet without emotional or psychological subtleties, without an axe to grind, but occupied with simple, elemental feelings. He himself claimed in an unpublished fragment of autobiography, that "matters most interesting to me are those belonging to man, in his life of body, mind and soul, so in his speech, manners, laws and works." Barnes never strayed outside his native valleys to pursue this study, and it is with deep and benevolent satisfaction, not rapture, that he surveys the prospects around him. The men and women with whom he daily associated are the centre of his world, and he sees nature through them. The interdependence of man and nature, not on the spiritual level that Wordsworth describes it, but tangibly in every action of the countryman, has never been more acutely realized. Out of doors in the May sunshine that Barnes loved so dearly there is harmony between the earth and its inhabitants:

An' vields where chaps do vur outdo
The Zunday sky, wi' cwoats o' blue;
An' maïdens' frocks do vur surpass
The whitest deäsies in the grass.

The first poems Barnes wrote were in ordinary speech, and throughout his life he continued to produce such poetry side by side with his dialect poems, and with no more pretensions to an elevated style or theme. He claimed that he wrote in dialect because he could not help it. "It is my mother tongue and is to my mind the only true speech of the life that I draw." It is very probable, however, that the spirit of the philologist caused him to write in Dorset. Unlike Doughty, who consciously attempted to re-create sixteenth-century English, and failed, Barnes, although starting as a perversity, ended by using it so naturally that he even preached in the dialect.

There is an astonishing unity in a poem by Barnes. It is impossible to capture the flavour of the whole from a few lines, and for this reason almost all those who have written about him either do not quote, or else reproduce an entire poem. No signal beauties arrest the reader, although the effect of the entirety is undeniably fine. This is caused largely by the rigidity of the form, coupled with the simplicity of the effect. It kept Barnes to a high, even standard of verse-making. He did not indulge in the visionary hit-and-miss brilliance of Clare, although there is a similarity to Clare's

I found the poems in the fields,
And only wrote them down,

in Barnes's assertion, "I write pictures which I see in my mind."

Harmony was Barnes's watchword; and his poems are consequently as indivisible as a fugue. He wrote for *The Gentleman's Magazine* on harmonic proportions as applied to churches, he bound his books harmonically, and he held that poetry must harmonize and conform to nature. His study of harmony led to his belief that nature never makes mistakes, and induced him to get together a collection of the tints that nature most frequently contrasts, which he attempted to introduce into both his painting (another of his pastimes) and his poetry. Consequently there is a frequent use of colour-words in Barnes's verse, often contrasted in pairs, but always simple; blue, yellow or white.

The gookoo over white-weav'd seas
Do come to zing in thy green trees;

or again in his description of "**The Water Crowvoot,**"

Thy beds o' snow-white buds do gleam
So feäir upon the sky-blue stream.

His colour descriptions are not so lavish as those of his contemporaries the Pre-Raphaelites, but there is an aloof calmness in his descriptions that elevates his poetry, despite its fetters of loam, above the normal run of nature poets.

In his article, "**Thoughts on Beauty and Art,**" Barnes repeats the wellknown formula, used indiscriminately by Pope, Cowper, and Wordsworth, "Nature is the best school of art," but adds as a corollary of his own, "and of schools of art among men those are best that are nature's best interpreters." His poetry is an able defence of his theory, and many vivid images, brilliant yet simple, spring to mind; the "loose-limbed rest of infants," "thin-heäir'd cows" that

up bezide the mossy raïls
Do stan' an' zwing their heavy taïls,

"the high-wound zongs o' nightingeäles," or the

whitest clouds, a-hangèn high
Avore the blueness o' the sky.

In Patmore's words, "the Life of Nature has seldom flowed with more surprising and enchanting freedom."

Not one of Barnes's poems is of any great length and none contains hidden meanings; they are all plain and downright. They depict the countryman in all the aspects of his life, at all seasons, working, courting, mourning, as he is still to be found in the flesh. Barnes's realism is never tempered by harshness, as is that of the poet of the East Anglian scene, Crabbe. He has no unkind words for anyone, largely because he does not sit in judgment. There is an utter lack of personal intrusion on the poet's part. He is always the sympathetic observer, watching the human kaleidoscope against a background of pastoral simplicity. Loss of intense power is inevitable, and whereas Barnes may be pathetic and charming in his descriptions, he never greatly moves one, and can but produce an evanescent delight. As he told the Bishop of Salisbury who visited him in his old age, all he had written was true of someone in the classes described in his poems, and he had painted from life even though the level might have been above the average.

The Welsh triad that Iolo Morganwg had long before advised the poets and critics of his generation to study was rediscovered by Barnes, who attempted to follow the discipline that is demanded of a man of *awen,* or poetic genius. Such a man, Iolo declared, must possess "an eye that can see Nature; a heart that can feel Nature; and a resolution that dares follow Nature." The triad did not require a poet to interpret nature; consequently Barnes is not often didactic, and then only unobtrusively. He will indicate his message (often using one of his characters to do this, not himself), but never press it.

An' vok' do come, an' live, an' goo,
But rivers don't gi'e out, John.

For the most part he sang for the pure joy of song. It was this aspect of his work that made Patmore draw a comparison between him and Theocritus—a comparison that had been lavished on Bloomfield forty years before. But Barnes does not describe a golden, pastoral age; his Muse is lowlier than the Sicilian's; it never soars so high. He was always unambitiously in command. Of Barnes's poems Hopkins said, "it is true they are not far-fetched or exquisite . . . but they are straight from nature and quite fresh."

There is no question that Barnes's dialect poems are those on which his fame most justifiably rests. We have already seen some of the perils that a dialect poet must face, avoiding preciosity on the one hand and incomprehensibility on the other. Relph being unknown, only the Scots had succeeded in making poetry out of local speech. Barnes was the first to prove that his Dorset dialect was more than an antiquarian curiosity. Hopkins, despite the lavish praise that he bestowed on Barnes's poetry, was not fully convinced that the dialect added to, or was even an integral part of, its poetic merit. "You may translate them and they are nearly as good," he claimed, and he agreed with Bridges that the dialect gave "a peculiar but short-lived charm." This might be true if Barnes had the slightest pretensions towards a poetic diction, but, unlike Wordsworth, his language was indeed the language of common speech. His lines cry out to be read with a West Country burr, regardless of whether the inflections are printed or imagined by the reader. The dialect is in large measure the very texture of the verse, and the colloquial passages in particular would be lost without it. The following lines, for example, it would be impossible to render into common speech without making them as bathetic as "Simon Lee" or "Alice Fell."

> The tiaties must be ready purty nigh;
> Do tiake oone up upon a fark an' try,
> The kiake upon the vier too's aburnen,
> I be afeärd: do run an' zee, an' turn en.

Although in the mechanics of poetry Barnes was a highly-trained artist, he had at the same time no artistic pedigree. As Patmore observed Barnes might well have written as he did had no other poet ever lived. But as he shunned fame, and had no gospel to preach (other than to his congregation at Winterbourne Came), he attracted no public notice until he was over sixty years of age, when he was rewarded by the admiring attentions of a small cabal of poets—Hardy, Patmore, and Hopkins—and a small pension of £70 a year. With this Barnes was perfectly content, nor did ambition stir within him. Duck and Bloomfield were lionized and perhaps spoilt as poets; Barnes continued to administer to his parish, scythe his lawn in a pale-blue dressing-gown, and pursue his studies in semantics.

So even was the tenor of his life that apart from his very earliest works it is impossible to trace any development in his poetry. Those poems that he wrote as a youth, felicitous in their descriptions of childhood and young love, are indistinguishable from those he continued to write into old age. He seems to have been born with this limited but perfect gift of expression, which persisted with as unwavering a flame as his own essential humanity. "There is no art without love," he wrote in that memorable essay on Beauty and Art, which contains his whole creed of aesthetics, "every artist who has produced anything worthy has had a love of his subject." Barnes's love was very deep, yet he never sentimentalizes, because of his detachment, and because of the gruff, earthy quality that dialectal good sense always creates. They are manly poems, albeit often exceedingly delicate, and they are poems that need to be sung; they are always (except certain of the humorous verses) of an entrancing lyricism. Hopkins sensed this when he set two of them to music. Barnes wrote to be read aloud: the printed word scarcely does him justice. The seeming cacophony of certain phrases does not occur in spoken Dorset, where speech is soft and burred, like humble-bees ("Dumbledores" in the Glossary) in a clover-field.

In speaking about Barnes I have not allowed Barnes to speak for himself. It is a significant fact, and one that Patmore also realized in his essay on the poet. The lack of illustrative quotations in these pages is primarily due to the unity of the poems; they do not present the critic with fragments that will fairly represent the whole. Barnes fashioned his work with such care and restraint, that in justice to him, and also to indicate a few of the innumerable ingenious rhythms and metres he employed, a few of his poems should be printed in their entirety. They are not necessarily the best, but they are representative of his outpourings.

"My Orcha'd in Linden Lea," familiar to many in its musical setting, is one of the loveliest of Barnes's descriptive poems, and expresses in its final verse the essence of his love of retirement.

> 'Ithin the woodlands, flow'ry gleäded,
>   By the woak tree's mossy moot,
> The sheenèn grass-bleädes, timber-sheäded,
>   Now do quiver under voot;
> An' birds do whissle auver head,
> An' water's bubblèn in its bed,
> An' there vor me the apple tree
> Do leän down low in Linden Lea.
>
> When leaves that leätely were a-springèn
>   Now do feäde 'ithin the copse,
> An' painted birds do hush their zingèn
>   Up upon the timber's tops;

An' brown-leav'd fruit's a-turnèn red,
In cloudless zunsheen, auver head,
Wi' fruit vor me, the apple tree
Do leän down low in Linden Lea.

Let other vo'k meäke money vaster
  In the aïr o' dark-room'd towns,
I don't dread a peevish meäster;
  Though noo man do heed my frowns,
I be free to goo abrode,
Or teäke ageän my hwomeward road
To where, vor me, the apple tree
Do leän down low in Linden Lea.

"Jeän" is one of the many autobiographical poems that Barnes wrote about his own wife. He wrote of young love, of married love, and the unhappy memories of a love who has departed, for Julia Barnes died thirty-four years before him. That her memory never left him may be judged from the constant record of his grief in his Italian diary. "Giulia" he wrote at the end of each day's entry after her death.

We now mid hope var better cheer,
My smilèn wife o' twice vive year.
Let others frown, if thee bist near
  Wi' hope upon thy brow, Jeän;
Var I vust lov'd thee when thy light
Young shiape vust grow'd to woman's height;
I lov'd thee near, an out o' zight,
  An' I da love thee now Jeän.

An we've a-trod the sheenen bliade
Ov eegrass in the zummer shiade,
An' when the leaves begun to fiade
  Wi' zummer in the wiane, Jeän;
An' we've a-wander'd droo the groun'
O' swayen wheat a-turnen brown,
An' we've a-stroll'd together roun'
  The brook, an' droo the liane, Jeän.

An' nuone but I can ever tell
Ov al thy tears that have a-vell
When trials miade thy buzzom zwell,
  An' nuone but thee o' mine, Jeän;
An' now my heart, that heav'd wi' pride
Back then to have thee at my zide,
Da love thee muore as years da slide,
  An' leäve thae times behine, Jeän.

There seems no obvious reason why **"Melhill Feast"** is written in Queen's English rather than in Dorset, but the verses from it that follow serve as an interesting comparison, and show how interchangeably Barnes's talents could be applied within the limited range of his subject-matter. The line, "By glittering gossamer and dew," might be objected to as too consciously poetic. Nevertheless, in this instance and elsewhere

the words employed are of Saxon origin, and foreign importations, which Barnes hated, are rigorously excluded from his writings. This limits his vocabulary, but it is also a form of insurance. The words he does employ are more absolute in their meaning, more appropriate when applied to the protagonists of the poems, and have a wholesomeness and honesty about them that a mixed vocabulary might mar. Barnes's purpose in simplifying was also to unify the English tongue, and his is perhaps the ideal compromise between the languages of high and low life in limiting the vocabulary when writing about "low" subjects to words that are in common use by the characters, the author and the reader.

Aye, up at the feast, by Melhill's brow,
So softly below the clouds in flight,
There swept on the wood, the shade and light,
Tree after tree, and bough by bough.

And there, among girls on left and right,
On one with a winsome smile, I set
My looks; and the more, the more we met
Glance upon glance, and sight by sight.

The road she had come by then was soon
The one of my paths that best I knew,
By glittering gossamer and dew,
Evening by evening, moon by moon.

Sweet were the hopes I found to cheer
My heart as I thought on time to come,
With one that would bless my happy home,
Moon upon moon, and year by year.

A final example of Barnes's craft as a poet is one of his humorous verses. He was a skilful raconteur, and in this instance his brilliant use of idiom and childlike artlessness make a very happy parable from the recollected incident.

When I wer' still a bwoy, an' mother's pride,
A bigger bwoy spoke up to me so kind-like,
"If you do like, I'll treat ye wi' a ride
In theäse wheel-barrow here." Zoo I wer'
  blind-like
To what 'e had a-workèn in his mind-like,
An' mounted vor a passenger inside;
An' comèn to a puddle, perty wide,
He tipp'd me in, a-grinnèn back behind-like.
Zoo when a man do come to me so thick-like,
An' sheäke my hand, where oonce 'e pass'd
  me by,
An' tell me he would do me this or that,
I can't help thinkèn o' the big bwoy's trick-
  like.
An' then, vor all I can but wag my hat
An' thank en, I do veel a little shy.

Barnes's poetry is the embodiment of a way of life, and in a tradition that we cannot hope to share. Inevitably we read him at a remove, for to analyse it minutely is only to destroy "the many-coloured thing." Barnes nevertheless deserves to be read, though we must expect to lose much of the bloom in gathering the fruit. It is not the difficulty of the language, which hardly interferes with fluent reading at all, but something more subtle; an attitude of mind. Barnes's poetry demands of the reader a compatibility of simplicity and dignity, enthusiasm without patronage, and a sincere parochial love of humanity. Neither the reader nor the poet is expected to do more than watch the scene sympathetically. The poetry does not induce tears or emotion, but it warms one with unaffected delight.

William Turner Levy (essay date 1960)

SOURCE: "The Dorset Poet," in *William Barnes: The Man and the Poems,* Longmans (Dorchester) Ltd., 1960, pp. 1-152.

[*In the following excerpt, Levy discusses the importance of nature in Barnes's poetry.*]

Nature

Emerson calls the sky the daily bread of the eyes, and so it and all present nature were to Barnes. He did not write of the sea nor of great mountains, for he was not familiar with them. Rather, he selected those details on which with delicacy of perception he lovingly lingered, and composed them into vignettes of unmistakable authority. They have the freshness necessary to arrest the most jaded and outrageously stimulated city dweller, and their accuracy stems from a desire to present without diminution of the Creator's intention those works for which man is not responsible: to capture, if possible, the "calm of blest eternity."[1] These songs of purity and innocence are not naive; they contain power enough to give man a serene and nourishing contact. The sanity of the countryman grows from his balanced conservatism and radicalism. Carl Van Doren has put it this way: breaking the soil, felling trees, wrenching a livelihood from the earth, makes one radical, and the repetitive march of day and night, of the seasons, keeps one conservative. One learns what must be done and what cannot be done. Nature establishes itself for man only when man acknowledges that it does so, and men approach it with different attitudes and carry away different lessons. The book is the same, but some read it immaturely, others with arrogance, some romantically; many see only what, consciously or not, they want to, and in their reports we see more of them than of the subject, or, more precisely, they become the subject. Barnes, like Constable (but we must not count Constable's last years), was in love with his subject and lost himself in its contemplation; nevertheless,

both men are present in their work: in the selection, the composition, the tone, in what they do not say more than in what they say: that is why it is so unmistakably theirs.

For Barnes, man, possessed of a consciousness including memory and imagination, is superior to nature, and turns to nature because she is the expression of that which is superior to her. What we recognize in azalea blossom or flinty hillside is a rightness not of its own choosing. God's closeness to man; man's distance from man; man's aloneness—are realistically presented in this poem, which avoids pitfalls of sentimentality and forced conclusions by virtue of its author's tact:

"Vields By Watervalls"[2]

When our downcast looks be smileless,
  Under others' wrongs an' slightèns,
When our daily deeds be guileless,
  An' do meet unkind requitèns,
You can meäke us zome amends
Vor wrongs o' foes, an' slights o' friends;—
O flow'ry-gleäded, timber-sheäded
Vields by flowèn watervalls!

Here be softest aïrs a-blowèn
  Drough the boughs, wi' zingèn drushes,
Up above the streams, a-flowèn
  Under willows, on by rushes.
Here below the bright-zunn'd sky
The dew-bespangled flow'rs do dry,
In woody-zided, stream-divided
Vields by flowèn watervalls.

Waters, wi' their giddy rollèns;
  Breezes wi' their plaÿsome wooèns;
Here do heal, in soft consolèns,
  Hearts a-wrung wi' man's wrong doèns.
Day do come to us as gaÿ
As to a king ov widest swaÿ,
In deäisy whitèn'd, gil'cup-brightèn'd
Vields by flowèn watervalls.

Zome feäir buds mid outlive blightèns,
  Zome sweet hopes mid outlive sorrow,
After days of wrongs an' slightèns
  There mid break a happy morrow.
We mid have noo e'thly love;
But God's love-tokens vrom above
Here mid meet us, here mid greet us,
In the vields by watervalls.

1. Seasons

And the variety within the whole is right. "Our climate," Barnes writes to an American correspondent, "is mild, our south-west and west winds are moist, as coming over the Atlantic, and our east wind is cold.

Our spring begins at the latter end of March, which is mostly a time of dry bracing winds, and our winter begins in November, usually a windy and rainy month. May is a charming month, in which our dry downs are covered with sheets, as it were of silver and gold, in daisies and buttercups. June is our hay month."[3] It is characteristic of Barnes that he should respond in turn to the gifts of each season. In **"The May-Tree"** he impartially discovers its appearance at all seasons, and in **"The Year Clock"** he utilizes the fable his aunt tells to confect a series of clock faces, painted impressions at once artificial and accurate. He prefers the meadow in the Spring and welcomes the mild weather ecstatically:

> Come out o' door; 'tis Spring! 'tis Maÿ![4]

but there is pleasant excitement in looking forward to the rigors of winter when

> vrosty sheädes do lie below
> The winter ricks a-tipp'd wi' snow;

and there is no reason for the girls to stay at home:

> You got noo pools to waddle drough,
> Nor clay a-pullèn off your shoe:

so, come out, come,

> Vor young men's hearts an' maïden's eyes
> Don't vreeze below the cwoldest skies.[5]

Barnes enjoys **"Zummer Thoughts in Winter Time,"** and the merging of seasons which T. S. Eliot perceives more importantly and uses to powerful purpose in his *Four Quartets* finds a minor statement in **"Zunsheen in the Winter"**:

> The birds do sheäke, wi' plaÿsome skips,
> The raïn-drops off the bushes' tips,
> A-chirripèn wi' merry sound;
> While over all the grassy ground
> The wind's a-whirlèn round an' round
>   So softly, that the day do seem
>   Mwore lik' a zummer in a dream,
>   Than zunsheen in the winter.[6]

Summer Barnes finds particularly noteworthy for its may-scented, hay-scented wind gusts. Strangely enough, if the poet is on his way to a friendly house he does not feel the rain, and can be warm even on the snow-covered plain. He seldom paints a landscape without figures. He is acutely responsive to the influence (sometimes opposite to expectation) of season on man's inner weather, and in **"Grief an' Gladness"** is even aware of what might be called man's storms and calms. At the very least, men find the passage of time as mirrored in nature's motions a poignant backdrop:

"Zummer an' Winter"[7]

> When I led by zummer streams
>   The pride o' Lea, as naïghbours thought her,
> While the zun, wi' evenèn beams,
>   Did cast our sheädes athirt the water;
>   Winds a-blowèn,
>   Streams a-flowèn,
>   Skies a-glowèn,
> Tokens ov my jaÿ zoo fleetèn,
> Heighten'd it, that happy meetèn.
>
> Then, when maïd an' man took pleäces,
>   Gaÿ in winter's Chris'mas dances,
> Showèn in their merry feäces
>   Kindly smiles an' glisnèn glances;
>   Stars a-winkèn,
>   Day a-shrinkèn,
>   Sheädes a-zinkèn,
> Brought anew the happy meetèn,
> That did meäke the night too fleetèn.

If Barnes favored any time of the year—and if the most successful seasonal poem indicates the greatest partiality—it was surely

"Fall Time"[8]

> The gather'd clouds, a-hangèn low,
>   Do meäke the woody ridge look dim;
> An' raïn-vill'd streams do brisker flow,
>   Arisèn higher to their brim.
> In the tree, vrom lim' to lim',
>   Leaves do drop
> Vrom the top, all slowly down,
> Yollow, to the gloomy groun'.
> The rick's a-tipp'd an' weather-brown'd,
>   An' thatch'd wi' zedge a-dried an' dead;
> An' orcha'd apples, red half round,
>   Have all a-happer'd down, a-shed
> Underneath the trees' wide head.
>   Ladders long,
> Rong by rong, to clim' the tall
> Trees, be hung upon the wall.
>
> The crumpled leaves be now a-shed
>   In mornèn winds a-blowèn keen;
> When they wer green the moss wer dead,
>   Now they be dead the moss is green.
> Low the evenèn zun do sheen
>   By the boughs,
> Where the cows do swing their taïls
> Over the merry milkers' païls.

The second half of the first stanza contains a skillful employment of consonants, from the clear *l*'s in *lim'* down through the plosives *t* and *d* to the lowest sound in the plosive, *r* colored *g* of *groun'*. The leaves fall in these consonantal sounds by stages through the line and rhyme movement. The word *slowly* perfectly placed to trace the manner; the leaves hitting the ground on the first and settling flat on the second syllable of *Yollow*. The second stanza gains effect through the crunchy sound of *thatch'd* and the onomatopoetic *a-happer'd*. The drawn out *l*'s give height to *Ladders long,* while *Rong by rong* indicates the tedious climbing, and the line end pause between *tall* and *Trees* accentuates the height. The last stanza turns from the yellow of the first and red of the second to green—the hopeful color of life. On that note of promise the attention lowers from the trees to the mirthful scene at the close of the day's labor, and the last line of the poem is the quickest (quicker even than the flow of the streams that interested us before we turned to watch the Fall time of the tree), for we turn away and the scene is closed. The eye moved easily from one to another of these aspects of Fall. The stanzas, too, were linked—by sounds: the *down* rhyme of the first becoming the *brown'd* of the second; the *dead* rhyme of the second becoming the *shed* of the third.

2. Day and Night

Looking at half of Barnes's poems we could make an excellent case for the fact that day pleased him most. We could make the same case for night by looking at the other half. It is not that he liked either less, but that he was catholic in his likes. The daily, common sights and sounds of each nourished him and led him to contemplate the material and spiritual—the two worlds into which he was baptised:

> Zoo teäke, vor me, the town a-drown'd,
> 'Ithin a storm o' rumblèn sound,
> An' gi'e me vaïces that do speak
> So soft an' meek, to souls alwone;
> The brook a-gurglèn round a stwone,
> An' birds o' day a-zingèn clear,
> An' leaves, that I mid zit an' hear
> A-rustlèn near, when birds be still.[9]

The most delicate of these sounds and sights might be found at night, but many were then missing that he enjoyed by day. Certainly, as we see in the above lines and in **"Linden Lea,"** he chose between country and city. Living in pastoral scenes might seem a form of escape to city dwellers; for Barnes it was an escape to reality:

> Waters, drough the meäds a-purlèn,
> Glissen'd in the evenèn's light,
> An' smoke, above the town a-curlèn,
> Melted slowly out o' zight;
> An' there, in glooms
> Ov unzunn'd rooms,
> To zome, wi' idle sorrows frettèn,
> Zuns did set avore their zettèn.[10]

Our age has the opportunity to prove that greatly imaginative town planning (experimented with by the Earl of Dorchester when in 1786 he rebuilt, charmingly, Milton Abbas, feeling that the old village crowded too closely upon the Abbey) could approach a meaningful balance between the two. The touted conveniences of the city shift to burdens when too many people are in one place, and it may be dangerous to be packed so closely with our fellow men that we begin to think of them as numbers. We may forget who they and we are, just as we may forget our dependence on the soil we do not see.

It is sunset, early twilight, **"The Turn of the Days"** that Barnes elected as the best time of day and night. It must always have been so for him, the hour when work was completed, the time of relaxation, the welcome close to what had been a welcome day. In muted monosyllables, he gives dramatic freshness to that hour in

"Good Night"[11]

> While down the meäds wound slow,
>   Water vor green-wheel'd mills,
> Over the streams bright bow,
>   Win' come vrom dark-back'd hills.
> Birds on the win' shot along down steep
> Slopes, wi' a swift-swung zweep.
> Dim weän'd the red streak'd west.
> Lim'-weary souls "Good rest".
>
> Up on the plough'd hill brow,
>   Still wer the zull's wheel'd beam,
> Still wer the red-wheel'd plough,
>   Free o' the strong limb'd team,
> Still wer the shop that the smith meäde ring,
> Dark where the sparks did spring;
> Low shot the zun's last beams.
> Lim'-weary souls "Good dreams".
>
> Where I vrom dark bank-sheädes
>   Turn'd up the west hill road,
> Where all the green grass bleädes
>   Under the zunlight glow'd.
> Startled I met, as the zunbeams plaÿ'd
> Light, wi' a sunsmote maïd,
> Come vor my day's last zight.
> Zun-brighten'd maïd "Good night".

Painfully, sometimes awkwardly, these lines convey with disturbing accuracy Barnes's mood. Lullaby-like the close of each stanza seeks to soften the frightening quality of what precedes. The extra foot in the fifth line of each stanza is unnerving. The birds (to refer to the first stanza) do fly that way the last flight of the day, but must he remind us of their violent urgency: *shot, steep/Slopes,* their mechanical *swift swung zweep?* The *dark-back'd hills* seem really to have backs, and red is the only color—blood red. And when we turn from that, the ominous sound of three *still*'s, and the word *Dark* where it appears. Even with the relief of emergence into somewhat brighter light—we seem almost to have fled the dark—*glow'd* is too unnatural to be welcome. *Startled:* the word we feared from the first! It's all right. We are not alone . . . but we have had enough alien beauty for one day—or night!

3. Birds

Barnes, who distinguishes one bird from another with nicety, took an interest in them at an early age:

> in bwoyhood I did rove
> Wi' pryèn eyes along the drove
> To vind the nest the blackbird meäde
> O' grass-stalks in the high bough's sheäde:
> Or clim' aloft, wi' clingèn knees,
> Vor crows' aggs up in swayèn trees,
> While frighten'd blackbirds down below
> Did chatter o' their little foe.[12]

A good variety appear in his pages: the thrush, the martin, the dove, the nightingale, the swan, and the ubiquitous geese (whenever he needs white on green). Here we find three in one stanza:

> Ov all the birds upon the wing
> Between the zunny show'rs o' spring,—
> Vor all the lark, a-swingèn high,
> Mid zing below a cloudless sky.
> An' sparrows, clust'rèn roun' the bough,
> Mid chatter to the men at plough,—
> The blackbird whisslèn in among
> The boughs, do zing the gayèst zong.[13]

No observer of the lark has failed to comment on the great height the bird rises to:

> the lark, in flight,
> Did zing a-loft, wi' flappèn wings,
> Tho' mwore in heärèn than in zight;

Barnes notes this and then watches two boys:

> Then woone, wi' han'-besheäded eyes,
> A-stoppèn still, as he did run,
> Look'd up to zee the lark arise
> A-zingèn to the high-gone zun;
> The while his brother look'd below
> Vor what the groun' mid have to show.

One occupied himself with the bird he could never catch, the other searched for its nest. The poet reflects:

> But, aggs be only woonce a-vound,
> An' uncaught larks ageän mid sound.[14]

The bird's outstanding characteristic is again expressed in **"Spring"**:

> An' the springèn
> Lark's a-zingèn,
> Lik' a dot avore the cloud,
> High above the ashes sh'oud.[15]

John Burroughs—during an English October—encounters larks:

> The song disappointed me at first, being less sweet and melodious than I had expected to hear, indeed I thought it a little sharp and harsh,—a little stubbly,—but in other respects, in strength and gladness and continuity, it was wonderful. And the more I heard it the better I liked it, until I would gladly have given any of my songsters at home for a bird that could shower down such notes, even in autumn. Up, up, went the bird, describing a large easy spiral till he attained an altitude of three or four hundred feet, when, spread out against the sky for a space of ten or fifteen minutes, or more, he poured out his delight, filling all the vault with sound . . Away he goes on quivering wing, inflating his throat fuller and fuller, mounting and mounting, and turning to all points of the compass as if to embrace the whole landscape in his song, the notes still raining upon you as distinct as ever, after you have left him far behind.[16]

The enormous number of birds of all varieties in England amazed Burroughs. Barnes, knowing only those he could not have avoided seeing and hearing, was certainly no bird-watcher. Nor does he seem to have kept a pet bird, though he has an amusing poem about one. The swallow was common, and he must have often watched its identifying flight:

> And then some swallows floated by,
> All sweeping out their airy bow,
> And rising up from low to high,
> Or sweeping down from high to low.[17]

He likes the blackbird's song the best, but it is the rook,[18] most common of all, he paints most tenderly, both for its own sake and for the pictorial and sorcerous possibilities it affords:

"The Rooks"[19]

> (1) Ay! when the sun is near the ground,
>   At evening, in the western sky,
> From west to eastward, all around,
>   The gathered rooks begin to fly.
>
> (2) In wedgelike flock, with one ahead,
>   They flap their glitt'ring wings in flight;
> But did you ever hear it said
>   Whereto they take their way at night!

(1) At Akdean wood, folk say they meet,
    To fold at night their weary wings,
And roost, with little clenching feet,
    On boughs that nightwind softly swings.

(2) O yes, at Akdean's shadowy ground
    Are broad limb'd oaks, and ashes tall;
Black pines, and aspen trees that sound
    As soft as water at a fall.

(1) There I have spent some happy hours,
    Where yellow sunshine broke through shades
On blue-bell beds and cowslip flow'rs,
    And us among them, in the glades.

4. Beasts

A familiar scene for Barnes would be "that of a herd of red-and-white Shorthorns grazing in an intensely green and kingcup-yellow water-meadow by the river's bank with the big chequer-board pattern of spring agriculture on the high Dorset downs as a background the sort of picture that owed almost everything to colour, and the colour was brightened and intensified by April sunshine, which seems to possess special qualities for this effect." This observation by a knowledgeable present-day countryman[20] reminds us that little in Barnes's poems dates. At that same time of the year a hundred years before (and might it not have been a thousand?), Barnes observed

> where the brook
> Do creep along the meäds, an' lie
> To catch the brightness o' the sky;
> An' cows, in water to theïr knees,
> Do stan' a-whiskèn off the vlees.[21]

His diction is capable of admitting all his subject matter, from nightingales to fleas; and his observation of the cow—while not equal to Gisborne's[22]—includes its activity as well as its passivity:

> Then I do dreve the cows across
>   The brook that's in a vog,
> While they do trot, an' bleäre, an' toss
>   Their heads to hook the dog.[23]

Nanny's Cow we could positively identify:

> Her back wer hollor as a bow,
> Her lags wer short, her body low;
> Her head wer small, her horns turn'd in
> Avore her feäce so sharp's a pin:
> Her eyes wer vull, her ears wer thin,
>   An' she wer red vrom head to taïl,
>   An' didden start nor kick the païl,
>   When Nanny zot to milk her.[24]

In these lines, Barnes's preoccupation with the creatures closest to man creates a familiar, crowded, *mille-fleur* tapestry background:

>   the woäk, wi' spreadèn head,
> Did sheäde the foxes' verny bed;
> An' runnèn heäres, in zunny gleädes,
> Did beät the grasses' quiv'rèn' bleädes;
> An' speckled pa'tridges took flight
> In stubble vields a-feädèn white;
> Or he could zee the pheasant strut
> In sheädy woods, wi' païnted cwoat;
> Or long-tongued dogs did love to run
> Among the leaves, bezide his gun.[25]

With quiet glance he sees the spider's silver web, and with greater interest watches the fish leap out of the water to catch the wheeling gnats over the stream. In **"Dobbin Dead"** the loss of his old mare reduces the tranter to a pitiful economic condition. The nag was too stiff of limb to climb after choice blades of grass, but climb it did until it lost its footing and fell to its death. **"The Heare"** is a breathless, humorous description of a hunt. Of the three who are watching the chase, two have a bet on. The third is a little slow at locating the hounds, asks where they are:

> (I) Why, out in Ash Hill, near the barn,
>   behind Thik tree.
>   (3) The pollard? (I) Pollard! no, b'ye
>   blind?
> (2) There, I do zee em over-right thik cow.
> (3) The red woone? (I) No, a mile beyand her
>   now.
> (3) Oh! there's the heäre, a-meäkèn for the
>   drong.

the suspense mounts:

> He's gwäin to groun'.
> (3) He is! (I) He idden!

the hare finally escapes:

> (I) He's geäme a-runnèn too. Why, he do
>   mwore
>   Than eärn his life. (3) His life wer his
>   avore.[26]

Although there is the story of the boy William adventurously floating down the Stour in a tub, towing a terrified cat behind in a wooden bowl, dogs that could accompany him on his long walks were Barnes's preference. He used to tell the story of one of his dogs (the incident dated from the days at Chantry House) that, pushing with its forepaws, turned its kennel completely around in order to face the door away from a storm. Using contrast, he wrote freshly of another dog, "Cara":

"I and the Dog"[27]

As I was wont to straggle out
To your house, oh! how glad the dog,
With low-put nose, would nimbly jog,
Along my path and hunt about;
And his great pleasure was to run
By timber'd hedge and banky ledge,
And ended where my own begun,
At your old door and stonen floor.
And there, as time was gliding by,
With me so quick, with him so slow,
How he would look at me, and blow,
From time to time, a whining sigh,
That meant, 'Now come along the land,
With timber'd knolls, and rabbit holes,
I can't think what you have on hand,
With this young face, in this old place.

Originally written in dialect (as is clear from the manuscript)[28], the poem is nimbler in expression in the Common English version. This is one of the poems that allows us to agree with Hardy that the dialect militated against Barnes's art: "As long as the spelling of standard English is other than phonetic it is not obvious why that of the old Wessex language should be phonetic, except in a pronouncing dictionary." Had Barnes, Hardy feels, devoted himself to standard English it "could soon have been moulded to verse as deftly as dialect by a man whose instinct it was to catch so readily the beat of hearts around him." Hardy sees his choice as unfortunate, since he was not "a spontaneous singer of rural songs in folk-language like Burns, or an extemporizer like the old balladists," but rather "an academic poet akin to the school of Gray and Collins."[29] This, of course, is not the same thing at all as saying that his Common English poems as they exist are comparable to his dialect poems. What Hardy is doing is hazarding the well-founded guess that a poet of Barnes's stature, had he so decided, would have accomplished equally fine things in the language which he knew as well as he knew the dialect.

5. Trees

We have seen that the memory of his mother knitting beneath it enhanced Barnes's regard for **"The Girt Woak Tree That's in the Dell."** He is passionately attached to the memories and to the tree as tree:

An' oh! mid never ax nor hook
Be brought to spweil his steätely look;
Nor ever roun' his ribby zides
Mid cattle rub ther heäiry hides;
Nor pigs rout up his turf, but keep
His lwonesome sheäde vor harmless sheep;
An' let en grow, an' let en spread,
An' let en live when I be dead.[30]

A monumental stability even more than tree shapes and seasonal beauties renders them significant in a way that defies definition. It is not too fanciful to imagine that as we walk among trees of sufficient age we retrospectively move through the forests in which man, in most countries, had his first home. Our senses have never become dulled to the enchanting play of light and shade through the protective arms of trees; we are safer there than in the open field, and if we cannot see far, then we will look within. Trees foster thought, but what we think may depend upon where we walk—under maples? among birch? by willows? Trees also have ages that we recognize. The "girt elem tree" is felled and the whole landscape is changed, and there was danger as he fell

An' as we did run vrom en, there, clwose at
our backs,
Oh! his boughs come to groun' wi' sich
whizzes an' cracks![31]

Barnes knew that **"Trees Be Company,"** and he felt a sympathy for their solitary, unregarded struggles on a stormy night. He could admire the tall, shining ash trees, but he felt the presence of those now departed when he stood beneath an ancient oak. (How he—who commissioned the ill-fated local artist Thorne to paint trees for him—would have stood enthralled before Crome's great *Poringland Oak* in the National Gallery!) When maple leaves turned yellow, he would hasten out to enjoy the last god weather before winter, and when the leaves fell, he pondered their fate:

The leaves that through the spring were gay,
Were now by hasty winds that shook
Them wither'd off their quiv'ring spray,
All borne away along the brook,
Without a day or rest around
Their mother tree, on quiet ground.
But cast away on blast and wave,
To lie in some chance grave.[32]

But as always in Barnes, nature keeps its place, however endearing that place may be:

"The String Token"[33]

'If I am gone on, you will find a small
string'—
Were her words—'on this twig of the oak by
the spring'.
Oh! gay are the new-leaved trees, in the
spring,
Down under the height, where the skylark may
sing;
And welcome in summer are tree-leaves that
meet
On wide-spreading limbs, for a screen from
the heat;

And fair in the fall-tide may flutter the few
Yellow leaves of the trees that the sky may
   shine through.
But welcomer far than the leaves, is the string
On the twig of the oak by the spring.

And in delineating the feminine trees, he compares them with girls:

"A Brisk Wind"[34]

The burdock leaves beside the ledge,
The leaves upon the poplar's height,
Were blown by windblasts up on edge,
And show'd their undersides of white;
And willow trees beside the rocks,
All bent grey leaves, and swung grey boughs,
As there, on wagging heads, dark locks,
Bespread red cheeks, behung white brows.

—these, he seems to say, these trees, these girls, are the beauties that fill the world.

6. Flowers

The calendar of the countryman's year is decorated with what Barnes calls "season tokens": dusky-red clover, yellow-fringed dandelion, pale-green grass, purple-studded thistle. Democratic in his flower preferences, he sprinkles his verse with daisies and buttercups. Tall elms rise "in steätely ranks" from "yollow cowslip-banks,"[35] and butterflies pursue their choosy ways. He is sure that the wild ivy with its freedom has advantage over the cloistered garden rose. "We are rich in wild flowers," he writes in an April letter from Came Rectory, "the snowdrop comes up in January; daffodils are now going off, and primroses are now coming into full bloom, and will soon be followed by cowslips and anemones or windflowers. On the Frome in May will bloom in snow-white patches the water crowfoot, or water ranunculus, a charming sight, with the water tinted blue from the sky . . . The river Stour bears the yellow water-lily, *Nuphar Lutea,* which we call the clote. Our hedges, as the summer goes on, are tinted with the blossom of the blackthorn, whitethorn, honeysuckle, wild rose, and briony, goosegrass, and other plants."[36] He favored the oxslip, planted it in the garden at Came, and would walk down from the verandah to look at its pale yellow blossoms when, at greatly advanced age, he was strong enough to do little else. We are reminded of Francis Darwin's sentence about his father—who as an old man looked rather like Barnes, and shared his qualities of dignity, curiosity, simplicity and humility—"I used to like to hear him admire the beauty of a flower; it was a kind of gratitude to the flower itself, and a personal love for its delicate form and color."[37] Barnes was also fond of the smell of mint, always carrying a spring in his pocket.

Barnes never poetically uprooted a flower he admired from its setting:

Where glossy red the poppy head
  'S among the stalks so brown, O.[38]

We would be almost distracted from the clote by its surroundings were it not for the rich music of the final line:

The grey-bough' withy's a-leänèn lowly
  Above the water thy leaves do hide;
The bendèn bulrush, a-swaÿèn slowly,
  Do skirt in zummer thy river's zide;
    An' perch in shoals, O,
    Do vill the holes, O,
Where thou dost float, goolden zummer
  clote![39]

The water-lilies with their broad glossy leaves thrilled Barnes, and he was careful to make distinction between the clote of the Stour and the water crowfoot of the Frome. The yellow clote roots in mud, the water crowfoot (*Ranunculus peltatus*) is a true non-rooting water plant, not a lily at all, with a white blossom less than an inch in diameter and somewhat geranium-shaped leaves a little over an inch across. The clote has come to stand for purity of heart.

"The Water Crowfoot"[40]

O small-feäc'd flow'r that now dost bloom
To stud wi' white the shallow Frome,
An' leäve the clote to spread his flow'r
On darksome pools o' stwoneless Stour,
When sof'ly-rizèn aïrs do cool
The water in the sheenèn pool,
Thy beds o' snow-white buds do gleam
So feäir upon the sky-blue stream,
As whitest clouds, a-hangèn high
Avore the blueness o' the sky;
An' there, at hand, the thin-heäir'd cows,
In aïry sheädes o' withy boughs,
Or up bezide the mossy raïls,
Do stan' an' zwing their heavy taïls,
The while the ripplèn stream do flow
Below the dousty bridge's bow;
An' quiv'rèn water-gleams do mock
The weäves, upon the sheäded rock;
An' up athirt the copèn stwone
The laïtren bwoy do leän alwone,
A-watchèn, wi' a stedvast look,
The vallèn waters in the brook,
The while the zand o' time do run
An' leäve his errand still undone.
An' oh! as long's thy buds would gleam
Above the softly-slidèn stream,
While sparklèn zummer-brooks do run
Below the lofty-climèn zun,

I only wish that thou could'st staÿ
Vor noo man's harm, an' all men's jaÿ.
But no, the waterman 'ull weäde
Thy water wi' his deadly bleäde,
To slaÿ thee even in thy bloom,
Fair small-feäced flower o' the Frome.

The reader of this poem is given line by line all he needs to partake of what the poet has, with unobtrusive skill, prepared for him. No monotony is tolerated: tones of light fascinate him, simple colors please him, his eye lingers on arresting textures, he recognizes the poet and himself in the boy, he accepts the cruelty of necessity.

There is fortuitousness in the way we associate flowers with persons or times, but once an impression has been made on us, the elements become inextricable:

"The Lilac"[41]

Dear lilac-tree, a-spreadèn wide
Thy purple blooth on ev'ry zide,
As if the hollow sky did shed
Its blue upon thy flow'ry head;
Oh! whether I mid sheäre wi' thee
Thy open aïr, my bloomèn tree,
Or zee thy blossoms vrom the gloom,
'Ithin my zunless workèn-room,
My heart do leäp, but leäp wi' sighs,
At zight o' thee avore my eyes,
For when thy grey-blue head do swaÿ
In cloudless light, 'tis Spring, 'tis Maÿ.

'Tis Spring, 'tis Maÿ, as Maÿ woonce shed
His glowèn light above thy head—
When thy green boughs, wi' bloomy tips,
Did sheäde my children's laughèn lips;
A-screenèn vrom the noonday gleäre
Their rwosy cheäks an' glossy heäir;
The while their mother's needle sped,
Too quick vor zight, the snow-white thread,
Unless her han', wi' lovèn ceäre,
Did smooth their little heads o' heäir;
Or wi' a sheäke, tie up anew
Vor zome wild voot, a slippèn shoe;
An' I did leän bezide thy mound
Ageän the deäsy-dappled ground,
The while the woaken clock did tick
My hour o' rest away too quick,
An' call me off to work anew,
Wi' slowly-ringèn strokes, woone, two.

Barnes is not a nature poet—whatever that may be. Nature assumes a large place in his poetry because of its relation to the human scene. We might almost say it is the air which Barnes's subjects breathe. It also provides the symbols in which he thinks, and a man-made object of considerable familiarity may blend into the landscape and assume the quality of natural background:

Why thik wold post[42] so long kept out,
Upon the knap, his eärms astrout,
A-zendèn on the weary veet
By where the dree cross roads do meet;
An' I've a-come so much thik woy,
Wi' happy heart, a man or bwoy,
That I'd a-meäde, at last, a'most
A friend o' thik wold guidèn post.

and create a drama all its own:

Poor Nanny Brown, woone darkish night,
When he'd a-been a-païnted white,
Wer frighten'd, near the gravel pits,
So dead's a hammer into fits,
A-thinkèn 'twer the ghost she know'd
Did come an' haunt the Leyton road;
Though, after all, poor Nanny's ghost
Turn'd out to be the guidèn post.[43]

His primary interest is in human emotion, but there is no resentment at anything that emotion acknowledges in the plangent life of the world:

"The Zilver-Weed"[44]

The zilver-weed upon the green,
    Out where my sons an' daughters plaÿ'd,
Had never time to bloom between
    The litty steps o' bwoy an' maïd.
But rwose-trees down along the wall,
    That then wer all the maïden's ceäre,
An' all a-trimm'd an' traïn'd, did bear
    Their bloomèn buds vrom Spring to Fall.

But now the zilver leaves do show
    To zummer day their goolden crown,
Wi' noo swift shoe-zoles' litty blow,
    In merry plaÿ to beät em down.
An' where vor years zome busy hand
    Did traïn the rwoses wide an' high;
Now woone by woone the trees do die,
    An' vew of all the row do stand.

The lack of resentment is due to what we have earlier called his recognition of the rightness of what is. That rightness points on to its living Cause, and in it, as his faith defines it, he rests.

We have seen in this short section that the final subject matter of the best poems is not easily to be defined. This is our assurance of the presence of a true poetic strain, however minor. "It is conceivable that all good poems say the same thing, and that this thing is what poetry was designed to say. But if there is sense in so broad a statement, then the thing said by poetry must be an abstraction unmanageable in words. And it is. The words of a great poem are concerned with more than their ostensible content. It is not the words so much as the passion behind,

them, the loving care with which they have been maneu-
vered into position, the envelope of sincerity and significance which they carry with them like an atmosphere, the
conviction they have of being at the centre of the unalterable human world, by which we know ourselves in the
presence of a good poet."[45] The words are Mark Van
Doren's. . . .

Notes

[1] William Wordsworth, *Upon The Sight of A Beautiful
Picture.*

[2] *Poems*, p. 401.

[3] *Life*, p. 345.

[4] *Poems*, p. 20.

[5] *Ibid*, p. 105.

[6] *Ibid.*, p. 112.

[7] *Poems*, p. 391.

[8] *Ibid.*, p. 407.

[9] *Poems*, p. 248.

[10] *Ibid*, p. 251.

[11] *Poems*, p. 361.

[12] *Poems*, p. 11.

[13] *Ibid*, p. 10.

[14] *Ibid.*, p. 345.

[15] *Poems*, p. 252.

[16] John Burroughs, *Winter Sunshine*, Boston, 1889, pp.
183-4.

[17] *Selected Poems*, p. 277.

[18] The rook is, like the crow it resembles, a member of the
genus *Corvus*, and is the more common in England. Other
English members of the genus are the jackdaw and the raven.

[19] William Barnes, *A Selection from Unpublished Poems*, Dorchester, 1870, p. 21.

[20] Major C. S. Jarvis in the magazine *Country Life*, 7
May 1948, London, p. 919.

[21] *Poems*, p. 21.

[22] Rev. Thomas Gisborne (1758-1846), *Walks in a Forest.*

[23] *Poems*, p. 88.

[24] *Ibid.*, p. 147.

[25] *Ibid.*, p. 228.

[26] *Poems*, p. 328.

[27] *Common English*, p. 30.

[28] The impossible final line of the original version
was: Wi' thease. young feace, in thease wold pleace.

[29] Proof sheets from Oxford University Press, 11 June
1917, *William Barnes*, Ward's English Poets, essay by
Thomas Hardy, Collection of the Dorset County Museum.

[30] *Poems*, p 15.

[31] *Ibid.*, p. 16.

[32] *Common English*, p. 23.

[33] *Common English*, p. 97.

[34] *Ibid.*, p. 36.

[35] *Poems*, p. 21.

[36] *Life*, p. 345.

[37] Curtis and Greenslet, *The Practical Cogitator*. Boston, Houghton, Mifflin Co., 1945, p. 200.

[38] *Poems*, p. 76.

[39] *Ibid.*, p. 64.

[40] *Poems*, p. 254.

[41] (The last four lines of the poem are omitted.) *Poems*.
p. 255.

[42] This post stood near an old house called Shirley
House, at Bagber.

[43] *Poems*, p. 166.

[44] *Ibid*, p. 409.

[45] Mark Van Doren, *The Private Reader*. New York.
Henry Holt, 1942 p.10. . . .

Bernard Jones (essay date 1962)

SOURCE: Foreword to *The Poems of William Barnes*.
Volume 1, edited by Bernard Jones, Centaur Press,
1962, pp. 3-22.

[*In the following foreword to* The Poems of William Barnes, *Jones surveys Barnes's life and work as a philologist and poet, particularly studying the nature of his dialect eclogues set in his native Dorset.*]

Since the publication of **Poems of Rural Life in the Dorset Dialect** in 1844, the name of William Barnes has seldom for long dropped out of publishers' lists. New editions of this book were published in 1847, 1862 and 1866. In 1846 his **Poems Partly of Rural Life in National English** was brought out; in 1859 **Hwomely Rhymes. A Second Collection of Poems in the Dorset Dialect,** which went into a second edition in 1863; in 1862 **Poems of Rural Life in the Dorset Dialect. Third Collection,** which went into a second edition in 1869; in 1868 **Poems of Rural Life in Common English;** in 1870 what Barnes would have called a bookling under the heading of **A Selection from Unpublished Poems;** and between 1878-81 a little Bible play on Ruth. These last two were printed and published—if they can be said to have been published at all—in Dorchester. Finally, in 1879, the three collections of dialect poems were published as one volume, and this went on being issued into the twentieth century, until, indeed, it was replaced by two selections, the one made by the poet's elder son and the other by Thomas Hardy.

Such a record represents a solid poetic achievement, and to it should be added the American editions of **Hwomely Rhymes** in 1864 and of **Poems of Rural Life in Common English** in 1869.

But poetry was not Barnes's only interest. As a schoolmaster he seems to have found it just as cheap to write and have printed his own text books, and as a townsman of Dorchester he was able to express himself on almost any matter in the local press. His essays, short or long, began in the local papers in the 1820's, steered their way through a long association with the *Gentleman's Magazine,* then through the short life of the revived *Retrospective Review* to the highly respectable pages of *Fraser's Magazine, The Reader* and *Macmillan's Magazine.* The archæological and philological societies asked for his contributions, and, in later life, he even wrote for the *Ladies' Treasury* and the *Leisure Hour.* Not everyone took to his prose style, though Carlyle did, and so some of his articles had to appear in rather unlikely company.

Such essays must have made him known to a great body of readers. However, more important than his periodical contributions was a series of books of historical, archæological and philological gleanings. **Se Gefylsta** (1849—second edition 1866), which is a sensible Anglo-Saxon primer; **A Philological Grammar** (1854), which is grounded on over sixty languages; **Notes on Ancient Britain and the Britons** (1858); **Views of Labour and Gold** (1859); **Tiw or A View of the Roots and Stems of the English as a Teutonic Tongue** (1862); **A Grammar and Glossary of the Dorset Dialect** (1863), which he revised from the editions of his poems published in 1844 and 1847 and which he much more thoroughly revised in 1886; **Early England and the Saxon-English** (1869); **An Outline of English Speech-Craft** (1878); and **An Outline of Rede-Craft (Logic)** (1880) make up a weighty mass of a self-taught man's questionings and answers to matters which came to interest the nineteenth century. His answers were not always right. He was taken in for instance by the forgeries of Iolo Morganwg, the learned stonemason who invented the gorsedd rites and then grafted them on to the Welsh Eisteddfodau, of which they have become a central feature: but so too were most Welsh scholars until the twentieth century. His studies in philology were spoken of with contempt by Skeat—yet Barnes began his studies single handed long before the combined operations of the countless literary societies of Furnivall. And although all his answers may not have stood the tests of later scholarship, they tell not a little about William Barnes. And many of those who so enthusiastically corrected the opinions of this 'untaught' man have, in their turn, also suffered correction.

But although, like Morris, Barnes was in the habit of talking of his poetry as only a pastime, it is the poetry which has given him his claim on later times. It is true that Lucy Baxter, his daughter, entitled her biography *The Life of William Barnes, Poet and Philologist* (1887), but since his death in 1886 interest has centred almost wholly on his poetry.

Nor has this interest been as thin as the general interest in Victorian poetry. Apart from Lucy Baxter's book, there were warm tributes by Thomas Hardy, Patmore, Gosse and Palgrave; in 1888 C. J. Wallis wrote about his early life; in 1891 a selection of his poems was appreciatively prefaced by Charles Sayle in Miles's *Poets and Poetry of the Nineteenth Century;* and in 1906 a selection of uncollected poems was published in Dorchester. All this time the volume of 1879 had been kept in print. Then in 1908 Thomas Hardy chose and introduced **Select Poems of William Barnes** at the request of Sir Walter Raleigh. This edition was twice reprinted later. **Select Poems of Rural Life in the Dorset Dialect** edited by the poet's son, the Reverend William Miles Barnes, was published the next year. In 1916, in Ward's *English Poets,* Hardy again introduced another selection of Barnes's poems; in 1925 John Drinkwater introduced **Twenty Poems in Common English;** in 1934 Sir Arthur Quiller Couch printed a lecture on Barnes—a very inaccurate one in the biographical parts—in *The Poet as Citizen;* in 1950 Mr. Grigson introduced and edited **Selected Poems of William Barnes;** *William Barnes Linguist* by Mr. Willis D. Jacobs was published in 1952; *William Barnes of Dorset,* a biography by Giles Dugdale, in 1953; and *William Barnes, the Man and the Poems,* by Mr. William Turner Levy, in 1960.

Such lists are by no means complete, yet they show quite clearly that Barnes has never wanted readers, even in the twentieth century, and that it has always been possible to get hold of at least a handful of his poems. The reasons are not hard to find. Without the slightest knowledge of the man's life a reader can draw from his poems something of the essence of a personality full of gentle compassion and delight. For although his lines do not burst forth with speculative discoveries of truth, they convey even more surely the quickness of his own kind of truth, the shy truth of the years upon years of the hedgerows with all their tiny details and absolute rightness, of the haymakers about their old wagon with its ages old tackle, of times of day or night:

> While rise or sink the glittering stars
>   Above dim woods, or hillock brows,
> There, out within the moonpaled bars,
>   In darksome bunches sleep your cows.

There is no straining after the unusual image. Barnes, with quiet tenderness, simply takes what lies about him in the life of the land and its folk. This life he understood so deeply that he seems part of it, and his word music and word pictures seem part of its natural means of expression.

The appearance and behaviour of his landfolk are those of the Vale of Blackmore in the early nineteenth century. Their homes, their work and play are such as Barnes remembered from early life. Nevertheless, he made his picture, his rising vision as he might have called it, by the most thoughtful looking into this world around him. But although it is part of a poet's task to shew his mind to his readers, the reader of Barnes never feels that he has been pressed to see things in a certain way. For Barnes took much care to ensure that the thoughts in his poetry arose naturally from its images and that the latter were not contrived or contorted to demonstrate an argument. These images did not just come. Barnes's mind and imagination selected and created them. But his skill in selecting and creating was such as to conceal the work required, and it is this skill which produces the almost invariable harmony and sweetness of his poetry. Of the fundamental brainwork which Rossetti thought needful to all poetic creation Barnes was fully aware, but he sought to shew the indwelling poetry of things and to hide the signs of the hard work. When he writes in **"The Rooks"**:

> *(1)* At Akdean wood, folk say they meet,
>   To fold at night their weary wings,
> And roost, with little clenching feet,
>   On boughs that nightwind softly swings.

> *(2)* O yes, at Akdean's shadowy ground
>   Are broad limb'd oaks, and ashes tall;
> Black pines, and aspen trees that sound
>   As soft as water at a fall.

the sense of fitness is fully satisfied.

It might be thought odd that a poet for whom such claims can be made—and no less were made for him by Patmore, Hopkins and Hardy—should never have had all his poems collected until now. Two reasons come to mind at once. Although Barnes was the kind of person who had Tennyson and Patmore—and even Martin Tupper—visit him, and although he was a parson, the general picture of him as a peasant poet, which arose naturally enough from his poetry, was never really shewn up as the deception it was. Since his death this difficulty has been prolonged by the often well meant efforts to keep up the tradition of Barnes as simply and exclusively 'the Dorset poet.' But to keep Barnes for Dorset is to set greater store by birthplace than by poetry. Barnes, it is true, helped 'the Dorset poet' school by writing almost invariably about Dorset. But if birthplace, upbringing and subject matter are taken as the ruling facts, Barnes is not even 'the Dorset poet': he is 'the poet of Blackmore Vale.' All such limitations are, in a sense, accidental, and should not be given weight enough to withhold from Barnes his rightful place among the English poets. Barnes's English is not always standard English, for he often chose to write in the English of Dorset, and this is the second reason why his poems have had to wait so long for gathering in. Yet his Dorset English is as near to standard English as Spenser's English, or Burns's or T. E. Brown's, and gives no ground for ranking Barnes with the many quaint provincial versifiers of his day.

Both the dialect in which many of his poems were written and the places and manners they set forth have held up wider knowledge and love of his work. No-one who knows Dorset would wish that Barnes had written of other scenes. But for some time the great need has been that Barnes should be read as one of the English poets and not as 'the Dorset Poet,' and the gathering together of all his poetry should help towards this adjustment.

Barnes himself would have been rather bemused by such talk. He had a shrewd knowledge of what his poetry was worth, and in his own modest way he delighted in friendly reviews. But although he enjoyed such fame as his poems brought him, he would have thought it unseemly in a poet to strive for it. Indeed fame may have been to him rather an airy abstraction, for no poet ever kept his eyes upon the object more untiringly.

He was no mere recorder, however. Most of the things that went into his poetry had been stored in his mind many years before they were given new life by his own original imagination. And so, although he left his Blackmore farmstead before he was twenty, for between sixty and seventy years he shewed in his poetry vision after vision of the life of the vale.

Barnes was born at Bagber near Sturminster Newton, the head town of the vale, in 1801. The family, once small land-owners, had come down in the world and the wartime and post-war farming conditions brought them still lower. Barnes's mother died when he was five and he spent most of the rest of his childhood with his father's sisters. He was first taught at a dame's school and then at the Church school at Sturminster, and at the age of thirteen or fourteen became clerk to a solicitor there. The solicitor died in 1817 and the next year Barnes took a similar appointment in Dorchester. There he first met Julia Miles, the daughter of an excise supervisor. Her father thought Barnes's income not enough for marriage and in 1823 Barnes gave up his clerkship and went to Mere in Wiltshire to run a school. This he must have done well enough, for in 1827 he and Julia Miles were married. They had the Chantry House at Mere as school and home until 1835, when Barnes, hoping for some kind of advancement that would enable him the better to bring up a growing family, returned to Dorchester. There he ran schools in three different buildings before he retired in 1862. By then, however, Julia had been dead ten years.

As early as 1838 he put his name on the boards as a ten years man at St. John's, Cambridge. He was admitted to the B.D. degree in 1850, but he had already been ordained in 1847, and he served as curate at Winterbourne Whitcombe until his wife became ill in 1852. The ten years which followed ended with some financial difficulties which were solved partly by a civil list pension, but mainly by the gift of the living at Winterbourne Came with Whitcombe. The family moved out to the thatched rectory of Came, and Barnes the schoolmaster became the parson, whom until lately not a few Durnovarians could bring back to mind from childhood days. In 1885 Hardy moved into his new house at *Max Gate,* which is only a few hundred yards from Barnes's rectory. But Barnes died in the next fall.

Apart from some natural sorrow, loss and pain, it was a seemingly uneventful life which, to a fair degree, allowed him to spend his time as he would most have wished. His many books and papers shew that his interests were about as wide as anyone's could be, and that such of his time as was not given up to pupils and parishioners was not wasted in idleness.

Now that all his poems have been brought together, it is possible to say a few words about the growth of his skill and insight. Readers who begin with the early poems will find few tokens of the kind of poetry Barnes wrote in middle life. These early poems, indeed, are often very slight things, and it should not be forgotten that some of them were published when Barnes was only nineteen years of age, and that others are from letters and were not meant for publication at all. *Orra,* however, which was probably written in his twenty-first year, shews more than a little promise, and a number of the poems which went into the book of 1846 belong to the thirties. The poem which is printed at the end of the early poems, and which is here reprinted for the first time since 1840, **"Thoughts Suggested at the Bazaar at Kingston House,"** however, shews Barnes at ease in the measured, easy-paced style he was to make thoroughly his own. It must be allowed that the moralising at the end, one of Barnes's less pleasing habits in the eyes of after times, is a little clumsy, but the poem conveys the very tones of Barnes's own poetic voice, moves with his own gait and to his own music, and in 'airy Paladour' gives a foretaste of a magic which he was able later to call upon at will.

"Thoughts Suggested at the Bazaar at Kingston House" was written in common English. By the time he wrote it, however, Barnes had written a number of poems in the Dorset dialect, and it would seem likely that it was the practice of writing in the dialect which really made him aware of his insight and skill. It has often been said that Barnes himself spoke the Dorset dialect. He did—as a performance. Everything, including the memories of a number of people who heard him speak, shews that he spoke common English, though most of those who remember or remembered his voice recall that the sound of the letter *'r'* was lightly trilled. This must have been noticeable, for several people carried it in mind for over sixty years. As a young man around Sturminster Barnes must have spoken with the Vale accent, but among the Latinizations of solicitorial English his speech must have moved towards the polite manner of the day, and the latter, as spoken by the cream of Dorchester society, was probably his ideal in early manhood. His accent certainly did not upset Miss Miles. Thereafter he must have busied himself teaching standard English to his many pupils.

Teaching, indeed, was the experience which turned his mind towards the practical importance of philology. He had worked at the classical languages in youth and natural taste later led him to study others. But with his pupils he faced for the first time the difficulty of trying to explain English in terms of the classics, and the difficulty of trying to teach with a kind of English that was a muddle of derivations from non-Saxon speeches. As years went by he believed more and more strongly that Saxon speech is the speech best understood by Saxons, and he Saxonized his prose to the height of his belief. In understanding his poetry, however, the theories he practised later are of less weight than the fact that teaching fixed his mind upon the central problem of how to make a speech immediately understandable among Saxons used to various social conventions of speech.

The situation had come home to him when he visited Wales in 1831. There he found that one form of speech is understood by all classes. Today the people of North Wales cannot always hide their mirth at the speech of their brethren from the south, but Welsh is, and in 1831 it must have been much more so, the speech of the people as a whole. Barnes thought that this was brought about by its comparative purity, and he called with all his might for a purer Saxon English which should be to the Saxons as Welsh was to the Welsh. In short, he wanted a speech which could be wholy understood by humble folk and children. He turned his thoughts to dialects, above all to those of Dorset, and found that many a dialect word and idiom which seemed out of place in polite society could claim a pure Saxon pedigree.

Why his first pieces of dialect writing should have been eclogues is not known. He had had a comedy and a farce produced locally in 1831—both are lost, apart, perhaps, from an **"Address,"** which is printed in this edition—and in Wales he may have been amused by the interludes of Twm o'r Nant. He may also have seen that the Welsh art of pennillion singing calls for a skill not unlike that called for in what in Dorset is known as 'running down.' This art Barnes defined as:

'To depreciate; to find fault with; to speak ill of.

The Dorset dialect often affords excellent examples of *running down,* particularly of work; not from the ill-nature of its speakers, but from a wish to show their own discrimination. . . . 'What did ye gi'e var they vish?' 'Two-pence a-piece.' 'Lar! how dear tha be. Why I wou'den gi'e a penny var the lot. Why tha be a-ponted an' a-squotted al to pieces: tha woon't keep till to-marra.'

And, of course, he knew the pastoral eclogues of classical and European poetry. But Barnes's reason for writing about the landfolk in the fall of 1833 and after is quite clear.

In an essay in *Two Cheers for Democracy* Mr. E. M. Forster suggests that for all the effect it had on his poetry Barnes might never have heard of the uprisings of 1830, and in *Unprofessional Essays* the late John Middleton Murry wrote of Clare as if no-one else had shewn up the effects of the enclosure acts in poetry. It never seemed likely that a man like Barnes should be unaware of such things and it is now possible to shew that he took the closest interest in them. The social agitation of 1830, indeed, turned his mind to the lives of the working classes of landfolk around him and led

him to write a series of eclogues of the greatest importance to the social historian and to anyone who would understand the making of William Barnes the poet.

There has always been some confusion about these poems because Lucy Baxter, who wrote the life of her father while she was living in Florence, did not have all the information needed for making a clear statement about them. Over seventy years later it is still impossible to claim that all the information is available, as files of old country newspapers often enough lack one or two issues here and there. Nevertheless, it is possible to give a much fuller account of this part of Barnes's creative life.

Barnes's insights into social change and upheaval in the 1830's are found in six eclogues—

> **"The Common A-Took In"**
> **"The 'Lotments"**
> **"Rusticus Emigrans or Over Sea to Settle"**
> **"Rusticus Res Politicas Animadvertens. The New Poor Laws"**
> **"The Unioners"**—the poem was later called **"The Times"**
> **"Two Farms in Woone."**

As these poems are now first brought together, it is worth spending a little time on them one by one, although really full consideration of them will have to await the publication of the book on Barnes's life and work.

"The Common A-Took In" first appeared in 1834 as **"Rusticus Dolens;/ or, Inclosures of Common./ A Dorsetshire Eclogue in the Dorset Dialect, by a Native of the County."** John is on his way to market to sell his geese, and he fears he will soon have to sell his cow, for, as he tells his neighbour Thomas:

'. . . they be guoin to close the Common, I do hear.'

Thomas says that John may get 'a lotment,' but this, says John, would not be 'so handy' as use of the common. They agree that the advantages of common land were fuel, fodder and giblets. Thomas laments:

'. . . if a poor man got a bit o' bread They'll try to tiake it vrom en.'

but ends with the hope:

'That they be got into a way O'letten bits o' ground out to the poor.'

John is less hopeful and would like 'a lotment,'—

'Or I must goo to Workhouse I do fear.'

The ill effects of enclosure on the landfolk may be studied in the writings of many later social historians. Barnes never forgot them and in the 1860's he held forth about them in a paper written for the royal commission enquiring into the employment of women and children in agriculture.

"The 'Lotments" shews John less fortunate than Richard in having failed to rent a patch of land from the squire. They talk of the store of food even a small plot can give. And if father owns a bit of land, the children too can help. Richard believes he is well in pocket by the deal, but John says that his family is

'. . . a starven nearly, an' we'd goo
To 'merica, if we'd enough to car us.'

As he cannot afford passages, he has to 'live on the parish,' cracking stones and taking outdoor relief, a disgrace which he thinks he could have warded off if only he had had 'a 'lotment.'

The movement for letting plots of ground to the poor began in the hard times of the French wars. However, it was slow to take root, and, sadly enough, the machine wrecking of 1830 did more to quicken its growth than thirty years of abstract philanthropy.

"Rusticus Emigrans" shews Robert asking Richard about emigration. Richard has sent his family off to London to join the boat, and he is about to beg lifts on the road to join them. He loves his own birthplace, but:

'. . . a man can't get a luoaf to veed en . . .
'Tis hard that if he'd work there's noo work
    var'n,
Or that his work woon't bring enough o'
    money
To keep en . . .
There's noo work here at huome that I can
    come at,
And zoa I'll goo abroad and try var
    some'hat.'

It is perhaps odd that in 1834 Barnes should write of emigrating to Van Diemen's Land, for the convicts of the 1830 riots had been shipped there and martyrs of Tolpuddle were packed off to Australia in the very year of the eclogue. The miseries of transportation were well enough known, but perhaps the presence of Dorset folk in such far off places gave them an imaginative reality for Dorset folk at home, and Barnes may have leant upon this for poetic purposes.

In **"Rusticus Res Politicas Animadvertens"** the two neighbours share the hope that they will keep out of the workhouse and discuss the system of the new poor law. The law of 1834 was an attempt to cut the poor rate. Outdoor relief was reduced until the only way a poor person could get relief was by entering the 'union,' a workhouse serving a union of parishes and known to the poor as a Bastille, a term still used by Thomas Hughes in *The Scouring of the White Horse* in 1859. The aim of the system was to make the supervisor of relief the hardest taskmaster and worst paymaster possible. There was to be neither beer nor speech at meals, and wives and husbands were to be separated. Barnes gives a sympathetic discussion of the sense and nonsense of the law.

"The Unioners," which was later called **"The Times,"** deals with another problem of the 1830's. The neighbours John and Tom must have known the fate of the Tolpuddle martyrs, for their conversation took place in 1838. But something simply has to be done when

'Bread is so high an' wages be so low
That a'ter worken lik a hoss, you know
A man can't yarn enough to vill his belly.'

John has little faith in politics and tells Tom, who has learnt his chartist catechism from Henry Vincent, that he

'. . . don't understand how this is yable
To put a jinte o' beef upon my tiable,
Or buy me flick to grease my tiaties.'

Nor does he think much of these fine chartist leaders:

'D'ye think, if we should meet em in the
    street
At Bath ar Lunnon, that tha'd stan' a treat?'

They had better look to the parson and squire rather than to outsiders for help. Tom, however, resents the charity of the gentry and says his friends will have their rights, and that it must be every man for himself. That may be all right for chartists, says John:

'But God ya know is var us al.'

The struggle for the right to form unions was important in the local history of Dorchester in 1838. In a wider sense this eclogue shews that Barnes had a good understanding of the interweaving social movements of *the times*—those of the unioners, leaguers and chartists.

The discussion in **"Two Farms in Woone"** turns again upon the hardships of the landfolk. Thomas's employer is to be turned out of his farm by the landlord, who for some time has been calling in leases:

'. . . In theäse here pleäce there used to be
Eight farms avore they were a-drow'd
    together,
An' eight farm-housen. Now how many be
    there?
Why after this, you know there'll be but dree,'

says Thomas's friend Robert. By letting the houses fall down the landlord lowers his repairs bill, and by using machinery he can cut his wages bill by sacking his labourers. And, looking back on former days, the landfolk see:

> ' . . . many that wer little farmers then,
> Be now a-come all down to leäb'ren men.'

These eclogues seen as a whole give a most true and detailed picture of social conditions and of the society of the landfolk. It is for this reason that so much space has been given to them here. For they shew that what is often rather sentimentally called the sweetness of Barnes's poetry was grounded on close and clear knowledge of the lives of his landfolk and not upon unwillingness to look upon the sorry scheme of things.

By writing the eclogues Barnes learnt where his greatest strength in poetry lay, and thereafter was able to write in Dorset or English speech the poetry by which he is best known. But the importance of the eclogues in the growth of Barnes as a poet does not mean that they are necessarily his best poems. Some readers think they are; others would choose his humorous verses. Barnes preferred his pathetic pieces, of which many new examples will be found in this edition. But no matter what the reader's preferences, they must be the offshoot of Barnes's experience of writing these early eclogues. Before them, his poems were mostly in the shape of personal reflections. After them, it became clear that he had found the dramatic mask which enabled him to behave as an instrument recording and interpreting the delicate shades and changes of the world of his youth in song after song.

At first, a part of this mask was the use of the Dorset speech. Later, he was able to write without it, and for the last eighteen or nineteen years of his life he wrote almost wholly in common English. From 1834 to 1867, however, his poetic instrument was mostly dialect, and as this has been a hindrance to the gathering together of his poetry, the nature of Barnes's Dorset dialect is, as he would have said, markworthy.

The most important thing to be said about it is that no reader who is willing to read the poems for ten minutes can fail to hear their music, and at the end of half an hour the poems will read themselves naturally enough. The aim should not be to speak 'Dorset-like,' but to listen to Barnes's Dorset speech. Barnes himself has made things difficult by saying that dialect was his mother speech. There is clearly some truth in this, as far as it goes, but it has been shewn already that Barnes spoke standard English. He used standard English in all the poetry he wrote before he reached the aged of thirtytwo or three and in almost all the poetry he wrote after he had reached the age of sixtysix, and he wrote his own varying kinds of standard English prose throughout his life. Mr. Grigson, therefore, thinks that the writing in the Dorset dialect was a learned perversity which Barnes was able to carry off because he had been brought up with the dialect. And, allowing for the importance of the early eclogues in the making of the poet, it would seem that although the words 'learned perversity' sound rather harsh they do tell some of the truth about the dialect used by Barnes and his way of using it.

The first difficulty is deciding what the Dorset dialect is. The dialect in Hardy's novels does not sound much like the dialect in Barnes's poems. But then Hardy was a Dorchester man, and by the time Hardy was born Barnes had more or less decided that the towns spoke a vulgar mongrel jargon and not the pure Dorset dialect. The dialect Barnes had in mind when writing the dialect poems was that spoken around Sturminster Newton in the early years of the century. Even today there is a great difference between the speeches of Dorchester and Sturminster. Dorchester has a more staccato manner, Sturminster a flowing and melodious music, to be heard in the market place and over the counter, so it is not surprising that Hardy and Barnes wrote their different kinds of dialect speech. But Barnes's delving into his memories of childhood to bring to life a passing kind of speech cannot have been a simple exercise, and his ideas of what had been spoken, or, rather, of what he thought ought to have been spoken, seem to have undergone some alteration in the passing of years. The details of such alterations can be traced in the different editions of the poems. An instance of Barnes's handling of the dialect is his treatment of what is still a common phrase in Dorset. A Dorset speaker today who had been refused a request would report the fact by saying, 'He woulden *gi'e it to I.'* This was printed a number of times in early editions of Barnes's poems. In later editions, however, he altered the phrase to *'gi'e it to me.'* Likewise the phrase *'wi' we'* of the early editions he altered later to *'wi' us.'* It is possible, of course, that in making such alterations he was only straightening out his memories of the Vale speech. But there are two far more likely reasons for the alterations. As a philologist Barnes was keen to shew that the Dorset speech was derived from Anglo-Saxon, and when he sought to understand the Dorset dialect more fully he did so with the Teutonic framework in mind. Above all, the more he became aware of his standing as a poet, the more shrewdly and confidently he wrought the instrument to his needs. So the Dorset dialect in which most of Barnes's dialect poems are written is a speech which Barnes thought the Blackmore landfolk would have spoken if their speech had grown by its own laws from the times of Alfred, and a speech which made possible the poems of Barnes in the Dorset dialect.

It must not be thought the dialect has wholly gone from Dorset, and, indeed, people there are very sensitive about it. A few years ago the present writer wrote a dialect poem as part of an appeal for money to repair a Dorset church. A parochial meeting voted that before the poem could be approved it should be sub-titled: 'In the style of William Barnes,' lest it were thought that the poem made fun of those it was meant to help. The speech of Barnes's poems is certainly not very close to anything that can be heard in the county now. Indeed it is mostly a highly personal kind of speech. For whereas a few of the dialect pieces of the 1830's seek to use the current idiom in the same way as Burn's dialect poems use the Scots idiom of his time, the later pieces mould the language to their needs in a manner which recalls Spenser's handling of ordinary English. It would be unwise to force the parallels too strongly. Spenser had a general manner of handling English which was clear enough to his own ear and imagination, no matter how troublesome to later generations of schoolchildren. Barnes, however, had a clearer awareness of his own handling of English and the effect is naturally less congested. But if eccentrics like Stanyhurst and Doughty are left aside, Spenser and Barnes may well be the two English poets who have succeeded in creating out of common English the most essentially personal forms of poetic speech.

Eccentricity, of course, is a matter of personal taste. There are fine passages in both Stanyhurst and Doughty, and the linking of Barnes and Spenser as creators of essentially personal forms of speech must bring to the minds of many readers the poems of Hopkins. Hopkins never met Barnes, but he had a high opinion not only of Barnes's poetry but also of his seeking to Saxonize modern English. A lot has been said, most of it admiringly, of Hopkins's taking into his poetry the features and shapes of Anglo-Saxon and Welsh verse. Yet he was only in his second year when Barnes's 1846 volume, which contains his adaptations of Anglo-Saxon alliteration, came out; only in his twelfth when **"My Orchet in Linden Lea,"** with its well known burden in Welsh cynghanedd, first came out; only in his fourteenth when Barnes had published his main essays on Welsh poetry in **Notes on Ancient Britain and the Britons;** and still only in his twentythird when Barnes's essay on **"The Old Bardic Poetry"** was printed in *Macmillan's Magazine*. The description of the sea translated from Japix's Friesic version of the psalms as:

> The souse-rush-brush-hollow-bulgy-hopping
>   top

is among Barnes's papers, not Hopkins's. This way of handling words is so often found in Hopkins's poetry, as in the following lines from *The Windhover:*

> I caught this morning morning's minion, king-
>   dom of daylight's dauphin, dabble-dawn-
>   drawn Falcon, in his
>   riding

> Of the rolling level underneath him
> steady air,

that it is widely held as his invention or innovation. But similar effects are found in Barnes's poems, as when he writes of a horse as:

> A cunning jade, that now would find
> Out all my roads if I were blind,
>   By winding ways, on-wand'ring wide,
>   Or wilder waste, or wind-blown wood.

Indeed, although Barnes seldom left Wessex, his mind ranged widely among the speeches and lives of peoples of many parts of the earth. At Mere he translated a number of Italian poems, mostly Petrarch's. Some of his translations from Persian poetry were printed in *Nine* in 1956. And apart from his knowledge of Anglo-Saxon and Welsh he had a wide knowledge of oriental literatures and made translations of the Psalms and other pieces of Bible poetry. Some passages from his translations of the Psalms were printed in the *London Quarterly* in 1960. He also corresponded with the committee which revised the Authorized Version of the Bible.

Although Barnes seldom tried merely to reproduce the effects of other literatures in his own poetry, the influence of his knowledge of them can be seen very often. The occasional use of Welsh cynghanedd—the exact matching of consonants in the two halves of a verse, as in the burden: **"Ellen Brine ov Allenburn"**—is handled so discreetly that it might often pass unnoticed. Perhaps the most striking of his borrowings are those from the Persian, as in the well known poem **"Woak Hill,"** which has a measure that Hardy found useful for *The Dynasts*.

Detailed discussion of Barnes's handling of such things will have to await the publication of the book on his life and work. His skill went on growing long after the time of the early eclogues. He was at that time already a fine painter of a scene, with good eyes for colour. Some time in middle life, however, he made a detailed study of colours and shapes of things and movements as they are found in nature, and the poems written after that study, among which are many of those now gathered for the first time, have a new freshness. Whereas the poems written up to almost 1860 might well be illustrated from the paintings of Morland, much of the later poetry has the visionary innocence of the work of Samuel Palmer. Sometimes, as in **"Rings,"** it is the shape itself which forms the theme of a poem, and which burgeons into the most fitting pattern of images. In other poems colour takes a part similar to that there taken by shape, as in **"White and Blue"** and **"Green."** Here Barnes again came close to Hopkins, whose understanding of what he called inscape was grounded on studies of nature not unlike those which Barnes had undertaken before him.

Barnes's skill was well enough known among the poets of his day. Allingham claimed to have brought his work to the notice of the Brownings, Tennyson, Clough and Rossetti; Patmore, Palgrave, Kingsley, Hopkins, Gosse, Hardy, and Quiller-Couch all appreciated his work, and most of them thought it worth while to seek him out personally. Barnes always found, therefore, a fit audience, though few. But his poetry appeals not only to the poet and critic. It conveys to anyone who cares to know it the gentleness and keenness of his insights in the tones of the poet's own voice:

> The children's light feet had climb'd the
> treads
>   Of stairs that to them are high and steep,
> And lay on their darksome little beds
>   With white little eyelids shut in sleep.

There are many such beautiful moments of peaceful restraint. But even apart from the delicacy of the handling there is much in Barnes's scene which might appeal to after times. The output of Victorian rural verse was both vast and varied, and the temper of Barnes's mind and the tones of his voice lacked the strident gestures popular at the time. But even though poets and critics were shrewd enough to see that Barnes's poetry was like nothing else ever written, the common reader of the time may be forgiven, perhaps, for thinking it a part of the overwhelming outpouring of rural verse. Today, however, the common reader will nowhere find a truer or more moving picture of how our forefathers dwelt until not so long ago. Their ways, the sights they saw and sounds they heard are all in the poems, which now have a new interest as part of the truth lying behind the bare facts of history. To an age which has seen so many and such great changes, the poems of Barnes are a glimpse into the heart of one aspect of Christendom as it had grown up through centuries. Not everything about it was good, yet, such as it was, it can be known in Barnes's poetry. And underlying its presentation of a particular part of England in a particular period, the movements of human feelings known to all ages are always there, always gently suggested in a way that must persuade anyone who reads them that the poems of William Barnes reach out beyond Dorset and the nineteenth century to offer an endless wellspring of clear refreshment.

Philip Larkin (review date 1962)

SOURCE: "The Poetry of William Barnes," in *Required Writing: Miscellaneous Pieces, 1955-1982,* Farrar, Straus, Giroux, 1982, pp. 149-52.

[In the following excerpted review of The Poems of William Barnes, *originally published in 1962, Larkin discusses the positive aspects of Barnes's use of dialect in his poetry.]*

It is little short of astonishing that we should have had to wait seventy-five years for the complete poems of William Barnes[1]. When he died in 1886, as old as the century, his work was known and admired by Tennyson, Patmore, Hardy, Allingham, Gosse, Palgrave and Quiller-Couch, and when Bridges made a characteristic sneer at 'the supposed emotion of peasants', his correspondent, Gerard Manley Hopkins, replied sharply: 'I hold your contemptuous opinion an unhappy mistake: [Barnes] is a perfect artist and of a most spontaneous inspiration.' Nor was his appeal limited to men of letters: 'an old Domestic Servant' wrote to him in 1869, having found his poems among some books she was dusting: 'Sir, I shook hands with you in my heart, and I laughed and cried by turns.' Nor has time devalued these tributes. Barnes's work is still acknowledged as a unique part of the variegated richness of nineteenth-century English poetry. His view of nature is clear, detailed and shining, full of exquisite pictorial miniatures: his view of human life is perceptive, compassionate and sad. Yet the time when he is read as an English and not a Dorset poet had been slow in coming—if, indeed, it has come at all.

The obstacle, of course, is the Dorset dialect. It is not so much that the eye is put off by Barnes's attempt to render it phonetically ('Lwonesome woodlands! zunny woodlands!'); nor that, once a few simple rules are grasped, it is particularly difficult to follow (not that an age so determined to make hard work out of reading poetry should mind if it were); it is rather that nowadays we are impatient of dialect as such, and regard efforts to perpetuate it as affectation, a futile attempt to deny the historical necessity of usage that a real artist turns to his own ends. We cannot see why Barnes deliberately made his poems to all intents and purposes unreadable: what prompted, in Mr Geoffrey Grigson's phrase, this 'learned perversity'.

Barnes, a schoolmaster for most of his life, was certainly learned: according to Willis D. Jacobs (*William Barnes, Linguist,* Albuquerque, N. Mex., 1952) he knew upwards of sixty languages, 'from Hindustani, Persian, and Russian, to early Saxon, Welsh, and Hebrew'. And like many a polyglot he was also a philologist, the kind that deplores the 'corruption' of English by Greek and Latin borrowings, and advocates such coinages as 'two-horned rede-ship' (dilemma) and 'pushwainling' (perambulator). His love of Dorset dialect was strong and unaffected: he saw it as a kind of Doric English, 'bold and broad', and although when Hardy made a selection of his poems in 1908 he could see this championship as an utterly lost cause, dialect may well have seemed to hold a much more impregnable position in Barnes's early lifetime, before halfpenny newspapers, the Education Act of 1870, and even the railways.

But his use of it was not a mere schoolmasterly fad. Barnes was a remarkable man, a kind of successful Jude Fawley, who began life as the son of a poor smallholder and gradually made his way from village school to town school, a B.D. at Trinity College, Cambridge, and the living of Winterborne Came, near Dorchester. It would have been easy for him to go to London—even the unambitious Hardy managed that—but he seems not to have wanted to. Nor did his education set him at odds with his environment. He liked his family, his neighbours, and the scenes that surrounded them. He saw nothing out of the way in writing poems called '**Grammer A-Crippled**' and '**Uncle an' Aunt**': Kilvert reports him as saying 'that there was not a line which was not inspired by love for and kindly sympathy with the things and people described'. This being so, it was natural that he should find these things and people indivisible from their own language. If he wrote of joy and sadness, it was their joy and sadness; if it was his own, it came more easily in their accents:

> Since I noo mwore do see your feäce,
>   Up steäirs or down below,
> I'll zit me in the lwonesome pleäce,
>   Where flat-bough'd beech do grow;
> Below the beeches' bough, my love,
>   Where you did never come,
> An' I don't look to meet ye now,
>   As I do look at hwome.

Barnes chose to write in dialect, in short, because it was inextricably bound up, emotionally, with the subjects that moved him to write. Not that he used it exclusively. There are in the present edition some 400 pages of poems in 'national' English against 500 pages of Dorset ones, and in many cases a version in each of the same poem. Comparison of them is interesting, because it shows that while dialect may be antipathetic to us, it carries one unexpectedly modern virtue—that of naturalness, the natural words in their natural order:

> Our minds could never yield the room for all
> Our days at once; but God is ever kind . . .

> Our minds ha' never room enough to call
> Back all sweet days at oonce, but God is
>   kind . . .

Here the dialect is not only smoother, but has the clearer meaning. Barnes liked the colloquial, but he matched it with the artificial: as he chose narrow limits for his life, so he sought intricate stanza forms and devices of rhyme and alliteration from the Welsh and Hebrew. The result is a unique blend of nature and art:

> Aye, at that time our days wer but vew,
> An' our lim's wer but small, an' a-growen;
> An' then the feäir worold wer new,
> An' life wer all hopevul an' gaÿ;
> An' the times o' the sprouten o' leaves,
> An' the cheäk-burnen seasons o' mowen,
> An' binden o' red-headed sheaves,
> Wer all welcome seasons o' jaÿ.

> Then the housen seem'd high, that be low,
> An' the brook did seem wide that is narrow,
> An' time, that do vlee, did goo slow,
> An' veelens now feeble wer strong . . .

This is a fair sample of Barnes's most characteristic mood, for though, as Mr Jones points out, he was by no means unaware of the decline in agricultural conditions (**'The Common A-Took In'**) nor devoid of humour, his sense of the melancholy stealth of time was almost as keen as Hardy's and took precedence. Indeed, the imaginative delicacy of his conceptions (**'Woak Hill'**) at times was superior to Hardy's, though if his work has a deficiency, it is in lacking Hardy's bitter and ironical despair: Barnes is almost too gentle, too submissive and forgiving. . . .

Notes

[1] *The Poems of William Barnes,* edited by Bernard Jones, 2 vols. (London: Centaur Press, 1962).

R. A. Forsyth (essay date 1963)

SOURCE: "The Conserving Myth of William Barnes," in *Victorian Studies,* Vol. VI, No. 4, June, 1963, pp. 325-54.

[*In the following essay, Forsyth probes Barnes's theme of the preservation of rural simplicity.*]

> *The view that a group of people hold towards their past is one of the controlling factors in their morals, religion, art, and intellectual pursuits, to say nothing of the sights, sounds, and actual feel of their daily experience.*

> Charles Frankel, "Explanation and Interpretation in History," in *Theories of History,* ed. Patrick Gardiner

> *I need not insist upon the social, ethical, and political significance of an age's image of man, for it is patent that the view one takes of man affects profoundly one's standard of dignity and*

the humanly possible. And it is in the light of such a standard that we establish our laws, set our aspirations for learning, and judge the fitness of men's acts. . . . Nor is it simply a matter of public concern. For man as individual has a deep and emotional investment in his image of himself . . . [and he] has powerful and exquisite capacities for defending himself against violation of his cherished self-image.

Jerome S. Bruner, "Freud and the Image of Man," in *Freud and the Twentieth Century,* ed. Benjamin Nelson

I

It is a byword that the Victorians responded in many different ways to finding themselves on "a darkling plain." This diversity indicates not only the complexity of their situation, which resulted from the scientific and industrial revolution that transformed English life during the century, but also the characteristic vigour of their efforts to disentangle and comprehend it. These ranged from Charles Kingsley's muscular embrace to Matthew Arnold's fastidious fortification against anarchy. Others were attracted by the ritualistic fervour and traditionalism of Newman, the semi-religious enthusiasm of the Pre-Raphaelites, or the individualism of Mill; still others looked for some effective way of combining these positions.

By contrast with these earnest efforts the response of the Dorset poet, William Barnes, appears at first sight to be simply a nostalgia for the peace of the "good old days," which it seemed had been replaced almost traumatically by the insecurity of a withered faith and a permeating materialism. Certainly Barnes looked back persistently, both in his poetry and at many other levels in his creative and personal life, to his own youth in the countryside and the rural ethos it typified. I want to suggest, however, that viewed properly within the total complex of his personality, this backward-looking habit of mind, which dictated his particularity of selection and treatment of country life and its virtues, did not result from a sentimental evasion of contemporary issues, but amounted rather to a conscious criticism unwaveringly aimed at those very issues. I think one may go even further by suggesting that Barnes's work, more especially his poetry, constituted a myth of minor though not insignificant proportions, and of a thoroughness and consistency to be measured by the graceful strength of his verse. And Barnes's achievement is enhanced in that it stands in direct opposition to the idea of progress—which became identified with technical advances and was increasingly regarded, therefore, as mechanically inevitable—an idea which more than any other characterized the popular conception of the age as it went spinning "down the ringing grooves of change," urged

on by the conviction "that the Heavenly City is at this moment having its building plots laid out on earth."[1]

Many Victorian poets spent their inheritance of Romantic idealism in striving, for the most part unsuccessfully, to find an intellectual faith through a sort of argumentative lyricism. The source of that inheritance was, of course, the revolt of the intuitive imagination against Augustan rationalism and empiricism, the attempt to comprehend imaginatively a mechanistic and materialistic view of the universe. This led to the rediscovery of an organic relationship between man and the dynamic force of nature which took on religious overtones that were translated into poetic myth. But Barnes's myth resulted, not from an involvement in revolutionary adaptation, but from a desire to preserve; he is not a nature poet in the sense commonly applied to Wordsworth, for example. His religion is immovably Episcopalian, and he rarely philosophizes or moralizes in his poetry about the "Spirit of Nature." As Tennyson commented after a conversation, their only one together, about Darwinism and pantheism—near sacrilege for the good parson—"he is not accustomed to strong views theologic."[2]

Barnes's "myth," to use T. S. Eliot's definition, is the "manipulating [of] a continuous parallel between contemporaneity and antiquity . . . a way of controlling, or ordering, of giving a shape and a significance to the immense panorama of futility and anarchy which is contemporary history."[3] His parochial isolation was not simply a regionalist limitation. It was, rather, a considered and coherent attempt to preserve an imaginative Eden—with all the emotional and religious overtones of his own youth in the vale of Blackmore—as well as the people's traditional life in "England's green and pleasant land" from what seemed to him to be the disastrous degeneration of that ethos into the "futility and anarchy" of the "dark Satanic Mills" of Coketown. That Barnes's poetry is concerned largely with recording the annals of the village is clear enough. But it seems to me that his writing about this rather circumscribed topic is obliquely also a commentary on his own life, symbolizing the virtues of a rural existence in the context of the cultural revolution which Ruskin characterized as the "storm cloud of the nineteenth century." It is Barnes's imaginative comprehension of those virtues, his accommodation of his individual talent to an ancient tradition, which is the basis of his art and of his validity as a poet of the countryside. As Hardy observed, he held "a unique position [as] probably the most interesting link between past and present forms of rural life that England possessed," and that position constituted the "world of circumstance," to use Keats's formulation of the spiritual struggle of man, in which Barnes discovered his "sense of identity."[4] For, as Hardy continues, the uniqueness of his position resulted not only from the great span of his life—

it was, for instance, "a day almost within his remembrance when . . . a stagecoach made its first entry into Sturminster-Newton"—but also from the "remoteness even from contemporary provincial civilization, of the pastoral recesses in which his earlier years were passed—places with whose now obsolete customs and beliefs his mind was naturally imbued."[5]

What I am suggesting in no way denies, of course, that Barnes's excessively modest and retiring temperament found complete satisfaction in living in the countryside, nor that the creative and personal sides of his life were, as a result, aligned. As Hardy justly observed of him, "the poetic side of his nature . . . was but faintly ruled by the practical at any time, [and] his place-attachment was strong almost to a fault" (p. lvii). But to conclude that this satisfaction was the motivating source of his poetry is both negative and tautological, leaving completely out of account, for instance, that the real significance of his many personal and creative activities lies in their knitted inter-relationship. His archaeological investigations, to take an example, led him not only to refute "the common view that our prehistoric colonists were a pack of H. G. Wellsian savages," but also directly to evolve a "theory of the origin of poetry and music as a trilogy of song-tune-dance . . . found . . . in Stonehenge—Chorea Giganteum, the song-dance of the giants."[6]

Such a conclusion also leaves out of account his extended attempts to restore the language to its pristine Anglo-Saxon health, as well as, more obviously, his writing much of his best poetry in a dialect of which he said, "It is my mother tongue, and is to my mind the only true speech of the life that I draw."[7] The close association here between language and a particular way of life is important because it points to his continual concern with an organic wholeness of sensibility, whose image is the compactness and coherence of his conserving myth. It may be true, as Geoffrey Grigson says in the Introduction to his selection of Barnes's poetry, that, "In the narrow sense, there are not art-and-society reasons for urging that Barnes should be read" (Grigson, p. 29). I would emphasize, however, a notion expressed earlier in the same excellent essay, that Grigson "may have suggested, wrongly . . . that Barnes was indifferent to the times, or separated from them entirely" (p. 27). Coventry Patmore too seems to me to be, even in the narrowest sense, wide of the mark when he writes, "Mr. Barnes, in his poems, is nothing but a poet. He does not there protest against anything in . . . the arrangements of society."[8]

II

Barnes was a countryman born and bred, and because his poetry is always about scenes and events and people he knows intimately, it has a quality of authenticity which can be derived only from first-hand experience.

As Hopkins rightly pointed out, "the use of dialect to a man like Barnes is to tie him down to the things that he or another Dorset man has said or might say, which though it narrows his field heightens his effects."[9] It would be false, however, to think of him as an untutored yokel, for he was in fact an educated and well-informed person of wide interests. Besides being a parson and schoolmaster, he was an accomplished linguist, a somewhat eccentric philologist, a competent wood-carver; he dabbled in etymology and archaeology, invented a quadrant and an instrument for describing ellipses, played the flute, violin, and piano, sang and composed songs, and was an expert in Welsh and Persian prosody. The list could be extended; but enough has been given to establish the point and to dispel any illusion about the quality of his reclusiveness. Nor did he have, as Patmore caustically remarked, "the advantage of being able to demand the admiration of the sympathizing public on the score that he is a chimney-sweep, or a rat-catcher, and has never learned to read" (p. 155).

It is clear that a person of such varied interests, and the exuberant participation in life that they suggest, was not one who, for instance, refused until middle-age to go to London, or to try to make his literary way, out of a sense of personal limitation. And more important is the implication, tacit in much of his prose, that the talented diversity of his activities, many of them rooted in the ancient soil of folk-lore, and all of them stressing the primacy in artistic creation of "fitness" or harmonious proportion of form, constitutes an oblique criticism of what he regarded as the straggling and fragmentary quality of many city-dwellers' lives.

The fading rural civilization, in many of its aspects, lived richly in Barnes's imagination, particularly through boyhood memories of the prosperous market town of Sturminster-Newton, which, two miles from his home across Bagber Common, was where he received his only schooling up to the age of thirteen. For it was there, as Giles Dugdale notes, that deep into the century "most of the articles of equipment needed in the daily lives of the country folk living many miles around . . . which, elsewhere, the Industrial Revolution was accustoming Englishmen to buy from the large towns, were still made locally by skilled craftsmen."[10] Even the knowledge necessary for effective participation in country children's games—"We . . . braided fishing lines of white horsehair, and made floats for them, and hung them on a peeled withy wand, and made small rush baskets for our fish"—Barnes regarded as one "level of folk-lore."[11] The inclusive scope and intimacy of the relationship between his creative life as an artist and what could almost be called its prerequisite, the rural ethos, comes out in a letter of Sophia Williams to Barnes's son after the poet's death: "The increase of ready-made articles and of contrivances to save trouble did not commend themselves to him. He said it destroyed invention and self-reliance in childhood, weakened the sense of responsibility in later life, and reduced things to a standard of mere money cheapness, which he thought involved cheapness of character too" (in Dugdale, p. 185).

The Rev. O. P. Cambridge, in a memorial tribute, observed of Barnes, "His life forms a harmonious whole such as the world rarely sees."[12] And in the opinion of Rayner Unwin, he approached "in his activities . . . the complete man of the Renaissance."[13] It is this quality of fulfilment which should warn us against taking too literally the poet's own statement, echoed by those not fully aware of the disciplined construction of his verse, that his poetry was a "leisure" activity, "simply a refreshment of mind from cares and irksomeness" (in Dugdale, p. 207). This view seems incongruous in the light of those frequent first-hand accounts in which one sees not a simple country parson, but a man profoundly involved in creation. There is, for example, his daughter's recollection of the poet's habit of sitting in his garden "with his eyes closed and face upturned into the sunlight . . . for an hour at a time, sometimes brooding poetry through the medium of visions, sometimes thinking out a deep question of ethics or philosophy, or perhaps puzzling with a new metre" (in Dugdale, p. 180). The significant issue for us at this point is that though by far the most important of his many imaginative activities, poetry was not an exception to, but an integral part of his creative personality. And that personality gained its coherence, as inevitably as did the rural sensibility he typified, from the sense of community that crowned a country upbringing. In Barnes, microcosm and macrocosm were harmoniously integrated.

III

Barnes's alert awareness of contemporary problems of living, and his distinctive response to them, is well illustrated by his little-known work on the emergent science of economics, entitled *Views of Labour and Gold* (1859). There his concern was "to show the possible effect of the increase of great working-capitals and monopolies on the labourer's freedom or welfare."[14] One could hardly describe the work as a devastating criticism of the "dismal science," nor were his recommendations sufficiently practicable to suggest how current hard times might be alleviated. Yet the views expressed in it are so germane to the pattern of Barnes's thought and life that, despite the seemingly obsolete premises from which he reasons, one must give due weight to the earnestness of his argument and not dismiss the book as the uninformed ramblings of a crank. There is, after all, nothing more inherently sensible in the "humanity" of Sissy Jupe, or in the pathos of Stephen Blackpool, or yet again, in Tennyson's resolution of his conflict in

"The Two Voices," than in the values of honesty and honourableness in commercial transactions which Barnes realised had been supplanted by the Utilitarianism of Bounderby and Gradgrind. And it was honesty and honourableness which he wished to see restored.

For Barnes, what was cardinal irreplaceable was the functioning at all levels of human intercourse of Christian ethic and morality, and he seems not to have been merely timid or sentimental in holding out no great expectations that they could flourish except within the conservative guarantee of small and simply organized communities. For as R. H. Tawney has pointed out, one of the major revolutions through which the human spirit has passed was the abdication by Christian churches in the nineteenth century of "one whole department of life, that of social and political conduct." As a result, they acquiesced "in the popular assumption that the acquisition of riches was the main end of man, and confined themselves to preaching such personal virtues as did not conflict with its achievement."[15] Barnes clearly perceived this revolution and refused to compromise his deep sense of democracy in the village community against which it offended. He clung, rather, to the "old-fashioned" idea that labour was the measure of commercial value and repudiated the usurious exploitation of money which transformed it from a token into a self-generating commodity bearing more money. Of course, the primitive labour-barter economy he envisaged as ideal was thoroughly inadequate to the needs of an expanding industrial economy, but the following homely anecdote, which he quoted with relish, suggests his awareness of the money morality, an inherent aspect of the Manchester School, and its human implications: "Patoo Mata Moigna, a Tonga chief, and his wife, went with an English ship to Botany Bay, where he saw people eating in a cookshop, and he thought the good housefather was sharing out food in the Tonga fashion, and went in with the claim of hunger, but was speedily kicked out with the foot of the man who had been born in the land of the Bible."[16]

Barnes's ideal emerges as a type of Christian "noble savage." By formulating it in this way, one may best understand his desire to incorporate in an organic unity the virtues of Christian morality and the dignity and health, both physical and spiritual, which to his mind resulted from the varied activities and sense of community and continuity making up the rural life. Industrialism and vast urban development had made that unity difficult to attain. The moral of the anecdote about the "noble Tongan" is that he would never have behaved in the same way as the civilized "Christian," because his way of life was rooted in the soil and in the traditions of people who had not been corrupted by worshipping Mammon. In that idolatry, Barnes perceived, lay a moral trap into which economists such as

Ricardo had fallen. It resulted from the false elevation of statistics to the status of "Natural Law," by which industrial capitalists were able to claim as inevitable and unalterable, indeed as part "of the nature of things," their treatment of workers under laissez-faire. Barnes's exposure of this moral dishonesty was as forthright as that which gave Marxism its apocalyptic force, though its impact was blunted because he did not share with Engels the advantage of being able to retaliate with the very argument of statistical analysis in terms of which the situation was being condoned and applauded. He had grasped, however, the essential danger in the flux of contemporary life—the emergence of a new avarice which used the mechanical inventions of the age of steam to achieve its ends and, as it discovered the massive strength of machines, became increasingly impatient of traditional religious and ethical safeguards against economic exploitation of those who operated them.

Barnes tends, admittedly, to reduce human existence to the simplicity of an isolated and static Christian community, where "The labour of man . . . is the making of his gear for the winning of his food" (*Views of Labour and Gold,* p. 1). But one should not be diverted from the burden of his criticism by his quaintness of orientation or expression, or the seeming obsolescence of his retaliation. For when, in the same strain of argument, he perceptively urges that "labour is both the action of the body or mind, *and* the reaction of the work on the body or mind" (p. 31; my italics), one ought to hear as a chorus of agreement the more sophisticated complaints of later writers who inherited the culture that Barnes criticized in its early stages of growth. There is William Morris's quiet lament, implying a state of affairs that had dissolved with the advent of the division of labour and mass production: "Time was when everyone that made anything, made a work of art besides a useful piece of goods; and it gave them pleasure to do it."[17] And complementary to it, the frustrated outcry from D. H. Lawrence on his return home to Derbyshire in 1915, when he observed the mining people from whom he had sprung: "These men, whom I love so much . . . they *understand* mentally so horribly: only industrialism, only wages and money and machinery. They can't *think* anything else . . . only this industrial-mechanical-wage idea."[18] Both Morris and Lawrence would accept the implication of Barnes's statement that labour is best when it provides harmonious balance of body and mind.

Barnes's book, then, is not an academic refutation of current economic practice which had acquired scientific status through the pragmatic deductions of Adam Smith, Malthus, and Ricardo. The book really constituted a rejection of the concept of the "economic man." And his rejection rests on sound if somewhat neglected values, which he regarded as imperative for the health of the whole man. It is a plea against fragmenting the manifestly composite stability of rural life into meretricious divisions to be either separately catered to, or ignored, in what was for him the urban chaos. His view here, as elsewhere, is considered, and when he writes, for instance, that "it is more healthy to rack one's mind in effectual devices to win a skilful end, than to work as a machine without a free aim or thought" (*Views of Labour and Gold,* p. 91), he is making not only a plea for the creative dignity of labour, but also very pertinent "criticism of life."

IV

Geoffrey Grigson is right when he says that "In English poetry, [Barnes's] own practice was based on the Enlightenment" (*Selected Poems,* p. 16). From another viewpoint, however, I would suggest that his poetry may be profitably regarded as reflecting both an ancient and multifarious, though uncomplex folk-culture, and the bleak age of revolution which destroyed it. This formulation points up the importance of the observation in the Preface to his *Poems of Rural Life* (1844), where, referring to himself, he writes, "As he has not written for readers who have had their lots cast in town-occupations of a highly civilized community, and cannot sympathize with the rustic mind, he can hardly hope that they will understand either his poems or his intention; since with the not uncommon notion that every change from the plough towards the desk and from the desk towards the couch of empty-handed idleness is an onward step towards happiness and intellectual and moral excellence, they will most likely find it very hard to conceive that wisdom and goodness would be found speaking in a dialect which may seem to them a fit vehicle for the animal wants and passions of a boor" (in Dugdale, p. 113). It is apparent from this that Barnes was aware not only of the scope and standard of his audience, but also that his function in the community was defined by the demands of the lives and language of its members. An observation earlier in the Preface further illuminates the issue: "As increasing communication among the inhabitants of different parts of England, and the spread of school education among the lower ranks of the people tend to substitute book English for the provincial dialects, it is likely that after a few years many of them will linger only in the more secluded parts of the land, if they live at all" (in Dugdale, p. 112). Barnes's underlying concern here is clearly similar to that which led Wordsworth to make his famous attempt in the *Lyrical Ballads* to employ "a selection of language really used by men." That attempt was largely unsuccessful, but the opposite is true with regard to the impressive mass of Barnes's dialect poems. Indeed they may fairly be regarded as the practical demonstration of Wordsworth's justification of his choice of "humble and rustic life," and his adoption of a diction purified from defects "because such men hourly communicate with the best objects from which the best part of language is originally derived." And language, for Barnes, was essentially speech, which he described as "shapen of the breath-sounds of speakers, for the ear of hearers, and not from speech-tokens [letters] in books."[19] The "beau ideal" was the speech of his youth in Blackmore Vale—a language firmly rooted in the oral tradition of the folk, and therefore untrammelled by the literary associations and importations of National English. His struggle for its continuance was life-long—"I have done some little to preserve the speech of our forefathers . . . [as it was] spoken in my youth" (in Dugdale, p. 226), was his comment on receiving a few months before his death the author's copy of his *Glossary of the Dorset Dialect.*

We read elsewhere in the Preface to his *Poems* that those members of the community he had in mind as audience were people like the ploughman and his wife. Coventry Patmore elaborates on this: Barnes's "humble glory was to recite to delighted audiences of farmers and ploughmen and their wives and sweethearts a series of lyrics, idylls, eclogues, which, being the faultless expression of elementary feelings and perceptions, are good for all but those in whom such feelings and perceptions are extinct."[20] Hardy suggests, in keeping with this picture of Barnes, that "the enthusiasm which accompanied" these readings was probably "more grateful to him than the admiration of a public he had never seen" (p. lvi). Furthermore, he published his poems in book form only relatively late, after he had for years contributed to the "Poet's Corner" in the local newspaper. A consideration of these facts shows that his poetic function in the community was an issue consciously thought about, and one which formed an integral part of his artistic intention, as well as confirming his mode of life. This view is supported not only by the main subject of his poetry and by his use of dialect, but also by his deep and technically informed interest in old bardic poetry, many of the characteristics of which he experimented with, eventually incorporating them as basic aspects of his poetic talent. Had Barnes's interest been only historical and philological, it would have been incidental to his purpose. However, in the light of his own poetical practice, the issue takes on a central importance because of his statement in the illuminating article, **"The Old Bardic Poetry,"**[21] that his interest in the techniques of that poetry stems from their enabling a "bookless and unwriting" people to remember better their lore in "verse-locks." For such people, "verse is rather a need than a joy"; it is indeed their "history." From this central assertion, Barnes proceeds to describe the various techniques which ancient bards, and he also to a large degree, used, "to keep together the true text, and fasten it on the learner's mind." His knowledge was based with typical thoroughness on a study of Welsh, Irish, Anglo-Saxon, and Persian bardic writings. Many of Barnes's contributions to the "Poet's Corner" were brief experiments resulting from his acquired knowledge, and the frequent recurrence in the

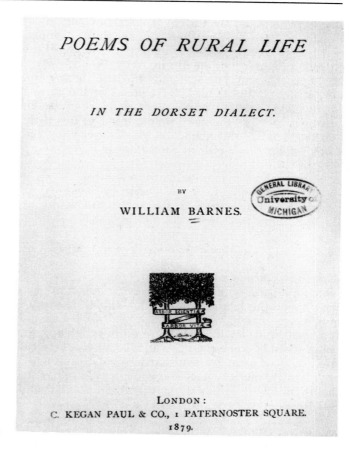

POEMS OF RURAL LIFE

IN THE DORSET DIALECT.

BY

WILLIAM BARNES.

LONDON:
C. KEGAN PAUL & CO., 1 PATERNOSTER SQUARE.
1879.

body of his writing of these ancient techniques relates closely to his consciousness of the intention he expounded in his article.

The following brief examples will help to indicate the nature of "bardic" techniques and Barnes's use of them in his poetry. Firstly, there is "cymmeriad . . . or the keeping of the same word through sundry verses, for the sake of oneness of time, or subject or thought," as it occurs in **"Went Hwome,"** where each of the three stanzas ends as follows:

> As noon did smite, wi' burnén light,
> The road so white, to Meldonley.
>
> As I did goo, while skies wer blue,
> Vrom view to view, to Meldonley.
>
> Till I come down, vrom Meldon's crown
> To rufs o'brown, at Meldonley.[22]

Here the repetition of "Meldonley," effectively supported by the internal rhymes, heightens the warmth of his "welcome hwome" by accentuating the close relationship for Barnes of domesticity and specific locality. The rhyming in these lines also derives from "bardic" practice, for in ancient Irish poetry the rhyming of a word at the end of a line with one in the middle of the following line was known as "union." Then there is the Celtic "cynghanedd" or consonant rhyme, as in **"In our abode in Arby Wood,"** where the repeated consonants in the two parts of the line are: u, r, b, d / u, r, b, d. Next there are the various highly complicated rhyme schemes which comprise the **"Englyn."** One of the more simple forms of this is the "awdlau," or one-rhyme lines, as Barnes uses it in **"The Cock,"** after the Welsh of Siôn Powel,

> I heard the homely cock by fits to crow,
> With golden wings, ere dawn began to glow,
> And sing his cheery sounds from high to low,
> Mild in the morn, amid the glitt'ring snow.

(Grigson, *Selected Poems,* p. 282)

Also to be considered among the "verse-locks" through which the bard, with intricate security, hoped to "fasten . . . on the learner's mind" his simple "history," are "metre [which] where it is true, will forbid a word to be put in for another of less or more syllables," the conventional "voice-rhyme, which keeps many words from displacement by any but those of like sound," and, finally, the less well-known "clipping-rhyme, or the rhyming of articulation, or alliteration" (**"Old Bardic Poetry,"** p. 306).

Aspects of Barnes's writing less specifically technical than those just listed show equally the conscious intention and scope of his association with "bardic" practice. The persistent lack of metaphorical elaboration in his "history" of the old civilization, for instance, might perhaps be seen as more than the result of restrained "fitness," in the light of his observation that "the poet can relieve the flatness of such historical truths, as Homer did the roll of his ships, or leaders, only with a few epithets" (p. 308). Considering Welsh bardic poetry, he refers to Llywarch Hen, who had coined compound epithets such as "greyhound-hearted," "brushfire-hearted," which are frequently used with a similar "instressed" precision by Barnes as in "dark-treed night," "peäle-twinklén stars," or "hedge-climb'd hills." Also, it is surprising to discover that lines such as "or as a short-stand-quick-night-watch foreflown" and "which at early morn with blowing-green-blithe bloom" are not discarded exercises by Hopkins, but translations from Old Friesian by Barnes (see *The Harp of Aeolus,* p. 122).

One must, then, disagree with Grigson that it is "curious to find him down in his Dorset isolation writing that 'the measures of song . . . may themselves be measured, not only by the steps of the dramatic dance, but by the steps of a march, or by the strokes of oars, as in the Tonga songs of the kind called Towalo or paddle songs, which Mariner says are never accompanied with instrumental music, but which are short songs sung in canoes while paddling, the strokes of the paddles being coincident with the cadence of the tune" (*Selected Poems,* p. 16). It is not at all curious—because Barnes's interest in this type of folk-song springs directly from his deep concern with its intimate and accepted association with the declining folk civilization he wished to preserve. Folk-songs such as those Barnes here describes are an integral part of any rural community; they are, as James Reeves observes, "the result of oral tradition in a rural society."[23] The English equivalents in song to dramatic dance, or the steps of a march, or the strokes of oars, were for Barnes part of the continued security of the rural way of life; and their slowly falling into disuse, or being supplanted by more lurid city-ballads, became for him a painful and continual reminder of transformation. This was so, furthermore, not only because those songs frequently accompanied some traditional craft or piece of work which might now have been displaced, but also because, as was acknowledged by Cecil Sharp (whose salvaging interest in the whole process was, by contrast, merely antiquarian) "the folk-singer attaches far more importance to the words of his song than to its tune" (Reeves, p. 11). It is no exaggeration, therefore, to regard these songs as a vital part of the simple "history" of country folk. H. J. Massingham even asserts of Barnes that "His verse is the old communal folk-song made the vehicle of an individual spirit whose reinterpretation of it was an act of genius" (p. 125).

V

Another important aspect of Barnes's presentation of his countryman's world is the relationship between his extensive description of the natural scene and his aesthetic theory. We have already noted the general absence of moralizing, philosophical speculation, or visionary insight in his treatment of nature; and his delineation of the natural world of sight and sound is a logical extension of this. While taking an intense delight in natural beauty, Barnes never submerges his personality in it. One finds in his poetry, therefore, no attempt to create luxuriant or picturesque effects. He adopts a sane countryman's attitude of objectivity and directness, and his descriptions are characterized by a sparse, fastidious selection of particular detail which precludes much metaphorical elaboration. Associated with this simplicity of line is Barnes's uncomplicated use of colour. He invariably uses, often in contrast, bright heraldic colours which stand out like symbols of his honest observation in the uncomplicated world of peace and certainty he cherished. These qualities of simplicity and colour may be seen in the following typical passage:

> I love the narrow lane's dark bows,
> When summer glows or winter blows;
> Or in the *f*all, when leaves all *f*ade,
> Yet *f*lutt'ring in the airy shade,

And in the *sh*elter'd *sha*w the blast
Has *sha*ken down the green-cupp'd mast,
And time is *bl*ack'ning *bl*ue-skinn'd sloes,
And *bl*ackberries on bramble bows,
And *r*ipening haws are growing *r*ed
A*r*ound the grey-rin'd hawthorn's head,
And hazel *br*anches, *br*okentipp'd
And *br*own, of all their nuts are stripp'd,
And in the leazes, *wh*iffling *wh*ite,
The *wh*irling thistle seeds alight
In sunshine, *st*ruck from bents' brown *st*alks
By *st*rolling girls in Sunday walks.

("The Lane," Barnes's italics; II, 665)

These aspects of Barnes's observation are closely related to his aesthetic theory, which is Christian in origin and application. In his **"Thoughts on Beauty and Art"** (1861), he bases his definition of Beauty on the accepted deterioration of Man and Nature after the Fall. In his view, "the beautiful in nature is the unmarred result of God's first creative or forming will" (in Dugdale, p. 276). Furthermore, because of their innate perfection, interference with any forms of Divine creation amounted to marring them; so "if an ash-tree is polled, there grow out of its head more young runnels than would have sprouted if the work of God's first will had not been marred by the man-wielded polling-blade" (p. 277). In light of this it is no surprise to see flourishing, admittedly amidst pragmatically observed detail, the perennial yet elusive dictum, "Nature is the best school of art" (p. 287). However, his use of "Nature" is not as vague as its blunt statement here might lead one to fear; for through a variation of Platonism, in which the exclusive presence of uncorrupted forms associated "Heaven" with prelapsarian Nature, he suggests that the devout may yet perceive, or construe from only partially deformed examples, the "beau ideal" of God's will, the "seeking and interpreting" of which, "and a working with His truth," become the priestlike "aim of high art" (p. 293).

Barnes's poetic practice is clearly related to his aesthetic theorizing, particularly with regard to the bare directness of the "unmarred" objectivity of his observation. What he is, in fact, frequently attempting in his poetry is to set down pictures of those original pure forms untrammelled by any embellishment or personal interpretation. And in doing this he was not merely being pious. For in his discovery and accurate recording of the "beau ideal," he is not only creating beauty and praising his God, but also "preserving" from disruptive man-made forces the pristine glory of God-created rural England, where "God's untarnished earthly good" is mainly to be found. In his view, the age had become one of "falsehood and sham" because most of "the beauty of God's primary work . . . [unmarred forms] in plants, animals, and man" (p. 277) was almost by definition to be found in the countryside and in the lives of the inheritors of the ancient folk civilization; and all this had been replaced by its perversion in urban existence: "we have deal painted and veneered into an imitation of more costly wood . . . cloth shown to our neighbours for leather; paste for gems; imitations instead of nature's truth," produced by artisans radically different from "the old workmen [who] were faithful and wrought to God, or art, or conscience, rather than to Pluto" (p. 294). He substantiates fully, in his terms, the validity of his world by criticizing the limitations of the city, which define by contrast the "wealth" of the disintegrating rural ethos, when he observes that in the "great towns . . . much of the beautiful in nature must be far forlorn by many of working people. Many a plain wall rises high between the workman and the glory of the passing sun, and has shut out his window-framed piece of blue sky, and the cheering whiteness of the flying cloud. Many a day of smoke has blackened the clearness of the sweet springtide; many a bright-leaved tree has heretofore given way to crowded shades of narrow rooms. Many a rood of flowery sward has become rattling streets, where, for songs of birds, they have the din of hammers. Many a cheek has been paled, and lovely piece of childhood marred, by longsome hours of over-work" (p. 294). Moreover, he extends his concept of "beauty" to include moral actions for "the winning of God's first given, and since forlorn good" (p. 292)—an extension exactly paralleled and illumination by Sir Joshua Reynolds' elaboration (in the *Discourses*) of his idea of Nature to comprehend "not only the forms which Nature produces, but also the nature and internal fabric and organization, as I may call it, of the human mind and imagination."[24] Barnes's criticism in this context as elsewhere, then, is broadly based not in sentimental retreat from the great "march of mind," but in a liberal and humane concern with the conditions of life most conducive to spiritual and moral health.

VI

There is a further aspect of Barnes's aesthetic theory worth considering—the influence of the tradition of natural theology, best represented for our purposes by William Paley's *Natural Theology* (1802), which the poet probably read as a prescribed text while a "Ten Year Man" at Cambridge in 1847. We have seen that Barnes's assumption concerning the superiority of the rural life rested on the belief that it offered the possibility of more constant contact with the greatest number of unmarred forms created by God, that the "forms and colours of objects in a landscape [reveal] a fitness and harmony of the good of God's formative will. . . . The beautiful is also the good by reason of a fitness or harmony which it possesses" (in Dugdale, pp. 288, 278). This attitude rests on a basic assumption of Paley's Natural Theology: "that in a vast plurality of instances in which contrivance is perceived, the design of the contrivance is beneficial."[25] John Stuart Mill, however, was to suggest that if Darwin's theory of the "survival of the fittest" proved to be correct, it would provide a radically different account of the appearances of benevolent contrivance in Nature, and "would greatly attenuate the evidences for it."[26] Darwinism seemed to imply that the traditional religious view of a universe contrived and regulated by divine omniscience would increasingly be replaced by new visions of a universe ordered by laws of physics or of the jungle, by human intelligence or the lawlessness of blind chance. Barnes's response to these implications is clearly one more of the elements that went into the making of his mythical world.

Natural theologians were mainly concerned to show God's beneficence towards the animate creatures of the universe by exhibiting for rational judgment evidence that inanimate creation had been adapted to their needs and gratification. And this argument for the existence and "continuing care . . . of a ruling Providence," as Paley stated, was of necessity based on the Newtonian "established order of nature which we must suppose to prevail, or we cannot reason at all upon the subject" (II, 190, 155). Frequently Paley's "evidences" to prove that "design must have had a designer. That designer must have been a person. That person is God" (II, 130), rest on a simple presupposition of the very benevolence of the Designer whose existence they are supposed to prove. At one important point, for instance, in considering the sensuous delights offered in Nature to men, he argues that this need not have been the case, for God might have made "everything we tasted, bitter; everything we saw, loathsome; everything we touched, a sting; every smell, a stench; and every sound, a discord" (II, 150). By referring comprehensively to "everything," he tacitly ignores in his listing the actual and inconvenient presence of these qualities in many natural phenomena. It is a similar sort of "fitness" that Barnes discovers when contemplating "the forms and colours of objects in a landscape." For he finds "evidence" of "God's formative will" in the "green of the earth, and the blue of the sky [which] are less wearisome and destructive to the sight than would be a world of red or white, and blinds our eyes more slowly than would an earth of silvery brightness, or a lasting vision of blood" (in Dugdale, p. 288). The conclusions drawn from such characteristic statements by Barnes and those of Paley and the natural theologians generally are identical.

The retention of this established order of nature, as opposed to the emergent one propounded by Darwin, was imperative for the continuance of the world of imaginative reality Barnes created in his poetry. And it was equally important to his aesthetic, which formed a bridge between that world and the daily duties as a country parson which in Dugdale's opinion were his

"true vocation" (p. 122). For as Paley had stated, if one laid Natural Theology as "the foundation of everything which is religious . . . the world henceforth becomes a temple, and life itself one continued act of adoration" (II, 199). Of course, Barnes was free to choose with Disraeli the angels rather than the apes, but the point of interest here is that his choice seems to have been dictated not only by his Christian convictions, but also by his artistic realization that his myth would no longer have been viable had he chosen the latter. The evolution of a "chance good" in a dispensation where "God and Nature" were "at strife" was for Barnes a degradation of that pristine and harmonious "fitness" of "unmarred forms" created by "God's formative will" through which by contrast he criticized the new cosmology and its implications. In his single poem explicitly on evolutionism, **"The Happy Days When I Wer Young,"** where he writes on "what's a-talked about/By many now—that to despise/The laws o' God an' man is wise" (I, 171), Barnes feels no need to re-justify to men the ways of an inscrutable God. The usual backward-looking title of the poem heightens his sense of the immemorial sanity of rural life, thereby endorsing his belief in the justice of the natural order; and he is led to repudiate Darwinism in a significant phrase—as he did in his review of "Patmore's Poems"[27]—as "venom": the serpent in his Eden, in fact. It was a serpent brought "To kill our hope an' taint our thought." The ideas were, with an almost predatory pervasiveness, intruding on the stable perfection of his world.

VII

As stated earlier, there is no philosophizing or moralizing about the "Spirit of Nature" in Barnes's poetry. His prime concern is with the activities and the relationships, both amongst themselves and with their environment, of country people, and only indirectly with the natural world as such. In relating Barnes's treatment of country folk to his overally mythopoeic activity, however, one must from the outset have clearly in mind the anomaly that, although he was almost exclusively a rural poet, Barnes was never an intimate acquaintance of the local rustics; and until he achieved some renown in later life, he was scorned as an eccentric by the "upper class." He was no Stephen Duck or Robert Bloomfield ("literary" peasants who misguidedly tried to adopt an urbanity that ill suited their unsophisticated origins and talents). Nor can the anomaly be explained by reference to Barnes's acknowledged shyness; indeed that only complicates the issue if we place in the context of the spiritual and intellectual loneliness that must have characterized his years of greatest creativity, the observation by an ex-pupil that Barnes was "nearly isolated" socially.[28] Furthermore, aside from scything his own grass in summer, he took no part in agricultural labour; yet the exactness of his knowledge about such matters and rural life generally (as, for instance, in his article **"Dorset Folk and Dorset"**[29]), is manifest throughout his work.

These biographical details throw into illuminating relief the very obvious limitation of scope in Barnes's treatment of country people in his poetry. Rayner Unwin surely exaggerates when he writes that Barnes's poems "depict the countryman in all the aspects of his life" (p. 158). Unlike Hardy and George Borrow, he shows no interest, for example, in the picturesque fringe of rural society composed of pedlars, tinkers, and gipsies. Also he has only a single poem, **"Culver Dell and the Squire,"** on a member of the gentry, all others treating of the working people. And even in that exception the squire is an ideal, if not idealized, figure. Again, except for a solitary poem, **"The Love Child,"** there is no suggestion of cruelty or immorality in the countryside. And this was hardly because of Barnes's ignorance of such aspects of rural life. He was probably quite aware, for instance, of the fearful and loathsome scenes of drunkenness and domestic misery which "Rabin Hill," a contemporary dialect poet of nearby Sturminster-Newton, was later to recall as being fairly common when he and Barnes were both young (see Dugdale, p. 22). Furthermore, besides the evidence to the contrary Barnes provides in his pamphlet, *Humilis Domus: Some Thoughts on the Abodes, Life and Social Conditions of the Poor, Especially in Dorsetshire,*[30] there are his concluding remarks to the otherwise glowing account of **"Dorset Folk and Dorset"**: "If I have painted a picture of Dorset life that is light, I have not given light where there is none; but I ought to say that there is among us darkness as well as light, and that you may too readily pitch on a man who is a shame to us." For a reader of his poetry, however, there is no such man, or woman, to "pitch on."

It is not coincidence that the most considerable of Barnes's poems on a particular topic of social interest, **"The Common a-took in,"** is concerned with enclosure; for as George Sturt stated in his invaluable record of the changing village, it was this more than any other single factor that was thought to have altered the appearance of the countryside and brought about the rapid deterioration of what he called the ancient "folk civilization." The Enclosure Acts covered the period of rapid industrialization which transformed "a social system of eight hundred years' duration"[31] into one which, in Hardy's words, served "smoke and fire rather than frost and sun."[32] The transformation resulted in what the Hammonds aptly described as "a world in disorder" (p. 233). Yet this was ostensibly also the world presented by Barnes in his poetry. He was probably unaware, for instance, of the actual statistics showing that by 1851 in almost all the great towns the migrants outnumber the people born there,[33] or that between 1792 and 1831 Poor Law expenditure in the

County of Dorset increased 214 per cent and expenses for prosecutions for crime 2,135 per cent, while the population had increased by only 40 per cent.[34] But he could hardly have been unaware of the general cultural changes which were so radically altering the world he had grown up in. E. M. Forster points to a particular instance when he observes, "He could live through the Labourers' Revolt in 1830 without its shadows falling across his verse" (in Dugdale, p. 89). It is not only that Barnes's range in portraying the life of a world he knew intimately is restricted, but also that his presentation is limited to a particular type of observation and treatment. The result is a picture of country life that is curiously distorted, one which, if not idealized, was at least selected to illustrate and corroborate specific sentiments and beliefs about that life. The attempt to "explain" this selectiveness (even granting fully the autonomy of the creative artist to plot his own area of imaginative activity) by saying that "His mind was attuned to harmonies, not discords" (Cambridge, p. xx), or that he was "a sundial recording only the shining hours" (Dugdale, p. 22) ignores the positive aspects of his achievement. It seems more accurate to state that in presenting his selective treatment of country life and its virtues, as in other fields already considered, he was motivated by a very real awareness of the contemporary cultural revolution.

VIII

The sphere of living to which Barnes devotes most attention is the family. This is the stable axis about which spin rural activities and pastimes within the confined circle of the immediate neighbourhood, and it is a reasonable preoccupation of one born and bred in the tight isolation of a small community. His stress on warm, intimate relationships within the domestic group and among close friends is consonant with his temperament and his artistic intention. Barnes writes consistently about such relationships, and although his dignified restraint largely forestalls sentimentality, they are invariably happy. The quiet and peace of rural domesticity he saw as a complementary commentary on the whole of rural life, whose excellence made it possible. But his attitudes here emerge not only from personal experience with his wife Julia, or from a thoughtful countryman's awareness of the family's importance in a daily routine unrelieved by much entertainment. For, on turning to the pamphlet *Humilis Domus* mentioned earlier, one finds a wider intellectual conviction based, in contrast with the conditions of the rustic poor, on the overcrowding and slums inevitable in expanding industrial cities, from which, he thought, "there must follow a train of moral evils too loathsome for a mind brought up in moral purity to behold in imagination" (p. 4).

But Barnes was not only concerned with the home as a sanctuary for preserving "the most lovely social

Christian graces"; he also regarded it in a broader perspective as the greatest safeguard against political disruption in a revolutionary situation. He feared what in fact has subsequently happened, though not as dramatically as he had anticipated—that the family with its multiple functions would become devitalized in the more fluid social structure of large cities, especially when people lived in congested slums away from ancient rural sanctions. Joseph Ashby, a true villager, believed that in the lean years that followed on the Enclosures, the labourers in his village of Tysoe "kept to the straight way because the village had been once a true community."[35] And as late as 1902 Rider Haggard's exhaustive investigation into the desertion of the countryside and the decline of husbandry led him to the "modest statement [that they] can mean nothing less than the progressive deterioration of the race."[36] Barnes would have agreed with Hardy that "This process, which is designated by statisticians as 'the tendency of the rural population towards the large towns,' is really the tendency of water to flow uphill when forced."[37] Barnes was painfully aware that the countryman suffered irreparable loss by his migration. The point is nicely made in the following passage where he is ostensibly writing about impoverished Dorset rustics, but with the consoling implication that the *rural* slum-dweller still had the protection of a conservative social structure and the solidarity of a traditional ethos to guard him from the ravages which would undermine his urban counterpart: "the true school for the training of good national subjects is the good father's roof: and a house training under the law of the house's head, is the only one to which we have good grounds to look for the rearing of good lawbound citizens; and the weaker may be the law of the house, the more bloody must be the law of the land; and if the social atoms of the nation are not gathered into family crystals by the house association, no monarch can afterwards form them into the strength of a sound political body" (*Humilis Domus,* p. 3).

Barnes's attitude toward domesticity in country life is best observed, however, in his treatment of women. It is noteworthy, in the first place, that the vast majority of people he writes about are women and children— **"The Maid o' Newton," "Jessie Lee," "The Motherless Child,"** for example, and the list could be greatly extended. Men are most frequently seen, anonymously, at such work as felling trees, or else as husbands who return to the domestic hearth at sunset. Furthermore, the virtues in women which he admires most are the reliable homely ones which make for domestic stability, and his admiration is always restrained and unimpassioned. This is particularly noticeable in his love poems, which are most often not concerned with present passion, but with the expectation of happiness deferred until marriage unites the pair by the hearth of their own home, thereby establishing them as a social unit. And parallel to this, there is a considerable number of poems, such as **"A Little Lost Sister," "Meäry Wedded," "Jenny Away from Home,"** based on familial relationships and the distruption of these by death, departure, or even marriage.

Clearly Barnes's treatment of women in his poetry is based on the correlation of the virtuous life and domestic happiness. These were the inseparable elements in the traditional structure of rural society. But he is concerned not only to commemorate the way of life he knew and admired, but also to deny its viability in an urban context, thereby implying that the good life crumbled with the dislocation of the rural ethos. This he frequently attempts to do by contrasting the "accepted" excellence of the rural character with the corrupting wealth, vice, and vanity which he imputes to the urban environment. Opposed, therefore, to his estimate of unsophisticated country people, there are frequent derogatory references in the poetry to a vain, superficial, and amorphous nobility. The unreality of these personages is the measure of his elevation of the "folk." For no allusion is made to the local gentry as one might expect if Barnes was just being assertively democratic in an age which saw the rise of the proletariat and the establishment of the first Agricultural Labourers' Union under Joseph Arch, or fervently regionalist over the principled heroism of the Tolpuddle martyrs. Thus it is that he "do little ho vor goold or pride,/ To leäve the plain abode where love do bide" (**"Knowlwood,"** I, 283). And Jeäne sits like some rustic Cleopatra, "steätely as a queen o' vo'k" (**"The Bwoate,"** I, 343); Poll the milkmaid walks, "Wi' her white pail below her eärm/ As if she wore a goolden crown" (**"The Milk-maid o' the Farm,"** I, 80); and the poet asserts that even were he extremely wealthy, and "as high in rank/ As any duke or lord," he would remain uncorrupted in his choice of mistress though she were "a leäser in the glen" (**"My Love is Good,"** I, 455). Tacit criticism of the city also underlies his joy in **"Ellen Dare o' Lindenore,"** whose charm results directly from the rustic modesty and tranquillity of her way of life, and the beauty of her home's natural surroundings, which are the opposite of the distracting city's "Swift bwoats, wi' water-plowén keels," its "broad high-roads a-wore/ By vurbrought trav'lers' cracklén wheels," its "crowds a-passen to and fro,/ Upon the bridge's high-sprung bow." The mutually enhancing interaction between **"Lindenore"** and **"Feair Ellen Dare"** substantiates the perfection of each. Imperceptive and hurrying "town-vo'k ha' but seldom calls/ O' business" on fair Ellen, but Barnes, by contrast, appreciates how she epitomizes saner values, like "Calm air do vind the rwose-bound door/ Ov Ellen Dare o' Lindenore" (**"Lindenore,"** I, 405). It is pertinent to note however that Barnes married neither **"Ellen Dare"** nor milkmaid, but the daughter of the middle-class Supervisor of Excise in Dorchester.

IX

It might be thought from the continual presence of hostility between rural and urban life in Barnes's poetry and thinking generally, that he could best be understood in terms of literary history as either a pastoralist or a regionalist. In fact neither category applies. Regionalism, as recently defined, "establishes a comparison between the rural world, seen in terms of its richly picturesque local traits, and the complex industrial society of today, just as the old pastoral established a comparison between peasant life and the court"; it exploits, then, an historical contrast similar to that found in pastoral, "by looking back from a present of advanced technology to the period, still not very far away, when the roads were dirt lanes, farmers walked behind horse-drawn ploughs, and the rural community depended pretty much on its own produce."[38] But Barnes looks back neither from corrupt court nor complex city. Although he accepts in its Christian version the pastoral concept of the restoration of some Golden Age men have forfeited through sin or abusive folly, he never as a result views rural life from the vantage ground of urban sophistication on which both he and his audience live. For his perspective is governed by his faith in the exclusive value of the rural ethos, so that past and present become telescoped into the ritualistic recurrence of the seasons.

The authority of his poetry is not thereby diminished as would be the case if his method were the subtle ironies of contrast. There is no equivalent to the Forest of Arden in Barnes's presentation; his criticism is, rather, overt, in that he asserts imaginatively those very elements which give his art and personal life their mutually enhancing validity. And the historical significance of his criticism becomes clear if one realises that it was being undertaken concurrently with the transformation of those dirt lanes into roads and the replacement of horse-drawn ploughs by such strange machines as the "horse-drill" Donald Farfrae introduced to a Casterbridge, "where the venerable seed-lip was still used for sowing as in the days of the Heptarchy."[39]

As might be expected, it is the apparent immutability of rural life that Barnes cherished greatly—perhaps even more than the peace and honest living he associated with the countryside. This was the source of his regret at any change that occurred, from death or decay, in the established pattern of relationships and activities.

In many of Barnes's poems, then, such as **"Hallowed Places," "The Voices that be Gone," "Joy Passing By,"** there is a nostalgic regret at the passage of time and the changes it has brought about. It is invariably associated with his strong countryman's sense of place, and it is this association which makes remarkable an otherwise common enough sentiment. Pertinent here is the Rev. Francis Kilvert's diary record of a conversation with the poet whom he visited in 1874: "He said that some of the names of people and places mentioned in his [poems] are fictitious, but they all represent real places and persons. The real name of Ellen Brine of Allenburn, he said, was Mary Hames, and the poem was true to the life. In describing a scene he always had an original in his mind, but sometimes he enlarged and improved upon the original. 'For instance,' he explained, 'sometimes I wanted a bit of water, or wood, or a hill, and then I put these in. **"Pentridge by the River,"** was a real place. The river was the Stour'" (in Dugdale, p. 203). It is from such remembered localities and activities that Barnes constructs much of his rural world. For the permanence or decay of individual objects in a particular locality is not only commemorated in itself, but becomes also a symbol of the continuity or collapse of rural life as a whole. Seen in relation to past generations and the regular flow of country traditions, local objects become on the one hand touchstones of certainty and continuity in a changing world, and on the other, depressing signs of change in the structure of living. Thus it is that he frequently mourns the decay of houses (Pentridge House, for instance) which are, in their relation with domesticity, richly suggestive for him of a previously secure and beautiful life now crumbling under the weight of intrusive events. The disintegration brought about by the passage of time is to some extent, however, redeemed for Barnes by the continuity of the seasons through which he as a countryman measures it, correlating the cyclic regularity of the fugitive, recurring seasons with the activities appropriate to each being performed by the younger generation who thereby continue the established tradition. Thus even though "My season-measur'd time's a-vled" (**"Zummer Stream,"** I, 462), and "we ourselves do vollow on/ Our own vorelivers dead an' gone" (**"Our Be'th Place,"** I, 275), it is nevertheless satisfying to see country life still following its ancient pattern, of a necessity which is an inherent part of its excellence:

> 'Tis good to come back to the pleäce,
> Back to the time, to goo noo mwore;
> 'Tis good to meet the younger feäce
> A-mentén others here avore.

("Zummer Stream")

Barnes, then, in re-creating his own "youth" through a presentation of remembered scenes, activities, people, and houses was not just furnishing idly with nostalgic memories an ageing man's recollection of happy bygone days, but was presenting in living terms, heightened by the productive diversity of his own life, his Christian aesthetic and the "actuality" of his remembrances, an allegory of the new Fall of Man. This was how he viewed the Victorian cultural revolution. He immersed himself in past events, or those hallowed by ancient practice or seasonal recurrence, not simply because he was by poetic temperament a recorder and not a creator of images and symbols, but rather because by "manipulating a continuous parallel between [the] contemporaneity" of his own long life, and the "antiquity" of an incorruptible Eden resurrected from his innocent rural youth, he was attempting to create a stable defence amidst the "immense panorama of futility and anarchy" of a world rapidly "maturing" into the confusion of industrial society. And for Barnes the symbol of this confusion and spiritual desolation came to be the city because it stood "outside" Nature, and in seeming opposition to the ancient sanctions that hallowed rural life. This was his real perception, incandescent with moral and imaginative vigour, withholding the encroaching shadows caused by a change visibly effected in the spreading towns and devitalized villages. The city was to become the image, not only of "man's inhumanity to man"; it was also inextricably associated with the romantic turbulence of the search for individual values and a sense of identity in a world made increasingly alien, not only by materialism and rationalism, but also, and more important for Barnes, because the established incorporation of man in the ancient cosmological trinity with God and His Nature had been disrupted. Barnes's world, through which he presents his image of Man, is his defence against this "city of dreadful night."

That image is persuasively delineated in the quality of Barnes's serene liberty when he wrote **"My Orchard in Linden Lee,"** with the well-known lines:

> Let other vo'k meäke money vaster
> In the air o' dark-room'd towns,
> I don't dread a peevish meäster;
> Though noo man do heed my frowns,
> I be free to goo abrode,
> Or teäke ageän my hwomeward road
> To where, vor me, the apple tree
> Do leän down low in Linden Lea.

(I, 234)

The stanza, and the whole poem, derive from his obvious satisfaction in sitting in his orchard. But the issues raised for Barnes by this typically rural activity are rather more complex than a simple gloating would imply. For through his sitting in the orchard, unlike the less fortunate townsman who is "fairly bound to yield to a clock-service," Barnes it able to participate in the cyclic ritual of the seasons, whose unfailing bounty is suggested by the apple tree that "Do leän down low in Linden Lea." And his mental and physical peace is contrasted implicitly with the restless turbulence, and "sudden fits of crowd-moodiness [and] acts of violence" which result from the "spiritual destitution" he associates with "the thick herding of

people in houses" in cities (*Views of Labor and Gold*, pp. 112-115). Their money-grubbing and economic slavery, their "hirelingship" (p. 68), must lead to a spiritual subservence that is dehumanizing in contrast to the freedom of spirit he experiences. Such moments as these, amidst, and made possible by, the beneficence of "God's untarnished earthly good," release Barnes from the enervating struggle in the cultural prison of what Lionel Trilling has called the "opposing self"; for here he experiences that liberation of complete identity with self founded in a satisfying mode of life such as Huckleberry Finn experienced on escaping to the river from the feuding shore, discovering that "there warn't no home like a raft, after all."

When, in *The Mayor of Casterbridge*, Farfrae says that the new mechnical horse-drill would "revolutionize sowing hereabout," Elizabeth-Jane comments, "Then the romance of the sower is gone for good. . . . 'He that observeth the wind shall not sow,' so the Preacher said; but his words will not be to the point any more. How things change!" (ch. xxiv). In an analogous way Barnes clung to what he conceived to be an untranslatable "language" in communicating with the deepest and most abiding sources of spiritual and moral well-being. In earlier times the presence of a beneficent order had been manifest in the appearance and regulation of the scheme of things, and was reinforced by the intricate set of correspondences between man and nature which was the rationale of the great unifying chain of being. In the emergent urban world, however, characterized to an ever-growing degree by uncertain values and a complex loneliness, the serene unity of man in God's love which had led him to "green pastures" was dissipated in spiritual exhaustion. In attempting to justify a dispensation where God's Nature was found to be "red in tooth and claw," and Himself, therefore, either malicious or illusory, Tennyson, for instance, at a moment of deepest despair quite naturally expressed his sense of destitution in terms of urban desolation:

> He is not here; but far away
> The noise of life begins again
> And ghastly thro' the drizzling rain
> On the bald street breaks the blank day.

(*In Memoriam*, vii)

It is not, of course, just a case of facilely observing the urban "tenor" of the image, to use I. A. Richards' term, but rather to remark the fact that in the central, and to most contemporaries, consoling poetic statement of the age, the poet frequently uses as the "vehicle" of his imagery what Dickens referred to as "the shame, desertion, wretchedness and exposure of the great capital."[40] Many sensitive people found themselves living between two worlds where, from one point of view, nature was being increasingly conquered and manipulated for man's material aggrandizement; but from another, metaphysical, aspect, nature was through that process having its cosmological role adapted to the new man-made setting. Thus the removal of nature from the prime and immediate context of human life led men to translate optimism in a rational dispensation into faith in progress in an industrialized environment, bringing about a radical dislocation of traditional values and standards, and replacing them, ineffectually for many, with the iron restriction of Necessity and the earth-bound aspiration of social perfectibility. This change of role resulted in a situation infinitely more perplexing than implied in the simple opposition of "God made the country, and man made the town"; it became commensurately more difficult to believe, in what seemed to Barnes and many of his contemporaries the worst of all possible worlds, that "He prayeth best, who loveth best/ All things both great and small." The difficulty is dramatized with terrifying effect by James Thomson. In his wanderings through the "City of Dreadful Night," whose ruin is suggested by the rubble of Love, Faith, and Hope, triple pillars that had supported a God-oriented cosmos, he meets a degenerate and forlorn man who hopes with grotesque improbability to find his way "From this accursed night . . . to *Eden's* innocence in *Eden's* clime" (Sec. xviii). By contrast, the world of William Barnes embodies a way of life, an attitude of mind, rooted firmly in his efforts to conserve the "Eden innocence" of rural Dorset—whose "life and . . . landscape," as Hopkins expressed it, "had taken flesh and tongue in the man" (p. 221)—from degenerating into such an "accursed night." Those efforts are the medium of his mythopoeic activity—his "powerful and exquisite [capacity] for defending himself against violation of his cherished self-image"—and constitute, in fact, the very "art-and-society reasons for urging that Barnes should be read."

Notes

[1] S. E. Hyman, "Psychoanalysis and the Climate of Tragedy," in *Freud and the Twentieth Century,* ed. Benjamin Nelson (New York, 1957), p. 170.

[2] Hallam Tennyson, *Alfred, Lord Tennyson. A Memoir* (London, 1897), I, 514.

[3] Quoted in William Van O'Connor, *Sense and Sensibility in Modern Poetry* (Chicago, 1948), p. 18.

[4] *The Letters of John Keats,* ed. M. B. Forman (Oxford, 1935), pp. 334-337.

[5] Thomas Hardy, "The Rev. William Barnes, B.D.," reprinted in Lionel Johnson, *The Art of Thomas Hardy* (London, 1895), p. 1.

[6] H. J. Massingham, *The English Countryman* (London, 1943), p. 127.

[7] Quoted in *Selected Poems of William Barnes,* ed. Geoffrey Grigson (London, 1950), p. 10.

[8] "William Barnes: the Dorsetshire Poet," *Macmillan's Magazine,* VI (1862), 155.

[9] *The Letters of Gerard Manley Hopkins to Robert Bridges,* ed. C. C. Abbott (Oxford, 1955), p. 88.

[10] *William Barnes of Dorset* (London, 1953), p. 21.

[11] Quoted in Dugdale, p. 20, from Barnes's "Foresay" to Judge Udal's *Dorsetshire Folklore.*

[12] "In Memoriam Rev. William Barnes, B.D.," *Procedings of the Dorsret Natural History and Autiquarian Field Club,* VIII (1887), xviii.

[13] *The Rural Muse* (London, 1954), p. 152.

[14] Quoted in Geoffrey Grigson, *The Harp of Acolus* (London, 1947), p. 121.

[15] *The Acquistive Society* (London, 1933), pp. 231-233.

[16] *Views of Labour and Gold* (London, 1859), p. 12.

[17] Quoted in Montague Weekley, *William Morris* (London, 1934), p. 134.

[18] *The Letters of D. H. Lawrence,* ed. Aldous Huxley (London, 1932), p. 300.

[19] Quoted from Barnes's "Foresay" to *An Outline of English Speech-craft,* in *The Harp of Aeolus,* p. 111.

[20] "An English Classic, William Barnes," *Fortnightly Review,* XL (1886), 664.

[21] *Macmillan's Magazine,* XVI (1867), 306.

[22] *The Poems of William Barnes,* ed. Bernard Jones (London, 1962), I, 392. All citations of Barnes's poetry will be from this edition, unless otherwise noted.

[23] *The Idiom of the People* (London, 1958), p. 30.

[24] "Discourse VII" (1776), quoted in H. A. Needham, *Taste and Criticism in the Eighteenth Century* (London, 1952), p. 135.

[25] *Natural Theology: Or the Evidences of the Existence and Attributes of the Deity* (London, 1802), II, 143.

[26] *Three Essays on Religion* (London, 1885), p. 174.

[27] *Fraser's Magazine,* LXVIII (1863), 130-134.

[28] C. J. Wallis, "Early Manhood of William Barnes," *Gentleman's Magazine,* CCLXV (1888), 29.

[29] This article is not listed in Dugdale's bibliography (pp. 237-244). It originally appeared in *The Leisure Hour* for 1883 (which I have not been able to consult). A copy of the article in pamphlet form, presumably reprinted from *The Leisure Hour,* appears among Barnes's papers in the Dorset County Museum. It has apparently not been reprinted since.

[30] This pamphlet is among Barnes's papers in the Dorset Museum. It was probably privately printed as a pamphlet by Barnes in 1849 from the *Poole Herald,* where it first appeared.

[31] Thomas Edwards Kebbel, "English Farmers," *Blackwood's Magazine,* CXLV (1889), 135.

[32] Quoted in J. L. and L. B. Hammond, *The Rise of Modern Industry* (London, 1930), p. 3.

[33] J. L. and L. B. Hammond, *The Bleak Age* (New York, 1947), p. 34.

[34] G. M. Trevelyan, *English Social History* (London, 1945), pp. 475-476.

[35] Mabel Kay Ashby, *Joseph Ashby of Tysoe, 1859-1919* (Cambridge, 1961), p. 285.

[36] Quoted in Douglas Brown, *Thomas Hardy* (London, 1954), p. 38.

[37] "The Dorsetshire Labourer," *Longman's Magazine,* II (1883), 269.

[38] J. F. Lynen, *The Pastoral Art of Robert Frost* (New Haven, 1960), pp. 57-58.

[39] Thomas Hardy. *The Mayor of Casterbridge* (London, 1912), ch. xxiv.

[40] Quoted in Frank Kermode, *The Romantic Image* (London, 1957), p. 5.

C. H. Sisson (essay date 1965)

SOURCE: "William Barnes," in *Art and Action,* Methuen, 1965, pp. 30-46.

[*In the following essay, Sisson examines Barnes's life, his writings on language, and his poetry of rural life.*]

I

William Barnes came of the best blood in England, being the son of a small farmer in the West Country.

Like many another in that countryside, the family was "down-start"—in his own language—being an off-shoot, or so he thought, of a gentleman's family of Gillingham in Dorset. That matters little enough, one way or the other. What does matter is that Barnes came from a stock neither high nor low, grown into the country like a tree-root. All distinctions of origin are on the way to being effaced, but there are still those who understand the intense pride of such birth, the furthest possible removed from pretension. In rural society it was a middle station; the gentry were above it, the labourers below, and its members no more aspired to be taken for the one than they feared being mistaken for the other. Snobberies are the product of an urban confusion, now spread too over an urbanised countryside. But before that happened the classes were an order of nature, worth nobody's while to question; a barrier of sorts, but not one that obscured the sottishness or other quiddity of the man on the other side—rather a setting against which his qualities could be shrewdly estimated and tartly commented. The tendency of social distinction to obscure personal worth is a phenomenon of dissolution, when members of different classes find themselves in competition in a world of supposed equalities.

The place of Barnes's birth was Bagber in the parish of Sturminster Newton, where his father had a poor farm and his uncle and aunt, across the common, a better one, until the fortunes of rural life turned against them and they had to sell up. The language spoken in this little world in 1801—the year of Barnes's birth—was a Dorset untroubled by the mobility of populations or an excess of reading matter: "the speech of our forefathers", as he is recorded as having said eighty-four years later, which in time would "be scarcely remembered" and none would "be found to speak it with the purity" he had heard it spoken with in his youth. He did "some little to preserve the speech", but while we are considering origins, rather than directions, it may be well to reflect that it was some such speech—in different but related dialects—that Shakespeare and Raleigh spoke as boys and there will have been more than a trace of it even in the speech which Raleigh used at Court. The Vale of Blackmore, whose capital Sturminster Newton is, must in 1801 have been a remote pastoral valley, the life of which was nearer to that which the Elizabethans knew—and which in the sixteenth century ran to the fringes of London itself—than to the almost universally suburban life of our own time. In Sturminster Newton things were still made by hand which elsewhere were already being made more numerously, and worse, by machine, and the equipment of farms and cottages was the stools and pots and pans and benches of an earlier age. These things matter the more, in Barnes's growth and development, because he was not one who was sent away to school at Eton or Winchester, or to college at Oxford or Cambridge, but found his education on his doorstep. A world of selection tests and scholarships may be surprised that he found it at all. There was, however, a good church school, and the curate at Sturminster Newton was one of those illustrations—which do not always spring to light when one scrutinizes the countryside of the time—of Coleridge's thesis as to the benefits conferred by a Church which sought to put a scholar and a gentleman in every parish. Barnes was fortunate in his clergy, both in Sturminster Newton and later, in Dorchester, and it was under these benign auspices that he grew up. He left school at thirteen to go into a solicitor's office. As things went in his world, he was favoured.

Although his studies had made a fortunate start in Sturminster Newton, Barnes needed a more metropolitan scene and at the age of seventeen he moved from the capital of the Vale of Blackmore to the capital of Dorset itself. In an age when every illiterate youth has to be transported to Paris or Barcelona before he has left school the movement may seem a modest one, but it answered to the natural need of a boy of Barnes's age to turn his back on his origins. Dorchester was the right field of force. It showed Barnes a little of what is called the world, but against a background which he perfectly understood. It was the resort of farmers on market days and the Tunbridge Wells of the local county families. Once again he had a sympathetic employer—another solicitor—and a clergyman who helped him with his studies. It is extraordinary how the vigour and range of those studies grew. Barnes was not put in for examinations but had a natural taste for learning. He made progress in classical and modern languages. He became a highly competent engraver, for he was a man of his hands as well as of his head. He also fell in love with an exciseman's daughter whom he was not to be able to afford to make his wife for nearly ten years. One would give a lot to be able to meet the Barnes of those days. The evidence is that he was a young man of great charm and eagerness of spirit. By the time he was twenty he had printed a pamphlet of verses (in Dorchester of course); one of these published poems celebrated a Julia (the actual name of the girl who became his wife) whose father

he lik'd the pecun'ary ore.

That must have caused a titter in the town. He went through a normal adolescent comedy with Julia's parents; he was snubbed when he tried to write or visit, and ignored the exciseman in the streets. At twenty-two he was no nearer an income he could marry on and went off to Mere in Wiltshire to take up school-mastering. E. M. Forster charges Barnes with a lack of sentiment about the Labourers' Revolt of 1830. The lowest middle classes have always lacked sentiment about the condition of the workers. They understand the troubles of poverty too well. It is the Schlegels (of *Howard's End*) and the Shelleys of

real life who get excited. Barnes could be accused of lack of sympathy with the labourers only by someone with a very politicised notion of sympathy.

Barnes was to go on schoolmastering for nearly forty years. He had not, by the move to Mere, acquired a salary. He was trying to collect pupils and to get fees out of reluctant payers. The society he lived in was not one that readily offered security. Going to Mere meant turning his back on the intellectual stimulations of Dorchester. He had few social diversions, and used his leisure for study—mathematics as well as languages—and he continued to engrave. He was an ingenious and original schoolmaster, and gentle in an age when gentleness in schoolmasters was by no means to be taken for granted. He unaffectedly tried to impart something of his own diversity of interests. The school at Mere did at last enable him to marry, when he was twenty-six. In 1835 he returned to Dorchester and opened school there. The success of the boarding establishment depended quite largely on Julia, and when she died in 1852 a certain listlessness set in. But the intervening years were years of active poetical production. His verses appeared in the *Dorset County Chronicle* and the first volume was published in London in 1844. Barnes says that he wrote for recreation in the evenings after his days of school-mastering. He certainly did not organize his life for poetry. His most conscious efforts were for the support of his family and the pursuit of a remarkable variety of studies, linguistical, philological, mathematical and archaeological. The poetry came "naturally as the leaves of a tree", as Keats said it should. But it is not unrelated to his more time-consuming studies, and tricks from the Welsh and the Persian are concealed in his indubitably spontaneous verses. During these years in Dorchester he also collected pictures—a Gainsborough and a Richard Wilson among them—excusing the expense which he felt should rather have been on his numerous family by saying that he spent nothing on wines or tobacco. He was not what you could call *maudit*.

It is characteristic of the slow but persistent movement of Barnes's career that at the age of thirty-six he put his name down at St. John's College, Cambridge, in order to be able, under a statute then in force, to take his degree of B.D. ten or more years later. He was ordained in 1847 and was given the care of the tiny parish of Whitcombe, detached from another for the purpose. It was not a living; it brought him thirteen pounds a year and he walked out from Dorchester to serve it. He would have liked, but did not get, the headmastership of Dorchester Grammar School, and the diminution of his own school in Dorchester after his wife's death made him seek employment elsewhere. It is of interest that, with all his intellectual attainments, some reputation as a writer, a public and impeccable rectitude and intense application to whatever duties he undertook, he obtained none of the employments he sought, perhaps because his ferocious spirit of independence allowed him to take none of the steps that are normally taken in these matters. It was not until he was over sixty, at a time when his financial anxieties were acute, that he was offered the living of Winterborne Came, the parish near Dorchester which included his old church of Whitcombe. It was this that made possible the patriarchal flowering of his later years.

Few men could have been better suited to the work of a parish priest; it is hard to conceive of anyone better suited to that work in the Dorset of that time. In temper and in learning, Barnes was Herbert's *Country Parson;* he had the super-added advantage of an intimate sense of the ways of his flock which the years at Bagber had given him. Though the bibliography of the last twenty-five years of his life shows a continuous literary production, particularly but by no means exclusively prose, he was out every morning visiting his parishioners, with his prayerbook and his pocket full of sweets for the children. Travelling on foot in a widely-scattered parish, he reckoned to visit everywhere once a fortnight. The muse came to him less frequently as he grew old, and he never pretended that she was there when she was not. She never withdrew her favours. Barnes could have said with Malherbe

> Je les possédai, jeune, et les posséde encore
> A la fin de mes jours.

At eighty-five, in the year before his death, he dictated his lovely verses of **"The Geäte A-Vallen To."** On the very eve of his death verses escaped him, in the same breath as the Third Collect at Evening Prayer.

II

Such was the life and death of William Barnes, a figure of the sixteenth century rather than of the nineteenth, not through any literary affectation but because his social origins, and his absolute truth to them, made any such affectations unnatural to him. E. M. Forster says that Barnes's "prose-intelligence was provincial", which may be admitted, if we admit also that his attention to his subject, and his ignorance of cultural drifts, remind us of Selden or Camden.

The list of prose works is formidable—perhaps thirty books, to say nothing of papers and essays not collected, on philology, grammar, applied mathematics, archaeology and social matters. Most of them are odd little books, such as no publisher would look at now and few wanted then. They are home-made things, with a complete lack of pretension. In a sense they belong to the Barnes who kept school in Dorchester rather than to Barnes the poet—a few because they are schoolmasters' books, if not school-books, but more because

they show what were the day-to-day workings of the mind of one in whose ordinary life poetry appeared, to those who knew him, to play only a small part. Yet they are certainly not without relevance to the work of the poet. It is not merely that passages here and there confirm the facts on which the poems are built, as this account of a sale:

> My uncle was a farmer in the West of England, but became insolvent from the depression of the agricultural interest after the French war. My aunt had a numerous family, and her long exercised solicitude as a mother, and her continual struggles against misfortunes, had nearly brought her with sorrow to the grave; she was calm, and it was only when either of her daughters passed her, that a tear rolled down her sallow cheek. The young men were in that severe and reckless mood in which young men are frequently thrown when assailed by misfortunes they can still resist. The girls were bewildered, and scarcely knew what happened to them; then were driven away the cows under which the weeping milkmaid had so often sung the simple songs of the country; then went the waggon in which the merry haymakers had so many times ridden in to the feast of harvest-home; and in short, then every thing that was dear from familiarity was taken away, and my uncle, as he looked on the fields he had so long cultivated with hope, and of which he had taken the produce in grateful joy, sighed and dropped a tear as if he had said "Dulcia linquimus arva."[1]

Nor is it merely that the prose works illustrate the learning and industry of the author, though the reader of the poems may well reflect that the author's acquaintance with the sixty or seventy languages from which the "principles and forms" of the ***Philological Grammar*** were drawn does not suggest that Barnes wrote in the Dorset dialect through any narrowness of linguistic scope. He wrote in it because he was celebrating the virtues of the ordinary population of a fortunate countryside. If he did not notice the Labourers' Revolt (as the social historians see it) he noticed the labourers, and cared in his writings as in his life for the families which grew up around him on a bare subsistence. If like Herbert's parson he makes "a hook of his charity", saying "I give you this for the good you have done or followed", he also cares that every family shall have a house, denounces the long hours, lack of holidays, and the restrictions of industrial life which deprive a man of the chance of "a break for half-an-hour's talk with a welcome friend." He is acutely aware of "the tyranny of a great working capital" and of the damage done by excessive division of labour, which may make a girl "a fitting companion only to the frame and the bobbin." He exhibits the prejudices and loyalties of a race untouched by liberal delusions, and introduces his note on the **"Character and Intelligence of the Britons"**[2] by saying in reply to Horace's accusation that the Britons were cruel to foreigners most likely we English, though we may deem ourselves men of a more refined life, should be found quite as warlike and bloodthirsty . . . if another race were to bring the sword against us.

He might be that yeoman in Fuller's *Holy State,* who "goes not to London, but . . . seeing the King once, he prays for him ever afterwards."

The most interesting of Barnes's prose works, to the reader of his poetry, may be thought to be the grammatical and philological works, though a certain dryness and laboriousness of analysis is to be expected. Different versions of ***The Glossary of the Dorset Dialect*** were produced in 1844, 1863, and 1886, and the subject matter of the book was throughout his central preoccupation, even if not always in the analytical form in which it is there presented. In a sense Barnes's books on language are a disappointment; it is as if they were always approaching a point they never quite reach. But they are genuinely thrown up by his life-long meditation on language as he had found it used, and they express by implication a profound dissatisfaction with the thinner speech that the multiplication of means of communication and the mobility of populations were already making. The language Barnes spoke in his boyhood was a genuine common store, made to express what those who spoke it could understand. Each man took as much of it as answered to his share of the world, what he had directly by sight and hearing and touch. It is as far as possible from the meretricious speech of public and commercial media which all but the most sophisticated are now ashamed not to talk. In taking the spoken Dorset speech for the solid base of his work, Barnes was turning his back on the literary effects of "the money-making mind, which looks on the work of God mainly, if not only, as sources of wealth." His translation into Dorset dialect of one of the contemporary Queen's Speeches[3] to Parliament is a piece of social criticism as well as literary criticism. His radical approach made him a literary innovator of the most unselfconscious kind. He did not merely react against the increasingly pervasive influence of commerce, as some of the best urban minds of the century did; he was moving surely, on his own, in a direction which would be seen to be a right one when many more blatantly advertised paths had ended in nothingness. Certain Scotch writers of our own day have had recourse to dialect as a means of detaching themselves from the corrupt speech of the time, and the exercise has enabled the best of them to return to current English and renew it. Some of Barnes's later English poems are in a tone and manner which he might never have attained if he had not first acquired sureness in a speech that the more sinister contemporary influences could not touch. But his dialect was not synthetic. More fortunate in his birth than MacDiarmid, he inhertied a speech and was not driven to invent one.

It must be admitted that Barnes's exercises in the purification of language led finally to ludicrous excesses of Saxonising, of which ***English Speech-Craft*** (1878) contains instructive illustrations. But this theoretical aberration never upset the balance of the language he used in his verse, for which he had a true touchstone in his early memories. In any case, saxonising is not the only, nor perhaps the most important aim of Barnes's linguistic studies. The ***Philological Grammar*** (1854) is nothing less than an attempt to analyse the essential content of all language; to define, for example, the series of relations which grammatical cases convey, whether indicated by case endings, by prepositions, or in some other way. It is the essential movements of the human mind that Barnes is seeking to define. This objective is perhaps most clearly seen in ***Tiw or A View of the Roots and Stems of English as a Teutonic Tongue*** (1862), which is said to have been a favourite with him among his books. In this book he tries to reduce the English language to "about fifty primary roots", reached "through English provincial dialects and other Teutonic speech-forms". The roots are given in the form of the initial and final consonants, as for example "Pring", which is said to mean

> To put forth, in a striking form, to any sense or to the mind as to—
> The feeling—in upstickingness;
> The taste—in sharpness;
> The sight—in prinking gaiety of colours or clothing;
> The mind—in mind-striking action, or upstickingness of behaviour."[4]

Various terminations, such as -nk, or -k or (more remotely) -m, -d, or -n, are substituted for the final -ng, and this brings into relation such words as "prang" (western dialect, finely clad), "prong" (as used in haymaking), "prick", "perk up", "prim" (eastern dialect for the spindle tree), "prune" (as of trees). The result is to reduce all speech to a small number of basic physical apprehensions, a conception which throws great light on the language of the poems, and on the prominence in them of physical movement, sometimes of a boisterous kind.

In his study of archaeology Barnes prided himself on "a careful use" of his "little knowledge of the British language, which . . . Antiquaries have too often neglected", and there is no doubt that for him an appreciation of language was a *sine qua non* of such understanding as we may have of human life. But the study of language took him back to physical apprehensions, and an esthetic ideal of the physical man and woman was never far from the mind of this majestic parson with long beard and flowing cassock:

> the beautiful in nature [he says in his ***Thoughts on Beauty and Art***] is the unmarred result of God's

first creative or forming will, and . . . the beautiful in art is the result of an unmistaken working of man in accordance with the beautiful in nature.[5]

Barnes had spoken in **Labour and Gold** of feeding like squirrels and exercising like monkeys, and in his **Thoughts on Beauty and Art** he spoke of the beautiful in man being the state in which "there should not be a spot on his body where . . . an insect or prickle might hold itself, so that it could not be reached by the fingers of one of the hands." As for animals, so for man, beauty is "fitness for the good continuance of the animal as such."

III

Barnes called his poems "of rural life", whether they were in the Dorset dialect or in common English, and the label has been read by an urbanised literary world to mean that they are of a limited and specialized interest. Barnes wrote about rural life because his life was in fact rural, and he used the material that came to hand as much as Baudelaire did when he wrote about Paris. What is disconcerting, because it was so rare in poets of his century, as indeed of ours, is his contentment within the order of nature, an order of nature capped by grace, for the church is as much part of his countryside as the "wide-horned cattle" and the "cracklen waggon",

> a pleäce, where we mid seek
> The gifts o' greäce vrom week to week.

Barnes celebrates the life of the English countryside as Shakespeare in *Henry V* celebrated our national wars. There is more to be said about both than is contained in Barnes or in Shakespeare, much of it less agreeable than what is to be found in those writers, but that does not detract from the truth of the elements they presented, one might say created. Barnes's theme—so far as a poet can be said to have a theme apart from the poems he writes—is nothing less than what is fit "for the good continuance" of the human animal. His personal griefs—and they are as poignantly expressed as those of anyone who has written in English—are felt against a larger background of natural growth and decline, with this world—however unpalatable the notion maybe—completed by the next. Children occupy a prominent place in his scheme of things, not as beastly little Peter Pans but as people setting out on the journey others are already far advanced in, their needs providing a motive for their elders' continuance, while

> livèn gifts o' youth do vall,
> Vrom girt to small, but never die.

It is not the "individual", that insecure invention of liberal romanticism, that is here in play. What William

Barnes does is part of the action, not only of his contemporaries who crowd in to Shroton fair, but of the "vorevathers" and descendants. His view of things is far removed from that typical contemporary mixture of extreme subjectivism and mechanism—of overweening awareness of one's own wants and rights and smartness about the operation of determinism in others. He is not solipsist and mechanical but one of a company, natural and theological. By the same token he inhabits a more permanent world than that of modern politics, and for him the first meaning of "our own free land" is the few fields a man may manage to own, as in his Dorchester days he bought a few symbolic acres at Bagber.

The best known of Barnes's poems are some of those lyrics he wrote after the death of his wife. These verses are not the simple product of the emotion of that time. Barnes does not present his grief in the setting of the school in Dorchester, in the running of which his wife gave him the most practical help, but identifies himself with the countryman taking "the bit he can avword" out under the beeches, so that the predicament is no longer merely his own. No distress could darken his sense of the existence of others, and the scrupulousness which made him lug the most inconveniently shaped purchases back to his rectory rather than trouble the Dorchester tradesmen to deliver them, enabled him to enter into the feelings of labourers and small farmers, whether as the subjects of his poems or as his parishioners. The transference of his observations into verse was made easier by the use of dialect, for he was a listener and it is in the turns of language that people most plainly reveal themselves.

> Good morn t'ye, John. How b'ye? how b'ye?
> Zoo you be gwain to market, I do zee.
> Why, you be quite a-lwoaded wi' your geese.

It is the very inflection of ordinary speech, and where else would you look for that in the verse written in England in 1833? It is not in the odd line or two that Barnes has caught it; all the eclogues in his first volume of Dorset poems have it throughout, combined with an utter sureness in the handling of metre. This represents an immense technical liberation, and the poetry of the nineteenth century suffered a progressive softening through lack of attention to it. It should not be supposed that an achievement of this kind would come inevitably, and as it were in the course of nature, to anyone writing in dialect. A glance at the Dorset verse of William Holloway (1761-1854) will show that that is not the case; or you may look at the "Northern Farmer," which Tennyson is supposed to have written, after seeing Barnes's poems, to see what could be made of the speech of the north. Barnes was always happy with the eclogue as a form, for it suited his sense of the plurality of lives about him, and it is marvellous what differences of tone and manner he catches—a girl with "sca'ce a thing a-left in pleäce" when she comes out of the crowd at Shroton Fair; two men discussing the advantages of a "little bit o' land" beside one's house; waggoners arguing about a load. For sheer technical proficiency in the handling of dramatic variations the last poem in the collected volume of Dorset poems (**"A Lot o' Maïdens a-runnèn the Vields"**) is incomparable, though the material of it is slighter than that of some of the others.

Had Barnes merely achieved lucidity and variety in dramatic dialogue that would have been one of the more notable achievements of the century, more particularly since he showed in the 1868 volume that he could do the same thing in common English when he chose, and if some richness is lost in that speech it is only because it was less his own than the language of Bagber. But Barnes could carry this conversational tone into the most intense lyric and into the most elaborate rhyme-scheme, and combine it with a sweetness of refrain which is almost painful, like Spenser's refrain in *Prothalamion*. For sheer verse-craft, you will scarcely find in the nineteenth century the equal of **"Shaftesbury Feäir"** or **"The Wold Wall"**—

> To Paladore. Aye, Poll a dear,
> Vor now 'tis feäir

or

> Ah! well-a-day! O wall adieu!
> The wall is wold, my grief is new.

Such is Barnes's skill that the reality of the voice is enhanced, not lost, amidst intricacies of rhyme and metre, as in **"Grammer a-crippled:"**

> "But oh! though low mid slant my ruf,
>   Though hard my lot mid be,
> Though dry mid come my daily lwoaf,
>   Mid mercy leäve me free!"
> Cried Grammer, "Or adieu
>   To jaÿ; O grounds,
>   An' bird's gaÿ sounds
> If I mus' gi'e up you,
> Although 'tis well, in God's good will,
> That I should bide 'ithin a wall."

IV

That Barnes has been undervalued many people are now willing to admit. It may be a long time before the Dorchester Museum does more than exhibit his buckle shoes and a school-desk in a corner of the Hardy room, but there are poets who look on him as one of the great masters, and the critics will follow. It will not be in a resuscitated dialect that his influence will be shown.

He was not a local poet except by accident. He did not seek out a language to give himself idiosyncracy, but exploited the natural speech of his boyhood. This enabled him to escape from the literary foibles of his time more quickly and completely than he could otherwise have done, as a comparison of the poems in the 1846 volume in "national English" with the Dorset poems of the same time shows. His use of dialect probably also enabled him to maintain his liberty of feeling amidst the uncomprehending pressures he must have faced from his social superiors. Barnes is not there to encourage a factitious oddity, but on the contrary to demonstrate that the poet has to develop in a straight line from his origins, and that the avoidance of literature is indispensable for the man who wants to tell the truth.

Notes

[1] *Labour and Gold,* 1859, p. 146.

[2] *Notes on Ancient Britain,* 1848, p. 79.

[3] See the preface to *A Glossary of the Dorset Dialect,* 1886.

[4] *Tiw* (1862), p. 44.

[5] An article in Macmillan's Magazine, 1861. Printed as an appendix to Giles Dugdale's *William Barnes* (1953).

James W. Parins (essay date 1984)

SOURCE: "Poetry," in *William Barnes,* Twayne Publishers, 1984, pp. 16-68.

[*In the following excerpt, Parins explores Barnes's poetic technique and surveys his love and religious poetry, as well as his folklore verse and "homely rhymes."*]

Barnes as a Dialect Poet

Barnes established himself as a writer of dialect poetry in 1844 with the publication of **Poems of Rural Life in the Dorset Dialect.** Here he turned to what he knew best for the subject matter of his art—the region and people of Dorset—and used as poetic language for those subjects the only appropriate one—the local dialect. Like Robert Burns, Barnes was an originator and a preserver of local tales and legends. The Dorset poet uses the dialect to produce atmosphere and to enhance the local color of his region as well; his language furnishes his descriptions of the countryside with a fresh point of view. His humor, highlighted with quaint expressions, pokes gentle fun at the foibles and vanities of the country folk. Appropriately enough, Barnes's style is low-keyed and folksy, due in large measure to his use of the rural speech patterns. The use of the Dorset language, too, makes poignant his depictions of country people suffering from unjust social and economic conditions and policies.

The decision to write in the dialect was appropriate for Barnes for other reasons as well. His deep interest in antiquarianism, natural philosophy, and philology doubtless played a major part. Barnes's inclination toward history, especially in the past of Dorset, led to a natural attraction for old folktales, customs, and legends. These, handed down in the local dialect, often became the subjects of his poetry. His lifelong love of the outdoors, and his corresponding curiosity for natural phenomena, prompted him to examine closely his surroundings in the Vale of Blackmore and to use this as the setting for most of his work. The Dorset settings undoubtedly influenced the choice of writing in the Dorset dialect. Finally, his passion for philology and the study of language led to his analysis of the local dialect and to the discovery of its poetic possibilities. Like Hopkins after him, Barnes was quick to realize the value of older, less familiar words in literary diction. This tendency toward the fresh and original was, in large measure, responsible for Barnes's choice of language.

Poetic Techniques

While it was Barnes's intention to write "homely rhymes," those which praised the life and values of the simple, hard-working rural Englishman and those written in such language that the subjects of the poems could understand them, the poet used many sophisticated poetic devices in his verse. Many of these devices Barnes gleaned from his readings in the literatures of other cultures; some of the more arcane techniques he adopted for his own poetry are probably employed there for the first time in English. These devices are common in both Barnes's dialect verse and those poems written in "common English."

A good example of such a device is his poem **"Green"** which is an imitation of the Persian poetic form called a *ghazal*, a lyric varying in length from five to fifteen couplets, all with the same rhyme:

> Our summer way to church did wind about
> The cliff, where ivy on the *ledge* was *green*
> [my italics].
> Our summer way to town did skirt the wood,
> Where shining leaves, in tree and *hedge*, were
> *green*.[6]

Another device borrowed from the Persian involves the matching of sounds in half lines. An example of this occurs in Barnes's poem **"The Wold Wall"** when the persona exclaims, "Ah! well-a-day! O was adieu!" This punlike refrain unfortunately is repeated at the

end of each stanza in the poem, providing proof once again that not all prosodic experimentation is successful.

Barnes borrowed from the Hebrew, as well. A device called "psalmic parallelism" is used in **"Melhill Feast"**:

> Then by the orchards dim and cool,
> And then along Woodcombe's elmy side,
> And then by the meads, where waters glide,
> *Shallow by shallow, pool by pool* [my italics].
>
> And then to the house, that stands alone,
> With roses around the porch and wall,
> Where up by the bridge the waters fall,
> *Rock under rock, and stone by stone.*
>
> (*P*, 738)

As Geoffrey Grigson points out, Barnes also used another Eastern form called "adorning."[7] This device involves the matching of each word in a line with another in the next line. The matching may be in rhyme or metrical quantity as in "As trees be bright / Wi' bees in flight."

But the poet's interests were not confined to the Middle East. His involvement with linguistics and history led him to the study of medieval and older literature. Always experimenting, Barnes's work with old texts spilled over into his own poetry. In **"The Lane,"** for example, he uses an alliterative formula reminiscent of Old English poetry:

> And where the ashes white bough whips
> The whistling air with coal-black tips;
> And where the grassy ground, beside
> The gravel-washing brook lies wide,
> And leaping lambs, with shrill-toned throats,
> Bleat loudly in their first white coats.
>
> (*P*, 644-65)

He borrows from the Irish, too, adopting the medieval device of "underrhyme," as in **"Times of the Year"**:

> Soon shall grass, a-vrosted *bright* [my italics]
> Glishten *white* instead of green,
> An' the wind shall smite the *cows*,
> Where the *boughs* be now their screen.
> Things do change as years do vlee;
> What ha' years in store vor me?
>
> (*P*, 415)

Barnes has a special interest in Welsh, probably because the language survived so well, and because it was still a vital tongue and not just an object of curiosity. The old Celtic bards were an important area of his studies; it was from them that he took the convention of "cymmeriad," or resumption. This is the repetition of a word or thought at the beginning of a verse or stanza, analogous to the refrain, which repeats words at the end of the verse. Barnes adopted this device in poems such as **"The Rest,"** calling it "versehead."

The Dorset poet anticipates Hopkins in his use of another Welsh device, *cynghanedd,* which is a consonantal sound pattern set up in a line—or adjacent lines—of poetry. A good example of Barnes's use of this occurs in **"My Orcha'd in Linden Lea."** The line "Do leän down low in Linden Lea" establishes the sound pattern *L N D N L* in the first half of the line and repeats it in the second.

The Welsh art of *pennillion,* or what the medieval Scots poets called *flyting,* is reflected in Barnes's *running down.* Running down—a popular Dorset pastime, according to the poet—is basically deprecation of a person, object, or idea, as in "that contract is not worth the paper it's written on." The speaker is not, most often, being unfriendly, but is attempting to establish his or her good taste or judgment. An example in Barnes's poetry can be found in **"Woak Wer Good Enough Woonce,"** in which the poet complains that while good English oak was once used as the basic building material, now people are not satisfied unless mahogany and other more exotic woods are used. He deprecates the new woods and the new habits and says that he will stick to his old standby, oak.

The willingness to experiment technically, to adapt conventions and techniques from other literatures to his own work was one of the main reasons that other poets were attracted to his verse. Patmore and Hopkins, both experimenters themselves, were among Barnes's most fervent admirers. And Thomas Hardy, a pioneer in both poetry and prose, learned much from Barnes's example.

Barnes's Language, Genres, and Subjects

Barnes's first book was **Poetical Pieces,** self-published in 1820 and consisting of ten poems written in what the poet came to call national English. Two years later, he brought out **Orra: A Lapland Tale,** a romantic narrative involving the search of a young girl for her lover. Both of these were printed in Dorchester and distributed locally. While he continued to write poetry, he did not bring out another volume of verse until 1844, when **Poems of Rural Life in the Dorset Dialect** was published. This achieved some degree of popularity, as new editions were brought out in 1847, 1862, and 1866. All of his work was not in the Dorset dialect, however, and his 1846 volume, **Poems Partly of Rural Life in National English,** was written in standard English. In 1859, Barnes published **Hwomely** [sic] **Rhymes: A Second Collection of Poems in the Dorset Dialect;** a second edition of this work was printed four years later. By 1862, he had added enough verses to bring out **Poems of Rural Life in the Dorset Dialect:**

Third Collection, which was reprinted later in 1869, a year after his second collection of standard English poems, **Poems of Rural Life in Common English.** The 1844, 1859, and 1862 dialect collections were brought together in one volume, **Poems of Rural Life in the Dorset Dialect** (1879), and reissued several times afterward. Bernard Jones, who collected all the poetry in 1962, comments, "Such a record represents a solid poetic achievement, and to it should be added the American editions of **Hwomely Rhymes** in 1864 and of **Poems of Rural Life in Common English** in 1869" (**P,** 3).[8]

While he did continue to write and to publish poems in standard English after bringing out his dialect poems, Barnes is noted today almost exclusively for the latter. Indeed, during the nineteenth century, too, his fame rested on the poetry written in the rural tongue; the volumes which Coventry Patmore enthusiastically sent to Gerard Manley Hopkins in 1886 were the three editions of poems in the Dorset dialect.

In commenting on Barnes's use of the dialect, a choice which probably made his poetry difficult for the average reader and thus limited his potential for popularity, Thomas Hardy says that Barnes "couldn't help it."[9] The implication seems to be that since the Dorset dialect is the language the poet grew up with, it became the natural vehicle for his creative expression. Others, including Geoffrey Grigson[10] and Barnes's biographer-daughter,[11] disagree, citing the poet's philological studies as the main impetus for his choice. His linguistics studies led him to consider the Dorset speech as being more forceful and more poetic than the corrupted national English; as such, he saw it as appropriate to poetic expression, being a pure form of the language inherited from King Alfred and his forebears:

> Thus derived, the Dorset dialect is a broad and bold shape of the English language, as the Doric was of Greek. It is rich in humour, strong in raillery and hyperbole; and altogether as fit a vehicle of rustic feeling and thought, as the Doric is found in the *Idyllia* of Theocritus. Some people, who may have been taught to consider it as having originated from corruption of the written English, may not be prepared to hear that it is not only a separate offspring from the Anglo-Saxon tongue, but purer and more regular than the dialect which is chosen as the national speech; purer, inasmuch as it uses many words of Saxon origin, for which the English substitutes others of Latin, Greek, or French derivation; and more regular, inasmuch as it inflects regularly many words which, in the national language, are irregular. In English, purity is in many cases given up for the sake of what is considered to be elegance.[12]

It is clear that Barnes considered the use of Dorset not so much a break from tradition as a continuation of it. The poet seems more at ease with the dialect, too.

Some of the common English poems—there are some notable exceptions—lack enthusiasm and even, at times, conviction. Other marked dissimilarities are apparent; for example, the dialect poems usually have an easily discernible dramatic structure. A persona can usually be identified, and he or she is usually speaking from a clearly marked setting, sometimes even from an actual geographic locality. An auditor is often present, as well; the resulting dramatic monologues do as much as the landscapes of John Constable to capture the life of country folk in nineteenth-century rural England. "Uncle Out O' Debt an' Out O' Danger" and "The Settle an' the Girt Wood Vire" use this dramatic technique. The majority of the common English poems, on the other hand, are presented from the point of view of the poet-persona, there is no identifiable audience, and in many instances the setting is not as readily apparent or vividly portrayed; "Season Tokens," and "The Parrock" are good examples. While many of the national English poems have been taken from earlier dialect versions, those verses which are "translated" from Dorset to national English lose something—perhaps authenticity.[13]

The dialect Barnes used when writing the dialect poems was that spoken around Sturminster Newton in Dorset during the early nineteenth century. According to authorities, there is a distinct difference between the speeches of Sturminster and of Dorchester, the latter, of course, being the one which Thomas Hardy used in his work (cf. *P*, 17). Bernard Jones describes the language of Sturminster as flowing and melodious, while that of Dorchester, he says, is more staccato. Barnes imitates the Dorset speech of his particular locality while at the same time applying the laws of language as he understands them from his philological studies. The fact that some Dorset expressions are revised from one edition to the next suggests that Barnes changed some of his concepts concerning Dorset as time went on (cf. *P*, 18).

Always the experimenter, the poet tried a number of genres for his poetry. Since he was an admirer of Petrarch all his life, it was natural for him to write Italian sonnets. We find several sonnets among the early pieces, like "I Saw A Boy" and "Two Trees Were We," and they are sprinkled among the later national English poems as well. "In Ev'ry Dream Thy Lovely Features Rise" and "In Tenderness To Me Whom Thou Didst Spurn" are examples of later sonnets. It is clear that Barnes shared Hopkins's feeling that this verse form offered an opportunity for that perfect blend of structure and expression. Among the dialect poems, though, we find few sonnets, perhaps because Barnes felt they were inappropriate. Instead, he turns to the eclogue, in many cases, in his attempts to re-create conversations between the simple folk of Dorset. He presents monologues in the dialect, too, sometimes in a dramatic setting with a clearly identifiable auditor,

other times as a rustic soliloquy in which the speaker reflects and comments on his life or environment. He experimented early with the romance in *Orra: A Lapland Tale* and later with the drama when he wrote *Ruth,* a short Bible play. He composed hymns to be used in his services, as well as some verses he calls "Sabbath Lays" which are short, Psalm-like poems which extend the idea of an epigraph quoted from scripture. In his first volume of poems written in national English, he follows Boccaccio and Chaucer in offering a "tale of tales," in which several narrators recount episodes in verse of a long story. Like Hopkins, Barnes seems content to confine his experimentation to language—diction and syntax especially—and to prosody; neither poet seems inclined to attempt the invention of new forms.

In terms of content, Barnes's poems can all be assigned to one of some six classes, each reflecting a subject of the poet's interest. The subjects of the groups are autobiography and love, social issues and politics, nature, religion, folktales and legends, and homely subjects. The last classification takes a name used by the poet himself which is used to signify those verses that describe the rural life. Naturally, there is some overlap; a love poem may have some homely aspects, for example, or a religious poem may include some natural description. But since the poems do seem to fall into one or another of the categories, this system, an artificial one like any other, will help discussion of the works.

Poems of Love and Bereavement

The first group—poems of autobiography and love—is comprised of two topics which are inextricably welded together in Barnes's poetry, love and bereavement. The man had one great love affair, that one with his wife, Julia. He had met her when he was a young man in Dorchester, she having moved there at age sixteen when her father was transferred in his position of exciseman for the government. Barnes claimed that he fell in love with Julia Miles upon first setting eyes upon her; he took great delight in later years in telling his children that at their first meeting in 1818 he knew she was to be his wife. By 1820, he had published in the *Weekly Entertainer* "To Julia," a poem which publicly declared his love for the young lady. They did not immediately marry, however, because his position as a lawyer's clerk did not provide him with enough salary to support a wife. In 1823, a schoolmaster's position became vacant at Mere, a town in the vicinity; Barnes applied and was accepted. While the new position made it necessary to leave Dorchester and Julia, Barnes took it on since it offered better pay and a chance in the future for the young couple. After four years the waiting was over; William and Julia were married and settled down in Mere in 1826. Their marriage was a happy and productive one, both of them working hard to provide for their six children and to carry out the duties of operating a school. This contented life went on until 1853 when Julia died after an illness, leaving William still a relatively young man with children to raise. The death was a great shock, of course, and Barnes never quite got over it. His journals, but most of all his poems, remind us that he missed her a great deal.

His love poems reflect his love for his wife and later, his sense of bereavement. Many of the verses seem to be autobiographical in that so many female characters in or objects of his poems take on qualities he attributes to Julia. In **"The Maid Vor My Bride,"** for instance, a young man enumerates the qualities of the girl he is in love with. These qualities are ones which he admired in his wife and, indeed, in all women. She is meek, kind, good, but not scatterbrained. The girl, "is little lik' too many maïdens bezide," a real rarity, and she is "Not branten [brazen], nor spitevul, nor wild; she've a mind / To think o' what's right, an' a heart to be kind (*P*, 187). The paragon of probity and virtue, the lass nonetheless is physically attractive, with white skin, peachlike cheeks, and a lithesome figure: 'She's pretty a-zitten; but oh! how my love / Do watch her to madness when woonce [once] she do move" (*P*, 188). Many of the other love poems follow the pattern of the enamored rustic raising paeans to the object of his affection, Barnes's obvious—and successful—attempt to adapt the pastoral eclogue to a Dorsetshire setting. The attributes of a number of young women, named variously Jennie, Jeanie, and Fanny, are praised in vivid dialect verse by moonstruck young men. But the love poems contain more than just representations of dairymaids, too; courtship is described, successful marriages are discussed, promises are made, and betrothals are broken. Love and marriage are examined from the point of view of both partners, and occasionally, Barnes uses a female persona. Most often, though, the point of view is that of the male lover, as in the dialect poem **"In the Stillness o' Night."**

Here, courtship, or at least the early stages of it, is described by the young man who travels

> A-hoppen over geätes an' bars,
> By twinklen light o' winter stars,
> When snow do clumper to my shoe;
> An' zometimes we do slyly catch
> A chat an hour upon the stratch,
> An' peärt wi' whispers at the hatch
>   In the stillness of the night.

(P, 173)

The dialect makes the innocence even more poignant, it seems, just as it adds to the earnestness of the young beleaguered lover in **"A Zong."** Here, that age-old dilemma faced by young lovers—demands of the family in the choice of mate and the resultant loyalty crisis—is apparent. The problem is succinctly put:

> My kinsvo'k would faïn zee me teäke for my
>   meäte
> A mäid that ha' wealth, but a maïd I should
>   heäte;
> But I'd sooner leäbour wi' thee vor my bride,
> Than live lik' a squier wi' any beside.

Barnes's persona rejects the cold logic of Tennyson's new style northern farmer, and demonstrates his old-fashioned reluctance to break a promise:

> My head's in the storm, but my root's in the
>   rock.
> Zoo, Jenny, don't sobby! vor I shall be true;
> Noo might under heaven shall peärt me vrom
>   you.

(P, 187)

Love like this, Barnes knew, does not fade with marriage although it might change directions; the mature relationship is often strengthened by adversity. In **"Jeane,"** the husband, after recounting the blissful courtship, tells of the evolution of a ten year marriage:

> An' nwone but I can ever tell
> Ov all thy tear that have a-vell
> When trials meäde thy boson swell,
>   An' nwone but thou o' mine, Jeäne;
> An' now my heart, that heav'd wi' pride
> Back then to have thee at my zide, Do love
>   thee mwore
> as years do slide,
>   An' leave them times behine, Jeäne.

(P, 214)

As an observer of the human scene, though, the poet knew that lovers do not always live happily ever after. In **"Meary Wedded,"** Barnes tries to depict the desolation left behind when a young swain's loved one goes off to marry another. The pathetic fallacy, mainstay metaphor of the adolescent heart, is much in evidence as the young man views his world. He echoes Mariana in the moated grange as he looks around the seemingly empty farmstead saying, "Our's is now a lifeless pleace." Even the animals are affected:

> The dog that woonce wer glad to bear
> Her fondlen vingers down his heäir,
> Do leän his head ageän the vloor,
> To watch, wi' heavy eyes, the door . . .

(P, 216)

Barnes's use of dialect and rhyme contribute to the overall bathetic effect of this portrait of the self-indulgent teenager. He treats more seriously, though, the plight of a young girl deserted by her lover. While it is not explicitly stated, perhaps Barnes is sympathizing with the vulnerability of an unmarried woman in a small conservative community who has succumbed to the charms of an unfaithful man. Jane of Buckley-hill is one such maiden who is deserted so that the man is free to marry a woman "with gold":

> For she had walk'd with him, poor maid,
> Word-trusting down to the grove's dim shade,
> And lov'd him, since she thought him true.
>
> (*P*, 648)

Many of Barnes's love poems are a direct reflection of the loss of his wife, Julia. **"Plorata Veris Lachrymis"** is a good example. The speaker, clearly the poet, says that life has lost "its hope and zest" since the bride's death, and that sights which brought pleasure when they were together now bring only pain. He concludes this painful, sincere, but conventional poem by remarking that he does not care about his own life's waning if this means that their souls will meet again. **"My Dearest Julia"** continues in this sentimental but doubtless therapeutic vein. Here the persona, again clearly the poet, admits that sometimes he is distracted from his loss:

> where joyful faces crowd
> And merry tongues are ringing loud,
> Or where some needful work unwrought
> May call for all my care and thought,
> Or where some landscape, bath'd in light,
> May spread to fascinate my sight,
> Thy form may melt awhile, as fade
> Our shades within some welkin shade.
>
> (*P*, 703)

But when he realizes this distraction, the persona says that he feels chastened, that he seems to hear Julia's voice admonishing him for forgetting his loss, even momentarily, in the light of all her years of work and care during their marriage. If this is not a pose—and Barnes is not a poseur—then the supposed admonishment displays an attitude toward his bereavement which is so scrupulous that it borders on the morbid. Guilt is obvious here, while the basis for guilt is obscure. In none of the biographical material—although the major source of the details of his life is Lucy Baxter, a daughter and scarcely an objective critic—is there any hint of enmity or even tension between William and Julia. While psychological analysis is clearly outside the province of this work, it should be noted here that Barnes's mother, like Julia an intelligent, strong, and capable person, died when he was very young, too young, perhaps, for him to frame his sorrow in appropriate conventional devices such as elegiac poems. The almost overscrupulousness of the mourning for the wife could be explained by a nagging feeling of inadequateness about the mourning for the mother. This speculation is fueled by another poem, **"The Morning Moon."**

In this poem, the persona—the poet—relates the story of an early morning walk which takes him to the house, now deserted, where his mother had lived. The house reminds him of his mother and what she had meant to him:

> And she, dear soul, so good and kind,
> Had holden long, in my young mind,
> Of holy thought, the highest place
> Of honour, for her love and grace.

But then some new thoughts enter in:

> But now my wife to heart and sight
> May seem to shine a fuller light;
> And as the sun may rise to view,
> To dim the moon from pale to blue,
>   My comely bride
>   May seem to hide
> My mother, now my morning moon.
>
> (*P*, 771-72)

The traveler then vows never to let his affection for his wife obscure the memory of his dead mother. The poem is interesting in that it indicates a link, perhaps a tension, existing between the feelings for his mother and those for his wife. This link was no doubt strengthened after Julia's death when Barnes once again was left alone.

His sense of loss doubtlessly contributed to the beauty of some of his best poetry. **"The Leady's Tower,"** written shortly after Julia's death, is a look at his own grief seen through the eyes of a fellow Dorsetman. The persona describes a walking tour taken with a local clergyman. The clergyman, a Mr. Collins, is a character in many of Barnes's dialect narratives, depicted as a gentle, intelligent commentator upon country scenes and events. He serves as an advisor to the Dorset folk; doubtless Barnes considered him to be a model of the rural preacher or schoolmaster.

In this poem, the narrator and Mr. Collins have come to the top of a hill where they find a tower, apparently not noticed previously by the speaker, as he asks the preacher, "'What is it then theäse tower do meän / A-built so feäir, an' kept so cleän?'" The good parson answers that it is grief that has caused the building to be erected. He goes on to say that the owner, a squire, has all the earthly accoutrements anyone could want; he is not happy, though, because "His woone true friend, his wife, is dead." The squire has erected the tower to show his grief. Mr. Collins explains it like this:

> Zoo now her happy soul's a-gone,
> An' he in grief's a-ling'ren on,
> Do do his heart zome good to show

His love to flesh and blood below.
An' zoo he rear'd, wi' smitten soul,
Theäse Leädy's Tower upon the knowl.

(*P*, 253)

"The Leady's Tower" takes grief for a loved one as its subject, as does "My Darling Julia," but there are striking differences in the two poems. "The Leady's Tower" is written in the Dorset dialect and narrated by a persona who is clearly sympathetic yet not involved directly in the squire's grief. "My Darling Julia" is much more personal in that the persona is the grieved one, yet the grief is as intense in the poem in which it is demonstrated as it is in the one in which it is stated.

Nowhere is Barnes's love for his wife and his grief for her loss shown more poignantly than in the companion pieces, "Wife A-Prais'd" and "The Wife A-Lost," both written in dialect. The first, as the title suggests, praises the wife not only for her comeliness, but also for her good humor, her grace, and "busy hands a-tweilen [toiling] on." The persona speaks of his attraction for the young woman who seems to effuse a Wordsworthian harmony with the natural surroundings:

An' there, wi' heäir o' glossy black,
Bezide your neck an' down your back,
You rambled gaÿ a-bloomen feäir,
By boughs o' maÿ a-bloomen feäir;
An' while the birds did glitter nigh,
An' water weäves did glitter nigh,
You gather'd cowslips in the lew,
  Below the vallèn dew.

(*P*, 332)

The attraction that the persona feels for the girl does not dissipate with age; after they are married, the woman's mature attributes come into bloom:

An' now, while you've a-been my bride
As years o' flow'rs bloom'd an' died,
Your smilen feäce ha' been my jöy;
Your soul o' greäce ha' been my jöy;
An' wi' my evenen rest a-come,
An' zunsheen to the west a-come
I'm glad to teäke my road to you
  Vrom vields of vallen dew.

(*P*, 333)

But in the companion piece, "The Wife A-Lost," Barnes describes the reluctance of the bereaved husband to stay in the house that the couple shared, indeed, his reluctance to visit places where they had been together. Now, the persona says, he would rather be in a place "Where you did never come" (*P*, 334).

. . . . .

Religious Poetry

As a member of the clergy, it was natural for Barnes to write poetry which is religious in nature. The religious poems can be described as being homiletic or liturgical; in addition, Barnes wrote a drama in verse, "Ruth, A Short Drama From the Bible."

The homiletic poems are verses written on religious subjects which illustrate a theological or ethical point or elucidate a scriptural passage. A good example of the illustrative homiletic verse is "The Railroad," divided into two parts, each of which demonstrate Barnes's scientific as well as his religious interests. Part 1 begins with a description of how a person, when traveling across the terrain in a swiftly moving conveyance such as a railroad train, receives two distinct visual impressions. One is the sensation that objects close to the observer are flashing past; the other is that celestial objects much further away, like the sun, seem to travel along with the observer. Barnes uses this familiar visual phenomenon in a metaphor in which the scenery flashing by is compared to the passage of time, and the seeming constancy of the sun is compared to the presence of God in our lives:

An' zoo, while time, vrom stage to stage,
Do car [carry] us on vrom youth to age,
The e'thly [earthly] pleasures we do vind
Be soon a-met, an' left behind;
But God, beholden vrom above
Our lowly road, wi' yearnen love,
Do keep bezide us, stage by stage,
Vrom be'th to youth, vrom age to age.

(*P*, 309)

"The Railroad," part 2, is similar in its structure and intent. Here, the traveler, when passing a park, trains his eye on a single distinctive oak tree within the grove. As the carriage moves on, all the other trees seem to wheel around the oak. Barnes uses this phenomenon to construct a metaphor in which the oak represents the single purpose which should be the center of concentration for each good Christian. Everything else—especially "e'thly pleasures"—must wheel about this single point:

Zoo while our life do last, mid nought
But what is good an' deär be sought,
In word or deed, or heart or thought,
An' all the rest wheel round it.

(*P*, 310)

Mr. Collins, the character introduced in "The Leady's Tower," appears in some of the religious poems, "The Thorns in the Geate," for example, and "Good Measter Collins." In the former, the kindly clergyman joins a group of farm folk who have climbed a hill to view the progress of the newly sown grain. The speaker recounts how the fields have been plowed, rolled, and harrowed, the seed planted, and the bird boys assigned to protect the seed with shrill voices and clackers. Now, he says, the corn is "up ancle high" and all there is to do is to wait for harvest, trusting in providence and the weather. A row of thorny wood has been placed in the gate to ward off cattle from the young tender blades of grain. Mr. Collins comments on the thorns in the gate, placed there to insure that the corn will be unmolested during the ripening process, then takes the opportunity to deliver a religious message to the assemblage. The grain situation parallels the human one, the preacher says. Just as the farmer, once his planting is done, must trust in God for the fate of his corn, so must the Christian, once his or her religious duty is done, trust in God for the fate of the soul.

> in life let us vulvil [fulfill]
> Whatever is our Meäker's will,
> An' then bide still, wi' peacevul breast,
> While He do manage all the rest.
>
> (*P*, 355)

The gifts of God—the only valuable ones, he says—are free and distributed equally to all His children.

Barnes wrote a series of six verses which he called **"Sabbath Lays."** These homiletic poems are numbered but untitled, and each is introduced by a scriptural quotation except for number 4. The poems then provide a commentary on the biblical message. Numbers 3 and 4, for example, present contrasting thoughts on the question "Why hast thou forsaken me?" from Mark 15:34.

Number 3 is a prayer from one who is on the verge of despair, who cries out to his maker for some sign of recognition or relief. The persona feels "cut off from human ways" and "number'd with the dead." He asked if this pain is sent to purify him as "silver in the fire." The question, written in the year of Gerard Manley Hopkins's birth, parallels a question that poet asks years later in the poem known as "Carrion Comfort." Hopkins asks, "Why wouldst thou rude on me / Thy wring-world right foot rock?" In both poems, too, the process of purgation is compared to the threshing of wheat, the separating of grain from chaff, and in both cases the rod of God is accepted as chief authority. Barnes describes his condition thus: "my soul in fear and pain / Is peaceless as the sea," while Hopkins also describes suffering and dread like a sailor in a storm: "O in turns of tempest, me heaped there; me frantic to avoid thee and flee?" The only vision of God Barnes's persona sees is a fearful one. He is "Before Thy frowning face, O God!" just as Hopkins's persona in the third stanza of "The Wreck of the Deutschland" sees "The frown of his face / Before me." The Hebrew words *Lama Sabachthani* are used as a refrain at the ends of each of the three stanzas; the issue is not resolved until we read lay number 4, which presents the soul as having passed out of its trial, now imbued with fresh faith.

Barnes's liturgical poems are written for specific church occasions; even the hymns celebrate particular activities, for example, a club service and harvest thanksgiving. Other liturgical poems were meant to be recited at services like baptisms, marriages, or church openings, with the poem's purpose stated in the title. Most of these are simple and conventional, aimed as they are at a conservative country audience. We can get a hint from many of these, however, why Barnes was so beloved in his native Dorset; he obviously turned his poetic talents to use in his church, honoring the recipients of holy sacraments from time to time not only with the rites that he was bound to give as a minister of God, but with the gift of his literary talent as well.

"Ruth, A Short Drama From the Bible" is a play in verse written for the parish stage. It is a fictionalized account of the Bible story, meant for both entertainment and instruction and supported by a choir singing psalms. Barnes keeps close to his source, explaining esoteric references in the stage directions for the benefit of the cast or in the dialogue for the audience. One is reminded of the medieval dramatic pageants of which Barnes was doubtless aware; the author even appends an epilogue to the play in the manner of the doctor's concluding speech in many of the biblical plays of the Middle Ages. Like the epilogues in the early dramas, Barnes intends that the message of the play be explicit as possible. He writes, "The history of Ruth shows the blessings of God on true-hearted love and kindness. From her faithfulness to Naomi she became a foremother of Kings David and Solomon; and in David and his offspring of the manhood of the Son of man" (*P*, 619).

The religious poetry is easily read and easily understood; it is appropriate to its audience in that it is written in simple language, it relates to the problems members of his parish would be likely to encounter, and it uses metaphors and images that persons of that place and time would readily identify or even use themselves.

Dorset Tales

As interested as he is in language and the oral tradition, it is no wonder that Barnes takes as subject matter for his own poetry the folk tales and legends of his native Dorset. As one might expect, most of these are told in the dialect, an attempt, no doubt, at retaining as much of the original flavor of the local legends as possible. Some of the tales seem peculiar to the region, while others are adaptations of stories told in other times and other places as well as in Dorset. In addition, Barnes tells some tales which seem to be his own fictional creations.

A good example of the pure Dorset tale is the one concerning the building of a church in one of the small communities of the region. This poem, **"The Beam in Grenley Church,"** recounts the story of a strange man who worked with the laborers building the structure. He is described as being meek, cheerful, and strong—so strong

> that all alwone,
> He lifted beams an' blocks o' stwone,
> That others, with the girtest païns,
> Could hardly wag wi' bars an' chaïns;
> An' yet he never used to staÿ
> O' Zadurdays, to teäke his paÿ.
>
> (*P*. 203)

The rest of the men took little note of their volunteer companion until the morning after a particularly exasperating day. All day the men had worked hard hewing timbers and fitting blocks of stone; but late in the day, perhaps out of sheer exhaustion, a beam was cut too short to fit the structure, causing the men to leave the beam and retire for the night. The next morning when the crew returned to work, they found the beam not on the ground where they had left it, but in position high on the walls, somehow now the correct length. The stranger was nowhere to be seen, nor did he appear in the area ever again. There is much speculation among the people "whether he mid be a man / Or angel, wi' a helpen han', / Or whether all o't wer a dream" (*P*. 204), but the truth of the matter was never discovered. The story lives on in local legend and is perpetuated by Barnes's use of it in his poem.

Other local legends include those involving witches and fairies. An eclogue aptly named **"The Veairies [fairies]"** depicts a conversation between two Dorset locals, Simon and Samel, who are discussing the appearance of circular patterns in the grassland vegetation that the local population have named "fairy rings." There are two theories, Simon says, about what causes the phenomenon—lightning or the tracks left by fairies as they dance in their nocturnal festivities. The local system of beliefs concerning the little people is then explored, from the instruments used to produce music at the fairy ball—

> There's nar a fiddle that's a-heär'd at all;
> But they do plaÿ upon a little pipe,
> A-meäde o' kexes [stems of hemlock or cow
>   parsley] or o' straws, dead ripe,
> A-stuck in row (zome short an' longer zome)
> Wi' slime o' snaïls, or bits o' plum-tree
>   gum,—

to the kinds of dance steps they use—"jigs to fit their little veet," not "The dree an' vow'r han' [three and four hand] reels that we do sprawl / An' kick about in" (*P*. 134).

The eclogue entitled **"A Ghost"** recounts many of the ghost stories of the Dorset countryside in much the same manner. Jem and Dick, the two speakers, are walking together on a dark evening and naturally enough begin to talk about the various apparitions that have been sighted over the years in their locality. They compare notes on the poltergeist which haunts a particular house, changing shapes ranging from a six-feet tall model in white with burning coals for eyes to a smileless lady dressed in silk, all the while slamming doors and moving furniture in ghostly fashion. Dick then tells the story of Jack Hime who was returning home after an all-night party at which he "mid a-took a cup / Or two o' eäle [ale] a-keepen Chris'mas up" when he came upon a great dog on the road. Intending to send the dog home to its master, Jack took a stick in his hand and began to beat the animal; instead of hitting it, though, the stick broke into four pieces which then flew over his head and came down to stick into the ground at the four points of the compass. Jack's hand got numb, his arm began to swell, and later his skin began to peel, proving once again that strange dogs should be left to lie whether they are sleeping or not. In addition to this obvious truth, Barnes no doubt repeated the story as a bit of a temperance lecture, even if the force of this is lost on Dick and Jem (*P*. 184-86).

As an example of the ubiquitous folk story, versions of which are told in many cultures, Barnes offers the dramatic monologue **"A Witch,"** wherein the narrator whispers gossip to a companion concerning Molly Brown, a neighbor who is passing by. The speaker alleges that Molly is a witch who possesses the evil eye, and denies that the old woman is being defamed by lies and made-up stories. He or she then goes on to tell a story—one which the speaker has heard repeated—concerning Molly and Farmer Gruff's family, how the Gruffs denied a request to borrow some unremembered object, and how they were rewarded by a series of misfortunes allegedly brought forth by the woman's "pow'r." The Gruff's milk and ale turned "zour," the "aggs" addled, and the cheese turned back to curds and whey, reversing several natural chemical reactions in the process; the animals all got sick or, like the little pigs, "turned their snouts [or noses, or bills] to the sky," "gave a little grunt [or bray, or quack], and died." All efforts to stop the curse, including nailing a horseshoe over the farmhouse door and ostracizing Molly, proved fruitless. Finally, the farmer's wife, in an apparent attempt at a countercharm, tried to draw blood from Molly's body by "dawking" needles and pins through "her wold hard wither'd skin." Even this failed, the narrator says, because the sharp instruments all broke before piercing the old lady's hide; in fact, this last operation had the opposite of its intended effect since it "Did meäke the hag bewitch em woo'se" (*P*. 224-25).

Of course, the Gruff's cruelty to the old woman is not lost to the reader even if it is to the narrator. Through his skillful reporting of this speech, Barnes shows that he is capable of producing all the subtle irony that the dramatic monologue is famed for. His skill in exposing small-minded rural hypocrisy through the use of dramatic forms and dialect speech was admired by his countryman Thomas Hardy. Hardy's "The Ruined Maid" is a good example of his emulation of Barnes in this regard.

Another universal tale Barnes tells is that of **"The Weepen Leady,"** a variation of a folk story told in many places around the world at many different times. The legend tells of a weeping lady who at certain times haunts an old house. The figure that appears on moonlit nights is believed by the natives to be that of a woman long dead. The woman had given birth to a son out of wedlock, leading her father to offer her two equally dreadful alternatives: either she must leave that country forever, or her son must be sent away "a thousand mile." The lady, Barnes reports, chose to leave herself and "Left the hwome ov all her pride / To wander drough the worold wide / Wi' grief that vew but she ha' tried." Later, "she wither'd wi' the deadly stroke" and died; now she returns to her formerly happy home

> To zee her father dead and gone,
> As if her soul could have noo rest
> Avore her teary cheäk's a-prest
> By his vorgiven kiss.

(P. 171)

Thus Barnes treats the often repeated tale of the woman whose restless spirit is doomed to return to familiar earthly scenes until whatever is bothering it is removed. England has several of these female apparitions, variously given names like the "Green Lady" and the "Lady with the Lantern;" even northeastern Wisconsin has its "Lady in Red."

While Barnes uses familiar folk tales as material for his work, he sometimes creates fictions of his own as well. The subtitle to his **"Erwin and Linda"** is given as "A Tale of Tales." The poem is not a retelling of a preexistent folktale, but rather the poet's attempt at spinning a yarn using a *Decameron*-type of setting. The first verse paragraph—written as is most of the rest of the poem in iambic pentameter couplets—sets up the scene: several neighbors have gathered for a winter's evening before a warm fire "Each ready as his turn might come, to hold / The others' minds with tales as yet untold."

Mrs. Fanny begins with her tale of Erwin's childhood. If it were not for Barnes's subtitles—"Mrs. Fanny's Tale," "Mr. John's Tale," etc.—the seven narrators would be indistinguishable from one another. Each in turn picks up the thread of the story, continues for an episode, and passes it on. The tale is a well-worn one, involving an orphan boy who is tricked out of his inheritance, but who through good-natured hard work, thrift, and even some heroics, manages to regain his fortune along with the hand of a girl he has long worshipped from afar but has been afraid to approach because of his reduced circumstances. The story is complete with a profligate brother who foolishly spends his and Erwin's inheritance and a villain named Wingreed who does his best to thwart Erwin's climb back to respectability.

We can guess that **"Erwin and Linda"** was originally written as a children's story purely for entertainment. Bernard Jones reports in his notes to the poem that fragments of the manuscript show that the hero was at first not named Erwin, but rather Egbert, the name of Barnes's younger son. Further, there is a distinct lack of subtlety about the poem. It is fast-paced and full of action with two rescue scenes—one involving a flood, the other a fire. There is a simple, clear moral tying in with the defeat of the bad guys by the good guys at the end. Finally, the episodic nature of the poem makes it very conducive to reading to children at bedtime.

Homely Rhymes

The term "homely rhymes" is one Barnes uses himself to designate verses written to describe the rural life and to depict its day-to-day occupations, reminiscences of country childhood, customs and holidays in the rural shires, rustic humor, and plain, honest country wisdom. It was his conservationist tendencies as much as anything else which prompted these poems. Barnes probably had two major specific aims for these works, the first being simply the recording of English rural life before it was buried under the landslide of time and change which he knew to be threatening his peaceful Dorset valleys. The second aim was more didactic. Barnes wished to portray the simple country life as an exemplar for Victorian society. He saw that the way out of many of the social, political, and spiritual dilemmas of the day was for people to turn back to the old values and traditions, to those attributes which were still practiced and preserved in pockets of English countryside.

Some of these poems deal with rural occupations and agricultural practices; at times, Barnes even seems to be following the example of the classical georgic, in which directions in or descriptions of specific tasks are given. The poet knew Hesiod's *Works and Days* and Virgil's *Georgics* and was no doubt impressed by their emphasis on the dignity of labor and their praise of the simple country life. The dialect poem **"Vellen O' the Tree"** is a good example of a description of a specific task. The speaker first describes the tree as it was before being approached by the cutters, remembering how it provided shade and a resting place for mowers.

Then the approach of the felling crew and its operations are described. First, a rope is attached "At the top o'n, wi' woone end a-hanged to ground," and a cut is made "near the ground" until "his girt [great] stem a'most drough." At this point, the crew leaves off its cutting, and all the men begin to tug at the rope, dictating the direction of fall. Giving in to the pressures above and below, the tree "swaÿed all his limbs, an' he nodded his head, / Till he vell away down like a pillar o' lead" (*P*, 183). Some sadness is expressed for the passing of the great tree as well as awe for its enormous size on the ground. Stanza one deals with the tree as it was in the past while providing a concise, specific description of the mowers' occupation and appurtenances. Stanza 2, on the other hand, treats the subject of the tree in the present while providing the reader with a description of the craft of tree-cutting.

"Hay-Meaken" and **"Hay-Carren,"** too, are in the georgic mode, being descriptions of those processes which their titles suggest. Again, the descriptions are quite specific in the manner of Virgil's instructions on grafting fruit trees in book 2 of the *Georgics*. In **"Hay-Carren,"** for example, the proper method of loading hay onto a wagon is given.

> The bwoy is at the hosse's head,
> An' up upon the waggon bed
> The lwoaders, strong o' eärm do stan',
> At head, an' back at taïl, a man,
> Wi' skill to build the lwoad upright
> An' bind the vwolded corners tight;
> An' at each zide o'm, sprack [lively] and strong,
> A pitcher wi' his long-stemmed prong.
>
> (*P*, 116)

Haying is the subject of another occupational poem, the eclogue entitled **"The Best Man in the Vield,"** in which two haymakers argue about who is better at his work. Other specialties are treated, too, in poems such as **"The Milk-Maid O' the Farm," "Fiddler Bob,"** and **"Thatchen O' the Rick."** These poems, perhaps again showing the influence of Virgil, offer panegyrics to country life, recognizing that in it lies what remains of the golden age.

The brightest gold, though, belongs to the child growing up in the countryside. Barnes's poetry contains many reminiscences of children's games, of solitary explorations of nature during boyhood, and of other youthful experiences. **"Grammer's Shoes"** and **"The Settle and the Girt Wood Vire"** are good examples of childhood memories preserved in poetry. The first poem describes how the children used to gather around their grandmother at Christmas time begging her to

open her chest of ancient treasures to show her wedding shoes and dress. This was done to the accompaniment of stories "O' the merry wold soul how she did use / To laugh an' to dance wi' her high-heel shoes." The second poem, too, features a speaker who remembers similar simple country pleasures. He addresses a friend who had been his companion as a boy, and asks if he remembers the great fireplaces and mantles the houses had when they were young. He compares the old settle, its bacons curing and bags of herbs drying alongside great racks of plates and pewterware, with the newer version:

> a little hole
> To tëake a little greäte o' coal,
> So small that only twos or drees
> Can jist push in an' warm their knees.
>
> (*P*, 174)

The childhood poems extol the virtues of country living while they recognize and exclaim against the changes which were occurring in agricultural communities all across England. These things are true, too, about the homely rhymes which Barnes writes about the customs and holidays of the rural Dorset communities. The traditional holidays are treated in poems like **"Easter Zunday," "Keepen Up O' Christmas,"** and **"Guy Faux's Night,"** but the local holidays are not ignored. In the two **"Shrodon Feair"** poems, the narrator relates the events surrounding that rural celebration, the country fair. The first poem describes the excitement of the people as they ready themselves—"Dick and I did brush our hats / An' cwoats, an' clean ourzelves lik' cats"—and the arrival at "Shrodon seäfe and sound / Astrutten in among the rows / O' tilted stannes [market stalls] an' o' shows." The speaker tries to capture the atmosphere of the fair through his description:

> An' girt long booths wi' little bars,
> Chock'vull o' barrels, mugs, and jars . . .
> Where zellers bwold to buyers shy
> Did hollow round us, "What d'ye buy?" . . .
> An' horns did blow, an' drums did rumble,
> An' bawlen merrymen did tumble. . . .
>
> (*P*, 154)

The second Shrodon Fair poem continues with the description of the fair, the characters meeting friends from other districts, shaking dice for a gingerbread treat, and returning home. Barnes's careful attention to detail in his depictions of what he saw to be a rural institution endangered by modernization indicates that he was attempting to preserve the memory of this important social event.

But Barnes writes of less convivial customs than attending fairs, the keeping of Christmas, and **"Zitten Out the Wold Year." "Leady-Day an' Ridden House"** describes the all too common scene in which a farm family loses its lease and is forced to leave for another location. Lady Day, 25 March, ends the first quarter of the new year. As such, it was traditionally the day on which yearly leases ran out, necessitating the removal of tenants, or "ridden house." The speaker in this poem gives all the details of his melancholy task, providing the reader with a veritable catalog of nineteenth-century household goods: firedogs, copper kettles, the butter-barrel and cheese wring, the salt box, as well as miscellaneous chairs and stools. The poem ends with the old wagon loaded and the family waiting while the speaker makes one last round, checking "In fusty holes an' darksome nooks, / To gather all I still mid vind." He confesses sadness at leaving "the he'th / An' ruf" that once made him happy, and does not linger long in the now deserted house. The poem closes with his stoic comment, "Zoo ridden house is such a caddle [confusing plight], / That I would rather keep my staddle" (*P*, 75). A staddle is the set of footings upon which the hayrick sits; in the farmer's mind, it is the symbol of the stable axis of the farm, much as the hearth is seen as the center of the household. The "caddle" of the situation, of course, is not just the confusion surrounding moving household goods, but the loss of equilibrium which accompanies such uprootings. Barnes's sympathetic treatment of this subject is such that one might dare say that ridden house was not one of the country customs he was intent on preserving.

Most of the subjects of the homely rhymes, though, are happy ones. He sees generally that these folk customs are important in that they provide both stability and continuity to the lives of the people. Poems like **"Harvest Hwome"**—a description of the great feasts which traditionally follow a cooperatively brought in harvest—and **"Minden House"**—a demonstration of the practice of petitioning the father for a young woman's hand in marriage—give the reader an indication of the central role custom and tradition played in the rural society Barnes was writing about.

Dialect literature has long been used as a source of humor. Chaucer himself makes effective use of dialect to produce laughter in the "Miller's Tale" and elsewhere; dialect humor continues in the English and American literary traditions, reaching a peak during the nineteenth century. Barnes does not overlook this use of local speech; much of his work contains good-natured humor.

The eclogue **"A Bit O' Sly Coorten"** is an example of one kind of humor to which lovers are so often prone. Here John has waited for Fanny arriving late for their meeting and is further put out by her attentions to another man. Fanny, for her part, plays John's jealousy for all that it is worth and, while feigning innocence, cunningly fuels the fire with lines like "If

he kiss'd me dree times, or a dozen, / What harm wer it? Why idden [isn't] he my cousin?" (*P*, 96).

Practical jokes have their appeal to some, and Barnes uses these as subjects for his humorous verse, too. In **"Polly Be-en Upzides Wi' Tom,"** the female speaker tells how she, in the best tradition of Sut Lovingood, the American prankster, found Tom Dumpy's coat where he had removed it in order to do some work. Polly confesses to taking the coat, sewing shut the sleeves and collar, and then returning it to where its owner had left it. A group of young people subsequently gathered to watch Tom try to put on the garment when he came in from the field; the company, of course, laughed uproariously at his misfortune. By the end of the poem, Polly tells the boy to whom she has given such attention that she hopes he has learned his lesson; she says she hopes he's learned

> He mussen [mustn't] think to peck
> Upon a body zoo, nor whip
> The meäre to drow me off, nor tip
> Me out o' cart ageän, nor slip
> Cut hoss-heäir down my neck.
>
> (*P*, 128)

Practical jokes other than those of the adolescent romance are depicted as well. In **"What Dick and I Did,"** the speaker tells of two boys who are resentful at not being asked to attend a "randy," or party, at the Brown's house. As a result, they sabotage the gathering. Just when the party has reached its height, the pair take a small grinding stone and use it to stop up the chimney. Those inside scamper out while the delighted jokers watch:

> The maïdens cough'd or stopped their breath,
> The men did hauk and spet
> The wold vo'k bundled out from he'th
> Wi' eyes a-runnen wet.
>
> (*P*, 167)

Riddles, too, are among the subjects for the humorous poems; the dialogue poem **"Riddles: Anne and Joey A-Ta'ken"** is one of these. Here, two country people try to stump one another with riddles such as this one describing a wheelbarrow.

> A two lagg'd thing do run avore
> An' run behind a man,
> An' never run upon his lags
> Though on his lags do stan'.

Barnes's humor is usually gentle, but at times his wit is barbed, as when he gives us the wonderful situational comedy of **"The Waggon A-Stooded."** Here, the rustics who have allowed a loaded wagon to become stuck in the mud are depicted as buffoons, shouting orders and recriminations at one another, and generally behaving like Keystone Cops. **"Gruffmoody Grim"** paints an exaggerated picture of the local grouch in which Barnes makes fun of all bad-humored people.

The homely rhymes as a group, though, are intended to demonstrate some simple truths; the dignity of work, the innate wisdom and intelligence of the poor but honest farmer, and the superiority of the country life. In **"The Lew O' the Rick,"** for example, a farmer sits with his haystack shielding him on a cold and windy evening, his mind "in vaïceless thought." He surveys his little world, his musings turning to eternity and his place in it. **"Tweil [Toil]"** is a similar poem representing a farmer's thoughts on work. He sees labor as what gives structure and substance to his life. What threatens him is not toil or its inevitability, but rather the chance that he might be deprived of the opportunity to work.

The importance of the past, of recognizing the value of past works and deeds, is demonstrated in **"Our Father's Works."** Here, the speaker describes the works of former generations, the bridges that were built, the ground that was cleared, the structures that were erected. The speaker, in a statement which is indicative of Barnes's philosophy, entreats the reader not to neglect the lessons of the past.

> Zoo now mid nwone ov us vorget
> The pattern our vorefathers zet;
> But each be faïn to underteäke
> Zome work to meäke vor others' gaïn,
> That we mid leäve mwore good to sheäre,
> Less ills to bear, less souls to grieve,
> An' when our hands do vall to rest,
> It mid be vrom a work a-blest.
>
> (*P*, 270)

The homely rhymes are representative of all of Barnes's poetry, indeed, of all of his work. They are learned, yet simple, sensible, yet compassionate, and while they appeal to a wider audience, are addressed to the simple country folk who make up their substance. They are full of hope, confidence, grace, and good cheer. While those attributes might be considered gauche in our modern poetry, it is yet refreshing to look back to a time when the possibility of an uncomplicated, essentially happy society was held out.

Notes

6 *The Poems of William Barnes,* ed. Bernard Jones (Carbondale, 1962), p. 743; hereafter cited in the text as *P*.

7 Geoffrey Grigson, *Selected Poems of William Barnes* (London, 1950), p. 19.

8 Information on the publications of Barnes's poetry is based on Jones's forewords to the poems.

9 Grigson, *Selected Poems,* p. 10.

10 Ibid., p. 10.

11 Baxter, *Life,* p. 84.

12 Ibid., p. 84.

13 Grigson, *Selected Poems,* p. 12. . . .

Alan Chedzoy (essay date 1985)

SOURCE: *"Poems of Rural Life: 1844-1846,"* in *William Barnes: A Life of the Dorset Poet,* The Dovecote Press, 1985, pp. 106-22.

[*In the following essay, Chedzoy studies Barnes's* Poems of Rural Life in the Dorset Dialect, *recounting the subject matter, technique, and critical reception of this collection.*]

The culmination of Barnes's life as a poet came as early as 1844 when the ***Poems of Rural Life in the Dorset Dialect*** was first published. Though he was to write much more poetry, and was to make second and third collections of his ***Hwomely Rhymes***, the nature and range of his art as a dialect poet was substantially established by 1844. The first edition ran to 373 pages of which 240 were devoted to the dialect poems, but they were sandwiched between a 37 page Dissertation and nearly 100 pages headed '**A Glossary of the Dorset Dialect of the English Language.**' Every page bespeaks a profound and an original mind, which combines a knowledge of curious lore with a deep familiarity with the life and language of Blackmore people.

The spirit of the book was antagonistic to that of the age. In a year which saw the publication of Chambers' *Vestiges of Creation* the poems celebrate ancient pieties. While Thomas Cook was planning his first travel excursions Barnes's poems depict the merits of a settled community. While Bradshaw issued his *Railway Guide* and the network of track stretched out to the borders of Dorset itself, the scale of Barnes's concerns is that of the distances people could walk. His themes are those of hearth, home and rural customs. Much of the material would have seemed absurdly antiquated to the new men of the age, for whom the steam engine was transforming the dimensions of life.

In the Preface to the second edition of the *Lyrical Ballads* in 1800, Wordsworth expressed his concern at the effects of the new sensationalist publications upon rural communities. He observed that a 'multitude of causes, unknown to former times . . . (was) . . . now acting with a combined force to blunt the discriminating powers of the mind.' The opening words of the Dissertation to the ***Poems of Rural Life in the Dorset***

Dialect echo some of Wordsworth's concern. But it quickly becomes apparent that Barnes is not offering his poetry as some sort of therapy for the treatment of cases of exposure to mass media, as Wordsworth was. Rather was he engaged upon the task of linguistic conservation:

> 'As increasing communication among the inhabitants of different parts of England, and the spread of school education among the lower ranks of our population, tend to substitute book-English for the provincial dialects, it is likely that after a few years many of them will linger only in the more secluded parts of the land, if they live at all; though they would give valuable light to the antiquary as well as the philologist, of that increasing class who wish to purify our tongue and enrich it from its own resources.'[1]

Poems are normally offered to the public as items of intrinsic aesthetic interest. Barnes's Dissertation casts doubt upon his primary intentions in presenting the poems; are they to be regarded as works of art, or merely as specimens of a language artificially preserved in poetic form for the benefit of the antiquarian and philologist? There can be no doubt that a number of readers regarded the book chiefly as a repository of rural phrase and expression for, on May 7 1844; John Russell Smith, the London publisher of the book, wrote to Barnes to observe that he had not yet sold many copies and that 'those who want only the Glossary and Dissertation think 10/- too much.' There is, in the Dorset County Museum, a second edition of the book with the Glossary removed. The early philological readers thought of the poems as no more than illustrations of the usage of words explained in the Glossary and of the linguistic theories outlined in the Dissertation. To readers interested in poetry, the Glossary was no more than necessary footnotes to the poems.

Neither view is adequate. The originality of the *Poems of Rural Life in the Dorset Dialect* lies in the fact that art and scholarship are related in its pages. The book combines Barnes's growing interest in philology with his quick observation, with ear and eye, of Dorset life. It unites his total seriousness of purpose with his buoyant sense of humour; his knowledge of ancient tongues with his familiarity with the vernacular. It is at once erudite and popular, esoteric and homely, and is, therefore, a just image of the idiosyncratic mind that produced it.

The Dissertation is a curious amalgam of history, philology and poetics in which Barnes traces the history of the West Saxons from whose language he believed the Dorset dialect to be derived. He claims for the dialect that it is 'a broad and bold shape of the English language, as the Doric was of the Greek'. It is 'rich in humour, strong in raillery and hyperbole; and, alto-gether, as fit a vehicle of rustic feeling and thought, as the Doric is found in the *Idyllia* of Theocritus'. Barnes is especially dismissive of those who consider the dialect to be a corruption of written English. Dorset, he argued, was richer and purer than 'that dialect which has been chosen as the national speech', purer in that it employed many words from the Saxon while English coined new names from foreign tongues, richer in that Dorset had names for many things which, in English, could only be referred to by the use of an entire phrase.

Barnes develops his argument by the suggestion, familiar from his *Gentleman's Magazine* pieces, that French expressions such as 'tout ensemble' and 'coup-de-grace' along with all other 'continental phraseology' should be rejected in favour of words formed from the native stock. As an example he points out that the name of the plant 'sorrel' has been formed from the word 'sour' because of the nature of the plant. Thus the poems themselves became demonstrations of the range of expression available in the dialect and, therefore, the indigenous Saxon speech forms.

When the first of his Dorset poems had appeared in *The Dorset County Chronicle* they had been regarded by their readers as jokes. Not only was the local speech a matter for amusement but the farm-worker himself was an object of ridicule to those who took their words and ways from genteel urban sources. Nearly forty years after the publication of Barnes's book, Thomas Hardy was still defending the Dorsetshire labourer against those who regarded him as a comic 'Hodge', a 'degraded being of uncouth manner and aspect, stolid understanding, and snail-like movement.'[2] It is true that Barnes in these poems delights in the verbal humour of his rustics but he laughs with them and not at them. The Dorset dialect is for him the medium of humour not the object of it. His characters are often amusing because they are strong in raillery, not because they are intrinsically ridiculous either as farm labourers or as dialect speakers.

Furthermore, the poems are not merely written *about* Dorset people, he claims to be writing *for* them. His audience, he says, is not cast among those with town occupations. The poems are offered to 'the happy mind of the milkmaid with her cow, or the dairy farmer's son in the hayfield' or 'the innocent evening cheerfulness of the family circle on the stone floor.' Even in 1844, however, he cannot resist a note of Victorian moralising by adding that the poems are 'free of slang or vice' and strive chiefly to utter the 'happy emotions' with which the mind contemplates the 'charms of rural nature'. Some readers may have noticed a contradiction between the determination to write *for* the rural audience and the provision of a Glossary of their language. Barnes probably hoped to be read among his fellow Dorset men and women but included the scholarly apparatus both to bolster the claims of the poems to be worthy of publicaton, and to appeal to a select circle of genteel and even academic readers.

None of the poems bears on any part of his life after he left Blackmore in 1818. It is as if he had subconsciously decided that only the earliest portion of his life—with the brief exception of his courting of Julia—was worth writing about. There are no poems about the life of a clerk in a provincial town, his work as a schoolmaster for forty years or his later life as pastor to a country flock. It is Blackmore that made him a poet and it is from recollections of Vale life that he took his subject matter. The whole of his adult life was an experience in prose. His debt to the Vale of Blackmore and its people is made quite explicit in his Dissertation to the poems, which, he says, 'are written from the associations of an early youth that was passed among rural families in a secluded part of the county'. With a rather selective memory he praises the 'sound Christian principles, kindness and harmless cheerfulness' of the people he represents. He is more accurate concerning the language of the poems:

> 'The dialect in which he (the poet) writes is spoken in its greatest purity in the villages and hamlets of the secluded and beautiful Vale of Blackmore.'[3]

The *Poems of Rural Life in the Dorset Dialect* was first published in the spring of 1844 by John Russell Smith of London and George Simonds of Dorchester. A second edition appeared in 1847[3], corrected and expanded to 411 pages. The title page bore an epigraph from Columella and the scholarly appearance of the book was designed to reassure the reader that it was not the work of an unlettered ploughboy. The poems were arranged in a seasonal scheme: Spring, Summer, Fall and Winter, perhaps, influenced by such works as John Clare's *The Shepherd's Calendar* which appeared in 1827. Not all the poems fitted easily into the frame and Barnes was obliged to include a fifth section entitled 'Miscellaneous Pieces' in the first edition. Interestingly, by 1847 and the second edition, Barnes was progressively more teutonic in thought so that the final section was then named 'Sundry Pieces'. The first reviewer in *The Dorset County Chronicle* picked up Barnes's philological intentions by observing that readers of the poems in his newspaper had eagerly turned to 'Poet's Corner' to enjoy 'another tit-bit in their own native Saxon tongue.'[5]

Because Barnes chose dialect poetry for his medium, there is always, in these poems, the sound of a speaking voice and, therefore, of human personality and dramatic situation. Sometimes we are able to identify the name, sex and age of the speaker but at times we have to fill in the details from our own imagination. Even when the identity of the speaker is shadowy, however, there is always a point of view taken and

expressed with a vigorous sense of the appreciation of life. An example is to be found in **"Bob the Fiddler"**:

> Oh! Bob the fiddler is the pride
> O' chaps an' maïdens vur an' wide;
> They can't keep up a merry tide,
>   But Bob is in the middle.
> If merry Bob do come avore ye,
> He'll zing a zong, or tell a story;
> But if you'd zee en in his glory,
>   Jist let en have a fiddle.
>
> Aye, let en tuck a crowd below
> His chin, an' gi'e his vist a bow,
> He'll dreve his elbow to an' fro',
>   An' playe what you do please.
> At Maÿpolen, or feäst, or feäir,
> His eärm wull zet off twenty peäir,
> An' meäke em dance the groun' dirt-beäre,
>   An' hop about lik' vlees.[6]

In many of Barnes's poems the true object of attention is not the apparent topic—in this case Bob himself—but the character of the speaker. As readers we must imagine a situation, perhaps a chance reference to Bob, or perhaps an actual performance which we attend, when an old admirer, perhaps some old labourer with his alepot, insists on buttonholing us so that he may pour the praises of Bob into our ears. The energy and vigour of the account re-enacts the stamping boisterousness of many a country 'randy' where Bob has played. When we read the poem we remember that, for hundreds of years, remote rural communities were entirely dependent upon itinerant fiddlers for social music. Both Thomas Hardy and his father walked the country roads to fiddle at local 'tides'.

The *Poems of Rural Life* contain many such portraits of country people: Moll Brown, the witch who lives along the lane; Uncle and Aunt; 'Grammar' telling tales to the children while musing over her old shoes; faithless Jeane of Grenley Mill. Each poem is animated by the attitude of the narrator, whether it be one of censure, affectionate recollection, or personal grief. Each character is placed firmly in the context of country life so that, to read the poems is to sketch in an entire village community of pre-enclosure times.

The seasonal frame Barnes chooses for the poems ensures that a full record is presented of the various times of the country calendar. There are poems of Eastertime and 'club-walking' at Whitsun; of hay-making, thatching, mowing, harvest-time, Guy Fawkes night and Christmas revels; there are incidents from country life: such as driving the common, consulting gypsies for predictions, playing ghosts in the moonlit threshing floor and going to Shrodon Fair. The folk-history preserved in the poems is sometimes rendered in meticulous detail. In **"Leady-Day, an' Ridden House,"** for example, we learn exactly how a wagon was packed with the family's household goods, when the farm-worker moved to another farm:

> Well, zoo, avore the east begun
> To redden wi' the comen zun,
> We left the beds our mossy thatch
> Wer never mwore to overstratch,
> An' borrow'd uncle's wold hoss *Dragon,*
> To bring the slowly lumbren waggon,
> An' when he come, we vell a-packen
> The bedsteads, wi' their rwopes an' zacken;
> An' then put up the wold eärm-chair,
> An' cwoffer vull ov e'then-ware,
> An' vier-dogs, an' copper kittle,
> Wi' crocks an' saucepans, big an' little;
> An' fryen-pan, vor aggs to slide
> In butter round his hissen zide,
> An' gridire's even bars, to bear
> The drippen steäke above the gleäre
> O' brightly-glowen coals. An' then
> All up o' top o' them ageän
> The woaken bwoard, where we did eat
> Our croust o' bread or bit o' meat,-
> An' when the bwoard wer up, we tied
> Upon the reäves, along the zide,
> The woaken stools, his glossy meätes,
> Bwoth when he's beäre, or when the pleätes
> Do clatter loud wi' knives, below
> Our merry feäces in a row;
> An' put between his lags, turn'd up'ard,
> The zalt-box an' the corner cupb'ard.
> An' then we laid the wold clock-ceäse,
> All dumb, athirt upon his feäce,
> Vor we'd a-left, I needen tell ye,
> Noo works 'ithin his head or belly.
> An' then we put upon the pack
> The settle, flat upon his back;
> An' after that, a-tied in pairs
> In woone another, all the chairs,
> An' bits o' lumber wo'th a ride,
> An, at the very top a-tied,
> The children's little stools did lie,
> Wi' lags a-turn'd toward the sky:[7]

Because Barnes was reworking the memories of a quarter of a century past, a prevailing theme of the poems is that of reminiscence and a common tone that of nostalgia. Memories could be re-awakened in him by a familiar landscape, a well-loved name or a commonplace object such as an old wagon. Indeed, in the poem **"The Wold Waggon"** he not only described in detail the appearance of the wagon itself, but recalled the diverse characters of the horses that pulled them:

> Upon his head an' tail wer pinks,
> A-païnted all in tangled links;
> His two long zides wer blue,—his bed
> Bent slightly upward at the head;

> His reäves rose upward in a bow
> Above the slow hind-wheels below.
> Vour hosses wer a-kept to pull
> The girt wold waggon when 'twer vull:
> The black meäre *Smiler,* strong enough
> To pull a house down by herzuf,
> So big, as took my widest strides
> To straddle halfway down her zides;
> An' champen *Vi'let,* sprack an' light,
> That foam'd an' pull'd wi' all her might:
> An' *Whitevoot,* leäzy in the treäce,
> Wi' cunnen looks an' snow-white faäce;[8]

Like Hardcastle in *She Stoops to Conquer,* Barnes loved things that were old, 'old friends, old times, old books', though not old wines for he was an abstemious man. He disliked new-fangled inventions and in the poem **"The Settle and the Girt Wood Vire,"** the speaker, who is an old man, confides to a crony how much he prefers the settle and open fire to the more modern sofa, armchairs with their anti-macassars, and the small Victorian firegrates. In **"Woak were good enough Woonce,"** Barnes declares in favour of furniture made from native wood to that fashioned from imported mahogany. The elegiac note in his poetry is most often heard in memoirs of old friends and old times, in the faces and the voices that are gone:

> What tender thoughts do touch woone's soul,
>   When we do zee a meäd or hill
> Where we did work, or playÿ, or stroll,
>   An' talk wi' vaïces that be still;
> 'Tis touchen vor to treäce, John,
> Wold times drough ev'ry pleäce, John;
>   But that can't touch woone's heart so much,
> As zome wold long-lost feäce, John.[9]

Barnes's poems have been celebrated chiefly for their love of nature and descriptions of trees, flowers and river-side scenes. Though these things are important in the poems, they are made so because each natural object evokes human associations and memories in the poet. The accuracy of Barnes's descriptions of natural history cannot be compared to that of a poet such as Clare. Barnes's primary interests are human and dramatic, as in the tale of Meary-Ann's child who dies in the night, in the story of the beam in Grenley Church which was placed there overnight by a mysterious workman, in the political eclogues, and in the humorous poems such as **"A Bit O' Sly Coortin"**—a popular favourite when he came to give readings of his poems.[10]

Yet Barnes himself preferred his 'pathetic' poems to his comic ones. Many of these treat of the loss of the loved one through death or other cases. Such poems poignantly anticipate the death of Julia Miles and it may be that her recurrent illnesses led Barnes to assuage his dread of her death by incorporating it into his verse.

The Dorset poems exhibit a considerable amount of technical variation in rhyme scheme, stanza form and parallelisms. The early eclogues which are included in the *Poems of Rural Life* are written in iambic tetrameter, as also are the 'folk' poems such as **"Leady-Day, an' Ridden House'"** and **"The Wold Wagon."** These poems are invariably cast in rhymed couplets which enabled Barnes to add afterthoughts and little touches of detail if he wanted to, but render them repetitive in the development of their thought and rather abrupt and inconsequential in their endings.

Barnes's studies in philology brought new variations to his writing, however, and his readings in other languages did not omit a study of their poetry. Astonishingly, this English dialect poet, who had never been abroad nor learned a foreign language in school or university, began to employ poetic devices culled from many languages. William Turner Levy has identified in his work such effects as the Norse half-rhyme or 'skot-hending', the Persian 'eekfa' or vowel rhyme, the Irish 'cumharda' or correspondence device, the Welsh 'cynghanedd', and many other such figures as well as the more familiar chiasmus and alliteration.[11] An examination of his finest poetry does indeed reveal a complexity of crafting which is probably unsuspected by the casual reader:

"Evenen in the Village"

Now the light o' the west is a-turn'd to
  gloom,
  An' the men be at hwome vrom ground;
An' the bells be a-zenden all down the
  Coombe
  From tower, their mwoansome sound.
    An' the wind is still,
  An' the house-dogs do bark,
An' the rooks be a-vled to the elems high an'
  dark,
  An' the water do roar at mill.

An' the flickeren light drough the window-
  peäne
  Vrom the candle's dull fleäme do shoot,
An' young Jemmy the smith is a-gone down
  leäne,
  A-playen his shrill-vaïced flute.
    An' the miller's man
  Do zit down at his ease
On the seat that is under the cluster o' trees,
  Wi' his pipe an' his cider can.[12]

The language of this poem is endearingly homely ('at hwome vrom ground') and the sharpness of observation of such things as the height and darkness of the elms and the exact tone of Jemmy's flute are perfectly judged. But the delicacy of this poem and its fineness of perception are products of its intricate stanzaic form

and its almost unnoticed rhyme-schemes. In each verse the latter four lines are so paced as to slow down the verse so that the echoes and images they evoke can settle into our minds. There are lovely undulations of the chain-rhymes such as 'peane', 'fleame', 'leane' and 'A-playen'. Thomas Hardy thought that though Barnes was 'Primarily spontaneous, he was academic closely after' and concluded that 'he (Barnes) would at times allow art to overpower spontaneity'. Not even in Burns was there 'such searchings for the most cunning syllables.'[13] Geoffrey Grigson went further than this by arguing that far from being a 'spontaneous act', Barnes's writing of dialect poetry was a product of his philological studies; it was 'a learned perversity' which once attempted he found he could do by nature.[14] In fact, the early eclogues precede his serious philological enquiry. As we have seen in **"Evenen in the Village"** it is the combination of the apparent naïvete of dialect with the subtlety of stanzaic and rhyme effects which endows his verse with its most characteristic note.

The *Poems of Rural Life* were immediately successful with local critics in Dorset. *The Dorset County Chronicle,* in which they had first appeared—some in the agricultural columns, others in 'Poet's Corner'—naturally gave them considerable attention and, with almost parental pride, offered two long reviews on 16 May, just after the book came out, and again on 16 October 1844:

'this is real poetry, a description so full of truth and feeling that each resident in the county will at once fancy it the picture of his own home, every line conveying to his own mind what he sees, hears and feels in his evening walk through the village at this time of year.'

The *Chronicle* reviewer regarded the poems chiefly as exhortations to contentment and respectability: 'the poems of Mr Barnes are free of any coarse vulgarity and urge the village labourer in the words of Bishop Hacket to 'Fear God and be cheerful'.' The October review takes the odd notion that not even 'the warmest admirers of Dorset will . . . claim for it any characteristic share of beauty.' Deprived of the Wordsworthian beauties of mountain, lake and forest, Barnes had the more difficult task to find pleasure in more gentle scenery.[14]

The *Chronicle* reviewer considered that Barnes had successfully employed language in producing 'a series of portraits of which (though we never saw the individuals) we seem to know the originals.' In case there should be any doubt about the social and political implications of the poems the *Chronicle* repeated its view that the chief effect of the verses was to enjoin the peasant reader to obedience and contentment and to place the blessings of his position before the man who: 'was, perhaps, before, hardly conscious how many were the advantages he possessed: he was not alive to the real dignity of his simple position.'[15]

The *Chronicle's* radical rival, the *Sherborne and Yeovil Mercury* was equally enthusiastic about the poems:

> 'Since the days of Burns we believe that no provincial dialect has been honoured by becoming the vehicle of true poetry, in any degree approaching this, and we have every reason to hope, that Mr Barnes's simple lays will embalm the good old-fashioned language of Dorsetshire, and secure it a memorial as long as the Doric and Scotch shall be unforgotten.'

Like the *Chronicle,* the *Mercury* reviewer assumed the 'simplicity' of the poems and it was many years after their first publication that critics such as Gerard Manley Hopkins, Hardy and Geoffrey Grigson first identified their metrical artfulness. The *Mercury,* as was to be expected, differed from the *Chronicle* on the social value of the poems, praising them for keeping alive 'the interest in the affairs of the poor' and for supplying to farmers and landlords 'a more intimate acquaintance with their (the poor's) feelings and habits and a more sincere sympathy with their wants.'[16]

The poems received attention in some national journals as well. *The Literary Gazette* concluded that the book must have been produced by one of extensive scholarship, which presumably indicates that the reviewer was impressed by the Dissertation and Glossary even if he could not make much of the poems.

The most extensive review in a national journal came in Barnes's old favourite, *The Gentleman's Magazine.* The December edition contained an article of fourteen pages which quoted many extracts and no fewer than fifteen poems full length. The unsigned article was given prominence by its placing at the front of the journal, which had the effect of pronouncing the publication of the poems to be a major literary event, which was no doubt the intention of the editor, Barnes's old friend Gough Nicholls. The reviewer explained to the reader that he did not know the poet personally but, Nicholls found himself bound to add in honesty, that the poet had been a contributor to the magazine for many years. This extremely perceptive review was the first to note a significant element in Barnes's claim to be a major poet, that the poems were entirely original in thought and language:

> 'Poets like all other persons, must have their thoughts strongly affected and acted on by the sympathies of their own times, and by the minds of their contemporaries . . . But we are bound in fairness to say that in Mr Barnes's poems we can trace no footsteps of the submissive or sequacious follower of any poetic school or model, but that of true nature and passions. The poet's heart is at home—his scenery is all domestic—his circle of description of home growth, confined to his own fields and boundaries; and the little village scenes, the household cares, and employments, the innocent pleasures, the gentle sorrows and joys, the rural pastimes, the business and amusements—he places before us, and throws into dramatic form, and invests with personal interest, are all drawn from the characters familiar to him.'[17]

But the sales of the poems were disappointingly slow in the spring and summer. *The Gentleman's Magazine* article appeared too late in the year to bolster the early sales. What Barnes needed in April and May was a patron, some friend at the court of literature, willing and able to push poetry in genteel society where reputations needed to be made. His publisher, John Russell Smith, wrote to him in May to complain that the poems are 'hardly known' in London and that he has sold very few copies. He advised that a little money might be spent on advertising.

Barnes's first and only excursion into literary society came with an invitation to a house party at Frampton House, the home of Richard Brinsley Sheridan, the grandson of the dramatist. The party was to include two of his three beautiful sisters, known locally as the 'three graces', in this case, Lady Dufferin and the Hon Mrs Caroline Norton. There were to be, in addition, the Dean of Westminster, two bishops, an archdeacon, and the editors of the *Royal Agricultural Journal* and the *Examiner.* At first, Barnes refused the invitation, on the ground that he was 'unaccustomed to society' but was subsequently persuaded. Julia, it seems, was not invited. Sheridan afterwards recollected that Mr Barnes had much impressed 'all the distinguished persons . . . by the simplicity, varied knowledge, and information he imparted on so many subjects of interest'.

Caroline Norton was particularly struck with him. It was she who had so earnestly pleaded with her brother to invite the obscure Dorchester schoolmaster. Barnes, the worthy and piously-respectable young schoolmaster of Norman's House, was dazzled and gratified by the notice of this society woman. Caroline Norton, an early feminist, a poetess, and a nationally-controversial figure, was touched and secretly flattered by Barnes's evident admiration. Her career was a matter of public record. In 1827 she married the Hon George Norton, an indolent barrister who had turned out to have a violent temper and a dullness of intellect. Caroline had prevailed upon her friend, the then Home Secretary, Lord Melbourne, to find a job for George and he had indeed been awarded a metropolitan police magistracy. However, in 1836, Norton had brought an action against Melbourne for seducing his wife. The action was dismissed and the defence let it be known that they considered the whole thing to be a

Tory plot to discredit Melbourne so that he might not become the Prime Minister to the new Queen. Thereafter, Norton and his wife lived apart but he constantly harassed her by denying her the right to the custody of her own children and even to her own income. He earned very little, whereas she was receiving £1,500 a year from the royalties on such ballads as "The Arab's Farewell to his Steed" and "Not Lost but Gone Before." Eventually, Caroline's passionate writings in her own defence directly influenced new legislation which much improved the rights of married women. Caroline died in 1877, and in 1885, George Meredith fictionalised her life in *Diana of the Crossways.*

From the time of their meeting at Frampton House, Caroline Norton appointed herself Barnes's friend and patron. She set herself to promote his poems among her influential friends in London. The effect she had may be deduced from the change in the publisher's letters to Barnes. In August he wrote to say that he was quite sold out of the **Poems of Rural Verse** and would Barnes send fifty more copies. Caroline invited her protege to visit her in London, and he did so later in the month on the pretext of visiting his publisher. They visited Professor Wheatstone, who demonstrated the workings of his galvanic telegraph between Slough and London. Barnes was much excited by the exhibition and stored up as much of the information as he could to communicate to his pupils. After an early dinner at 6.30pm, Mrs Norton took him to the opera. He enjoyed the performance but was rather shocked that the social events continued into the sabbath day. In November, Caroline Norton wrote to say that she had discussed his work with the Rev John Mitford at the home of the poet, Rogers, and Mitford had spoken highly of the Dorset poems. Barnes was so taken with Mrs Norton's flattering attention that he addressed a sonnet to her:

"To the Hon Mrs Norton, the Poetess, on Meeting Her at Frampton House"

When first I drew, with melting heart, alone,
  (O gifted vot'ry of the tuneful nine,)
  Entrancing melody from songs of thine,
Sweet echo'd words of one as yet unknown;
How much I wonder'd what might be the tone
  Of her true voice, as yet unansw'ring mine,
  And what the hue with which her eyes
    might shine,
And what the form in which her soul was
    shown

To sons of men. How busy fancy brought
  Before me lineaments of love and grace;
    But who can tell what joy was mine at
      last,

When I beheld the object of my thought,
  In bright reality before my face,
    And found the fairest of my dreams
      surpass'd.[18]

History does not record the comments of Mrs Barnes on this poem.

Caroline Norton not only attempted to promote the poems, she attempted to influence their form. In this respect she was one of the first to try to persuade Barnes to change his manner of writing. She wrote to him:

> 'I much wish you would put some of them into more Cockney English. Perhaps you would let me send a list of those which are most liked, and would easiest bear the transmuting power proposed to be applied to them. Then you would judge if we were right in our selection.'

Twenty years later Alexander Macmillan, the publisher, was communicating to him similar sentiments from a reader: 'What a pity Mr Barnes *will* write that dialect! I really cannot, even after much pains, get at the meaning, and the effort too often exhausts the interest.'[19] Despite this, local audiences were beginning to receive performances of the dialect poems with delight. In the winter of 1844, for instance, the Rev W. Henning read some of them at the Sherborne Literary Institution to an appreciative audience. Nevertheless, Caroline kept up the pressure. She wrote in November to ask 'Have you given up thoughts of rendering some of them (the poems) more easy for the common English reader?'

It would have seemed ungrateful for him to ignore the advice from kind friends. In 1846 appeared **Poems Partly of Rural Life in National English,** published again by John Russell Smith in London and George Simonds in Dorchester. The book contained sixty-four poems and cost five shillings. Unlike the dialect poems, which ran to four editions and three expansions, the poems in national English were never reprinted, a fact which bears upon the wisdom of Caroline Norton's enthusiasm for his poems in national English.

The English poems mark a clear falling off of poetic talent. Barnes's peculiar gifts are rarely evident in standard English. Of the national English poems only one, **"Rustic Childhood"** is truly effective and this poem, as expected, derives from his recollections of Blackmore:

No city primness train'd our feet
To strut in childhood through the street,
But freedom let them loose to tread
The yellow cowslip's downcast head;
Or climb, above the twining hop
And ivy, to the elm-tree's top;
Where southern airs of blue-sky'd day

Breath'd o'er the daisy and the may.
I knew you young, and love you now,
O shining grass, and shady bough.[20]

Most of these poems in national English might well have been written by any one of a number of minor Victorian poets. They employ no distinctive speaking voice as do the dialect poems. The themes remain constant but they lack the vigour, humour and bite of the originals. The poems in national English are, in truth, the conventional musings of a Victorian schoolmaster concerned to find favour with an audience of genteel readers. Mrs Norton was wrong. Though she was most helpful in attempting to publicise his poetry, she was no judge of its merits and, therefore, became a harmful influence upon it. Some years later Barnes published a second volume in National English but, like the first, it was not reprinted. Meanwhile the Dorset poems gradually attracted the genuine admiration of poets with a national reputation.

Notes

[1] See the 'Dissertation' to the *Poems of Rural Life in the Dorset Dialect,* John Russell Smith, London, and George Simonds, Dorchester, 1844, p. 1

[2] See Hardy, Thomas 'The Dorsetshire Labourer' in *Longman's Magazine* for July 1883, reprinted in Orel, op. cit. pp. 168-191.

[3] 'Dissertation' to *Poems of Rural Life*

[4] The DCM [Dorcet County Museum] possesses two editions of the *Poems of Rural Life* (second edition), one dated 1847 and the other 1848.

[5] DCC [Dorcet County Chronicle] 16/5/1844

[6] Jones, Bernard (Ed.), *The Poems of William Barnes*, Centaur, London, 1962, p. 88. According to Barnes's *Glossary of the Dorset Dialect,* a 'crowd' is a fiddle, while the 'tides' or times of the year 'were formerly given by the times of some of our great fairs.'

[7] Jones 1 pp73-4. Lady Day, Old Style, was April 6th, when such removals took place. See Hardy in Orel, op.cit., pp. 176-80, also Orel's note p. 275.

[8] Jones 1 pp. 194-5

[9] Ibid. I p. 198

[10] See Grigson G. (Ed.), *William Allingham's Diary,* Centaur Press, Fontwell, 1967 p. 109.

[11] See Levy pp. 160-164, for an account of Barnes's metrical experiments.

[12] Jones 1 p. 86

[13] See Hardy, Thomas, Preface to his *Select Poems of William Barnes* 1908 pp. ix & x.

[14] See Grigson G. (ed.) Introduction to *Selected Poems of William Barnes* pp. 10-11.

[15] DCC 16/4/1844 and 16/10/1844

[16] *The Sherborne and Yeovil Mercury,* December 1844

[17] GM [*Gentlemen's Magazine*] December 1844

[18] Jones 11 p. 693

[19] Baxter, Lucy *The Life of William Barnes: Poet and Philologist,* Macmillan, London, 1887, p. 242

[20] Jones 11 p. 643

Alan Hertz (essay date 1986-7)

SOURCE: "Exile in Eden: William Barnes's Lyrics of Romantic Encounter," in *University of Toronto Quarterly,* Vol. 56, No. 2, Winter, 1986-87, pp. 308-18.

[*In the following essay, Hertz analyzes the imagery and versification of Barnes's romantic lyric poems.*]

Despite its overwhelming lushness, a poem by William Barnes often seems strangely artificial, a kind of verbal topiary. Isolated in an anthology, its self-consciously limited vocabulary and rich, stylized imagery can appear merely an eccentric and unproductive impoverishment of the medium. Seen in the proper context, however, it stands revealed as part of a large and interesting literary enterprise. The poems I call lyrics of romantic encounter—those about unexpected meetings with irresistible women—undergo just such a transformation. On their own, they seem no more than highly wrought curiosities, but the appearance of superficiality is misleading, for beneath the pruned and polished surface lie deep emotion and profound thought. These lyrics are easy to undervalue because so much of their force derives from imagery and techniques of versification established and endowed with significance elsewhere in Barnes's works. Thus, like his other poems, they are flowers best appreciated in their peculiar native habitat, and I begin with an analysis of the soil in which they naturally grow.[1]

Barnes is a poet with a method: he uses a set repertoire of images and prosodic techniques to present the Blackmore Vale (the part of Dorset where he was born) as stable, prosperous, and uniquely suited to human settlement. His best-known poem, '**My Orcha'd in Linden Lea,**'[2] exemplifies this strategy:

'Ithin the woodlands, flow'ry gleäded,
  By the woak tree's mossy moot,
The sheenen grass-bleädes, timber-sheäded,
  Now do quiver under voot;
An' birds do whissle over head,
An' water's bubblen in its bed,
An' there vor me the apple tree
Do leän down low in Linden Lea.

When leaves that leätely wer a-springen
  Now do feäde 'ithin the copse,
An' païnted birds do hush their zingen
  Up upon the timber's tops;
An' brown-leav'd fruit's a-turnen red,
In cloudless zunsheen, over head,
Wi' fruit vor me, the apple tree
Do leän down low in Linden Lea.

Let other vo'k meäke money vaster
  In the aïr o' dark-room'd towns,
I don't dread a peevish meäster,
  Though noo man do heed my frowns;
I be free to goo abrode,
Or teäke ageän my homeward road
To where, vor me, the apple tree
Do leän down low in Linden Lea.

Although Barnes often varies the rhyme scheme, he uses this stanza form (an iambic tetrameter octet divided in half and ending in a refrain) more often than any other. In the first four lines, he characteristically employs complex sound patterns as the aural counterpart of his lush imagery. Just as lines 2-4 elaborate the image of shady meadows presented in line 1, so the elongated vowels and multiple consonants of 'woodlands, flow'ry gleäded' are transformed and echoed in the words that follow: 'woak tree's mossy moot' and 'grass-bleädes, timber-sheäded.' Even the caesura in line 1 is duplicated in line 3. The reader picks his way through this intensely harmonious verse just as the speaker moves attentively and lovingly through the woods.

This movement, however lingering, is not purposeless. In the second quatrain the pace quickens as the speaker nears his goal and the stanza approaches its refrain. The echoes and harmonies persist: the interweaving of *b* and *w* in lines 5-6; the internal rhyme in line 7. But the diphthongs disappear, the repeated conjunctions give the reader no pause, and the absence of a verb or end-stop in line 7 forces him to hurry on. The *cynghanedd* of the refrain is a suitable climax to this crescendo of consonance. The sound patterns make the orchard strangely magnetic: the closer it is, the more reader and narrator alike feel—or rather hear—its power. To summarize, the exquisite craftsmanship of this stanza has two functions: to emphasize the peace and prosperity of the Vale; and to make the orchard the pole to which its owner and his audience are irresistibly drawn.

The imagery of these lines is as carefully orchestrated as their versification, but its function can only be fully understood by reference to other poems. Shade, the dominant motif, is not peculiar to Linden Lea; the final stanza of '**The White Road up athirt the Hill**' (pp 90-1) shows that all Blackmore, as Barnes conceives it, is unusually sheltered:

What peacevul hollows here the long
White roads do windy round among!
Wi' deäiry cows in woody nooks,
An' haÿmeäkers among their pooks,
An' housen that the trees do screen
From zun an' zight by boughs o' green!

The essential elements of this strange landscape are practically invisible: roads nestle in hollows; people disappear in the shadows of haystacks; livestock and cottages are hidden by greenery and enclosed by hills. Similarly, the narrator of '**Hill or Dell**' (pp 521-2) contrasts dank, secluded bottom land with the bracing freedom of life in the surrounding hills, concentrating almost exclusively on the *lewth* (shelter) offered by each. The dry, sandy, exposed upland cannot support large trees; its furze and scrub give adequate cover only to small birds. The speaker rejects it, however rich and healthy its inhabitants may be, because they inevitably feel naked and insecure. The psychological benefits of lewth outweigh all other considerations.

In '**My Orcha'd in Linden Lea,**' Barnes uses such imagery emblematically. The poem celebrates the economic independence of the old-fashioned yeoman farmer, and its emotional climax comes in the third stanza, a triumphant rejection of the modern, urban, commercial world. That rejection is founded on the speaker's absolute confidence in the livelihood provided by his orchard. The landscape provides a striking emblem of that security: the apple tree—giving shelter, offering fruit, bowing in almost feudal submission—is itself surrounded and protected by a wood. For people as anxious to avoid disturbance as the shyest birds, the double seclusion of Linden Lea provides an ideal nest. To natives of Barnes's Blackmore, this shade enclosed in shade must come as close to paradise as the sublunary world can. Significantly, the place name which the refrain so insistently repeats combines the name of a shade tree, a pun on 'lee,' and an echo of Eden.

Another prominent feature of Linden Lea is the river 'bubblen in its bed,' and this too has a symbolic dimension more clearly visible in other poems. While the Vale's hills and trees give protection, its ever-audible streams promise fertility. In **'Sound o' Water'** (pp 311-12), the weary labourer is refreshed by this pledge of eventual reward:

> An' when the zun, wi' vi'ry rim,
> 'S a-zinken low, an' wearen dim,
> Here I, a'most too tired to stand,
> Do leäve my work that's under hand
> In pathless wood or open land,
> To rest 'ithin my thatchen oves,
> Wi' ruslen win's in leafy groves,
>   An' sounds o' flowen water.

These lines do not diminish the harshness of farm work; even the sun seems exhausted after a day in the fields. But at least they secure the fruits of toil. The noises which penetrate the protective thatch of the labourer's cottage—the breeze in the grove, the gurgling brook—reinvigorate him by renewing his confidence that nature will keep him safe and prosperous. In **'Rivers Don't Gi'e out'** (pp 112-13), the refrain, at first merely a repetition of the title, modulates at the end to 'His goodness don't gi'e out,' thus underwriting this promise with a religious sanction. The stream running noisy with spring rains through Linden Lea is a similar if less explicit pledge of an ample harvest. It makes the dry, silent autumn of the second stanza restful rather than threatening. In short, the blooming confidence of Linden Lea's owner is rooted in a landscape of implicit comfort and latent promise.

The embodiment of divine good will in common topographical features can give even Barnes's briefest lyrics an extraordinary, mysterious intensity. **'Evenen in the Village'** (p 86) is a powerful example:

> Now the light o' the west is a-turn'd to
>   gloom,
>   An' the men be at hwome vrom ground;
> An' the bells be a-zenden all down the
>   Coombe
> From tower, their mwoansome sound.
>   An' the wind is still,
>   An' the house-dogs do bark,
> An' the rooks be a-vled to the elems high an'
>   dark,
>   An' the water do roar at mill.
>
> An' the flickeren light drough the window-
>   peäne
> Vrom the candle's dull fleäme do shoot,
> An' young Jemmy the smith is a-gone down
>   leäne,
>   A-playen his shrill-vaïced flute.
>   An' the miller's man
>   Do zit down at his ease
> On the seat that is under the cluster o' trees,
>   Wi' his pipe an' his cider can.

Barnes's contemporaries would no doubt have called this poetry of the Dutch school, and it resembles the landscapes of van Ruisdael and Cuyp in its technical sophistication, its modest subject, its restful tone. The use of assonance, for example, is at once deft and reticent. In lines 3-4, long *o* and *ou* sounds echo like the bells they describe without becoming crudely onomatopoeic. At the end, the shift from the *m* and flat *a* of 'An' the miller's man' to the sibilants and long *e* of the next two lines is neatly resolved in 'cider can,' simultaneously completing the alliteration, assonance, and rhyme. To me at least, the effect is delightfully calming.

The real force of the poem, however, lies in its imagery. The conventional details reassure the experienced reader of Barnes that this moment of hard-earned leisure will be savoured in peace. Church-bells, for instance, frequently act as emblems of a traditional and universal religious faith. But the sound of a particular set of bells can also mark the boundaries of community, the limits of allegiance; anyone out of earshot is in a foreign land. Thus these villagers are doubly comforted: they enjoy the companionship of lifelong neighbours and the protection of a God at home everywhere. The 'house-dogs' are further evidence of well-protected domesticity, and as in the poems already discussed, the roaring water of the millrace and the lewth of the overhanging elms are symbols of a divinely guaranteed plenty and security. Like the owner of Linden Lea, the miller's man can find the perfect balance between freedom and safety by a Blackmore stream in the protective custody of Blackmore trees.

In such a poem, the contentment of the Vale seems beyond disruption; a stable social order, a fertile environment, and a benevolent God combine to preserve and enhance it. In others, however, this Edenic equilibrium is broken, even destroyed, and Barnes's characters then feel an alienation as intense as their normal peace of mind. The three principal causes of crisis are socio-economic change, bereavement, and—most peculiarly—sexual passion, my concern in the rest of this essay. But the uncontrollable, bewildering emotion of the lyrics of romantic encounter—like the political discontent of the eclogues and the overwhelming grief of the elegies—is best seen against the background of prelapsarian peace and prosperity celebrated in **'My Orcha'd in Linden Lea'** and **'Evenen in the Village.'**

Poems which describe falling in love at first sight are surprisingly rare in English. Our best-known love poems, whether by Shakespeare, Donne, or the Brownings, explore established, intimate relationships. Only in those drawing on pastoral or troubadour conventions, like Keats's 'La Belle Dame sans Merci,' does *le coup de foudre* have much poetic impact. Barnes's emphasis is unusual and reflects the peculiarity of his literary enterprise. For sudden passion—the urgent need to rely on another, fundamentally unreliable human being—poses one great threat to the fragile sense of stability which, according to Barnes, is the essence of human happiness.

One striking encounter is with '**The Maïd o' Newton**' (pp 258-9):

> In zummer, when the knaps wer bright
> In cool-aïr'd evenen's western light,
> An' haÿ that had a-dried all day,
> Did now lie grey, to dewy night;
> I went, by happy chance, or doom,
> Vrom Broadwoak Hill, athirt to Coomb,
> An' met a maïd in all her bloom:
> The feäirest maïd o' Newton.
>
> She bore a basket that did ride
> So light, she didden leän azide;
> Her feäce wer oval, an' she smil'd
> So sweet's a child, but walk'd wi' pride.
> I spoke to her, but what I zaid
> I didden know; wi' thoughts a-vled,
> I spoke by heart, an' not by head,
> Avore the maïd o' Newton.
>
> I call'd her, oh! I don't know who,
> 'Twer by a neäme she never knew;
> An' to the heel she stood upon,
> She then brought on her hinder shoe,
> An' stopp'd avore me, where we met,
> An' wi' a smile woone can't vorget,
> She zaid, wi' eyes a-zwimmen wet,
> 'No, I be woone o' Newton.'
>
> Then on I rambled to the west,
> Below the zunny hangen's breast,
> Where, down athirt the little stream,
> The brudge's beam did lie at rest:
> But all the birds, wi' lively glee,
> Did chirp an' hop vrom tree to tree,
> As if it wer vrom pride, to zee
> Goo by the maïd o' Newton.
>
> By fancy led, at evenen's glow,
> I woonce did goo, a-roven slow,
> Down where the elems, stem by stem,
> Do stan' to hem the grove below;
> But after that, my veet vorzook
> The grove, to seek the little brook
> At Coomb, where I mid zometimes look
> To meet the maïd o' Newton.

Like '**Evenen in the Village**,' the beginning of this poem describes the pleasures of well-earned rest. But here the speaker is not content with the limited, communal comforts of his native parish. He deserts the familiar shades of Broadwoak Hill, and, like many unprotected travellers in Barnes's poetry, so discovers his own immense emotional vulnerability. As soon as he sees the maid, he begins to behave oddly, addressing her in language he can neither remember nor explain. Such linguistic loss of control is ominous in a poetic persona, who after all exists only in words; the confusion this visionary girl creates is evidently neither superficial nor temporary.

In the last two stanzas, the speaker's emotional dislocation can be measured in his changed response to his surroundings. He wanders through a typical Blackmore landscape, complete with sheltering hills, a screen of trees, and a stream. But this normally restorative terrain merely disorients him further. Even the birds seem to sing for her. The final lines emphasize that this change, of fundamental importance to any Barnes character, is permanent. Like the owner of Linden Lea, this narrator was once drawn to and comforted by a specific group of trees. Now he cannot walk where he chooses—his feet involuntarily forsake the grove—but only where the maid draws him. The victim of a new and irresistible magnetism, he is an exile in his own home. Unsurprisingly, he is not sure whether seeing the maid was 'a happy chance, or doom.'

This pattern is elaborated in '**Jessie Lee**' (pp 322-3):

> Above the timber's benden sh'ouds,
> The western wind did softly blow;
> An' up avore the knap, the clouds
> Did ride as white as driven snow.
> Vrom west to east the clouds did zwim
> Wi' wind that plied the elem's lim';
> Vrom west to east the stream did glide,
> A-sheenen wide, wi' winden brim.
>
> How feäir, I thought, avore the sky
> The slowly-zwimmen clouds do look;
> How soft the win's a-streamen by;
> How bright do roll the weävy brook:
> When there, a-passen on my right,
> A-walken slow, an' treaden light,
> Young Jessie Lee come by, an' there
> Took all my ceäre, an' all my zight.
>
> Vor lovely wer the looks her feäce
> Held up avore the eastern sky:
> An' comely wer the steps her peäce
> Did meäke a-walken slowly by:
> But I went east, wi' beäten breast,
> Wi' wind, an' cloud, an' brook, vor rest,
> Wi' rest a-lost, vor Jessie gone
> So lovely on, toward the west.
>
> Blow on, O winds, athirt the hill;
> Zwim on, O clouds; O waters vall,
> Down maeshy rocks, vrom mill to mill;
> I now can overlook ye all.

But roll, O zun, an' bring to me
My day, if such a day there be,
When zome dear path to my abode
Shall be the road o' Jessie Lee.

Once again the speaker meets his nemesis in open, unfamiliar country. Indeed the lack of shelter is emphasized from the start: the trees are below the speaker and so cannot protect him; the brook is ruffled by the wind and bright with direct sunlight; the clouds are in plain view. Until Jessie Lee appears, the narrator finds this terrain exhilarating. he feels in tune with nature as he moves in the same direction as the wind, the clouds, and the stream. The intricate sound patterns of lines 5-8 (in particular the repetition of *s, m,* and *w,* and the internal rhyme of 'plied,' 'glide,' and 'wide') ostentatiously emphasize this harmony. The second stanza continues the prominent alliteration of *s* and *w,* but caesuras in lines 13-14 slow the pace, anticipating Jessie Lee's entrance.

Even her name is slightly dissonant, for it begins with the first soft *g* used in the poem.[3] Visually, too, she is disruptive; her beauty reduces the landscape to background. The end of the third stanza compresses this transformation into four magnificently dense lines which echo and invert lines 5-8. Having passed Jessie, the man continues eastwards, accompanied by the symbolic comforts of nature. But everything now of value to him—his heart, his peace of mind, the woman who has bewitched him—moves inexorably in the other direction; and these things of value—'breast,' 'rest,' and 'Jessie'—are intextricably linked to 'west' by internal rhyme. The last stanza is a coda similar to the end of 'The Maid o' Newton.' The speaker apostrophizes the landscape only to dismiss it as worthless. He too will remain an exile in his own home unless this literally distracting woman returns.

Perhaps the finest of these lyrics is **'The Bwoat'** (pp 343-4):

Where cows did slowly seek the brink
O' Stour, drough zunburnt grass, to drink;
Wi' vishen float, that there did zink
 An' rise, I zot as in a dream.
The dazzlen zun did cast his light
On hedge-row blossom, snowy white,
Though nothen yet did come in zight,
 A-stirren on the strayen stream;

Till, out by sheädy rocks there show'd
A bwoat along his foamy road,
Wi' thik feäir maïd at mill, a-row'd
 Wi' Jeäne behind her brother's oars.
An' steätely as a queen o' vo'k,
She zot wi' floaten scarlet cloak,
An' comen on, at ev'ry stroke,
 Between my withy-sheäded shores.

The broken stream did idly try
To show her sheäpe a-riden by,
The rushes brown-bloom'd stems did ply,
 As if they bow'd to her by will.
The rings o' water, wi' a sock,
Did break upon the mossy rock,
An' gi'e my beäten heart a shock,
 Above my float's up-leäpen quill.

Then, lik' a cloud below the skies,
A-drifted off, wi' less'nen size,
An' lost, she floated vrom my eyes,
 Where down below the stream did wind;
An' left the quiet weäves woonce mwore
To zink to rest, a sky-blue'd vloor,
Wi' all so still's the clote they bore,
 Aye, all but my own ruffled mind.

The initial harmony of movement in **'Jessie Lee'** is here succeeded by an equally intense harmony of mood. The speaker identifies with the river so thoroughly that he refers to 'my withy-sheäded shores.' Like all other living things, he basks in a sun-kissed pastoral calm where even his dreamy indolence apparently prospers. The Vale's birds have been lulled into silence, and the fish lack the energy to strike; lack of shelter has evidently reduced all life to somnolence. The words which set the sleepy mood—'slowly seek,' 'zunburnt grass,' 'zink an' rise,' 'dazzlen zun'—establish the dominance of *s* and *z,* setting up the richly alliterative final line of the first stanza.

From this thicket of sibilants, heralded by a startling fanfare of long *o* sounds, appears no ordinary boat but a rustic descendant of Cleopatra's barge. A mysterious, nameless girl, with suitably queenly posture and splendid costume, is rowed majestically into view. As with Jessie Lee, the quality of her movement sets her apart. Before she arrives, nothing stirs on the river, and all activity seems an effort. In contrast, she sails by without exerting herself at all. This seeming exemption from the natural order is reflected in the obeisance of the stream and rushes in lines 17-20. This motif has long been a pastoral commonplace, but I think Barnes has Pope's lines, made famous by Handel, specifically in mind:

Where'er you walk, cool gales shall fan the
 glade,
Trees, where you sit, shall crowd into a shade:
Where'er you tread, the blushing flow'rs shall
 rise,
And all things flourish where you turn your
 eyes.[4]

Barnes's maid, compared to a passing cloud, also brings refreshment and momentary relief from the sun in her wake. His rustic angler stands beside Mark Antony and Alexis in a tradition of lovestruck heroes who ascribe divine qualities—notably the ability to create shade—to women.

The third stanza ends with the only sound reported in this luxuriously aural poem; the explosive 'sock' of the boat's wash hitting the bank is also the shock of Cupid's dart striking home. In another sweet irony, the fisherman's float leaps as if he had a bite; in fact, he is the one hooked by the maid's 'floaten scarlet cloak.' As the boat moves inexorably on, reeling his captured attention behind it, the river recovers its glassy, sunstruck stillness. But to the narrator, himself utterly transformed, it will never be the same. To Antony and Enobarbus, Cleopatra is Egypt; to the fisherman who once identified himself with it, 'thik feäir maid at mill' has become the Stour. In future, the river should always 'show her sheäpe a-riden by'; the 'sky-blue'd vloor' of the final stanza is less peaceful than heartbreakingly empty. Again a woman has come between a Barnes narrator and his personal source of peace and strength. However many fish he catches, the stream can no longer yield him anything of value. In the last line, only his mind is 'ruffled'; the harmony of man and environment has been replaced by an uneasy dissonance. A rarity in Barnes's meticulously regular verse, the last line does not readily scan; in its 'ruffled' rhythm, sound again echoes sense.

Barnes flaunts his marvellous technical facility in the lyrics of romantic encounter, but they are more than verbal exercises. In fact, the flamboyant workmanship can sometimes distract the reader from their underlying emotional complexity. The poems should not be read merely because they sound splendid. More significantly, they invert patterns and subvert symbols Barnes developed in dozens of other poems. The helplessness of the lovers is highlighted by the inability to find comfort as their neighbours do. One peek from the dank shadows of Blackmore, one moment of daring and curiosity, and lightning strikes. Then they wander disconsolate, disoriented, confused through the Vale's idyllic landscape, hoping to recover or replace the sense of stability and security it once provided. To me, this exile in a bucolic Eden is one of the most troubling images of alienation in Victorian poetry.

Notes

[1] Most criticism of Barnes is so impressionistic as to be almost useless, but the chapter in W.J. Keith's *The Poetry of Nature* (University of Toronto Press 1980) is a recent, valuable exception. I make no such claims for my own 'The Hallowed Pleäces of William Barnes,' *Victorian Poetry,* 23 (Summer 1985), 109-24.

[2] Bernard Jones, ed, *The Poems of William Barnes* (London: Centaur Press 1962), I, 233. I have incorporated into the text other references to this volume, the only complete modern edition of the dialect poems. Unfortunately the proofreading was poor, so I have silently corrected a few minor and obvious errors. As copies are quite rare, I have quoted in full all the poems I discuss in detail.

[3] This bizarre device is one of Barnes's favourites. Lines 3-18 of 'My Orcha'd in Linden Lea' contain no long *i* sounds. Barnes thus gives the self-assertion of 'I don't dread a peevish Meäster, / Though noo man do heed my frowns' the heaviest possible emphasis, the poetic equivalent of a crash of cymbals.

[4] From 'Summer, or Alexis.' Herbert Davis, ed, *Pope: Poetical Works* (London: Oxford University Press 1966), pp 74-5.

Peter Levi (essay date 1996)

SOURCE: "Hardy's Friend William Barnes," in *Celebrating Thomas Hardy: Insights and Appreciations,* edited by Charles P. C. Pettit, Macmillan Press Ltd., 1996, pp. 68-89.

[*In the following essay, Levi describes Barnes's life and the enduring power of his poetry.*]

That Wessex which we call Hardy's Wessex is only an idea of course. There is something magical or fey about the maps of it that Hardy began to publish in 1895, but they do represent something real—a dialect, the boundaries of a way of life—and it was undoubtedly that deeply original, deeply provincial poet William Barnes who first established it as a literary province. Tennyson talked of Wessex dialect: he got some notes on it from Thomas Hughes of Uffington, and used them in the dialect scenes of his play *Becket,* where they make a preposterous impression, which the dialect poems of Barnes never did. I have argued in a life of Tennyson[1] for the virtual certainty that it was Barnes who inspired Tennyson in 1861 to the first of his own Lincolnshire dialect poems. Thomas Hardy grew up very conscious of his provincial origins, in the shadow of Barnes who was the monarch of literary Wessex and a successful poet, one of whom there was a cult when Hardy was born. Hardy, in his early poems, followed Barnes in dialect verse, and in his Welsh and Persian tricks also. And Hardy never lost a certain respect, admiration, affection for the old man, although there were some forty years between them, thirty-nine between Barnes's birth at Rushay in 1801 (or possibly 1800) and Hardy's in 1840, and forty-two between Barnes's death at Winterborne Came in 1886 and Hardy's at Max Gate in 1928. They were both antiquarians, both excited by the dialect, on which Barnes did serious work and which Hardy carefully observed, but Barnes's world was all but confined to the Blackmoor Vale, and Hardy's went further so that his limits had to be more deliberately defined. There is something entrenched about Hardy's idea of Wessex, whereas Barnes's Blackmoor Vale is even today rather unselfconscious and innocent.

It is not a moral or an intellectual matter; it is the luck of the generations. In 1847 the railway arrived at Dorchester, but Barnes's golden age was before Waterloo, and he remembered the coming of the first stage-coach at Sturminster Newton. Hardy heaved himself up by the bootlaces to become an architect and a writer, and middle class: in his writing nothing came easily to him, they say. His ancestors and his claim to be from what used to be called a county family were fantasies: his true lineage is from an honourable and interesting line of stone-masons. But Barnes was painted by Thorne of Sturminster for the Revd Mr Lane Fox, his ancestry goes back through farmers and landowners to a grant of land from Henry VIII in 1540, and perhaps to a servant of King John. His life was a struggle almost more titanic than Hardy's, because the land went in his grandfather's day. His father died in William's childhood; his uncle was a tenant farmer who crashed soon after Waterloo. He became a clergyman from being a schoolmaster by taking a degree at Cambridge as a 'ten year man', that is, keeping his name on the College books with a minimum of formalities for ten years. He went on after his BA to get a BD, and that was the key to Winterborne Came. They were both self-taught, though Barnes was more ferociously intellectually ambitious; that also was a matter of generation. Barnes's father had a small-holding on Bagber Common, near Sturminster Newton. Mr Lane Fox as the Vicar spotted young William, who was the fifth of six motherless children, and tutored him a little in Latin and Greek, and lent him books.[2] Barnes found a job at 13 under Mr Dashwood, the lawyer, but when Dashwood died he moved hopefully to Dorchester: he already had literary pretensions.

In 1821 when Alfred Tennyson was a boy being tutored by his father, young Barnes was printing his own poems in a book and in the local papers, studying French, playing duets with a friend, learning music from an organist, learning to engrave on copper and wood, reading the classics with the Revd H. J. Richman of Dorchester, and courting Julia Miles, whose father was dubious about his prospects. He sold drawings, engravings, visiting cards, and a narrative poem called *Orra: a Lapland Tale*, which he printed in 1822. At Christmas the two young people got secretly engaged, and William went to Mere, at the other end of the Blackmoor Vale, to take over as village schoolmaster in a loft above the Market House where the inscription now is, while Julia taught little girls in Dorchester. So far, the story is typical of the early nineteenth century: the poems were on the

whole embarrassing, but the drawings and engravings were remarkably able. In 1825 the hostile Mr Miles was transferred as a customs officer to Nailsea, where Julia hated the smoke of the glassworks. William was paid for engraving by a Blackmoor man in bookbinding and cheese: he thought of setting up in Bath, and applied for a teaching post at Plymouth and a clerkship in a Dorchester bank, then in 1827 he managed to rent the Chantry at Mere for £20 a year and open a boarding school, and with this prospect Mr Miles accepted him and he married Julia. Their love letters from 1820 to 1827, with some poems, engravings and drawings, were edited by Charlotte H. Lindgren for the Dorset Record Society in 1986, and Barnes's lovely drawing of the fifteenth-century stone Chantry house where the boarding school was, a building put up by the royal architects and masons for the chantry priests at Mere in 1425, has been printed at Wincanton for the friends of that church.

In 1835 they moved back to Dorchester and opened a school in Durngate Street. Two years later it was in South Street and in 1847 they were at number 40; by the time he was ordained (1847) they had seven children, six of them alive; but in 1852 Julia died and was buried in Dorchester. His *Poems of Rural Life in the Dorset Dialect* came out in 1844, but more were to come. In 1862 his school had its greatest success. A boy who was a natural linguist came first in all England in an examination for the Indian Civil Service, and when this news hit *The Times* Barnes got shoals of letters of application: but he had just closed down his school, and retired to be Rector of Winterborne Came. His strategy of being a clergyman headmaster had indeed been a success, but very late in the day. He was now a distinguished man of letters all the same. Hardy was 22 and proud to know him. Barnes had written a great number of philological and antiquarian books and a terrifying number of articles: and he had translated The Song of Solomon into the Dorset dialect for the English Dialect Society. He lived on at Winterborne Came for 24 years of tranquil eccentricity. He complained of the word 'bicycle' for example; he thought 'wheel-saddle' would have been better. For 'forceps' he proposed 'nipperlings', for 'bibulous' 'soaksome', for 'botany' 'wortlore', for 'meteor' 'welkin-fire', and for 'telegraph' 'spell-wire'. He was proud of the four Dorset demonstrative pronouns and the numerous Dorset words for the parts of a tree. Yet his Dorset poetry was not a didactic exercise, it was not pedantic in any way. He just wrote it, as he told Hardy, because he had to. His last words spoken to Hardy were these: 'The sparrows are pulling my thatch to pieces. I shall have to have it attended to I'm afraid.' Old age and pallor overtook him, but here he is in Hardy's eyes in the vigour of his early eighties:

Until within the last year or two there were few figures more familiar to the eye in the county town of Dorset on a market day than an aged clergyman, quaintly attired in caped cloak, knee-breeches, and buckled shoes, with a leather satchel swung over his shoulders, and a stout staff in his hand. He seemed usually to prefer the middle of the street to the pavement, and to be thinking of matters which had nothing to do with the scene before him. He plodded along with a broad, firm tread, notwithstanding the slight stoop occasioned by his years. Every Saturday morning he might have been seen thus trudging up the narrow South Street, his shoes coated with mud or dust according to the state of the roads between his rural home and Dorchester, and a little grey dog at his heels, till he reached the four cross ways in the centre of the town. Halting here, opposite the public clock, he would pull his old-fashioned watch from its deep fob, and set it with great precision to London time. This, the invariable first act of his market visit having been completed to his satisfaction, he turned round and proceeded about his other business.[3]

When he died he was 85, and that is the beginning of his obituary by Hardy. The splendidly mordant drawing of the portrait gives it a certain authority, though Leader Scott, the pen-name of Barnes's daughter Lucy Baxter, adds in her charming and informative life of the poet that his pockets would be stuffed with sweets to give children, 'or now and then a doll might be seen with its head peering out of the clerical pocket'.[4] As for the strange clothing, he adopted it only when the plum of the Rectory of Winterborne Came dropped in his lap (the advowson was Colonel Damer's, and his cousin had luckily resigned the parish), so that Barnes's teaching days were over: 'Cassock and wide-brimmed hat, knee breeches and large buckles on his shapely shoes. He had passed through many phases of costume before finally adopting this one, which he deemed enjoined by the ecclesiastical canons.' At one time he wore a poncho, at another a Scottish plaid. He liked a red cap: the first a Basque beret someone brought home from the Pyrenees, after that a Turkish fez, and finally something made by his daughters. 'Comfort or utility was always his object, united very often with a total disregard of appearance.'[5] He was the sweetest of men and of a ripe eccentricity.

It is not my purpose to expound his intellectual views, which were wide-ranging and quite as peculiar as his dress: but there is an analogy between his intransigent views of philology and Anglo-Saxon, entailing his opposition to Latin or Greek words in English, and his stunning originality as a Dorset poet. In 1831 he went to Wales, and it was his experience of Welsh literature and language that started him off as a philologist: he had a bit of Persian and Sanskrit, which he used for coaching pupils for the Indian army or civil service; then the Persian and Welsh came together to suggest

new formal tricks or devices in his lyric poetry. He became extremely sensitive to the uses of alliteration and half-rhyme and internal rhyme within a tight stanza form. When this new and pleasing style was used in Dorset dialect it was very beautiful in the ear. In common English poems he used it more sparingly and it is less successful. It does not matter that we do not observe what rules he applied to his stanzas—he invented them and they were not written down; it matters even less to us where he got them. All that matters is how wonderfully they work: they are a rediscovered element in the sweet, traditional harmony of verse. They are often mistaken for some intrinsic quality of Dorset dialect: not so. That gleam of his language is invented and applied by him to the dialect, which in itself is no more musical than any other.

Barnes loved Dorset dialect and it set something free in him. When he read or heard Tennyson's Lincolnshire dialect verse he was horrified, because he felt in it a mockery of the people and a lack of that love which he himself so intensely felt, and which inspired him both as a priest and as a poet. He is wrong about Tennyson, or the difference is a class difference. William Barnes is much closer to the innocence, both as a poet and as a man, of Charles Tennyson, who was also a country vicar. His first use of Dorset dialect was because he thought it was like Doric, a pure and antique country speech such as he conceived Theocritus to have used.[6] He was not a great Hellenist but that was his impression, so that although the philologist in him was never absent in his Dorset poems, and although he issued them with a glossary and a dissertation on Anglo-Saxon, he remained true to his idea. Dorset dialect set him free in poetry to express his own golden age, his Blackmoor Vale world of before Waterloo, which it is true to say largely survived his lifetime and faintly echoes in ours. In the early Dorset poems he alludes to Virgil by calling them eclogues, and in his prose he quoted and imitated Virgil's eclogues more than once. **'The Common a took in'** was called **'Rusticus dolens'** in the *Dorset County Chronicle,* **'The Lotments'** was **'Rusticus gaudens'**; others were **'Rusticus Domi/ Emigrans/Rixans/Procus'** (**'A bit of sly courting'**) and **'Rusticus Res Agrests animadvertens'** (**'Two Farms in Woone'**). In 1833-4 they caused a small stir, and there was a little flurry of correspondence in the papers.

There is no doubt that he was a Blackmoor Vale man at heart. When he saw a marquee at Cambridge put up for a visit of the Prince Consort, he wrote home to say it was 'as large as the shed of our railway station'. He saw the whole congregation slipping out one by one to fight a rickfire, until the parson was left preaching alone. Indeed in Dorchester he saw the whole congregation gassed by underfloor heating, first the children, then the youths, then the adults, with only the preacher high in his pulpit left exhorting them. And however learned the circumstances of his dialect poetry were, it was still true that 'I wrote them so to say as if I could not help it. The writing of them was not work but like the playing of music'[7]—something which of course involves all kinds of trade secrets, which the listener need not notice. On the other hand it is as mistaken to say of him as it was of Shakespeare: 'Sweetest Shakespeare, Fancy's child / Warbles his native wood-notes wild'.[8] His poetry was intricate by skill, as Shakespeare's lyrics also are. Hardy was not far wrong in writing that Barnes 'really belonged to the literary school of such poets as Tennyson, Gray, and Collins'.[9] He was not quite right, because the intellectual force and research that went into Barnes's dialect poetry were not classical but entirely his own, and he was not as smooth as Gray or Collins. However that may be, Hardy feels and Tennyson suggests that he was recognised in 1844; Hopkins was crazy about him in his day (later), and Auden adored him. The high-minded Bridges disapproved, and when Eliot says of Kipling that people resent poetry they are unable to understand, and despise poetry they easily understand—alas, he hits Barnes with both barrels.

And yet one only needs to pick up a poem by Barnes to be bewitched. One does not need to have learnt the principle of Anglo-Saxon alliteration from Dasent's Rask's *Icelandic Grammar* to hear the particular music when William Barnes combines it with stanzaic verse and a faint undertone of the hymn tune, in a poem to an elm tree. It is just a little like the elm of dreams in the sixth book of the Aeneid:

> But when the moonlight marks anew
> Thy murky shadow on the dew,
> So slowly o'er the sleeping flow'rs
> Onsliding through the nightly hours,
> While smokeless on the houses height
> The higher chimney gleams in light
> Above yon reedy roof . . . [10]

This is not Barnes at his best because it is in standard English, just a little enlivened by a device that pleases him: moonlight, marks, murky; slowly, sleeping, onsliding; houses, height, higher . . . and so on. But the form is sentimental, it derives from middle-class drawing-room poems and songs of the 1820s as early Tennyson does; only with Barnes, he speaks middle-class poetic common English as if it were a foreign language, as if it were stiff and not native to him. The all-important tension between vernacular rhythm and the demands of metre gets lost. So do his patterns and devices. Lucy Baxter offers **'Clouds'** as a good example of how his Dorset poems translated into common English ones without loss. Yet in the first stanza, for 'A-shiftèn oft as they did goo / Their sheäpes vrom new ageän to new', he translates 'For ever changing as they flew / Their shapes from new again to new'. But the alliteration of

'shiftèn sheäpes' has got lost, and 'oft' is better than 'for ever'. Yet we must not exaggerate: of course nineteenth-century dialect is an obstacle to many people, and fine translations of Barnes can still be made into easier and excellent English. Pauline Tennant has done it. Further, Barnes's own 'National English' poems, as they were entitled, can be wonderful: or at least the music is wonderful though the words may be less so. Take **'Melhill Feast'**:

> Aye up at the feast, by Melhill's brow,
> So softly below the clouds in flight,
> There swept on the wood the shade and light,
> Tree after tree, and bough by bough.
>
> . . . . .
>
> Then by the orchards dim and cool,
> And then along Woodcombe's elmy side,
> And then by the meads, where waters glide,
> Shallow by shallow, pool by pool.
>
> And then to the house, that stands alone,
> With roses around the porch and wall,
> Where up by the bridge the waters fall,
> Rock under rock, and stone by stone . . .

The alliterations and near rhymes are intricate and subtle: I am not sure that I can unravel them: 'Melhill's brow   softly below . . . clouds in flight   swept wood   shade bough . . . house   roses . . . ' and so on. It is easy to hear how the words run and I am very fond of the 'meads, where waters glide', but it is wellnigh impossible to reduce this beautiful behaviour of the commonplace language to a set of rules.

I have chosen to discuss this kind of poem first because it is easier to dissect than the Dorset dialect poems. There is one more stage before we get to those: I have said that young Hardy imitated the famous and elderly poet. One can observe it superficially in his poem in Sapphics 'The Temporary the All', the first poem in his first volume *Wessex Poems,* and again in 'Postponement' in the same volume. In 'Valenciennes' he adopts the accent and dialect of Dorset. In 'The Alarm', there are Barnes-like oddities of speech: 'skyway' for example:

> In a ferny byway
>   Near the great South-Wessex Highway,
> A homestead raised its breakfast-smoke
> aloft;
> The dew-damps still lay steamless, for the sun
> had made no
> skyway,
>   And twilight cloaked the croft.

Hardy clearly admired the strange knobbly quality of Barnes's language. In 'A Sign-Seeker', 'the nightfall shades subtrude', and in 'Friends Beyond' we have 'mothy curfew-tide', while the title of another poem is 'In a Eweleaze near Weatherbury'. 'The BrideNight Fire' is in much solider dialect than 'The Alarm', so much so that it needs a glossary. This poem is a short story, with touches of humour, written in 1866 and first published in a magazine in 1875. It is unique in Hardy's work, I believe, and most fully justifies the title *Wessex Poems*. Barnes himself was not above the same kind of poem, though they are not often reprinted. Hardy's **Select Poems of William Barnes** (1908) sternly declares that dialect is not comic and that the lyrics should be taken seriously, and that has set the tone of how Barnes's lyrics have been treated: but it may be thought that the atmosphere of solemn sweetness has done no service to his reputation. Certainly Hardy's dialect poem is wonderfully lively and unsolemn, and the line 'Her cwold little figure half-naked he views' has been altered for publication. It should read 'Her cwold little buzzoms half-naked he views'. Barnes is equally a master of the vernacular, but less daring, I suppose.

In his dialect poems it is possible sometimes to see the banality of an idea through the disguise of reality that the dialect may give it. In **'The Woody Hollow'** for example, he casts a wonderful garment over what is utterly simple, and one can hardly resist reading him in an uncritical frame of mind. In the end this poem records a frank attempt to become 'as little children', but it works truthfully enough: one must remember that essentially Barnes is an earlier poet than any Victorian: it would be easier if he were two hundred years earlier, because one feels there is something wilful about the sentiments of 1820 dressed up in a provincial past we never knew. We must try to know it, as we try to know Hardy's early days:

> When evenen's risèn moon did peep
> Down drough the hollow dark an' deep,
> Where gigglen sweethearts meäde their vows
> In whispers under waggen boughs;
> When whisslen bwoys, an' rott'len ploughs
>   Wer still, an' mothers, wi' their thin
>   Shrill vaïces, call'd their daughters in,
>   From walken in the hollow . . .

Barnes was a perfectly genuine man and in his poetry the smaller the vignette he offers the sharper and more genuine it will be. **'Vellen o' the Tree'** for example is a perfect poem that Edward Thomas or Charles Cotton might have written. It is quite unpretentious, like a watercolour by Peter De Wint.

'Evenen in the Village' has the same quality, yet in **'Evenen Twilight'** the reader has to make a positive effort to see in what kind of world words so conventional were perfectly genuinely said: it is a poem that remembers older days than its own, but the refrain is not insistent and none of its moods is false:

> How sweet's the evenen dusk to rove
> Along wi' woone that we do love!
> When light enough is in the sky
> To sheäde the smile an' light the eye
> 'Tis all but heaven to be by;
>   An' bid, in whispers soft an' light
>   'S the russlen ov a leaf, 'Good night',
>   At evenen in the twilight.

I think that, being in dialect, the poems are careless of convention as they are of dignity. The dancers 'hop about lik' vlees . . . An' cows, in water to their knees / Do stan' a-whisken off the vlees', and the conventional white road up the hill is just a fact of life. His eclogues, and a poem like **'Whitsuntide an' Club Walken'**, which he also wrote about in prose, can give a thrilling insight into an age that is over, and institutions few alive can have known. I do remember the club walk with the band and the church service in Lancashire in 1959, but alas I never took part in the celebrations that rocked the fells later in the day. Barnes disapproved of the drink and the fighting in Dorset: 'Zoo in the dusk ov evenen, zome / Went back to drink, an' zome went hwome'. Not that Barnes is unrough. The smockfrocks chase the skirts, and there are fights and poking of boys down holes:

> There I do vind it stir my heart
> To hear the frothen hosses snort,
> A-haulen on, we' sleek-heäir'd hides,
> The red-wheel'd waggon's deep-blue zides.
> Aye; let me have woone cup o' drink,
> An' hear the linky harness clink
> An' then my blood do run so warm . . . [11]

In all these poems, as in similar work by John Clare, it is the unexpected collocations of the simple observer that catch one and make the poems very memorable. They may begin quite simply, like Be'mi'ster with green woody hills around it, high hedges, 'a thousan' vields o' zummer green' and elms and hedge-flowers: that is memorable enough, but then:

> Where elder-blossoms be a-spread
> Above the eltrot's milk-white head,
> An' flow'rs o' blackberries do blow
> Upon the brembles, white as snow,
> To be outdone avore my zight
> By Jeäne's gaÿ frock o' dazzlen white.[12]

When we read in the **'Eclogues'** about the new Poor Laws or the Common taken in, we are perhaps less excited: because we have heard all that before so many times, and we have ourselves seen bad days, and had some taste of what Barnes's worse days must have been like. It is as if he wrote just enough poems of that kind to be politically correct: a concept of which his happy age of the world was innocent. His instincts indeed were conservative, he saw a role for the gentry and wished they fulfilled it. It is true that of the two voices, John Clare is incomparably more plaintive. Barnes's peasants see ruin coming, but Clare is really ruined. Virgil's 'Eclogues' lie at the back of Barnes's: in particular the first where one of the herdsmen has lost his land and must go into exile. It is not really at all a close analogy with anything Barnes suffered: and I do not think he would be a better poet if he were unhappier or less sweet-natured than he is. He carries, as only those with happy childhoods can do, the sweetness of his nature in a kind of time capsule that nothing can disturb. He is really a most remarkable human being, of a kind that has almost never become a writer in the last 350 years. Indeed I suspect we have all known people as devoted, as sweet-natured (more usually women) and as undisturbed. One of their characteristics is that they express themselves quite unselfconsciously in conventional terms. The difference with Barnes is that his intimate vernacular was the Dorset dialect, and that was in the time capsule that came from his early childhood, when his father was a smallholder on Bagber common. He was obsessed with the place, and bought two fields there himself when he was a grown man. He just loved the business of having a tenant, and arguing with him against the polling of elm trees.

I do not feel I have been able to characterise William Barnes centrally: he is in his dialect verse more deeply what it appears he was in life, and he is that by entering into a countryman's life both his and not his, with a life-giving warmth. He gets out of his conventional poems what he consciously puts into them, but something more important emerges from his commerce with the dialect. For one thing, he is really more rustic than he knows: he is not *rusticus dolens,* he is deeply a nineteenth-century Blackmoor Vale man, Christian only in the sense that the gravestones, with their sternness, their Roman stoicism and their childish clarity, are Christian. There is a restraint about his poems, but we feel strongly what he restrains. This queer kind of Christian rustic stoicism is present in the use he makes of the simplest conventions he adopts. Because he is more rustic than he realises the dialect is very revealing, not of him personally, but of meadows and lanes full of characters, a whole world that we have no other means of reaching. The dialect is a kind of fondling of once familiar things, eltrots and greggles (cow parsley and bluebells), and people. He is not a Virgilian poet, and not Theocritean: the only touch of Theocritus is a cage he made out of rushes as a child, and that may easily be coincidence: Theocritus had one for catching crickets. He is more like Horace trying to re-write Virgil's 'Eclogues' in the style of the satires.

His longest political argument is in that able eclogue 'The Times' about the position of small farmers and labourers (one man of course could be both) in hard times, and it contains some zany arguments against the Corn Laws. We know there were country riots against those laws, which kept the price of bread high and kept out foreign grain; indeed I am told I had an ancestor hanged by a mob over the Corn Laws, and I certainly have a friend whose great-grandfather was burned in effigy on his own lawn by his own parishioners. Barnes is comparatively low-toned. One of his people says he would like to see England double the size; the other answers:

> But if they were a-zent to Parli'ment
> To meäke the laws, dost know, as I've a-zaid,
> They'd knock the corn-laws on the head;
> An' then the landlords must let down their
>   rent,
> An' we should very soon have cheaper bread:
> Farmers would gi'e less money vor their
>   lands.

It seems a highly unlikely series of conclusions, but no doubt it represents the level of real rustic arguments in Barnes's day about the market economy. The eclogue ends in a fable about the pig and the crow. It is Horatian and very well told, but I am not certain how it applies, except through a certain ominous and suspicious country wisdom. The poem ends:

> Ah! I do think you mid as well be quiet;
> You'll meäke things wo'se, i'-ma-be, by a
>   riot.
> You'll get into a mess, Tom, I'm afeärd;
> You'll goo vor wool, an' then come hwome a-
>   sheär'd.

Is this some suppressed memory of the Tolpuddle martyrs? There is a lot of shifting of blame onto agitators who come from elsewhere. The poem and its date and the precise local conditions are worth more study than I can offer.

But I had promised you a certain enchantment to be found in these poems. It is most obviously seen where Ralph Vaughan Williams spotted it, in 'My Orcha'd in Linden Lea':

> 'Ithin the woodlands, flow'ry gleäded,
>   By the woak tree's mossy moot,
> The sheenen grass-bleädes, timber-sheäded,
>   Now do quiver under voot;
> An' birds do whissle over head,
> An' water's bubblen in its bed,
> An' there vor me the apple tree
> Do leän down low in Linden Lea.
>
> When leaves that leätely wer a-springen
>   Now do feäde 'ithin the copse,

An' painted birds do hush their zingen
  Up upon the timber's tops;
An' brown-leav'd fruit's a-turnen, red,
In cloudless zunsheen, over head,
Wi' fruit vor me, the apple tree
Do lean down low in Linden Lea.

Let other vo'k meäke money vaster
  In the aïr o' dark-room'd towns,
I don't dread a peevish meäster;
  Though noo man do heed my frowns,
I be free to go abrode,
Or teäke ageän my homeward road
To where, vor me, the apple tree
Do leän down low in Linden Lea.

They are not writing poems quite like that any more. The plot is so simple it hardly exists: a countryman, a free labourer who may wander if he chooses, is coming home at the end of summer through the woods (a mossy moot is the trunk of a felled tree), the leaves are changing colour, the birds have lost their voices, it is late September and the early apples are ripe. The technique of the poem is not a formal pattern of alliteration but there is a lot of stray alliteration, and even more half-rhyme and internal rhyme: 'dark-room'd towns . . . don't dread', and 'vo'k . . . dark-room'd towns . . . don't . . . noo man . . . frowns'. These are not tricks applied to the language, they are not predictable, they are used instinctively, by a kind of second nature. Did Hopkins learn some of the philological oddities of his verse from habits that to Barnes were second nature?

And flockbells off the aerial
Downs' forefalls beat to the burial . . . [13]

Barnes's habit of joining two words in a new word attracted notice in his lifetime, but Hardy inherits it, and as for Hopkins, what about 'baldbright' and 'hailropes', 'heavengravel' and 'wolfsnow', all in one stanza? The later poets lack Barnes's simplicity, which can seem almost like a riddle, as in **'A Brisk Wind'**:

The burdock leaves upon the ledge,
The leaves upon the poplar's height,
A-blown by wind all up on edge,
Did show their underzides o' white;
An' withy trees bezide the rocks
Did bend grey limbs, did swaÿ grey boughs,
As there, on waggen heads, dark locks
Bespread red cheäks, behung white brows.

The shock to the senses of these sharp, primary observations is like that of primary colours, with which the poem ends. It is all like a series of linked haiku.

There are poems by Barnes like a bucket of extremely cold water, but there are others with an exquisite and trailing kind of music where what the poem says seems determined by its metrical pattern. 'A Winter Night' for example is like that, and at first reading you might have sworn it was a poem by Thomas Hardy:

It was a chilly winter's night;
  And frost was glitt'ring on the ground,
And evening stars were twinkling bright;
  And from the gloomy plain around
    Came no sound,
But where, within the wood-girt tow'r,
The churchbell slowly struck the hour;
As if that all of human birth
  Had risen to the final day,
And soaring from the wornout earth
  Were called in hurry and dismay,
    Far away;
And I alone of all mankind
Were left in loneliness behind.

This scary but perfect little poem surprises one several times: first by not being about Christmas, then by the ghostly flitting rather than general resurrection, and then most of all by the single figure left alone in the empty graveyard. If Hardy had written if, there might have been more verses, as there are in 'Channel Firing'. I do not think it was influenced by that much younger master, but Barnes may have sown a seed in Hardy's mind. When Hardy, hardly above school age, read to better himself and kept word-lists, Barnes was one of the authors he studied; he even fancied an amour with Lucy Barnes, but she was too shy for him. That must have been when he was eighteen or so, since she was three years older than he was; it must have been in the last years of the school, before Barnes moved out to Winterborne Came in 1862, with his daughters acting as curates, and one of his sons in the end as Rector of Winterborne Monkton, which was the next parish.

The most famous poem of his last years was **'The Geäte a-Vallèn To'**, one of the last few poems he dictated, in October 1885, about a year before he died. It is a poem that melts in the mouth, neatly enough executed but not strongly enough incised to be by Horace. The openings of each stanza are in the same magical version of the vernacular as Thomas Moore's *Irish Melodies,* which must lie somewhere among his forgotten models. Moore himself lay buried not far from Barnes's youthful horizons in a country churchyard not far from Bath:

In the zunsheen ov our zummers
  Wi' the haÿ time now a-come,
How busy were we out a-vield
  Wi' vew a-left at hwome . . .

     . . . . .

There's moon-sheen now in nights o' fall
  When leaves be brown vrom green . . .

and finally . . .

> To hear behind his last farewell
>   The geäte a-vallèn to.

In the end he becomes a patriarchal figure, prophetic and so distant in his old age as to be terrifying, dressed in fur-lined crimson to the waist, crouching in his chair over the fire and discussing Tennyson. I prefer him in the days of his riper eccentricity. If you want to recall that dead world, just remember how Tennyson was planting out primulas when he met the Irish poet Allingham whom he greatly liked, and swept him up to visit Winterborne Came. They got to Lymington at once, and then sat through a long hot day in a train while Tennyson smoked that filthy tobacco he liked, puffing out smoke like the engine. A man got into their compartment who was a professional clock regulator for the Great Western Railway, and at every station (this train stopped at every station) he got out and corrected the clock by his watch to London time. In the evening they got to Dorchester and next day they walked to Lyme Regis sending on their luggage by a coach, because Alfred wanted to carry out a pilgrimage to Jane Austen. On the night they spent in Dorchester they walked out to Winterborne Came, and saw old Barnes—a little earlier Barnes had called on Tennyson at Farringford. (On that occasion Barnes had gone to bed earlyish, as Tennyson was in full cry after Darwinism and pantheism and so on, being a thorough liberal: Barnes had little taste for 'speculation in matters theological'.) But the person in this rambling story who most embodies the age is surely the railway company's regulator of clocks. There was universal mechanical time, and we would never be free of it again. As C. H. Sisson has written in words well applied by Robert Nye to the poetry of Barnes: 'The man that was the same in Neolithic and in Roman times, as now, is of more interest than the freak of circumstances. This truth lies at the bottom of a well of rhythm.'[14]

It is in the freedom of his rhythms that you immediately know William Barnes for what he was: I mean their vernacular freedom, as in **'Black and White'**:

> When you stroll'd down the village at
>   evening, bedight
> All in white, in the warm summer-tide,
> The while *Towsy,* your loving old dog, with
>   his back
> Sleeky black, trotted on at your side:
> Ah! the black and the white! Which was
>   fairest to view?
> Why the white became fairest on you.
>
> At the end of the barton the granary stood,
> Of black wood, with white geese at its side,
> And the white-winged swans glided over the
>   waves
> By the cave's darksome shadows in pride:

> Oh! the black and the white! Which was
>   fairest to view?
> Why the white became fairest on you.

There is something more spirited or more developed, more intricate than a lilt in this poetry. The paradox is that where Tennyson places every footstep faultlessly like a man crossing a marsh, Barnes, having once digested his far-ranging examples and become able to produce them by second nature, can be perfectly, easily fluent. One would be wrong to say too fluent, because his easy voice, the easy sway of his voice, is an essential element in the enchanting effect of his poetry. Many things lay beyond his range, but he could do what was traditionally done and is not done now, and was not done in his time:

> O spread ageän your leaves an' flow'rs,
>   Lwonesome woodlands! zunny woodlands!
> Here underneath the dewy show'rs
>   O' warm-aïr'd spring-time, zunny
>   woodlands! . . .
>
> O let me rove ageän unspied,
>   Lwonesome woodlands, zunny woodlands!
> Along your green-bough'd hedges' zide,
>   As then I rambled, zunny woodlands!
> An' where the missen trees woonce stood,
> Or tongues woonce rung among the wood,
> My memory shall meäke em good,
>   Though you've a-lost em, zunny
>   woodlands![15]

One despairs in the attempt to construct a paper about anything so fragile: it is like snow, it is only made of pure water and it runs out of your hand. But Shakespeare would have recognised it as poetry, Milton would have envied it as poetry, Chaucer would have smiled at it, Donne would have been interested, no one would have thought it uninteresting until after the Civil War. It may be the Blackmoor Vale is in this sense prelapsarian, it has something about it continous with the days before the Civil War. The world of Barnes's eclogues is not in the least timeless, but the time they belong to might as easily be before the Civil War, that great divide and loss of English innocence. They are the only world of poetry for more than a century that Charles Cotton and Izaak Walton could have entered into without a qualm.

His rhymes can be playful and his verse is never full-toned as Shakespeare's is, but it perfectly fits the world and the people it reveals. In **'Shaftesbury Feäir'** he calls the place Paladore, not a new name in his day:

> As you did look, wi' eyes as blue
> As yonder southern hills in view,
> Vrom Paladore—O Polly dear,
>   Wi' you up there,
> How merry then wer I at feäir.

Yet taken together his poems carry the weight of life in their good-natured and reticent way, and somehow of the life of whole villages, a whole way of life. They are not essentially poems about the past even though it helps to know that they arise from the genius of a little child before Waterloo. If they were not in some way frozen there, they would not be as powerful as they are; but they are not about their period, that is only their condition, which so long afterwards it is useful for us to notice. Their subject is life, which is surely the subject of all true poetry, and it is surprising how much they carry of the experience of life at their simple level. It is not a life that ever touches the newspapers, and history hardly touches it even at Waterloo: hardly touches it at all I suppose until 1914 when the whole rural youth of England were taken away to another country and shot. That disaster is the foundation of the modern world. But when William Barnes thinks at all about English history it is to tell his daughter on his death-bed after having dictated **'The Geäte a-Vallèn To'**, "Observe that word 'geäte'. That is how King Alfred would have pronounced it, and how it was called in the *Saxon Chronicle,* which tells us of King Edward, who was slain at Corfe's geäte." After a pause he continued, "Ah! if the Court had not been moved to London, then the speech of King Alfred of which our Dorset is the remnant—would have been—the Court language of today, and it would have been more like Anglo-Saxon than it is now".'[16] That is exactly how a scholar of Shakespeare's day would have considered things, in just the same spirit. It is freakish enough of course, but it rouses one's affection for the good old poet. His vein of eccentricity was golden.

Twenty years ago I had the honour of reprinting his version of the **'Song of Songs'**, published in 1859 with many others in various dialects by the English Dialect Society under the patronage of Lucien Bonaparte.[17] The entire enterprise was rich in comedy, and in the Bodleian Library the only way to find Barnes's contribution used to be to look under SAL for Salamonis, as Biblical books in whatever language were under their first authors in Latin. Yet the effect, extremely queer as it undoubtedly is to most ears, is not without beauty.

> I be the rwose o' Sharon, an' the lily o' the valleys.
> Lik' a lily wi' thorns, is my love among maïdens.
> Lik' an apple-tree in wi' the trees o' the wood, is my love among sons. I long'd vor his sheäde, an' zot down, an' his fruit wer vull sweet to my teäste.
> He brought me into the feäst, an' his flag up above me wer love.
> Refresh me wi' ceäkes, uphold me wi' apples: vor I be a-pinèn vor love.
> His left hand wer under my head, an' his right a-cast round me.

When it came to translating from the Old Friesian, Barnes was less restrained. It is there he introduces the compound 'blowinggreen lithebloom', which prefigures Hopkins. Yet as a young man in 1826, thirty-three years before, he translated a sonnet of Petrarch with an icy neoclassic perfection such as he never attained in his own poems in common English. He was a man like Edward Lear in whom translation or pastiche might set free powers that would surprise him and still surprise the world. They are quite different in the case of the dialect version of the **'Song of Songs'**, which is a beautiful and most restrained piece of work, much better than the other dialect versions, as far as I remember them, and in the case of Petrarch:

> And those two lovely eyes that lit my track
> Are gone, and reason in the waves is
> 　drowned.

One would not imagine they could have been written by the same person.

Thomas Hardy said goodbye to them both. It was after a walk with Hardy in freezing, unexpected rain that Barnes took to his bed. In 'An Ancient to Ancients' Hardy does not mingle Barnes's name with those of Etty, Mulready, Maclise, Bulwer, Scott, Dumas and Sand:

> The bower we shrined to Tennyson,
> 　Gentlemen,
> Is roof-wrecked; damps there drip upon
> Sagged seats, the creeper-nails are rust,
> The spider is sole denizen;
> Even she who voiced those rhymes is dust,
> 　Gentlemen!

In the next to last stanza of that poem he turns the tables on the young:

> Sophocles, Plato, Socrates,
> 　Gentlemen,
> Pythagoras, Thucydides,
> Herodotus, and Homer,—yea,
> Clement, Augustin, Origen,
> Burnt brightlier towards their setting-day,
> 　Gentlemen.

That I take to be something he learnt from Barnes, who was dead when Hardy wrote it. But the poem of farewell is the one annotated '11 Oct. 1886 . . . Winterborne Came Path' and not published until more than thirty years afterwards. It is moving enough to conclude with, and words like 'yew-boughed' and 'grave-way' derive from Barnes's English. The little poem certainly does follow Barnes in its technique. How curious it is after all if we are right in supposing that Barnes only ever had two disciples who were poets: but those two were Gerard Manley Hopkins and Thomas Hardy.[18]

The Last Signal
(11 Oct. 1886)
A Memory of William Barnes

Silently I footed by an uphill road
That led from my abode to a spot yew-
    boughed;
Yellowly the sun sloped low down to
    westward,
    And dark was the east with cloud.

Then, amid the shadow of that livid sad
east,
    Where the light was least, and a gate stood
    wide,
Something flashed the fire of the sun that was
    facing it,
    Like a brief blaze on that side.

Looking hard and harder I knew what it
meant—
    The sudden shine sent from the livid east
    scene;
It meant the west mirrored by the coffin of
    my friend there,
    Turning to the road from his green,

To take his last journey forth—he who in
his prime
    Trudged so many a time from that gate
    athwart the land!
Thus a farewell to me he signalled on his
grave-way,
    As with a wave of his hand.

Winterborne-Came Path

It is an implacably melancholic poem, but so restrained—so much is not said—that we must take it
as the most personal of tributes.

Notes

Quotations from Barnes's poems are taken from *The
Poems of William Barnes,* ed. Bernard Jones (London: Centaur Press, 1962). Quotations from Hardy's
poems are taken from *The Complete Poems of Thomas Hardy,* ed. James Gibson (London: Macmillan,
1976).

[1] Peter Levi, *Tennyson* (London: Macmillan, 1993).

[2] Lane Fox's role as mentor is attested by Barnes's
daughter in her biography of her father (see note 4
below). However, Alan Chedzoy in his *William Barnes:
A Life of the Dorset Poet* (Stanbridge: Dovecote
Press, 1985) p. 23 suggests that Barnes's acquain-
tanceship with Lane Fox began at a later date.

[3] Thomas Hardy, 'The Rev. William Barnes, B.D.'
[obituary in:] *Athenaeum,* 16 October 1886, pp.
501-2; reprinted in H. Orel (ed.), *Thomas Hardy's
Personal Writings* (London: Macmillan, 1967) p.
100.

[4] Lucy Baxter ('Leader Scott'), *The Life of William
Barnes: Poet and Philologist* (London: Macmillan,
1887) p. 201.

[5] Ibid., p. 209.

[6] Ibid., p. 84.

[7] Ibid., p. 277.

[8] Milton, *L'Allegro.*

[9] Preface to *Select Poems of William Barnes,* ed. Thomas Hardy (London: H. Frowde [Oxford University
Press], 1908) p. ix.

[10] 'The Elm in Home-Ground'.

[11] 'Hay-Carren'.

[12] 'Be'mi'ster'.

[13] Gerard Manley Hopkins, 'The Loss of the Eurydice.
Foundered March 24 1878'.

[14] Original quote by C. H. Sisson is from *Art and
Action* (London: Methuen, 1965). Quoted by Robert
Nye in his Introduction to *William Barnes: A Selection of his Poems* (Oxford: Carcanet Press, 1972) p.
14.

[15] 'The Woodlands'.

[16] Baxter, *The Life of William Barnes,* p. 317.

[17] Peter Levi, *The English Bible 1534-1859* (London:
Constable, 1974). Barnes's translation is entitled 'The
Zong o' Solomon' and the quoted extract is from 'Song
of Songs II'.

[18] This fact was first pointed out by Geoffrey Grigson
in an article in *Lilliput* in the 1940s.

Andrew Phillips (essay date 1996)

SOURCE: "Society" and "Politics," in *The Rebirth of
England and English: The Vision of William Barnes,*
Anglo-Saxon Books, 1996, pp. 55-68 and 83-93.

[*In the following excerpt, Phillips looks at the social and political views Barnes expressed in his
poetry and prose writings.*]

Society

> Ill fares the land, to hastening ills a prey,
> Where wealth accumulates, and men decay.

> Oliver Goldsmith, *The Deserted Village*

> The enclosing of the commons robbed the country folk in England of leisure and independence, the coming of the factories took them from the fields and the old communities, and flung them into the new ones, which were allowed to grow up anyhow, without art, without thought, without faith or hope or charity, till the face of the land was blackened, and the soul of the land under a cloud.

> John Masefield, *St. George and the Dragon*

. . . Barnes' values were to a great extent shaped by his upbringing in the Blackmore Vale. True of his artistic values, his attitude to Nature and to Art, true of his attitudes to Marriage, this is also true of all his social values. His fathers and forefathers had all been rooted in the land, the pre-Enclosure, pre-industrial rural way of life. Indeed, despite moving to Dorchester, Barnes later bought (thanks to his wife's frugality, as he acknowledges) a small piece of land in the Vale, as recorded in his poem, **'I Got Two Vields'**, thus somehow joining his forebears in their way of life. His forefathers were yeomen, self-reliant, self-sufficient, self-improved and self-educated smallholders—like Barnes himself. Barnes, as Hardy said, was a great example of self-help, a genius who had risen from nowhere. He was in favour of self-help not, however, for the sake of money or greed but for the sake of self-respect.

Barnes expressed his social views in several works and poems quite outspokenly. Notably he opposed the Enclosures in several Eclogues such as, **'The Common A-Took-in'**, **'The Times'**, **'The 'Lotments'**, **'Two Farms in Woone'**, **'Father Come Hwome'** or **'The New Poor Laws'** and in a poem **'The Leane'**. Despite being disguised in dialect and in imitation of Virgil's Eclogues, these poems were in fact quite radical political statements—they were written after rioting among farmworkers, especially in Dorset, and at the time of the injustices inflicted on the Dorset Tolpuddle Martyrs in 1834. As regards emigration for example, even in the form of transportation, Barnes considered it unfair that criminals could emigrate, whereas honest farmworkers, living in conditions of starvation, could not. Of this he wrote in one Eclogue, **'Rusticus Emigrans'**, where a desperate labourer says, 'If 'twerden var [it weren't for] my children and my wife, I wou'dent gi' zixpence var my life'.

His Eclogues especially have led several commentators to compare Barnes with Cobbett.[1] But Barnes, though often *radical* was not at all a *Radical,* if anything his views could be compared to those of Ruskin and Morris, with the important difference that Barnes preceded them—he was a forerunner. In fact Barnes would have agreed with Cowper: 'God made the country, man made the town'. The mere thought of what men had done in towns saddened him: 'Many a plain wall rises between the workman and the glory of the passing sun, and has shut out his windowframed piece of blue sky, and the cheering whiteness of the flying cloud. Many a day of smoke has blackened the clearness of the sweet spring-tide; many a bright-leaved tree has heretofore given way to crowded shades of narrowed rooms. Many a rood of flowery sward has become rattling streets, where for songs of birds, they have the din of hammers. Many a cheek has been paled, and lovely piece of childhood marred, by longsome hours of over-work'.[2] He found it unnatural that man should work by night and sleep by day; in the country, 'we don't grow up pe,le an' weak But we do work wi' health an' strength' (**'Sleep Did Come Wi' The Dew'**). And in **'Open Vields'** he wrote:

> Well, you mid keep the town an' street,
> Wi' grassless stwones to beät your veet,
> An' zunless windows where your brows
> Be never cool'd by swaÿen boughs;
> An' let me end, as I begun,
> My days in open aïr an' zun.

Barnes was a traditionalist, yearning for the pre-industrial past which he had known in his childhood.[3] And here he professed a certain regional patriotism, for Dorset after all had for long been bypassed by the Industrial Revolution, remaining uncontaminated by grasping industrialism. There was no doubt in Barnes' mind that the country was superior to the town, and he expressed it in poems like **'Praise O' Do'set'**, **'Farmer's Sons'** or **'The Farmer's Woldest Da'ter'** [Oldest Daughter], **'Blackmwore Maidens'**, **'John Bloom in Lon' on'** or **'My Orcha'd in Linden Lea'**. But in reality it is implicit in his whole work, both poetry and prose. In general he could not understand why the vital activity of agriculture was not more highly valued. If then we are to look at Barnes' social values, we are to look first at his critique of the new nineteenth century society, the urbanised society of the Industrial Revolution.

Perhaps the first tangible results of the changes that came to Dorset were the Enclosures and the merging of farms. The enclosures effectively pauperised the rural classes, for farms were brought up by a few large owners and as a result, 'now they don't imploy so many men Upon the land as work'd upon it then', as Barnes wrote in his Eclogue, **'Two Farms in Woone'**. This merging of farms meant the capitalisation and industrialisation of farming. Barnes defined such merging as: 'The kindness which is done by capital when it affords employment to people from whom, by a monopoly, it has taken over their little business is such as one might do to a cock by adorning his head with a plume of feathers pulled out of his own tail'.[4] The aim of the merging of farms was not to continue the traditional, contented, self-supporting, village community, but to maximise output and profits at its expense. It also took away any opportunity and motivation for the thrifty labourer to save enough to one day work his own farm, a theme that was close to Barnes' heart and as early as 1829 he had written to the Dorset County Chronicle speaking of this. Poverty and distress grew and Barnes talked of it quite openly. Thus in **'The Hwomestead a-Vell [Fallen] Into Hand'**, where out of eight farms only three were left, he wrote:

> An' all the happy souls they ved
> Be scattered vur [far] an' wide.
> An' zome o'm [some of them] be a-wanten
>   bread,
> Zome, better off, ha' died,

This can be compared with the former state of the smallholder, for example in his poem, **'The Hwomestead':**

> An' I be happy wi' my spot
> O' freehold ground an' mossy cot,
> An' shoulden get a better lot
> If I had all my will.
> I'm landlord o' my little farm,
> I'm king 'ithin my little pleäce;
> I don't break laws, an' don't do harm,
> An' ben't [aren't] afeärd o' noo man's feäce.

[At this point it might be worthwhile making a small digression: if Barnes thought this of the result of the merging of smallholdings in the nineteenth century, what would he have thought of the unemployment caused by the emergence of multinational corporations since the Second World War, the takeover and merger fever since the 1960's, the advent of the Superstore, or for that matter the development of customs unions, fashionably called 'trading blocs', with their 'single markets'?].

Barnes saw the baneful effects of the Enclosures and industrialisation in the rise in crime-rates in his own day, as we have seen in the above-quoted **'The Hwomestead'**. In his **'Views of Labour and Gold'** he demonstrated statistically that crime actually rose in proportion as farms grew in size. Of the impossibility for the labourer to better himself by saving and starting his own 'farmling', he said: 'The result is that the possession of property, whether to a large or small amount, retains a man from breaking the laws of his country'.[5] He went on to demonstrate that crime rose even more with urbanisation, quoting statistics for Liverpool and Manchester, where the amount of crime was 'ten times that which pre-

vails in the yeomanry counties'.[6] Since Barnes considered that much crime was a result of poor social conditions, it was to some extent a social responsibility. But, having said this, we should not think of Barnes as some kind of 'softee'. Barnes was never negligent and considered leniency to criminals a great mistake. Wrongdoers had to be punished, the innocent had to be protected. There was no reason to be kind to rogues, all had to see that honesty paid, and he thought it unmerciful to the victim to leave the wrong done to him unrighted. However, with his usual balance Barnes was not only against punishment out of cruel vengefulness, but also against the do-gooder who pays more attention to attempting to reform the criminal than to helping the victim. Although Barnes understood the responsibility of society, he also understood the importance of personal responsibility for one's acts.[7] Indeed this same notion of personal responsibility and self-discipline or moral training was the very foundation of his pacific teaching methods.

Some of Barnes' social thought is contained in articles he wrote for the local *Poole and Dorset Herald* in 1849, under the collective title, **'Humilis Domus'**, subtitled, **'Some thoughts on the Abodes, Life and Social Condition of the Poor, especially in Dorsetshire'**. (Some of these thoughts were reprinted later in his *Views of Labour and Gold*). Here he raised a critique against the social changes in English society at the time. Objecting to the National Debt, he considered that its existence causes every worker to have to work longer hours in order to pay it off. Although Barnes was hardly opposed to work as such, he did object to overwork, 'workaholism' as we might now call it. The overworked had no time for his family and children, ' . . . no time to solace himself with the gifts of God . . . no time to enlighten and purify his soul by a peaceful reading of the word of life . . . While moderate labour is wholesome to the body and good to the mind, excessive daily toil is fraught with evil to the body and soul . . . The holy affection of kindred for kindred grows out of the happier hours of freedom and rest in house life'.[8] He considered that long working hours were baneful for family life: 'These graces [a happy house-life], therefore, grow out of incidents and services for which some time, with freedom from toil, is needful. Good fathers and mothers (and there are good ones among the poor, and would be more with a happier house-life) are the best teachers of children, and a good home is the best school for the formation of the mind'.[9] Regarding a not unconnected field, slavery, Barnes was of the opinion: 'Slavery is as destructive to its masters as to its slaves'.[10]

On the other hand Barnes was equally against enforced idleness, and would certainly have wanted to replace 'welfare' with 'workfare': 'It is better for paupers themselves that they should do something rather than nothing for their money towards the amelioration of the life of men'.[11] However, he is equally stern with the idle rich, living off unearned income, whom he sees as little more than parasites: 'The consumption of a gay and insolvent spendthrift is most awfully large: his horse and carriage, and wine and grogs, and meats and cigars, and clothing, and firing, and travelling, are all most costly . . . The consumption of a portion of the nation's wealth by unproductive spendthrifts, and reckless insolvents . . . is as much a loss to the community as would be the destruction of it by fire, or locusts, or any other unproductive consumer'.[12] 'The Christian law is that if any man will not work, neither should he eat'.[13] Moreover, the existence of the idle rich, said Barnes with prophetical (but much disregarded) common sense, could be politically dangerous: ' . . . in a community of many rich idlers, care should be taken of the honest working classes, or else they will become degraded and dangerous'.[14] Elsewhere[15] he adds: 'Disdain of labour and pride of wealth are breeding among us great evils of social life'. (Some might wonder if these words were really written in 1859 and not perhaps in the 1990s).

Moreover modern industrialism may have produced quantity, but it did not produce quality; modern goods were decadent and shoddy. 'Primitive' peoples in the Sandwich Islands were able, says Barnes, to make clothing of a skill and grace that no machinery could make. And Indians made rush baskets so water-tight that they were waterproof, and Hindu cooks with hardly any tools will cook a better meal that 'will allow little glory to our load of cooking gear'.[16] In poems like **'The Stwonen [Stone] Porch'** or **'The Girt Wold [Great Old] House O'Mossy Stwone'** he criticised modern buildings, which are too small, do not let sunshine in, have thin deal doors, are made of brick not stone, 'wi' yards a-sprinkled wi' a mop, Too little vor a vrog to hop'. Barnes cries: 'But let me live an' die where I Can zee the ground, an' trees, an' sky'. On the same theme Barnes was greatly alarmed at the plight of the poor who were badly housed and considered it only natural that every family have its own house and that the children of each sex have its own room.[17] Worse still was the fate of those who went to the workhouse, where orphans lived in misery and where wives were separated from husbands contrary to Christian marriage: 'They mid [might] as well, I think, each wi' his bride Goo back to Church an' have their knot untied', he wrote in **'The New Poor Laws'**. Barnes' general feeling was that social life was suffering from 'Progress' (a feeling widespread at the end of the twentieth century too): 'I believe that most of our so-called improvements either displace a good, or bring in their train some evil, and that our true progress in wellbeing is only the difference of good of the so-called improvement and the good displaced by it or the evil which follows it'.[18] He expressed this most effectively and pithily in a poem, **'The Cost of Improvement'**, written in 'National' English:

For aught that's nice
You pay a price . . .
The higher has become your speed
The stronger are your calls for haste;
Wealth's quicker streams in more ways waste,
The more you have the more you need.
Your fathers trode on English dust,
And while you, o'er the world, will roam,
The more you roam, the more you must,
From irksomeness of any home.
Whatever changes you may choose,
And something gain, you something lose . . .
Fell woods, your shield from wind and heat,
And you must meet the weather's strokes;
Or turn the oak-grove to a street,
And smoking tuns will cost the oaks.
Give night with day to toil for wealth,
And then your gain will cost your health.
To buy new gold
Give up some old.

We have come across little in the 1990's more pertinent or topical to today's situation than this, written nearly six generations ago.

William Barnes then was very critical of the social results of the processes of industrialisation and urbanisation proceeding in Victorian England. Moreover, he put forward ideas as to where solutions might be found. Firstly, he was resolutely opposed to largeness and agglomerations which he saw as socially and spiritually unhealthy: 'Another evil of congregated labour is . . . an outfalling from the ordinances of grace . . . being collected from sundry places, they sink into a godless and dark-minded form of life'.[19] Barnes' ideal, when not in the smallholder or yeoman-farmer, was certainly in cottage industry, the cottage economy: 'The cutting of the Bohemian glass is, I believe, carried on by men who work each in the quiet of his own house, which may be in the pretty nook of a village dell; and the carding and spinning of wool, and buttoning, were formerly home-work in this country'.[20] But who would govern this mass of cottage-workers and peasant-farmers?

In his largely linguistic and historical work of 1869, ***Early England and the Saxon-English,*** Barnes, speaking of instances of nineteenth century hooliganism, wrote: 'The mindstrength and body worksomeness [mental and physical strength] of the Saxon, which are of great might for good when well spent, need a training in wisdom to keep them from mischief. The Saxon's mind, and above all in the young, is destructive, and his sprackness [energy] wants the guidance of refined thought'.[21] Barnes preached this idea of refining the 'Saxon' mind as part of his lecturing for educational and mutual improvement associations. For example, according to a newspaper report on a lecture given in Corfe (and no doubt repeated elsewhere): 'He reminded those present, as Anglo-Saxons, that (to use a homely expression) they had the 'stuff' in them to make great men, and exhorting them so to study God's Word, and to train their minds they might really become good men, and above all, good Christians'.[22]

In other words Barnes deemed that English folk needed to be governed by some hierarchy. Given that in any society, a hierarchy is inevitable, he came to the logical conclusion that this hierarchy must be enlightened, to justify its privileges, it also had to carry out burdensome but needful duties. His solution was this: 'There should be some classes free of handtoil [manual work], that they might purify and adorn the nobler element of man, their mind, with the graces and excellence of a free and intellectual life, and let their life of intelligence shine for the good of the darker-minded sons of toil. Every community needs men who . . . might be the better qualified to effect man's well-being either as clergy, legislators, magistrates, lawyers or otherwise . . . The squire and his lady are a great social good when they live among the poor, and keep before their eyes the graceful pattern of a Christian life, and raise their tone of feeling by kindness and sober bearing'.[23] Barnes hope was then in an enlightened squirearchy. This was not imagination, this was his childhood from which he recalled the toast of the Harvest Home:[24]

> Here's a health unto our meäster,
> The founder of the feäst;
> And I hope to God, wi' all my heart,
> His soul in heaven mid rest.
> That everything mid prosper
> That ever he teäke in hand.
> Vor we be all his sarvants,
> And all at his command.

Indeed he actually portrayed this class in his poetry, for instance in **'Culver Dell and the Squire'** (from which, significantly, was taken the verse in praise of Barnes himself on his statue in Dorchester) the squire is one who knows the poor, sympathises with them and above all helps them:

> An' all the vo'k did love so well
> The good wold [old] squire o' Culver dell . . .
> Vor he did know the poor so well
> 'S [As] the richest vo'k in Culver Dell.

In **'The Leane'**, written against the Enclosures, the same much respected and loved squire appears again, letting trespassers off with a smile and 'mild words' which 'cut 'em like swords': his authority alone is enough to shame the lawbreaker. In one of his Eclogues **'The 'Lotments'**, he again praised the squire: 'Why 'twer the squire, good now! a worthy man, That vu'st [first] brought into ouer pleäce the plan; He zaid he'd let a vew odd eäcres O' land to us poor leäb'ren men'.

And in another poem, **'Herrenston'**, he describes a Christmas party given to villagers by the local Herrenston squire and his good lady:

> Zoo then the leady an' the squier,
> At Chris'mas, gather'd girt [big] an' small,
> Vor me'th [mirth] avore their roaren vier
>   [fire],
> An' roun' their bwoard, 'ithin [within] the
>   hall; . . .
> Zoo peace betide the girt vo'k's [rich folk's]
>   land,
> When they can stoop, wi' kindly smile,
> An' teake a poor man by the hand,
> An' cheer en [him] in his daily tweil [toil].
> An' oh! mid [might] He that's vur [far] above
> The highest here, reward their love,
> An' gi'e [give] their happy souls, drough
>   [through] greace,
> A higher pleace than Herrenston.

Now if we consider these words and thoughts in the context of Barnes' life and philosophy, then what he is saying is quite remarkable. We know that Barnes was himself of the people, whose speech and folklore he admired and described both in poetry and in learned articles. It might therefore have seemed curious that he should write of the 'Saxon's' (i.e. English countryman's) destructiveness, and how he needed a refining example from above. In fact we can only understand this seeming paradox if we take into account his linguistic views which we shall describe in detail in Part Two of this book. For Barnes' fundamental intuition was that the English language suffered from the fact that all its learned vocabulary concerning for example, administration, government, military affairs, technology, was Norman-French or Latin in origin. The learned 'Saxon' compounds of English had virtually all been lost with the Norman Conquest. As he had written as long ago as 1832: 'The English are a great nation; and as an Englishman, I am sorry that we have not a language of our own; but that whenever we happen to conceive a thought above that of a plough-boy, or produce anything beyond a pitch-fork, we are obliged to borrow a word from others before we can utter it, or give it a name'.[25] But just as England had lost an elite language with the Norman Conquest, so it had also lost its social elite.

In wishing for an enlightened squirearchy, what Barnes really wanted was the restoration of the patriarchal 'atheldom' or nobility of Saxon 'folk' England—that which had perished at the Battle of Hastings, or been dispossessed by Norman warrior and fled into exile abroad. The promotion of a governing class, sympathetic to the poor, was certainly part of Barnes' message given in his constant lecturing in the West Country. Indeed this is even one of the fruits of Barnes' dialect poetry, as one sympathetic reviewer wrote: 'This, we would trust, may be among the consequences of the present publication, to keep alive, in some measure, the interest in the affairs of the Poor . . . If the Landlords and upper classes generally may thus be led to a more intimate acquaintance with the feelings and habits (of the poor) and to a more sincere sympathy with their wants, and hopes, and fears; if they may be taught in any degree to have a respect for their homely and household prejudices which are far too frequently violated and despised, we are convinced that Mr. Barnes will feel that his poems have aided in a work whose success he would value far above any fame or emolument that may accure to himself . . . All the poor want is to be known and to be communicated with directly . . . instead of being left to the tender mercies of an ill-educated class, whose own bargains have been often hardly driven, and whose prosperity, therefore, depends upon oppression and illiberality. Against this treatment their only weapon is deceit; and the consciousness of deceiving produces a savage gloom in their character and a suspiciousness of the upper classes'.[26]

In other words what Barnes was seeking in an enlightened squirearchy was none other than the restoration of a social system which had certainly been greatly shaken, though not altogether destroyed, with the imposition of a foreign and unsympathetic ruling class onto it centuries before. This is why he could write of the need for a refining influence on 'the Saxon mind'; Saxon England had lost not only the learned compounds used by its elite, but also, through massacre, exile or dispossession, the elite itself. Since then the relation between landed and landless, rich and poor had been unsteady, divisive, first on account differences of race and language between English and Norman, then on account of the differences of class and culture. Wittingly or unwittingly, Barnes was promoting in both his poetry and prose works not only the speech of rural, pre-industrial England, which harked back to the speech of Saxon, pre-Conquest England, but also the social attitudes, structures, patterns of thought and expectations of rural, pre-industrial England, which ultimately harked back to those of Saxon, pre-Conquest England. What at heart Barnes wanted to see was the restoration of the paternalism of the Saxon hall and church, whose descendants he instinctively, though probably at first unconsciously, saw in the enlightened nineteenth century squire and 'parson'. The images and even words of his poem **'Herrenston,** 'Vor me'th, avore their roaren vier, An' roun' their bword, 'ithin the hall', describe not so much a nineteenth century Dorset village feast as the festive board of a paternal, patriarchal, protective Saxon lord as he made feast with his folk. Barnes wanted the gentlefolk of England to be Christian and cultured, to be with the people, and to use their positions and wealth in charity towards their fellows. Elsewhere in an Eclogue, **'The Times'**, he wrote:

> If we've a-got a friend at all,
> Why who can tell—I'm sure thou cassen
>   [canst not]—
> But that the squier, or the pa'son,
> Mid [Might] be our friend, Tom, after all?

Barnes' vision was that of the rural community of the paternal and therefore respected Saxon lord and lady with his hall and Saxon priest with his church, which had officially disappeared with the imposition of Norman feudalism and the Norman Church, a foreign Establishment elite. At first unconsciously as a village boy, later consciously as a linguist, Anglo-Saxonist, antiquarian, teacher, polymath and polyglot, he preached the restoration of this social ideal of Saxon England, transposed into his own age, into the community of the enlightened squire and the country rector.

Thus the seemingly backwards-looking traditionalism of William Barnes was in fact a radical and revolutionary social philosophy, which challenged the ultimately Norman-English class conflict of English society and called for the governing class to overcome it. And this relevance for the present should hardly surprise us, who have witnessed the tragic consequences of class divisions in English society into Establishment and People, Management and Unions, 'them and us', especially in recent years. At a time when large corporations all revere the ideas of teamwork, quality circles, total quality and the importance of social responsibility, at a time when Taylorism is dead and management gurus predict 'flat' companies without hierarchies thanks to the triumph of the 'knowledge worker', at a time when politicians of left and right talk freely of 'communitarianism' and the 'social market', how can we not find Barnes' insights relevant?

And if we are surprised by the relevance of Barnes' social vision, then we can do no better than read once more the words of Barnes' daughter in her biography of her beloved father: 'Some men live before their age, others behind it. My father did both. in action he was behind the world, or rather apart from it; in thought he was far before his time . . . A great and deep student of the past, he drew from it inferences and teaching for the future'.[27]

Notes for "Society"

[1] For Comparisons with Cobbett, see especially Ruffell, pp.227-30 and Wrigley, 'William Barnes and the Social Problem', *Dorset Natural History and Archaeological Society, Proceedings for 1977*, pp. 19-27.

[2] Thoughts on Beauty and Art, *Macmillan's Magazine* June 1861, p. 134.

[3] Colloms, p. 129 and Forsyth, especially pp. 147-50.

[4] *VLG [Views of Labour and Gold]* p.69

[5] op. cit. pp. 71-2

[6] op. cit. pp. 72-3

[7] *Notes on Ancient Britain,* pp. 73-8

[8] *Poole and Dorset Herald* (PDH), 26/4/1849

[9] *VLG* p. 171

[10] Professor Charlotte Lindgren in *Proceedings of the William Barnes Society* 1983-92, Vol I, p.43.

[11] PDH 3/5/1849

[12] op. cit. 24/5/1849

[13] *VLG* p. 96

[14] op. cit. p. 163

[15] op. cit. p. 97

[16] op. cit. p. 111

[17] op. cit. pp. 181-2

[18] op. cit. p. 155

[19] op. cit. pp. 114-5

[20] op. cit. p. 115

[21] *Early England and the Saxon English,* pp.63-4.

[22] Scrapbook II, p.32, in the Dorset County Museum

[23] *VLG* pp. 172-3

[24] Lucy Baxter, p.7

[25] 'On Compounds in the English Language', *Gentleman's Magazine* 1832, Supplementary Volume CII, p.593

[26] Quoted in Hearl, pp. 180-1

[27] Baxter, Preface

. . . . .

Politics

> For what is England that she should be dear to me, but that she is the land that owns my county? Why should I love my county, but that it contains the village of my birth? Why should that village be hallowed in my mind, but that it holds the home of my childhood?

> William Barnes, **'Humilis Domus'**

> Imperialism is a depraved choice of national life, imposed by self-seeking interests which appeal to the lusts of quantitative acquisitiveness and of forceful domination surviving in a nation from early centuries of animal struggle for existence. Its adoption as a policy implies a deliberate renunciation of that cultivation of the higher inner qualities which for a nation as for an individual constitutes the ascendancy of reason over brute impulse. It is the besetting sin of all successful States, and its penalty is unalterable in the order of nature.

> J. A. Hobson, *Imperialism a Study,* 1902

. . . It might perhaps seem strange to talk of the political views of Rev. William Barnes, for he did not like political parties, never belonged to one, and it would be pointless to comb through his writings in search of some directly political comment or an indication of how he may have voted at elections. Barnes disliked both power and money—the two main preoccupations of politics and politicians, and he called himself a 'political heretic'. Indeed he spent a part of his life hovering on the edge of poverty and seems to have been despised by the local Dorchester Establishment for his selfless lack of ambition. On the other hand, there are many implications or comments in his works which have indirect bearings on Barnes' political orientations. Let us first, however, try to uncover Barnes' attitude to his own country, then the most powerful in the world, and its actions and influence outside its own borders.

Firstly it is quite clear that Barnes disliked Imperialism—a policy pursued by both the political parties of his day. This is clear as early as 1849 when he spoke forthrightly against the occupation of the lands of other peoples, justified by some by the Biblical text that man should multiply and replenish the earth: 'We are fearful that the logic by which we take the lands of others under this authority, is not perfectly sound. The truth is that the red men of America, and the darker ones of Australia and New Zealand, are children of Adam, and therefore *they* are bidden with *us* to replenish the earth, and are fulfilling the injunction till we go and stop them, by the occupation of the lands over which they might be spreading'.[1] What Barnes is saying is astoundingly modern, for he is saying that all men are sons of Adam, not just Western Europeans. In so doing he unmasks the deeply unpleasant racist arrogance of those who justified Imperialism which was implicit in their whole ideology, which asserted that Western man and culture were inherently superior to all others and that the 'coloured savages' of the Americas, Africa, Asia and Australasia were really no better than animals since they were not really human. He criticises the idea that Christians, simply because they were Christians, had the inherent right to seize the lands of non-Christians: ' . . . as if Christians could draw from the positive precept, the new commandment of their Divine Saviour 'to love one another', the negative one that they might plunder all men not yet within the fold of the Church. It is to be feared that as a nation, we have to answer for much unrighteousness towards weaker tribes'.[2]

With these few, seemingly moderate words, Barnes denounces the whole, many-centuried process of Empire-building, beginning with the Crusades, which Western Powers justified through their distortions of the Christian Faith. In his 'Views of Labour and Gold', as we have already mentioned, Barnes had condemned the Opium Wars and Western Imperialism in China. Of the West Indies he spoke of a writer who justifying the sugar and rum trade, 'has stated, seemingly without any misgivings of conscience, that he himself had worked slaves eighteen hours a day at cropping time'.[3] Barnes' views on slavery were quite clear; he considered it to be as destructive to its masters as to the slaves. Perhaps, however, the clearest and most extraordinary (for the period) denunciation of the Imperialist mentality came two years before the publication of **'Views of Labour and Gold'**, when on seventh October 1857 he preached in Dorchester's main church—no doubt in front of the town's social elite. This was the Day of Humiliation, the Day of National Mourning for those massacred in the Indian Mutiny. Since it is such an important statement of Barnes' position, we shall quote from it at some length:

> 'Was this day of humiliation to own ourselves as sinful as a nation, and yet not to try our behaviour by the pattern of the mind that is in Christ? What is the high place to which we as a nation have been too often going for ages? Dominion. Land. Gold. In one word: Mammon . . . the first danger is pride. The tokens of our pride are seen in our writings in which we see Englishmen arrogantly boasting of England's might instead of yearning with fear for her godly use of it. Another danger is injustice, or when dominion or wealth can be won with ease, a selfish readiness to mistake the opportunity of taking it for God's call to it; and justify our taking it by worldly maxims, instead of the law of Christ . . . Look at the power we hold in India, and the evil that has notwithstanding arisen against us . . . There is a doctrine which is nevertheless a dangerous one. It is that the Lord of the Earth has given to us, the English nation, a wide dominion, so that inasmuch as we hold a pure form of faith our sword may make way for the Gospel . . . Has no Englishman, standing proudly on the power of England, behaved among men of another religion as if our own had

been wanting in the power of hallowing his heart? If we are guilty in these cases, how will it help us that we have a pure form of Faith? We want pure hearts, pure lives . . . One of the un-Christian maxims so common among us is often taken up not only against weaker tribes, but against men of a lower status of life—that they cannot appreciate kindness, but mistake it for weakness, and therefore we cannot be too severe, too cruel with them. It is a Satanic argument to reconcile the conscience to injustice and cruelty . . . Missionary work will never be done by the sword, the sceptre, nor the civil power of itself. They may make thousands of hypocrites, but no conversions. Conversion must be the work of the word and the spirit . . . Let us be sure we do our missionary work with a missionary spirit, and that if we strive for the conversion of the heathen it is for their good, and not for our gain in a freer and easier form of trade. They who have taken the sword will perish by the sword. There was no need for our Saviour to take the form of man to teach him to avenge his wrongs. the worst of men did it before the Incarnation . . . My work is peace and salvation . . . Remember as a warning that though a people may gain in dominion, in population, in land, in wealth by a sinful act, they are by that act weaker than they were before it'.[4]

Thus Barnes condemned the ethnocentric arrogance of the Western Powers to other cultures, which in fact was a mere camouflage for lust for power, land and gold, and which had existed 'for ages', as he said in this sermon.

The arrogance condemned here was arrogance to others who lived in the same historical era. He also, however, condemned the arrogance of the West towards its own past, implicit in its belief in progress. In his **'Notes on Ancient Britain and the Britons'**, written in 1858, he wrote: 'Some of our school-books tell their readers that the Britons wore the skins of beasts, as it were a token of great misery; but . . . a fur coat is no token of misery . . . in an English railway carriage through a snowy day!'.[5] Combining criticisms of attitudes to both the past and to other cultures he wrote that the Ancient Egyptians, 'were a nation learned in the sciences when the inhabitants of Europe were wild in the woods, and . . . the Hindoos applied a system of fluxions of their own to the quadrature of the circle before Sir Isaac Newton or Leibnitz was born'.[6]

Barnes' denunciation of arrogance, both in time (towards past history) and space (towards contemporary peoples and cultures) would most certainly have alienated him from the Imperialist wings of the Tory Party and also the Liberal Whig Party of his day which found that Imperial trade justified colonial aggression and war (the Crimean War, the Opium Wars, the Balkan Wars of Muslim Turkey with their horrific massacres of Balkan Christians, and later, it must be said, the Boer War and the First World War). On the other hand,

and this may at first seem paradoxical, Barnes, as a patriot and an Anglican priest who disliked Non-Conformism, and wrote against the Disestablishment of the Church of England, both of which he thought weakened the unity of Church and Nation, was therefore in some way a member of the Establishment, an antidisestablishmentarian. How can this seeming contradiction be accounted for? I think that if we define Barnes' patriotism, then we shall understand that there is no contradiction in reality.

Barnes' patriotism was in fact local, it was home-love, England held 'the home of his childhood', as we have quoted above. He loved the place where he had met God in his blissful childhood. And that childhood had not been spent in the slumdom of Manchester or London but in the virtually untouched, millennial Dorset countryside. This was a regular theme in his poetry. In **'Praise O' Do'set'**, he wrote:

> We Do'set, though we mid [might] be
>   hwomely,
> Ben't [Aren't] asheam'd to own our pleace
>   . . .
> Friend an' wife,
> Fathers, mothers, sisters, brothers,
> Happy, happy be their life!
> Vor Do'set dear,
> Then gi'e woone cheer;
> D'ye hear? woone cheer!

And in **'The Girt Woak Tree That's In The Dell'** he described how he would fight for his country, but standing on ship's planks made from the favourite oak tree of his childhood:

> An' I upon his planks would stand,
> An' die a-fighten vor the land,—
> The land so dear,—the land so dear,—the land
>   so free,—
> The land that bore the girt woak tree.

Barnes then was a local patriot, a 'home-lover': 'It is to the house that we must look for the growth of many of the most lovely social Christian graces: the affections of kindred, a reverence for the kindly feelings, and a love of home, which in its full outgrowth, becomes that bulwark of the safety of a community and constitution, 'amor patriae', the love of one's fatherland'.[7] He was also a highly cultured and intelligent man. He was in no way a nationalistic 'patriot', a jingoist, an attitude which at the time must have cost him dear, in part certainly the rejection of the social elite of Dorset. Thus to call Barnes a 'Little Englander', though an anachronism since the expression dates from 1890, would seem to us the most exact definition of his position. He was a local patriot, one who loved only the beauty and good and truth in the England he knew—and not the soul destroying Mammon-worship of tradesmanship, of Victorian industrialism with its ragged, urban proletariat, worker exploitation, colonial rape and all its hypocritical justifications for its sins.

The closest Barnes ever came to a political statement was in his Eclogue **'The Times'**, where he wrote against the Chartists—'the socialists of those days'. Here his character John (bearing the same name as Barnes' commonsense yeoman father) speaks against Tom: 'Ah! I do think you mid as well be quiet; You'll meäke things wo'se, i'-ma'-be [it maybe], by a riot'. Barnes considered that the intervention of the townee Chartist would make the situation of the farm-labourer even worse than before. However he later regretted these political statements in this Eclogue, thinking poetry the wrong place for politics. It is therefore all the more interesting to discover the original version of the Eclogue was even more political and had to be quite radically changed, not least because the Tory editor of the Dorset Country Chronicle objected[8]. Thus in the original version, John praises the charity of the parson and the squire and their good ladies in typical Barnesian fashion . . . :

> Var thee dost know the pa'son an' the squier
> Do git us coals to miake a bit o' vire,
> An' gi'e us many a meaty buone to pick,
> An' zend us medicine when we be zick,
> An' then ther liadies, bless their lives,
> Do come an' gi'e things to our wives . . .

But John goes on to warn Tom:

> You'll blunder out o' water into mud:
> A civil war wo'd be noo benefit
> To noobody, an' ef a man can't git
> Good bread by zweat,'e woon't, I think, by
>   blood.

Tom goes on to defend his viewpoint, with which John disagrees:

> . . . Ev'ry oone is var hizzell, mind John.
> Zoo be the men that ya da'pend upon;
> But God ya know is var us al'.

Given Barnes' total lack of support for party politics, it may seem pointless to wonder whom he would vote for at an election, were he alive today. Nevertheless it may help us to put him into perspective.

His rejection of Tory Imperialism would certainly have made him no friend of their opportunistic, ideological heirs on the left of the contemporary Conservative Party, the pro-Europeans. Barnes was too patriotic, too pro-English, nay, too pro-Dorset, to have become pro-European. Barnes had principles, he disliked capital, 'gold'. He disliked extremes of rich and poor: 'It is true that a man may now leave his wife a million of money earned for him by workmen in the service of his capital, but then fewer men out of every hundred in his trade may leave their children a hundred pounds'.[9] On the other hand his rejection of Big Business, of the division of labour and of Free Trade, and advocacy of Protectionism (the lack of which caused so much suffering in the rural society of nineteenth century England through the import of cheap corn from the vast prairie-lands of North America) would put him very far from free-marketeers on the right of the contemporary Conservative Party.

Would Barnes then, with his paternalism, his hope for social justice and the importance he placed, as a pedagogue, on Education, have found himself on the left of the political spectrum? After all, did he not preach 'Small is Beautiful' and the values of cottage industry?

We think not. Barnes could scarcely have been on the left. As we have seen, he was opposed to the Chartists. He felt that the Chartists would unsettle Dorset farmworkers without actually solving their problems. Thus he would have been against the organisation of Trade Unions, fearing their militancy; he believed strongly in self-help not State intervention—though it is true that he would have liked a national system to replace the Poor Laws. He did not believe that an idle man should receive money, but that he should work for them—he believed, not in welfare, but in workfare. He also disliked secular education, wanting a strong Church influence on the educational system. He felt that social injustice could be resolved without militancy. Moreover, though Barnes saw the need for social justice, he saw it as coming from 'the law of Christian kindness', not from the works of humanistic and often atheistic thinkers, the most extreme of whom was Marx. Moreover, his Christian faith, though making him want social justice, also made him conservative, or rather traditional, in terms of personal morality and responsibility. He was opposed to divorce and we can imagine that he would have rejected outright even the possibility of abortion, let alone other morally permissive legislative changes. And, significantly, these have been introduced in our own times in a consensus by both Conservative and Labour governments, as if to demonstrate how little difference there is between them at least in this field.

Would then Barnes have found a place as a centrist? We think not, for Barnes was never wishy-washy. He was a man of deep principles, traditional in family matters, but looked for balance and justice in social and economic affairs—and as we have already mentioned, he saw this balance coming from an enlightened—Christian—squirearchy.

We have in fact then confirmed our initial intuition that speculation as to how Barnes would vote were he alive today, is indeed pointless. What then can be our conclusion of Barnes' political views?

Barnes was too deep and principled a thinker to feel comfortable in a political party. He was a man of tradition, not simply a conservative, though we might on the one hand be tempted to call him a Christian or High Tory in the sense that he believed in paternalism—source of social justice. But then, on the other hand, Barnes' paternalism was such that we might be tempted to call him a 'proto-socialist'. His politics were not so much linear as circular, for his Old Tory paternalism was that of social justice. Indeed in modern jargon, were he alive today, he might perhaps have been called a 'communitarian', but in a much deeper and sincerer sense than those who glibly label themselves with this term today—as we have seen in his original version of **'The Times'**: 'But God ya know is *var us al*'. What can be more communitarian than this? The Fatherhood of God brings the Brotherhood of Man. Again in his poem **'Fellowship'** he wrote of this sense of community so much stronger among the poor than among the rich:

> But we, wherever we do come,
> Ha' fellowship o' hands wi' lwoads,
> An' fellowship o' veet on roads,
> An' lowliness ov house an' hwome,
> An' fellowship in hwomely feäre,
> An' hwomely clothes vor daily wear;
> An' zoo mid [so might] Heaven bless the mwore
> The worken poor wi' fellowship.

As we have already seen, Barnes regretted the loss of the Old English elite, the 'atheldom' or nobility of Saxon England, who, alone respected and were respected by the Saxon folk. And much of the tragedy in English society was the absence of an elite organically—racially—linked to the people and the presence of a foreign elite, an ultimately Norman-imposed Establishment. Not, after eight centuries, Norman by race, but Norman by value. One writer and poet working a full generation after Barnes' death, Maurice Hewlett, put it thus: 'The governing class is by race even now preponderatingly Latin-French with a Scandinavian admixture; by tradition, breeding and education it is entirely so. All the apparatus, all the science, all the circumstances of government are still Norman'.[10]

Barnes in fact envisioned a society so traditional that there would be no need for socialism; the folk of England would have found it in the 'law of Christian kindness' as applied by the protective lord of the Saxon hall and the fatherly married priest of the Saxon church, both lost with the imposition of feudalism, the Norman baron with his castle and the Norman warrior-bishop with his palace. For the spiritual rebirth of Saxon lords and Saxon priests Barnes looked to an enlightened nineteenth century Christian squirearchy and clergy. In fact Barnes' politics were Saxon politics. This is why he can in no way be fitted into the party political system, either of his time or of ours. This is why he can be called both a populist and a traditionalist. Barnes was outside the system, and probably felt politics to be needless. Social and economic justice would not be delivered by political hacks (and it is true that they never have been) but only by an elite of 'squires' and clergy incarnating 'the law of Christian kindness'. His Saxon social and economic values amounted to Saxon politics, which can perhaps be best summed up by his own thoroughly unpolitical confession of faith: 'My work is peace and salvation'.[11]

Politically Barnes confessed a strand of English patriotism that runs discreetly and often unseen throughout English history, culture and thought. As a postscriptum to this overview of Barnes' political vision and values, it is not without interest to ask whether he has any followers today. Curiously enough, and only recently, one Member of Parliament has spoken in a way which reflects some considerable part of Barnes' views. A contemporary rebel, Sir Richard Body, has written thus: 'Surely Englishness is grounded on Anglo-Saxon values. Before the Normans came to conquer and corrupt, England was far more democratic than today; everyone's voice was heard in a society of plain living and plain speaking, where extremes of personal wealth and poverty were not permitted, and where personal freedom abounded, blended with a sense of community. The Anglo-Saxons were libertarian, and believed in vigorous freedom of speech, which led to truth in a trial by jury, as much as in the Witan (the Anglo-Saxon Parliament) . . . Snobbish, conformist, pageant-adoring and hard of heart, the Normans introduced a contrast . . . the Norman tradition—conformist, regulated and authoritarian'.[12] . . .

Notes for "Politics"

[1] 'Humilis Domus', *Poole and Dorset Herald* (PDH), 24/5/1849

[2] op. cit.

[3] *Views of Labour and Gold (VLG)*, p.58

[4] Sermon on the Day of Humiliation, p.39, Scrapbook 2 in the Dorset County Museum Barnes Archive.

[5] *Notes on Ancient Britain and the Britons*, p.13

[6] Education in Words and in Things, *Gentleman's Magazine* January, p.22

[7] *VLG* p.170

[8] Bernard Jones, *The Poems* Vol.I, pp. xiii-xv

[9] *VLG* p.70

[10] Maurice Hewlett, Preface to 'The Song of the Plow', 1916

[11] Sermon on the Day of Humiliation

[12] *New Statesman & Society*

FURTHER READING

Biographies

Badham-Thornhill, D. G. B. *William Barnes of Dorset.* Beaminster, Dorset: J. Stevens Cox, 1964, 19 p.
   Brief sketch of Barnes's life.

Baxter, Lucy. *The Life of William Barnes: Poet and Philologist.* London and New York: Macmillan and Co., 1887, 98 p.
   Biography by Barnes's daughter which endeavors to explore both the scholarly and poetic sides of his character.

Colloms, Brenda. "The Rev. William Barnes: Parson, Poet and Philologist, 1801-1886." In *Victorian Country Parsons*, pp. 124-51. Lincoln: University of Nebraska Press, 1977.
   Details Barnes's life and the critical reception of his works.

Hardy, Thomas. "The Rev. William Barnes, B. D." *The Athenaeum* 2, No. 3077 (October 16, 1886): 501-02.
   Laudatory biographical sketch by Barnes's fellow Dorset poet.

Hearl, Trevor W. *William Barnes, 1801-1886: The Schoolmaster.* Dorset: Longmans (Dorchester) Ltd., 1966, 355 p.
   Discusses Barnes's career as an educator, presenting "a livelier, if more complex, personality than that popularly associated with the gentle and aged poet of nature."

Jacobs, Willis D. *William Barnes Linguist.* Albuquerque: University of New Mexico Press, 1952, 87 p.
   Biography that focuses on Barnes's extensive philological research and writings.

Wallis, C. J. "Early Manhood of William Barnes, the Dorset Poet." *The Gentleman's Magazine* CCLXV (July-December 1888): 23-40.
   Biographical sketch covering the years from Barnes's birth until 1840, primarily focused on the poet's marriage and early career as a schoolteacher.

Criticism

Davies, Aneirin Talfan. "William Barnes: Friend of Thomas Hardy." *Monographs on the Life, Times and Works of Thomas Hardy*, No. 30 (1967): 1-12.

Concentrates on Barnes's lifelong interest in Welsh language, literature, and history.

Gachelin, Jean-Marc. "The Ultimate Purist." *English Today*, No. 10 (April-June 1987): 34-36.

Focuses on Barnes's disdain for the English adoption of French, Latin, and Greek words rather than of Anglo-Saxon vocabulary.

Heath-Stubbs, John. "The Regionalists—The End of a Tradition." In *The Darkling Plain: A Study of the Later Fortunes of Romanticism in English Poetry from George Darley to W. B. Yeats*, pp. 62-97. London: Eyre & Spottiswoode, 1950.

Briefly mentions Barnes as part of a survey of regional English poets.

Jacobs, Willis D. "A Word-Hoard for Folkdom." *The Arizona Quarterly* 15, No. 1 (Spring 1959): 157-61.

Recounts Barnes's protest of Latinized English vocabulary.

Jones, Bernard. "William Barnes on Lindley Murray's English Grammar." *English Studies* 64, No. 1 (February 1983): 30-35.

Remarks on Barnes's critique of Murray's *English Grammar Adapted to the Different Classes of Learners* (1795) in Barnes's own *Philological Grammar*.

Keith. W. J. "Thomas Hardy's Edition of William Barnes." *Victorian Poetry* 15, No. 2 (Summer 1977): 121-31.

Examines Hardy's editorship of *Select Poems of William Barnes* and discusses what Hardy's deletions suggest about the opposing worldviews of both writers.

Lindgren, Charlotte. "Barnes and Whittier, Early Folklorists." *Tennessee Folklore Society Bulletin* LXVII, No. 2 (June 1981): 67-75.

Investigates the parallel roles of Barnes and John Greenleaf Whittier as poetic preservationists of folklore.

Patmore, Coventry. "An English Classic, William Barnes." *The Fortnightly Review*, No. CCXXXIX (November 1, 1886): 659-70.

Survey of Barnes's poetry occasioned by his death, in which Patmore suggests that the Dorset poet's works should be hailed as classics of English literature.

Powys, Llewelyn. "William Barnes." In *Thirteen Worthies*, pp. 193-208. New York: American Library Service, 1923.

Emphasizes the gentle pathos and loveliness of Barnes's verse.

Quiller-Couch, Sir Arthur. "William Barnes." In *The Poet as Citizen and Other Papers*, pp. 174-96. Cambridge: Cambridge University Press, 1934.

Evaluation of Barnes's poetry that praises his poetic celebration of rural speech.

Sutton, Max Keith. "Truth and the Pastor's Vision in George Crabbe, William Barnes, and R. S. Thomas." In *Survivals of Pastoral*, edited by Richard F. Hardin, pp. 33-59. Lawrence: University of Kansas Publications, 1979.

Includes a discussion of the harmonious influence of the pastoral tradition in the poetry of Barnes.

"William Barnes, the Dorsetshire Poet." *Macmillan's Magazine* 6, No. 32 (June 1862): 154-63.

Divides Barnes's poetry into lyrics, idylls, and eclogues, while discussing the advantages offered by the Dorset dialect in these works.

Zietlow, Paul. "Thomas Hardy and William Barnes: Two Dorset Poets." *PMLA* 84, No. 2 (March 1969): 291-303.

Studies Barnes's influence on Thomas Hardy and compares the work of both poets.

Additional coverage of Barnes's life and career is contained in the following source published by The Gale Group: *Dictionary of Literary Biography,* Vol. 32.

Hugh Blair

1718-1800

Scottish preacher, professor, rhetorician, and literary critic.

INTRODUCTION

Hugh Blair is known primarily for his book *Lectures on Rhetoric and Belles Lettres* (1783), which originated as a series of lectures on composition and rhetoric that he delivered at the University of Edinburgh for almost a quarter-century. *Lectures* was translated into many languages, becoming an internationally acknowledged text used to educate generations of students. Blair also took center stage in the literary controversy of the day, garnering dubious honors for his essay *A Critical Dissertation on the Poems of Ossian, the son of Fingal* (1763), in which he staunchly, but erroneously, defended the authenticity of the poems translated by James Macpherson. Blair was one of the leading members of the Moderate clergy and was considered to be the most popular preacher of eighteenth-century Scotland. His sermons were valued for their warmth, eloquence, and sound morality; several volumes of his *Sermons* (1777-1801) were published worldwide. The overwhelming success of *Lectures* and *Sermons* ensured that Blair's views on matters of literature, morality, and taste held sway well into the nineteenth century.

Biographical Information

Born on April 7, 1718 in Edinburgh, Scotland, Blair was the only child of John Blair and Martha Ogston. At the age of eight, Blair attended the High School of Edinburgh, undertaking a rigorous five-year course of study that included grammar, Latin, and classical rhetoric. In the autumn of 1730, he entered the University of Edinburgh, where he eventually earned a Master of Arts degree. In 1741, the Presbytery of Edinburgh licensed Blair to preach, and he was soon called to serve in a number of prominent churches. Blair married his cousin and childhood companion, Katherine Bannatine in 1748. He kept company with the leading literary men of Edinburgh, becoming friends with David Hume, Adam Smith, Alexander Carlyle, and Henry Home, Lord Kames. Intent on advancing cultural interests, they formed various literary organizations such as the Select Society, the Royal Society of Edinburgh, and the spirited Poker Club. At the age of forty, Blair became the Minister of the High Church of St. Giles in Edinburgh, the most distinguished pulpit in eighteenth-century Scotland. In 1759 Blair began his public lec-

tures on composition and rhetoric in Edinburgh, and soon established his reputation as a teacher. King George III, impressed by Blair's achievements, appointed him the first Regius Professor of Rhetoric and Belles Lettres at the University of Edinburgh in 1762. Blair delivered his lectures to eager students for the next twenty-one years. Shortly after Blair's retirement in 1783, incomplete and often inaccurate copies of students' notes of the lectures began to circulate, so he determined to publish them as *Lectures on Rhetoric and Belles Lettres* in order that they might be preserved in their entirety. Despite Blair's advancing years, he continued to assist aspiring writers who came to him for advice or judgment of their work, including poet Robert Burns. Blair died after a short illness on December 27, 1800. He is buried near Greyfriars Church.

Major Works

Blair's *Lectures on Rhetoric and Belles Lettres* is comprised of forty-seven lectures that cover such topics as taste, language, style, eloquence, critical analysis, and the rules of composition. Blair distilled the teachings of such writers as Aristotle, Longinus, Cicero, and Quintilian and merged them with his own thoughts, maintaining that while the lectures were not "wholly original," neither were they merely a compilation of others' work. At a time when interest in literature and the teaching of writing and speaking were piqued, Blair's lectures offered the most comprehensive view of the subject. Blair also embarked on a number of literary projects, editing an eight-volume edition of the *Works of Shakespear* (1753), the first to be issued in Scotland, as well as the volume *Sermons on Several Important Subjects* (1753), a collection of the late Frederick Carmichael's sermons. In 1763, Blair found himself embroiled in the authorship controversy that surrounded James Macpherson's translations of the poems of Ossian, a third-century Scottish poet. Blair had previously edited Macpherson's *Fragments of Ancient Poetry*, and had provided him with financial support to further his search for Gaelic poetry. Convinced of the Ossian poems' authenticity, Blair defended their beauty and antiquity in *A Critical Dissertation on the Poems of Ossian, the son of Fingal* (1763), going so far as to compare them to the works of Homer. The debate raged on, however, and Blair further attempted to sway the naysayers by expanding his original text and adding an appendix which contained the results of an inquiry he had conducted and vouchers of Ossianic authenticity. His new *Dissertation* (1765) was published with the second edition of *Ossian*. The poems were later found to have been the work of Macpherson. In 1762, Blair supervised the forty-four volume edition of *The British Poets*, an anthology that contained works by twenty-one representative poets, including Milton, Swift, and Addison, among others. By 1777, Blair had published his first volume of *Sermons*. Three more volumes soon followed. At the age of 82, Blair recomposed many of his sermons for a fifth volume of *Sermons*, which was printed posthumously in 1801 as part of a five-volume set.

Critical Reception

Translated into French, German, Italian, Dutch, and Spanish, Blair's *Lectures* became an internationally known textbook on rhetorical theory and literature. Indeed, more than one hundred and thirty editions were published after 1783. In spite of the book's popularity, many critics have faulted Blair's lack of originality and failure to develop his own rhetorical theory. While George Saintsbury praised Blair's survey of Belle Lettres as "ingenious and correct," he assailed Blair's general view of literature, claiming that "the eighteenth-century blinkers are drawn as close as possible," and accused him of "positive historical ignorance." Harold F. Harding, however, has defended Blair's elementary approach, pointing out that his task

was a limited one—to help students become proficient in the art of writing—and that he "knew he was speaking to college students, most of whom were lads of fifteen or a little older." Moreover, in response to insinuations that Blair plagiarized the lectures of Adam Smith, which Blair had attended in 1748, Harding has argued that although striking similarities between Blair's notes and Smith's lectures exist, the differences in content and style are significant enough to negate such charges.

Despite the heated debate over the authenticity of the Ossian poems, Blair's *Critical Dissertation on the Poems of Ossian* was held in high esteem at the time it was published; in fact, it made him famous throughout Europe. But G. H. Cowling echoed the sentiments of most critics when he stated that Blair had defended the poems "with more patriotism than judgement and with more enthusiasm than taste. . . ." Saintsbury further condemned Blair's *Dissertation* as "absolutely uncritical," faulting him for failing to examine any evidence regarding the authenticity of the Ossian poems. Nevertheless, the essay is still included as a preface to most editions of Macpherson's *Poems of Ossian*.

Blair's five volumes of *Sermons*, advocating tolerance, politeness, and the gospel of sensibility, were counted among the century's best sellers not only in Scotland, but in England and America as well. Numerous editions were published and many nineteenth-century anthologies reprinted individual sermons. Critic John Dwyer has attributed Blair's popularity as a Scottish moralist to "the fact that [his] pulpit discourse hit the mood and fashion of the times." His sentimental sermons, however, fell out of favor with the advent of the Victorian era's religious fervor.

PRINCIPAL WORKS

A Poem Sacred to the Memory of the Reverend Mr. James Smith, Principal of the University of Edinburgh, and one of the Ministers of the City (poem) 1736
Dissertatio Philosophica Inauguralis, De Fundamentis & Obligatione Legis Naturae: . . . (essay) 1739
The Wrath of Man Praising God (sermon) 1746
The Resurrection [with George Bannatine under the joint pseudonym William Douglas, M.D.] (poem) 1747
The Importance of Religious Knowledge to the Happiness of Mankind (sermon) 1750
The Works of Shakespear 8 vols. [editor] (drama) 1753
Sermons on Several Important Subjects [editor] (sermon) 1753
Observations on a Pamphlet, entitled An Analysis of the Moral and Religious Sentiments contained in the

Writings of Sopho, [ie. Lord Kames], *and David Hume, Esq; &c.* (essay) 1755

Objections against the Essays on Morality and Natural Religion Examined (essay) 1756

Fragments of Ancient Poetry, collected in the Highlands of Scotland and translated from the Galic or Erse Language [editor] (poetry) 1760

*A Critical Dissertation on the Poems of Ossian, the son of Fingal (criticism) 1763

The British Poets [editor] (poetry) 1773

Sermons Vol. I-IV (sermons) 1777-94

Lectures on Rhetoric and Belles Lettres 2 vols. (lectures) 1783

The Compassion and Beneficence of the Deity (sermon) 1796

Sermons 5 vols. (sermons) 1801

*A revised version of *A Critical Dissertation on the Poems of Ossian, the son of Fingal,* in which Blair expanded the text and added an appendix, was published with the second edition of Macpherson's *Ossian* in 1765.

CRITICISM

Anonymous (essay date 1800)

SOURCE: "Dr. Hugh Blair," in *Public Characters, or Contemporary Biography*, Bonsal and Niles, 1803, pp. 237-49.

[*In the following excerpt, originally written in 1800, the author describes the development of Blair's career as a preacher and a scholar, noting that he was "regarded as one of the rising literary ornaments of his country."*]

He [Dr. Hugh Blair] was completely and regularly educated at the University of Edinburgh, where he took his degree of M. A. and entered into orders in the year 1742. The medical sciences, even before that period, had begun to be taught in that illustrious school with eminent ability and success. Pure and mixed mathematics were then recommended to students by the genius and scientific ardour of Maclaurin, the friend of Newton, and the best interpreter of the Newtonian phIlosophy. Logic, ethics, the principles of classical and elegant literature, as well as theology, were, perhaps, explained with inferior ability and reputation. But all these last mentioned branches of knowledge had been already illustrated by great writers in the English language, whose works were admired and fondly studied by every *ingenious* scholar among the Scots. This was, indeed, the very æra at which the Scots in general first began to discard their own dialect from all their more elaborate compositions, and to aspire to write solely in pure and clas-

sical English. Arbuthnot, Thomson, Mallet, and several other natives of Scotland, whom the fortune of life carried to fix their residence in England, had distinguished themselves in the very foremost ranks of English literature: and all the studious youth of Scotland were not eagerly fixing their eyes on these great examples, and aspiring to emulate their fame. David Hume, the historian, and Henry Home, Lord Kaimes, published about this time, their earliest works. It was at this æra, too, that the Latin language began to give place to the use of the English, in the academical *prelections,* and in the mutual converse between the professors and their pupils at all the Scottish Universities.

Blair, as was related by an old fellow-student of his who is since dead, did not particularly distinguish himself during the first years of his residence in the University by any uncommon literary enthusiasm, or singularly intense application. But soon after he had entered upon the study of theology, his genius began distinctly to *unfold* itself, and to assume that peculiar bias under which it was to act in its *future* exertions. His first exercise in theology displayed an elegance of composition and a justness of taste and sentiment which excited the emulation of the most eminent among his fellow-students. Success inflamed that enthusiasm. In the farther progress of his studies, the correctness of his judgment, the refinement of his taste, the vivacity of his fancy, and the general elegance of his genius, became continually more conspicuous.

At the time when he was licensed as a preacher of the presbyterian church of Scotland, even the first discourses which he delivered in public from the pulpit, were at once reckoned to excel almost every thing of the same kind that had been hitherto heard in Scotland.

It must indeed be owned that, until Blair and some of his contemporaries arose, the style of preaching which was most prevalent in the Scottish pulpits, did not very widely differ from that of the famous *Friar Gerurd.*

It was common for the Scottish clergy to value themselves upon the length, the loudness, the extemporary effusion, the mingled mysticism and vulgarity, the canting recitation of their sermons, much more than upon any of those qualities which can alone gain the approbation of rational piety and true taste. The congregations to which those sermons were addressed agreed in the estimation of their merits. A considerable share of fortitude and manliness of mind that could scorn injudicious censure or applause, was therefore requisite in the young preacher who aspired to distinguish himself by a more legitimate excellence. There was manly virtue, no less than taste and genius, in the choice of Mr. Blair. He quickly found his reward in the approbation of all the best judges of pulpit eloquence. He was regarded as one of the rising literary ornaments of his country; and, in the year 1742 was presented to the rural benefice of Collessie, in the county of Fife.

The ardour with which many of the Scottish clergy applied to study in their earlier years is entirely relaxed as soon as they obtain a *living* in the church. Blair's successful promotion augmented his diligence, and enlivened his desire to arise to more eminent distinction by the culture of pulpit-eloquence and polite literature. About this time he renewed and made more intimately familiar his acquaintance with the Greek and Roman classics, read, with the care of emulation, the most eloquent sermons of the divines of France and England, and endeavoured anxiously to furnish himself with a rich store of genuine English phraseology, by the diligent perusal of the writings of the classical Atterbury, Swift and Bolingbroke. But of all the helps to excellence which he now cultivated, it is probable that the most useful was his confining himself rigorously to do upon all occasions of composition and of preaching, his best; never to suffer sloth, a presumptuous confidence in his talents, nor scorn for those before whom he was to make an effort, to betray him into negligence. This honest and manly care soon became, with him, a fixed and predominant habit: and to it, more perhaps than to any thing else, is to be attributed the greatness of his subsequent success.

From Collessie he was in a short time translated to be minister of Cannongate, in the city of Edinburgh. From Cannongate he was afterwards translated successively to those other ecclesiastical charges in the city, which were accounted more easy, more honourable, of higher emolument, till in the year 1758, he was appointed first minister of that which is called the *high church,* the most respectable clerical situation in the kingdom.

About this time he received the compliment of the degree of D. D. from the University of St. Andrew's, the oldest University in Scotland; and in the year 1761, he was created a Professor in the University, and began to read almost the first course of *Lectures upon the Principles of Literary Composition,* which were delivered in Scotland. Only Dr. Adam Smith, the celebrated author of the Wealth of Nations, had read to a respectable audience a series of discourses not very dissimilar to those of Blair upon *Rhetoric and elegant Literature.* Smith had discontinued the prosecution of this undertaking, and had been appointed to the professorship of moral philosophy in the University of Glasgow, before Blair had began to read his **Lectures on Rhetoric and Belles Lettres** in Edinburgh. Blair's undertaking was patronised, as it deserved, by all those persons in Edinburgh who were the most eminent for science, taste, and high rank.

The celebrated Henry Home, Lord Kaimes, and David Hume, the historian, were among the most zealous of those who laboured to promote the lecturer's success. His Majesty was soon after induced to endow a professorship of rhetoric and belles lettres in the University of Edinburgh, and to nominate Blair the first professor. The number of the students who resorted to hear his lectures continually encreased. His classroom was usually crouded; and it was universally allowed that no course of lectures delivered in the University could be more beneficial to the hearers.

He from this time continued, agreeably to the general practice of the University, to deliver them every winter, for above twenty years, till, for the reasons given in the Preface to his printed **Lectures,** he chose to resign, and became *professor emeritus.*[1]

While he continued to discharge the duties of one of the ministers of the city, and professor of rhetoric and belles lettres in the University of Edinburgh, he was at length encouraged to court the suffrages of the British Public, in the character of an author. His first publication was *A Critical Dissertation on the Poems of Ossian.* These poems are fragments of ballads in the *Scoto-Celtic* language, and of uncertain antiquity. It is now generally believed, that Macpherson, the translator and publisher of these Fragments, must have altered them, in his publication, with a very improper and unfaithful licence, which leaves it almost impossible to distinguish what parts of his translation are genuine, and what parts forged by the pretended translator. But whatever might have been done, Blair engaged himself in the controversy, and became the avowed champion of Macpherson. Blair's dissertation simply illustrates beauties in these poems, of which the existence was never questioned, but of which the nature was never more happily explained. This **Dissertation on the Poems of Ossian** is, perhaps, the finest critical composition in the English language. It combines the precision and acuteness of Aristotle with the eloquence of Longinus. No critic was ever more remarkable than Dr. Blair in this Essay, the great sublime which he draws. It has passed through many editions, and is now usually prefixed to the *Poems of Ossian.*

In the year 1777, he published a volume of sermons, universally admired as they were delivered from the pulpit. His sermons had already become the objects of very general imitation among the younger clergy of the Scottish church. In combination with his lectures, they had begun to accomplish a general change in the character of the pulpit-eloquence of Scotland.

Blair sent the manuscript to a celebrated Bookseller of London (Mr. Strahan) who, after keeping it some time, wrote a letter to him, discouraging the publication. This is one of the many instances of the unpropitious state of the most successful books that have appeared. Mr. Strahan by some accident lent one of the sermons to

Dr. Johnson for his opinion; and, after his unfavourable letter to Dr. Blair had been sent off, he received a note from Johnson, of which the following is a paragraph:

I have read over Dr. Blair's first sermon, with more than approbation; to say it is good is to say too little.

Very soon after this time Mr. Strahan had a conversation with Dr. Johnson concerning them, and then he very candidly wrote to Dr. Blair, enclosing Dr. Johnson's note, and agreeing to purchase the volume, for which he and Mr. Cadell gave *fifty pounds.* The sale was so rapid and extensive, and the approbation of the Public so high, as more than to gratify the Bookseller's warmest hopes of profit from it: to their honour be it recorded, they made Dr. Blair a present of fifty pounds some time after its publication.

The Public in general no sooner saw these sermons in print, than they were all of the same mind as Dr. Johnson in regard to their merit. Her Majesty having heard one of Dr. Blair's Sermons read to her by the late excellent Earl of Mansfield, the great patron of Scottish genius, was pleased to settle on the author a pension of 200*l.* sterling per annum: At the time when he retired from the discharge of the public duty of lecturer in the University of Edinburgh, an addition of 100*l.* a year was added to his pension.

The first edition was quickly sold. It became *fashionable* with all ranks, with both sexes, even with those who scarcely read any other books on the subject of morality and religion, to read, with real or affected eagerness, the *Sermons of Blair.* New editions were rapidly multiplied. The Clergy of the Church of England were induced, in many instances, to read these discourses to their congregations from the pulpit, instead of new compositions of their own. Such success made the Bookseller solicit, with great eagerness, other sermons from Blair for publication. In compliance with these solicitations, and with the general voice of all that was respectable in public opinion, Dr. Blair published a second volume for which he received 200*l.* copy-money. Since that time the whole sum for both these volumes was made up 500*l.*

When he proposed a third volume of sermons, the Booksellers at once offered him 600*l.* for the copyright of that single volume. It is also confidently reported, that for the fourth volume he received 2000*l.* sterling. These volumes have had an astonishing success, not only in Great Britain, but all over Europe. There have been frequently surreptitious editions reprinted, in their original language, in both Ireland and America. In the French language there are two editions of them; one in the Dutch; one in the German, by Mr. Sach, Chaplain to the King of Prussia;[2] one in the Sclavonich, or Hungarian: and there is at this time a translation in considerable forwardness in the Italian.

About the year 1783, Dr. Blair, who was then considerably advanced in years, was, at his own desire, as before stated, permitted to retire from the exercise of his duties as Professor of rhetoric and belles lettres, but his salary was continued for life. Upon this event he began to revise and prepare his *Lectures* for publication from the press, as several imperfect copies of them, composed chiefly of notes taken by students who heard them read, were circulated; and, to prevent their being sent into the world in an imperfect or erroneous form, he was induced to publish them.

"In composing them," he says, "as a public professor, he thought it his duty to communicate to his pupils not only original, but useful matter." The world received them with the same eager curiosity and approbation with which they had been heard in his classroom. It was universally confessed that no language, ancient or modern, possessed among the stores of its literature a system of critical rules and of principles for the formation and the direction of taste, at once so judicious, so comprehensive, and so faultlessly elegant. These *Lectures* were soon translated, like Dr. Blair's other works, into several other European languages, and reprinted in America and Ireland, as well as in Britain. They have passed through six successive editions in the hands of the original publishers. They have been abridged and extracted into a number of compilations, possessing no other merits of such utility as that which is derived from them. No work has been hitherto produced in English to supersede or rival them. They display sometimes originality, always justness of thought, without being deformed by any excess of ornament. They are written in the most ornate style that the *didactic* species of composition can legitimately employ. There is no other book which will afford a more comprehensive view to persons who are studying *to correct a bad taste, or to form a good one* for the beauties of composition or public speaking. Dr. Blair received for the copy-right from Mr. Cadell 1500*l.* sterling.

In 1796, Dr. Blair published *The Compassionate Beneficence of the Deity,* a Sermon preached before the Society instituted for the benefit of the Sons of the Clergy of the established Church of Scotland, price 1s. 6*l.* but since prefixed to the fourth volume of his Sermons. This elegant discourse appeared with the peculiar advantage of a strong prepossession in favour of the writer. It was expected, as coming from Dr. Blair on so interesting an occasion, to be an excellent discourse: nor has the public been disappointed. The representation here given of the character of the Almighty, as the friend of the distressed, is very impressive; and unequivocal recommendation is bestowed on it when it is pronounced, that this sermon, instead of diminishing [will] add additional lustre to the author's merit as an author of sermons. . . .

Notes

[1] Among many distinguished persons who failed not to attend Dr. Blair's lectures in rhetoric was the Prince d' Aschoff, of Russia, son to that lady whose name makes a distinguished figure in the history of those intrigues which placed the late Empress Catharine on the Russian throne. This young nobleman, with his mother, the Princess d'Aschoff, resided some time at Edinburgh, while the Prince went through a course of study in the University. Dr. Blair's politeness made him duly attentive to these illustrious strangers.

[2] Dr. Blair's writings have been no where more highly admired than among the Germans. The late amiable Dr. Zimmerman, whose fine work upon Solitude is universally known and admired, bestows the most impassioned praise upon the effusions of the genius of Blair, and quotes his works as models of the most perfect literary excellence.

George Saintsbury (essay date 1900-04)

SOURCE: "Blair," in *A History of Criticism and Literary Taste in Europe: From the Earliest Texts to the Present Day*, William Blackwood & Sons Ltd., 1949, pp. 462-5.

[*In the following excerpt, originally written between 1900 and 1904, Saintsbury praises Blair's* Lectures on Rhetoric and Belles Lettres, *but finds his view of literature to be narrow.*]

Hugh Blair, . . . in 1759, started . . . the teaching of modern literature in his own country. He had the advantage, as far as securing a popular audience goes, of lecturing in English, and he was undoubtedly a man of talent. The **Lectures on Rhetoric and Belles Lettres**,[1] which were delivered with great *éclat* for nearly a quarter of a century from the Chair of their subject, are very far, indeed, from being devoid of merit. They provide a very solid, if a somewhat mannered and artificial instruction, both by precept and example, in what may be called the "full-dress plain style" which was popular in the eighteenth century. They are as original as could be expected. The critical examination of Addison's style, if somewhat meticulous, is mostly sound, and has, like Johnson's criticisms of Dryden and Pope, the advantage of thorough sympathy, of freedom from the drawback—so common in such examinations—that author and critic are standing on different platforms, looking in different directions, speaking, one may almost say, in mutually incomprehensible tongues. The survey of **Belles Lettres** is, on its own scheme, ingenious and correct: there are everywhere

evidences of love of Literature (as the lover understands her), of good education and reading, of sound sense. Blair is to be very particularly commended for accepting to the full the important truth that "Rhetoric" in modern times really means "Criticism"; and for doing all he can to destroy the notion, authorised too far by ancient critics, and encouraged by those of the Renaissance, that Tropes and Figures are not possibly useful classifications and names, but fill a real arsenal of weapons, a real cabinet of reagents, by the employment of which the practitioner can refute, or convince, or delight, as the case may be.

But with this, and with the further praise due to judicious borrowings from the ancients, the encomium must cease. In Blair's general critical view of literature the eighteenth-century blinkers are drawn as close as possible. From no writer, even in French, can more "awful examples" be extracted, not merely of perverse critical assumption, but of positive historical ignorance. Quite early in the second Lecture, and after some remarks (a little arbitrary, but not valueless) on delicacy and correctness in taste, we find, within a short distance of each other, the statements that "in the reign of Charles II. such writers as *Suckling and Etheridge* were held in esteem for dramatic composition," and later, "If a man shall assert that Homer has no beauties whatever, that he holds him to be a dull and spiritless writer, and that he *would as soon peruse any legend of old knight-errantry* as the *Iliad,* then I exclaim that my antagonist is either void of all taste," &c. Here, on the one hand, the lumping of Suckling and Etherege together, and the implied assumption that not merely Suckling, but Etherege, is a worthless dramatist, gives us one "light," just as the similar implication that "an old legend of knight-errantry" is necessarily an example of dulness, spiritlessness, and absence of beauty, gives us another. That Blair lays down, even more peremptorily than Johnson, and as peremptorily as Bysshe, that the pause in an English line may fall after the 4th, 5th, 6th, or 7th syllable, and no other, is not surprising; and his observations on Shakespeare are too much in the usual "faults-saved-by-beauties" style to need quotation. But that he cites, with approval, a classification of the great literary periods of the world which excludes the Elizabethan Age altogether, is not to be omitted. It stamps the attitude.

These same qualities appear in the once famous but now little read **Dissertation on Ossian**.[2] That, in the sense of the word on which least stress is laid in these volumes, this "Critical Dissertation" is absolutely *un*critical does not much matter. Blair does not even attempt to examine the evidence for and against the genuineness of the work he is discussing. He does not himself know Gaelic; friends (like Hector M'Intyre) have told him that they heard Gaelic songs very like *Ossian* sung in their youth; there are said to be manuscripts; that is enough for him. Even when he cites and compares parallel passages—the ghost-passage and that from the book of Job, Fingal's "I have no son" and *Othello*—which derive their whole beauty from exact coincidence with the Bible or Shakespeare, he will allow no kind of suspicion to cross his mind. But this we might let pass. It is in the manner in which he seeks to explain the "amazing degree of regularity and art," which he amazingly ascribes to Macpherson's redaction, the "rapid and animated style," the "strong colouring of imagination," the "glowing sensibility of heart," that the most surprising thing appears. His citations are as copious as his praises of them are hard to indorse. But his critical argument rests almost (not quite) wholly on showing that *Fingal* and *Temora* are worked out quite properly on Aristotelian principles by way of central action and episode, and that there are constant parallels to Homer, the only poet whom he will allow to be Ossian's superior. In short, he simply applies to *Ossian* Addison's procedure with *Paradise Lost*. The critical piquancy of this is double. For we know that *Ossian* was powerful—almost incredibly powerful—all over Europe in a sense quite opposite to Blair's; and we suspect, if we do not know, that Mr James Macpherson was quite clever enough purposely to give it something of the turn which Blair discovers. . . .

Notes

[1] The first ed. is that of Edinburgh, 1783: mine is that of London, 1823.

[2] I have it with *The Poems of Ossian*, 2 vols., London, 1796. Blair had taken Macpherson under his wing as early as 1760.

G. H. Cowling (essay date 1925)

SOURCE: "The English Teaching of Dr. Hugh Blair," in *Anglica: Untersuchungen zur englischen Philologie,* Mayer & Muller, 1925, pp. 281-94.

[*In the excerpt below, Cowling lauds Blair's method of literary criticism and his approach to teaching English composition.*]

Dr. Hugh Blair (1718-1800), a graduate of Edinburgh and minister of St. Giles' Church, was the arbiter of taste in polite literature in the northern capital, and the friend of Robertson, Hume and Adam Smith. The most celebrated preacher of his day, he published several volumes of sermons, praised most highly in that age for their sound morality and their 'continuous warmth', and valued even more perhaps for their graceful eloquence. He was appointed the first Professor of Rhetoric and Belles Lettres in the University of Edinburgh in 1762, and signalized his accession to the chair by his *Critical Dissertation on the Poems of Ossian* (1765),

in which with more patriotism than judgement he defended the authenticity of the poems, and with more enthusiasm than taste ascribed to that mythical bard "the two chief ingredients in poetical genius", namely strength of feeling, and ability to describe naturally.

For twenty one years he lectured to appreciative audiences, composed not entirely of undergraduates, for Dr. Blair had more than a local reputation, witness the visit which Dr. Samuel Johnson paid him; and visitors of many kinds, graduates, advocates, parsons, Englishmen on their travels, and so forth, were attracted to his lectures. When on his retirement from the chair of Rhetoric and Belles Lettres in 1783 Dr. Blair published his *Lectures* in three volumes, their success was immediate. They passed through twelve editions between 1783 and 1812, and a thirteenth edition in one volume was published in 1830. But they were overwhelmed by the flood tide of the romantic movement, and during the nineteenth century the name of Blair was forgotten except to vilify. Yet Blair's *Lectures on Rhetoric and Belles Lettres* are not without interest, and the book has several positive merits. It is the first published record of the modern academic teaching of English. It is moreover a good example of that formal and regular code of literary criticism which commended itself to the common-sense minds of the eighteenth century, and may prove a wholesome influence still.

Englishmen bred in the romantic tradition were fortunate indeed, if they were not taught to regard the literary judgement of the age of reason and enlightenment as shallow and pedantic; but, happily, fashions change in literature as well as in dress, and in this twentieth century, to most of us, the romantic and impressionistic critics of the nineteenth century are no longer so comprehensive and authoritative, nor the disciples of Aristotle and Quintilian so superficial, as once they seemed. Even in England the principles of literary theory and of literary criticism are being again stated by Lascelles Abercrombie, Middleton Murry, and T. S. Eliot; and it is not unlikely therefore that Blair's *Lectures* may find an interested audience once more. Indeed, in spite of the views of publishers, I think the time is ripe for another edition, or at least a selection of the *Lectures,* if only for their historical importance. For there is much to be said in favour of Dr. Blair. He said gracefully what he meant, and he meant exactly what he said. No teacher ever made the study of English Composition more pleasant, nor the principles of literary criticism more rational.

As specimens of the beginnings of the teaching of English Language and Literature in the University of Edinburgh, these lectures have an historical importance. Dr. Blair taught English as a delicately precise means for the elegant representation of sane and suitable thoughts. The language was presented, not primarily as a subject of historical interest or scientific investigation, but as an artistic medium for the exercise of good taste in prose or verse composition; and as a means for the expression of that "internal sense of beauty" upon which, according to Blair, taste is founded. Though in his preface he claims that: "He consulted his own ideas and reflections, and a great part of what will be found in these lectures is his own"; he followed the orthodox tradition, adapting Quintilian's principles of composition and structure to the English language and to English eloquence; selecting for his lectures those doctrines and disciplines by which his students might benefit, and rejecting over-elaborate and unprofitable refinements. In composition he recommended perspicuity of thought and expression; and "purity, propriety, and precision" of language, cemented by unity of design. In style he admired that neatness, which, though less plain than the dry style, is yet more elegant than the flowery. His very formality itself induced a certain clear and consistent eloquence which is still pleasing.

His ideal in prose was what he describes as "the neat style". "A writer of this character shews", he tells us in Lecture XVIII, "that he does not despise the beauty of language . . . But his attention is shown in the choice of words . . . rather than in any high efforts of imagination, or eloquence. His sentences are always clean, and free from the incumbrance of superfluous words; of a moderate length; rather inclining to brevity, than a swelling structure; closing with propriety; without any tails or adjections dragging after the proper close. His cadence is varied; but not of the studied musical kind. His figures, if he uses any, are short and correct; rather than bold and glowing". Such a style is Blair's own agreeable mode of expression. His style is the polite English prose of his age, and in his idiom it became a clear and yet vigorous instrument, eminently suitable both for the unostentatious adequacy of his learning, and for the engaging charm of his acknowledged power as a lecturer. Blair's **Lectures on Rhetoric** are for English students a study of the principles of composition, admirable in design and precise in expression, which may still be read with advantage by those who wish to recover the secret of the dignity and elegance of polite English prose.

As a critic, Blair is typical of his age. We can not accept his principles without restatement, but they are not without historical importance. A man of common sense, he stood for the sound taste of the average educated man, rather than for the intense aesthetic experience or the personal impression of a professional book-worm. He was not an appreciator, but a critic. Dr. Blair's is the criticism of urbane common sense. He rejected individual eccentricity. He would have agreed with Addison that: "human nature is the same in all reasonable creatures; and whatever falls in with it will meet with admirers amongst readers of all qualities and conditions". He assumed a general faculty of taste, common to all educable minds, which,

by recognising excellence when it is presented to it, makes a general agreement of opinion possible. "The public", he tells us in Lecture III, "is the supreme judge, to whom the last appeal must be made, in every work of taste; as the standard of taste is founded on the sentiments that are natural and common to all men." The general mind may err for a time, but in the end "the judgement of true criticism and the voice of the public, when once become unprejudiced and dispassionate, will ever coincide at last". "That which men concur in most admiring", he says in Lecture II, "must be held to be beautiful. His taste must be esteemed just and true which coincides with the general sentiments of men. In this standard we must rest. To the sense of mankind the ultimate appeal must ever lie, in all works of Taste." So that, to Blair, the expression of licentious or perverse instincts was mere depravity. "If any one should maintain that sugar was bitter and tobacco was sweet, no reasonings could avail to prove it. The Taste of such a person would infallibly be held to be diseased, merely because it differed so widely from the Taste of the species to which he belongs." It may be that tastes differ, and ought to differ, more than Blair imagined; but he speaks surely as a prophet of democracy. If we disagree with the criticism of common sense, and it is not unlikely that we do, can we agree with him that the public is the supreme judge to whom the last appeal must be made?

He regarded taste as the natural sentiment of mankind, governed by reason, common to all, and as widespread amongst mankind as its sister the moral conscience; differing in degree undoubtedly in different individuals, but in all essentially cultivable by reading and its exercise. Criticism, he tells us in Lecture III, is the application of taste and good sense to literature. Its principles are based on the observation of such excellences as have been found to please mankind generally. Its rules are designed chiefly to show what faults are to be avoided, and its object is to distinguish what is beautiful and what is faulty. And just as, no doubt, he regarded expediency as the basis of moral judgement, so he declared utility to be the test of good literature. "The ultimate end of all poetry, indeed of every composition, should be to make some useful impression on the mind." He held that literature is good in so far as the writer's idiom achieves clearness and grace, and in so far also as the writer's subject and his treatment of it tend to the cultivation of his readers' imagination and power of expression, and to the inculcation of virtue. According to Blair, the greatest literature is that which most enriches the mind.

He had little sympathy with misty theosophy and vague mysticism. He liked perspicuity and precision. "Upon no subject ought any man to write", he declares in Lecture X, "where he cannot think clearly. His ideas indeed may, very excusably, be on some subjects incomplete or inadequate; but still, as far as they go, they ought to be clear; and wherever this is the case, Perspicuity in expressing them is always attainable. The obscurity which reigns so much among many metaphysical writers is, for the most part, owing to the indistinctness of their own conceptions." Philosophers will smile at this, and doubtless the poets will object with some heat; but we must remember Blair's standpoint: he is as a critic associating himself with the average reader, and regarding the author as an artist who is to be judged upon the merits or failings of his work; he never pretends to be an interpreter, understanding and pardoning. He judged in accordance with what were, to him, common sense principles; and he preferred to test the poets by his general principles, rather than to make individual exceptions and special rules for each.

The direct aim of poetry, "the language of passion or of enlivened imagination", is to quicken and to delight the mind. "The primary aim of Poet", he says in Lecture XXXVIII, "is to please, and to move; and therefore it is to the Imagination, and the Passions, that he speaks." But if cultivation of the poetic imagination and fictitious emotions is the direct aim, virtue is an indirect aim of poetry. Blair would not indeed put virtue first. He refused to accept René Bossu's theory of the moral and allegorical origin of epic poetry. A writer who thinks first of the moral "might write, perhaps, useful fables for children", he says in Lecture XLII, "but as to an Epic Poem, if he adventured to think of one, it would be such as would find few Readers".

Nevertheless the poet, according to Blair, should be a virtuous man. "He may, and he ought to have it in his view to instruct and to reform; but it is indirectly, and by pleasing and moving, that he accomplishes this end" (Lecture XXXVIII). He regarded excellence as the child of virtue, and goodness as the natural and fertile soil for the cultivation of the fine flower of beauty. What Blair said, following Quintilian, of the dispositions of orators in Lecture XXXIV, he might have said *mutatis mutandis* of poets. "The sentiments and dispositions particularly requisite for them to cultivate are the following: The love of justice and order, and indignation at insolence and oppression; the love of honesty and truth, and detestation of fraud, meanness, and corruption; magnanimity of spirit; the love of liberty of their Country and the public; zeal for all great and noble designs, and reverence for all worthy and heroic characters. A cold and sceptical turn of mind is extremely adverse to Eloquence: and no less so, is that cavilling disposition which takes pleasure in depreciating what is great, and in ridiculing what is generally admired . . . A true Orator should be a person of generous sentiments, of warm feelings, and of a mind turned towards the admiration of all those great and high objects, which mankind are naturally formed to admire."

Blair's method of literary criticism was formal. He classified the various traditional forms of poetry and prose, and then described of each its particular qualities, its difficulties, and possible excellences; and characterises the work of the chief writers in that form. He rightly saw that sound criticism may not be based on the literature of one age, or on the style of one period. In search of principles thesefore he surveys the works of the poets and writers of "the four ages", the Grecian, the Roman, the Renaissance, and the Augustan. In this critical survey he says much that is sound and well expressed, but little that is surprisingly wise. He has but little to say about the Elizabethans. Shakespeare enters Lecture XLVI as an example of a poet possessed of more genius than taste,— "it is a genius shooting wild; deficient in just taste, and altogether unassisted by knowledge or art . . . All these faults however, Shakespeare redeems by two of the greatest excellences which any Tragic Poet can possess; his lively and diversified paintings of character; his strong and natural expression of passion. These are his two chief virtues; on these his merit rests." Milton takes a higher rank in Blair's opinion, because his taste is equal to his genius; and, as Blair reminds us, "Taste consists in the power of judging; Genius in the power of executing." Milton shows "a grasp of genius equal to every thing that is great; if at some times he falls much below himself, at other times he rises above every poet of the antient or modern world". His "great and distinguishing excellence is his sublimity. In this, perhaps, he excels Homer; as there is no doubt of his leaving Virgil, and every other Poet, far behind him . . . His style is full of majesty, and wonderfully adapted to his subject. His blank verse is harmonious and diversified, and affords the most complete example of the elevation which our language is capable of attaining by the force of numbers . . . Paradise Lost is a poem that abounds with beauties of every kind, and that justly entitles its Author to a degree of fame not inferior to any Poet." Blair surveys the classics of the ancient and the modern world, and yet his criticism of English poetry is almost confined to the writers of the Augustan age from Dryden to Pope. Even Goldsmith appears to be unknown, and Dr. Johnson is only appealed to as a contemporary whose criticisms appear in foot-notes in order to add weight to Blair's own judgements.

In his criticism of individual writers, Blair's method was to construct the "character" of the object of his criticism. As a method of descriptive criticism it is somewhat cold and impersonal, and bears an analogy to a scientific process of analysis and dissection. It lacks of course the poetic fascination of a modern critical fiction which claims to be an "interpretation" of a poet's mind. It lacks even the biographical interest of Dr. Johnson's *Lives of the Poets*. Blair's method was to observe the characteristics of an author in his various works, in his use of literary forms, in his style, and in the individual quality of his mind, and to assemble from these detached observations a critical judgement made in the form of a character, descriptive of the author's qualities, excellences, and defects. Criticism of this academic kind still has its merits, if not as a descriptive formula, as an intellectual exercise. It is observant and analytic, and moreover it avoids undue egoism. It is elementary of course, but it is no demerit that it is within the powers of most students of literature. Imaginative critics may to their own satisfaction, not without fiction and charm, "explain" the significance of artistic personality and the influence of environment, or "interpret" the psychology of poetic experience; but their aim is generally to show how much their thought differs from, not how much it has in common with, that of the average educated man. Dr. Blair assumed that the qualities and excellences which he observed are obvious to all.

As an example of Blair's method of common sense criticism we may refer to his character of Alexander Pope in Lecture XL. "In the enthusiasm, the fire, the force and copiousness of poetic genius, Dryden, though a much less correct Writer, appears to have been superior to him. One can scarce think that he was capable of Epic or Tragic Poetry; but, within a certain limited region, he has been outdone by no Poet. His translation of the Iliad will remain a lasting monument to his honour, as the most elegant and highly finished translation that, perhaps, ever was given of any poetical work. That he was not incapable of tender Poetry, appears from the Epistle of Eloisa to Abelard, and from the verses to the Memory of an Unfortunate Lady, which are almost his only sentimental productions; and which indeed are excellent in their kind. But the qualities for which he is chiefly distinguished are, judgement and wit, with a concise and happy expression, and a melodious versification. Few Poets ever had more wit, and at the same time more judgement, to direct the proper employment of that wit. This renders his Rape of the Lock the greatest masterpiece that perhaps was ever composed in the gay and sprightly Style; and in his serious works, such as his Essay on Man, and his Ethic Epistles, his wit just discovers itself as much as to give a proper seasoning to grave reflections. His imitations of Horace are so peculiarly happy, that one is at a loss whether most to admire the original or the copy; and they are among the few imitations extant that have all the grace and ease of an original. His paintings of characters are natural and lively in a high degree; and never was any Writer so happy in that concise and spirited Style, which gives animation to Satires and Epistles. We are never so sensible of the good effects of rhyme in English verse, as in reading these parts of his works. We see it adding to the Style an elevation which otherwise it could not have possessed; while at the same time he manages it so artfully, that it never appears in the least to encumber him; but on the contrary, serves to increase the liveliness of his manner."

This is a mode of criticism which is at once judicious and judical. It knows its aim, and it carries straight to the mark without a random shot. It has the weight and the completeness of the summing-up of a judge. It is as clear as a creed. Nevertheless it was somewhat narrow, more cognizant of incorrectness and departure from tradition, than appreciative of positive merits and adventurous originality. Of mediocrity it was tolerant, but it tended to be suspicious of original genius, and antagonistic to the warm enthusiasms of youth. Perhaps its greatest defect was that its standard of common sense is inadequate when measured against those idealists who "would rather go to hell with Plato and Lord Bacon" than stoop to conquer heaven with Paley and Sydney Smith. It soars like a kite, bound to earth. "If we are obliged to follow a writer with much care", he says in Lecture X, "to pause, and to read over his sentences a second time in order to comprehend them fully, he will never please us long. Mankind are too indolent to relish so much labour. They may pretend to admire the author's depth, after they have discovered his meaning; but they will seldom be inclined to take up his work a second time." In that respect, Blair was the child of his age, and we now know better than to agree with him; but in spite of his obvious limitations, he has still, I think, something to teach us.

We can no longer accept Blair's neat and pragmatic judgements as the last word in criticism; but his analytic and comparative view of literature is sound, and even his doctrine of common sense may be a wholesome corrective to individualistic and esoteric appreciation. There will always be personal criticism, let us hope; and it has its value as a stimulus to study, and as a delight; but, by reason of its very individuality, its validity is determined solely by the learning and the personality of the critic. For example, what is the value of the statement that the poet X "has a delicacy, when he chooses to be delicate, which is quintessential"; or that the poem Z is "by no means despicable", or has "very high merit". I attack no particular critic: I merely parody a method. For academic purposes, it seems to me, this method has no value. Applied by students, it leads easily to a facile expression of self-satisfied egoism, which is the negation of knowledge. This "drawing-room talk" about authors and books is interesting, and has its place in life no doubt; but it is an unintellectual method of criticism. Nor is the historical method, valuable though it is, wholly satisfactory. To explain the taste of an age in terms of its social history, is merely a disguised form of the materialistic interpretation of history. Accepted wholly, it makes inspiration purely a secular hint. It neglects the essential spirituality of great poetry.

For academic teaching, for the purpose of training students to study literature, do we not need a method which will regard literature as an object of understanding, as well as of taste? And can we not best obtain this academic approach by asking the student to take first an objective view of literature, to rule out personal feeling, and to read an author or a particular work simply as an ordinary reader, endowed only with the common instincts, feelings, likings and aversions of common humanity? I hesitate to dogmatize in a world where dogmatism has little place, and therefore I will speak only in general terms; but the preliminary of criticism, it seems to me, is not so much the gathering of an impression, as an investigation. After reading a work, his desire to understand it should lead the student to study the personality of its author, through biography and letters, in search of the quality and characteristics of his mind. He now begins to delve more deeply than the average reader, but with the same objective view he pursues the intention and purpose of the author, and traces as far as possible the author's conception of his work from the inspiring hint to the final form. He examines the choice of form, and the method of treatment of the subject. He examines the author's idiom, characterises its style, and describes its effects and its qualities. He may compare, if comparison seems worth while, either the characteristics of his author or his work with those of another who offers a likeness or a contrast. He may point out excellences or defects in conception, form, or style, by reference to approved standards of excellence; and finally, after tilling the field, he may reap the crop, which is his own personal estimate of the work, based, not on a whimsy, but on understanding, rational examination, and comparison.

This is a mode of criticism which is at once descriptive and judicial,—descriptive, after examination, of the meaning, conception, form, and intention of the subject; and judicial by reference to common standards of literary excellence. It is elementary, of course, and not final. The student of literature may become a literary historian, or a philosophic critic with methods of his own. He may even become an interpreter, and may criticise with the sympathetic insight of a poet. But these are the winning-posts of a critic's career, and not the starting-points. It is a good thing to learn the value of discipline, not as an end in itself, but as a means to an end. The heritage which the impressionist critics have left us, is that we should begin with "appreciation" and forsake formal criticism. This is to begin at the wrong end. Fine appreciation of literature is the consummate reward of study and developed taste. It is utterly beyond the reach of most young students. In any case the student's appreciation can not be universal. The same mind on the same examination-day ought not to appreciate with equal gusto, and with equal adulation, Shakespeare, Milton, Pope, Wordsworth, Shelley, and Browning. The very supposition is dishonest, and we do wrong to expect it.

Blair founded the teaching of English with excellent intentions. He combined language, composition, and literature. His teaching was practical. His aim was to present English as the material for the use of writers and public speakers, and to describe the principles of selection and arrangement which must be followed, in order to produce the polite style of his age, neat, lucid, and persuasive. The individual mode of expression, the idiom which is the man himself, he wisely left to his students. And in the teaching of composition also, he has still something to say. He stands for well ordered structure, lucidity of expression, and persuasiveness. I cannot help thinking that many of our modern English prose writers would write better after the instruction and discipline of Dr. BLAIR. We have all but lost the secret of the classical English prose style. Much of our contemporary prose is written either anyhow, or with excess of mannerism. The good old ideal of perspicuity is almost forgotten, and our punctuation and our arrangement of words are as haphazard as is our feeling for rhythm and balance. We are in danger of losing the sense of structure in sentence and paragraph. We have no modern English standard prose style, nothing comparable to the conversational prose of the Elizabethans, or to the golden style of English prose. We have merely the individual idioms, some of them good, some of them slipshod, of a miscellaneous crowd of individuals. Now we do not want to make every historian write like Gibbon, and every novelist like Goldsmith or Smollett, and we could not if we would; but in lacking a style,—a temporary and yet distinctive manner of writing,—we lack something which is worth having, if only as a gesture of courtesy. It is a good thing to have an ideal of style,—of style, not of individual idiom, which is something different;—and the acquirement by practice of lucid and just expression, and of the minor arts of arrangement, paragraphing, and punctuation is a discipline which the writer may neglect only at the peril of his art.

The more we try to form an English prose style which is, in Blair's phrase, "neat", and keep our minds set towards precision of word, rhythmical flow of sentence and paragraph, and persuasiveness of form, the greater is the chance which our English has of being forceful and fine. Let even genius learn the drill of composition. After that it may walk as it pleases, but it will walk with an alert step and a free swing. We believe in a standard of spoken English. Why do we fear an ideal of style? I think it must be because we have got into a habit of confusing style with individual idiom. . . .

E. C. Knowlton (essay date 1927)

SOURCE: "Wordsworth and Hugh Blair," in *Philological Quarterly*, Vol. VI, No. 3, July, 1927, pp. 277-81.

[*In the essay below, Knowlton asserts that Wordsworth followed Blair's suggestions for revitalizing pastoral poetry as set forth in the latter's Lecture XXXIX of* Lectures on Rhetoric and Belles Lettres.]

In earlier papers I have set forth suggestions concerning Wordsworth's relations to the type of literature which has been denominated "pastoral."[1] The term has narrow as well as broad meanings. It may be used to include any literature connected primarily with country life. It may refer to the sort of treatment which shepherds and other herdsmen received from Theocritus in his *Idylls,* from Virgil in his *Eclogues,* and from some of their imitators. The atmosphere herein is southern or Italian; the topic is often love; set amid rural scenery, the machinery is often amœbæan and employs nymphs and satyrs. Or the term may be used whenever the literature of any country deals with the life of people like shepherds.

The course of pastoral in the eighteenth century is as familiar to scholars as it was to Wordsworth. That great poet wished to renew the force of the type, to revitalize it for English service.[2] Similar attempts had been made before sporadically; the aridity into which pastoral had fallen from strict imitation of the Greeks and Romans was well known at the time of Pope and Gay. Goldsmith, however, by modifying its scope in *The Deserted Village,* incurred the rebuke of Crabbe, who decided to tell the actual truth about hamlets. Crabbe in turn won the displeasure of Wordsworth, who felt that he misused facts.[3]

A more acceptable critic was Hugh Blair (1718-1800), a professor of rhetoric at the University of Edinburgh from 1760. Not only were his **Sermons** popular from the time of their publication in 1777, but his **Lectures on Rhetoric and Belles Lettres** went through many editions subsequent to their first appearance in print, 1783.[4]

In **Lecture XXXIX** Blair[5] treated at length the nature of pastoral. He gave three purposes for the author of such work: to treat the present reality, to give an imaginary picture of an earlier golden age, to attempt (what is impossible) to combine a picture of that simple and aureate past with the manners of the present, highly cultivated (aristocratic) society. In tracing the history of pastoral in Theocritus, Virgil, Sannazarius, Pope, Phillips, and Gray, he adopted about the same position concerning them as Wordsworth took later.[6] He praised Shenstone. In addition he recommended the reënlivening of pastoral, opposing close imitations of classical models:

> For why may not pastoral poetry take a wider range? Human nature, and human passions, are much the same in every rank of life; and wherever these passions operate on objects that are within the rural

sphere, there may be a proper subject for pastoral. One would indeed choose to remove from this sort of composition the operations of violent and direful passions, and to present such only as are consistent with innocence, simplicity, and virtue. But under this limitation, there will still be abundant scope for a careful observer of nature to exert his genius. The various adventures which give occasion to those engaged in country life to display their disposition and temper; the scenes of domestic felicity or disquiet; the attachment of friends and brothers; the rivalship and competition of lovers; the unexpected successes or misfortunes of families, might give occasion to many a pleasing and tender incident; and were more of the narrative and sentimental intermixed with the descriptive in this kind of poetry, it would become much more interesting than it now generally is, to the bulk of readers.

In a footnote he declared, "The above observations on the barrenness of the common Eclogues were written before any translation from the German had made us acquainted in this country with Gessner's *Idylls,* in which the ideas that had occurred to me for the improvement of pastoral poetry, are fully realized."[7]

The program thus suggested by Blair was much the same as that fulfilled by Wordsworth.[8] The history of pastoral, as I have indicated, is substantially identical for both. The plea for a wider field in which genius might exercise itself was of a kind congenial to a poet who analyzed the function of genius as Wordsworth did in the *Essay Supplementary* of 1815. In treating the passions—a subject of constant interest to him—he laid stress on those consistent with "innocence, simplicity, and virtue," as in *Michael* and in *The Leechgatherer.* The dominant note is by no means jocund, even when the poet praised a Stoic endurance or derived encouragement from unexpected places. *The Idle Shepherd-Boys* shows a sudden turn in events that for youth seems nearly tragic. In fact, the scope may be widened to include *Ruth,* where the main theme falls in line with Blair's desire, because the more sinister or violent aspects of passion remain in the background. Wordsworth similarly pictured scenes of domestic felicity or disquiet; the attachment of brothers, as in *The Brothers;* the unexpected misfortunes of families. Rivalry in love Wordsworth omitted, but the Lucy poems as an elegiac group dwelling on the theme of love and picturing the girl "beside an English fire" are not in conflict with Blair's recommendations. The poet likewise emphasized the narrative element, and, if I understand the sense of the adjective as Blair used it, the sentimental element. That is, he paused for sympathetic reflection or meditation on the circumstances and offered suggestions for the reader's reaction (like those of a Greek chorus). Thus the program supported by Blair was, to a large extent, executed by Wordsworth. At times, to be sure,

Wordsworth went beyond the limits of the tentative program that Blair offered. For instance, the point of view taken resulted in hints for reaction scarcely to be foreseen. A case of this nature is *The Cumberland Beggar,* where the author employed an unhappy situation in individual experience and in social economy, and extracted therefrom the comfort that those who give to the beggar really offer testimony that there are some people who have kindly feelings of a sort which expresses itself in action. And again the poet deepened the poignancy of certain episodes until they became tragic, and at times intimated, as in the last Lucy poem, the vastness of the somewhat impersonal earth on which we live.

That Wordsworth knew Blair's work at first hand is uncertain, but probable.[9] Aside from the evidence that he read the critical theories of Great Britain in the eighteenth century,[10] and aside from his study of the poets of that age, he was an ardent reader who felt that he must have access to a good library. The fact that he collected many books himself is an indication of the tendency, and we know that he went beyond what was in his own collection. The popularity of Blair for sermons and for criticism renders it likely that Wordsworth had considered his opinions, especially on a subject which interested him, such as that of the pastoral. Nevertheless, Blair's program,[11] as I have called it, was really expressing what hung in the air, and Wordsworth may have caught it thence.

It is important to note that the novelty of Wordsworth's pastoral had support in a popular critic of the eighteenth century who in a sense helped to prepare part of the public to receive Wordsworth's creative work with something like appreciation. It is further important to perceive that Wordsworth with his pastoral tendencies was not in isolation. By later papers, I intend to point out through a study of Southey, the writers of eclogues from about 1800 to 1825, Landor, and others, what became of pastoral after 1800.[12] The study will have a bearing on dramatic monologues like those of Tennyson and Browning.

Notes

[1] "The Novelty of Wordsworth's *Michael* as a Pastoral," *P.M.L.A.,* XXXV, 432 ff.; "Pastoral in the Eighteenth Century," *M. L. N.,* XXXII, 471 ff.

[2] The problem was observed in France by J. F. de la Harpe, *Lycée ou Cours de la littérature ancienne et moderne,* 12 vols., Toulouse, 1813-14 (first published 1789-1805), I, 518-519; he emphasized the change in manners and climate from the southern countries, and thus pointed out that whenever the same machinery is employed in the north, the bucolics of the latter region are but "jeux d'esprit." He established

his premise all the more forcibly by a parallel asserting a greater frequency of songs and dances in Provence than in northern France.

[3] *Letters of the Wordsworth Family,* ed. Wm. Knight, Boston, 1907, 3 vols. I, 376.

[4] A one-volume edition appeared in Philadelphia, 1784; a Philadelphia edition in two volumes (1804) derives from a ninth London edition. There are early versions in Spanish and Italian. Blair first lectured in 1759. He was overlooked by M. K. Bragg, "The Formal Eclogue in Eighteenth-Century England," *U. of Maine Studies,* 2d. Ser., No. 6. Orono, 1926.

[5] Attention has recently been directed to Blair by G. H. Cowling, "The English Teaching of Dr. Hugh Blair," *Palœstra,* No. 148, Brandl-Festschrift, Band II. Blair offered interesting criticism on Addison's style. He also urged Macpherson to bring out his Ossianic compositions. In *Camb. Hist. Eng. Lit.,* X, 257, W. P. Ker defended his sense for style (and Goethe's) in admiring the product of his fellow Scotsman. It may be noted that the style shows not only traces of Biblical influence but effects from the Swiss Gessner; see B. Reed, *The Influence of Salomon Gessner upon English Literature,* Philadelphia, 1905, pp. 7-8, 38, as to Blair's opinion of Gessner. John Hill wrote *An Account of the Life and Writings of Hugh Blair,* Philadelphia, 1808.

[6] *Essay Supplementary,* p. 38. Blair found that Addison, in comparing Tasso and Guarini, betrayed that he had not read the former carefully and followed an error of Bouhours in his *Manière de bien penser dans les ouvrages d'esprit.*

[7] James Beattie in his *Remarks on the Usefulness of Classical Learning* included in the 3d. edit. (corrected) of his *Essays on Poetry and Music,* London, 1779, p. 484, hints at a breadth in the term "pastoral" thus: "And those foreigners must entertain a high opinion of our Pastoral poetry, who have seen the Latin translations of Vincent Bourne, particularly those of the ballads of *Tweedside, William and Margaret,* and Rowe's *Despairing beside a clear stream;* on which it is no compliment to say, that in sweetness of numbers, and elegant expression, they are at least equal to the originals, and scarce inferior to any thing in Ovid or Tibullus." Beattie expresses himself on pastoral elsewhere, p. 493, and also in the chief essay of the volume, pp. 109-110. Cf. the approval of Blair's views in Alexander Jamieson, *Grammar of Rhetoric and Polite Literature,* 4th edition, New Haven, 1826 (introduction dated 1818).

[8] The contrast between Blair and Samuel Johnson will become evident if one reads *The Rambler,* Nos. 36 and 37, and the *Lives of the Poets,* references to pastorals in his discussion of Thomson, Ambrose Phillips, Gay, Congreve.

[9] The argument that since Wordsworth was silent in the matter we must therefore presume ignorance is well known to be untenable in his case. I find no direct record in his works, none observed by K. Lienemann, *Die Belesenheit von William Wordsworth,* Berlin, 1908, and none in the Rydal Mount Library Catalogue, *Transactions of the Wordsworth Society,* No. 6.

[10] Wordsworth's study of the eighteenth-century theorists as to art, literature, and ethics (besides Godwin and Rousseau) has received much emphasis recently from O. J. Campbell, "Sentimental Morality in Wordsworth's Narrative Poetry," *U. of Wisconsin Studies in Language and Literature,* Madison, 1920, pp. 21 ff.; Arthur Beatty, "Wordsworth and Hartley," *Nation* (New York), XCVII, pp. 51 ff.; and "William Wordsworth, His Doctrine and Art in their Historical Relations," *U. of Wisconsin Studies,* Madison, 1922. Dr. Campbell points out relations to Hartley (as does Dr. Beatty).

[11] Though Blair makes no claim to originality, and may have read Fontenelle's "Discours sur la nature de l'églogue," (*Poésies Pastorales,* 3d edit., Paris, 1708), he appears definitely to have gone beyond the French author. The same may be said as regards Marmontel, *Œuvres Complètes,* Paris, 1787, *Elémens de Littérature,* III, 68 ff., "Eglogue," IV, 134 ff., "Idylle"; *Poétique Françoise,* 2 vols., Paris, 1763, II, ch. xviii, 483 ff., "De l'Eglogue."

[12] At this round date of 1800 critics are accustomed to say that save for elegy, pastoral disappeared. If pastoral must include the pagan machinery of classical Greece and Rome, the conventional view is right. If pastoral during the latter part of the eighteenth century came to include and to suggest something else for England, we must see that the form did not die about 1800 and that it may be traced in the nineteenth century. Some of the puzzles here have been discussed by M. H. Shackford, "A Definition of the Pastoral Idyll," *P.M.L.A.,* XIX, 583 ff.; R. F. Jones, "Eclogue Types in English Poetry of the Eighteenth Century," *Jour. Eng. Germ. Philol.,* XXIV, 33 ff. That the range is wide is further shown by the article on *Pastoral* in the *Encyclopaedia Britannica,* and by some corresponding encyclopedias in foreign languages. Simple illustrations are idyls by George Sand and Björnsen. Or again, we may take Platen's *Eklogen und Idyllen* (dated 1827-33), such as *Die Fischer auf Capri, Amalfi, Hirte und Winzerin, Das Fischermädchen in Burano.*

R. W. Chapman (essay date 1931)

SOURCE: "Blair on Ossian," in *The Review of English Studies,* Vol. VII, No. 25, January, 1931, pp. 80-3.

[*In the following essay, Chapman examines correspondence written by Blair and London bookseller Thomas Becket, which discusses the terms of payment and final corrections for the publication of* A Critical Dissertation on the Poems of Ossian, Son of Fingal.]

The correspondence printed below, which came lately into my possession, does not seem to have been published. It perhaps deserves record for its Ossianic interest and as pleasing evidence of the manners of the age.

Macpherson's first Ossianic publication, *Fragments of Ancient Poetry, Collected in the Highlands of Scotland, and Translated from the Galic or Erse Language,* was a kite. It was published anonymously (Edinburgh, G. Hamilton and J. Balfour, 1760), and the *Preface* of six pages by Hugh Blair was also unsigned. In the same year appeared a second edition, containing a new *Advertisement,* in which the public are informed that "measures are now taken" for "recovering and translating the heroic poem mentioned in the preface."

This was *Fingal,* which was handsomely printed in quarto for T. Becket and P. A. De Hondt in the Strand (best known as publishers of the *Sentimental Journey*), and published in 1762. It was followed by a second edition in quarto in the same year, and in 1763 by *Temora,* again in quarto.

In 1763 Becket and De Hondt published in the same style:

> **A Critical Dissertation on the Poems of Ossian, the Son of Fingal** [ornament, *vide infra*]. London: Printed for T. Becket and P. A. De Hondt, at *Tully's*-Head, in the *Strand.* MDCCLXIII.

There is no name on the title-page; but in the *Advertisement* (printed on the second leaf) the author is identified as having lectured "in Rhetorick and Belles-Lettres, in the University of Edinburgh."

My first document is addressed To Mr. Thomas Becket, Bookseller, London, and is endorsed "Ed: Aug. 19, 1762, Dr. Blair."

> Sir
>
> I am Sorry, that as you desired to have my MSS., and asked me to name any terms for it I pleased, I should have named a Sum which you think too high. I thought my self perfectly secure not to have over-stretched matters, when I rested upon the opinion of two such allowed good Judges of the value of Literary property to a Bookseller, as Mr. David Hume & Dr. Robertson; and when a few days before I sent it away, Mr. Balfour bookseller in Edinburgh, offered me the same or even a higher price than what I mentioned to you. I did not indeed imagine that by one separate impression of it you could make much profit; but as the property of it remained with you to be imployed in what ways you

pleased for advancing the sale of Fingal, and might afterwards make a part of the Volume, I thought your Bargain was pretty safe.

However as I have now sent it up to you, and as it was not, assuredly, the view of making [much *erased*] money by so small a performance that induced me to put pen to paper, but a Zeal to make Ossian's works be more thoroughly understood & Relished, it is not worth while to stickle about terms; and therefore I give it to you; and leave it wholly to your self to make what terms you think proper. I think a Critical Dissertation in favour of Ossian should naturally belong to the Proprietor of the Works of Ossian.

Only one thing, I think it ought by no means to be published till the beginning of November when the Town turns throng; otherwise it will run the risque of being entirely overlooked, & not having fair play; which will be good neither for you nor me. I give it to you as the Proprietor, not as my Publisher merely. I am

Sir

Your most obed^t humble

Servt

Ed^r

19th Aug^t

HUGH BLAIR.

We may suppose Balfour to have resented the flight of Ossian to the metropolis, and to have made an attempt to improve his position by securing the copyright of the **Dissertation.**

The draft of Becket's reply is written on the third page:

REV. SIR

Your very obliging fav^r of the 19th I rec^d by the hands of Mr Macpherson. Your presenting me with your MSS. is extremely kind, and I have no other way to return the obligation but by assuring you that the profits it may produce shall be yours, and I hereby oblige myself to it. I think it an honour and a Credit to publish any thing of yours—it is all the reward I wish.

I shall print it handsomely, and intirely agree with you not to publish it till the Parliament meets.

I am with the utmost Respect
Rev. Sir,
Yours &c.
T. B.

The next letter is endorsed "Edinb. 10 & 30th Decb. 1763, Dr. Blair. Ans^d & sent his Copies. Jany. 25. 63." But the letter on which this is written is that of December 30; the letter of December 10 is to seek:

DEAR SIR

I Inclose the last half sheet & title page, corrected. I cannot agree to make any change in the Title-page. I think the Simpler a Title-page is, the better. I would even wish the little ornament you have putt in it to be taken away; and the Lines spread more open. What you would have in the title page is mentioned immediately after in the advertisement, and as it belongs only to the introduction to the work, has no proper place in the Title.

Please make my Complim^{ts} to Mr. Macpherson; being in a hurry just now to catch the post I have no time to write him, but shall do it soon. In the meantime, I have made such alterations in the Passages he has excepted to, as I imagine will satisfy him. As this has occasioned a pretty long alteration in the last Paragraph, pray attend that this be correctly printed; & desire Mr. Macpherson to take the trouble to revise the last sheet for that end. I have sent your letter to Mr Hume. Your time of Publication seems very well judged. Let the Copies be sent to Edinb^r as soon as possible; and pray omitt not those to my Friends at London, Mr Elliot, Mr. Oswald, Dr. John Blair, Mr. John Hume 2 Copies, Mr. Shaw, Mr. Macpherson. I am

Dr Sir
Your most obed^t Servt
HUGH BLAIR.

30 Dec^r

This letter has no address; no doubt it was enclosed with the proofs (title-page and *Advertisement* two leaves, and L², pp. 73-76).

The "last paragraph" is in praise of Ossian, who though "exhibited in a literal version, still has power to please as a poet; and not to please only, but often to command, to transport, to melt the heart"; and of Macpherson, whose translation is pronounced "elegant and masterly." But the emphasis is on the merit of the original; a place is claimed for Ossian "among those, whose works are to last for ages."

We may be surprised to find the Professor of Rhetorick and Belles-Lettres then deferring to the "exceptions" of his protégé. But it must be remembered that Macpherson was a power in politics.

Morley J. Mays (essay date 1942)

SOURCE: "Johnson and Blair on Addison's Prose Style," in *Studies in Philology*, Vol. 39, No. 4, October, 1942, pp. 638-49.

[*In the following excerpt, Mays summarizes Blair's criticism of Joseph Addison, illustrating Blair's methods of literary analysis and principles of style.*]

Of the critics in [Joseph] Addison's own century who pronounced on his style none was more approving or more exhaustive in his treatment of it than Dr. Hugh Blair. Blair was the minister of the most distinguished pulpit of eighteenth century Scotland, that of St. Giles' Cathedral, or, as it was commonly known, the High Church, in Edinburgh, and *arbiter elegantiarum* of Scottish letters in the latter half of the eighteenth century. On December 11, 1759, Blair began to read in the University of Edinburgh a series of lectures on rhetoric,[22] which became a permanent part of the work of the institution for the next twenty-four years when the Town Council appointed Blair the first Professor of Rhetoric and Belles Lettres less than a year later.[23] As a class exercise Blair asked his students to examine and analyze the first four of Addison's eleven papers on the pleasures of the imagination in the *Spectator* (nos. 411 to 421). He hoped that the assignment would help purge the students' speech of the broader traces of Scottish dialect.[24] Some of the students' suggestions were incorporated into Blair's own observations on the same papers, which constituted **Lectures XX to XXIII,** inclusive, when the lectures were committed to print in 1783 under the title **Lectures on Rhetoric and Belles Lettres.** It is a curious fact that Blair was induced to have the lectures published by the appearance of his comments on Addison without his approval in the *Biographia Britannica.*[25] Consequently, we may assume that his criticism of Addison in the printed lectures may comprise even firmer statements of his intention than those which were given orally in the classroom. The four lectures devoted exclusively to Addison consist of a running commentary on the four *Spectator* papers, sentence by sentence. Addison seemed an especially suitable writer for this purpose because Blair found Addison's writings to combine both great excellencies and palpable inaccuracies of style. Blair expressed his attitude in this manner:

> Without a free, impartial discussion of both the faults and beauties which occur in his composition, it is evident, this piece of criticism would be of no service: and, from the freedom which I use in criticizing Mr. Addison's Style, none can imagine, that I mean to depreciate his writings, after having repeatedly declared the high opinion which I entertain of them.[26]

To reproduce these criticism in detail would be an endless task. Moreover, a knowledge of the terms which Blair uses in them will make them readily intelligible.

Not only did Blair conduct the minute analysis of the four Addison papers on the pleasure of the imagination, but he found it possible in the ten preceding general lectures, which advance a systematic treatment of style, to categorize Addison's style quite precisely. The meanings of the terms in both places are the same, and they can be discovered by a study of the framework of concepts in which the terms appear. As a result, we must approach them by means of a prior investigation of the premises from which they flow. It will become apparent that Blair manages his analysis in essentially the same way that Johnson does, but with far greater complexity.

Underlying and unifying all of Blair's discussion of style is the figurative analogy that style is to the writer's manner of thought as an image is to its object.

> Style has always some reference to an author's manner of thinking. It is a picture of the ideas which rise in his mind, and of the manner in which they rise there; and, hence, when we are examining an author's composition, it is, in many cases, extremely difficult to separate the Style from the sentiment.[27]

Psychology and rhetoric are complementary sciences. As one man's or one nation's peculiar manner of thought varies from another's, style progresses through an infinite number of modes. So directly related are these two factors that the denominations customarily given to style, like "nervous," "feeble," and "spirited," are equally applicable to thinking. Theoretically at least, one should be able to trace characters of style back to corresponding characters of thought; and, on the other hand, knowing a person's manner of thought, one should be able to predict with considerable accuracy the nature of the reflection in writing. That is, Blair's principles of style have a psychological origin. The analogical manner in which Blair manages this basic premise adumbrates the whole discussion of style, and we shall see that he constantly is working with pairs of terms, the distinctions between which are not strict and inviolable, but fluid and interacting. We may well expect, therefore, that what he will have to say about Addison's style will not be in terms of absolutes but in terms of relative qualities united in pairs and sharing degrees of assimilation between them.

Given the substance of thought, a person may conceive of the thought according to degrees of accuracy and also according to degrees of strength. The appropriate characteristics of style which rise from each of these respective modes of thought are perspicuity and ornament, perspicuity implying the more strictly intellectual management of the thought and ornament the sentiment or passion which gives thought its force. These approximate the twin purposes of writing so commonly expressed in the eighteenth century of instruction and pleasure. In perspicuity, the more fundamental of the two modes, one may distinguish contraries to which Blair gives the names precise and merely perspicuous or loose. They are occasioned by "an author's spreading out his thoughts more or less."[28] Addison's style may be located somewhere between these extremes, generally approaching the looser. Precision is not "the prevailing character of Mr. Addison's Style,"[29] but "he is not so deficient in this respect" as Archbishop Tillotson and Sir William Temple.[30] Nor, moreover, is Addison so diffuse as Lord Shaftesbury, whose faults are not only more prodigious than Addison's but more unpardonable "because he is a professed philosophical writer; who, as such, ought, above all things, to have studied Precision."[31] As a relatively loose stylist, Addison, we may infer, bears some of the marks of merely perspicuous writers. He has likely chosen the proper words and placed them in their proper order, but the ideas which they represent may not have been crystal clear in his mind. More probably, since the looser style usually arises from a mismanagement of words, Addison did not have "an exact and full comprehension of the force of those words which he employs."[32] In an attempt to be more precise, inexact thinkers frequently multiply words in the hope of hitting upon the exact one at one time or another. However, even so-called synonoymous terms diverge ever so slightly among themselves by reason of their accessory ideas, and the forced attempt at precision yields only a profusion of words which weaken and confuse one another and throw "a certain mist, and indistinctness"[33] over the style. Swift is the almost absolute example of the precise style, his every word sharply coinciding with his thought. He shares honors with such writers of antiquity as Tacitus and, especially, Aristotle, and with the French philosopher, Montesquieu.

Just as Blair found a principle of designating styles in the relative clearness with which thought is conceived, he also set up another classification on the degree of sentiment and passion expressed in writing. In these two faculties stylistic ornament has its genesis. "Real and proper ornaments of style . . . ," Blair says, "flow in the same stream with the current thought."[34] They may consist either in the "graceful, strong, or melodius construction of words"[35] or in the coloring of a figurative language. Again there are contraries of style, but in this scheme stages of relative variation in between are discernible. The result is a scale of styles based on the amount of ornament in proportion to the thought which a particular author's style may incorporate. At one extreme is the dry style, which is destitute of all ornament whatsoever. Aristotle is the "thorough example of a Dry Style";[36] "he writes like a pure intelligence, who addresses himself solely to the understanding, without making any use of the channel of the imagination."[37] Then succeed three intervening denominations of style, the plain, the neat, and the elegant, in the order of their increasing use of ornament. At the other extreme is the florid style, which is a false luxuriance of words, dazzling and gaudy, lacking any foundation in the imagination or passions. The elegant style, which stands next to the florid, is that into which

Addison's style falls, along with that of Dryden, Pope, Temple, Bolingbroke, Atterbury, and a few others whom Blair does not name. This style implies a balance between perspicuity and ornament, between the informative work of the understanding and the beautifying work of the imagination. There is a "harmonious and happy"[38] arrangement of words and a judicious use of figurative language. Without falling into the excesses of the florid style, Addison's style is "full of those graces which a flowery imagination diffuses over writing."[39]

So long as Blair confined himself to the direct relation between a writer's manner of thought and his expression, the two classifications which we have just examined are exhaustive. However, one may look at writing not only for evidences of the writer's workmanship but also for revelations of his total character. Now we see the man and not the writer, and we are introduced to the final pair of contrary terms, simplicity and affectation. Cutting across both the previous classifications, these have as their principle the genuineness of the expression in writing and a lack of effort in producing it. The implication, of course, is that the simple style is preferable. Simplicity, therefore, is not opposed to ornament, but to affectation of ornament. It is not synonymous with immaturity, but presupposes some aptness for writing. Intellectual and imaginative defects of style may even exist, but they are superseded if the manner is strongly expressive of great goodness and worth. Considering the approximation of writing to the man, it becomes increasingly important that he be possessed of virtue and religion. It is as a simple writer that Blair ascribes to Addison the highest praise: "Of . . . the highest, most correct, and ornamented degree of the simple manner, Mr. Addison is, beyond doubt, in English Language, the most perfect example. . . ."[40]

It is obvious that Blair's categories of style are not exhaustive, but only functional. It would be impossible to isolate all the available degrees of style in all three classifications. The discussion is profitable in enabling us to see writers in relative terms. It is only with Blair's system in mind that the terms emerging from all three classifications become intelligible in his longest abstract statement about Addison's style:

> Perspicuous and pure he is in the highest degree; his precision, indeed, not very great; yet nearly as great as the subjects which he treats of require: the construction of his sentences easy, agreeable, and commonly very musical; carrying a character of smoothness, more than of strength. In Figurative Language, he is rich; particularly, in similes and metaphors; which are so employed, as to render his Style splendid without being gaudy. There is not the least Affectation in his manner; we see no marks of labour; nothing forced or constrained; but great elegance joined with great ease and simplicity. He is, in particular, distinguished by a character of

modesty, and of politeness, which appears in all his writings. No author has a more popular and insinuating manner; and the great regard which he every where shews for virtue and religion, recommends him highly. If he fails in any thing, it is in want of strength and precision, which renders his manner, though perfectly suited to such essays as he writes in the Spectator, not altogether a proper model for any of the higher and more elaborate kinds of composition. Though the public have ever done much justice to his merit, yet the nature of his merit has not always been seen in its true light: for, though his poetry be elegant, he certainly bears a higher rank among the prose writers, than he is intitled to among the poets; and, in prose, his humour is of a much higher, and more original strain, than his philosophy.[41]. . . .

Notes

. . . [22] Alexander Grant, *The Story of the University of Edinburgh During Its First Three Hundred Years* (London, 1884), II, 358.

[23] Andrew Dalzel, *History of the University of Edinburgh from Its Foundation* (Edinburgh, 1862), II, 428-29. There are two contemporary biographies of Blair, one by James Finlayson (1801) and one by John Hill (1807).

[24] Hugh Blair, *Lectures on Rhetoric and Belles Lettres* (London, 1783), I, 430 *n*. All page references to the *Lectures* which follow are to this edition.

[25] I, iii.

[26] I, 409.

[27] I, 183-84.

[28] I, 371.

[29] I, 192.

[30] *Ibid.*

[31] *Ibid.*

[32] I, 202.

[33] I, 195.

[34] I, 365.

[35] I, 272.

[36] I, 380.

[37] *Ibid.*

[38] I, 383.

[39] I, 409.

[40] I, 394.

[41] I, 394-95.

Robert Morell Schmitz (essay date 1948)

SOURCE: "Chapter Two," in *Hugh Blair*, King's Crown Press, 1948, pp. 17-38.

[*In the excerpt below, Schmitz describes Blair's role as the editor of Frederick Carmichael's* Sermons *and of the first complete edition of the* Works of Shakespeare *published in Scotland.*]

Vita Sine Litteris Mors

One should not assume for a moment that a clergyman of the "Moderate" persuasion would confine himself to church matters. The "Moderates" were devotees of the many-sided life, and were anxious to display their intellectual wares. "Moderate" clergymen essayed poetry, history, philosophy, mathematics. The Scottish literary revival of the eighteenth century is crowded with their names: Beattie, Blacklock, Blair, Campbell, Carlyle, Ferguson, Fordyce, Greenfield, Home, Jardine, Logan, Reid, Robertson, Watson. There was hardly a minister among the "Moderates" who, if he expected to make a figure among his fellow clergy, would not essay at least one of the cultural pursuits outside divinity. For the most part they accepted as truth the motto of the minister, educator, and historian, William Robertson: *Vita sine litteris mors.*

Blair's interest in the cultivation of letters began quite early in his career. His work upon the paraphrases was, in fact, partly the result of a literary interest in sacred poetry. He was particularly pleased when Lowth's Oxford lectures on the poetry of the Hebrews were published in 1753, and thereafter he accepted Lowth as the final word upon the subject.[12] He was among the numerous and fashionable audience which heard Adam Smith's lectures on literary criticism during the winter of 1748. The 1740's were also the years in which he was cultivating the company of the leading literary men at Edinburgh, in and out of the church. By 1753 Blair came full swing into the field of letters as an editor, with an eight-volume *Works of Shakespeare,* and an edition of *Sermons* by the late Frederick Carmichael, minister at the New Greyfriars Church.

Carmichael

As for the *Sermons,* Blair found himself in "an immense deal of trouble" over their preparation, but it was a labor of love for a fellow minister whose death had left a family in very straitened circumstances.

Though a number of Carmichael's friends in the ministry had planned the publication, the editorial preparation of the *Sermons* devolved entirely upon Blair. That work must have been tedious indeed, for Blair found Carmichael's papers "in prodigious disorder; and his compositions not at all accurate."[13] Nevertheless, he managed to pull the sermons into such shape that they would display "those things in which [Carmichael] had real merit." Blair then wrote the preface which gave Carmichael credit for "an excellent strain of rational devotion, sound thought, and clear reasoning."[14] The volume was of sufficient interest to run into a second edition in 1757.

Shakespeare

Both the *Sermons* and the edition of *Shakespeare* came from the press in July, 1753.[15] Though neither of the works carried Blair's name, there is no doubt about their being his. Blair's own correspondence tells of the Carmichael publication, and the *Shakespeare*, after running through four anonymous editions, was finally identified in the fifth (1795) as "by Dr. Hugh Blair."[16]

The reasons why Blair remained anonymous are not difficult to arrive at. In editing the sermons of Carmichael, he would not wish to place his name alone to a work which was presumably the effort of many friends who had projected the issue. His anonymity as "Scots Editor" of *Shakespeare* was, however, thrust upon him by other circumstances.

The motives for the undertaking were frankly commercial. Towards the mid-century Scottish printers were beginning to offer strong competition to the English publishers, and were particularly eager to capture some of the lucrative business in cheap editions of Shakespeare. The London presses of Walker and Tonson were flooding the market with such wares, and the serious Scottish competition began in 1752 when a Glasgow printer started to issue reprints of the separate plays in Pope's edition. Blair's *Shakespeare* of 1753 was, however, the first to be expressly edited for the Scottish trade, and the first complete *Shakespeare* issued in Scotland. Publisher Kincaid was probably the man who approached Blair and, finding him willing to undertake the work, outlined roughly what the booksellers wanted. At all events, the character of Blair's *Shakespeare*—its make-up, format, the size of the volumes, and the price at 3 s. the volume—bespoke a "trade" edition. Blair himself, in the capacity of "Scots Editor," confirmed the motives for the undertaking when he wrote of "the great demand for . . . [Shakespeare's] works among the learned and polite, and the laudable zeal for home manufactures."[17] Under the circumstances, the Edinburgh publishers wanted a "Scots" editor for the Scots trade, and Blair fell in with their "laudable zeal" at the expense of his personal reputation.

Blair produced a workmanlike and very saleable edition, in which prospective purchasers were offered a *Shakespeare*, "In which the Beauties observed by Pope, Warburton, and Dodd are pointed out. Together with the Author's life; a Glossary; copious Indexes; and, a list of the various readings." All this Blair accomplished to the greater glory of the Scottish booksellers who were to make a very good profit from the edition and its reprintings for half a century.

As a textual editor, Blair was systematic but unsure—or perhaps too sure. He was the sixth of the modern textual editors, following Rowe (1709), Pope (1725), Theobald (1734), Hanmer (1744), and Warburton (1747). Blair proposed to consult them all, and to insert into his text "not a single line, not even a single word . . . but what is warranted by the authority of the preceding editors."[18] His allegiance to the critical dicta of the Rev. William Warburton was, however, so strong that the editors before Warburton were given short shrift. Both Blair and Warburton show the same contempt for the seventeenth century Folios which they both refer to as the "Vulgar" editions. Blair sat in judgment upon approximately 1000 disputed passages, but Warburton won almost all the decisions. He also contributed most of Blair's explanatory footnotes.

Whenever Blair came upon the problem of what constituted interpolations or "players' trash" he was not long in finding an answer, but at one point we find him perfectly spitted upon both horns of a dilemma. Pope and Warburton, it will be recalled, degraded to the bottom of the page such passages as they held suspect. Blair, following their lead, degraded to the foot of the page seven passages of "Romeo and Juliet" which he considered unworthy of Shakespeare. One of these passages was Capulet's angry speech, dismissing Tybalt with: "You are a princox; go!" Pope had ruled that passage out of the text as an interpolation. Warburton had, however, thought it very fine and had blessed it with the double commas, insignia of the "beauty." Blair, seeing his two authorities completely at odds and being unwilling to risk any conjecture himself, degraded the passage in obedience to Pope, but printed the rejected passage in all the glory of its double commas. Here indeed was "Moderate" literary criticism.[19]

After 1753 it became more and more difficult to distinguish the minister from the man of letters. In some ways Blair's literary life was beginning to overshadow his ministerial duties, though it should not be forgotten that the ministry was his chief concern. . . .

Notes

[12] Blair later devoted an entire lecture to Lowth's commentary. See Lecture XLI, *Lectures on Rhetoric and Belles Letters.*

[13] All the information available about Blair's preparation of the sermons is contained in a letter to George Sinclair of Ulbster, 24 September, 1753, MS. B. M. Addit. 11,679.

[14] *Sermons on Several Important Subjects,* 2nd edition (Edinburgh, 1757), preface.

[15] The announcements in *The Scots Magazine,* XV (1753), 368, follow one immediately upon the other:

The Works of Shakespear. 8 vols. 12mo. 1 £ 4s. Sands, Hamilton & Balfour, Kincaid & Donaldson, Hunter, Yair, Gordon, and Brown.

Sermons on Several Important Subjects. By the late Mr. Frederick Carmichael, one of the ministers of Edinburgh. 5s. in boards. Kincaid & Donaldson.

[16] *The Works of Shakespeare* (Edinburgh: Bell & Bradfute, Dickson, Creech, Fairbairn, Duncan, 1795), verso of titlepage, reads:

This edition of Shakespeare *is correctly printed from the famous edition 1753, by Dr. Hugh Blair.*

Though the ascription of the work to Blair hangs entirely upon the two printed lines of the 1795 edition, the identification is now commonly accepted. See *British Museum Catalogue of Printed Books;* Jaggard, *Shakespeare Bibliography;* Boswell's *Letters,* ed. C. B. Tinker (Oxford, 1924), I, 185; Boswell's *Hypochondriack,* ed. Margery Bailey (Stanford, Calif., 1928), II, 220. The *Cambridge Bibliography of English Literature,* while accepting Blair as editor, unfortunately omits listing the identifying edition of 1795.

[17] "Scots Editors Preface," *The Works of Shakespeare* (Edinburgh, 1795), I, 1.

[18] *The Works of Shakespeare* (Edinburgh, 1795), I, vi.

[19] For a more complete description of Blair's edition see R. M. Schmitz, "Scottish Shakespeare," *The Shakespeare Association Bulletin,* XVI (1941), 229-236.

Harold F. Harding (essay date 1965)

SOURCE: Introduction to *Lectures on Rhetoric and Belles Lettres,* by Hugh Blair, edited by Harold F. Harding, Southern Illinois University Press, 1965, pp. vii-lx.

[*In the essay below, Harding outlines the main ideas in Blair's lectures and appraises the man and his work from a twentieth-century perspective.*]

For well over a century beginning about 1760 Hugh Blair markedly influenced writers and speakers, teachers and students in Great Britain and in America. He was well known as a university lecturer on rhetoric and belles lettres, as a preacher to a fashionable Edinburgh congregation, as an editor and literary taste maker, and indeed as the shaper of the style of generations of readers. In republishing his ***Lectures on Rhetoric and Belles Lettres,*** it is fitting that we should appraise the man and his work in the light of what we of this generation know.

Although Blair's reputation today may have slipped from the high favor of the early nineteenth century it is still certain that he did more to interpret and make known the rhetorical theory of the ancients than any other British or American rhetorical writer. He was a conveyer of excellence in both written and spoken style. In fact, he wrote for his age the kind of a book Quintilian produced for the first century A.D. Blair selected and restated the teachings of writers like Aristotle, Longinus, Cicero, and Quintilian. He then exemplified their theories by the use of passages from English writers. These include among others Addison's *Spectator* papers, Swift's writings, and Bishop Atterbury's sermons.

Blair's ***Lectures*** has been alternately praised and scorned. The editor of the London, 1863 edition, Dr. Thomas Dale, Canon Residentiary of St. Paul's Cathedral felt impelled to warn that the work retained its "high position in popular esteem, notwithstanding the questionable character of some of the Author's canons of criticism, and the occasional contradiction of his own rules for style and structure in his own sentences."[1] Sir Richard C. Jebb, the classical scholar, states in his *Brittanica* article that "the popularity enjoyed by Blair's ***Rhetoric*** in the latter part of the 18th and the earlier part of the 19th century was merited rather by the form than by the matter." But when we now add up all the effects of Blair's precepts upon students, teachers, and preachers in Britain and in the colleges of the eastern United States it would seem that Blair's popularity was merited by both the form and the matter. His ***Lectures*** and his ***Sermons*** were widely published, read, and studied in ways that would make writers of today envious. In any history of rhetorical criticism they cannot be ignored.

Boswell on Blair

The best known portrayer of the literary activity of the time of Blair is his fellow Scotsman, James Boswell. His *Life of Johnson* and his *London Journal 1762-63* are full of references to the discussions about the writers, speakers, and actors of the day. Boswell reveals in lively style his own ambitions to speak and act. He carries on these conversations with Thomas and Frances Sheridan, David Garrick, Edmund Burke, David Hume, Lord Chesterfield, George Dempster, William Robertson, Blair, and others. The charm of Boswell's writing may indeed be due to his early study of rhetoric and criticism.

In the summer of 1761, Thomas Sheridan, father of Richard Brinsley Sheridan, came to Edinburgh to give a course of lectures on elocution. Boswell attended. He was twenty-one years old at the time. He had studied rhetoric with Adam Smith. He had already heard Dr. Blair preach and lecture. His literary aspirations were taking shape and he was cultivating those who could help him.

Henry Home, Lord Kames, author of the *Elements of Criticism,* 1762, was one of Boswell's friends. In the early fall of 1762 when young Boswell accompanied Lord and Lady Kames on a tour of Southern Scotland there must have been frequent conversation about authors and their merits.

By the time Boswell reached London in November 1762 to seek his fortune he already had a well stocked mind with ideas about taste, style, criticism, genius, and writing in general. He was becoming a man of discrimination.

Dr. Johnson and Boswell met for the first time on 16 May 1763. Some six or seven weeks before that event Dr. Blair came to visit in London. He had been appointed Regius Professor of Rhetoric and Belles Lettres at the University of Edinburgh in April of the year before. Boswell records how he and Blair dined together, took long walks, went to church, and engaged in serious talk. The *Journal* entry for 6 April 1763 reads as follows: "Blair is a very amiable man. In my earliest years I admired him while he was Minister in the Canongate. He is learned and ingenious, and has a degree of simplicity about him that is extremely engaging."[2]

Blair's Career

The foregoing quotation is a valuable appraisal made long before Blair became famous. It is well worth remembering as we proceed with more details about his qualifications as a teacher of eloquence and as an arbiter of taste. He was born in Edinburgh on 7 April 1718, the only child of John and Martha Blair. At 13 he matriculated at the University of Edinburgh. For nine years he studied the Humanities, Greek, Logic, and Natural Philosophy. He took his Master of Arts degree in 1739. It was probably Professor John Stevenson, his teacher of rhetoric, who shaped Blair's thinking and led him to the study of letters. One of Blair's classmates was John Witherspoon, author of a set of lectures on rhetoric and later president of what is now Princeton University, as well as a signer of the Declaration of Independence.

In October 1741 when Blair was twenty-three the Presbytery of Edinburgh licensed him to preach. A

year later he was ordained and in February 1743 he was elected to preach at the Canongate Church in Edinburgh. He served there until 1754.

Blair's eight-volume edition of the **Works of Shakespear,** labored over in these formative years, came out in 1753 and also his edition of the **Sermons** of Frederick Carmichael, the preacher of New Greyfriars Church. His second call was to Lady Yester's Church where he preached for four years (1754-58). In this period and later Blair joined and took part in discussions of the Select Society, the St. Giles Society, and the *Belles Lettres* Society. In 1762 the celebrated literary group called the Poker Club was formed. The original members all became distinguished. They included Blair, Alexander Carlyle, Lord Kames, Adam Ferguson, and William John Stone.

In June 1757 the University of St. Andrews conferred on Blair the honorary Doctor of Divinity degree. A year later, at the age of forty, he became Minister of the High Church of St. Giles, the most influential in Edinburgh. It was while here that he attracted the favorable attention of the faculty of the University of Edinburgh. In December 1759 he began his Edinburgh lectures, at first sponsored by the town and held outside of campus grounds. For a dozen years ever since hearing Stevenson and Adam Smith (1748) lecture on rhetoric, Blair had been reading, taking notes, and reflecting on what should go into his own course of lectures. By 1762 his trial teaching had attained such a reputation that King George III created for him a Regius Professorship at an annual salary of £70. He distinguished himself in that chair until retirement in 1783. In that year he helped to found the Royal Society of Edinburgh and became one of the four chairmen of the literary section of the society. Blair's preaching and writing did not cease although his health gradually declined. Even in his final year, at the age of eighty-three, he was full of activity. Among other projects he recomposed a number of his sermons for a fifth volume, published in 1801.

Blair died on 27 December 1800. He lies buried near Greyfriars Church. As the plaque on the wall of the church states in Latin he was a good man, a loyal friend, a learned teacher and critic, and a bulwark of the University of Edinburgh for nearly sixty years.

Blair's Purpose

In the latter half of the eighteenth century more than fifty textbooks, essays, lectures, and treatises on rhetoric and literary criticism by thirty different writers were published in England, Ireland, and Scotland.[3] Interest in literature and the teaching of writing and speaking ran high. As Blair noted: "Next to speech, writing is beyond doubt, the most useful art which men possess." He set about to help students become proficient in the art. He conceived his task to be that of "the initiation of youth into the Study of Belles Lettres, and of Composition. . . . He hopes that to such as are studying to cultivate their Taste, to form their Style, or to prepare themselves for Public Speaking or Composition, his Lectures will afford a more comprehensive view of what relates to these subjects, than, as far as he knows, is to be received from any one Book in our Language."[4]

The lectures of these two volumes were read continuously for twenty-four years. We can take Blair's word that he made few revisions before publication. If we remember this fact and think of the work as having been completed around 1760 we can discount the more common criticisms—about the author not being up to date, not sufficiently aware of later works on genius and taste, and often being too elementary in his outlook. Professor Blair knew he was speaking to college students, most of whom were lads of fifteen or a little older.

Conceptions of **Rhetoric and Belles Lettres**

In the preface, Blair admits his work is not wholly original, but it is not, he insists, a compilation from the writings of others. Indeed, on every topic he has thought for himself, consulting his own ideas and reflections.

The forty-seven lectures are of nearly equal length and closely retain the form and content of the course as delivered at the university. Blair, like Quintilian, was forced to publish, he says, because imperfect copies in note-form were circulating and being offered for sale in the bookstores of Parliament Close.[5]

Following the introductory lecture, we find four lectures on *Taste,* four on *Language,* fifteen on *Style,* and ten on *Eloquence.* The final thirteen lectures are devoted to a "critical examination of the most distinguished *species of composition* both in prose and verse." For students of speech and of rhetorical theory especially, some twenty lectures have most to offer: 10-19, dealing with Style, and 25-34, covering "Eloquence properly so called, or public speaking in its different kinds." Lectures 20-24 consist of critical examinations of certain of the *Spectator* papers and of a passage from Swift's "Proposal for correcting, improving, and ascertaining the English tongue." The last thirteen lectures, 35-47, concern criticism in the broadest scope. They touch upon historical writing, philosophical writing, poetry, tragedy, and comedy. These discourses represent Blair, the literary critic, as a judge of what he has chosen to call authors whose works examplify taste and genius, or as in the case of Shakespeare of "genius shooting wild."[6]

We turn now to the early lectures to survey their main ideas. Taste, "the power of receiving pleasure from the beauties of nature and art,"[7] is reducible to two characters, delicacy and correctness.[8] It is a faculty composed of "natural sensibility to beauty, and of improved understanding"[9] and may be greatly aided by exercise. Without an "internal sense of beauty"[10] however, study will avail little. There are, of course, "principles of reason and sound judgment" which can be applied to matters of taste.[11]

What is the standard for determining good taste? There can be but one court of appeal—universal acceptance of the past. "That which men concur the most in admiring must be held to be beautiful. His taste must be just and true which coincides with the general sentiments of men."[12]

Criticism is the habit of applying taste and good sense to the judging of the fine arts.[13] When we have accumulated data on a sufficient number of particular instances, we can then "ascend to general principles" of beauty as found in works of genius. Genius is a talent or aptitude for excelling that we inherit from nature. It may be improved but cannot be wholly acquired by art and study.[14]

There are, according to Addison, three primary sources of the pleasures of Taste: *beauty, grandeur,* and *novelty,*[15] and these qualities Blair adopts adding a fourth of his own, *imitation.* Melody, harmony, wit; humour, and ridicule also belong to Taste. Poetry, eloquence, and good writing receive their power not from any one of these pleasures, but from all.

The sublime in writing may be said to center upon vigorous conciseness and simplicity.[16] We find the sources of the sublime "everywhere in nature."[17]

Language is the "expression of our ideas by certain articulate sounds, which are used as the signs of those ideas."[18] From the four lectures devoted to the rise and progress and the structure of language we derive what is the core of a main topic, the analysis of Style. Blair's definition of style is "the peculiar manner in which a man expresses his conceptions by means of Language."[19] Perspicuity and ornament are the two heads under which good style may be classified. In accordance with the dictum of Quintilian's *Institutio,* perspicuity is really the fundamental quality of the two. Again, following classical predecessors Blair discusses perspicuity with regard to words and phrases and concludes that three qualities are essential: purity, propriety, and precision.[20] In similar fashion, the demands of perfect sentence structure are four: clearness and precision, unity, strength, and harmony.[21] "The fundamental rule of the construction of Sentences, and into which all others might be resolved, undoubtedly is, to communicate in the clearest and most natural order, the ideas which we mean to transfuse into the minds of others."[22]

The ornamental feature of Blair's stylistic scheme rests almost entirely on a rather small number of figures, of which Metaphor, Hyperbole, Personification, Apostrophe, Comparison, and Antitheses are most important. Figures as a class are prompted either by the imagination or by the passions.[23]

In general, figures perform four functions: 1] they enrich language and make it more copious, 2] they confer dignity upon style, 3] as Aristotle points out, they let us see one thing in another, and 4] they give "us frequently a much clearer and more striking view of the principal object, than we could have if it were expressed in simple terms, and divested of the accessory idea."[24] In addition, we can always heighten the emotion by the figures we introduce.

Lectures 18 and 19 set forth the general characteristics of style. "The foundation of all good Style, is good sense accompanied with a lively imagination."[25] Among the practical directions that Blair offers for forming a proper style are: 1] study your material, 2] practice composing frequently, 3] read the best authors, 4] do not imitate servilely, 5] adapt according to the subject and the demands of hearers, 6] do not sacrifice clear thought to ornamental style.[26]

By "Eloquence" Blair means the art of persuasion.[27] It is therefore rhetoric in Cicero's[28] sense. But when Blair uses the term "rhetoric," he seems to have in mind written composition. Of the ten lectures (25-34) on eloquence, or public speaking, as he occasionally refers to the topic, two are devoted to the history of the subject, three to the different kinds of speaking: before popular assemblies, the bar, and the pulpit, two to the parts of the oration, and one to delivery. One lecture on means of improving in speech and another on the criticism of a sermon of Bishop Atterbury complete the section on style.

The purposes of eloquence are these: 1] to please, 2] "to inform, to instruct, to convince,"[29] 3] to arouse the passions. If criticism is taste plus good sense, eloquence is good sense and solid thought.[30] And likewise, if good style is founded on perspicuity, "in all kinds of public speaking nothing is of greater consequence than a proper and clear method."[31]

We commonly think of the latter half of the eighteenth century as the beginning of a golden age of British eloquence, but it was far from that to Blair. England, he says, has the vital elements for great oratory: "free and bold genius of the country" and popular government, but where are the orators? Historians and poets there are of first rank, "but of orators and public speakers, how little have we to boast?"[32] As for good preaching, the practice then current, Blair declares, of reading sermons, has practically ruined the development of any great pulpit oratory.[33]

Throughout the lectures on speaking Blair repeatedly shows his dependence upon two classical sources, Cicero and especially Quintilian. But he refuses to use their classification of the kinds of oratory and prefers to base his discussion on what he terms "the great scenes of eloquence, popular assemblies, the bar, and the pulpit."[34] The summary of Blair's remarks on popular eloquence so accurately and concisely represents his philosophy of speech preparation and presentation as a whole that I shall give the excerpt in full:

> The sum of what has been said is this: The end of Popular Speaking is persuasion; and this must be founded on conviction. Argument and reasoning must be the basis, if we would be Speakers of business, and not mere Declaimers. We should be engaged in earnest on the side which we espouse; and utter, as much as possible, our own, and not counterfeited Sentiments. The premeditation should be of things, rather than of words. Clear order and method should be studied: the manner and expression warm and animated; though still, in the midst of that vehemence, which may at times be suitable, carried on under proper restraints which regard to the audience, and to the decorum of character, ought to lay on every Public Speaker: the style free and easy; strong and descriptive, rather than diffuse; and the delivery determined and firm. To conclude this head, let every Orator remember, that the impression made by fine and artful speaking is momentary; that made of argument and good sense, is solid and lasting.[35]

This same set of directions holds true for eloquence at the bar (Lecture 28) and eloquence of the pulpit (Lecture 29). These particular observations may be added: forensic eloquence is founded on a lawyer's reputation and this in turn rests upon his own legal acumen.[36] Eloquence suitable for the bar whether in written brief or oral argument ought to be "of a calm and temperate kind and connected with close reasoning."[37] Distinctness is the advocate's greatest asset. It should show itself in the stating of the question, next in the statement of the issues, and finally in the order and arrangement of the parts of pleading.[38] In all speaking ethical appeal is paramount. Nothing can take the place of a speaker's reputation "of probity and honour."[39]

Persuasion is also the object of the pulpit orator. The preacher's aim should be "to persuade men to serve God and become better men"[40] and in so doing he may instruct, teach, reason, and argue. The preacher himself must always be a good man.[41] The two features which distinguish pulpit eloquence from other kinds of Public Speaking are gravity and warmth.[42] What are the characteristics of a good sermon? Five stand out: 1] unity, 2] particularizing of the subject, 3] selection of material, 4] adaptation to audience interest, 5] unwillingness to imitate the passing fashion in preaching.[43] Moreover, good preaching demands perspicuous style.[44] In general, a lively and animated style is well suited to the pulpit. The careful preacher never employs "strong figures or a pathetic style except in cases where the subject leads to them."[45] Whereas to Blair a French sermon is "a warm animated exhortation," an English sermon is "a piece of cool instructive reasoning." The perfect sermon, he thinks, would combine the qualities of the two types.[46]

Lecture 30 distinguishes the good and the bad in Bishop Atterbury's celebrated sermon on Praise and Thanksgiving. It is a critique of a preacher and his composition. The next two lectures take up in detail the "conduct of a discourse" or the parts of the oration from the introduction to the peroration. Throughout his treatment of this subject Blair restates classical precepts. Gain the good will of your hearers. Compose in an easy and natural style. See that the expression is correct. Be modest. Speak in a calm manner. Don't rush into your main topic. Such is the gist of the advice on the Introduction.[47] After you have stated the proposition, you may or may not "lay down heads," that is, reveal a division. In the case of sermonwriting Blair opposes the declaration of Fénelon in his *Dialogues on Eloquence* and commends the practice then current in British preaching of announcing heads.[48]

Logical and Emotional Appeals

In treating the argumentative part of a discourse three things are necessary: the invention of the arguments, their disposition and arrangement, and last, clothing them in effective style.[49] Blair casts aside as too technical Aristotle's system of *Topoi* or Commonplaces and in their stead suggests two methods for reasoning: the Analytic, in which the orator builds up his proofs by successive points, and the Synthetic, when the point to be proved is announced and a series of arguments are arranged for its support.[50] This latter method is most suited "to the train of Popular Speaking."

For his discussion of the Pathetic, Blair again rejects Aristotle, or rather his treatment of the passions as found in Book 2 of the *Rhetoric,* and for practical reasons prefers to follow Quintilian's *Institutio,* Book 6.[51]

As for the Conclusion, the great rule is to place last whatever point will determine the balancing of a decision.[52]

Delivery

The four chief requisites of good "Pronunciation, or Delivery" (Lecture 33) are: 1] proper loudness of voice, 2] distinctness, 3] slowness, and 4] propriety of pronunciation.[53] These matters are fundamental. Refinements of delivery focus on 1] proper emphasis, 2] pauses, 3] tones, and 4] gestures.[54] Of these, the study and exercise of good tone is probably the most impor-

tant. And to this end Blair says, "the greatest and most material instruction which can be given . . . is to form the tones of Public Speaking upon the tones of sensible and animated conversation."[55] The same standard applies for action. "A public speaker must take that manner which is most natural to himself."[56] For specific advice on delivery the student is urged to consult the final chapter of the *Institutio,* Book 11. But even the rules there laid down, Blair believes, are of little use unless demonstrated in the presence of the student speaker.

Further Training

Lecture 34 on Means of Improving in Eloquence is little more than a collection of Greek and Roman maxims on the speaker and the speech. The true orator is a virtuous man,[57] a man of generous sentiments and warm feelings,[58] endowed with a proper mixture of courage and modesty.[59] Next to these moral qualifications he must possess a fund of knowledge.[60] The aspiring speaker will not neglect the general circle of polite literature.[61] Study and enthusiastic application are always important.[62] Attention to the best models greatly aids improvement.[63] Frequent practice in composing and in speaking is necessary.[64] For gaining experience before audiences debating societies are excellent training places. Properly conducted they enable the student to acquire that *copia verborum* which the ancients deemed so vital in the equipment of the speaker.

Appraisal

We have now scanned the twenty lectures that relate to rhetorical theory. One finds, of course, other places in the remaining twenty-seven lectures where Blair deals with speaking, but in these lectures he writes mainly as a critic and as a literary historian. His treatment of language in Lectures 6-9 is of interest to specialists in linguistics just as those on poetry, Lectures 38-47, have attraction for students of poetics.

Considering therefore the twenty lectures surveyed here, what special merit do they possess for the rhetorician and the student of eloquence? What is the reason for Blair's great vogue in his lifetime, and how do we account for the use of his book throughout most of the next century? A favorable or complimentary answer to the first part of that question should help to explain the second part.

Blair considers his lectures on oratory or public speaking to constitute a sort of system.[65] His main emphasis, more than half of his effort, goes to the details of Style. He is almost contemptuous of Invention and Disposition as set forth in Aristotle's *Rhetoric.* Memory is barely touched upon. Every speaker must decide for himself whether to memorize, read, or speak extempore. Delivery gets compressed into one lecture. It states in effect: follow nature, be earnest and occupied with your subject, and your previously formed habits will take care of everything.[66] And so, compared with any of the great classics, Aristotle's *Rhetoric*, Cicero's *De Oratore*, or Quintilian's *Institutio Oratoria*, Blair's "system" is a mere outline. What Blair has in fact done in his *Lectures* has been to digest and adapt some of the more important classical theories that applied to the needs of eighteenth-century speaking. He did not undertake the exhaustive cento of ancient rhetorical precepts that we find in John Ward's lectures. Blair was selective and discriminating. He emphasized what was important to him. Like every good teacher he had his students and their needs in mind.

After a restatement of Greek and Roman principles we find added the doctrine of "good sense." That expression is repeated at regular intervals throughout the work. Unfortunately, what is "good sense" in respect to style or taste in one generation is not always so in another. "Follow nature" is another of Blair's favorite injunctions—one that is generally more difficult to comply with than to write about. "Be clear" in meaning of words and in structure of sentences is also a main feature of Blair's teaching. In this respect he is repeating a leading precept of the *Institutio*. So we see, in matters of rhetorical theory, Blair may have, as he says, thought for himself, but in reality he is seldom original. He has, however, written understandingly and with an old-fashioned charm. His own long experience in the pulpit and his weekly exercise in composing sermons unquestionably gave to the *Lectures* a partical consideration they might not otherwise have had. When we read them we "listen" to a speaker and not a theorizer. We should put ourselves into the mental outlook of the college students of Scotland from about 1760 to 1784.

The Value of Blair's Lectures

What was Blair's value in the latter half of the eighteenth century? How did it come, as a recent writer says, that "half the educated English-speaking world studied"[67] his famous book? The answer is found in Blair's reputation as a preacher. His church, the High Kirk, was the most prestigious in Edinburgh at the time.[68] His congregation was composed largely from the gentry and the learned community. His speaking style was unaffected. His sermons were thoughtful essays. he himself was a scholar, the friend of Hume, Ferguson, Alexander Carlyle, and Principal Robertson. In the pulpit Blair seems to have put into effect the theories of his classroom.[69] Dr. Samuel Johnson boasted that he was the first to give a stamp of approval to Blair's sermons.[70] That in itself was almost the acme of recognition. Once Blair's reputation as a preacher and later as a man of letters was created, its own momentum carried it along. Young authors brought

him their manuscripts for criticism and he came to be regarded as "the literary accoucheur of Scotland."[71] Blair's *Critical Dissertation on the Poems of Ossian* (1763) made him a principal in the greatest literary controversy of the day. Strangely enough, Blair's own speech delivery did not seem to detract from his popularity. His platform manner is described as unforceful, his speech was said to be marked by a strong provincial dialect, and his general attitude indifferent.[72] But in spite of shortcomings Blair, the preacher, was a notable success. Judged by the sale of his *Lectures* and the size of his classes he was likewise a success as a writer on rhetoric. The man was heard and his books were read. What forms of acceptance are more convincing?

The Universities

We cannot forget the high standards of the Scottish universities in the reign of George III. Their chairs were filled with first-rate scholars whose influence extended far beyond their classrooms.[73] Their glory and deserving fame is the more pronounced when the comparison is made with the low state of scholarship and teaching that prevailed at Oxford and Cambridge in the same period.[74] Besides the awakening at the Scottish universities there were many signs of a genuine revival of intellectual interest among the educated Scots classes. Ability to write and speak correct English, of a sort free from provincialisms, was earnestly sought by the cultivated. Beattie and Hume, for example, collaborated in compiling a list of Scotticisms to be carefully avoided.[75] In the process of helping their countrymen acquire "Received" English Blair and Campbell, Kames, and Monboddo had a significant part.

Blair as Professor

Blair's fame as a writer of sermons established and strengthened his reputation as a lecturer and writer on rhetoric. For this reason his lectures, both when delivered and when published, enjoyed a great patronage. The classes in rhetoric at the University of Edinburgh had been taught by the professor of logic from 1708 to 1760 and were seldom attended by more than a handful of students a year. But Blair had classes of 60 or more and when his successor, William Greenfield, took over in 1784 the attendance dwindled to twenty or less.[76] In his *Dictionary of Eminent Scotsmen* (1863) Robert Chambers tells us that so great was the interest aroused by Blair's lectures that impecunious students wrote out their notes and sold them to booksellers, who freely exhibited them for re-sale. These facts, supported by the scores of printings and editions for nearly a century after the two volumes of *Lectures* were first published in 1783, attest to the influence of Blair in his generation and afterwards. Judged by the standards of today, one may have to look hard to justify their high popularity. We can say, however, that before Campbell and Whately published their rhetorical works nothing as useful was available in English.

Blair's Sources

There is need for a word about Blair's sources. What writers did he rely upon? Were they ancient or modern? Are they mentioned or do we have to search for parallels? The problem is really not difficult. Blair is explicit. Quintilian, he says at the close of the section on eloquence "has digested into excellent order all the ancient ideas concerning rhetoric and is himself an eloquent writer." Few books, he continues, "abound more with good sense and discover a greater degree of just and accurate taste" than the *Institutio*.[77] Hence, that work has his highest approval. He cites it or borrows from it some fifty-odd times and more than from any other work. There are many more references to Quintilian than the Index lists. Next, in influence, comes Cicero. But Blair usually regards Cicero as an orator rather than as a writer on oratory and thus seems less indebted to him for theory. Aristotle has but slight appeal, although there is admission that in his *Rhetoric* he "laid the foundation for all that was afterwards written on the subject."[78] Plato's rhetorical dialogues are not mentioned and it can be argued that Blair owes little to the *Gorgias* or the *Phaedrus*. Among modern writers, Vossius is so full and ponderous that his work "is enough to disgust one with the study of eloquence."[79] Several French writers, Rollin, Batteaux, Crevier, Gibert and others, are mentioned, but Fénelon deserves special merit for his *Dialogues sur l'Eloquence*.[80] For his general ideas on taste Blair depended on the *Elements of Criticism* by Lord Kames. Actual citation of the book is limited to two instances,[81] but a comparison of the two authors reveals similarities in their conceptions of the elements of taste, the difficulty of analysis, and the standard for appeal. The Rev. Dr. George Campbell had published his *Philosophy of Rhetoric* in 1776, but Blair, as far as I can judge, uses that work in no substantial way.

James Burnett, Lord Monboddo, dealt with rhetoric at great length in his 6-volume work, *Of the Origin and Progress of Language,* 1773-1792. But when we recall that Blair's lectures were largely finished in 1758-59 and not substantially changed when published in 1783, it is understandable why Monboddo is mentioned only in a footnote in Blair's **Lectures.** Blair was apparently not as interested in the judgments of his colleagues as modern scholars usually are. He was lecturing to college students and he was much more concerned with giving them what they needed to know to become good stylists.

Blair and Adam Smith

The publication in 1963 of the notes of Adam Smith's *Lectures on Rhetoric and Belles Lettres* has revived the age-old controversy of the originality of Blair and how much he owed to others. Since we know that Blair attended Smith's lectures in Edinburgh (1748) and that he read Smith's notes before beginning his own course in 1759 there has been a presumption that Blair borrowed from Smith. John Rae, Smith's biographer, states: "The lectures Smith then delivered on English literature were burnt at his own request, shortly before his death. Blair, not only heard them at the time, but got the use of them, or at least part of them. . . . It has been suggested that they are practically reproduced in the lectures of Blair." Earlier Rae had said that Blair does not "seem to have borrowed anything but was the commonest property already" and then adds contemptuously "to borrow even a hat to any purpose, the two heads must be something of a size." The present editor of Smith's lecture notes, Professor Lothian aptly says, "with the discovery of Smith's lectures, it will now be possible to measure the two heads."[82]

I believe that Rae's insinuations of plagiarism by Blair are overdrawn. It is true that there are a number of points of similarity between the student's notes on Smith and Blair's **Lectures.** The two men touch upon many of the same subjects, they refer to several of the same authors as models of good form, and on the surface they appear to have the same standards of taste. But there are notable differences that should be explained. Here are a few:

> 1. The notes in Lothian's 1963 edition are oral remarks made in a classroom in 1762-63, long before accurate reporting was in use. Even if they represent the gist of Smith's ideas we cannot be sure that they represent his actual sentences. They may or may not represent what Smith wanted to convey. "The writing, the gaps in the text, and the existence of certain comments, seem to suggest that these are the original notes written at speed in the lecture room, and not a fair copy." Most lecturers want to alter words and phrases or to delete before going into print. The fact that Smith ordered his notes destroyed would argue that he was unwilling to give them his unreserved approval:

> 2. As the notes reveal, Smith is sketchy and suggestive. Blair is detailed and even discursive. He provides more than is needed and often repeats ideas. Whereas Blair's style is usually precise we have to compare it with a probably imperfect paraphrase of what Smith said. It is a case of lining up what one man wanted to say with what someone thought another man wanted to say. The comparison is to the disadvantage of Adam Smith.

> 3. Blair was really interested in teaching students how to write (composition) and how to appreciate good literature (belles lettres). Practical speaking in the sense of pleading cases, presenting arguments

in parliament, or delivering ceremonial addresses gets surprisingly little attention in either Smith or Blair. But Smith was mainly interested in style. "Indeed, in Smith style alone is the pressing concern of rhetoric and the area of greatest artistic latitude. His view is belletristic in that he extended the scope of rhetoric to literature and literary criticism, treating historical, didactic, and rhetorical composition as well as forensic, epideictic, and deliberative public address." Blair gives a broad treatment in his 47 lectures. They divide themselves, as he explains at the end of the first lecture, into five parts: 1] the Nature of Taste, 2] Consideration of language, 3] of style, 4] of eloquence, and 5] a critical examination of the species of composition. Smith's 29 lectures cannot be so easily classified. He gives headings to four and leaves the others untitled. Following the Introduction we find three lectures on language, three on words and figures of speech, and four on the style of Swift, Lucian, Addison, Lord Shaftesbury, and Virgil. Lectures 12 to 17 deal with composition, 18 to 20 with historians and their works. The poets are discussed in Lecture 21. Lectures 22 to 24 concern various kinds of oratory. Invention and arrangement are combined in Lecture 25. The final five lectures, 26-30, touch upon the orations of Cicero, Demosthenes, Thucydides, and a few British orators before the bar.

It is clear that Smith neither covers the variety of topics Blair does nor does he cover them as fully. Perhaps this is because he refrained from using notes during the delivery of his lectures. Perhaps, too, he regarded Rhetoric as an avocation and devoted his best scholarly efforts to Economics and Jurisprudence.

4. Smith admired the Greek writers and referred to them frequently. Blair, except for Demosthenes, seldom does. Smith, however, does not seem to know Aristotle's *Rhetoric* or Plato's rhetorical dialogues. He does not mention them. Blair relies heavily on Cicero and Quintilian. Smith knows Cicero's orations but makes little use of the *De Oratore, Brutus,* or *Orator*. His references to the *Institutio Oratoria* are so slight that we can only conclude that Smith failed to discover the merits of Quintilian. In fact, the differences in the attitudes of Smith and Blair towards Quintilian may be their sharpest area of contrast. Blair has several faults but a failure to appreciate the work of the first Roman public professor of rhetoric is not one of them.

It is probably safe to say that Blair owes to Smith the idea of combining the study of Belles Lettres with Rhetoric. He seems to have followed Smith in his analysis of writers like Swift and Addison, Temple, Pope, Lord Clarendon and Lord Shaftesbury. Both writers cite the orations of Demosthenes and Cicero as models for study. Both are fond of the French writers

La Bruyère, Fénelon, Rapin, and Voltaire. Like Smith, Blair refers several times to Dionysius of Halicarnassus, Lucian, Thucydides, Herodotus, Polybius, Livy, and Caesar. Unlike Smith, Blair devotes several pages to French preachers. He mentions Saurin, Bourdaloue, Massillon, Bossuet, and Flechier.

It is easy to see broad topical similarities in the lectures of Blair and the lecture-notes of Smith—especially in the way they treat in detail the subjects of language, style, the writings of Swift, Demosthenes, Cicero, and the ancient historical writers.

It is not easy to prove that Blair adopted in wholesale fashion the ideas of Adam Smith. What each wrote had been commonly discussed in the Edinburgh literary clubs for years. Blair actually delivered a better set of lectures than his teacher delivered. But Smith, the versatile man and better scholar, was also interested in jurisprudence, ethics, and economics. We remember him today for the *Theory of Moral Sentiments* and his *Wealth of Nations* and not as a lecturer on rhetoric. Blair spent a lifetime teaching his subject, practicing it, and indeed, trying to save souls by it. It is natural, therefore, that his published lectures gained fame for him. Smith's unpublished notes come down to us two centuries later as a literary curiosity. They are like the first draft of a Greek tragedy. We see the power of the dramatist, we sense his abilities, we wish he could have completed his task.

Summary and Conclusion

In the universities of Britain in the second half of the eighteenth century the rhetorical teachings of John Ward, Hugh Blair, and George Campbell predominated. For all three, style, of both written and spoken discourse, was most important. Although speaking *practice* both by the recitation of "elegant extracts" and by the giving of original declamations persisted in the schools and academies, it does not appear to have extended to the universities. Students may have gained practice at informal literary societies and debating clubs, as at Trinity College, Dublin, but it is doubtful if instruction in speaking with an instructor-critic in charge as we know it today was very prevalent. The evidence shows that Blair and his contemporary professors customarily read their lectures and then set their students adrift to gain practice by whatever means they could find.

This survey of Blair makes some conclusions apparent. As a writer on Rhetoric he was neither original, comprehensive, nor profound. His own style is clear, but not especially distinguished. He often becomes prolix and belabors the obvious. His principal contribution to the art of rhetoric seems to be in his classification of speeches—before the bar, at popular assemblies, and in the pulpit. In the main Blair has adapted the tenets of the Scottish Common Sense School of Philosophy to the speaking situations of his time. He knows the ancient rhetorical lore, but believes it is too cumbersome and technical for his purposes. He is especially insistent that the classical devices for finding and stimulating ideas under Invention, *topoi* or *loci communes,* are not practical. They may, Blair believes, actually stifle ideas and curtail inventiveness. Likewise, Blair discounted the values of developing emotional appeals that Aristotle and other considered so fully.

Quintilian is clearly Blair's ideal and his master. He leaves no doubt about his high esteem for the *Institutio Oratoria.* That Blair's *Lectures* continued to be published, imitated, praised, studied, condensed, and reissued for several generations after his death is understandable.[83] The work is easy to grasp and immediately useful as a guide. It was written by a respected churchman whose sermons enjoyed the reputation of high excellence. College teachers, and especially those in the new colleges of the eastern United States, regarded Blair as scholarly and sound. His popularity in American classrooms continued unabated until the appearance of Whately's *Rhetoric* in 1828.[84]

Although in some respects Blair follows the strictly classical tradition laid down by John Ward in his *System of Oratory* (1759) in reality he goes beyond Ward in breadth of view and scope of generalization. Blair's chair at Edinburgh obliged him to pay more attention to criticism and the study of polite literature, or, as he says, to "distinguishing false ornament from true." His *Lectures* are the most detailed, suggestive, and helpful work on *belles lettres* which the group Bosker[85] calls "The Champions of Teste" produced. Blair's ambition to set forth a more comprehensive view of taste, style, public speaking, and composition than that found in any other one book does not fall so far short of its mark. Leslie Stephen, Edmund Gosse, and others have sneered at Blair for his lack of originality.[86] But that attitude is not entirely reasonable. The best of Blair's precepts have sound classical origins. What he says about composition is clearly stated and with the good sense of a man who knows from experience. In final judgment, Blair's reliance upon the practical wisdom of Quintilian saves him from the absurdities which less careful writers lapsed into in their efforts to be original.

Notes

[1] Hugh Blair, *Lectures on Rhetoric and Belles Lettres,* Thomas Dale, ed. (London, 1863), p. vii.

[2] James Boswell, *London Journal, 1762-63,* F. A. Pottle, ed. (New York, 1950), p. 234.

[3] H. F. Harding, *English Rhetorical Theory, 1750-1800.* Unpublished Ph.D dissertation, Cornell University, 1937.

[4] Hugh Blair, *Lectures on Rhetoric and Belles Lettres,* 2 vols. (London, 1783), I, iv-v. Future references in this edition will be indicated in this fashion. Pages will follow the volume number. In his valuable book, *Hugh Blair* (New York, 1948), Robert M. Schmitz lists 26 British editions of the *Lectures on Rhetoric and Belles Lettres* published to 1863, two continental editions in English, 37 American editions between 1784 and 1853, 13 translations in French, Italian, Russian and Spanish between 1797 and 1855, and 52 Abridgments of the *Lectures* between 1787 and 1911. Schmitz also adds seven textbooks, which use Blair's *Lectures* in part and two published "Questions for the Lectures." No other book on rhetoric in English approaches a record of this kind.

[5] Blair, *Lectures,* I, iii.

[6] *Ibid.,* II, 523.

[7] *Ibid.,* I, 16.

[8] *Ibid.,* I, 23.

[9] *Ibid.,* I, 21.

[10] *Ibid.,* I, 30.

[11] *Ibid.,* I, 31.

[12] *Ibid.,* I, 30.

[13] *Ibid.,* I, 36.

[14] *Ibid.,* I, 41.

[15] *Ibid.,* referring to Addison's "Essay on the Pleasures of the Imagination" in Vol. 6 of the *Spectator.* I, 44.

[16] *Ibid.,* I, 66, 70.

[17] *Ibid.,* I, 75.

[18] *Ibid.,* I, 98.

[19] *Ibid.,* I, 183.

[20] *Ibid.,* I, 186.

[21] *Ibid.,* I, 209.

[22] *Ibid.,* I, 245.

[23] *Ibid.,* I, 275.

[24] *Ibid.,* I, 287.

[25] *Ibid.,* I, 402.

[26] *Ibid.,* I, 402-7.

[27] *Ibid.,* II, 3, 8. For other meanings of the term "eloquence," see J. W. Bray, *A History of Critical Terms* (Boston, 1898), p. 96.

[28] *De Inventione,* I, 5, 6; *De Oratore,* I, 31, 138.

[29] Blair, *Lectures,* II, 5.

[30] *Ibid.,* II, 49. Compare II, 233: "Good sense and knowledge are the foundation of all good speaking."

[31] *Ibid.,* II, 53.

[32] *Ibid.,* II, 39.

[33] *Ibid.,* II, 43 Also II, 118. At II, 102, Blair complains that "we have a great number of moderately good preachers, . . . but few who are singularly eminent."

[34] *Ibid.,* II, 42.

[35] *Ibid.,* II, 61.

[36] *Ibid.,* II, 78.

[37] *Ibid.,* II, 81.

[38] *Ibid.,* II, 82-83.

[39] *Ibid.,* II, 85.

[40] *Ibid.,* II, 125.

[41] *Ibid.,* II, 106.

[42] *Ibid.,* II, 107.

[43] *Ibid.,* II, 107-14.

[44] *Ibid.,* II, 114.

[45] *Ibid.,* II, 115.

[46] *Ibid.,* II, 119.

[47] *Ibid.,* II, 158-69.

[48] *Ibid.,* II, 170.

[49] *Ibid.,* II, 179-80.

[50] *Ibid.,* II, 193-99.

[51] *Ibid.,* II, 193-99.

[52] *Ibid.,* II, 200.

[53] *Ibid.,* II, 206.

[54] *Ibid.,* II, 210-22.

[55] *Ibid.,* II, 218.

[56] *Ibid.,* II, 222.

[57] *Ibid.,* II, 228. See also Herman Cohen, "Hugh Blair on Speech Education," *Southern Speech Journal,* 29 (1963), 1-11.

[58] *Ibid.,* II, 232.

[59] *Ibid.,* II, 232.

[60] *Ibid.,* II, 233.

[61] *Ibid.,* II, 237.

[62] *Ibid.,* II, 236.

[63] *Ibid.,* II, 236.

[64] *Ibid.,* II, 239.

[65] *Ibid.,* II, 246.

[66] *Ibid.,* II, 246.

[67] William Charvat, *The Origins of American Critical Thought, 1810-1835* (Philadelphia, 1936), p. 44.

[68] H. G. Graham, *Scottish Men of Letters of the Eighteenth Century* (London, 1901), p. 121. Speaking of Blair's sermons as essays, composed by a professor of rhetoric to illustrate the principles of his art, see Leslie Stephen, *English Thought in the Eighteenth Century,* 2nd ed. (2 vols., London, 1881), II, 346. Elsewhere Stephen says Blair is like a "declaimer, whose rhetoric glides over the surface of things without biting into the substance." *Ibid.,* II, 215. As a theologian Blair was "a mere washed out retailer of second-hand commonplaces who gave the impression that the real man had vanished and left nothing but a wig and gown." *Ibid.,* II, 347.

[69] See James L. Golden, "Hugh Blair: Minister of St. Giles," *The Quarterly Journal of Speech,* 38 (1952), 155, 60. Also his 1948 Ohio State University Master's essay on Blair's practice in sermon writing.

[70] Graham, p. 128. The sermons were published in five volumes from 1777-1801. Blair received £200 for the first volume, £200 for the second, and £600 for the third. When Lord Mansfield read selections from them to King George III, the King expressed a wish that every youth in Britain might own a copy of the Bible and of Blair. See Boswell's *Life,* Chap. 3, p. 104 where

Johnson says: "Dr. Blair is printing some sermons. If they are all like the first, which I have read, they are *Sermones aurei, ac auro magis aurei.* It is excellently written as to doctrine and language." Also: "Please to return Dr. Blair thanks for his sermons. The Scotch write English wonderfully well." *Ibid.,* Chap. 3, p. 109.

[71] Graham, p. 128.

[72] Sir Alexander Grant, *The Story of the University of Edinburgh,* 2 vols. (London, 1884), I, 357. Quoting from Bower's *History University of Edinburgh,* Chap. 3, 17. Also Graham, p. 124.

[73] J. H. Millar, *Scottish Prose of the Seventeenth and Eighteenth Centuries* (Glasgow, 1912), p. 177.

[74] See A. D. Godley, *Oxford in the Eighteenth Century* (London, 1908), Chaps. 3 and 4; Christopher Wordsworth, *Scholae Academicae: Some Account of the Studies at the English Universities in the Eighteenth Century* (Cambridge, 1877).

[75] See Hume's *Essays,* Green and Grove, eds. 4 vols. (London, 1874), II, 46.

[76] Sir Alexander Grant, *The Story of the University of Edinburgh,* I, 350. At the request of Lord Kames, Adam Smith had given a course of lectures in rhetoric at the University of Edinburgh in 1750-51, I, 276. Blair tells us that he borrowed and studied Smith's manuscript notes. John Rae, *Life of Adam Smith* (London, 1895), p. 32. For the best recent account of Blair's life see Robert M. Schmitz, *Hugh Blair,* Chaps. 3-6. Also see John Hill, *An Account of the Life and Writings of Hugh Blair* (Edinburgh, 1807), and the biographical sketch by James Finlayson, in Blair's *Sermons* (London, 1826). See also Alexander Carlyle's *Autobiography,* 3rd ed. (London and Edinburgh, 1861), pp. 201-4 and *The European Magazine,* 4 (1783), 201-2.

[77] Blair, *Lectures,* II, 244-45.

[78] *Ibid.,* II, 242.

[79] *Ibid.,* II, 243.

[80] *Ibid.,* II, 242.

[81] *Ibid.,* II, 243.

[82] Adam Smith, *Lectures on Rhetoric and Belles Lettres,* John M. Lothian, ed. (London, 1963), p. xxi. Lothian uses the quotations from Rae's *Life of Adam Smith.*

[83] See Charles A. Fritz, on "The Content of the Teaching of Speech in the American Colleges before 1850: With Special Reference to the Influence on the Current Theories." New York University Ph.D. dissertation, 1928; Donald Hayworth, "The Development of the Training of Public Speakers in America," *Quarterly Journal of Speech,* 14 (1928), 489-502; Warren Guthrie, "The Development of Rhetorical Theory in America, 1635-1850," *Speech Monographs,* 15 (1948), 61-71; William Charvat, *The Origins of American Critical Thought, 1810-1835* (Philadelphia, 1936).

[84] For contemporary reviews of Blair's *Lectures,* see *The Monthly Review,* 68 (1783), 489-505; 69 (1783), 186-92; 70 (1784), 173-83; *The European Magazine,* 3 (1783), 433-35; 4 (1783), 33-34; 113-14; 197-202; *The English Review,* 2 (1783), 18-25; 81-95; *The Gentlemans Magazine,* 53 (1783), 684, 756.

[85] A. Bosker, *Literary Criticism in the Age of Johnson* (Groningen, 1930).

[86] Some seventeen adverse criticisms of Blair's *Lectures* have been assembled in the excellent monograph by Douglas Ehninger and James Golden, "The Intrinsic Sources of Blair's Popularity" in *Southern Speech Journal,* 21 (1955), 12-30. The authors give five good reasons for Blair's popularity. Their account should be read as the best modern explication of the *Lectures.* It serves to re-establish Blair's place in the history of rhetorical theory.

Herman Cohen, Edward P. J. Corbett, S. Michael Halloran, Charles W. Kneupper, Eric Skopec, Barbara Warnick (essay date 1986)

SOURCE: "The Most Significant Passage in Hugh Blair's *Lectures on Rhetoric and Belles Lettres,*" Rhetoric Society Quarterly, Vol. XVII, No. 3, Summer, 1987, pp. 281-304.

[*In the collection of essays below, originally presented at the 1986 Speech Communication Association convention, six experts on Blair discuss what they feel is the most significant passage in his book* Lectures on Rhetoric and Belles Lettres.]

Herman Cohen, The Pennsylvania State University

The passage which I have chosen as the most significant in the works of Hugh Blair is one which might seem very obvious. It occurs at the beginning of Lecture X. It reads as follows:

> It is not easy to give a precise idea of what is meant by style. The best definition I can give of it, is the peculiar manner in which a man expresses his conceptions by means of language. It is different from mere language or words. The words which an author employs may be proper and faultless and his style may, nevertheless, have great faults. Style always has some reference to an author's manner of

thinking. It is a picture of the ideas which rise in his mind, and of the manner in which they rise there; and hence when we are examining an author's composition, it is, in many cases, extremely difficult to separate the style from the sentiment. No wonder these two should be so intimately connected, as style is nothing else, than that sort of expression which our thoughts most readily assume.[1]

This passage is important because it represents a key (perhaps *the* key) to all that Blair has to say on language and style.

Before I explicate this brief text it may be useful to place this passage in context and remind ourselves of some apparent (and even obvious) characteristics of Blair's rhetoric. A good deal has been written and spoken about the question of whether Blair's *Lectures* are stylistic, managerial or epistemological. These taxonomies may be useful or they may merely be matters of academic convenience. Nonetheless, whatever other kind of rhetorician Blair was, he was most certainly a writer fundamentally and principally concerned with matters of language and style. Let us remind ourselves again concerning the format of the *Lectures.* Before Blair turns to the treatment of any specific literary or rhetorical genres he devotes more than half of his lectures to the treatment of the general foundational concerns with taste, language and style which will be applied to the treatment of specific genres later in the work. Twenty-four of the forty-seven *Lectures* are devoted to such matters. Of those twenty-four *Lectures,* twenty (Lectures IV and VI-XXIV) are concerned with linguistic matters. In contrast, in the *Lectures* in which Blair applied the principles enunciated in the earlier portion of the work, nine *Lectures* are devoted to public speaking and fourteen to various literary genres. In addition, we should remember that much of the later portion of the *Lectures* is concerned with the language and style of public speaking, historical and philosophical writing, poetry and drama. Thus we must recognize that Blair's interest in, even preoccupation with, matters of language and style is not only significant; it is the foundation of his rhetorical and literary theory and Blair's treatment of language must be understood if one is to understand his rhetorical theory in its entirety. Therefore, if as I believe, this passage is the key to Blair's treatment of language and style, it is the most significant passage in the *Lectures.*

But what is the significance of the passage itself? Is it anything more than a restatement of fairly standard eighteenth century doctrine concerning style? Even if it is a standard restatement, it is a very clear and cogent one, but it goes beyond a routine doctrinal statement and contains significance in itself.

The first significant element in the passage is to be noted in the definition which Blair gives of style. When he defines style as " . . . the peculiar manner in which a man expresses his conceptions by means of language," Blair departs from much eighteenth century doctrine, and, indeed, from some of his own positions including his own doctrine of taste. In most of his literary and rhetorical theory, Blair, in good eighteenth century fashion, seeks to find universal and elements common to all mankind. For example in Lecture II Blair says of taste, "The foundations upon which they rest, is what has been founded to please mankind universally."[2] "In every composition, what interests the imagination and touches the heart, pleases all ages and all nations."[3]

In contrast, Blair's definition of style, and the discussion which follows is based on individual differences, not on the common characteristics of mankind. It is important to note that the entire passage, I have cited, except for the last sentence is written in the third person singular. If Blair's perspective were entirely Neo-Classical he might well have written " . . . The manner in which men express their conceptions by means of language." Instead, he wrote " . . . the *peculiar* manner in which *a man* expresses *his* conceptions by means of language." (Emphasis added.) He goes on to speak of "the words which *an author* employs," "*an author's* manner of thinking," "the ideas which rise in *his* mind." Only in the final sentence does he speak of "that sort of expression which *our* thoughts must readily assume." (Emphasis added.) Blair's individualistic perspective toward language and style is demonstrated in numerous places in the succeeding *Lectures.* In Lecture XVIII Blair makes the point that the ability to use figurative language is dependent on individual power of imagination " . . . without a genius for figurative language, none should attempt it. Imagination is a power not to be acquired; it must be derived from nature. Its redundancies we may prune, its deviations we may correct, its sphere we may enlarge, but the faculty itself we cannot create; . . . "[4]

Similarly, in the same Lecture when Blair begins his discussion of the "General Characters of Style," he relates style very closely to the individual author's mode of thought and expression . . . " words being the copies of our ideas, there must always be a very intimate connexion between the manner in which every writer employs words, and his manner of thinking; and that from the peculiarity of thought and expression which belongs to him, there is a certain character imprinted on his style, which may be denominated his manner."[5]

Blair follows the same theme in Lecture XXVII when he explicates the style of "Eloquence of Popular Assemblies," when he writes "the great rule here, as indeed in every other case, is to follow nature: never to attempt a strain of eloquence which is not seconded by our own genius. . . . to attain the pathetic and the sublime of oratory, require these strong sensibilities of mind, and that high power of expression which are given to few."[6]

Although Blair's concern with style is individualistic and, even though it seems to have an almost Pre-Romantic strain, we must recognize that his treatment of language and style is also reflective of a pervasive eighteenth century preoccupation—the nature vs. art dispute. Throughout the *Lectures,* Blair attends to the question of the respective contributions of our natural endowments (nature) and education and culture (art).

Blair's criteria for the standards of taste are firmly rooted in the sentiments of mankind. "That which men concur the most in admiring, must be held to be beautiful. His taste must be esteemed just and true which coincides with the general sentiments of mankind. In this standard we must rest. To the sense of mankind the ultimate appeal must ever lie, in all works of taste."[7] Nevertheless, as in style, Blair understands that "the power of receiving pleasure" is not equal in all humans. "But although none may be wholly devoid of this faculty, yet the degree in which it is possessed are widely different."[8] "This inequality of taste among men is occurring, without doubt, in part to the different forms of their natures."[9]

In Lecture III when Blair treats of "Genius," he also recognizes the importance of nature. "This talent or aptitude for excelling in someone particular is, I have said, what we receive from nature. By art and study, no doubt, it may be greatly improved; but by them alone it cannot be acquired."[10]

We may thus speculate that Blair's concern with nature in the nature vs. art controversy caused him to give precedence to nature in his definition of style while he had assigned it a more equal role in his discussion of other matters.

We should also note the distinction between language and style which Blair makes in his definition. To Blair, language and style are not at all synonymous. Style is the product; language the means. He speaks of style as " . . . the particular manner in which a man expresses his conceptions, by means of language. It is different from mere language or words." In effect, Blair is saying that language is *merely* language and that words are *merely* words. Only when the thoughts and sentiments of a writer or speaker are expressed by means of language does "style" result. Thus style is always the product of the use of language in a "peculiar manner" by a particular human being. Style cannot be separated from the individual.

"Style has always some reference to an author's manner of thinking. It is a picture of the ideas which rise in his mind, and of the manner in which they rise there. . . . " For Blair, then, style is more than the mere clothing of thought. It is "a picture of the ideas." The representation of thought comes through style and not through language by itself. Language as a means is universal but style as an end is personal and individualistic.

But style is related not only to thought but to sentiments as well. Blair writes that, " . . . it is in many cases extremely difficult to separate the style from the sentiment." Not only is style reflective of the individual sentiments of humans, it is also reflective of various ethnic characteristics. "Hence, different countries have been noted for peculiarities of style, suited to their different temper and genius."[11] In the case of individuals, "In giving the general characters of style, it's usual to talk of a nervous, a feeble, or a spirited style; which are plainly the characters of a writer's manner of thinking, as well as expressing himself so; so difficult is it to separate these two things from one another."[12]

The passage which I have chosen as Hugh Blair's most significant is important because it is a key to the bulk of Blair's *Lectures,* especially the *Lectures* dealing with language and style. It emphasizes the individuality of style, its reliance on nature, and its relationship to ideas and sentiments.

. . . . .

Edward P. J. Corbett, Ohio State University

The passage that I nominated as the most significant in Blair's text occurs in Lecture 32, which deals with the argumentative part of a discourse. Let me read you that passage:

> The Grecian sophists were the first inventors of this artificial system of oratory; and they showed a prodigious subtlety and fertility in the contrivance of these *loci.* Succeeding rhetoricians, dazzled by the plan, wrought them up into so regular a system that one would think they meant to teach how a person might mechanically become an orator without any genius at all. They gave him recipes for making speeches on all manner of subjects. At the same time, it is evident that though this study of commonplaces might produce very showy academical declamations, it could never produce discourses on real business. The *loci* indeed supplied a most exuberant fecundity of matter. One who had no other aim but to talk copiously and plausibly, by consulting them on every subject and laying hold of all that they suggested, might discourse without end; and that, too, though he had none but the most superficial knowledge of his subject. But such discourse could be no other than trivial. What is truly solid and persuasive must be drawn *"ex visceribus*

causae" ["from the very bowels of the case"], from a thorough knowledge of the subject and profound meditation on it. They who would direct students of oratory to any other sources of argumentation only delude them; and by attempting to render rhetoric too perfect an art, they render it, in truth, a trifling and childish study.

The explanation of my choice of that passage is tied up with the story of my fortuitous discovery of Blair during the first year of my teaching career. I was searching desperately and randomly in the college library for help in dealing with prose essays in the classroom. Because of the heavy dosage of the New Criticism in my graduate courses at the University of Chicago, I knew how to analyze the form as well as the content of a poem, but because I could not recall anything from my formal training that would enable me to talk about the form of a prose text, I was reduced to talking only about the Scanning the rows of books on the shelves, I spotted a calfskin-covered book bearing the title ***Lectures on Rhetoric and Belles Lettres.*** When I took the book down from the shelf, it broke open at one of the lectures in which Hugh Blair was analyzing the style of one of Joseph Addison's *Spectator Papers*. I stood there and read through the whole lecture. Never before or since did I encounter the kind of sentence-by-sentence analysis of the style of a whole essay that Blair was engaged in. I was enraptured by his skillful analysis of one of the formal aspects of a literary text that was written in prose. Looking at the intriguing titles of other lectures in the book, I realized that my experience that day was going to be my classic example of serendipity. I took Blair's book home with me, and before the end of that day, the future of my professional career was cast. I discovered more than Blair that day; I was launched into my discovery of the whole tradition of rhetoric, which went back to fifth-century Athens.

It was not long before I learned that Blair came along at the *end* of the tradition of classical rhetoric that was fostered by rhetoricians such as Aristotle and Isocrates. Blair represented the "new rhetoric," a rhetoric that, among other changes, was expanding its purview to include a study of contemporary belletristic texts. I had dipped into Blair just at the point that represented his major interest among the five traditional canons of rhetoric. Blair devoted fifteen lectures to a discussion of style, more lectures than on any other subject.

It was not until much later that I realized how revolutionary the passage I just read to you was. That passage articulated the whole Romantic rejection of the canon of rhetoric that had been the primary one for most of the classical rhetoricians: the canon of invention. Like the Romantic poets who were about to proclaim the primacy of imagination and taste and originality in the creative process, Blair here expresses his disdain for the mechanical nature of the topics. That disdain presaged the disappearance of the formal study of invention from the curriculum of rhetoric for more than a century. Consequently and subsequently, speech courses concentrated on the elocutionary aspects of speech-making, and composition courses in English departments were preoccupied with the linguistic and stylistic aspects of prose texts. Blair's text fostered that narrowing of the traditional concerns of rhetoric in American colleges during the nineteenth century. His influence was understandable but regrettable. Should we forgive him for what he wrought?

. . . . .

S. Michael Halloran, Rensselaer Polytechnic Institute

> Exercises of speaking have always been recommended to students, in order that they may prepare themselves for speaking in public, and on real business. The meetings, or societies, into which they sometimes form themselves for this purpose, are laudable institutions; and, under proper conduct, may serve many valuable purposes. They are favourable to knowledge and study, by giving occasion to inquiries, concerning those subjects which are made the ground of discussion. They produce emulation, and gradually inure those who are concerned in them, to somewhat that resembles a public assembly. They accustom them to know their own powers, and to acquire a command of themselves in speaking; and what is, perhaps, the greatest advantage of all, they give them a facility and fluency of expression, and assist them in procuring the 'Copia verborum,' which can be acquired by no other means but frequent exercise in speaking.

> But the meetings which I have now in my eye, are to be understood of those academical associations, where a moderate number of young gentlemen who are carrying on their studies, and are connected by some affinity in the future pursuits which they have in view, assemble privately, in order to improve one another, and to prepare themselves for those public exhibitions which may afterwards fall to their lot. As for those public and promiscuous societies, in which multitudes are brought together, who are often of low stations and occupations, who are joined by no common bond of union, except an absurd rage for public speaking, and have no other object in view, but to make a show of their supposed talents, they are institutions not merely of an useless, but of an hurtful nature. They are in great hazard of proving seminaries of licentiousness, petulance, faction, and folly. They mislead those who, in their own callings, might be useful members of society, into fantastic plans of making a figure on subjects, which divert their attention from their proper business, and are widely remote from their sphere in life.

Lecture XXXIV
"Means of Improving in Eloquence"

LECTURES

ON

RHETORIC

AND

BELLES LETTRES.

By HUGH BLAIR, D.D. and F.R.S. Edin.

ONE OF THE MINISTERS OF THE HIGH CHURCH, AND PROFESSOR
OF RHETORIC AND BELLES LETTRES IN THE
UNIVERSITY OF EDINBURGH.

SIXTH AMERICAN,

FROM THE LAST EDINBURGH EDITION.

NEW-YORK;

PUBLISHED BY RICHARD SCOTT.

NO. 276 PEARL-STREET.

1815.

The societies of which Blair speaks in this passage were a prominent feature of what Davis McElroy calls "Scotland's Age of Improvement." In addition to the student groups and "public or promiscuous societies" mentioned by Blair, there were societies for professionals in various specialties and, most important of all, literary and debate societies for the intelligentsia and the social elite. Blair was himself a director of the most famous of these, the Select Society for Promoting the Reading and Speaking of the English Language in Scotland, or, as it was better and more simply known, the Select Society. The general purpose served by all these societies was improvement of Scottish life in all aspects: agriculture, commerce, morality, conversation, oratory, literary taste and authorship. They adopted English models in their improving efforts, suggesting a kind of national inferiority complex, a sense that to improve Scottish manners would be to make them indistinguishable from those of the English.

What I find significant in this passage is Blair's aversion to the "public and promiscuous societies," and the language in which he expresses it. According to McElroy, these societies were simply "democratic offshoots" of the more elite societies, made necessary by their reluctance to admit persons of the middle classes. Some of these democratic offshoots were as much concerned with public entertainment as with improvement, and they were "promiscuous" to the extent that some even admitted women. One, the Bachelor Club, included the young poet Robert Burns in its relatively small membership, and its by-laws and minutes suggest a somewhat liberal leaning on political and social questions. Perhaps it was one or another of these instances that made Blair see in them potential "seminaries of licentiousness, petulance, faction, and folly."

Whatever specific excesses he may have had in mind, the language of Blair's short diatribe against these societies betrays the fundamental elitism of his own social vision. He sees the members of these societies—merchants and farmers, most likely—as being lead astray from "their own callings . . . their proper business . . . their sphere in life." The same sense of a neatly ordered society in which each person occupies a clearly defined and more or less permanent niche applies to the students for whom Blair recommends the academic speaking societies. These students are "connected by some affinity in the future pursuits which they have in view," and their exercises will prepare them for what will "afterwards fall to their lot." A place for everyone, and everyone in his place. The vision of a stable social hierarchy that ought not to be disturbed is, in my view, central to Blair's Lectures. It pervades his views on taste, composition, eloquence, and all the other topics of the Lectures, but it becomes particularly clear in his

attack on the non-elite speaking societies. It is for this reason that I nominate this passage as "most significant."

. . . . .

Charles W. Kneupper, University of Texas at Arlington

Before I deal specifically with the passage(s) which I recommend for your consideration as the most significant, enduring, intriguing and perhaps precocious, yet antiquarian in Blair's *Lectures,* I wish to make several preliminary remarks regarding the contextual significance of Blair and concerning my intent and method.

First, while Blair is sometimes not considered an intellectual of the first rank and his theoretical contributions to rhetoric are minimized, it is widely conceded that his lectures were among the most popular and widely read in Britain and America of the so-called British triumvirate (Blair, Campbell and Whately). Despite this his influence on rhetorical theory is often not thought significant, this position is often taken in part because his positions are in many respects derivative (at times strongly echoing, but as often providing a Romanticist and/or pedantic distortion of classical rhetoric) and in part because of the peculiar attitude which Blair displays throughout the text in which he to some extent distances himself from "the rhetoricians." However, if one takes a wider view of the historic influence of Blair's *Lectures,* particularly their influence on American education, then it seems clear that Blair by far outdistances the social and institutional significance of Campbell or Whately. Put simply, Blair's *Lectures* are a blueprint for the 20th century American Department of English. And while a direct causal link between Blair's *Lectures* and the development of American English departments might be difficult to establish, the parallels between the structure and curriculum and even attitudes of English departments and the lectures are striking—the concerns for language in general, composition, literary genres and critically informed taste.

Second, I feel it desirable to describe my method in selecting "a most significant passage." Put simply, I reread Blair's *Lectures* twice making notes and transcribing passages which simply seemed noteworthy, interesting, well-phrased or quotable. The usefulness of this simple approach depends on the assumption that a reader is armed with sufficient tacit knowledge from immersion in the field to make intelligent selections, even though all the criteria for selection are not specified in advance. (Polanyi) The two readings produced a list of about fifty selected passages. I then attempted to look for a passage which might summarize the theory behind the work. This was problematic—I doubt that there is any general theory informing Blair's *Lectures* beyond the minimal sense that improvement in language facility is transferable between the rhetorical and literary spheres. And while, there is some truth in this insight, it far from provides a useful or principled integration for Blair's *Lectures,* which if I may follow a hyperbolic analogy from the Wizard of Oz's description of the tin man, might be characterized as a "clinkering, clattering, contiginous conglomeration." After not finding a usable synecdoche, I considered a second alternative which was essentially to choose one of the many passages which I would be inclined to take issue with and decry Blair's pernicious influence. Blair's romantic devaluation of invention, his pedantic view of style, his implicit attitudinal devaluation of rhetoric and superior evaluation of *Lettres,* or to make the last point again in different terms, his privileging of the aesthetic over the pragmatic, all reflect theoretical and practical problems with which rhetoricians in general contend. This is particularly the case in English departments, where rhetoricians have been or still are contending such issues among their colleagues in literature and often among themselves. While I think there is much to condemn in Blair, I rejected this course of selection insofar as it seemed to me that there is no need for one more attack on "the current traditional paradigm" even if in terms of its historic roots and influences (see Berlin). At this point, there are very few passages left to select from and none seems to be central to Blair's decentered thought or even the main outlines of those thoughts. Rather, there are comments on issues of continuing theoretical interest and there are noteworthy asides—the significance of which is not developed in Blair's lectures. My final and somewhat arbitrary choice was among these noteworthy asides—which does seem of greater merit than any other passages of the text. So somewhat paradoxically, my perspective of the most significant passage(s) in Blair's *Lectures* is not significant for understanding his *Lectures* as a whole, nor have these passage(s) been historically influential in a way traceable to Blair's work, and in a certain sense they are the passages in which Blair may realize his role in continuity of the rhetorical tradition, but in which he has failed to realize the significance of his own words.

Thus, my nominations are from Lecture 1:

> One of the most distinguished privileges which Providence has conferred upon mankind, is the power of communicating their thoughts to one another. Destitute of this power, reason, would be a solitary, and, in some measure, an unavailable principle. Speech is the great instrument by which man becomes beneficial to man: and it is to the intercourse and transmission of thought, by means of speech, that we are chiefly indebted for the improvement of thought itself. Small are the advances which a single unassisted individual can make towards perfecting any of his powers. What

we call human reason, is not the effort or ability of one, so much as it is the result of the reason of many, arising from lights mutually communicated, in consequence of discourse and writing.

I cannot read this selection without hearing an echo of Isocrates, and while Blair does not acknowledge a debt to Isocrates, he essentially continues an insight long rooted in the rhetorical tradition. In the *Antidosis,* Isocrates writes:

> . . . because there has been implanted in us the power to persuade each other and to make clear to each other whatever we desire . . . we have come together and founded cities and made laws and invented arts, and, generally speaking there is no institution devised by man which the power of speech has not helped to establish . . . With this faculty we both contend against others on matters which are open to dispute and seek light for ourselves on things which are unknown; for the same arguments which we use in persuading others when we speak in public, we employ also when we deliberate in our own thoughts; and, . . . if there is need to speak in brief summary of this power, we shall find that none of the things which are done with intelligence take place without the help of speech, but that in all our actions as well as in all our thoughts speech is our guide, and is most employed by those who have the most wisdom. . . .

The point behind both Isocrates and Blair concerns the social/intellectual significance of communication. For Isocrates social institutions and "things done with intelligence" are consequences of communication. Blair seems less explicit than Isocrates in stating that "social reality is a rhetorical product"—to use a modern paraphrase. But, Blair is quite clear in viewing reason as profoundly a social/collective activity—and that the improvement of thought is rooted in the communication processes. And since this much seems obvious, the mighty question of SO WHAT? looms before us.

Isocrates and Blair's thought predate that of such linguists as Sapir and Whorf, whose hypothesis of linguistic relativity and linguistic determinism reach convergent insights, and as importantly predate Mannheim's early formulations of the sociology of knowledge. Certainly, Sapir, Whorf (see Kneupper, 1975), and Mannheim's thought were not directly influenced by Blair. The point of this predating game is essentially to point out that there is rooted in the classical rhetorical tradition a relatively underdeveloped sociolinguistic/sociological aspect of rhetoric. While the sociological dimension in rhetorical theory does not seem carefully articulated in Blair or most of the traditional theories of rhetoric, and is somewhat obscured in the emphasis of the writer or speaker, it is critically important to recognize that a sociology of rhetoric is always immanent in the concern for audience and in the rhetorical characterization of the dimensions of persuasive appeal to audiences: ethos, pathos, logos, style. Yet, the modern sociology of knowledge is philosophically grounded in a Kantian psychology of "constitution" and a Marxist privileging of economic and class structure without recognition of "communication" as a social activity which creates both "socially shared constitutions" and economic and class structures. While linguistics at least in its Chomskian backwash, still seeks a Platonic version of linguistic structure, instead of attempting to account for a rhetorically evolving social life world in which language use changes phonetically, semantically, pragmatically and even structurally. In Sassurean terms it is *parole* which is real and *langue* which is always a fiction and contrary to prevailing opinion, it is *parole* which provides the possibility for *langue* as a meaningful abstraction and not langue which provides the possibility for the communicability of language. Interpretation of rhetoric (parole) is dialectical and evolving and influenced situationally and semiotically as well as linguistically. All of these factors occur in a social context, which is itself a rhetorical product and a material context which may be partially a rhetorical product.

Despite this mild diatribe on linguistics and the early sociology of knowledge, which might be extended to other "human or social sciences" whose conceptual evolution seems more tied to the philosophic than the rhetorical tradition—and that includes much work in speech communication which has abandoned a rhetorical framework to adopt the concepts of other disciplines, the question of SO WHAT? looms large again. So what if rhetoricians had this insight first, so what if there are immanent in standard rhetorical treatises concepts and approaches which other disciplines have neither recognized nor absorbed. Is this anything more than the recognition that over the last 300 years in the wake of Ramian reforms, Rhetoric as a formal discipline has dropped out of intellectual dialogue and the social prestige it enjoyed in antiquity? Is it anything more than the fact that Rhetoric no longer has sufficient power to get other disciplines to speak or even carefully attend to its concepts and theoretical formulations? Indeed, it is the last 300 years that need to be overcome. But in grand terms the consequences are equally grim for other disciplines of the loss of a dialogue with Rhetoricians. I read and hear much these days about the turn to the rhetorical on the contemporary intellectual scene. Rhetoricians in Speech Communication and English often see in philosophers such as Rorty, critical theorists such as Habermas, or in such writers as Gadamer, Foucault or even Derrida a turn to the rhetorical. And yet, while this turn might be explained due to the increasing recognition of the bankruptcy of the dominant philosophical tradition,

this turn supposedly to the rhetorical occurs without careful attention to scholarship in the classical rhetorical tradition or any attempt to explicitly relate to it. My point, simple as it is, is that application of traditional rhetorical concepts or theories has simply not yet been attempted and that at the very least it is a potentially significant road not taken, which rhetoricians might now take since at least there is a potentially interested intellectual audience beyond rhetorical specialists. The last 300 years of intellectual history might have been very different had the rhetorical partner of the dialogue maintained a prominent position (see Ijssérling). The "turn to consciousness" might have taken a much less introverted direction.

But, while some potential here is clear, I suppose I still need to face the big SO WHAT? in regard to Blair. And, I would like to attempt that briefly by reflecting on a second passage which I believe contributes to the illumination of the first. In Lecture 6, Blair writes: "This artificial method of communicating thought, we now behold carried to the highest perfection. Language is become a vehicle by which the most delicate and refined emotions of one mind can be transmitted, or, if we may so speak, transfused into another." I am particularly interested in the tossed off metaphor of transfusion, because even though he does absolutely nothing with the concept, I think it has significant implications for the understanding of rational thought. From here on, you are getting Kneupper reading immanent meanings into Blair's transfused. While a modern reader might immediately interpret "transfuse" only in regard to a blood transfusion—it is not certain that Blair had this metaphor in mind. The *Oxford English Dictionary* notes three nuances with historical reference to the time of Blair's writing. Only one of these relates to our notion of blood transfusion. The other two nuances of transfuse are described as "to pour (a liquid) from one vessel or receptacle to another" and the other which seems related to but more abstract as "to cause to 'flow' from one to another, to transmit; to diffuse into or through something; to cause to permeate, to instill" (261). Even more interesting than the indicated meanings of the verb form is that the noun form transfusion also had the meaning of translation (OED, 261). And the root verb of fuse, held a metallurgical sense of melting and mixing of metals to unite them and might abstractly be seen as creating a unity by fire. If we allow a confluence of these verb and noun and root meanings available in the late 1700 and early 1800s, then we can ask what difference between transmit and transfuse might Blair be suggesting?

To transmit is to "carry language to" another—the verb transfuse can carry a synonymous meaning, but probably not in a sentence apparently drawing a contrast or extension. While as a verb analogous to our sense of blood transfusion to transfuse is "to let language flow from one living being into another living being with whom a fusion of language and self will occur." Meaning is not carried in the language but produced through fusion within the living being. Through communication in speaking, reading and writing, meanings occur through transfusion. Words are always potentially capable of a meaningful "fusion" with the human being. Human thought advances not through the solitary and inherently anemic "fusions" of disconnected individuality, but through the historic and continuous "transfusions" which speech and inscription enable. As long as communication continues, the transfusion of thought continues and through this interaction the "fusions" of human thought are coordinated and can thereby develop and advance. When communication stops human beings lose engagement with the oriented and coordinated "fusions" of the historically evolving traditions of human thought; individual reason becomes con-fused; in the sense of not-fused with social thought; experience becomes isolated and becoming reifies into solitary being and the Death of man as a social being.

Or noting the relation of the noun "transfusion" with translation, there may be implied a notion that a meaning is fused with language within a person and that meaning/fusion is communicated to introduce that form into others to create within them a meaning/fusion. Translation is, in effect, a transformation of the fusion—and while this is not impossible to do approximately—it is difficult and perhaps impossible to accomplish in totality. This interpretation suggests that form and meaning cannot be separated and is allied with at least one contemporary linguistic theory (Pike).

While these readings may be influenced by distant readings of Kierkegaard, Heidegger, Sartre, or more recent ones of Kenneth Pike, I hope it at least suggests that we can read documents from the history of rhetoric not only to inquire what they meant in their time, or what historic influence they may have had, but to inquire what they can mean to us theoretically, humanistically, heuristically, and rhetorically today. Or to follow Blair's metaphor—to "transfuse" with them anew in the fullness of who we are now, in the fullness of where we are now and in the fullness of the other concepts, theories and issues of today. Such a reading of documents from the history of rhetoric may remind us of "our roots" and from such a knowledge not return us into the past, but provide us with an unexplored though anciently rooted direction for the future (see Kneupper, 1985). Such an approach to scholarship is not a replacement for traditional historical scholarship, it is however one approach by which traditional rhetorical theory can be brought to bear on contemporary theoretical issues in a vital and interesting way—to show the

relevance of the past on the present and to produce a "fusion" of horizons which may lead us into the future (Gadamer).

. . . . .

Eric Skopec, University of Southern California

I found selecting a passage to nominate for consideration on this panel to be a surprisingly difficult task. Of course, you could attribute this difficulty to my preoccupation with more contemporary matters, but I prefer to attribute it to certain peculiarities in the *Lectures* themselves. As you know, I am not the only person to have had difficulties deciding just what to make of the *Lectures.*

Written for a select group of eighteenth-century school boys, the *Lectures* became one of the most popular works on rhetoric ever published. Alternately read as the high watermark of neoclassicism and the harbinger of the emerging romantic movement,[13] the *Lectures* feature a theory of taste simultaneously acclaimed as a substantial addition to the theory of rhetoric and condemned as superficial and incoherent.[14] Moreover, while the *Lectures* may well have set a record for longevity in the textbook market, critical reactions have never been all together favorable.[15] Most critics agree that they were "neither original, comprehensive, nor profound." Less favorable critics have found them to be "empty, insipid, and loquacious."

While I have struggled with these peculiarities, I also recognize that they give me considerable license. Capitalizing on this freedom, I have chosen to nominate a passage from the midst of a doctrine which Howell says demonstrates that "Blair's rhetorical theory must be said to lack penetration and insight at a crucial moment in its development."[16]

With this introduction, let me set the stage for the passage I nominate. Blair's grand plan for his lectures calls for discussion of five general topics: taste, language, style, eloquence, and critical examination of distinguished compositions. Dealing with the first three topics in lectures two through twenty-four, Blair opens his discussion of "eloquence properly so called, or publick speaking" with the twenty-fifth lecture. Before discussing specific characteristics of the art, he proposes to "take a view of the nature of Eloquence in general" to insure that his readers have "a just idea of the perfection of the art." This is particularly necessary in discussing eloquence, he says, because false notions commonly held make it seem to be "a very contemptible art" "of varnishing weak arguments plausibly; or of speaking so as to please and tickle the ear." Contesting this popular view, Blair defines eloquence as "the Art of Speaking in such a manner as to attain the end for which we speak," argues that speaking to influence action or conduct is its highest form, and concludes that "Eloquence may, under this view of it, be defined, [as] The Art of Persuasion." From this it follows, Blair says, that the requisites of persuasion are "solid argument, clear method, a character of probity appearing in the Speaker, joined with such graces of Style and utterance, as shall draw our attention to what he says." This is the point at which Blair makes the statement I nominate as the most significant passage in the *Lectures.*

> Good sense is the foundation of all. No man can be truly eloquent without it; for fools can persuade none but fools. In order to persuade a man of sense, you must first convince him; which is only to be done, by satisfying his understanding of the reasonableness of what you propose to him.[17]

As many of you recognize, this passage invokes a linear adjunct theory of persuasion according to which a speaker must first sway the audience's critical judgment and then invoke the audience's emotions in support of his cause. This doctrine informs much of what Blair says about eloquence and, in more general terms, represents his position on a matter of continuing interest.

There can be little doubt that the linear adjunct theory of persuasion informs Blair's rhetorical theory. Examples are numerous and Blair frequently remarks that "reason and argument make the foundation . . . of all manly and persuasive eloquence" (II, 179; compare II, 189 and II, 233). He takes particular care in using the doctrine to describe eloquence of popular assemblies and of the pulpit.

Persuasion is the end of speaking in popular assemblies, he says, and then notes that "in all attempts to persuade men, we must proceed upon this principle, that it is necessary to convince their understanding" (II, 48). Summarizing his remarks about deliberative speaking, Blair restates his case noting that "The end of popular speaking is persuasion; and this must be founded on conviction. Argument and reasoning must be the basis, if we would be Speakers of business, and not mere declaimers" (II, 61).

With regard to the eloquence of the pulpit, Blair begins by dismissing the objection that rhetoric has no place in preaching. This argument would have merit, he says, if eloquence were only an "ostentatious and deceitful art . . . calculated to please and to tickle the ear." Fortunately, this is an inappropriate conception and Blair argues that "eloquence is the art of placing truth in the most advantageous light for conviction and persuasion" (II, 104). Since the end of every sermon is to persuade men to be good, he says, it follows that "every sermon . . . should become a persuasive oration . . . founded on conviction" (II,

105). This line of reasoning is followed by a frequently quoted passage in which Blair maintains that persuasion must begin with conviction if speakers want to make a lasting impression on the heart.

Blair's use of the linear adjunct theory of persuasion also is relevant to a problem of continuing interest. Comprehensive rhetorics authorize appeals beyond those arising from analysis of the subject. For example, Aristotle's doctrine of proof draws materials from the subject of dispute, the character of the speaker, and the emotions of the audience. In contrast, narrow or specialist rhetorics limit the range of factors to which a speaker may legitimately appeal.

Much of the history of rhetoric, and of the dispute between rhetoric and philosophy, can be written in terms of the range of appeals considered acceptable. Rationalists have maintained that emotional responses should be irrelevant and the fact that speakers appeal to the passions has long been grounds for condemning rhetoric. Slightly less extreme positions authorize a rhetoric devoid of emotional appeals. Witness Bacon's purified rhetoric enlisted to unite reason and imagination against the passions.

At the other extreme, antirationalists bordering on mysticism could maintain that reasoning is necessarily fallible and that the emotions are our only reliable guide. Such theorists write fewer books than the rationalists and have not fared as well historically. However, the common sense movement in Blair's own era produced a number of treatises that come close to the extreme antirationalist position. In this contest, Blair's contemporary Thomas Reid adopted a relatively moderate course maintaining that reason and the emotions are both God-given faculties. Each is supreme in its own domain and education should teach us which one to attend to under particular circumstances.

In this contest, Blair chose to present a comprehensive rhetoric but could not fully escape the prejudices of his age. Reason and emotion are both important in his system, but they are not presented as autonomous sources of proof. For Blair, appeal to reason alone is appropriate for didactic purposes, but appeal to the passions alone is never appropriate unless one is a "mere declaimer" who is satisfied to "raise transient emotions, or kindle a passing ardour; but can produce no solid or lasting effect" (II, 105).

. . . . .

Barbara Warnick, University of Washington

One aspect of Blair's *Lectures* which has been remarked upon is his theory of style. Schmitz calls Blair's analysis of the categories of style "the most complex of his time."[18] Howell labels Blair's decision to depart from the ancient doctrine of the three major styles "a decision of some consequence."[19] Blair proposed two systems for classifying style. One, which is standard, is according to the degree of ornament contained within discourse.[20] The other, which is unique, is in accordance with the extent and manner of expression of meaning.[21] Here Blair proposes a continuum between the diffuse or feeble style on one hand and the concise or nervous style on the other. Diffuse or feeble expression distributes thoughts generally and indistinctly within discourse, while concise or nervous styles give a strong impression of meaning and express thoughts with energy and acuity.

What led Blair to rank precision of expression so highly that he constructed a new category scheme in accordance with it? And why was he so preoccupied with proposing a complete theory of style? I believe he was motivated by a belief that the thoughts we have and the words in which we express them are so closely related that we can improve the quality of our thoughts by improving the quality of our expression. Blair wanted the students of his lectures and the readers of his work to concentrate upon style as a means to an end, that end being the improvement of their ability to conceive and reason about the matter at hand. In Blair's system, then, language use had an inherently epistemological function.

The passage which expresses Blair's view on this subject most forthrightly is in the first lecture. Here Blair says that "by putting our sentiments into words, we always conceive them more distinctly. Every one who has the slightest acquaintance with composition knows, that when he expresses himself ill on any subject, when his arrangement becomes loose and his sentences turn feeble, the defects of his style can, almost on every occasion, be traced back to his indistinct conception of the subject: so close is the connection between thoughts and the words in which they are clothed."[22] In Blair's view, the process of forming thoughts is inextricably bound up with the act of expressing them. Not only does this mean that faulty expression can be traced to faulty conception. It also works the other way; improving expression can lead to an improvement in the quality of our thought. The desire to improve thought by improving its expression explains Blair's attention to style, particularly to stylistic precision.

The term "precision," central to Blair's theory of style, implies the mechanism by which thoughts and their expression are to be linked. Blair notes that the etymological origin of precision is "precidere," to cut off, which "imports retrenching all superfluities, and pruning the expression so, as to exhibit neither more nor less than an exact copy of his idea who uses it."[23] Therefore, a conception that a writer or speaker has

and the term which he uses to express it must exactly match; Blair's view of language function is strictly referential.

I believe that Blair's conception of linguistic reference can be traced to the Cartesian emphasis on clear and distinct ideas laid out in Arnauld's *Art of Thinking*.[24] In that work, precise reference was crucial to the rational method. Arnauld viewed reasoning as a progression of connections expressed linguistically. (An example of this sort of connection is the transference we make in a syllogism via the middle term.) Since language provides the medium in which connections are made, precise reference is essential. Ideas must be both clear and distinct so that language can precisely refer to them. A clear idea as described by Arnauld is one in which we recognize all the constituent parts which make up the idea; a distinct idea is one where we recognize all the aspects a referent has which it shares with other referents. An idea is clear when we recognize everything which can be included with it; it is distinct when we recognize all its external applications. For example, our conception of a triangle is clear when we recognize such aspects as "three-sided," "three-angled," "two dimensional figure," etc. It is distinct when we can differentiate a triangle from the rest of reality.

Although Blair cites neither Descartes nor Arnauld explicitly, he does repeatedly use the terms "clear" and "distinct" to refer to conception. He ardently believed one must first have a clear and distinct conception of the idea to be expressed and then must locate and apply the term which refers precisely to the idea. His view of this procedure is made most clear when he describes how it can go wrong. In Lecture X, he claims that "the words, which a man uses to express his ideas, may be faulty in three respects: They may either not express that idea which the author intends, but some other which only resembles or is akin to it; or, they may express that idea, but not quite fully and completely; or they may express it, together with something more than he intends."[25] What clearer call for conceptual clarity and referential precision could we ask for? A given term should match up perfectly with its referent as conceived by speaker and audience. It should never match up with an idea different from what was intended. Furthermore, a term must cover all characteristics and aspects of its referent excluding none of them, and it should include no aspects external to the conception.

Blair, then, sees communication as a process of transfusion wherein a source must accurately and precisely transfer a clear and distinct conception of an idea to the mind of another. He concludes his discussion of style by claiming that "the fundamental rule . . . is, to communicate, in the clearest and most natural order, the ideas which we mean to transfuse into the minds of others . . . we may rest assured, that, whenever we express ourselves ill, there is . . . some mistake in our manner of conceiving the subject. Embarrassed, obscure, and feeble Sentences, are generally . . . the result of embarrassed, obscure, and feeble thought. Thought and Language act and re-act upon each other mutually. Logic and Rhetoric have here . . . a strict connection."[26]

Blair's approach to style in his lectures is intriguing. He proposes stylistic classification based on the acuity and precision used by a speaker or author to express himself, thereby departing from treatments of style based solely on ornamental features of discourse. Blair emphasizes developing style as a means of improving one's ability to conceive and reason about a subject. His criteria of conceptual clarity and referential precision seem to be drawn directly from Arnauld's system of logic, a system which emphasized the mutual dependence of thought and expression, of logic and rhetoric. Blair viewed as the function and purpose of language the portrayal of concepts and ideas so clearly that they could easily be conceived by an audience in the way the speaker intended. The significance of this view is its emphasis on the connection between logic and its expression, a connection Blair viewed as vital to his system of rhetoric.

Notes

[1] Hugh Blair, *Lectures on Rhetoric and Belles Lettres,* London, William Sills, pp. 115-116.

[2] *Ibid.,* p. 20.

[3] *Ibid.,* p. 22.

[4] *Ibid.,* pp. 229-230.

[5] *Ibid.,* p. 230.

[6] *Ibid.,* p. 348.

[7] *Ibid.,* p. 20.

[8] *Ibid.,* p. 12.

[9] *Ibid.,* p. 12.

[10] *Ibid.,* p. 27.

[11] *Ibid.,* p. 116.

[12] *Ibid.,* p. 116.

[13] For review of this issue, see Douglas Ehninger, "Campbell, Blair, and Whately: Old Friends in a New Light," *Western Speech,* 19 (1955), 263-269; and "Campbell, Blair, and Whately Revisited," *The Southern Speech Journal,* 28 (1963), 169-182.

[14] Contrast Herman Cohen, "Hugh Blair's Theory of Taste," *The Quarterly Journal of Speech,* 44 (1958), 265-274 with John Waite Bowers, "A Comparative Criticism of Hugh Blair's Essay on Taste," *The Quarterly Journal of Speech,* 46 (1961), 384-389.

[15] James Golden and Douglas Ehninger describe the *Lectures* as a "first-rate literary curiosity—a wholly mediocre and pedestrian work which, in spite of its evident deficiencies and of the sustained barrage of epithets hurled at it by critics, gained a secure place among the best selling and most widely influential textbooks of all time." For review of the issues involved and a summary of critical commentaries, see "The Extrinsic Sources of Blair's Popularity," *Southern Speech Journal,* 22 (1956), 16-32, and "The Intrinsic Sources of Blair's Popularity," *Southern Speech Journal,* 21 (1955), 12-30.

[16] Wilbur Samuel Howell, *Eighteenth-Century British Logic and Rhetoric* (Princeton: Princeton University Press, 1971), p. 655.

[17] *Lectures on Rhetoric and Belles Lettres* (London: W. Strahan and T. Caddell, 1783), II, 3. Remaining citations of this edition are in the text.

[18] Robert Morrell Schmitz, *Hugh Blair* (Morningside Heights, NY: King's Crown Press, 1948), 105.

[19] Wilbur Samuel Howell, *Eighteenth-Century British Logic and Rhetoric* (Princeton: Princeton University Press, 1971), 653.

[20] Hugh Blair, *Lectures on Rhetoric and Belles Letters* ed. Harold F. Harding (Carbondale, IL: Southern Illinois University Press, 1965), 1: 379-400.

[21] Blair, I: 371-77.

[22] Blair, I: 7.

[23] Blair, I: 189.

[24] Antoine Arnauld, *The Art of Thinking,* trans. James Dickoff and Patricia James (New York: Bobbs-Merrill, 1964), 51-88.

[25] Blair, I: 189.

[26] Blair, I: 245-6.

References

James Berlin. *Writing Instruction in Nineteenth Century American Colleges.* Carbondale, IL: Southern Illinois University Press, 1984.

Hugh Blair. *Lectures on Rhetoric and Belles Lettres.* Philadelphia: Hayes and Zell, 1856.

Jacques Derrida. *Of Grammatology*. Trans. Fayatri Spivak. Baltimore: Johns Hopkins University Press, 1976.

Michel Foucault. *The Archaeology of Knowledge*. Trans. A. M. Sheridan Smith. New York: Harper and Colophon, 1972.

Han-Georg Gadamer. *Philosophical Hermeneutics*. Trans. and Ed. David E. Linge. Berkeley: University of California Press, 1977.

Jurgen Habermas. *Legitimation Crisis*. Trans. Thomas McCarthy. Boston: Beacon Press, 1975.

Jurgen Habermas. *Communication and the Evolution of Society*. Trans. Thomas McCarthy. Boston: Beacon Press, 1979.

Martin Heidegger. *The End of Philosophy*. Trans. Joan Stambaugh. New York: Harper and Row, 1973.

Martin Heidegger. *Being and Time*. Trans. John Macquarrie and Edward Robinson. New York: Harper and Row, 1962.

Samuel Ijsseling. *Rhetoric and Philosophy in Conflict: An Historical Survey*. The Hague: Martinus Nijhoff, 1976.

Isocrates. *Antidosis*. In Thomas W. Benson and Michael H. Prosser. *Readings in Classical Rhetoric*. Bloomington: Indiana University Press, 1972.

Charles W. Kneupper. "Language and Thought: Rhetorical Implications." *Etc.—A Review of General Semantics,* 32 (1975), 304-315.

Charles W. Kneupper. "Rhetoric as a Modern Discipline: Lessons from the Classical Tradition." *Oldspeak/ Newspeak: Rhetorical Transformations*. Ed. Charles W. Kneupper. Arlington, Texas: Rhetoric Society of America, 1985, pp. 110-118.

Karl Mannheim. *Ideology and Utopia*. New York: Harcourt, Brace, Jovanovich (first printed 1936) reprinted 1985.

Kenneth Pike. *Linguistic Concepts: An Introduction to Tagmemics*. Lincoln: University of Nebraska Press, 1982.

Michael Polanyi. *Personal Knowledge: Towards a Post-Critical Philosophy*. Chicago: University of Chicago Press, 1962.

Richard Rorty. *Philosophy and Mirror of Nature*. Princeton: Princeton University Press, 1980.

John Dwyer (essay date 1989)

SOURCE: "Clio and Ethics: Practical Morality in Enlightened Scotland," *The Eighteenth Century: Theory and Interpretation*, Vol. 30, No. 1, Spring, 1989, pp. 45-72.

[*In the following excerpt, Dwyer discusses Blair's sermons in light of his influential role as a Moderate preacher and champion of sensibility.*]

Recent work on eighteenth-century Scottish culture demonstrates the significance of practical moral concerns within a relatively backward economy experiencing the tensions associated with modernization. In his magisterial *Church and University in the Scottish Enlightenment*, Richard Sher argues that the Moderate clergy of the Church of Scotland helped to formulate that ethic of polite Stoicism which simultaneously reinforced personal integrity while it encouraged tolerance and benevolence towards one's fellows.[1] Sher and others also remark upon the renewed vitality of the civic tradition in late eighteenth-century Scottish society and its contribution to the enlightened but conservative Scottish consciousness.[2] Adopting a flexible definition of this same civic tradition, Nicholas Phillipson attempts to document the Scottish search for a *virtú* which made sense within a modern commercial polity.[3] These writings, by challenge and implication, have stimulated a new appreciation of eighteenth-century Scottish culture—one which avoids such increasingly anachronistic perspectives as the Scottish contribution to historical materialism or to the discipline of sociology.[4]

Research into the specifically Scottish variations on civic humanist and stoic themes, as well as those critiques which emphasize civil jurisprudence, illuminates the enlightened Scottish consciousness as a complex, multidimentional, and, above all, practical one. The purpose of this essay is to explore some hitherto overlooked facets of this consciousness and to assess their significance for those moralists who sought to provide their countrymen with an ethical temperament better suited to an increasingly refined and intricate society. I will examine the moral discourse of such ignored yet influential propagandists as Hugh Blair and other Moderate preachers. . . . In particular, I will emphasize their treatment of sensibility, or that polite and controlled fellow feeling which supposedly characterized the interaction of men in the modern age and differentiated the tone and texture of their manners from societies in the past. For it was their appreciation of the attributes of human sensibility which permitted the Scots to re-align ethics to a complicated and differentiated modern world.

. . . . .

Hugh Blair's sermons, in particular, numbered among the century's best sellers and described the appropriate manners of a Christian gentleman in the age of enlightenment and improvement. At the same time, they demonstrated an acute awareness of the relation between sensitivity, religion and historical change.

As a popular teacher, artful diplomat, and elder statesman of the Moderate cause, Blair provided the model for and link between a number of Scottish preachers who advocated the historical gospel of sensibility. His friend John Drysdale's sermons were highly recommended in the Scottish press for shunning dogma and advocating charity.[47] Two of Blair's young protégés, Samuel Charters and Thomas Somerville, published volumes of sermons of their own. Charters's sermons were touted for their pathetic qualities and were even recommended by Adam Smith to his London publisher.[48] Thomas Somerville, who enjoyed Blair's confidence and friendship, is best known to modern readers for his recollections of Scottish society in *My Own Life and Times*. In his own day, Somerville was a preacher of some repute, and a number of his sermons, including "A Sermon on Alms" and a "Discourse on the Duty of Making a Testament," were frequently reprinted.[49] The Reverend John Logan was yet another student and ally of Blair's, acting as a propagadist for the latter's writings in his capacity as editor of the *English Review*.[50] His volumes of sermons, which were published posthumously, reflected many of the same themes and subjects as those of his mentor.

For these Moderate preachers, religion itself was not immune to the historical principle. The Book of Genesis, for example, was primarily a description of "human manners in their primitive simplicity, before the arts of refinement had polished the behaviour."[51] The Bible as a whole traced the development of society and civilization "from rude beginnings in every corner of the earth; and gradually advancing to the state in which we now find them."[52] As society developed, so too did Christianity change. Its initial role was that of brining the "rude multitudes" together in acts of worship; to "restrain them from violence"; and to "train them to subordination." Later on, religion played a more positive role than mere social control, for it "humanized and polished manners" and "strengthened the social connections."

Hugh Blair and his Moderate colleages wanted to differentiate refined Christian manners from that "mere felicity of nature, or an external accomplishment of manners" which preoccupied the "bulk of men." John Drysdale, for example, distinguished between "keeping the heart" and "the external appearances and behaviour," arguing that manners should be firmly grounded in a basic human sensibility.[53] It was this same sensibility that prompted the individual to "enter into the feelings of mankind" and "to desire their happiness." Samuel Charters described man's "common sensibility to pain and sorrow," as "the strongest

social connection."[54] This refined capacity for sympathy, he described simply as "humanity." In what was perhaps his most popular and significant sermon, **"On Gentleness,"** Hugh Blair defined sensibility as "that unaffected civility which springs from a gentle mind" and which was very different from the "studied manners of the most finished courtier."[55] Indeed, he argued, it was "native feeling heightened and improved by principle. It is the heart which easily relents; which feels for every thing that is human; and is backward and slow to inflict the least wound." Although it was based upon native sentiment, sensibility was capable of a considerable degree of cultivation. Christianity, rightly understood, had played and would continue to play a critical role in supporting that "gentleness," "affability," and "unaffected ease" which not only supported the social bond but were the bases of morality.[56]

To the Moderates's way of thinking, "true religion" had a far greater impact than either government or law. Drysdale dismissed laws as "a kind of props devised to support a tottering edifice" and opposed these to the natural power of Christian benevolence.[57] The latter, he maintained, softened the heart "into sympathy and the tenderest affections for our neighbors." John Logan, in the first two of his own published sermons, argued that while primitive men responded mechanically to the authority of the law, true Christianity represented a more complex "mode of communication by discourse in public assemblies" which gradually molded men's manners into a subtler form.[58] Moderate Christianity, he added elsewhere, did not burn heretics; it encouraged its adherents to become "better neighbours" and "better friends."[59] For Thomas Somerville, too, the "enlightened Christian" no longer viewed the laws as sufficient supports for the peace and order of the world.[60] Instead, he regarded the religion of Jesus as "the most social and beneficent, the most conductive to the dignity and improvement of the individual, and to the peace and happiness of mankind." Even the "mildest and most auspicious model of human laws," he maintained, could never eliminate the "miseries occasioned by hardheartedness and oppression."[61] These could only be alleviated by a religion which encouraged us to "cultivate the society and friendship of good men."[62]

Hugh Blair's sermons made a similar distinction between a *mechanical* and an *organic* society. "Mere law, among men," he wrote, "is rigid and inflexible."[63] Not only did it fail to take into account the subtle feelings and intentions of men, but it made no allowance for particular situations. Gentle Christian manners, on the other hand, were always reflective of "the humane and generous liberality of sentiment."[64] They, not the laws, were the real cement of British society. On sensibility itself, Blair asserted that "whatever is amiable in manners or useful in society naturally and easily engrafts itself upon it. . . . It is the chief ground of mutual confidence and union among men." "In proportion as manners are vicious," he added elsewhere, "mankind are unhappy."[65]

Blair and his fellow Moderates, therefore, laid considerable emphasis upon refined sensibility as the foundation of ethics in modern life. While their treatment of the human sentiments was considerably more sophisticated than much of the commonplace sentimentalism of the day, the popularity of Scottish moralists was obviously tied to the fact that their pulpit discourse hit the mood and fashion of the times. James Boswell, who was justly terrified of orthodox Calvinism, thought that Blair's sermons "lighted things up so finely, and you get from them such comfortable answers," while the editor of the *Scots Magazine* claimed that they were popular precisely because "they were adapted to the very tone of public taste, humour and judgment."[66] Blair and his colleagues would have been gratified by such remarks; they were proud to be associated with polite society and the gospel of sentiment. Blair himself was an avid reader of sentimental French sermons and a truly modern literary form—the novel. Indeed, he was *avant garde* in Scottish literary circles in regarding the best examples of this literary *genre* as excellent "channels for conveying instruction, for painting human life and manners, for showing the errors into which we are betrayed by our passions, for rendering virtue amiable, and vice odious."[67] Like his allies in the *Scots Magazine* and the Mirror Club, Blair saw positive attributes in the modern world, its literature and its discourse.

At the same time, Blair and his friends believed that the popular propagandization of sensibility could be, and often was, carried too far. He expressed this concern in a sermon entitled **"On Sensibility."** Here he outlined the common theory of the passions derived from Scottish moral philosophy. Since man was too inclined to self-love, he argued, the temper of mind known as "sensibility" was given to him as a social creature. It was this temper of mind that "interests us in the conerns of our brethren; which disposes us to feel along with them, to take part in their joys, and in their sorrows."[68] Such a temperament, he maintained, was the "chief improvement" of which "modern times" could rightfully boast. At the same time, "excessive softness" and "sentimental language" often covered an unfeeling and calculating heart. It was important, therefore, always to distinguish "native affection" from "exterior manner" and truly feeling individuals from those who professed their sensibility "on every trifling occasion."

A chief concern of Blair's—and of many Scottish writers on ethical subjects—was that, while modern manners exhibited a finer degree of refinement and a better understanding of the workings of human nature, they were at the same time subject to the "dissimulation" and "insincerity" of a highly individualistic and selfish modern world.[69] While men's understanding of manners and sentiment were becoming ever more subtle and precise, they were simultaneously being detached from their natural moral source. Thus separated from "virtue and moral worth," they lost their effect upon the social community. They dwindled into "despicable talents, which have no power to command the hearts, nor to ensure the respect and honour of mankind." Politeness, courtesy, ease and gentleness—the supposed characteristics of a modern refined society—were being transformed into an artificial system which hid a designing, rather than reflected an engaging, heart. Exposed to such a selfish system, a naive and crude sociability could result in the unwary individual's moral destruction. "We naturally mould ourselves on the pattern of prevailing manners," wrote Blair, "and corruption is communicated from one to another."[70] The world, advised his friend John Drysdale, tended "so directly to strengthen a selfish and interested disposition," that moralists, educators and parents needed to be vigilant in making the proper distinctions between good and evil for minds not "well informed and ripened."[71] "That softness and politeness, which characterize the manners of our age," asserted Thomas Somerville, "are certainly carried too far, when promiscuously extended to men of every description and character."[72] Refined or *gentle* sensibility was no crude outpouring of fellow feeling; it needed to be carefully cultivated by those who best understood man's nature and his history. . . .

Notes

[1] Richard B. Sher, *Church and University in the Scottish Enlightenment: The Moderate Literati of Edinburgh* (Princeton, 1985), esp. 175-86. On the stoic tradition generally, see Gerhard Oestreich's *Neostoicism and the Early Modern State* (Cambridge, 1982).

[2] *Church and University in the Scottish Enlightenment,* 187 ff. Sher is particularly informative about the civic humanism of Adam Ferguson. See also *New Perspectives on the Politics and Culture of Early Modern Scotland,* ed. John Dwyer, Roger Mason and Alexander Murdoch (Edinburgh, 1982), and John Robertson's *The Scottish Enlightenment and the Militia Issue* (Edinburgh, 1985). On the significance of civic humanism in eighteenth-century British thought generally, see J. G. A. Pocock's *The Machiavellian Moment: Florentine Political Thought and the Atlantic Republican Tradition* (Princeton, 1975).

[3] See, for example, N. T. Phillipson, "Towards a Definition of the Scottish Enlightenment," *City and Society in the Eighteenth Century,* ed. P. Fritz and D. Williams (Toronto, 1973), 125-47; and "Adam Smith as Civic Moralist," *Wealth and Virtue: The Shaping of Political Economy in the Scottish Enlightenment,* ed. Istvan Hont and Michael Ignatieff (Cambridge, 1984), 179-91.

4 For these older viewpoints, see especially Ronald Meek, *Social Science and the Ignoble Savage* (Cambridge, 1979); Gladys Bryson, *Man and Society: The Scottish Inquiry of the Eighteenth Century* (Princeton, 1945); and Andrew Skinner, "Economics and History: The Scottish Enlightenment," *Scottish Journal of Political Economy* 12 (1965):1-22. . . .

47 *Scots Magazine,* August 1793. See also Thomas Somerville, *My Own Life and Times* (Edinburgh, 1861), 60-61. For William Robertson's praise of Drysdale's sermons, see Ian Clark, "Moderatism and the Moderate Party in the Church of Scotland, 1752-1805" (Cambridge, 1963), 125.

48 *The Correspondence of Adam Smith,* 269.

49 See the long review of Samuel Charters's sermons in the *Scots Magazine,* January 1786.

50 Edinburgh University Library, Laing MS., LA II, 419, letter 8.

51 Hugh Blair, *Sermons* (Edinburgh, 1777), vol. 1, sermon 13.

52 Ibid., sermon 19.

53 John Drysdale, *Sermons* (Edinburgh, 1793), sermons 1 and 4.

54 Samuel Charters, *Sermons* (Edinburgh, 1786), sermon 8.

55 Blair, *Sermons,* vol. 1, sermon 6.

56 Ibid., vol. 1, sermor 11.

57 Drysdale, *Sermons,* vol. 2, sermon 1.

58 John Logan, *Sermons* (Edinburgh, 1826), sermon 1.

59 Ibid., sermon 2.

60 Thomas Somerville, *Sermons* (Edinburgh, 1813), 39.

61 Ibid., 15 ff.

62 Ibid., 198.

63 Blair, *Sermons,* vol. 3, sermon 10. The terms *mechanical* and *organic,* of course, are borrowed from the corpus of the great French sociologist, Emile Durkheim, who used them to distinguish between traditional and modern societies.

64 Blair, *Sermons,* vol. 2, sermon 10.

65 Ibid., vol. 3, sermon 18.

66 See Schmitz, 1, and the *Caledonian Mercury,* 17 January 1801. For an earlier and long assessment of Blair's claim to fame, see "An Account of Dr. Blair's Sermons," in the *Caledonian Mercury,* 17 February 1777, which also praises other Moderates such as Ferguson, Robertson and Carlyle.

67 John Hill, *An Account of the Life and Writings of Hugh Blair* (Edinburgh, 1807), 200. See also Hugh Blair, *Lectures on Rhetoric and Belles Lettres* (London, 1783), 2:303-4. Blair held Henry Mackenzie's *The Man of the World* in particularly high esteem; see Henry Mackenzie, *Anecdotes and Egotisms,* ed. Harold Thompson (Oxford, 1927), 189. For another moralist's, James Fordyce, praise of good novels, see the *Scots Magazine,* October 1766. The brother of the Scottish moral philosopher David Fordyce, James Fordyce was a friend of Blair's and an important moral propagandist in his own right.

68 Hugh Blair, *Sermons,* Vol. 3, sermon 2. See also a sermon of Somerville's which was included as the final selection in Charters's volume, in which the former argued that there were certain "principles" and "dispositions" which "formed the heart to friendship" and which were the "most deserving of the approbation of others" and "the most rational and pure enjoyment of the individual who has cultivated them." In another place, he paraphrased Scottish moral philosophy in his discussion of the ways in which "we intutively discern, in the moral world, 'right' and 'wrong', 'merit' or 'demerit', attached to particular actions." See Somerville, *Sermons,* 42.

69 Blair, *Sermons,* vol. 5, sermon 17.

70 Ibid., vol. 4, sermon 19.

71 Drysdale, *Sermons,* vol. 1, sermon 2.

72 Somerville, *Sermons,* 200. . . .

Thomas Frank (essay date 1990)

SOURCE: "Hugh Blair's Theory of the Origin and the Basic Functions of Language," *Papers from the 5th International Conference on English Historical Linguistics,* Cambridge, 6-9 April 1987, edited by Sylvia Adamson, Vivien Law, Nigel Vincent and Susan Wright, John Benjamins Publishing Company, 1990, pp. 165-87.

[*In the following essay, Frank examines Blair's ideas on the nature, history, structure, and development of language.*]

In the history of English studies, the figure of Hugh Blair, the Scottish divine and prominent member of the

Edinburgh literati of the second half of the 18th century is of particular interest. When he was appointed Regius Professor of Rhetoric and Belles Lettres in the University of Edinburgh in 1762, the institutional study of what later became the English Language and Literature course can, in a very real sense, be said to have been initiated. It should perhaps be pointed out that, provided this interpretation of Blair's role is accepted, England was well over a century behind Scotland in setting up comparable chairs either in the ancient universities or in the more recently founded 19th century institutions. My claim is this: in courses like that taught by Blair at Edinburgh, or by Adam Smith in Glasgow[1], by Robert Watson[2] at St. Andrews or James Beattie[3] in Aberdeen, we have the nucleus of what in time became what I would like to call the 'Oxford model' of the English Language and Literature course. I am not concerned here with the 'belles lettres' or strictly rhetorical aspect of these courses, though the subject is by no means devoid of interest. In saying that this tradition goes back to Blair, I am not claiming that he was the first to lecture on the subject in a Scottish university: even before Smith became Professor of Logic at Glasgow, he had lectured in an informal capacity on rhetoric in Edinburgh[4], and according to John Millar (quoted by Dugald Stewart, Stewart, 1795: 274) he completely transformed the barren course of logic offered by his predecessors at Glasgow "illustrating the various powers of the human mind . . . from the several ways of communicating our thoughts by speech." It is a curious sidelight on the culture of 18th century Scotland, that the author of *The Wealth of Nations* in some of his earliest published work concerned himself with the problems of language, and in fact his *Considerations Concerning the First Formation of Languages and the Different Genius of Original and Compounded Languages* (a greatly expanded version of the language part of the Rhetoric lectures) first appeared in 1761. It is noteworthy that Blair acknowledged his debt both to Smith's published treatise on language and to his unpublished lectures on rhetoric[5]. As is well known[6], a MS of these lectures was discovered as recently as 1961 and first published in 1963. But Smith's was by no means the only treatment of language with the Scottish rhetoric courses. Watson's lectures at St. Andrews consisted basically of a digest of Harris's *Hermes* and there is evidence that this work was studied at Edinburgh too[7], and even Leechman's lectures on pulpit oratory[8] at Glasgow contained observations on linguistic matters.

Blair tells us in the Preface to his *Lectures* (Blair I 1785: iv) that the text now published represented the lectures he had been delivering at Edinburgh over the previous twenty-four years, and it is clear that during this period of time his ideas on language, as on other subjects, must have matured considerably. A synopsis of the *Lectures* (Blair 1777) had already appeared six years before their publication in book form and there are numerous MS student notes preserved in the Edinburgh University Library. He considered his *Lectures*

> neither as a work wholly original, nor as a Compilation from the writings of others. On every subject contained in them, he thought for himself. He consulted his own ideas and reflections; and a great part of what will be found in these Lectures is entirely his own. (Blair 1785 I: iv)

Perhaps it is precisely this capacity as an expounder of received ideas, his exposition of a 'consensus' view of the subjects he treats—we may remember that Blair was one of the leading moderates within the Church of Scotland at the time—that accounts for his extraordinary popularity not only in the English-speaking world, but also throughout Europe. Within a few years of the first publication of the *Lectures,* there appeared translations into French, German, Italian, Dutch and Spanish. To mention only those I am most familiar with: I have counted no fewer than twenty different editions or adaptations of the Italian translation[9], published between 1801 and 1859 in five different Italian cities, but the list is almost certainly incomplete. Let us put it this way: Blair's *Lectures* became an internationally acknowledged textbook and we may therefore assume that generations of students were brought up not only on his digest of classical rhetorical theory and on his comments on the great authors of the past, but also on his ideas on the nature, history and structure of language.

Let us now look at these ideas a little more closely. I have mentioned what I called the 'Oxford model' of the English syllabus and its development from the end of the 19th century onwards. The language part of this was—and, to some extent still is—largely concerned with the historical study of the English language, with some Gothic and Old Norse thrown in for good measure. We all know this, since I suppose most of us were brought up on it. Blair's language sections (Lectures 6-9, but there are passages of considerable interest for linguists also in Lectures 10-16, i.e. those dealing with rhetorical theory) partly also deal with historical matters, though much of this is what in the 18th century was known as 'conjectural history', a term I shall return to shortly. His brief account of the origin and history of the English language, whose "irregular grammar" is said to be due to the fact that English is of hybrid origin, is disappointing and shows little direct knowledge of the earlier phases of the history of our tongue. Blair is far more interested in language as a general phenomenon of human societies than in any particular language. In choosing this approach, he is squarely within the tradition of 18th century rational grammar, a philosophical rather than a philological discipline, although he complains that "few authors have written with philosophical accuracy on the principles of General Grammar, and what is more to be regretted, fewer still have thought of applying those principles to the English Language" (Blair I 1785: 172-73), unlike the French who have "considered its construction and determined its propriety with great accuracy" (Blair I 1785: 174). Some attempts have been made, but much remains to be done. I am not concerned here with refuting Blair's claim that little had been written on general grammar in English, though this would not be difficult, bearing in mind influential authors like Harris, Smith or Priestley, but I do want to go back for a moment to the concept of 'conjectural history', because I believe this is central to our understanding of how Blair, like most of his contemporaries, approached the study of language. The term, which came to be widely used of all forms of history, was coined by Dugald Stewart in talking about Smith's *Considerations*

> In this want of direct evidence we are under a necessity of supplying the place of fact by conjecture; and when we are unable to ascertain how men have actually conducted themselves upon particular occasions, of considering in what manner they are likely to have proceeded, from the principles of their nature, and the circumstances of their external situation. In such enquiries, the detached facts which travels and voyages afford us, may frequently serve as landmarks to our speculations, and sometimes our conclusions *a priori* may tend to confirm the credibility of facts, which on a superficial view, appeared to be doubtful or incredible.

(Stewart 1975: xli-xlii)

If this was true in general of human history, it was true in particular of the history of language: an account of the history of human speech is above all an account of its nature, and vice versa, the nature of language can be understood by reconstructing not its more or less documented stages, but by an *a priori* reasoning, on 'how it must have happened', where 'must' is to be interpreted in terms of an objective rather than subjective epistemic modality, since the facts described arise out of considerations based on the general principles of communication, which give the term 'conjectural' objective validity. To a considerable extent, this explains the recurrent concern of 18th century writers on language, both in France and in Britain as well as in Germany (we remember Herder's prize-winning essay for the Berlin Academy in 1771) with the question of origins. It was a subject that loomed as large in most 18th century accounts of language as it is conspicuous by its absence in practically all contemporary writing on the subject. I am not sure that I would go all the way with Aarsleff's interpretation of the origins question, when he affirms that what these authors were interested in was a model, rather than a historical state of things

the philosophical question of the origin of language first formulated by Condillac sought to establish man's linguistic state of nature in order to gain insight into the nature of man . . . the search for origins concerned the present state of man, not the establishment of some 'historical' fact or 'explanation' of how things actually were at some point in the past.

(Aarsleff 1974: 107-8)

Blair of course cites Condillac among his sources, together other French authors like the Port-Royal grammarians, Du Marsais, Beauzée, Batteaux, de Brosses, Girard, Rousseau as well as English works like those of Adam Smith and Harris, and in a long note in Lecture 7 he discusses Monboddo's account of "some of the first articulate sounds" of certain primitive tongues, in which he accepts Monboddo's contention, in its turn based on a hypothesis enunciated by Smith and ultimately traceable to Condillac, that they

> denoted a whole sentence rather than the name of a particular object; conveying some information, or expressing some desires or fears, suited to the circumstances in which that tribe was placed, or relating to the business they had most frequent occasion to carry on; as the lion is coming, the river is swelling & c.

(Blair I 1785: 176)

It is certainly true that much of the discussion of the origins of speech is conducted in philosophical terms. For Condillac, as for Rousseau and Monboddo, arises in response to human need, primitive men

> n'ont pas dit, *faisons une langue:* ils ont senti besoin d'un mot, et ils ont prononcé le plus propre à représenter la chose qu'ils vouloient faire connaître

(Porset 1970: 162-63)

Beauzée too talks of *sociabilité* as the source of the universal phenomenon of human language, emphasizing that the elements that all human languages have in common are far more numerous and basic than the superficial elements of time, place and custom that determine the difference between individual tongues, an idea that we also find in other 18th century philosophers: Blair, for example, would have found it in the writings of the most prominent Scottish philosopher of his time, David Hume, and another Scot, Thomas Reid, distinguishes between 'natural' and 'artificial' signs (Reid 1764: 103), a distinction much insisted upon also by Monboddo when he talks of the 'language of nature' vs. the 'language of art': it is only the latter which has the full status of language, since the former, especially in Reid's formulation, is nothing but the direct expression of the passions not mediated by the double articulation characteristic of human speech.[10]

But let me return to my previous point: Aarsleff's 'metaphorical' reading of 18th century concerns with origins. Since the subject is not dealt with in detail by Blair, I will limit myself here to saying that the interest shown in Britain by such writers as Monboddo or in France in the numerous accounts of the customs and speech of primitive tribes (echoed, for example, in de Brosses) is surely proof that these 18th century scholars were concerned not merely with the general principles of human speech, which is undeniable, or with primitive languages as somehow representing the basic functions of language, which too I believe to be beyond doubt, but that they sought to provide a concrete and empirically verifiable account of what the speech of primitive man was actually like. I do not believe one necessarily excludes the other, though in the case of Blair the philosophical as opposed to the empirical interest appears to be predominant.

There are several aspects of the origin question that were widely debated and that Blair too is concerned with. I shall not deal with the vexed question of whether language was of human or divine origin (Blair is inclined to accept the latter view), since this is not my central concern here. Blair, like Rousseau, whose *Discours sur l'origine de l'inégalité parmi les hommes* he quotes, is caught up in what we might roughly call the chicken or the egg dilemma, i.e. of whether we can conceive of a society prior to the 'invention' of language, or whether language is a condition necessary to the existence of society:

> So that, either how Society could form itself, previously to Language, or how words could rise into a Language previously to Society formed, seem to be points attended with equal difficulty.

(Blair I 1785: 126)

Since there is no obvious answer to this question, Blair skates over the problem in order to consider just what this language must have been like. Like most of his contemporaries, he identifies the 'language of nature' with the grammatical category of interjections, which must therefore have been the first words, though the term 'word' may be inappropriate for such direct expressions of the passions. "Those exclamations, therefore," he affirms, "which by Grammarians are called Interjections, uttered in a strong and passionate manner, were beyond doubt, the elements of beginnings of Speech" (Blair I 1785: 128-29). Like de Brosses, Blair rejects a purely arbitrary origin for the first linguistic signs, for

> To suppose words invented, without any ground or reason, is to suppose an effect without a cause. There

must have always been some motive which led to the assignation of one name rather than another

(Blair I 1785: 128-29)

although he concedes in a different passage that sound symbolism can have affected only a very limited sphere of the vocabulary.[11]

The problem is twofold: what words were first 'invented' and how did they develop in the course of human history to form the languages of the polite nations of Europe, which are now greatly refined and not only have words for all the objects of the world, but also a series of ornaments, a state of affairs which has been in existence "among many nations for some thousand years" (Blair I 1785: 124). In the second place he sought to ascertain how these words were arranged in structures to convey propositional, not merely atomistic meanings. It is to these two subjects that I now wish to turn my attention.

Early man had few words at his disposal, since his experience of the world was limited and he therefore had to help himself out by an abundant use of metaphor, since Blair, like practically all his contemporaries, holds that abstract terms all have their origin in concrete nouns denoting the objects of the world:

> The names of sensible objects were, in all languages, the words most early introduced, and were by degrees, extended to those mental objects, of which men had more obscure conceptions, and to which they found it more difficult to assign a distinct name

(Blair I 1785: 353)

so that primitive speech was

> strong and expressive . . . (and) could be no other than full of figures and metaphors, not correct indeed, but forcible and picturesque . . . Mankind never employed so many figures of speech, as when they had hardly any words for expressing their meaning

(Blair I 1785: 141)

That the men of letters of the Enlightenment were fascinated by 'primitive' (or what they believed to be primitive) poetry is a commonplace: as is well known, Blair was one of the chief defenders of the authenticity of Macpherson's *Ossian,* which he considered to be the perfect example of primitive, but powerful poetry. Like other writers on rhetoric, Blair is distinctly wary of the use of figures of speech, which must be strictly subordinate to the supreme requirement of clarity, or as the oft quoted Quintilian had put it, "nobis prima sit virtus perspicuitas" (*Inst. Or.* VIII, ii, 2).

Figurative language is associated with primitive societies, whereas "Language is become, in modern times, more correct indeed, and accurate, but however less striking and animated" (Blair I 1785: 157). Ours is, in other words, an age of reason and philosophy, not of poetry and oratory. I do not know if Matthew Arnold knew this passage of Blair's; it would certainly have been grist to his mill in his contention that the 18th century was essentially an age of prose.

The earliest vocal sounds were interjections, but the first real words were

> substantive nouns, which are the foundation of all Grammar, and may be considered as the most antient part of Speech; For, assuredly, as soon as men got beyond simle interjections, or exclamations, of passions, and began to communicate themselves *(sic)*, they would be under a necessity of assigning names to the objects they saw around them; which, in Grammatical Language is called the invention of substantive nouns.[12]

(Blair I 1785: 176)

The idea that the naming process is the basis of all language goes back at least as far as the mediaeval so-called 'modistae' school of grammarians, who insisted on the primacy of the 'modus entis' over the 'modus esse'. In English linguistic theory this is particularly evident in Wilkins's *Essay,* where everything, except the purely grammatical operators called 'particles', is reduced to the basic category of the noun. In Blair this must be seen in his almost Bloomfieldian account of the first linguistic utterances, which are treated in terms of stimulus and response[13]. However, unlike his 17th century predecessors, who in one way or another tend to subsume the verb in the naming process, for Blair

> Verbs must have been coëval with men's first attempts towards the formation of Language

(Blair I 1785: 203)

and, following Smith's suggestion (Smith 1983: 215-16), as we have already had occasion to mention, he opines that impersonal verbs must have been the first to appear, so that the origin of speech must be seen not in the mere naming process, envisaged as a mythical savage pointing to a tree laden with apples and uttering the word 'apple', but in 'event verbs' in elementary one argument propositions like 'it is raining'.

Blair follows Harris's scheme of dividing lexical words into substantives and attributes, and he is of the opinion that since adjectives, the simplest form of attributes, are found in all languages, they must have been among the first words to be invented, whereas adverbs, which can generally be reduced to nouns plus prepositions

may be conceived as of less necessity, and of later introduction in the System of Speech, than any other classes of words

(Blair I 1785: 210)

In other words, for Blair, most ancient means most essential or necessary. The whole concept of the 'necessary' elements of a language is fully developed in Beauzée, who mentions "éléments necessaires" on the very title-page of his Grammar. Shortage of space does not permit me to go into Blair's many points of contact with this influential French work, published some 16 years prior to the *Lectures.* Necessary is seen in terms of basic, so we come back once again to the idea that, at least to some extent, and in the case of Blair rather more so than in an author like Monboddo, the origins question is intimately connected with what are seen to be the basic structures of language: richness of vocabulary, elegance, harmony, ornament are the additions of a politer age, which make language suitable for scientific and philosophical discourse, but do not constitute the essential categories that serve to convey meaning as invented by the first men. To what extent we are justified in equating these basic categories with our contemporary concept of deep structure is a question I would like to leave open for the time being, but I suspect it may well be possible to draw some sort of parallel between the two.

Finally, I would like to turn to the question of how words are arranged in sentences so as to convey propositional rather than purely lexical meaning. The problem of word order, i.e. the order of words considered to be most natural, was much debated during the 18th century. That word order constitutes one of the principal criteria of modern typological studies hardly needs emphasizing.[14] The problem was seen in terms of rigid as opposed to (comparatively) free word order, with particular attention to the position of the subject. Girard, whose *Les vrais principes* is cited by Blair among his list of sources, had divided languages into 'analogous' and 'transpositive' types, roughly what later linguists called 'analytic' and 'synthetic' languages, and this division is followed, among others, by Beauzée in France and in Britain by the anonymous author of the article on 'Language' in the first edition of the *Encyclopaedia Britannica* (1771). In both cases, analogous languages are said to respect the order of nature. Beauzée calls this the "analytical order" or "analytical succession of ideas", since according to him

> La succession analytique des idées est le fondement unique & invariable des loix de la Syntaxe dans toutes les langues imaginables

(Beauzée 1947: 467-68)

and Du Marsais, another much quoted author in English treatments of the subject, in his article for the *Encyclopaedie* (Porset 1970: 232) is of much the same opinion. A full examination of word order as treated by 18th century grammarians and philosophers (but there is often little difference between the two) would be out of place here. I have referred to it since Blair approaches the question from a rather different point of view. Word order, like the question of word categories, is seen in terms of origins:

> Let us go back . . . to the most early period of Language. Let us figure to ourselves a Savage, who beholds some object, such as fruit, which raises his desire, who requests another to give it to him . . . He would not express himself, according to an English order of construction, 'Give me fruit', 'Fructum da mihi': For this plain reason, that his attention was wholly directed towards fruit, the desired object

(Blair I 1785: 148-49)[15]

In other words, Blair is concerned with a psychological as opposed to a logical succession of ideas, an order which he calls "though not the most logical . . . the most natural order (Blair I 1785: 149), and in view of the importance focusing has acquired in recent linguistic theory, this dichotomy of natural (i.e. psychological) vs. logical order is of considerable interest. This question had been the cause of controversy between Beauzée and Batteaux, another French source quoted by Blair, and nearer home, Campbell in his highly influential *The Philosophy of Rhetoric* (1776), a work Blair greatly esteemed, had talked of a grammatical vs. a rhetorical order, ascribing universal status to the latter, but only local and particular validity to the former

> I imagine that the only principle in which this subject can safely rest, as being founded in nature, is that whatever most strongly fixes the attention, or operates on the passion of the speaker, will first seek utterance by the speaker . . . In these transpositions, therefore, I maintain that the order will be found, on examination, to be more strictly natural than when the more general practice in the tongue is followed.

(Campbell 1850: 357-58)

Within the context of 18th century Enlightenment culture the question could not but be seen in terms of the superiority of the classical languages as compared with their modern successors, or vice versa. Unlike some of his contemporaries, who came down very decidedly on the side of the moderns[16], Blair tries to reconcile the two positions in some way: Latin order is said to be "more animated", English "more clear and distinct",

the Latin order reflecting the succession in which ideas rise in the speaker's mind, ours "the order in which the understanding directs those ideas to be exhibited (Blair I 1785: 153)[17].

The above remarks by no means aim to give an exhaustive account of Blair's ideas on the nature, structure and development of language: there are a great many points, both in the chapters strictly concerned with language and in his treatment of the laws of rhetoric, that would repay much more detailed study, especially within the wider framework of the contribution of the thinkers of the Scottish Enlightenment to linguistic theory, than is possible in a short paper. In conclusion, I would not claim any great originality for Blair's ideas, but I do think that it was precisely because he was *not* original that he became so popular and that both as the first Professor of Rhetoric and Belles Letters and as the author of an internationally acclaimed text-book he deserves more than an honourable mention in the history of English Studies.

Notes

[1] Smith was appointed Professor of Logic and Rhetoric at Glasgow in 1751 and following year he succeeded Thomas Craigie as Professor of Moral Philosophy. The rhetoric lectures, as they have come down to us in the Glasgow University Library MS, go back to the session 1762-63, but according to Bryce (in Smith 1983: 9) he began lecturing on rhetoric as soon as he took up his appointment in Glasgow.

[2] Robert Watson was appointed to the Chair of Logic at St. Salvator's College, St. Andrews in 1756 and Principal of the same in 1778. There are five sets of student notes of his lectures on universal grammar delivered at St. Andrews preserved in the University Library dating from between 1758 and 1778. With the exception of MS PN 173, they are substantially identical and consist of an abstract of Books I and II of Harris's *Hermes*. Watson never published anything on the subject.

[3] James Beattie was appointed Professor of Moral Philosophy and Logic at Marischal College, Aberdeen in 1760. The following year he was elected member of the Aberdeen Philosophical Society, of which George Campbell, Principal of Marischal College, was a founder member. Though Rule 17 of the statutes of the Society states that "all Grammatical Historical and Philological Discussion being conceived to be foreign to the Design of this Society", Campbell certainly read a number of papers on rhetoric to the Society. These papers were later transformed into *The Philosophy of Rhetoric,* and there are other contributions on such matters as the word order of the ancient compared with those of the modern languages (George

Skene), the characteristics of a polished language (James Dunbar) or writing systems (Thomas Gordon). See Aberdeen University Library MS 539, reprinted in Humphries 1931. Beattie's *The Theory of Language* too is based on lectures delivered at Aberdeen. Copies of the Session Journals of Marischal College preserved in the Aberdeen University Library give a very clear idea of how his Rhetoric course was structured.

[4] In 1748 at the suggestion of Lord Kames. At the time Smith was 25 years old. Cf. Bryce in Smith 1983: 8.

[5] Smith's *Considerations* are mentioned among his sources in Lecture V, whereas in Lecture XVIII we read: "On this head . . . several ideas have been taken from a manuscript treatise on rhetoric, part of which was shewn to me many years ago, by the learned and ingenious Author, Dr. Adam Smith; and which, it is hoped, will be given by him to the Public" (Blair II 1785: 24).

[6] Cf. Introduction to Smith 1983: 1.

[7] For example there is a notebook (MS 3125) in the National Library of Scotland entitled 'Universal Grammar written by James Trail' which is very similar to the Watson notes in the St. Andrews University Library. James Trail was educated at Edinburgh, but the notes were apparently originally taken down by his brother David, who was a student at St. Andrews. It would therefore appear that Watson's Universal Grammar course, based on Harris, was also in use at Edinburgh. There are frequent echoes of Harris in Blair's treatment, for example his division of words into substantives and attributives in Lecture VIII or his definition of adjectives in the same Lecture.

[8] 'Lectures on Composition by the Reverend Mr. Leechman'. The parts that have some linguistic interest are Lectures 11-18. Leechman (1706-1785) was appointed Professor of Divinity in the University of Glasgow in 1743 and Principal in 1761. He gave lectures on composition and the Evidences of Christianity in alternate years (Wodrow I 1779: 49).

[9] *Lezioni di Retorica e Belle Lettere di Ugone Blair . . . Tradotte dall'Inglese e commentate da Francesco Soave C.R.S.*, Parma: dalla Real Tipografia MDCCCI-MDCCCII.

[10] In case it may be thought that I am arbitrarily using contemporary concepts and terminology (e.g. double articolation) in referring to different ways of conceptualizing these matters, I would refer the reader to Monboddo's extended treatment of the enormous conceptual jump represented not only by the use of sounds to symbolize ideas, as compared with the direct expression of the passions which are said to their origin in animal cries, but by what he calls the *matter of* language, i.e. the sound system and the development of articulate, that is to say significant sounds, which in Monboddo's view provide the real dividing line between true language and the *language of nature*.

[11] "natural connexion (i.e. sound symbolism) can affect only a small part of the fabric of language; the connexion between words and ideas may, in general, be considered as arbitrary, and conventional, owing to the agreement of men among themselves" (Blair I 1785: 123). Even the most outstanding exponent of the view that there exists a natural correspondence between certain sounds and some of the basic human needs or sentiments like de Brosses (e.g. "Dans tous les siècles et dans toutes les contrées on emploie la lettre de lèvre ou à son default la lettre de dent, ou tous les deux ensemble, pour exprimer les premieres mots enfantins papa et maman" de Brosses 1798 I: 222) has to accept that conventional words are far more numerous than 'natural' words.

[12] Cf. Smith's much fuller account of the origin of common nouns: "Those objects only which were most familiar to them, (i.e. to the first men) and which they had most frequent occasion to mention, would have particular names assigned to them. The particular cave whose covering sheltered them from the weather, the particular tree whose fruit relieved their hunger, the particular fountain whose water allayed their thirst, would first be denominated by the words *cave, tree, fountain* . . . Afterwards when the more enlarged experience of these savages had led them to observe, and their necessary occasions obliged them to make mention of other caves, and other trees, and other fountains, they would naturally bestow, upon each of those new objects, the same name, by which they had been accustomed to express the similar objects they were first acquainted with. The new objects had none of them any name of its own, but each of them exactly resembled another object, which had such an appellation . . . And thus, those words, which were originally the proper names of individuals, would each of them insensibly become the common name of a multitude" (Smith 1983: 203-204).

[13] Like Bloomfield in his account of Jack and Jill and the apple tree (Bloomfield 1935: 22), he talks of a savage who desires a fruit.

[14] Among recent treatments, see for example the special issue on typology of *Folia Linguistica*, Plank 1986.

[15] Condillac in the chapter entitled "Des Mots" discusses the question of 'natural' word order at some length: "l'ordre le plus naturel des idées vouloit qu'on mit le régime avant le verbe: on disoit, par example, *fruit vouloir* . . . les mots se construissoient dans la même ordre dans lequel ils se régissoient; unique moyen d'en faciliter l'intelligence. On disoit *fruit vouloir*

Pierre pour *Pierre veut du fruit;* & la premiere construction n'étoit pas moins naturelle que l'autre l'est actuellement" (Condillac 1792: 263-64). The example, it will be noted, is almost identical to Blair's, but Condillac's reason for preferring OV order is grammatical-conceptual, whereas Blair's is psychological.

[16] For example Beauzée and even more strongly the anonymous author of the above-mentioned article on "Language" in the first edition of the *Encyclopaedia Britannica*.

[17] Cf. "Le français suit l'ordre de l'intelligence, mais le latin suit l'ordre du sentiment et des mouvements du coeur" (de Brosses I 1798: 71). Beauzée dedicates a great deal of space to refuting Batteaux's thesis that languages like Latin represent the order in which ideas arise in the mind, since his interest is not so much in the input as in the output of language. As to ornament or elegance "l'ordre analytique peut donc être contraire àl'éloquence sans être contraire à la nature du Langage, pour lequel l'éloquence n'est qu'un accessoire artificiel" (Beauzée II 1974: 530).

References

Aarsleff, H. 1974. 'The Tradition of Condillac. The Problem of the Origin of Language in the Eighteenth Century and the Debate in the Berlin Academy before Herder'. In D. Hymes, ed. *Studies in the History of Linguistics,* 93-156. Bloomington: Indiana University Press.

Batteaux, Charles. 1764 (1746). *Traité de la Construction Oratoire.* Vol. 5 of *Principes de la Litterature.* Nouvelle Edition. Paris: Desaint & Saillant.

Beattie, James. 1788. *The Theory of Language.* London: A. Strahan. Microfiche reproduction in *English Linguistics 1500-1800.* Menston: Scolar Press, 1968.

Beauzée, Nicolas. 1974 (1767). *Grammaire générale ou exposition raisonnée des éléments nécessaires du langage.* Nouvelle impression en facsimile de l'édition du 1767 avec une introduction par Barrie E. Bartlett. 2 vols. Stuttgart-Bad Caunstatt: Fromman.

Blair, Hugh. 1777. *Heads of the Lectures on Rhetoric and Belles Lettres in the University of Edinburgh.* Edinburgh: W. Creech.

————. 1785 (1783). *Lectures on Rhetoric and Belles Lettres.* 3 vols. Second edition corrected. London: W. Strahan and T. Cadell; Edinburgh: W. Creech.

Bloomfield, L. 1935 (1933). *Language.* Revised British edition. London: Allen & Unwin.

de Brosses, Charles. 1798 (1765). *Traité de la formation méchanique des langues.* Paris: chez Terrelonge.

Burnett, James (Lord Monboddo). 1773-1792. *On the Origin and Progress of Language.* 6 vols. Edinburgh: Kincaid & Creech; London: T. Cadell. Microfiche reproduction in *English Linguistics 1500-1800.* Menston: Scolar Press, 1968.

————. 1779-1799. *Antient Metaphysics.* 6 vols. Edinburgh: J. Balfour; London: T. Cadell. Both works were published anonymously.

Campbell, George. 1850 (1776). *The Philosophy of Rhetoric.* London: W. Tegg.

Condillac, Etienne Bonnot de. 1792 (1746). *Essai sur l'origine des connoissances humaines.* Troisième Edition revue & augmentée. Paris: chez le Libraires Associés.

————. 1775. *Cours d'étude pour l'instruction du Prince de Parme.* In Porset 1970: 149-211.

Du Marsais, César Chesneau. In porset 1970: 210-301.

Encyclopaedia Britannica. 1771. "by a Society of Gentlemen in Scotland". 3 vols. Edinburgh: Bell & Macfarquhar.

Frank, T. 1979. *Segno e significato. La lingua filosofica di John Wilkins.* Napoli: Guida.

Girard, Gabriel. 1747. *Les vrais principes de la langue françoise.* 2 vols. Paris: Le Breton.

Harris, James. 1751. *Hermes; or a Philosophical Inquiry concerning Language and Universal Grammar.* London: H. Woodfall. Microfiche reproduction in *English Linguistics 1500-1800.* Menston: Scolar Press, 1968.

Herder, Johann Gottfried. 1772. *Abhandlung über den Ursprung der Sprache.* English translation by A. Gode, *Essay on the Origin of Language.* Chicago: Chicago University Press, 1986.

Humphries, W.R. 1931. 'The First Aberdeen Philosophical Society'. *Transactions of the Aberdeen Philosophical Society,* 5.203-38.

Lancelot, Claude and Antoine Arnauld. 1660. *Grammaire Générale et Raisonnée.* Paris: Presse Le Petit. Repr. Menston: Scolar Press, 1968.

Leechman, William. 1779. *Sermons.* London: A. Strahan & T. Cadell; Edinburgh: E. Balfour & W. Creech.

———. c. 1770. Glasgow University Library MS Gen 51. The last six leaves of this contain an abstract of Harris's *Hermes.*

———. 1770 (but delivered 1754-55). 'Lectures on Composition'. Edinburgh University Library MS Dc.7.86. Student notes.

Plank, F. (ed.) 1986. *Folia Linguistica. Special Issue.* 20/1-2.

———. 'The Smith-Schlegel Connection in Linguistic typology: forgotten fact or fiction?'. To appear in *Zeitschrift für Fonetik, Sprachwissenschaft und Kommunikationsforschung.*

Porset, C. 1970. *Varia Linguistica.* Bordeaux: Ducros.

Quintilian (M. Fabius Quintilianus). *Istituto Oratoria,* ed. H.E. Butler. London: Heinemann, 1921.

Reid, Thomas. 1764. *An Inquiry into the Human Mind on the Principles of Common Sense.* London: A. Millar; Edinburgh: Kincaid & Bell.

Rousseau, Jean-Jacques. 1755. *Discours sur l'origine et les fondements de l'inégalité parmi les hommes.* English transaltion by M. Cranston, *A Discourse on Inequality.* Harmondsworth: Penguin Books. 1984.

Smith, Adam. 1983. (1762-63?). *Lectures on Rhetoric and Belles Lettres,* ed. J. Bryce. Oxford: Clarendon Press.

———. 1761. *Considerations Concerning the First Formation and the Different Genius of Original and Compounded Languages* in Smith 1983.

Soublin, F. 1976. 'Rationalisme et grammaire chez Dumarsais' in H. Parret ed. *History of Linguistic Thought and Contemporary Linguistics,* 383-409. Berlin-New York: de Gruyter.

Stewart, Dugald. 1795. *An Account of the Life and Writings of Adam Smith LL.D.,* published as an introduction to Smith's *Essays on Philosophical Subjects.* London: T. Cadell Jun. & W. Davies; Edinburgh: W. Creech.

Watson, Robert. Student notes on Watson's lectures on universal grammar delivered at St. Andrews University and preserved in the St. Andrews University Library:

1. MS PN 173 (1762).

2. MS 36978 (1776).

3. MS BC 6 W1 (1776).

4. MS BC W2 (1778).

5. MS PN 173 (1758) contains an earlier version.

Wilkins, John. 1668. *An Essay towards a Real Character and Philosophical Language.* London: Gellibrand. Microfiche reproduction in *English Linguistics 1500-1800.* Menston: Scolar Press, 1968.

Wodrow, James. 1779. *Life of William Leechman* in Leechman 1779 I: 1-102.

H. Lewis Ulman (essay date 1994)

SOURCE: "Words as Things: Icons of Progress in Blair's *Lectures on Rhetoric and Belles Lettres,*" in *Things, Thoughts, Words, and Actions: The Problem of Language in Late Eighteenth-Century British Rhetorical Theory,* Southern Illinois University Press, 1994, pp. 117-45

[*In the following essay, Ulman analyzes Blair's rhetorical theory, paying particular attention to his presentation of language and his view of words as "things," such as "objects of art and icons of aesthetic, intellectual, and cultural progress."*]

> Whether we consider Poetry in particular, and Discourse in general, as Imitative or Descriptive; it is evident, that their whole power, in recalling the impressions of real objects, is derived from the significancy of words. As their excellency flows altogether from this source, we must, in order to make way for further enquiries, begin at this fountain head.
>
> It appears, that, in all the successive changes which Language has undergone, as the world advanced, the understanding has gained ground on the fancy and imagination. The Progress of Language, in this respect, resembles the progress of age in man. The imagination is most vigorous and predominant in youth; with advancing years, the imagination cools, and the understanding ripens. . . . Language is become, in modern times, more correct, indeed, and accurate; but, however, less striking and animated: In its antient state, more favourable to poetry and oratory; in its present, to reason and philosophy.
>
> —Hugh Blair, ***Lectures on Rhetoric and Belles Lettres***

In contrast to George Campbell's *Philosophy of Rhetoric,* which grew out of a set of philosophical discourses presented to a private literary society, Hugh Blair's ***Lectures on Rhetoric and Belles Lettres*** (1783) originated as a more or less complete set of public lectures first delivered during the winter of 1759-60 under the auspices of the University of Edinburgh and thereafter for nearly a quarter-century to students at the university. According to Blair's preface, this pedagogical setting influences the scope, content, form, and style of the published volume of lectures: "[The lectures] were originally designed for the initiation of Youth into the study of Belles Lettres, and of Composition. With the same intention they are now published; and, therefore, the form of Lectures, in which they were at first composed, is still retained" (iv). He goes on to explain his selection and treatment of materials in light of his "duty as a Public Professor." While he admits that the lectures are not "wholly original," he also maintains that they are not merely "a Compilation from the Writings of others." Rather, he claims to have "thought for himself" about his subject, adopting the views of others and adding his own reflections according to the principle that he should "convey to his Pupils all the knowledge that could improve them; to deliver not merely what was new, but what might be useful, from whatever quarter it came" (iv). Following this approach, Blair does not present a philosophically profound treatment of rhetoric, but he does provide a carefully drawn and richly detailed map of the realms of belles lettres and composition, as he conceived of them, tracing connections among doctrines of taste, language, style, eloquence, and belles lettres as he lays before his students various rules of composition and criticism. Moreover, perhaps in part because he was mindful of the need to motivate his young charges, Blair keeps before his listeners and readers a telos for the study of rhetoric and belles lettres: throughout the lectures, he implicitly and explicitly links the progress of society, language, taste, and the arts to the improvement of individuals.

Language plays a key role in Blair's rhetorical theory and mythos of progress, serving both as the material cause of oratory and written composition and, more importantly, as material evidence of the progress of society. Yet while Campbell links principles of language to principles of thought and logical truth throughout his argument, Blair never provides a rigorous epistemological account of language. Rather, he asserts a link between language and various faculties of mind, then develops that link primarily within his mythos of progress; he explains how language and knowledge have developed in concert but says little of the principles governing their interaction.

This tendency poses an interpretive problem somewhat different from the task of tracing and clarifying the philosophical analysis of language in Campbell's *Rhetoric*. As Vincent Bevilacqua notes in "Philosophical Assumptions Underlying Hugh Blair's *Lectures on Rhetoric and Belles Lettres*," Blair does not examine in his lectures many of the assumptions upon which he builds his theory of rhetoric: "unlike Kames

and Campbell, Blair did not develop systematically as a distinct and related part of his theory of rhetoric the various philosophical and epistemological assumptions from which he reasoned in the lectures. Rather, Blair left such presuppositions for his audience to provide from their own philosophic frame of reference, assuming that as orthodox eighteenth-century notions about human nature they would be readily understood and accepted" (151). Bevilacqua and others have done much to recover for twentieth-century readers the underlying epistemological assumptions that Blair shared with his eighteenth-century colleagues and readers. But as I noted earlier, relatively little has been done to recover Blair's philosophy of language. That task requires us to ask how Blair "thought for himself" about the resources of eighteenth-century language theory and wove his assumptions about language into a set of lectures on rhetoric and belles lettres. Even though his treatment of language is less thorough and ambitious than Campbell's, and therefore yields a less richly detailed model for articulating philosophies of language and theories of rhetoric, Blair offers a useful complement to Campbell because he draws more often on a different alchemic opportunity for overlapping the generating principles of this study. While Blair subscribes to the Lockean doctrine that words are signs of ideas, and he believes that the chief end of eloquence is to move others to action, the perspective that most consistently informs his treatment of language and rhetoric presents words as things—objects of art that reflect the intellectual and social circumstance of individuals and cultures.

To trace Blair's *Lectures* back to these generating principles, this chapter first sketches the scenes of his theory building, the public lectern and the lecture halls of the University of Edinburgh. The next section examines how Blair presents language as the material foundation of eloquence, and the final section assesses his view of words as things—more specifically, as objects of art and icons of aesthetic, intellectual, and cultural progress.

Rites of Initiation and Improvement

Blair's lectures provided his public audience and his students not only with the principles and precepts of oratory and composition but also with an argument for the importance of those arts in the improvement of society and, more particularly, in the education of those who wish to speak in, or write for the, public; "to support a proper rank in social life"; and to improve their understanding of human nature (1: 9-10). Accordingly, before considering more specifically the role of language in Blair's lectures, I will outline the place of rhetoric and belles lettres in the curriculum of the University of Edinburgh and note how Blair addresses the aspirations and expectations of his students.

The Institutional Role of Rhetoric at Edinburgh

Blair's lectures are significant not only because of their influence on the teaching of rhetoric but also because of the circumstances under which they were delivered. From 1762 to 1783, Blair served as Regius Professor of Rhetoric and Belles Lettres, holding the only chair of rhetoric and belles lettres established in a Scottish university during the eighteenth century.[1] In "The Formation of the Regius Chair of Rhetoric and Belles Lettres at the University of Edinburgh," Paul Bator presents a detailed account of the social milieu, university *curriculae,* and intellectual traditions that provided the contexts for Blair's appointment as Regius Professor. Bator and others demonstrate clearly that the Regius Chair was the "logical outcome" of a host of factors, including "attitudes toward scholarly and vernacular language, achievements in the polite arts, and a general spirit of curricular reform" (40).

In 1708, the University of Edinburgh followed several Continental universities in "fixing" the professorial positions at the university to particular fields of study. Previously, regents had taught individual classes throughout their arts curriculum. The professorships at Edinburgh included Greek, moral philosophy, natural philosophy, and logic, but the distinctions among the areas were not sharply delineated. In these circumstances, Bator notes, rhetoric "found itself attached to various disciplines and professorial holds" (51). For instance, subjects treated in Blair's lectures were taught at Edinburgh during the first half of the century by professors of both logic and moral philosophy (Bator 51-56). Also, from 1748 to 1751 Adam Smith delivered to the *literati* of Edinburgh a set of public lectures on rhetoric and belles lettres, which Blair attended.[2] Sometime after Smith was appointed professor of logic at Glasgow in 1751, Robert Watson continued Smith's course until he left Edinburgh in 1756 to occupy the Chair of Logic at St. Andrews (in which capacity he would teach rhetoric and metaphysics).

In addition to teaching rhetoric and belles lettres in their classes, Scottish professors were writing books about the subject. Roger Emerson has determined that of publications by Scottish university professors serving between 1691 and 1800, "The various categories of *belles lettres* which prior to 1746 accounted for a mere 2% of the titles in the latter period rose to 19%, an impressive demonstration of the success of the efforts to make the universities seats of polite learning" (Emerson, "Scottish Universities" 460). This phenomenal increase in treatises concerning rhetoric and belles lettres during the second half of the century occurred throughout Great Britain and Ireland. The most influential British rhetorical treatises published during the eigh-

teenth century—other than Blair's—that originated as courses of academic lectures include John Lawson's *Lectures Concerning Oratory* (1758; delivered at Trinity College, Dublin); John Ward's *System of Oratory* (1759; delivered at Gresham College, London); and Joseph Priestley's *Course of Lectures on Oratory and Criticism* (1762; delivered at Warrington Academy).[3]

Blair's lectures were first delivered publicly during the winter of 1759-60.[4] He read the lectures at the university with the approval of the Edinburgh Town Council, but the lectures were not officially part of the university curriculum, nor was Blair a member of the faculty. So successful were the lectures, however, that the following year the council named Blair "Professor of Rhetorick" without salary. As a result, after 1760 his lectures were restricted to university students. During the negotiations leading up to his appointment as Regius Professor in 1762, Blair took steps to ensure that his course was established on what he considered sound academic grounds. He was first offered a salary of £100 on the condition that he not charge students to attend his course. In response, Blair proposed that he be given a salary of £70 and the right to charge fees, arguing that students would commit themselves more fully to a course for which they had paid. Blair's biographer, Robert Schmitz, reports that Blair rejected a proposal in 1767 to open his lecture again to the public, citing the same reasons for which he rejected the initial proposal to offer a free class (63). Both the Town Council and Blair's sponsors for the Regius Professorship believed that his lectures would attract students to the university, as they apparently did—Schmitz reports that Blair's classes enrolled fifty to sixty students each session (63).

Blair's other significant contribution to the definition of his chair was the suggestion that "Belles Lettres" be added to the title. Bator demonstrates that Blair had "a host" of models for combining rhetoric and belles lettres, including the work of previous professors at Edinburgh and various French treatises on eloquence (63-64n95). However, Bator cautions against seeing Blair's Chair of Rhetoric and Belles Lettres as "a signal institution for either the discipline of rhetoric or the nascent discipline of English literature and literary criticism," for it was not part of any comprehensive plan to integrate rhetoric and belles lettres into the curriculum—indeed, Blair's course was not required for a degree at Edinburgh (58). Rather, Bator views Blair's course as "one of the results of an ambitious reform of the curriculum that took place in all the Scottish universities during the mid-eighteenth century" and "as a fitting feather for the cap of the Edinburgh *literati,* who strove to promote polite literature in town and university" (58). It was, in other words, part of larger movement of cultural and personal improvement in which language and discourse were understood to play a central role.

The Aspirations and Expectations of Blair's Student Audience

Though a broader and more mature segment of Edinburgh's polite society served as the audience for Blair's original public lectures, university students were the exclusive audience for the lectures during Blair's active years on the faculty at Edinburgh. Moreover, as we have seen, Blair takes particular notice of his student audience in the volume of lectures eventually published in 1783. Who were those students, and, perhaps more to the point, how did Blair conceive of them?

In *A Short History of the University of Edinburgh, 1556-1889*, D. B. Horn cites studies demonstrating that Edinburgh University graduated 343 of the 2,500 university-educated men born between 1685 and 1785 who are listed in the *Dictionary of National Biography*—more than all other Scottish universities combined (63-64). "Most of them," Horn notes, "are clergymen, teachers, physicians, or lawyers; some are statesmen, inventors, reformers, and authors" (64). During roughly the same period, Edinburgh produced more of the scientists listed in the *DNB* than Oxford and nearly as many as Cambridge (64). These numbers support the generalization that Edinburgh was training Scotland's future leaders.

How did Blair articulate the role that he envisioned for rhetoric and belles lettres in the education of such men? Having in his preface to the published lectures identified his intended audience as those who "are studying to cultivate their Taste, to form their Style, or to prepare themselves for Public Speaking or Composition" (iv), Blair treats in his first lecture several "general topics" that place these communicative practices in the contexts of culture, education, and human nature.

Blair argues that human reason, though a faculty of mind, is intimately linked to language and discourse: "What we call human reason, is not the effort or ability of one, so much as it is the result of the reason of many, arising from lights mutually communicated, in consequence of discourse and writing" (1: 1). Accordingly, he maintains, curiosity about the means of improving discourse is a universal feature of human culture and is developed most fully in the most civilized countries. Bringing his point closer to home, Blair asserts "that in all the polished nations of Europe, this study has been treated as highly important, and has possessed a considerable place in every plan of liberal education" (1: 2). From the outset, then, Blair appears to link his subject to a cultural hierarchy. Yet neither he nor his audience was necessarily smug about that hierarchy. Throughout the eighteenth century—Scotland's "age of improvement"—Scottish *literati* worried about bringing letters in Scotland up to the standard of England and France.

There were of course many venues for such improvement, including private study, literary magazines, and the scores of literary, philosophical, and student debating societies established in Scotland during the century, but Blair takes pains to describe for his particular audience the role of rhetoric and belles lettres in "academical education." He acknowledges the disdain of "men of understanding" for the "artificial and schol`astic rhetoric" taught in the past but promises to establish "good sense as the foundation of all good composition" (1: 3). He does so in the first instance by turning the commonplace separation of thought and language—a traditional reason to distrust rhetoric—to his advantage, employing one of his favorite evaluative metaphors: "Knowledge and science must furnish the materials that form the body and substance of any valuable composition. Rhetoric serves to add the polish, and we know that none but firm and solid bodies can be polished well" (1: 4). Though it might be tempting to emphasize that such metaphors establish a close relationship between rhetoric and reason, they nevertheless distinguish substance from polish (or the body from the dress of discourse) and, I believe, more accurately reflect the role that Blair envisions for rhetoric in education. In his lectures, Blair never systematically examines the principles or methods by which we come to know the substance of things, assigning that task to philosophers rather than rhetoricians.

Further, Blair discusses the pedagogical role of rhetorical training from two perspectives more specifically related to the aspirations of his audience. Those preparing to "communicate their sentiments to the Public" must study rhetoric and belles lettres in order to "do justice" to their thoughts, cultivate their reason, and adapt to "the taste and manners of the present age" (1: 5-7). Those with no aspirations as speakers or writers will nevertheless benefit from such study by becoming conversant with the concerns of polite society and improving their understanding of human nature, in particular "the operations of the imagination, and the movements of the heart" (1: 8-10). Speaking generally of the "happy effects" of the "cultivation of taste," Blair prefigures his students'' future circumstances, whether they will engage in "serious professions" or be favored with "the most gay and flourishing situations of fortune." In either case, there will be "unemployed intervals" in which "the entertainments of taste, and the study of polite literature" will provide a means of improvement and a guard against dissipation: "He who is so happy as to have acquired a relish for these, has always at hand an innocent and irreproachable amusement for his leisure hours, to save him from the danger of many a pernicious passion. . . . He is not obliged to fly to low company, or to court the riot of loose pleasures, in order to cure the tediousness of existence" (1: 11). Blair complements the overt and simplistic moralizing in this passage by tying his argument to commonplace assumptions about human faculties, arguing that the pleasures of taste occupy "a middle station between the pleasures of sense, and those of pure intellect" (1: 12). Of course this analysis still reflects a hierarchical ordering of the faculties, from the "low" senses through taste and imagination to the "high" region of the understanding: "We were not designed to grovel always among objects so low as the former; nor are we capable of dwelling constantly in so high a region as the latter. The pleasures of taste refresh the mind after the toils of the intellect, and the labours of abstract study; and they gradually raise it above the attachments of sense, and prepare it for the enjoyments of virtue" (1: 12).

Thus, Blair overlays his hierarchical analysis of the faculties with parallel analyses of communicative practices and the "duties" and "pursuits" of life. Near the end of his introductory lecture, he aligns these analyses in an apologia for the role of rhetoric and belles lettres in the education of his students:

> So consonant is this to experience, that in the education of youth, no object has in every age appeared more important to wise men, than to tincture them early with a relish for the entertainments of taste. The transition is commonly made with ease from these to the discharge of the higher and more important duties of life. Good hopes may be entertained of those whose minds have this liberal and elegant turn. Many virtues may be grafted upon it. Whereas to be entirely devoid of relish for eloquence, poetry, or any of the fine arts, is justly constructed to be an unpromising symptom of youth; and raises suspicions of their being prone to low gratifications, or destined to drudge in the more vulgar and illiberal pursuits of life. (1: 12)

Apologias for the study of composition and literature are familiar features of our own textbooks, and in any given period such arguments can help us understand the ways in which "higher" levels of literacy were viewed and valued. To the historical record of their middle-class status and considerable achievements, Blair's treatment of his students' aspirations and expectations adds rich detail about the intellectual and moral dimensions of their training in rhetoric and belles lettres.

The Foundation of Eloquence

After the initial lecture discussed above, Blair devotes four lectures to the general topic of taste, a faculty whose development and operation he later links intimately to language. Though he later describes these lectures as "introductory to the principle subject" of his lectures (1: 97), he explains their importance by noting that taste is the "faculty which is always appealed to in disquisitions concerning the merit of discourse and writing" (1: 15). Blair's definition of taste—"The power of receiving pleasure from the beáuties of

nature and of art" (1: 16)—leads him to two assertions concerning human nature and taste that will determine much of his approach to language and style, the foundations of his rhetorical theory. First, he distinguishes between taste and reason while relating their operations: "Though taste, beyond doubt, be ultimately founded on a certain natural and instinctive sensibility to beauty, yet reason . . . assists Taste in many of its operations, and serves to enlarge its power" (1: 16-17).[5] Though Blair acknowledges that reason "assists" taste, his readers should not forget that from the outset he aligns "disquisitions concerning the merit of discourse and writing" fundamentally with sensibility. Second, he analyzes the differences or inequalities among people with regard to taste. He argues first that "in the powers and pleasures of Taste, there is a more remarkable inequality among men than is usually found in point of common sense, reason, and judgment" (1: 18). He offers no grounds for this analysis beyond the assertion that in "the distribution of those talents which are necessary for man's well-being" a benevolent "Nature hath made less distinction among her children" (1: 18). Even greater sources of "this inequality of Taste among men," he claims, are education and culture. However, he welcomes this characteristic of taste, for it means that "Taste is a most improveable faculty," a fact "which gives great encouragement to such a course of study as we are now proposing to pursue" (1: 19).

As further support for this key assertion, Blair offers a parallel, hierarchical analysis of the differences among cultures and the differences among individuals within any given society:

> Of the truth of this assertion we may easily be convinced, by only reflecting on that immense superiority which education and improvement give to civilized, above barbarous nations, in refinement of Taste; and on the superiority which they give in the same nation to those who have studied the liberal arts, above the rude and untaught vulgar. The difference is so great, that there is perhaps no one particular in which these two classes of men are so far removed from each other, as in respect of the powers and the pleasures of Taste: and assuredly for this difference no other general cause can be assigned, but culture and education. (1: 19)

One can detect in this argument two rather shaky assumptions that underlie Blair's mythos of progress. First, Blair does not consider the possibility that he might just as well reverse his causal argument and assert that "civilized" societies give a liberal education to those whose class or family have already been deemed superior. (To be fair to Blair's context, however, I should note that eighteenth-century Scotland made greater provisions for general education than its European neighbors.) More importantly, we should recognize that in Blair's system there is no test of taste independent of the culture and education that fosters it. Blair's argument doubles back on itself by conflating specific cultural forms with supposedly universal or "natural" mental faculties.

Other aspects of Blair's argument participate in the larger debate over the effects of nature and art in human affairs. Identifying the two sources of improvement in taste as frequent exercise of the faculty and "the application of good sense and reason to the objects of Taste," Blair claims that "in its perfect state, [Taste] is undoubtedly the result both of nature and of art" (1: 23). Accordingly, he defines the two "characters" of taste in relation to nature and art. "Delicacy of Taste," he asserts, "respects principally the perfection of that natural sensibility on which Taste is founded" (1: 23). "Correctness of Taste," by contrast, "respects chiefly the improvement which that faculty receives through its connexion with the understanding" (1: 24). In sum, he writes, "The former is more the gift of nature; the latter, more the product of culture and art" (1: 25). Though eighteenth-century authors typically consider the understanding a natural faculty, they also consider it a foundation of art. Thus, Blair argues that natural sensibility is to the understanding as Taste is to reason and nature is to culture or art.

After establishing the nature and characters of taste, Blair turns to the problem of determining a standard for taste. Acknowledging that the variation in taste among individuals and nations has led some to reject any standard beyond "whatever pleases," Blair attempts to counter with an argument *ad absurdum:* "For is there any one who will seriously maintain that the Taste of a Hottentot or a Laplander is as delicate and as correct as that of a Longinus or an Addison? or, that he can be charged with no defect or incapacity who thinks a common news-writer as excellent an Historian as Tacitus?" (1: 27). However, this ploy smacks of gratuitous ethnocentrism and class bias. Whom, after all, do we suppose Blair is asking to compare the journalism of early English newspapers to Latin historiography and the taste of Hottentots and Laplanders to Roman and British authors? Surely he is addressing people whose "culture and education" has naturalized them to a particular standard of taste.

Granting that taste "admits of latitude and diversity of objects," Blair nevertheless defines a standard of taste intended to resolve disagreement over the merits of any given object of taste: "His Taste must be esteemed just and true, which coincides with the general sentiments of men" (1: 30). Implicitly, this attempt to appeal to the Taste not of individual humans or groups but of "human nature" detracts from the importance of particular cultures or classes, and Blair almost immediately qualifies his definition. First, he rejects the notion that a quantitative assessment of the "approbation of the majority" can settle matters of taste, maintaining that arguments concerning taste must employ

"reason and sound judgment" and appeal to principle. Second, he specifies that "the concurring sentiments of men" refers not to "rude and uncivilized nations" but to "the sentiments of mankind in polished and flourishing nations" (1: 32). Even in such nations, he acknowledges, "accidental causes may occasionally warp the proper operations of Taste," in which cases we must trust to the test of time (1: 33).

Having proposed a standard of taste, Blair proceeds to define criticism, which strives "to distinguish what is beautiful and what is faulty," and genius, or "the power of executing" (1: 36, 41). With these basic terms in hand—*taste, criticism,* and *genius*—he next presents a long survey of the sources of the pleasures of taste. Most of the lectures devoted to this subject concern the sources of sublimity and beauty. Under the former head, he first discusses the sublimity of objects and sentiments, then turns to the sublime in writing. Here we encounter an important, if implicit, assumption about language.

Blair tells us that he deals with the subject of sublimity in writing under the general heading of taste rather than in later lectures on eloquence and composition because "the Sublime is a species of Writing which depends less than any other on the artificial embellishments of rhetoric" (1: 57). Indeed, his discussion of the sublime in composition downplays attention to the textual features of sublime discourse, emphasizing instead the concise and simple presentation of sublime objects.[6]

In his discussion of beauty, Blair follows a similar pattern. He first treats the beauty of objects (color, figure, motion), of qualities of mind (high and great virtues, social virtues), and of fitness and design. This last species of beauty he identifies as particularly important in composition, but when he turns explicitly to "Beauty as it is applied to writing and discourse," he says little more than he said in regard to the sublime in writing: beauty in writing is associated with the same emotions aroused by beautiful objects and sentiments.

Everything that Blair has said so far in his lectures on taste, except for the two sections devoted specifically to sublimity and beauty in writing, could apply to any object of taste. It is for this reason that he considers these lectures as "introductory to the principal subject" of the course—"poetry, eloquence, and fine writing." Turning to his "chief subject" near the end of lecture 5, Blair asserts that writing and discourse "have power to exhibit, in great perfection, not a single set of objects only, but almost the whole of those which give Pleasure to Taste and Imagination" (1: 93). And of all the productive arts that present to us objects of taste, eloquence and composition are the most "full and extensive":

Now this high power which eloquence and poetry possess, of supplying Taste and Imagination with such a wide circle of pleasures, they derive altogether from their having a greater capacity of Imitation and Description than is possessed by any other art. Of all the means which human ingenuity has contrived for recalling the images of real objects, and awakening, by representation, similar emotions to those which are raised by the original, none is so full and extensive as that which is executed by words and writing. Through the assistance of this happy invention, there is nothing, either in the natural or moral world, but what can be represented and set before the mind, in colours very strong and lively. (1: 93)

In this key passage, Blair clearly reveals his representationalist view of language and his conviction that language is the most powerful semiotic system available to humans. Taste, in this view, is doubly related to language: first, the refinement of taste requires reason and, therefore, language; second, language is the richest source of art and, therefore, of the objects of taste.

Before turning his full attention to language, however, Blair relates discourse to other arts in terms of two semiotic principles: imitation and description. Imitation, he asserts, "is performed by means of somewhat that has a natural likeness and resemblance to the thing imitated, and of consequence is understood by all; such are statues and pictures" (1: 94). Description, by contrast, "is the raising in the mind the conception of an object by means of some arbitrary or instituted symbols, understood only by those who agree in the institution of them; such are words and writing" (1: 94). Though he suggests that writing may imitate actual speech and, in a special sense, "the course of nature," he views discourse as an art built upon a primarily descriptive symbolic system (1: 95n). Yet more important to him than the particular principle by which language signifies objects and sentiments are the medium of language itself and the ends toward which it can be employed: "Whether we consider Poetry in particular, and Discourse in general, as Imitative or Descriptive; it is evident, that their whole power, in recalling the impressions of real objects, is derived from the significancy of words. As their excellency flows altogether from this source, we must, in order to make way for further enquiries, begin at this fountain head" (1: 96). At this point in his argument, Blair leaves his introductory material behind and turns in lecture 6 to language, shifting his metaphor for language from the fountainhead of meaning to "the foundation of the whole power of eloquence" (1: 97).

Blair's fairly conventional definition of language follows the operational principle introduced at the end of lecture 5—description by means of arbitrary symbols—but adds to that formulation explicit mention of the concept of ideas:

Language, in general, signifies the expression of our ideas by certain articulate sounds, which are used as the signs of those ideas. . . . How far there is any natural connexion between the ideas of the mind and the sounds emitted, will appear from what I am afterwards to offer. But as the natural connexion can, upon any system, affect only a small part of the fabric of Language; the connexion between words and ideas may, in general, be considered as arbitrary and conventional, owing to the agreement of men among themselves; the clear proof of which is, that different nations have different Languages, or a different set of articulate sounds, which they have chosen for communicating their ideas.[7] (1: 98)

This definition applies only to the present state of language, however, and Blair's larger project requires that he turn first to consider the rise and progress of language before analyzing further the current structure of language. While such speculative history may have little immediate application to the formal rules of style, it does establish the relationship of linguistic style to cultural history, thus contributing a significant hortatory element to Blair's argument.

Blair sidesteps the question of whether language was a divine gift or human invention by observing that whatever its origin, language must have existed first in an imperfect state suited to the "circumstances of mankind" at the time, leaving it up to mankind "to enlarge and improve it as their future necessities should require" (1: 100-101). This is the history that interests Blair, a history that he promises will be "curious" in its own right and "useful in our future disquisitions" (1: 101).

He provides separate histories of speech and writing, following a pattern that informs much of the course. In his account of speech, he first considers the transformation of words from imitations to arbitrary symbols. Assuming that language originated in the "cries of passion" that "nature teaches all men," Blair asserts that exclamations or interjections must have constituted the "first elements" of speech. When such limited natural signs proved inadequate for changing social circumstances, humans developed names for objects assigned at first by imitation or natural relations of sound, noise, or motion. Later, through analogy, words associated with natural objects were applied to moral ideas, for example, "stability" or "fluidity." Thus, Blair's history challenges the theory that language was "altogether arbitrary in its origin" (1: 101-4). As language progressed, however, words, "by a thousand fanciful and irregular methods of derivation and composition," lost their relationship to their "natural" origins (1: 105). Consequently, according to Blair, "Words, as we now employ them . . . may be considered as symbols, not as imitations; as arbitrary, or instituted, not natural signs of ideas" (1: 106).

Turning to changes in the "style and character of Speech," Blair speculatively examines three characteristics of early speech. First, in line with his earlier argument, he claims that primitive language was more picturesque or imitative. Second, he reasons that early speech must have been accompanied by more gestures and more and greater inflections of voice, both strategies for overcoming the limitations of language in its formative stages. To this characteristic he traces the origin of several features of more polished language: of ornament to the "fire and vivacity in the genius of nations" (1: 105) who retained these embellishments after they were no longer necessary; of prosody to exaggerated tones; and of theatrical delivery to exaggerated gestures. Third, he argues that early speech must have been more figurative in order to compensate for the barrenness of a limited lexicon and to accommodate the dominion of imagination and passion over reason in earlier stages of society.

A similar argument informs Blair's survey of shifts in "the order and arrangement of words." Here he argues that ancient languages were characterized by inversion—subjects in the initial position—and other variations in word order that emphasized objects and their effects on the imagination. Animation was the most important principle of arrangement. In modern languages, he maintains, this "order of the imagination" has given way to the "Order of Understanding" or "the order of nature and of time" (1: 120). The new principle of arrangement is "clearness in communication" (1: 121). Blair identifies "differences in termination" (i.e., inflection) as the key to this structural shift. The earlier order, he maintains, favored poetry and oratory, while our present arrangement favors reason and philosophy. Oddly enough, he ignores the obvious objection that Western philosophy emerged in ancient Greece.

In sum, Blair's history of speech identifies three causes of change in language: the material and social "circumstances of mankind," the "genius" of particular nations, and the relative importance of imagination and understanding in human society.

Turning briefly to the history of writing, Blair again couches analysis in the context of a narrative of progress. He traces the nature and development of two sorts of written characters, signs for things and signs for words. The former, associated with rude societies and ancient languages, Blair assigns to three principles of signification: pictures signify by representation, hieroglyphics by analogy, and nonalphabetic symbols by institution or convention.[8] By contrast, signs for (spoken) words, which he associates with civilization and more modern languages, consist of wholly arbitrary alphabetic symbols.

Comparing speech and writing as he closes his account of the rise and progress of language, Blair observes that both speaking and writing reveal parallel shifts

from natural to artificial forms, though speaking retains the more natural signs of "tones of voice . . . looks and gesture" (1: 136). These features of spoken language, he argues, "remove ambiguities . . . enforce impressions; [and] operate on us by means of sympathy, which is one of the most powerful instruments of persuasion" (1: 136). Thus, he concludes, while writing is best suited to instruction, speaking is requisite for "all the great and high efforts of eloquence."

While shifting emphasis from the development to the structure of language, Blair's two lectures on general grammar and on English grammar are still organized according to his mythos of progress. He analyzes the parts of speech, which he takes to be the same in all languages, in order of their supposed appearance: substantive nouns, pronouns, adjectives, verbs, prepositions and conjunctions (1: 138ff.). Blair acknowledges that the traditional division of the parts of speech "is not very logical," but he adopts the convention for convenience, "as these are the terms to which our ears have been most familiarized, and, as an exact logical division is of no great consequence to our present purpose" (1: 139). He does not clarify his purpose in this passage, but he devotes more time to description and prescription in his treatment of grammar than to logical analysis. Indeed, after asserting that "there are few sciences, in which a deeper, or more refined logic, is employed, than in Grammar," Blair begs off any detailed grammatical inquiry: "I do not propose to give any system, either of Grammar in general, or of English Grammar in particular. A minute discussion of the niceties of Language would carry us too much off from other objects, which demand our attention in this course of Lectures" (1: 137-38). Accordingly, Blair offers no discussion of such key theoretical problems as the relationships between usage and grammar, grammar and verbal criticism, and grammar and rhetoric. Given the superficiality of his treatment of "general grammar," his apologia at the end of this section falls a bit flat:

> [D]ry and intricate as [grammar] may seem to some, it is, however, of great importance, and very nearly connected with the philosophy of the human mind. For, if Speech be the vehicle, or interpreter of the conceptions of our minds, an examination of its Structure and Progress cannot but unfold many things concerning the nature and progress of our conceptions themselves, and the operations of our faculties; a subject that is always instructive to man. (1: 168)

For Blair's students and readers, this observation remains little more than a recommendation for further study.

Turning to the structure of English, Blair provides a brief historical account of English and discusses the compound nature of the language (i.e., its mixture of Saxon, Danish, Norman, and Latin influence), the national characteristics of the English-speaking people ("gravity and thoughtfulness"), and the flexibility of English (in terms of its lexicon, possibilities of arrangement, and variety and quality of sound). This section establishes two important principles linking the formal study of language to the arts of speaking and writing. The first relates to avoiding error. Blair argues that the more elaborately inflected classical languages required attention that constituted them as "objects of art":

> [Language] was reduced into form; a standard was established; and any departures from the standard became conspicuous. Whereas, among us, Language is hardly considered as an object of grammatical rule. We take it for granted, that a competent skill in it may be acquired without any study; and that, in a syntax so narrow and confined as ours, there is nothing which demands attention. Hence arises the habit of writing in a loose and inaccurate manner.[9] (1: 179)

On a more positive note, Blair draws his students' attention to "The flexibility of a Language, or its power of accommodation to different styles and manners, so as to be either grave and strong, or easy and flowing, or tender and gentle, or pompous and magnificent, as occasions require, or as an author's genius prompts," noting that such flexibility is "a quality of great importance in speaking and writing" (1: 175). In terms of the *practical* benefits of the study of language to the student of rhetoric and belles lettres, Blair's comments are thoroughly conventional. He stresses avoiding error and making effective choices among the options allowed by the language.

Blair turns next to style, and, while he does not forge a theoretical link between language and style as explicitly as did his fellow rhetorician George Campbell, he does not leave his theories of language completely behind. Without explicitly alerting the reader to the fact, however, he shifts the substantive and pedagogical emphases of the lectures. In the middle of the final paragraph of his lecture on the structure of English, Blair still invokes the mixed audience of writers and speakers characteristic of the lectures on language: "Whatever knowledge may be acquired by the study of other Languages, it can never be communicated with advantage, unless by such as can write and speak their own Language well" (1: 181).[10] By the end of the paragraph, he is referring primarily to writers: "The many errors . . . which are committed by writers who are far from being contemptible, demonstrate, that a careful study of the Language is previously requisite, in all who aim at writing it properly" (1: 182). In the lectures on style, Blair refers almost invariably to "authors" and "writers," and of

course his examples are all of written discourse. This shift from spoken to written language may explain in part why Blair's lectures on language appear less fully integrated into his lectures than, say, Campbell's treatment of similar issues.

In moving from the consideration of language to style, Blair also shifts the emphasis of his lectures from description, narration, and critical commentary to prescription. The first sentence of the first lecture on style quietly effects the transition: "Having finished the subject of Language, I now enter on the consideration of Style, and the *rules* that relate to it" (1: 183; emphasis added). Throughout the lectures on style, specific rules accompany discussions of particular aspects of style. With this shift to a more didactic delivery, Blair moves from the "foundation" of his subject to its superstructure.

That transition is further marked by his definition of style:

> [Style refers to] the peculiar manner in which a man expresses his conceptions, by means of Language. It is different from mere Language or words. The words, which an author employs, may be proper and faultless; and his Style may, nevertheless, have great faults. . . . Style has always some reference to an author's manner of thinking. It is a picture of the ideas which rise in his mind, and of the manner in which they rise there. . . . Style is nothing else, than that sort of expression which our thoughts most readily assume (1: 183-84).

Blair's distinction between language and style, however, is blurred. According to his doctrine, language, too, reflects the mind. The more important distinction developed at least implicitly in the lectures is that the rules of language and the rules of style are not coterminous. Moreover, style distinguishes patterns of individual choice from the resources supplied by language.

Blair divides his treatment of style according to two chief qualities: perspicuity and ornament. He considers perspicuity in terms of the choice of words and phrases and the construction of sentences, both areas of style that overlap with traditional grammar. In his discussion of perspicuity in words and phrases, Blair identifies three subordinate qualities—purity, propriety, and precision—that build directly on the foundation supplied by language. Purity he defines as "the use of such words, and such constructions, as belong to the idiom of the Language which we speak; in opposition to words and phrases that are imported from other Languages, or that are obsolete, or new coined, or used without proper authority" (1: 187). Similarly, propriety refers to "the selection of such words in the Language, as the best and most established usage has appropriated to those ideas which we intend to express by them. It implies the correct and happy application of them, according to that usage, in opposition to vulgarisms, or low expressions; and to words and phrases, which would be less significant of the ideas that we mean to convey" (1: 187). As Blair is quick to note, both of these qualities raise the question of standards: "There is no standard, either of Purity or of Propriety, but the practice of the best writers and speakers in the country" (1: 187). Of course this criterion is not particularly helpful, for it leaves open the question of who constitutes the "best" speakers and writers? Blair reveals his biases in his choice of examples, but he never warrants his choices further. Moreover, he neglects in this instance to raise the complicated issues related to such standards, issues that he addressed in greater detail in his discussion of taste.

The final quality related to perspicuity—precision—constitutes "the highest part of the quality denoted by Perspicuity" (1: 188) and "imports retrenching all superfluities, and pruning the expression so, as to exhibit neither more nor less than an exact copy of his idea who uses it" (1: 189). Again, Blair develops his subject by precept rather than principle. He does not consider the problems with the notion of communicating an "exact copy" of ideas through words, problems to which Campbell devotes much thought.

At this point in his lectures, Blair has begun to move beyond stylistic choices dictated by grammatical and semantic convention. He moves further beyond "mere Language or words" when he turns to perspicuity in sentences, setting forth rules governing the length and variety of sentences in extended discourses as well as various other "qualities that are required to make a Sentence perfect" (1: 208): clearness and precision, unity, strength, and harmony of sound. Discussions of sentence variety, unity of scene and topic, emphasis within sentences, and rhythm appeal more to aesthetics, text conventions, and reading habits than to any strictly grammatical concerns.

Neither is any explicit connection with his earlier treatment of language apparent in Blair's definition of ornament or figurative language: "some departure from simplicity of expression" in order to "render the impression more strong and vivid" (1: 273). However, in the course of discussing the origin and nature of figurative language he argues again that figurative expression is *natural* and characteristic of early speech (1: 274). Also, he associates figurative language with the imagination and the passions and notes that figures render language more copious, thus linking ornament in these ways to his earlier account of the history of language and society (1: 275).

When Blair turns next to consider general characters of style—diffuse, concise, feeble, nervous, dry, plain, neat, elegant, and flowery—he no longer considers linguistic conventions as constraints but focuses on patterns of linguistic choices that reveal or embody individual genius: "Of such general Characters of Style, therefore, it remains now to speak, as the result of those underparts of which I have hitherto treated. . . . Wherever there is real and native genius, it gives a determination to one kind of Style rather than another. Where nothing of this appears . . . we are apt to infer . . . that he is a vulgar and trivial author, who writes from imitation, and not from the impulse of original genius" (1: 368-69). This transition marks a pivotal point in Blair's lectures, for it indicates that the "foundation" or "underparts" provided by his discussion of language is complete. Up to this point, his argument has focused on natural faculties and artificial conventions that make it possible for language to be intelligible, vivid, and moving—that is, that link language to the understanding, imagination, and passions. From this point forward, Blair builds upon this foundation by analyzing general characters of style and types of discourse according to new criteria: individual genius and the occasions and subjects of eloquence and composition. However, the foundation provided by his lectures on language determines the shape of the superstructure built upon it.

Several implicit connections link the lectures on language with Blair's treatments of eloquence and composition—that is, his inquiry proceeds in similar ways even when he makes no explicit reference to the lectures on language. At the most general level, Blair's separate treatment of public speaking (lectures 25-34) and composition (lectures 35-47) mirrors his separate consideration of the rise and progress of speech and writing. Near the end of his lectures on eloquence, lamenting the "very few recorded examples of eloquent Public Speaking" and urging caution when imitating the style of a favorite author for the purpose of public speaking, Blair draws attention to the differences between written and spoken language:

> We must attend to a very material distinction, between written and spoken Language. These are, in truth, two different manners of communicating ideas. . . . In books, we look for correctness, precision, all redundancies pruned, all repetitions avoided, Language completely polished. Speaking admits a more easy copious Style, and less fettered by rule; repetitions may often be necessary, parentheses may sometimes be graceful; the same thought must often be placed in different views; as the hearers can catch it only from the mouth of the Speaker, and have not the advantage, as in reading a book, of turning back again, and of dwelling on what they do not fully comprehend. (2: 237-38)

This passage also articulates the principle behind Blair's shift to written discourse and his presentation of prescriptive rules in his lectures on style. Other implicit connections to the lectures on language inform more local emphases in the later lectures. Early in his lectures on eloquence, Blair maintains that eloquence is natural to mankind (2: 4); that degrees or kinds of eloquence—aimed at pleasing, instructing, and moving—are linked to the faculties of imagination, understanding, and passion (2: 4-6); and that the most effective kind of eloquence is linked in part to the conditions of society as well as to particular ends and occasions (2: 8-9). Further, the lectures on eloquence and composition each open with comparisons between the ancients and moderns (2: 44ff.; 2: 246ff.). Finally, Blair draws a comparison between social history and personal history analogous to the comparison he drew between the history of language and the growth of individuals: "To return to our comparison of the age of the world with that of a man; it may be said . . . that if the advancing age of the world bring along with it more science and more refinement, there belong, however, to its earlier periods, more vigour, more fire, more enthusiasm of genius (2: 254). In sum, a host of themes first raised in the lectures on taste and language continues to inform the lectures: the relationships between nature and art, mind and language, speech and writing, society and individuals, the ancients and the moderns, the conditions of society and the standards of taste, language, style, and discourse.

Throughout the lectures on eloquence and composition, Blair also makes several explicit references to his lectures on language, but these tend not to be systematic, that is, they do not determine the direction of his inquiry. For instance, in his review of the history of eloquence, Blair argues that the early state of language favored poetry over reasoning and debate:

> There is reason to believe, as I formerly showed, that the Language of the first ages was passionate and metaphorical; owing partly to the scanty stock of words, of which Speech then consisted; and partly to the tincture which Language naturally takes from the savage and uncultivated state of men, agitated by unrestrained passions, and struck by events, which to them are strange and surprising. In this state, rapture and enthusiasm, the parents of Poetry, had an ample field. But while the intercourse of men was as yet unfrequent, and force and strength were the chief means employed in deciding controversies, the arts of Oratory and Persuasion, of Reasoning and Debate, could be but little known. (2: 10)

Explicit references to the language of nature also appear frequently in a lecture on pronunciation (lecture 33), linking intelligibility to qualities of loudness, distinctness, slowness, and propriety of pronunciation, or establishing a natural foundation for the artistic uses of emphasis, pauses, tones, and gestures. However, these and other explicit references to the lectures on language do not extend Blair's theory of language or the themes outlined above.

This overview of Blair's lectures on language and their place in the larger course of lectures illuminates two ways in which Blair presents language as the "foundation" for the study of eloquence and composition: first, as a resource for and constraint on the chief end of eloquence, "to speak to the purpose" (2: 2); second, as a source of knowledge about two of the most important focuses of inquiry in the Scottish Enlightenment, the mind and society. In order to compare Blair's articulation of language and rhetoric with others' attempts, however, we must now look more closely at two global aspects of his theory of language: the status he assigns to language in terms of the matrix of generating principles adopted at the beginning of this study and the mythos of progress that informs his analyses of taste, language, style, eloquence, and composition.

Words as Things: Language as an Object of Art and an Icon of Progress

Along with most of his contemporaries, Blair defines language in terms of a relationship between signs and thoughts: "Language . . . signifies the expression of our ideas by certain articulate sounds, which are used as the signs of those ideas" (1: 98). More particularly, he bases much of his analysis on the relationship of various features of language and style to the several faculties, and he stresses the importance of sentiment over expression in discourse. Though he believes that thought and expression are distinct, Blair see them as interdependent: "it is to the intercourse and transmission of thought, by means of speech, that we are chiefly indebted for the improvement of thought itself" (1: 1). Elaborating on this interdependence, he asserts that "when we are employed . . . in the study of composition, we are cultivating reason itself. True rhetoric and sound logic are very nearly allied. The study of arranging and expressing our thoughts with propriety, teaches to think, as well as to speak, accurately. . . . so close is the connection between thoughts and the words in which they are clothed" (1: 6-7).[11] In all these general doctrines, there is little to distinguish Blair from other late eighteenth-century British rhetoricians such as Campbell, Priestley, and Smith.

Metaphorically, Blair sometimes constitutes thought and language as closely related objects, as he does in the passage quoted above, using the familiar metaphor of language as the dress of thought. Elsewhere, as we have seen, language becomes almost a quality of thought: "Knowledge and science must furnish the materials that form the body and substance of any valuable composition. Rhetoric serves to add the polish, and we know that none but firm and solid bodies can be polished well" (1: 4). Again, both of these metaphors seem quite conventional, maintaining the traditional priority of thought over language while illustrating their interdependence. However, Blair never examines the relationship between linguistic signs and ideas in any depth; for him (and, thus, for his audi-

thus, for his audience) that relationship constitutes a doctrine, not a philosophical problem.

Blair also views language from the perspective of action, as illustrated by his particular analyses of the uses of language in rude and civilized societies and by his general definition of eloquence in which he argues that "as the most important subject of discourse is Action, or Conduct, the power of Eloquence chiefly appears when it is employed to influence Conduct, and persuade to Action" (2: 2-3). In such passages, however, Blair views action as the end of discourse, and language as a means to that end. Accordingly, he most consistently views language as an object, a system of *sensible* signs whose formal qualities make them ideal for expressing thought and feeling.

This emphasis appears, for instance, in Blair's discussion of the natural language of gestures, cries of passion, and facial expressions that artificial language first imitated. Later, he claims, words imitated the nature and qualities of "sensible objects," either by representing sound, noise, motion, or some other principle of correspondence.[12] As language evolved, these words for sensible objects and their qualities were transferred by analogy to "moral ideas" (1: 103). At the end of his survey of the rise and progress of speech, Blair seems quite well aware of his focus on language as a system of sensible signs: "Thus I have shewn what the natural Progress of Language has been, in several *material articles* . . . it appears, that Language was, at first, barren in words, but descriptive by the sound of these words; and expressive in the manner of uttering them, by the aid of significant tones and gestures" (1: 124; emphasis added).[13] Much later in the course of lectures, after his detailed analysis of the structure of language, of perspicuity, and of the origin and nature of figurative language, Blair pauses to praise the instrumentality of language: "What a fine vehicle is it now become for all the conceptions of the human mind; even for the most subtile and delicate workings of the imagination! What a pliant and flexible instrument . . . prepared to take every form which [one] chuses to give it!" (1: 289). This focus on form recalls an earlier passage near the end of his lectures on language, in which he praises a particular formal characteristic, flexibility, which gives language "its power of accommodation to different styles and manners" (1: 175). In that passage, Blair maintains that the flexibility of language depends upon three qualities: (1) lexical copiousness; (2) syntactic variation; (3) phonetic richness. His emphasis on such formal characteristics of language help Blair to portray language as both a rich resource for human communication and, as we shall see, an icon of progress.

It is not Blair's *belief* in progress that distinguishes his rhetorical theory from those of his contemporaries but the manner in which he weaves language and arts of

discourse into his mythos of progress. In his introductory lecture, Blair introduces and links together three broad themes of progress that he develops throughout the lectures: the progress of society from rudeness to civilization, of language from barrenness to copiousness and flexibility, and of individual reason and sensibility from callowness to mature understanding and discriminating taste. Linked in turn to all three of these themes is the "improvement of thought itself," accompanying the progress of society and language, and improvement in the arts and sciences as mankind's knowledge and experience grow.

Given Blair's topic, it is natural that he adopts "improvement of discourse" as his central theme, arguing that attention to the "grace or force" of expression is not only a universal concern of human societies but a measure of their progress toward civilization and a mark of every civilized person's education: "But, among nations in a civilized state, no art has been cultivated with more care, than that of language, style, and composition. The attention paid to it may, indeed, be assumed as one mark of the progress of society towards its most improved period. . . . Hence we find, that in all the polished nations of Europe, this study has been treated as highly important, and has possessed a considerable place in every plan of liberal education" (1: 2). Having established three themes related to language and the arts of discourse, to the progress of society, and to liberal education, Blair elaborates on these themes—particularly on the theme of liberal education—throughout his introductory lecture.

Blair's mythos of progress also includes a familiar compensatory theme first introduced in his lectures on taste. Early on, he argues that in rude and uncivilized nations "taste has no materials on which to operate," that it improves as arts, science, and philosophy improve (1: 32). Nevertheless, he allows that genius may offset deficiencies of taste "in the infancy of arts" (1: 42). Indeed, he suspects that the circumstances of mankind in rude and uncivilized nations may favor sublimity more than polite society:

> I am inclined to think, that the early ages of the world, and the rude unimproved state of society, are peculiarly favourable to the strong emotions of Sublimity. The genius of men is then much turned to admiration and astonishment. Meeting with many objects, to them new and strange, their imagination is kept glowing, and their passions are often raised to the utmost. They think, and express themselves boldly, and without restraint. In the progress of society, the genius and manners of men undergo a change more favourable to accuracy, than to strength or Sublimity. (1: 60-61).

Because of this sea change in the genius of language and humanity, Blair later maintains that we are at somewhat of a disadvantage in the art of oratory relative to the ancients (2: 44). It is beside the point to dwell on how fanciful this historical narrative appears to us. In the context of Blair's argument, this compensatory theme allows him to account for the literary merits of the Bible, the *Iliad,* and the works of Ossian, thus complicating without directly contradicting his overall mythos of progress in language and society (1: 61-66).[14]

The invention of language poses a similar problem, for this greatest of inventions appears to be the product of "rude" ages (1: 99). Blair states the problem as follows:

> One would think, that in order to any Language fixing and extending itself, men must have been previously gathered together in considerable numbers; society must have been already far advanced; and yet, on the other hand, there seems to have been an absolute necessity for Speech, previous to the formation of Society. For, by what bond could any multitude of men be kept together, or be made to join in the prosecution of any common interest, until once, by the intervention of Speech, they could communicate their wants and intentions to each other? (1: 100)

Blair dodges this problem by entertaining the notion that language originated in "divine teaching or inspiration" but was given to mankind in a state suited to their needs at the time, obliging them to "enlarge and improve it as their future necessities should require" (1: 101). Thus, Blair settles for a mythos in which mankind continually shapes language to meet changing material and cultural circumstances, ignoring the fact that he has figured language as God's chief agency for shaping human society. In spite of this suggestive speculation (and in either case—whether God or humanity invented language), Blair's theory of language does not allow the possibility that this great agency of progress could turn on its creators/improvers, becoming an agent capable, in twentieth-century parlance, of inscribing them.[15]

All the same, while language may not serve as the *agent* of social change in Blair's mythos of progress, it does provide perhaps the most revealing evidence of that change. As we have seen, Blair devotes much of his discussion of language to tracing those changes, including the transformation of the *lexicon* from barrenness to copiousness; of the *character of speech* from picturesque, demonstrative, and figurative to discriminating and accurate; of the *arrangement of words in sentences* from the order of the imagination to the order of understanding; of *writing* from signs of things to signs of spoken words; and of the *structure of language* from isolated interjections and names to precisely related parts of speech. Perhaps Blair's most reflective statement concerning his use of language as evidence of progress occurs in his consideration of "the order and arrangement of words," the history of which

he claims will "serve to unfold farther the genius of Language, and to show the causes of those alterations, which it has undergone, in the progress of Society" (1: 117). In reviewing those alterations, he again conflates—or, more precisely, links without thoroughly explaining the relationships among—changes in linguistic form, "advancement" of the world, shifts in the relative operation of mental faculties, and "the progress of age in man":

> It appears, that, in all the successive changes which Language has undergone, as the world advanced, the understanding has gained ground on the fancy and imagination. The Progress of Language, in this respect, resembles the progress of age in man. The imagination is most vigorous and predominant in youth; with advancing years, the imagination cools, and the understanding ripens. Thus Language, proceeding from sterility to copiousness, hath, at the same time, proceeded from vivacity to accuracy; from fire and enthusiasm, to coolness and precision. . . . Language is become, in modern times, more correct, indeed, and accurate; but, however, less striking and animated: In its antient state, more favourable to poetry and oratory; in its present, to reason and philosophy. (1: 124-25)

Though the analogy between the progress of language and society and the progress of age in man is an eighteenth-century commonplace, it appears no less implicated here in the occasion of Blair's lectures to university students. More generally, Blair's influential presentation of words as icons of mental and social progress constitutes an important chapter in the history of the subtle relationships among the forms of academic discourse, the perceptions and measurements of mental ability, and the markers of social standing that form the nexus of our own debate over literacy and education.

Finally, it is important to note a tension in Blair's theory of language related to his use of words as icons of progress, a tension that dogs any study of rhetorical history. As Wilbur Samuel Howell has pointed out, Blair's comparison of ancient and modern oratory invokes contradictory principles (656-59). On the one hand, Blair holds forth Demosthenes and Cicero as timeless standards of oratorical perfection. On the other hand, he defends modern orators for not hewing to that standard but rather addressing their times in ways appropriate to their audiences. He also warns students not to follow inappropriate, outmoded models. His argument, in short, is stretched between static and dynamic principles of rhetorical practice. A similar tension vexes several aspects of his language theory. In his analysis of inflection, for instance, he seems to present flexibility based on "differences in termination" as an ideally economic linguistic principle, yet he also praises the shift to an "order of understanding" occasioned by the emphasis on word order rather than inflection in English. It does not occur to Blair that the grammatical principles that we call inflecting and isolating (in which word order determines grammatical relationships) might be equally capable of embodying a range of mental functions. In a mythos of progress such as Blair's, conflating linguistic and discursive forms with the intellectual and social functions of language seems inevitably to lead to tension between ideal relationships among these elements and their dynamic interplay. More than any other aspect of his *Lectures,* it is this perspective that distances Blair's work from much twentieth-century literary and rhetorical theory. A measure of the difference between Blair's articulation of language and rhetoric and much modern rhetorical theory is the body of research that suggests that semiotic, cognitive, and social systems do not "track" one another according to some internal logic, that is, particular linguistic forms do not *exclusively* embody the uses to which they are put by particular social groups or the intellectual capabilities of individuals who belong to those groups. A measure of the influence of the mythos in which Blair worked, however, is the continuing pressure to insist that language, thought, and society should march to a standard step.

In terms of my generating principles, whereas Campbell's treatment of words as thoughts often emphasizes principles that drive ongoing practical adaptation and theoretical innovation, Blair's treatment of words as things or objects of art tends to reify written and even spoken language as fixed systems that embody equally stable truths and virtues, thus constituting the historical culmination of a mythos of progress. And whereas Campbell's philosophical inquiry into language complicates his compromise between empiricism and Scottish Common Sense realism by distancing an analogous world of words and thoughts from the world of things, Blair's treatment of words as icons of progress employs only those aspects of eighteenth-century realism that allow language to be viewed as material evidence that the achievements of eighteenth-century British science, art, and society are uniformly based in a knowable reality.

Notes

1 Blair retired from lecturing in 1783. However, Paul Bator notes that from 1784 until 1799 Blair shared the appointment with William Greenfield, who delivered his own lectures. After Greenfield's dismissal in 1799, Blair was again designated the sole professor in the Chair until his death the following year (58).

2 Smith's course of lectures was not offered under the auspices of the university, and records of the circumstances surrounding the lectures are sketchy. For a review of the evidence, see Bator (54-55). Also, for overviews of the controversy concerning the degree to which Blair's lectures borrow from Smith's, see

Harding (xxii-xxv) and Lothian (xxi). Blair acknowledges his debt to Smith for his discussion of the general characters of style (1: 381n).

3 Other figures, most notably Adam Smith and James Beattie, also delivered very influential courses of lectures in rhetoric.

4 Except where noted, my account of Blair's public lectures and subsequent appointment as Regius Professor follows Bator (56-58).

5 On this point, in the first of several bibliographic footnotes, Blair fulfills the promise he made in his preface to cite his sources. He refers the reader to Alexander Gerard's *Essay on Taste* (1759), Jean d'Alembert's "Reflections on the Use and Abuse of Philosophy In Matters that are Properly Relative to Taste" (originally delivered to the French Academy 14 March 1757; Blair cites the translation appended to Gerard's *Essay*), Alembert's *Réflexions sur la poésie* (1760), Lord Kames's *Elements of Criticism* (1762), David Hume's essay "On the Standard of Taste" (1757), and Edmund Burke's *Philosophical Inquiry into the Origin of Our Ideas of the Sublime and Beautiful* (1756). Obviously, taste was a hot topic in the 1750s and 1760s. Blair might also have mentioned William Hogarth's *Analysis of Beauty* (1753).

6 After reviewing various definitions of the sublime, Blair determines that the "fundamental quality" of the sublime is "mighty force or power" (1: 56).

7 In a bibliographic note to the opening paragraph of lecture 6, Blair cites Adam Smith's *Treatise of the Origin and Progress of Language;* James Harris's *Hermes;* Condillac's *Essai sur l'origine des connoissances humaines;* Marsais's *Principes de grammaire;* President de Brosses's *Grammaire generale & raisonnée* and *Traité de la formation mechanique des langues;* Rousseau's *Discours sur l'inegalité parmi les hommes;* Beauzee's *Grammaire generale;* Batteaux's *Principes de la traduction;* Warburton's *Divine Legation of Moses;* and Abbé Girard's *Sanctii Minerva, cum notis Perizonii* and *Les vrais principes de la langue Françoise.*

8 Though the accuracy and derivation of Blair's ideas about language are not immediately germane to this study, I should note that his examples of writing are drawn from a wide range of Old World and New World writing systems, including Egyptian hieroglyphics, Chinese characters, Mexican "historical pictures" and "hieroglyphical characters," Peruvian knotwriting, and Arabian "cyphers."

9 Blair notes that Bishop Lowth makes this same argument in the preface to his *Introduction to English Grammar.* For readers who want more help avoiding

error, Blair recommends Lowth, Campbell's *Philosophy of Rhetoric,* and Joseph Priestley's *Rudiments of English Grammar.*

[10] In fact, Blair devotes more space in the lectures on language to speech than to writing.

[11] Blair repeats this argument in lecture 12, on the structure of sentences: "Thought and Language act and re-act upon each other mutually. Logic and Rhetoric have here, as in many other cases, a strict connection; and he that is learning to arrange his sentences with accuracy and order, is learning, at the same time, to think with accuracy and order" (1: 245-46)

[12] In a long footnote, Blair cites President de Brosses's work on naturally significant sounds: "Some of the radical letters or syllables which he supposes to carry this expressive power in most known Languages are, St, to signify stability or rest; Fl, to denote fluency; Cl, a gentle descent; R, what relates to rapid motion; C, to cavity or hollowness, &c." Blair also discusses John Wallis's work on the sounds of English, which, according to Wallis, expresses "the nature of the objects which it names, by employing sounds sharper, softer, weaker, stronger, more obscure, or more stridulous, according as the idea which is to be suggested requires. . . . Thus; words formed upon St, always denote firmness and strength, analogous to the Latin *sto;* as, stand, stay, staff, stop, stout, steady, stake, stamp, stallion, stately, &c." Blair concludes that these arguments "leave no doubt, that the analogies of sound have had some influence on the formation of words. At the same time, in all speculations of this kind, there is so much room for fancy to operate, that they ought to be adopted with much caution in forming any general theory" (1: 104n). As he often does, Blair "skips a step" in the conventional Lockean analysis of language to which he at least in part subscribes. If words are signs of *ideas,* de Brosses's principle would require that our *ideas* also materially resemble the objects of which they are signs, farfetched as that seems. In context, however, it is clear that Blair is primarily interested in these theories as historical rather than epistemological principles.

[13] Though "material," as used here, carries a double meaning—"important" and "having to do with physical matter"—the context emphasizes the latter sense of the word.

[14] Blair championed the works of Ossian in his *Critical Dissertation on the Poems of Ossian* (1763), and he edited an eight-volume edition of *The Works of Shakespear* (1753). In the *Lectures,* he offers Shakespeare along with Homer as proof of his assertion that "in the infancy of arts . . . Genius frequently exerts itself with great vigour, and executes with much warmth; while Taste, which requires experience, and improves by slower degrees, hath not yet attained its full growth" (1: 42).

[15] Though it would be anachronistic to argue that Blair figures language as an *agent* of thought, he appears in several places to flirt with the notion because he so often incorporates linguistic forms and mental faculties into metaphors open to such interpretation. Thus, when Blair claims that "it is to the intercourse and transmission of thought, by means of speech, that we are chiefly indebted for the improvement of thought itself," modern readers will ask—though Blair does not—whether such transmission necessarily determines the nature of what gets transmitted (1: 1). Again, he argues that by speech and writing "men's thoughts are communicated, and the foundation laid for all knowledge and improvement," and modern readers will ask to what degree the foundation determines the superstructure built upon it (1: 135).

Works Cited

Bator, Paul G. "The Formation of the Regius Chair of Rhetoric and Belles Lettres at the University of Edinburgh." *Quarterly Journal of Speech* 75 (1989): 40-64.

Blair, Hugh. *Lectures on Rhetoric and Belles Lettres.* 1783. 2 vols. Ed. Harold F. Harding. Carbondale: Southern Illinois UP, 1965.

Campbell, George. *The Philosophy of Rhetoric.* 1776. Ed. with a new introduction by Lloyd Bitzer. Carbondale: Southern Illinois UP, 1988.

Horn, D. B. *A Short History of the University of Edinburgh, 1556-1889.* Edinburgh: U of Edinburgh P, 1967.

Howell, Wilbur Samuel. *Eighteenth-Century British Logic and Rhetoric.* Princeton, NJ: Princeton UP, 1971.

Schmitz, Robert Morell. *Hugh Blair.* Morningside Heights, NY: King's Crown Press, 1948.

FURTHER READING

Biography

Hill, John. *An Account of the Life and Writings of Hugh Blair, D. D.* Philadelphia: James Humphreys, 1808, 229 p.
    Discusses Blair "as a *Critic,* as a *Preacher,* and as a *Man*" and compares him to other distinguished preachers in Great Britain and France.

Schmitz, Robert Morell. *Hugh Blair.* Morningside Heights, N.Y.: King's Crown Press, 1948, 162 p.

> Standard biography that includes an account of Blair's role in the authorship controversy that surrounded James Macpherson's translations of the poems of Ossian. Contains a comprehensive bibliography of references and the canon of Blair's work.

Criticism

Berlin, James A. "John Genung and Contemporary Composition Theory: The Triumph of the Eighteenth Century." *Rhetoric Society Quarterly* 11, No. 2 (Spring 1981): 74-84.

> Maintains that Genung, a teacher of literature and composition at Amherst from 1882 to 1917, relied on the work of Blair, George Campbell, and Richard Whately for both his conception of rhetoric and the content of his textbook, *Practical Elements of Rhetoric,* which serves as a model for contemporary college texts.

Covino, William A. "Blair, Byron, and the Psychology of Reading." *Rhetoric Society Quarterly* 11, No. 4 (Fall 1981): 236-42.

> Contrasts Blair's "principles of unity, perspicuity, and closure" with the "systematic aversion to any unified literary form" demonstrated in Byron's epic poem *Don Juan.*

Warnick, Barbara. "Charles Rollin's *Traite* and the Rhetorical Theories of Smith, Campbell, and Blair." *Rhetorica* 3, No. 1 (Winter 1985): 45-65.

> Discusses Rollin's seventeenth-century rhetorical theory and examines its influence on the works of his English successors Adam Smith, George Campbell, and Blair.

Matthias Claudius

1740-1815

German poet, journalist, critic, and letter writer.

INTRODUCTION

Now regarded primarily for his idyllic poetry, Claudius was known during his lifetime as editor of such newspapers as *Der Wandsbecker Bote,* to which he made numerous contributions. These pieces were collected in a series of eight books titled *Asmus omnia sua secum portans* (1775-1812), which greatly influenced the *Sturm und Drang* movement and, later, Romanticism. Although critical responses to Claudius have been decidedly mixed, his acquaintance with many of the leading literary figures of the day as well as what many are beginning to see as his innovations, particularly with fictional correspondence and the folk song, are generating a new interest in Claudius as an important writer of late-eighteenth- and nineteenth-century Germany.

Biographical Information

Claudius was born on 15 August 1740 in Reinfeld in Southeast Holstein. His father was one in a line of seventeen Protestant pastors, and he instructed Claudius in classical languages, mathematics, and the Christian religion until his confirmation. From 1755 to 1759, Claudius and his brother Josias attended the Latin School in Plön, where they continued their study of Latin and Greek and began to learn Hebrew in order to pursue careers in theology. Afterward they studied at the University of Jena in Thuringia, where Claudius attended lectures by both the orthodox Christian and the philosophical schools represented there. However, neither Lutheran orthodoxy nor theological rationalism appealed to him and, ostensibly due to a chest ailment, Claudius decided against further pursuing theology and turned to the study of law. Claudius's professional studies failed to interest him, however, and he began to nurture his enthusiasm for literature; he joined the *Teutsche Gesellschaft* ("German Society"), an organization devoted to the study and improvement of German language and literature, through which he became acquainted with critic Jakob Friedrich Schmidt and writer Heinrich Wilhelm von Gerstenberg, who would later become a major figure in the *Sturm und Drang* and whose *Tändeleien und Erzählungen* Claudius would imitate.

In 1762, Claudius returned to Reinfeld without completing his studies. There, he befriended Gottlob

Friedrich Ernst Schönborn, a career diplomat who introduced Claudius to William Shakespeare and the Greek poet Pindar, and furthered his study of Friedrich Gottlieb Klopstock, Rene Descartes, Isaac Newton, and Francis Bacon. During a short tenure in Copenhagen as secretary to Count Johann Ludwig Holstein, an advisor to the Danish crown, Claudius became acquainted with several members of the literary elite, including Klopstock. After another stay in Reinfeld, Claudius travelled to Hamburg in 1768, where he became active in literary circles and established many friendships, most notably with Johann Gottfried Herder. While in Hamburg, Claudius also met Polykarp August Leisching, a prominent relative of Klopstock who hired Claudius to assist in the editing of his two newspapers, the *Hamburgische Neue Zeitung* and its regular supplement *Adreâ-Comptoir-Nachrichten.* Shortly thereafter, Claudius was given sole editorship of the *Adreâ-Comptoir-Nachrichten,* which he infused with his own commentary, most often in the form of fictional correspondence and dialogues.

In 1771, Claudius left his position, possibly due to a falling out with Leisching, and became the editor of *Der Wandsbecker Bote,* a newly founded newspaper in nearby Wandsbeck. Appearing four times weekly, the paper consisted of three pages of news and one of feuilleton, which during the next four and a half years Claudius filled with poems by some of the most famous writers of Europe. Claudius also began to write for the paper in the guise of the Wandsbeck Messenger (later named Asmus), his cousin, and a silent character named Andres; through these characters Claudius wrote fictional letters, verse, reviews of recently published books, and criticism on topics such as philosophy, music, and politics.

During this time, Claudius met and married Rebekka Behn, the daughter of a local craftsman. Their growing family—Rebekka had twelve children—soon demanded that Claudius seek a new position through which he could financially support them. Despite its popularity in cultivated circles, the appeal of the *Der Wandsbecker Bote* was too narrow to support either Claudius or the paper itself and, shortly after Claudius left in June 1775, the publication ceased. In an effort to bolster his income, Claudius collected his works for publication, but despite its positive reception, Claudius continued to face financial troubles until, through Herder, he secured a post in 1776 with Baron Friedrich Karl von Moser, first minister of Hesse-Darmstadt. Claudius first served on the agricultural commission and was later appointed editor of its *Hessen-Darmstädtische privilegirte Land-Zeitung,* which included not only news on land management and governmental reforms but also some of Claudius's fictional contributions.

Weakened by the Darmstadt climate and disenchanted by the relationships with his bureaucratic peers, Claudius shortly resigned and, after a bout with pleurisy, returned to Wandsbeck, where Claudius spent most of his later life. There he continued to publish volumes of his collected writings, translated a number of works, and privately tutored the sons of the elite classes, including those of Friedrich Heinrich Jacobi. In 1788, he was named First Inspector of the bank in Altona, near Hamburg, by the Crown Prince Frederick of Denmark. In his declining years, Claudius maintained a number of correspondences and engaged in private study, particularly of contemporary works of German literature. He remained in Wandsbeck and received many visitors there until 1813, when the Napoleonic Wars forced him and his wife to spend the following year moving from place to place. After his return to Wandsbeck, Claudius's health slowly deteriorated. He died in Hamburg in 1815.

Major Works

Many critics have noted a marked difference in tone between Claudius's early and later works. Although many of his early poems comment directly or indirectly on contemporary social issues, the young Claudius is known primarily as a lyric poet; *Tändeleien und Erzählungen* (1763) draws extensively on folk songs in its portrayal of country life. The first two books of his *Asmus omnia sua secum portans, oder Sämmtliche Werke des Wandsbecker Bothen,* which appeared in 1775, contain ninety-four pieces collected from his newspaper work; they differ widely in theme and form but most are infused with humor and idyllic pictures of rural life. In successive volumes of *Asmus,* however, Claudius's positive Christianity comes increasingly to the fore; the books gradually become less comic, contain fewer poems, and rely more heavily on prose pieces devoted to religion and politics. Claudius's later works comment extensively on contemporary events, with numerous treatises and correspondences, including *Auch ein Beytrag über die Neue Politick* (1794), in which he criticizes the French Declaration of Human Rights, and *Von und Mit* (1796), in which he disparages rationalistic theology. A recurring theme in such religious writings is humankind's self-imposed separation from God and the moral attitude engendered by the direct experience of God's power. The personal nature of religious revelation and the morality generated by a close relationship with God animate such later works as *An meinen Sohn Johannes* (1799) and *Einfältiger Hausvater-Bericht über die christliche Religion an seine Kinder* (1804), in which Claudius examines the instructive value of Christianity by a close reading of Bible stories interspersed with personal confessions of faith.

Critical Reception

Claudius was a highly respected and recognized figure in the literary avant-garde of Europe during the 1770s, and he formed a number of friendships—personally and through correspondence—with many of the leading writers of the day, including Schmidt, Gerstenberg, Klopstock, and Herder. His newspapers, particularly *Das Wandsbecker Bote,* were favorably regarded by the cultural leaders of Germany, and the collection of his work in the *Asmus omnia sua secum portans* was widely praised, most notably by Johann Wolfgang von Goethe and C. M. Wieland. As the times changed, exponents of the Enlightenment and Classicism largely ignored Claudius, but he was warmly received by many of the Romantics, including Philipp Otto Runge, F. W. J. Schelling, and Friedrich Schlegel, who asked Claudius to contribute to his *Deutsches Museum;* Austrian composer Franz Peter Schubert later immortalized Claudius by setting a number of his poems to music. But since the time of Claudius's first publication, literary critics have responded ambivalently to his writings. In 1796, German philologist and diplomat Wilhelm von Humboldt remarked to German writer Friedrich von Schiller that Claudius deserved none of his attention, and later anthologizers often felt the need to explain the inclusion of Claudius among the works of such figures as Schiller and Goethe. But recently, especially in Germany, a body of secondary literature has grown, as well as a number of reprints of his published works, newspapers, and letters. Critics have begun to discover the contributions Claudius made to the development of modern literature—his innovative use of fictional dialogue and correspondence, his mastery of the folk song and hymn, his satirical engagement with contemporary events—which has led to a reevaluation of the work of an often overlooked writer.

PRINCIPAL WORKS

Ob und wie weit Gott den Tod der Menschen bestimme, bey der Gruft seines geliebtesten Bruders Herrn Josias Claudius (treatise) 1760

Tändeleien und Erzählungen (poetry and prose) 1763; second edition, 1764

Eine Disputation zwischen den Herren W-. und X-. und einem Fremden über H. Pastor Alberti "Anleitung zum Gespräch über die Religion" und über H. Pastor Goeze "Text am 5ten Sonntage nach Epiphanias" (treatise) 1772

Asmus omnia sua secum portans, oder Sämmtliche Werke des Wandsbecker Bothen Vols. 1 and 2 (poetry, prose, and criticism) 1775

Asmus omnia sua secum portans, oder Sämmtliche Werke des Wandsbecker Bothen Vol. 3 (poetry, prose, and criticism) 1778

Asmus omnia sua secum portans, oder Sämmtliche Werke des Wandsbecker Bothen Vol. 4 (poetry, prose, and criticism) 1783

Zwey Recensionen etc. in Sachen der Herren Leâing, M. Mendelssohn, und Jacobi (treatise) 1786

Der Küster Christen Ahrendt, in der Gegend von Husum an seinen Pastor, betreffend die Einführung der Speciesmünze in den Herzogthümern Schleswig und Holstein (prose) 1788

Politische Correspondenz zwischen dem Küster Ahrendt und dem Verwalter Olufsen insonderheit die Kriegssteuer betreffend (prose) 1789

Asmus omnia sua secum portans, oder Sämmtliche Werke des Wandsbecker Bothen Vol. 5 (poetry, prose, and criticism) 1790

Auch ein Beytrag über die Neue Politick (treatise) 1794

Von und Mit dem ungenannten Verfasser der "Bemerkungen" über des H. O. C. R. und G. S. Callisen Versuch den Werth der Aufklärung unsrer Zeit betreffend (treatise) 1796

Urians Nachricht von der neuen Aufklärung, nebst einigen andern Kleinigkeiten (poetry) 1797

Asmus omnia sua secum portans, oder Sämmtliche Werke des Wandsbecker Bothen Vol. 6 (poetry, prose, and criticism) 1798

An meinen Sohn Johannes (treatise) 1799

Fénelons Werke religiösen Inhalts [translator; from the religious writings of François de Salignac de la Mothe Fénelon] 3 vols. (treatises) 1800, 1809, 1811

Asmus omnia sua secum portans, oder Sämmtliche Werke des Wandsbecker Bothen Vol. 7 (poetry, prose, and criticism) 1803

Einfältiger Hausvater-Bericht über die christliche Religion an seine Kinder Caroline, Anne, Auguste, Trinette, Johannes, Rebekke, Fritz, Ernst und Franz (treatise) 1804

*Zugabe zu den Sämmtlichen Werken des Wandsbecker Bothen; oder VIII Vol. 8 (poetry, prose, and criticism) 1812

Predigt eines Laienbruders zu Neujahr 1814 (sermon) 1814

Claudius; or the Messenger of Wandsbeck, and His Message [translated anonymously] (poetry, prose, criticism, and treatises) 1859

Matthias Claudius: Werke 10th ed. (poetry, prose, criticism, and treatises) 1879

Matthias Claudius: Briefe an Freunde (letters) 1938

Matthias Claudius schreibt an die Seinen. Familienbriefe (letters) 1955

All Good Gifts around Us [translated by Jane M. Campbell] (poetry, prose, criticism, and treatises) 1977

*This work is the eighth volume of Asmus omnia sua secum portans, oder Sämmtliche Werke des Wandsbecker Bothen, a series that was originally intended to be seven volumes.

CRITICISM

Herbert Rowland (essay date 1982)

SOURCE: "Matthias Claudius's *Paul Erdmanns Fest* and the Utopian Tradition," in *Seminar: A Journal of Germanic Studies,* Vol. XVIII, No. 1, February, 1982, pp. 14-26.

[*In the following essay, Rowland positions Claudius's* Paul Erdmanns Fest *in the utopian tradition and interprets it as a critical tool "designed to elucidate society's essential elements and possibilities so that they might better be realized by those with the power to do so and to the extent possible in an imperfect world."*]

I

When Matthias Claudius published **Paul Erdmanns Fest** in Book IV of his **Sämtliche Werke** in 1783, he entered into a tradition which already had a quite varied, if relatively brief history in modern Europe. The sixteenth century made the first attempts to recover the concept of utopia, largely lost since classical antiquity.[1] In the seventeenth century there was a veritable eruption of utopian writing, which produced all the forms which were to become characteristic of later utopias, from the progressive, regressive, the totalitarian and republican on down to the fantastic and dystopian, all reflecting an overriding concern for institutional organization.[2] The eighteenth century narrowed its focus somewhat to the communitarian ideal which arose in the wake of Fénelon and Rousseau but was all the same little less than profligate in its production of utopias.[3] No exact count exists to my knowledge, but in France alone there were periods when as many as thirty new ones appeared annually.[4]

While the burgeoning of the form in the seventeenth and eighteenth centuries offered contemporaries various visions of socio-political alternatives, it has presented scholars with seemingly insuperable problems of definition. There is no definitive comprehensive study of the many aspects of the complex and thus neither an Aristotelian definition nor even an ideal type of the utopian state and its mode of presentation.[5] In view of this state of affairs one seems obliged to plead helplessness and to rely chiefly on more limited formulations.

The definition used here proceeds from that of Negley and Patrick: 'a utopia is first a fictional work (thus distinguished from political tracts and dissertations); it describes a particular state or community, even though that may be as limited as a small group or so extensive as to encompass the world or the universe (thus a statement of principles or procedural reforms is not a utopia); its theme is the political structure of that fictional state or community (thus a mere Robinsonade, adventure narrative, or science fantasy does not qualify as utopian).'[6] The relationship between a utopia as fiction and socio-political reality is given greater precision by Gustaffson, who describes a utopia as 'einen außerhalb der historischen Erfahrung liegenden Gesellschaftszustand.'[7] In this connection, Vaihinger and Frye view the utopia anthropologically as one of the myriads of fictions through which man attempts to understand himself and his world.[8] The particulars of external form, left untouched by these characterizations, are surveyed by Biesterfeld and will be considered where appropriate.[9]

Outside the small circle of scholars devoted to his work, Claudius seems to be known today primarily as a lyric poet of religious and familial experience and of social conviviality, who successfully cultivated the traditions of the folk song and the Protestant hymn. As a political being he is known mainly through his criticism of general evils in such pieces as **'Der Schwarze in der Zuckerplantage'** and **'Kriegslied.'** Less recognized is his lifelong social and political engagement, which found expression in many other poems, in essays, fictional correspondences and conversations, and open letters. In these works he addressed himself to specific

local and international issues of the day, ranging from the introduction of a new currency and a war tax in Schleswig and Holstein to the French Revolution and the English blockade of Danish ports during the Napoleonic Wars.[10]

Claudius was not at all unfamiliar with the more visionary forms which socio-political reality assumed in the utopian tradition. He reviewed Klopstock's *Die deutsche Gelehrten-Republik* in *Der Wandsbecker Bote* and translated works by Twiss, Terrasson, and Ramsay, which were inspired by Fénelon's *Télémaque,* a *Fürstenspiegel* itself related to the utopia.[11] He himself wrote a highly original mirror for princes in his **Nachricht von meiner Audienz beim Kaiser von Japan.**[12] And in **Paul Erdmanns Fest** he gave poetic expression to his ideal state and at the same time contributed a unique work to the utopian tradition. While the ideal quality of the work has been recognized, **Paul Erdmanns Fest** has to my knowledge not been discussed in its most relevant literary context.[13] My specific aim here is to describe the formal and thematic relationship of the work to its tradition with a view ultimately towards answering the questions why it is the kind of utopia it is and how it bears upon contemporary reality, which, as we shall see, are essentially one. More broadly, I hope to contribute to a better understanding of the interface between religion and enlightenment in Claudius's thought and work.

II

Paul Erdmanns Fest is basically a dramatic narrative, composed roughly of two-thirds dialogue, including two songs, and one-third narration; it covers sixty-five pages or a full quarter of the original edition of Book IV of Claudius's collected works, which suggests its importance among Claudius's typically short prose works.

During a stopover in a small village two travellers learn that the jubilee of a local farmer's tenancy is to be celebrated the following day. They join other farmers, the local gentry, and some visiting nobility in the celebration, which centres around a festive meal and table conversation and comprises the remainder of the work.

We have seen that fictionality is a primary characteristic of utopias. In this connection the appearance of **Paul Erdmanns Fest** in Claudius's **Sämtliche Werke** must be considered. The full title of the collected works is **Asmus, omnia sua secum portans oder Sämtliche Werke des Wandsbecker Boten.** *Asmus* and *Der Wandsbecker Bote* refer to the main persona, first of Claudius's famous newspaper (1771-5) and later of his works (1775-1812), which Claudius created under the influence of the moral weeklies. *Asmus* and his *Vetter* are alter egos both of each other and of Claudius himself. They serve, among other things, to present the contents of the works in a certain tone and from a certain point of view within the framework of a fictitious circle of friends. Thus, they set out on their journey from an already explicitly fictional world and on reaching Paul Erdmann's village enter a realm which exists at a third remove from reality.

Their peregrination bears all the earmarks of the imaginary voyages of their utopian colleagues. They begin their journey for no loftier a reason than 'die Welt und ihre Berge und Gewässer zu sehen.'[14] Only after three days do they consider a more specific purpose. The *Vetter* suggests that they make *le grand tour,* which he describes as 'Immer vorwärts, so wie der Wagen dasteht, bis wir herumkommen auf denselben Fleck; und denn zu Hause' (p. 188)—which is more an ironic jibe at the often self-indulgent practice of young noblemen than a serious suggestion. They then travel for three or four weeks, 'immer so vor uns hin, die Kreuz und die Quere, wo uns der Weg hinführte' (p. 189), before reaching the village where the jubilee takes place.

Even their visit here is more a matter of chance than design. They happen to hear of the forthcoming festivities during their stopover and decide to stay. However, their driver demands that they proceed to their destination as stated in his orders, and the *Vetter* is forced to write a note proving that they had actually been in the coach. These tribulations, on top of the first driver's falling beneath the horses and losing a leg, form a light-hearted parody of the often shallow romance of the *Reisebeschreibung* and suggest that something more significant may be expected. They humorously heighten the geographical vagueness of the journey and the village and in part justify designating the work, both spatially and generically, as (a) utopia—that is, nowhere.[15]

Two other events which occur during the initial journey are important for our purposes. On reaching a beautiful area early one morning, the *Vetter* dreams of settling down with Asmus and another of their fictional friends. Asmus, taken for a moment by mock-heroic whimsy, declares, 'Ich bin willens, von dieser Gegend Besitz zu nehmen . . . Ich zieh meinen Hirschfänger heraus, und haue in alle vier Winde, und rufe überlaut, daß ich hiemit Besitz nehme; und denn gehöret die ganze Gegend meine mit allem was darin ist. So haben es ja die Europäer in andern Weltgegenden gemacht, und es ist reüssiert' (p. 188). The *Vetter* responds that the circumstances were different then, and later, on seeing Asmus's awe before the rising sun, continues, 'Sie haut nun in alle vier Winde, und nimmt von dieser Halbfläche der Erdkugel Besitz!—Und das, Vetter, ist dir doch ein rechter Besitz-nehmer! Er bringt und nimmt nicht!' (p. 189). In nature, then, the *Vetter* sees a model of benevolent authority not without a political dimension. Further along, the travel-

lers stand in wonder before what they perceive as the beneficent infinitude of the sea, and the *Vetter* asks Asmus if he has ever dreamed of it. Asmus replies, 'Einmal; und da hatte sie der liebe Gott so in der hohlen Hand mit allen Inseln und Schiffen, und sah darauf, und die Schiffer merkten es nicht,' to which his cousin responds, 'Gut geträumt, Vetter' (p. 189). In terms of this most traditional symbol of human life Asmus and his cousin see man and nature, with its overtones of political benevolence, in direct relationship to and dependence on God. This relationship is fundamental to the model society and state which manifest themselves later in the work.

One might rightly wonder how Claudius develops an ideal community from the meagre material of a farmer's jubilee. The answer is suggested by a plate which Chodowiecki etched at Claudius's wish and which accompanied the work in the *Sämtliche Werke.*[16] The plate depicts two main groups, the farmers along with Asmus and his cousin, and the nobility with Herr von Hochheim, the local landlord, in a prominent position. Situated in a large square room in Paul's modest home, the two parties stand around tables of equal size at right angles to the viewer, facing each other and slightly toward the foreground. Here, Paul stands as one of the farmers, hat in hand like them, head slightly bowed, and offers a toast to von Hochheim and the other gentry. Several farm hands, standing in the background with scythes held above their heads, complete the picture. The plate represents the final scene and climax of the celebration and in its formal symmetry suggests both the relationship of the groups and individuals to each other and the ritualized nature of this relationship and its narrative-dramatic presentation. Indeed, this ritualization begins as soon as Paul receives his first guests: 'Gegen zehn kamen die Nachbaren, immer Mann und Frau zusammen, einer nach dem andern an; und Paul empfing jedweden mit einem Handschlag, und hieß sie niedersitzen. Einige brachten auch einen Sohn oder Töchter mit' (p. 191). The guests come in family groups and range from children to adults of various ages, from the expectant mother Liese Westen to Jost, the eldest of the village. Paul greets each warmly but formally and, after all have arrived, gives a festive speech befitting the occasion. Around noon, von Hochheim and his guests appear: 'alle Bauern gingen heraus vor Pauls Hofe ihm entgegen, und führten ihn herein. Zu beiden Seiten auf dem Hofe standen eine Partie Knechte und strichen die Sicheln, und Paul stand in der Mitten' (p. 193). Paul greets von Hochheim with the formality due his position, which includes the farmers' festive *Feldmusik,* and welcomes each of the new guests in his warm manner. Since his own guests are unexpected and would be an additional burden to Paul, von Hochheim and his visitors sit apart from the farmers and eat their own food. He suggests that each table choose a speaker, for 'wir können uns nicht bequem übersehen' (p. 195). Paul then offers a table prayer, and the meal begins. During its course the farmers sing two songs and drink a number of healths, the last one to von Hochheim at the high point of the celebration.

The ritual character of the festive meal, frozen at its climax in Chodowiecki's plate, reveals the general contours of the social and political relationship between the farmers and nobility—their fundamental separateness as well as their mutual dependence and respect. Other events and the table conversation bring these contours into sharper focus.

Having just spoken of his infirmity, old Jost continues, 'Ich bin am besten in meinem Lehnstuhl hinterm Ofen, aber ich sollte und mußte herkommen,' to which von Hochheim responds, 'Freilich! Ihr seid unser Großpapa, und unser Großpapa muß ja bei uns sein solange er noch da ist' (p. 194). Jost clearly recognizes and fulfils his duty to the community as its eldest father, a role which von Hochheim, as a member of the community, warmly acknowledges. The bonds between the farmers and nobility find further expression when von Hochheim has half of his servants wait on the farmers (p. 195) and when one of the ladies asks to share their food (pp. 195-6). At one point the farmers request permission to sing their 'Kartoffellied,' a celebration of their simple fare, to which von Hochheim responds, 'Ihr habt alle Freiheit' (p. 199). Indeed, von Hochheim had himself asked them to compose the song.[17] Later, he asks them to sing 'Das Bauernlied,' which they had written on their own initiative to express their gratitude to God for the benevolence shown them in nature (p. 206). For this occasion they have added a few stanzas to thank God for his goodness to Paul and von Hochheim.

Prior to his other guests' arrival Paul speaks to Asmus and his cousin 'von seinem gottesfürchtigen Edelmann und was der durch seine Vorkehrungen und sonderlich durch sein eignes Exempel für gute und fromme Gesinnungen bei jung und alt ausbreite' (p. 191). Later, the farmers include von Hochheim as the greatest among God's many gifts to them (pp. 192-3). Asmus and his cousin are astounded to hear such sentiments: 'Mein Vetter und ich waren wie vom Himmel gefallen, denn solche Bauern waren uns noch nicht vorgekommen' (p. 193). They have never seen such farmers, nor, by implication, such a nobleman.

Herr von Saalbader, whose personality is suggested by his name, is perhaps the most colourful figure in the work, adding by contrast to the impression created by the community.[18] A portly young man who has just returned from *le grand tour,* he and his wizened elderly mother arrive after all the other nobility, inspiring the *Vetter* to comment, 'diese zwei gehören nicht zu den übrigen, oder ich hänge alle Physiognomie am Nagel. Gebt Ihr acht, Vetter' (p. 194). Von Saalbader

unwittingly compromises his credibility at every step, from his irreligiousness to his empty aestheticism and sensuality, all results of a serious case of francomania contracted during his travels abroad. His mockery of the farmers endears him to no one. After listening to him for some time, one of the farmers muses, 'Von Saalbader! von Saalbader! Den Namen habe ich nie gehört. Wo ist er her? Hier aus dem Lande kann der nicht sein' (p. 197). Von Saalbader can poke fun at sovereigns himself but is anxious that the farmers respect the prerogatives of the nobility.

Following one of von Saalbader's more offensive outbursts of prurience, Asmus says, 'Sprechen Sie nicht so, Herr v. Saalbader. Vielleicht sind Sie darum ein Edelmann, weil Ihr Urgroßvater seinerzeit ein unschuldiges Mädchen großmütig vom Verderben gerettet und im Guten erhalten hat . . . Sie sollten die bessere Liebe Kennen, und das Gefühl vor Großmut und Edelmut . . . Sie sind ein Edelmann; und so mu Ihnen ein jedweder Vater 'n Freund sein, und ein jedes Mädchen ist die Tochter Ihrer Freundin! Wofür wären Sie sonst ein Edelmann?' (p. 203). Von Saalbader responds to this question with one of his own: 'Zum Henker, was ist denn ein Edelmann?' Here, Asmus tells the following tale:

> Es war in einem Lande ein Mann, der sich durch hohen Sinn, durch Rechtschaffenheit, Uneigennützigkeit und Großmut über alle seinesgleichen erhob, und um alle seine Nachbaren verdient machte; dieser Zirkel war aber nur klein, und weiterhin kannte man ihn nicht, sosehr man sein bedurfte. Da kam der Landesherr, der mit der goldnen Krone an seiner Stirn, und nannte diesen Edlen öffentlich seinen *Angehörigen,* und stempelte ihn vor dem ganzen Lande als einen Mann, bei dem niemand je gefährdet sei, dem sich ein jedweder, Mann oder Weib, mit Leib und Seele sicher anvertrauen könne—und das ganze Land dankte dem Landesherrn, und ehrte und liebte den neuen *Edelmann.*
>
> Und weil der Apfel nicht weit vom Stamme fällt, und der Sohn eines edlen Mannes auch ein edler Mann sein wird; so stempelte der Landesherr in solchem Vertrauen sein ganzes Geschlecht in ihm mit, legte ihm auch etwas an Land und Leuten zu, wie Eisenfeil an den Magneten, daß seine wohltätige Natur, bis er ihn etwa selbst brauche, daran zu tun und zu zehren habe. (Pp. 203-4)

To the perplexity of von Saalbader and the indignation of his mother, Asmus then states that a common man can be noble and a nobleman common, indeed, that a commoner can be ennobled and a nobleman abased. In any event, each must *be* noble, either to receive or to retain the formal distinction. Out of reverence for the king, everyone must respect a nobleman as a noble man, whether he is or not, until the king himself decides to nullify the abused privileges (pp. 204-5).

Nobility and farmers alike join in approbation of Asmus's story, and the work ends with the festive toast to von Hochheim and all other noblemen who make the story reality. The von Saalbaders must resign themselves to the realization that their views are foreign to this society. The French spoken frequently by the local gentry, distinguished in its urbanity from von Saalbader's affected speech, cannot conceal their deep spiritual and emotional affinity with the farmers, who express themselves in simple and often sentimental German. For the community is at its core an extended family, in which relationships in both the private and public spheres are determined by a patriarchal principle accepted as self-evident. Asmus's tale of the noble man suggests that this community is a miniature of society as a whole and, in the context of the entire work, of the cosmos as well: we recall at this point Asmus's dream of God holding the world and humanity in His hand, and his cousin's vision of the sun as a benevolent natural ruler. In Paul Erdmann's world both are realized. God, as the father of mankind, reveals his love in the abundance of nature and in the natural, beneficent example of His representative. The farmers fulfil their filial duty by cultivating the land and following their nobleman in appreciation of the paternal gifts, while von Hochheim meets his obligation by observing the full significance of his name.

Paul Erdmann's community is structured according to a principle which informs the universe, nature, and man with meaning.[19] All its members live out their lives in analogy to this principle, with regard both to the phenomenal and spiritual worlds. Even in their village they experience pain as well as joy. The pregnant Liese Westen finds sitting difficult, and her husband cannot hide his fear of the impending birth (p. 206); old Jost is weary of life and waits every day for the end to come (p. 194). But pain and death are accepted as a matter of course in the security of living in a meaningful world.

III

Significantly, Claudius portrays this divinely sanctioned, patriarchal society as a utopia. The community exists in one fictional world enframed in another and in a geographically unspecifiable location. The travellers have never seen such people in their own world, and another visitor, representing ideas characteristic of this world, finds a cool reception. The sociopolitical ideal of the community is presented in the form of a story, which, beginning with the words 'Es war in einem Lande,' echoes the opening of the fairy tale and thus places the ideal at an even farther remove from reality. And the enthusiasm attending the final celebration of this ideal, in which even von Saalbader participates, is qualified in the words 'als ob die Empfindung epidemisch würde und Recht'nmal

Recht bleiben wollte' (p. 212), which casts an elegiac note over the whole work. Paul Erdmann's community exists indeed beyond historical experience.

Claudius's ideal polity proceeds, of course, from the ancien régime as it had developed through the centuries up to his own day. In its emphasis on the obligations of the powerful to their subjects and its imperative that the first man in the land also be the best, it closely resembles the state of an enlightened despot. The resemblance is not fortuitous, for Claudius was born in 1740, the year in which Frederick the Great ascended the Prussian throne, and himself experienced something of the widespread infatuation with this 'first servant of the people' during the Seven Years' War.[20] Claudius took the ideal seriously and even saw it realized in his own homes Reinfeld and Wandsbek. However, the mode of its presentation in *Paul Erdmanns Fest* clearly indicates his scepticism regarding the realization of the ideal on a large scale.

Recent historiography justifies Claudius's pessimism and explains in large part why his ideal assumed the form of a utopia. According to Krieger, historians since the 1930s in general no longer subscribe to enlightened despotism in the nineteenth century's literal historical sense of a distinctive phase of absolutism dominant in Europe during the second half of the eighteenth century.[21] Due in part to the actual varieties of practice during the period, even in the hands of rulers presumably uniform in their enlightenment, they posit an extremely tenuous relationship between enlightenment and absolutism within both the theory and the practice of enlightened absolutism (Krieger, pp. 19 and 26).

Within the realm of theory Krieger suggests that this uneasy marriage derives primarily from a shift during the eighteenth century from the genetic to the telic concept of authority, or from authority based on origins to authority based on goals (Krieger, pp. 52-3). In seventeenth-century natural law the right to rule was founded on a contract, whereby the community vested its rights to self-help in the sovereign, either in analogy to the structure of the cosmos (Grotius) or for reasons of self-preservation (Hobbes). By the mid-eighteenth century, however, certain political writers posited the idea of an authority grounded in the capacity of rulers to fulfil social purposes as *the* criterion of valid government; from this new idea derived the necessity of enlightened rulers (Krieger, p. 55). Indeed, these writers combined the telic and genetic concepts of authority. Krieger summarizes the theoretical result as follows: 'The upshot of the uneven combination was to make the independent authority of the government, addressed to social ends which only a rationally minded government could pursue, continuous with the derivative authority of the ruler which was a function of the collective power mandated to him via contract by the community' (Krieger, p. 56). In effect, this illogical combination transferred the sanctity of rule from the sovereign office to the character and policies of the ruler himself, dismissed traditional built-in limitations on the office-holder, and subjected the common welfare to the possible vagaries of the individual ruler. For Krieger (p. 85), 'Enlightenment thus became the modern practical equivalent of old-style paternalism, and the despot the modern active equivalent of the old-style ordained autocrat.'

The rationale for this leap in logic is located in the gradual realization of men such as Sonnenfels, Pestalozzi, and others that despotism, with all its shortcomings, was *the* primary fact of practical political life and that only the truly enlightened despot could connect this fragmented and contradictory political life with the order of nature perceived as being equally real (Krieger, p. 87). Krieger suggests that the few theorists of enlightened despotism were closer to the attitudes of the masses than their liberal constitutional colleagues and implies that they were closer to the realities of political life as well (Krieger, pp. 89-90).

Claudius's scepticism was indeed justified, for enlightened despotism existed in theory only as a logically necessary principle of reason and in fact only in the most isolated instances. Claudius did not suffer from the vicissitudes of secularized theory which plagued some of his contemporaries. For him, sovereign authority rested neither on a contract between community and ruler nor on the ruler's capacity to provide benevolent government and the concomitant need to connect the two. The arbitrariness of such an idea was unthinkable to him. Rather, God provided the original sanction which itself mandated a telos of benevolence. For the believer in old apostolic Christianity, sacred history as a closed system offered a hallowed and at the same time more logical connection between origin and goal than could open-ended secular history. While untouched by theoretical considerations, however, Claudius stood before the same disparity between ideal and reality as the theorists of enlightened despotism—between a universal principle and unprincipled rule. How were the two to be made one? Certainly not by legitimizing unprincipled rule, much less by introducing the equally unprincipled, institutionalized anarchy and vacillation which he saw in democracy. Claudius did not believe in man's ability to rid himself of his evil propensities simply by eliminating the traditional forms through which they functioned—in modern idiom, by legislating morals. If the old system, with its ideal of a benevolent absolute ruler and obedient community, had been estranged from its source and subjected to abuse, it still reflected its source in its form and thus retained both the sanction and the potential provided by the source. Claudius's answer, then, was to impress upon his contemporaries both the origin of the old system and its present potential.

This he did in the indicative mood throughout his work.[22] In *Paul Erdmanns Fest,* perhaps the most comprehensive and definitive poetic expression of his views on society and politics, he presented the origin and potential of the old system, as it were, in the conditional, as a utopian ideal. Despite his convictions and hopes, Claudius was far too aware of the extremes of human nature and the historical and contemporary abuses of the old system to believe in the tale of the noble man and Paul Erdmann's community as categorical, factual truth. Moreover, he was far too convinced of the gulf between the realms of spirit and phenomena to entertain the possibility that the ideal could ever be fully realized.[23] Consequently, he looked at his society and its tradition for their most significant elements and, in the manner of similar, grand fictions, ritualized them in order to show what this society would be if these elements *were* fully realized.[24] He thereby indicated at once the distance of the ideal from reality, the conditionality of its realization, and its spiritual and practical legitimacy. His utopia is thus not a specific goal of action but rather an informing power of the mind. It is designed to elucidate society's essential elements and possibilities so that they might better be realized by those with the power to do so and to the extent possible in an imperfect world.[25] Seen in this light, *Paul Erdmanns Fest* assumes an original and valid, if modest, position in the utopian tradition and in the history of religious, social, and political thought.

Notes

1 For an overview of the utopia of antiquity see Glenn Negley and J. Max Patrick, 'Classical Utopias: 900 B.C. - 200 B.C.,' in *The Quest for Utopia: An Anthology of Imaginary Societies* (New York: Henry Schuman, 1952), pp. 251-9.

2 Negley provides a brief survey of the historical continuity of utopian writing in *Utopian Literature: A Bibliography* (Lawrence, Kansas: Regents Press of Kansas, 1977), pp. xiv-xix.

3 Olga von Hippel surveys a number of Rousseau's German followers in connection with the farmer as noble savage in *Die pädagogische Dorf-Utopie der Aufklärung,* Göttinger Studien zur Pädagogik, 31 (Langensalza: Julius Beltz, 1939).

4 Werner Krauss, ed., *Reise nach Utopia. Französische Utopien aus drei Jahrhunderten,* 1964 (see Wolfgang Biesterfeld, *Die literarische Utopie,* Sammlung Metzler, M 127 [Stuttgart: Metzler, 1974], p. ix).

5 See, for example, Negley, *Utopian Literature,* pp. xi-xiv, Biesterfeld, in *Utopie,* p. 44, and Frank E. Manuel, *Utopias and Utopian Thought* (Boston: Houghton Mifflin; Cambridge: Riverside Press, 1966), pp. vii-xxii.

[6] This definition is presented in Negley, *Utopian Literature,* p. xii, and is an elaboration of the one offered in Negley and Patrick, *The Quest for Utopia,* p. 3.

[7] Lars Gustaffson, 'Utopien,' in *Utopien. Essays,* trans. Hanns Grössel et al. Reihe Hanser, 53 (Munich: Hanser, 1970), p. 82.

[8] H. Vaihinger, *Die Philosophie des Als-Ob. System der theoretischen, praktischen und religiösen Fiktionen der Menschheit auf Grund eines idealistischen Positivismus* (Berlin: Reuther & Reichard, 1911), pp. 36-8; Northrop Frye, 'Varieties of Literary Utopias,' in *Utopias and Utopian Thought,* pp. 25-49.

[9] Biesterfeld, *Utopie,* pp. 5-7, 11-12.

[10] See Matthias Claudius, *Sämtliche Werke,* ed. Jost Perfahl, Wolfgang Pfeiffer-Belli, and Hansjörg Platschek (Munich: Winkler, 1969), especially 'Der Küster Ahrendt,' pp. 902-12, 'Politische Korrespondenz,' pp. 913-32, 'Über die neue Politik,' pp. 416-43, and 'Schreiben eines Dänen,' pp. 959-62.

[11] Richard Twiss, *Travels Through Portugal and Spain in 1772 and 1773* (London: Robinson, 1775); Jean Terrasson, *Sethos, histoire ou vie tirée des monuments anecdotes de l'ancienne Égypte* (Paris: Guerin, 1731); Andrew Michael Ramsay, *The Travels of Cyrus* (London: Woodward, 1727). Claudius's translations appeared in 1776 with Weygand in Leipzig, and in 1777-8 and 1780 with Löwe in Breslau, respectively.

[12] *Sämtliche Werke,* pp. 131-49.

[13] Berglar mentions this ideal quality in his discussion of the piece in *Matthias Claudius,* Rowohlts Monographien, 192 (Reinbek: Rowohlt, 1972). Zimmermann uses the expression 'christliche[n] Utopie liebreich-patriarchalischer Sozialverhältnisse' to describe the ancien régime threatened by the French Revolution, yet without elaborating on the concept or mentioning *Paul Erdmanns Fest* in this connection ('Matthias Claudius,' in *Deutsche Dichter des 18. Jahrhunderts. Ihr Leben und Werk,* ed. Benno von Wiese [Berlin: Erich Schmidt, 1977], p. 440).

[14] *Sämtliche Werke,* p. 188. From this point on references to the work will be included in the text as page numbers in parentheses.

[15] Asmus and his *Vetter,* like the inhabitants of the village, speak German (and French), and the episode with the Jewish pedlar indicates clearly that the village is 'auf deutschem Boden' (p. 201). However, location of the utopia in the native land, rather than on a distant island, is not unusual, if at the same time not typical. See Biesterfeld, *Utopie,* p. 38, and von Hippel, *Dorf-Utopie.*

[16] See letter from Claudius to Chodowiecki, 3 October 1782 (Matthias Claudius, *Botengänge. Briefe an Freunde,* ed. Hans Jessen, 2nd ed. [Berlin: Eckart, 1965], pp. 329-31).

[17] The introduction of the potato as a staple food for farmers during the second half of the eighteenth century was of course one result of enlightened agricultural policy.

[18] One should remember that 'Saalbader,' like 'Hochheim' a 'sprechender Name,' means 'long-winded bore.'

[19] See Gordon Schochet, *Patriarchalism in Political Thought: The Authoritarian Family and Political Speculation and Attitudes Especially in Seventeenth-Century England* (New York: Basic Books, 1975), esp. pp. 10-16.

[20] See, for example, 'Cissides und Paches,' in *Sämtliche Werke,* p. 713, probably inspired by Ewald von Kleist's heroic poem with the same title.

[21] Leonhard Krieger, *An Essay on the Theory of Enlightened Despotism* (Chicago and London: University of Chicago Press, 1975). From this point references to the work will be indicated in the text in parentheses.

[22] See, for instance, 'Kron und Szepter, 1795' and 'Über die neue Politik,' in *Sämtliche Werke,* pp. 543 and 416, respectively.

[23] 'Der Mensch ist für eine *freie Existenz* gemacht, und sein innerstes Wesen sehnet sich nach dem Vollkommnen, Ewigen und Unendlichen, als seinem Ursprung und Ziel. Er ist hier aber an das Unvollkommne gebunden, an Zeit und Ort; und wird dadurch gehindert und gehalten, und von dem väterlichen Boden getrennt' (ibid., p. 541). Passages such as this are found throughout the work.

[24] See Vaihinger, *Die Philosophie des Als-Ob,* pp. 36-8, and Frye, 'Varieties of Literary Utopias,' in *Utopias and Utopian Thought,* p. 26.

[25] Frye, 'Varieties of Literary Utopias,' p. 36.

Herbert Rowland (essay date 1983)

SOURCE: "The Major Motifs: Religion: Self-Imposed Separation," in *Matthias Claudius,* Twayne Publishers, 1983, pp. 33-55.

[In the following excerpt, Rowland explores the major themes that recur in Claudius' writings, including his treatment of man's self-imposed separation from God, the relationship of man and God through nature, his ambivalent feelings toward death, the centrality of love, his political views, and his comments on the artistic process.]

In an introductory study such as the present one there is no room for an exhaustive treatment of any of Claudius's motifs, least of all religion.[1] A brief summary of the religious substance of many complete pieces, not to mention countless passages and allusions in other texts, would itself fill a volume. On the whole, Claudius's beliefs coincide with those of all Christianity and may thus be assumed to be familiar. However, his emphasis of certain of them lends his faith a quite personal character. Moreover, he applied their consequences in a remarkably consistent manner to all other areas of concern, which appear as the remaining motifs of his work. These facts suggest the need to point out here and in the following section at least two of the dominant features of his religion.

Claudius's deep sense of man's self-imposed separation from God was especially significant, both in primarily religious and more mundane matters. For Claudius, man's very real but imperfect communion with God, which has existed at all times, results in a certain relativity in any expression of divine awareness. The experience of God's existence, for example, engenders a need to live in accord with its content. It changes man inwardly, manifesting itself in a way of life and an attitude toward life.[2] That is, it leads to morality. The key words here are "way" and "attitude." The highly personal nature of religious experience creates a broad range of possible moral behavior, which due to its origin will nevertheless be essentially the same. The general way of life and the attitude toward it are thus more important than any codified rules of conduct. In the final analysis morality is for Claudius a derivative of religious experience, not an end in itself, which explains in part his rejection of Kant's categorical imperative.[3]

This relativity extends to all historical, institutionalized expressions of religious experience—to all the religions of the world, including Christianity, as well as to all their holy ceremonies and scriptures. The insight into this relativity gave Claudius a keen sense for the symbolic nature of all such manifestations and for the truth behind them all as well. He once described the world's religions as children of one father, differing in appearance but bearing familial traits, and was tireless in combating religious and confessional zealotry.[4] Time and again he stressed the importance of liturgy and revelation as sensual and thus comprehensible signs of the spiritual and ultimately incomprehensible.[5] Just as often and frequently in the same passages, however, he underscored his view that these are "news of the thing," not the thing itself.[6] The form is always arbitrary, but the essence made palpable by it is not.[7]

Claudius's attitude toward general expressions of religious experience determined his response to those of individuals of both past and present. In contrast to many of his contemporaries he was unwilling to exclude "heathens" from the possibility of salvation; in Socrates and other representatives of classical antiquity he indeed saw models of "Christian" conduct.[8] While retaining his affiliation with the Protestant church throughout his life, he was always able to praise Catholics and criticize members of his own confession.[9] His long life and activity in the world of letters brought him into contact with men of widely varying religious persuasions and occasionally of none at all. He met each individually and sought out his approach to life rather than any formal allegiance.[10]

Like his writing, Claudius's tolerance was a living reality. When Friedrich Leopold von Stolberg converted to Catholicism in 1800, his old, enlightened friends Jacobi and Voß scorned his presence and vented their indignation and, one must add, sincere despair in the harshest words.[11] Even Klopstock would receive him only on the condition that the conversion not be mentioned. While not enthusiastic about the step, Claudius on the other hand maintained the old warm relationship with his friend for the rest of his life. Claudius's tolerance reached an end only where intolerance toward the religious experience and expression of others began.

While certainly influenced in varying degrees by the main religious currents of his time, Claudius was no orthodox, Rationalist, Pietist, or Mystic. One might best describe his religion as a very broadly conceived and personally accentuated version of Luther's own faith. Claudius parted ways with his precursor in his emphasis on the primacy of experience and rebirth. However, he shared with him belief in the fundamental separation between God and man and the role of Christ and grace in the process of reunion. The most appropriate label for his attitude is perhaps Dietrich Bonhoeffer's term "Christian worldliness."[12]

Reason and Philosophy: Pretenders to the Throne

Claudius's work abounds with direct and indirect statements on the place of reason and philosophy in life. When considered together, they disclose a basic concern for and attitude toward the possibility and nature of knowledge, or what may without undue exaggeration be called Claudius's epistemology. This concern and attitude grew organically out of his faith; indeed, many of the most important expressions are made in connection with religion.

Claudius's views on epistemology proceed from his belief in the presence of divinity in the human soul. He felt that man can gain direct knowledge of God's existence and being *only* through this link. Such knowledge is for him experiential in nature and manifests itself as feeling, emotion, or instinct, terms which he uses interchangeably.[13] Yet, the impressions of the soul are subject to the influence of multitudinous earthly stimuli, so that the knowledge thus obtained is imperfect.[14] Aside from the soul man possesses nevertheless no faculty for immediate perception of absolute truth. In this most essential regard knowledge derived from reason and philosophy is secondhand.[15]

The key to understanding Claudius's position, however, lies not in the proposition "either faith or reason," religion or philosophy, but rather in what he felt was the proper relationship between the two. As early as the *Adreß-Comptoir-Nachrichten* he says that head and heart should work together, illustrating their mutual dependence in the metaphor of the Houses of Lords and Commons.[16] Commons introduces all legislation, but Lords must give it the seal of approval. He later described their complementary nature in the image of a man and wife, who must remain together if legitimate children are to be born.[17] The offspring of this marriage are commonsense actions, a brood for which Claudius had the most paternal feelings. Thus, reason played a very important role in organizing and guiding knowledge obtained from the ultimate source.

However—a word encountered frequently in the present context—while head and heart *should* walk hand in hand, they usually do not. More often, the husband is a wife-beater, and in London Lords is at Commons's throat. In this abuse and usurpation Claudius saw both effrontery and danger. If the in part supernatural soul itself is numbed by the sensual world, how completely anesthetized must reason be, which is totally at the mercy of nature's quackery?[18] Moreover, such arrogance leads man away from his most primary concerns into false security. For the way to religion does not pass through metaphysics, and there is no necessary relationship between formal learning and a moral life or final healing.[19] Both religion and life were wholes for Claudius which cannot be separated from their source without losing much of their substance.[20]

Nature and Earthly Life: The Faces of Janus

Claudius possessed an unusual ability to bring life to a near standstill, to live close to the passing moment, and then to capture its joy in the language of immediate experience or of reflection. In **"Täglich zu singen"** [**To be sung daily**] he sings,

> Ich danke Gott, und freue mich
>   Wie's Kind zur Weihnachtsgabe,
> Daß ich bin, bin! Und daß ich dich,
>   Schön menschlich Antlitz! habe;[21]

> (I thank God and am as glad
>   As a child with a Christmas present,
> That I am, am! And that I have you!
>   Fair human countenance.)

The vibrancy of such lines derives in the main purely from the human creature's momentary transport with the rush of life. Yet, it stems in part from a sense of intimacy with a meaningful universe as well. The relationship of God and man through nature implicit in this piece permeates numerous others, chief among them the various **Bauernlieder** ("farmers' songs"). In **"Das Bauernlied,"** for example, Claudius writes the lines,

> We plow and we scatter
>   The seed upon the land;
> But their growth and flourishing
>   Lie not in our hand.
> All good gifts
> Come from above, from God,
> Down from the beautiful blue sky.[22]

However, Claudius's presentation of this cosmic triangle is not always as positive as these pieces would seem to indicate. **"Frau Rebekka mit den Kindern, *an einem Maimorgen*"** [**Frau Rebecca with the children, on a May morning**], which expresses in general the theme of the **Bauernlieder,** ends with the following reference to God and nature:

> He dwells himself unseen within,
>   And is hard to discover.
> Be pious, and seek him with all your heart,
>   To see whether you may find him.[23]

We shall see that even **"Abendlied,"** supposedly a consummate expression of unity, is far from unproblematic. Indeed, many of Claudius's works reveal a pessimism toward nature and earthly existence, a literal God-forsakenness, as abject as any encountered in the seventeenth or twentieth centuries. In the early **Impetus philosophicus** (1775) he writes,

> but the heart . . . seeks to return to *Eden* and thirsts and longs for it. And a veil was bound about *Psyche's* eyes, and she was led out to play blindman's buff. She stands and listens beneath the veil, runs toward every sound, and spreads out her arms. I implore you, daughters of Jerusalem: if you find my friend, tell him that I am lying sick with love.[24]

Book IV of the collected works contains two other prose pieces of great significance in this regard. In **Der Besuch in St. Hiob zu ** [**The visit to St. Job in **] Claudius gives an unusually objective and dark account of an imaginary call paid to an establishment for the physically and mentally ill.[25] When asked how he could bear to see such misery every day, an attendant replies, "Would there be less of it if I did not see it? And can it be seen here alone?" This answer and the allusiveness of the name of the institution suggest the general character of the statement made by the work. Claudius more than once symbolized the world as a hospital, in which the afflicted are cared for until their recovery in death.[26] The work immediately following bears the title *Verflucht sei der Acker um deinetwillen etc.* **[Cursed is the ground for thy sake etc.]** and represents a commentary on Genesis 3:17-19.[27] Claudius described the anguish of life so vividly here that the philosopher of pessimism, Arthur Schopenhauer, later recommended the piece as an expression of the essentially pessimistic spirit of Christiantiy.[28]

Like so many readers, Schopenhauer "received" Claudius selectively, isolating those works which tended to support his own view of the world. However, he deserves credit for having seen in Claudius and Christianity what many others overlooked. Claudius's response to nature and earthly life was highly ambivalent and proceeded from a very real potential in Christianity, especially Protestantism. Despite the inner relationship between God and man and the possibility of communion between them, the distance separating them and the final uncertainty of grace could be overwhelming. For Claudius, the sense of union is not an ever-present state of being but rather a fleeting occurrence to be striven after constantly.

Claudius once wrote that the divine spirit is stamped in all matter and thus can be perceived in it.[29] Nature is a writing, and each creature, man the most important of them, is a letter. Each bears a trace of God and serves as his messenger to remind us of or tell us something about him. The senses themselves are seemingly unending sources of pleasure. As phenomena, however, nature and all creatures and their sensual experience carry their fundamental flaw within. They can provide no direct knowledge of God or overcome radical evil. Like all religions and religious scriptures and ceremonies, they are not the essence but only an ambiguous means to it. This attitude had a profound influence on Claudius's literary style.

Death

Aside from the awareness of divine presence and its promise the fact of physical death was Claudius's most central experience. Death cast a long shadow over his entire life; one might say that he lived each of his days with one eye upon it. The intimate relationship between life and death in his personal existence is mirrored in their proximity as motif within his literary production. His work reveals the same ambivalence toward death as toward life and nature, and for the same reasons.

In many pieces Claudius presents death positively as a transition to external life, which reflects back on earthly existence as an ephemeral but highly meaningful interlude. In 1772, while still a young man, he described his joy at attending funerals: "When I see wheat being sown, I begin to think already of the stubble and the harvest dance. . . . It is a moving, sacred, beautiful sight to look a corpse in the face. But it must have no finery. The quiet, pale form of death is its adornment, and the traces of decay its necklace and the first cockcrow to resurrection."[30] In other works, however, the promise of future bliss fades tonally in the moan of earthly misery. Even in the early *Parentation über Anselmo* **[Eulogy for Anselmo,** 1778] Claudius can write the lines, "Everything is vain and transient after all, worry, fear, hope, and finally death!—The time will come, Andres, when they wrap us too in linen and lay us in a coffin. Let us do, my friend, what we would wish to have done and place our trust in God!"[31]

In still other pieces on death the prospect of eternal life holds no comfort or does not exist at all. In **"Das betrübte Mädchen" [The sorrowful maiden],** which appeared still earlier in the *Tändeleien und Erzählungen,* the vision of her lover's being with God offers no consolation for the grief-stricken young girl, who feels that he cannot possibly be happy without her.[32] And during the period of his greatest public activity in 1772 Claudius addressed a poem on Bernstorff's death to Schönborn, which contains the following lines:

> They've buried him, too, with the others,
>   And he'll come to us never again!
> He's lying now in the grave and moldering,
>   And he'll come to us never again!
> And so they will all be buried,
>   And molder in the grave to dust!
>
> . . . . .
>
>   Oh! S., if, oh! if they buried you, too,
> And I sought and couldn't find you!—
> I'll offer him sacrifice and implore,
>   That death may long spare you.[33]

The pieces and tendencies discussed to this point represent extremes in Claudius's experience and work; they are constitutive elements but not the entire edifice. A look at additional writings reveals a fundamental attempt, not to reconcile his ambivalence toward death, but rather to accept it and to make it constructive. This endeavor is apparent early in Claudius's treatment of the figure of death.

The Grim Reaper first comes into full view in the dedication to Books I and II of the collected works, which was reproduced in part in Chapter 1. Claudius was well aware of other figures of death. In *Wie die Alten den Tod gebildet* [How the ancients represented death] Lessing had suggested that *Mors,* the beautiful Greek youth with the lowered torch, represented the serenity offered by Christianity better than the Grim Reaper.[34] Herder had agreed.[35] Claudius was attracted to the figure as well as to its counterpart, *Somnos*

("Sleep"), as the dedication indicates. However, he retained the medieval representation. Having accompanied him throughout his childhood and youth, it had acquired very personal significance for him. Moreover, it embodied a side of death which *Mors* did not, namely, the terrifying side. For Claudius the Christian, death entailed the fulfillment of a meaningful life and reunion with God. It also brought an end to the anguish accepted as an unavoidable companion along the way to the goal. For Claudius, the Protestant waiting for grace, however, death possessed an element of uncertainty, which tended to vitiate the sense and suffering of life within the universal scheme. And the very real wordly joys as well as the basic drive to live made their claims on Claudius, the human being.

Consequently, Claudius chose to live with death in all its dimensions. Only by coming to terms with its negative aspects could he devote himself to the positive. This was a lifelong process, and the balance was always precarious, now gravitating to one side, now to the other. In any case, his approach to death had a formative effect on his life. With his physical end and its questions ever in mind he developed a delicate sensibility for all the movements of the heart and for the real, if not ultimate, value of life. Their presence enabled him to mold his life optimally as a justification of having existed and gave him a sense of mission. He once wrote,

> Death is a peculiar man. He strips the pied clothing from the things of this world and opens the eye to tears and the heart to sobriety! One can of course be bewildered by him and do too much of a good thing, and that is usually the case when one has done too little up to that point. But he is a peculiar man and a good professor of morality! And it is of great profit to do everything one does as if one were sitting before his lectern and eyes.[36]

Claudius's attitude toward death exerted a creative influence on his work as well. Not least of all, it led him to a symbol of death unique in literature, *Freund Hain.*

Recognition of the darker side of Claudius's view of life and death should not lead one to question his religious faith.[37] As we shall see, his literary style itself forbids such doubt. His works must be read as responses of a long, highly sensitive life to a wide range of experience, each of which reflects a moment in the mood of the poet and man. In the final analysis, the Claudius *mit seinem Widerspruch* ("with his contradiction") is at least as sympathetic as either the idylist or the secret skeptic.[38]

Love

In Chapter 1 we had the opportunity to observe the importance of marriage and family in Claudius's life.

Few German poets have drawn on their rich sources so often or expressed their joys and sorrows so compellingly. These wells of experience were for him perhaps the least troubled of all. Like the rest, however, their origin and ultimate meaning lay in the realm of spirit.

Little is known of Claudius's youthful affairs of the heart. Whatever his real or imagined experiences may have been, his early work from the *Tändeleien und Erzählungen* to Books I and II of *Asmus* is replete with variations on the motif of "romantic" love. Most do not rise above the emotional threshold or the occasional charm of Anacreonticism. A few criticize humorously the extravagances of related feelings, as does "Fritze," which appeared immediately after the review of Goethe's *Werther:*

> Now I don't want to go on living,
>   The light of day is vile to me;
> For she has given Franz some cookies,
>   But none to me.[39]

Still others, such as the three letters to the moon, themselves luxuriate in high sentimentality.[40]

Yet, by the time of *Der Wandsbecker Bote* other tones can be heard. In 1772 Claudius comments on Genesis 1:27, **"Er schuf sie ein Männlein und Fräulein" ("Male and female created he them"):** "What strengthens my assumption is the peculiarity and incomprehensibility of love. You stand there and tremble speechlessly, and your heart begins to pound and your cheeks to glow, and you don't know how or why. And right where philosophy founders and reason has to scratch its head, where you hear a rustling but don't know where it's coming from or going, right there I sense the hand of God."[41] And following the birth of his first daughter he wrote **"Als er sein Weib und's Kind an ihrer Brust schlafend fand" [On finding his wife and his child sleeping at her breast]:**

> Das heiß ich rechte Augenweide,
> 's Herz weidet sich zugleich.
> Der alles segnet, segn' euch beide!
> Euch liebes Schlafgesindel, euch![42]

> (Now I call that a feast for the eyes,
> The heart shares in it, too!
> May he who blesses all bless you both,
> You sweet sleepyheads, you!)

Over the years Claudius wrote a number of pieces celebrating the life and love he shared with Rebekka. The vision of the son he did not yet have and weddings and births in the families of friends and relatives provided the impulse for several joyous occasional poems. The deaths of loved ones in his own family and more distant circles moved him to write some of his most beautiful and significant works. He treated marriage and family in various connections throughout his work. As in the commentary on the passage in Genesis, however, Claudius always returns directly or indirectly to the spiritual realm. In *Neue Erfindung* [New creation] he describes his attempt to attune his family to the eternal process of birth, death, and rebirth by celebrating with them a festival for each season of the year.[43] For in the love of man and woman and of parents and children he saw a reflection of divine love for all mankind. His *Einfältiger Hausvater-Bericht* contains the words, "we know well, when we feel charitable, benevolent stirrings and sentiments in our heart, that somewhere there must be a wellspring of love, an essential benevolence, a *loving father.* . . . "[44] The nature and extent of this love are perhaps most apparent in the short poem **"Die Liebe"** [Love]:

> Die Liebe hemmet nichts; sie kennt nicht Tür
>   noch Riegel,
>   Und dringt durch alles sich;
> Sie ist ohn Anbeginn, schlug ewig ihre Flügel,
>   Und schlägt sie ewiglich.[45]

> (There's nothing hinders love; it knows no
>   lock or key,
>   And passes through all things;
> It is without beginning, ever beat its wings
>   and
>   Shall beat them endlessly.)

In the *Antwort an Andres auf seinen letzten Brief* [Answer to Andres's last letter] Asmus expresses admiration for his friend's ability to lose sight of his worldly happiness while viewing the stars: "It gladdens my soul every time I hear of a man who keeps his head in spite of his passions and can forget bride and groom for something better."[46] Claudius stops, looks, and dwells on all manifestations of love. At the same time he sees them within the context of eternity, where their importance, like that of all temporal things, becomes relative. Nevertheless, earthly love is for him the closest approximation to divinity possible in life and is thus the least problematic of all areas of his experience.

Society and Politics: ordo amoris

The political Claudius, like the religious Claudius, has been claimed by proponents of various ideologies as one of their own. He has been called everything from a German patriot and slave of princes to a precursor of National Socialism and, more recently, of socialism.[47] As is so often the case, lines taken out of context can appear to support completely contradictory conclusions. However, such misunderstandings at least have the virtue of pointing out the important role of sociopolitical thought in Claudius's life and work, which all too often has been forgotten in the

myth of the idylist. Claudius devoted many entire pieces to society and politics and touched on these subjects in many others. In them he dealt with numerous general and specific issues of his time. He had very definite views on these subjects, which can be clearly discerned and placed historically. Yet, as unequivocal as they are, they require interpretative care to avoid false generalizations such as those above, not least of all due to the literary form in which Claudius cast them. And like all other positions on topics of major importance to man, they proceed from his religious world view.

Claudius's outlook on the history of mankind is illuminating in this regard. The eighteenth century witnessed the beginnings of recognizably modern historical thinking, and Claudius's friendship with Herder brought him close to its source in Germany. In *Auch eine Philosophie der Geschichte zur Bildung der Menschheit* [Another philosophy of history concerning the development of mankind, 1774] Herder argued against the Enlightenment's equation of historical development with progress.[48] At the same time, however, he attempted to show that man had been in a process of perfection since the age of the patriarchs according to God's plan. Claudius reviewed the work the year it appeared.[49] While expressing general approval and acknowledging Herder's teleological view of history, he suggests significantly that one should perhaps seek God's plan synchronically rather than diachronically. For him, truth has always been the same in one guise or another, and God's plan for mankind lies outside human history. He backs away from the breach between sacred and secular history potential in Herder's philosophy and manifest in Voltaire's.

Claudius's notion of the essential immutability of human history is complemented by his view of the basic unchangeability of human nature. This idea is implicit in his indirect comparison of Rome before the fall and the present age in **"Ein Versuch in Versen"** [An essay in verse] in 1773.[50] It is explicit in the preface to the third volume of his translation of Fénelon's religious works (1811), where he states, "Since human nature is always the same, however, and its possibilities, needs, and flaws are always identical or at least similar, aside from some regional and individual circumstances, man's consolation and counsel must naturally always be identical or similar as well."[51]

Traces of historical consciousness appear occasionally in the work. There is something of Rousseau in the suggestion that the ancients possessed more courage and energy than modern men.[52] On the whole, however, Claudius's understanding of man's walk through the ages is ahistorical. Indeed, he employs history to deny historicity.[53] For him, secular history is merely an extension of sacred history and its story of salvation.

This is apparent as early as 1778 in the sketch of the origin and nature of social and political life contained in *Nachricht von meiner Audienz beim Kaiser von Japan* [Report on my audience with the emperor of Japan], both thematically and formally one of Claudius's major works.[54] Here, Asmus says that God made all men brothers and that all are equal in death and in his eyes. He placed them on earth temporarily to live accordingly. Because of their natural weakness, however, they were unable to do so. Consequently, he chose the best and noblest among them to represent him as fathers to all other men. These are the emperors, kings, and princes. The subject owes his ruler the unconditional and unquestioning obedience due a father. The ruler, by the same token, is entrusted with the well-being of his subject both in this world and the next.

The social and political relationship outlined here reveals the interpenetration of sacred and secular history in Claudius's world-view and is as clear an expression of divine-right patriarchalism as one is likely to find. It also represents Claudius's understanding of the foundation and structure of the *ancien régime* in Europe. Claudius was acutely aware of the faulty construction of this edifice, as both this and other works indicate—a fact both under- and overestimated in critical commentary. The secular order presented in the work is an ideal rather than a literal description of reality. It is this ideal which underlies all his statements on society and politics. He harbored it years before accepting the sinecure from the Danish court and before the ideas of progress and perfectibility reached their first culmination in 1789. His rejection of the French Revolution and its ideals reflects no shift of position but rather a response to a menace to principles long cherished and asserted. The prospect of changing the sociopolitical form through which God's plan had apparently functioned over the centuries seemed ominous to Claudius indeed.

Auch ein Beitrag über die neue Politik is Claudius's most direct discussion of the events in France and one of his most systematic and important statements on politics and life in general. Here, as elsewhere, one may fault his premises; his faculty for historical thought and political detail was limited. However, he often made much of very little. He finds the individual articles of the Declaration of Human Rights generally true but in their generality too vague and open to later interpretation and abuse to serve as positive laws. They say everything and nothing and take with one hand what they give with the other. He is most convincing when reflecting on human nature in connection with politics. He says at one point that political institutions alone can make man neither happy nor good. Human evils cannot be eradicated simply by eliminating the forms in which they have traditionally appeared. He believes that man is too weak to govern himself, for there remains an unbridgeable gulf between even the best will and the corresponding action, both in the state and the individual. For Claudius, true freedom is spiritual rather than political in the first place. One can work toward this kind of liberty under any system and with no understanding of politics at all. If the individual begins the process of reform within himself, the reform of the state will evolve as a matter of course.

In the *Gespräche, die Freiheit betreffend* [Conversations on Freedom], published even earlier in Book V and another major work on politics, Claudius centers his concept of freedom more directly within its spiritual context.[55] Even in the most reasonable form of government there are obstacles to pragmatic political freedom. They stem from the finitude of man and earthly life on the whole. Essential freedom, "the real England," lies in release from the flesh and union with God.

Precisely because he took his spiritually founded sociopolitical ideal so seriously, Claudius was far from advocating the *ancien régime* as it actually existed and had existed in most places. He understood himself as a friend and defender of the weak and abused, and his work abounds with criticism of the misuse of power. This criticism assumes various forms. He aims humorous but pointed barbs at the injustices of the strong in a number of fables and verse narratives. And in the newspaper he edited in Darmstadt the simple, loyal subject Görgel reminds his ruler of his duty indirectly by addressing him as if he already governed as he should.[56]

Claudius's sympathy for the downtrodden could lead him to strong attacks on political oppression. In the report on his visit to Japan, Asmus's discovery of a human skull and the vision of its living owner's torment elicit helpless rage.[57] However, it was the outbreak of the War of the Bavarian Succession in 1778 that inspired his most moving indictment. In a poem bearing the ironic title "Kriegslied" [Song of war], he included the verses,

> There's war! There's war! Oh angel of God
> impede it,
> And intercede for us!
> Alas, there's war—and I desire
> That I not be to blame.
> What should I do, if in my sleep with sorrow
> And bloody, wan, and pale,
> The spirits of the slain came to me,
> And wept before me, what?
>
> . . . . .
>
> What value crown and land and gold and
> honor!
> They could not gladden me!
> Alas, there's war—and I desire
> That I not be to blame.[58]

While the misuse of power provoked language such as this, benevolent rule prompted words of praise. When Frederick the Great and Maria Theresa ended the war over the Bavarian throne in 1779, Claudius published a poem in which he attributed their action, idealistically or in subtle suggestion, to concern for their subjects and reflection on their true duties.[59] And when the Austrian empress died the following year, he celebrated her as a peacemaker.[60]

Claudius's criticism and praise of the powerful, which have elicited such contradictory reactions, stem neither from a belief in mankind's maturity nor from an acceptance of carte-blanche authority. He was neither a revolutionary nor a lip server. They sprang basically from a deep, personal love for all mankind, a true humanism, which was at the same time a reflection of divine love. For Claudius, the family of man extended from the spiritual realm on down to the individual home and included both the single state and the different nations of the world. Nowhere in his work is there a sign of the nationalism of the nineteenth- or twentieth-century kind. What has been interpreted as such—his Bardic songs, for example—are expressions of patriotism in the sense of a love for familiar, German variations of universal human values. Claudius soon enough turned against even the Bardic movement, itself more culturally than politically nationalistic. He advocated war only in self-defense. His approach to the relationship of nations was fundamentally cosmopolitan, his criticism of France and England directed in part against precisely their breach of cosmopolitanism.[61] His divinely sanctioned sociopolitical ideal derived essentially from his concern for the material and spiritual welfare of all men.

From the distance of nearly two hundred years it is easy enough to say that Claudius should have been more farsighted and recognized the need for fundamental social and political change, especially given his Christian Humanism and keen awareness of current and past abuses of the *ancien régime*. It is not difficult to point out that he, unlike myriads of others, had the good fortune to live under relatively benevolent rulers. When immersed in the torrent of the time itself, however, an individual's vision is not infrequently less than clear. Many other Germans and Europeans repudiated the revolution in France, although at times for reasons different from those of Claudius. After welcoming its outbreak enthusiastically, Klopstock, Goethe, and most leading artists and intellectuals shuddered at its progress. Along with Wieland, Claudius was one of the few who immediately recognized its possible consequences. Given its course of development and the events of the war years, his conviction that man had not yet reached majority and his affirmation of a system which reflected this belief are entirely understandable. One may well be inclined to respect his sense for the fragility of all

social and political life. Claudius's disregard for the influence of political form on human life is at least counterbalanced by his championing of living content.

Poetics: Trimming, Child's Play, and a Cup of Cold Water

Claudius never wrote anything remotely resembling a systematic exposition of artistic principle. His gifts and interests were primarily of a creative rather than an analytical nature. However, he was not at all without critical reflection. His numerous reviews of contemporary works in the newspapers and in the first books of *Asmus* reveal a fine and certain instinct for literary values. These and other works contain statements on and allusions to art, language, genius, and the artist, which allow one to deduce a coherent aesthetic attitude.

The term "sensibility," understood as "a reliance upon the feelings as guides to truth and conduct as opposed to reason and law as regulations both in human and metaphysical relations," goes a long way toward expressing a basic premise of the literary and intellectual avant-garde of the time with respect to both literature and life.[62] If we bring Claudius's epistemology to bear on it, the concept also goes a long way toward explaining his position in the discussion on poetics.

Man has access to ultimate truth for Claudius, we recall, through that remnant of divine nature resting in his soul since the fall. The knowledge thus acquired manifests itself experientially as intuition or emotion. When this experience finds appropriate linguistic expression, it assumes the form of metaphors, symbols, and all the other figures of poetry and prose which flow from and address primarily the senses and feelings.

Claudius himself employs such language in a very revealing piece entitled *Über das Genie* [**On genius**], which first appeared in *Der Wandsbecker Bote* in 1771.[63] Here, he writes, "In idle hours I often picture a language as a bundle of sticks, to each of which a spellbound princess or an unhappy prince has been affixed by magic."[64] Claudius's usage of imagery drawn from the fairy tale suggests his awareness and affirmation of the figurative and emotive dimension of language. It soon becomes clear that he finds the cognitive referents of words—the sticks themselves and their naming function—less attractive. Further along the reason for his preference is apparent: "It is said that in real sorcery, if one understands the craft, a princess can be released from her spell and a goblin or elf enchanted onto the stick in her place. It is certainly the same with languages. . . ."[65] From this imagery emerges Claudius's view of the power of figurative language to express truth and beauty, which are identical, and to distinguish them from their opposites.

The emotional nature of truth charmed by such language and its ultimately divine source are revealed in Claudius's enthusiastic review of Klopstock's *Oden* [Odes], both of which appeared in 1771.[66] After reproducing stanzas from his friend's "Der Erbarmer" [Father of mercy], in which Klopstock praises God ecstatically for saving mankind, Asmus asks, "Now is that foaming, *Vetter?* How do you feel after reading it? How do I feel? A *hallelujah* stirs in me, too . . . I'd like to tear the stars from the sky and strew them at the feet of the Father of Mercy and sink into the earth. That's how I feel!"[67] His cousin is somewhat less enraptured earlier in the review, where Asmus reports his idea that poems "must be clear, like a drop of dew, and heartfelt, like a sigh of love, especially since the whole value of contemporary poetry rests in this dew-drop clarity and the warm breath of emotion."[68] In a brief history of music which came out the same year Claudius objectively presents his belief in the original unity of divine inspiration, poetry, and music.[69] He was firmly convinced of the truth and moral power of all art forms.

However, poetic language need not be hieroglyphic to be true. Claudius felt that the simple phrases and figures, rhythms, and motifs of the folk song, as it had been transmitted over the centuries, had borne and were still capable of bearing nature or truth. He cultivated them on a high level throughout his life; indeed, the folk song and related Protestant hymn were his major poetic forms. He also had great respect for everyday, colloquial speech and its reproduction in literature. In the humorous dedication of **Wandsbeck, eine Art von Romanze** [Wandsbeck: a kind of romance] to the Emperor of Japan he makes the serious statement, "Should His Majesty hear . . . the comment that my verses are strewn rather carelessly, I graciously request He bear in mind that they are intended to be strewn carelessly."[70] He himself spoke Low German at home and with friends. While only one complete work is written in dialect, he sprinkled expressions from his native tongue and various colloquialisms from the adopted High German throughout his work.[71]

For Claudius, as for his contemporaries, nature was a very broad concept. It could encompass at different levels all aspects of both the phenomenal and spiritual realms. The soul and emotion provided the connection between the two, as we have seen. Their linguistic expression, even in the most commonplace form, could thus be at once "natural" and true on both higher and lower planes. Consequently, Claudius very consciously cultivated colloquial language in his writings. This fact is important for a proper understanding of his stylistic change and his later prose works.

Claudius frequently expressed admiration for men who possessed the ability to fashion a language which could move their reader or spectator emotionally to recogni-

tion of truth. In **Über das Genie** he describes the man who recognizes the emotive power of language as a "Sunday's child, who can see spirits, while the other sees the stick and nothing more."[72] And when the Emperor of Japan asks what poets are, Asmus replies, "Bright, pure pebbles, which the beautiful sky and the beautiful earth and holy religion strike together so that sparks fly."[73]

Given Claudius's attitude toward language, art, and the artist discussed so far, it is not surprising that he rejected the normative-systematic poetics of Neo-Classicism. In a piece entitled **Steht Homer z. Ex. unterm Spruch des Aristoteles & Compagnie? [Does Homer, e.g., stand under the judgment of Aristotle & company?]** he answers his own question by referring to Christian Felix Weiße's *Romeo und Julia:*

> The question seems to me as comical as if it had occurred to someone, when the thrill and clamor of love and despair had grown quiet and the unfortunate enthusiast had died, to knock on the door of the tomb and to ask . . . whether Miss Juliet had played her role with expression and according to the rules of art. . . . A bunch of art critics and a year's worth of journalists piping wisdom must be dirt under the feet of the man who has a warm heart, wants earnestly to be useful, and has what it takes.[74]

Along with Klopstock's circle and the *Sturm und Drang* writers Claudius defended the concept of artistic freedom insofar as this meant the artist's right to depart from canons of rules for poetic creation. Such catalogs represented for him an impermissible rationalization of a basically emotional process. The individuality of emotional experience brings with it an individuality of expression, which should not be constrained by any preconceived, immutable laws. Rather than depending on such codified rules, the poet should rely on nature in the fullest sense of the word; for nature is the proper source and object of art. If the artist is true to his own response to nature, his expression will emerge of itself. Claudius's criticism of literature followed from these principles and is itself highly intuitive and individualistic.

At this point we must pause for a moment to note that the picture of Claudius's poetics drawn so far is only half complete. He indeed believed that art and the artist possessed significant potential and found this potential realized in works of all ages. At the same time he felt that both were subject to severe inherent limitations. These must be sketched if his views on the subject are to be fully understood.

We recall Claudius's belief that human emotions can be addressed not only by the soul but by all earthly phenomena. This interference impairs their capacity to communicate the originally clear impulses from the spiritual realm and thus makes them imperfect like all other things of this world. It follows that linguistic expression of emotional experience, itself an entirely temporal appearance, must be flawed as well. This idea permeated Claudius's attitude toward poetics from early on.

Claudius made an important general statement in this connection in the *Morgengespräch zwischen A. und dem Kandidaten Bertram* [Morning conversation between A. and the student Bertram] in Book VIII of the collected works: "For words are words, and one cannot be on one's guard enough against them. When they have *real* objects, everything goes fairly well and safely. But when they deal with abstract concepts the matter becomes thorny."[75] He then draws on a pertinent, systematic discussion by Bacon to support his contention and concludes, "And here words and phrases are the little Cartesian devils incarnate."[76] Language is relatively reliable where it reflects the objective and the close at hand. When it seeks to go beyond, however, whether in theology and philosophy as here or in literature, its inadequacy (indeed, its harmfulness) is everywhere apparent.

Claudius was highly skeptical of literary language, once referring to it as an "infamous funnel in which wine becomes water."[77] Even in the eulogy for Josias in 1760 he spurns the flourishes of the orator, saying that a sigh or tear speaks more eloquently; the first line of one of the poems written on this occasion reads, "Today I wish not to appear in poetic garb."[78] Such complaints about the impotence of poetic language were common in an age of sensibility. With Claudius and others as well, however, they were a matter of principle. In a letter to Andres in Book V Asmus says, "You write that he [John the Baptist] seems so great to you and yet you can't quite say why. That's really good, Andres. One often knows most just when one can't quite say why."[79] Language may proceed from ideas or emotions—from realities—but it is never identical with them. The objectivity of language itself precludes such identity, and there always remains an essential difference between them.[80]

Moreover, many poets seem to be unaware of this difference, equating their poetic productions with truth. Claudius may well have clapped his hands with glee on reading and later translating Socrates' words on poets. After going among them in his search for wisdom and knowledge, the sage says to his fellow Athenians, "But I am ashamed to tell you . . . that they wrote . . . not from the inspiration of wisdom but rather from a natural inspiration in a kind of enthusiasm like the prophets and soothsayers. For these, too, say many beautiful things but understand nothing of what they say. . . . At the same time I noticed, too, that because of their rhyming they believed themselves to be wise men in other things as well, but they were not."[81]

Not only do they fail to recognize the yawning gap between experience and language; poets frequently take it upon themselves to write in the absence of any experience at all. In *Ernst und Kurzweil, von meinem Vetter an mich* [Earnestness and pastime, from my cousin to me] in Book IV, for example, Asmus's cousin offers some comic exempla to show the difference between emotional earnestness and pastime. In one he writes,

> The sea is stormy . . . and the ship to the left [of a sketch included in the piece] . . . is about to sink. You are on the other ship and see your poor neighbors stretching out their hands and crying for help. Now, if you're an aesthetic soap boiler, then sit down and write an elegy on the sinking of the other ship together with how the people screamed and the kind of sympathy you felt, etc. But if your sympathy is earnest, then go to the skipper and ask him to risk the lifeboat. Hang the poet to the mast, so that he won't get in the way when you lower the boat, and climb in quickly and joyously with the other sailors to retrieve the poor people.[82]

Worst of all, many poets, even the best of them, lose all sight of the content of art and create a cult of form. In his review of Wieland's *Der neue Amadis* in 1771 Claudius cannot but acknowledge his bedazzlement at the author's stylistic virtuosity.[83] However, he absolutely rejects what he perceives as the immorality and even mockery of virtue in the work. Such considerations underlie his position in the heated controversy over Goethe's *Werther* during the early 1770s and his condemnation of Goethe and Schiller, the "aesthetic bagpipes," and their ideas during the late 1790s.[84] For Claudius, the content of literature, as of religion, politics, and all other areas of life, is far more important than form. And there is subject matter both proper and improper for literary treatment. Artistic freedom does not entail the liberty to be immoral. For this reason Claudius can criticize formally free works, such as Klinger's *Das leidende Weib,* and praise more conventional pieces, such as Lessing's *Emilia Galotti.*[85]

In view of the fundamental inadequacy and widespread abuse of the written word Claudius frequently recommends the self-sufficiency and purposefulness of silence. He fairly demolishes a contemporary, formal laudation of Christ: "Herr Bastholm asks right at the beginning, 'May I speak, when the seraphim are silent?' What good is the question? Why did he not remain silent instead? The silence of the seraphim is the true laudation of the Messiah, it or none at all. Anything else is sickening water soup. . . . "[86] To say many things is to profane them. Truth and language are of two entirely different orders of being, and silence is often the ultimate sign of reverence and wisdom. We shall see that Claudius was in this regard truly reverent and wise, for much of his work is an expression of meaningful silence.

Claudius's basic pessimism toward language is as pervasive as that of Maurice Maeterlinck or Hugo von Hofmannsthal in more recent times. In view of this skepticism one may well wonder why he wrote at all. When asking this question, one should of course remember that neither Maeterlinck nor Hofmannsthal ceased to write because of their insight into the insufficiency of language. Yet, the latter did in fact give up one form of expression for another. And Claudius, too, altered his style in his later work. However, this shift resulted not from any change in his poetics, but rather from what he saw as a threat to it. A closer consideration of his view of the purpose of art will demonstrate this fact.

Our reading of Claudius indicates that the core of his poetics can be understood entirely in terms of the Horatian dictum "Et prodesse volunt et delectare poetae" ("Poets want both to instruct and to delight"). To be sure, he interpreted Horace in a different sense from many of his contemporaries. Rationalists saw the instructive function of literature as lying in part in the transmission of rationally conceived truths. The pleasure of literary art derived from the intellectual comparison of the artist's imitation of truth with truth itself. Literature and truth were thus two distinct entities, and literary form served the didactic purpose of conveying truth as well as activating the intellect of the reader as the faculty for perceiving it.

Claudius, on the other hand, found both the instructional and entertainment value of literature in its cultivation of sensibility. For he felt that the emotions are at once the bearers of truth and the source of pleasure. Literature fulfilled its raison d'être by evoking the truth and enjoyment of feeling and by exercising man's capacity to experience them. No less than the Rationalists, however, he saw an essential difference between literature and truth. For him, unlike the Classicists and Romantics, there is not truth inherent in artistically formed language. Words are entirely neutral and can be used for both the good and the bad. Moreover, the emotions themselves are not infallible and can be led astray as well as along the right path.

Consequently, everything depends on the thematic content of literature. Claudius's criticism of Wieland and Goethe and Schiller, indeed, his statements on form and content in all contexts, indicate that he was far more interested in what literature *does* than in what it *is*. His works disclose a keen sense for the interplay of form and content. However, literary form is legitimate for him only to the extent that it supports by enlivening literary content or truth. Claudius's approach to literature is thus as didactic, if in a different way, as that of Gottsched or, for that matter, of Goethe and Schiller. Like the former and contrary to the latter, in any case, he "commits" what New Criticism condemns as the "affective fallacy" and what some recent critics praise as engagement.[87]

While Claudius's attitude toward literary form and content is manifest in his early work, it is especially visible in his later writings. In the preface to Book VIII Asmus writes, "Readers will have to be content with word and expression. One can't help no longer being young when one is old. But as regards the content, which is after all the main thing in a writing, I think I've kept my word."[88] And in the **Valet an meine Leser [Farewell to my readers]** in Book VII Claudius alludes both to the dedication in Books I and II and Matthew 10:42: "Most of it is *trimming and child's play,* wound like a garland round my *'Cup of Cold Water,'* so that it might strike the eye more pleasantly."[89]

Claudius wrote for the sake of the cup of cold water, which he felt was increasingly being contaminated by the spirit of the time. Completely aware of his own limitations and those of his enterprise he understood himself more and more as a messenger and defender of religious truth.

Not only the cup of cold water, but the trimming and child's play as well were being defiled by the times. Consequently, Claudius turned increasingly from the predominantly figurative language and the frequently fragmented, impetuous syntax of his youth, which had proven particularly subject to abuse. In his later work he made a concerted effort to unite the language of emotion with the more measured idiom of natural, everyday language. Each was capable of bearing truth when used alone. How much more effective might they be if employed together?

Notes

[1] See Friedrich Loofs, *Matthias Claudius in kirchengeschichtlicher Beleuchtung: Eine Untersuchung über Claudius' religiöse Stellung und Altersentwicklung* (Gotha, 1915), especially pp. 11-12, 22-28, 41-49, 117-44.

[2] See "Vom Gewissen" and "Valet an meine Leser," *Matthias Claudius: Sämtliche Werke,* ed. Jost Perfahl, Wolfgang Pfeiffer-Belli, and Hansjörg Platschek (Munich, 1972), pp. 679, 601-2, respectively.

[3] See "Von und mit," ibid., pp. 393-99, and the letters to Jacobi, Matthias Claudius, *Botengänge: Briefe an Freunde,* ed. Hans Jessen, 2d ed. (Berlin, 1965), pp. 372, 379, 382.

[4] See "Eine asiatische Vorlesung" and "Nachricht von meiner Audienz beim Kaiser von Japan," *Sämtliche Werke,* pp. 531, 140, respectively.

[5] See the reviews of Herder's *Älteste Urkunde des Menschengeschlechts* and Goethe's *Zwo wichtige biblische Fragen* as well as "Übungen im Stil" and

"Briefe an Andres," ibid., pp. 35-38, 837-38, 467, 482-84, respectively.

[6] See "Einfältiger Hausvater-Bericht" and the review of *Die Taufe der Christen,* ibid., pp. 573, 862-63, respectively.

[7] "Einfältiger Hausvater-Bericht," ibid., p. 592.

[8] "Hinz und Kunz" and the review of *Neue Apologie des Sokrates,* ibid., p. 791, the corresponding note on p. 1045, and pp. 22-23, respectively. The question was then very current.

[9] See the review of *Hirtenbrief S. H. G. des Bischofs von Speyer an seine Geistliche* and "Das heilige Abendmahl," ibid., pp. 822, 615-17, respectively.

[10] See "Zwei Rezensionen etc. in Sachen der Herren Lessing, M. Mendelssohn, und Jacobi" and the review of *Anleitung über die Religion vernünftig zu denken,* ibid., pp. 348-60, 813, respectively.

[11] Johann Heinrich Voß, "Wie ward Fritz Stolberg ein Unfreier?," *Voß: Werke in einem Band,* ed. Hedwig Voegt (Berlin and Weimar: Aufbau, 1966), pp. 293-395, and *Bestätigung der Stolbergischen Umtriebe, nebst einem Anhang über persönliche Verhältnisse* (Stuttgart: Metzler, 1820); see also portions of letters from Jacobi to Stolberg in Urban Roedl, *Matthias Claudius: Sein Weg und seine Welt* (Hamburg, 1969), pp. 297-98.

[12] Dietrich Bonhoeffer, *Widerstand und Ergebung: Briefe und Aufzeichnungen aus der Haft,* ed. Eberhard Bethge, 2d ed. (Munich: Kaiser, 1970), p. 257f.

[13] See "Über die Unsterblichkeit der Seele," "Zwei Rezensionen," "Von und mit," and "Über einige Sprüche des Prediger Salomo," *Sämtliche Werke,* pp. 286, 357-58, 397, 245-46, respectively.

[14] See "Morgengespräch zwischen A. und dem Kandidaten Bertram," ibid., p. 654.

[15] "Zwei Rezensionen," ibid., p. 357.

[16] "Eine Abhandlung vom menschlichen Herzen, *sehr kurios zu lesen,*" ibid., pp. 760-63.

[17] "Übungen im Stil," ibid., p. 462.

[18] "Morgengespräch" and "Geburt und Wiedergeburt," ibid., pp. 654, 659-61, respectively.

[19] See, for example, the reviews of *Philosophie der Religion* and *Discours sur les fruits des bonnes études,* ibid., pp. 826, 56-57, respectively.

[20] "Morgengespräch," ibid., p. 649.

[21] Ibid., p. 149.

[22] Ibid., pp. 207-8.

[23] Ibid., p. 447.

[24] Ibid., pp. 16-17.

[25] Ibid., pp. 257-59.

[26] See, for example, "Parentation über Anselmo, *gehalten am ersten Weihnachttage,*" ibid., pp. 177-78.

[27] Ibid., pp. 259-61.

[28] Rolf Siebke, "Arthur Schopenhauer und Matthias Claudius," *Schopenhauer-Jahrbuch* 51 (1970): 24-25.

[29] "Morgengespräch," *Sämtliche Werke,* pp. 654-57.

[30] "Was ich wohl mag," ibid., p. 17.

[31] Ibid., p. 178.

[32] Ibid., p. 716.

[33] "An S. bei———Begräbnis," ibid., p. 80.

[34] Gotthold Ephraim Lessing, *Sämtliche Schriften,* ed. Karl Lachmann & Franz Muncker, 3d ed. (Stuttgart: Göschen, 1895), 11:55.

[35] Johann Gottfried Herder, *Sämmtliche Werke,* ed. Bernhard Suphan (Berlin: Weidmann, 1891), 5:656.

[36] "Über einige Sprüche des Prediger Salomo," *Sämtliche Werke,* p. 242.

[37] See Rolf Christian Zimmermann, *Deutsche Dichter des 18. Jahrhunderts: Ihr Leben und Werk,* ed. Benno von Wiese (Berlin, 1977), p. 440.

[38] This is part of a phrase made famous by Conrad Ferdinand Meyer, who included it in the motto to his *Huttens letzte Tage.*

[39] *Sämtliche Werke,* p. 44.

[40] Ibid., pp. 57, 84, 87.

[41] Ibid., pp. 806-7.

[42] Ibid., p. 25.

[43] Ibid., pp. 220-22.

[44] Ibid., p. 579.

[45] Ibid., pp. 473-74.

46 Ibid., p. 128.

47 Examples of such distortions are found in Hans Jessen and Ernst Schröder, "Einleitung," *Matthias Claudius: Asmus und die Seinen, Briefe an die Familie* (Berlin, 1940), pp. 5-16; F. J. Curt Hoefer, "Der Wandsbecker Bothe: Ein Beitrag zur Geschichte der Deutschen Publizistik des 18. Jahrhunderts," Ph.D. diss., Leipzig, 1944; and Günter Albrecht, "Einleitung," *Werke des Wandsbecker Boten* (Schwerin: Petermänken, 1958), 1:9-50, especially p. 32.

48 *Herders Sämmtliche Werke,* 5:475.

49 *Sämtliche Werke,* pp. 108-9.

50 Ibid., p. 83.

51 Ibid., pp. 639-40.

52 Ibid., p. 514.

53 This is especially true of "Eine asiatische Vorlesung" and "Über die neue Politik," ibid., pp. 499-535, 416-43, respectively.

54 Ibid., pp. 144-45.

55 Ibid., pp. 294-310.

56 Ibid., pp. 119-24.

57 Ibid., p. 143.

58 Ibid., p. 236.

59 Ibid., p. 218.

60 Ibid., p. 230.

61 See "Schreiben eines Dänen an seinen Freund," ibid., pp. 959-62, which Claudius wrote in response to the English blockade of Danish ports in 1807.

62 William Flint Thrall, Addison Hibbard, and C. Hugh Holman, *A Handbook to Literature,* rev. ed. (New York: Odyssey, 1960), p. 448.

63 The work appears in altered form in the *Sämtliche Werke,* pp. 25-26.

64 Ibid., p. 25.

65 Ibid.

66 Ibid., pp. 50-53.

67 Ibid., p. 51.

68 Ibid.

69 Ibid., pp. 46-49.

70 Ibid., p. 851.

71 See "An den Naber mit Rat," ibid., pp. 951-58.

72 Ibid., p. 25.

73 Ibid., p. 136.

74 Ibid., p. 70.

75 Ibid., p. 647.

76 Ibid., p. 648.

77 Letter to Herder, 18 April 1776, *Botengänge,* p. 193.

78 *Sämtliche Werke,* pp. 887, 725.

79 Ibid., p. 367.

80 See the review of Herder's *Abhandlung über den Ursprung der Sprache,* ibid., pp. 78-80, where Claudius agrees largely with his friend's pertinent remarks on language.

81 Ibid., p. 319. Also see p. 881.

82 Ibid., pp. 225-26.

83 Ibid., pp. 792-95, 44-45.

84 See the reviews of Friedrich Nicolai's satire of *Werther* in *Freuden des jungen Werthers* and of the attack on Goethe's critics in Heinrich Leopold Wagner's *Prometheus, Deukalion und seine Rezensenten,* ibid., pp. 876, 877, respectively; also see the works from p. 938 to p. 946.

85 Ibid., pp. 881-82, 90-92, respectively.

86 Ibid., p. 819.

87 William Wimsatt, *The Verbal Icon: Studies in the Meaning of Poetry* (Lexington: University of Kentucky Press, 1954), pp. 21-39.

88 *Sämtliche Werke,* p. 606.

89 Ibid., p. 599.

Herbert Rowland (essay date 1987)

SOURCE: "Matthias Claudius and Science: A Footnote on an Eighteenth-Century Figure and Theme," in *Modern Language Notes,* Vol. 102, No. 3, April 1987, pp. 655-62.

[In this essay, Rowland explores Claudius's interest in science and its thematic expression in his writings, and positions him in the Enlightenment tradition.]

The use of science as theme and motif in German literature has been studied systematically for only two literary periods. Walter Schatzberg has examined the Enlightenment through 1760, while Alexander Gode von Aesch has investigated Romanticism.[1] Scholarship has yet to inquire thoroughly into the intervening time and, indeed, will still require specialized discussions before a synthetic treatment can be undertaken.[2] Matthias Claudius is one of the writers who have not yet been considered in this context. The present note is therefore intended in part to help prepare the way for a comprehensive study of the subject.

Claudius is typically portrayed as standing to the side of the multifarious developments associated with the Enlightenment and clinging to a naive faith in old-style apostolic Christianity.[3] In point of fact, he had a lifelong interest in science and mathematics and early became acquainted with the work of Bacon, Newton, and Boyle.[4] The translator of St. Martin's mystical *Des erreurs et de la verité* also translated from the religious writings of these giants of science.[5] In his capacity as newspaper editor Claudius reviewed a number of publications by or about scientists, and his own oeuvre abounds with references to science and its methodology.[6] If one understands "science" in the broad, contemporary sense of "natural philosophy," indeed, it joins with religion to form his major theme.[7] Even in the more narrow, modern sense science furnishes the thematic and metaphoric substance of several works. While none remotely resembles a systematic statement of principle, two of these mutually illuminating pieces are especially suited both to exemplify Claudius' literary usage of science and to suggest the nature of his essentially positive relationship to the Enlightenment.

The first, later entitled **"Brief über den Durchgang der Venus,"** deals with a subject which requires some introductory commentary.[8] The transits of Venus in 1761 and 1769 held out the prospect of a momentous advancement of knowledge of the universe. Scientists felt that they offered the means of determining one of the basic natural constants of physical astronomy, namely the solar parallax, or the mean distance of the earth from the sun, and thus the fundamental unit of solar measurement. It was believed that global observation of inner contact between Venus and the sun during the planet's ingress or egress would lead to differences in the duration of time which the planet appeared to spend upon the sun, from which the solar parallax could be accurately calculated. In 1761, accordingly, one hundred twenty observers traveled to sixty stations all over the world, while in 1769 one hundred thirty-eight journeyed to sixty-three different points. If the enterprise ultimately failed to produce the anticipated result, it nonetheless represented a grand union of mathematics and astronomy with the principles of the Enlightenment and a large-scale attempt to complete the Newtonian system of the world by ascertaining its actual dimensions and thereby to solve the "final" problem of astronomy.

Claudius' **Brief** appeared somewhat less than two months before the transit of June 3rd, 1769, at a time when preparations and hopes of improving on the observations of 1761 were at a high pitch. The core of the piece is formed by a short treatise entitled **"Von dem Durchgange der Venus durch die Sonnenscheibe am bevorstehenden 3. Jun."**[9] It was perhaps written by Johann Elert Bode, later the prolific, highly regarded director of the Berlin Observatory and then the youthful prodigy of German astronomy, whom Claudius may have met in the circle around Samuel Reimarus in Hamburg.[10] In any case, it handles the imminent event in a straightforward, largely non-technical style accessible to the educated layman.

The author initially discusses the phenomenon of planetary transits in general. He then traces the history of scientific observation, especially of the rare transits of Venus, and emphasizes the importance of observing the forthcoming one. Indicating the time at which the transit can be seen in Hamburg, he explains what and how one must observe and recommends appropriate instruments. After urging his readers to participate, he mentions a number of benefits to be derived for both astronomy and the public at large. In conclusion, he expands on optical instruments and offers his services in procuring ones of unquestionable quality for those interested.

While notable as a document of the significance accorded the transit and of contact between the scientific and lay communities, the treatise itself possesses no inherent literary worth. It acquires such value only in connection with the introductory **Brief**. Claudius published the piece in the feuilleton of the *Hamburgische Adreß-Comtoir-Nachrichten,* which he edited from 1768 to 1770. In the manner of the moral weeklies he occasionally presented his contributions in the guise of various fictitious correspondents. Certain of these closely resemble the ingénue Asmus of **Der Wandsbecker Bote** and the **Sämtliche Werke,** and it is this mask that Claudius dons in the present letter.

The persona begins,

> Mein Herr! Es ist mir gerade so beim Durchgange der Venus durch die Sonne den 6. Jun. 1761 gegangen wie es Ihnen itzo geht, ich hörte viel und oft davon sprechen, sprach auch wohl selbst mit davon, ohne im geringsten zu wissen, was es heiße: die Venus geht durch die Sonne.[11]

Feeling that one should have some understanding of a matter about which one so often hears and wants to speak, he determined, "den Mund nicht wieder von der Venus aufzutun," before having read and understood some book on astronomy (741). He continues,

> Stellen Sie sich die Sache nur nicht so schwer und gefährlich vor, es geht alles ganz natürlich zu und ich denke, dass die Gelehrten sich und andern manchmal eine Sache schwerer und gefährlicher machen, als sie ist.
>
> (741)

He then proceeds to explain the nature of planetary transits, particularly that of Venus, in the same conversational style as in his prefatory comments. By way of illustration he writes,

> Sie haben doch wohl ehedem, den leidigen hölzernen Esel angesehen, der Ihnen tagaus tagein in die Fenster guckt. Wenn Sie in Ihrer Haustüre stehen, sehen Sie ihn gerade gegen die Wache, gehen Sie aber linker Hand weg, verändert er seine Lage gegen die Wache, bis er endlich, wenn Sie in Ihrer Gartentür stehen, Ihnen gegen das Haus Ihres Nachbars des Apothekers erscheinet. Wäre der Esel näher an die Wache, so würde er seine Lage gegen dieselbe weniger, wäre er Ihnen aber näher so würde er dieselbe merklicher verändem, wenn Sie verschiedene Standpunkte annehmen. Ebenso ist es mit der Venus, doch alles sans comparaison, denn ich habe wahre Achtung für die Himmelskörper.
>
> (742)

In view of the preceding he indicates the necessity of sending expeditions to various parts of the world as well as the scientific value of the observations and concludes, characteristically, "Wollen Sie noch mehr von diesen Sachen lesen und gelehrter werden als ich bin, so lege ich Ihnen eine kleine Abhandlung bei, darin allerlei steht, das ich Ihnen nicht sagen konnte, weil ich es nicht wußte" (743).

The persona of the **Brief** covers essentially the same material as the author of the treatise, yet how different the nature of his language. It diverges not only in its colloquialism, even artlessness, but here and there in its tone as well. This is especially apparent in the passage where the persona provides a concrete example of the need to observe the transit from various points around the world. The "leidige[n] hölzerne[n] Esel" refers to a kind of wooden horse which soldiers in particular were forced to "ride" as punishment for minor offenses.[12] "Die Wache," of course, designates the building or place where soldiers stood watch. Both through its specific meaning and its associations with fabular and popular tradition the *Esel* contrasts ironically with the phenomenon it ostensibly serves to illuminate, or, rather, it illuminates the phenomenon by travestying it. It is in this spirit that one must understand the transition from illus-

tration to matter at hand. One has little other choice than to view the passage and the authorial statement expressed in it as criticism of some kind.

And yet Claudius and his persona obviously find the transit worthy of the quite serious treatise, which, after all, represents the lion's share and primary raison d'être of the piece. They clearly feel that it merits the attention of the public in a form less *schwer* and *gefährlich* than the terminologically inflated works of many scholars. And the treatise indeed furnishes greater knowledge of the transit than the introductory **Brief.** How is one to account for this close proximity of travesty and objective earnestness? In other words, in what light does Claudius' irony place the scientific event?

An answer is suggested by **"Ein Brief, von C. an D.,"** another fictional letter employing science as a motif, that appeared in the *Adreß-Comtoir-Nachrichten* shortly before the piece on the transit of Venus.[13] C. requests that the jack-of-all-trades D. quickly make him a machine, "die ohne Aufhören rundgeht," which he wants to send to England to be placed in a monument on Harvey's tomb (739), for he has recently read that Harvey discovered the circulation of the blood and "daß der Tropfen der itzt in der Spritze [sic] meiner Nase ist, nach einiger Zeit durch meinen ungestalten großen Zehen laufe" (739). He finds it "wunderbar" that a man in England knows more about what occurs in his body than he himself: "Auf die Weise kann darin noch allerlei passieren" (739). The idea of circulation pleases him exceedingly and makes him think of "den ewigen Jäger," who also rides incessantly throughout the world (740). But, he continues,

> daher mag's auch wohl kommen, daß wir Menschen so wunderlich sind, unser Blut ist immer auf der Reise, und kann nie recht zur Besinnung kommen. Ich denke itzo darauf hie und da in meinem Körper Schlagbäume anzulegen—coelum non animum mutant, qui trans mare currunt
>
> (740)[14]

In conclusion, he asks that D. send the machine soon, for he cannot rest until he has paid tribute to Harvey. He then signs, "Ihr Diener, in dem das Blut bis dato noch immer zirkuliert" (740).

C. is an even more full-blown example of the ingénue than the persona of the later **Brief,** witness his naive excitement over learning of Harvey's discovery almost a century and a half after its announcement.[15] If the irony created by this wise fool appears more calculated and reveals the manipulating author more clearly, it is also more telling and, indeed, controls the entire piece.

C.'s description of the blood coursing from the tip of his nose through his misshapen big toe reflects on the phenomenon of circulation in a way that Harvey would likely have found less than flattering and is reminiscent in its effect of the *Esel* of the other **Brief.** Consequently, his expression of admiration of the foreigner's farsightedness sounds a self-vitiating note, as does his reference to the as yet unknown ramifications of circulation for his body. In fact, C.'s envisioned tribute to Harvey is ambiguous at best, for the device he requests is in essence a perpetual motion machine, based on a concept that as early as the third quarter of the eighteenth century was generally dismissed as scientifically unsound.[16] Claudius himself treated it as an example of *Projektmacherei* in a piece entitled **"Von Projekten und Projektmachern,"** which he published in the *Adreß-Comtoir-Nachrichten* in 1770.[17] Needless to say, Harvey's discovery suffers in the oblique comparison.

The circulation of the blood appeals to C. not because of the mechanistic view of man that it represents here but by virtue of images and associations of an entirely different order which it calls forth. The eternal hunter, a traditional figure of death, evokes a frame of reference in which Harvey's finding and all human endeavor become relative. The vision of peripatetic blood, with its pre-modern spiritual connotations, suggests the inconstancy and insensibility of the soul. These reflections lead to C.'s characteristically whimsical notion of erecting barriers in his body, for, after all, according to Horace, external change does not transform the inward man.

While ironic in one sense, C.'s desire to pay homage to Harvey, mentioned again at the end of the piece, is quite literal in another. For the idea of circulation has caused him to meditate on the central problem of human existence—man's spiritual nature within the context of physical death. Bearing this in mind, his apparently fanciful closing has the ring of a personal confession of one still in search of the essential.

Now, what does all this have to do with Claudius' piece on the transit of Venus? The basic attitude toward science and the function of travesty are the same in both works. The transit promised to do for science precisely what the discovery of circulation had done—namely, to provide a significantly greater understanding of a major realm of physical being. Given the fact of the feuilleton and its generally positive tenor, one can only conclude that Claudius regarded the phenomenon and scientists' preparations favorably. By extension, his treatment of the event counterbalances the ambiguous impression created by the piece on circulation. In his critique of *Projektmacherei,* indeed, he writes, "das Perpetuum mobile mag wohl ein Projekt sein; daß indes eine Aufgabe noch nicht aufgelöst worden, ist kein Beweis gegen die Auflösung," thus implying an openmindedness toward both this scheme and scientific progress on

the whole (72). Claudius' travesty does not touch the intrinsic value of the transit and science's perspectivistic methodology. Rather, it presents them from another point of view. By employing this device, Claudius demystifies the event, reduces its dimension, and suggests that one not attach more consequence to it than it warrants. Horace's words apply here as well as in the other work and all related contexts. Progress in the sciences and all physical change occupy a valid place within human concern, but such externals of life have no bearing on the soul and things of final importance.

In his fascination with nature Claudius was very much a child of his enlightened age.[18] He was drawn particularly to its empirical and utilitarian currents.[19] While finding the senses more reliable than reason, he also acknowledged the power of mind within what he perceived as is proper purview, the domain of the empirically verifiable.[20] However, his enthusiasm was born of that early phase of the Enlightenment associated with Brockes, Haller, and the mathematician-theologian Johann Lorenz Mosheim, who saw in nature ultimately a revelation of divinity and halted reverently before its mysteries. If the variously critical tone of Claudius' two *Briefe* later grew sharper and more prevalent, it is not because of any change in his position. It is due, instead, to the radicalization of the Enlightenment during the last quarter of the eighteenth century, a time, as Claudius might have said, when Horace's admonition fell increasingly on deaf ears.

Notes

[1] See Walter Schatzberg, *Scientific Themes in the Popular Literature and the Poetry of the German Enlightenment, 1720-1760,* German Studies in America, 12 (Berne: Herbert Lang, 1973), and Alexander Gode von Aesch, *Natural Science in German Romanticism* (New York: Columbia UP, 1941).

[2] Letter received from Walter Schatzberg, 20 February, 1986.

[3] See, for example, Fritz Martini, *Deutsche Literaturgeschichte von den Anfängen bis zur Gegenwart,* 13th ed., Kröners Taschenbuchausgabe, 196 (Stuttgart: Kröner, 1965) 214.

[4] Wolfgang Stammler, *Matthias Claudius der Wandsbecker Bothe: Ein Beitrag zur deutschen Literatur- und Geistesgeschichte* (Halle: Waisenhaus, 1915) 9 and 30.

[5] See, for example, "Das letzte Kapitel aus dem unvergeßlichen und vergessenen Werk es Großkanzlers Franz Baco v. Verulam: De dignitate et augmentis scientiarum," "Aus Newtons Observationen zum Propheten Daniel, das 11. Kapitel, *darin er die Zeiten der Geburt und der Leiden Christi zu bestimmen sucht,*" and "Eine asiatische Vorlesung," Matthias Claudius, *Sämtliche*

Werke, ed. Jost Perfahl, Rolf Siebke, and Hansjörg Platschek, 5th ed. (Munich: Winkler, 1984) 552, 569, and 526, respectively. Contrary to Gode von Aesch's assertion (*Natural Science in German Romanticism* 114, note) *Des erreurs et de la verité* is the only work by St. Martin which Claudius translated; see, for example, Karl Goedeke, *Grundriß zur Geschichte der deutschen Dichtung,* 3rd ed. (Dresden: L. Ehlermann, 1916), vol. IV, pt 1 973-983, especially 980.

[6] See, for example, the reviews of Sandel's *Von Schwedenborg,* Lavater's *Physiognomische Fragmente,* and Johann Georg Büsch's *Enzyklopädie der historischen, philosophischen und mathematischen Wissenschaften, Sämtliche Werke,* 73, 116, and 882, respectively.

[7] See Ernst Cassirer, *Die Philosophie der Aufklärung* (Tübingen: J. C. B. Mohr [Paul Siebeck], 1932) 488-122, especially 50-56.

[8] *Sämtliche Werke,* 741. The work appeared in two parts in numbers 31 and 32 of the *Hamburgische Adreß-Comtoir-Nachrichten* on April 20th and 24th, 1769, not on April 20th alone, as stated in the *Sämtliche Werke,* 1043. I am indebted here to Harry Woolf, *The Transits of Venus: A Study of Eighteenth-Century Science* (Princeton, N.J.: Princeton UP, 1959).

[9] *Sämtliche Werke,* 743.

[10] cf. Bode's lengthier and more sophisticated but still popular *Deutliche Abhandlung nebst einer allgemeinen Charte von dem bevorstehenden merkwürdigen Durchgang der Venus durch die Sonnenscheibe am 3ten Junii dieses 1769sten Jahrs* (Hamburg: D. A. Harmsen, 1769), especially 5-6 and 43-44. A number of textual similarities, among them the resemblance between the titles, and Claudius' acquaintance with Bode speak for common authorship. The only pertinent biographical information available to me is found under "Bode (Jean-Elert)," *Grand dictionnaire universel,* ed. Pierre Larousse, II (Paris: Administration du Grand dictionnaire universel, 1796), 850.

[11] *Sämtliche Werke,* 741. All future quotations are drawn from this edition and are cited in the text as page numbers in parentheses.

[12] See *Grammatisch-kritisches Wörterbuch der Hochdeutschen Mundart mit beständiger Vergleichung der übrigen Mundarten, besonders aber der Oberdeutschen,* ed. Johann Christoph Adelung, 2nd ed., I (Leipzig, 1793, rpt. Hildesheim and New York: Georg Olms, 1970), 1969.

[13] *Sämtliche Werke,* 739.

[14] "coelum non animum . . .": "den Himmelsstrich, nicht die Stimmungen der Seele und des Geistes verändern die, die über das Meer fahren," ibid., note to 739, 1043.

[15] Harvey's finding was generally accepted as medical fact during his own lifetime; see Mark Graubard, *Circulation and Respiration: The Evolution of an Idea* (New York and Burlingame: Harcourt, Brace and World, 1964) 173-176. By the mideighteenth century it had become common knowledge; see, for example, "BlutKreis," *Grosses vollständiges Universal-Lexikon,* ed. Johann Heinrich Zedler, IV (Halle and Leipzig, 1733; rpt. Graz: Akademische Druck- und Verlagsanstalt, 1961), cols. 241-242, and "Circulation," *Encyclopédie, ou dictionnaire raisonnédes sciences, des arts et des métiers,* ed. Denis Diderot and Jean Le Rond d'Alembert, III (Paris: n.p., 1753), 467-470.

[16] See, for example, "Movement," *Encyclopaedia Britannica, or A Dictionary of Arts and Sciences, Compiled Upon a New Plan* (Edinburgh: A. Bell and C. Macfarquhar, 1771), III, 312-313. In 1775 the French Academy of Sciences passed a resolution in which it refused to entertain any further communications concerning perpetual motion, "Perpetual Motion," *New Encyclopaedia Britannica: Macropaedia,* 1982 ed., XIV, 105.

[17] *Sämtliche Werke,* 71.

[18] See Annelen Kranefuss, *Die Gedichte des Wandsbecker Boten,* Palaestra, 260 (Göttingen: Vandenhoeck and Ruprecht, 1973) 123-146, and my *Matthias Claudius,* Twayne's World Authors Series, 691 (Boston: Twayne Publishers, 1983), 36-38.

[19] See "Übungen im Stil" and the review of Büsch's *Enzyklopädie, Sämtliche Werke,* 462 and 882, respectively.

[20] See the letter to Friedrich Heinrich Jacobi of March 19th, 1792, Matthias Claudius, *Bogengänge: Briefe an Freunde,* ed. Hans Jessen, 2nd ed. (Berlin: Eckart, 1965) 382.

Herbert Rowland (essay date 1997)

SOURCE: "Dualistic Analogues: Claudius's Notion of Language and Its Relationship to His View of Nature and Man," in *Matthias Claudius: Language as "Infamous Funnel" and Its Imperatives,* Fairleigh Dickinson University Press, 1997, pp. 17-53.

[*In the following essay, Rowland examines the theoretical implications of Claudius's writings for a philosophy of language and attempts to position him in the history of semiotic thought, describing Claudius's attitude toward language as "a compound consisting of an Augustinian base, an element of Lutheran biblicism, another of Pietist inwardness, and a healthy dose of Enlightenment skepticism."*]

1

Since the 1960s, literary study in America and Europe has been dominated by theoretical considerations that aim at a methodological synthesis founded on the study of language structure and its function.[1] These considerations have assumed the form of a debate between two schools of thought. Semiotics, in Seeba's words, "appears to dissect the whole world into systems of signs, as if it were a network of traffic signals and directional signs regulating all behavior"; in semiotics, the "sign is independent of thought, assigned thereto only subsequently and arbitrarily for purposes of communication."[2] Hermeneutics, on the other hand, "tries to explain the entire world as though it were a comprehensible text whose meaning is apparent to the practiced reader almost without effort"; in hermeneutics, "the word is taken as constitutive for the organization of thought."[3] These characterizations offer something of both the substance and the tenor of the debate. However one views the polarization—as unavoidable, unnecessary and unproductive, or indicative of broader social currents—, it should come as no surprise that the present study begins with an examination of language.[4] The inherent relationship between language and knowledge, on the one hand, and view of the world and man, on the other, makes such an investigation indispensible with regard to literary figures. Claudius's notion of language is intimately bound up with his understanding of nature and mankind and thus provides a key to his work.

Not surprisingly, the debate between adherents of semiotics and hermeneutics has extended to students of eighteenth-century German literature. After all, the roots of modern hermeneutics can be traced to Johann Gottfried Herder; while the semiotic tradition goes back at least to Plato, John Locke has been called the philosophical father of semiotics, and Gotthold Ephraim Lessing played an important role in its development in Germany.[5] A prominent theme in recent discussion has been the awareness in eighteenth-century Germany of the problematic nature of signification. One thinks in particular of David Wellbery's book on Lessing's *Laokoön*.[6] The acuteness of this awareness is due to the gradual process of secularization over the course of the century, more specifically, to the "unplaiting of hermeneutics from theology" in the various disciplines, above all philosophy, as well as the persistence of a number of theological and religious traditions.[7] In any case, recognition of the complexity of semiosis is by no means limited to major thinkers such as Lessing or to masterworks of theory or criticism. At a time when the formal study of language was in its infancy, many insights into the constitution of meaning lay implicit in occasional writings—reviews, essays, and the like—composed by various authors dealing with then more current topics. Claudius and his prose provide a case in point.

Claudius was not a rigorous thinker and never developed a *theory* of signs. Perhaps for this reason, scholarship has yet to produce a systematic study of his view of language, limiting itself largely to pertinent comments in other contexts.[8] However, his work is replete with theoretical *implications*. The essay **"Über das Genie"** [hereafter **"On Genius"**], an essay in the original sense of the word, reveals a relatively coherent and, at least in the expression, original attitude toward the question of signification. It therefore receives special emphasis here and serves as both a point of departure and a point of reference for a consideration of numerous random, yet often explicit comments on language strewn throughout the work, comments that add substance as well as nuance to the poet's concept of semiosis. Claudius's notion of language and view of nature and man are mutually illuminating. Accordingly, their interrelationship undergoes close scrutiny, both for its own sake and in order to establish a context for treatment of related concerns in subsequent chapters. Finally, an attempt to locate Claudius's position in the history of semiotic thought affords an opportunity to determine his attitude toward language with greater precision.

Claudius's essay **"On Genius,"** which first appeared in 1771, has been called an indirect commentary on Johann Adolph Schlegel's "Vom Genie in den schönen Künsten" [On Genius in the Fine Arts], a treatise appended to the third edition of his translation of Charles Batteux's *Les Beaux-arts réduits à un même principe* [The Fine Arts Reduced to a Single Principle] in 1770.[9] In his influential work, Batteux had defined genius as the imitation of "belle nature" [beautiful nature], that is, the rational ability to comprehend and depict the order behind an apparently chaotic universe.[10] Through a continuous process of purification the intellect strips nature of its particular and contingent features and retains only its most beautiful parts. From these it constructs a perfect whole, more perfect than nature itself, without ceasing to be natural. While originating in sensual experience, this "idée de la raison" [idea of reason] or "idée factice" [factitious idea] is ultimately a figural or symbolic representation that rests on the tacit assumption of an unproblematic relationship between sign and referent. By describing genius as a matter of discovery, rather than of invention, Batteux in effect denies the concept of creative imagination as genial, that is, "engendering" faculty.

Schlegel's definition of genius, on the other hand, is predicated on the notion of imagination. For him, genius consists "in einer sehr lebhaften Einbildungskraft, die mit einer natürlichen zarten Empfindsamkeit des Herzens, oder . . . mit einer sehr weichen Reizbarkeit der Empfindungen und Affecten verbunden ist . . ." [of a very vivid imagination that is combined with a natural, delicate sensitivity of heart or with a very sensitive responsiveness of feeling and emotion].[11] Making another start, he describes genius "als eine warme Einbildungskraft, welche durch die Werke, die sie hervorbringt, ihre Wärme andern mitzuteilen vermag" [as a warm imagination that is able to communicate its warmth to others through the works it produces].[12] In his emphasis on imagination and emotion in the creation and reception of art as well as in his criticism of slavish adherence to neoclassical rules and recognition of the *je ne sais quoi*, Schlegel marks a departure from Batteux toward an expressivist aesthetics and an orientation toward signification associated above all with Herder. Nevertheless, the inconsistencies and *esprit de système* characteristic of his approach obscured his divergence from most contemporaries and made him appear more indebted to Batteux than he in fact was. This was apparently the case with Claudius, whose essay bears a Latin motto that translates "It has a certain smell of dependence and not of independence" and whose own concept of genius and language differs from those of both Batteux and Schlegel (1,002).

Claudius's essay begins as follows:

> Ich stelle mir oft bei müßigen Stunden eine Sprache als ein Bündel Stäbe vor, wo an jedweden Stab eine verwünschte Prinzessin angezaubert ist, oder ein unglücklicher Prinz; und der Mann, der die Sprache versteht, wäre denn ein Sonntagskind, das Geister sehen kann, unterdes der andre den Stab sieht und nichts weiter. Man sagt, daß in der eigentlichen Zauberei, wenn einer das Handwerk versteht, eine Prinzessin vom Zauber erlöset, und statt ihrer ein Alp und Kobold an den Stab festgezaubert werden kann; bei den Sprachen geht's gewiß so her, und beides die Stäbe und die Geister sind sehr der Veränderung unterworfen. (25)

> [In idle hours I often picture a language as a bundle of sticks, to each of which a spellbound princess or an unhappy prince has been affixed by magic. And the man who understands the language would be a Sunday's child that can see spirits, while another sees the stick and nothing more. It is said that in real sorcery, if one understands the craft, a princess can be released from her spell and a goblin or elf enchanted onto the stick in her place. It is certainly the same with languages, and both the sticks and the spirits are quite subject to change.]

The passage clearly evinces a semiotic notion of language as a matter of a priori existant signifieds and arbitrarily related signs, that is, of the disjunction between word and referent and the concomitant, problematic relationship between the two. The prince and princess are "an-*gezaubert*," spell*bound to* the sticks, that is to say, ultimately distinct from them. For this reason, attending to the latter does not necessarily lead to comprehension of the former: the Sunday's child may make the connection, but the other person does

not. The power of the "magic wand" evoked here to release a princess in exchange for an elf or goblin suggests the potential of language to express beauty and truth and to distinguish them from their opposites. On the other hand, the comical sense of hocus-pocus also created by the motifs tends to vitiate their positive thrust. The double-edged nature of these and subsequent motifs enables Claudius to advance an argument while ironicizing notions with which he is at odds, here, the rationalist poetics of Batteux and Schlegel and the extravagant claims of original genius.[13] In addition to the problem of disjunction, the passage indicates that signifier and signified are subject to change, both in principle and, as we soon learn, over the course of history. On balance, emphasis lies on the desystematization of semiosis and a shift to the contingent historicity of meaning, which bring with them the potential for flawed discourse.

But perhaps the terms *comprehension* and *discourse* are inappropriate in the present context, at least to the extent that they suggest the prevalence of intellect in the process of signification with Claudius. In the eighteenth century, the term *Geist* [spirit, essence] was a common expression for the referent of a word, whatever its nature. Given the evocation of the fairy-tale world in our passage, however, *Geister* [= plural] would seem to refer not to abstractions, but to experience, and would appear to submit not to mental grasping or discursive thought, but rather to imagination and intuition. Clearly, language and experience, too, have a troubled marriage. However, it can be stated here, in anticipation of subsequent discussion, that the language of Claudius's essay is itself a kind of response to the more fluid, protean state of affairs.

Meanwhile, it will be well to direct attention back to the notion of genius, for despite appearances the basic purpose of the passage at hand is to illuminate the concept. The Sunday's child is so called, we remember, because it is able to understand the magical language, and this ability sets it apart from its fellow. Command of this language—implicitly, with all its limitations—is thus a characteristic of genius and of a person who possesses it. Genius is rare, however, as Claudius indicates: "Die Geschichte dieser Veränderungen und Sukzessions [of *Stäbe* and *Geister*] ist ein sehr feines Studium. Sie erfordert ein philosophisches Fühlhorn, das nicht jedermanns Gabe ist . . ." (25) [The history of these changes and successions (of sticks and spirits) is a very *subtle* field of study. It requires a philosophical feeler that is not everybody's gift . . .]. Having established the appropriate frame of reference and broached his subject in this manner, Claudius now proceeds to the heart of his endeavor.

Claudius looks first at the word *genium* in connection with Socrates and his admirers. He suggests that the Greek sage and the many who have spoken of a genius after him compare to each other like an old bard and prophet to the minstrels and balladmongers of England to whom Queen Elizabeth said, "'Alle Zigeuner, Landstreicher und Minstrels kommen in das Zuchthaus nach Neumünster'" (26) [All gypsies, vagrants, and mistrels go to jail in Neumünster].[14] Perhaps not, on the other hand, for no one really knows what Socrates and the many mean. Almost all who have written about Socrates's genius have stumbled "entweder in die Marschländereien mondsüchtiger Phantasten . . . oder in die dürre Sandwüsten der Wolffischen Philosophie und der mathematischen Lehrart" (26) [either into the marshlands of moonstruck fantasts . . . or into the arid deserts of Wolffian philosophy and the mathematical method]. It may be that only one who possesses a similar genius can say anything about it, and such an individual may be as reticent regarding the subject as Socrates. Speaking for this is a common experience among men, according to which "ein Säugling der Venus Erycina im ersten platonischen Paroxysmo der zarten Leidenschaft stumm ist, und in der Tiefe des einsamsten Waldes den Namen des *Idol suo* kaum aussprechen darf" (26) [a child of the Venus of Eryx, in the first Platonic paroxysm of the tender passion, is silent, and, in the depths of the most solitary forest can scarcely speak the name of its idol]. Accordingly, one should not expect to learn much about Socrates's genius from other people. "Es sei also in Ansehung seiner genung," the retrospect concludes, "in einer sanften Mondnacht mit gewaschenen Händen und einem Schauer von Ehrfurcht und Eifersucht Blumen für den Mann hinzulegen, der ihn hatte, und für den, der ihn hat . . ." (26) [let it suffice, on a softly moonlit night, with clean hands and a thrill of reverence and envy, to lay down flowers for the man who had it and for the one who has it]. Claudius then shifts his focus with the words, "und nun herunter zum modernen Genius oder zum Genie" (26) [and now *down* to the modern genius or man of parts], that is, down from Socrates to the balladmongers—from Klopstock to his imitators.

At this juncture it should be pointed out that Claudius's essay first appeared in *Der Wandsbecker Bote* [hereafter *The Wandsbeck Courier*] in five parts interspersed over a space of five weeks. The modified version published in the first volume of the **Collected Works** in 1775, which serves as our text, retains something of the original journalistic flavor, since the portion already discussed is separated from the rest by several poems. In both the paper and the works, more importantly, Claudius employed a number of personas in the manner of the moral weeklies.[15] The first part of the essay is the work of a character most often referred to as Asmus's *Vetter* [cousin], a learned, if whimsical fictionalization of the author actually identified in the **"Dedikation"** of the volume as "Matthias Claudius" (13). The remainder is written by the ingenuous Asmus, Claudius's chief spokesman and, at base, a variation of the wise fool.[16]

Asmus relates that his cousin was taken by a new fancy and left completion of the essay up to him. Although Asmus protested that he understood nothing of the matter, his cousin responded, "'Desto besser werdet Ihr davon schreiben, Vetter, es ist vieles in der Natur verborgen'" (28) [You'll write about it all the better, Cousin. There's much lies concealed in nature], and Asmus must now try his luck willy-nilly: "Wenn einer 'n Buch geschrieben hat, und man liest in dem Buch und 's würkt so sonderbar als ob man in Doktor Fausts Mantel davon sollte, daß man aufsteht und sich reisefertig macht, und, wenn man wieder zu sich kommt, dankbar zum Buche zurückkehrt; dann, sollt ich glauben, habe der Autor mit Genie geschrieben" (28-29) [When someone has written a book, and you read in the book, and it affects you so oddly that you feel you're about to take off in Doctor Faust's cloak, that you get up and get ready to travel, and, when you come back to your senses you gladly return to the book, then I should think that the author has written with genius]. Anticipating the objection that he has merely stated who possesses genius and not what it is, Asmus takes another tack:

> Das Genie also ist—ist—weiß nicht—ist 'n Walfisch! So recht, das Genie ist 'n Walfisch, das eine Idee drei Tage und drei Nächte in seinem Bauch halten kann und sie denn lebendig ans Land speit; ist 'n Walfisch, der bald durch die Tiefe in stiller Größe daherfährt, daß den Völkern der Wasserwelt 'n kaltes Fieber ankommt, bald herauffährt in die Höhe und mit Dreimastern spielt, auch wohl mit Ungestüm aus dem Meer plötzlich hervorbricht und große Erscheinungen macht. (29)

> [Genius is thus—is—I don't know—is a whale! Right, genius is a whale that can hold an idea in its belly for three days and three nights and then spew it living onto the land. It's a whale that now swims along through the deep in quiet grandeur, giving the multitudes of the watery world a cold fever, now surges upward and plays with three-masters, also suddenly bursts forth impetuously from the sea and makes a great spectacle.]

Nongenius, by contrast, is the skeleton of a whale, driven to and fro over the water by the wind, emitting scent for black and white bears—"(Journalisten und Zeitungsschreiber)" (29) [journalists and newspapermen]—who come across the ice and gnaw on it. Asmus then proceeds along still another line:

> Der menschliche Körper voll Nerven und Adern, in deren Centro die menschliche Seele sitzt, wie eine Spinne im Centro ihres Gewebes, ist einer Harfe zu vergleichen, und die Dinge in der Welt um ihn den Fingern, die auf der Harfe spielen. Alle Harfensaiten beben und geben einen Ton, wenn sie berührt werden. Einige Harfen aber sind von einem so glücklichen Bau, daß sie gleich unterm Finger des Künstlers sprechen, und ihre Saiten sind

so innig zum Beben aufgelegt, daß sich der Ton von der Saite losreißt und ein leichtes ätherisches Wesen für sich ausmacht, das in der Luft umherwallt und die Herzen mit süßer Schwermut anfüllt. Und dies leichte ätherische Wesen, das so frei für sich in der Luft umherwallt, wenn die Saite schon aufgehört hat zu beben, und das die Herzen mit süßer Schwermut anfüllt, kann nicht anders als mit dem Namen *Genie* getauft werden, und der Mann, dem es sich auf'n Kopf setzt, wie die Eule auf'n Helm der Minerva, ist ein Mann, der Genie hat. . . . (29)

[The human body, full of nerves and veins, in the middle of which the human soul sits like a spider in the middle of its web, is comparable to a harp, and the things of the world around the body are like fingers that play the harp. All the harp strings vibrate and create a tone when they are touched. However, some harps are of such felicitous construction that they immediately begin to speak under the finger of the artist, and their strings are so intensely disposed to vibrating that the tone breaks loose from the string and forms a light, ethereal essence of its own that floats around in the air and fills hearts with sweet melancholy. And this light, ethereal essence that floats around in the air so freely and alone when the string has already stopped vibrating and that fills hearts with sweet melancholy cannot be christened with any name other than *genius,* and a man on whose head it alights, like the owl on Minerva's helmet, is a man who possesses genius. . . .]

While originally a gift of nature, genius is molded and either fostered or suppressed by the particular circumstances in which the individual develops. School philosophy is especially adept at suppressing it: "Die Herren Philosophen, die von Allgemeinheiten gehört haben, die tief in der Natur verborgen liegen sollen und durch Hebammenkünste zur Welt gebracht werden müssen, abstrahieren der Natur das Fell über die Ohren, und geben ihre nackte Gespenster für jene Allgemeinheiten aus . . ." (30) [Philosophers who have heard about universals that are supposed to lie deeply concealed in nature and have to be brought into the world through the artifices of the midwife abstract nature's hide over its ears and give their naked specters out for those universals]. Those who listen to such philosophers and grow accustomed to their phantoms gradually lose the gift of receiving impressions from the world: "Alle Hacken ihrer Seele, die an die Eindrücke der wirklichen Natur anpacken sollen, werden abgeschliffen, und alle Bilder fallen ihnen nun perspektivisch und dioptrisch in Aug und Herz, usw" (30) [All the hooks of their souls, which are supposed to catch hold of the impressions of true nature, are worn down, and all images now fall into their eyes and hearts perspectively and dioptrically, etc.].

Here, Asmus halts abruptly with the words, "Aber das kostet Kopfbrechen, von einer Sache zu schreiben, von

der man nichts versteht" (30) [But it gives you a headache to write about something you know nothing about], and rests from his labors by writing a letter to his friend and former schoolmate Andres. Enthusiastic about a book he is currently working on, Asmus suggests that Andres attempt one himself and offers some advice. Andres could perhaps publish his recipe for corn plasters together with a disquisition on its origin and some errata. After all, the content of a book is not so important; as long as there is black on white somebody will praise it. Recalling Andres's difficulty with punctuation in school, Asmus concludes, "Sieht er, Andres, wo der Verstand halb aus ist, setzt er ein Komma; wo er ganz aus ist, ein Punctum, und wo gar keiner ist, kann Er setzen, was Er will, wie Er auch in vielen Schriften findet, die herauskommen" (30) [You see, Andres, when the sense (of a sentence) is halfway down (on the paper), you write a comma; when it's all down, you write a period; and when there's none at all, you can write whatever you want, as you'll find in many writings that come out].

The connection between the magic sticks of the introductory paragraph and the punctuation rules of the last may not be self-evident, but it exists nonetheless. As stated earlier, the body of the essay is throughout an attempt to come to terms with the problematic view of language expressed at the beginning. Following his comparison of man to a harp, Asmus writes, "und der geneigte Leser wird nun hoffentlich besser als ich wissen, was Genie ist" (29) [and the kind reader will now know, hopefully better than I, what genius is]. As elsewhere in this and other works, Asmus's humorous self-deprecation is both artless and totally honest, for he in fact does *not* know what genius is, at least not in the conventional sense of the word. Aside from his association of genius with a peculiar facility with language, neither, for that matter, does his cousin. Owing to his insight into the nonsystematicity and historicity of verbal meaning, he reflects on Socrates's *genium* and its usage over the centuries, but his musing yields nothing in the way of a positive definition of the term. He concludes that the meaning of genius cannot be captured in language and rejects vain attempts at conceptualization in favor of reverent silence.

The conclusion reached by Asmus's cousin discloses an axiom of Claudius's notion of language, which, as we shall see, is manifest in numerous works. Genius belongs to a class of the most profound ineffables, which not only elude linguistic reduction but are profaned by efforts to render them as language. For this reason, Asmus's *Vetter* turns completion of the essay over to the man of nature Asmus himself, his confidence in his cousin's ignorance expressed, contrary to appearances, in all earnestness.

Asmus's cousin's faith in him proves to be well-founded. To be sure, Asmus soon confesses that he has been reading his cousin's papers and has done "wie die andern: Fremd Kraut, und meine Brühe drüber" (29) [like the others: someone else's cabbage, and my broth over it].[17] Far from reflecting the true state of affairs, however, his candid admission represents another ironic innuendo aimed at the intellectual dependence of rationalist aestheticians such as Schlegel.[18] For the "simple" Asmus in fact goes beyond his learned cousin in his endeavor to define genius. Witness the ingénue's reference to Faust's cloak in the old chapbook and its magical ability to transport and make invisible, in a figurative as well as literal sense. His comparison of genius to a whale is both comically burlesque and richly evocative. With its initial appearance of nonsensicality, on the one hand, it continues the travesty of derivative rationalist poetics. On the other hand, it elicits associations with myths of creation, particularly, as has been pointed out, with the story of Jonah and Christ's allusion to it when foretelling his resurrection.[19] Certainly, the allusion involves the idea of "poetic inspiration."[20] It suggests the ultimate source of inspiration—and genius—and thereby pairs its travesty with a corrective. However, the device goes beyond inspiration per se to embrace the whole notion of creativity and its power, especially in view of the whale's surge to the surface and play with the three-masters, its sudden emergence from the depths and "great spectacle"—and, on a more mundane note, the meaning of the Indo-European root gên- and its descendents, "to produce" or "to beget," which echoes with particular intensity at this point of this essay on genius. The reference to sacred history, specifically to this central aspect of it, is, as we shall see, not fortuitous. Finally, Asmus's likening genius to the tone of a harp calls forth a sense of responsiveness, beauty, delicacy, and emotiveness.[21]

Asmus does not *comprehend* genius; nor, however, does he try to. Rather, he seeks to suggest what genius *is* in terms of what it *does*—the manner in which the comparisons as a whole affect the reader and, more specifically, the way in which the magic cloak carries one away, the whale causes a cold fever, and the harp's tone fills hearts with sweet melancholy. Through the guileless Asmus, Claudius indicates that knowledge of immediate and ultimate truth occurs at the level of imaginative and emotional, that is, intuitive, experience. A language capable of bearing such knowledge will therefore proceed from and address intuition. While imperfect, like all verbal expression, the language most appropriate to the task is that of metaphor, and it is precisely this figural language that Claudius employs in his, by implication, admittedly circumscribed and circuitous endeavor to confront the problem of signification, here, to bridge the gap between the sign "genius" and what it signifies.[22] For those unable or unwilling to perceive the truth of his view, Claudius always has recourse to corn plasters and other basic elements of travesty.

2

At least six main themes pertinent to language theory emerge from Claudius's essay **"On Genius."** An examination of them as treated in numerous works over the course of the author's life reveals a unified attitude toward signification that differs only in completeness and emphasis from that expressed in the essay.

1. First and foremost among these themes is the disjunction between signifier and signified. Claudius broaches the idea implicitly in his mildly critical review of Herder's *Abhandlung über den Ursprung der Sprache* [Treatise on the Origin of Language] in *The Wandsbeck Courier* in 1772. Employing his favorite weapon of criticism, travesty, he depicts the discussion on the origin of language as a medieval joust and presents the competition sponsored by the Academy of Sciences in Berlin as a challenge to scholarship either to produce a new Don Quixote or to reequip one of the old ones and to provide him with a Sancho Panza. Beginning the next sentence with the words, "Herr Herder kam" (79) [Mr. Herder came], he then relates Herder's view of the human origin of language and the organic relationship between word and referent, much in his friend's own manner. Claudius proceeds less circuitously in his **"Korrespondenz zwischen mir und meinem Vetter, die Bibelübersetzungen betreffend"** [Correspondence between My Cousin and Me Concerning Bible Translation] of 1774, which he probably wrote in response to Karl Friedrich Bahrdt's controversial paraphrase of the Bible, *Die neuesten Offenbarungen Gottes* [The Latest Revelations of God] (1,011). Explaining the difficulty involved in understanding and translating, "sonderlich wenn ein warmer hoher Geist in das Sprachstückchen gelegt ist" [especially whenever a warm, lofty spirit has been placed in the writing], Asmus's cousin employs a familiar motif: "Denn der läßt sich ohne sympathetische Kunststücke nicht herausbannen . . . und wenn einer die nicht hat und doch bannt; so kommt der Geist nicht selbst, sondern schickt einen kurzen pucklichten Purzelalp mit hoher Frisur und Puder, die Leute zu äffen" (86) [For it cannot be conjured up without sympathetic ploys . . . and if one does not possess them and still conjures, then the spirit doesn't come itself but rather sends a hunchbacked little shrimp of a goblin with hair powdered and coifed high to make fun of the people].

In **"Eine Korrespondenz mit mir selbst"** [A Correspondence with Myself] of 1790, Claudius criticizes the "spirit of scribbling" of his time, specifically the habit of dressing up old ideas in new garb. In this context he allows Asmus to write, "Aber sieht Er, Schreiben ist Schreiben . . . Und wenn die Sachen so recht in die Feder treten, so pflegen sie aus dem Menschen heraus zu sein. Und der dagegen meint, wenn sie auf dem Papier stehen, so hätte er sie" (310) [But, you see, writing is writing . . . And when things step right into the pen they tend to step right out of the person. And he, on the contrary, thinks that, if they're down on paper, he possesses them]. He varies this idea in his moral testament to his eldest son, **"An meinen Sohn Johannes 1799" [To My Son Johannes, 1799]**, where he states, "Worte sind nur Worte, und wo sie so gar leicht und behende dahinfahren; da sei auf Deiner Hut, denn die Pferde, die den Wagen mit Gütern hinter sich haben, gehen langsameren Schrittes" (546) [Words are only words, and where they go along lightly and nimbly be on your guard, for horses that have wagons with goods behind them walk at a slower pace]. In both passages Claudius points out the possibility of volarizing sign over signified, which is inherent in their disjunction, as well as the attendant dangers relating to moral conduct. A potentially even greater hazard arises when language is applied to the concerns of philosophy and theology, as Claudius makes clear in **"Morgengespräch zwischen A. und dem Kandidaten Bertram" [Morning Conversation between A. and the Licentiate Bertram]** (1812): "Uberhaupt Worte sind Worte, und man kann dabei nicht genug auf seiner Hut sein. Wo sie *würkliche* Gegenstände haben, da geht alles ziemlich gut und sicher; wo sie aber mit abstrakten Begriffen umgehen, da wird guter Rat teuer" (647) [After all, words are words, and one cannot be on one's guard enough against them. When they have *real* objects, everything goes fairly well and safely. But when they deal with abstract concepts the matter becomes thorny], for "hier sind Worte und Phrasen die leibhaften Cartesianischen Teufelchen" (648) [here, words and phrases are the little Cartesian devils incarnate].

Claudius stresses the referential nature of even sacred writing. In **"Briefe an Andres" [Letters to Andres]** in Part IV of the ***Collected Works*** (1783) he states that all the wonderful stories of Christ in the Bible are not he himself, but only "Zeugnisse von ihm" (261) [evidence of him]. One cannot treasure the Bible highly enough, he says in **"Einfältiger Hausvater-Bericht über die christliche Religion" [A Simple, Fatherly Account of the Christian Religion]** (1803), yet it goes without saying that the Bible is "immer nicht die Sache, sondern nur die Nachricht von der Sache" (573) [not the thing, but only news of the thing].[23] Claudius also speaks of religious rites such as baptism as *Zeichen* [signs] (862-63) and implies the figural character of religion itself (610). As suggested above, Claudius has the greatest respect for these signs. In **"Übungen im Stil" [Exercises in Style]** (1798) he writes, "Zeremonien können gute Rührungen veranlassen, und auf gute Gedanken bringen. Auch sind sie bisweilen ein Fähnlein über dem Wasser, das uns anzeigt, wo der Schatz gewesen und versunken ist" (467) [Ceremonies can cause good feelings and bring good thoughts to mind. Sometimes, they are also a little flag over the water that shows us where the treasure was and was sunk]. However, external form has only relative significance. In the telling **"Korrespondenz zwischen mir und meinem Vetter" [Correspondence between My Cousin and Me]** of 1790 Claudius criticizes the modernization of traditional church songs: "Das Kleid macht . . . den Mann nicht; und wenn der Mann gut ist, so ist alles gut . . . Man ist einmal daran gewöhnt, und oft steckt's grade darin und muß so sein" (344) [Clothes don't make the man, and if the man is good then all is well . . . One is used to them, and often everything depends on that, and it has to be that way]. One clings to the old form not for the sake of any ultimate value it might possess but because of the personal, experiential meaning it has acquired over the years.

The discontinuity between word and referent is most crucial in the context of last things. Claudius expresses his view of the matter with greatest cogency in the essay **"Geburt und Wiedergeburt" [Birth and Rebirth]** of 1812:

> Wenn wir wirklich etwas von der *unsichtbaren Welt* verstünden; so müßten wir noch, um davon verständlich und bestimmt sprechen zu können, eine eigene Sprache haben. Unsere gewöhnliche Sprache, die in der *sichtbaren Welt* zu Hause ist, wird, wenn man sie auf die *unsichtbare* anwendet, eine bloße Hieroglyphe, die ein jeder nach der Analogie deutet, *wie er will* und *kann*, um den korrespondierenden Begriff zu finden. (661)

> [Even if we really understood something of the *invisible world*, we would still have to have a special language to speak of it comprehensibly and distinctly. Our customary language, which is at home in the *visible world*, becomes, when applied to the *invisible one*, a mere hieroglyph that everyone interprets according to the analogy *as he wants* and *can* in order to find the corresponding concept.]

The gap between sign and signified represents both the gulf between ignorance and knowledge of absolute truth and the source of much idle speculation and confusion.

2. Closely related to the theme of disjunction in **"On Genius"** is that of the historicity of meaning. In certain fundamental respects Claudius viewed the world ahistorically. This is evident in the essay **"Über die Unsterblichkeit der Seele" [On the Immortality of the Soul]** (279-91) of 1790, in which he argues against the theory of organic evolution advanced by the French naturalist Jean Baptiste de Lamarck, a precursor of Darwin. It is also manifest in the preface to the third volume of his translation of *Fénelons Werke religiösen Inhalts* [Fénelon's Works on Religion] (1811), where he writes that since "die menschliche Natur immer dieselbe ist, und ihre Zufälle, Bedürfnisse und Gebrechen, einige Lokal- und individuelle Umstände abgerechnet, sich immer gleich oder doch wenigstens ähnlich sind; so muß natürlich auch der Trost und

Rat sich immer gleich oder ähnlich sein" (639-40) [human nature is always the same, and its possibilities, needs, and flaws are always identical or at least similar, aside from some regional and individual circumstances, man's consolation and counsel must naturally always be identical or similar as well]. Claudius even employs history to deny historicity, as in **"Eine asiatische Vorlesung"** [A Lecture on Asia] (1803; 499-535), in which he surveys the religions of the Orient in order to show their similarity to Christianity and the essential identity and truth of all religions. For Claudius, secular history was merely an extension of sacred history. Thus, in his review of Herder's *Auch eine Philosophie der Geschichte zur Bildung der Menschheit* [Another Philosophy of History Concerning the Development of Mankind] (1774) he counters his friend's notion of historicity with the words, "Vielleicht ist auch gar der Plan Gottes nicht der *Länge* sondern der *Quere* nach zu suchen. Es ist nämlich die Wahrheit zu aller Zeit in der Welt gewesen, so oder anders gekleidet" (109) [Perhaps one should seek God's plan not diachronically but synchronically. For truth has always been in the world in one guise or another]. One might summarize Claudius's general attitude toward history by calling to mind the old saw, "the more things change, the more things stay the same."

However, Claudius acknowledged that many aspects of life, semiosis among them, are subject to change through time. He implies as much in numerous remarks concerning the disjunction of letter and spirit. As far as I can see, he does not comment specifically on the historic contingency of meaning outside of the essay on genius. However, he displays a lucid awareness of the historicity of the products of language. In his review of *Bekehrungsgeschichte des vormaligen Grafen und königlich dänischen geheimen Cabinetsministers Joh. Friedrich Struensee* [Story of the Conversion of the Former Count and Royal Danish Privy Councillor Joh. Friedrich Struensee] (1772), for example, he writes, "Fast alle Systeme, die Menschen sich von *Gut* und *Böse* machen, sind Ephemera, Kinder des gegenwärtigen Zustandes, mit dem sie auch wieder dahinsterben . . ." (55) [Almost all systems of good and evil that men make themselves are ephemeral, children of the present situation, with which they also die away . . .]. More pointed still is his comparison of human knowledge to the omniscience of Brahma in *Übungen im Stil* [Exercises in Style] (1798): "Mit unsrer Wissenheit ist es anders beschaffen. Sie ist von der Stirne bis zur Brust unterworfen und abhängig, und ihre Füße liegen in dem *Stock* der Zeit und des Raums" (462-63) [With our knowledge it is different. It is subservient and contingent from brow to breast, and its feet lie in the *stocks* of time and space].

3. The essay on genius also thematicizes the idea that knowledge of the most important truths in life comes by way of intuitive experience, an idea that is prominent in Claudius's work from the early prose on.[24] In the epistle **"Über den Ausdruck: 'Stilles Verdienst'"** [On the Expression "Silent Virtue"], published in the *Adreß-Comtoir-Nachrichten* [hereafter *Registry Office News*] in 1769, the young editor writes, "Man könnte sagen, daß der Mann, dessen Seele groß und edel genug ist, nach allen Verdiensten zu dürsten, durch eine Art von Sympathie bei den Worten besonders affiziert werde, und daß diese Empfindung mehr wert sei, als eine lange Abhandlung über diese Materie" (748) [One could say that a man whose soul is great and noble enough to thirst for all virtue is, through a kind of sympathy, especially affected by hearing the words and that this feeling is worth more than a lengthy treatise on the subject]. A particularly felicitous expression of the notion appears in **"Brief an Andres"** [Letter to Andres] in *Collected Works I-II* (1775), where Asmus says in his characteristic manner, "und oft wenn ich 's Nachts unterwegen an den *Rabbuni* denke . . . , überfällt mich ein Herzklopfen und eine so kühne überirdische Unruhe, daß ich würklich manchmal denke, ich sei zu etwas Besserm bestimmt, als zum Brieftragen . . ." (97) [and often, when I'm underway at night and think of the *Master*, my heart starts beating, and such a bold, unearthly restlessness comes over me that I sometimes really think I was born for something better than carrying mail]. In a similar context in the later **"Briefe an Andres"** [Letters to Andres] of *Collected Works-IV* (1783) Claudius concedes that "solche Empfindungen" [such feelings], much like the Bible and religious ceremonies, are not "die Sache" [the thing] itself (272). However, it is clear that he places greater store in this medium of knowledge than in any other. Witness his use of the words *ahnen* [to sense, intimate] and *fühlen* [to feel], *Ahndungen* [intimations] and *Ideen* (in the sense of *Ahnungen*), *Erfahrung* [experience] and *Gefühl* [emotion] in comparable passages throughout the work beginning with Part IV.[25] In **"Morgengespräch zwischen A. und dem Kandidaten Bertram"** [Morning Conversation between A. and the Licentiate Bertram] he states in no uncertain terms, "Religion *ist die sie ist*. Sie ist eine lebendige Kraft . . . Wo sie nicht *erfahren* wird, da ist und bleibt sie unbekannt" (649) [Religion is *what it is*. It is a living force . . . Where it is not *experienced* it is and remains unknown].

4. As the essay on genius makes clear, Claudius was not at all insensible to the capacity of language to express beauty and truth. In his critical review of W. A. Teller's *Versuch einer Psalmenübersetzung* [An Essay to Translate the Psalms] (1773) he writes in the manner of Herder,

So nach dem Klange und der Buchstabenzahl—jeden Vers—aus einer Sprache wie die orientalische—aus dem Geist der Dichtkunst, wo alles hervorgedrungen—frei—göttlich—unerschöpflich ist—nicht übersetzen und hinüberströmen, sondern auf-und nachzählen, dünkt uns, wo nicht unmöglich, so wenigstens oft zwangvoll und unvorteilhaft. Riese Goliath in eine enge Schnürbrust eingespannt, was kann ihm sein Weberbaum helfen? (853)

[To enumerate and tally, rather than to translate and stream over, according to the sound and number of letters—every verse—from a language like the eastern—from the spirit of poetry, where everything wells up—is free—divine—inexhaustible—seems to us, if not impossible, then at least often forced and disadvantageous. Goliath the giant squeezed into a tight waistcoat—what good can his weaver's beam do him?]

Claudius also has words of recognition for purely discursive language. Fundamentally ill-disposed toward Voltaire, he nonetheless criticizes the author of *Voltaire der Reformator* [Voltaire the Reformer] in 1772 for his invective against the Frenchman, asserting that one must address the reader's intellect with strong, credible arguments (824-25). He frequently alludes to the accomplishments of scholarship, as in **"Passe-Temps"** [Pastime] (1783), where he states, "Allerdings ist die Welt der Gelehrsamkeit viel schuldig, und was in ihr nützlich und ausgemacht ist, wer wird das nicht mit Dank annehmen und mit Dank erkennen?" (255) [Of course, the world owes much to scholarship, and who would not gratefully accept and acknowledge what is useful and certain in it?]. Indeed, Claudius kept abreast of developments in various fields of learning, especially theology, and employed biblical exegesis in his own writings.[26] Moreover, he often acknowledges the driving force behind erudition, reason, which, he writes, God gave man as a "Vorzug vor andern Geschöpfen auf dem Erdboden" (812) [distinction above other creatures on earth]. Elsewhere, however, he is not so generous. In the preface to his translation of Louis Claude de St. Martin's *Des erreurs et de la vérité* [On Errors and Truth] (1782), for example, he labels learning as "ein nützliches Hausgerät, ein honetter Filzhut auf dem Gelehrten ihn wider Frost und Kälte zu decken" (213) [a useful household utensil, a respectable felt hat *on* the scholar's head to protect him from cold and frost]. Worse yet, as the passage continues, learning can also become "ein Paradehut, und zuweilen gar ein Chapeaubashut mit dem er vor dem Bassa wedelt und sich beliebt macht" (213) [a showy hat, and sometimes even a gaudy one with which he (the scholar) wags his tail before the pasha and tries to gain favor].

5. Such flamboyance is particularly out of place since, as Claudius suggests in **"On Genius,"** language is ultimately powerless to tell man what he most wants and needs to know. One recognizes this idea as early as the review of Herder's *Älteste Urkunde des Menschengeschlechts* [Oldest Record of the Human Race] of 1774, where Claudius's admiration of his friend's poetic style does not pre-

vent him from questioning the view of revelation it expresses: "Ein dergleichen orientalischer Laut ist nun diese Schrift, und ist, man mag dem Verfasser recht geben wollen oder nicht, immer eine schöne Erscheinung hoch in der Wolke und ein Weben des Genies" (35) [Now, this writing is such an Oriental sound, and, whether one agrees with the author or not, is still a beautiful apparition high in the clouds and a stirring of genius]. Without doubt, Claudius is harshest vis-à-vis the linguistic handiwork of reason. In a monosyllabic review of a book entitled *Die Philosophie der Religion* [The Philosophy of Religion] (1772) he states, "Der Titel wäre nicht viel sonderbarer wenn er umgekehrt würde, und die Religion der Philosophie hieße. Der selige Mosheim sagt an einem Ort, wo er von dem Gebrauch der Vernunft in der Theologie spricht: 'Man solle die Magd ausstoßen die gar zu gerne Frau im Hause sein will'" (826) [The title would not be much more peculiar if it were reversed and read *The Religion of Philosophy*. Our late Mosheim says in a passage where he speaks of the use of reason in theology, "One should fire a maid who wants too much to be the woman of the house"]. Claudius's terseness is attributable not least of all to his perception of the discontinuity between discursive thought on the one hand and will and action on the other (433).

Given this state of affairs, Claudius more than once draws the conclusion reached by his cousin in the essay on genius and recommends silence as the most appropriate response.[27] As we shall see in detail in chapter 2 and as Asmus avers in the **Brief an Andres** [Letter to Andres] on John the Baptist (1790), silence is often a positive quality: "Du schreibst, daß er Dir so groß vorkömmt, und Du kannst Dir doch nicht recht sagen warum. Das ist recht gut Andres. Man weiß oft grade denn am meisten, wenn man nicht recht sagen kann warum" (367) [You write that he seems so great to you and yet you can't quite say why. That's really good, Andres. One often knows most just when one can't quite say why]. Claudius affirms this dimension of silence most forcefully, perhaps, in his review of a book bearing the title *Lobrede auf den Messias* [Laudation of the Messiah] (1772):

Der Herr Bastholm frägt gleich anfangs "darf ich wohl reden, wo Seraphim verstummen?" wozu die Frage? warum verstummte der Herr Magister nicht lieber? So ein Verstummen, wie die Seraphim verstummen, ist die eigentliche Lobrede auf den Messias, die oder gar keine, alles übrige ist ekele Wassersuppe, und Magister Bastholms Lobrede ist Wassersuppe, wenn sie auch nur auf Alexander den Großen wäre. (819)[28]

[Mr. Bastholm asks right at the beginning, "May I speak, when the seraphim are silent?" What good is the question? Why did he not remain silent instead? The silence of the seraphim is the true laudation of the Messiah, it or none at all. Anything else is sickening watery soup, and Master Bastholm's encomium would be watery soup even if it were addressed only to Alexander the Great.]

As damning as this verdict is, it was in his letter to Herder of 18 April 1776 that Claudius made his most laconic and most memorable observation on the impotence of language, to which we alluded earlier: "Die Schriftsprache ist ein infamer Trichter, darin Wein zu Wasser wird" (*Botengänge,* 193) [Written language is an infamous funnel in which wine turns to water].[29]

6. In **"On Genius"** Claudius tacitly proposes the language of metaphor as that most adequate to the task of spanning the gap between signs and signifieds of a more spiritual nature. He had proceeded in a similar fashion a year earlier in a feuilleton entitled **"Ein defekter locus communis" [A Defective Commonplace].**[30] Here, he relates the story of a man who paid tribute to the memory of several geniuses of high order by erecting statues of them in an oak grove. Following the man's death, his successor replaced the statues with ones of Cupid. Now, the story continues, a long white figure walks around the wood on moonlit nights, angrily knocking the statues to the ground. Claudius closes with the words, "Mir gefällt die Sage so sehr, daß ich meinen Lesern zumute sie zu glauben, und dadurch die Gesetze der gesunden Vernunft zu übertreten, wie ich hier die Gesetze eines *locus communis* übertreten habe" (759) [I like the story so much that I suggest that my readers believe it and thereby transgress the laws of common sense, as I have transgressed the laws of a commonplace here]. He renews the proposal made in the essay on genius in his review of Johann Salomo Semler's *Paraphrasis Evangelii Johannis* [Paraphrase of the Gospel of St. John] (1772), one of the seminal works of modern theological hermeneutics. He devotes most of his space to an evocation of his experience of reading the Gospel, for example, "In ihm ist so etwas ganz Wunderbares—Dämmerung und Nacht, und durch sie hin der schnelle zückende Blitz! 'n sanftes Abendgewölk und hinter dem Gewölk der große volle Mond leibhaftin!" (18-19) [In it is something so thoroughly wondrous—twilight and night, and through it the rapidly flashing lightning! Soft evening clouds and behind the clouds the full moon as large as life!]. He turns to Semler's book only in the last sentence, which, however, speaks eloquently: "Des Herrn Verfassers Erklärung ist sehr gelehrt, dünkt mich, und ich glaube, daß man wohl zwanzig Jahr studieren muß, eh man so eine schreiben kann" (19) [The author's explanation is very learned, I think, and I believe one would have to study twenty years before one could write one like it]. Claudius employs figurative language all the way to his last work in prose, ***Predigt eines Laienbruders zu Neujahr 1814* [Sermon of a Lay Brother on New Year's Day, 1814],** in which he uses timeworn yet time-honored metaphors to describe the possible fruit

of God's *Züchtigung* [chastisement] of Europe during the Napoleonic Wars, namely, a world that would be "eine Herberge . . . , wo man sich behilft, und nur an die weitre Reise und an die Heimat denkt . . ." (700) [a refuge where one makes do and thinks only of the rest of the trip and home]. Of course, he relies heavily on such language in his lyric poetry, as we shall see in the next chapter.

However, Claudius was acutely aware of the problems involved in interpreting verbal meaning, whatever the vehicle of expression. In the short text **"Über ein Sprichwort"** (*"man soll auf einem Grabe nicht schlafen,"* 183) **[On a Proverb; one should not sleep on a grave]** from the year 1783, he states in general fashion, "Wenn ein Spruch tiefsinnig ist, so schwimmt der Sinn nicht obenauf; und denn pflegt er ziemlich sicher zu sein" (183) [When a saying is deep, its meaning doesn't float on the surface, and then it's usually pretty safe]. He expands upon this idea by alluding to a recent naval disaster involving a British ship that had sunk up to its top-mast: "Das Fähnlein züngelt da über dem Wasser, daß man wohl sieht: es sei im Grunde etwas vorhanden; wer aber den 29. August nicht in Portsmouth war oder sonst des Wesens kunding ist, der wird dem Feind nicht viel von dem Royal George verraten" (183) [The pennant is waving there over the water so that you can tell something is on the bottom. But anyone who wasn't in Portsmouth on August 29th or isn't otherwise knowledgeable about the matter won't betray much about the Royal George to the enemy]. That is to say, the problem lies in part in the nature of the medium of meaning itself. However, as Claudius continues, "Ein Umstand ist bei solchen Auslegungen noch zu bemerken, der manchem sonderbar dünken möchte, der nämlich: daß der letzte Ausleger allemal der klügste ist, und daß seine Vorgänger immer herhalten müssen. Dafür muß er aber zu seiner Zeit wieder herhalten, und so ist das Gleichgewicht hergestellt" (183) [I should mention another circumstance surrounding such interpretations that may seem odd to many, namely, that the last interpreter is always the best and that his predecessors always have to suffer. On the other hand he has to suffer when his time comes, and thus the balance is restored]. In this passage, Claudius implies not only the historicity of meaning but also its relativity, which is due to the subjectivity of perception. As if to demonstrate the veracity of his assertions, he then proceeds to give three possible interpretations of the proverb. The metaphorical language he employs in the text clearly identifies at least one of the relevant problems, but it is unable to provide a solution.

As suggested earlier, the limitations imposed on understanding by the complexity of signification become most critical with regard to the spiritual. In the preface to his translation of André Michael Ramsay's *Voyages de Cyrus* [The Voyages of Cyrus] (1780) Claudius writes,

"Sieh, es ist nur *ein* Gott, so wie nur *eine* Natur ist; also kann davon auch nur *eine* Lehre sein die wahr ist . . ." (237) [Look, there is only *one* God, just as there is only *one* nature. Thus, there can be only *one* doctrine about him that is true . . .]. So far so good. However, as he continues, "alle Lehre davon . . . muß, sie sei wo sie wolle, sowohl vor als nach dem Babylonischen Turmbau, inwendig einerlei sein . . ." (237) [every doctrine about him, wherever it might be, both before and after construction of the Tower of Babylon, has to be the same inwardly]. In the current state of post-Babylonian polyglotism, understood in a figurative sense, it is precisely *das Inwendige* [the inward] that resists even the reduction of metaphor. In his commentary on Genesis 3:17-19, "Verflucht sei der Acker um deinetwillen etc." [Cursed is the ground for thy sake etc.][31] (1783), Claudius declares, "Man mag das Paradies und seine vier Ströme und seinen Baum des Lebens und des Erkenntnisses etc. so oder so auslegen, und die wahre Erklärung mag sein welche sie will; so ist und bleibt der Inhalt klar und außer allen [sic] Zweifel: Der Mensch war glücklich! Und er machte sich elend!" (259) [One may interpret paradise and its four rivers and its tree of life and knowledge, etc., this way or that, and the true explanation may be whatever it may be, the content is and remains clear and beyond any doubt: man was happy! And he made himself miserable]. Through the Bible and one's own experience, as we shall soon see, one can gain an accurate general notion of the human condition. However, the particulars and above all the remedy remain a mystery. The Bible may be "das Beste was wir auf Erden haben" [the best we have on earth], but it amounts ultimately only to "Glöcklein am Leibrock" (261) [little bells on the dresscoat].

For this reason, and in order to close the ultimate gap, Claudius recommends not language at all, but rather a certain inner state. In his **"Valet an meine Leser" [Farewell to My Readers]** (1803), he describes this state as "eine gewisse Gestalt des inwendigen Menschen . . . eine gewisse innerliche Denkart, Fassung, Haltung etc. die man sich vorsetzen und darnach man streben muß" (601) [a certain condition of the inner man . . . a certain inner way of thinking, state, attitude, etc., that one must resolve upon and strive after]. If man is in the final analysis incapable of helping himself, as Claudius writes in the preface to his translation of Fénelon (1800), "so kann er sich doch, durch eine gewisse fortgesetzte Behandlung und Richtung Seiner-Selbst, empfänglicher machen, und der fremden Hand den Weg bereiten" (542) [he can still make himself more receptive and even the way for the foreign hand through a certain, permanent management and dressing of himself]. Elsewhere, he specifies this openness as the positive force of faith. In **"Geburt und Wiedergeburt" [Birth and Rebirth]** (1812) he says that anyone who is to be helped must want and believe in help: "Und zwar muß dies Wollen und Glauben nicht

etwa ein Gedanke, eine Betrachtung *im* Herzen, sondern eine Fassung, ein Zustand *des* Herzens sein" (665) [And this *wanting* and *believing* must not be, for instance, a thought, a reflection *in* the heart, but rather a state, a condition *of* the heart]. Through faith, he states in another passage, "kann der Mensch . . . eine Krisis zuwege bringen, und an seiner Reinigung und Herstellung arbeiten" (663) [man . . . can bring about a *crisis* and work toward his purification and restoration].

Based on Claudius's **"On Genius"** and related writings, one has no alternative but to characterize his attitude toward language as radically skeptical. For him, the desystematization of semiosis and the historicity of meaning render language incapable of capturing immediate and ultimate truth, primarily because of the pre-rational nature of man's imperfect knowledge of such truth. This holds particularly for discursive language but applies in the final analysis to figurative language as well. As the essay on genius and other works indicate, skepticism pervades Claudius's notion of language from early on. If its tone becomes darker after around 1780, it is due not to any shift in his view of language, but rather to the gradual radicalization of the Enlightenment, which represented an increasing threat to his beliefs and led to his decision to confront the enemy head-on.[32] One must view the growing spiritualization of his treatment of language from about this time on in the same light. Indeed, many of his later comments on linguistic themes have as much bearing on other areas of concern as on language per se. Owing to this close interrelationship, as stated at the outset, Claudius's notion of language provides a key to his understanding of nature and man. It is to this understanding that we now turn our attention.

3

The ontological underpinning of Claudius's view of nature and man is Christian in the sense of old-style apostolic Christianity. Its essence can be subsumed under two of the similarities between Eastern religions and Christianity presented in **"Eine asiatische Vorlesung" [A Lecture on Asia]**: "'*Alle nehmen ein erstes unbegreifliches unerforschliches höchstes Wesen . . .* an'" ["All presuppose a prime, incomprehensible, unfathomable, highest being"] and "'*Alle sind übermenschlichen Ursprungs,* und durch ein himmlisches Wesen geoffenbaret und mitgeteilet worden . . .'" (531) ["All are of transcendental origin and are revealed and communicated by a heavenly being"].[33] Claudius describes the nature of the highest being in **"Einfältiger Hausvater-Bericht über die christliche Religion" [A Simple, Fatherly Account of the Christian Religion]:** "Wir wissen wohl, wenn wir die sichtbaren vergänglichen Geschöpfe ansehen, daß ein unsichtbarer unvergänglicher Schöpfer sein müsse; wir wissen wohl, wenn wir milde wohlwollende Bewegungen und Gesinnungen in unserm

Herzen fühlen, daß irgendwo eine Urquelle der Liebe, ein wesentliches Wohlwollen, ein *lieber Vater,* sein müsse . . ." (579) [We know well, when we look at visible, transient creatures, that there must be an invisible, intransient creator; when we feel charitable, benevolent stirrings and sentiments in our heart, that somewhere there must be a wellspring of love, an essential benevolence, a *loving father* . . .]. Claudius's notion of God as a loving father is accompanied by his belief in the existence of a divine plan, mentioned already in the review of Herder's *Auch eine Philosophie der Geschichte zur Bildung der Menschheit* [Another Philosophy of History Concerning the Development of Mankind] (109) and portrayed at length in his **"Einfältiger Hausvater-Bericht" [Simple, Fatherly Account].** However, his view of the matter is not as unproblematic as it might at first appear, for the passage in **"Einfältiger Hausvater-Bericht"** quoted above continues with the words, "aber wir sehen ihn [God] nicht und hören ihn nicht, und erkennen ihn nicht" (579) [but we do not see him (God) and do not hear him, and do not grasp him]. This passage contains in a nutshell the basic problem of Claudius's life and work—man's uncertain but compelling knowledge of a God from whom he exists in radical isolation. Claudius's understanding of human existence in the original sense of the word, to step or stand out, led him to inquire into man's means of apprehending God and overcoming the gulf separating them. It is from this point that his meditations on nature and the soul depart.

Claudius refers to the epistemic dimension of nature from his early work on. In his review of Herder's *Älteste Urkunde* [Oldest Record] (1774), for example, he questions whether the origin of the similarities among ancient religious scriptures lies where the author finds it or "im Schematismus des Universi und in den vestigiis creaturae a creatore impressis" (38) [in the scheme of the universe and in the traces that the creator stamped onto his creation]. In his review of *Abhandlung über den Ursprung der Sprache* [Treatise on the Origin of Language] (1772), he asks whether Herder believes that all language originated in the way described, "oder ob er eine Sprache ausnimmt . . . , die . . . eine warme Übersetzung ist aus der Originalsprache, darin ein milder unerschöpflicher Schriftsteller den großen Kodex Himmels und der Erden en Bas Relief und ronde Bosse für seine Freunde geschrieben hat" (80) [or whether he excludes a language which . . . is a warm translation from the *original language* in which a gentle, inexhaustible *writer* has written the great codex of heaven and earth *in low relief* and *full relief* for his *friends*]. Here, Claudius participates in the physico-theological tradition, which portrays God as the author of the universe, nature as his book, and the things of the world as his language.[34] One finds countless passages of this sort all the way up to *Predigt eines Laienbruders zu Neujahr 1814* [Sermon of a Lay Brother on New Year's Day, 1814], where we read, "Auch kann ein reines Auge die sichtbare Natur nicht ansehen, ohne ihn [Christ] zu finden und an ihn zu glauben. Ihn predigen Himmel und Erde, und alle Körper und Erscheinungen in der sichtbaren Natur sind Glöcklein am Leibrock, die *ihn* und *seinen Gang* verraten" (692-93) [Also, a pure eye cannot look at visible nature without finding him (Christ) and believing in him. Heaven and earth proclaim him, and all substances and phenomena in visible nature are little bells on a dresscoat that betray *him* and *his passage.*][35]

Beginning with Part V of the **Collected Works** in 1790, however, passages such as the following, drawn from **"Eine asiatische Vorlesung" [A Lecture on Asia]** and **"Valet an meine Leser" [Farewell to My Readers]** become ever more frequent:

> Gott kann nur aus Gott erkannt werden; nichts kann von ihm einen *wahren* Begriff geben, als er selbst. Alle Eindrücke, Ideen und Begriffe, die seine sichtbaren und sinnlichen Werke auf uns machen, sind nur Begriffe von endlichen und unvolkommenen Dingen; die können keine Erkenntnis des *Unendlichen, Vollkommenen* geben. . . . (526)

> [God can be known only from God; nothing can provide a *true* concept of him but he himself. All impressions, ideas, and concepts that his visible and sensual works give us are only concepts of finite and imperfect things; they cannot provide knowledge of the *infinite,* perfect. . . .]

> Diese Welt und die Dinge die darin sind und zu ihr gehören, liegen uns *nahe,* und die *Natur* hängt sich gerne an und sammlet sie; aber sie sind nur ein luftig Wesen und ein trüglicher Schatz. Auch das Zeitliche und Sichtbare an uns selbst hat nicht Bestand und Wert, ist nur ein brechlicher Verschlag und inwendig wohnen *wir.*

> Was unsichtbar und geistig ist, das nur ist fest und ewig. Und *der* Art sind auch die rechten Schätze, die der Rost nicht frißt. . . . (601)

> [This world and the things that are in it and are part of it are *close* to us, and *nature* clings to them and collects them. However, they are an airy thing and a deceptive treasure. What is temporal and visible in us is also without endurance and value, is but a flimsy shed, and within it *we* reside.

> Only what is invisible and spiritual is sure and eternal. And true treasures, the ones rust does not corrode, are of *that* kind. . . .]

Wherever nature appears in a favorable light, it is almost always immediately overshadowed by qualifications such as those expressed in the preceding passages. Did Claudius fall victim to a contradiction or undergo a fundamental change of mind? Not at all. Despite its beauty and suggestiveness, nature was for him *ultimately* never more than a sign and therefore never possessed more than referential power.[36] It could neither provide a clear idea of God nor bring man closer to salvation. As mentioned with respect to his view of language, the change of tone and emphasis in his later writings represents his response to the march of the Enlightenment, in this context to the rapid spread of "natural" religion and its pantheistic tendency to valorize nature at the expense of the spiritual in a traditional sense. How could he do otherwise, since for him nature, as opposed to man, and divinity are of two entirely different ontological orders?

To be sure, Claudius had no illusions about man himself.[37] In **"Über die Unsterblichkeit der Seele" [On the Immortality of the Soul],** much as in the passage from **"Valet" [Farewell]** cited above, he carefully distinguishes between the spiritual and natural aspects of man: "denn das *andre Etwas* sind eigentlich wir, und das übrige von uns ist nur unser Gehäuse . . ." (283) [for *we* are actually the *other something,* and the rest of us is only our shell . . .]. While having no direct effect on man's spirit, however, nature has a major impact on the shell and therefore exerts an indirect influence on the soul as well. Consequently, nature and spirit lie in eternal struggle against each other within man. In **"Geburt und Wiedergeburt" [Birth and Rebirth]** Claudius articulates his view of the human condition with greater clarity:

> Die sinnliche Natur im Menschen wird in ihm von ihres gleichen *unmittelbar* berührt; sie liegt gleichsam nach außen, und umschließt das *Verständige* in ihm, wie die Hülse den Kern, wie das Weiße im Ei den Dotter. Was um uns her sichtbar und *sinnlich* ist, sehen wir, wahrnehmen und empfinden wir *in und an sich selbst,* und genießen es ungehindert und ohne Mühe.

> Nicht so das *Verständige;* das wird in uns von seines gleichen nicht *unmittelbar* berührt. Wir nehmen es nur wahr *in und an seinen Wirkungen;* und zwischen dieser Wahrnehmung und der unmittelbaren Berührung ist eine große Kluft, die erst überstiegen werden muß. (661)[38]

[Sensual nature in man is affected *directly* only by *its own like.* It is directed outward, as it were, and envelops the understanding within itself like a hull the kernel, like the white of an egg the yoke. What is visible and *sensual* around us we see, perceive, and sense *in and of itself,* and we enjoy it undisturbed and without difficulty.

Not so with the understanding. It is not affected *directly* in us by *its own like.* We perceive it only *in and through its effects,* and between this perception and direct contact there is a great cleft that must first be bridged.]

Claudius treats the origin of the cleft and its consequences most extensively in **Einfältiger Hausvater-Bericht über die christliche Religion [Simple, Fatherly Account of the Christian Religion].** Written in response to his daughter Anna's request for a spiritual vade mecum on leaving home and four years in the making, the work must be considered a definitive statement. It presents a narrative overview of sacred history according to the Bible from the Garden of Eden to Pentecost and concludes with reflections on salvation. In the midst of the narrative, Claudius quite consciously and characteristically enlarges upon original sin and its ramifications in the sense of Pauline anthropology, as renewed by Luther, with its distinction between the divinity of the spirit and the corruption of the flesh. He quotes at length from Luther's preface to the Epistle to the Romans as well as from the central Pauline text, Romans 7 (579-80). So pervasive is his sense of man's sinfulness that it outweighs his awareness of divine love and the role of Pentecost.[39] Apparently originating in his youth, his assumption of man's dual nature and *natürliches Verderben* (578) [natural depravity] explains why he devotes almost the final third of the work to the inner transformation of the individual prerequisite for salvation.[40]

Throughout the work of his middle and later years, Claudius continually affirms the superiority of the soul over nature as a medium of apprehending the divine and, of course, as the place of redemption. In the **Briefe an Andres [Letters to Andres]** of 1798, for example, he makes the following characteristic statement:

> Offenbar muß man von Erde und Himmel und von allem, was sichtbar ist, die Augen wegwenden, wenn man das Unsichtbare finden will. Nicht, daß Himmel und Erde nicht schön und des Ansehens wert wären. Sie sind wohl schön, und sind da, um angesehen zu werden. Sie sollen unsre Kräfte in Bewegung setzen, durch ihre Schöne an einen, der noch schöner ist, erinnern und das Herz nach ihm verwunden. Aber, wenn sie das getan haben, denn haben sie das Ihrige getan, und weiter können sie uns nicht helfen.

> Der Mensch ist reicher als sie, und hat, was sie nicht geben können . . . Er sieht in der sichtbaren Natur nichts als *Zeit* liches und *Ört*-liches; und *er* weiß von einem Ewigen und Unendlichen. (483).

[Apparently, one must turn one's eyes away from heaven and earth and everything that is visible if one wants to find the invisible. Not that heaven and earth are not beautiful and worth looking at. They *are* beautiful and are there to be looked at. They should set the powers within us in motion and, through their beauty, remind us of someone who is even more beautiful and make our hearts sore for him. But after they have done that, they have done what they were meant to do and cannot help us any further.

Man is richer than they and has what they cannot give him . . . In visible nature he sees nothing but things that are temporal and spatial; and *he* knows of someone who is eternal and infinite.]

A few lines later he continues even more cogently: "Selbst die Weisheit und Ordnung, die der Mensch in der sichtbaren Natur findet, legt er mehr in sie hinein als er sie aus ihr herausnimmt. Denn er könnte ihrer ja nicht gewahr werden, wenn er sie nicht auf etwas, das er in ihm hat, beziehen könnte" (484) [Even the wisdom and order that man finds in visible nature he projects into it more than he extracts it from it. For he could not become aware of it if he were unable to relate it to something he already has within himself]. In **"Morgengespräch zwischen A. und dem Kandidaten Bertram" [Morning Conversation between A. and the Licentiate Bertram],** Claudius makes his most positive statement concerning the transparency of nature as sign, drawing on the famous passage regarding the Godlikeness [*Ebenbildlichkeit*] of all creation in Hamann's *Aesthetica in nuce* for support (654-56).[41] Even here, however, he takes with one hand what he gives with the other. Calling man the first and most important *Buchstabe* [letter] of all, he writes, "Jedermann, wenn er von Gott forschen und sagen will, wendet sich an sich selbst; und das mit Recht. Denn im Menschen ist ein unsterblicher Same und Keim, in dem die Schätze der Wahrheit, und Erkenntnis Gottes verborgen liegen . . ." (656) [Everyone, whenever he wants to search for and talk about God, turns inward, and rightly so. For in man there is an immortal seed and bud in which the treasures of truth and knowledge of God lie concealed . . .). In contrast to **Briefe an Andres [Letters to Andres],** cited above, Claudius states here that the seed requires a "Reaktion von aussen" (656) [reaction from without] in order to germinate. Changing metaphors, however, he still clearly distinguishes between the "mirroring" power of nature and the soul: "In der physischen Natur spiegeln sich einzelne Kräfte, und im Menschen spiegelt sich die Gottheit selbst" (656) [In physical nature individual forces reflect each other, and in man divinity reflects itself]. With man's sinful state in mind, he then continues, "Nur in uns, so wie wir hier sind, ist der Spiegel so verbogen und unrein, daß das Bild nur verstellt und wie in Nebel gehüllt ist" (656) [Only in us, the way we are here, the mirror is so crooked and impure that the image is distorted and as if veiled in mist]. Clearly, Claudius focuses on the positive dimension of nature in certain writings; as indicated earlier, he was not a systematist and never wrote a thoroughly methodical exposition of his thought. However, his work discloses an overwhelming preoccupation with the sinfulness of man's postlapsarian condition, due to his inner dualism, and with the soul as his only means of immediate communion with God and salvation.[42]

From his own lifetime to the present day, Claudius's assumption of an essential relationship between God and the soul and his resulting attitude toward nature and introspection have raised the question of his relationship to mysticism.[43] This is not the place to ascertain his position in the complex crosscurrents of theological thought in the eighteenth century. The difficulty of the task is suggested by the fact that no theologian or literary historian has yet undertaken an exhaustive investigation.[44] Surprisingly, perhaps, in view of the familiar image of Claudius, Schröder and, more recently, Fechner stress the poet's debt to the Enlightenment, and we ourselves shall see numerous instances of this debt further along in this study, particularly in chapters 3 and 5.[45] In one of the most substantive inquiries in recent years, however, Görisch observes "the extensive loss of futuristic, eschatological quality" visá-vis Claudius's attitude toward resurrection, immortality, and the kingdom of God, which is consistent with the subjectivism of mysticism.[46] In the most important older study, to be sure, Loofs only grudgingly concedes the influence of mysticism on the late Claudius.[47] All the same, the four basic elements of mysticism that he mentions for purposes of comparison warrant attention:

> *First,* the assumption of an essential relationship between the true, innermost essence of man and God. *Second,* the idea that the sensual world round about us, indeed, our own external, sensual part, is something heterogenous to the divinity within us that draws us away from God. *Third,* the assertion that it is man's task to strive for union with God by turning away from this ungodly something and turning inward to one's innermost self. And *fourth,* finally, the conviction that this union, which man can only prepare for, comes about only through God's *immediate* influence on man's innermost self. (122-23)

In light of the discussion over the last several pages, the passage requires no commentary. While to my mind Claudius's mystical inclinations are patent, I would add two qualifying considerations.

Claudius was obviously deeply concerned with the possibility and circumstances of *Herstellung* [restoration] during earthly life.[48] However, his work discloses extreme pessimism in this regard.[49] In his reflections on the phrase "Zu uns komme dein Reich!" [Thy kingdom come!] in **"Vom Vaterunser" [On the Lord's Prayer]** (1812), for example, he declares unequivocally, "Dies *Reich Gottes* kann auch zu den Menschen auf Erden kommen . . ." (643) [This *kingdom of God* can come to men on earth, too]. Nevertheless, he adds that one must pray for it to come and closes with the words, "Die nun, zu denen es kommt, die erfahren, wie Christus es in dieser Bitte mit uns meint, und kennen dies Reich. Aber, bis es gekommen ist, kennen wir es nicht, und wissen nur halb was wir beten" (643-44) [Now, those to whom it comes learn what *Christ* has in mind for us with this request and know this kingdom. But until it has come, we do not know it and know only halfway what we are praying]. In **"Vom Gewissen: In Briefen an Andres" [On Conscience: In Letters to Andres]** (1812), he makes a similar statement with respect to those, "die . . . wirklich *hergestellt* sind. *Dahin* kann der Mensch kommen; und *dazu* ist er auf Erden.—*Aber dahin kommen wenige!*—" (680) [who are truly *restored.* Man *can* get there, and he is on earth *for that reason.*—*However, few are those who get there!*—]. Moreover, one does not have to go far to find comments that can be understood only in a futuristic, eschatological sense. As early as in **"Passe-Temps" [Pastime]** in Part IV of the *Collected Works* (1783), Claudius writes, "Dazu bleiben wir nicht ewig unter den Sternen und unser Erdenleben ist nur eine ganz kleine Strecke auf der ganzen Bahn unsrer Existenz . . ." (256) [In addition, we do not remain eternally under the stars, and our earthly life is only a very short stretch on the whole road of our existence . . .]. As late as **"Predigt eines Laienbruders zu Neujahr 1814" [Sermon of a Lay Brother on New Year's Day, 1814]**, he can say of man, "Er ist nicht für diese vergängliche Welt beschieden, sondern nur auf eine kurze Zeit hieher getan, daß er . . . für eine unvergängliche zubereitet und tüchtig gemacht werde. Da wird er ewig sein und bleiben . . ." (698) [He is not destined for this *transient* world but is placed here for only a short time so that he can be prepared and made fit for an *intransient* one. There he will be and remain eternally]. It is not at all clear to me that Claudius's work supports Görisch's assertion of an extensive loss of eschatological substance.[50] There no doubt exists a strong tension between the claims of the present and hopes for the future. On balance, however, Claudius's intense introspection would appear to signify *preparation* for receiving grace in the here and now and for eternal life in the hereafter. In any case, his experience and notion of communion with God fall well short of the *visio et fruitio et unio Dei* [the sight and enjoyment of and union with God] that represent the cardinal features of true mysticism.[51]

Unlike Pietists, furthermore, Claudius was quite content to remain within the established Lutheran Church and to observe the positive forms of its faith. While viewing the Bible as a *Nachricht* [news] and not the *Sache* [thing] itself, as we have seen, he felt that he ultimately had no choice but to take it at face value, as he relates in the *Briefe an Andres* [Letters to Andres] of 1783: "Wenn wir ihn nicht selbst sehen können, Andres; so müssen wir denen glauben die ihn gesehen haben. Mir bleibt anders nichts übrig" (261) [If we cannot see him ourselves, Andres, we have to believe those who have seen him. I have no other choice]. Apparently suffering from the onslaught of rationalist theology, he writes to Andres in the *Briefe* [Letters] of 1798:

Alles muß allerdings zusammenhängen, und wird sich auch wohl reimen lassen, wenn die data bekannt

sind. Die Spekulanten lassen es sich nicht träumen, daß das brillanteste Feld der Spekulation hinter der Kirchmauer liege.

Doch, dem sei wie ihm wolle, Andres; wir glauben der Bibel aufs Wort, und halten uns schlecht und recht an das, was die Apostel von Christus sagen und setzen.

Die ihn selbst gesehen und gehört haben . . . die sind ihm doch näher gewesen, als wir und die Glosse. (479)

[Of course, everything must hang together and will surely make sense when all the data are known. The speculators have not the least inkling that the most splendid field of speculation lies behind the wall of the church.

But be that as it may, Andres, we'll take the Bible at its word and cling purely and simply to what the apostles say and write about *Christ.*

Those who saw and heard him themselves . . . were closer to him, after all, than we and any annotation.]

Later in this series of letters, he speaks of Christ's works and miracles as visible signs of greater ones yet to come (486-87). The tension between the subjective and positive aspects of Claudius's faith mentioned above finds perhaps clearest expression still further along in the same work, where he writes of religious mysteries, specifically Holy Communion, as follows: "wer sie aber zu verdienen sucht und sich den Besitzer zum Freunde zu machen weiß, der erfährt sie bisweilen. Darum wollen wir ehrerbietig und demütig *vor der Tür* dieses hochheiligen Geheimnisses stehenbleiben, und die *Außenseite* ansehen, schlecht und recht und wie die Bibel sie gibt" (488) [However, someone who seeks to deserve them and is able to make a friend of their owner experiences them at times. Therefore, we will remain standing reverently and humbly *before the door* of this holiest of mysteries and look at the outside, purely and simply and the way the Bible shows it].[52]

In light of Claudius's notion of language, nature, and man, his reaction to the radicalization of the Enlightenment in theology and philosophy after about 1780 is entirely understandable.[53] More than once he illustrated his view of the ideal relationship between experience and reason in the metaphor of marriage, as in **"Übungen im Stil" [Exercises in Style]**: "Nur trenne sie nicht; denn sie sind Mann und Frau, und müssen beisammen sein zu einer vernünftigen Haushaltung und wenn legitime Kinder sollen geboren werden" (462) [Only don't separate them, for they are man and wife and must stay together if they're to have a sensible household and if legitimate children are to be born].[54] As early as his review of Goethe's *Zwo wichtige biblische Fragen* [Two Important Biblical Questions] (1773), however, he indicates his preference, should the need arise to choose between the two: "Es gibt in der Religion auch Scylla und Charybdis—Schwärmerei und kalte räsonierte Dogmatik . . . Wenn doch eins sein muß, ist's noch fast besser der Schwärmerei zu nahe zu kommen. Die kann noch durch die Gärung ihren trüben Bodensatz niedersetzen, und helle werden, aus der andern wird gar nichts" (837) [In religion there is also Scylla and Charybdis—fanaticism and cold, reasoned dogmatism. But if I have to choose between them it's almost better to come too close to fanaticism . . . Through its agitation its cloudy sediment will settle, and it will become clear. Nothing comes of the other]. As in the case of nature and the soul, he virtually always acknowledges the power and achievements of reason, only to qualify them with an *aber* [but]. For Claudius, reason belongs entirely to the order of nature and is totally subject to its stimuli, whereas experience can emanate from the soul and partake of its riches. As the final quarter of the century advanced, moreover, it gradually became evident to him that reason, the husband, was turning into a wife-beater. In view of this abuse, he devoted much of his later work to advocacy for spiritual experience.

In its (for all practical purposes) thorough dualism, Claudius's conception of nature and man is indeed analogous to his notion of language. In varying ways and degrees, all three entities represent signs that refer to a realm of spirit from which they are separated by a wide gulf. Through faith and grace man has the possibility of bridging the gulf in the sense of Romans 7:6: "But now we are delivered from the law, that being dead wherein we were held; that we should serve in newness of spirit, and not *in* the oldness of the letter." For Claudius, however, in contrast to the classical and romantic generations, there is no "salvation" for nature or the word. Capable of magnificent flights on the wings of metaphor, language must always eventually return to earth. Despite his love for the Gospel of St. John, Claudius was in this regard, as in others, strictly Pauline.

4

It is beyond the scope of this chapter to determine the precise historical locus of Claudius's view of language. Based on preceding discussion, however, some general conclusions can be drawn that may serve as a framework for future inquiry.

The essay **"On Genius,"** like much of the early work, creates a deceptive initial impression. The poetic figures related to metamorphosis and creativity, the desystematization and historicization of meaning as well as the recognition of the influence of physical and cultural environment on genius—indeed, the con-

cern with genius itself—all summon up the milieu of Hamann and Herder and mark Claudius as a child of the 1770s. While similarities of idiom and other secondary likenesses certainly obtain, however, they emerge from radically different spiritual and conceptual frames of reference. This is suggested already by Claudius's diplomatic criticism of Herder's works of the seventies as well as by the allusion to Johannine and Pauline notions of language above. Herder's idea of signification is characterized by the unity of word and referent.[55] Emotion and metaphor, far from possessing a distinct "bridging" function, are both subsumed under a broadened concept of rationality.[56] As indicated earlier, Herder had little understanding for Claudius's mystical tendencies and allowed their relationship to cool during the eighties and nineties. To his mind, truth comes from God but can assume only human form.[57] Gaier implies the anthropocentric nature of Herder's whole philosophy with reference to *Eine Metakritik zur Kritik der reinen Vernunft* [A Metacritique of the Critique of Pure Reason]: "With the linguistic conditionality of intellect, the linguicity of reason, and the determination of language as being dependent on experience, relative to interest, historically conditioned, and changeable, first of all, a metacritical argument is again found. For, taking this into consideration, an a priori truth cannot even be conceived of with regard to content, much less formulated."[58] Like Claudius, Herder was aware of the limits of language. However, his love for the word never permitted him to criticize it seriously; rather, he typically emphasized its potential and achievements.[59] Moreover, his interest in language was far broader than Claudius's. He pursued the study of language within a general theory of knowledge that he applied to a number of the humanities and social sciences. As we have seen, Claudius openly acknowledged the successes of reason and discursive language in these fields of endeavor, even in certain areas of theology. The question of signification became problematic for him and thus thematic in his work only in connection with areas of profound experience such as genius, love, and divinity.

In view of Claudius's relationship to Herder, it is clear that he did not stand in the line of development that led to Wilhelm von Humboldt and the early Romantics Novalis and Friedrich Schlegel, who also proceed from the unity of sign and signified on the way to varying notions of semiosis.[60] However, his prominence in the essays of Eichendorff—indeed, Eichendorff's work itself—suggest one possible link with the future.[61] In chapter 2 we shall see that there is also a bridge to the symbolism of the late nineteenth and early twentieth centuries.

Scholarship typically represents Claudius as being spiritually and intellectually more akin to Hamann than to Herder, and with good reason.[62] Most importantly, perhaps, their shared belief in man's dependence on God led to a common struggle against rationalism and its faith in man's autonomy, which is discernible to a degree even in Herder.[63] With regard to language theory, however, as suggested earlier, the question of relationship becomes problematic. The difficulty lies primarily in the fact that there is as yet a wide variety of opinion concerning Hamann's view of language, a circumstance due not least of all to the opacity of his style, which even minds of the caliber of Lessing and Kant found obscure.[64] Nevertheless, general agreement exists with respect to his belief in the godlikeness of all creation and its consequences for his theory of language.[65]

Ruprecht writes, "The origin of language [with Hamann] is thus divine, because the living word proceeds from God as logos. However, it is at the same time human insofar as logos-endowed man speaks the originally divine speech further in a human manner and in the process develops it into human language."[66] This divine-human origin of language guarantees the unity of *Buchstabe* [letter] and *Geist* [spirit], as with Herder. Indeed, Frank argues against the customary view of Herder's dependence on Hamann, pointing out that Hamann's theory of language became focused only after he read *Abhandlung über den Ursprung der Sprache* [Treatise on the Origin of Language] and that he expressed agreement with Herder's thought after his friend ceased insisting on a purely human origin of language.[67] In response to the rationalism of the times, mainstream scholarship tells us, Hamann placed a particularly high premium on man's sensual nature and therefore asserted the power of the poet and his idiom to "translate" the "damaged" book of nature, which, for reasons left unclear, is not directly accessible to man as revelation.[68]

Although deeply rooted in positive Christianity, Hamann's anthropology and conception of language would appear to bring him in close proximity to Herder and in diametrical opposition to Claudius. As we have seen, Claudius was highly skeptical of the "flesh" and everything related to it. Suspicious of all literary language, he criticized any glorification of the word for its own sake and during the nineties mounted an earnest, if futile, campaign against the alleged empty aestheticism of Weimar classicism.[69] However, Hoffmann's interpretation of Hamann's philology, should it gain wide currency, could necessitate reconsideration of the relationship. In his view, Hamann's idea of participation in divine truth through the Bible reveals a spontaneous, prerational basis that manifests both aesthetic-literary and religious features.[70] Furthermore, he finds that Hamann's epistemological skepticism results ultimately in the negation of hermeneutics in favor of the "appearance of the content of the religious referent," that is, immediate experience of the divine.[71]

Surprisingly, perhaps, given Claudius's virtually canonical association with Hamann, Herder, and the Storm and Stress, a survey of contemporary linguistic thought discloses that his concept of language is structurally closest to that of the Enlightenment. Christian Wolff and his adherents also posed the question of signification as a matter of signs, referents, and a gap between them that must be bridged.[72] With Claudius, one finds no parallel to Wolff's view of the soul as an organ of representation, duplicating—read "abstracting"—the things of the world apprehended directly through intuition. However, he shared the enlighteners' belief in the epistemological primacy of immediate experience and their concomitant skepticism toward the sign as an intrinsically valueless medium to be overcome. His attitude toward metaphor also resembles their idea of its "bridging" function.[73] On the other hand, Claudius certainly did not understand absolute knowledge in the sense of a "post-semiotic experience of the world as logical structure."[74] His notion of language differs from that of the Enlightenment most fundamentally in its firm anchorage in traditional Christianity.

To find the origin of Claudius's view of language one must delve still further into the past. Given its ubiquitous presence in the **Collected Works,** the spirit of Martin Luther automatically suggests a possible source. Claudius had the greatest respect for Luther and drew upon his ideas and words frequently and in significant contexts, for example, his discussion of sin in **"Einfältiger Hausvater-Bericht" [Simple, Fatherly Account].** With regard to language, there are many areas of agreement. Both looked askance at literature and felt that the spoken word possesses greater signifying force.[75] In contrast to Hamann they recognize not all language but only holy scripture as revelation.[76] Claudius was not an uncritical student of Luther, however, and in certain basic respects the two go separate ways.

Wolf writes, for example, "At bottom, Luther is concerned . . . with the interdependence of divine word and human word . . . To his mind both belong together because the language lent man by God through the incarnation of Christ has experienced, as it were, a back-coupling and serves as the bearer of mediation."[77] This Johannine view of language led Luther to attach enormous importance to the word. It also caused him to seek the middle path in the debate between literalists and spiritualists, who found divinity in either the sign or the signified alone.[78] If he leans slightly toward one side or the other, it is toward that of the literalists, for he consistently asserts the authority and dignity of "the outer word" and places great weight on philological precision in dealing with canonical documents.[79] He feels that the Bible is "comprehensible in itself in its literal historical meaning" and therefore only occasionally requires "sympathetic projection founded on belief" of the faithful.[80] As we have seen, Claudius places the accents differently. Quite apart from his contrary view of signification, he does not accord the

Bible the same degree of transparency or the same exclusive status as Luther. Perhaps owing precisely to its lack of complete transparency for him, he emphasizes that inner space within the soul where innate knowledge of God exists and imperfect yet true communion with him is possible.

The ultimate origin of Claudius's attitude toward language would appear to lie at the very wellspring of Christian linguistic reflection, that is, in the work of St. Augustine. Schmidt underscores the Pauline character of the church father's anthropology: "Augustine's doctrine of sin and grace is surely more strongly influenced by Paul than any other between Paul himself and Luther."[81] Probably due to his strong sense of man's sinfulness Augustine distinguishes carefully between the outer word—the sign—and the inner word, or spirit.[82] Moreover, he also differentiates between "hearing" and "understanding." Accordingly, the inner word may or may not accompany the outer word. The discontinuous relationship between sign and referent leads Augustine to stress the experiential aspect of comprehension, that is to say, it results in a spiritualization of semiosis.

St. Augustine's relative devaluation of the outer word underwent radicalization in the theology of medieval mystics such as Meister Eckhart, spiritualists on the order of Luther's contemporary, Sebastian Franck, and the Pietists of the seventeenth and eighteenth centuries.[83] His thought probably reached Claudius closer to its original form through Pastor Claudius, whose Lutheran faith was colored, but not determined, by Pietism.[84] As indicated earlier, Pietism had a significant but limited impact on Claudius's religion and little, if any, on his formal religious practice. Nevertheless, his notion of signification more closely resembles the Augustinian model likely transmitted by Pietism than any other.

It is certainly easier to say what Claudius's view of language is *not* than to say what it *is*. His attitude toward language clearly represents a unique combination of several historical traditions. One could describe it positively, if inexactly, as a compound consisting of an Augustinian base, an element of Lutheran biblicism, another of Pietist inwardness, and a healthy dose of Enlightenment skepticism. As we shall see in the next three chapters, Claudius's skepticism is perhaps the most decisive feature of his notion of language with respect to his literary work. He would certainly have approved of Wittgenstein's statement, "What one cannot speak of one should keep silent about"; a number of his own statements indeed amount to as much.[85] With the reply, "What one cannot speak of one can write poetry about," however, he would have agreed only in a certain, restricted sense.[86] Significant portions of his lyric poetry and areas of his prose as well can be characterized as linguistic expressions of meaningful silence.

Notes

[1] See, for example, Hinrich C. Seeba, "Word and Thought: Herder's Language Model in Modern Hermeneutics," *Johann Gottfried Herder: Innovator Through the Ages,* ed. Wulf Koepke and Samson B. Knoll, Modern German Studies, 10 (Bonn: Bouvier Verlag Herbert Grundmann, 1982), 35.

[2] Ibid., 35.

[3] Ibid.

[4] Wilkinson, for example, argues against the necessity of the dispute; Elizabeth M. Wilkinson, "The Inexpressible and the Un-speakable: Some Romantic Attitudes to Art and Language," *German Life and Letters* 16 (1962-1963): 308-20. Eagleton places the controversy in the context of large-scale cultural developments; Terry Eagleton, *Literary Theory: An Introduction* (Minneapolis: University of Minnesota Press, 1985).

[5] Seeba, "Word and Thought," 36; 38-39.

[6] David E. Wellbery, *Lessing's "Laokoön": Semiotics and Aesthetics in the Age of Reason,* Anglica Germanica Series, 2 (New York: Cambridge University Press), 1984.

[7] Volker Hoffmann, *Johann Georg Hamanns Philologie: Hamanns Philologie zwischen enzyklopädischer Mikrologie und Hermeneutik,* Studien zur Poetik und Geschichte der Literatur, 24 (Stuttgart: Kohlhammer, 1972), 160.

[8] Some of these, however, are quite useful. See particularly Annelen Kranefuss, *Die Gedichte des Wandsbecker Boten,* Palaestra, 260 (Göttingen: Vandenhoeck & Ruprecht, 1973) and Reinhard Görisch, *Matthias Claudius und der Sturm und Drang: Ein Abgrenzungsversuch. Vergleiche mit Goethe, Herder, Lenz, Schubart und anderen am Beispiel eschatologischer Vorstellungen im Kontext des Epochenbewußtseins,* European University Papers, I: 357 (Frankfurt am Main: Lang, 1981).

[9] Wilhelm Flegler, ed., "Anmerkungen," *Matthias Claudius' ausgewählte Werke,* Reclams Universal-Bibliothek, 1691-1695 (Leipzig: Reclam, 1882), 501.

[10] See Jacques Chouillet, *L'esthétique des Lumières,* Littératures Modernes, 4 (Vendôme: Presses Universitaires de France, 1974), 59-63.

[11] Johann Adolf Schlegel, trans. and ed., "Vom Genie in den schönen Künsten," *Einschränkung der schönen Künste auf einen einzigen Grundsatz: Aus dem Französischen übersetzt und mit Abhandlungen begleitet,* by Charles

Batteux, 3d ed., 2 vols. in 1 (1770; reprint, Hildesheim and New York: Olms, 1976), 2:10.

[12] Ibid.

[13] While the essay is indeed a persiflage, as Görisch indicates, it is also much more than that. Görisch sees bardic poetry, rather than the Storm and Stress, as the object of Claudius's irony throughout the essay; *Matthias Claudius und der Sturm und Drang,* 299.

[14] I do not know the source of Claudius's quote.

[15] See, for example, my *Matthias Claudius,* Twayne's World Authors Series, 691 (Boston: Twayne, 1983), 11, 13, and 56-60.

[16] For other usages of the wise or holy fool see the discussion of "Eine Disputation" [A Disputation] and especially "Der Besuch im St. Hiob zu **" [The Visit to St. Job in **] in Chapters 5 and 7 of this study, respectively.

[17] Kranefuss's suggestion that the *fremd Kraut* refers to Hamannian ideas, while plausible for stylistic reasons, is problematic for others; *Die Gedichte des Wandsbecker Boten,* 205, note 11; 206-7. Claudius does not say all that he knows or thinks about language or any major concern in any given work. We shall see that his view of language and other central issues precludes dependence on Hamann.

[18] Claudius mocks *das Bardenwesen* [bardism] in a more conventional manner when he allows Asmus to begin his new charge with the words, "Will nur zuvor den letzten Perioden nachlesen: 'und nun herunter zum modernen Genius oder zum Genie'—herunter denn, und gleich im Fallen angefangen. Empfange mich, du lieblicher Hain am Helikonberg! Ich komme gefallen, zu hören deinen Silbersturm und dein sanfteres Geräusche, und ihr im leichten Rosengewand, mit dem blassen Munde, der so holdselig sprechen kann, Gesellen des Hains! seid mir gegrüßt—Ha! der Schwindel ist über, und ich habe wieder festen Grund unter'n Füßen" (28) [Beforehand I would just like to read over my last periods: "and now down to the modern genius or man of parts"—well then, down, and let me begin while falling: Receive me, thou lovely grove at the foot of the Helicon! I come falling to hear thy silvery storm and thy softer rustlings. And ye in the light rosy gowns, with the pale mouths that can speak so sweetly, companions of the grove, I greet ye—Ha! My dizzy spell is over, and I have firm ground under my feet again].

[19] See Jonah 2 and Matthew 12:38-42 and Luke 11:29-32, respectively, as well as Kranefuss, *Die Gedichte des Wandsbecker Boten,* 204-5. Görisch undervalues the allusion in his criticism of Kranefuss's assessment; *Matthias Claudius und der Sturm und Drang,* 300, note

360. As explained above, Kranefuss's shortcoming lies only in her failure to draw all the appropriate consequences from her quite accurate insight.

[20] Kranefuss, *Die Gedichte des Wandsbecker Boten,* 205.

[21] In limiting the meaning of the allusion to poetic inspiration, Kranefuss interprets the whale literally, that is, allegorically rather than metaphorically, and overlooks what it does. She also neglects important aspects of the allusion, i.e., Jonah's conversion of the Ninevites, that is, his "creation" of new life, to which Christ refers in addition to the whale and his own resurrection and "re-creation" of mankind. Furthermore, her view of the whale and harp as religious and psychological "possibilities of interpretation" of genius "which do not contradict but perhaps vie with each other" and "between which the reader may choose" posits an equivalence that does not necessarily obtain in this essay, when considered in isolation, and that certainly does not hold, as subsequent discussion indicates, when seen within the context of the entire work; *Die Gedichte des Wandsbecker Boten,* 205-6. The two motifs are equal only in their usage as metaphorical means of describing genius.

[22] Kranefuss comes to similar conclusions by way of Claudius's poetics, which she characterizes "as the difference between 'corporeality and meaning,' life and art, word and reality"; *Die Gedichte des Wandsbecker Boten,* 200.

[23] Claudius borrowed the expression from his friend, the popular philosopher and writer Friedrich Heinrich Jacobi. An overview of their relationship is found in Siobhán Donovan and Annette Lüchow, "'Viel Wahres und viel Scharfsinniges': Matthias Claudius und die 'Vermischten Schriften' von Friedrich Heinrich Jacobi," *Jahresschriften der Claudius-Gesellschaft* 2 (1993): 5-19.

[24] This theme and related ideas are treated in chapter 3 of the present study in connection with Claudius's prose satire.

[25] See, for example, "Passe-Temps" [Pastime], "Über die Unsterblichkeit der Seele" [On the Immortality of the Soul], "Zwei Rezensionen" [Two Reviews], "Eine Korrespondenz zwischen mir und meinem Vetter" [A Correspondence between My Cousin and Me], "Vom Gewissen" [On Conscience], and "Predigt eines Laienbruders zu Neujahr 1814" [Sermon of a Lay Brother on New Year's Day, 1814], *Sämtliche Werke,* ed. Jost Perfahl, Rolf Siebke, and Hansjörg Platschek, 6th ed. (Munich: Winkler, 1987), 252, 284 and 287, 349, 456, 678, and 699, respectively.

[26] See Wolfgang Freund, "Matthias Claudius: Eine Untersuchung zur Frömmigkeit des Wandsbecker Boten

und dessen Stellung in der Zeit" (Ph.D. diss., University of Jena, 1988), 146.

27 A feuilleton entitled "Ein defekter locus communis" [A Defective Commonplace], which appeared in the *Registry Office News* in 1770, represents an earlier stage of Claudius's musing on genius and may have served as the point of departure for "On Genius." Here, too, Claudius advocates silence before geniuses of high caliber: "Ich weiß nur wenige Namen zu nennen, und auch die verschweige ich, daß ich sie nicht entweihe und ihren Manibus ein minderes Opfer bringe, als ein bescheidenes Stillschweigen ist, wenn der Gedanke an sie lauten Ausruf gebeut" (759) [I know only a few names to name and shall pass over them, too, in silence, so as not to profane them and bring their spirits a lesser sacrifice than an humble silence, when the thought of them demands a loud cry].

28 In the years following publication of the work (which was written in German) in 1770 Christian Bastholm (1740-1819) became a prominent theologian in his native Denmark. See Vilhelm Andersen, *Den danske Litteratur i det attende aarhundrede*, vol. 2 of *Illustreret Dansk Litteraturhistorie*, ed. Carl S. Petersen and Andersen (Copenhagen: Gyldendalske Boghandel-Nordisk Forlag, 1934), 622-24.

29 That Claudius accorded the spoken language greater, if still limited, signifying power is suggested by the fact that he cultivated a conversational style in much of his prose (and verse) throughout his life, even in many of the late sermonic writings.

30 See note 27 above.

31 Unless otherwise indicated, English-language quotations from the Bible are drawn from the King James Version, which is closer to the tone and style of the Luther-Bible than more modern versions.

32 For details, see my *Matthias Claudius*, Autorenbücher, 617 (Munich: C. H. Beck, 1990), 91-94.

33 The historical inaccuracy of the sources from which Claudius quotes is less important for our purposes than the fact that they reflect in nuce his own Christian ontology. See Christel Matthias Schröder, *Matthias Claudius und die Religionsgeschichte* (Munich: Ernst Reinhardt, 1941), 11-14.

34 See, for example, Görisch, *Matthias Claudius und der Sturm und Drang*, 298.

35 Also see, for example, "Ein Lied vom Reifen" [A Song of Frost], "Neue Erfindung" [New Invention], "Von und mit" [From and With], and "Rebekka mit den Kindern, *an einem Maimorgen*" [Rebecca with the Children, *on a May Morning*]; *Sämtliche Werke,* 184, 221, 397, and 446, respectively.

36 In this sense, in contrast to Kranefuss's view, Claudius does reduce ("verkürzen") nature to a sign; *Die Gedichte des Wandsbecker Boten,* 190.

37 For a more specifically theological discussion of Claudius's anthropology see Wolfgang Freund's very useful study, "Matthias Claudius: Eine Untersuchung."

38 In light of this statement and many others like it I must disagree with the assertion made by Görisch and Kranefuss that Claudius's view of nature was unproblematic; *Matthias Claudius und der Sturm und Drang,* 312, and *Die Gedichte des Wandsbecker Boten,* 177. Kranefuss in particular far overestimates the value of nature in Claudius's work; see especially 169-82.

39 The following passage is particularly telling: "Die *Heilige Schrift* hat uns zwar dies Rätsel unserer Natur, dies Für und Wider zugleich in *einem* Wesen, aufgelöst; denn die göttliche Natur ist das Gute, die Weisheit, die Gerechtigkeit, die Liebe, das Erkenntnis und alle Vollkommenheiten auf einmal und in eins und sie kann, wo sie auch ist, sich nicht verleugnen. Aber dadurch wird unser Unglück, wenn's möglich ist, nur noch größer. Und kann es einen Jammer geben, der *dem Jammer* gleich wäre: mit dem Bedürfnis und Drang zu Erkenntnis und Licht, *im Dunkeln;* mit dem Bedürfnis und Drang zum Guten, im *Bösen;* mit dem Bewußtsein eines Herrscherwerts und -berufs in *einer schmählichen Knechtschaft, in ewigem innerlichen Unfrieden und Furcht des Todes* zu sein; und nun dazu noch zu wissen: daß wir selbst an unserm Unglück *schuld* sind und es so ganz anders hätten haben können, daß wir den Zorn eines *gerechten und allmächtigen Herrn* auf uns geladen, einen *liebreichen Vater* beleidigt haben, und keine Hoffnung haben, sein Angesicht wiederzusehen" (581) [The *Holy Scripture* has certainly resolved this enigma of our nature, this for and against in one being, for us. For divine nature is the good, wisdom, justice, love, knowledge, and all perfections at once and in one and cannot deny itself, wherever it is. But for that reason our misfortune is, if possible, all the greater. And can there be a wretchedness equal to this: with the need and thirst for knowledge and light, to be *in the dark;* with the need and thirst for the good, to be in *evil;* with the awareness of having the worth and calling of a ruler, to be in *ignominious bondage, in eternal inner discord and fear of death;* and now, in addition, to know that we ourselves are to blame for our misfortune and could have had it so totally differently; that we have laden ourselves with the anger of a *just and almighty Lord,* offended a *loving father,* and have no hope of seeing his countenance again]. For a brief statement on the sanctifying influence of the Holy Spirit, see *New Jerusalem Bible,* New Tes-

tament, 279, note m. With regard to man's sinfulness Herbst writes, "Scarcely anyone had a deeper sense of the misery of the fall and of sin than Claudius; hardly anyone of his time expressed this sense as movingly"; Wilhelm Herbst, *Matthias Claudius der Wandsbecker Bote: Ein deutsches Stilleben,* 3rd ed. (Gotha: Perthes, 1863), 383-84. According to Wolfgang Freund, Claudius experienced man's dualistic nature as a cleft not only between God and man but also within man himself, while Luther acknowledged such a cleft in the "natural" man only to a limited extent; "Matthias Claudius: Eine Untersuchung," 50-51; 126, note 97. Referring to Görisch's *Matthias Claudius und der Sturm und Drang,* 109, Freund comments prudently, "that for Claudius the dualism of the two natures does not constitute man absolutely . . . but rather is fundamentally nullified by God's act of salvation in Christ" and that the expression "'dualistic anthropology'" is therefore "appropriate only within limits . . . to characterize Claudius's view of man accurately" (119). However, Claudius's faith in this theological principle and its factual operation in his view of man cannot conceal his fundamental experience of dualism. It is in recognition of this circumstance that Freund retains the term "dualistic anthropology," "since it . . . underscores the pronounced manner in which Claudius emphasized the efficacy of sin in his work and thereby sought to resist its minimalization" (119). More recently, Donovan speaks of Claudius's "trichotomous" anthropology, suggesting that he viewed both body and soul as purely human and distinct from the holy spirit; Siobhán Donovan, "Christlich-theologische und philosophische Anthropologie bei Matthias Claudius," *Anthropologie und Literatur um 1800,* ed. Jürgen Barkhoff and Eda Sagarra (Munich: iudicium verlag, 1992), 113-16.

[40] See Görisch, *Matthias Claudius und der Sturm und Drang,* 15.

[41] Kranefuss relies heavily on this work in her attempt to demonstrate the significance of nature in Claudius's thinking; *Die Gedichte des Wandsbecker Boten,* 188-91. However, she overlooks his relativization of the whole notion of godlikeness later in the work, not to mention other texts discussed here, and draws insupportable conclusions.

[42] Relevant comments are found in the following works: "Von und mit" [From and With], "Über die neue Politik" [On the New Political System], "Eine Korrespondenz zwischen mir und meinem Vetter" [A Correspondence between My Cousin and Me], "Bedenklicher Stil" [Dubious Style], "Vorrede zu der Übersetzung von Fénelons Werken religiösen Inhalts" [Preface to the Translation of Fénelon's Religious Works], "An meinen Sohn Johannes 1799" [To My Son Johannes, 1799], "Über die neue Theologie" [On the New Theology], "Valet an meine Leser" [Farewell to My Readers], "Das heilige Abendmahl" [The Lord's Supper], "Vom Gewissen: In Briefen an Andres"

[On Conscience: In Letters to Andres], and "Predigt eines Laienbruders zu Neujahr 1814" [Sermon of a Lay Brother on New Year's Day, 1814]; *Sämtliche Werke,* 393-99; 433-34 and 439-40; 456-57; 462-63; 541-43; 545-46; 597; 599-602; 609-10; 677-78 and 681-82; entire work.

[43] See, for example, Stammler's comments regarding Voss and Herder; Wolfgang Stammler, *Matthias Claudius der Wandsbecker Bothe: Ein Beitrag zur deutschen Literatur- und Geistesgeschichte* (Halle: Waisenhaus, 1915), 125-26. Claudius's translation of St. Martin's *Des erreurs et de la vérité* [On Errors and Truth] has often been offered as evidence of the poet's mysticism. Whatever the case may be, Gründer shows that Claudius's translation at least exercised an influence on a branch of the Christian cabalistic tradition that extended into the twentieth century; Karlfried Gründer, "Aufklärung und Surrogate," *Aufklärung und Haskala in jüdischer und nichtjüdischer Sicht,* ed. Gründer and Nathan Rotenstreich (Heidelberg: Lambert Schneider Verlag, 1990), 101-22.

[44] Among the myriad religious writings on Claudius only a handful are of a scholarly nature. The following are the most thorough and useful: Friedrich Loofs, *Matthias Claudius in kirchengeschichtlicher Beleuchtung: Eine Untersuchung über Claudius' religiöse Stellung und Altersentwicklung* (Gotha: Perthes, 1915); Görisch, *Matthias Claudius und der Sturm und Drang;* and Freund, "Matthias Claudius: Eine Untersuchung."

[45] See Schröder, *Matthias Claudius und die Religionsgeschichte,* and Jörg-Ulrich Fechner, "Literatur als praktische Ethik: Das Beispiel des *Wandsbecker Bothen* von Matthias Claudius," *Aufklärung und Pietismus im dänischen Gesamtstaat 1770-1820,* ed. Hartmut Lehmann and Dieter Lohmeier (Neumünster: Wachholtz, 1983), 217-30.

[46] See *Matthias Claudius und der Sturm und Drang,* 184. Görisch discusses this notion more recently in "'Der Mensch ist hier nicht zu Hause,'" 119-23.

[47] *Matthias Claudius in kirchengeschichtlicher Beleuchtung,* 117-41.

[48] Stolpe formulates a major principle of Claudius's religious thought in the words, "The highest he (man) can experience on earth is total rebirth in the spirit"; Albert Stolpe, "Das Christsein des Wandsbecker Boten," *Schleswig-Holstein* (Sept. 1990): 17. He then cites a passage from the poet's review of *Bekehrungsgeschichte des . . . Joh. Friedrich Struensee* [Story of the Conversion of . . . Joh. Friedrich Struensee], where Claudius describes the phenomenon of rebirth as "jene merkwürdige katholische transzendentale Veränderung, wo der ganze Zirkel unwiederbringlich zerrissen wird und alle Gesetze der Psychologie eitel und leer werden, wo der Rock von Fellen ausgezogen wenigstens umgewandt

wird und es dem Menschen wie Schuppen von den Augen fällt . . ." (55) [that remarkable, catholic, transcendental change in which the whole circle is irreparably torn and all laws of psychology become vain and empty, in which the coat of skins is taken off or at least turned inside out and it is as if blinders fall from the person's eyes . . .]. See Wolfgang Freund for a discussion of the role of human will in Claudius's view of *Herstellung* [restoration], which reveals a subjective tendency reminiscent of mysticism; "Matthias Claudius: Eine Untersuchung," 57-58.

[49] Frühwald writes, "Skepticism and mysticism, the two complements of a modernity that is skeptical toward language, are already found in the work of the Wandsbeck Courier. However, the skepticism, which occasionally bursts out in despair, outweighs the mystical experience of the world—even in the sense of an experiential knowledge of God—by far"; Wolfgang Frühwald, "Der Sonne und des Mondes Philosoph," 24. Further along, to be sure, he stresses the role of mystical union in Claudius's faith (27).

[50] For purposes of balance, one should note the following comment by Görisch: "Despite that reinterpretation of eschatological conceptions the hope for eternity in an authentically futuristic sense naturally remains an intrinsic component of Christian faith for Claudius"; "'Der Mensch ist hier nicht zu Hause,'" 123. However, Claudius's use of metaphors such as *das gelobte Land* [the Promised Land] and *das Land des Friedes und der Glückseligkeit* [the land of peace and bliss] for the kingdom of God has less to do with any "inward relation" (123)—many pertinent passages in Claudius's work can be read both immanently and futuristically—than with the ineffability of such a concept, as discussed in this chapter and especially in the next.

[51] See Kurt Dietrich Schmidt, *Grundriß der Kirchengeschichte,* 5th ed. (Göttingen: Vandenhoeck & Ruprecht, 1967), 239-43.

[52] For additional comments related to the Bible and faith see the review of Jacob Jochims's *Anleitung über die Religion vernünftig zu denken* [Guide to Thinking Rationally about Religion], "Eine asiatische Vorlesung" [A Lecture on Asia], "Einfältiger Hausvater-Bericht" [Simple, Fatherly Account], and "Geburt und Wiedergeburt" [Birth and Rebirth]; *Sämtliche Werke,* 812; 515; 584 and 589-90; and 662-65.

[53] See my *Matthias Claudius* (1983), 26-30.

[54] Also see "Postskript an Andres" [Postscript to Andres], 572. Wolfgang Freund writes, "Using precisely Newton and Bacon as examples, Claudius demonstrates that for him reason, as the capacity for plumbing the mysteries of the world, can ideally stand in a complementary relationship to experience as the means of awaking to the mystery of religion"; "Matthias Claudius: Eine Untersuchung," 28. Freund also discusses the relationship between reason and experience in religious-theological matters (29-34).

[55] For a brief overview of Herder's philosophy of language see James W. Marchand, "Herder: Precursor of Humboldt, Whorf, and Modern Language Philosophy," *Johann Gottfried Herder: Innovator Through the Ages,* ed. Wulf Koepke and Samson B. Knoll, Modern German Studies, 10 (Bonn: Bouvier Verlag Herbert Grundmann, 1982), 20-34.

[56] See Michael M. Morton, "Herder and the Possibility of Literature: Rationalism and Poetry in Eighteenth-Century Germany," *Johann Gottfried Herder: Innovator Through the Ages,* 48.

[57] See Wulf Koepke, "Truth and Revelation: On Herder's Theological Writings," *Johann Gottfried Herder: Innovator Through the Ages,* 139.

[58] Ulrich Gaier, *Herders Sprachphilosophie und Erkenntniskritik,* Problemata, 118 (Stuttgart-Bad Cannstatt: Frommann-Holzboog, 1988), 209.

[59] See Marchand, "Herder," 28.

[60] With regard to Humboldt see Roger Langhorn Brown, *Wilhelm von Humboldt's Conception of Linguistic Relativity,* Janua Linguarum: Series Minor, 65 (The Hague: Mouton, 1967). The early Romantic concept of sign and metaphor is treated by Winfried Menninghaus, "Die frühromantische Theorie von Zeichen und Metapher," *The German Quarterly* 62 (1989): 48-58.

[61] See my "Eichendorff's Critical View of Matthias Claudius in *Der deutsche Roman des 18. Jahrhunderts,*" *Michigan Germanic Studies* 11 (1985): 50-61.

[62] See, for example, Görisch, *Matthias Claudius und der Sturm und Drang,* 296.

[63] Ibid., 294-96. Also see Johannes Herzog, *Claudius und Hamann: Ihr Kampf gegen den Rationalismus und ihr Vermächtnis an unsere Gegenwart* (Leipzig and Hamburg: Schloeßmann, 1940), 10. Herzog is far less useful and comparative than one would expect, given the title of his book.

[64] See, for example, Sven-Aage Jørgensen, *Johann Georg Hamann,* Sammlung Metzler, M 143 (Stuttgart: Metzler, 1976), 71 and 42.

[65] See Peter Meinhold, "Hamanns Theologie der Sprache," *Acta des Internationalen Hamann-Collo-*

quiums in Lüneburg 1976, ed. Bernhard Gajek (Frankfurt am Main: Vittorio Klostermann, 1979), 59.

[66] Erich Ruprecht, "Die Frage nach dem Ursprung der Sprache: Eine Untersuchung zu J. G. Hamanns Wirkung auf die deutsche Romantik," *Acta des Internationalen Hamann-Colloquiums in Lüneburg 1976*, 311.

[67] Luanne Frank, "Herder and the Maturation of Hamann's Metacritical Thought: A Chapter in the Pre-History of the *Metakritik*," *Johann Gottfried Herder: Innovator Through the Ages*, 178, 180.

[68] See, for example, Görisch, *Matthias Claudius und der Sturm und Drang*, 255.

[69] For a general overview of Claudius's poetics see my *Matthias Claudius* (1983), 48-55. Chapter 5 of the present volume treats the problematic relationship between Claudius and C. M. Wieland, whom Claudius considered guilty of aesthetic immoralism. His attack on the Weimar classicists took the form of the "Rezension der Xenien von Goethe und Schiller" [Review of the Xenia of Goethe and Schiller] in 1796 and "Einige andere Kleinigkeiten" [Some Other Trifles] in 1797; *Sämtliche Werke*, 943 and 938, respectively.

[70] *Johann Georg Hamanns Philologie*, 190.

[71] Ibid., 213. It is worth noting here that Büchsel refers to Hoffmann's book as epoch-making; Elfriede Büchsel, "Geschärfte Aufmerksamkeit: Hamann-Literatur seit 1972," *Deutsche Vierteljahrsschrift* 60 (1986): 381.

[72] Wellbery provides a survey of Enlightenment semiotics in *Lessing's "Laokoön."* Fechner posits a relationship between Claudius and German Enlightenment theology, particularly the neology of Johann Gottlieb Töllner, who speaks of a dichotomy between scripture and the word of God in the Bible; "Literatur als praktische Ethik," 222.

[73] See Wellbery, *Lessing's "Laokoön,"* 77-80.

[74] Ibid., 42.

[75] See Herbert Wolf, *Martin Luther: Eine Einführung in germanistische Luther-Studien*, Sammlung Metzler, M 193 (Stuttgart: Metzler, 1980), 22, 21.

[76] See Karl Otto Apel, *Die Idee der Sprache in der Tradition des Humanismus von Dante bis Vico*, Archiv für Begriffsgeschichte, 6 (Bonn: Bouvier, 1963), 267.

[77] *Martin Luther*, 21. Also see Friedhelm Debus, "'ein ittliche sprag hatt ir eigen art'": Zur Sprachauffassung Martin Luthers," *Sandbjerg 85: Dem Andenken von Heinrich Bach gewidmet*, ed. by Debus and Ernst Dittmer (Neumünster: Wachholtz, 1986), 213-16.

[78] See Wolf, *Martin Luther*, 22.

[79] See Apel, *Die Idee der Sprache*, 256, and Meinhold, *Luthers Sprachphilosophie* (Berlin: Lutherisches Verlagshaus, 1958), 15.

[80] Wolf, *Martin Luther*, 22.

[81] *Grundriß der Kirchengeschichte*, 115.

[82] Schmidt elaborates on St. Augustine's view of sin, ibid., 115-18, while Meinhold discusses his concept of signification, *Luthers Sprachphilosophie*, 53-55.

[83] With regard to medieval mysticism and Pietism see Schmidt, *Grundriß der Kirchengeschichte*, 239-43 and 414-31, respectively. Concerning Franck, see Meinhold, *Luthers Sprachphilosophie*, 21-25.

[84] See Stammler, *Matthias Claudius*, 3.

[85] Ludwig Wittgenstein, *Tractatus logico-philosophicus* (London: Routledge and Kegan Paul, 1961), 150.

[86] See Marchand, "Herder," 28.

FURTHER READING

Rowland, Herbert. "Matthias Claudius and C. M. Wieland." In *Christoph Martin Wieland: North American Scholarly Contributions on the Occasion of the 250th Anniversary of His Birth*, edited by Hansjörg Schelle, pp. 181-94. Tübingen: Max Niemeyer, 1984.

Surveys the views shared by Claudius and C. M. Wieland, specifically by examining their reviews of each other's works and their correspondence.

————. "Eichendorff's Critical View of Matthias Claudius in *Der Deutsche Roman des Achtzehnten Jahrhunderts*." *Michigan Germanic Studies* XI, No. 1 (Spring 1985): 50-61.

Examines Joseph von Eichendorff's treatment of Claudius in his later criticism in an effort to elucidate Eichendorff's own religious views and Claudius's literary influence.

————. "Topical Conservatism and Formal Radicality: The Fables and Verse Narratives of Matthias Claudius." *Lessing Yearbook* XVIII (1986): 151-77.

Claims that Claudius fuses idyllic portrayals of religion and nature with topical discussions of contemporary theology, philosophy, politics, and art.

————. "Matthias Claudius's *Critical Don Quixote*: A Footnote on Cervantes in Eighteenth-Century Germany."

Romance Notes XXIX, No. 1 (Fall 1988): 3-8.
  Examines Claudius's "A Letter on the Notion of Writing a *Critical Don Quixote*" in an effort to illuminate *Don Quixote*'s presence in eighteenth-century Germany and to provide insight into Friedrich Schlegel's conception of the novel.

Additional coverage of Claudius's life and career is contained in the following source published by The Gale Group: *Dictionary of Literary Biography*, Vol. 97.

Timofei Nikolaevich Granovskii

1813-1855

Russian historian.

INTRODUCTION

Granovskii was one of the most renowned and complex intellectuals of 1840s Russia, an era often referred to as the Remarkable Decade, as it encompassed the first flowering of the intelligentsia during the reign of Nicholas I. Granovskii's approach to history as an instrument of enlightenment broadened the scope of the discipline into such arenas as the political and social constitution of Europe. With his liberal humanist stance and keen interest in Western European history and law, Granovskii provided a moderate view of the ideological conflicts of his time, and his influence on Russian and Soviet historians remains unparalleled.

Biographical Information

Granovskii was born on March 9, 1813, in Orël to a wealthy family. His childhood schooling was erratic; he studied with various foreign tutors, becoming fluent in English and French, and read extensively, particularly literature and history. In 1826 Granovskii entered a Moscow boarding school, where he developed an interest in poetry. He was also, even at a young age, intensely attentive to moral character. These attributes, combined with Granovskii's weak health, have led many biographers, including Patricia Reynolds Roosevelt, to represent his early life as imbued with romanticism. After a short period in Moscow, Granovskii spent the remainder of his adolescence at his parents' home, ending his early formal education. His intellectual life was now restricted to a small group of tutors and writers. At the age of eighteen he entered the civil service in St. Petersburg, where he lived with relatives. Already he was distinguished from his colleagues as an intellectual, even though his schooling had been brief, and as a Westernizer for his love of European literature. In 1831-32 he worked at the Ministry of Foreign Affairs as a translator, but by the spring of 1832 decided to enter the recently established University of St. Petersburg. Granovskii's mother—who had cultivated his sense of moral virtue and his religious faith—had recently died, and Granovskii suffered his first major episode of depression, which would continue to plague him throughout his life. His family's wealth considerably dissipated by his father's gambling and spending habits, Granovskii was forced to live in some poverty through his university years. In September of 1832 he entered the Faculty of Law, where he encountered rigid and repetitive teaching and instead derived intellectual stimulation outside of the classroom, in his own reading and discussion with other students. Around this time he began to read not only romantic literature but also history, especially Augustin Thierry, the French romantic historian. Gradually Granovskii joined the circle of the intelligentsia in St. Petersburg, where he met Yanuarii M. Neverov, Mikhail Bakunin, Vissarion Grigoryevich Belinski, and Nikolai Stankevich. In 1836 Granovskii was sent to Germany for graduate study at state expense. His three years abroad amplified his affinity for Western culture and enhanced his intellectual foundation in history; he studied with Leopold von Ranke and Friedrich von Savigny, among others. His study in Berlin also provided him with a "cosmopolitan veneer," in Roosevelt's words, that considerably aided his professorial success. Upon his return, Granovskii embarked on a career as a professor of history at Moscow University, the most prestigious of Russian institutions, where he increasingly used historical scholarship as "a medium for the enlightenment of Russia," according to Derek Offord. His early interest in literature and poetry remained strong, and he was particularly interested in history as a form of art. His enthusiasm and command of the language contributed to his growing popularity as a lecturer, and in 1843-44 he delivered a series of public lectures that were attended by a wide spectrum of Muscovites and became the most famous of Granovskii's contributions to the development of the intelligentsia and public discussion of political and philosophical issues. In 1841 he married Elizaveta Bogdanovna Mülhausen, a young Russian who embodied Granovskii's conservative social ideal: religious and devoted, she also fulfilled Granovskii's need for a morally virtuous confidant. Political problems within the university and ill health dampened Granovskii's success, and his own views on the Slavophile-Westernizer controversy, the role of state authority, and spirituality cost him some of his closest intellectual ties. In the early 1850s he despaired of the decline of the intellectual life that had flourished in Russia during the previous decade. In October, 1855 he died, succumbing to a weakness in his chest that dated from childhood and had been aggravated during his time in Berlin.

Major Works

Granovskii's most extended work is in the form of lectures, which survive primarily in the form of students' notes. In these lectures, he treated history not only as a retelling of the past, but also as lessons for enlightenment. This approach to history was therefore intimately entangled with the moral, political, and social issues of the day; Granovskii's views came to be regarded as dangerous to the authoritarian government of tsarist Russia, although he was never officially reprimanded. He was particularly interested in individuals in history, including Peter I and Charlemagne, which reflects both his early romantic/militaristic ideals and his study of Georg Wilhelm Hegel. Granovskii is commonly characterized as a Westernizer, but his views were moderate in comparison to those Westernizers who opposed themselves to the emergent Slavophile movement. Suspicious of fanaticism of any variety, Granovskii negotiated a middle ground between these two extremes: although he was firmly convinced of the need for individual freedom, he also believed that the tsarist state could support rather than hinder the fulfillment of this ideal. His lectures demonstrate a pronounced humanism, which denounced the injustice of despotism and rigid class lines, but he opposed radical political activism and social reform. He also emphasized the need for education, including the study of Western literature and history. Granovskii's rejection of the Slavophile position derived from his impatience with the glorified image of Russia's past; however, he remained convinced of the importance of Christianity for its mitigation of state authority with moral standards. He was passionately interested in nobility of character and brought this interest to bear not only on his scholarship, but in his relationships with students and other members of the intelligentsia. Late in his life he began to work on a textbook of history—he had for many years criticized the available textbooks at the university—that would model a "scientific" approach, a study that would "extract eternal laws from known, already completed phenomena," in his own words from an 1850 proposal for the textbook. The textbook remained incomplete—only the introduction, the chapter on Chinese history, and drafts of chapters on ancient history had been written by the time of Granovskii's death. Granovskii's letters reflect the quality of his personal relationships with leading Russian intellectuals of the day as well as his more intimate correspondence with family members. These documents display his command of political and philosophical ideas, his adeptness with language, and his increasing discouragement with the political and intellectual climate in Russia. His moderation, as well as his ability to apply Western philosophy of history to Russian society and politics, are also strongly evident in his work.

Critical Reception

During his lifetime Granovskii was revered as a lecturer by his students and remained in the thick of intellectual discussions in Moscow. His moderate views distanced him from Slavophiles, such as Kireyevsky, and ardent Westernizers, such as Aleksandr Herzen and Belinski; as the university came under scrutiny from the monarchy, Granovskii's liberalism eroded his popularity. Since his death, his political position and scholarship have been variously characterized by Russian, Soviet, and Western historians. Yet he is perhaps most commonly considered to embody the ideal of the noble intellectual, morally serious and politically engaged. Many scholars consider him to manifest the sometimes contradictory aspects of the intelligentsia of the 1840s, a period of transition for Russia particularly and a time of great political upheaval in Europe generally. Fedor Dostoevsky, himself leaning toward conservative Slavophilism, explicitly used Granovskii as a model for his character Verkhovensky, a rationalist liberal and Westerner, in *The Possessed* (1872). This critical portrait, skeptical of the seeming nobility of the intellectual, has influenced subsequent interpretations of Granovskii. Roosevelt has claimed that Granovskii's legacy lies in his ability to bring history to bear on present debates and in his liberal philosophy of history, not easily categorized under any major methodology. A major figure of the Remarkable Decade, Granovskii has become, as Martin Katz has argued, "an intellectual hero of radicals and liberals alike," and a seminal scholar in Russian historiography.

PRINCIPAL WORKS

"Granovskii Timofei Nikolaevich (Aftobiografia)" (autobiography) 1855
Sochineniia [*Works*] 2 vols. (history) 1897
T. N. Granovskii i ego perepiska [*T. N. Granovskii and His Correspondence*] 2 vols. (letters) (edited by A. V. Stankevich) 1897
Polnoe Sobranie sochinenii [*Complete Collection of Literary Work*] 2 vols. (essays, lectures) (edited by N. F. Mertts) 1905

CRITICISM

Leonard Schapiro (essay date 1967)

SOURCE: "Granovsky Between East and West," in *Rationalism and Nationalism in Russian Nineteenth-Century Political Thought*, Yale University Press, 1967, pp. 59-84.

[*In the essay that follows, Schapiro traces the conflict between Slavophiles and Westernizers in Moscow intellectual circles of the 1840s, and the path Granovskii threaded between these two extreme positions in his philosophy of history.*]

In one of the most fascinating of the many intellectual autobiographies in which the Russian nineteenth century is so rich, P. V. Annenkov has left us a portrait of what he called the "Remarkable Decade." This decade, from the end of the thirties until the period of reaction which set in after 1849, produced a short intellectual awakening after the deathly silence which followed the executions and condemnations of the Decembrists. During this decade the seeds of much of later political speculation were sown. The issue that dominated this time of intellectual ferment in the discussion circles of Moscow and Petersburg was the question of Russia and the West, which had been raised so dramatically by the publication in 1836 of Chaadaev's "First Philosophical Letter." It was a decade of high emotional pitch and of intellectual extremism, which ended with the separation of the intellectuals into the (much-publicized, and much-exaggerated) division into Slavophiles and Westerners—or broadly the Moscow and the Petersburg groups.

It was not surprising that Russian intellectual life should have been characterized by this uncompromising extremism. The world of the intellectuals was small and inbred, drawn mostly from the same social class, the nobility, with few outlets for mental energy other than the private circles where talk was furious, passionate, and interminable. The age of the periodicals and the universities, of the influx of men from a new social class to swell the ranks of the intellectuals, was only beginning as the Remarkable Decade drew to its close. Moreover, the alienation of the intellectual from the state, which had already become apparent by the end of the eighteenth century, and which in one sense had contributed to the Decembrists' desperate action, became even more intense and marked after the failure of the revolt and after the revenge which the Emperor exacted on those who took part in it. Henceforward the number of those who could overcome this alienation, in the sense of not allowing themselves to be drawn to one extreme or another, was to be very small indeed. One of this small number was Granovsky with whom we shall be concerned in this chapter.

The ideological pabulum on which the participants of the discussion circles were nurtured was all of Western importation. In the thirties it was the Germans, and especially Hegel. In the forties the stockpot was enriched by the addition of the French Utopians, as Marx and Engels, the great high priests of Utopia, so quaintly named the French socialist thinkers. In the numerous groups and societies of France the socialism of Fourier and Considérant was in the course of the thirties replacing the elitism of Saint-Simon and his disciples, and its repercussions were soon to be felt in the first revolutionary group to appear in Russia after 1825, that of Butashevich-Petrashevsky.

In the thirties the intellectual stage was completely dominated by N. Stankevich. Stankevich was essentially non-political, and above all a philosophical rationalist—the last of the Alexandrine rationalists, perhaps. "Reason and the Spirit reign in this world," he is quoted as saying on one occasion; "this consoles me for everything." He was outspokenly critical of nationalism in every form, and a lover of the universal, and few, if any, in his circle would have disagreed with him at that date—it would all be very different in the forties. Writing in 1837 he has this to say about *Volkstum,* or *narodnost,* that elusive term for which English has no equivalent: "Why are people busying themselves with *narodnost?* One must strive toward the all-human, one's own will then get its due without special effort . . . To invent or think up a character for a nation out of its old customs, its ancient activities, is to wish to prolong for it the period of its childhood." Gershenzon, one of the most sensitive and learned historians of Russia's intellectual path, says that even Konstantin Aksakov, the most extreme of the Slavophiles in the forties, would have subscribed to these words of Stankevich in 1837.[1] Annenkov, indeed, goes so far as to say that there was no such being as a *Russian* intellectual in 1840—he was either French or German in tendency, or at all events European.[2] It was not to be expected that this denial of national identity would remain unchallenged.

Stankevich's discussion circle in the thirties in Moscow included both Belinsky and Granovsky. The other main Moscow circle was that headed by Herzen and Ogarev. All these could properly be described as "Westerners" in outlook, though the term "Westerner" was not yet current and did not become current until the "Slavophile" challenge made its appearance. The pattern of the circles had changed by 1840, and the change in itself indicates the developments in thought that were imminent. Stankevich, who had left Russia for Germany and Italy on grounds of health in 1837, was dead; Belinsky had left Moscow in the autumn of 1839, to join the editorial board of what was soon to become the leading liberal—or as we should now say, left-wing progressive—journal. Granovsky was now a member of the circle headed by Herzen and Ogarev; but a new circle already existed in Moscow as well as that of Herzen, and it was from this new circle that the Slavophiles were soon to emerge, passionate in their defense of that very *narodnost* which Stankevich had dismissed as irrelevant.

There were perhaps three reasons which explained the birth of nationalist feeling among the intellectuals. First, there was the effect of several shocks to national pride and self-respect—among them Chaadaev's "First Philosophical Letter" in 1836, and the publication in 1843 of de Custine's *Russie en 1839* were perhaps the most severe. Second was an increasing interest in the study of Russia's past, to which the Decembrists, for all their rationalist predilections, had already given so substantial an impetus, as had also Karamzin. But the Decembrists looked to history to support a case which they drew from rational analysis; the Slavophile faith was directly acquired in the course of study of history.

But perhaps the most powerful cause of the division in intellectual life in the forties was a reaction against both Belinsky and the official doctrine which Belinsky set out to oppose. The "doctrine," as it is called, would be better described as lines of officially sponsored and subsidized propaganda. These were aimed at the defense and justification of the autocratic system against what the authorities believed were the foreign, subversive, and atheistic, or at all events non-Orthodox, ideas which had culminated in the Decembrist rising; and which, if not kept in check, would threaten to become active again. While in its crude form, as financed by the government on the pages of the "Northern Bee" (published in St. Petersburg as a newspaper after 1831), this propaganda was of a very low intellectual content, the general nationalist, religious, and anti-revolutionary message could quite properly appeal to all conservative patriots who feared change as a threat to the national Russian heritage. As for Karamzin a generation earlier, for the conservative patriot this heritage primarily meant autocracy of the Russian type. Unless we ourselves wish to become the victims of propaganda, there is every reason, in our pursuit of Russian intellectual history, to distinguish between such sincere and relatively independent-minded scholars and publicists as Shevyrev and Pogodin, on the one hand, and government hacks like Grech or Bulgarin on the other—even though all of them supported certain basic views on the Russian state. Central to these was reverence for the autocratic power, as it emerged after the reforms of Peter I. This was conceived of as the only possible system for Russia, which required no reform. The true needs of the people were safeguarded by the Emperor's responsibility to God. The function of the nobility was to find their true mission in service to the State. The people were linked by love and trust, through the bonds of orthodoxy and nationality, to the Emperor, and the peace and harmony which this produced in the state could only be disturbed by alien influences and by dangerous and wicked ideas imported from outside.

The influence of V. G. Belinsky (1811-48) was at its height between 1839 and 1846, when he was writing for the *Annals of the Fatherland.* Through the medium of his long literary articles he propagated a passionate, Western-oriented, radical progressiveness. Verbose and diffuse, and now, at all events, largely unreadable, he made an enormous impact on the intellectuals of his day through the dissemination of all the advanced ideas of his time, within the limits of literary criticism; and with the aid of what has since

become the traditional Russian aesopian language which was intended to, and often did (and does) fool the censors, but was clear to his readers. Belinsky represented not so much a system of ideas as an attitude, a rallying point for those whose liberal temperament and repugnance to official hypocrisy cried out for a language they could accept. It was perhaps not so much that his readers agreed with what he said as that he reinforced them in their sense of alienation from the official state regime, and relieved them of the sense of accepting even tacitly the views expressed by a Grech or a Bulgarin. Perhaps the most typical illustration of this was the enormous success of his attack on Gogol in 1847 in the form of an open letter. Gogol had been accepted by the intellectuals as an ally, because *Dead Souls* had been interpreted, no doubt erroneously, as an attack on life in Russia under Nicholas I. When Gogol's published *Correspondence* revealed an essentially mystical, religious, and patriarchal attitude to Russian society, Belinsky, who in 1842 had welcomed *Dead Souls* as the Russian *Iliad,* now denounced the author as the "Champion of the knout, apostle of ignorance . . . and obscurantism"—to the universal approbation of the entire liberal intelligentsia. But by this date another group had grown up among the intellectuals, in part at any rate as a reaction against the violence of Belinsky, the Slavophile group. Repelled by the rationalism of the "Westerners," the Slavophiles, though deeply nationalist, were equally repelled by much, or most, of the official doctrine.

It is of some importance to note that it was not until the early forties that the Slavophile point of view emerged into the open. Most competent contemporary observers are agreed that until the early years of that decade there was in general little disagreement on basic issues between a future Slavophile and a future Westerner. Of course, political ideas are not formed all at once overnight, and are in any case in large measure the reflection of temperament. Hence it is not surprising to find that many of the leading Slavophiles, as they were later to be known, were defending in the privacy of discussion views which were eventually to set them worlds apart from their friends. We observed in the last chapter how Khomiakov drew fire from Pushkin in 1833 for what were regarded as his eccentric nationalist views, and another contemporary records how, in the same year, Khomiakov found himself in a minority of one when defending the need for an indigenously national (*samobytnoe*) development for every people. Rationalism was rejected in favor of faith by Ivan Kireevsky as well as by Khomiakov by 1838, at any rate; and Kireevsky was emphasizing the importance of the peasant commune, which was to play such a vital role in the political doctrine of the Slavophiles, in 1839.[3] Nevertheless, it required the impetus of Belinsky's vigorous onslaughts to cause the Slavophiles to formulate their doctrines openly and as a group. It is this fact, the fact that they emerged as a movement of defense, which may explain some of the extremism and exaggeration of their position.

The center of the Slavophiles was Moscow, where they had their circle and a platform in the shape of a journal, *Moskvitianin,* which was to become essentially the vehicle for their views. It was on the pages of *Moskvitianin* that there appeared in 1845 what was probably the earliest complete exposition of Slavophile doctrine, by Ivan Kireevsky. This was primarily an explanation of the reasons why Russia, in the main because of the fact that her historical development was different from that of Catholic Western Europe, was able to preserve *within the people* the orthodox way of thought. This way of thought, says Kireevsky, "did not become bemused by the one-sidedness of syllogistic constructions [*scilicet* which are characteristic of the Western Catholic form of thought] but constantly adhered to that fullness and wholeness of outlook which constitutes the distinctive feature of Christian philosophy." By Christian, in this context, Kireevsky apparently meant Orthodox Christianity, or perhaps Christianity before the division took place between the East and the West. Thus his theme was primarily related to his views of the history of religion. But in expounding what he believed to be the distinctively orthodox Christian way of thought for the purpose of proving his thesis, Kireevsky at the same time had to expound, if only in rudimentary form, many of the ideas on the political order which were to become central before long to the Slavophile philosophy—the cult of unanimity, as against majority decision, for example, or the elevation of society above the state.

The Slavophile political philosophy can be fairly reduced to three main elements, though needless to say the individuals to whom the term Slavophile was applied did not all think alike or accept the same basic ideas as true. But it is probably true to say that all of them would have accepted the following three propositions.

First was a belief in the primary importance and virtue of what they called *samobytnost,* the word which has no equivalent in English. It means literally something like "one's own way of being," and is used to describe the indigenous way of life, being oneself without imitating others, the traditional and national way of living as opposed both to some invented or devised way of life, and to some imitated, imported, or foreign, non-national way of life. The great lexicographer Dal' says of this word that "strictly speaking" it can be applied only to God, and he is presumably right insofar as no man can live uninfluenced by other men outside his own immediate patch of home territory at some period of his history. Indeed, as used

by the Slavophiles, the word is more of a protest word than a strictly defined political concept.

Secondly, all Slavophiles believed that only in the orthodox Church and its faith, in which all of them without exception devoutly lived, could there be a "completely sincere sense of brotherhood." These words are taken from a "Message to the Serbians," dated 1860, which, although written by Khomiakov, was subscribed to by ten others, including the brothers Ivan and Konstantin Aksakov, and can therefore be regarded as a kind of highest common factor of Slavophile doctrine. The passage from which the above words are taken continues: "Not without reason are the commune, the sacredness of the *mir* judgment and the unconditional subordination of everyone to the unanimous decisions of his brothers preserved only in the orthodox lands." This emphasis on the unanimity of the decision of the *mir* (the peasant meeting which is part of the administration of the commune) reflects a very important element in Slavophile thought—the rejection of counting of votes as a method of arriving at decisions. The unanimity of the *mir* was often contrasted by them with the dissensions that rend Western political assemblies, which are not imbued with the spirit of orthodox Christianity. To continue with the "Message to the Serbians":

> From the Germans came to the Slavs the custom of counting votes, as if wisdom and truth always belonged to the greater number of votes, when actually a majority very often depends on chance . . . If it is not possible to arrive at a unanimous decision, it is better to pass over the matter to the decision of one man favored by the whole meeting. The conscience and intelligence of a man honored by common confidence is more hopeful [*scilicet* of arriving at a sensible result] than the game of counting votes.

Thirdly, the Slavophiles rejected Peter I and all his works as foreign importation, alien to the spirit and traditions of Russia. "The whole Russian land was changed," says the "Message to the Serbians" (by Peter I) "into a ship in which only German words of command were to be heard." This rejection of Peter is of vital importance as an element of Slavophile political thought both because it determined the whole of their theory of autocracy, and because it formed a certain touchstone for distinguishing the true Slavophile from the ordinary conservative, like Shevyrev. At the center of the Slavophile view of true autocracy lay the belief that it consisted of rule by the monarch in complete harmony with the wishes, traditions, and interests of the people, not of imposition by the autocrat of his will *upon* the people. It is necessary to examine this more closely, because all their doctrine on the nature of government, law, and freedom flowed from this belief.

Thus, it is plain that the autocracy in which they believed was very far from identical with the autocracy which actually existed in the Russia of their day. In fact the Slavophiles abhorred the post-Petrine form of autocratic government, with its elaborate (as they saw it) bureaucratic machine and its emphasis on a system of service to the state leading to rewards, in contrast, as they saw it, to the more personal and patriarchal relations of the nobles to the Tsar of Muscovite Russia. They applied to the modern form of state the term "absolutism," which they used as a term of opprobrium; the pre-Petrine system was praised by them as "autocracy." "Absolutism" for them was an evil system of foreign, European origin, and quite alien to the traditional Russian form of rule. In this new, evil form, as they saw it, the Tsar is hedged around and fenced in by a wall of bureaucracy, which grows like a cancer and increasingly divides him off from the people. According to some Slavophiles, at any rate, the state under "absolutism" becomes a police state, in which everything is subsumed in obedience to the Emperor's command. "The motto of the bureaucracy," wrote one of the Slavophiles, "is not *divide et impera, but impera quia divisi sunt.*" Neither faith nor conscience nor patriotism can exist in such a society as individual emotions, as individual experiences—I think what they meant by this was that if you are told all the time what to do and what not to do, what to praise and what to condemn, then you lose all genuine sense of individual judgment and responsibility as a citizen.

Their ideal state was based on their somewhat romanticized picture of pre-Petrine Russia. As they saw it, the Tsar received the surrender of all political power from the people once and for all, who then faded from the scene, except occasionally to make their collective view known in a gathering of the Russian land, the *Zemsky sobor.* The people have no interest in government, which is in any case an evil thing in itself. The notion that government was the consequence of man's sinful nature and the fall is of course common in medieval political thought, and central, for example, to the view of Saint Augustine. The Slavophiles also regarded the actual act of governing as a sin, and (again, like Saint Augustine) looked upon the assumption by the Tsar of the powers of autocrat as a self-sacrificial act, which warded the sin off from his people. The reason why political rights are unnecessary for the people is that the faith and the moral aims and the interests of Tsar and people are identical: they are all united by their common Christian orthodoxy and by their shared traditions. According to Konstantin Aksakov, who was eccentric even among the Slavophiles, political rights are not only unnecessary so far as the people is concerned, but positively harmful:

> every striving of the people after state power deflects it from its inner moral path, and, by means of political external freedom, undermines the freedom of the inner spirit. To exercise political

power becomes, as it were, an aim for the people, and the highest aim disappears—inner truth, inner freedom, the spiritual act of life. If the people is sovereign, if the people is the government, then there is no people.

The attitude of the Slavophiles to law was perhaps the most distinctive part of their doctrine. In the main they denied the scientific nature of law, and rejected law in favor of custom as a formal framework for social obligation. For custom they had, as one would expect, a deep veneration. They did not believe that it was or should be immutable, but that it should change slowly and naturally in accord with the wishes and habits of the people. "The inner sense of the people alone," says the "Message to the Serbians," "serves as a gauge of the legality and necessity of the gradual changes." Khomiakov, in particular, praised England for what he regarded as the ability of its people to build anew, while yet preserving the best of what had grown up over the ages. "Yes, in England they know how to respect the work of time. Today's invention does not berate what has been created by long centuries. The English know how to build, but what is built must respect what is grown up." For Khomiakov law is a meaningless abstraction until incarnated in custom. There can be no such thing as an independent science of law: there can only be law based on this or that philosophy, or this or that religion, because the whole idea of legal obligation must be founded on the general belief which an individual holds on eternal truth, whether his ideas be religious or philosophical. Therefore all legislation is formal, abstract, impersonal rationalism as contrasted with custom, which is ever alive and ever creative.

> Custom [says Khomiakov] is law. But it is distinguished from law by the fact that law is something eternal, something which has accidentally become mixed up with life, while custom is an inner force which penetrates the whole life of a people, and enters into the conscience and thoughts of all its members. The aim of every law . . . is to be transformed into custom, to enter the flesh and blood of the people, and to have no need for written documents.

It was consistent with these views of the Slavophiles that they should have rejected outright any form of constitution, and indeed any form of legal limitation of the plenitude of the monarch's power. There can be no legal limits over what the people has offered up to the Tsar, over that of which it has divested itself. There can be no room for legal guarantees where the unity of Tsar and people is based on love and trust, on custom, and on identity of faith and of moral aims. Konstantin Aksakov boldly faced the obvious objection to this view, namely, that however desirable it may be as an ideal, the political order in practice has to provide for all contingencies. If, he says, government in Russia rests upon mutual faith and trust between Tsar and people, as the Slavophiles assert, then it will be objected that "either the people or the state power[4] will prove false to the other," and that therefore there is need for some kind of guarantee. Aksakov rejects this argument: "There is no need for any guarantee! Every guarantee is evil. Where it exists there can be no virtue. It were better that life in which there is no virtue should collapse than that it should be shored up with the aid of evil."

And lastly, let us consider the Slavophile attitude to individual freedom. Whatever may have been their views on the nature of legal guarantees, there can be no doubt of their complete commitment to the freedom of the individual in his thought, his speech, and his conduct. They were tireless advocates of the emancipation of the serfs, and one of their number, Yuriy Samarin, played an important part in its practical achievement. They were bitter critics of all forms of legal inefficiency and corruption. They advocated freedom of the press and freedom of speech, drawing upon themselves the ire of the authorities in the process. This freedom of expression was for them a very essential part of their faith: without it, how could the Tsar know the thoughts and opinions of his people, and achieve that unity of moral purpose and harmony of aims with them which was the Slavophile ideal? Indeed it was precisely because they feared that this moral unity and harmony of aims would be imperiled by them that they rejected Western notions of the legal and constitutional protection of individual civil rights. To quote from a Memoir addressed by K. Aksakov to the Emperor in 1855, they believed that the political order should leave to the government "the unrestricted freedom of governing, for that is its exclusive concern." But the people, under the protection of the government, should have "complete freedom both in their external life and in their inner life. That is the Russian form of social order."[5]

It should be apparent by now that there was a world of difference between the view of the Slavophiles and the tenets of the official doctrine of autocracy, orthodoxy, and nationality. It is important to emphasize this because their political opponents found it a very convenient polemical device to try to identify the views of the Slavophiles with those of the government-sponsored propagandists. Historians have on occasion also failed to see the distinction between the two political outlooks, though without the justification of the exigencies of party polemics. In the first place, the Slavophiles rejected the post-Petrine state, and with it, for good or ill, the whole process of modernization upon which Russia had been launched by Peter. For them this had been a wrong move, a foreign, un-Russian incident, which had turned Russia away from her traditional patriarchal form of autocracy, to which they believed she should return.

Even more important perhaps was the fact that for the Slavophiles the source of all authority was the people, from whom the Tsar derived all his power by their act of surrender. Plainly, the implications of this for the source of the monarch's legitimacy were enormous. If his power did not derive from God alone, as official doctrine maintained, then all kinds of consequences could follow—even if the Slavophiles did not always draw the conclusions from their own doctrine. One of these consequences, which was the one drawn by the exponents of Natural Law (as Kunitsin had done in his lectures at the Tsarskoe Selo Lycée), was that the rights of the ruler were strictly limited by the object for which those rights came into being—the welfare of the ruled. The Slavophiles would not have expressed this thought in the language of rights and contract, but it is not very far off from what they believed. Finally, the Slavophile defense of freedom was completely at variance with the arbitrary despotism of the Russia of Nicholas I. Perhaps the clearest proof of the fact that the Slavophiles were no slavish admirers of nineteenth-century autocracy was the fact that they were subjected by the Russian authorities to the persecution of censorship and repression as often as their radical adversaries.

Of course the Slavophiles were eccentric in their views, and sometimes in their behavior, to the point of absurdity. (It was Chaadaev who said of Konstantin Aksakov that he dressed so much like a Russian of the Muscovite period that he was mistaken for a Persian.) But to see them in perspective it is necessary to remember two facts: first, that their views were formulated in response to rationalist, radical views often as extravagant as their own, and in the course of quite violent polemics against opponents as youthful and as excited as themselves; secondly, that allowance must be made for national pride which had been deeply wounded by attacks on the backwardness of Russia by such critics as Chaadaev and Custine. As Adam Ferguson has remarked, "No nation is so unfortunate as to think itself inferior to the rest of mankind: few are even willing to put up with a claim to equality." To accept the argument that the only way for Russia was the way of Western Europe meant accepting the fact that Russia, as compared with Western European countries, was backward; and that her only hope of progress was to catch up with them as soon as possible, and in the same manner. This view would have been accepted, however reluctantly, by the majority of the Decembrists, to some extent by Pushkin, by Chaadaev, by Granovsky, Boris Chicherin, and Ivan Turgenev, by all the early Marxists, at any rate, and by the majority of the twentieth-century liberals.

But it was obviously much more satisfying to national pride to believe that Russia was different from and indeed morally superior to the countries of Western Europe; and perhaps understandable enough to reject in the process not only those features of Western European civilization which it was right to condemn, but in one sweep those, like liberty under the law, which were worthy of imitation. It was certainly the appeal to national pride inherent in Slavophile doctrine which ensured that, in one form or another, it should never really have died out on the Russian intellectual scene. Indeed, its recognition of the element of national peculiarity and tradition, of *samobytnost*, as an essential ingredient of political order taught a lesson which could only be ignored at the price of disaster. To this theme it will be necessary to return more than once. But we must first consider the thought of some of those who were able to integrate the nationalist element in a different, less extreme form. One such was Granovsky.

T. N. Granovsky (1813-55), perhaps the most brilliant star of the period of the Remarkable Decade, does not readily fall into any category—rationalist or nationalist, Slavophile or Westerner. In a period of polarization and extremism in thought, he stood for synthesis and balance. After Belinsky's move to St. Petersburg in 1839, Granovsky belonged to the circle of Herzen and Ogarev, both at that time rabid Westerners. As Granovsky's correspondence shows, there was a very close personal attachment among the three. Yet by 1846 a breach had opened between Granovsky and his friends. The immediate issue was the atheism and materialism of Herzen and Ogarev, which Granovsky could not accept. But even before then Annenkov had noted a growing estrangement between the three men on another issue, that of revolution and socialism. Herzen was deeply immersed in the new socialist doctrines blowing from France. Granovsky saw danger in what he believed was socialist contempt for political life because of the preeminence which this doctrine attached to social life. "Socialism is very harmful," he said, "because it teaches people to seek the solution of the problems of social life not in the political arena, which it despises, but on the side from it. By this means it undermines both itself and the political arena."[6]

There was, however, another, deeper ground for the growing division among the three friends. Granovsky viewed the prospect of revolutionary upheavals in Europe, which appeared imminent, with apprehension and with deep pessimism as to their outcome. Herzen, on the other hand, like Belinsky, without wishing for revolution, faced the advent of it with confidence and felt no horror at the prospect of the destruction which revolution in Europe would bring in its train. Both Herzen and Belinsky believed that out of the ruins of the old order a new and better order would arise, like a phoenix from the ashes, and would become the crowning achievement of European civilization. Belinsky did not live to see the effects of the revolutions of 1848. Herzen, who witnessed them, emerged

bitterly disappointed and crushed, to seek consolation in the innate and as yet untapped socialism of the Russian peasant which he now discovered. The interest of this clash of temperaments lies in the fact that it was an early instance of the parting of the ways on the issue of revolution which was to characterize Russian political thought thereafter, and especially during the age of reform inaugurated by Alexander II.

However, Granovsky was not primarily concerned with political issues, but with the philosophy of history and with the question of Russia's place in Europe. After studying in Russia and in Germany, he became Professor of History at the University of Moscow in 1839 and exercised a profound influence on the generation of the forties. His public lectures (in 1843-44, 1845, and 1851) were regarded as outstanding intellectual events, the more so as they followed upon a period when the intellectuals had been starved of all stimulus during the dark years of the thirties. Granovsky had a very remarkable and original mind, as is evident even from the very small amount of his writings which has survived—some lectures and notes of lectures, a few reviews, and some correspondence.[7] When he made his debut in Moscow Herzen, then an enthusiastic Westerner, welcomed him as a recruit in the battle with the group of Slavophiles which was then just emerging. But Granovsky was not a man to take sides in the squabbles of intellectual cliques. He was in general endowed with what is supposed to be the Anglo-Saxon veneration for both sides of a question, and little inclined toward the extremism of thought which characterized his generation. This was very evident in the closing words of his first public lecture in 1845, which Herzen recorded in his diary: "Let us devote our studies to the analysis of, to the service of Russia—Russia as she issued from the hands of Peter I. Let us keep ourselves equally clear of the biased slanders of foreigners, and of the senile and decrepit desire to restore ancient *Rus* in all its one-sidedness."

Granovsky's main contribution to the development of the social thought of his period falls under two heads: his criticism of determinism in history; and his assessment of Russia's place in Europe. The belief that the development of human societies is subject to laws which the actions of individuals cannot evade or even alter, was, along with rationalism, a heritage of the eighteenth century. Even Montesquieu would have nothing to do with chance as a factor in history.

> It is not chance which rules the world . . . There are general causes, be they moral or physical, which operate in every monarchy . . . ; all the accidents are subject to these causes; and if it should happen that the chance of a battle should bring about the downfall of a state, there was a general cause which required that this state should perish as the result of a single battle: in a word, the main force draws along with it the individual accidents.[8]

That all-devouring Sphinx, the Spirit of the Age, and the uniformity of political development in which the Alexandrines believed, were a part of this search for universal, ineluctable laws of human society.

Granovsky certainly believed in the individual character of nations, in the influence of their history and environment. He also accepted that "a nation is collective in its nature," and that its collective nature required a great man of a special sensitiveness in order that its collective thought and will be given expression. One can observe a move away from his German influences, particularly that of Savigny, in Granovsky's thought on this question of the importance of *Volkstum* in history. In 1839 he was still arguing that the living force of a people is its "national spirit," which in spite of the great variations in individuals, maintains one "overall direction" and which "appropriates and puts its imprint on all that takes place outside it as lord and master." Eight years later, in the maturity of his thought, these influences were wearing thin, and many passages testify to his increasing stress on individuality. For example it was in 1847 that he criticized Montesquieu for having brought "the idea of the dependence of man on climate to such an extreme point as to sacrifice to this idea the independent activity of the human spirit."

At the same time he believed, with Hegel, in the unity of world history and in the universality of the purpose of mankind. This he saw as the uninterrupted approximation to the highest moral purpose. He believed that there certainly existed observable laws of history. But this only meant for him that the ultimate *aim* is fixed: the *road* toward that aim is not fixed, and divine Providence leaves to each individual, or to each class or nation, the choice of the road. "The life of mankind," he wrote in 1847,

> is subject to the same laws as those to which the whole of natural life is subject, but the law does not fulfil itself in the same way in the two spheres . . . [History] is subject to a law of which the fulfillment is unavoidable, but nothing is laid down about the time for fulfillment—ten years, or ten centuries, it is all one. The law stands as an aim to which mankind is moving ineluctably; but this law is not concerned by what path it moves toward the aim, and how much time it spends on the way. Here it is that the individual personality comes into its full rights.

And again, in 1852: "History has two sides: on one side appears the free creative activity of the human spirit, on the other the conditions for this activity, laid down by nature and independent of this free spirit."

Thus, according to Granovsky, the universality of the aim meant that all individuals, classes, and nations are imbued with one spirit, and the history of mankind is therefore the history of its moral growth. This was very close to the views of Chaadaev, as expressed in his "Second Philosophical Letter" (in the edition of Gershenzon; in fact the Sixth): "We should strive toward the elucidation of the moral meaning of great historical epochs; we should try to define precisely the features of each age in accordance with the laws of practical reason." But for Chaadaev this moral meaning always signified the degree to which that epoch had served the progress of Christianity. Thus he esteemed the age of Islamic dominance above the Homeric age because Islam had at all events propagated basically Christian principles. Granovsky's conception of moral meaning was less closely tied to Christianity.

In no sense, in Granovsky's thought, is the action of the individual determined by laws of history. Such universal, all-embracing laws do not exist and have been invented in order to evade responsibility. It is indeed in the very nature of the laws of history that the sphere of their fulfillment, which is moral progress, lies inside the individual consciousness. This factor also to some extent limits the individual's responsibility, as he explained in his lecture on Louis IX in 1851:

> The great actors in history and the small, who are not visible to the naked eye, are alike bound by the duty to labor in the sweat of their brow. But they bear responsibility only for the purity of their intentions and for their zeal in carrying them into effect, and not for the remote consequences of the labor which they perform. Their actions enter history as mysteriously as a seed falls in the soil. The ripening of the harvest, the time of harvesting and its yield all belong to God.

But the individual cannot be seen apart from his environment in society. In this sense the historical process is the process of the liberation and enlightenment of individual consciousness. The mass, unlike the individual, is both good and savage at different times, but without sense of purpose: its spiritual life is completely determined by the environment—by natural conditions and by the historic past. Only the individual and not the mass can achieve liberation from the power of the historic past. Nevertheless the individual is heavily influenced by the form of the society in which he lives. Hence the purpose of history is the attainment of "a moral and enlightened individual personality, independent of fatalistic categories; and of a society which is appropriate to the demands of such a personality." In this sentence the kernel of Granovsky's thought is summed up.

Granovsky's second main contribution to the development of Russian political thought was on the one question which in the forties was animating all minds—the place of Russia in Europe. Granovsky's position on this issue was crystal clear and very balanced. He ridiculed the Slavophile and ultranationalist attempts to portray Russia as something quite different from and outside the European community, on the basis of historical mythology of their own making. At the same time he had no patience with those Russians who were merely slavish apers of the Western way of life, and whom the foreigner scoffed at for their "irresponsible copying of Western forms." Russia must learn from the rest of Europe: but it is not the externals that matter. Crying for the past was equally ridiculous to Granovsky, especially where the "past" was largely the product of the imagination. He deplored "the senile complaints of those who love not the real, living Russia, but an ancient ghost, summoned by them from the grave; and who dishonor themselves by bowing down before an idol which their own idle imagination has created." There was never any doubt in his mind that the main achievements of Western civilization lay in Western Europe. But Russia is a part of Europe, and a member of the brotherhood, though a younger brother, with both rights and duties in the family. Thus in 1849, while the older European countries were absorbed in their revolutions and had little time for history, he commented: "They have left this task to us, the younger brother in the European family, who is not involved in the strife in which his elders are engaged." Moreover he thought that Russia had a valuable role to play in the study of history precisely because of her position on the fringe of Europe.

> A great and splendid field of activity lies open to us Russians. We stand as observers on the threshold of Europe, removed from this fray. At the same time we are not idle observers: the movements of European life find their echoes in our midst too, and we try to understand them and to extract from this understanding of them instructive lessons. This is the essence of the Russian view of history. But this does not, of course, mean that we approach the history of the West from a petty, exclusively nationalist point of view.

Russia was indeed fortunate, he thought, in being able to receive much of European civilization ready made, with the benefit of the experience of the older countries. But there was no doubt that Russia must ultimately follow the same pattern as the other European countries, if not necessarily in exactly the same way. National traditions and the national spirit will of course have the effect of producing individual variations in the general pattern. But the general pattern exists, and is basically the same for all countries of the same broad type, such as Russia and the rest of the countries of Europe, as distinct from the patriarchal despotisms of the Orient. This view led him to the conclusion, for example, that industrialization would come about in Russia in much the same way as in the Western Euro-

pean countries, and with similar consequences. "Following the paths of development [he wrote in 1847] which have been trodden by all societies in historical times, with the exception of the patriarchal states of the East, it has proved impossible to escape a proletariat."

Granovsky introduced a note of balance and calm into Russian political thought which it had hitherto lacked. It is impossible to assess his influence in any direct sense; and it is true that balance and calm were not to be the most marked characteristics of many of the thinkers who succeeded him. But political thought was never to be the same after Granovsky. He put the issue of Russia's place in the European community into the kind of perspective which satisfied the instinctive "Westerner." But at the same time he recognized the important place in Russian political thought which ought to be assigned to the peculiar, national element and which had been neglected by the rationalist, universalist school of thought. Moreover, by his emphasis on the uniformity of the history of civilized man, and the universality which he saw in the ultimate aims of all history, he laid the foundation for those who would in the future argue that, whatever might be the peculiarities of Russia and the distinctiveness of her development, she must ultimately go the same way as the rest of Europe.

Most important, and probably most directly influential on those who came after him, was Granovsky's emphasis on the importance of the individual, as the bearer of culture and the instrument of progress, and as a responsible actor on the stage of history. He rescued the individual both from historical determinism and from national anonymity. For the individual is liable to be ground between the two great millstones, rationalism and nationalism: the universal laws of the rationalist, for whom the individual becomes an atom driven by ineluctable laws and forces which he cannot control; and the mystical unity of the nationalist, which subjects man to the equally ineluctable laws of blood, or race, or the mortmain of the past. The nineteenth-century Russian thinkers who were to look to the individual as the main force for cultural progress, such as Pisarev, Lavrov, or Mikhailovsky, were in this sense the direct heirs of Granovsky.

If Granovsky may thus be said to have attempted to make some kind of synthesis of the two broad trends or temperaments which are in this study described as the rationalist and the nationalist, his friend and contemporary Alexander Herzen (1812-70) tended to oscillate between the one and the other. During the period of his friendship with Granovsky, Herzen was a fervent Westerner, a socialist on the French model, much influenced first by Saint-Simon and then by Fourier. His diary and writings of the period while he was still living in Russia (he left in 1847) show no particular emphasis on the peculiarities of the Russian predicament. Nor are they concerned with the relevance of Russian traditions to the problem of grafting Western European institutions on her, beyond the sense that Russian backwardness had to be overcome, common to all thinkers of the rationalist type at the time. He was a revolutionary by temperament, at any rate to the extent that he accepted the fact that revolution might become inevitable and was confident that its results could only in the long run prove beneficent—it will be recalled that it was to some extent upon this issue that the parting of the ways between him and Granovsky took place.

But after witnessing the revolutions of 1848, and incidentally describing them with sublime skill, he turned against his former Westernism. In his bitter disappointment with the European revolutions, which, in his view, had in the end merely strengthened the bourgeois order, he now turned with a new hope to Russia, perhaps a Russia of his own imagination, but one in which he now saw new grounds for faith that within her lay the possibility for the regeneration of the world. Russia for Herzen was instinctively socialist, as exemplified by the traditional institution of the peasant commune, to which new attention had recently been drawn by the Prussian observer, Haxthausen. Moreover in Herzen's eyes the simple Russian people was fortunate in being unimpeded by the legal formalism and duplicity which bedeviled the countries of Western Europe; even after over fifteen years' life in England Herzen never succeeded in grasping the role which law performs in society, or the relationship between law and liberty. Russia was for Herzen also blessed by the fact that she was free from the cancer of modern industry, which had made mid-Victorian England so repellent for Herzen (as well it might for anyone not blind to social inequality and injustice). Russia, Herzen believed, would now be able to point the way toward the regeneration of Europe in spite of, indeed in many ways precisely because of, the backwardness in her development. She would give the lead to a new type of socialism, and would thus redress the wrong which had resulted from the revolutions in Western Europe.

There are obviously certain elements in these views of Herzen of the fifties which are reminiscent of the Slavophiles, and especially the inordinate importance attached to the commune. Herzen has indeed occasionally been described as a Slavophile. The short analysis attempted above of Slavophile doctrine should be sufficient to show how erroneous such a view is. In the first place Herzen was all his life an atheist and a materialist, the Slavophiles were above all Orthodox Christians. It makes little sense, in discussing political theorists, to class together those who start from a denial of the moral and philosophical imperatives dictated by the acceptance of a religious faith and those whose views on human conduct and political obligation are based on certain spiritual premises and religious loyalties.

Secondly, in contrast to the Slavophiles, Herzen accepted the Petrine reforms as a positive stage in Russian history. This difference of approach was not merely a disagreement on some point of interpretation of Russian history. It was fundamental to the attitude adopted to the whole civilization of Western Europe. The Slavophiles turned their backs on it; Herzen did not. For him it still remained the fountain of all rational progress, even if Europe had temporarily lost its way. I use the term "rational" advisedly, because Herzen remained a rationalist, for all his infatuation with the commune. He was a revolutionary by temperament, even if not always a consistent or enthusiastic advocate of revolution—a subject to which it will be necessary to return. He hated kings, priests, churches, and religion, and was drawn irresistibly to the new world of organization and science. He was a rationalist as Pestel was a rationalist. And, like Pestel, he drew on national tradition and peculiarity in order the better to promote his rationalist utopia. At best he was a nationalist malgré lui.

As Herzen himself records, it was upon the recollection of his old arguments with the Slavophiles that he drew when the time came for him to assess anew the Westernism which he had once so passionately defended. For all their eccentricity and exaggeration, the Slavophiles touched a chord which was to find an echo thereafter in the breast of the Russian intellectual throughout the century. In its extreme form, as formulated in the forties and fifties, their doctrine was short-lived. But the wider issues they raised, the claims of Russian national peculiarity and the significance of Russian institutions for political progress, were destined to recur again and again. In the spheres of philosophy and religion the central problem which beset the Slavophiles—that of Russia's place in Europe—was to occupy such giants as Dostoevsky, Leontiev, and Vladimir Soloviev. Their contribution to this problem is outside the narrow scope of an analysis of purely political thought. But in the realm of political speculation, as the century advanced and as thought of revolution and of its alternative, reform, came to dominate the mind of the intellectual, the heritage of the Slavophiles or, more accurately, the permanence of the problems with which they were preoccupied, became increasingly apparent.

In the pages which follow [this essay] we shall have occasion to return to some of the Slavophile formulations at three important crossroads on the path of Russian politics. First, in the nineties, when Western rationalist Marxism clashed with traditional national populism, which sought to turn its back on Western European development, seeking salvation in an indigenous national Russian solution. Then again a decade later, when the Marxists themselves were to divide into those who sought to continue along the rationalist and Western lines which had shaped the doctrine when it first took root in Russia, and those who tried to go back to older Slav roots, and to blend the indigenous and national with the alien, Western, and rational. And finally, on the eve of the revolutionary year of 1905, when the young liberal movement was faced with a choice between a complete breach with the whole traditional system of autocracy and a compromise proposed by the last of the Slavophiles, who sought to modify the autocracy while preserving intact what they believed to be its essential national form.

In the end politics is not about Masses or the People or Movements or Classes—though that is how men have often talked about it and will no doubt continue to do. Politics is about institutions. In the end a political process is always bound to reflect the realities of the existing institutions, whatever the hopes and intentions, or promises, of those who engage in the political process. In Russia, throughout the period we are engaged in considering, the institutional reality was the autocracy and little, if anything, else. In order to have any practical validity all political speculation had to face this problem of the autocracy, whether the aim was to preserve it, or modify it, or destroy it, or capture it. Speculation about replacing it with institutions which did not exist and which could not be created overnight, like that of the Decembrists, or of the early Westerner radicals, was idle dreaming. This at all events the Slavophiles understood, for all their unpractical and even somewhat ridiculous romanticism. It was to become the central problem after the period of the Reforms was inaugurated in 1861.

Notes

[1] M. O. Gershenzon, *Istoriia molodoi Rossii* (Moscow, 1908), p. 202, and cf. p. 85.

[2] P. V. Annenkov, *Literaturnye vospominaniia* (Moscow, 1960), p. 200.

[3] These early instances of distinctive Slavophile opinion have been collected by Peter K. Christoff in his *An Introduction to Nineteenth-Century Russian Slavophilism, A Study in Ideas,* Volume I: *A. S. Xomiakov* (The Hague, 1961). This work, together with a study by N. Ustrialov, "Politicheskaia doktrina v slavianofil'skoi postanovke," in *Vysshaiia Shkola v Kharbine: Izvestiia iuridicheskogo fakul'teta* (Harbin, 1925), I, 47-74, has been of great value to me in preparing this section on the political views of the Slavophiles.

[4] Note that "power" in this context means *potestas,* not *potentia:* the English word does not make this clear.

[5] The "Message to the Serbians" is quoted from the translation printed in Christoff, pp. 247-68. Other quotations are mainly my own translation from the works of Konstantin Aksakov and Ivan Kireevsky, published respectively in Moscow in 1886-87 and 1911.

[6] This conversation is quoted by Annenkov in his *Remarkable Decade—* see p. 273.

[7] The extant works of Granovsky, apart from two volumes of correspondence, include some notes of lectures on the Middle Ages delivered in 1848-49 (published in Moscow in 1961, edited by S. A. Asinovskaiia); and several editions of *Collected Works* which include texts of lectures on Universal History, on Tamerlane, on Alexander the Great, Louis XI, and Francis Bacon; an article on the Jewish people; reviews and articles mainly on medieval themes; and his doctoral dissertation on Suger, the 12th-century statesman, historian, and Abbot of Saint Denis.

[8] *Grandeur et decadence des Romains,* Chap. XVIII. See also Robert Shackleton, *Montesquieu: A Critical Biography* (Oxford, 1961), pp. 166-69.

Martin Katz (essay date 1973)

SOURCE: "Timofei N. Granovskii: An Historiographical Interpretation," in *Canadian Slavonic Papers: Revue Canadienne des Slavistes,* Vol. XV, No. 4, Winter, 1973, pp. 488-96.

[*In the following essay, Katz considers Granovskii's significance as a historian in the estimation of liberal and radical scholars from his contemporaries to the present.*]

The major evaluations of the liberal Westernizer and professor of universal history at Moscow University in the nineteenth century, Timofei N. Granovskii, provide evidence of the interest shown toward him not only by his own, but by future generations of public figures and historians as well.

This paper does not pretend to be an exhaustive examination of the literature concerning Granovskii, but rather a representative sampling of liberal and radical views concerning his importance as a historian and also as a public figure. It purposely does not treat the views of conservative and reactionary historians since they are well known to students of Russian history. What is of interest, however, is the manner in which Granovskii has been eulogized by both liberals and radicals, including Soviet historians (especially those writing in the post-Stalinist period). The paper is divided into the following sections: views of Granovskii by his contemporaries, by later generations within the Imperial period, by Soviet historians in the Stalinist period, by

Soviet historians in the post-Stalinist period, and finally by present-day Western historians.

Granovskii's fame derived not only from his lectures in universal history at Moscow University, but also from his public lectures to the enlightened Moscovite society of his day. He was a very complex figure, a Westernizer with many points of contact with the opposing Slavophiles. It was only the exponents of Official Nationality such as Pogodin, Shevyrev and Davydov who were his lifelong enemies. His short life is significant, not so much by what he wrote, but rather by his influence on his own and future generations.

References to Granovskii are to be found in the numerous memoirs and biographies of his contemporaries. Among the most important are the memoirs of P. V. Annenkov and the biography of Granovskii by A. V. Stankevich (the brother of the famous N. V. Stankevich who was founder of the Moscow circle bearing his name and a close friend of Granovskii). Annenkov dispassionately recounted the views of his friend Granovskii. He pointed out the moderate position assumed by the Moscow professor and the splintering of the Westernizer camp when Granovskii could no longer sympathize with the thought of Belinskii and Herzen. One of the primary points of friction between the moderate Granovskii and the radical Herzen and Belinskii was the question of socialism. Annenkov quotes a conversation with Granovskii in which the latter said, "Socialism is extremely dangerous . . . in that it teaches one to look for solutions to the problems of social life, not in the arena of politics, which it despises, but apart from that arena, whereby it undermines both it and itself."[1] It is this statement more than any other which makes it so difficult to comprehend the popularity that Granovskii enjoyed among the radicals of his own and future generations in Imperial times and among Soviet scholars as well.

Granovskii, the moderate synthesizer, is revealed clearly in A. V. Stankevich's biography of him. Stankevich was perhaps the most important biographer of Granovskii as well as one of the Moscow professor's staunchest apologists. Stankevich provides a detailed sympathetic view of Granovskii's childhood, youth and adult life, and attempts to paint his subject as a person who overcame adversity with strength and with a strong element of humanism. The latter trait was revealed in Granovskii's constant effort at reconciliation of seemingly irreconcilable personalities and ideas:

> It is impossible not to note that already in school Granovskii was distinguished by the ability to be a center of unity, a conciliator of hostile inclinations and directions, which remained with him thoughout life.[2]

This attempt to achieve synthesis was later recalled by another biographer, D. M. Levshin, and more recently by the British historian Leonard Schapiro, both of whom will be discussed later.

An early exception to the praise which Granovskii was receiving from all but the extreme Right, came from one of the Moscow professor's old classmates at St. Petersburg University, V. V. Grigor'ev. Here faint praise is mixed with condemnation. Grigor'ev found that Granovskii's popularity stemmed from his moral qualities and artistic nature; ". . . from behind the artist there appeared a good, warm, gentle man, distinguished by the absence of any pedantry and egoistic irritability, a man noble both in aspirations and in deeds . . ."[3] But the criticism follows:

> Many consider Granovskii a scholar. Of course how is one to define scholarship. In my opinion, broad erudition does not at all give one the right to the title scholar. From a scholar, I demand that he should not only know much, but that he should know critically, that he should process the material which he has obtained and transmit it to others in a comprehensible form, enriched or refined by his own thinking. Granovskii in lectures and in some of his work is almost completely a passive transmitter of material learned by him, not the judge of affairs, but the reporter of facts and views worked out by others. I do not find in him independence even less originality of thought.[4]

The views of Granovskii's most notable contemporary and former colleague, Herzen, were extremely perceptive. Herzen and Granovskii remained close friends even after their ideological split in the 1840's. Few opinions of Granovskii were as well stated as those made by Herzen.

> Granovskii reminds me of a number of the calm, reflective preachers and revolutionaries of the Reformation—not those fierce, turbulent spirits who "feel their life fully in their wrath" like Luther . . . certainly Granovskii in all the harmonious moulding of his soul, in his romantic bent, in his dislike of extremes, might more readily have been a Huguenot or a Girondist than an Anabaptist or a Montagnard.[5]

The men of the sixties as well as those of the forties took an interest in Granovskii and came to have a heartfelt respect for him both as a public figure and as a scholar. Perhaps the most important thinker of that time, N. G. Chernyshevskii, praised Granovskii as an original mind who in Russia had no rivals.[6]

However, such positive views were not without their negative counterparts. Dostoevsky in his notes for the character Stepan Trofimovich Verkhovenskii in the novel *The Possessed* portrayed Granovskii in the following manner:

T. N. Granovskii

A portrait of a pure and idealistic Westernizer in his full splendor. Perhaps he is living (in Moscow) in a provincial capital. *Characteristic traits.* That aimlessness and lack of firmness in his views and in his emotions, which have dominated his whole life, used to cause him suffering before, *but have now become his second nature* (his son makes fun of this tendency)[7]

Undeniably Granovskii was admired by his students. But the manner in which his lectures reflected Acsopian propaganda is perhaps best revealed by the statement of a former student on this subject. Thus R. Krylov wrote:

This was a happy time for students: The students left the lecture hall with new thoughts and with noble souls, such was the force of challenging historical events [in the lecture], that it became easy to understand the very laws of history: after a short while, almost half an hour into the lecture, the students felt somehow the possibility to explain other events about which they had not even heard in the lecture . . . Thus Granovskii so possessed the secret of history that he was the master in its field.[8]

Granovskii's influence on his contemporaries was not limited to abstract humanism or concern with the lower classes in history. He also inaugurated the statist school in Russian historiography, whereby political improvements were seen to derive from the state. Among his most notable intellectual disciples in this direction were S. M. Solov'ev, Chicherin and Kavelin.[9]

Some of the most provocative and penetrating biographical work on Granovskii has been done by those who were removed from him by a generation or two, and thus were free of the contemporary polemics that raged around the Moscow professor during the time of Nicholas I. Ch. Vertinskii (Vas. E. Cheshikhin) has provided a relatively favourable view of Granovskii from the vantage point of the nineties. Though relying heavily on the earlier biography by A. V. Stankevich, Vetrinskii arrived at his own conclusions concerning Granovskii as both a public figure and an historian. Vetrinskii pointed out the rather amorphous nature of Granovskii's thought, which was opposed to fatalism while initially supporting a kind of determinism derived from the Hegelian dialectical view of history. Vetrinskii also indicated that Granovskii believed that one of the salient aims of universal history was to reveal the laws of history. Granovskii was valued for his honesty and determination to improve his own and future generations through enlightenment during the dark days of *Nikolaevshchina.* Vetrinskii found a motto for this monumental mission in the words of Shakespeare: "There is no time so miserable, but a man may be true."[10]

Another historian who commented on Granovskii toward the end of the Tsarist regime was N. Kareev. He was primarily concerned with Granovskii's historical world outlook. Kareev perceptively showed how Granovskii, while being an aesthetic orator, nevertheless placed history in the category of a science rather than an art by the development of a "unity of science" (*edinstvo nauki*).[11] Granovskii, in a manner not dissimilar to that of the famous French historian of the Middle Ages—Marc Bloch—, hoped for a rapprochement between history and the other social sciences which would reveal the moral laws of mankind to his university students and to the whole of educated Moscow society. Kareev sympathetically noted that Granovskii showed a disregard for political economy, mainly because the " . . . historical school of political economy was born at the time that the historical world outlook of Granovskii was just taking shape . . . the economic direction, which made itself successful in historical scholarship in our day, came only after the death of Granovskii . . ."[12] Though stating that Granovskii was not indiscriminately eclectic, Kareev noted that Granovskii borrowed from each direction that which was most valuable.[13] Referring to Granovskii's adherence to the Hegelian system in the first part of his career, Kareev indicated that "Granovskii understood the regularity of history in the sense of its organic nature."[14]

One of the most outstanding Russian historians, Kliuchevskii, also expressed unqualified praise of Granovskii as a teacher and public figure:

It was Granovskii who taught his audience to value scholarship as a social force. Since his time and since the time of his public lectures, Moscow University became the focal point of the best expectations and designs for the education of Russian society.[15]

An interesting analysis of Granovskii's desire to synthesize opposing ideas was written by D. M. Levshin. His biography of Granovskii was an early, primitive attempt to fathom the psychological depths of Granovskii's character. Levshin pointed out that Granovskii's personality represented the dominance of that which he called Granovskii's "emotional I" over his "intellectual I," but Levshin qualified his opinion.

By this, however, we do not want to say that his intellectual "I" was absorbed by his emotional one but only that the equilibrium of mind, will and feelings, which constituted the ideal of psychological organization, was upset in Granovskii by the predominance of feelings over the remaining elements of his soul.[16]

In the Stalinist period Soviet historians placed Granovskii somewhere between "bourgeois-pomeshchik liberalism" on the Right and "revolutionary democracy" on the Left. Herzen's description of Granovskii as a latter day "Girondist" was generally accepted by Soviet historians of this period when they mixed praise for Granovskii's firm stand against serfdom with blame for his not going as far as Herzen and Belinskii.[17] In the early Stalinist period some excitement was generated by a newly discovered letter of Granovskii which concerned the events in France during the summer of 1848. The Soviet historian V. Nevskii took the position that the controversial letter, which Granovskii had written to his friend Mme. Chicherina, did not represent a shift in Granovskii's views from liberalism to radicalism, but rather indicated the Moscow professor's humanism with regard to the lower classes.[18] The letter in question contained the following lines:

> Again the case-shot triumphed, the oppressors are triumphant. They think of returning the workers and the proletariat to their former slavery. Again the bourgeoisie gathers forces, but the oppressed do not sleep. They cover Paris with barricades, and this was in the full sense a class rising of the proletarians.[19]

V. Nevskii maintained that Granovskii did not understand the term "proletariat" in the same sense as did Karl Marx, and thus the moderate convictions of the Moscow professor had not really changed.

> First of all, from the text of the letter it is evident that Granovskii differentiates between two concepts: "workers" and "proletariat." If by the word "proletariat" Granovskii meant the "working class," then there would be no need for this word to be placed next to another word "workers." We know that not only Granovskii, but his friends, gave another meaning to the word "proletariat" than we give it. For him the "proletariat" is that large stratum of the urban poor, among which a large part is composed of the petty urban bourgeoisie and above all by people living by intellectual toil.[20]

With respect to the post-Stalinist Soviet period, no sharp distinction can be found between the views expressed in the Stalinist period and those of S. A. Asinovskaia who is presently engaged in the compilation of Granovskii's work on the Western Middle Ages. Asinovskaia indicates that Granovskii's courses on this period were in the form of Aesopian propaganda directed against the "feudal-serf order" of Russian reality during the reign of Nicholas I. Nevertheless, she chastised Granovskii for his "liberal narrow-mindedness" which she believed contradicted his scholarly views. Asinovskaia, in a manner not unlike that of Granovskii's contemporary Herzen, indicated that Granovskii expressed more sympathy for the Girondists than for the Jacobins, and that when treating the Reformation, Granovskii found the radical Thomas Münzer to be a frightening figure.[21]

Recently the Soviet historian S. S. Dmitriev has provided a much more positive view of Granovskii than that of Asinovskaia:

> The names of certain persons are indissolubly linked with events and institutions. In the public memory are inseparable Lomonosov and the Academy of Sciences, Peter I and St. Petersburg, Schliemann and Troy, Lenin and October. These are examples of historical symbiosis, cultural-historical unity.
>
> Granovskii and Moscow University is a model of such unity.[22]

Dmitriev cites the words of Herzen, that Granovskii "thought history, studied history and consequently with history made propaganda."[23] Throughout his article on Granovskii. Dmitriev stated nothing derogatory about the professor of the forties.

Writing in the same study as Dmitriev, E. V. Gutnova discussed Granovskii's merits as a historian. One of her main conclusions was that Granovskii was a truly independent and seminal thinker, not merely a transmitter of the ideas of others.[24] In this respect she is diametrically opposed to Grigor'ev, the contemporary of Granovskii who was discussed earlier. Gutnova indicated that for Granovskii, the history of the Middle Ages was " . . . not a dead collection of confused facts, but a laboratory of the historical and political experience of different peoples, the study of which, in his opinion, explained much concerning the fates of contemporary Western Europe and the future Russia."[25]

Among modern Western historians who have commented on Granovskii, Leonard Schapiro warrants attention. Schapiro, in a manner not dissimilar to earlier evaluators of the Moscow professor, placed Granovskii as a public figure between the Westernizers and the Slavophiles, thus attempting a synthesis of opposing viewpoints. He indicated that Granovskii's " . . . main contribution to the development of the social thought of his period falls under two heads: his criticism of determinism in history, and his assessment of Russia's place in Europe."[26] With respect to Russia's place in Europe, Schapiro indicated that Granovskii " . . . ridiculed the Slavophile and ultranationalist attempts to portray Russia as something quite different from and outside the European community, on the basis of historical mythology of their own making."[27] With reference to Granovskii's criticism of determinism, Schapiro showed how Granovskii moved from a more deterministic position based on "the laws of history" to a less deterministic one which placed the individual beyond such "laws."[28] Without specifically mentioning Granovskii's adherence to Comtian positivism, Schapiro nevertheless viewed such adherents of Comte as Pisarev, Lavrov and Mikhailovskii as " . . . direct heirs of Granovskii."[29]

James H. Billington, the American historian, viewed Granovskii as being in the mainstream of the Russian liberal tradition, a tradition which was strengthened by the work of university professors to a greater extent than other currents of political thought in the nineteenth century.

> The most influential university professor tended to sympathize with liberalism from the time when Professor Granovsky first tried to present some of its salient ideas in his lectures at Moscow University in the 1840's. Granovsky, the spiritual father of the original Westernizers, was the first to lecture in detail to Russians on the historical development of laws and liberties in the democratic West.[30]

Billington took G. Fischer to task for not including Granovskii in the latter's work on Russian liberalism.[31]

In conclusion, it can be seen that Granovskii became an intellectual hero of radicals and liberals alike. Each political direction emphasized different aspects of his thought which coincided with their own ideological and attitudinal positions. The most recent Soviet interest in Granovskii possibly reflects the effects of the post-Stalinist thaw in a way that is not unlike the recent treatment of Shakespeare's Hamlet.[32] One can only hope that the kind of Soviet humanism shown by Dmitriev in his evaluation of Granovskii will continue.

Notes

[1] Arthur P. Mandel, ed., *The Extraordinary Decade: Literary Memoirs by P. V. Annenkov* (Ann Arbor: 1968), p. 141.

[2] A. V. Stankevich, *T. N. Granovskii i ego perepiska* (Moscow: 1897, 2nd ed.), Vol. I, p. 9.

[3] V. Grigor'ev, *T. N. Granovskii do ego professorstva v Moskve* (Moscow: 1856), p. 84.

[4] *Ibid.*, p. 86.

[5] Alexander Herzen, *My Past and Thoughts: The Memoirs of Alexander Herzen* (London: 1968), Vol. II, p. 500.

[6] N. G. Chernyshevskii, *Izbrannye filosofskie sochineniia* (Leningrad: 1950), Vol. II, p. 19; in E. V. Gutnova, "Granovskii kak Istorik," *Granovskii, Timofei Nikolaevich,* ed. by S. S. Dmitriev (Moscow: 1969), p. 45.

[7] F. Dostoevsky, *The Notebooks for the Possessed* (London: 1968), p. 82.

[8] R. Krylov, "Moi vospominaniia o Granovskom i Kudriavtsev . . ." *Zhurnal dlia Vospitaniia* (1858), III, p. 249.

[9] For the contribution of Granovskii to the statist school see Anatole G. Mazour, *An Outline of Modern Russian Historiography* (Berkeley: 1939), *passim.*

[10] Ch. Vetrinskii (Vas. E. Cheshikhin), *T. N. Granovskii i ego vremia: istoricheskii ocherk* (Moscow: 1897), p. 319.

[11] N. Kareev, *Istoricheskoe mirosozertsanie T. N. Granovskago* (St. Petersburg: 1905, 3rd ed.), p. 16.

[12] *Ibid.*, p. 24.

[13] *Ibid.*, p. 35.

[14] *Ibid.*, p. 51.

[15] V. O. Kliuchevskii, *Sochineniia* (Moscow: 1959), Vol. VIII, p. 391.

[16] D. M. Levshin, *T. N. Granovskii (Opyt istoricheskogo sinteza)* (St. Petersburg: 1902, 2nd ed.), pp. 192-93.

[17] "Granovskii, Timofei Nikolaevich," *Bolshaia Sovetskaia Entsiklopediia* (Moscow: 1952, 2nd ed.), Vol. XII, pp. 445-48.

[18] "Granovskii o revoliutsii 1848 goda: novoe pis'mo Granovskogo." *Literaturnoe Nasledstvo* (1933), No. 7-8, p. 51.

[19] *Ibid.*, p. 53.

[20] *Ibid.*, p. 51.

[21] S. A. Asinovskaia, ed., *Lektsii T. N. Granovskogo po istorii srednevekov'ia* (Moscow: 1969), pp. 3-6, 9.

[22] S. S. Dmitriev, "Granovskii i Moskovskii Universitet," *Granovskii, Timofei Nikolaevich: Bibliografiia (1828-1967)* (Moscow: 1969), p. 3.

[23] *Ibid.*, p. 19.

[24] E. V. Gutnova, "Granovskii kak Istorik," *Granovskii . . . Bibliografiia (1828-1967)*, p. 45.

[25] *Ibid.*, pp. 49-50.

[26] Leonard Schapiro, *Rationalism and Nationalism in Russian Nineteenth-Century Political Thought* (New Haven: 1967), p. 75.

[27] *Ibid.*, p. 78.

[28] *Ibid.*, pp. 76-77.

[29] *Ibid.*, pp. 80-81.

[30] James H. Billington, *The Icon and the Axe: an Interpretive History of Russian Culture* (New York: 1966), p. 450.

[31] *Ibid.*, p. 755.

[32] Arthur P. Mendel, "Hamlet and Soviet Humanism," *Slavic Review* (December: 1971), Vol. XXX, No. 4, pp. 733-47.

Nicholas S. Racheotes (essay date 1978)

SOURCE: "T. N. Granovskii: On the Meaning of History," in *Studies in Soviet Thought*, Vol. 18, No. 3, August, 1978, pp. 197-221.

[*In the excerpt that follows, Racheotes examines the intellectual affinities between Granovskii and German philosophers of history, principally Ranke, Schelling, and Hegel.*]

The life of T. N. Granovskii, which spanned the years 1813 to 1855, has been seen by Soviet historians of thought in various perspectives. His career as a teacher of medieval and world history at Moscow University between 1839 and 1855, his few publications, and most of all, his friendships with N. V. Stankevich, A. I. Herzen, V. G. Belinskii, and N. P. Ogarëv have attracted the comments of Soviet scholars. Despite their differing vantage points, they have gradually fashioned a consistent view of the significance to be accorded to Granovskii's life.

The present inquiry has been designed to focus attention upon the following general areas: the extent to which Granovskii's philosophy of history was related to that of Leopold von Ranke, the definition of 'universal history' to which the former subscribed, and the influences which the German philosophers, Schelling and Hegel, exerted upon Granovskii. Finally, a suggestion will be made as to Granovskii's impact upon Soviet historiography.

In modern biographies, Granovskii has been acclaimed as the representative of Hegelian thought in Russia, as the founder of Russian historiography concerned with medieval Europe, and as a highly politicized, though cautious, intellectual.[1] Moreover, one of the outstanding characteristics which Soviet observers attribute to Granovskii stems from their contention that he employed the writing and teaching of history as a means of propaganda. They are fond of citing A. I. Herzen to this effect.[2]

The article on Granovskii in the *Filosofskaja enciklopedija* lies within the established Soviet tradition. As is appropriate in an encyclopedia, the treatment is concise but noteworthy, especially insofar as it touches upon Granovskii's philosophy of history.

Sharing many of the ideas of Hegel's philosophy of history, albeit that Granovskii regarded it critically during the years [1836-1839] of study in Germany, Granovskii continued the tradition of the representatives (N. Polevoi, K. Lebedev, K. Zelenetskii, Chaadaev) of the idealistic (and partially dialectical) philosophy of history on Russian soil.

The article goes on to discuss Granovskii's search for the underlying causes of historical development:

Granovskii formulated and evolved a theory of historical development: "the origin which lies at the foundation of this (historical) development is the infinite mind"; the history of mankind which possesses "its stages of development", its goal which is freedom, is the aggregate history of separate peoples.

Hinting at the interdisciplinary approach to which Granovskii subscribed, the article continues:

Granovskii noted the role of the geographic milieu in historical development which, in the struggle with fatalistic conceptions, he regarded dialectically as a struggle of heterogeneous, including social, forces.

Turning to the question of Granovskii's 'historical organicism', the unidentified author writes:

Granovskii considered one age to be separated from another by a 'sharp differentiation'—revolution (for example, the conquest of the ancient Germans, the French revolution at the end of the eighteenth century, and others) which resolved "the contradiction which can be annihilated only by force". Granovskii asserted that historical development was endless, inasmuch as "the antitheses are eternally new and as they never return to previous points, from their struggle there emerge eternally new results".

Implying a transformation in Granovskii's view of the world, the article states:

The evolution of Granovskii's views is characterized by a gradual breaking down of idealism on account of an ever-increasing recognition of the dependence of history upon nature, of historical science upon natural science and especially on account of his striving towards the realization of the role of material factors, the role of the people, and of separate individuals in history. This tendency manifests itself above all in the concrete analysis of historical materialism, principally the history of Rome and feudalism, which was carried on in university lectures and a few published works ('Concerning the Contemporary Condition and Significance of Universal History', 1852). It is possible to number Granovskii among those historians who, as Engels puts it, were striving towards the discovery of a materialistic understanding of history (K. Marx and F. Engels, *Selected Letters,* 1953, p.471.)[3]

Despite the wooden manner in which it is phrased, the passage just cited raises several issues of interest. What is meant when Granovskii is described as a 'critical Hegelian'? What did Granovskii have in mind when referring to the 'eternal mind' as the guiding force of history? Exactly what part did geographic factors play in Granovskii's definition of history? How did he differentiate between historical eras? Did Granovskii consider history to be directional, dialectic, repetitive, and strife-ridden? How did he perceive the dependence of history upon Nature, the physical sciences, popular movements, and individual personalities? Lastly, is it justifiable to label Granovskii as a materialist?

The first step in answering such a panoply of questions may be taken when it is pointed out that Granovskii was profoundly influenced by a few of the German historians active during the first half of the nineteenth century. Laboring in their shadow, he was, in actuality, led away from historical materialism. His German training prodded Granovskii to search for central ideas and cultural developments as historical turning points.

It follows that in an attempt to assemble the various strands of reasoning which Granovskii wove into his conception of history, one must turn to the creators of German 'scientific' history. From them and from their intellectual disciples, he learned his craft. In general, the emergence of 'scientific' history in Germany placed its emphasis upon objectivity, the critique of historical sources, and the examination of the causes which underlie events. Of especial importance in this regard were the writings and teaching of Barthold Niebuhr (1776-1831) and Frederic von Savigny (1779-1861). These scholars insisted upon the necessity of a philological approach to historical documents and stressed the value of looking far back into a nation's past to discover the origins of its culture and its legal system.

Of the many German influences upon him, those of Georg Friedrich Hegel (1770-1831) and Leopold von Ranke (1795-1886) were the most pronounced. Moreover, Granovskii was taken by the concept, current during his lifetime, of *Einfühlungsvermögen* which referred to man's ability to empathize with institutions and ideas belonging to the remote past.[4] Thus a good historian had to envision the past in its most vivid actuality and he had to will himself free from the pull of his own era.

Like Niebuhr, von Ranke emphasized the value of a historian's critical study of historical monuments. He strove to work toward the sound generalization by discovering the significance of an event within its immediate context, after which he would proceed to the discovery of its broader implications.[5] Writing in 1838, von Ranke listed the characteristics which a historian must possess in order to produce works of high quality. He urged all historians to seek well-founded generalizations and to perfect the following abilities:

(1) The pure love of truth.

(2) . . . a documentary, penetrating, profound study . . .

(3) A universal interest.

(4) Penetration of the causal nexus. [The historian must realize that the causes of events are more complex than man's passion or lust for power.]

(5) Impartiality.

(6) Conception of the totality. [The historian must strive to see the whole universe simultaneously and with perfect clarity, although God alone succeeds at this.][6]

Both Ranke and Hegel believed in historical progress, but unlike Hegel, Ranke did not see the historical process as dialectical.[7] According to Ranke, man did not always advance. He insisted that when mankind did progress, it was not necessarily because of a natural gravitation toward higher forms of civilized existence. Instead, the reasons for advancement might be traced back to the rivalry among nations for territory and power. To Ranke, these international rivalries generated universal tendencies which are at odds with the distinguishing features of each nation involved in a particular struggle. In his words:

> The history of each separate nation throws light on the history of humanity at large; . . . there is a general historical life, which moves progressively from one nation or group of nations to another.[8]

It may be observed, then, that Ranke joined Hegel in seeing conflicts as fomenting historical progress and promoting historical universality, but von Ranke refrained from mapping this process in the way that his compatriot did.

For his part, Granovskii had to blend the Rankean approach to historical causality with the Hegelian idea of transitional epochs in history so that he could refine his own definition of historical progress. Therefore, some space will have to be devoted to the relevant aspects of Hegel's philosophy and the success with which Granovskii synthesized Hegel's philosophy of history and Ranke's historiography.

Two of the pertinent elements which combined in Ranke's definition of history were his preoccupation with measuring historical progress and his wish to demonstrate the validity of 'universal history'. He had become convinced, as Granovskii would be subsequently, that every age was the cultural beneficiary of its predecessors. Here Ranke took the path which led away from Hegel who maintained that the cultural advances of a given epoch negated those of its forerunners.[9] Ranke preferred to believe that mankind accumulated a sort of cultural treasury throughout the ages. The historical legacy, Ranke contended, had manifested itself in material, social, cultural, and religious advances. As he put it:

> One portion of this heritage, the most precious jewel of the whole, consists of those immortal works of genius in poetry and literature, in science and art, which, while modified by the local conditions under which they were produced, yet represent what is common to all mankind.[10]

Expressing his devotion to broadening and clarifying his conception of 'universal history', von Ranke had written in a manuscript which dates from the 1830s:

> I am of the opinion, rather, that historical science at its best is both called upon and able to rise in its own way from the investigation and contemplation of the particular to a general view of events and to a recognition of their objectively existing relatedness.[11]

Half a century later, he returned to the same subject and elaborated:

> Universal History, as we understand the term, embraces the events of all times and nations, with this limitation only, that they shall be so far ascertained as to make a scientific treatment of them possible. . . . A collection of national histories, whether on a larger or a smaller scale, is not what we mean by Universal History, for in such a work the general connections of things is liable to be obscured. To recognise this connection, to trace the sequence of those great events which link all nations together and control their destinies is the task which the science of Universal History undertakes.[12]

In a recent collection of essays, Peter Gay touched upon one of the essential ingredients in the Rankean approach to history, namely, the infusion of history with scientific rigor:

> . . . the methods and results of Ranke's way as a historian were aimed straight at science, the systematizing of research, the withdrawal of the ego from presentation, the unremitting effort at objectivity, the submission of results to critical public scrutiny.[13]

In addition, Gay observed that Ranke considered both the good and evil in history to be part of God's grand design. It was the historian's duty to trace and present God's design to his readers.[14] To put it another way, historians had the didactic mission of interpreting the lessons of the past for mankind. As will be shown, this idealization of the historian's calling is rich with implications.

There is much solid evidence on which to base the contention that Ranke imparted many of his ideas to Granovskii. Uppermost among these were Ranke's definition of 'Universal History', historical causality, and the proper function of the historian. In fact, it may be confidently asserted that the German historian was the single most important influence upon Granovskii's philosophy of history. While a student in Berlin, Granovskii participated in von Ranke's research seminars from which so many historians were propelled to scholarly eminence. However, Granovskii was especially enthusiastic about Ranke's lectures. To his close friend, Ia.M. Neverov, he wrote,

> . . . his [von Ranke's] lucid, vivid, poetic view of science will charm you. He understands history. . . . Many find that he is dry because he is not in the habit of amusing his students with anecdotes. I am in ecstasy from his lectures.[15]

What is more, in his own lectures, he relied heavily upon von Ranke's writings.[16]

Of course, Granovskii imbibed more than the Rankean philosophy of history during the years spent in Berlin. One of his instructors at Berlin University was the Hegelian, Heinrich Werder (1791-1869), with whom Granovskii and N. V. Stankevich studied Hegel's philosophy. Therefore, the process of combining Rankean and Hegelian notions began during Granovskii's years of study abroad.

Gradually, he took possession of the opinions to which his instructors clung. He became convinced that history was directional. He grew to have faith in the idea that mankind progressed through the ages. In Granovskii's view, there existed laws of historical behavior which the historian had to attempt to discover.[17] Pressing the point still further, he came to argue that historical laws and historical progress were connected.

To Granovskii, as to von Ranke, the most accurate measurement of historical progress could be found within the realm of ideas. As generations passed, man became better educated and augmented his culture. In its turn, this improvement enhanced the quality of man's life by checking the uncivilized elements which belonged to mankind's instinctive nature.[18] In order to uncover the laws which governed this whole process, Granovskii believed that the historian must proceed as Ranke and Hegel had recommended. First, he must explore the histories of individual nations and then decide which features they had in common. All the while, he must be keeping an eye upon each nation's contribution to the evolution of humanity.[19] In this connection, Granovskii credited Johann Gottfried Herder with the discovery that even national peculiarities were of value to historians.[20]

However, Granovskii admitted that historians could not proceed directly from the individual histories of particular nations to the general history of the whole world wherein human behavior was largely regulated. When describing the treachery of this route, he had recourse to phrases which were stylistically reminiscent of Hegel's:

> The recognition of the individual peculiarities of national characters instead of an abstract conception of general human nature, the source of which is an animated, according to internal law, developing force which in union with circumstances determines the course of events instead of a simple external causality, finally, the comprehension of universal history as the comprehension of the progress of forces and forms, but not the accumulation and legacies of external means—these contemporary ideas are common to all historians.[21]

As far as he was concerned, the characteristics which dwell below the surface of each event and the confluence of these characteristics with those underlying another event made generalizations possible. Once generalization was possible so was a philosophy of history. The phenomological issue was resolved by turning to monism.

> The simple foundation upon which the philosophy of history is based is that which has already been articulated: the coincidence of the visible and the invisible, Nature with Spirit, the object of the real with the ideal, existence with thought. It is only the two sides of existence which has sprung up from the same root—from the absolute or from understanding, or, better to say, this self-absolute, revealing itself in a phenomenon, creates and composes the impatient forces of history and Nature; the subject, Spirit, and world is subordinate to the same law. They create one in the same process of development.[22]

This causal monism, taken together with Granovskii's exaltation of intellect, conclusively demonstrates that he had hit upon a keystone of Schelling's and Hegel's philosophies, because both German thinkers devised their 'historiosophic' systems with these two properties in mind.[23]

At this point, one must become cautious. Obviously, Granovskii's mental capacity was not on a par with the cerebral powers of these gifted German philosophers. In day to day practice, he lacked the time, energy, ability, and inclination to incorporate these considerations in his work. As a result, while he held up the German philosophical approach as ideal, he could not adhere strictly to it.

Rather than devote himself to the search for the material dynamics of historical progress, Granovskii endeavored to merge intellectually with the past as Herder and Ranke had enjoined. He strove to be merciful to the victors and victims found in the various historical episodes about which he wrote.[24] Granovskii believed that each generation represented an advance over its predecessors. He joined Herder in seeing each generation's dependence upon the past as obliging it to be sympathetic rather than contemptuous of the past.[25]

Resembling von Ranke, Granovskii argued that the historian's calling carried with it some important demands. Immersed in the past, the historian had an instructive function which he could carry out only by regarding the past objectively.[26] Inevitably, notions derived from a historian's own era came into play. In order for history to instruct the present, its lessons would have to be influenced by the ideas of the present.

> For its content, history much more than other sciences must accept contemporary ideas. We cannot perceive the past except from the point of view of the present. In the fate of our predecessors we seek, for the most part, an explanation of our own.[27]

Basing their argument upon declarations like the foregoing. Soviet historians emphasize Granovskii's role as a propagandist and play down his devotion to objectivity. This interpretation of Granovskii's significance has been derived from perhaps the most widely circulated and laudatory evaluation of his career as a popularizer. It was N. G. Chernyshevskii, writing in the 1850's, who praised Granovskii for building a bridge between scholarship and the Russian people.[28]

P. Miliukov has offered a more sober estimate of Granovskii's attraction to history. At the same time, Miliukov hinted at its somewhat dilettantish character.

> In reality he always loved the poetry in history independently of the philosophical thought of history. . . . If he is carried away with Ranke's lectures, it is because his [Ranke's] enlightening, animated, poetical conception of science infatuated him. If he wishes to praise [Barthold] Niebuhr, it is not his critical analysis, not the heralded historical critique which elicits Granovskii's sympathy. . . . In Niebuhr, Granovskii values the bold synthesis, on

the basis of which the law is given to the historian, his knowledge of life. In his view of history, Granovskii sees poetry.[29]

In his definition of history, Granovskii also left room for the moral considerations which are attendant upon historical perspective. Those individuals who led lives of historical moment were not always appreciated by their contemporaries. In Granovskii's view, one of the historian's most vital functions was to examine and correctly appraise the records which fashioned the reputations of great men:

> He [the historian] must bring to view forgotten merits and he must expose law less claims. This is the moral, in the highest sense of the word, juridical part of his work. . . . Judgment must be founded upon a true and frank study of the matter. It is pronounced not with the object of disturbing the sepulchral repose of the adjudged, but to strengthen the moral sense of the living subjected to innumerable temptations; to strengthen their wavering faith in the good and the true. Let each be given according to his deserts: gratitude to the various toilers working by the sweat of their brows for humanity, satisfying somebody's needs; stern judgment for men who deceive their contemporaries. . . . There is something profoundly comforting for mankind in the possibility of such judgment. The thought of it gives the tired soul new strength for the quarrel with life.[30]

In one of his articles, Granovskii discussed the elusiveness of historical perspective. He sensed that the nineteenth century was an age of rapid industrial progress and abundant scientific discoveries. In the face of such progress, he found himself having to argue that even during an age in which mankind was preoccupied with the advancements made by the physical sciences, there would always be a place for history. In the course of this argument, he dealt with historical perspective as it concerned the secrets of Nature. Unlike so many of the Romantic thinkers, poets, and composers of music in the nineteenth century, Granovskii believed that man's victory over Nature was almost complete.

> The old conflict of Man with Nature has almost concluded. Nature has surrendered its secrets and its strength to him.

This momentous victory should have altered not only Man's view of science and social well-being, but his attitudes toward life itself.

Yet, mankind had moral needs which even his triumphs over Nature could not satisfy. Like the *philosophes* of the 'Enlightenment', Granovskii believed that in every respect, man was nature's superior. It followed that the struggle between mankind and cosmic forces was a struggle between unequals:

> It [Nature] is only history's pedestal upon which Man's great achievements are accomplished; where he himself appears as the architect and as the material.[31]

History could satisfy these moral demands which the natural sciences ignored. It followed that, because each generation sought the lessons of history, because each generation could not resist bringing its own ideas, its own anxieties, and the questions generated by its own era to the study of history, in the hope that history could resolve them, every generation wrote history for itself. Therefore, the actual questions which each generation asked of the past were to Granovskii as revealing as were the facts which each generation derived from its study of the past. The modes of historical inquiry, varying from age to age, explained why there were differing schools of historiography and why the study of these schools by means of surveying their literature was interesting.[32]

By insisting upon the interconnectedness of past and present, Granovskii reminds one of the well-known phrases which von Ranke incorporated into his inaugural lecture at Berlin University.

> A knowlege of the past is imperfect without an acquaintance with the present; there is no understanding of the present without a knowledge of earlier times. The one gives to the other its hand; neither can exist or be perfect without the other.[33]

The German scholarship which both shaped and stimulated Granovskii's thought conveyed certain antinomies. In choosing examples, one need only point out that from Hegel and Schelling Granovskii inherited conflicting notions of history, which was either bound by laws or shaped by the spontaneous actions of great men. From J. G. Herder and Karl Ritter, the geographer, he learned of the polarity between national character and general history. His fondness for Hegel's ideas meant that Granovskii would have to wrestle with dialectical notions of historical progress. The result was his being attracted to the study of epochs during which great historical transitions occurred. Finally, his exposure to the Germans, especially Hegel, caused Granovskii to think about the function of a philosophy of history.

For guidance in these area, Granovskii relied heavily upon Hegel's *The Philosophy of History*. Hegel had attributed to 'Spirit' an existence independent of matter. When matter combined with 'Spirit's' consciousness of itself, there resulted freedom for 'Spirit'.[34] Thereupon, Hegel could reduce world history to a phrase:

> The history of the world is none other than the progress of the consciousness of freedom of Spirit conscious of itself and thus conscious of its own freedom.[35]

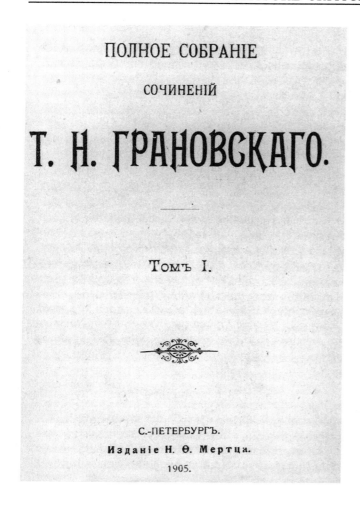

ПОЛНОЕ СОБРАНІЕ

СОЧИНЕНІЙ

Т. Н. ГРАНОВСКАГО.

ТОМЪ I.

С.-ПЕТЕРБУРГЪ.

Изданіе Н. Ѳ. Мертца.

1905.

deduced from it. Each period is involved in such peculiar circumstances, exhibits a condition of things so strictly idiosyncratic, that its conduct must be regulated by considerations connected with itself, and itself alone.[39]

Briefly stated, and with apologies to Hegel, these are the Hegelian conceptions in which Granovskii was most keenly interested.

Some of the features of Friedrich Schelling's thought must be added to what has already been said. Like his student, Hegel, Schelling believed that the world was moving towards increased freedom. As for nature, he defined it as the combination of the real and the ideal. Nature and mind were united and, as absolutes, were self-revelatory.[40] Nature was defined further as the self-objectivization of God.[41] Therefore, scientific knowledge was the understanding of nature. This knowledge was universal and a path to knowledge of God. According to Schelling, God was also revealed through history, particularly in those ages of freedom between the world's great ages.[42] This was the first allusion to the historical transitional era, a notion which Granovskii would find so attractive.

Granovskii adopted only the aspects of Schelling's philosophy which dealt with history and which either echoed Herder or were echoed by Hegel. For example, Herder's view of history as transitional but monolithic and progressive is worth recalling in this connection because it was shared, in part, by both Schelling and Hegel. Specifically, all three philosophers believed in historical progress. During his mature years, Granovskii was acquainted with the writings of these men. Consequently, their ideas impressed him both directly and indirectly inasmuch as these thinkers influenced Leopold von Ranke.[43]

Neither von Ranke nor Granovskii agreed with Hegel that mankind refused to learn from history.[44] Whereas Ranke believed that historical perspective conveyed the essence of the past to the present, Granovskii preferred to view the past as an organic whole tied to the present by living sinews. To him, the link between past and present was general, moral, and, in some respects, susceptible to the dictates of law. While at the height of his intellectual powers. Granovskii wrote on this subject:

Man's history was simply a mental process. Greatness was proportional to the extent to which an individual's goals coincided with those of the 'World Spirit', although the individual himself was unaware of its existence and was conscious only of his own selfish goals.[36]

According to Hegel, the state was 'divine'. It was the only source of true freedom and reason in the world.[37] Since the historical process was dialectical, in Hegel's view, 'Spirit' was at war with itself in realizing the goal of freedom. History was progressive, because each of its great ages—that of classicial Greece, for example—made its special contribution to man's attaining freedom.[38] History was determined because it, somehow, unfolded dialectically and it was universal because 'spirit' played its part in a theater the size of the whole universe. However, Hegel was convinced that man could not study history in order to speed up its process because he had shown his incapacity to learn from it:

. . . what experience and history teach is this—that peoples and governments have never learned anything from history, or acted on principles

Already it appears to us that the use of history does not refer to applying the examples of the past, but a wholistic and vivid understanding of the past, to the present. Such an understanding, based upon a long discourse with by-gone centuries and peoples, brings us to the realization that over all the laws of historical development uncovered by science, reigns one supreme law, that is the moral law, in the realization of which consists the ultimate purpose of humanity on earth. Consequently, the loftiest use of history consists in this, that it informs us with reasoned beliefs in the inevitable triumph of good over evil.[45]

Granovskii was bold enough to seek the precarious balance between historical laws and human spontaneity. Like Hegel, he believed that mankind's increased consciousness was one form in which progress appeared. Moreover, it was the human element which knit the past and present together tightly.

> In trying to divorce themselves from the present, the majority of historians look upon the past as something which existed separately, as something cut off, so to speak, from the present time. They look upon ancient and medieval man as one who is defined by a known political situation, by a certain store of ideas and so forth, so that in the forms of the definitions, the essence itself is pushed into the background, that is, man himself; and in such a way the historical actors, the people whose actions constantly change as a consequence of the change of ideas, but who always remain people with the same passions and with a constant striving toward one great goal, are pushed out of view. So that faced with one and the same goal, only the paths are different—more or less conscious in one era or another—so that the whole progression of history is summed up in the fact that man becomes more conscious and the goal of his existence becomes clearer and more definite.[46]

Granovskii detected a universal yearning for progress. However, paradoxical as it may seem, he also discovered that one form of progress threatened the foundation of historiography, its didactic mission. Granovskii was as enthralled with this aspect of history as Ranke had been. It followed that he became quite disappointed at the manner in which the inhabitants of rapidly industrializing nations seemed to be turning their backs on the lessons of history. In 1847, as part of his continuous reaction to what he considered to be Hegel's assertion, not regret, that mankind did not learn from history, Granovskii wrote:

> Despite the splendid progress which has been accomplished by historical science during our century, perhaps never was the practical use of the study of history subjected to such doubts as it is at present. Hegel's paradox, which stated that history never taught anything to anybody, and which was evoked by the pedantic claims of Johann Mühler and his school, found great sympathy especially in that part of the public which rejoices in each justification of its intellectual laziness. The authority of the great thinker finally took away from it [the public] the obligation to waste time on the study of a science which is fruitless in its application. On the other hand, the rapid change of events, the number of phenomena which so unexpectedly and sharply change the character of European societies led many thinking people of the better sort to reflection. The question of the connection of the past with the present in the age of bitter attacks upon historical tradition has confronted them as an insoluble and terrible problem. The trust in the experiences of personal life having been fulfilled, they doubted the possibility of profiting from the centuries of all humanity's experiences. [It has been said] frankly that now a well-ordered factory would be more instructive to the people than all of history. And this opinion, coarse to the point of cynicism, which reveals a rare narrowness of understanding and feeling, was, however, accepted by many with approval. But, incidentally, very few events are distinguished by being entirely new and unprecedented phenomena; for the majority there exist instructive historical analogies. In the ability for grasping these analogies, not stopping upon one formal correspondence—the ability to recognize, under the changing cover of current events—the smoothed out features of the past, is contained in our opinion the highest indication of living historical feeling which is, in its turn, the highest fruit of science.[47]

The Mühler to whom Granovskii referred was Johann von Mühler (1752-1809), a Swiss medieval historian, writing in the 'Enlightenment' style of universal history, whose works influenced Schiller's 'William Tell' and von Ranke's notion of general history.

Granovskii could set down such windy pronouncements on the lessons of history and their practicality, because he was convinced that laws existed which governed historical causality. This position forced him to reject eighteenth-century historiography for what he felt to be its overreliance upon capricious and particularistic, rather than schematized and general, causes for events.

> Historians of the eighteenth century tried to explain important events by means of trivial reasons. In such intimacies was expressed not only the wit of the writers but also the sincere thought of a century which did not believe in the limited life of a mankind that had subordinated its fate to the capricious influence of personal will and personal passion. Proceeding from this beginning, it was not difficult to arrive at the conviction that in history, which is entrusted to the rule of chance, there is nothing unrealizable; that for whole peoples there are possible *salti mortali*—jumps from one order of things to another order which is separated from it by a long series of stages of development.

To Granovskii, there was the proof of man's intellectual evolution, for the haphazard attribution of historical causes had yielded to the proposition that historical causality was governed by laws.

> Our age has ceased believing in the mindless control of chance. The new science, the philosophy of history, has set up in its place law, or, better to say, necessity.

Although every nation advanced, history had ordained that some advance more quickly than others. The determinations of history were inevitable. They supplanted man's will. Yet, Granovskii refused to discount completely the historic role of the individual.

> Together with chance, the separate personality has lost the greater part of his significance in history . . .

The development of science with its discoveries of the laws which embraced the behavior of natural phenomena represented a precision which forced historians to seek laws determining past human behavior.

> We will not deny the merits of the new view, which is certainly more intelligent than what preceded it, but we cannot ignore the fact that it is just as dry and one-sided. The life of humanity is subordinated to the same laws as the life of all Nature, but the law is not realized in the same way in these two spheres. The phenomena of Nature occur more distinctively and regularly than do the phenomena of history. The plant blooms and gives fruit at a given time known to us in advance; a living thing can neither extend nor shorten the extent of its own lifetime. There is no such regular, determined development in history. Law is given to it [history], the fulfillment of which is inevitable, but the period of its fulfillment is not stated—ten years or ten centuries—it is all the same. The law stands as a goal towards which mankind moves irrepressibly. But it neither matters to him which road he takes nor whether he loses time on the way.

The speed at which each nation traversed the path to progress was left for its great men to set.

> It is precisely here that the separate personality enters into all its rights. Here the personality appears not as a tool, but on its own, as a supporter or an opponent of historical law and taken upon itself by right, responsibility for the whole orders of events which have been summoned or suppressed by it. This is why its [the personality's] character, its passions, its internal development become for the thinking historian an important and deeply absorbing subject of study[48]

Statements like those just cited furnish one with the opportunity to define the limits which Granovskii imposed upon deterministic history. He held himself back from unreserved historical determinism when he admitted that the historian's findings were characterized by an unavoidable inexactitude. Furthermore, he was too much of a humanist to abandon himself utterly to conceiving of history as strictly bound by laws. Yet, as he delineated the force of historical laws, Granovskii, likewise admitted that the individual possessed restricted power to hasten historical development.

> Man is impatient; he believes that with the fall of one age a better one begins immediately, but history

is unhurried. Destroying one order of things, it allots time for its ruins to decay, and the destroyers of the previous order never see with their own eyes the goal toward which they moved. Consequently, we see in modern history the steady, uninterrupted battles between the elements which remain intact from the Middle Ages, new demands, new scholarship, and new ideas.[49]

Thus Granovskii was very far from taking the cataclysmic view of history which Soviet historians have ascribed to him.

During a short series of public lectures which he delivered in 1851, Granovskii payed some attention to the part which great men played in history. He argued that men became great when they were selected by history for some purpose. It must be observed that here, as throughout Granovskii's discussion of the meaning and function of history, he attached an animate quality to both scholarship and the historical process itself. One might even go so far as to say that for Granovskii, the concept of *History* became synonymous with God and connoted the interaction of man and Deity. This is the case in what follows.

As defined by Granovskii, the 'great man' necessarily produced effects which outlasted his lifetime and was somehow the incarnation of 'Spirit'.

> A people is something collective. Its collective idea, its collective will ought, for self-discovery, to be transformed into the thought and will of one person endowed with an especially sensitive moral ear, with an especially keen intellectual eye. Such people wrap in a living expression what was concealed to us in the thought of the people and express in a visible feat the obscure strivings and desires of their compatriots or contemporaries.

Having captured the spirit of their times, great men become the symbols of an entire people. However, they do not appear accidentally.

Granovskii returned to one of his favorite themes, the minimal impact of chance upon history.

> But with the opinion which I have previously expressed is associated another groundless one which we may do without, according to which great people appear somehow by chance. We notice upon this occasion that the great role of chance is tolerated only in ages of intellectual and moral decay, when man stops believing in the lawful movement of events; when he loses sight of the divine tie which binds the whole life of mankind.

Like Hegel and Schelling, Granovskii had become convinced that nineteenth-century man would not be content with anything short of laws which accounted for the phenomena of this world. Resembling both the *philosophes* and these two German philosophers, he envisioned God as at the zenith of world order, as its first cause, and as its architect. By implication, knowledge of the world was knowledge of God. In this regard, Granovskii's ideas merged with von Ranke's.

Moreover, both he and von Ranke believed that past and present were linked because the latter was both the product of and instructed by the former.

> Of course, the place belonging to the great man in the chain of events is not always clear to us; the object of his activity is not always clear. Centuries go by, but he remains a bloody and mournful riddle, and we do not know why he came; why he stirred up nations. The rumors evoked by him are to such an extent mutually contradictory that we may not, with any precision, delineate the influence manifested by him. Must that which we do not understand today remain not understood tomorrow? Must not each new event shed light upon events apparently completed long ago and isolated? The meaning of isolated events is sometimes disclosed only in the course of centuries and even of millenia. In such cases, scholarship is not in a position to outstrip life itself and must patiently await new facts, without which the cycle of well-known developments would be incomplete.

Granovskii realized that time was the historian's most faithful ally because it permitted him to see events in perspective. Enumerating the other facets of historical perspective, Granovskii argued that the great man was inextricably bound to his own era, nation, and circumstances. He must be understood against this background.

> For the study of each great man we must turn our attention to his personality; to the land upon which he grew; to the time in which he acted. His life and activity is composed of this three-fold character. . . . In the presence of attentive contemplation of great personalities, they appear to us as revelations of an entire nation and an entire age. For whatever reason they were called to the earth, for good or for ill, in any case, they stand not apart, not independently, but strongly and closely linked with the earth upon which they grew and with the time in which they acted.[50]

Calling to mind the Soviet characterization of Granovskii as a sort of forerunner of historical materialism, one must underscore the significance of the fact that in establishing the context within which the historical personality must be understood, Granovskii made no provision for economic or class status. . . .

Notes

[1] Among the works from which these opinions have been distilled are: S. A. Asinovskaja, *Iz istorii peredovyx*

idej v russkoj medievistike: T. N. Granovskij, (Moscow, 1955), 119-124; I. N. Borozdin, 'K voprosu ob u ennyx raznoglasijax russkix medievistikov sorokovyx godov XIX veka', *Srednie veka,* (1955), 345-356; the introductory essays in S. S. Dmitriev, *Granovskij, Timofej, Nikolaevi : Bibliografija (1828-1967),* (Moscow, 1969); M. M. Grigor'jan, 'Filosofskie i sociologi eskie vzgljady T. N. Granovskogo', *Russkaja progressivnaja filosofskaja mysl' XIX veka 30-60 e gody* (Moscow, 1959), 33-120; E. V. Gutnova, *Istoriografija istorii srednix vekov* (Moscow, 1974), 246-254; L. E. Kertman, 'Evoljucija istori eskix vzgljadov T. N. Granovskogo', *Nau nye zapiski Kievskogo Universiteta,* Vyp. 1,6 (1947), 91-126.

[2] L. S. Cetlin, *Iz istorii nau noj mysli v Rossii* (Moscow, 1958), 197; E. A. Kosminskij, *Problemy anglijskogo feodalizma i istoriografii srednix vekov (Sbornik statej),* (Moscow, 1963), 426; O. A. Vajnštejn, *Istoriografija srednix vekov v svjazi s razvitiem istori esk oj mysli ot na ala srednix vekov do našix dnej* (Moscow-Leningrad, 1940), 298.

[3] *Filosofskaja enciklopedija* (5 v., Moscow, 1960-1970), I, 402-403.

[4] T. H. von Laue, *Leopold Ranke: The Formative Years* (Princeton, 1950), 116.

[5] *Ibid.,* 122-123.

[6] Leopold von Ranke, 'On the Character of Historical Science', in Leopold von Ranke, *The Theory and Practice of History* (Georg G. Iggers and Conrad von Moltke, eds., New York, 1973), 39-44.

[7] Leopold von Ranke, 'On Progress in History' (a lecture delivered in 1854), *Ibid.,* 51-55.

[8] Leopold von Ranke, *Universal History: The Oldest Historical Group of Nations and the Greeks* (G. W. Prothero, ed., New York, 1885), XII.

[9] G. W. F. Hegel, *The Philosophy of History* (Carl J. Friedrich, ed., J. Sibree, tr., New York, 1956), 250.

[10] Leopold von Ranke, *Universal History* XIII.

[11] Leopold von Ranke, 'On the Relations of History and Philosophy', *Theory and Practice of History* 30.

[12] Leopold von Ranke, *Universal History* X-XI.

[13] Peter Gay, *Style in History* (New York, 1974), 68.

[14] *Ibid.,* 80-85.

[15] T. N. Granovskii to Ia. M. Neverov, winter, 1836-1837, reprinted in Ia. M. Neverov, 'Timofei Nikolaevich

Granovskii professor Moskovskogo Universiteta, 1834-1856', *Russkaia starina* 27 (1880), 746. See also T. N. Granovskii to V. V. Grigor'ev, February 3, 1838, *Shchukinskii sbornik* (10th ed., Moscow, 1912), 92, in which Granovskii expressed similar feelings.

[16] For example, see *Lekcii T. N. Granovskogo po istorii pozdnego srednevekov'ja (zapiski slušatelej s avtorskoj pravkoj),* (S. A. Asinovskaja and L. A. Nikitina, eds., Moscow, 1971), 331.

[17] *Lekcii Granovskogo po istorii srednevekov'ja* (S. A. Asinovskaja, ed., Moscow, 1961), 35; 37-38.

[18] *Ibid.,* 40.

[19] *Ibid.,* 36.

[20] Johann Gottfried Herder, 'Ideas for a Philosophy of History of Mankind', in J. G. Herder, *On Social and Political Culture* (F. M. Barnard, ed. tr., London, 1969), 291.

[21] Lekcii Granovskogo (1961), 40.

[22] *Ibid.,* 41.

[23] See the introduction to Friedrich Schelling, *The Ages of the World* (Frederic DeWolfe Bolman, ed., New York, 1942), 14-17.

[24] For additional commentary on this point, see. V. Buzeskul, *Vseobš aja istorija i ee predstaviteli v Rossii v XIX i na ale XX veka* (Leningrad, 1929), 63.

[25] Compare J. G. Herder, 'On Social and Political Culture', 188 with T. N. Granovskii, 'Chetyre istoricheskie kharakteristiki Timur, Aleksandr Velikii, Ludovik IX, Francis Bekon', *Sochineniia Granovskogo* (2d ed., 2v., Moscow, 1866), I, 341. Unless otherwise stated, all citations are drawn from this edition.

[26] N. I. Kareev, *Filosofiia istorii v russkoi literature* (St. Petersburg, 1912), 23.

[27] T. N. Granovskii quoted in *Ibid.,* 50.

[28] S. A. Asinovskaja, *Iz istorii peredovyx idej,* 149, relies upon Chernyshevskii who wrote of Granovskii that "He was one of the strongest intermediaries between scholarship and our society. . ." See N. G. Chernyshevskii, 'Sochineniia Granovskogo, tom pervyi, Moskva, 1856', (a review) N. G. ernyševskij, *Polnoe sobranie so inenij* (15 v., Moscow, 1939-1953), III, 352-353.

[29] P. Miliukov, *Iz istorii russkoi intelligentsii, Shornik statei i etiudov* (St. Petersburg, 1903), 262.

[30] T. N. Granovskii, 'Abbat Sugerii', *Sochineniia Granovoskogo* I, 240-241.

[31] T. N. Granovskii, 'Istoricheskaia literatura vo Frantsii i Germanii v 1847 godu', *Ibid.,* II, 190-191. The image of man as the material, the builder, the architect, and changing user of the mutating edifice of universal history is explored in George Dennis O'Brien, *Hegel on Reason and History: A Contemporary Interpretation* (Chicago, 1975), 98.

[32] The above is a paraphrase of T. N. Granovskii, *Ibid.,* 192.

[33] Leopold von Ranke as quoted by Herbert P. Adams, 'Leopold von Ranke', *Report of the Proceedings of the American Historical Association,* Vol. 3, No. 1 (1889), 109.

[34] G. W. F. Hegel, *The Philosophy of History,* 19.

[35] *Ibid.*

[36] *Ibid.,* 30.

[37] *Ibid.,* 39.

[38] *Ibid.,* 258.

[39] *Ibid.,* 6. George O'Brien offered the following reading of this passage: "It is not that the lessons are there but we are too sluggardly to apply them. The message is much more radical: there are no *lessons* of history in a conventional sense, and that is what makes the use of history for pointing political or moral examples so useless". George O'Brien, *Hegel on Reason and History,* 7.

[40] Friedrich Schelling, *The Ages of the World,* 14-17.

[41] *Ibid.,* 20.

[42] *Ibid.,* 60.

[43] For the manner in which Ranke reacted to Hegel's philosophy, see, T. H. von Laue, *Leopold Ranke,* 31;96; 111; 116-117; 123.

[44] *Ibid.,* 71ff.

[45] T. N. Granovskii, 'Soderzhaniia uchebnika vseobshchei istorii: vvedenie', *Sochineniia Granovskogo* (4th ed., 2v., Moscow, 1900), II, 605.

[46] *Lekcii Granovskogo,* (1961), 90.

[47] T. N. Granovskii, 'Reforma v Anglii', *Sochineiia Granovskogo* II, 242-243.

[48] *Ibid.,* 250-251.

[49] *Lekcii Granovskogo* (1961), 33. For Granovskii's views relative to the fusion of Roman and Germanic cultures during the Middle Ages, see the same, 145.

[50] Granovskii expressed his views on the personality most completely in, 'Chetyre istoricheskie kharakteristiki, Timur, Aleksandr Velikii, Ludovik IX, [Francis] Bekon', *Sochineniia Granovskogo* I, 331-333. George O'Brien explained the notion that the great man was, for Hegel, the sum of a society of free individuals: "In the final stage, as in the primary stage, the society is focused in the person of a particular individual". George O'Brian, *Hegel on Reason and History,* 124. . . .

Derek Offord (essay date 1985)

SOURCE: "Timofey Nikolayevich Granovsky (1813-1855)," in *Portraits of Early Russian Liberals: A Study of the Thought of T. N. Granovsky, V. P. Botkin, P. V. Annenkov, A. V. Druzhinin and K. D. Kavelin,* Cambridge University Press, 1985, pp. 44-78.

[*In the excerpt that follows, Offord discusses Granovskii's intellectual influence and provides a detailed account of his liberalism, Westernism, and humanism, as well as his deep-seated belief in the importance of moral character in the political arena.*]

Granovsky's status in the intelligentsia and the reasons for his neglect

In October 1855 Turgenev addressed to the editors of the journal *Sovremennik* an obituary notice, which was headed by an epigraph from Schiller, *'Auch die Todten sollen leben'* ('the dead must also live'), and began with an account of a funeral Turgenev had attended the day before:

> Yesterday Granovsky's funeral took place. I am not going to describe to you how much his death affected me. His loss may be reckoned society's loss and will be received with bitter perplexity and grief in many hearts throughout Russia. His funeral was a moving and deeply significant occasion; it will remain an important event in the memory of everyone who took part in it. I shall never forget the long procession, the coffin gently rocking on the shoulders of the students, the bare heads and young faces ennobled by an expression of honest and sincere sorrow, nor how many people in spite of themselves tarried among the scattered graves of the cemetery even when everything was over and after the last handful of earth had fallen on the remains of the beloved teacher . . . [1]

The occasion was not the pretext for an overtly political demonstration, as the funerals of prominent figures in the Russian intelligentsia were later to become. But

in the dignified mourning described by Turgenev there was expressed a sense of loss which was both a more fitting tribute than public disorder to the man who was being buried and a more telling indication of his significance in the national life. A man had been lost who had not only established himself, during fifteen years as Professor of World History at the University of Moscow, as the most revered teacher of his generation but who had also been, in Herzen's words, one of 'the most luminous and remarkable personalities'[2] in the intellectual life of Russia in the 1840s, itself remembered as a 'marvellous decade'.[3]

However, by comparison with Belinsky and Herzen, with whom contemporaries tended to rank him as an equal, Granovsky has received little attention from students of Russian thought.[4] There are perhaps three reasons for this comparative neglect. The first lies in the volume and nature of Granovsky's work itself. Granovsky published relatively little, and those monographs on universal history which we do have, ranging from his master's dissertation on medieval Pomeranian cities and his doctor's dissertation on the French Abbot Suger to essays on Alexander the Great and Tamburlaine, relate only obliquely to the Russian intellectual life of his time. His lectures to his students and his public lectures, for the most part, were not published, and, although substantial parts of his courses on ancient and medieval history have been reconstructed from the notes of students[5] (who must have been extremely diligent and nimble), such transcripts must obviously be treated with some caution. Most of his own manuscripts have been lost; in any case the mature lecturer tended to extemporise even on those rare occasions when he came to the lectern equipped with a lecture written out in its entirety, and it seems that the full force of his lectures was lost in the transcription.

The second probable reason for Granovsky's neglect lies in the nature of the intellectual life of his time. For, in spite of the dynamic growth of publicism, intellectual authority tended, in the 1840s at any rate, to derive as much from the stature of an individual in the circle of his intimates as from his public utterances. This stature, moreover, owed much in circles still imbued with notions of moral nobility to personal qualities with which Granovsky was richly endowed. 'One comes across few such loving, sincere, saintly and pure natures', wrote Belinsky in 1840; Granovsky had a 'pure, noble soul', an engaging innocence and a warmth that instantly conveyed itself to others.[6] To Herzen too Granovsky was an 'affectionate, serene, indulgent spirit', who possessed a 'wonderful power of love' and a nature 'so remote from the irritability of diffidence and from pretentiousness', 'so pure, so open' that he was extraordinarily easy to get on with.[7] Indeed, all sources describe him as a gentle, compassionate and conciliatory man who lived for others rather than for himself and gave generously of his time to those who came to him for help and advice. But these qualities are less manifest to subsequent generations than the persuasiveness of ideas committed to print and there is therefore some force in Panayev's warning that it is almost impossible to explain the reputation of Granovsky to those who had not known him.[8]

A third reason for the relative neglect of Granovsky, however, undoubtedly lies in the complexion of his thought. For although he died in 1855, just before the period in which many Russian writers and thinkers felt obliged to make a choice between what might be broadly termed liberalism and socialism, nevertheless in essence Granovsky had already made his own choice, in favour of liberalism. His thought is therefore naturally less attractive to Soviet scholars than that of his contemporaries Belinsky and Herzen, whose more revolutionary leanings were in the second half of the 1840s already becoming a source of friction among the so-called Westernisers. Admittedly Granovsky continues to be respected in Soviet historiography as a scholar and, more importantly, as a humanitarian intellectual who, because of his premature death, never had the need or the opportunity to translate his views into explicitly political terms. He cannot therefore be deemed to have reneged on an earlier commitment to opposition to the Russian autocracy or be tainted by association with the critics of those radicals who began in the late 1850s to lay the theoretical foundations for a socialist revolutionary movement. But the fact remains that his outlook is in many respects very close to that of Botkin, Annenkov and Kavelin—with all of whom he had been on intimate personal terms—who did in the second half of the 1850s become leading representatives of a liberal tendency in Russian thought that was scorned by Chernyshevsky and that has been despised ever since by Russian socialists as half-hearted, ineffectual and hypocritical.

It is the purpose of this chapter to attempt to re-establish the fact, which has thus become rather obscured, that Granovsky did indeed play one of the most important roles in Russian intellectual life in the 1840s and thereby to account for the high regard in which he was held by his contemporaries. This purpose may best be served not by giving a strictly chronological survey of his work but by dealing with each of the three main aspects of his contribution to Russian intellectual life— as historian, as a leading 'Westerniser' and as a thinker occupying a liberal position on the political spectrum. Admittedly Granovsky's thought did undergo certain changes or was modified in the course of time, but not so much as to make this thematic approach unsatisfactory in his case; indeed, the tenor of his thought, like its tone, remained remarkably stable in a period when others, particularly Belinsky and Herzen, were prone to more or less abrupt changes of course.

. . . . .

Granovsky's Westernism

What values, though, did Granovsky contrive to express in his lectures and writings which could give rise to these extravagant expressions of gratitude and enthusiasm? On the broadest level there was in Granovsky's scholarship a warm, compassionate humanism that posed an implicit challenge to a brutish and obscurantist régime. Reviewers immediately noted this quality. 'What roundedness in each lecture, what a broad view and what humanity!' wrote one of those present at the public lectures; 'this is a work of art, a story full of love and energy'. A 'broad and much encompassing love' informed the lecturer's words, wrote another commentator, 'love for what is arising, which he joyfully greets, and love for what is dying, which he buries with tears'.[38] It was a quality on which his devoted biographer, A. V. Stankevich, younger brother of the Hegelian to whom Granovsky had been so close in his youth, chose to dwell in the concluding passage of his work.[39] Granovsky, then, belongs to that long and broad humanist tradition in European culture which dates back as far as the Renaissance and whose representatives take a warm and catholic interest in all man's religious, artistic, scientific and political strivings.

On another level there is in Granovsky's work a vein of social protest which could easily be detected by a public already adept at the elucidation of allegory and which humanitarian men of his generation were bound to welcome. Some of his passages on the Middle Ages, for example, had a special pertinence for an educated class which believed their own country had in many respects not progressed beyond those times. Relations between lord and serf in Western Europe in the feudal period had much in common with relations between landowner and peasant in the Russia of the 1840s—a relationship which was beginning to attract the attention of imaginative writers but which the government, having refused to contemplate the abolition of serfdom, considered too sensitive an issue to be allowed open discussion. The rights of the lord over his serfs in Western Europe in the tenth and eleventh centuries, Granovsky proclaimed in his lectures, were not yet defined by law. The lord had the right of life and death over his serfs, took money and other taxes from them and could try and sentence them at will. His authority was the most severe and dismal despotism. From the unlimited power of one individual over a herd of people—and the 'slaves' of feudal times merited that description—there naturally developed a mocking and wilful attitude of lord to common man, a contempt for human dignity.[40] Never was the condition of the masses more burdensome and degrading, never did individuals or a social group as a whole achieve such unbridled freedom.[41] In Granovsky's doctoral dissertation too there are references, which have an equally transparent application to the Russia of his time, to the 'predatory' feudal lord or the lawless barons who considered social order incompatible with their personal rights and civilisation with oppression.[42] Elsewhere Granovsky condemns tyrannical institutions and underlines the harmful effects of their barbarousness. The Spanish Inquisition, for example, is held responsible for the decline of Spain's prosperity and the coarsening of her people, who were naturally noble and gifted.[43]

There was, however, yet another, equally important level of meaning in Granovsky's historical scholarship, beyond its broad humanism and its obvious implicit condemnation of the Russia of the 1840s with her irresponsible arbitrary government and her serf-owning lords bound by no law. For this scholarship reflected the broader concern of the intelligentsia in the age of Nicholas I to establish Russia's national identity and thence to plot her destiny (which in fact radical thinkers were rather prone to depict as no less glorious than, if different from, the destiny conceived by conservatives). To a large extent, of course, the search for an answer to the riddle of Russia's national destiny was carried out in imaginative literature, and indeed the blossoming of that literature was one indication of the growth of a distinctive consciousness. But the search could also be conducted in the field of history. Like other European peoples who were becoming conscious of their nationhood during the Romantic period, the Russians began in the 1820s, 1830s and 1840s to develop an interest in their historical past, which found expression in their enthusiasm for the historical novels of Zagoskin and Lazhechnikov, in the *Philosophical Letters* of Chaadayev and in the earnest if fanciful researches of the Slavophiles. And Granovsky, even though his field was universal and, in particular, medieval Western European history, used the discipline to make one of the most serious contributions to the debate which these researches generated.

It is worth emphasising at the outset that Granovsky was no more an advocate of indiscriminate aping of things foreign than other major so-called Westernisers, such as Belinsky and Herzen. He complains, for example, in a review of a book by a fellow historian, Kudryavtsev, of the latter's needless introduction into his work of linguistic borrowings from Western European languages, such as *shef, fortuna* and *traditsiya.*[44] Nor is he any less conscious than the Slavophiles of his Russianness or less determined than they to fulfil a patriotic duty. He looks on the connection with the native land as the basis of a people's morality, and agrees with a correspondent that 'real activity' is possible 'only on one's native soil'.[45] He possesses that same 'sense of duty' which compels all his contem-

poraries to attempt to serve their country in whatever sphere circumstances might permit[46] (and which it is tempting to trace to the more general notion of service which it was incumbent on the noble to give to his sovereign). He complains of the ignorance of Russia which he encounters in his travels abroad. (A young German woman had asked him during his stay in Berlin, for example, whether it was true that outside St Petersburg and Moscow Russian women still wore Tartar costume. 'Not exactly', Granovsky had replied, 'for our provincial ladies have as clothes the furs of wild animals which they kill themselves in the hunt.')[47] Finally, and in a different key, in a speech delivered to his students in 1845, shortly after his defence of his master's dissertation, Granovsky anticipates 'noble' and 'long' service of 'our great Russia', Russia which strides forward with contempt for the slanderous foreigners—he is no doubt referring to Custine, among others—who see in Russians 'only frivolous imitators of Western forms without any content of [their] own'.[48] He is therefore surely foremost among those Westernisers of whom Herzen was thinking when he conceived his felicitous image of the double-headed eagle which looked in different directions, East and West, for its inspiration, but in which there beat the same Russian heart.

Nevertheless Granovsky was also scathingly critical of those people—and he had the Slavophiles in mind—who loved 'not the living Rus, but a decrepit phantom summoned by them from the tomb', people who profanely worshipped an idol created by their own fanciful imagination.[49] As early as 1839 he emphatically rejects the main Slavophile propositions, concerning the decay of the West, the wisdom of the writings of the fathers of the Greek Orthodox Church and the damage supposedly done by Peter the Great in tearing away the Russians from their own historical heritage. Kireyevsky was saying these things in prose and Khomyakov in verse. It was irritating that they were gaining a following among the students; indeed, 'Slavonic patriotism' was regnant in Moscow, Granovsky lamented. He intended, however, to rebel against it from the rostrum.[50] His master's dissertation too contains implicit criticism of the Slavophiles, in so far as they are equated in it with those historians who 'remould the past in accordance with personal whim or national vanity'. Granovsky examines the existing body of knowledge on the medieval Pomeranian townships of Jomsborg and Wollin. Medieval chroniclers and writers of the age of the Reformation had tended to confuse these two townships, the first of which was a Norman fortress on the Baltic and the second a Slavic settlement in the same region. Popular imagination and later historical scholarship had gone even further and had fused the two settlements into a myth of the magnificent city of Vineta, a northern Venice which had been engulfed by the sea in divine retribution for its pride in its wealth and the ruins of which were said to be sometimes visible beneath the waves off the Pomeranian shore. This glorious legendary city, however, existed only in the imagination of misguided scholars, Granovsky contended; it had no more basis in historical fact, we are intended to infer, than the similarly romantic fantasies of the Slavophiles.[51]

It was in the history of the West rather than in a supposedly more glorious Russian national past that Granovsky thought the key to Russia's destiny should be sought, and in his writings and lectures on Western Europe in the Middle Ages he outlined the heritage which Russia seemed to lack. In the first place, of course, the West had enjoyed a vigorous intellectual tradition. The medieval schoolmen, for instance, for all their shortcomings, had exuded a healthy confidence in the power of human reason; their conviction that the truth could be taken by storm like a medieval castle might have been naïve, but they had lent the European mind a noble curiosity and developed in it considerable powers of logic.[52] In the second place, the West had a democratic tradition which Russia lacked. Western European peoples had long since promoted concepts of freedom and constitutional forms of government. Spanish history, for instance, offered examples as early as the fourteenth century which greatly interested Granovsky. 'A wonderful people!' Granovsky wrote of the Spaniards.

> They understood constitutional forms at a time when people didn't have any conception of them anywhere else. In 1305 the Spanish Cortes had laid down that during their sessions the King's troops should leave the town: otherwise votes would not be free. They had many such laws. Present-day Europe is still fighting for what they had then.

And it was as a result of his interest in this subject that Granovsky was in 1838 considering the formation and decline of free urban communes in the Middle Ages as a possible theme for a master's dissertation.[53] He also greatly admired the Quakers, whose social and moral theories, he believed, were based on a deep respect for human dignity, and he praised their democratic community, their egalitarianism and their practice of settling matters by discussion among elected representatives.[54]

In the third place, the West had greatly benefited—so Granovsky believed, unlike the Slavophiles—from aspects of classical civilisation which had been passed on to medieval Europe through the Roman Empire, notably the institutions and experience of civilian administration and Roman law.[55] One example of the wisdom of Roman legislation—and an example of which Nicolaevan Russia, with its inequality before the law, would do well to take note—was the *lex frumentaria,* according to which the poorest citizens were entitled to a monthly allowance of grain at a quarter of the going rate.[56] Granovsky also noted that even in feudal times individuals were to be found who had improved their own imperfect societies by instilling in them certain principles inherited from the ancient world. Louis IX of France, for example, by his own sense of law and by the introduction into his courts of jurists imbued with the ideas of Roman legislation, had invested monarchic authority with the 'moral radiance of incorruptible justice' and had disposed the people to see the king as a dispassionate judge.[57]

It is worth pausing briefly at this point to emphasise the cardinal importance of Granovsky's admiration of the heritage of Roman law in Western Europe (even though that admiration is only succinctly expressed) and to underline the significance that the concept of legality had for the liberal political philosophy which we find in an embryonic form in Granovsky's historical scholarship. Owing to the lack of interest, within the Orthodox Church, in the pursuit of rational as opposed to spiritual wisdom, and as a result too of the relatively late beginning of the attempt substantially to secularise her culture, Russia lacked a strong and ancient tradition of jurisprudence just as she lacked a related history of philosophical and political speculation of the sort that had flourished in Western Europe since the Renaissance. Enlightened individuals such as Radishchev, who himself had a legal training, did from the time of Catherine II bemoan the absence in Russia of the concepts to which such a tradition might have given rise. Radishchev found no sense of natural justice or legality in the Russian administration either at national or local level or indeed on the estates of the gentry who, like Russian officials, are able throughout the *Journey from St Petersburg to Moscow* to commit acts of callousness and brutality with impunity. And yet even within the intelligentsia the supporters of Western legal concepts still had their powerful detractors in the 1840s and '50s. To the Slavophiles in particular Roman law and the Western system of formal, secular justice operating on the basis of statute as well as custom seemed a manifestation of pernicious rationalism, a corrupting influence on Christianity. For them the moral law laid down in Christianity in its Orthodox form was absolutely binding and for the purpose of regulating everyday conduct in the community it required the support of convention, not legislation and highly developed secular judicial agencies. Granovsky, then, in commending the concept of a temporal law to which all were subject, irrespective of their social standing, was again implicitly attacking both tsarist society and the opponents of his Westernism within the intelligentsia. The former was indefensible because its members' accountability for their conduct tended to vary in relation to their social status and because examples of arbitrariness were legion; and the latter were to be reproached for showing less interest in the physical protection of the individual citizen and the definition of his rights than in the preservation of his supposed moral and spiritual well-being. At the same time, however, Granovsky was raising a subject of particular importance to men of liberal outlook. For a sense of legality in society was a necessary adjunct to the liberty which liberals hoped the individual (or the enlightened individual, at least) would enjoy. Like the other Russian Westernisers of the 1840s Granovsky was concerned, as we shall see, to free the individual from the various forms of oppression which had stifled him. But once the iron grip of the autocratic state had been loosened, once the individual had broken away from Aksakov's 'moral choir' and marked himself off from the uniform community, he would need certain indefeasible rights and liberties and the protection of the law if he were to pursue his interests in safety and without hindrance.

It is characteristic, however, of the thought of the Westernisers of the 1840s, with their interest in ethical questions, that Granovsky should have attached great importance not only to the intellectual vitality and the democratic and legal traditions of Western Europe but also to its Christian ethos, which, he believed, had exercised an immense civilising influence. For one thing the Western Church, he contended, had directly helped to improve the condition of the serfs, by giving them shelter, accepting them into its ranks and conferring on those who lived on church lands greater rights than those enjoyed by serfs living on the lands of laymen. More importantly, the Church had indirectly mitigated the evil of serfdom by instilling moral ideals in the representatives of secular authority.[58] The moral education of the monarchy is the major theme of Granovsky's doctoral dissertation on the twelfth-century Abbot Suger, who in his capacity as representative of the Church and through his close personal relationship with Louis VI gave the secular powers a conception of their purpose and duty which they had hitherto lacked. From the time of Suger the monarchy had begun to restrain the centrifugal forces of feudal society, subordinating separate baronial interests to the general weal of the state, and to strengthen the moral bases on which society rested and which gave rise to a deep sense of law. Seen in this light the Church was not an instrument of oppression in the service of the state; rather the state was the agent of the Church in the defence of those who had been oppressed by feudalism in the course of its long ascendancy.[59]

There is one further respect in which religious or moral ideas seemed to Granovsky to have conferred on Western civilisation benefits which Russia had not enjoyed. They acted as a cohesive force, they lent societies a certain unity which was attractive to men of cosmopolitan and liberal temper, such as Granovsky, who hoped for the erosion of the more blatant divisions in Russian society and wished to avoid the conflicts to which such divisions might shortly give rise. Therefore Granovsky, like Chaadayev in his *Philosophical Letters,* admires those men who by their vision and will had created the conditions in which such unifying ideas could be disseminated. Above all he praises Charlemagne, to whom one of the most memorable lectures of his public series of 1843-4 was devoted. By stopping tribal migrations, by bringing separate peoples under a single administration and by giving them a common law and religion, Charlemagne had laid the foundations for a great civilisation which, in spite of all its subsequent schisms, had retained something common to all its disparate constituent parts.[60] Not that Granovsky considers Christian doctrine the only source of unifying ideas, or Western European monarchs the only men capable of promoting them: he also offers a favourable assessment of Alexander the Great's pre-Christian vision of universal empire, his attempt to merge victorious Greek and vanquished Persian into one nation and his creation of the possibility, through the foundation of the city of Alexandria, of a confluence of the ideas of East and West.[61]

It is in the light of Granovsky's emphasis on the unifying role of the great historical individual, inspired by some profound moral idea, that we should consider his admiration for Peter the Great, the ruler who more than any other had attempted to bring Russia into the mainstream of European civilisation. Whilst the Slavophiles viewed Peter with hatred as being chiefly responsible for the divorce of Russia from her sacred past, Granovsky looked on him as the only Russian ruler who had been capable of giving his country a sense of high national purpose. As early as 1839 Granovsky complains that Peter is not understood in Moscow circles, where he is not regarded with the gratitude due to him.[62] Much later, in 1854, he rebukes Herzen for casting aspersions on Peter. 'The longer we live', wrote Granovsky, 'the more the image of Peter towers before us.'[63] And in 1855 he describes his awe of a portrait of Peter, painted just after the ruler's death, which he had seen during a visit to Pogodin's house. He had almost sobbed contemplating this 'divinely beautiful face'. The 'tranquil beauty of the upper part' was impossible to describe: only a 'great, infinitely noble and holy idea' could have laid on its brow the 'stamp of such tranquillity'. But the lips were tight with grief and anger, as if they were still trembling, still involved in the cares and anxieties of life. What a man was Peter, who had given Russia a 'right to a history' and who almost single-handed had announced Russia's historical mission.[64] Like Chaadayev, then, Granovsky looked on Peter as the great man who had thrown down for Russia the 'cloak of civilisation'.[65] Like Chaadayev too he seems not to have baulked at the ruthlessness with which such rulers as Charlemagne, Alexander and Peter set about translating their vision into reality, even though in the process they crushed those hapless individuals, such as the 'poor Yevgenity' of Pushkin's *Bronze Horseman,* whose interests and dignity Granovsky was at the same time so anxious to protect.

The spirit of chivalry

There is another manifestation of Granovsky's reverence for Western European civilisation, besides his interest in its law, its liberties, its Christianity and its sense of moral unity, which deserves particular attention, namely his enthusiastic appraisal of the institution of knight-errantry. Like Roman law, the Western Church and the figure of Peter the Great, this institution excited animosity among the Slavophiles; I. Kireyevsky, for instance, on more than one occasion devoted bitterly critical passages to it. Granovsky, on the other hand, regarded the institution and its representatives with something akin to awe. Partly inspired perhaps by the novels of Walter Scott, which he first read at an early age and for which he retained a lifelong fondness,[66] he returned repeatedly to the subject with an almost juvenile relish, devoting articles full of sympathy and enthusiasm, for example, to the Castilian hero celebrated in the epic *El Cid* and to the late fifteenth- and early sixteenth-century French knight, Pierre Terrail de Bayard, the knight *'sans peur et sans reproche'*.[67] The institution of knighthood, Granovsky argues, reflected the ennobling influence of the Catholic Church on Western European civilisation. Numerous practices and qualities of the knighthood, he contends, emanated from the Church—for example, fasting, prayer, chastity, renunciation of material concerns, abhorrence of avarice, the concept of service to a master or mistress, the defence of the weak, such as widows and orphans. Thus within feudal society, which was based on the oppression of the weak by the strong, there arose its very antithesis, an institution dedicated to the defence of the otherwise defenceless.[68]

On one level, of course, the knighthood was an expression of the spirit of the Middle Ages and, together with the Church which had moulded its character, the finest achievement of that time, the product of a quest for moral improvement.[69] But it is also tempting to interpret the institution, as it is presented by Granovsky, in a very loose sense, as a model for or moral example to men of another time who found themselves in a society not altogether dissimilar to the feudal order in which the institution of knighthood had originated. There was after all a distinctly chivalric quality in the Russian circles of the late 1830s and 1840s with their cult of the *'schöne Seele'* (the impeccable spirit), and with their admiration of Schiller. Indeed, the group of Westernisers of the 1840s, among whom Granovsky was one of the lu-

minaries, was explicitly likened by Annenkov to a 'knightly brotherhood, a fighting order' with no written code but a unity that was clearly understood.[70] And Granovsky in particular appears to have been governed both in private and his public life by precisely such a chivalrous code. He was saddened to think, as he wrote, for example, to his fiancée in June 1841 shortly before their wedding, that so many marriages which had begun with true love on both sides became a source of unhappiness for both partners when love degenerated into a 'kind of indifference' and when the remnants of mutual affection were sustained only by habit. Such a marriage was not for him: 'I should prefer to lose you straightaway', he told his fiancée,

> rather than come to this point of *Spiessbürgerthum* [philistinism] in marriage. It would be death for me if I had to replace the bonds which at present unite us by those of egoism and habit.

And he reassured himself with the thought that love could not be worn out except in a heart 'devoid of all other serious and noble interest'. If a man had a 'beautiful vocation', if he and the wife of his choice were 'moral beings' and intent on their moral improvement, then love would last as long as life itself.[71] His own marriage, to a woman ten years his junior, seems by all accounts to have lived up to these idealistic expectations and to have benefited from the same spirit of generosity and altruism which Granovsky brought to his teaching career and which earned him such affection and popularity among his students.

The same quixotic attitudes came to the fore in a curious episode which took place in Moscow University in 1848. Granvosky and some of his colleagues took exception to the conduct of one Professor Krylov who had publicly execrated his wife for her liaisons with his students. Krylov, in acting as his wife's 'executioner', seemed to be behaving in a manner unworthy of a university teacher, who, Granovsky felt, should set a moral as well as intellectual example to his students. Unfortunately Krylov stubbornly refused to vacate the post which he was held to have brought into disrepute, whereupon Granvosky and his colleagues tendered their resignations in the hope that their example might show future students that a professor could not be 'vicious with impunity'. As a matter of fact, even this stratagem failed in Granovsky's case; he was forbidden to take early retirement on the grounds that he would have to remain at his post for at least a further two years in order to redeem the cost of his stay as a student in Germany in the 1830s.[72] But the episode did clearly reveal a way of looking at the world which always affected the actions and coloured the thought of the 'men of the 1840s' and of which we need to be aware if we are fully to understand their lives and work. Nor was this quixotism without value, even though some of its manifestations were plainly absurd and its application in the Krylov affair of doubtful worthiness. For it indicated the existence of and encouraged a moral commitment, that love of some ideal outside oneself for which Turgenev, himself a member of Granovsky's generation and circle of friends, was later to praise Cervantes' tragi-comic hero in his famous essay, 'Hamlet and Don Quixote'.[73] It persisted beyond the 1840s, too, finding expression in Botkin's admiration for the Spanish *caballero* and even in Druzhinin's commendation of the English gentleman, and coming to the surface again in the avowedly chivalric idealism of the Populists of the Chaykovsky circle of the early 1870s.[74]

Granovsky's moderation: sources of friction with Belinsky, Herzen and Ogaryov

In the atmosphere of the Russia of the 1840s, where ideas and convictions were defended with passion, even ferocity, it was perhaps inevitable that Granovsky's relations with the Slavophiles, several of whom were his close personal friends, would sooner or later deteriorate as a result of his attacks on their views and his enthusiasm for aspects of Western culture. A reconciliation was attempted at the end of his course of public lectures in 1844 and a dinner arranged at which Westernisers and Slavophiles embraced and kissed one another; but the effusive expressions of friendship, as Herzen drily noted, did not prevent those who had been present from disagreeing more than ever only a week later.[75] Passions were inflamed by a lampoon written by Yazykov in which Granovsky was addressed as an ' . . . eloquent bibliophile, The oracle of young ignoramuses, . . . the frivolous companion Of depraved ideas and hopes.'[76] Granovsky's relations with P. Kireyevsky deteriorated to such a point that the two men almost came to a duel. K. Aksakov, sensing that differences were now too great to be overcome, called on Granovsky in the early hours one morning, woke him up, threw his arms round his neck and bid him a tearful farewell.[77] In 1847 Granovsky became embroiled in an ill-humoured polemic with Khomyakov on the abstruse historical question of the moral calibre of the Franks, whom Khomyakov had called a 'corrupt tribe' and whom, as a non-Slavonic race, he was eager to portray as truculent, mendacious and perfidious.[78] And as the years went by Granovsky spoke of the Slavophiles with increasing bitterness.[79]

However, it was not only the Slavophiles from whom Granovsky grew apart as a result of the clarification of his views on Russia and the West in the 1840s. For as they defined their own response to Slavophilism, so the Westernisers began to become aware of differences among themselves too. At first these differences seemed relatively superficial, but their seriousness increased as external circumstances began to change and eventually they proved to be fundamental.

There is no doubt but that temperamental differences, perhaps as ever, played some role in producing this split within the ranks of the Westernisers and in determining the stance of Granovsky in particular. Granovsky had by all accounts a peaceable and instinctively conciliatory nature. In Herzen's words, he 'often brought together in their sympathy with him whole circles that were at enmity among themselves, and friends on the brink of separation'[80] Fine qualities he would recognise and acknowledge wherever he found them, regardless of partisan considerations. He was therefore quite able to respect the Kireyevsky brothers and even at a time when he disagreed profoundly with their views to say that he saw in them more 'holiness, straightforwardness and faith' than he had ever seen in anyone else.[81] Similarly, after his disagreements with Herzen in the mid 1840s he could still write to him, in 1847: 'I remain an incurable Romantic . . . I am an extremely personal man, that is to say I value my personal relationships, and my relationship with you has not been easy of late. Give me your hand, *carissime!*'[82] This strength of personal attachment, what he himself called a 'sacred corner' of his heart, was something Granovsky could not give up.[83] It was perhaps the source of the defence of the dignity of the individual in Granovsky's writings; but it also precluded the extreme ideological commitments and animosities which revolutionary socialism was shortly to require. Granovsky belonged very clearly to the generation of the 'fathers' who in Turgenev's novel could not subordinate things which were sacred to them—love, friendship and art—to a new social and political outlook supposedly underpinned by science.

Granovsky's conciliatory temperament contrasted vividly with that of Belinsky, who was given to fanatical enthusiasms and tacked wildly between opposite intellectual havens. It was characteristic of him, for example, that he could write in 1839, at the time of Belinsky's reconciliation with reality: 'Our convictions are absolutely opposite, but that doesn't stop me from loving him for what is in him . . . '[84] All the same Granovsky did already criticise Belinsky for 'judging and laying down the law about everything in a dictatorial manner',[85] while in 1843 Belinsky tells Botkin that the one thing wrong with Granovsky is his 'moderation'.[86] (Interestingly Belinsky uses the word based on the French, *moderatsiya,* rather than *umerennost'*; it was as if the phenomenon of 'moderation' were itself of foreign origin and not to be confused with *umerennost'*, the virtue of non-commitment extolled by Griboyedov's bureaucrat, Molchalin, and later ridiculed by Saltykov-Shchedrin.)

This temperamental incompatibility naturally gave rise to differences of opinion between Granovsky and Belinsky. Their convictions—and in this both men agreed—were 'diametrically opposed' so that what was white for Granovsky was black for Belinsky and *vice versa*.[87] This difference found expression in an early, and as it turned out portentous, dispute of 1842 on the subject of the French Revolution. In a letter to Botkin—which the latter, according to the custom of the time, promptly read to Granovsky—Belinsky had expressed enthusiasm for Robespierre and the methods of Jacobin dictatorship. The millennium would be brought about on earth, Belinsky wrote, 'not by the honeyed and rapturous phrases of the perfect and fair-souled members of the Gironde, but by the terrorists—by the double-edged sword of the word and deed of the Robespierres and Saint-Justs'.[88] Granovsky replied that Robespierre was the 'shallow' and 'worthless' instrument of other people's will. Belinsky was no doubt attracted to him because Robespierre's revolutionary violence swept away so many members of that class, the aristocracy, which Belinsky detested. But how many petty personal impulses had lain behind Robespierre's actions? He was inferior to Saint-Just, a 'limited fanatic, but a noble and deeply convinced man', and his eloquence could not compare with that of the Girondins, not to mention Mirabeau. As a statesman, moreover, he was 'insignificant'. Admittedly Robespierre was a 'practical person' inasmuch as he was able to 'vulgarise' the larger questions of historical destiny which were at issue by interpreting them in the particular interest of himself and his party. But he lacked the vision of the Girondins, who understood that the purpose of the revolution was not merely to change external political forms but also to solve all the social problems and tensions which had been afflicting the world for so long. The Girondins had defined and drawn attention to all the questions which Europe was now pondering half a century later and they had declared that the revolution was not a 'French event' but a universal one. They had gone to their graves 'pure and holy' having fulfilled their mission on the theoretical level. Robespierre, on the other hand, had looked on the revolution as an exclusively political and an exclusively French event (although he said he believed the opposite to be the case). And it was he, finally, who had given the bourgeoisie a secure position from which it could be dislodged only by a new revolution.[89]

We may surmise that another early manifestation of Granovsky's moderation was his reluctance to follow his defence of the rights of women to its logical conclusion. He believed, his biographer A. V. Stankevich tells us, 'in the possibility of woman's high moral and intellectual development' and was always glad when he found women who were entitled to claim equality with men within the intelligentsia. (Granovsky's own wife, Herzen's wife and Panayeva had attained to this level of development; Yelagina, mother of the Kireyevsky brothers, played an important role in the intellectual life of the late 1830s and early 1840s as hostess of a famous salon, and Yelena Shtakenshneyder had a similar func-

tion in the late 1850s and early 1860s.) This approval of women's aspirations to intellectual equality with men, however, by no means implied a belief that women should enjoy full social equality, as the radicals of the late 1850s and 1860s were to demand. The notion that women should have made careers in business, trade or the law, for example, Granovsky appears to have found distasteful: 'I don't like women who know the laws', he is reported to have said on one occasion *à propos* of a woman who had successfully conducted some litigation. His attitude towards women, then, revealed the broad humanism that was characteristic of the Westernist intelligentsia in the 1840s and a certain gallantry that was typical of Granovsky in particular; nevertheless beneath this idealism there remained a strong respect for social convention, a view of woman as first and foremost wife, mother and, if domestic circumstances allowed, philanthropist in the local community.[90]

By the mid 1840s such differences between Granovsky and more radical contemporaries had begun to multiply and to take on a larger significance. One exchange, after which relations between the antagonists seem never to have been quite the same again, took place between Herzen and Granovsky in 1846 at Sokolovo, an idyllic spot just outside Moscow where in the summer of 1845 both men and their families had rented accommodation which in the following year once more became a meeting place for the leading Westernisers. Herzen's growing interest in the natural sciences and his reading of Feuerbach's *Essence of Christianity* led him towards a philosophical materialism incompatible with the preservation of religious faith. Science, Herzen claims to have observed at Sokolovo, obliged one to accept certain truths whether one liked them or not. Granovsky, however, refused to accept Herzen's 'dry, cold idea of the unity of soul and body' and clung instead to his cherished belief in the immortality of the soul.[91] This belief almost certainly provided Granovsky with some consolation after the loss of people very dear to him, particularly Stankevich and his own two sisters. But it is tempting also to surmise that Granovsky defended such a belief because he already sensed, as Dostoyevsky was to do in the 1860s, that without it man's life on earth would seem intolerably devoid of meaning. Man could not get by without some concepts or notions of 'some higher force, some law of being', he once wrote.[92] That is not to say that Granovsky found arguments to refute Herzen's new materialism; but he had powerful reasons of his own for refusing to accept it.[93]

Other sources of friction with members of the Westernisers' circle confirm Granovsky's moderation, his reluctance to follow the circle's more militant members to extreme conclusions. In January 1847, for example, he rebukes Ogaryov for intolerance, a subject vigorously debated by Botkin and Belinsky in the same year. He had a 'really profound hatred for any intolerance', Granovsky wrote, which did not respect views seriously arrived at by a thinking person. Intolerance was valuable and excusable, he felt, only in the youth who thought he had mastered the truth because he had read and taken to heart an intelligent and noble book, or in people with 'limited and crude' minds, such as the Protestant theologians of the seventeenth and even nineteenth centuries. The more limited a person was intellectually, the more easily he absorbed any little conviction which might enable him to sleep easily. Granovsky realised that his 'scepticism' might be seen as something 'unhealthy' or even a 'sign of weakness', but he was grateful to it for cultivating in him a 'true, humane tolerance'. It was a natural product of his study of history, for there was no science 'more inimical to any dogmatism'. (Whatever one might say about the natural sciences, they would never give one that 'moral strength' which history furnished.)[94]

At the same time Granovsky had to defend himself against renewed criticisms from Belinsky, who was embittered by what he saw as the failure of Granovsky and others to give sufficient support to *Sovremennik*. Indeed, Belinsky even accused Granovsky of trying to ruin *Sovremennik* by continuing to contribute to its main rival, *Otechestvennyye zapiski*. That Granovsky was prepared to write for two journals at the same time and that he was indeed pleased that there were two of similar orientation—such lack of partisanship was incomprehensible, almost offensive, to Belinsky.[95] Again, like Botkin, Granovsky disliked Herzen's *Letters from the Avenue Marigny,* in which Herzen condemned the bourgeois order he found in Paris in 1847. The letters were 'very intelligent in places', Granovsky commented, but there was 'too much *frivolous* Russian superficiality' in them. They reminded Granovsky of the way in which Frenchmen (he no doubt had Custine in mind) wrote about Russia.[96] As for the proletariat, whose suffering inspired the sympathy of Herzen for their cause, Granovsky appears to have looked on this class dispassionately as an inevitable by-product of the development of all 'historical societies' except the patriarchal states of the Orient.[97] He could acknowledge the right of the proletariat, which was just making its clamorous entry on the historical stage, to a higher standard of living. He was also fully aware of the potential of the working class as a historical force and was wont by 1849 to express his feeling that the old world, faced with the emergence of this force, was doomed to decay by quoting a quatrain of Goethe's:

> Komm her! Wir setzen uns zu Tisch,
> Wen möchte solche Narrheit rühren!
> Die Welt geht auseinander wie ein fauler
> Fisch,
> Wir wollen sie nicht balsamieren.[98]

On the other hand, Granovsky was doubtful, as the air of resignation which he shared with Goethe suggests, whether the triumph of the proletariat would produce a wholly better society; indeed, he feared it might mark the ruin of modern civilisation just as the barbarian invasions had brought to an end the Roman era. In particular, he suspected that conditions in a socialist society might not allow the enlightened individual to flourish (and for Granovsky the enlightened individual was not so much a member of an aristocratic minority pursuing refined pleasure as a seeker after elevated moral truths that were valuable to mankind as a whole). Granovsky clearly perceived, then, that the reactionary forces in Western society had themselves underlined the obsolescence of the *anciens régimes* when they had resorted to violence to sustain those régimes. But at the same time he believed that European civilisation was too closely connected with those obsolescent orders for one to be able to predict with certainty what would become of it if they collapsed or for one to relish the prospect of quick and easy success for the new radicalism.[99] It is worth noting, finally, that this ambivalent attitude of Granovsky's towards current events in Western Europe in the late 1840s was quite consistent with his interest as a historian in transitional epochs in the development of societies—a subject on which he read a paper at the home of Count Uvarov in 1849. He valued the youthful optimism of great historical movements as they first manifested themselves; but he also keenly sensed a tragic element in the decline of orders which had once been glorious.[100]

Granovsky's reluctance to embrace the new materialism or to condone intolerance towards the ideological enemy, his refusal wholeheartedly to welcome Herzen's attack on the Western European bourgeoisie—all of these reservations about the movement of Belinsky and Herzen towards a more uncompromising radical position were of a piece with Granovsky's larger objections to the socialist outlook. Western European socialism he saw as a phenomenon which could not be ignored by the historian or the thinking person; but with its utopian insights into the future this socialism was also a 'disease of the century'. It was harmful because it encouraged one to seek solutions to social problems outside the political arena; that is to say, outside the arena in which the liberal expected to be able to determine the course of historical development. As for the violence which would probably be necessary to usher in the socialist utopia—and which Herzen and Belinsky were able to contemplate with equanimity—Granovsky no more approved of it than of the abolition of those old values incompatible with the new socialist outlook. . . .[101]

Notes

[1] I. S. Turgenev, *Polnoe sobraniye sochineniy i pisem,* 28 vols., Moscow-Leningrad, 1960-8, VI, p. 371.

[2] Herzen (A. I. Gertsen), *My Past and Thoughts: The Memoirs of Alexander Herzen*, trans. by Constance

Garnett, revised by Humphrey Higgens, 4 vols., London, 1968, II, p. 499.

[3] The phrase belongs to Annenkov, being the title of his best known memoirs (*Zamechatel 'noye desyatiletiye*); see his *Literaturnyye vospominaniya*, Moscow, 1960, pp. 135-374.

[4] Most of the main Russian works on Granovsky are pre-revolutionary. See esp. A. V. Stankevich, *T. N. Granovskiy i yego perepiska*, 2nd ed., 2 vols., Moscow, 1897 (hereafter Stankevich, I, and Stankevich, II; vol. I is a biography, vol. II contains Granovsky's correspondence, which is an invaluable source of information on his life and thought). See also N. I. Kareyev, *Istoricheskoye mirosozertsaniye Granovskogo*, St Petersburg, 1896; Ch. Vetrinsky [V. Ye. Cheshikhin), *V sorokovykh godakh: Istoriko-literaturnyye ocherki i kharakteristiki*, Moscow, 1899, pp. 62-95; and M. Gershenzon, *Istoriya molodoy Rossii*, Moscow, 1908, pp. 202-43, where the influence of Granovsky's personality, as opposed to his scholarship, is rightly emphasised. In the Soviet period material on Granovsky has been published by, among others, V. P. Buzeskul, 'Vseobshchaya istoriya i yego predstaviteli v Rossii v XIX i nachale XX veka', part I, in *Trudy komissii po istorii znaniy*, VII, Leningrad, 1929, pp. 47-64; I. Ivashin, 'Rukopis' publichnykh lektsiy T.N. Granovskogo', *Istoricheskiy zhurnal*, 1945, nos. 1-2 (137-8), pp. 81-4; and S. A. Asinovskaya, *Iz istorii peredovykh idey v russkoy mediyevistike (T. N. Granovskiy)*, Moscow, 1955. There is also an exhaustive bibliographical work on Granovsky by S. S. Dmitriyev, ed., *Granovskiy, Timofey Nikolayevich. Bibliografiya, 1828-1967*, Moscow, 1969.

For discussion of Granovsky in English, see Leonard Schapiro, *Rationalism and Nationalism in Russian Nineteenth-Century Political Thought*, New Haven, Conn., 1967, pp. 73-81; and esp. the long monograph by Priscilla R. Roosevelt, 'Granovskii at the lectern: a conservative liberal's vision of history', *Forschungen zur osteuropäischen Geschichte*, XXIX, Berlin, 1981, pp. 61-192, where attention is focused primarily on Granovsky's university lectures on world history.

[5] See Asinovskaya, ed., *Lektsii T. N. Granovskogo po istorii srednevekov'ya*, Moscow, 1961; idem, *Lektsii T. N. Granovskogo po istorii pozdnego srednevekov'ya*, Moscow, 1971. See also P. Milyukov, *Iz istorii russkoy intelligentsii*, 2nd ed., St Petersburg, 1903, pp. 212-65; and 'Neizdannyye universitetskiye kursy Granovskogo', introduced by M. N. Kovalensky, in *Golos minuvshego*, Moscow, 1913, no. 9, pp. 210-33.

[6] V. G. Belinsky, *Polnoe sobranie sochineniy*, 13 vols., Moscow, 1953-9, XI, pp. 456, 494, 377.

[7] Herzen, *My Past and Thoughts*, II, pp. 499, 489.

[8] I. I. Panayev, *Literaturnyye vospominaniya*, Leningrad, 1950, p. 230. . . .

[38] Stankevich, I, p. 127.

[39] *Ibid.*, p. 283.

[40] See Milyukov, *Iz istorii russkoy intelligentsii*, pp. 252-3.

[41] See Asinovskaya, *Lektsii T.N. Granovskogo po istorii srednevekov'ya*, p. 169.

[42] Granovsky, *Soch.*, pp. 203, 206.

[43] *Ibid.*, p. 555.

[44] *Ibid.*, p. 419.

[45] *Ibid.*, p. 414; Stankevich, II, p. 419.

[46] Stankevich, II, p. 420.

[47] *Ibid.*, pp. 176-7.

[48] *Ibid.*, I, p. 138.

[49] *Ibid.*

[50] *Ibid.*, II, pp. 369-70.

[51] Granovsky, *Soch.*, pp. 134-71, esp. 154, 162.

[52] *Ibid.*, p. 266.

[53] Stankevich, II, pp. 351, 412-13.

[54] Granovsky, *Soch.*, p. 562.

[55] Asinovskaya, *Lektsii T. N. Granovskogo po istorii srednevekov'ya*, p. 100.

[56] Granovsky, *Soch.*, p. 456.

[57] *Ibid.*, pp. 273-4.

[58] *Ibid.*, pp. 190, 193.

[59] *Ibid.*, pp. 180-2, 225.

[60] Milyukov, *Iz istorii russkoy intelligentsii*, p. 246; see also Granovsky, *Soch.*, p. 536; Annenkov, *Literaturnyye vospominaniya*, p. 214.

[61] Granovsky, *Soch.*, pp. 256-7.

[62] Stankevich, II, p. 370.

[63] *Ibid.*, p. 448.

[64] *Ibid.*, pp. 437, 453.

[65] Chaadayev, *The Major Works of Peter Chaadayev*, trans. by Raymond McNally, Notre Dame, Ind. and London, 1969, p. 38.

[66] See Stankevich, II, p. 439.

[67] Granovsky, *Soch.*, pp. 420-37, 540-50.

[68] Asinovskaya, *Lektsii T. N. Granovskogo po istorii srednevekov'ya*, p. 174.

[69] Granovsky, *Soch.*, p. 268.

[70] Annenkov, *Literaturnyye vospominaniya*, p. 270.

[71] Stankevich, I, pp. 184-5.

[72] *Ibid.*, II, pp. 450-1.

[73] Turgenev, *PSSP*, VIII, pp. 171-92.

[74] See N. V. Chaykovsky, 'Cherez polstoletiya: Otkrytoye pis'mo k druz'yam', *Golos minuvshego na chuzhoy storone*, 3 (16), 1926, p. 183.

[75] Herzen, *My Past and Thoughts*, II, p. 545.

[76] N. M. Yazykov, *Polnoye sobraniye stikhotvoreniy*, Moscow-Leningrad, 1964, p. 394.

[77] Annenkov, *Literaturnyye vospominaniya*, p. 226.

[78] See Granovsky, *Soch.*, pp. 517-35.

[79] See e.g. Stankevich, II, p. 457.

[80] Herzen, *My Past and Thoughts*, II, p. 499.

[81] Annenkov, *Literaturnyye vospominaniya*, p. 291; Stankevich, II, pp. 402, 415, 442.

[82] Stankevich, II, pp. 445-6.

[83] *Literaturnoe nasledstvo*, LXII, p. 94.

[84] Stankevich, II, p. 363.

[85] *Literaturnoe nasledstvo*, LVI, p. 132.

[86] Belinsky, *PSS*, XII, p. 132.

[87] *Ibid.*, XI, p. 377; Stankevich, II, p. 363.

[88] Belinsky, *PSS*, XII, p. 105. See also *Literaturnoe nasledstvo*, LVI, p. 80.

[89] Stankevich, II, pp. 439-40.

[90] See *ibid.*, I, pp. 194-5.

[91] Herzen, *My Past and Thoughts*, II, p. 586; Annenkov, *Literaturnyye vospominaniya*, pp. 274-5.

[92] Granovsky, *Soch.*, p. 472.

[93] The same reluctance on Granovsky's part to abandon notions which warmed human life is apparent in his belief in the hortative potential of historical scholarship and in the existence of pattern in history. In the preamble to his doctoral dissertation, published when his differences with Herzen had come to a head, for example, he declares that historical judgement is pronounced not in order to disturb the peace of the dead but to strengthen the moral sense of the living and to bolster 'their shaky faith in good and truth . . . In the possibility of such judgement there is something profoundly comforting for man.' It gives the 'weary soul new strength for its quarrel with life' (*Soch.*, p. 174). And in the introduction to the first of a new series of public lectures delivered in 1851 he talks of periods of intellectual and moral weakening when man ceases to believe in the 'legitimate movement of events' and loses sight of the 'divine link, which embraces the whole life of mankind'. But in fact the sense of events does at last become clear even if it is not revealed for thousands of years (*ibid.*, p. 242).

[94] Stankevich, II, pp. 448-9.

[95] Belinsky, *PSS* XII, pp. 406, 428.

[96] Stankevich, II, p. 424.

[97] Granovsky, *Soch.*, p. 447.

[98] See Stankevich, I, p. 219. The quatrain is from Goethe's *Zahme Xenien*, V, and appears in *Goethes Werke*, Weimar ed., 1887-1919, section I, vol. 3, p. 325. The last two lines also appear as Paralipomenon 62 of *Faust* (*ibid.*, I, 14, p. 313). A literal translation of the quatrain would be: 'Come! Let us sit down to dine./Who would be moved by such folly!/The world is coming apart like a rotten fish./We shall not embalm it.

[99] Stankevich, I, pp. 218-19.

[100] *Ibid.*, p. 246.

[101] Annenkov, *Literaturnyye vospominaniya*, pp. 273-4. . . .

Priscilla Reynolds Roosevelt (essay date 1986)

SOURCE: "The Public Lectures of 1843-44," in *Apostle of Russian Liberalism: Timofei Granovsky*, Oriental Research Partners, 1986, pp. 72-93.

[*In the following excerpt, Roosevelt discusses Granovskii's role as the "voice of the intelligentsia" in Moscow, as particularly reflected in his celebrated public lectures of 1843-44.*]

In the fate of our forefathers we seek, for the most part, an explanation of our own.

Granovsky, *Lectures on the Middle Ages*

Shortly after Granovsky's marriage his old friend V. V. Grigoriev visited him in Moscow. Grigoriev, a Slavophile in the making, bristled upon seeing the company Granovsky was keeping. Grigoriev's observations were symptomatic of the rift developing among the Moscow intelligentsia. "Granovsky is very happy with his little German," he told a mutual friend. "The best Moscow geniuses gather *chez lui*—they are men of feeling, of intelligence, but for some reason they do not please me. They talk a lot, drink a lot, but do little. Among them there are youths of great promise, but filled with a dreadful amount of egoism. The word "Fatherland" rings hollow in their minds—it does not sink into their breasts."[1] Grigoriev's perception of the Westerners' alienation was accurate, but his criticism of their idleness and lack of patriotism was unfair. The reign of Nicholas offered few outlets for talent and energy. The Moscow intelligentsia felt involuntarily isolated; this was one of the factors uniting it against official Russia. Wounded patriotism, not the lack of it, inspired both Westerners and Slavophiles to search for an historical explanation of their disaffection, and for an historically justifiable course for Russia to pursue. But from this search two very different views of national history and national purpose arose, neither of which was acceptable to the government. In 1843 Granovsky would become the voice of the intelligentsia, bringing the quarrel into the open in a sensational course of public lectures. Their success would at first cause general jubilation: through Granovsky the intelligentsia would speak out, and find that it had a receptive audience in the Moscow public. Yet only a short time later this mood of unity and celebration would dissolve in bitterness and recrimination.

In 1842 few could have predicted this outcome. In the nostalgic view of one student in the early 40s, this was "a time of more or less courteous tournaments and battles between Slavophiles and Westerners. It was a joyous period, when the tournament was not ridiculous, and sincere disagreement among thinking people was possible."[2] A tournament requires two opposed sides, each with its credo and champions, and an audience. By 1842 all were in place. A distinguishing feature of the Remarkable Decade was the growth of an audience for the ideas of the intelligentsia. In the mid-1830s, at the height of its popularity, the crypto-

liberal *Moscow Telegraph* had maintained a circulation of a mere 500. A decade later its successor, *Notes of the Fatherland,* had 2,000 subscribers, and an ideological competitor in the *Muscovite.* In the early 40s too, salon life in Moscow expanded. Almost every evening was preempted: the Elagins received on Sundays, Chaadaev on Mondays, the Pavlovs on Tuesdays, the Sverbeevs on Fridays. At least in the beginning, much the same group could be found at all of them, discussing the latest articles, arguing the issues, listening to public readings of newly discovered authors such as Gogol. Periodicals and salons were the twin forums in which the ideological wares of the day were packaged and sold, and where rivalries were paraded.

The least constrained arenas for debate were the salons and the university. In both places Granovsky found the Slavophile point of view amazing and somewhat amusing, hardly to be taken seriously. Nonetheless he felt it his duty to stake out his own position in private conversations and at the lectern. Shortly after his arrival in Moscow in September of 1839 he had written Stankevich,

> You cannot imagine what kind of philosophy [the Slavophiles] have. Their main positions are: the West has become stagnant and nothing can come of it; Russian history has been ruined by Peter; we have been torn forcibly from our historical roots and are living on luck . . . all human wisdom springs from the creations of the Holy Fathers of the Greek church after the schism with the West. One need only study them; there is nothing to add, everything has been said. They condemn Hegel for his disrespect for the facts. Kireevsky says these things in prose, Khomiakov in verse.[3]

In November he announced to Stankevich that he was "rising up against . . . Slavic patriotism . . . from the podium, without, of course, straying from the confines of my subject. They reproach me for being partial to the Germans. It is not a question of the Germans, but of Peter the Great, whom they do not understand here."[4] Granovsky was preoccupied with getting established at the university, not to mention affairs of the heart. Bakunin, whose judgment Granovsky did not entirely trust,[5] tried to force him to take sides, but he refused to let the disputes rule his social life.

> He gave me to understand that I am acting badly by visiting the Kireevskys . . . I know the weak side of the Kireevsky brothers very well; their convictions do not agree with mine; I even consider them harmful—and in my given sphere of activity I fight them. As a teacher I shall always attack such opinions; as a writer (if I write) as well; but as a private person I spend time with them with pleasure . . . And why not? Because people have different opinions should I cut myself off from

them? Perhaps there would be something lofty in that, but this loftiness is higher than I. I have not yet reconciled myself to moral disgrace in whatever form it may appear, but I think that a man may be better than his opinions . . . You know [Ivan Kireevsky] yourself. It saddens me to see his deviation from the truth; it sickens me to see his influence on young people. However, I respect his nobility and his independence of character (of which I have seen proof), united with his warm spirit.[6]

For the chivalrous Granovsky and his supporters, morality was the central issue. As Annenkov remarked, "The whole circle unconditionally concurred . . . in certain principles: all took the moral factor as the starting point for any activity, whether in life or in literature."[7] So did the Slavophiles. While they might dismiss their opponents with the derogatory term "Westerner", and insist that any criticism of Russian culture amounted to a surrender to alien principles, they were very much like the Westerners in their moral censure of Nicholaevan Russia. In Moscow, the only intellectuals satisfied with the status quo in this respect were Pogodin and Shevyrev.

Neither side had a journal for its views. *Notes of the Fatherland,* published in St. Petersburg, tended to be viewed as the Westerners' house organ, but the editor, A. A. Kraevsky, published their work primarily because it sold, not for the ideas. Throughout the decade the Westerners made repeated attempts to get permission for a truly partisan journal, but all their requests were denied. Similarly, the *Muscovite* published Slavophile articles, but was in the hands of Pogodin and Shevyrev, loyal defenders of the regime. The feud between the two journals which began in 1842 was waged chiefly between their two literary critics, Belinsky and Shevyrev. Shevyrev initiated hostilities with an article in which he called Belinsky a "knight without a name" who had stolen the limelight from the "clown" Senkovsky; Belinsky, according to Shevyrev, was a "loner" with "conviction" emblazoned on his shield and a mighty sword recklessly cutting down everything in his path.[8] Shevyrev claimed that only the foolish young listened to this Don Quixote who was in reality an arrogant ignoramus. From St. Petersburg Belinsky replied with a diatribe against Shevyrev's scholarly pretensions entitled "Pedant." Henceforth this term would become the Westerners' code for the "Muscovites," as they termed Pogodin, Shevyrev, and their allies. The following year Pogodin added fuel to the fire by issuing a manifesto committing the *Muscovite* to resolute struggle against "unconditional worship of the West."

In the midst of these hostilities, in 1842 Granovsky, though identified with the Westerners, managed to hold a mediatory position. Not only was he on good terms with the leading Slavophiles, he also tried, for obvious reasons, to maintain harmonious relations with Pogodin. Early on, Pogodin had asked him and Evgenii Korsh, the university librarian, to be regular contributors to the *Muscovite.* Granovsky turned him down, for one thing, because he and Korsh were just then assembling the program for a journal of their own. But at the end of 1841 he wrote a short review of a textbook on medieval history for the *Muscovite.* And early in 1843 the journal published his long review of G. A. Stenzel's *Geschichte des Preussischen Staates.*[9]

Innocently, Granovsky inquired whether Belinsky, now in St. Petersburg, had read the article. The reply could not have been more hostile. "I am a Jew by nature," Belinsky wrote Herzen, "and cannot eat at the same table with Philistines . . . Granovsky wants to know if I read his article in the *Muscovite?* No, and I will not read it; tell him that I do not like to be seen with friends in inappropriate places, or to arrange meetings with them there."[10] Belinsky's painful conversion to a radical, Left Hegelianism was now complete, and he would not condone any fraternizing with the opposition. But it was the more amiable Herzen who would draw Granovsky into a battle which forced a break first with the *Muscovite,* and then with his Slavophile friends.

Herzen had taken up residence in Moscow in July of 1842, having finally received permission to return from exile from the Third Section, but he was still under police surveillance. The frustrations of his position must have been enormous. Intellectually he was poles away from the Herzen whom Granovsky had met in 1839, still happily adrift in romantic idealism, and his personal life had changed for the worse. Ogarev's passivity towards life, a paralysis brought on by his marital unhappiness, angered Herzen and strained their friendship. His own holiest of marriages had suffered from the stillbirths of several children, and an infidelity with a serf-girl in Vladimir. He was unable to understand Natalie's consequent depression and disillusionment or to sympathize sufficiently with her distress. While Natalie had enjoyed the tranquility of Vladimir and disliked the bustle of Moscow society, Herzen threw himself into it, immediately making the rounds of the regular evening gatherings.

Herzen and Granovsky were drawn to each other at once. Later Herzen would write,

> Granovsky was endowed with an incredible tact of the heart. With him everything was so far from pretensions, so pure, so open, that it was very easy to be with him. He did not bind friendship, but loved strongly.[11]

Gershenzon has suggested that part of Granovsky's attractiveness to Herzen was his "feminine" nature, reminiscent of the absent Ogarev.[12] But the two were also natural intellectual allies. Herzen had finally read Hegel during the preceding year, and gleaned from this the philosophical rationale for the activist position he had espoused much earlier. Back in the center of Russian intellectual life, he was in a combative mood. No one among his Moscow friends was in a better position than Granovsky to satisfy this urge for a good fight over principles, which was, under the circumstances, the most activist role available.

By 1842 Granovsky was a prominent figure in the Moscow circles. His coherent view of history, which lent philosophical and scholarly support to the Westerner position, his eloquence, his personal charm, and his identification with the much-loved Stankevich had given him formidable stature. Moreover, as professor he had a lectern to use as a forum for the views of the Westerners. Nikitenko's diary for 1841 provides an interesting insight into the position and power of a professor at this time, when university lectures were—aside from salon conversation—virtually the only open forum for ideas. Ruminating on changes he was contemplating in his lectures, Nikitenko, terming himself a "public figure," noted that he had a "natural inclination to turn the lectern into a tribunal. I want more to affect the feeling and will of men than to lay out before them a theory of knowledge . . . For me, knowledge is a means, not an end."[13]

Like Nikitenko, Granovsky was well aware of his potential power as an uncensored voice in a closed society. Nikitenko thought seriously that winter of giving a course of public lectures, but did not. It was Granovsky who would become a "public figure" in 1843-44, at the urging of Herzen, who wanted to put his friend's eloquence and knowledge to service publicly smiting their ideological opponents.

With no lectern at his disposal, Herzen spent much of 1843 writing four articles outlining his philosophical position which were published under the collective title, *Dilettantism in Science*. In them Herzen sketched out the main features of Left Hegelianism, with all its radical implications. Discussing the historical process as being the Absolute's striving for increasing consciousness, Herzen stressed that each new stage of knowledge brings man more freedom. "Without knowledge, without complete consciousness, there is no truly free action."[14] The insistence on constant historical evolution, and on the consequent historical relativity of social and political institutions and values, had revolutionary undertones. The cosmos the articles present is a unity of "being" and "consciousness," of nature and reason. Thus, there can be no ideas, religions, or philosophies external to man, not subject to his reason and to historical circumstances. Hegel had also insisted on the immanence of the universe, but he valued Christianity as a symbolic expression of the Absolute,

while Herzen did not. In *Dilettantism* he implicitly rejected faith in an afterlife, a religious tenet very important to Granovsky.

In the last of the four articles Herzen attacked the "Buddhists of science", those orthodox Hegelians, German or Russian, who claimed that the dialectical process of development had come to an end, that absolute consciousness had been achieved, that reality was rational. Hegelianism itself was proof, Herzen declared, that reason had at last become immanent; therefore the time had come to turn from thought to action, from philosophy to propaganda.

Herzen recorded in his memoirs that the success of *Dilettantism in Science* was "a source of childlike joy" for Granovsky, who was by now fully co-opted to the cause of combat with his ideological foes. By 1843 the joyful tranquility of the days after his marriage had given way to another attack of gloom and despair. When his brother-in-law returned from a trip to Berlin bringing greetings from Werder, Granovsky unburdened himself in a bitter letter to his old teacher:

> "If anyone in Russia remembers me"—these words could only have come to you in a gloomy hour, and you were not thinking of me then. If you only knew how ever present for me Berlin life and Berlin friends are, and how longingly I recall them all the time! I have lived through so much in these four years, so many joys and pains, have lost and won so much, that I have become a different person. I have never so well understood what you often counseled me then: work, and renounce! In the end, there is nothing else to be done . . . I feel strongly that my heart is becoming old and tired. It is a sad time, ours, especially in my country. One has nothing to do, and one searches for inner peace. Stressful activity would have done much less to me than this nameless and pointless distress . . . I am working, by the way, as much as it is possible to work in Russia, and believe strongly in a better future, not for me personally, but for those who come into the world later. They will have it good and cheap.[15]

What had gone wrong? For one thing, both Granovsky's sisters and his ne'er-do-well but beloved younger brother Platon had died within a year of each other. Varvara, he wrote Grigoriev, had been his "best friend, the most beloved member of our family."[16] Secondly, the intellectual atmosphere of Moscow was becoming decidedly more heated. People were being forced to take sides, old friendships were being threatened, and Granovsky could no longer maintain the aloof stance he preferred. But there is some evidence he no longer wanted to. Since Herzen's arrival in Moscow the two had grown very close; to judge from Granovsky's letter to Werder, some of Herzen's eagerness for action had rubbed off on him. Herzen may also have made

Granovsky reflect ruefully on the smallness of the part history had assigned to him. While he was more fortunate than most in having an active part to play, as a professor he could hardly hope to have the impact he had dreamed of in Berlin. The one effort he had made to reach a wider audience—his plan to start a journal with his old friend Evgenii Korsh—had thus far come to naught. All these factors may have played a part in his decision to give public lectures.

Such lectures would serve two purposes. The first was intellectual: his ideas, the "new" view of history, would be broadcast widely and, perhaps, cause his audience to think about Russia's position. The lectures would also relieve this "pointless distress." Granovsky, unlike Herzen or Belinsky, who were activist by nature, needed an obstacle or outside stimulus to get himself going. "Without them I would perhaps just fall asleep," he had confided to his cousin in 1839, characterizing his temperament as a "melange of laziness and opinionatedness."[17] The rumor that Pogodin and Shevyrev were going to try to work against his lectures in some way made him angry. Shortly before the lectures began he told Ketcher that he had no desire to make peace with the "Muscovites," and called them "real Tatars." He even showed some belligerence:

> I hope not to fall on my face in the mud, and to express to my hearers *en masse* that which I would not be able to say to each of them alone. In general I want to polemicise, scold, and insult. Elagina said to me not long ago that I have many enemies. I do not know where they have come from; I have hardly insulted anyone personally, and consequently the source of the enmity is in the opposition of opinions. I will try to justify and deserve the enmity of my enemies.[18]

About the same time Herzen also wrote Ketcher, explaining that the lectures would be a joint effort against the "Muscovites": he would reinforce the lectures with accounts summarizing and emphasizing the main points which would be published in *Moscow News,* the official organ of the university.[19] For Herzen as for Granovsky, the lectures would serve public and private goals.

It is symbolic of the voicelessness of the intelligentsia of the Remarkable Decade that no notes of these lectures, the very heart of the decade's achievements, have survived. We are left with Granovsky's outline, submitted to Golokhvastov in September for approval.[20] This outline's striking similarity to the structure of Granovsky's university courses, and the fact that he did little extra preparation for the public course, justify our turning to his recently published university lectures as our source for those ideas which held Moscow spellbound in the winter of 1843-44.

Granovsky's "superlative" introductory lectures, as we know from Chicherin, contained an overview of historiography and described his own methodology. In them he typically stressed the unity of the life of the "spirit" and historical life; the applicability of the theory of organic development to all world-historical peoples; the inevitability of progress; and the supremacy of ideas as forces in history. All of these concepts were key aspects of the "modern" approach to history. Granovsky begins by hailing the principle of organic development as the most fruitful concept ever to be applied to history, and declares that it applies not just to national but to world history, for "if parts live organically, then the whole does also."[21] This alerts his audience to the notion that Russia, as a world-historical nation, is intimately related to its European counterparts. From contemporaneous accounts it is clear that Granovsky made an elegant case for the Hegelian approach to history, even while downplaying Hegel's own *Philosophy of History.* It was the application of Hegelian principles to the actual course of historical events which appealed to Granovsky, and which he set before his audience.

The Hegelian dialectic posits that in any given period of history, there is a close correlation between ideology, religion, political forms, and social conditions; when the underlying ideas are challenged by new ones, a battle ensues which changes the old forms and which results in historical progress. The task of the philosophy of history, Granovsky declares, is to extract the general principles at work in history, "to show that what has happened ought to have happened because of an internal, logical law, to justify history."[22] But Granovsky warns that the historian pursuing these general principles or laws must rely on the factual evidence and proceed through "normal reflection", not abstract thought.

Granovsky's periodization, which dictates the organization of his courses, reveals his fascination with the internal dynamics of history. He appears to have accepted Guizot's hypothesis that periods of expansion alternate with periods of concentration in European history, a concept Comte also adopted (following Saint-Simon), dividing history into "critical" and "organic" epochs. Granovsky is particularly fascinated by "critical" or transitional epochs, which he expands in his own course in such a way as to eliminate any periods of historical stasis. He declares that dividing European history into periods or by nations is fundamentally deceptive. He insists, for instance, that beginning medieval history with the fall of the Western Roman empire is a form of vivisection, for "the transitions from one [way of] life to another occur gradually and slowly and constitute special, instructive epochs in history."[23] In his view, the slow triumph of Christianity over paganism, which occupied the entire period from the fall of the Roman republic to

Charlemagne, constitutes the content of a large transitional epoch. Catholicism gave the medieval world an "internal link", but this link tenuously bound together a host of conflicting elements. Hence, Granovsky asserts, "on a larger scale one can say that the whole medieval period is a transitional one between ancient and modern times."[24] The end of the Middle Ages, traditionally dated to the Age of Exploration and the Reformation, for Granovsky begins in the 13th century and continues into the 16th, "while the last three centuries are transitional from that order to another which we still do not understand."[25] Thus while Granovsky identifies two "organic" epochs, the Roman republic and medieval Europe of the 11th and 12th centuries, he spends far more time on those elements at work undermining the essential elements of each than he devotes to the epochs themselves.

For Granovsky, transitional epochs are key to the discovery of historical laws, for it is here that the historian can observe the historical process at work. But he warns his audience that the pace and direction of change can be deceptive, particularly for first-hand observers. A joyous spirit of challenge and discovery, he tells his audience, accompanied the transition from medieval to modern times. This spirit perished in the bloody and barbaric conflicts of the 16th and 17th centuries. At such times it might seem as though history's forward momentum has been stopped. Not so, Granovsky assures his listeners. "History does not hasten. In destroying one order of things it allows time for the ruins to rot away, and the destroyers of the former order never see with their own eyes the goal towards which they have been moving."[26]

Sometimes only force can be the midwife of change. Speaking of the fall of Rome Granovsky talks about revolution in general:

> In the history of humanity there are such unhappy epochs in which reform cannot be accomplished by so-called regular development, in which there exists between the demands of the new time and the demands and pretensions of the completed historical residuum a contradiction which can be annihilated only by force. Such force was employed in the ancient world by the Germans, in the eighteenth century by the French Revolution.[27]

Though Granovsky may term such periods "unhappy," he does not condemn force per se, particularly when his sympathies lie with the conquering principles. But sometimes he sympathizes with the vanquished. In his public lectures Granovsky followed his description of the victory of Philip the Fair over the Knights Templar with the following observation: "In modern history as well, we frequently foresee the inevitability of the victory, but we cannot withhold sympathy for the vanquished, nor contempt for the victor"[28]—a remark which

his audience might well have taken as an allusion to the Decembrists. Thus periods of apparent historical regression are really, Granovsky insists, periods of latency.

Granovsky's emphasis on the power of ideas to alter the status quo, and on history's constant forward movement towards its "higher moral goal" of freedom and justice, was subversive and uplifting. In addition, Granovsky's presentation of European history was replete with Aesopian analogies to the Russian past and present which threw into question Slavophile claims that Russia was unique and Official Nationalist glorification of the status quo. His view of Russia as one part of an organic European whole was in itself a challenge to the Slavophile point of view. Beyond this, in his discussion of the history of European politics, society, and culture he frequently passed implicit judgment on the Russian present.

Granovsky's analysis of European political development emphasized the necessity of a proper balance between the needs of the state and the rights of the individual, a balance best achieved, in his view, when the laws and policies of a state are firmly grounded on moral principle. Granovsky pointed out in his lectures that immoral laws such as Tiberius' decree on *lésé majesté,* and immoral institutions such as the Spanish Inquisition, the English Star Chamber or, by implication, the Third Section in Russia, may temporarily corrupt society but do not endure.[29] The political model Granovsky seems to have had in mind was the *Rechtstaat:* the strong state based on law and justice which, to the mind of his generation, was the best guarantor of the rights of the individual. As Richard Wortman has pointed out, the Hegelian training of the Moscow "youngsters" had imbued them above all with a veneration for legalism and justice, neither of which were evident in the Russia of their time.[30]

Granovsky repeatedly asserts that civil rights are fundamental to a properly constructed polity. Early in his lectures Granovsky warns against simplistic analogies between Roman plebeians and the European proletariat. Whereas the Romans were content with the charity of the state, the European proletariat's struggles are "the natural desire of an oppressed class to better its position, for equality of rights, to obtain those benefits without which there is no full civil life."[31] When Granovsky describes "the struggle of abstract opposites" in the Middle Ages, of "separate forces and tendencies in society, in which each put forth its egotistical demand for a separate existence,"[32] he overtly invites comparison with the present. For he goes on to say that at that time "there had not yet arisen the understanding of full, harmonious life for all the elements which make up society—an understanding which belongs exclusively to our times."[33]

Sometimes Granovsky seems to hint that the modern concept of full civil rights includes the right of popular representation. Speaking, for instance, of the reign of Henry IV of France, he applauds this strong monarch's efforts to reestablish order but deplores his subversion of French representative institutions. "When he died, there were only two elements in France: on the one hand, the King; on the other, the people. But no proper relationships existed between them."[34] In the eyes of the Westerners, Nicholas's bureaucratic police state likewise lacked any proper bridge between monarch and people. Earlier Granovsky had asserted that "by a state we mean an organic whole, in which every member has his obligations, his rights."[35] His audience undoubtedly interpreted such statements as a plea for a pluralist political structure in Russia.

Certainly there could be no "full, harmonious life" nor a "proper relationship" between the state and the individual in Russia without the abolition of serfdom. Granovsky's description of Roman slaves and of medieval serfs clearly invited comparison with this most reprehensible of Russian institutions. While slavery was a prerequisite for Roman culture and material prosperity, according to Granovsky, he also notes that slave labour eventually undermined the economic structure of the empire. Here Granovsky seems to be commenting on the fact, increasingly discussed in enlightened circles, that serfdom was retarding economic development in Russia. But it is chiefly his humanitarian instincts which are offended by Roman prohibitions on marriages between non-household slaves, and by the degrading conditions in which they lived.[36] The same humanitarianism is evident in his description of medieval serfdom. Most of Granovsky's audience no doubt had first-hand experience of situations similar to Granovsky's description of the feudal baron's "egotistical individualism" which led him to impose a host of "senseless . . . and petty obligations"[37] on his serfs merely to increase his own feeling of power. Granovsky points out that until the 13th century the villeins or *servi* had no avenue of appeal against such injustice. "Never perhaps in all history has man been subjected to such a humiliating position as that of the rural classes under the rule of the feudal order," he pointedly remarks.[38]

Among the most obvious parallels Granovsky draws between medieval and Russian serfdom are the lack of legal definition of a lord's power over his serfs, the meliorating influence of the church and the better lot of its peasants, and an individual's occasional escape from the system through being given the land he worked or through purchasing his freedom.[39] These serfs were the ancestors of the European proletariat; when Granovsky tells his audience that the proletariat's origins is "one of the most acute questions of contemporary scholarship"[40] he is reminding it of the urgency of the peasant question.

The "youngsters" were committed not merely to the intellectual awakening of their students but to their moral training for their future responsibilities. For this reason Granovsky's description of education in imperial Rome, a thinly disguised attack on contemporary Russian practice, has particular significance. He begins by attacking the emphasis on rhetoric, a "holdover from the old order which was entirely inappropriate to the new order, but which society could not relinquish—a typical phenomenon."[41] In the heyday of the Roman republic the study of rhetoric had been put to good use, for young men often began their careers by denouncing corrupt officials. In the Imperial period, however, Granovsky notes, the art of rhetoric was used against private citizens for personal rather than civic ends. Roman parents, he says, no longer cared whether their sons acquired a sense of moral and civic duty from their education, and thus a new class arose in Rome: the *delatores,* who were eloquent, ambitious, and thoroughly immoral informers.[42] In this instance we know exactly whom Granovsky had in mind, for he wrote a friend during the public lectures that he had "already brought Shevyrev on stage a few times. I pointed at him when I spoke of men who deny the philosophy of history, I spoke of him with regard to the orators of the fourth and fifth centuries."[43]

Moving from the results of a morally insufficient curriculum to the plight of those forced to teach in such a system, Granovsky notes that in Imperial Rome "the honest teacher had to remain silent about the most important things touching mankind and the state."[44] Since he did not believe in the official dogmas he was forced to parrot, "between him and the students there was always something half-spoken, half-understood, half-uttered."[45] This could only be a commentary on Granovsky's own position, for even at the university there was much he could not say. Noting the high suicide rate during the twilight of Imperial Rome, Granovsky relates it to the educational system and to a general moral decline.

> In the life of man there are such times, when he becomes bored with life and dies with a readiness which is astounding to us. Life in Rome was unhealthy, full of disease, lack of faith and convictions, principles without which man is weak . . . There was much education, but it was not useful and only increased the susceptibility [to moral disease]. Education is useful if it produces noble impressions; but the educated Romans just sensed the social ills more strongly.[46]

We know that in these lectures Granovsky intended to "scold and insult" his opponents. Herzen at the time, and Chernyshevsky after him, hailed Granovsky's approach to history as propagandistic denunciation of contemporary evils. In the last analysis, however, save for the few occasions when he trots despicable opponents on stage, Granovsky appears less eager to draw specific analogies between the European past and Russian present than to promote enthusiasm for three large moral desiderata: justice towards one's fellow man; intellectual freedom (because it is vital to the search for truth and to progress); and a sense of principle and legalism in government. These were the elements Granovsky most desired to see in his own society, and which his presentation of history as progressive and providential assured his audience would in time come to pass. To judge from the comments of contemporaries on these lectures, their high moral tone was one of their most striking features. It was a tone well suited both to Granovsky's nature and to the mission of his generation. While the intimates to the Moscow quarrels privately raged or reveled in every political nuance of the lectures, the public at large was captivated by Granovsky's intellect, artistry, and particularly his empathy with his subject.

Granovsky's first public lecture was delivered November 23, 1843, to an overflow audience Annenkov later described as comprised "not only of men of science, all the literary factions and his usual rapturous listeners—the university youth, but also the entire educated class of the city—from old men who had just left the gaming tables to young girls still flushed from their triumphs on the dance floor, from government officials to non-service noblemen."[47] According to Herzen, tickets to the lectures were soon fetching enormously inflated prices, as it became fashionable to attend. Granovsky himself noted in the audience "more than fifty women belonging to the highest society," which made him feel that he was *"boeuf à la mode"* in Moscow.[48] During his first lecture he was interrupted twice by applause, and after the third his audience applauded long after he had left the hall.[49]

After the first lecture Herzen noted in his diary, "Superlative. What noble, beautiful language, precisely because it expresses noble and beautiful thoughts."[50] And to Ketcher he wrote, "I was always convinced that he would lecture beautifully, but I must confess that he surpassed my expectations. Although his voice is weak, although he speaks hesitantly while lecturing he has an absorbing talent for excellence of speech . . . What fullness in each lecture, and what humanity; it is an artistic, energetic, and love-filled discourse."[51] Annenkov speaks of Granovsky's historical portraits as the "artistic product of a master's brush," Chicherin of "vivid oratory . . . to the point, refined, freeflowing."[52]

But to his diary Herzen also confided the other, more pointed and polemical significance of the lectures: "How contemporary they are, what a stone hurled at the heads of the narrow nationalists."[53] Granovsky was drawing praise from the leading Slavophiles,

but Pogodin and Shevyrev were enraged. Pogodin's diary entry for November 23 noted, "Attended Granovsky's lecture. Such mediocrity that it was wretched. This is not a professor but a German student who has read French newspapers. So many omissions, what contradictions. As if Russia did not exist in history . . . He is giving the psalter of the West."[54] In December Granovsky wrote Ketcher that "the frenzy of the Slavs is growing every day; they ridicule me not for what I am saying, but for what I am silent about. I am lecturing on the history of the West, but they say, 'Why does he not speak about Russia!'"[55] A week later he departed from his lecture to ask his audience why, in fact, he ought to hate the West, and why, if he detested the path of development it had taken he would bother to lecture on its history. The answers were obvious. He brought down the house with his closing remarks: "I am accused of using history only to express my views. This is partially right; I have convictions and I express them in my lectures. If I did not have them, I would not appear before you publicly in order to recite, in more or less interesting fashion, a series of events."[56] Granovsky's public defense of his point of view made Herzen ecstatic.

> Looking at the scene and the noise, my heart beat and blood rushed to my head from sympathy. Perhaps after this the authorities will bring down their fists, the course will be shut down, but the deed is done: a new form of university influence on the public has been revealed, the possibility of publicly defending oneself against absurd charges has been demonstrated, and the possibility of unanimous approval, of stirring up sympathy for such an event, has been confirmed.[57]

This defense had become necessary because of Stroganov's reaction to the battle in ink which had been raging between Herzen and Shevyrev since the beginning of the lectures. Their articles are a classic illustration of the Aesopian mode of communication characteristic of the times, as well as of the significance the two sides attributed to the lectures. Herzen had wasted no time in dashing off a first article for *Moscow News,* in which he faithfully adhered to Stroganov's admonition that Hegel's name not be mentioned. He hailed the course as a "beautiful and deeply significant phenomenon" which had attracted a "brilliant" audience. "The stronger a greedy taste for the past develops, the more clearly it is visible that the past prophesies, that, trying to look back, we, like Janus, look forward."[58] The public, in other words, was urged to consider European development relevant to Russian experience, to listen to Granovsky's remarks on the fate of Europe with their own in mind.

Beyond reminding his readers to look for such analogies, Herzen urged them to take pride in Granovsky's

"Russian" interpretation of European history. Periodically in his courses Granovsky took time to point out that the Russian perspective on European events was bound to differ from that of the Europeans themselves, and that it was possibly superior in being based on "unselfish" interest, and hence more objective.[59] Such statements were a measure of Granovsky's pride in the recent accomplishments of his profession, and a novel idea for his audience.

Herzen intended this article as the first round of a lengthy barrage against the opposition. Herzen's opponents, meanwhile, dismayed by Granovsky's initial success, were readying their own ammunition. Pogodin had already begun to think about "anti-Western lectures;"[60] and Shevyrev immediately prepared an article attacking Herzen's in no uncertain fashion. When he sent it to Pogodin for publication in the Muscovite, even his ally was upset by its tone. Treat Granovsky as young and inexperienced, he urged; condescend to him rather than attacking frontally. Shevyrev, insulted, replied that he had to write the way he knew how. He seems, however, to have paid some attention to the cogent view of Nikolai Melgunov who wrote, "In my opinion, it would be better if you softened or even omitted the polemic against Herzen's article. You have a pack of literary enemies even without that; why increase their number needlessly? . . . They will think that you take praise of Granovsky as a personal insult to yourself."[61]

In truth, there was a measure of wounded vanity which demarcated Shevyrev's attitude from Pogodin's. Pogodin was on the eve of retirement after a long and distinguished career at the university. Shevyrev was closer to being a contemporary, and in a sense Granovsky had replaced him as the most popular teacher. Some observers, in fact, considered the rivalry between the two to be largely a popularity contest, despite their wellknown ideological differences.

Shevyrev's article appeared in the December issue of the Muscovite. Somewhat toned down, it still came close to accusing Granovsky of treason. In Herzen's diary for December 11 he had written,

> The ignobleness of the Slavophiles of the Muscovite is great; they are voluntary assistants of the gendarmes. They are dissatisfied with Granovsky because he does not lecture about Russia (when he is lecturing about the Middle Ages in Europe), he does not touch on Orthodoxy, they are dissatisfied that he is on the side of Western science (when there is no Eastern science at all), and that he says little about Christianity in general. All this would be their own business; but they are shouting about it so much that Filaret [metropolitan of Moscow] has begun to talk, they want to print in the Muscovite that he is lecturing on Hegel etcetera . . . Watch, they will close down the lectures.[62]

Shevyrev's article confirmed his fears. It focussed on Granovsky's unpardonable subordination of "all schools, all views, all great works . . . to one name, one system, namely to Hegel." Insisting that Western scholars had already gone beyond Hegel, Shevyrev warned that "such one-sidedness threatens us simply with European China-ism."[63] How, Shevyrev sardonically enquired, could the historical process consist of growth and progress if Prussia had reached the stage of decrepitude? Here Shevyrev capitalized on Granovsky's error (also noted by Herzen) of interpreting Hegel's view of Prussia's "final" historical stage as that of old age rather than maturity.

Herzen, seeking a way around the prohibition on mentioning Hegel, had criticized Granovsky for, "by old habit," overemphasizing Herder (the originator of the organic view of history) to the detriment of Schiller, the poet of freedom and human dignity. This was as close as he could come to Hegel: Schiller's Letters on the Aesthetic Education of Humanity had adumbrated many of the ideas of Schelling and Hegel in poetic form.[64] Shevyrev in response praised Herder's "broad view, . . . his feeling of universal humanism," contrasting it to Hegelian narrowness. In Russia particularly, history should be broad and many-faceted, a four-sided lantern shining in all directions, he insisted.[65] Granovsky's narrowness, his sacrifice of everything to Hegel, including his own teachers Ranke and Raumer, was the deed of an impetuous youth who with time would come to his senses. "He will show us that he, like a Russian bee, has gathered honey from all his teachers."[66] This was an intentional insult: the journal the Westerners most loathed was Bulgarin's Northern Bee.

Herzen's response was a second article, far more polemical than the first. His fear that the lectures were doomed gave his second "Letter from Moscow" its peculiar compound of polemic and apologia: he wanted to defend Granovsky's position in the most convincing way, yet not yield any ground to Shevyrev.

Shevyrev had hinted that the turnout for the lectures, with women actually outnumbering men in the audience, proved it was chiefly a diversion for the idle rich. "We are convinced that the educated Moscow public . . . will not turn a deed of science into the whim of willful fashion," he pontificated.[67] That was another insult. Herzen's generation of Westerners, devouring the novels of George Sand, had become converts (at least on an intellectual level) to feminism, long a cause célèbre in Europe. The time for denying the mental capabilities of women had passed, Herzen proclaimed; "truth and talent belong to men and women alike."[68] Then Herzen turned on the Slavophile view of history. Shevyrev had claimed that Heinrich Leo along with Savigny and Eichhorn was a major influence on Granovsky's interpretation of the Middle Ages. Denying this, Herzen declared that Leo's worship of the perfection of the Catholic Middle Ages had blinded him to the last three centuries. No reader could miss the implicit comparison to the Slavophiles' worship of pre-Petrine Russia. Granovsky's historiographical sketch had been eminently balanced, Herzen insisted. "It was noticeable that Granovsky, well-acquainted with the writings of the great German thinkers, is not overwhelmed by them. He views Hegel as an historical stage in knowledge . . . which one cannot pass over but also at which one must not remain forever."[69]

A main task was to explain that Granovsky was a Left Hegelian, not a Buddhist, as Shevyrev had tried to make him out. Herzen accomplished this by rebutting Shevyrev's emotion-charged accusation that Granovsky had ignored Slavic contributions to history. Had not Granovsky mentioned Cieszkowski's treatise *Prologomena zur Historiosophie* in his discussion of the philosophy of history?, Herzen asked his readers. In bringing up Cieszkowski he reminded those who knew the treatise of the radical implications of the dialectic for Russia's future. Cieszkowski, in perhaps the first Left Hegelian interpretation of the dialectic, had maintained that if the past of the Absolute were discoverable through the dialectical method, it followed that the future was as well. Hence Hegel's logic should not have led to such conservative conclusions about his own society. No admirer of Cieszkowski would uphold the view that the "real was rational" in contemporary Russia.

Granovsky, Herzen could now demonstrate, was offering an Aesopian critique of his own society. Herzen began by quoting "practically word for word" Granovsky's introduction to his fourth and fifth lectures on the end of the pagan, and beginning of the Christian, world.

> Viewed from the outside, the ancient world still shone with the reflection of its former greatness; it evidently still possessed all the conditions for might and development . . . But looking more closely at this huge mass, we see that it is suffering from terrible sores[70]

Herzen found Granovsky's remarks to be a commentary on the "irony of the superficial might of the empire which concealed despairing impotence," an impotence most clearly displayed in late Imperial poetry, which consisted mainly of "lowly panegyrics, rhetorical phrases" empty of meaning. Whom could Granovsky more clearly have had in mind than the Official Nationalists? To drive the point home, Herzen noted Granovsky's characterization of the leading exemplar of this pagan school as a specialist in "pedantic" praises of "pedant" professors. Like Shevyrev's reference to bees, the insult was unmistakable.

The article, dated December 15, just before Granovsky's public defense of his views, was never published. The open discussion of Hegel virtually ensured that Stroganov would stop it. After a long conversation with the count, Herzen concluded, "perhaps he is right; the fear of outcries, of priests, of denunciations is justified."[71]

Stroganov was in an awkward position. On the one hand, Granovsky was his own appointee and a great enhancement to the university's reputation. But Stroganov was already in trouble with the Ministry of Education for tolerating Hegelianism in the curriculum. He had the university's future, and his own, to worry about if the lectures got out of hand. In January he summoned both Herzen and Granovsky for interviews in which he clearly defined the limits of the acceptable. To Herzen he said on January 7, "I will oppose Hegelianism and German philosophy by all possible means. They are opposed to our religion . . . I will not even support the position which advertises the reconciliation of science with religion: religion is fundamental."[72] Stroganov threatened to resign or to abolish certain chairs at the university if things did not go his way. A week later he called in Granovsky. After the interview a shaken and angry Granovsky wrote Ketcher that he would probably have to retire or at least transfer.

> Stroganov is demanding the impossible. Yesterday I had a serious, harsh discussion with him. Perhaps I was foolish to speak directly and openly, but I do not regret it. He told me that with such convictions I cannot stay at the university, that he needs orthodox [teachers] etcetera. I replied that I do not talk about the existing order, and that my private beliefs are not his concern. He answered that a negative relationship was not sufficient, that he required love for the existing [order], in short, he demanded an apology . . . in the form of a lecture. The Reformation and [French] Revolution ought to be presented from the Catholic point of view, as steps backward. I suggested not lecturing at all on the Revolution. I could not give up the Reformation: what kind of history would that be. He concluded with the words, 'there is a good which is higher than knowledge; one must guard it, even if for this it were necessary to shut down the universities and all schools.'[73]

Stroganov's volte-face was hard to explain. Granovsky assumed that someone had gotten to him, but absolved Shevyrev, who, he noted, had "himself now changed his tune and is demanding freedom of thought, for without this he cannot annihilate his opponents. I suspect that . . . Davydov is responsible."[74]

We do not know whether Granovsky altered his usual description of the Reformation or made some other gesture of reconciliation to Stroganov. The lectures continued to their conclusion in March without further ado. Herzen used Granovsky's concluding remarks as the introduction to his third article. "I thank you again, I thank those who, in sympathy with me, shared the honesty of my scholarly convictions; I also thank those who, not sharing them, . . . directly and nobly expressed their opposition to me!", Granovsky said to a storm of applause.[75] Herzen's last article incorporated some of the points of the unpublished December review: Granovsky's championing of the rights of women, his independence from any one philosophical formula, and his concern about the ease with which history can be turned into propaganda. Granovsky, Herzen stressed, had particularly distinguished himself for extraordinary "humaneness," for his ability to withhold emotional judgment on the past without concealing his emotional involvement in it. Granovsky's lectures evinced

> a broad and far-reaching love, love for the arising, which he joyfully greets, and love for the dying, which he buries with tears. Nowhere was a word of dislike expressed for anything . . . he walked past the graves, pointed them out, but did not insult the deceased. To be able, in all centuries, among all peoples, in all phenomena, to find, lovingly, that which is related to oneself, the human, to turn not away from one's brothers, no matter how tattered they are or in what unreasonable age we find them; to see, through the cloudy mists of the temporary, the light of an eternal principle, an eternal goal is a great thing for an historian.[76]

Reproaching the Slavophiles, Herzen noted that not once did Granovsky "bear into the catacombs of others' ancestors a single word, a single remark from the present quarrels of their heirs."[77]

Since Stroganov's change of heart, the pages of *Moscow News* had been closed to Herzen. It is testimony to the importance both sides granted to the lectures that this article appeared in the *Muscovite,* that "voluntary assistant of the gendarmes." To indicate that its views were not their own, the editors printed it with the notation, "communicated." From Petersburg Belinsky violently denounced Herzen's apparent compromise. He was being "seen in public" with the enemy. Moreover, he had not openly pressed the Left Hegelian viewpoint, and therefore had not taken issue openly with the problem of Granovsky's idealism, his refusal to become a "fierce immanent" (as Khomiakov had termed those Westerners who, like Herzen and Belinsky, had abandoned religion.) "In my opinion," Belinsky wrote, "it is shameful to praise that which you are not allowed to criticise; that is why your articles on Granovsky's lectures did not please me."[78]

Granovsky's idealism would shortly become a real problem for the "fierce immanents," but at the moment Belinsky's carping could not lessen the triumphant mood in Moscow. Khomiakov, the very dean of the Slavophiles, had expressed the consensus on Granovsky's achievement, calling the lectures "the best display of Moscow life . . . We have not had such lectures since the time of Kalita himself,"[79] and comparing them favourably to European lectures. Granovsky had won over his audience by his style and by the substance of his lectures. His language had been "severe, extremely grave, full of force, daring, and poetry, which vigorously jolted his hearers and woke them up."[80] But Granovsky's habitual mild demeanor had concealed his daring, so that, while he made no compromises with conviction, "he escaped the consequences of his boldness."[81] Granovsky refrained from hammering home the moral of his lectures, but led his listeners to find it themselves, thereby proving he had learned much from Ranke's lectures on the French Revolution. "As he laid the events of history before his audience, grouping them artistically, he spoke *in them* so that the thought, unuttered but perfectly clear, . . . seemed to be their own thought."[82]

Herzen's memoirs describe the astounding demonstration at the conclusion of the lectures.

> When at the end, deeply moved, he thanked the audience, everyone lept up in a kind of intoxication, ladies waved their handkerchiefs, others rushed to the platform, pressed his hands and asked for his portrait. I myself saw young people with flushed cheeks shouting through their tears, 'Bravo! Bravo!' It was impossible to exit. Granovsky stood white as a sheet, with his arms folded and his head a little bent; he wanted to say a few words more but could not. The applause, the shouting, the fury of approbation doubled, the students ranged themselves on each side of the stairs . . . Granovsky made his way, exhausted, to the council-room; a few minutes later he left it, and again there was endless clapping; he turned, begging for mercy with a gesture and, ready to drop with emotion, went into the office. There I flung myself on his neck and we wept in silence.[83]

The lectures had been a celebration of the coming of age of Russian intellectual life. They were a signal that the Russian educated public, the group interested in ideas and change, had expanded to such an extent that it could hardly be contained within officially prescribed boundaries. To Annenkov, the fact that such a diversified audience all acclaimed Granovsky was highly remarkable, a "political event."[84] Chaadaev too termed them of historic significance. In a state where all public meetings and statements were as carefully controlled as under Nicholas I, the very fact of such a gathering in support of Granovsky and the realm of ideas had political import. When, back in 1839, Granovsky had outlined the idea behind the journal he hoped to start, he had proclaimed his goal to be the "spreading of *Humanität.*"[85] He hoped, he said, to enlist "all respectable people in Russia from the new generation" to the cause.[86] This was, in the largest sense, what his public lectures, perhaps the high point of the Remarkable Decade, accomplished. . . .

Notes

[1] Cited by [N.] Barsukov, *Zhizn' [i trudy M. P. Pogodina* (St. Petersburg, 1891-1910)], Vol. VI, p. 325.

[2] Vladimir A. Cherkassky, "Studencheskoe vospominanie," in: *Kniaz Vladimir Aleksandrovich Cherkasskii: ego reachi i vospominaniia o nem* (Moscow, 1897), vii-viii.

[3] Granovsky to N. V. Stankevich, Moscow, November 25, 1840, [*Pesepiska Nikolaia Vladimirovicha Stankevicha, 1830-1840*, edited by A. V. Stankevich (Moscow, 1914)], pp. 369-70.

[4] *Ibid.*, p. 370.

[5] "A strange man, this Bakunin: intelligent as few are, with a deep interest in knowledge—but without any sort of moral beliefs." Granovsky to Ya. M. Neverov, Pogorelets, July 19, 1840, *Perepiska*, p. 403.

[6] Granovsky to N. V. Stankevich, Moscow, February 12, 1840, *Perepiska*, p. 381.

[7] P. V. Annenkov, "Zamechatel'noe desiatiletie" [*Literaturnye vospominaniia*, pp. 135-376. Ed. V. P. Dorofeev. Moscow, 1960,] p. 212. English: [A. P. Mendel, ed. *The Marvelous Decade*. Tr. I. R. Titunik. Ann Arbor, 1968,] p. 79.

[8] "Vzgliad na sovremennoe napravlenie russkoi literatury," *Moskvitianin*, 1842, No. 1, pp. XXVII-XXIX.

[9] *Moskvitianin*, 1843, part II, no. 4, pp. 441-463.

[10] Cited by [A.I.] Herzen, *Byloe i dumy* [(Moscow, 1968)], p. 122.

[11] *Ibid.*, p. 90.

[12] M. Gershenzon, *Istoriia molodoi Rossii* (Moscow, 1908), p. 222.

[13] [A.V.] Nikitenko, *Dnevnik* [(3 vols., Moscow, 1955)], May 28, 1841, Vol. I, p. 235.

[14] Herzen, *Polnoe sobranie sochineniia*, ed. Lemke, Vol. III, p. 230. See Martin Malia, *Alexander Herzen and the Birth of Russian Socialism* (New York, 1965), pp. 236-50 for a full discussion of "Dilletantism in Science."

[15] Granovsky to K. Werder, Moscow, October 4, 1843, *Perepiska*, pp. 440-441.

[16] Granovsky to V. V. Grigoriev, Moscow, autumn, 1842, *Shchukinskii sbornik* [(ed. P. I. Shchukin, Moscow, 1912)], Vol. X, p. 107.

[17] Granovsky to A. E. Kromida, Moscow, December 19, 1839, *Perepiska*, p. 182.

[18] Granovsky to N. Kh. Ketcher, Moscow, November 15, 1843, *Perepiska*, p. 459.

[19] A. Herzen to N. Kh. Ketcher, Nov. 18, 1843; cited by A. G. Dementiev, "Granovskii i Shevyrev," *Uchenye zapiski Leningradskogo gosudarstvennogo universiteta, seriia filologicheskikh nauk*, 1939, no. 46, p. 330.

[20] T. N. Granovsky to D. P. Golokhavstov, September 12, 1843, Tsentral'nyi gosudarstvennyi arkhiv, *fond 459, opis' 2, ed. khr. 573;* cited by Racheotes, "The Gentle Granovskij [*:An Intellectual Biography of Timofej Nikolaevic Granovskij 1813-1855*]" [(Boston College, 1975)] pp. 100-101.

[21] *Lektsii T. N. Granovskogo po istorii srednevekov'ia*, ed. S. A. Asinovskaia (Moscow, 1961), p. 47.

[22] *Ibid.*, p. 41-42.

[23] *Ibid.*, p. 91.

[24] [*Polnoe sobranie sochinenii*, ed. N. F. Mertts, 2 vols. (St. Petersburg, 1905)], Vol. II, p. 285.

[25] *Lektsii po istorii srednevekov'ia*, pp. 92-93.

[26] *Ibid.*, p. 33.

[27] P. N. Miliukov, "Universitetskii kurs Granovskogo," *Iz istorii russkoi intelligentsii* (St. Petersburg, 1902), p. 221.

[28] Cited by Dementiev, "Granovskii i Shevyrev," p. 334.

[29] Roosevelt, *Granovskii at the Lectern*, p. 151.

[30] See his *The Development of a Russian Legal Consciousness* (Chicago and London, 1976), Ch. 8: "The Emergence of a Legal Ethos," especially pp. 223-229.

[31] *Sobranie sochinenii*, Vol. II, p. 299.

[32] Miliukov, "Universitetskii kurs Granovskogo," p. 219.

[33] *Ibid.*

34 *Lektsii T. N. Granovskogo po istorii pozdnego srednevekov'ia*, ed. S. A. Asinovskaia (Moscow, 1971), p. 299.

35 *Ibid.*, p. 28.

36 *Sobranie sochinenii*, Vol. II, p. 308.

37 *Lektsii po istoriia srednevekov'ia*, p. 163.

38 *Ibid.*, p. 164.

39 [P.R.] Roosevelt, *Granovskii at the Lectern* [*: A Conservative Liberal's Vision of History* (Berlin, 1981)], p. 141.

40 *Sobranie sochinenii*, Vol. II, p. 308.

41 M. N. Kovalensky, "Neizdannye universitetskie kursy Granovskogo," *Golos minuvshego*, 1913, No. 9, p. 224.

42 Roosevelt, *Granovskii at the Lectern*, p. 146.

43 Granovsky to N. Kh. Ketcher, Moscow, beginning of December, 1843, *Perepiska*, p. 460.

44 Kovalensky, "Neizdannye kursy Granovskogo," p. 224.

45 *Ibid.*

46 *Sobranie sochinenii*, Vol. II, p. 342.

47 P. V. Annenkov, "Zamechatel'noe desiatiletie," p. 213. English: p. 81.

48 Granovsky to M. V. Kromida and N. V. Charnysh, Moscow, December 13, 1843, *Perepiska*, p. 311.

49 Granovsky to N. Kh. Ketcher, Moscow, December 14, 1843, *Perepiska*, pp. 460-462.

50 Herzen, "Dnevnik 1842-45," *Sobranie sochinenii v tridtsati tomakh* (Moscow, 1954-1968), Vol. II, November 24, 1843, p. 316. Henceforth, *Dnevnik*.

51 A. I. Herzen to N. Kh. Ketcher, Dec. 2-3, 1843, in Herzen, *Sobranie sochinenii*, Vol. XXII, pp. 159-160.

52 Annenkov, "Zamechatel'noe desiatiletie," p. 214; English: p. 82; [B.N.] Chicherin, *Vospominaniia* [(2 vols., Moscow, 1929)], Vol. II, p. 8.

53 Herzen, *Dnevnik*, November 24, 1842, p. 316.

54 Cited by Barsukov, *Zhizn' Pogodina*, Vol. VII, pp. 115-116.

55 Granovsky to N. Kh. Ketcher, Moscow, December 14, 1843, *Perepiska*, p. 462.

56 Cited by A. Stankevich, *T. N. Granovskii i ego perepiska*, Vol. I, p. 130.

57 Herzen, *Dnevnik*, pp. 319-320.

58 "Publichnye chteniia Granovskogo," in Herzen, *Sobranie sochinenii*, Vol. II, p. 112.

59 In the introduction to his lectures on medieval history, for example, speaking of French and English efforts to demarcate the boundary between ancient and medieval times, Granovsky declared, "At present we Russians, non-participants in the movement of western life, are able to judge this question more dispassionately." *Sobranie sochinenii*, Vol. II, p. 292.

60 Barskuov, *Zhizn' Pogodina*, Vol. VII, p. 116.

61 Cited by Dmitriev, "Granovskii i Shevyrev," p. 333. Melgunov was a friend of Pogodin and a contributor to the *Muscovite*. After Granovsky's death, however, he expressed shock at V. V. Grigoriev's attempt to denigrate Granovsky.

62 Herzen, *Dnevnik*, December 11, 1843, p. 320.

63 S. Shevyrev, "Publichnyia lektsii ob istorii srednykh vekov g. Granovskago," *Moskvitianin*, 1843, no. 11, part IV, pp. 525-526.

64 Herzen, 'Publichnye chteniia Granovskogo," p. 113. Herzen termed Schiller's *Letters* "a colossal step in the development of the idea of history." *Ibid.*

65 Shevyrev, "Publichnyia lektsii," p. 528.

66 *Ibid.*, pp. 528-529.

67 *Ibid.*, p. 524.

68 I. Ptushkina, "Neopublikovannaia stat'ia A. I. Gertsena," *Novyi Mir*, 1962, no. 3, p. 234.

69 *Ibid.*, p. 235.

70 *Ibid.*, p. 236.

71 Herzen, *Dnevnik*, December 17, 1843, p. 319.

72 *Ibid.*, January 7, 1844, p. 324.

73 Granovsky to N. Kh. Ketcher, Moscow, January 14, 1844, *Perepiska*, pp. 462-463.

74 *Ibid.* Granovsky thought he might have to transfer from Moscow to St. Petersburg.

75 Cited by Herzen, "O publichnykh chteniakh g-na Granovskogo (Pis'mo vtoroe)", *Sochineniia* (Moscow, 1954), Vol. II, p. 12.

[76] *Ibid.*, p. 150.

[77] *Ibid.*, pp. 124-125.

[78] V. G. Belinskii, *Polnoe sobranie sochinenii v 13-ti t.* (Moscow, 1953-59), Vol. III: "Pis'ma," p. 86.

[79] Cited by Barsukov, *Zhizn' Pogodina,* Vol. VII, p. 113.

[80] Herzen, *Byloe i Dumy,* p. 430.

[81] *Ibid.*

[82] *Ibid.*

[83] *Ibid.*, pp. 430-431.

[84] Annenkov, "Zamechatel'noe desiatiletie," p. 213; English: p. 81. Chaadaev's comment is cited by Herzen, *Byloe i dumy*, p. 430.

[85] Granovsky to N. V. Stankevich, Moscow, March 4, 1840, *Perepiska*, p. 386.

[86] *Ibid . . . .*

FURTHER READING

Barghoorn, Frederick C. "Russian Radicals and the West European Revolutions of 1848." *The Review of Politics* 11, No. 3 (July 1949): 338-54.

> An account of the response of the Russian intelligentsia to the 1848 European political turmoil.

Brown, Edward J. "Letters to Granovsky." In his *Stankevich and His Moscow Circle, 1830-1840,* pp. 115-19. Stanford, Calif.: Stanford University Press, 1966.

> Discusses the exchange of letters between Nikolai Stankevich and Granovskii, which contain informal considerations of Russian intellectual life of the time.

Walicki, Andrzej. "Slavophiles and Westernizers." In his *The Slavophile Controversy: History of a Conservative Utopia in Nineteenth-Century Russian Thought,* translated by Hilda Andrews-Rusiecka, pp. 394-455. Oxford: Clarendon Press, 1975.

> Traces the nineteenth-century development of the Slavophile-Westernizer conflict.

Additional coverage of Granovskii's life and career is contained in the following source published by The Gale Group: *Dictionary of Literary Biography,* Vol. 198.

Sarah Josepha Hale

1788-1879

(Born Sarah Josepha Buell) American journalist, biographer, novelist, short story writer, and poet.

INTRODUCTION

Author of one of the most famous children's poems ever written ("Mary Had a Little Lamb"), Hale fell into obscurity after her death and for most of the twentieth century. Her authorship of "Mary Had a Little Lamb" was both challenged and forgotten, and her other work was mostly ignored until feminist scholars rediscovered her in the 1990s. Recent critics have viewed Hale as a writer and editor who had a great deal of influence in the nineteenth century, and her opinions on the role of women, the slavery question, and morality have undergone serious study.

Biographical Information

Hale was born on a farm in Newport, New Hampshire, the daughter of Gordon and Martha Buell. She was educated at home, at first by her mother and later by her brother Horatio, who tutored her in the courses he was studying at Dartmouth College. Between the ages of eighteen and twenty-four she taught school in Newport, giving up that profession when she married David Hale, a lawyer, in 1813. Her husband continued her education, studying history, French, and botany with her, and also encouraging her to write. She published a few poems and stories during this time but only turned to writing seriously after her husband died suddenly in 1822, leaving her with five children to support. In the next year, she published poems and stories in a variety of magazines and also completed her first book, *The Genius of Oblivion and Other Original Poems* (1823). After the publication of her novel *Northwood* (1827), she was offered the editorship of the new *Ladies' Magazine*, beginning a fifty-year career as an editor. In 1837 the *Ladies' Magazine* merged with Louis Godey's *Lady's Book*, and Hale became editor of the new publication, a post she held until 1877. In her role as editor, Hale contributed editorials, columns, and book reviews to the two publications. She also continued to write fiction and poetry, and published cookbooks, etiquette manuals, and her monumental *Woman's Record* (1853), a collection of biographies of notable women from the time of Eve until the mid-nineteenth century. Her most popular work was "Mary Had a Little Lamb," originally called "Mary's Lamb" (1830); it was frequently reprinted during her lifetime, though

often without crediting her as the author. Two years before her death, her authorship of the poem was questioned by Mary Sawyer Tyler, who claimed to be the original Mary and who said a classmate of hers had written the verses. In the 1920s, Tyler's claim won the support of Henry Ford, the automobile manufacturer, but there has never been any evidence for it, and modern scholars agree that the poem was indeed written by Hale.

Major Works

Hale wrote a large number of works in a wide variety of genres, including novels, short stories, poems, plays, biographies, cookbooks, etiquette manuals, and journalistic contributions to the two magazines that she edited. Despite exploring these different genres, Hale's basic aim remained the same throughout her writings: to give advice and moral guidance. Even "Mary Had a Little Lamb" ends with a moral about being loving and kind to animals, and her novels and short stories tend to be didactic vehicles for her views on social issues and life in general. For instance, her novel *Northwood* promotes the New England virtues of hard work and domesticity as opposed to the supposed idleness and undisciplined leisure of the American South. Her novel *Liberia* (1853) advocates the emigration of slaves to Africa as a solution to the slavery problem. Her short story "The Catholic Convert," originally published as "The Unknown" (1830) asserts the shortcomings of celibacy and convent life, as opposed to marriage. In providing this sort of advice, Hale was acting in accordance with her philosophy as presented in *Woman's Record*: that it is the role of women to provide moral and spiritual leadership. Hale believed that although men were superior to women physically, women were superior morally, and it was women's duty to provide guidance to men and to refine men's "brute" natures. She maintained that it was also specifically women's duty to Christianize the world, for she saw Christ and the Christian virtues of meekness, mercy, purity, and charity as being essentially feminine. Hale was a believer in the doctrine of separate spheres for men and women; men were to engage in industry, business, and politics, while women were to be teachers, writers, and mothers.

Critical Reception

In her own day, Hale was known primarily as an editor who campaigned for women's rights—especially a woman's right to be educated—and for other causes, such as the institution of a national Thanksgiving Day holiday. After her death, she fell into obscurity, but in recent years has been the subject of several studies, mostly by feminists seeking to establish her relation to feminism. Even in her own day, though, this relationship was seen as complicated; Hale campaigned for certain women's rights but opposed the vote for women and the notion that women should seek to do "men's work." As a result, a women's rights society stated after her death that Hale "mingled . . . the spirit of progress with true conservatism." Some later critics have portrayed Hale as militantly feminist and anti-slavery, while others have seen her as anti-feminist and sympathetic to slavery (because she preferred emigration to abolition as a solution to slavery). Although one modern commentator has described her as a liberal in conservative clothing, it is clear that Hale does not easily fit into conventional categories.

PRINCIPAL WORKS

The Genius of Oblivion and Other Original Poems (poetry) 1823
Northwood: A Tale of New England (novel) 1827; revised edition, 1852
Sketches of American Character (short stories) 1829
Poems for Our Children (poetry) 1830
Traits of American Life (short stories) 1835
Ormond Grosvenor (drama) 1838
The Good Housekeeper; or, The Way to Live Well and To Be Well While We Live (handbook) 1839
Alice Ray: A Romance in Rhyme (poetry) 1845
Three hours; or, The Vigil of Love and Other Poems (poetry) 1848
The Judge (drama) 1851
Liberia, or Mr. Peyton's Experiments (novel) 1853
Woman's Record; or, Sketches of All Distinguished Women, from "The Beginning" Till A.D. 1850 (history and biographies) 1853; revised editions, 1855, 1870
Mrs. Hale's Receipts for the Million (handbook) 1857
Manners; or, Happy Homes and Good Society All the Year Round (handbook) 1868

* Includes the poem "Mary's Lamb," more commonly known as "Mary Had a Little Lamb."

CRITICISM

Ruth E. Finley (essay date 1931)

SOURCE: "Chapter XVI: A Female Writer" in *The Lady of Godey's: Sarah Josepha Hale*, J. B. Lippincott Company, 1931, pp. 263-78.

[*In the following excerpt, Finley surveys Hale's writings, discussing her style, her attitudes, and her subject matter.*]

Of the many poems written by Sarah Hale only a few are remembered. These few, however, have become part and parcel of American ballad tradition, so much so that scarcely any one ever asks the name of the author. What modern stops to wonder who wrote **"If Ever I See," "Our Father in Heaven," "It Snows," "Mary Had a Little Lamb"**?—even though for the past few years the authorship of the last named verses has been figuring somewhat in the news.

This consigning of a creator to oblivion the while his creation endures in full flush of appeal is, in a true sense, the highest compliment posterity pays an artist—a compliment won by some through works of exceeding beauty. How many persons can reply offhand to the question—who painted Mona Lisa, the exquisite lady whose inscrutable smile has become proverbial? Sarah Hale won the compliment with a handful of nursery rhymes.

Mrs. Hale has been dead for half a century. The magazine she edited so long has passed with the needs of yesterday. All the many books she wrote are out of print. No attempt was ever made to collect the great mass of her prose and verse that lies scattered, not only through fifty years of the *Lady's Book,* but in scores of other publications—the dailies, weeklies, monthlies and annuals of her era. Effort now to assemble her magazine and newspaper contributions, were there point to the undertaking, would be doomed to failure; for, as she said in **Woman's Record,** her writings often were printed unsigned, in accordance with the haphazard custom of the day. Even in the *Lady's Book,* where she was careful to credit the work of others, many an article, story and poem of her own was printed anonymously. At other times she was content with the initials "S. J. H." or simply "The Editor."

Enormous was her output. Now it survives only in its original printing—all except a poem or two written with modest simplicity for grown-ups and the handful of little lilting rhymes for children, rhymes that almost sing themselves. These, remaining dear to each succeeding generation, have been reprinted a thousand times—in school-book after school-book, in anthologies without end—even unto now.

But fundamentally Sarah Hale was an editor, not a writer. She wrote, to be sure, wrote without ceasing, but as an editor writes—for the day.

Almost from the outset her prose showed a strong journalistic bent, reason of itself why none of it survives. In addition, it was marred by many of the stilted mannerisms of the eighteenth century. For, though as an editor she came to inveigh against prolixity, it was her own worst fault for many years. Never did she wholly overcome a fondness for big words and involved sentences. It will be remembered that, in the autobiographical sketch telling of her hours of study with her husband, she confessed that her "early predilection was for the pompous words and sounding periods of Johnson—the sublime flights and glittering fancies of Counsellor Phillips," and that her husband labored to persuade her that these models of her girlhood study were "sublime nonsense."

Only her first prose, **Northwood,** shows full results of his teachings. Written unhurriedly and with apparent care, its style departs farther from Addisonian standards than does that of her later writings. Had financial necessity not sidetracked her into the exacting time limits set on editorial work, she might well have developed a thoroughly readable style. For the praise accorded **Northwood** by contemporary critics was deserved. It displays, not only a command of "pure idiomatic English," but a structural aptitude, especially in the combining of narrative and dialogue, that up to that time had characterized only one American, James Fenimore Cooper.

However, when confronted with the imperative rush of getting a magazine out on time, she unconsciously dropped back into emulation of the diligently studied writers of her youth. From then on, for years, her prose was ponderously Georgian, filled with "sounding periods," though happily devoid of "glittering fancies." Against the latter her husband's warning must have been most emphatic, since never did she indulge in the "sublime flights" so dear to tongue as well as pen throughout the eighteen-hundreds. Herein the nineteenth century outdid its predecessor.

But with the rest of the Victorians she was guilty of stodginess and shared even their conviction that the one sure way to be impressive was to call on God. Following the line of least resistance, she, too, threw the heft of the rhetorical burden on the Almighty. For this she should not be too harshly criticized. She was, in fact, a deeply religious woman, a devout Episcopalian and so truly a Christian that she came closer to loving her neighbor as herself than is vouchsafed most humans. Besides, everybody called on God, from preachers to politicians. Any one wading through old Congressional Records is puzzled, indeed, to know whether it was sermons or speeches then being delivered in the country's law-making halls. Even as late as the turn of the century Bryan's cohorts agitated free silver in the name of the Lord, while Republican orators assured voters that William McKinley and Heaven would fill all dinner-pails. These indiscriminate references to Deity, in season and out, indicated neither conscious sanctity nor unconscious blasphemy. It was a fashionable rhetorical habit—and that was all.

Turning out numerous "annuals," two anthologies, cookbooks, translations and much verse in addition to editing *Godey's,* Mrs. Hale had little time during the forties and fifties for finished writing. But about 1860 her style changed for the second time, becoming more straightforward and thereafter reproducing much of the vivid quality of the earlier **Northwood.**

Not solely because it exemplifies the happiest prose style of its author is **Northwood** interesting. Published in 1827, it was one of America's first attempts at novel-writing, and as such has been accorded far less attention by literary historians than it deserves. Charles Brockden Brown had offered the public his essay-like fiction from 1798 until his death in 1810. William Wirt had published *The British Spy* in 1803; and by 1821 Cooper with *The Spy* was well on his literary career. But this was about the sum total of American novel-length fiction.

Northwood has three other claims to fame:

It was the first American novel of consequence written by a woman.
It was the first novel—by either man or woman—to deal with the question of slavery.

It is the most accurate and detailed picture of the domestic habits, customs and manners of the post-Colonial period contemporaneously recorded.

In the last respect, the author, being a potential editor, knew precisely what she was doing. Her eye on the "century hence" when "this unpretending book may be a reference," she went into such minutiæ as the color of decorative paint, "coffee and toast" for breakfast and the correct apparel for "bridesmen" at weddings.

While dealing primarily with the problem of emancipation, *Northwood* displayed a range of interests as wide as the activities of its times. Nor did it stop there; repeatedly it anticipated attitudes more characteristic of the twentieth than the nineteenth century. Into the mouths of her characters the author put her own ideas on education, feminism, child-training, sumptuary laws, industrialism, immigration, centralized government, international relations. She foresaw the United States as a world power and as such extending association to Great Britain—this last a rather amazing conception in view of the animosity then still fostered between the lately severed countries. But Mrs. Hale had a faculty for stripping facts of emotions as well as for taking into account those natural laws which in the final analysis so inexorably govern. In blood of race she sensed the functioning of one of these laws, and so, though born out of the prejudices of the Revolution, she could yet look for an inevitable drawing together of the two great Anglo-Saxon nations for the protection of their common institutions, liberties and culture.

> "Great Britain once called herself our mother," she caused a *Northwood* character to say, "and though far from being an indulgent one we do not deny her maternity; but there is a period when nations as well as individuals quit their minority, and if the parent country would continue the parallel of relationship which subsists in families, she will not consider her independent offspring as her natural enemy. . . .

> "And do we not see instances where the mother finds not only a useful friend in the child she once discarded, but a support in age—one who will afford an asylum when no other protector is to be found?

> "When Alexander sacked Tyre the Carthaginians conveyed many of the Tyrians to a place of safety: they remembered they were descendants of a Tyrian colony. . . . And will Great Britain be exempted from the operation of those universal laws of nature which have governed all created things on this globe and their works? . . . The nations of Europe will band against her, for she has trampled them

down in her day of triumph; and she has the light of freedom which tyrants hate. The nations will gather against her and she will be sore beset.

> "And then will America remember. . . ."

America remembered on the sixth of April, 1917, ninety years after *Northwood* was written.

There is much wisdom to be gleaned from this early American novel. The woman who wrote it, inexperienced as she then was, had done some exceptionally clear thinking. She knew, for instance, that "the art of self-government is indispensable to woman's felicity." She had learned that "persons who dare not commune with their own hearts, are not only dependent on society for their pleasures, but must seek it as a refuge from anxiety and remorse." She faced poverty for herself and children fearlessly, because she had already observed that "excessive luxury and rational liberty were never yet found compatible." Though the complacent artificiality of Victorianism was to cozen most people, she had long viewed "selfishness as an insidious passion, mingling itself with motives, and inspiring actions which claim to proceed from holy and benevolent feelings."

And, above all, she held to the following:

> There can be no excellency attained without industry. The mind of the idle, like the garden of the slothful, will be overgrown with briars and weeds; and indolence, under whatever fashionable name . . . , is a more dangerous enemy to practical goodness and to moral and intellectual improvement, than even dissipation. . . . Those who tread a devious path may possibly retrace their steps, or by a circuitous route finally reach the goal; but those who never stir, how can they win the race!

She "stirred." And, if for herself she avoided devious paths, she retained nonetheless enough of eighteenth-century broadmindedness to keep her charitable in the midst of obduracy, charitable enough to set genius above weakness, befriending such men as Dr. William Morton and Edgar Allan Poe.

But *Northwood* is far from a dry and didactic volume. It contains many a sly dig that even yet brings a smile. Who could help chuckling over the sentence, "You may easily tell a rich Yankee farmer—he is always pleading poverty."

Mrs. Hale had the keenly observant mind of the true journalist. Hers was that sensitivity which registers both the little and the big—the homely, human interest of every day, on the one hand; and, on the other, the wider events of social import. So that, while she could wax editorially enthusiastic over the trim of a bonnet, it was never all chit-chat with the magazines she edited. At a time when there was little dissemination of news and smaller interpretation of it, she subjected public affairs to a running fire of comment, not only as these affected women and the home, but in respect to the big thing she called "our American experiment." In an age when public prints dealt most effectively with trivialities, she was acutely conscious of movements and trends; witness her early sensing of the menace of slavery. She searched for the meaning of events, trying always to calculate what they might portend. An editor's greatest gift, appreciation of the *significance* of facts, was hers.

Thus she is found sending Eliza Leslie to Niagara Falls in pursuit of a descriptive story with which to bait the reader by amusing him, while she herself sat at her desk attempting to figure out just how important steam as applied to overland transportation was likely to prove, how it would affect the growth of the country commercially, what relation it was going to have to education and the home.

Illustrative of the journalistic aptitude of Sarah Hale is her book of essays, *Traits of American Life,* published in 1835. The following selections have been culled at random:

> To speak without metaphor—the engrossing pursuit of Americans is wealth.

> What in the rising man was industry and economy, becomes in the rich man parsimony and avarice.

> Any man who has money may obtain the reputation of taste by the mere purchasing of works of art.

> Political controversies are never entered into with any wish to gain knowledge, but only a triumph for the party.

> We shall never be *free* in spirit, while bigotry and intolerance are cherished among us.

> Americans have two ardent passions; the love of liberty and the love of distinction.

> Few individuals enter into public life who would not be wealthier and happier as private citizens— but then they would not be known, would not see their names in the newspaper, except for raising a curious calf, or a mammoth cabbage.

> There is small danger of being starved in our land of plenty; but the danger of being stuffed is imminent.

> This is a speculating and selfish age; and to think "money will answer all things" is too much the characteristic of Americans. . . . God of my country! is there no word of power that can exorcise this demon from among us!

> We are aware that a certain class of political economists affect to believe that luxury is beneficial to a nation—

but it is not so. The same reasoning which would make extravagance in dress commendable, because it employed manufacturers and artists, would also make intemperance a virtue in those who could afford to be drunk, because the preparation of the alcohol employs laborers, and the consumption would encourage trade.

> The glories of conquests and the luxuries of wealth alike tend to make the few masters, and the many slaves.

As a good journalist must, she spoke her mind—did Sarah Hale. But seldom did she preach. She was not a Puritan, unbelievable as it may seem to the twentieth century that any one Victorian in point of time could be otherwise.

As she wrote Matthew Vassar, she "did not believe in sumptuary laws." She had faith in the midst of Victorianism's most pedantic and reactionary mandates that right conditions would create uprightness of mind, body and heart. Possessing the editor's knowledge that there are two sides to every question, she was liberal to a degree uncharacteristic of her times.

"I can tolerate anything better than the puritanical zeal which exalts itself at the expense of every social virtue and innocent enjoyment" are words spoken by a character in *Northwood.* The author of *Northwood* made those words a precept of her editorial life.

The tolerance of Mrs. Hale is well exemplified in her books on etiquette. She wrote several. Coming out of a social order that stressed recreative restraint, they are unique. She devoted whole chapters to games, dancing and like "frivolities." Especially did she go to lengths to devise **"Happy Sundays for Children,"** as she entitled one chapter wherein she said:

> There is something monstrous in linking Sunday and sadness in the brain of a child. . . . We all teach our children and hold for ourselves that Sunday is a "day of rest." So it is. But upon this subject it seems to me there is a mistaken view. The word "rest" implies not idleness or tedious vacuity of thought, but a rest from the wearying secular cares of earth and from physical toil. . . . We are far from meaning that the day should not be marked to children as something distinct from other days; but let it be by linking holiness with happiness, by changing their amusements, not annihilating them.[1]

Fully aware of the war then waging between Jacksonian scorn of form and manner and Victorian worship of them, she had as little use for one extreme as for the other. Yet, for all his bluff disdain, the democrat, she suspected, was the more worth saving. So her appeal here was to sincerity.

While other social arbiters were concerned over such momentous questions as whether a "genteel female" should insist upon a gentleman's wholly "restraining himself in demonstrations of affection," Mrs. Hale was insisting on essentials:

> Rules of courtesy are necessary in every family and for all stations of life in our country, because here all have a chance for improvement.

> The first mark of a well-bred person is a sensitive regard for the feelings of others.

> The first indispensable requisite of good society is education.

> The most welcome guest in society will ever be the one to whose mind everything is a suggestion, and whose words suggest something to everybody.

> Society appears to impose on its members a number of arbitrary rules which continually restrict them in their actions. It tells them how they must eat and drink and dress and walk and talk and so on. . . . But if the ordinances of society are examined it will be found . . . that they all tend to one end—the preservation of harmony, and the prevention of one person from usurping the rights, or intruding on the province of another.

These sayings are quoted from Mrs. Hale's most popular book on etiquette, *Manners, or Happy Homes and Good Society All the Year Round.* It ran through many editions; and, while it fully explained why one should eat with a fork instead of a knife, its real object was to convince a sprawling pioneer America that "a certain formality of manner, or etiquette as it is usually called, is both a mark of respect for others and of one's own self-respect" and that correct conduct is predicated on right feeling.

But more important than manner to Sarah Hale was achievement. Of all her prose works the one she considered most important was *Woman's Record or Sketches of All Distinguished Women from "The Beginning" till A.D. 1850. Arranged in Four Eras. With Selections from Female Writers of Every Age. Illustrated by Two Hundred and Thirty Portraits Engraved on Wood by Lossing and Barritt.* It was first published in 1853.

The thing is stupendous. It begins with Abigail, wife of King David of Israel, and ends with a list of contemporary women "labouring with their husbands in foreign mission fields." The index contains more than two thousand names. The purpose of the undertaking was, as usual with the lady editor, the glorification of woman. Most enthusiastically received, *Woman's Record* was considered a standard work for many

years. It still has value in that it is the only compilation including the name of every American woman who had the slightest claim to fame prior to 1850.

A biographical sketch of Mrs. Hale herself appears along with the rest. It quotes, however, from her verse only, for, as she naïvely pointed out, "sufficient specimens of my prose will be extant in this work." Of the poems she selected only one is remembered to-day, **"It Snows,"** first printed in the *Lady's Book* for January, 1837, and gaining an immediate popularity. It was reprinted in many journals and in various annuals and almanacs, and became a favorite piece in *McGuffey's Fifth Reader.* The first of its five stanzas reads:

> "It Snows!" cries the School-boy—"hurrah!" and his shout
>   Is ringing through parlor and hall,
> While swift, as the wing of a swallow, he's out,
>   And his playmates have answered his call:
> It makes the heart leap but to witness their joy—
>   Proud wealth has no pleasures, I trow,
> Like the rapture that throbs in the pulse of a boy,
>   As he gathers his treasures of snow;
> Then lay not the trappings of gold on thine heirs,
>   While health, and the riches of Nature are theirs.

In truth, Mrs. Hale rather fancied herself as a versifier; and time has not wholly gainsaid her. But, as against the few of her rhymes that have survived, literally reams of them have perished. Yet in her day she was widely acclaimed as a "poetess."

It was a rhythmical age. People loved the measured sound of iambic and trochee feet wholly aside from content. To the primitive taste of a mass mind that possessed no criteria of its own, any verse, if only it held an ear-tickling swing, was satisfying. Rhyme and meter were the "jazz" of Victorianism. Writers sat up nights evolving new forms, new rhythms to attract, even so great a poet as Poe catering to his rub-a-dub public—

> Keeping time, time, time,
> In a sort of Runic rhyme
> To the tintinabulation that so musically wells
> From the bells, bells, bells, bells,
> Bells, bells, bells—
> From the jingling and the tinkling of the bells.

Poe did it supremely, of course. So did Longfellow, who, discarding the accepted form of blank verse, as in the "Song of Hiawatha" and "Evangeline," managed without rhymes to endow old cadences borrowed from the ancient Greek with modern charm.

While some of the best American poetry was written between 1830 and 1880, it is also true that during that span of fifty years more metered trash was published in this country than ever before had been recorded in all the history of the ages. Every crossroad boasted a local "poet" or half a dozen "poetesses." The latter in particular inundated press and public with their burblings. Small was their grammar, through no fault of their own, and consequently poetic license was requisitioned to cover a multitude of rather elementary lacks. Anyway, to jingle was the thing; so jingle they did—these crossroad poets, male and female. As for the poetesses, had not most of them been presented by friends and admirers with gold pens especially destined for literary purposes? And was it not obligatory that they so use them?

From about 1840 on the *Book* carried advertisements that read like this:

> Rapp's Gold Pens: Goose Quill size, $2; Swan Quill size, $2.50; Condor Quill size, $5. Without holders.

Technically pens were sized according to these standards until close to the year of the Centennial. The holders that were extra—bone, onyx, silver, pearl, ivory, gold—are not so long gone out of general use but that even yet one is occasionally seen.

Of course, Mrs. Hale, who started life with a mere goose quill, acquired a gold pen. Did she not in *Godey's* for April, 1845, print **"The Gold Pen—A Poem, Inscribed to the Gentleman Who Presented the Gift,"** and sign same with her full name, a most unusual indulgence in her own magazine? She certainly did. But even so she was not one of the jinglers.

Neither was she a poet, in the true sense. Her work in the rhythmical medium of her period resulted in verse, not poetry—some of it very good. All of it was better than the average of the bulk then being produced, though none of it equaled the best. In any case, she possessed not a little facility for manipulating form to produce pleasing effects; and, as it was the common habit of many rhymsters to copy any new and happy structural combination, much of her verse *sounds* familiar, as the result of its rhythm having been imitated by others, even though the actual words she wrote may have gained no lasting currency. A case in point is her **"Christmas Hymn,"** first published in *Godey's* for February, 1841—"music by G. Kingsley." It had been composed for a children's festival. The first and last stanzas were:

> Hail, hail the happy morn
> When Christ our Lord was born!
>   Sound, sound His Praise!
> The Prince of Righteousness,

> He came our world to bless,
> The glorious hymn of "Peace"
>   On earth to raise.

> Sound, sound the loudest strain!
> Let earth and sky and main
>   The anthem raise!
> Father, Thy love we bless,
> Saviour, we ask Thy peace,
> Spirit, we beg Thy grace,
>   When God we praise.

An old favorite unblushingly borrowed without credit by many a vellum- or plush-bound annual or gift book of nineteenth-century vintage, originally appeared in *Godey's* for January, 1850—under the New Hampshire-inspired title **"Our Granite Hills."** It has been reprinted under a dozen different headings since. The opening stanza will suffice to recall it to mind:

> What glowing thoughts, what glorious themes
>   To mountain-tops belong!
> The law from Sinai's summit came;
>   From Sion, sacred song;—
> And Genius, on Parnassian heights,
>   His banner first unfurled;
> And from the Seven-hilled city waved
>   The sword that swayed the world!
> Then let us raise the hymn of praise—
>   To us the hills are given;
> And mountain-tops are altars, set
>   To lift the soul to heaven.

Taste changes with the times, as Mrs. Hale herself suggested in the preface to her **Dictionary of Poetical Quotations,** published in 1850, a revision of the work of one John F. Addington done some twenty years before. After explaining that, as Addington antedated most of the modern poets, they were of necessity omitted from his compilation, she cited as further ground for the revision this: "The old dramatic poets wrote according to their lights," and, therefore, Addington's selections were not "always in accordance with the present standards of public taste"—a truism even more pertinent now than then. The nineteenth century wrote according to its lights; new lights illumine the new century. Rightly or wrongly, every year all but the very best of the old slips further into the background.

It was Mrs. Hale's first slender book of children's songs, **Poems for Our Children,** that contained the verses of hers which, taking their place as nursery classics, have resisted time. The three best known are **"Mary's Lamb," "Birds"** and **"Prayer."** *McGuffey's Second Reader* for 1857 used **"Birds"** as Lesson V, giving it a new title, **"The Bird's Nest,"** and adding a third stanza not appearing with the two originally printed; **"Mary's Lamb"** was Lesson XLVII.

"Prayer" was used in the first (1836) edition of the *Second Reader* as Lesson LXII. None was signed, of course. *McGuffey's,* like the almanacs, did not take the trouble to note authors' names—not until the dignity of the famous *Fifth Reader* was reached. There **"It Snows"** was credited to "Mrs. Hale."

"Birds," the first poem of *Poems for Our Children,* read originally as follows:

> If ever I see,
>   On bush or tree
> Young birds in a pretty nest,
>   I must not, in my play,
>   Steal the birds away,
> To grieve their mother's breast.
>
>   My mother I know
>   Would sorrow so,
> Should I be stolen away—
>   So I'll speak to the birds,
>   In my softest words,
> Nor hurt them in my play.

"Prayer," the final poem of the little book, came to be included, it seems, in every nineteenth-century collection of children's verse. And there is many a youngster even yet taught this easily memorized version of the Lord's Prayer:

> Our Father in heaven,
>   We hallow thy name!
> May thy kingdom so holy,
>   On earth be the same—
> O, give to us, daily,
>   Our portion of bread!
> It is from thy bounty
>   That all must be fed.
>
> Forgive our transgressions,
>   And teach us to know
> That humble compassion
>   That pardons each foe—
> Keep us from temptation,
>   From weakness and sin—
> And thine be the glory
>   Forever—Amen!

Notes

[1] *Manners* by Sarah J. Hale, Boston, 1868.

Ruth E. Finley (essay date 1931)

SOURCE: "Chapter XVII: Mary's Lamb and Mr. Ford" in *The Lady of Godey's: Sarah Josepha Hale,* J. B. Lippincott Company, 1931, pp. 279-305.

[*In the following excerpt, Finley discusses the controversy surrounding Hale's authorship of the poem "Mary Had a Little Lamb."*]

"Mary Had a Little Lamb," the most famous children's poem in the English language, was first printed in 1830. It was signed by Sarah Hale. Now Mrs. Hale's authorship of the first half of the poem has been challenged by Mr. Henry Ford, who has given credence to an old claim first made public in the late eighteen-seventies by a Mrs. Mary Sawyer Tyler. Mrs. Tyler asserted that she was the "Mary" of the poem, that it originally consisted of but twelve lines and was written by one John Roulstone, a youth who died in 1822.

"Mary's Lamb," as the poem was titled in Mrs. Hale's little volume of verse, *Poems for Our Children,* published by Marsh, Capen & Lyon of Boston some time subsequent to May 1, 1830, the date attached to the preface of the book, also was printed in the same year in a bi-monthly magazine for children called the *Juvenile Miscellany.* One of the earliest attempts to produce a child's periodical, the *Miscellany* was published in Boston by Putnam & Hunt, which firm also published Mrs. Hale's *Ladies' Magazine,* and lived from September, 1826, until about 1835. On page sixty-four of its issue for September-October, 1830, **"Mary's Lamb"** appeared, signed, as Mrs. Hale signed so much of her fugitive writing, with the initials "S. J. H."

Whether the book *Poems for Our Children* came out before the magazine publication of the rhyme, or *vice versa,* is not entirely clear. Though the book's preface is dated May 1, there is to be found on page 198 of the November-December number of the *Miscellany,* the issue following the one that printed the poem, an announcement of the publication of '*Poems for Our Children'* by Mrs. Sarah J. Hale." In either case, the important point now is that Sarah Hale, not only published **"Mary's Lamb"** in her first book of children's verse, but gave it separate, signed publication in a magazine in the same year.

That she chose **"Mary's Lamb"** for the *Juvenile Miscellany* was perhaps sheer chance, though it might be argued that such choice indicated a particular liking on the part of the author for that particular poem. That she should have picked the one poem, out of the fifteen in the book, which above all her other work was later to become famous, is at least significant of her sure instinct as an editor. And happily she signed it—S. J. H.

Poems for Our Children, of course, was signed in full—on the title page, "Mrs. Sarah J. Hale"; and at the end of the preface, "Sarah J. Hale." The preface follows:

> *To All Good Children in the United States.*
>
> DEAR CHILDREN,
> I wrote this book for you—to please and instruct you. I know children love to read rhymes, and sing

little verses; but they often read silly rhymes, and such manner of spending their time is not good. I intended, when I began to write this book, to furnish you with a few pretty songs and poems which would teach you truths, and, I hope, induce you to love truth and goodness. Children who love their parents and their home, can soon teach their hearts to love their God and their country.

I offer you the First Part of Poems for Our Children—if you like these I shall soon write the Second Part, and perhaps I shall make a larger book.

SARAH J. HALE.
Boston, May 1, 1830.

The promised "larger book" appeared in 1834, published by Allen & Ticknor of Boston.

The
SCHOOL SONG BOOK
Adapted to the
SCENES OF THE SCHOOL ROOM
Written for
American Children and Youth
BY MRS. SARAH J. HALE
Editor of the Ladies' Magazine, and author of
"Floria's Interpreter," etc., etc.
BOSTON:
ALLEN & TICKNOR
1834.

So read the title page, while the preface follows:

TO THE PUPILS OF————SCHOOL

A new book-I hope, my young friends, that you will find it *a new pleasure.*

Some time ago I wrote a little book, naming it "Poems for Our Children." A number of these poems have been set to music by Mr. Mason; and if you have never seen the book, you have probably heard or sung

> "If ever I see
> On bush or tree,"
> or
> "Our Father in heaven,
> We hallow thy name," etc.

I was told these songs were very popular with the young; and this encouraged me to write this book for your gratification. I have included in this book all the *favorites* from the other, and added others which I hope will *become* favorites.

MRS. HALE.
Boston, May 1, 1834.

The Mr. Mason referred to by Mrs. Hale was Dr. Lowell Mason, the first well known American composer. Dr. Mason's contribution to American music was principally hymns—and the first songs for elementary schools. Living in Boston when Mrs. Hale arrived there in 1828, he was eager to experiment with the use of music in connection with inculcating ideas in the child mind. It was inevitable that their common interest in education, particularly child education, should draw Sarah Hale and Lowell Mason together, They became life-long friends. He died in 1872, five years before Mrs. Hale.

It was Lowell Mason's idea really that prompted the writing of *Poems for Our Children.* He wanted some simple verses suitable for setting to music, the words and precepts of which would be comprehensible to little people. He asked Mrs. Hale to write a series of such poems. She complied. He set them to music, **"If Ever I See," "Mary's Lamb," "My Country"** and **"Our Father in Heaven"** gaining the widest immediate popularity. By the following year, 1831, these songs were fairly well circulated throughout New England. For they were unique, an innovation, and represented the first step toward wide-spread musical education. Lowell Mason and Sarah Hale had set American children singing.

"Mary's Lamb" again appeared under Mrs. Hale's signature in 1841, in a new edition of her *School Song Book,* published this time, not by Allen & Ticknor, but by James B. Dow of Boston under a new title, *My Little Song Book,* though still carrying the 1834 copyright. The author's "Remarks" at the beginning of this book stated that the reason for a new edition was the increasing popularity of "vocal music as a branch of school education."

Thereafter a general—and uncredited—lifting of Mrs. Hale's little poem ensued. For instance, in the writer's possession is an old book—the first ever owned by her mother, who is still living and to whom it was given on her fifth birthday, in 1855, as a reward for having learned her letters. It is a compilation of children's poems called *Songs for the Little Ones at Home.* The cover is gone; the title page is gone; the first legible page is number 70; the last legible page is 212. How many pages the book had seventy-six years ago when presented to its original owner, who compiled it, or what other poems of Mrs. Hale's it may have contained is not to be determined. But on page 79 is **"If Ever I See"**; on page 119, **"Mary's Little Lamb"**; and on 206, **"The Thunder Storm"**—all three originally published in *Poems for Our Children.* None is credited to its author; but at the end of **"Mary's Little Lamb"** is printed in small type *Songs for Children,* indicating that it, at least, had been included in a former compilation, where doubtless it had also been used without credit.

Certain it is that in the case of *Songs for the Little Ones at Home* authors' names were few and far between; Mrs. Hale was not the only one who suffered. "How Doth the Little Busy Bee," on page 109, was signed "Watts"; but "Twinkle, Twinkle, Little Star," on page 196, was not credited even to a previous collection. Its author had been dead since 1824, and few were the people around 1855 who knew, just as few know now, that this lovely bit of children's verse was written by a woman named Jane Taylor.

By about 1855 all of Mrs. Hale's own books containing **"Mary's Lamb"** were out of print. In a letter written October 17, 1858, to Rufus W. Griswold concerning the biographical sketch which was to appear in the forthcoming third edition of his *Female Poets of America,* a work kept in revision as late as 1892, Mrs. Hale discussed which of her poems should be chosen as examples of her work and spoke of her book of children's songs published in Boston. She said:

"It is now entirely out of print. But most of the songs have been set to music and many have been copied into other works. . . . "[1]

In short, inadequate copyright laws, coupled with the general literary confusion and loose publication practices of the times, made it possible for compilers of anthologies "annuals," school-books and the like to reprint favorites at will, with or without credit. And so it was that **"Mary's Lamb,"** not unlike many another familiar poem, slipped into the language uncredited, easy prey to theft of ideas, verbal plagiarism and even bodily appropriation.

But it was reserved for one William H. McGuffey to accomplish the definitive anonymous broadcasting of **"Mary's Little Lamb."**

During the period that Mrs. Hale and Lowell Mason were encouraging music in the schools, the early thirties, McGuffey was busy compiling the first edition of his renowned *Eclectic Series. McGuffey's First* and *Second Readers* were originally published in 1836; the *Third* and *Fourth Readers* came out in 1837, and the *Fifth Reader* in 1844. They, too, were an innovation, and for more than half a century remained the standard textbooks in America's common schools. As such they became one of the country's most deeply entrenched institutions. In 1901 they were revised for the fifth time, and in 1911 were still being used in the West and South.

It is impossible to estimate how great a part these readers played in forming the literary tastes of nineteenth-century America. Suffice it to say they were memorized from cover to cover, and that every word they contained became a part of the individual mental equipment of the grandparents of all of us, the parents of many of us and in some instances of our own selves.

Mrs. Hale's contribution to *McGuffey's* included, among other selections, **"Mary's Lamb,"** printed as Lesson XLVII in the 1857 edition of the *Second Reader*—the edition that was to prove classic and which Mr. Ford has had reprinted. As Lesson XLVII **"Mary Had a Little Lamb"** went fully into the consciousness of the people—unsigned. For, as has been previously pointed out, *McGuffey's First, Second, Third* and *Fourth Readers* gave no credits.

Though through the years innumerable Marys owned pet lambs and all of them learned the famous poem out of their *McGuffey's Reader,* more than one believing herself to be the original Mary of the poem, there was no question raised as to the verses' authorship until a Mrs. Mary Sawyer Tyler of Somerville, Massachusetts, asserted in 1878, not only that she was the original Mary, but that a certain John Roulstone, known to her, had written the first half of the poem. There are further claims now that Mrs. Tyler had made this statement before 1878. Possibly, probably even, she did. If she did, the assertion gained her only local reputation. Either way makes no difference. But the publicity given the statement she made in 1878 did make a difference, and, as a result of Mr. Ford's interest in the case, continues to.

Mrs. Tyler, it appears, was visiting in Boston during the fall and winter of 1877-78. At the moment, there being danger that a famous Boston landmark, the Old South Church, would be razed to give place to business, a great Fair, or series of bazars, was being held in an effort to raise money to save the ancient edifice from destruction. These bazars—one at least was a "Spinning Bee," which the *Boston Transcript* of February 14, 1878, reported Mrs. Tyler attended the day before—seem to have been continued intermittently for months. There was much excitement over the proposed vandalism, and everybody was asked to help avert it. Mrs. Tyler's donation was an ancient pair of woolen stockings. The stockings, she said, had been knit for her as a child, by her mother, from the first fleece sheared from her pet lamb. This lamb, she further asserted, was the original of the **"Mary's Lamb"** poem—a poem written, she stated, around 1816 about her and her pet, the original script of which, consisting however of only twelve lines, was presented her by its author, John Roulstone.

Such a statement was sure to attract attention. The stockings were raveled out, and bits of the wool were attached to cards inscribed in Mrs. Tyler's handwriting:

> Knitted yarn from the first fleece of
> Mary's Little Lamb
> Mary E. Sawyer Tyler
> Somerville [and the date]

The cards were then sold as souvenirs, apparently over a period of several years. The date of the card in the possession of a nephew of Mrs. Hale is May 13, 1878; the card reproduced in a booklet sponsored by Mr. Ford, "The Story of Mary's Little Lamb," is dated January 27, 1880.

The fact that these cards were originally sold in connection with the patriotic movement to save to posterity the historic Old South Church lent to Mrs. Tyler's statement nation-wide publicity. Immediately protests arose. For close to fifty years the authorship of "Mary's Lamb" had been credited, when it was credited, to the well known woman editor of *Godey's Lady's Book,* who, it was clear, had signed the poem upon its first appearance in print. Details of Mrs. Tyler's claim were asked for by newspapers and magazines and these she supplied as follows:

That she, born Mary Elizabeth Sawyer on March 22, 1806, in Sterling, Mass., had attended what was known as the Redstone District School;

That from the time she was nine years old until she was thirteen she had owned a pet lamb, which upon a certain occasion had followed her to school;

That on the day of the lamb's escapade the school had a visitor in the person of John Roulstone, a lad born in 1805, who at the time was residing in the home of his uncle, the Reverend Mr. Lemuel Capen, minister at Sterling, and being prepared by Mr. Capen to enter Harvard;

That young Roulstone was greatly amused by her embarrassment over her pet's following her to school;

That the next day he returned with a poem of twelve lines, which, she said, was identical with the first twelve lines of the famous "Mary's Lamb."

This twelve-line poem, according to Mrs. Tyler, was written on a slip of paper which young Roulstone gave to her.

Mrs. Tyler never produced the slip of paper or any witness who had ever seen it. The writing which she said the piece of paper contained was never printed prior to publication of Mrs. Hale's "Mary's Lamb"; and Mrs. Tyler did not claim it had been so printed.

Consequently, granting any portion of the poem existed before publication of "Mary's Lamb" by Mrs. Hale in 1830, the only way it could have come to her attention was by word of mouth. This would have meant a wide verbal circulation of the poem, in which case many persons beside Mrs. Hale would have become familiar with it. There is not now and has never been any evidence that there were such persons.

At the time the Tyler-Roulstone claim was made public in Boston, Mrs. Hale was in her ninetieth year. She had just retired to private life, having laid down the editorship of *Godey's* in December, 1877. What was done at that time by way of affirming her authorship of "Mary's Lamb" and replying to the implied accusation that she had plagiarized the first twelve lines, is best told by her son Horatio Hale, the world-eminent ethnologist and philologist, whose signed statement appeared in the *Boston Transcript* for April 10, 1889. He said in part:

> I am asked for a statement of the facts relating to the authorship and first publication of the well-known poem "Mary's Lamb." This poem was written sixty years ago by my mother, Mrs. Sarah J. Hale. It was first published . . . in her little book entitled "Poems for Our Children." This book—which is now before me—comprises only twenty-four duodecimo pages in a stiff paper cover. It is not a compilation, but an original work, composed throughout by Mrs. Hale. This fact is stated, as clearly as words can express it, in the introductory address prefixed to the poem.

Mr. Hale then set forth the preface earlier quoted in this chapter. After discussing the poem from a literary standpoint, showing how in content it met the intention of his mother's book as set forth in her preface—"poems which would teach truths . . . and induce . . . truth and goodness"—he continued:

> With regard to the story of Mrs. Tyler and young John Roulstone, it is certain that Mrs. Hale knew nothing of it until many years after her poem was published. On this point I may adduce some letters written at my mother's request in the year 1878—the year preceding that of her death. In October of the former year a letter was received by her at her home in Philadelphia from a lady of Boston connected with a popular periodical, informing her of an impression existing in that city that the first three quatrains of "Mary's Lamb" were written by a Mr. Roulstone about the year 1817, and asking for the "real facts," to be embodied in an article on the subject. One of my mother's children, at her request, replied in the following terms:

> "Your courteous letter of inquiry addressed to my mother, Mrs. Sarah J. Hale, relative to the authorship of the poem known as 'Mary's Lamb,' was duly received, but my mother has not been well enough to reply to it. On her behalf I beg to say that the poem in question first appeared in a book of twenty-four pages, published in Boston in 1830 by Marsh, Capen & Lyon, entitled 'Poems for Our Children, by Mrs. Sarah J. Hale.' My mother states that every poem in this book was of her own composition. What can have given rise to the impression that some part of this particular poem was written by another person she does not know. There is no foundation for it whatever."

This letter brought another, enclosing some newspaper slips which comprised the now familiar "Tyler and Roulstone" story, making Mrs. Tyler (when she was little Mary Sawyer) the heroine of the poem, and John Roulstone, a student of sixteen or seventeen, the composer of the first part of it in her honor. To this letter the following reply was made:

"My mother knows nothing of the incident referred to in the extracts which you send. There would seem, however, no reason to doubt that good Mrs. Tyler has given a truthful account of her recollections. She is merely mistaken in regard to the verses. Pet lambs are common enough, and the incident of one of them following its little mistress to school may have happened on more than one occasion. It did actually happen to my mother. She was a farmer's daughter, and had several pet lambs at different times. One of these once followed her to the school and lingered about the door, precisely as she has recorded in the poem. If a young collegian like Mr. Roulstone, with a turn for poetry, happened to be present when Mary Sawyer's lamb came into the schoolhouse, it would be very natural that he should compose some verses about it. But it is quite certain that these were not the verses which my mother published many years afterward, in her little book of 'Poems for Children.' These verses, like all the other poems in the book, were entirely of her own composition."

Here it should be noted that in the second letter quoted by Horatio Hale the statement is made by one of Mrs. Hale's children that the poem was founded on a personal experience. The Ford arguments have laid special stress on the fact that certain of Mrs. Hale's grandchildren have said that their grandmother told them there had been no personal experience back of the poem, that the verses employed an imaginary incident. Were this definitely established, it would afford no evidence that Mrs. Hale was other than full author of the poem. Most poetical work is imaginative. But Mrs. Hale was reared on a farm, and during her girlhood lambs were widely used as children's pets. Certainly her background was such as to suggest that the incident might well have been drawn from her own experience. Moreover, as her children were members of her household at the time **"Mary's Lamb"** was published, any statement made by one of them relative to the circumstances of the poem's composition must carry weight. On the other hand, there need be no doubt that her grandchildren, greatly delighting in her juvenile verse, questioned her about this particular poem and that any report made by them is in accordance with their memory of her answers.

To the letters quoted by Horatio Hale in 1889 must be added one penned in 1879 by Mrs. Hale's daughter, Mrs. Frances Ann Hunter, to a Miss Brown in reply to an inquiry made in behalf of *Wide Awake,* a then well known children's periodical. This letter is of special importance because it was dictated by Mrs. Hale herself. It reads:[2]

1413 Locust street, Philadelphia.
April 26, 1879.

DEAR MISS BROWN:

The poem **"Mary Had a Little Lamb"** I wrote early in the year 1830 at the request of Mr. Lowell Mason who desired me to write some poems for children to be set to music. It was published in May, 1830, by Marsh, Capen & Lyon of Boston in a small volume called **"Poems for Our Children"** and was in three stanzas.

The first of these little poems was for boys **"The Bird's Nest"** [the name McGuffey's gave to **"Birds"**], "If ever I see—on bush or tree."

The book is now out of print, but Mr. Nahum Capen who is living in Dorchester may perhaps furnish you with a copy.

With much regard,
Yours truly

(Signed) F. A. HUNTER for MRS. SARAH J. HALE.

Mrs. Hale died four days after this letter was written.

Now why, in view of Mrs. Hale's clearly authenticated authorship of **"Mary's Lamb,"** is there present call for discussion of the claim of Mary Sawyer Tyler? There would be none except for the fact that Mr. Henry Ford, in his laudable endeavor to collect and preserve for America early historical objects, is perpetuating the claim in a permanent memorial.

Having previously restored and opened to the public the old Wayside Inn at Sudbury, Mass., made world-renowned by Longfellow in his "Tales of a Wayside Inn," Mr. Ford purchased in 1926 in the town of Sterling, Mass., the Redstone School House, in which Mrs. Tyler's lamb episode was supposed to have taken place, moved it to Sudbury, restored it, and caused two bronze memorial tablets to be placed on great bowlders near the school door. One is a facsimile of the pages in *McGuffey's Second Reader* that contain **"Mary's Lamb."** The other reads as follows:

IN HONOR OF THE CHILDREN'S CLASSIC
"MARY HAD A LITTLE LAMB"
and of
MARY ELIZABETH SAWYER—1806-1889—the
"Mary" of the Poem
REBECCA KIMBALL, the Teacher
JOHN ROULSTONE, Author of the First Twelve

Lines
SARAH JOSEPHA HALE, Whose Genius Completed
the Poem
in Its Present Form

This Building Incorporates the "Redstone" School House, Scene of the Poem, Which Stood in the Second District of Sterling, Massachuetts. It Was in Use from 1798 to 1856 and Was Removed to This Spot for Its Preservation by

MR. AND MRS. HENRY FORD
January 1927

Thousands of tourists from every state in the Union visit the Wayside Inn every year, see the schoolhouse, read the tablets, and in many cases buy from the person in charge the little book of forty pages called "The Story of Mary's Little Lamb as told by Mary and Her Neighbors and Friends—To which is added a critical analysis of the Poem. Published by Mr. and Mrs. Henry Ford, Dearborn, Michigan, 1928."

This booklet reprints, in an expanded form, an unsigned article, "The True Story of Mary's Little Lamb," first published March 26, 1927, in Mr. Ford's magazine, the *Dearborn Independent.* It was in December of the same year that Mr. Ford discontinued his publication of the *Independent,* having previously issued a statement through Mr. Arthur Brisbane, printed in the *New York Times* for July 8, 1927, in which, after telling of a personal survey he had made of certain of the magazine's articles, not including, however, the one on **"Mary's Lamb,"** he said with admirable frankness:

"As a result of this survey I confess that I am deeply mortified that this journal, which is intended to be constructive and not destructive, has been made the medium for resurrecting exploded fictions."

No one will deny the charm of the thought that prompted preservation of the little old schoolhouse, with its worn stone step and quaint unpainted desks polished smooth by generations of children's hands. It stands a little way from the Inn, by the side of a narrow, briar-lined road—on a slight rise of ground and in the midst of trees. An invitingly informal path, between rocks and carpeted with pine needles, leads to its door. It is the very essence of Whittier's well loved poem:

> Still sits the schoolhouse by the road,
>   A ragged beggar sunning;
> Around it still the sumachs grow,
>   And blackberry-vines are running.

> Within, the master's desk is seen,
>   Deep-scarred by raps official;

> The warping floor, the battered seats,
>   The jackknife's carved initial;

> The charcoal frescoes on its wall;
>   Its door's worn sill. . . .

All—just as Whittier described a typical nineteenth-century New England schoolhouse—is there, made visible and real to hurrying twentieth-century eyes by Mr. Ford. And whether it is the real **"Mary's Lamb"** schoolhouse or not, it is still a symbol of the beginnings of that education Sarah Hale spent her life to win for boys and girls.

One of the specially stressed arguments made by the Ford booklet in support of Mrs. Tyler's claim concerns the circumstantial atmosphere with which Mrs. Tyler told the story of her lamb: That in March, which is the usual lambing time, a lamb born on her father's farm proved a weakling; that she begged to be allowed to try to save it, and that it was given to her; that she took it into the farm kitchen, warmed it and fed it hot milk and catnip tea prepared by her mother; that the little creature thrived, became her special pet and followed her about the farm, in one instance following her to school; that it lived some four years in all, bore three offspring of its own, including one pair of twins, and came to an untimely end—gored by a cow.

This story is sufficiently reasonable. Not one incident of it, save the lamb's following its mistress to school, is other than what happened yearly on thousands of farms. Seldom a lambing season passed without one or more weaklings being born in a flock. Now heated barns or lambing sheds are available; but formerly young animals born in delicate condition were taken to the heat of the farm kitchen, there to be saved if possible. So were young fowls, particularly turkeys. Circumstances such as these are familiar enough to all who have lived on farms. Even the catnip tea is in character—it was the farm-wife's prime remedy. And as to the lamb's following Mary to school—undoubtedly. It would follow her whenever and wherever it had the chance—a well known trait of pet lambs.

Surely there is no reason to question either the possibility or probability of Mrs. Tyler's story, up to and including the arrival of her pet lamb at school.

Putting the age of Mary Sawyer at the time of the lamb incident at ten or eleven years and that of John Roulstone at eleven or twelve, the booklet goes on to assert that there is "no manner of doubt that there was a John Roulstone and that he lived in Sterling." But here again no occasion for doubt arises. There was certainly a John Roulstone, Jr., son of that Captain John Roulstone whose portrait still hangs on the walls of Faneuil Hall; and undoubtedly he spent some time with his uncle in Sterling. He died, a Freshman at

Harvard, on February 20, 1822, aged seventeen. That he had an unusually attractive personality is attested by the fact that soon after his death a sixteen-page tract was printed in Boston by one John Cotton, Jr., entitled "Tribute of Affection to JOHN ROULSTONE, JR."

And was he capable, between the ages of ten and fourteen—he was born in 1805 and his uncle's ministry in Sterling lasted only from 1815 to 1819—of writing verse? Very likely. Many children at that age do write rhymes, and John seems to have been a fairly precocious boy in an era when all children matured early. Girls frequently married at fifteen; David Hale entered West Point at fourteen.

Did he, while living in Sterling, visit the school, witness the lamb incident later related by Mrs. Tyler, and write some verses to her? He could have and perhaps he did. At least he seems to have done something to impress his personality on Mary Sawyer's mind, though the mere fact of his presence in a rural community would have been enough. For John Roulstone, in addition to possessing an attractive personality, enjoyed two outstanding distinctions—the social prestige, and it was prestige in those days, of being the minister's nephew, and the intellectual superiority of preparing to enter Harvard. Also he was no country boy, but had come from the great city of Boston where his family were people of some consequence.

And if John wrote some verses, he certainly carried them to Mary Sawyer. He would have been less than human if he had not sought that much satisfaction as a reward for his poetical effort. What seems strange now is that, if he possessed a knack for versifying, it was not specially mentioned along with his other accomplishments and virtues in the tribute published after his death and written by his uncle and tutor, the Reverend Mr. Capen.

But, granting that John Roulstone wrote some verses about a lamb and took them to Mary Sawyer on some date between 1815 and 1819, it surely does not follow that they were the same twelve lines that constitute the opening stanza and a half of **"Mary's Lamb"** as published in 1830 by Sarah Hale. Of that sequence no evidence exists beyond the word of Mrs. Tyler, passed to the public fifty years later.

One cannot be sure, of course, of the date when Mrs. Hale's poem first came to Mrs. Tyler's attention. It could not have been before 1830, the year the poem was originally printed, and it may have been much later. Could she, in the necessarily long interval between her own lamb-at-school incident and her first hearing or reading of Mrs. Hale's poem, have forgotten the exact wording on the piece of paper handed her by John Roulstone? The answer must be, yes, she could have.

Was her first reading of the Hale poem from a printing thereof appearing under Mrs. Hale's signature? Not necessarily. The poem, as has been shown, soon received wide currency in reprints that gave no credit to its author.

Would the fact that Mary Sawyer had herself been the heroine of a lamb-at-school episode, and that her own name was the same as the one used in the poem, have enhanced her interest in the Hale verses? Most certainly.

Could she have confused the verses written by John Roulstone around 1817, when she was only eleven, with the poem published years later and perhaps first seen by her in an anonymous printing of still later date?

It is well known that memory can, and frequently does, produce just such confusion.

And, however sincere Mrs. Tyler may have been in 1878 when she publicly dramatized herself as the heroine of a famous poem, one is not impressed that hers was a mind practiced in exactness of thinking.

The Ford booklet quotes a letter she wrote September 8, 1879, in which she says the poem handed her by John Roulstone, "being the first three stanzas of the Poem as now printed," was written in "blank verse." Facing the fact that Mrs. Hale's poem is not written in blank verse, the booklet says that probably Mrs. Tyler meant the twelve lines were not broken into stanzas. This explanation may be correct. But, if so, it serves only to illustrate Mrs. Tyler's inexact mode of thought. Again, in this same letter she says: "I am ignorant how the Poem got into print." Nor is there anything to show that she made inquiry as to this, despite the amazement that must have been hers when she discovered that the very verses she believed were written about her as a child and actually given her on a piece of paper by their author were being circulated in printed form.

And now, sifted down, what is the evidence that John Roulstone wrote the first twelve lines of **"Mary's Lamb,"** or, indeed, any lines about any lamb? That Mrs. Tyler said so, is the sole evidence offered. She told a great many people the story and they repeated it. But every particle of attempted proof goes back to her bare word in the matter and nothing else.

The "critical analysis" of **"Mary's Lamb"** offered by the Ford booklet contends that the poem itself discloses a "double nature of composition"; that the first twelve lines narrate an incident, while the last twelve, conceded by the booklet to have been written by Mrs. Hale, point a moral. The "critical analysis" holds that the style of the first twelve lines evinces "artless naturalness" which in the thirteenth line "gives way to artificial and moralistic imaginativeness."

All this ignores the form of the poem as originally published by Mrs. Hale. Had not the uncredited reprint contained in *Songs for the Little Ones at Home* divided the poem's three eight-line stanzas into six four-line stanzas, perhaps even *McGuffey's* would never have thought of doing so, so correct technically was the original structure. But when the printer who made up this old collection of children's verses reached the bottom of page 119, there was room for the first four lines of **"Mary's Lamb,"** and no more; so to meet the exigencies of make-up the first stanza was split. It was logical then, for the sake of uniformity, to split the two remaining stanzas. Consequently the poem as printed in *Songs for the Little Ones at Home* appears in quatrains.

By a curious coincidence the printer who made up *McGuffey's Second Reader* for 1857 faced precisely the same problem as had the printer of the earlier *Songs for the Little Ones at Home*. He, too, reached a page, which happened to be ninety-nine, where there remained room only for the first four lines of the poem; and he solved his problem in the exact fashion of his predecessor, by printing **"Mary's Lamb"** in quatrains.

As for the combination of incident and moral in a poem written in the first half of the nineteenth century, that surely should occasion no bewilderment. More surprising, indeed, would be the lack of that combination, for such was the literary fashion of the day. Practically every climax was a "moral." Furthermore, if "critical analysis" of a nursery rhyme must be indulged in, the first twelve lines of **"Mary's Lamb"** leave an abrupt, unfinished piece of work, offering no excuse for their having been written. Viewed in this light, they represent only the first step and part of the second step of accepted structure.

In Mrs. Hale's poem the time-honored structure is flawless. The first stanza presents a problem—the abnormality of a lamb in a schoolroom:

> Mary had a little lamb,
> 　Its fleece was white as snow,
> And everywhere that Mary went
> 　The lamb was sure to go;
> He followed her to school one day—
> 　That was against the rule,
> It made the children laugh and play,
> 　To see a lamb in school.

The second stanza develops the action—the lamb being turned out by the teacher and waiting for the appearance of his one sure friend, Mary, to whom he immediately runs for protection:

> And so the Teacher turned him out,
> 　But still he lingered near,
> And waited patiently about,
> 　Till Mary did appear;
> And then he ran to her, and laid
> 　His head upon her arm,
> As if he said—"I'm not afraid—
> 　You'll keep me from all harm."

The third stanza is the conclusion, the logical result or outgrowth of the problem and its development—a "moral," the precise moral Mrs. Hale had had in mind from her very first line:

> "What makes the lamb love Mary so?"
> 　The eager children cry—
> "O, Mary loves the lamb, you know,"
> 　The Teacher did reply;—
> "And you each gentle animal
> 　In confidence may bind,
> And make them follow at your call,
> 　If you are always *kind*."

Structurally the poem as written by Mrs. Hale defies criticism.

But why did not Mrs. Hale come out in the newspapers in 1878 and deny the Tyler-Roulstone claim?

First, she was very old and had just completed fifty years of exceedingly active and strenuous work. Secondly, she knew the verses really were her own. Why should she be concerned? Also by that time she was accustomed to the peculiar temptation the poem seems always to have offered. College and army songs and parodies innumerable had been based on it. *Godey's* had published some of them, but finally seems to have grown thoroughly sick of all Marys and the whole race of lambs. In August, 1872, Mr. Godey, seated in his "Arm Chair," announced:

"The following are selected from about one hundred verses received and are all we intend to publish about **'Mary and Her Little Lamb':**

> Mary had a little lamb,
> 　'Twas subject to the gout;
> At last she got disgusted,
> 　And put it up the spout."

In the third place, having been required all her editorial life to protect her magazine from that peculiar phase of neurosis rampant in the nineteenth century which impelled certain types of mentality to seek notoriety by fair means or foul, Mrs. Hale long before 1878 had adopted a policy—a policy best explained in her own words as published in the July, 1863, issue of the *Lady's Book:*

"BORROWED FEATHERS—Certain pretenders to literary talent seem to be afflicted with a disease that, for want of a definite name, we will call the *mania of appropriation.* When a real poet has won popular applause, these pretenders to genius endeavor either to imitate or plagiarize a portion of the successful poem; and in some instances they even appropriate or claim the whole. The young lady who announced herself as the writer of 'Nothing to Wear' is a distinguished instance of this kind of *mania.* . . . The real author is never injured in these cases; on the contrary a poem worth stealing, or imitating, is immediately vested with superior merits. . . .

"In our long course of editorial duty we have had many scores of imitations and plagiarisms sent us. . . . One of these appeared in our April number. . . ."

After which followed the usual editorial apology to the real author.

A surprisingly large number of such corrections are to be found in all publications of the times. The embarrassment was not *Godey's* only. Just what caused this inclination to seek vicarious fame, a tendency which seems to have been peculiarly feminine, is hard now to understand. Perhaps the explanation may be that for the first time in history it was possible for woman, who in the former order of things ordinarily had lived and died obscurely, to win more or less of renown. Nineteenth-century women seem to have craved the lime-light, and, if records of news events are to be trusted, went to strange lengths to gain notice. Education has since done much to free society of this form of egomania.

But absurdly enough the following appeared in the *New York Times* for May 29, 1931, practically as these words are written:

MARY, OWNER OF FAMOUS LAMB,
MARKS 90TH BIRTHDAY IN WALES
By The Canadian Press

London, May 28.—Mrs. Mary Hughes, who is stated to be the Mary of the nursery rhyme, **"Mary Had a Little Lamb,"** to-day celebrated her 90th birthday at her home, Ty Issa farm, Llangollen, North Wales, and received congratulations from children in all parts of the world.

"Mary," who is blind and suffers from chronic rheumatism, delights to relate how years ago her little lamb was turned out of school. The lamb had followed her from her father's farm two miles away. The rhyme was written by Miss Sarah Buell, who was staying at the farm at the time.

Here, then, is another claim that has been going the rounds of the newspapers for years. The *Boston Post* for May 19, 1929, quoted Mrs. Hughes as saying:

"It is true that America claims that the incident happened at Redstone Hill, Sterling, U. S. A., and that the poem was written by the wife of Horatio Hale, the American ethnologist. The details of the story are given in the Encyclopedia Britannica, where it is stated that Hale married Miss Sarah Josepha Buell, and I have only to add that this lady I have reason to believe was the Miss Buell who stayed with my father and mother at the farm in the spring of 1849 when the lamb (named Billy) followed me to school. I possess a letter written to my mother by Miss Buell after her return to London. After her death there was some controversy as to the authorship of the poem, and her son wrote a letter which appeared in the *Boston Transcript* of April, 1889, that his mother had definitely asserted shortly before her death that she was the author of the poem. . . ."

This is about as garbled an account of fact and fancy as could well be conceived. Without attempt to unscramble Mrs. Hughes' understanding of relationships in the Hale family, it need only be said that Mrs. Hale was not in England in 1849 and that **"Mary's Lamb"** had been in print eleven years before Mrs. Hughes was born.

Nor is Mrs. Hughes the only Briton to seek approbation through Sarah Hale. Mrs. Hale's verse was always being purloined. **"It Snows,"** for instance, originally published in *Godey's* in January, 1837, was later reprinted in England under another signature.[3]

Another claimant to the honor of being the original "Mary" was a Mary Dale. Her claims are to be found in New York and Boston newspapers of 1903.

And now did or did not Sarah Hale write **"Mary's Lamb"**? Was she or was she not capable of plagiarizing the first twelve lines? Is she or is she not the sole author of this best known child's poem in the English language?

The Ford booklet's final argument as to fact says:

"No letters have been produced as from her [Mrs. Hale's] hand. The volume of 1830 and the statements of her descendants as to their recollections of her poem constitute the available material now at hand."

Ordinarily, the signature of a professional writer of recognized integrity is sufficient testimony of authorship, and must stand unless conclusive evidence is adduced to the contrary. And are not the statements of Mrs. Hale's own children living at the time their mother composed the famous veres equal in credibility to those of a woman who claimed that a boy dead eight years when the poem was first published had written something on a slip of paper which itself was never produced?

And would Sarah Hale have stooped to make even imitative use of another's work—let alone plagiarize it?

In the January number of the *Ladies' Magazine* for 1828, two years before her poem **"Mary's Lamb"** was even thought of, she made clear her reaction to this nineteenth-century weakness. In a review of an "annual" called the "Token" she said in part:

"The poetry in especial we are sorry to pass over, for we see much to praise, except the frequent imitation of Mrs. Hemans. We entirely disapprove of all imitations; they are the bane of all real excellence."

But it is no longer accurate to say that "the volume of 1830 and the statements of her [Mrs. Hale's] descendants as to their recollections of her poem constitute the available material now at hand." In the first place, it is now established that there was separate, signed publication of the poem in the *Juvenile Miscellany* the same year the book was issued. In the second place, there is the letter Mrs. Hale herself dictated to the *Wide Awake* magazine. And, finally, examination of the files of *Godey's Lady's Book* discloses a statement direct from Mrs. Hale's own hand. In the *Book* for January, 1875, she reprinted **"Mary's Lamb,"** in her editorial column, together with an explanation of her purpose in writing the poem. Her comment follows:

> "About forty years ago, when my home was in Boston, an effort was made to introduce vocal music as one of the lessons to be taught in all the primary schools of that city. The leader of this novel measure was Professor John Mason ["John" is either a typographical error or a slip of Mrs. Hale's pen, Professor Mason's given name being Lowell as Mrs. Hale knew], eminent as an instructor in the art of psalmody, and highly esteemed for his abilities and success in the profession which he seemed to love as the means of doing good. He held the faith that all children who could talk could be taught to sing, and that it was the duty of those who had care of the young to have all taught the art of psalmody. He said that the simplicity of harmonious sounds, united with words and thoughts which *morally* educated the young mind in the knowledge of truth and goodness could never be wholly forgotten, and that rhyme and reason were important aids to memory.

> "Professor Mason thus gave his views when requesting that I would help his plan by writing 'Little Songs for Little Children,' which he would set to music. I knew he was master of the art he taught, and that his motives were worthy of success. The songs were written; his plan was faithfully carried out and with wonderful effect."

Commenting next on the proficiency in choral music later attained in Boston and on a "triumph of choral voices at the Boston Colosseum," Mrs. Hale proceeded:

> "We did not have the privilege of enjoying this pleasure, but the report brought to mind the small beginnings forty years ago. We thought of the good professor who struck the first chord of this wonderful creation of choral voices which had made the men and women of Boston thus happy and glorious, as it were, in the possession of a new faculty both of giving and enjoying pleasure.

> "Our mention of the 'Little Song Book' was not to claim any part in the success, but to do honor to a good and faithful man, whose work has borne such precious fruit. And then we wanted to interest those who are in earnest to promote improvement in the free schools to introduce vocal music as the best method of securing attendance of pupils without compulsion. If the little songs we put before the little folks have any part in hastening this era of vocal music in the free schools, we shall be richly compensated for our part in the good work."

Whereupon she printed the words of two of her best known songs, **"Winter Joys"** and **"Mary's Lamb."**

. . . . .

"Still sits the schoolhouse by the road"—the little old schoolhouse across whose threshold, it is said, children's feet tramped in and out from 1798 to 1856, when as a school the building was discarded. Now children's feet again skip over the uneven sill and echo on the warped floor. Since Redstone Schoolhouse was moved to Sudbury, it again "keeps school," its pupils the children of employees on the Ford property and of neighboring farmers. And all this is as it should be. It is fitting that to-day should be so physically linked with yesterday.

But the schoolhouse is what it is, nothing less and nothing more—quaint, charming, inspiring in the heart and mind of every visitor new patriotism and pride in what it stands for, that bygone century which saw the working-out, slow and faltering at first, of "our American experiment." It is an emblem of a great achievement, and it is good that it should be preserved.

But it is not good that it should perpetuate an extraneous error. The tablet placed at its door reads, "Mary Elizabeth Sawyer . . . the 'Mary' of the Poem . . . John Roulstone, Author of the First Twelve Lines."

Here is a statement made as fact where there was never more than an unsubstantiated claim. Here is a lasting record that sets forth with color of finality a judgment flagrantly at variance with the evidence. Here is accepted the uncorroborated word of a woman whose only bid to fame was her own assertion as against the accomplishments of one to whom America still owes more in the way of those fundamentals which background modern life than to any other single woman.

And it is peculiarly ironical that the little old school-house at Wayside Inn, the most characteristically American memorial yet raised to education, should cast—however unwittingly—aspersion on the name of one who stood above all else for education, who, seeing into the heart of childhood, hastened our great to-day that with lavish hand offers schooling to every American boy, rich or poor, and to every American girl.

Nothing can take away the legacy Sarah Hale left her country. Each year the states will join in keeping Thanksgiving Day; Vassar and her sister colleges will go on and more will join them; women physicians will continue to learn the art of healing and carry it to those who need; abuse of children is tabooed; for half of our citizenry sex no longer bars the door of economic opportunity. These consummations Sarah Hale fought for, and they will remain. Bunker Hill Monument now indissolubly "stands on Union"—the Union she so loved. And the shrine at Mount Vernon which she helped to save continues as the symbol of freedom. Things tangible and intangible she gave-institutions, aspirations and dreams.

What can this twentieth century, for which she planned and builded so well, do for Sarah Hale? A little nursery rhyme, unimportant of itself, but which has found its way into the memory of every man and woman who speaks the English tongue, might be restored to her—its author.

Notes

1 This letter is the property of the Historical Society of Pennsylvania.

2 Courtesy of Richard W. Hale, Esq.

3 *Godey's Lady's Book,* June, 1839.

William R. Taylor (essay date 1961)

SOURCE: "Point Counterpoint" in *Cavalier and Yankee: The Old South and American National Character,* George Braziller, 1961, pp. 122-41.

[*In the following excerpt, Taylor discusses Hale's views regarding the ideal American character and the contrast between North and South as exhibited in her short stories and her novel* Northwood.]

The Yankee Ethos in Limbo

The very fact of the novel [**Northwood**] is a puzzle. What had made a busy and hard-pressed widow living in a small provincial town sit down in the winter of 1826 and fill page after page with the story of Sidney

Romilly? Why should she have concerned herself, as she did, with the South? Her whole life of thirty-eight years had been spent in and near the small town of Newport, New Hampshire. She knew as little about the South as she did about the Antipodes. She had evidently set out to paint an agreeable picture of the small provincial world she had known since her childhood. She had wanted to show that the village of Northwood, New Hampshire, where her story was set, was, like her own Newport, a society of independent, industrious and virtuous freemen or, as she put it, a society "of contented minds and grateful hearts."[47] In Northwood a man might live by the labor of his hands in peace and plenty. To James Romilly, Sidney's father, his happy provincial home on a winter evening was a safe haven, almost womblike in its protectiveness.

> Indeed, few conditions in this world of care can be imagined more enviable than that of Mr. Romilly, when of a winter evening, with every chore done, he seated himself before a "rousing fire," "monarch of all he surveyed," and listening to the roaring of the tempest without, contrasted it with the peace, plenty, and security reigning within.[48]

Such a situation seemed to provide everything a man could wish for. Why should anyone want to emerge from it? Why would Sarah Hale herself be willing to leave her own village? Why would she send Sidney Romilly forth to become a gentleman and a planter in a South she did not know?

The one thing Northwood did not provide was opportunity. Northwood, she observed, "offered few temptations to the speculator" and its soil, unlike that of the South and the West, "promised no indulgence to the idle."[49] If her young men and young women were to better themselves, as she believed Americans characteristically did and should, they would have to go elsewhere to do it. But how could they go elsewhere without being false to the values of Northwood? Since America in her eyes was characterized by its Northwoods, how could a young man from the provinces rise and become successful without in a sense betraying both his family and his country? How was it possible to make a Yankee provincial into a gentleman and a Southerner? Harvey Birch into General Washington?

The problem fascinated, almost obsessed, her. For [Daniel] Webster's selfless devotion to Union, Sarah Hale substituted a selfless devotion to her family and to her sex. To young women, she recommended the same kind of selfless devotion to family. To young men, she recommended a more difficult combination of benevolence and ambition, a balanced diet of give and take. For the Yankee who had left the provinces, the solution to the problem of emergence lay, as for Webster, in adopting a mask of selflessness. But where could the emergent Yankee best find an opportunity to play his selfless role? Though the answer she gave was hedged about with all kinds of qualifications and punctuated with warnings, she nonetheless answered: "In the South."

The South which Sarah Hale created as an antipode to her North is less a place than a moral climate: an expression of what the North lacked and what the emergent Yankee needed. In 1829 she published her first collection of stories, or, as she preferred to call them, "sketches." These sketches, taken together, go a long way toward explaining why Sarah Hale felt driven to invent a South that was different from the Northern world she was every day evoking in this early writing. The problem which she encountered was certainly not the one she had consciously in mind as she set out to describe her country and her countrymen. Everything about these first inventive efforts suggests that she wanted above all else to write "realistically," as we would say, about America. Sarah Hale's sense of realism may seem stylized and cloudy to modern readers, but she entertained the greatest scorn for writing that was derivative and European in flavor. She always insisted on a certain American verisimilitude. Her intention, she announced, was to write only about what "gives to Americans their peculiar characteristics."

> To exhibit some of those traits, originated by our free institutions, in their manifold and minute effects on the minds, manners, and habits of the citizens of our republic, is the design of these Sketches.[50]

The titles which she gave to collections of these sketches are further evidence of this concern. The first of two volumes was published under the title *Sketches of American Character.* The second volume, published six years later in 1835, was entitled *Traits of American Life.* For Sarah Hale, as for Webster, the word "character" was more normative than descriptive; it was more concerned with "should" than with "is." For both of them "character" meant restraint, self-control, self-discipline.

The need for character is precisely the point of the lurid tale, **"Wedding and Funeral."** James Murray, the hero of the story, is the pampered son of a rich New York merchant. The story begins with a village wedding in which James Murray marries a simple country girl, Lucy Marsh. One bystander at the wedding admires the obvious good fortune of the young couple.

> Few begin the world thus advantageously. They have health and beauty, wealth and reputation, and friends, and affection for each other.

Another bystander is more skeptical and cautious.

> Could you add one item more to the catalogue of advantages, the earthly picture would be complete.

> . . . How unfortunate that the absence of that one requisite, may, perhaps, render all the others nugatory.

When the skeptic is asked to name the missing "requisite" for happiness, he replies that James Murray, while otherwise blessed, seems to be without "self-control."[51]

He is certainly right. James Murray becomes a madman and a beast. Because he had no fortune to make and no purpose in life, he had begun to tipple in college while his poorer classmates studiously prepared themselves to read law and better their stations. After his marriage he becomes a habitual drunk, spends his fortune in debauchery and finally goes berserk altogether. He riots about the house, breaks all the windows, thrashes and beats the submissive Lucy, and at last, in a moment of rage, strikes and kills his small son. Overwhelmed with sorrow, he rushes out and drowns himself, while Lucy succumbs and dies of a "broken heart." Near the end of the story Mrs. Hale has one of her characters underscore the fact that the tragedy of James Murray is peculiarly American.

> When . . . men yield to temptation, to sin—suffering must follow. Indeed in our country, more than in any other on earth, deviations from morality and integrity are punished either with the loss of fame, fortune, or public confidence.[52]

Why was America so different? As this story suggests, there is more melodrama than one would suppose in Sarah Hale's *Sketches of American Character.* Every sketch was in some sense a recipe. You put together a little of this and a little of this and you get that. You put together a spoiled child, a great sum of money and a bottle of brandy, and you get violence and social chaos. You end up with "debauchery," "broken hearts" and "sorrow."

In writing about a man, you took his measure. When he went wrong, as Mrs. Hale's characters frequently did, you explained to your readers what mistakes he had made and, as a kind of *obiter dictum,* you told them how the mistakes might have been avoided. You said, "If Richard Woodcock had not bought the lottery ticket . . ." or "if Lucy Marsh had refused to marry a man who drank . . ." or "if James Murray's parents had taught him the meaning of honest labor. . . ." For every disastrous or regrettable occurrence there was a condition which would have made it avoidable.

The object of such a discussion was self-improvement and self-improvement was something in which Americans passionately believed. This is a form of speculation so foreign to our own thinking and, as we conceive of reality, so "unrealistic," that it is difficult to understand the significance that could once have been attached to it. It is difficult now to understand the amount of reality which the idea of self-improvement contained for nineteenth-century Americans; or, put in another way, it is difficult to understand today how much reality was itself defined by change. What one fact could have loomed larger than that of change in the minds of Webster or Sarah Hale? Americans conceived of their social and institutional life as in a state of flux which, if it promised almost unlimited individual opportunity, threatened to subvert all familiar forms of order. For them, nothing was impossible. It is difficult for us to realize that their superb optimism and their terrible anxiety were functions of the same human situation.

It seems apparent that Americans in the early part of the century were quite unprepared for changes of the order of those that they experienced in their personal lives and observed in the life about them. They were also uncertain about the direction in which things were tending. Sarah Hale felt these concerns and her fantasies come very close to the imaginative center of her time. Almost instinctively she fell into the kind of moralizing for which Americans hungered; her little sketches, like the historical legends of later decades, can be thought of as parables for survival. Her writings always concerned themselves with a world gone wrong through lack of character or a world *kept* right through the exertion of character at some crucial moment.

The sketches included in these volumes were written during the years in which Webster was working out his own defensive fiction of the disinterested American. Despite the fact that her sketches appeared in ladies' magazines, she revealed an anxiety about America that was very similar to Webster's. Beneath a surface of seemingly imperturbable optimism and dogmatic certainty ran a strong undercurrent of fear and uneasiness.

Sarah Hale's argument for the preservation of an ordered society is reiterated in story after story. In a world of flux and change, only character can preserve a man—or woman—from the ruin of a James Murray or a Richard Woodcock. Nothing is therefore more important to the future of the country than the formation of a stable American character. Again and again she made the point that character is formed in the home and by the parents. It is in the home and not at schools and colleges that the habits essential to survival can be developed and reinforced. James Murray is sent to college by his merchant father, but he has not been given the values that permit him to profit from the experience. He takes to drink, and college is simply a step in his disintegration.

In the tales of merchants' sons there are few happy endings. The surest way to work out your salvation in Mrs. Hale's America was to keep your hand on the plow and stay in the provinces. In a historical tale entitled **"The Silver Mine"** and set in the eighteenth century in her own Newport, this point is heavily un-

derscored. Deacon Bascom has a series of dreams in which he is visited by "a man clothed in black" who tells him he will find a silver mine under a rock near a blasted tree on nearby Sunapee Mountain. After much deliberation he yields to temptation and (like Hawthorne's Goodman Brown, whom he in some ways resembles) he leaves behind his "good wife" and threads his way through a dense wilderness to the indicated spot. Just as he is about to dig for the silver, he kneels to pray and finds the strength to leave the stone unturned and the silver unmined. Deacon Bascom is able to perform this heroic act of self-denial, he admits, only because at the crucial moment he suddenly remembered his children. Riches would ruin them. "I felt," he told his wife, "that should my children be corrupted by the riches I there sought, how terrible would be my guilt, and the accusations of my conscience!"[53]

The story has a further point that is less obvious. Sarah Hale appears to be saying that the Yankees should stay put. The wilderness through which Deacon Bascom has to make his way is described in a way that makes it appear allegorical. The wilderness is where a man goes to make his fortune; it is what separates him from his home; it is a place where a man can get lost. Like Harvey Birch, Deacon Bascom refuses wealth. As a result, "The children of that good couple were excellent men and women, and their descendents are worthy and respectable people."[54]

This curious story, which Sarah Hale referred to as an American fairy tale, is really a fairy tale *manqué*.[55] The American Cinderella *refuses* the glass slipper and lives happily ever after. Modern New Englanders, she interjects toward the end, show a falling off in character. Their one concern is riches and they leave home and sweetheart to seek their fortunes at the ends of the earth. Country society is thus deteriorating.

> Alack! what a change half a century has produced. Now our gentlemen are wholly engrossed with caring for their own dear selves; marriage is slavery, and a family a bill of cost. Our fine young men, who should be the glory and strength of New England, go to find their graves in the marshes of the south, or the prairies of the west; and our fair girls go— into the cotton factories![56]

A society, to remain stable, must also remain static. The frontiers of the West and Southwest were fully as threatening and perilous to her as the metropolis. Her ruined young men die as regularly of "yellow fever" in New Orleans as of intemperance in New York City. A land of plenty was indeed a fearful place.

In her fiction the ambitious young man who leaves the provinces does so at his peril. He may not meet the melodramatic ruin of a Richard Woodcock in **"The**

Lottery Ticket," but he is always punished in some way. With a good character and the best of intentions he may, like William Forbes in the story of that name, marry a rich and fashionable woman who makes him a stupid and uncompanionable wife; or he may, like the promising George Torrey in **"The Poor Scholar,"** die fighting a duel in Virginia. The only kind of migration that is permissible is backward migration. A young man may be sent back to the provinces.

A return to the provinces is, in fact, one prescription for saving the character of a merchant's son. **"Walter Wilson"** is the story of a rich merchant's son who is left penniless at his father's death. Far from being a disaster, this circumstance alone saves him. He is bound out to a "Puritan farmer" who teaches him the self-discipline of hard manual labor. He ends by marrying the farmer's daughter, Fanny, and settling in the country. The theater-going and sophisticated Owen Ashley in **"A Winter in the Country"** is saved in a similar way when his father, a rich Boston merchant, goes bankrupt. Ashley is sent to find work in a small village in Vermont. At first he despairs at the thought that he is being exiled to "Boeotia." Instead of the crudeness, rusticity and ignorance that he expected, he finds in Vermont a little Eden of self-sufficient and self-instructed yeomen. In letters written to a friend in Boston, Ashley describes the cultivation and leisure of a country winter where he does not find the contrast between effeteness and poverty which characterized life in the "metropolis." The story ends with his expected marriage to the daughter of an industrious Yankee farmer.

The problem of the merchant's son could not, however, be permanently solved by a winter in the country. Owen Ashley could not be expected to stay in Vermont any more than Sarah Hale could have stayed in New Hampshire. It seems clear from the title of the story that Ashley will return to Boston with his country wife, just as certainly as Daniel Webster had taken his own country wife to the same city. The country was a place of indoctrination. Merchant's son and farmer's son alike could there be introduced to the sobering self-discipline of work. Character could there be formed to a republican model. Sooner or later many provincials like George Ticknor, Sarah Hale and Daniel Webster would have to encounter the Great World and put their American virtue to the test. They would have to emerge from their provincial chrysalis and meet the test of the metropolis or the frontier. Sarah Hale knew very well that the American could not always leave his talent buried in the provinces like Deacon Bascom's silver.

Arthur Lloyd in **"The Lloyds"** had not had the "advantages" of a country childhood, but he had been provided with its moral equivalent by his rich but heroic father, another New York merchant. Arthur was never indulged or gratified in his selfish desires. He was always made to feel that a virtuous and useful life was a pleasure, not an obligation. But after all his instruction what, finally, does Sarah Hale have her faultless hero do? In a long story that is practically a novella, he does in fact very little, because there is very little he can do.

"The Lloyds" is a dull story and Arthur Lloyd, for all his careful nurture, is himself dull because nothing *can* happen to him. He already has his money. In Sarah Hale's world there is very little a rich man can do, unless he loses his money or goes to pieces and dies a suicide or an alcoholic. In her tales of rich and successful men she therefore encountered a problem she had not been forced to face in her stories of bankruptcy and moral disintegration. Everybody knew that "the wages of sin is death"; the wages of virtue, however, were another matter. Virtue inevitably brought financial success, but at a certain point in her scheme of things, financial success became a vice and the successful man became idle if he stopped earning money, and avaricious if he continued to do so. She therefore chose most often to skirt this problem and to write about poor boys who became rich, or rich boys who became poor or who came to no good. Arthur Lloyd is a stalemate. The best he can do is to practice negative virtues. By self-control he can hang on to his money, and by acts of benevolence he can maintain his unselfishness and self-control. In other words, he can live as though he were not rich and as though he were still in the competitive race. For such a character there was one other possibility. He could tackle the problem of living as a gentleman planter in the South.

From Yankee to Southern Cavalier

It was not easy to make out in the South. Sarah Hale's fiction is strewn with the corpses of those who had tried and failed. Her Yankees who visit the South do not all die violent deaths like George Torrey, who is killed in a duel. The experience of life there has, however, a crucial effect on all of them. Either it brings out the worst or the best in them. George Torrey's mistake is to forget that the transcendent Yankee is conservative of life just as he is conservative of money. His death is wasteful and spendthrift. Like Daniel Webster, he should have refused to risk his life so senselessly and stupidly. By becoming the inseparable companion of a brilliant and extravagant young Virginian, he is made to forget for a moment his own values. The mistake costs him his life. Sidney Romilly, Sarah Hale's most important hero, does better.

Sidney Romilly, like George Torrey, promised great things. He had been named for Algernon Sidney, English republican theorist, by his hopeful father. He possessed the Websterian assets of "an expansive forehead" and "large luminous eyes" which "gave promise of uncommon genius." He early took to books. "Literature," Sarah Hale comments, "is the star and garter of a Yankee. It claims precedence and gains privileges to which wealth alone is not entitled."[57] Among the Romilly children he was the one marked for emergence. Sidney's one fault was the curious one that he learned *too easily*. He responded too readily and passively to his surroundings. Thus, while the disciplined world of Northwood made him strong, the undisciplined and leisurely moral climate which he encountered in the South made him weak and ineffective.

Some twenty years before the opening of the story, Lydia Romilly, with whom Sidney goes to live, has married a Mr. Horace Brainard of South Carolina. Brainard exemplifies Sarah Hale's idea of the Southerner. When he visits Northwood, to see about adopting one of the Romilly children, he is carefully contrasted with James Romilly, Sidney's father. The contrast is an interesting one. The elder Romilly had made his own way; he is a devout Protestant and he believes in the virtues of work. Brainard had inherited his plantation and his wealth; he is a Roman Catholic; he lives a life of leisure. Romilly believes in the family and centers his own life there. Brainard believes in society and the Great World. Romilly has a large, happy family; the Brainards are childless. Brainard is nonetheless a sympathetic character in the novel. His errors are errors of weakness. His dissipations are those of his society and of his class. The race track, the billiard table and the theater symbolize the purposelessness of his life.

Brainard is also given many admirable traits. He is courteous and cultivated. He is a kindly and conscientious master to his slaves, and he considers them a trust, rather than an indulgence. In his other relationships he is charitable and yielding. Even his Catholicism is portrayed as a sympathetic trait when placed alongside the uninformed Protestant bigotry of his New England wife. Catholicism in this period did not yet have quite the associations it later had for middle-class Americans. It was still more associated with aristocratic George Calvert, the Carroll family and Baltimore, than with Paddy and Boston. A great many Protestant Americans, among them Harriet Beecher Stowe, felt attracted to Catholicism, if only as an antidote for an overdose of Calvinist austerity. They saw Protestantism as inclining toward Puritan fanaticism and self-righteousness, or toward the uncontrolled emotionalism of the revivals. Neither tendency could be sympathetically viewed. If Catholicism inclined toward indifference and passivity, the other face on the coin of Puritan fanaticism was Yankee hypocrisy; and emotionalism was too much associated with madness to find acceptance in an age that feared madness and the consequences of loss of control. Sarah Hale thought of Catholicism as a quiet, aristocratic religion which stood for tolerance, reason and moderation. In her personal

life she, like Harriet Stowe, compromised her early Puritanism by becoming an Episcopalian "convert." Such a conversion was in the pattern of emergence in both the North and the South.

The features of Sarah Hale's fantasy-South thus become a little clearer. If Northwood stood for the Protestant ethic, the South represented a set of compensatory possibilities. It stood for *noblesse oblige,* cultivated leisure and human sympathy. One tendency of Northwood was represented by the stock Yankee villains, Deacon Jones and Ephraim Skinner, who are revealed as fanatics, misers and hypocrites. In his attitude toward money, Brainard is again set off against such Yankees. He is portrayed as free from any taint of acquisitiveness. He spends his money grandly and generously, hardly noting the cost of what he does. He is finally ruined because he honorably takes the word of a dishonorable speculator. The Southerner, despite his weakness, could be a disinterested man of honor. The greatest liability of Southern character was its tendency toward idleness and self-indulgence, the cult of pleasure. The even greater liability of Northern character was its tendency toward selfish acquisitiveness and predatory greed. It is important to note that in Sarah Hale's eyes the weakness of the Yankee was a kind of strength; the weakness of the Southern gentleman was, alas, his weakness. In her world, only the salubrious North had bad men; only the debilitating South had bad air. In other words, only the Yankee could be a villain. The Southerner was marked for a victim.

> It is not the love of pleasure, the taste for amusements, that constitute the love of the world. It is the love of money, the craving desire to accumulate property, the entire devotion of the heart and soul, mind, might and strength, to the one object of increasing or preserving an estate, that bows down the lofty intellect of men, and makes their sordid souls as grovelling as the appetites of the brutes that perish. This inordinate thirst for riches is the besetting sin of Americans; situation, institutions, education, all combine to foster it.[58]

How, she asks, can you temper the acquisitiveness of the Yankee without destroying the strength which alone enables him to survive the competitive race? How could you salvage the disinterestedness and honor of the Southerner without having to accept his weakness into the bargain? Both strength and disinterestedness were requirements for a stable national character. How could they be combined?

The first attempt to superimpose the Cavalier gentleman on the Protestant Yankee almost results in Sidney's ruin. The Northwood he knew as a child was nearly all work; the Southern world into which he moved was nearly all play. He soon learned that as a young gentleman he could do exactly as he pleased. His foster parents competed for his favor; the Brainard slaves, who expected him to become their master, fawned over him and jumped at the chance to serve him. His Yankee tutor soon abandoned the hope of getting him to study. Once he found that he had no competitors, all his incentive to study and to excel left him. Why should he bother? Had he not been given Great Expectations? When Sidney was twenty his tutor was dismissed and he was introduced into Charleston society, where, it is implied, he soon cut a considerable figure. Only "those early lessons of sobriety and virtue" moderated his indulgence and prevented his becoming a rake.[59] "Sidney had never forgotten he was Yankee born, although half *raised* on a southern plantation."[60] Sidney is finally rescued from his hybrid impasse by another New Englander, who urges him to return home. At his friend's suggestion he finally returns, after seventeen years away, to visit his family in Northwood. This experience completes his re-education.

Once back in Northwood Sidney discovers at last what the Good Life really is:

> Till within a few months, pleasure has been the idol of my pursuit; and I have, I believe, sought it in every place except where alone it is to be found— in a virtuous home.[61]

His education is further aided by the accidental death of his father and the death of his stepfather, who dies a bankrupt. Sidney is left penniless and has to begin all over again. He runs the family farm, learns to work with his hands and successfully courts a virtuous Yankee girl. At this point, destiny steps in and saves Sidney for gentility. His wife-to-be becomes an heiress and Sidney mysteriously recovers Brainard's fortune. The novel ends as he once again leaves for the South to run Brainard's plantation and to become a virtuous Southern planter. This time, it is implied, Sidney has the character necessary to survive in the loose moral world of the South.

This ending is schematic and in many ways unsatisfactory, but Sarah Hale, almost inadvertently, uncovers a very serious problem in her thinking about American character. Sidney Romilly, by the end of the novel, is both an emergent Yankee and a merchant's son. He is both a young provincial on the way out and on the way up, and the rich young man whose character is saved by a reindoctrination in provincial virtue. It took two exposures to the disciplined life of Northwood to make Sidney Romilly into a gentleman who could be trusted to control himself. The first kept him from going utterly to seed during his education; the second instructed him in the responsible use of his money and his social distinction. Twice he emerged from the provinces, each time a little better able to control himself. At last, he emerged with his character formed and with the Hale stamp of approval. What was he equipped to do? The answer is simple. He had finally learned to say no. The emergent Yankee must learn to say no in order to succeed, but why must the gentleman say no? Why, in heaven's name, can he not at long last relax and enjoy himself? Why must he be continually bedeviled with tempters till the end of his days?

The Problem of American Gentility

The answer to these questions reveals the dimensions of Sarah Hale's problem. The idea of leisure was unacceptable to a great many Americans in the nineteenth century. Mr. Chapman, the Connecticut Yankee in "**The Springs**," a story set in Saratoga, had a go at leisure and the fashionable life of a spa and found the experience not to his liking. He believed in being useful, and leisure to him was a form of uselessness.

> I don't think those gentlemen and ladies there are so happy as the persons I left at work in my factory. They do not look half as cheerful and gay. Indeed, the observations I have made, have convinced me that employment, some kind of business, is absolutely necessary to make men, or at least our citizens, happy and respectable. This trifling away of time when there is so much to be done, so many improvements necessary in our country, is inconsistent with that principle of being useful, which every republican ought to cherish.[62]

The gentleman of leisure has little place in the fiction of this period, except as a warning. When he appears at all, he is apt to appear as a rake or a villain. Arthur Lloyd's gentility is proved by his ability to detect a false aristocrat, not by his ability to be one himself. He must go on saying no. At the same time an American was expected to distinguish himself somehow and his success was measured by the distance he could put between himself and his Northwood. If he must, in fact, rise, to what could he legitimately aspire? He could not aspire to become a gentleman of leisure, because to become one would be to betray the whole meaning of his life. He would have to begin saying yes. To accept a genteel status would mean accepting Europe and denying Northwood. If an American was to become a gentleman, he would have to become an American kind of gentleman. What did this involve?

Sarah Hale's fiction contains an answer to this question. Only a kind of social distinction which was consistent with the values of the emergent Yankee was acceptable to her. Her idea of the gentleman was an extrapolation from her idea of the successful man. To become a useful gentleman it was necessary for a man to act as though he were still in the competitive race. The emergent Yankee was expected to deny himself any indulgence and to put all his energy and his time to "use." The American gentleman was supposed to place "service" before everything. What "use" was to the Yankee, "service" was to the gentleman. There was, however, an important difference between becoming successful and becoming a gentleman. It was legitimate, even necessary, for the Yankee to be ambitious, if his ambitions were proper. The American gentleman, on the other hand, could not want anything, except to be of more service, to be more selfless. In public, Webster could only aspire to join the constellation of the Great and Disinterested Statesmen whom he tried to emulate. Only in private could he want power, money and the Presidency. He could transcend his own image, but he could not wish to rise. If the emergent Yankee had to deny his desires and say no, the gentleman was not supposed to have any desires to deny. The only kind of distinction which many Americans could imagine and accept was one of moral perfection. To be better, it was necessary to be perfect. Parson Weems sensed the meaning of distinction when he inserted the cherry-tree story in his life of Washington. Washington was not simply truthful. He *could not* tell a lie. . . .

A Division of Labor

. . . Sarah Hale appears to have had [Daniel Webster] very much in mind as she wrote *Northwood.* He was the plowboy become statesman, whom Sidney Romilly envied. He was the emergent Yankee. Sarah Hale was even for a time associated with Webster during the building of the monument at Bunker Hill, that monument to national harmony. In 1852, the year of Webster's death, she paid tribute to him again. That year she had revised and reissued *Northwood,* substituting for the old subtitle, "A Tale of New England," a new one, "Life North and South: Showing the True Character of Both." Her object in bringing out a new edition was to provide an answer to Harriet Beecher Stowe's disturbing novel, *Uncle Tom's Cabin,* published the same year, and to abolitionist arguments in general. In a brief foreword to this edition she made a plea for Union and praised the statesmen who had never been betrayed into divisive tactics. She identified herself with their cause:

> And from the glorious old Granite State, where the scenes of this novel begin, have come forth those great men, "Defenders of the Constitution",—who "know no North and no South",—but wherever the sacred Charter of Union stretches its cordon of brotherhood, and the Eagle and the Stars keep guard, is their country. In the same spirit our book goes forth.[64]

The Union, in other words, was a kind of family. She went on to emphasize the point that a war between North and South would be a war between brothers. "The great error of those who would sever the Union rather than see a slave within its borders, is, that they forget the *master* is their brother, as well as the *servant.*" She had made this point, she said, in 1827, and she had found it necessary to revise very little of what she had then said. Sidney Romilly, a Yankee, had become a Southerner and a gentleman. "The few additions made to the original work are only to show more plainly how the principles advocated may be effectually carried out."[65]

In 1826 Sarah Hale was living the isolated life of a provincial widow. She was poor and the race was ahead of her. Twenty-five years later she had achieved fame, success, influence—call it what you will. She had emerged, and she was living in Philadelphia, an editor, *the* editor really, of *Godey's. Godey's,* furthermore, had reached the peak of its influence. Thereafter it met increasing competition from such new publications as *Harper's Magazine,* founded in 1850, and the *Atlantic,* founded in 1857. Sarah Hale was sixty-four and, vigorous as she was, even she must have known that her life lay behind her. She could have looked back on her struggles and those of her hero with a certain detachment which would not have been possible twenty-five years before. Her knowledge of American life had, of course, increased immensely over the years, and America itself had changed, changed tremendously. The South, which was virtually unknown to her before, was now a part of her everyday experience as an editor of a national magazine with many Southern subscribers and contributors. She knew about it as a mother as well. Three of her children had made their lives, or part of their lives, in the South. The surprising thing, really, is not that she made changes in *Northwood,* but rather that she did not make more. The race, it appears, looked much the same from either end.

The first edition of *Northwood* had said little or nothing about Sidney's plans. The last chapter had ended with his departure for the South. The new chapter is much more specific. Sidney has adopted the view that slavery is sanctioned by the Bible. For the Negro slaves, slavery had been, in fact, a great opportunity. The Negro had become a Christian and he had been introduced to civilization in the most advanced nation the world had ever known. In America, however, the Saxon is destined always to be superior. The future of the Negro, therefore, lay in Africa. There he might carry Christianity and civilization to his less fortunate "countrymen." Sidney had thus been made a mouthpiece for the arguments of the American Colonization Society, an organization founded in 1817 with the purpose of sending Negroes back to Africa. Although its program was unacceptable to either abolitionist or fire-eater, and its activities limited, it had a considerable appeal in the border states and listed among its members the leading spokesmen of the Whig party, Henry Clay and Daniel Webster. Sidney had worked out a plan for permitting his slaves, Yankeelike, to earn their own emancipation.

The principal danger of slavery, Sarah Hale contended, was not its effect on the slave but its effect on the master. Planters tended to forget that in the absence of work, they must fill up their time with duties, that they must live a life of service. All too frequently, a young Yankee tutor wrote to Sidney, young Southerners returned from college "where they often give promise of great talent, to smoke cigars in a veranda, or lie in the shade reading *cheap* novels!"[66] The English language, he wrote, was being bastardized by a promiscuous association with Negroes, and lovely Southern women spoke in a "niggerish" way. There is a strong hint in this last chapter that more than language was being bastardized.

> Thus the system of slavery increases the temptations to sin, and only the most resolute courage in duty and humble reliance on Divine aid can struggle on successfully against the snares of evil around the slaveholder.[67]

Despite all these dangers and temptations, however, Sidney and his wife were completely happy in the South and fully up to its demands and its challenge. "Sidney and Annie Romilly are *at home!*" she wrote. "To them the word is full of meaning."[68] Surrounded by their own children and the numerous slave "children," they enjoy the satisfactions of an extended family. In such a family, the woman supplied the moral force while the man was kept busy with material concerns and with politics. Only the woman, she felt, could be really "disinterested," because only the woman was completely unconcerned with making money—and untempted by sensuality. In the North she must protect against overacquisitiveness, greed. In the South she must protect her family from falling prey to self-indulgence and idle pleasure. Southern men and Northern men must meanwhile work out a compromise which would hold the Union together, and combine the best features of both regions. "'Constitutions' and 'compromises' are the appropriate work of men; women are the conservators of moral power," she concluded. Surely she must have had Webster in mind as she went on to explain. Appropriately, she took her supporting text from John Bunyan's *The Pilgrim's Progress:*

> His hero Christian, with all the man's power, knowledge, and force of will, could hardly hold on his way to the "Celestial City". What doubts beset him! What dangers and delusions! He went *alone,* and only one soul joined him on the long pilgrimage. But when the *woman,* Christiana went, *she took the children with her.* She drew nearly all she met to join her, and angels led them on through pleasant ways to heaven and eternal life.[69]

Daniel Webster and Sarah Hale as Christian and Christiana went their separate ways. It is unknown if they ever met face to face. Still, there was a kind of marriage of purpose, and for a number of years they presided as master and mistress over the house of Whiggery. Between the two of them they also licked the platter clean.

Notes

[47] Sarah Josepha Hale, *Northwood, or Life North and South; Showing the True Character of Both* (New York, 1852), p. 7.

[48] *Ibid.,* p. 10.

[49] *Ibid.,* p. 7.

[50] Hale, *Sketches of American Character* (Boston, 1838), p. 8.

[51] *Ibid.,* pp. 52-53.

[52] *Ibid.,* pp. 67-68.

[53] Hale, *Traits of American Life* (Philadelphia, 1835), p. 110.

[54] *Ibid.,* p. 111.

[55] *Ibid.,* pp. 99-100.

[56] *Ibid.,* pp. 101-102.

[57] Hale, *Northwood,* pp. 9-12.

[58] Sarah Josepha Hale, *Northwood; a Tale of New England* (Boston, 1827), Vol. II, p. 146.

[59] Hale, *Northwood* (1852), p. 180.

[60] *Ibid.,* p. 235.

[61] *Ibid.,* p. 73.

[62] Hale, *Sketches,* p. 193. . . .

[64] Hale, *Northwood* (1852), p. iv.

[65] *Ibid.* These "few additions" are nonetheless very interesting. Many of the small changes she made suggest the years that had elapsed. Steam power and the telegraph had made their appearance (1827, vol. II, pp. 8-10; 1852, p. 219). A reference to Sir Walter Scott was dropped (1827, Vol. I, pp. 3-5); so were the references to the Scotch reviewers (1827, Vol. I, p. 206; 1852, p. 164). An "apprentice" has become a "clerk" (1827, Vol. II, p. 194; 1852, p. 356), and "females" have become "women" (1827, Vol. I, p. 12; 1852, p. 13). Coffee replaced tea in the Romilly household (1827, Vol. I, p. 118; 1852, p. 96) and beer was added to the list of drinks served (1827, Vol. I, p. 155; 1852, p. 124). The Episcopalian Church received some free

propaganda in the new edition. Sidney has become an Episcopalian like Sarah Hale herself, and Horace Brainard, it is implied, is about to leave the Catholic Church and join the church of his foster son (1852, p. 170). More significant, a reference to "American Liberty" was changed to "American Liberty and Power" (1827, Vol. I, p. 74; 1852, p. 60). Sidney's father has become an advocate of Manifest Destiny and a promoter of African colonization for Negro slaves (1852, Chap. XIV). The name of a Brainard Negro has been changed from "Cato" to "Tom" (1827, Vol. I, p. 26; 1852, p. 24). The family name, spelled "Romilee" in the first edition, has been changed to "Romilly" and stress was laid on the English ancestry of the family, despite the fact that the name Romilly had the same kind of ambiguous nationality as Sarah Hale's maiden name, Buell. A long discussion of the possible dangers and advantages of the new European immigration is entirely new (1852, Chap. XIV). So is the final chapter of the book, which describes Sidney's plans for operating the Brainard plantation and justifying his gentility (1852, Chap. XXXIV).

[66] Hale, *Northwood* (1852), p. 407.

[67] *Ibid.,* p. 401.

[68] *Ibid.,* p. 389.

[69] *Ibid.,* p. 402.

Nina Baym (essay date 1990)

SOURCE: "Onward Christian Women: Sarah J. Hale's History of the World." *New England Quarterly*, Vol. 63, No. 2, June, 1990, pp. 249-70.

[*In the following excerpt, Baym discusses Hale's views on the moral superiority of women as expressed in* Woman's Record.]

We know Sarah J. Hale as the editor, for almost half a century (1837-77), of *Godey's Lady's Book.* In that position she exercised considerable power (or, to use a word she would have preferred, influence) over emergent middle-class culture in the United States.[1] Dedicated above all to the cause of women's education, Hale approached social issues with strongly expressed convictions that authorize the critic of today to see her either as a profound conservative or equally as a progressive liberal. More often than not, however, she is interpreted as a retrograde force, a woman who impeded the development of egalitarian feminism through her espousal of the ideology of separate spheres for the sexes and who contributed to the weakening of an older, vigorously masculine cultural style through her successful championing of an alternative feminine (i.e., sentimental, consumerist) aesthetic sensibility.[2]

The energy, indeed pugnacity, with which Hale undertook to promulgate an ideology of feminine meekness may look like duplicity if not outright hypocrisy—but only if one holds a simplistic notion of the concept of women's sphere and only if one skims the surface of Hale's own productions.[3] Besides supervising and contributing to the *Lady's Book* (and the Boston-based *Ladies' Magazine* earlier on [1828-37]), she published several books of her own writings, of which the most impressive by far as well as the most fully expressive of her theory of womanhood is **Woman's Record.** First published in 1853 and again in a revised edition in 1855, the book is described in the *Oxford Companion to American Literature* as "a history of distinguished women" and in *Notable American Women* as "an ambitious biographical encyclopedia containing some 2,500 entries—an early effort to remedy the neglect of women in most such works." Neither description prepares a reader for the actual book, with its more than 900 pages of closely spaced double columns of type recounting the lives of some 1,650 women from all historical eras and nations, decorated with 230 engraved portraits, and organized within an elaborate historical narrative.[4]

In this, more than any other of her works, Hale comes forward in her own voice; at the same time, the volume's wide-ranging coverage publicizes numerous views at odds with her own, so that the effect of the whole is truly dialogic. The polyvocality is enhanced by Hale's inclusion of substantial extracts from the writings of literary women. Her own moral commentary is pervasive, yet **Woman's Record** is intended as a celebration of all the women it describes—even of Jezebel, whose story "shows the power of female influence" (p. 43).[5] Rejoicing in female energy and achievement wherever and however they are manifest, **Woman's Record** also situates women's lives in history in a way that precludes taking accounts of them as simple lessons in proper or improper female behavior. The biographies are sorted chronologically into four eras, each introduced by a controlling historical narrative that makes **Woman's Record** a work of history rather than a collection of biographies.

Moreover, far from aiming modestly to compensate for the absence of women from the conventional historical record, or to highlight their neglected presence in that record, or even to construct a self-contained history of women, the work attempts nothing less than to reconstitute world history around the figure of woman, to restructure world history *as* the history of women. In pursuit of this goal, Hale assumes the stances of the eulogist, the critic, the moralist, the scholar, the polemicist, and the disputatious theologian. At the back of the book she lists, in addition to personal interviews and private correspondence, 137 sources for **Woman's Record**—sources that include encyclopedias, histories, biographical dictionaries, individual biographies, memoirs, journals and newspapers, along with general books about the condition of women, in French and Italian as well as English. The character of the work itself gives no reason to doubt that Hale had in fact consulted, to some extent, all the works that she lists. As an example of what an educated Christian woman could achieve in the nineteenth century, **Woman's Record** declares itself a world event as well as a record of world events. In Hale's words, "I have sought to make *[Woman's Record]* an assistant in home education; hoping the examples shown and characters portrayed, might have an inspiration and a power in advancing the moral progress of society" (p. 687).

I stress the word *Christian* here, for Hale's vision of the progress of world history—and it is a progressive, even millennial, vision—conflates the progress of Christianity with that of women.[6] The supposed special bond between women and Christianity in nineteenth-century America has, of course, been much noted by students of American culture, many of whom have lamented this feminization of Christianity and some few others the co-opting Christianization of the feminine. In Hale's representation, the two themes cannot be disentangled because the Christian and the feminine are one. The Christian message is precisely the superiority of women, the destined mission of women is to Christianize the world, and the story of history is of inevitable progress toward a world dominated by Christian and Christianizing women. Without Christianity, women are underestimated, degraded, enslaved; without women, Christianity is misunderstood, devalued, corrupted. Hence, it is imperative that every woman be a Christian and that every Christian man learn to recognize women's superiority. When these two goals have been accomplished, the goal of history itself will have been achieved and history will presumably come to an end.

Woman's Record is meant in part to demonstrate that throughout history men have perceived and accepted the superiority of Christian women more readily than any other womanly type. The book is dedicated to the men of America, "who show, in their laws and customs, respecting Women, ideas more just and feelings more noble than were ever evinced by men of any other nation: May 'Woman's Record' meet the approval of the sons of our great republic; the world will then know the Daughters are Worthy of Honour."[7] Many women contemporaries come in for criticism in the pages of **Woman's Record,** but what Hale objects to is their ignorance not their morals—even in such egregious careers as that of George Sand. (The life of Mary Wollstonecraft, it is only fair to acknowledge, is not included in the book.) Women who do not recognize the tendency of the *zeitgeist* may act from the best possible motive—to advance womankind—and still do such silly and self-defeating things as wear men's clothes or advocate free love. Hale must have expected many of her targets to read **Woman's Record**

(as indeed they did); and no doubt she anticipated that the weight of evidence presented in the work would persuade many of them to change course (as, apparently, they did not).

The introduction to the second edition starts with two points: that "on the right influence of women depends the moral improvement of men; and that the condition of the female sex decides the destiny of the nation" (p. vii). Observing that the record she has compiled shows women in every age and nation winning their way to eminence without any special preparation and in spite of obstacles and discouragement, Hale then advances her gendered Christian argument:

> The Bible is the only guarantee of woman's rights, and the only expositor of her duties. Under its teachings, men learn to honour her. Wherever its doctrines are observed, her influence gains in power. . . . If the Gospel is the supreme good revealed to the world, and if this Gospel harmonizes best with the feminine nature, and is best exemplified in its purity by the feminine life . . . then surely God has, in applying this Gospel so directly to her nature, offices, and condition, a great work for the sex to do. [Pp. viii-ix]

In the general preface that follows her introduction, Hale defends the religious case for female superiority at considerable length and with what might be considered unfeminine tenacity. "I believe," she says—making no bones about the first-person speaker—" . . . and trust I shall make it apparent, that WOMAN is God's appointed agent of *morality,* the teacher and inspirer of those feelings and sentiments which are termed the virtues of humanity; and that the progress of these virtues and the permanent improvement of our race, depend on the manner in which her mission is treated by man" (p. xxxv).

This assertion is not advanced as poetic flight or metaphor; Hale follows it with several pages of biblical exegesis and theological interpretation (disputing male authorities in the process) that show a literal intention. "I entreat my readers, *men,* who I hope will read heedfully this preface, to lay aside, if possible, their prejudices of education, the erroneous views imbibed from poetical descriptions and learned commentaries, respecting the Creation and the Fall of Man. Go not to Milton, or the Fathers, but to the Word of God; and let us from it read this important history, the foundation of all true history of the natural character and moral condition of mankind" (p. xxxvi).[8] Hale reads Genesis to show that only Adam, and thus only the male sex, fell. Man—not woman—"was rendered incapable of cultivating by his own unassisted efforts, any good propensity or quality of his nature. Left to himself, his love becomes lust, patriotism, policy, and religion, idolatry. He is naturally selfish in his affections; and *selfishness* is the sin of depravity" (pp. xxxv-xxxvi).

But Eve, representative of all women, "was not thus cast down" (p. xxxi). St. Paul's assertion that woman was made for man, Hale grants, is true but "not in the sense that this text has heretofore been interpreted." If woman was destined to help man, she self-evidently had to be superior to him in whatever area she was supposed to provide aid. Manifestly, since she isn't as strong as a man, and lacks his "capacity of understanding to grasp the things of earth," she could not "help him in his task of subduing the world"; therefore, she must have been "above him in her intuitive knowledge of heavenly things; and the 'help' he needed from her was for the 'inner man'" (pp. xxxvi-xxxvii).

Since she did not imagine that there could be any dispute over whether in fact women are weaker than men, Hale turns a potential deficit to her advantage and presents it as a mark of superiority, as mind and spirit are superior to body. She then describes Christianity as the only movement historically successful in counteracting men's greater physical strength and hence in overcoming their ability to subjugate women as well as weaker persons of their own gender through mere brute force. Her differentiation between the quality of mind in men and women—women lack materialist, instrumental understanding of worldly things but possess spiritual intuition—argues one side of an issue that is still, in other terms, debated among feminists today, as in the question of whether women have a different morality from men, whether they see and speak "in a different voice." From a perspective more aligned with her own intellectual moment, we see Hale in the process of reconfiguring a conventionally contemptuous view of women's mental powers to align it with the Kantian-Coleridgean-transcendental distinction between Understanding and Reason, thereby making intuitional woman the repository of the higher forms of knowledge.[9] (Margaret Fuller, whose ideology of the feminine is occasionally contrasted to Hale's, as the radical versus the conservative, did much the same thing.)

Hale's insistence on approaching Scripture directly and without authorities of course invokes the whole weight of the Protestant, if not the Antinomian, tradition; but in quoting chapter and verse, meeting doctrinal objections with counter-argument, she behaves like a trained biblical scholar fully endowed with the masculine understanding to grasp the things of this earth. This readiness to contest male precursors might look like behavior that is inconsistent with Hale's feminine methods; but it looks equally like behavior enacting her conviction that educated Christian women have the right and obligation to speak out—to speak out because they are correct and because it is necessary for men to hear them. "One of the most subtle devices of the power of darkness to perpetuate sin," she observes, "is to keep women in restraint and concealment—hidden, as it were, behind the shadow of the evil world. They may not even express openly their abhorrence of vice—it is

unfeminine; and if they seek to promote good, it must be by stealth, as though it were wrong for them to be recognized doing anything which has a high aim." But since the Saviour, she goes on, "was constantly bringing forward female examples of faith and love, encouraging the exertions and commending the piety of his female followers" (p. 563), he evidently did not mean for women to keep silent in the face of moral wrong.[10]

Ceding the physical and material world to men, reserving the higher domain of morality, values, and meaning to women, Hale argues in the preface to *Woman's Record* and again in her biography of Eve—"the crowning work of creation, the first woman, the mother of our race" (p. 38)—that the Fall consisted in the splitting of an original and perfect human unity, symbolized by the couple, into better and worse parts, with the better part (woman) made subject to the worse (man). "While [Adam and Eve] were one, *Adam* was perfect. It was not till this holy union was dissolved by sin that the distinctive natures of the masculine and the feminine were exhibited" (p. 39). Now, if man's nature was higher than woman's, there would be nothing wrong with making woman subject to him. What has been wrong with the world since the Fall has been, precisely, that the fine has been subjected to the coarse—that brute strength has gained dominion over mental and moral powers—which is embodied in men's domination of women. This subjection, then, is the Fall itself, and historical progress toward a Christianized world involves the gradual overturning of this unnatural, or perhaps all-too-natural, state of things, until women everywhere finally take their rightful places as men's spiritual guides and intellectual leaders.

The four eras into which *Woman's Record* is divided are presented as stages in this inevitable, but by no means smooth and unimpeded, historical movement toward restoration of a prelapsarian human wholeness which coincides with the elevation of women and is embodied in a monogamous marriage where the wife is spiritual and moral leader of the husband. In each of these eras, as Christianity advances, so do women. And women advance in two ways: their own nature changes or, rather, historical circumstances shift in such a way that women's inherent natures are more free to develop and be expressed; and, their influence over the course of world events becomes greater. Because the two dimensions of women's advancement are mutually reinforcing, the pace of historical change increases over time, but some nations outstrip others and changes within a nation do not necessarily affect everyone equally. "Improvement is only where the Bible is read, and its authority acknowledged" (p. 152). Hence, although progress is inevitable, human beings can do much either to obstruct or to further it.

The four eras in *Woman's Record* are: from the creation to the birth of Christ; from 1 A.D. to 1500 A.D.;

from 1500 to 1850; and the era of living women. The general preface quickly outlines a historical story to which this periodization conforms. In the pre-Christian era, women "had only their natural gifts of a lovelier organization of form, and a purer moral sense, to aid them in the struggle with sin which had taken possession of the brute strength, and human understanding of men" (p. xl). After Christ, "woman had now the aid of the blessed Gospel, which seems given purposely to develop her powers and sanction her influence" (p. xli). Around 1500 the invention of printing gave a freedom to woman's mind that matched the earlier emancipation of her soul, so that now men who are philosophers, philanthropists, patriots, and Christians "all find in educated woman, as the Bible represents her mission, and this Record shows her influence and her works, their best earthly helper, counsellor, encourager, and examplar" (p. xli).

In the fourth era, the United States enters the narrative. "A new element of improvement, now in course of rapid development, is destined to have a wonderful effect on the female mind and character. This element is individual liberty, secured by constitutional laws" (p. xli). The last hundred years, Hale says later on, have been "remarkable for the development of genius and talent in a new race of women—the Anglo-Saxon" (p. 152). Later still she singles out the twenty million English Anglo-Saxons who "hold the mastery of mind over Europe and Asia; if we trace out the causes of this superiority, they would centre in that moral influence, which true religion confers on the female sex" (p. 564). And, she continues,

> there is still a more wonderful example of this uplifting power of the educated female mind. It is only seventy-five years since the Anglo-Saxons in the New World became a nation, then numbering about three millions of souls. Now, this people form the Great American Republic, with a population of twenty-three millions; and the destiny of the world will soon be in their keeping! The Bible has been their "Book of books" since the first Puritan exile set his foot on Plymouth Rock. Religion is free; and the soul, which woman always influences where God is worshipped in spirit and truth, is untrammeled by code, or creed, or caste. . . . The result is before the world,—a miracle of national advancement. American mothers train their sons to be Men! [p. 564][11]

Here as always Hale moves effortlessly between "true religion" and "the uplifting power of the educated female mind." But, obviously, this is not her only effortless move. When she presents the ongoing Christianization of the world through missionary effort as the great enterprise of the nineteenth century; when she takes the missionary as the highest development of the nineteenth-century male and the woman missionary (or the missionary's wife) as the highest

development of human character since Christ himself; when she asserts that this character development is found above all among the Anglo-Saxons; and when she places the United States ahead of Britain as the premier Anglo-Saxon nation—then she demolishes, inadvertently but irreparably, the very boundaries between the male political and material sphere and the female spiritual and moral sphere on which her argument has depended. Since the world that is to be spiritualized is, after all, a material world, while those doing the spiritualizing are material beings, Hale cannot ultimately avoid becoming conventionally political. And her politics are conventional: Anglo-Saxonist, expansionist, nationalist.[12]

Hale's four historical eras also rely on convention. The birth of Christ, the advent of the Reformation thanks to the invention of the printing press, and the establishment of a Protestant Christian republic in the United States are standard chronological markers in the "Universal History" that was narrated in variously authored American schoolbooks. These schoolbooks, too, were gendered—but the gender was male, with history unfolding as a series of wars, territorial conquests, and kingly successions. This masculine gendering appeared in textbooks whether the author was a man or a woman. Hale's presentation of world history as a woman's story does, then, constitute a radical narrative innovation. "Military force extinguishes moral feeling," she insisted, and in most of the world today, "Man the Murderer, Woman the Mourner, is still the great distinction between the sexes!" (p. 564).

Equally innovative, it would seem, was Hale's frank gendering of the Christian religion, including her fully articulated expression of female superiority.[13] The femininity of Christianity is argued along two lines. First, the Christian virtues—Christ's own nature—are feminine. "That the laws Christ enjoined on his followers are pre-eminently favourable to the development of [woman's] faculties, while they repress or denounce the peculiar characteristics usually called *manly,* is an irrefragable proof that her nature was the best" (p. xli); "The fact that the Saviour of the world, the Son of God, inherited his human nature entirely from his mother, can hardly be too often pressed on the attention of Christians" (p. 65). Hale's biography of the Virgin Mary makes this second point more emphatically:

> [Christ's] *human soul,* derived from a woman, trained by a woman, was most truly *womanly* in its characteristics. Examine the doctrines he taught, the duties and virtues he enforced, the examples he set—where, in any of these, are the distinctive traits men vaunt as proofs of masculine greatness? Physical strength, earthly honours, riches, wordly wisdom, even the gifts of intellect and the pride of learning, our Saviour put all these down far, far beneath *meekness, mercy, purity, patience, charity,*

humility; qualities and graces always considered peculiarly feminine; qualities and graces his blessed mother had displayed and commended. [p. 129]

Second, Christianity is a particularly feminine religion because so many of its followers, and most of its effective proselytizers from the beginning, historically have been women:

> The empress Helena has been widely celebrated for her agency in introducing Christianity into the Roman empire. It may not be as well known that many queens and princesses have the glory of converting their husbands to the true faith, and thus securing the success of the Gospel in France, England, Hungary, Spain, Poland, and Russia. In truth, it was the influence of women that changed the worship of the greater part of Europe from Paganism to Christianity. [p. 66]

Of course Christianity's attractiveness to woman is not accidental; rather, she is moved by and toward it precisely because it is congruent with her nature: "No wonder these honourable ladies were zealous in the cause of the religion which gave their sex protection in this life and the promise of eternal happiness in the life to come" (p. 66). That women are drawn to a high representation of their natures is simultaneously testimony both to the value of the religion that so moves them *and* to the fact that women's natures are, really, "high." Hale would not have been much surprised if men were not equally impressed by this line of argument. Their very callousness would show that even though they had made much progress, they were still spiritually and morally needy.

In fact, despite the importance that, in some contexts, Hale attributed to feminine tact, *Woman's Record* is astonishingly ready at every opportunity to take man to task for bad deeds, which include, significantly, attempts to conceal or appropriate the good deeds of women. In the pre-Christian era, "the licentious example was set by the men;—they made the laws; and always the women were better than the men of their time" (p. 18). In the days of the Roman Empire, it was not until "Roman men were banded together and absent from their homes in their long wars, thus losing the softening, purifying influence of their mothers, wives, and daughters, that the frightful demoralization of the nation was reached" (p. 18). Cleopatra, living in an age of crime, "was better than the men her subtle spirit subdued,—for she was true to her country. Never was Egypt so rich in wealth, power, and civilization, as under her reign" (p. 32). Delilah was far less culpable than Samson, "because she was his paramour, perhaps his victim, and he the heaven-gifted champion of Israel. Read the history as recorded in the Bible, not in Milton's 'Samson Agonistes,' where the whole is set in a false light" (p. 36). Granted that "Esther was

deeply indebted to Mordecai for his care and zeal in her education; still, had she not possessed, and exercised, too, the highest powers of woman's mind . . . the Jews must have perished" (p. 38). "Had [Julia] lived, there would not have been war between Caesar and Pompey" (p. 44). In a comparison of Isaac and Rebekah, "the wife is, morally, superior to her husband, and appears to have been specially entrusted by God with the agency of changing the succession of her sons, and thus building up the house of Israel" (p. 55).

Xantippe was a morose character, but "if we take into account this true love she felt for her husband, and consider what she must have suffered while he was passing his evenings in the society of the beautiful and fascinating Aspasia, we shall hardly wonder at her discontent." Indeed, had Socrates been a faithful husband to Xantippe, "he would have been a wiser and a better man" (p. 63). As for Aspasia, she surpassed all her contemporaries, male and female, in eloquence and has probably been victimized in history by the unjust aspersions of Aristophanes. Far from coming between husband and wife, she endeavored to impress on Socrates and Xantippe "the reciprocal duties of a married state" (pp. 26-27).

The simultaneous exoneration and indictment continues throughout the book. In the middle ages "truth was perverted by selfish men" (p. 66). "We cannot but consider the noble-hearted, though erring Heloise, a victim to the vanity of the selfish Abelard" (p. 110). Zenobia, "one of the most illustrious women who have swayed the sceptre," was "in every virtue which adorns high station, as far superior to Aurelian, as soul is superior to sense" (p. 150). "Compared with the men of her time, Charlotte Corday was like a bright star shining through noxious and dark exhalations of selfishness and wickedness" (p. 271). "It was to his wife that [Roland] owed his courage, and the power of his talents" (p. 491). And the African Princess Zinga—"a more odious spirit, licentious, blood-thirsty, and cruel, never inhabited the form of woman!"—nevertheless, "in understanding and ability, stepped far beyond her countrymen, and the circumstances under which she lived" (p. 560).

Nor does Hale confine her strictures to men of bygone times or non-Anglo-Saxon nations. "We read of colossal endowments by the British government, upon great generals; of titles conferred, and pensions granted, through several generations, to those who have served their country; of monuments erected by the British people to statesmen, and warriors, and even to weak and vicious princes; but where is the monument to Lady Mary Wortley Montagu?" (pp. 434-35). "Some masculine critics have pronounced it impossible that the classical allusions and quotations, interspersed through Mrs. Gore's works, should have proceeded from herself. The Latin and Greek of these gentlemen must have found very difficult access into their brains, but they may be assured such trifling accomplishments can be, and are, acquired every year by hundreds of school-boys, who would be entirely puzzled were a single chapter, such as the most indifferent of Mrs. Gore's works would furnish, to be expected of them" (p. 677). Reporting that Harriet Cheney's anonymously published *Sunday School, or Village Sketches* was stolen by a man who republished it under another title (and earned royalties from it), she comments that "this appropriation of the writings of women by men has been repeatedly done; thus Miss Hannah Adams was injured, and Miss Strickland plundered; while such men are usually the most authoritative in claiming for their own sex all the talents" (p. 826).

As can be seen from these entirely typical examples, the strategy of blaming men and praising women frequently requires *Woman's Record* to contest the historical, that is the male, record. If we judge Agrippina, the mother of Nero, "by the circumstances under which she lived, and with reference to the morality of her contemporaries," we see that she "rises immeasurably superior to the greatest men associated with her history." More: "Her faults belonged to the bad men and the bad age in which she lived—the worst on record: her virtues and her genius were her own" (pp. 21-22). "Virgil and others represent [Dido] as visited by Aeneas, after whose departure she destroyed herself from disappointed love; but this is a poetical fiction, as Aeneas and Dido did not live in the same age" (p. 37). "No individual charge can be substantiated against [Lucretia Borgia]. On the contrary, she is mentioned by contemporary poets and historians in the highest terms; and so many different writers would not have lavished such high praise on a person profligate and base as she has been represented. Many of the reports about her were circulated by the Neapolitans, the natural enemies of her family" (p. 86). Catherine of Russia's licentiousness is certainly inexcusable in a woman, "yet as a sovereign she is well entitled to the appellation of *great*" since "she established schools, ameliorated the condition of the serfs, promoted commerce, founded towns, arsenals, banks, and manufactories, and encouraged art and literature" (p. 253). Indeed, the only woman whose life seems to defy Hale's will to praise is Anne Hutchinson, of whom she writes with uncharacteristic terseness: "a woman who caused much difficulty in New England soon after its settlement. . . . She advocated sentiments of her own, and warped the discourses of her clergyman to coincide with them" (pp. 358-59). Perhaps this case came too close to home!

Finally, whenever possible, Hale constructs the historical, and especially the biblical, record to show that the survival of the human race, and particularly its Judaeo-Christian component, has depended on female heroism. Esther "saved her countrymen from total extermination" (p. 37), and Jochabed, the mother of Moses, did the same. "That the preservation of Moses, and his preparation for his great mission as the Deliverer of Israel, and the Lawgiver for all men who worship Jehovah, were effected by the agency of woman, displays her spiritual gifts in such a clear light as must make them strikingly apparent; and that their importance in the progress of mankind, will be frankly acknowledged by all Christian men, seems certain—whenever they will, laying aside their masculine prejudices, study the word of God" (p. 44). Without Mary, no Jesus; without Isabella, no Columbus; without Charlotte Corday, no end to the French terror; without Mrs. Mary Washington (the mother of George), perhaps no United States of America.

Although no doubt many contemporary egos were bruised by the critiques in *Woman's Record,* I would suggest that from Hale's own perspective her very decision to include particular women marked her admiration and high regard, her sense of their historical importance. The subtitle of *Woman's Record* is "Sketches of all Distinguished Women, from the Creation to A.D. 1854, Arranged in Four Eras." To be in the *Record* was to be distinguished. Furthermore, Hale's eagerness to debate her contemporaries in print inevitably circulated their points of view. Catharine Beecher's campaign for women's education, Elizabeth Blackwell's for women physicians, and Sarah Peters's to open a school of design (that is, a vocational school) for women are all strongly endorsed. The leading ideas of George Sand, Lydia Maria Child, Margaret Fuller, Harriet Martineau, Lucretia Mott, and Dorothea Dix are vigorously disputed; but stressing the high womanly motive behind what she considers a misguided project, Hale balances her strictures with a show of respect. Child was "true to the generous sympathies of her own heart" (p. 619); George Sand was a woman of "wonderful genius" (p. 642); Fuller was a woman of "exemplary qualities," whose meaning "was always honest and generous" (p. 666); Martineau had "excellent qualities and much benevolent feeling," was "earnest, enthusiastic and hopeful," and her faulty books "were yet far more candid in tone and true in spirit, than any preceding works of British travellers in America had ever been" (p. 739); in private life Lucretia Mott displays an "exemplary character" (p. 753); and Dorothea Dix, though devoting her energies to the wrong reform, "is a remarkable proof of the power of disinterested zeal concentrated on one purpose" (p. 864).

Whatever her intentions may have been, by arguing with her women contemporaries, Hale brought a female polyvocality into the public arena, instituting— for all her talk of "woman"—not woman's voice, but women's voices, at the center of contemporary history. To express this somewhat differently, in *Woman's Record* Hale represented the contemporary moment as one in which women were no longer willing to be silent. Instead of just speaking softly among themselves, women were now invited to address each other in public, within earshot of men. In *Woman's Record* women were given the power of the word.

Thus while it may seem hubristic for Hale to have included her own biography among the contemporary sketches, one might read this inclusion as her willingness to situate her own voice and achievement within history, just as she had situated others'. The biographical sketch is also metacommentary on *Woman's Record.* Hale defines herself as "Chronicler of my own sex" (p. 686) and attributes much of her lifelong inspiration to having read a novel—and of all novels, *The Mysteries of Udolpho!*—written by a woman. "I had remarked that of all the books I saw, few were written by Americans, and none by *women*. Here was a work, the most fascinating I had ever read, always excepting 'The Pilgrim's Progress,' written by a woman! How happy it made me! The wish to promote the reputation of my own sex, and do something for my own country, were among the earliest mental emotions I can recollect" (p. 687). That Mrs. Radcliffe should be described, in her own biographical entry, as "a celebrated romance writer, whose genius and amiability adds *[sic]* lustre to the glory of her sex" (p. 481) may well indicate the extent to which Hale is implicated in, party to, a middle-class commercializing of culture; but the account of her happy response to reading *The Mysteries of Udolpho*—a response that led eventually to the very public *Woman's Record*—does not support a New Historicist or Foucauldian interpretation of antebellum women as increasingly passive, compliant, and privatized consumers.

Nor does it support any particular totalizing representation of antebellum women—or of women from all times and places; rather, Hale's *Woman's Record* has material enough to support virtually any representation that an interpreter might choose to draw from it. "Woman," because she has not yet arrived at the state of her perfection, evades all attempts to be fully represented in any individual life or lives. Thus, notwithstanding the religio-cultural bias within which its women's history of the world is constructed, and which it is designed to extol, the *Record* goes on the record for the diversity, difference, endurance, and adaptability of specific and imperfect earthly women in historical situations that, since the Fall, have been defined by women's subjugation.

The crucial subtext of *Woman's Record*—that of women's continuous vulnerability to a superior male physical strength that is all too often manifested violently—is inferable throughout, even in Hale's own biography, which closes with acknowledgment of the "ready and kind aid I have always met with from those men with whom I have been most nearly connected." She remarks that her brother, who taught her Latin,

mathematics, and mental philosophy, "often lamented that I could not, like himself, have the privilege of a college education," while her husband—"a number of years my senior, and far more my superior in learning"—embarked with her on "a system of study and reading which we pursued while he lived" (p. 687). How few women, she implies, have had the good fortune to meet with such men. And how many more women like herself there would be were more men like these. If it seemed to Hale that the explanation for these men's behavior was their Christian faith, it is no wonder that she could not extricate a vision of women's future from the future of Christianity.

Notes

[1] In *The Poetry of American Women from 1632 to 1945* (Austin: University of Texas Press, 1977), Emily Stipes Watts quite sensibly assigns Hale an important role in the formation of an American women's poetic tradition through her selection of the poems printed in the magazines she edited (p. 68); but most critics downgrade Hale into Godey's subordinate—from Frank Luther Mott, in his *History of American Magazines,* 2 vols. (Cambridge: Harvard University Press, 1938), 1:580-94, to Cheryl Walker, in *The Nightingale's Burden* (Bloomington: Indiana University Press, 1982), where we are told that "although women like Sara *[sic]* Josepha Hale were nominal editors of the ladies' magazines, they were in fact controlled by their publishers, who were male" (p. 34). Mott simply did not consider the possibility of women holding cultural power; Walker, deploying a Gilbert-and-Gubartian paradigm of the silenced, anxious woman poet, considers but dismisses the possibility. However, a close look at the editorial pages of *Godey's Lady's Book* and correspondence surrounding the journal reveals conclusively that editorial policy and content were Hale's domain, while Godey attended to sales, format, and publicity. I am indebted to unpublished research by Patricia Okker for this point, as well as for the information that in her letters Hale always referred to the *Lady's Book,* not *Godey's.* Louis Godey's name does not appear in her biographical sketch in *Woman's Record* either. From the vantage point of the reading I give here, the division of responsibilities would correspond with Hale's idea of sexual difference: she was the mind and spirit, Godey the physical implementer, of the journal.

[2] In Susan Phinney Conrad's *Perish the Thought: Intellectual Women in Romantic America, 1830-1860* (New York: Oxford University Press, 1976), Hale figures throughout as a virtual allegory of American female anti-intellectualism; and similarly in Ann Douglas's influential *The Feminization of American Culture* (New York: Knopf, 1977) Hale is the ultimate spokeswoman for female softheads. Thus most scholars who do attribute power to Hale and women like her see it as bad power.

³ The first scholarship on "woman's sphere," emerging from the new academic feminism of the late 1960s, initiated a declension model of nineteenth-century womanhood, as in such works as Gerda Lerner's "The Lady and the Mill Girl: Changes in the Status of Women in the Age of Jackson" (*Mid-Continent American Studies Journal* 10 [1969]: 5-15), and Barbara Welter's "The Cult of True Womanhood: 1820-1860" (*American Quarterly* 18 [1966]: 158-74). These essays saw the concept of the separate spheres in practice as a co-optation of women, who were being removed from participation in the productive and egalitarian colonial economy and reinstalled in a class-bound and confining industrial order. But more recent research revises the picture. As Bruce Ronda summarizes this research, "few women were engaged in commerce, law, or medicine in the colonial period. The domestic round to which women were supposedly relegated in the nineteenth century had in fact always been their assignment." Moreover, "husbands and males in general demeaned women's work." In short, "across the classes, women's personalities and behavior were rigidly defined by their gender, long before the industrial revolution gave rise to a cult of domesticity" (Bruce A. Ronda, ed., *The Letters of Elizabeth Palmer Peabody, American Renaissance Woman* [Middletown: Wesleyan University Press, 1984], p. 50). Among important revisionary works are Nancy Cott's *The Bonds of Womanhood: "Woman's Sphere" in New England, 1780-1835* (New Haven: Yale University Press, 1977); Mary Beth Norton's *Liberty's Daughters: The Revolutionary Experience of American Women, 1750-1800* (Boston: Little, Brown, 1980); and Linda K. Kerber's *Women of the Republic: Intellect and Ideology in Revolutionary America* (Chapel Hill: University of North Carolina Press, 1980). See also Kerber's "Separate Spheres, Female Worlds, Woman's Place: The Rhetoric of Women's History," *Journal of American History* 75 (1988): 9-39, for a compelling argument that the "spheres" were and are rhetorical constructions rather than accurate descriptions of reality. Not only other facts, but other rhetorics, can be perceived in the era. Working with women's fiction of the Jacksonian and antebellum period, my *Woman's Fiction: A Guide to Novels by and about Women in America, 1820-1870* (Ithaca: Cornell University Press, 1978) observed that the protagonists of such fiction did not fit the "true womanhood" pattern, since they were much more energetic, independent, and strong-minded than the pure, passive, pious figure described by Welter. This observation has recently been confirmed and extended in Frances B. Cogan's *All-American Girl: The Ideal of Real Womanhood in Mid-Nineteenth-Century America* (Athens: University of Georgia Press, 1989), and Laura McCall's "'The Reign of Brute Force is Now Over': A Content Analysis of *Godey's Lady's Book*, 1830-1860," (*Journal of the Early Republic* 9 [1989]: 217-36). Notwithstanding, the more restrictive interpretation of the spheres and of women's situation in the antebellum nineteenth century continues appealing to inveterate denigrators of the middle class, and it is getting a second wind in Foucauldian New Historicist interpretations of antebellum culture.

⁴ The figure of 2,500 entries is a misreading of Hale's statement that the *Record* contains 2,500 *names*—which it does, more or less; but not all these names are accompanied by biographical entries. There are a number of one-sentence allusions to up-and-coming young writers as well as lists of the names of several hundred female missionaries. The biographies include one American Indian (Pocahontas); one African-American (Phillis Wheatley); and one African (Anna Zinga, a sixteenth-century princess). There are no representatives from any Asian nation. The selective principles of *Woman's Record* confirm its Eurocentric thesis that the advancement of women and of Christianity go in tandem.

⁵ My parenthetical citations are from the second edition of *Woman's Record* (New York: Harper & Brothers, 1855).

⁶ By *Christian*, Hale herself means a consensus form of evangelical Protestantism. She virtually dismisses Catholicism as a Christian religion because of its attitude toward women: "The Roman Catholic church degraded women, when it degraded marriage by making the celibacy of the priests a condition of greater holiness than married life. From this falsehood against the Word of God, came those corrupting sins which, at the close of our Second Era, seemed about to dissolve the whole fabric of civilized society, and spread the most polluting crimes of heathen nations over the Christian world" (p. 152). Because the Edenic human image was that of a couple, Hale takes monogamy as the divinely sanctioned human relation. There is virtually nothing about women in studies of American millennial thought and activity.

⁷ The dedication is set in several different, elaborate typefaces which my quotation cannot convey. *Woman's Record* is an object as well as an extractable text, prepared as material testimony to its ideal subject.

⁸ Those who have rummaged through standard antebellum American history textbooks will recognize that it is conventional to begin accounts of world (or universal) history with the Bible. In fact, many narratives of Universal History seem designed to demonstrate, through the convergence of biblical and secular historical reports, the validity of the Bible as history.

⁹ On the aptness of romantic values—introspection, intuition, feeling—for women, see Conrad, *Perish the Thought*, passim. See also Carol Gilligan, *In a Different Voice: Psychological Theory and Women's*

Development (Cambridge: Harvard University Press, 1982), and Mary Field Belenky et al., *Women's Ways of Knowing: The Development of Self, Voice, and Mind* (New York: Basic Books, 1986). But in striking contrast to a view that sees Cartesian logocentrism as woman's antagonist, Hale's approach requires the split between body and mind so as to devalue the body, which is associated with strength and hence with the male.

[10] Hale criticized women lecturers in a didactic novel of 1839, *The Lecturess; or, Woman's Sphere,* [not generally accepted as being by Hale] and elsewhere. Her position here may be inconsistent, or she may have been undecided or changed her mind. In *Woman's Record* there are many approving biographies of singers and actresses, as well as of a range of women reformers who spoke out—who had to speak out—in pursuit of their goals.

[11] Ever a daughter of New England, Hale identifies the origins of the nation with the settling of Plymouth Colony. The sentence with which this passage concludes echoes the comparison of American mothers with Spartan mothers that resounds throughout republican patriotic documents.

[12] Resistance to women's involvement in politics among what one might call "conservative" women took the form of opposition to the ballot and women officeholders, not opposition to women's interest in or holding and expressing opinions about politics. In the 1845 edition of her widely used school text, *History of the United States, or Republic of America* (New York: A. S. Barnes & Co.), Emma Willard observed that debates over the pet banks in the United States Senate "were exciting and attractive to such a degree, that the room for spectators was crowded at an early hour. Ladies, who assembled from every part of the Union, were so much fascinated, that they were often in waiting three hours, in order to secure seats" (p. 389). (Willard, too, was a "conservative" woman, and her textbooks are full of political opinions.)

[13] Of course, the idea of the superiority of women was (and is) implicit in a great deal of feminist discourse. Yet, according to Norton Mezvinsky, one of the few writers on the topic, "Although some early women reformers may have implied it, not until 1874 was the idea of feminine superiority expressed clearly and directly" ("An Idea of Female Superiority," *Journal of the Central Mississippi Valley American Studies Association* 2 [1961]: 17-26). To be sure, Hale's clear and direct expression of the idea did not connect it to social reform movements. The biographical organization of *Woman's Record* reflects her general opposition to reform organizations (except for missionary organizations) and invests reformist energy, like all energy, in *individuals*. Certainly a probable implicit target of this

biographical organization is the nascent Women's Rights Movement, which had held its first convention in 1848. As we know, many of the antebellum women activists opposed women's suffrage for a variety of reasons. Still, Hale's focus on individuals cannot be called "merely" conservative, since the supposedly radical transcendentalists also located all reformative and transformative powers in individuals. Attempts to attach today's rhetorical labels of liberal, conservative, radical, or reactionary to Hale only call attention to differences between the ways in which various intellectual positions converged and intersected then and the ways they do now.

Barbara Bardes and Suzanne Gossett (essay date 1990)

SOURCE: "Two Visions of the Republic" in *Declarations of Independence: Women and Political Power in Nineteenth-Century American Fiction,* Rutgers University Press, 1990, pp. 17-37.

[*In the following excerpt, Bardes and Gossett note the importance of community and comment on the role of women in Hale's novel* Northwood.]

Six years before Tocqueville makes similar observations on the status of American women, Squire Romelee, the voice of wisdom in Sarah Josepha Hale's **Northwood,** comments:

> I presume you will not find, should you travel throughout the United States, scarcely a single female engaged in the labors of the field or any kind of out-door work as it is called. And the manner in which women are treated is allowed to be a good criterion by which to judge of the character and civilization of a people. Wherever they are oppressed, confined, or made to perform the drudgery, we may be sure the men are barbarians. But I do not believe there is now or ever was a nation which treated their women with such kindness and consideration, tenderness and respect, as we Americans do ours. Here they are educated to command esteem, and considered as they deserve to be, the guardians of domestic honor and happiness, friends and companions of man.[1]

Although Romelee's analysis of woman's role makes no mention of political rights or the state, the appropriate status of women is clearly enunciated: women are equal (not oppressed), respected, and educated for a special place in the social order. They are to be "guardians of domestic honor" and, within that sphere, "companions" of their spouses. This passage briefly summarizes a set of political and social beliefs about the relative contributions of men and women to the American polity. In a sense, what is missing from the passage—overt political references—is as telling as what is included. The world of political ideas, which is discussed at length in *Northwood,* is the world of men.

Northwood, along with Catharine Maria Sedgwick's *Hope Leslie,* also published in 1827, demonstrates how fiction expresses the political culture of a period. Both novels are particularly concerned with the place of women within the political community. Comparison of the novels reveals that while both support the existing political system, *Hope Leslie* questions women's subordination to authority, which *Northwood* defends as essential to the success of the political order.

The two novels were both popular in their time. *Northwood,* Hale's first published work of fiction, led to her assumption of the editorship of the *Ladies' Magazine* later in 1827. *Hope Leslie* was Sedgwick's third novel and her greatest critical success.[2] . . . [Like *Hope Leslie,*] *Northwood* met the demand for patriotic literature; as the *Boston Spectator and Ladies' Album* put it, "*Northwood* is strictly an American novel, and relates only to the common events of life which are daily passing in our country. . . . We venture to say the taste that is not gratified with such scenes and characters . . . must have grown morbid by feasting too much on foreign production."[4]

Constructing the Political Culture

Through authorial comments, plots, approved characters, symbolism, and other devices, both of these early nineteenth-century novels participate in the dominant political culture of New England. In 1827, readers of Hale's fiction were likely to share certain tenets of that culture: reverence for the Founders, belief in the importance of the small property-owner, and the conviction that partisan politics was men's business. At the same time, certain subgroups within the society rejected aspects of the larger culture. For example, members of the flourishing Shaker communities practiced celibacy, held property in common, and subscribed to equality of the sexes.

The political culture of a society is maintained through the process of political socialization. Individuals "learn" the proper attitudes toward government and politics from several sources.[5] In the nineteenth century, novels such as *Northwood,* with its unqualified patriotism, functioned much as modern media do, as part of the socialization process.[6] Hale's statement of purpose reflects her understanding of this public role. In the opening to the first edition of *Northwood* she wishes the book's success to come from "the expression of sentiments which virtue will approve" (1:4). The epigraph reads, "He who loves not his country, can love nothing." Like other republican authors, Hale believed that the public good depended on private virtue. Neither Hale nor Sedgwick would have characterized herself as a political writer, yet their novels contribute to

the political instruction of their readers. Both novels delineate the character traits necessary to sustain the Republic, praise the fundamental political structures of the societies they portray, and reinforce the political beliefs of the reader by recalling the principles on which the nation was founded. Both narratives respond to the many demands of the day for distinctively American novels.[7]

The rapid growth and economic development of the United States subjected the dominant political culture to tension and conflict. Economic and social changes were sweeping the country as the commercial sector flourished, the cities grew, the pace of western expansion quickened, and immigration lessened the homogeneity of the society. Increasing urbanization and the introduction of factories widened class differences, although the political rhetoric emphasized increased opportunity for all. The widespread acceptance of political equality for all white males brought its own set of questions and fears. Reluctant democrats like Cooper questioned whether the common man could exercise complete self-government, while the foreign observer Tocqueville noted that the leveling effects of equality encouraged private, material motives in the citizens.[8] Both Cooper and Tocqueville called attention to a fundamental dilemma of the Republic: whether increased individual equality is compatible with order in the community.

Neither Hale nor Sedgwick attempted to address the leading controversies of Jacksonian democracy. In an era when party politics was becoming increasingly a social activity for men, it would have been inappropriate for a female novelist to consider such specific political issues as tariffs in her novel.[9] Nevertheless, both women responded to the general atmosphere of political change in the nation. The primary goal of each author is to present a vision of the Republic in keeping with the widespread movement to "restore" the virtues of the past in an age of rapid economic and social change.[10]

Hale does this directly. Northwood, the ideal homogeneous New England village, composed of the "yeoman farmers" so dear to Jeffersonian thought and bound together by shared belief in the Republic, is very similar to the vision held by Jackson himself. Marvin Meyers summarizes Old Hickory's ideal as a recollection of the revolutionary days of 1776-1800: "Laissez-faire notions were embedded in a half-remembered, half-imagined way of life. When government governed least, society—made of the right republican materials—would realize its own natural moral discipline."[11] Hale's community functions in like manner: each household contributes to the common good, and there are no true divisions of interest within the village.

Sedgwick, by setting her novel in the colonial period, is apparently equally patriotic, but she concentrates on the actions of individuals rather than on the political structure of the community as a whole. She creates in her heroine, Hope Leslie, a character whose highest value is freedom of conscience. In contrast to Hale, Sedgwick emphasizes individual judgment and personal liberty rather than the common good. The most striking feature of Sedgwick's attempt to "restore the republic" is that she expresses her belief in individual liberty primarily through female characters.

For both authors, the family and the position of women within it are central to the political order. The family, which holds distinct roles for men and women, is the building block of the democratic republic. This model is explicitly presented in both **Northwood** and *Hope Leslie*. That Hale and Sedgwick differ in their primary values is revealed in their treatment of women. For Hale, women play an important role in the Republic, but only in subordination to community and family needs. Sedgwick, while not directly attacking society or the family, exhibits her choice of liberty as the primary value through the creation of strong independent characters who defy the community for conscience's sake. Furthermore, Sedgwick reveals her own ambivalence about the position of women in an egalitarian society by using females to illustrate the tension between the individual and the community.

Hale's Vision of the Republic

Northwood is Hale's vision of the American republic as it functions in the New England town. It is the Republic writ small. Such a political society was patterned after the eighteenth-century understanding of the Hellenic republics: small, homogeneous polities governed by all the free citizens. As Gordon Wood points out, eighteenth-century American patriots understood that the highest goal of such societies was to provide for the public good. The individual citizens were free and possessed certain natural rights, but the common welfare superseded any individual's private demands.[12] In **Northwood**, Hale re-creates such a society and introduces, as the ideal type, Squire Romelee, who acts as a model and explains the system to the foreign visitor.

In republics, both ancient and modern, government officials are amateurs; the citizens take turns fulfilling their obligation to the community by serving in public office. Mr. Romelee has held a minor civil position and has served twice in the legislature: "he considered every freeman under sacred obligations to serve his country whenever and in whatever manner she required his services; and the confidence of his own townsmen placed him, almost every year, in some office, which, had he consulted his inclination or interest, he would unhesitatingly have refused" (1:10).

Maintaining such devotion to the public good is one of the most formidable challenges faced by any republic.

Wood notes that republics were dependent for their survival on the character and spirit of the people. Such character traits as "frugality, industry, temperance, and simplicity—the rustic traits of the sturdy yeoman—were the stuff that made a society strong."[13] Republics cannot depend on fear of the sovereign or an aristocratic class to elicit obedience to the laws, but as the Squire explains philosophically, the freemen of the United States are far more obedient to the laws than are the English masses. Every citizen holds himself "responsible for the execution of those wholesome regulations, he has either directly or indirectly contributed to make, and for the observance of the constitution" (1:164). The laws rest on popular sovereignty, and the citizens are active participants in the political process. The Squire describes all Americans, and Yankees in particular, as "fond of argument"; their debating skills are encouraged by frequent elections. Such public discourse is further enhanced by freedom of the press and the "circulation, too, of newspapers and other periodicals throughout every part of the country" (1:114). Widespread knowledge, public debate, and participation in elections make the citizens feel a greater commitment to the laws.

Every society must socialize its young into its values and cultural traditions; the means of doing so were widely discussed in the early years of the United States. **Northwood** addresses directly the question of how to sustain the character of the citizenry. Public education is seen as an important tool in creating democratic virtue. Romelee explains to the Englishman that "every child in the New England States has the privilege of attending our free schools," and little Mary has received the prize for being "at the head of my class" (1:142-143). The singling out of Mary reflects Hale's strong belief in the importance of female education, a crusade which she sustained in *Godey's* throughout her lifetime. Davidson, however, points out that female education was itself a form of socialization: "women . . . were a primary target of a conservative social message. They should be educated at public expense . . . but educated *to* a certain set of beliefs."[14]

The most important tool for inculcating virtue is the home. The Squire is teaching his children habits of prudence, love of literature and science, and "cherishing in their minds hopes of obtaining the highest honors and privileges their country could bestow" (1:167). The mother's role is to shape character. As Emma Willard said in 1819 in her request for support for a female seminary, the "prosperity [of the nation] will depend on the character of its citizens. The characters of these will be formed by their mothers; and it is through the mothers, that the government can control the character of its future citizens."[15]

This attention to the role of women in the Republic has been documented by a number of scholars. Mary Beth

Norton described the changes in women's own political consciousness that resulted from the American Revolution. Their participation in the war effort took specifically domestic forms, including the boycotting of British products and managing the family farm or establishment while their husbands took up arms.[16] According to Linda Kerber, the war increased the salience of politics for many colonial women but did not grant them any increased independence. Instead, as the necessity of creating and preserving virtue in the citizenry became an important issue, women "claimed a significant political role, though [they] played it in the home."[17] The republican mother had to be well educated and politically aware, although her only participation in political decision-making would be through others—her husband and sons.

This attitude prevailed for many decades. In 1852 Hale wrote in her "Editors' Table":

> How American women should vote: "I control seven votes, why should I desire to cast one myself?" said a lady who, if women went to the polls, would be acknowledged as a leader. This lady is a devoted, beloved wife, a faithful, tender mother; she has six sons. She *knows* her influence is paramount over the minds she has carefully trained. She *feels* her interests are safe confided to those her affection has made happy. She *trusts* her country will be nobly served by those whom her example has taught to believe in goodness, therefore she is proud to vote by her proxies. This is the way American women should vote, namely, by influencing rightly the votes of men.[18]

The implicit message of **Northwood** is the same. The Romelees' Thanksgiving feast exemplifies the way women are to support the political order. While at the table, the Squire and an English visitor discuss political topics: education, the self-sufficiency of the Republic, and relations with Great Britain. Mrs. Romelee and her daughters serve; their conversation is not reported. But their role is revealed when Frankford laughingly asks Romelee if he imagines that currant wine and ginger beer are connected to the preservation of liberty, and is sharply reminded of the place of tea in the Revolution. Everything at the feast has come from Romelee's farm and has been made by Mrs. Romelee and her daughters; thus, the women are fundamental to the political and economic independence of the United States, and their efforts allow men the luxury of political debate. They show their patriotism by carrying out their domestic duties.[19]

As the ideal of republican womanhood, Mrs. Romelee is far more important to Hale's novel than the romantic lead, Susan Redington. Mrs. Romelee's relationship to her husband exemplifies order in the family commonwealth. She is an intelligent woman, respected by her husband, but she does not consider disobeying him.

When Mr. and Mrs. Brainard ask to adopt one of the Romelee children, Sidney, Hale shows us a model discussion between the Romelee parents, and then gives Mr. Romelee the last word. After that, "Mrs. Romelee wept; but she urged no more objections" (1:40). Mr. Romelee's death in an accident reveals most about the position of women and the parameters of their freedom. Mr. Romelee is brought home wounded in a fall. When the doctor comes to examine him, Mr. Romelee urges his wife to leave the room, saying, "But you must . . . it will overcome you." She replies, "My husband . . . you must not bid me go; I cannot leave you" (2:117). In the phrase "you must not bid me go" is embodied a precise balance of her independent desires and her unwillingness to disobey her husband. When Romelee does succumb, almost his last words are "Sidney, be a father to these little ones, and protect your mother" (2:124). The father thus transfers protection of his wife to his eldest son, who will now represent the household. It is, in fact, the sons as a group who decide how to divide up the farm and care for the various family members.

Throughout **Northwood,** women left on their own have few resources. When Sidney, deceived by the villain's forged letters into believing that Susan has broken off their relationship, remains on his regained southern plantation, Susan promptly becomes ill and nearly dies. Another young woman, Zemira, when separated from her beloved, "seemed fast declining" (1:256). Susan's mother proudly supports her daughter for some years after her husband's death, but dies without really being able to provide for her. Mrs. Romelee requires her sons' assistance. Women are both praised and honored for their contribution to the Republic, but nowhere does Hale indicate any expectation of independence on their part.

Both the plot and the characters of **Northwood** are designed to show the contrast between the republican village and other ways of life. Like other commentators of the time, Hale believes that republics are threatened by heterogeneity, luxury, loss of virtue, and failure of equality—evils found in less fortunate places. To demonstrate, Hale sends her hero, Sidney Romelee, to the South as a young boy and gives Sidney an English friend who can be properly astonished at the virtues of New England life.

The slaveholding South is perceived as a threat to the achievements of northern society.[20] For example, Sidney, a promising scholar as a youth, once he reaches the South is idle. His southern family, a contrast to the Romelee household, does not teach him necessary virtues. Lydia Romelee, Sidney's aunt, is a negative example of womanhood. A beauty, Lydia was not taught self-government in her youth. Though she was engaged to a local farmer, on a trip to Boston she met Mr. Brainard, a plantation owner from South

Carolina, and soon married him. Her jilted lover attributed her fickleness "more to her injudicious education than to her heart" (1:19). She is, indeed, rather ignorant: not only is she unaware that her husband is a Roman Catholic, but in the South she is startled to find herself surrounded in her household by Negroes for whom her husband feels responsibility. Childless, she and her husband drift apart. Their activities illustrate the absence of community. They go separately to church, and he keeps himself busy with theater and other mild forms of dissipation. Much later in the novel, when Brainard, now a widower, dies during Sidney's trip up North, there is an implicit contrast with the death of Sidney's father. Romelee dies surrounded by his wife and children; Brainard dies quite alone.

Young Sidney falls in love with a beautiful girl named Zemira, who exemplifies the weaknesses of untrained young womanhood. When Sidney declares himself, she startles him by announcing that she is already secretly married and begging for his help. In comparison to her New England sisters, Zemira has little personal freedom and has developed little strength of character. The Romelee girls, and Susan, are rational creatures who can appropriately choose their own husbands. Zemira, instead, acts impulsively and nearly destroys her own happiness and her family's. At the same time Hale guarantees Zemira's future by making her secret lover none other than her New England schoolmaster, a man who can train her properly.[21] Sidney reads Stuart's letters to Zemira and concludes:

> He is worthy of her. . . . He sought her not as a toy for the moment, but to make her his friend, his companion through life. . . . I am not worthy of Zemira, for I could not guide aright her gentle spirit. . . . Why am I thus inferior to Stuart? . . . Had I remained in New Hampshire and won my way from the plough to the honors of a college, I should not now be envying the superior acquirements of even Stuart. . . . But luxury has undone me. (2:6-7)

In fact, the restoration of Sidney's virtue is completed when, due to his uncle's death, he himself becomes for a season a simple New England schoolmaster.

To symbolize the interdependence of family and community, Hale dovetails her plot with public occasions: a wedding, a Thanksgiving, a church service, and a funeral. Even such apparently private concerns as landscaping and house furnishing become public and patriotic: though the Romelees had at first planted "Lombardy poplars, an exotic" around their house, they "had already discovered their error . . . this was evinced by the young elms and maples planted between the poplars" (1:71). The chief ornament of the sitting room is "over the mantel piece, the eagle . . . in his beak he held a scroll, on which was inscribed the talisman of American liberty—E pluribus unum" (1:73-74).

The relation of the individual and society is symbolized by Sidney's dream. As a child Sidney almost drowns, but is saved by his father. After his father's death, when he despairs because "I am nothing, for I can do nothing; I am neither educated for a profession, nor have I habits of industry to gain a subsistence by labor" (2:131), he dreams his father again comes to rescue him, telling him to "do your duty; then may you expect happiness" (2:133). This dream implies that the individual can only become "something," rather than "nothing," by accepting his ties to his family and to the community values.

By drawing the parallel between Sidney's relation to his father and the central force of the community, Hale presents an essentially nostalgic vision of happiness. Virtue is seen as developing sequentially through the three levels of community organization—family, village, and country—and the basis of this virtue is family instruction. Women at home are essential to the whole system. The individual, male of female, supports the community and receives support in turn. The idealized village of Northwood is Hale's prescription for the concerns of the early Jacksonian era. If Americans would pay heed to her model household and village, the best features of the Republic could be preserved in the face of social and economic change. . . .

Northwood, in 1852, had its subtitle changed from A Tale of New England to Life North and South: Showing the True Character of Both. The main additions, apart from some name changes such as Romelee to Romilly and Susan to Annie, are a medial chapter entitled "The Destiny of America," largely concerned with slavery, and a final chapter that shows how Sidney assumes control of his plantation. Hale's position on slavery is quite clear: the best thing that can happen to the slave is to be converted to Christianity in the United States and then sent to Africa to establish a higher civilization. A year later, in a novel entitled Liberia, she again used fiction to give a fuller exposition of these views.

The 1852 additions are a natural extension of Hale's conviction that women must transmit the belief system of the community. Sidney instructs his new bride that she will be required to teach the slaves their religious duties. It is the job of woman to lead her husband and "her family on gently but surely to happiness and heaven." The Squire's posthumous journal, which Sidney and his bride read together, reminds them that "in this soul education pious women are the most efficient instructors."[52] The position of women in the South is thus an extension of the original concept of republican motherhood: women must inculcate the attitudes and beliefs of the larger culture in their slaves as in their children.

Strikingly, we never hear Annie's words on slavery or the duties assigned to her. The villain of the piece almost succeeds in breaking off the marriage by forging a letter from Annie in the North to Sidney in the South, in which Annie tells her fiance that she could not go south and "be a partaker in the sin of slavery." When the trick is cleared up, Sidney gives Annie a letter containing "a full confession" of his position as a slaveholder and asks her to be "as frank in expressing your own views." But narrative summary substitutes for Annie's voice. "Annie's reply was brief, but warm with sympathy for his feelings, and assurances of her co-operations."[53] There is no expectation that the heroine will or should express individual conscience against husband or established social codes; such stubborn insubordination, in fact, was the destructive tactic of the forged letter. Furthermore, by 1852 Annie's silence was itself a political statement, aligning her with women powerless to overturn slavery or to change their own position in society. . . .

Notes

[1] Sarah Josepha Hale, *Northwood* (Boston: Bowles and Dearborn, 1827), 1:187-188. Unless noted, all citations are to the first edition, which varies in many small details, including names, from the second (1852). All further citations to the first edition are found in the text.

[2] No precise circulation figures exist, and Nina Baym, in *Woman's Fiction: A Guide to Novels by and about Women in America, 1820-1870* (Ithaca, N.Y.: Cornell University Press, 1978), 300-301, has warned against trusting statements about sales and popularity. Nevertheless, the *Boston Spectator and Ladies Album* for April 28, 1827, reports that "Northwood is selling faster than any similar work, which has been for some years published in this city" (135), and Hale herself points out in the preface to the second edition that the book "was republished in London—at that time a very remarkable compliment to an American book" (*Northwood; or, Life North and South*, 2d ed. [New York: H. Long and Brother, 1852], iii). According to one source, this was its fifth U.S. edition (read printing) (Carol Dick Buell, "Sarah Josepha Hale, the Editor of *Godey's Lady's Book*," M.A. thesis, University of Chicago Graduate Library School, 1976, p. 17). . . .

[4] *Boston Spectator and Ladies Album*, February 24, 1827, 57.

[5] For discussion of the political socialization of adults as well as children, see W. Lance Bennett, *Public Opinion in American Politics* (New York: Harcourt, Brace, Jovanovich, 1980); Doris Graber, *Mass Media and American Politics* (Washington, D.C.: Congressional Quarterly Press, 1980); and M. Kent Jennings and Richard G. Niemi, *The Political Character of Adolescence: The Influence of Families and School* (Princeton: Princeton University Press, 1974).

[6] As Cathy Davidson puts it in *Revolution and the Word: The Rise of the Novel in America* (Oxford: Oxford University Press, 1986), "the novel served as a major locus of republican education" (70).

[7] Typical was the call of Sedgwick's friend William Ellery Channing in his remarks "On National Literature" (1830) for a literary Declaration of Independence. See Benjamin T. Spencer, *The Quest for Nationality: An American Literary Campaign* (Syracuse: Syracuse University Press, 1957), for a full discussion.

[8] Cooper's attitudes can be seen most clearly in his social novels, particularly *Home as Found* (1838). See also the discussion of *The Ways of the Hour* in chap. 3, below. For Tocqueville, see *Democracy in America*, trans. George Lawrence, ed. J. P. Mayer and Max Lerner (New York: Harper and Row, 1966), 638-639.

[9] Paula Baker, "The Domestication of Politics: Women and American Political Society, 1780-1920," *American Historical Review* 89 (1984): 620-647. Baker describes the development of the Jacksonian party system in terms of its social functions for the male citizens. As the vast majority of men gained the franchise during the 1820s, political participation became a "fraternal" and social practice.

[10] Marvin Meyers, *The Jacksonian Persuasian: Politics and Belief* (Stanford, Calif.: Stanford University Press, 1957).

[11] Ibid., 31.

[12] Gordon S. Wood, *The Creation of the American Republic, 1776-1787* (Chapel Hill: University of North Carolina Press, 1969), 55.

[13] Ibid., 52.

[14] Davidson, *Revolution and the Word*, 62.

[15] Emma Willard, "Plan for Improving Female Education," in Willystine Goodsell, ed., *Pioneers of Women's Education in the United States* (New York: AMS Press, 1970), 58.

[16] Mary Beth Norton, *Liberty's Daughters: The Revolutionary Experience of American Women, 1750-1800* (Boston: Little, Brown, 1980), esp. chap. 6, 155-194.

[17] Linda K. Kerber, *Women of the Republic: Intellect and Ideology in Revolutionary America* (Chapel Hill: University of North Carolina Press, 1980), 12.

[18] *Godey's Lady's Book* 44 (1852): 293.

[19] Hale carefully reveals the limits of these duties: the Romelee women work only in the house, and the poorest

farmer insists on hurrying home because "he feared his wife would work too hard, and women had never ought to do any thing out of doors" (2:224). Alexis de Tocqueville confirms that "you will never find American women in charge of the external relations of the family, managing a business, or interfering in politics; but they are also never obliged to undertake rough laborer's work or any task requiring hard physical exertion. . . . If the American woman is never allowed to leave the quiet sphere of domestic duties, she is also never forced to do so" (*Democracy in America*, 601).

[20] William R. Taylor claims, in *Cavalier and Yankee: The Old South and American National Character* (New York: George Braziller, 1961), that "the South which Sarah Hale created as an antipode to her North is less a place than a moral climate: an expression of what the North lacked and what the emergent Yankee needed" (123). According to Anne Norton, *Alternative Americas: A Reading of Antebellum Political Culture* (Chicago: University of Chicago Press, 1986), southerners defined themselves with a different set of cultural beliefs. As she contrasts the two regions, "While New Englanders were rocking in the bosom of Jesus, neither fed nor coddled, but rather weaned and selfless, Southerners were suckled by nature. Raised in a balmy climate, they were accustomed to regard nature as an indulgent and beneficent mother. . . . Puritan families were characterized by the absolute and arbitrary authority of the father. . . . Southern families, conversely, were characterized by indulgent and affectionate care of children" (106). Thus Norton sees southern culture as maternal, close to nature, and more self-expressive than the northern culture.

[21] See Norton, *Liberty's Daughters*, 62, for a discussion of how husbands advised wives on behavior and growth. . . .

[52] Hale, *Northwood* (1852), 392, 402.

[53] Ibid., 369, 390, 392. . . .

Nina Baym (essay date 1992)

SOURCE: "Sarah Hale, Political Writer" in *Feminism and American Literary History: Essays,* Rutgers University Press, 1992, pp. 167-75.

[*In the following excerpt, Baym discusses the political nature of Hale's writings and describes a shift she sees in them from an interest in general political issues to an emphasis on women's role in society.*]

Sarah Josepha Hale, author of poems, stories, sketches, a play, novels, and several home reference books, is remembered chiefly for her lengthy tenure (1837-77) as editor of *Godey's Lady's Book,* the most widely read women's magazine of its day. Using her position year after year to advance the doctrine of separate spheres for women and men, Hale is assumed by most critics to have exerted considerable influence on the gender ideology and cultural mores of the nineteenth-century American middle class.[1]

The doctrine of the separate spheres was once thought to reflect reality; now it is recognized as a rhetorical construct designed to intervene in cultural life but over whose content there was no consensus. Contemporary feminist scholars differ over their descriptions of the doctrine, their assessment of its liberating potential for women, and, therefore—explicitly or implicitly—their judgment of Hale's work.[2] Everybody agrees, however, that Hale was firmly committed to keeping women out of politics and that she used the concept of women's sphere to further this goal.

In *Declarations of Independence,* for example, Barbara Bardes and Suzanne Gossett cite an **"Editor's Table"** from the 1852 *Lady's Book* where Hale belittles the women's rights movement. Women should vote, she writes, "by influencing rightly the votes of men"; she quotes a woman "who, if women went to the polls, would be acknowledged as a leader," to the effect that, since she controls the seven votes of her husband and six sons, "why should I desire to cast one myself?"[3] Bardes and Gossett see the editorial as a non-political document opposing women's involvement in politics. But such a reading assumes in advance that casting a ballot is the only way to be political, which, I would argue, is precisely the view that Hale is attacking here. Her editorial can (and in my view should) be read as pragmatically insisting that any issue to be decided at the polls is better served by seven votes than by one. Hale implies that it is shortsighted, selfish, and just plain bad politics for one woman to insist on casting a ballot in person when she can deliver seven votes by staying home. The position advanced here is certainly controversial, arguably illogical, but thoroughly political.

Again, Nicole Tonkovich Hoffman, who argues that Hale's work for women's education and women's occupations should be recognized as political, insists at the same time that Hale resisted such mainstream political issues as abolition and women's rights.[4] I would argue contrariwise that these two issues were extremely important to her in the 1850s—the **"Editor's Table"** discussed above, after all, is written in opposition to women's rights. The mammoth biographical and historical compendium **Woman's Record** (1853) is also explicitly and implicitly directed against that movement. As for abolition, two of the books Hale published in the early 1850s—a revised version of her 1827 novel **Northwood** (1852) and a historical novel **Liberia** (1853)—explicitly attacked it and supported colonization. Therefore, if women's rights and abolition are ipso facto political issues, Hale was very much an active political writer, at least in the decade before the Civil War. The problem, of course, is that from "our" point of view she argued for the wrong side in both instances.

My hypothesis here is simply that Hale was a profoundly political writer throughout her career. Born in New Hampshire in 1787, she was shaped intellectually, ideologically, and politically by the agitations and values of New England during the early republican era. From first to last she wrote on behalf of a vision of the United States as a Christian republic destined to lead the world into the millennium. She was not an individualist; she defined women and men in relation to each other, to the nation, and to the nation's goals. While she assumed that many human tasks would necessarily be allocated according to gender in any nation, she also saw the United States as uniquely responsive to female participation in the polity—this, indeed, was one of its claims to greatness. One field in which women might contribute to the national well-being was literature; illustrious foremothers like Mercy Otis Warren, Hannah Adams, Sarah Wentworth Morton, and Judith Sargent Murray testified amply to the compatibility of a literary career and womanly republican duties.

These convictions remained constant in Hale's work; others changed over time. Her views of appropriate gender activities, her very definitions of *man* and *woman,* altered dramatically, along the lines of a transformation from Enlightenment to Victorian ideologies that I have discussed earlier in this volume. Hale's writing in the late 1820s defined *woman* as a rational being, like *man.* In the enlightened republican patriarchy that Hale took the United States to be, woman's main tasks—the socially subordinate duties of helpmeet and mother—followed logically from her reproductive capacity and bodily weakness. By the eve of the Civil War Hale had come to define *woman* as a spiritual being, not at all like man, who had now become purely material; woman's tasks—no longer socially subordinate—were to harness and guide his brute force, to provide moral leadership for the nation and the world. Rationality had more or less disappeared from this picture; the nation—whether or not it had ever in fact functioned as a harmonious, hierarchical commonwealth—was now perceived as a scene threatened by atomistic fragmentation and chaotic competition. In this scene *woman* was redefined as man's opposite and alternative; she was, therefore, enjoined from action that simply replicated his behavior. If, in cultural terms, Victorianism is supplanting Enlightenment thinking here, it is not difficult to infer specific historical and political pressures behind the transformation. National survival remains Hale's obsession.

In the discussion that follows I am going to talk about Hale's independent writings rather than her work as

editor of the *Lady's Book,* although I suspect that the journal would reflect similar continuities and changes. Her first novel, *Northwood, A Tale of New England* (1827), was about national identity and republican politics. It centers on the disparities and divisions between North and South and proposes to unite the nation by instituting a New England hegemony over the South. In line with the republican vision of a nation as constituted by the character and virtue of its citizens Hale assumes that the United States must have one character and identifies New England as the source of that character. The colonization of the South by New England is accomplished by sending the technical hero of the book, Sidney Romilly of New Hampshire, South to be adopted by a wealthy aunt and uncle.[5] The real hero of the book, however, is Sidney's father, Squire Romilly, the patriarch who embodies the ideal republican character. Allowing Sidney to go South is his rational decision to subordinate parental affection to Sidney's future welfare, since the family cannot afford to send him to college. But the nation is served as well: The underdeveloped South becomes a fair field for the industry and virtue of a surplus New England population, whose activity in turn incorporates it into the nation.

Northwood develops a bildungsroman around Sidney, who has to return North as a young man for further character development as well as to find a New England bride to help him plant a New England dynasty in the South; it also contains a few love stories. The first thirteen of the thirty chapters in the 1827 novel, however, contain little story material, and even the late-developing romances are subordinated to such discursive aims as describing the ideal American woman. Much of the book surveys New England life and character through a technique of interweaving narrator description and commentary with the male characters' political and patriotic discussion. As Lawrence Buell observes, its "return of the native" device creates a "comparatist but still essentially Yankee perspective" that allows Hale to anatomize "New England character and institutions from both an insider's and an outsider's angle of vision."[6] Moreover, since the returning Sidney is accompanied by an English friend, Hale is able to work her comparison three ways; if she partitions the nation to contrast North and South, she unifies it to contrast the United States with England.

Bardes and Gossett observe that "the world of political ideas, which is discussed at length in *Northwood,* is the world of men," and their point is well taken to the extent that the discussants of these ideas in the book are, indeed, male characters.[7] It is certainly reasonable to expect that, if a book is situating women within the field of politics, it will show them engaging in political discussion; this does not happen in *Northwood.* The lengthy encomiums on the female New England character focus on rationality, self-control, industry, frugality—to be sure, precisely the traits that are valued in men and hence not constitutive of sexual difference—but at no time do women appear to function in the public, political world. But Hale represents the domestic world within which women operate as resonant with political significance in every detail. The Romilly women, for example, enunciate political statements by wearing clothes made from American fabrics and preparing food and drink from native produce. When the Englishman Mr. Frankford laughingly asks Squire Romilly if he imagines "that currant wine or ginger-beer are at all connected with the preservation of your liberties," the squire reminds him of the significance of tea in American-English history (*Northwood,* 94).

More generally, republican ideology held obsessively to the conviction that luxury and extravagance were destructive to citizen virtue and national independence and believed that extravagant women in particular had been responsible throughout history for the fall of nations. (This point of view has not disappeared, as residual political criticism of Nancy Reagan's extravagance makes clear.) The prudent young American woman preserves and contributes to the national welfare when she is frugal and industrious in her home. And even more, when she chooses the true-hearted, hard-working American man of modest means over the leisured European aristocrat she stabilizes and perpetuates American values. In short, while it cannot be denied that Hale presents a fully domestic picture of American womanhood in *Northwood* and allocates specifically public concerns to men, it is also true that she politicizes and publicizes the domestic realm within which she situates her women characters.

There is also a second level on which women are implicated in American politics in *Northwood*—the level of discourse rather than story. The narrator of this book is clearly identified as a woman; Hale published the book under her own name. Her constant narrative interpolations alternate with the pronouncements of Squire Romilly and other men in the book, who are in any case her constructions and can speak only the words that she writes for them. Hale is thus writing men, and writing men's political discourse, staking out writing—and reading—as ways by which women could appropriate politics for themselves. Insofar as the public sphere is constituted by print, women are free to enter it. When we consider that the novel, as a genre, was already conventionally perceived as a female domain dominated by love and fashion we may think of *Northwood* as a counterstatement about what the novel—the American novel—and its American women readers might be or become. Their literary activity represents a public extension of the republican mother's home task of constructing the characters and value systems of her sons and embodies the cultural work of the "republican public mother." Thus, the national character as represented in *Northwood's* admirable

Squire Romilly is doubled and shadowed by a female version of the national character expressed as the figure of Hale the woman author, a figure who is equally politically engaged, savvy, and significant as the squire himself—a figure who authorizes the squire and thus in some sense is prior to him.

Hale was always opposed to slavery, but in the 1827 *Northwood* she approached it simply as one among many cultural sectional differences, showing less concern for the institution's disregard of the slave's human rights than for its bad effect on the slaveholder character. She saw in slavery the main explanation for the white Southerners' lack of (New England) moral fiber; the institution freed them from the healthy imperatives of the work ethic. It also puffed up their pride and gave them false—indeed, unAmerican—notions of class. Insofar as these criticisms implied an antislavery position, however, that position was qualified by a pragmatic sense that gradual emancipation was the only way to avoid secession or violence, either of which would terminate the union. She took refuge in the platitude that, since God had permitted slavery, he would end it in his own good time. She maintained that Africans could never become part of an American republic based in citizen equality because they could never become equal to whites. While believing that Africans probably *were* inferior to white people, she was more certain that white Americans would never *accept* blacks as equals, and so would always prevent blacks from functioning as citizens. Emancipated slaves, therefore, needed a republic of their own. From the first, accordingly, Hale advocated Liberian colonization and, in the Uncle Tom-inspired 1852 revision of *Northwood,* this political position became much more prominent.

Northwood, while only modestly successful, led to Hale's appointment as editor of a newly established Boston-based journal, the *Ladies' Magazine,* which continued until Louis Godey bought and merged the magazine with his *Lady's Book* in 1837. Hale wrote much of the material in the *Ladies' Magazine,* including a series of "American sketches" collected in *Sketches of American Character* (1829) and *Traits of American Life* (1835). These lightly narrativized essays furthered and sophisticated the discursive strategies of *Northwood,* whereby the authorial persona commented without gender embarrassment or disguise on a wide range of public and national topics. As *Sketches* announces in its preface, "it is the *free* expression of that spirit [the spirit of man], which, irradiated by liberty, and instructed by knowledge, is all but divine, that gives to Americans their peculiar characteristics. To exhibit some of these traits, originated by our free institutions, in their manifold and minute effects on the minds, manners, and habits of the citizens of our republic, is the design of these sketches."[8] In *Traits* a piece called "Political Parties" makes an important distinction between partisan politics and other political activity and identifies suprapartisan politics as particularly appropriate for women. "I do not say," the spokeswoman character explains to her two nieces, "that ladies should abstain from all political reading or conversation; that they should take no interest in the character or condition of their country." She continues, with characteristic rationalist aplomb: "I cannot think, in a land so favoured as ours, such indifference and ignorance is excusable in a rational being. But their influence should be expected to allay, not to excite animosities; their concern should be for their whole country—not for a party."[9]

Suprapartisanship in American life has always been a political strategy for assailing the other person's party, but for Hale it represented the essence of republicanism—a recognition that one's own interest should always come second to the interest of the whole. Over time suprapartisanship became her ever more gender-specific response to the dangers of disunion posed by North-South differences. If the men of the North and South could not agree, perhaps women's influence over them could keep the union together. For Hale, then, suprapartisanship was women's proper way of being political in the Unionist cause, not a sign of women's withdrawal from the political issues agitating the polity.

In 1838, a year after she became editor of the *Lady's Book,* Hale serialized her one historical closet drama in its pages. The subject of this five-act Shakespearean tragedy, **Ormond Grosvenor,** is nominally the American Revolution (according to the preamble it was written to "illustrate the spirit of the American Revolution, or the struggle between principles of civil Liberty—them first developing their power in this country—and the prescriptive privileges of aristocratic domination in the old world")[10] but is actually North-South relations. The action takes place in South Carolina and centers on a hero who rejects his English title and fights with the Americans. This story line, couched in blank verse, permits such lofty Enlightenment articulations of American republican ideals as the following:

> We'll raise, on Liberty's broad base,
> A structure of wise government, and show
> In our new world, a glorious spectacle
> Of social order. Freemen, equals all,
> By reason swayed, self-governed, self-
>   improved,
> And the electric chain of public good,
> Twined round the private happiness of each.[11]

The contrast between England and America tries to establish by implication that North and South are more like each other than either is like the nations of the Old World. The partnership of North and South is also expressed in prose, as a plain soldier from New England explains to his southern counterpart that "this war is permitted by an over-riding wise Providence, not only to make America free, but as all the states must unite to carry it on, we shall become, in a good measure, one people; and this we shall remain forever. All our perils will be shared together, and our glories must be enjoyed. . . . Like brothers, shoulder to shoulder, we will go on through this war, and then like brothers, hand in hand, will we proceed in the march of improvement."[12]

From the time that she became editor of the *Lady's Book,* however, Hale also increasingly focused on women as local agents in history as well as its recorders, commentators, and hero trainers. For example, she serialized much of Elizabeth Ellet's *Women of the American Revolution* before it appeared in book form. She also published many historical tales featuring female heroism.[13] Sensitive to emergent Victorian ideology, she also began to stress the moral efficacy of women's role, shifting from post-Revolutionary, rationalist theories of republican womanhood toward Victorian theories of intuitive womanly spirituality. Women began to occupy the center of her world's stage.

By the 1850s Hale's political work began oscillating—as it dealt with slavery, women's rights, and territorial expansion—between a residual republican rationalism and an essentialist gender theory identifying redemptive Christian spirituality with the feminine and looking to this spirituality for solutions to social ills. Behind the development of this essentialist view one senses not only the pressure of Victorian mores but also a loss of confidence in the power of reason to override sectional interests. Differently stated, Hale began to lose faith in the human nature on which her idea of the nation had been predicated. In attributing gender to traits that earlier she had taken as constitutive of general human nature, she was looking for a way to install in feminine nature a salvific force that she had not previously felt a need for.

After passage of the Fugitive Slave Law seemed to focus all the various disagreements and differences between North and South on the single issue of slavery, and abolitionism became more vocal and socially respectable in the North, Hale stepped up her campaign for colonization. When the women's rights movement—a movement affiliated from the first with abolitionism—got actively under way Hale conceded that it signified a new social awareness among women but deplored its private, selfish focus. For women to organize on their own behalf (or worse still, on behalf of a disunifying political project) seemed to her to be just the wrong thing. As for expansionism, she saw this movement alternately as capable of destroying whatever virtue was left in the American polity or—if women provided spiritual leadership—as destined to spread republican Christianity throughout the globe. These revisions in Hale's cultural practice were energetically expressed in 1852 and 1853. In 1852 she entered the lists against *Uncle Tom's Cabin* with a revision of **Northwood** which pointed up what Hale now claimed were her novel's original antiabolitionist, pro-union sentiments.

> **Northwood** was written when what is now known as "Abolitionism" first began seriously to disturb the harmony between the South and the North. In the retirement of my mountain home, no motives save the search for truth and obedience to duty prompted the sentiments expressed in this work; nor has a wider sphere of observation, nor the long time for examination and reflection changed, materially, the views I had then adopted. These views, based on the conditions of the compact the framers of the Constitution recognized as lawful, and the people of the United States solemnly promised to observe, have been confirmed by a careful study of the word of God, as well as of human history. (**Northwood**, iv)

The new **Northwood** presented an extraordinary millennial vision of American slavery as the seedbed of a Christian Africa that would be produced by emancipated, repatriated blacks. American slavery became a blessed, divinely ordained event—"The mission of American slavery is to Christianize Africa" (**Northwood**, 408). The paragon Squire Romilly was reconstructed as a deep thinker on the slavery question; the last chapter of the 1852 **Northwood** contains extracts from his newly created journal on such topics as "Of Slavery and its Reformers," "What the Bible Says of Slavery," "Is American Slaveholding Sinful?" "How the Slave Is to Be Made Free," and "Of the Bible and the American Constitution" (**Northwood**, 394-399). Sidney Romilly uses his father's journal as a virtual Bible when running his plantation; Hale thus covertly imbues her own written words with the power to unite the nation. To Sidney's wife she allocates a more conventional womanly task (though a task that, in southern political life, was illegal)—educating the slaves for freedom and Liberia. Even as she denies Africans a place in the American polity, Hale affirms European imigration: "Let them come. We have room for all, and food, too; besides, we want their work, and they want our teaching. We shall do each other mutual good" (**Northwood**, 165).

The revised **Northwood** did not expand on the Liberian alternative, so Hale followed it with a second antiabolitionist, pro-colonization work in 1853, **Liberia; or, Mr. Peyton's Experiments.** This book combined fiction, history, and geography to propagandize for Liberia. Hale went so far as to claim that the emigrating former slaves would not only bring Christianity to Africa; they would bring Christianity itself to a higher level of development than it had known among the Anglo-Saxons. How could this be achieved by individuals who were clearly inferior to Anglo-Saxon whites? she asked rhetorically: "Does the dark race, in all its varieties, possess a capacity for understanding and living out the deep laws of the world's ruler, Christianity, as the offspring of the followers of Odin never did and never can, understand and act it?" And she answered:

> If the old Egyptian Sesostris had paused to contemplate the illiterate wanderers of Greece, to whom Cadmus was just striving to make known the letters of Phoenicia, would not Plato and Aristotle have seemed as impossible to him as the existence in Africa of a higher Christianity than has yet been seen seems to us? Would not the present position of the Teutonic race have appeared equally incredible to the founder of the Parthenon, the loungers in the gardens of the Academy?[14]

One sees here a flourishing of historical knowledge typical of many republican women who, as I have argued in "From Enlightenment to Victorian," appropriated history as a sign of their mental equality with men. *Liberia* itself is in part a historical narrative, including a brief general history of Africa as well as a detailed history of the settlement of Liberia along with geographical segments detailing the country's climate and agricultural possibilities. The plot follows several emancipated African Americans as they undergo various humiliating defeats while attempting to live decent lives in the United States and Canada. They blossom out into full humanity only when they emigrate. One character says, "The first moment I stepped my foot on Liberia, I felt like a different man. . . . It is a blessed thing to be able to bring up a family of children where they need not be ashamed of their color, and where their feelings as well as their rights are respected" (*Liberia*, 219). Insofar as there is a main character, it is a black woman named Keziah, a strong-minded heroine whose force of personality and capacity for principled thinking makes her the leader of the group— a black, feminized version of the republican hero, leading her little band of pilgrims to the new New World.

On the penultimate page of **Northwood** in its 1852 version Hale parts with the reader, "in friendship, I hope," and continues:

> Mine is no partizan book, but intended to show *selfishness* her own ugly image, wherever it appears— north or south: and, also, to show how the good may overcome the evil.

> "Constitutions" and "compromises" are the appropriate work of men: women are conservators of moral power, which, eventually, as it is directed, preserves or destroys the work of the warrior, the statesman, and the patriot.

> Let us trust that the pen and not the sword will decide the controversy now going on in our land; and that any part women may take in the former

mode will be promotive of peace, and not suggestive of discord. (*Northwood,* 407)

Notes

[1] There are no recent biographies of Hale. Ruth E. Finley, *The Lady of Godey's: Sarah Josepha Hale* (Philadelphia: Lippincott, 1932); and Isabelle Webb Entrikin, *Sarah Josepha Hale and Godey's Lady's Book* (Philadelphia: Lancaster, 1946), are the most cited studies. Like virtually everything else written on Hale, they focus on the *Lady's Book* (which they call—what it was not called in its own time—*Godey's*). For scholars who see Hale as Louis Godey's silenced subordinate rather than a power in her own right, see Frank Luther Mott, *History of American Magazines* (Cambridge: Harvard University Press, 1938), 1:580-594; and Cheryl Walker, *The Nightingale's Burden* (Bloomington: Indiana University Press, 1982), 34. Critics who see her as perniciously powerful include Susan Phinney Conrad, *Perish the Thought; Intellectual Women in Romantic America, 1830-1860* (New York, Oxford University Press, 1976); Ann Douglas, *The Feminization of American Culture* (New York: Knopf, 1977); and David Leverenz, *Manhood and the American Renaissance* (Ithaca: Cornell University Press, 1987).

[2] Linda K. Kerber's "Separate Spheres, Female Worlds, Woman's Place: The Rhetoric of Women's History," *Journal of American History* 75 (1988): 9-39, is the best exposition of the position that the "spheres" were and are contested discursive formations rather than descriptions of reality. Influential feminist scholarship attacking while reifying the woman's sphere includes Barbara Welter, "The Cult of True Womanhood: 1820-1860," *American Quarterly* 18 (1966): 158-174, reprinted in *Dimity Convictions: The American Woman in the Nineteenth Century* (Athens: Ohio University Press, 1976), 21-41; and Gerda Lerner, "The Lady and the Mill Girl: Changes in the Status of Women in the Age of Jackson," *Mid-Continent American Studies Journal* 10 (1969): 5-15. Revisionary feminist scholarship discerning strength and value in the women's sphere includes Nancy Cott *The Bonds of Womanhood: "Woman's Sphere" in New England, 1780-1835* (New Haven, Conn.: Yale University Press, 1977); Mary Beth Norton, *Liberty's Daughters: The Revolutionary Experience of American Women, 1750-1800* (Boston: Little, Brown, 1980); Linda K. Kerber, *Women of the Republic: Intellect and Ideology in Revolutionary America* (Chapel Hill: University of North Carolina Press, 1980); Mary Ryan, *Cradle of the Middle Class: The Family in Oneida County, New York, 1790-1895* (New York: Cambridge University Press, 1981); Nancy A. Hewitt, *Women's Activism and Social Change: Rochester, New York, 1822-1872* (Ithaca: Cornell University Press, 1984); Mary Beth Norton, "The Evolution of White Women's Experience in Early America," *American*

Historical Review 89 (1984): 593-619; and Paula Baker, "The Domestication of Politics: Women and American Political Society, 1780-1920," *American Historical Review* 89 (1984): 620-647.

[3] Barbara Bardes and Suzanne Gossett, *Declarations of Independence: Women and Political Power in Nineteenth-Century American Fiction* (New Brunswick, N.J.: Rutgers University Press, 1990), 22.

[4] Nicole Tonkovich Hoffman, "Sarah Josepha Hale," *Legacy* 7 (1990): 51.

[5] In citing *Northwood* I use the more accessible revision: *Northwood; or, Life North and South* (New York: H. Long, 1852); when speaking of the 1827 version I use material in the 1852 edition retained from the earlier work. The 1827 subtitle, "A New England Tale," stresses the New England imperialism of Hale's original project. The revised version, and Hale's reasons for revision, are discussed below. Throughout I use the 1852 spelling of the chief characters' family name—Romilly—rather than the 1827 Romelee.

[6] Lawrence Buell, *New England Literary Culture: From Revolution through Renaissance* (New York: Cambridge University Press, 1986), 296. See also William R. Taylor, *Cavalier and Yankee: The Old South and American National Character* (New York: George Braziller, 1961), 96-133, for a discussion of Hale's representation of the southern male (the Cavalier) in contrast to the New Englander (the Yankee).

[7] Bardes and Gossett, *Declarations of Independence,* 17. They also write that *Northwood* addresses general issues of political culture rather than "the leading controversies of Jacksonian democracy" involving commerce (banks and tariffs), urbanization, territorial expansion, immigration, and the trade-off between individualism and order (19). Many of the issues are in fact coded in Squire Romilly's discourse; and it is not caviling to insist that the issue of the North-South divide implicates many or most of these concerns and constitutes, in its own terms, a political issue of the utmost urgency in antebellum America. Moreover, just as Hale's superficially nonpartisan campaign to make Bunker Hill a national monument was actually deeply implicated in Masonic—anti-Masonic politics (see Paul Goodman, *Towards a Christian Republic: Antimasonry and the Great Transition in New England, 1826-1836* [New York: Oxford University Press, 1988], 98), so numerous apparently bland details of *Northwood* might, upon closer study and further research, disclose political implications. Two suggestive instances occur when Squire Romilly opines on the local highway taxation system in a way that must have had immediate political resonance in its own day and when another character contrasts the grasping, money-grubbing Connecticut character to the truly republican New Hampshire type.

A long segment on how to organize and finance public education must have had at least local political resonance. Numerous English-American comparisons along with discussion of how the two countries should relate to each other would certainly have conveyed political meaning to New Englanders in 1827 as well as in 1852.

[8] Sarah Hale, *Sketches of American Character* (Boston: Putnam and Hunt, 1829), 8.

[9] Sarah Hale, *Traits of American Life* (Philadelphia: Carey and Hart, 1835), 127.

[10] Sarah Hale, *Ormond Grosvenor,* in *Godey's Lady's Book* 16 (1838): 33.

[11] Ibid., 50.

[12] Ibid., 146.

[13] See Laura McCall, "'The Reign of Brute Force is Now Over': A Content Analysis of *Godey's Lady's Book,* 1830-1860," *Journal of the Early Republic* 9 (1989): 231-232.

[14] Sarah Hale, *Liberia: or, Mr. Peyton's Experiments* (New York: Harper and Brothers 1853), 185; hereafter cited parenthetically in the text. . . .

Patricia Okker (essay date 1993)

SOURCE: "Sarah Josepha Hale, Lydia Sigourney, and the Poetic Tradition in Two Nineteenth-Century Women's Magazines," *American Periodicals: A Journal of History, Criticism, and Bibliography,* Vol. 3, 1993, pp. 32-42.

[*In the following excerpt, Okker examines Hale's views on women's poetry as reflected in her editing of* Godey's Lady's Book *and* Ladies' Magazine.]

No doubt in part because of her authorship of **"Mary Had a Little Lamb,"** Sarah Josepha Hale—editor first of the *Ladies' Magazine* and then for forty-one years of *Godey's Lady's Book*—is often described in the context of . . . [what Allison Bulsterbaum has called] "mawkish, moralistic poetry" (144). Specifically, Hale is remembered as one of the many nineteenth-century editors who promoted a highly restricted notion of women's poetry. In their respective studies of American women's poetry, in fact, Emily Stipes Watts, Cheryl Walker, and Alicia Suskin Ostriker all cite Hale's declaration in 1829 that "the path of poetry, like every other path in life, is to the tread of woman, exceedingly circumscribed" (*Ladies' Magazine* 2: 142).[2] In many ways, such statements place Hale in what Ostriker has described as the genteel tradition:

> What the genteel tradition demanded of the ladies was that they bare their hearts, gracefully and without making an unseemly spectacle of themselves. They were not to reveal that they had heads, let alone loins. They were not to demonstrate ambition. They were not to lecture on public issues or to speculate on philosophical or religious ones. (31)

Watts and Walker have offered similar characterizations of the genteel expectations of the woman poet, or "poetess." While socially revered, the poetess is bound by expectations of modesty, unassertiveness, and melancholy emotionalism. Denied ambition and rational thought, she is expected to produce poetry spontaneously and to strive for "light" verse (Watts 69; Walker 23-24). Never granted the status of a great poet, she is Mark Twain's Emmeline Grangerford, who produces endless elegies without even having to think and who, in the process, embodies and produces images of women's weakness and passivity.

While scholars have recently examined how some nineteenth-century women poets struggled to evade these poetic restrictions, no one has yet questioned whether Hale was in fact one of the editors/critics who promoted the restricted aesthetics of the poetess. Indeed it is my argument that, while Hale's declaration about the "path of poetry" being "exceedingly circumscribed" appears to endorse the genteel tradition, the body of Hale's periodical work suggests a quite different poetics. In contrast to those critics who expected women to assume the restricted role of the poetess, Hale used the pages of her magazine to expand and glorify women's poetic achievements.

In the essay from which Hale's oft-quoted remark about women's poetry being "circumscribed" comes, Hale does outline what seems to be a restrictive feminine poetic. In this 1829 review of *Guido, and Other Poems,* published under the name of "Ianthe" (and written, in fact, by Emma Embury), Hale contends that the woman poet

> may not revel in the luxuriance of fancies, images and thoughts, or indulge in the license of choosing themes at will, like the lords of creation. She must never for the sake of a subject, forget or forfeit the delicacy of her sex.

Exploring in more detail those themes inappropriate to women's poetry, Hale targets love as especially unsuitable. While she finds Ianthe's love poetry beautiful, Hale wishes the poet had "chosen different themes." In addition to raising thematic restrictions, Hale warns women writers to consider their motives: "Neither anger, ambition, or the love of *fun* must ever inspire a woman," Hale insists; the only appropriate motive is to be inspired by "some deep, affectionate impulse" (*LM* 2: 142-43).

However much Hale's caution about both the themes and motives of the woman poet recalls the genteel critical agenda described by Ostriker, Hale's understanding of women's poetry in the review as a whole challenges the basic assumption of that tradition—namely that women poets should aim for writing "light" verse. Hale's primary criticism of Ianthe's volume of poetry is that it trivializes women's emotional lives by emphasizing the romances of young women. "Love," Hale insists, "should not have been thus exclusively the burden of her song; it is not the sole business of life, nor is a disappointment of the heart the most terrible affliction that can befal [sic] the children of men." Critical of the focus on the "discarded lover" or the "disappointed damsel," Hale urges Ianthe to portray a much greater range of emotional experiences, such as "the kind husband who has an ill-tempered wife" or "the agony of feeling which the fond, faithful wife must endure who has a drunken husband" (*LM*2: 143).

Hale's suggestions for new themes are clearly limited to domestic—specifically marital—relations, but these suggestions also urge women poets to abandon a romantic tradition of defining women only in their obtainment of a husband. While traditional love poetry, in Hale's view, generally ends with the heroine's wedding, Hale encourages women poets to investigate marital life itself. No longer a "light" topic which ends predictably and blissfully, marriage in Hale's view becomes a complex subject more worthy of the woman poet's attention than the simple concerns of the forlorn lover. Hale's discussion of Ianthe's "The Mother's Farewell to Her Wedded Daughter"—a poem Hale praises—demonstrates the emotional richness that she expects from women poets. Rather than represent marriage as an inherently idyllic occasion, Ianthe's poem portrays the wedding as a time of considerable tension: the mother "fears" for her daughter's happiness and mourns her daughter's leaving, yet chooses not to "pale" her daughter's "cheek" with her concerns (qtd. in *LM*2: 143-44). The poet's decision to focus on the mother's point of view, rather than on the daughter's, further intensifies the challenge to the convention that the woman poet avoid emotional complexity. As Joanne Dobson has observed, few nineteenth-century texts by women focus on the full development of a woman's life past marriage (61), yet here Ianthe chooses the point of view of the older woman rather than the more conventional perspective of the blissful bride. While we might regret the implication here that marriage is a woman's destiny, this poem does break the conventional expectations of the poetess: the poem not only questions the happiness assumed in traditional love stories that end in marriage, but also insists that we consider the experiences of an older woman in a moment of considerable anxiety and ambivalence. While the genteel tradition demanded that the woman poet offer little more than simplistic visions of life, Hale praises a

woman poet for creating a moment of considerable conflict, which is itself never resolved.

The difference between Hale's understanding of women's poetry and the genteel tradition of many of her contemporary critics becomes apparent by comparing her review of Ianthe's *Guido* with a review of the same collection published in the *North American Review* in July 1829, just a few months after Hale's essay. While this reviewer is much more laudatory of Ianthe's *Guido* than is Hale, the *North American* praises the volume because—not despite—it is "light literature." As this reviewer explains, Ianthe's volume functions "simply and solely to please." A reader "hoping to see a strong light thrown down into the deep places of human nature, or to find glimpses of a high and far philosophy, would be disappointed." One expecting to "relieve himself of heavy thoughts," on the other hand, "will find them well fitted for his purpose." The lack of emotional depth, however, evidently caused this reviewer no concern, for he concludes the essay by expressing his "pleasure" and "pride" in the "productions of our fair country-women," who have taken "possession of the whole domain of *light* literature" (*NAR* 29:237,240-41; emphasis added). The lengthy discussion of the general aims of poetry that precedes the actual analysis of Ianthe's poetry reinforces the double association made here of "light literature" with women's poetry and great literature with men's. In a direct contradiction of the terms used to praise Ianthe's verse, the reviewer asserts generally that the aims of the great poet

> should be, not solely nor chiefly to bring before the mind pleasant associations and images and allusions, but something far higher,—to unfold to the mental vision, and to stamp upon the heart, the sublimest truths of moral and intellectual being. (*NAR* 29:232)

In contrast to Hale's review which insists that women's poetry be more than beautiful, light verse, this review clearly assumes a poetic hierarchy based on gender: men's poetry must express "the sublimest truths," but women's poetry can be praised simply for being "beautiful" and "light" (*NAR* 29:238).

Hale's later essays challenge even more directly the genteel tradition adopted by many of her contemporaries. In her essay **"Woman the Poet of Nature"** published in *Godey's Lady's Book* in 1837, Hale directly refutes the idea that women's poetic achievements were naturally inferior to men's, and in so doing, she advances a feminized critical discourse of poetry. Basing her argument on the premises that women were inherently more moral than men[3] and that poetry should aim to be moral, Hale concludes that women—not men—are "morally gifted to excel" as poets (*GLB* 14:194). The notion that women should serve as society's moral guardians is hardly unique to Hale, of course, but her use of these feminine terms to identify both women's and men's highest poetic achievements challenges the separate standards used by many other critics. In language remarkably similar to her descriptions of women as the world's moral guardians and instructors, Hale insists here in **"Woman the Poet of Nature"** that the "office of true poetry is to elevate, purify, and soften the human character, and thus promote civil, moral and religious advancement." While the *North American Review* implied that women's poetry is inherently "light," designed "solely to please," Hale insists that all poets—both women and men—have the same weighty responsibilities of individual and national achievement.

In defining poetry's aims in **"Woman the Poet of Nature,"** Hale offers her own narrative of poetry's history. According to Hale, poetry began as a male-dominated form and then blossomed under the influence of women. In the "heathen world," Hale argues, the woman poet had "no place": "Her harp cannot move stones, or tame beasts. She must wait till the flowers bloom and the birds appear." Thus, the greatest poets of this time were men, namely Homer and Virgil, who presented "the lofty and complete picture of national aggrandizement." In the Judeo-Christian world, where people founded pious poetry, the woman poet emerged. Celebrating the Bible as the first pious poetry, Hale notes the achievements not of David or of Solomon, but of Deborah: "The song of Deborah is one of the most beautiful and sublime poems to be found in holy writ" (*GLB* 14:193).

According to Hale's literary history, women's voices transformed and ultimately improved poetry:

> War, the chace [sic], the wine-cup and physical love are the themes of song in which men first delight and excel; nor is it till feminine genius exerts its power to judge and condemn these, always earthly, and often coarse and licentious, strains that the tone of the lyre becomes softer, chaster, more pure and polished and finally, as her influence increases, and she joins the choir, the song assumes that divine character which angels might regard with complacency. (*GLB* 14:194)

Hardly inferior to men, women have brought poetry to the apex of the genre's development. As she explains, "the poetry of man" focuses on the individual "intellect," "passions," and "pride," but the "poetry of woman" expresses the greatest human truths, including "impressions of the Beautiful and the Good," "the love of truth and nature," and "faith in God" (*GLB* 14:195). . . .

Notes

[2] The abbreviations for magazines used in the text are as follows: *LM* for *Ladies' Magazine, GLB* for *Godey's Lady's Book,* and *NAR* for *North American Review.*

[3] Hale frequently promoted this popular idea of sexual difference. In her *Woman's Record,* for instance, she declared that "WOMAN is God's appointed agent of morality, the teacher and inspirer of those feelings and sentiments which are termed the virtues of humanity" (xxxv). . . .

Works Cited

Bulsterbaum, Allison. *"Godey's Lady's Book."* American Literary Magazines: The Eighteenth and Nineteenth Centuries. Ed. Edward E. Chielens. New York: Greenwood, 1986. 144-50.

Dobson, Joanne. *Dickinson and the Strategies of Reticence: The Woman Writer in Nineteenth-Century America.* Bloomington: Indiana UP, 1989. . . .

Hale, Sarah Josepha. *Woman's Record: or, Sketches of All Distinguished Women from 'The Beginning' till* A.D. *1850.* New York: Harper, 1853.

Ostriker, Alicia Suskin. *Stealing the Language: The Emergence of Women's Poetry in America.* Boston: Beacon, 1986.

Walker, Cheryl. *The Nightingale's Burden: Women Poets and American Culture before 1900.* Bloomington: Indiana UP, 1982.

Watts, Emily Stipes. *The Poetry of American Women from 1632 to 1945.* Austin: U of Texas P, 1977.

Susan M. Ryan (essay date 1995)

SOURCE: "Errand into Africa: Colonization and Nation Building in Sarah J. Hale's *Liberia,*" *New England Quarterly,* Vol. LXVIII, No. 4, December, 1995, pp. 558-83.

[*In the following excerpt, Ryan discusses Hale's position, expressed in her novel* Liberia, *that the only way to solve the slavery problem was for the slaves to return to Africa.*]

To many white Americans before the Civil War, the idea of "returning" free blacks and manumitted slaves to Africa sounded like the perfect solution to the United States' increasingly rancorous and violent racial problems. Generally thought a moderate position in its day—compared to radical abolitionist and pro-slavery sentiments—colonizationism has since come to seem (as it seemed to most anti-slavery activists at the time) misguided at best, and venomous at worst, in its attempt to eliminate racial difference within the United States and so to evade the troubling issues such difference inevitably raised. It is no surprise, then, that Harriet Beecher Stowe's advocacy of African colonization near the end of *Uncle Tom's Cabin*—probably the plan's most famous articulation—has elicited innumerable condemnations, lamentations, and apologies in the more than 140 years since the novel's publication. . . .

If Stowe's colonizationist stance troubled anti-slavery activists, they must have been significantly more perturbed by a novel like Sarah J. Hale's *Liberia* (1853), whose portrayals were far more representative of white colonizationists' beliefs.[1] The fact that the book was not mentioned, as far as I have been able to discern, in three of the major anti-slavery periodicals (*Frederick Douglass's Paper,* the *Liberator,* and the *National Anti-Slavery Standard*) in the year of its publication or the year after, may owe something to this discomfort.[2] The April 14, 1854 issue of *Frederick Douglass's Paper* did, however, review two cookbooks that Hale had recently published, with the cutting implication that her attempt to enter into the debate over slavery (possibly in reference to *Liberia,* but more likely to a March 1853 piece in *Godey's Lady's Book* or to the 1852 edition of *Northwood*) was both unwelcome and illegitimate.[3] While the paper considered Stowe's voice acceptable despite her colonizationism, it wanted nothing to do with Hale's writings on slavery, even as positions against which to argue.[4]

This desire to keep Hale out of the conversation has persisted in twentieth-century scholarship. Nina Baym argues that scholars have been reluctant to identify Hale as a political writer, despite the fact that abolition and women's rights were issues of great importance to her, particularly in the 1850s. "The problem," Baym writes, "is that from 'our' point of view [Hale] argued for the wrong side in both instances."[5] Much is to be gained, though, from the exploration of political positions that now seem objectionable and embarrassing; not only do such investigations reveal the tactics and beliefs of important historical actors, but they often reveal unexpected commonalities with those positions we hold in higher esteem. Hale's *Liberia* is remarkable in its embodiment of the prejudices and agendas (hidden and overt) of a particular brand of white colonizationism, yet the novel also represents an apparently sincere and to a large extent religiously motivated reformist project—one strangely similar to the abolitionist fiction whose implications and goals it opposes. Critical investigations of that anti-slavery fiction—its tropes, rhetorical strategies, and political compromises—have helped to elucidate the cultural matrix we call "the slavery issue." I wish to explore that matrix from another perspective, using a text from a decade in which a great deal of fiction about slavery appeared and in which there was substantial belief in fiction's ability to do certain kinds of cultural, even political, work.[6]

Hale's treatment of colonization expresses much of what abolitionists deplored in the American Colonization Society—racism, condescension, fear of blacks, and the desire conveniently to be rid of the "race problem" by expelling non-whites from the United States. But Hale's project is not simply about displacing an unwanted population; she also conceived of it as a means of improving the status and condition of the "African race" as a whole. Colonization, Hale believed, would greatly increase opportunities for erstwhile American blacks to achieve a dignified self-sufficiency insofar as they would finally be relieved of the burden of their "inferiority" to whites and of the virulent racial prejudice that seemed to her irremediable within the United States. Even more compelling for the devoutly Christian Hale was the notion that colonization would provide a means of christianizing and civilizing "heathen" Africa.

Most notable, though, is Hale's incorporation of such widely held colonizationist points of view into a narrative that explores the meanings and possibilities of nationalism; she promotes African colonization as a means not only of preserving the Union as she conceives of it (that is, as Protestant and Anglo-Saxon) but also of replicating, among ex-slaves in a "new" country, American-style nation building, national identity, and citizenship, as she defines them.[7] Liberian colonization in Hale's novel becomes an unusual incarnation of colonialism, in that the departure of blacks from the United States results in two strong nations on the (white) American model rather than a racially and regionally divided (and possibly disintegrating) United States, on the one hand, and a heathen non-nation in Africa, on the other. The implications of such a strategy for both the emigrants and the African natives whose land they would "share" are disturbing indeed.

. . . . .

Liberia: or, Mr. Peyton's Experiments is both a fictional representation of Hale's proposed solution to the slavery question and a piece of pro-colonization propaganda.[8] It depicts a paternalistic Virginia landowner (the Mr. Peyton of the subtitle) who decides to free a number of his slaves for their years of faithful service, and particularly for their loyalty to his family during a threatened slave insurrection. Though several of Peyton's slaves accept his offer of emancipation with excitement, others make it clear that they prefer their present state. Clara, a household servant, remarks that "a nigger's nothing but a nigger, whether he is free or not," and she rejects Peyton's offer largely because she prefers labor in the home to labor on the land.[9] According to the narrator, "a desire for freedom, for its own sake, was too abstract and intangible a motive" to override her concerns for personal comfort (p. 72). Clinging more fervently to his slave status, Essex, the Peyton family's head waiter, declares that "as I came into this world, so I go out of it" (p. 52). Hoping to win over Southern readers who would be offended by a negative depiction of plantation life and perhaps also wanting to distance herself from other Northern authors who ardently opposed slavery, Hale presents a version of slavery so benign that it hardly seems to require abolishing.

Hale extols Peyton's liberality nonetheless, and in doing so she invites readers to identify with his efforts to do what is right—free his slaves—without creating a worse situation for them by doing so. He is especially concerned that his "servants" be able to support themselves once they move beyond his benevolent supervison.[10] There is a danger, according to Peyton's eminently sensible sister, that his slaves, once free, would become like the other "free negroes" in the area: "idle, degraded, and worthless men, a burden and a nuisance to every respectable person near them" (p. 46).

The "experiments" of the novel's subtitle, then, are Peyton's attempts to find or create a viable living arrangement for his former slaves—one that will prevent their becoming "burdensome." The first of these is to establish a group of freed slaves on their own farm. Peyton prefers to keep them nearby, however, because, he asserts, Southerners "are so familiar with their habits of improvidence and indolence, that it does not strike us with the same feelings of surprise and contempt that it does the thrifty Northerners" (pp. 47-48). Hardly a vote of confidence, but thus he initiates the project. His second "scheme for improvement," to use Hale's rhetoric of uplift, is to free a family of slaves and help them secure employment in Philadelphia. Both attempts at domestic emancipation—one Southern and rural, the other Northern and urban—fail miserably, and Hale concludes that freed slaves become "a drain" on American society "whenever the conduct of their life is given in their own hands." But, lest the first half of her narrative prove too pessimistic and frustrate any desire to pursue alternative solutions, Hale insists that her characterization applies only to "the masses": "noble exceptions . . . have risen up more quickly and in greater numbers than their best friends could have ventured to hope" (p. 127). These exceptions have not, however, been witnessed in America but only where the black man is "freed from the crushing superiority of the white man" (p. 127).

At first, Peyton's agrarian experiment goes well: "animated by the desire of proving themselves worthy of their liberty, all faithfully performed their part in the common task." During the first year, the former slaves "worked the land for Mr. Peyton," and Nathan, a particularly trusted member of the group, was "their overseer" (p. 57). Once they are on their own, however, most of the ex-slaves become lethargic, debt-ridden, and more willing to steal than to work. Having "tasted the pleasure of an indolent life," they are "not inclined to resume their old habits of active exertion" (p. 58). A select few—Nathan, Keziah, and

Polydore—do relatively well once Peyton relieves them of their communitarian pact with the rest and allows them to work their own parcel of land independently (in emulation of Hale's exemplar of individual responsibility, the Yankee farmer); the majority of Peyton's ex-slaves, however, are insufficiently ambitious or self-disciplined to work without coercion.

Having fully exploited the time-worn stereotype of the slow, shiftless rural "black" who cannot (or will not) "regulate" himself, Hale then draws on the popular image of the frivolous, pleasure-seeking, irresponsible urban "black."[11] Ben and Clara, who eschewed the farming option they were previously offered, want their freedom only if they can have it in a city, where they can indulge their love of spectacle and fine clothing. And indulge they do, as the narrator disapprovingly notes. They invest in expensive adornments for themselves and music lessons for their daughter Maggie, without a thought of saving their money or preparing for adversity. Criticizing the family's interest in cultural attainments—Clara's brother Americus's involvement in a literary discussion group and Maggie's music lessons—Hale implies that freed slaves should invest their time and money in things that will be "of use." She disapproves of their attempt to adopt the trappings of a bourgeois culture to which, because of their race, level of education, and economic status, she believes they have no legitimate claim.[12]

Although the family experiences prejudice, segregation, and violence in the city—Americus is assaulted at one point by a band of working-class whites—its members ultimately fail through a combination of misfortune and their own lack of foresight. When Ben becomes ill and loses his position as a coachman, the family soon faces destitution because no one has ever bothered to set aside any money. Clara takes in extra sewing in a desperate attempt to support the family, but, as Ben sinks into alcoholism and the family's standard of living falls drastically, "not poverty alone, but crime" comes to characterize their existence (p. 107). Hale borrows much from temperance literature in this segment of the novel: the family's situation improves only when little Maggie, filthy and pathetic, begs the assistance of two young women who alert a city missionary, Mr. Lyndsay, to their plight. Under this (white) missionary's watchful eye, Ben and Clara are restored to respectable self-sufficiency and no longer seek luxuries they do not deserve.

Unlike Stowe's George Harris, who as a free man "found constant occupation" and earned "a competent support for his family," Hale's freed slaves are a feckless lot, ill prepared for the responsibilities and complications of autonomy and dependent on the benevolence of white men to save them from themselves.[13] Hale does not, however, assert that blacks are beyond improvement, despite occasional essentialist claims as to "the indolent and docile nature of the African" (p. 94). Instead, she insists that blacks' servitude has engendered in them the lack of ambition and self-hatred that render them, in effect, helpless in a competitive, largely unsympathetic society such as America's. "The overpowering superiority of the white man in social and political advantages" crushes "every earthly aspiration" in both free black and slave and thus prevents them from altering their subservient position within the United States (p. 68). The very presence of whites constantly reinscribes the inferiority and degradation of former slaves.

Hale's assignments of blame and causality in the novel prove quite ambiguous. She indicts her "shiftless" black characters for their failures—almost gloating over their myriad missteps—but she also claims that their inadequacies are to a large extent imposed rather than inherent. The degree to which whites bear responsibility is unclear as well. Hale argues that the slavery system has robbed an entire population of its ambition, self-assurance, and autonomy, yet nearly all of the slaveowners she portrays (in *Northwood* as well as *Liberia*), with the exception of Keziah's first master, are benevolent souls who want only the best for their "dependents." Taken together, these portrayals in effect absolve the individual slaveholder from guilt for continuing to participate in an unjust system since he had not himself established the system but merely inherited it. All he need do is appear well intentioned.

Inconsistent, too, are Hale's attributions of power and powerlessness. African Americans inspire considerable fear in her narrative—the threat of a slave uprising at the beginning of the novel causes the area's white inhabitants to flee their plantations, and the black inhabitants of a Philadelphia slum terrify two young white women engaged in charity work. Nevertheless, Hale's frightening blacks are all anonymous, mentioned in the abstract or in the realm of possibility, while her individual black characters are generally ineffectual and never menacing. Even though Hale tends to treat the "African race" as a single, unified category, her characterizations are mutually exclusive. As Barbara J. Fields notes in her discussion of Southern planters' ability to believe simultaneously in their slaves' weakness and in their power, Hale's confusions were not unique: "attitudes are not discrete entities and people have no innate compulsion toward logical consistency."[14] Hale portrays blacks as both fearsome and pathetic, both culpable and victimized, presumably because she believes that all those descriptions are accurate; it is also true that such paradoxes serve her purpose. In order to promote colonization, she must present a population sufficiently helpless that its success in the United States is impossible but sufficiently powerful that its later achievement—the founding of a new nation—is credible.

Once Hale's former slaves cross the Atlantic, she suddenly shows them considerable respect and abandons her use of racial stereotypes. Instead of cataloguing their inadequacies, she now details their accomplishments; they tend their houses and lands with exemplary efficiency, she asserts, and she applauds Junius's missionary work and Keziah's attempts to educate native girls and women. Even the less outstanding colonists (among whom none of Peyton's ex-slaves is included) are described as succumbing only to "the natural desire that all people share for . . . self-indulgence" (p. 167); indolence is now a common, *human* (rather than a racial) trait. In Hale's America, whiteness is the standard, or universal, state, and so whites' attributes are human attributes (or else individual aberrations), whereas blacks as a minority are "nonstandard," "other," and are granted only group identity, with no access to universality or particularity. Once in Africa, where blackness is the standard, the emigrants' qualities are suddenly generalizable and human. This transformation from minority to majority status changes their self-concept; without the presence of the white population, Hale's colonists can "forget all about . . . color in a little while" and feel "more like men" (p. 224).[15]

One of emigration's most unusual outcomes is that the former slaves (with the exception of Polydore) lose their rural black English dialect and begin to use grammatically perfect, standard (white, northern) English: "Dey" becomes "they," "it don't" becomes "it does not," etc. In fact, their new speech patterns are practically indistinguishable from the narrator's, a transition that occurs without explanation or acknowledgment within the text. Landowners, teachers, missionaries, and colonizers, those once slaves now speak like Sarah Hale; emigration begins to close the gap between the educated, white, middle-class author and her black characters, as they prove in a sense "whiter" in Africa than they could ever have been in America.

The emigrants' family structures, too, adhere more closely to conventional white models once they arrive in Liberia—specifically, to the model of the white pioneer or independent farming family. Keziah and Polydore, who had formerly "kept company" in an informal, desexualized partnership, decide to marry; they select "a fine tract of land for themselves," build a cottage on it, and begin the work of clearing and planting (p. 167). Later, when they have moved several miles inland to a more advantageous spot, they build a sugar mill to increase their self-sufficiency and plant a thick hedge to maintain the privacy and impenetrability of their home. Some distance away, Nathan builds "a substantial farm-house" for his family and begins accumulating acreage at an impressive rate (p. 218). Male emigrants feel "more like men" because they are landowners and because they can provide their children with opportunities and inheritances—a far cry from their situation in the United States, where slaves could neither own property nor guarantee that their children would not be sold away from them. In Hale's Liberia private property, and privacy itself, become supremely important as each family, though friendly with other settlers, works (and uses cheap native labor) to better its own condition.[16]

American slavery was often criticized for destroying black family life. It separated family members, thus supposedly discouraging attachment, and by emasculating African-American men, left them unable to provide adequately for their families, to protect their wives from sexual violation by white masters, and to bequeath their children land and other material goods. Stowe focuses particularly on this assault on the slave family in *Uncle Tom's Cabin,* and her subsequent reconstruction of the Harris family and its emigration to Liberia, as Gillian Brown notes, "colonizes Africa for domesticity."[17] Hale engages in a similar project: the more conventional family arrangements among blacks in the Liberia section of the novel undo the dissolution (or at least the disorganization) of family life for which slavery was thought to be responsible. Hale, however, "colonizes Africa" for other cherished American ideals as well—namely, for private property and free enterprise.

As the momentum to "sell" the colonization project builds, Hale begins to lose sight of her characters' humanity. Any semblance of cohesive storytelling, character development, or interpersonal drama that exists in the American episodes is lost, and the writing becomes largely propagandistic and informational; snippets from Liberian documents and the exploits of historical figures such as Lott Cary and Elijah Johnson now compete with Hale's fictional characters for the reader's attention.[18] When those characters do speak, they often ventriloquize a hardsell of the colony, including favorable details of its climate, indigenous plants, and economic opportunities.[19] Though Hale proposes to the reader that emigration has allowed her black characters to become fully "human" or, more precisely, fully "civilized," it becomes clear that she cannot represent them as such, for they have no convincing subjectivity in the narrative, nor even any believable dialogue. Hale has remade the emigrants into familiarly structured families, like the hard-working Romilly family she portrays with such warmth in *Northwood,* but their lives have become unrepresentable in the process. In her attempts to make the former slaves as much like herself and her venerable pioneer ancestors as possible— to make them, in effect, the dominant social group in their environment—she is essentially (according to her belief system) making them white, or at least analogous to white people. But Hale can never quite forget that they are *not* actually white, and so she cannot sustain the characterization. Her efforts to normalize former slaves have a limit, as she stops short of portraying a level of intimacy among them that would seem, in fact, too close to home.

. . . . .

Imaginative failings aside, Hale does theorize how the ex-slave's transformation from social burden to community leader can occur. In a newly formed colony, the strongest blacks will "naturally" rise to power. Once free of whites' insults and socioeconomic superiority, the colonists have an incentive to achieve, a chance at and desire for self-improvement and advancement that they did not have in the United States. Hale's proposal sends manumitted slaves and free blacks to a place where, according to her standards of judgment, everything is so "backward," so uncompetitive, that they cannot help but seem superior. Nathan asserts proudly that in Liberia "the natives look up to us as something wonderful" (p. 220). She suggests that this perceived superiority then solidifies, over time, into reality. For Hale, who firmly believes in the inevitability of a gradation of status based on color, the best thing one can do for black Americans is to place them against a darker background.

Hale also implies, though, that it is the very experience of superiority that effects the emigrants' transformation. By the end of the novel it becomes clear that the absence of whites is a necessary, but not sufficient, condition for black actualization; the emigrants must also have a group of people whom *they* can dominate. The African natives, of course, serve that purpose.[20] Despite numerous battles with native tribes, the settlers soon have the upper hand in the colony—economically, culturally, and politically. Natives work for extremely low wages and often serve as the colonists' house servants. Junius, the missionary, considers the natives to be "sunk in the deepest ignorance and superstition," and he christianizes them by denouncing their faith "with the utmost boldness" while the natives listen "in meek submission" to his sermons and agree in time to replace their gods with his (pp. 231, 241). The natives not only accept the emigrants' religion, but also their laws. In a passage that Hale presents as historical rather than fictional, she claims that by 1852 a minority of eight thousand settlers in Liberia and the Maryland colony had "nearly two hundred thousand Africans living in their republic and submitting to their laws" (p. 229). She applauds the emerging hierarchies in Liberian society; for her, there must always be the teachers and the ignorant, the civilized and the savage, the patriots and the sluggards, the leaders and the led.

Liberian immigration is, for Hale, a civilizing process. In order for Africans to achieve status as "real," civilized men, they must have been colonized by white American society (through the institution of slavery), must have absorbed white values and, especially, white religion, and then must return to Africa to civilize and christianize their native "cousins."[21] Advocates of slavery had long justified it on the basis of its success in persuading African Americans to embrace Christianity, but Hale, like many fellow colonizationists, carried this line of reasoning a step further: by converting the colonized subject, the ex-American slave, into a colonist and a missionary, she not only solves the immediate problem of what to do with these social and economic outsiders but also assuages white America's collective guilt by re-defining the nation's participation in African slavery as providential. *Liberia* enacts Hale's declaration at the end of the 1852 *Northwood*: "Liberia has solved the enigma of ages. The mission of American slavery is to christianize Africa."[22]

By giving her emigrants an "errand," Hale casts them in the mold of America's founders. Like many of her era and region who considered American nationalism providential, she conflated Puritan and Pilgrim enterprise with the settlement of all of New England and saw New England as the "cradle" of the American Revolution.[23] As Lawrence Buell has noted, the legend of our "Pilgrim-Puritan origins was patently reductive" but nevertheless had great currency in the nineteenth century, perpetuating itself through "public speeches and patriotic festivals."[24] It is not surprising, then, that in her attempts to dignify the Liberian settlers' endeavor, Hale should call them "pilgrims," though her use of quotation marks implies a reluctance to see the two groups as equal (p. 145).[25] Nonetheless, similarities abound. Following an American pattern of settlement and expansionism, Liberian colonists procure and "improve" tracts of virgin land, that is, land unused or underused by European standards; moreover, their wars against native African tribes recapitulate the American colonists' Indian wars. Just as America's own natives had been vilified, so Hale's white nineteenth-century readers would have found much to despise in the native Africans, in part their continuing participation in the West African slave trade but, mostly, their "savage," non-Christian way of life. Hale makes much of the natives' "heathen rites" and violent customs, all of which serve to capture the moral high ground for her settler-conquerors.

Much of Hale's description of the Liberian experience has to do with nation building. She titles the first of the Liberian chapters "The Planting of the Nation" and uses Whittier's lines as an epigraph: "I hear the tread of pioneers, / Of nations yet to be . . ." (p. 128).[26] Hale also includes long passages on Joseph J. Roberts, Liberia's first president, and on the new nation's efforts to establish itself and to gain international recognition. Her fictional characters, not entirely forgotten among the historical details, express a growing patriotism: Nathan says that he does not believe "there ever was a nation before that has grown so rapidly," and he hopes that his son will become "a senator or a judge, if not a president" (p. 220).

Hale's notion of full citizenship, and the dignity that accompanies it, rests on an individual's ability to claim original status within a nation, at least among its "civilized" population. Nativism and racism intersect as she asserts the centrality of being a founder, or a descendant of one, a status uniformly unavailable to blacks in the United States, however, no matter how early their ancestors arrived, because they have historically had little access to the social and political power required for nation building. Hale's colonizationist stance, then, is not simply a plan for solving the race problem in the United States; it is a means, she suggests, of elevating blacks to the status of Anglo-Americans—perhaps even to the status of New Englanders. In her zealous (though hardly anomalous) patriotism, she believes that the American model of nation building, if applied in the right context, can transform even a previously "degraded" population like manumitted slaves. Her implied answer to Machiavelli's maxim, that "to make a servile people free, is as difficult as to make a free people slaves" (p. 128), is the American prescription for legitimacy and self-improvement: those unfortunates must find a country to call their own, force its inhabitants to bend to their will, and establish for themselves and their progeny the status of "founders."

A central question Hale's nationalistic program raises, though, is precisely when and how race matters. She advocates placing American-born blacks in a situation where they will not "have to be ashamed of their color," where, it would seem, race does *not* matter. But simply because they must escape to this site where race is supposedly irrelevant attests to its overwhelming, determining importance. And, further, it becomes clear that race, or something structurally very much like it, *does* matter in Liberia, as a hierarchical society begins to develop with American-born blacks (especially those born free) and their descendants occupying the upper echelons of society and native Africans occupying the lower. The historian Evelyn Brooks Higginbotham, among others, has argued convincingly that race should be conceived of as "a social construction predicated upon the recognition of difference," a difference arising from "the simultaneous distinguishing and positioning of groups *vis-à-vis* one another."[27] Race is neither an essential nor a stable category, and it becomes particularly unstable in the context of African colonization; as one (actual) Liberian settler noted in a letter to her former owner, the native Africans habitually "call us all white man."[28] But even if Hale were to recognize native Africans and American-born emigrants as belonging to different racial groups—which, of course, she does not—she would still see the emigrants as free of racial constraints in Liberia, for the privilege of having race "not matter" is intimately related, in her scheme, to the notion of citizenship. Part of founder's status, at least as it has been articulated in the United States, is the privilege of establishing one's own race as the nation's standard.[29]

Liberian colonization was, as abolitionists so vehemently argued, a racist and unworkable solution to the problems of slavery and racial difference in nineteenth-century America. Hale's colonizing plan is, in some ways, particularly troubling in that it seems to promise equality but the price exacted is greater than most African Americans were willing or able to pay: acceptance of the proposition that a country (in this case the United States), once claimed and "civilized," belongs to the race of those who staked that claim.

Although Hale takes great care to present the Liberian option in a positive light, presumably with the goal of encouraging blacks to emigrate, the extent to which she actually addresses African Americans is unclear. Her potential black audience would necessarily have been limited to a relatively elite group—those who were literate, had access to books published in the northeast, and were not enslaved (or whose owners could be convinced to emancipate them for the purpose of emigration).[30] In her preface, Hale implies, instead, that whites are her primary audience when she refers to "the African, who among *us* has no home, no position, and no future" (p. iv; italics mine). This collusive "us" appropriately sets the tone, for the question that governs the first half of the narrative—what to do with one's slaves—is a white man's question, and the Liberian solution of the second half originated among and was largely administered by whites. Moreover, Hale's colonizationism speaks directly to the concerns of mainstream (Northern) Anglo-Americans, who worried about the future of the Union and wondered how slavery could be eliminated without leaving hundreds of thousands of former slaves destitute, many of them "flooding" into Northern cities in search of work.

In some sense, then, the book is as much *about* Anglo-Americans as it is about African Americans; Hale is, to paraphrase Clifford Geertz, telling white America a story about itself. For Geertz, the Balinese cockfight about which he uses the phrase is "a kind of sentimental education"; the story that it tells the Balinese about themselves, though exaggerated and abstracted, is nonetheless somehow *true*.[31] The story Hale's text tells, however, is a wishful distortion. Not only has she manipulated historical representations (her slaveowners are far more benevolent and her colonists healthier and more successful than historical sources would support), but, more important, the attitudes, justifications, and emotions such representations engender are carefully controlled. Her book offers a flattering portrait of a well-intentioned "representative" white man who has earnestly sought a solution to the slavery problem and has found it in the replication of whites' own colonizing experience. Not only, then, have whites exonerated themselves for their participation in slavery by fashioning this satisfactory remedy, but they can also congratulate themselves for having given blacks

the training—christianizing and general "civilizing"—that assures its successful application.

Liberia's preface makes explicit these self- and group-justifications:

> And who can doubt that, in thus providing a home of refuge for "the stranger within her gates," our beloved Union was nobly, though silently, justifying herself from the aspersions of oppression and wrong so often thrown out against her?

> What other nation can point to a colony planted from such pure motives of charity; nurtured by the counsels and exertions of its noblest, wisest, and most self-denying statesmen and philanthropists; and sustained, from its feeble commencement up to a period of self-reliance and independence, from a pure love of justice and humanity? [P. iv]

Hale's is a story of white nobility and self-vindication, of which the transformation of slaves into colonists is merely the occasion. And, barely submerged in these celebratory variations on the colonial script is a reinforcement of the legitimacy of the United States' own founding and of its expansionist and white supremacist policies, for Hale presents colonization and nation building in entirely positive terms, with only benefits accruing to both colonist and "heathen" native.

A significant disjunction remains, however, between my critical reading of Sarah Hale's colonizationism—influenced as it is by late twentieth-century perspectives on colonialism and American race relations—and her expressed desire to aid African-American slaves (a desire whose genuineness I do not fundamentally question, though I maintain that it coexists with other, less admirable desires). Nevertheless, the assumptions on which her work rests—that African Americans are inevitably to occupy an inferior social position in the United States, that Christianity is the one, true religion and should be spread wherever possible, that ownership of private property is inherently superior to communitarian arrangements—are not, for Hale, or for many of her contemporaries, inconsistent with her benevolent impulses; in fact, they are essential to her expression of those impulses. Ultimately, the contradiction is mine and not Hale's.

Such difficulties are not, of course, exclusive to Hale; they inhere in any attempt to deal with nineteenth-century white Americans' writings on race. Even Stowe and Lydia Maria Child—authors whose anti-slavery stances make them more acceptable than Hale to twentieth-century readers—rely on racist and racialist assumptions that render their texts extraordinarily difficult to assess (and to teach). Clearly, to begin and end inquiries into the thought of these authors by simply plumbing the depths of their racism inexcusably reduces the richness and cultural relevance of their work; indeed, the very label of "racist" becomes all but meaningless in its ubiquity if we apply the standards of most late-twentieth-century academics to nineteenth-century writers. But neither does it seem sufficient to re-create, relativistically and nonjudgmentally, these authors' own conceptions of their projects.[32] What interests me, finally, is how their representations of racial difference and proposed solutions to the problem of slavery functioned; that is, what cultural work did they perform and whose interests were thereby served? Broadly speaking, how did these ideas circulate through what might be termed the racial economy of antebellum America? That economy cannot be understood without considering the writings of middle-class white women like Sarah Hale. The coexistence of their good intentions and their nonetheless damaging representations is a legacy that, however disquieting, we cannot afford to ignore.

Notes

[1] I call *Liberia* a novel (as does Nina Baym in *Feminism and American Literary History: Essays* [New Brunswick, NJ; Rutgers University Press, 1992]) despite the fact that it is more precisely a combination of novel, historical account, and propaganda tract. The fictional passages predominate, though, which I believe justifies the use of a somewhat reductive term. The original title page states that the book was "edited by" Hale, presumably because she collected a number of historical documents in the appendix.

[2] I qualify my assertion that abolitionist papers did not mention *Liberia* because it is difficult to have absolute confidence in a visual search of so much microfilmed material; in addition, some issues from the runs I searched were missing.

[3] After criticizing Hale's recipes for requiring "too much expenditure of *time* and *money*," the reviewer writes: "we should be deemed more egotistical than ever, were we to add that we have a strong idea of publishing something on this subject. . . . Amidst her domestic researches, Mrs. Sarah Josepha Hale found leisure to write a weak and diluted defence of the great Patriarchal domestic Institution of Slavery! So we don't see why we may not find opportunity to discourse on *French Flummery, Puff Paste, Apple Fool,* &c.! especially as we are peculiarly desirous to display our knowledge on this subject" ("Literary Notices," *Frederick Douglass's Paper,* 14 April 1854, p. 3). While I have no proof that Douglass and his associate Julia Griffiths (who wrote many of the paper's book reviews) were aware of *Liberia* and deliberately chose to review Hale's cookbooks in its stead, their hostility to her commentaries on slavery is obvious.

[4] On the response to *Uncle Tom's Cabin* in *Frederick Douglass's Paper,* see Robert S. Levine, *Martin Delany,*

Frederick Douglass, and the Politics of Representative Identity (Chapel Hill: University of North Carolina Press, 1997), pp. 71-90.

[5] Baym, *Feminism and American Literary History,* p. 168. Most scholarship on Hale focuses on her editorship of *Godey's Lady's Book* and, to a lesser extent, on *Northwood* and *Woman's Record,* a historical work Hale published in 1853; *Liberia* is usually mentioned briefly, if at all. An exception is Baym's chapter "Sarah Hale, Political Writer," which treats the novel in some detail (*Feminism and American Literary History,* pp. 167-82). Baym treats *Liberia* less extensively in *American Women Writers and the Work of History, 1790-1860* (New Brunswick, N.J.: Rutgers University Press, 1995). Patricia Okker's recent book, *Our Sister Editors: Sarah J. Hale and the Tradition of Nineteenth-Century American Women Editors* (Athens: University of Georgia Press, 1995), came to my attention while this essay was in press; although Okker takes Hale quite seriously as a literary figure and editor, she treats Hale's views on slavery and colonization only briefly.

Of course, scholars may have paid little attention to *Liberia* for reasons other than its embrace of colonization; by most academics' standards, it is not a particularly "good read." Nevertheless, I would argue that the novel's capacity to embarrass modern readers—and the fact that it does not fit neatly into the anti-slavery/pro-slavery binary—has discouraged close examination of it. . . .

[6] Hale's statement at the end of the 1852 *Northwood* illustrates her faith in fiction's power to effect change: "Let us trust that the pen and not the sword will decide the controversy now going on in our land; and that any part women may take in the former mode will be promotive of peace, and not suggestive of discord" (*Northwood: or, Life North and South* [1852; reprinted, New York: Johnson, 1970], p. 407). She is probably referring here to Stowe—whether or not the "little lady" in *fact* started the "big war," Hale seems to have feared the possibility. Such a direct reference is temporally plausible; the preface to the 1852 *Northwood* is dated 9 September, while *Uncle Tom's Cabin* was published in March of the same year and appeared in serial form even earlier. Rita K. Gollin notes in her introduction to the 1970 reprint of *Northwood* that Hale "offered her expanded novel as a peaceful if long-range alternative to Mrs. Stowe's abolitionism position" (p. xix). According to Angela Zophy, though, both Hale and Louis Godey denied that the republication of *Northwood* had anything to do with the recent appearance of Stowe's novel ("For the Improvement of My Sex: Sarah Josepha Hale's Editorship of *Godey's Lady's Book,* 1837-1877" [Ph.D. diss., Ohio State University, 1978], p. 98).

[7] On American Anglo-Saxonism, see Reginald Horsman, *Race and Manifest Destiny: The Origins of American*

Racial Anglo-Saxonism (Cambridge: Harvard University Press, 1981). See also Maggie Sale, "Critiques from Within: Antebellum Projects of Resistance," *American Literature* 64 [March 1992], pp. 695-701.

[8] The book's lengthy appendix contains white colonizationists' writings, Liberian documents, and letters from black emigrants. Hale presumably includes these letters—which surely were chosen carefully—because they present Liberia in a generally positive light, contradicting the unfavorable reports that anti-colonization groups were circulating in the United States. They also tend to mirror her narrative, as black settlers attest to their improved status and wider range of options in Liberia. Interestingly, Hale uses letters written by blacks to legitimate her story, just as the authors and editors of slave narratives often included letters by whites to assure readers of their authenticity.

[9] Sarah J. Hale, *Liberia: or, Mr. Peyton's Experiments* (1853; reprinted, Upper Saddle River, N.J.: Gregg, 1968), p. 53. All subsequent quotations are cited parenthetically in the text.

[10] The term "servant" was often used in antebellum America to refer to slaves, especially in the South. For a discussion of the social implications of this usage, particularly among white domestic workers, see David Roediger, *The Wages of Whiteness: Race and the Making of the American Working Class* (London: Verso, 1991), pp. 47-50.

[11] Hale's urban and rural stereotypes resemble the stock characters Zip Coon and Jim Crow of blackface minstrelsy; she sanitizes them, however, of the sexual suggestiveness common to such theatrical representations. It seems unlikely, though, that Hale was a devotee of the minstrel show; I assume that both she and blackface performers were drawing on well-established modes of representing African Americans.

[12] Such arguments are not, of course, the sole province of whites. Nearly half a century after the publication of *Liberia*, Booker T. Washington would make similar claims. Former slaves and their children, he believed, should not pursue culture; instead, industrial education and the attainment of basic economic independence would better meet their needs. Washington's most famous remark along these lines appears in *Up from Slavery*: "one of the saddest things I saw during the month of travel which I have described was a young man, who had attended some high school, sitting down in a one-room cabin, with grease on his clothing, filth all around him, and weeds in the yard and garden, engaged in studying a French grammar" (*Up from Slavery* [1901; reprinted, New York: Penguin, 1986], p. 122).

[13] Harriet Beecher Stowe, *Uncle Tom's Cabin: or, Life Among the Lowly*, ed. Kathryn Kish Sklar (New York: Library of America, 1982), p. 497.

[14] Barbara J. Fields, "Ideology and Race in American History," in *Region, Race and Reconstruction: Essays in Honor of C. Vann Woodward*, ed. J. Morgan Dousser and James M. McPherson (New York: Oxford University Press, 1982), p. 154.

[15] Several of the letters from Liberia in Hale's appendix reinforce this sentiment: one emigrant writes that "I have grown to be a man; in America I never could have been a man" (p. 253); another claims that, even if he were seventy years old, he would "come to Liberia and be a man, and no longer a nigger" (p. 256); and a third writes that "in America the free colored man can never be 'a man'" (p. 257).

[16] Hale's central characters learned the "lesson" of private property in their Virginia farming experiment, but there they were always in danger of being dragged down by their shiftless neighbors; in Liberia, such problems seem not to exist.

[17] Gillian Brown, *Domestic Individualism: Imagining Self in Nineteenth-Century America* (Berkeley: University of California Press, 1990), p. 31.

[18] Cary, a minister and former slave from Richmond, Virginia, and Johnson, an emigrant from New York, both assumed leadership roles early in the colony's history (James Wesley Smith, *Sojourners in Search of Freedom: The Settlement of Liberia by Black Americans* [Lanham, Md.: University Press of America, 1987], pp. 14-16, 22-26).

[19] Nineteenth-century representations of Liberia were contradictory and quite politicized. Predictably, colonizationists tended to present an idealized view of the settlement in order to encourage emigration, while anti-colonizationists often described the place as an unhealthful backwater where no informed person would settle by choice. For contrasting views, see William Nesbit's and Samuel Williams's accounts of their travels in Liberia (William Nesbit, *Four Months in Liberia: or, African Colonization Exposed;* Samuel Williams, *Four Years in Liberia: A Sketch of the Life of Rev. Samuel Williams.* Both have been reprinted in *Nesbit and Williams: Two Black Views of Liberia* [New York: Arno, 1969]). Hale's representation of the colony is not entirely positive—she mentions difficulties with pests and fever and the presence of some poorly adapted settlers—but it is far rosier than historical records support.

[20] Though Liberians worked to undermine the transatlantic slave trade that was still active on Africa's west coast, historical records indicate that some Liberian settlers kept natives as slaves, or at least as very badly treated "indentured servants." It also seems, though, that the Liberian government attempted to eradicate such practices. See Tom Shick, *Behold the Promised Land: A History of Afro-American Settler Society in*

Nineteenth-Century Liberia (Baltimore: Johns Hopkins University Press, 1977), p. 174; Nesbit, *Four Months in Liberia,* p. 15; Amos J. Beyan, *The American Colonization Society and the Creation of the Liberian State: A Historical Perspective, 1822-1900* (Lanham, Md.: University Press of America, 1991), pp. 127-31; Smith, *Sojourners,* p. 64.

21 Like others writing prior to late-twentieth-century concerns about sexist language, Hale ostensibly means both men and women when she writes "men." But, as is often the case, in a sense she really does mean *men.* Her depiction of the ex-slaves' increased status focuses largely on issues of political and economic power, which she considered unequivocally a part of the masculine sphere. Oddly enough, some anti-colonizationists used similar terms to criticize blacks who emigrated to Liberia. A piece that appeared in the *Liberator* decried black colonists as "utterly lost to every sense of manhood" ("Preamble and Resolutions of the Anti-Colonization Believers in Syracuse," *Liberator,* 15 April 1853, p. 58).

22 Hale, *Northwood,* p. 408. Daniel Webster, white Methodist minister John P. Durbin, and black nationalist Edward W. Blyden, among others, spoke of American slavery in providential terms, citing it as the means by which Africa was to be christianized. Other Liberian advocates did not push the issue as far; a white colonizationist's editorial, reprinted (with disapprobation) in the *Liberator,* argues that "It may be a compensation, that if Africa's children have been dragged through the horrors of the Middle Passage, that their descendants have been returned with the germs of civilization, acquired during their long servitude" ("Refuge of Oppression," *Liberator,* 9 December 1853, p. 191). Although this author is not willing to call American slavery *providential,* he is eager to assert that some good has emerged from injustice.

23 Nina Baym calls Hale "ever a daughter of New England" and asserts that she tended to identify "the origins of the nation with the settling of Plymouth Colony" ("Onward Christian Women: Sarah J. Hale's History of the World," *New England Quarterly* 63 [1990]: 260). Appropriately, Hale was active in the campaign to institutionalize the Thanksgiving holiday, a cause she pursued from 1846 until 1863, when President Lincoln made the observance official (Ruth E. Finley, *The Lady of Godey's: Sarah Josepha Hale* [Philadelphia: Lippincott, 1931], pp. 195-204).

24 Lawrence Buell, *New England Literary Culture: From Revolution through Renaissance* (Cambridge: Cambridge University Press, 1986), pp. 204, 197.

25 The final item in Hale's appendix to *Liberia* is a portion of the Reverend Dr. Scott's address to the Louisiana State Colonization Society in which he asserts that "the colony of Liberia has succeeded better

than the colony of Plymouth did for the same period of time"; he goes on to compare the African colony's prospects for success to the accomplishments of the United States (p. 303).

26 Hale's use of the staunch abolitionist Whittier is puzzling, given her usual distaste for such radicalism. She must have felt able to separate his poetry from his politics; the other possibility, that she quotes from his work in order to ally herself more closely with abolitionists, I find implausible.

27 Evelyn Brooks Higginbotham, "African-American Women's History and the Metalanguage of Race," *Signs* 17 (1992): p. 253. Along similar lines, Michael Omi and Howard Winant have written that "racial categories and the meaning of race are given concrete expression by the specific social relations and historical context in which they are embedded" (*Racial Formation in the United States: From the 1960s to the 1980s* [New York: Routledge, 1986], p. 60).

28 Bell I. Wiley, *Slaves No More: Letters from Liberia, 1833-1869* (Lexington: University Press of Kentucky, 1980), p. 57.

29 Liberians exercised this "right" in their 1847 constitution, which "excluded whites from citizenship" (Wiley, *Slaves No More,* p. 2).

30 A paragraph on *Liberia* in *Godey's* "Literary Notices" (surely approved, if not actually written, by Hale) describes the limitations of her appeal to African Americans in quite different terms, asserting that the work "commends itself not only to the attention of those who are anxious to benefit an unhappy race, but also to the serious consideration of such of that race as have sufficient intelligence to comprehend their true interests, and sufficient energy to follow their dictates" (*Godey's Lady's Book,* March 1854, p. 274). The notice's author effaces the constraints of illiteracy and enslavement, defining the book's audience instead according to innate intelligence and self-determined (and determining) "energy."

31 Clifford Geertz, "Deep Play: Notes on the Balinese Cockfight," in *Rethinking Popular Culture: Contemporary Perspectives in Cultural Studies* (Berkeley: University of California Press, 1991), p. 266.

32 What seems most useful here is a "strategic relativism," that is, a willingness temporarily to enter into the mind and value system of a historical figure for the purpose of understanding, but with the expectation of moving outside that world view once again in order to judge and analyze as a twentieth-century scholar with particular ethical and political commitments. (This coinage was suggested by Gayatri Spivak's notion of strategic essentialism. See her collection *The*

Postcolonial Critic: Interviews, Strategies, Dialogues, ed. Sarah Harasym [New York: Routledge, 1990], pp. 50-51.) Such a process is extremely difficult to enact with someone like Hale, whose racial attitudes differ so radically from those with which most twentieth-century academics feel comfortable; it is easier, perhaps, with Stowe and Child.

Barbara A. Bardes and Suzanne Gossett (essay date 1995)

SOURCE: "Sarah J. Hale, Selective Promoter of Her Sex" in *A Living of Words: American Women in Print Culture,* edited by Susan Albertine, University of Tennessee Press, 1995, pp. 18-34.

[*In the following excerpt, Bardes and Gossett explore Hale's views on women's roles, especially as reflected in her* Woman's Record.]

Interpretations of Hale's life and career have varied widely, depending largely upon the period and upon the interpreter's attitude toward powerful women. Yet as we survey Hale's works, the most consistent element, the invariable factor whether one considers Hale radical or conventional in her activities, is her dedication to the promotion of her own sex. Within her own ideologically inflected definition of what was appropriate, she unwaveringly favored women's activities and, specifically, their literary achievements. These ideals are continuously expressed from her earliest editorials in the *Ladies' Magazine* to her final revision of **Woman's Record,** her encyclopedia of women's achievements.

It is not surprising that those who compare Hale to other major nineteenth-century figures in publishing are most struck by what she was able to accomplish despite her gender. Mott, the historian of magazines, describes Hale simply as "a great woman" (583), praiseworthy especially for her commitment to female education (349). For Eugene Exman, writing about the house of Harper, Hale was "demonstrating how much a woman could do in a man's world" (237); and for James Playsted Wood her editorial achievements justify referring to her as "the stalwart feminist from Boston . . . the militant Sarah Josepha Hale" (54).

Since the beginning of the second feminist wave, however, interpretations of Hale have been more divided. The negative view is clearest in the writing of Ann Douglas, who while conceding that Hale was "the most important arbiter of feminine opinion of her day" (51), condemns her as the "chief exponent of the doctrine of the feminine sphere" (54), one who even when seeking partially feminist goals" does so by "largely anti-feminist means" (52). A more moderate analysis comes from Angela Zophy, who presumes that Hale's goal was to promote a traditional kind of "true womanhood" but nevertheless notes that in her monthly editorials Hale worked "to promote advances in women's education and employment opportunities" (1), and "used the concepts of true womanhood, woman's sphere, and woman's influence to broaden the scope of women's activities and interests to suit the times" (48).

Zophy, though more favorable than Douglas, denigrates Hale's accomplishments by asserting that Louis Godey was the controlling force at the journal and that, especially after Hale moved to Philadelphia in 1841, her "proximity to her publisher seemingly increased his influence over her and therefore over her formulation of editorial policy" (72). Consequently, Zophy concludes, by "following her publisher's policy of offending no one . . . Mrs. Hale tacitly accepted a diminished role as a lady-like reformer" (77). Cheryl Walker generalizes this picture, claiming that "women like Sara [sic] Josepha Hale . . . nominal editors of the ladies' magazines. . . . were in fact controlled by their publishers, who were male" (Walker 34). Such a structure would place Hale in a situation comparable to that which Susan Coultrap-McQuin argues obtained for most of the nineteenth century in the book publishing industry, a situation in which male publishers took a paternalistic attitude toward the female or feminized writers who worked for them and set the terms for their involvement in the literary marketplace (Coultrap-McQuin passim).

The view of Hale as Godey's puppet diminishes unjustifiably Hale's significance in the world of nineteenth-century publishing. Though Hale was no doubt grateful to Reverend Blake, the publisher of the *Ladies' Magazine,* for giving her the opportunity to enter the literary world as a professional (Martin 46), there is no proof that she adapted her opinions to suit him. It is true that the pages of *Godey's* have more fiction and more fashion plates than the *Ladies' Magazine,* but such marketing decisions did not force Sarah Hale to change her intellectual and political positions once she moved to the larger journal. Instead, Baym has argued, "editorial policy and content were Hale's domain, while Godey attended to sales, format, and publicity" ("Christian Women" 249n). Significantly, before Hale joined his operation, Godey's magazine had been largely made up of reprints from English publishers: it was Hale who once again insisted on an American magazine "made up of articles written by American authors on subjects of special interest to an American public."[1] And she chose those articles.

Furthermore, the extent to which Hale can be dismissed as an uncomplicated advocate of "true womanhood" has been challenged by Laura McCall's content analysis of *Godey's Lady's Book* from 1830 to 1860. Analyzing a random sample of 120 short stories chosen from among all those published over that thirty-year period, McCall tested the women characters in the stories for the four presumably cardinal feminine virtues: piety, purity, submissiveness, and domesticity.[2] She was surprised to find that the majority of women characters reflected no interest in piety, that many were openly erotic (in the Victorian mode), and that quite a few were admired for their intellect. McCall concludes that "the categories historians have formulated to describe the ideal woman were not prevalent in either the fiction or the editorials of *Godey's*" (235).

McCall's analysis of the fiction in *Godey's* complements several other revisionist interpretations of Hale's ideology. From a political point of view, we have argued elsewhere, Hale must be seen in a context more nuanced than feminist or antifeminist. *Northwood,* her 1827 novel, reveals her advocacy of a particular subset of activities for female citizens, undertaken in subordination to male authority and within the family, yet clearly understood as fundamental to the political order. This novel, typical of the "nationalist historical fiction" written by women in the 1820s (Baym, "Women Writing History" 24), makes manifest the bases of Hale's political attitudes throughout her life. As a proto-Victorian, Hale accepted the premise that the differences between men and women were both physical and moral, such that each sex had a different but essential role to play in the preservation of the republic. Deeply patriotic, in keeping with her view of woman's role in the republic, throughout her life Hale expressed her dedication to the national cause through such activities as her successful campaigns for a national Thanksgiving Day and for the completion of the Bunker Hill monument.[3] Others have extended the political analysis of Hale's early work: Nicole Tonkovich Hoffman, for example, sees Hale as "continually politically involved" (50).

In two recent articles, "Onward Christian Women: Sarah J. Hale's History of the World" and "Between Enlightenment and Victorian: Toward a Narrative of American Women Writers Writing History," Nina Baym points the way to analyzing Hale's compendium *Woman's Record* as an indication of her most profound beliefs. Here Hale attempts "nothing less than to reconstitute world history . . . as the history of women" ("Christian Women" 252). And rather than showing the contribution of true womanhood or the conventional female virtues to the advance of a civilization led by men, Hale demonstrates that progress in world history depends explicitly on the progress of women. As Baym summarizes the argument implicit throughout the encyclopedia, "the Christian message is precisely the superiority of women, the destined mission of women is to Christianize the world, and the story of history is of inevitable progress toward a world dominated by Christian and Christianizing women" (253). *Woman's Record* is thus typical of Victorian women's history because, unlike the Enlightenment historians of the late eighteenth and early nineteenth centuries, who believed that "mind has no sex and that language, by which mind makes itself known and effective, also has no sex" ("Women Writing History" 29), Hale rooted her understanding of women's mind in the weaker female body and argued that women, though inferior in physical strength to men, developed compensatory superior moral and spiritual senses (38).

Baym's analysis of *Woman's Record* focuses on its place in nineteenth-century women's historiography and on its vision of women's moral and religious power. She says little about the *form* of the work, a series of biographies, though she does comment that "from Hale's own perspective her very decision to include particular women marked her admiration and high regard, her sense of their historical importance" ("Christian Women" 267). While Baym notes with some astonishment a few of the women that Hale did include—Agrippina, mother of Nero; Lucretia Borgia; and the African Princess Zinga, "licentious, blood-thirsty, and cruel"—she does not pause over the women who are absent, with the exception of Mary Wollstonecraft ("Christian Women" 254).[4] Baym also says nothing about the work's persistent emphasis on woman as writer. The last section of the book, for example, is headed "Fourth Era. Of Living Female Writers." Yet we can learn much about the way that Sarah Hale promoted her sex, and about her commitment to seeing women into print, by following these two lines of analysis, biographical and literary. Believing that only women could provide the necessary moral and spiritual leadership for the young nation and for Western civilization in general, Hale used her position as an author, editor, and historian to advance the careers of women authors, to promote a few other occupations and activities for women, and to provide models for her readers to follow in their own lives. She did this by exclusion as well as inclusion, by selection among the biographical facts as well as by selection among the subjects of the biographies. The ideology of *Woman's Record* is profoundly tied to Hale's lasting commitment to the selective promotion of her sex and even more specifically to the selective promotion of women writers.

Throughout her life Sarah Hale used biography as a way to establish female role models and judged publication the most concrete measure of approbation. That there could be conflict between success in publishing and Hale's standards for women was something that she only gradually acknowledged. In 1834, in the seventh volume of the *Ladies' Magazine,* she announced a series of "female biography," which she promised would include those who "have been eminent for domestic virtues and benevolence, as well as those who have exhibited brilliant talents and literary excellence. We are by no means in favor of exalting intellectual attainments above moral virtues" (41).

This announcement, nineteen years before the appearance of *Woman's Record,* shows how early Hale began to accumulate her card files, with plenty of opportunity to add and delete.

She had, perhaps, borrowed the idea. As early as 1829, in volume 2 of the *Ladies' Magazine,* she reviewed Anna Maria Lee's *Memoirs of Eminent Female Writers,* which she calls a "manual of biography." She explains the interest of the book thus:

> The private histories of eminent persons are always sought after with eagerness; and were this passion for biographical literature, rightly fostered and directed, it would have a most powerful influence in promoting the intellectual and moral improvement of women. But to do this, greatness, in its worldly sense, either as applied to talents or station, must not be the object of eulogy; or rather, the domestic virtues must possess a prominence in the pictures which are held up for the admiration and consequent imitation of women." (393)

With this comment, Hale begins to outline her own ideal of womanhood. "We do not, in our country . . . want exhibitions of those talents and acquirements, which have fitted women to rule empires and manage state intrigues,—we want patterns of virtue, of intelligence, of piety and usefulness in private life." Still, Lee's book does include biographies of some whose fame "rests solely on the merit of their knowledge and writings." Hale's ambivalence about the respective importance of "virtue" and "intelligence," especially when that intelligence leads to publication, surfaces almost immediately, as she explains that she will reprint sketches of "two, eminent for profound and brilliant acquirements," and then add "specimens of that kind of eminence, which seems to have been the result of goodness of heart, rather than pride of understanding." Her purpose is to allow "our young ladies" to "decide in which class of these distinguished females, they should prefer to see their names enrolled." The first two are Madame de Chastelet, who studied philosophy with Voltaire and wrote about Newton, and Sappho; the others are Elizabeth Carter and Elizabeth Smith, both of whom wrote poetry, and Madame de Sevigné (2 [1829]: 395-400). That both exemplars of the first category, who are less notable for their character than for their accomplishments, are foreign and not Anglo-Saxon, is one of several patterns that would coalesce in *Woman's Record.*

Hale began her own sketches soon, and from the beginning they were not purely domestic. In 1832 the *Ladies' Magazine* carried one of Mrs. Fry, as an example of "just what our charitable ladies require, to invite them to act, as well as talk" (5 [1832]: 444). Fry, whose life was "devoted to acts of virtue," was a comfortable model for Hale because she combined religious devotion with a mission to women.

The sketch pointedly describes Fry reading the Bible in prison and helping female prisoners' children. In the years that Hale edited the *Ladies' Magazine,* she identified herself with many of the causes that she would advocate throughout her life—female education, temperance, female missionaries, the control of their own property by married women—and praised women like Elizabeth Fry who worked for these causes. In the *Ladies' Magazine* Hale also delineated the methods she preferred: "I am not advocating what is termed *blue-stockingism.* No one can dislike a thorough dogmatical, dictatorial, demonstrating, metaphysically learned female more sincerely than I. But it is necessary, if men would improve, that women should be intelligent" (2 [1829]: 377).

Among these intelligent women, preeminently, were women writers. Writing had been Hale's own road to independence, and she always justified publication as the way by which intelligent, moral women could contribute to society while carrying out their domestic responsibilities. She promoted women authors at every step of her career and missed few opportunities to remind her readers of her special attention to female writers. For example, in volume seven of the *Ladies' Magazine* (1834) she lists her contributors for the past six years, including "Sigourney, Sedgwick, Gilman, Embury, Smith . . . Child, Gould, Wells, Willard, Phelps, Locke" (48). In 1837 she published *The Ladies' Wreath,* a collection of poetry by women from England and America, once again proposing two grounds for her choices and ignoring any possible conflict between them: "Two principles have guided my selections; one, to admit no poetry unless its aim was 'upward and onward;' the other, to allow place to those writers only whose style had some peculiar stamp of individuality, which marked their genius as original" (4). Some of those included had appeared in the list in the *Ladies' Magazine*—for example, Lydia Sigourney, Caroline Howard Gilman, Emma Catherine Embury, Elizabeth Smith—and all but one of those in *The Ladies' Wreath* would appear again in *Woman's Record.*

During her years as editor of *Godey's Lady's Book,* Hale published at least three special issues that included only female writers. The January 1840 issue of *Godey's* contained articles and stories by Hale, Elizabeth Ellet, Harriet Beecher Stowe, Lydia Sigourney, and Mary Russell Mitford, all of whom would appear in Hale's *Woman's Record.* In the Editor's Table of the January 1843 issue of *Godey's,* which again contained only women writers, Hale described her magazine as "the only Periodical in the world which embodies the piety, genius, intelligence, and refinement of perfect womanhood" (58). Once again Hale's stated ideal of womanhood went beyond the domestic virtues to include intelligence; McCall's quantitative analysis of the fiction in *Godey's* demonstrates that Hale's selection of stories reinforced this attitude for her readers. Finally, in the July 1845 all-female issue Hale provides yet another statement of her goals for the periodical and for American women. She is defending her temporary exclusion of men: "We make this arrangement, not as disparaging our gentlemen contributors, but to show the great progress of female literature, and the vast moral influence the genius of woman is obtaining in our country" (284).

Thus *Woman's Record,* which appeared first in 1853, with a second edition in 1855 and a third in 1872, was the apex of Sarah Hale's lifelong career as the discriminating promoter and patroness of members of her own sex and especially of the writers among them. In publications and reviews in the *Ladies' Magazine* and in *Godey's,* in the special issues of *Godey's,* in the **Ladies' Wreath,** Sarah Hale had regularly had opportunities to choose which women to feature and which to ignore. Viewed from the perspective of its exclusions as well as its inclusions, **Woman's Record** culminates a lifework of ideological choices. The volume argues, as Baym has said, for the superiority of women and of Christianity, but it has other, specific targets. In it Hale has the last word in her disputes with advocates of women's rights and of abolition, reveals the lower standard of morality she required of women not fortunate enough to be Americans, and again demonstrates her profound belief that there was nothing more important for a woman to do than to write. Especially in the 1872 edition, completed in 1869 when Hale was over eighty years old, **Woman's Record** closes the canon of Hale's writing by creating a print canon of the women she wished to have remembered—or forgotten.

Woman's Record; or, Sketches of All Distinguished Women from the Creation to A.D. 1868 was far more than a reference work or dictionary of biography. The **Record** provides at least a short biographical sketch for more than 1,800 women in world history, and names, in toto, more than 2,500 outstanding women, including a list of female missionaries in the appendix. In the general preface to the first edition, in the introduction to the second edition, and in the prefaces to each era, Hale states her goals for the **Woman's Record** quite clearly. She begins with the statement, "The want of the world is moral power" (xxxv), and then proceeds to outline her thory that educated, intelligent women will provide that moral power to the world. Her compendium will both prove her theory and serve as an example to women for their own lives: "The wide field of my plan, gathering records of women from every age, country, condition and character, presents an opportunity, never before accessible, of ascertaining the scope of feminine talent, and the effect the cultivated intellect of the sex, when brought to bear on Christian civilization, would exercise" (xlvii).

The third and last edition of **Woman's Record** is the best place to study the progress of Hale's ideas over the years from the 1840s until 1869, when the third edition went to the publisher. In complications, second thoughts, divided opinions, Hale reveals much about herself, as the construction of the book demonstrates much about her purposes. **Woman's Record** is divided into four eras: from the Creation to the birth of Jesus Christ, from the birth of Christ to 1500, from 1500 to 1850 (that is, to appear in this section a woman must have died by 1850), and the contemporary era "of living female writers." At the end of the contemporary period, Hale added a section on young writers and others, arranged by nation, a section on benefactresses that includes both philanthropists and Dorothea Dix, yet another section of supplementary names, and lists of female American missionaries. In the 1872 edition, she added another seventeen women in a second supplement and some brief notes updating the activities of women previously profiled, as well as notes on female progress since the first edition.

When it comes to the world of the living, Hale is more interested in women who have distinguished themselves by writing than in those in any other field. Of the 119 women profiled in the fourth era, the period of Hale's younger contemporaries, more than 90 are writers— poets, playwrights, historians, and novelists. For these women writers the **Record** goes beyond biography: it is also an anthology and a handbook of criticism, printing selections of their work as well as Hale's often hard-headed reviews and analyses. For example, after noting that Emma D. E. Nevitte Southworth, known to readers as E.D.E.N. Southworth, was left destitute with two infants to support, Hale praises the author for her "great powers of the imagination, and strength and depth of feeling," but along with selections from Southworth's gothic novel, *The Deserted Wife,* comes criticism of Southworth's "wild and extravagant manner" and "fervid imagination," which carries her "beyond the limits prescribed by correct taste or good judgment" (794). In another case, like many Victorians Hale saw serious flaws in Charlotte Brontë's *Jane Eyre:* "Vigour, animation, originality, an interest that never flags, must be conceded to it. . . . But the hero of this book, Mr. Rochester, is a personage utterly distasteful and disagreeable." She even proposes that "the chapters which immediately follow Mr. Rochester's most singularly managed declaration of love . . . have the air of being a contribution from some male friend." On the other hand, though she recognizes it as a literary "digression," Hale praises the section of the novel where Jane runs a parish school for girls, because it exemplifies "what may be effected by an intelligent woman, in awakening the torpidity of those classes of her sex to whom knowledge has but few opportunities of 'unrolling her ample page'" (597-98).

It is when we examine closely the women who are not writers that the extent of Hale's quiet exclusion becomes most apparent. Included are famous actresses and singers (Jenny Lind among others), scientists such as Maria Mitchell, teachers, at least one preacher, several European revolutionaries, and women rulers (Victoria and the queens of Spain and Portugal). Most of these women could be best described as intellectuals who were also examples of domestic virtue.

Women carrying forward the Christianization of the world of course merit approbation: with the exception of Phillis Wheatley, who appears as a poet, those women of color who are included figure because of their active Christianity. These include Kamamalu, daughter of the king of the Sandwich Islands; Kapiolani, another Hawaiian who overthrew the "idolatrous worship of Pele"; Pocahontas, "the first heathen who became converted to Christianity by the English settlers"; and Catherine Brown, a half-blooded Cherokee who also "brought many to Christianity." Even the odious Zinga was "the first of her tribe who made any attempt to adopt Christianity."[5] Yet Hale does not entirely support the religious thesis of her preface in the majority of the biographies. Not only are several Jewish women included, among them an actress and a singer, but Hale rarely mentions the religious denomination of the women or their dedication to the work of church or parish. Most surprising, given the anti-Catholic sentiment of nineteenth-century American society, she never identifies the European women by baptismal affiliation.

Hale's deeper purposes emerge if we compare the list of women discussed by Susan Conrad in *Perish the Thought: Intellectual Women in Romantic America, 1830-1860* to the selections in Hale's fourth era. Only seven of the thirteen described by Conrad appear in *Woman's Record.* Hale writes biographies of Margaret Fuller, Lydia Maria Child (with a rebuke we will discuss below), Elizabeth Fries Ellet, Louisa McCord, Sarah Whitman Power, Elizabeth Peabody, and Elizabeth Oakes Smith. All were authors, and many were contributors to Hale's periodicals. A look at the women whom Conrad proposes as intellectual leaders but whom Hale excludes provides a strong indication of Hale's goals and standards: Sarah Grimkeé, Elizabeth Cady Stanton, Antoinette Brown Blackwell, Paulina Wright Davis, Caroline Dall, and Mary Booth do not appear. Except for Mary Booth, all of the excluded women were politically active, either for women's rights or abolition, or both.

Woman's Record is, among other things, a continuation of Hale's literary dialogue on the proper response to slavery in America. Early in her career she gave some indication of uncertainty, though later her opposition to the abolition movement hardened. In the first edition of ***Northwood*** (1827) slavery was acknowledged as a problem that the northern hero would face by moving south, but was not a major topic. Two years

later, while editing the *Ladies' Magazine,* Hale even reprinted a "southern lady's" appeal on behalf of the slaves (2: 515-17). Her comment, however, was not about the ethics of slavery but about the appropriateness of women's taking political action:

> We presume the writer had no idea of advocating female interference or usurpation of authority, in directing the affairs of state. . . . The establishment of "female emancipation societies," as has been suggested by the writer, would not, we think, be perfectly in accordance with woman's character. . . . The influence of woman, to be beneficial, must depend mainly on the respect inspired by her *moral* excellence, not on the political address or energy she may display. (515-16)

Nevertheless, she did reprint most of the appeal.

By the 1850s, Hale, like many Americans, had become more concerned about the issue, and her position had hardened. Typically, she engaged in the debate about slavery and abolition through fiction. As a response to *Uncle Tom's Cabin,* which had begun running in the *National Era* in 1851, Hale prepared a revision of ***Northwood: A Tale of New England*** with the new subtitle ***Life North and South: Showing the True Character of Both*** (1852). In the preface she insists that "the great error of those who would sever the Union rather than see a slave within its borders, is, that they forget the *master* is their brother, as well as the *servant*" (iv). In this version Hale concludes the novel with an additional chapter of twenty pages, in which the hero and his bride read his late father's journal instructing them on how to manage the plantation they inherit. The journal has a section on "slavery and its reformers," which expresses opposition to abolition by condemning the use of "*fraud, falsehood, or force,* rather than wait God's time for the liberation of the slave," and another on "What the Bible says of Slavery," which argues that slavery is not sinful, though undesirable (395). The wife's chief duty will be to Christianize the slaves, after which they may return to Liberia and spread the gospel they have learned.[6]

In 1852 *Uncle Tom's Cabin* appeared in a hardcover edition. Thomas Gossett comments that Hale's next response, ***Liberia, or, Mr. Peyton's Experiments*** (1853) is one of those "difficult to classify as pro- or anti-slavery" (235). The novel begins with a Negro uprising and, despite the sentimental portrait of some slaves devoted to one idealized master, is quite negative about the possibility that freed slaves will be able to handle independent life on this continent. Hale's eventual solution, repatriation to Liberia, connects her work with Stowe's, where George and Eliza, and eventually Topsy, choose to return to Africa as missionaries. However, by including a section on the unhappiness of freed slaves in Canada—where George and

Eliza do well—and another on their inability to manage their own farms, Hale deprecates all other possibilities that Stowe includes. Her conviction is that only in Africa can Africans take charge of their own destinies. The final section of **Liberia** is an "Appendix" in which she subjoins "documents for the most part written by colored persons from and about Liberia, showing the estimation in which that country is held by those who have the best opportunity of judging" (247). To these are added the Declaration of Independence of Liberia, its constitution, and a number of papers on colonization, as well as a statement of the failure of emancipation in the West Indies. This collection seems to be Hale's attempt to meet Stowe on the ground of documentation she had claimed as her own in *The Key to Uncle Tom's Cabin* (1853).

Given her attitude toward female public speakers and toward abolition, it is not surprising that in **Woman's Record** Hale exercises her editorial power to express disapprobation of female abolitionists. She excludes almost all the women active in the abolition movement from the compendium as she had excluded them from her magazine. Of the fifty-one women whom Blanche Glassman Hersh identifies as working for abolition during the period coinciding with Hale's fourth era, only six appear in **Woman's Record:** Elizabeth Blackwell, Lydia Maria Child, Julia Ward Howe (a brief mention under "Young Writers"), Lucretia Coffin Mott, Elizabeth Oakes Smith, and Jane Grey Swisshelm (mentioned in passing in a summary paragraph). Blackwell is excused because she is the model for female physicians, a career choice Hale strongly supported; Smith is praised for her intellectual achievements.

The portraits and editorial comments on Child and Mott, however, embody Hale's peculiar blend of praise and criticism and demonstrate her difficulty in setting boundaries for the action of the intelligent and committed women she admired. Hale devotes considerable space to Child and prints a number of passages from her writings. What Hale finds appealing is Child's "warm sympathy with the young," as shown in her editorship of *The Juvenile Miscellany*. She anthologizes a selection from a book for children, *Fact and Fiction*, claiming that it "discloses the impulse of [Child's] own nature, always seeking to do good." But Child's abolitionist sympathies do not escape Hale's sharp tongue. She concedes that "the design of the abolitionists, let us believe, is the improvement and happiness of the coloured race; for this end Mrs. Child devoted her noblest talents, her holiest aspirations. . . . The result has been, that her fine genius, her soul's wealth has been wasted in the struggle which party politicians have used for their own selfish purposes" (619-20). If, instead, Child had spent her energies on sending "free emigrants" to Liberia and working for schools there, Hale imagines "what blessed memorials" would have come to her. Thus Hale praises a

woman's character, rebukes her for her life choices, and promotes her own solution to the national problem within one profile. This mixed analysis characterizes many of the portraits of active women whose beliefs Hale did not share.

A particularly delicate problem for Hale was how to deal with Harriet Beecher Stowe. In this case the successive editions provided an opportunity for second thoughts. Hale includes a highly laudatory portrait of Catharine Beecher, Stowe's elder sister, in the first edition of the **Record**. Her profile of Stowe there is short, noting her first collection of stories, *The Mayflower*, and her promise as a young author; she had published Stowe herself, in *Godey's*. There is no mention of *Uncle Tom's Cabin*, though Forrest Wilson asserts that by November 1851 "the fame of the *National Era's* serial had penetrated into an elegant sanctum in Philadelphia. Harriet received a letter from Sarah J. Hale, asking for her daguerreotype and biographical facts about herself which Mrs. Hale could use in writing a compendious book about distinguished women writers of the earth" (274). Stowe may bear part of the responsibility for this omission—Wilson reprints her reply to Hale, in which she calls her life uneventful, uninteresting, and domestic, and adds in a postscript, "In answer to one of your enquiries, I would say that I have never published but one book, 'The Mayflower,' by the Harpers."

Yet Hale deliberately used her editorial expertise to evade consideration of *Uncle Tom*. In the 1872 edition she includes a brief update under the heading of "List of the living not Found in the 4th Era." Here she notes the novels Stowe had written "since *Uncle Tom's Cabin*" (902). However, in her summary at the end of the second supplement to the edition of 1855 she had commented, "But the book of the three years is, as all the world knows, 'Uncle Tom's Log Cabin.' . . . We have no room here for an analysis of the story or the history of its triumphs: these matters will be more suitably discussed ten years hence" (898). In this passage she also complained of "another work," presumably *The Key to Uncle Tom's Cabin*, which she claimed would "do more to lower the standard of [Stowe's] genius and destroy the prestige which her assumed philanthophy *[sic]* had given to 'Uncle Tom's Cabin.'" Thus by emphasizing the storm of criticism which greeted the *Key* in the second edition, and then in the third edition ignoring her own proposal to consider the major work after a suitable time lapse, Hale, the advocate of women writers, managed never to review or discuss the most important novel by an American woman in the nineteenth century.

If Hale disapproved of and therefore excluded female abolitionists, who presumably were working for the benefit of an oppressed race, her views on women who were active in the women's rights movement were even more hostile. In an editorial in the *Ladies' Magazine* of 1833, Hale issues her judgment: "the term *rights of woman* is one to which I have an almost constitutional aversion. It is a kind of talisman, which conjures up . . . the image of a positive, conceited, domineering wife, than whom scarce any object in nature can be more disgusting" (6 [1833]: 496). It is no surprise to find that of all the women involved in the planning of Seneca Falls or the first few national women's rights conventions, only Lucretia Mott is included in the *Record.* Yet given Hale's position in Philadelphia, her comments on Mott, and her penchant for updating her work, she cannot have been unaware of the women's rights movement or unable to include profiles of its leaders. Such omissions were certainly deliberate.

In her rather lengthy profile of Lucretia Mott, Hale praises her for attending well to the duties of motherhood and for her support of her husband. She shows her familiarity with abolitionist activities by crediting Mott with being the most able representative sent to the World Anti-Slavery Convention, notable particularly for her power of speech. However, rather than attack Mott on the issue of abolition, she criticizes the Quaker preacher for her stand on the rights of women, for her position on marriage, and for her erroneous views of woman's place in society. Hale comments, "It is evident that Mrs. Mott places the 'true dignity of woman' in her ability to do 'man's work,' and to become more and more like him. What a degrading idea; as though the worth of porcelain should be estimated by its resemblance to iron" (753). She summarizes her estimate of Mott as follows: "In short, the theories of Mrs. Mott would disorganize society. . . . Woman's 'best gifts' are employed to promote goodness and happiness among those whose minds take their tone from her private character. Measured by this standard, Mrs. Mott deserves an estimation higher than her public displays of talent or philanthropy have ever won" (753).

Mott was, at least, an American; *Woman's Record* culminates the nationalist vision Hale had first expressed almost fifty years earlier in *Northwood.* Baym believes that the *Record* is meant to show not only Christian but also American progress; in America, both women and Christianity are closest to Hale's ideal ("Christian Women" 261). Yet of the 119 profiles in the fourth era, 79 are of European and British women. Among those who are not American, Hale was willing to include a fair number whose morals she condemned—for instance, George Sand, Bettina von Arnim, and Maria Christina, dowager queen of Spain—as well as several women who fought for their countries in man's dress and a number of female monarchs. We can justify these choices and Hale's glossing over the political, social, and sexual behavior of such women only by assuming that she set a higher standard for Americans. No toleration of moral laxness or unseemly

political activism could be afforded American women because they were to be the model for all women; nevertheless, Hale's fascination with the foreigners she describes complicates any attempt to imprison her or her text within the limits of "woman's sphere."

Sarah Hale was not only the promoter of other writers, she was herself a boon to the literary markets of her era. *Godey's,* of course, was a continuing success. For her books Hale used and benefited publishers in different cities: for example, in Boston, Bowles and Dearbom for the first edition of *Northwood,* and Marsh, Capen and Lyon for *The Ladies' Wreath* and *Poems for our Children;* in New York, H. Long for the second edition of *Northwood;* in Philadelphia, first Grigg and Elliot, and then Claxton, Remsen and Haffelfinger for her *Complete Dictionary of Poetical Quotations.* She wrote and edited so many books that Paul Boyer concludes that "'Sarah Josepha Hale' eventually became a kind of trademark" (*Notable American Women* 2: 113).

Woman's Record was published by the largest publisher in America at the time of its appearance, New York's Harper and Brothers. In the same year, 1853, Harper also published *Liberia; or, Mr. Peyton's Experiments* by Mrs. Hale; they had previously published both *Keeping House and Housekeeping* and *Boarding Out; or, Domestic Life;* in addition, they took over Hale copyrights from Marsh, Capen, Lyon & Webb. The Harper historian, Eugene Exman, notes that *Woman's Record* was a "big book for Christmas sales" and that it "had a lead position in the 1853 catalogue" (330). But 1853 was also the year of the great fire that destroyed the entire Harper printing plant on December 10. J. Henry Harper reprints Hale's letter of condolence, dated ten days later, which conveys both sympathy and the conviction that "adversity, that tries the souls of good men . . . brings its own reward in ways that are often more really beneficial than continued prosperity would be" (103). Exman points out her adroitness in dealing with her publishers here: during the ten days prior to the fire "four new books had been dispatched to dealers to fill advance orders. Among them was *Liberia, or Mr. Peyton's Experiments* by Mrs. Hale, a fact, however, which she did not comment on when she sent a letter of condolence" (Exman 359). It was by practicing just this kind of apparent self-effacement, while busily promoting her own work and that of other literary women, that Sarah Josepha Hale maintained her position as the most famous female editor of the nineteenth century.

When viewed as a whole, Hale's writing and editorial decisions over half a century display an astonishing constancy of purpose. Imbued by a vision of woman's role in the republic and in the world, Hale used every outlet available to her to promulgate her ideology and to support women's progress toward achieving the position she envisioned for them. Her ideology was a product of American political culture and Victorian views of gender difference. Women, morally superior rather than physically strong, were charged with responsibility for the moral direction of the family and the society. When Hale opened *Woman's Record* with the claim that what the world needs is moral power, she meant the moral power of women.

However, because Hale so firmly believed that woman's moral power was rooted in her inherent, essential nature, she opposed any attempt by women to compete with men, to enter the public spheres of politics or economics, or, as her rebuke of Mott showed, to try to become like men. As American society changed, becoming urban and industrial, Hale broadened her definition of woman's role to meet the needs of the age. A single mother herself, she first identified writing and teaching as appropriate activities for women; later she became the preeminent supporter of female missionaries and physicians. After the Civil War she supported light industrial work, domestic work, and clerical work as occupations for women who needed to earn a living. As Zophy points out, Hale's careful selection of these pursuits for middle-class women unintentionally paved the way for job segregation and the accompanying low pay for women workers (176).

Although Sarah Hale continually emphasized the duties of wife and mother as paramount, even praising women with whom she differed philosophically if they fulfilled their domestic duties well, she needed to find a way for woman's influence to be spread beyond the family. She found it, of course, in her own career as writer and editor. Women could promote moral progress and Christian life far beyond their own households as authors and yet not neglect their primary responsibilities. In addition, women writers could inspire others of their sex to moral and intellectual improvement. Sarah Hale's own position as an editor gave her the resources to promote women authors and to use model biographies of outstanding women to encourage her readers in their own lives. *Woman's Record* thus stands both as an explication of Hale's philosophy and as an example of the means by which woman's influence would be felt.

Notes

[1] Finley 43; she points out that the first thirteen volumes were entirely English.

[2] See Welter for a full exposition of this thesis.

[3] For a full discussion, see Bardes and Gossett, *Declarations of Independence* 17-37, and passim.

[4] Douglas notes that a writer for the *New Englander* protested Hale's "whitewash job on Nero's mother"

but that Hale defended Agrippina because she was above all a mother (86-87).

[5] Hale doesn't think much of Wheatley's work: her "poems have little literary merit; their worth arises from the extraordinary circumstance that they are the productions of an *African woman;* the sentiment is true always, but never new" (553). No women of color appear in the fourth era.

[6] There is a fuller analysis of this novel in Bardes and Gossett, *Declarations of Independence.*

Works Cited

Bardes, Barbara, and Suzanne Gossett. *Declarations of Independence: Women and Political Power in Nineteenth-Century American Fiction.* New Brunswick, NJ: Rutgers UP, 1990.

Baym, Nina. "Between Englightenment and Victorian: Toward a Narrative of American Women Writers Writing History." *Critical Inquiry* 18 (1991): 22-41.

———. "Onward Christian Women: Sarah J. Hale's History of the World." *New England Quarterly* 63 (1990): 249-70.

Conrad, Susan Phinney. *Perish the Thought: Intellectual Women in Romantic America, 1830-1860.* New York: Oxford UP, 1976.

Coultrap-McQuin, Susan. *Doing Literary Business: American Women Writers in the Nineteenth Century.* Chapel Hill: U of North Carolina P, 1990.

Douglas, Ann. *The Feminization of American Culture.* New York: Avon, 1978.

Exman, Eugene. *The Brothers Harper.* New York: Harper and Row, 1965.

Finley, Ruth. *The Lady of Godey's: Sarah Josepha Hale.* Philadelphia: Lippincott, 1931.

Gossett, Thomas. *Uncle Tom's Cabin and American Culture.* Dallas, TX: Southern Methodist UP, 1985.

Hale, Sarah J. *The Ladies' Wreath.* Boston: Marsh, Capen & Lyon, 1837.

———. *Northwood: A Tale of New England.* Boston: Bowles and Dearbom, 1827; *Northwood; or, Life North and South: Showing the True Character of Both.* New York: H. Long, 1852.

———. *Woman's Record; or, Sketches of All Distinguished Women from the Creation to A.D. 1868.* 3d ed. New York: Harper and Brothers, 1872.

Harper, J. Henry. *The House of Harper.* New York: Harper and Brothers, 1912.

Hersh, Blanche Glassman. *The Slavery of Sex: Feminist-Abolitionists in America.* Urbana: U of Illinois P, 1978.

Hoffman, Nicole Tonkavich. "Sarah Josepha Hale 1788-1874 *[sic]:* Profile." *Legacy* 7 (1990): 47-55.

James, Edward T., Janet Wilson James, and Paul S. Boyer, eds. *Notable American Women, 1607-1950: A Biographical Dictionary.* 3 vols. Cambridge, MA: Belknap P of Harvard UP, 1971.

Martin, Lawrence. "The Genesis of Godey's 'Lady's Book.'" *New England Quarterly* 1 (1928): 41-70.

McCall, Laura. "'The Reign of Brute Force Is Now Over': A Content Analysis of *Godey's Lady's Book,* 1830-1860." *Journal of the Early Republic* 9 (1989): 217-36.

Mott, Frank Luther. *A History of American Magazines, 1741-1850.* New York: D. Appleton, 1930.

Walker, Cheryl. *The Nightingale's Burden: Women Poets and American Culture before 1900.* Bloomington: Indiana UP, 1982.

Welter, Barbara. "The Cult of True Womanhood, 1820-1860." *American Quarterly* 18 (1966): 151-74.

Wilson, Forrest. *Crusader in Crinoline.* Philadelphia: Lippincott, 1941.

Wood, James Playsted. *Magazines in the United States.* 3d ed. New York: Roland, 1971.

Zophy, Angela. "For the Improvement of My Sex: Sarah Josepha Hale's Editorship of *Godey's Lady's Book, 1837-1877.*" Diss. Ohio State U, 1978.

Patricia Okker (essay date 1995)

SOURCE: "From Intellectual Equality to Moral Difference: Hale's Conversion to Separate Spheres" in *Our Sister Editors: Sarah J. Hale and the Tradition of Nineteenth-Century American Women Editors,* University of Georgia Press, 1995, pp. 38-58.

[*In the following excerpt, Okker discusses what she sees as a shift in Hale's writings from a belief in the Enlightenment notion of equality between the sexes to the Victorian notion of separate spheres of endeavor for men and women.*]

Hale's writings during these early years [of her career] show little sign that she would eventually promote absolute notions of sexual difference and the idea of gendered separate spheres. Hale's novel ***Northwood: A Tale of New England,*** published in 1827, reveals her grounding in Enlightenment values. Though the novel does associate women with domesticity and men with politics, it repeatedly portrays ideal men and women as practically identical—rational, industrious, and frugal.[13] Hale's view of shared, rather than divergent, traits among men and women is particularly evident in the novel's exploration of marriage. Lydia and Horace Brainard are relatively unhappy together, precisely because Lydia's education neglected her intellectual abilities. Thus, when Horace's attempts at "rational conversation" with his new wife fail and he realizes that only "insipid, common-place chat" can entertain her, he reflects unhappily that "he must travel the journal of life with such a companion." In contrast, ideal marriages are presented as partnerships of similar individuals. Mrs. Romelee, for instance, is described as her husband's "helpmate" and "a tried and discreet friend," and the narrator later celebrates a wedding ceremony in which "two rational beings . . . voluntarily enter into a league of perpetual friendship."[14]

No doubt the rural setting of the novel contributes to the sense of men and women as more alike than different. In this world of small New England farms, men and women live and work together, not in separate worlds. While Victorian ideologies of separate spheres frequently delineated men's and women's work as properly public and private respectively, all members of Hale's ideal New England family contribute to the success of the family farm—itself inseparable from the domestic space. Several of the novel's women are noted for their abilities in running dairies, and the presentation of Mr. Romelee's cider and Mrs. Romelee's currant wine suggests that they share responsibilities for the family orchard. Just as the duties of running the farm are shared in Hale's novel, so too are responsibilities of raising children. Indeed, when Sidney Romelee first returns to his parents' home after an absence of nearly thirteen years, he finds his father—not his mother—sitting before the hearth, reading, with one of his daughters seated on his knee.

Though she would continue to rely on certain elements of Enlightenment ideologies throughout her editorial career, Hale started to shift toward Victorian notions of sexual difference soon after she turned to writing as an occupation. One sign of this change was Hale's new sense of her audience, specifically her increased submission to women's periodicals. In 1826 alone, Hale contributed twenty-one pieces to the *Boston Spectator and Ladies' Album,* and she won that magazine's literary prize for her poem **"Hymn to Charity."**[15]

Hale's self-definition as a woman writing for other women became even more pronounced when, based in part on the limited success of *Northwood,* publisher and clergyman John Lauris Blake offered Hale the position as editor of his new magazine.[16] The first issue of the *Ladies' Magazine* appeared in Boston in January 1828.[17] Hale edited the first few issues from her home in Newport, but she moved to Boston in April. Although the *Ladies' Magazine* was not, as some have suggested, the first women's periodical to be edited by a woman, it was the first such magazine to achieve any kind of success, surviving nine years.

During her editorship of the *Ladies' Magazine,* Hale vacillated between an Enlightenment emphasis on women's intellectual equality with men and a Victorian belief in women's moral difference from men. Initially, the magazine emphasized Enlightenment principles of women's intellectual equality and the importance of women's education. In this way, Hale's editorship of the *Ladies' Magazine* shared much with her previous work as a teacher. Just as she insisted that women's schooling be intellectually challenging rather than merely ornamental, so Hale rejected the idea that her magazine would simply entertain. Thus, in contrast to other early women's magazines—based on British models and noted for their distinctly anti-intellectual flavor and their emphasis on fashionable life—Hale's *Ladies' Magazine* focused on women's education, social reform, and American literature.[18] In the introductory issue, Hale explained that her intent was "to accelerate the progress of mental improvement," and she promised particular attention to "the cause of education" (*LM,* Jan. 1828, 1-2). In keeping with the educational tone of the magazine, its essays were generally serious and treated such topics as dueling, temperance, letter writing, suicide, and women's physical education. Essays arguing for an intellectually rigorous education for women were especially common, and Hale frequently used her editorial column to do a bit of teaching herself, often in regard to social issues, such as property rights for married women and increased work opportunities for women. She also used her editorial pages to endorse women's civic organizations, such as the Fatherless and Widows' Society and the Seaman's Aid Society, both in Boston.

Hale advocated a strong literary component as part of the intellectual and educational basis of the magazine. As she explained in her opening editorial, literature was necessary for any "mental improvement." In her support of literature, Hale abandoned the popular practices of so-called scissors editors, who reprinted material from other sources, mostly British. Hale instead insisted on original material, and the magazine's fiction and sketches emphasized American characteristics and settings. She also published book reviews and longer essays on such literary issues as novel reading, English poetry, and women writers. Biographical sketches of famous contemporary women were common.

Hale's reliance on Enlightenment rhetoric within this intellectual and educational focus is demonstrated by her introductory essay that opened the magazine in January 1828. Associating "the experiment of universal instruction" with the "perfection of our social happiness," Hale defined her own periodical project as part of that national experiment. She explained that the magazine was "designed to mark the progress of female improvement, and cherish the effusions of female intellect," and she portrayed the magazine as assisting women—specifically mothers—in fulfilling their republican duties: "It is that mothers may be competent to the task of instructing their children, training them from infancy to the contemplation and love of all that is great and good, and the practice of piety and virtue. Then the sons of the republic will become polished pillars in the temple of our national glory, and the daughters bright gems to adorn it." Hale's reliance here on republican ideology is also demonstrated by her specific addresses to men. While she did speak of women's "domestic duties" and women's "sphere," Hale did not really endorse the idea of either a physical separation or an essential difference between men and women, referring instead to woman as the "rational companion" of man. Furthermore, she insisted that although the *Ladies' Magazine* was "ostensibly designed for the ladies, [it] is not intended to be exclusively devoted to female literature." Hale "respectfully" invited the "gentlemen" to "examine its contents," and she devoted five full paragraphs to asking for their patronage. In keeping with her focus on this audience, Hale referred to women not as "our sex," as she would later do, but rather as "the sex" (*LM,* Jan. 1828, 1-3). Thus, although Hale did identify herself as a woman and did use some elements of the sisterly editorial voice in early issues of the *Ladies' Magazine* (including printing letters to the editor), she initially denied a strictly separatist identity for her magazine and avoided intimacy with her readers.

Still, the magazine was titled *Ladies' Magazine,* suggesting at least some elements of a separatist identity. Unlike later separatist rhetorics, which established women as the center of attention, however, Hale's limited use of separatism seems to have been motivated by her desire to avoid criticism. She willingly accepted a marginal position for herself and, to some extent, for other women. She credited men, after all, not women, with the "triumph" of improved education for women, and she even minimized the magazine's worth. "Competition," she insisted, "even were it *possible,* with any established literary journal, is neither wished nor intended" (*LM,* Jan. 1828, 1-4).

Hale's struggle to determine the appropriate degree of separatism is further revealed in her efforts to define her role as book reviewer. Although she published monthly book reviews, Hale repeatedly rejected the title of literary critic, which she associated with men. Instead, she identified herself as an "inspector" of literature and as a writer of "notices" (*LM*, Jan. 1828, 46; Nov. 1828, 522). Defining how such a position differed from that of a "critic," Hale explained her preference of "giving directions where the young may find what will improve their minds and confirm them in the love of virtue, rather than occupy their time with disquisitions on the structure of sentences or the rhythm of poetry" (*LM*, Jan. 1829, 38-39). Similarly, Hale informed her readers that she wrote "*notice* of books" rather than "*criticisms* in the *critical* acceptation of that learned word." As she explained, criticism noted "the faults of authors," while her "notices" identified "the beauties" (*LM*, Nov. 1828, 522).

At the basis of this distinction is gender: a "male critic," Hale wrote, was free "to criticise on style, or cut up books with the keen dissecting knife of ridicule, or triumph in the superior wit or argument, . . . or to 'deal damnation' on the dull." Such behavior did "not accord with the province of woman" (*LM*, Nov. 1828, 522). In many ways, Hale's editorial stance appears to be what Ann Douglas would call the amateurish pose of the professional.[19] When Hale insisted, for example, that a woman who practiced literary criticism had violated "propriety" and forgotten "the dignity" of her sex, she seemed to deny the possibility of a woman as critic. Similarly, by describing her judgments as especially appropriate for the "young," Hale appeared to renounce her ability to make intellectual, literary judgments. Indeed, she made such a claim quite explicit when she announced that she did "not feel qualified to perform the task" of the literary critic (*LM*, Nov. 1828; 522-23; Jan. 1829, 36-38).

Despite the appearance of self-effacement, Hale's comments indicate her positive self-identity as a woman critic. Rather than suggesting inferiority, Hale's position demonstrates the confidence necessary to condemn current practices in literary criticism. When she described how male critics practiced "the science of carping," she did not suggest that she might be incapable of such work, but rather that the male critics' attacks were inappropriate. Such behavior, according to Hale, was motivated not by love of literature but by selfishness. Suggesting that male critics found unnecessary fault only to boast of their abilities, Hale described "the hardihood of mind, which enables the male critic to depend on himself, and command the acquiescence of the world in his sentiments, more perhaps by his own boldness, than the real justness of his opinions" (*LM*, Nov. 1828, 522-23). A female critic could certainly judge the work, as did Hale throughout her editorial reviews, but the female reviewer, according to Hale, would

never celebrate in "triumph" upon finding artistic flaws, nor would she present unjust opinions simply to appear bold.

In distinguishing her work from that of the male critics, Hale also identified a positive sense of her function as editor. Hale's self-identity here suggests the beginnings of a shift toward Victorian ideologies of gender. Not willing to see all critics as identical, Hale began to articulate an essential difference between men and women editors. Significantly, Hale defined her own critical discourse in typically Victorian terms, with a special emphasis on morality. As she explained in 1829,

> It was never our design, when we undertook to conduct the *Ladies' Magazine,* to engage in those elaborate discussions, or profound researches which confer the title of scientific and learned on the work they occupy. Nor did we propose to be critical, in the sense the philologist would deem necessary, in that important department. We only intended to explain to our readers what we considered the *moral* tendency of the books we might notice, or more particularly their fitness for, and probable effect on female minds. We considered this course most appropriate for a woman, and the most likely to prove acceptable as well as beneficial to our own sex. (*LM*, June 1829, 282)

Rather than suggesting her limitations, then, Hale's testimony about not finding authors' faults is more accurately an attempt to define the kind of faults she would cite. Indeed, when describing her role as critic, Hale explained that she would criticize authors only when their "sins should be in *morals*" (*LM*, Nov. 1828, 522). Hale was not, of course, the only reviewer in the 1820s calling for moral criticism, but her version of moral criticism as gendered suggests her shift away from an Enlightenment emphasis on intellectual equality toward Victorian ideologies of essential sexual difference based on women's morality.[20]

The transition from an Enlightenment to a Victorian ideology of womanhood is evident within other features of her magazine as well. Beginning in 1830, for example, Hale's intermittent use of fashion plates—which were increasingly identified with the idea of a separate women's culture—suggests her experimentation with Victorian notions of gender.[21] Similarly, many of the magazine's essays began featuring Victorian rhetoric. Consider, for example, an 1831 essay titled **"Boarding Schools,"** which was unsigned but in all likelihood written by Hale. The essay began in fairly conventional Enlightenment terms, arguing the necessity "to instruct equally both sexes." Though defending that argument in part on the basis of the republican mother's influence on men, the essay itself interpreted that influence in ways remarkably similar to Victorian notions of essential sexual difference. Arguing that "till women are permitted to become rational, men will

Painted by J.C. Timbrell.   Engraved by J. Bannister

MATERNAL INSTRUCTION.

Engraved expressly for Godey's Lady's Book.

"Maternal Instruction," an engraving of domestic life from Godey's Lady's Book, *March, 1845.*

continue [to be] fools," the author of the essay defined fools "in the scriptural sense, meaning ignorant, weak, wicked, unstable, perverse." Though ostensibly supporting "equal" education, the writer suggested that men and women needed different educations: while both men and women must receive intellectual stimulation, men must also experience the influence of women. Education alone was insufficient for men's proper development. The implication clearly was that men and women had very different essential natures (*LM,* April 1831, 145).

In addition to implying an essential sexual difference, the essay suggested a shift toward Victorian notions of separate spheres. While the republican image of domestic space often focused on a woman's influence on her sons (assumed to be the next leaders of the republic), this essay focused almost exclusively on women and girls.[22] The emphasis here was not on a mother's teaching of her sons and daughters but on daughters alone. Similarly, the schools and the home were depicted as multigenerational worlds of women, with mothers responsible for transmitting female culture to their daughters. Although supporting formal education for young girls, for example, the essay recommended that girls from age twelve or fourteen continue their education at home so that the "mother [may] become the preceptress and companion of her daughter." The emerging vision of women's culture is also suggested in the idea that the "useful and ornamental in education, must be made to harmonize." Rather than rejecting the so-called ornamental arts, this essay insisted upon the value of women's learning housekeeping as well as music, sewing, drawing, and painting (*LM,* April 1831, 147-49).

No doubt many factors contributed to Hale's increasing reliance on Victorian notions of womanhood and women's culture. Certainly, Vicetorian rhetoric and images of a separate women's culture—including fashion plates—were proving popular in other women's magazines. Still, Hale's turn to Victorian ideologies of gender was probably not based solely on market forces. As an independent, unmarried woman eager to earn a living for herself and her children, Hale would have likely found republican ideologies of gender limiting, for such rhetorics tended to define women primarily as wives and mothers and as occupying the domestic space. Unable to earn her living within that space but still insisting on her identity as a mother, Hale needed—both professionally and personally—a rhetoric that fused womanhood with the public space, which, unlike the domestic sphere, offered financial remuneration for work. To a great extent, Victorian ideologies of gender provided just what Hale needed. Indeed, without undercutting the association of women as mothers and wives, Victorian notions of sexual difference offered women both

an image of a separate women's culture and, perhaps even more important, a rationale for their emergence into the public sphere.

Hale's conversion to a Victorian perspective on gender was sealed in January 1837, when she began editing Louis Godey's *Lady's Book,* later titled *Godey's Lady's Book.*[23] Before Hale's arrival, the *Lady's Book* had consisted primarily of reprints, engravings, fashion plates, recipes, and embroidery patterns and thus offered its readers a fare entirely different from that available in Hale's *Ladies' Magazine,* which focused on women's intellectual and moral strengths and original American literature. Suggesting the extent to which Hale and Godey combined their different approaches, Hale's inaugural essay for the *Lady's Book,* titled **"The 'Conversazióne,'"** depicted the magazine's transition as a "perfecting process" in which the two periodicals, with their "pleasant voices blended in one sweet melody," combined to create something new: "Though not a *new* work in name," Hale explained, the *Lady's Book* was "improved and beautified" (*GLB,* Jan. 1837, 1). Hale's image of two voices blending was an apt one, for the "new" *Lady's Book* continued to feature the often elaborate fashion plates, engravings, and needlework patterns— the so-called embellishments for which Louis Godey became famous. At the same time, Hale injected her own editorial interests into the new magazine. She emphasized women's education and original literature, as she had in the *Ladies' Magazine,* and she used her editorial pages to promote her patriotic and social causes, including a campaign to complete the Bunker Hill Monument, one to save Mount Vernon, and others to support such women's interests as the founding of Vassar College and the training of women as physicians.

Although some twentieth-century scholars have written that Louis Godey maintained most, if not all, editorial control of the *Lady's Book,* Godey and Hale seem to have had a clear sense of divided duties. Indeed, from the beginning of their partnership and throughout the more than forty years that they worked together, Louis Godey served primarily as publisher, and Sarah J. Hale was literary editor. In advertisements, Godey described the magazine's reading matter as "under the control" of Hale, and Hale in her closing editorial in 1877 described Godey as "the sole proprietor and business manager" and herself as "the literary editress" (*GLB,* Dec. 1877, 522).[24] The only feature that she evidently did not manage was fashion. Repeatedly reminding readers of this fact, Louis Godey instructed them to address material to the fashion editor in care of him.[25] These distinct duties are evident within the magazine columns as well. While Godey often used his column to advertise and boast the magazine's successes, Hale's "Editors' Table" generally focused on book reviews and editorial essays.

Though Louis Godey's and Sarah J. Hale's voices within the magazine did, at times, compete with one another, the magazine established by this merger did find a coherent identity, one that, significantly, celebrated Victorian ideologies of gender. Godey's expertise in the embellishments and Hale's interest in original literature and women's causes combined to create a strong sense of a separate women's culture. Hale's essay **"The 'Conversazióne'"** reveals her commitment to Victorian gender ideals. While in the *Ladies' Magazine* Hale focused on women's rational abilities as equal to men's, here she rigorously asserted an essential sexual difference. Arguing that there were "mental differences in the character of the sexes," Hale explained: "The strength of man's character is in his physical propensities—the strength of woman lies in her moral sentiments." In an even more detailed elaboration of her notion of essential sexual difference, Hale quoted at length a Professor Wilson, who deemed women "spiritual beings" and "pure as dew-drops, or moonbeams," but men "vile, corrupt, polluted, and selfish." Though Hale herself avoided complete agreement, on the grounds that she had "more sons than daughters," her attention to Wilson's claims functioned as an implicit endorsement of an absolute sexual difference (*GLB,* Jan. 1837, 1-3).

Hale, though, did not completely renounce her earlier assertions about women's intellectual equality with men. Indeed, what Hale did in this essay and what she tried to do throughout her editorial career was to combine Enlightenment and Victorian ideologies of gender. When explaining the Victorian belief in "mental differences" between men and women, Hale refused to give up the principle of equality: the difference of "the minds of the sexes," she insisted, "is not in strength of intellect, but in the manner of awakening the reason and directing its power." Similarly, as much as she associated women with moral influence, Hale continued to assert the importance of education, including the rational study of "mathematics, philosophy, and rhetoric" (*GLB,* Jan. 1837, 1-2).

In Hale's writings this blend of women's intellectual equality and moral difference proved a flexible—and powerful—rhetoric, and she repeatedly moved from one ideology to the other, without any apparent sense of contradiction. In **"The 'Conversazióne,'"** for instance, she defended her patronage of improved women's education on the basis of "the enlightened intellect of woman." Elsewhere in the essay, however, she employed the rhetoric of difference to claim her own authority as editor and the superiority of her periodical. Immediately after explaining the "mental differences" of "the sexes," Hale argued: "It is on these principles that the claim of superior excellence for 'The Lady's Book,' is founded. If men are, by their position and knowledge of the world, better qualified to instruct men, it can hardly fail to be conceded that a

woman is more susceptible of those delicate traits of feeling and sympathies of the soul which predominate in her own sex" (*GLB,* Jan. 1837, 2). The implication, of course, is that the *Lady's Book* had improved precisely because its editor was a woman.

In contrast, at the time that Hale began her editorship of the *Ladies' Magazine* she made no such claim. In her opening editorial in that publication, Hale explicitly asked for the patronage of men, and she granted men the authority to determine whether the magazine was appropriate for their wives, daughters, sisters, and lovers. Hale's opening essay in the *Lady's Book,* however, defines a space that is exclusively women's. Though she did acknowledge that "gentlemen" might be paying for the magazine, she granted women the right to "introduce" men to it. Hale's editorial voice in this *Lady's Book* essay is informal and reveals an intimacy with readers. In contrast to her earlier references to women as "the sex," here she relied on the more intimate "our own sex." Similarly, in elaborating on the essay's title, Hale relied heavily on the sisterly editorial voice, as she imagined the magazine to be equivalent to a party of women: "In short, we intend our work as a *'Conversazióne'* of the highest character, to which we invite every lady in our land—this 'Book' is the ticket of admission, and the first weekday in every month the time of attendance" (*GLB,* Jan. 1837, 1-2). As this passage suggests, Hale's "new" *Lady's Book* both depended on and helped to sustain a separate women's culture. Without an image of such a culture, Hale would have had no way of identifying an exclusively female audience. At the same time, the magazine itself was one of the elements of that culture. In the experience of receiving and presumably reading the magazine on the same day, Hale's readers would have likely had a sense of that shared culture.

The *Lady's Book*'s contributions to and dependence on a separate women's culture are also suggested in Hale's introductory essay in other ways. Again in contrast to Hale's claim in 1828 that her magazine would not be "exclusively devoted to female literature," here all the writers Hale promised her readers were women.[26] Similarly, though twentieth-century scholars have generally referred to the magazine as *Godey's* and have thus deemphasized its separatist identity, Hale declared the title *The Lady's Book* to be "perfect." Despite the subsequent title changes, in fact, both Hale and Louis Godey continued to refer to the magazine as the *Lady's Book,* or simply the *Book,* throughout their tenures at the magazine. In keeping with the designation popular in its own day and in order to suggest the magazine's image of itself as a woman-identified periodical, I will use the title *Lady's Book.*

Hale's transition to a Victorian ideology of gender and her corresponding sense of writing to an exclusively female audience are also suggested by her publications outside the two magazines that she edited. During her editorship of the *Ladies' Magazine,* Hale's publications generally depended on an Enlightenment philosophy. Like **Northwood** that preceded them, *Sketches of American Character* (1829) and *Traits of American Life* (1835), for example, featured republican virtues and rationality.[27] Significantly, both texts also assumed a general rather than a sex-specific audience. Though originally published as series of sketches in the *Ladies' Magazine,* **Sketches** and **Traits** did not focus specifically on women's issues. Rather, as the preface to **Sketches** explained, the focus was on "Americans" and their "peculiar characteristics," on "the minds, manners, and habits of the citizens of our republic."[28]

Hale increasingly turned her attention to more specialized audiences, and by the early 1830s she was well on her way to establishing a successful career in children's literature. Her **Poems for Our Children,** in which "Mary's Lamb" appeared, was published in 1830; **Flora's Interpreter; or, The American Book of Flowers and Sentiments,** which was intended to help educate children, appeared in 1832; and **The School Song Book** was issued first in 1834 and then again in 1841 as **My Little Song Book.** Hale also edited a number of works for children, including a ten-volume series, the Little Boys' and Girls' Library, and an abridged Bible for children, and she assumed Lydia Maria Child's editorial position of the *Juvenile Miscellany* from 1834 until April 1836, when it ceased publication.[29]

Although Hale continued to write children's literature throughout her life, she turned increasingly to writing for a specifically female adult audience in her book publications at the same time that she promoted the idea of a separate women's culture in her magazines. In the first year that she edited the *Lady's Book,* she published an anthology of poetry, her first clearly separatist book, **The Ladies' Wreath: A Selection from the Female Poetic Writers of England and America** (1837). In addition to singling out women writers, Hale defined her audience as primarily women. The title page declared that the book was "Prepared Especially for Young Ladies," and Hale explained in the preface: "I cannot but believe that this book will find favor in the eyes of my own sex. It is particularly intended for young ladies."[30] Many of her subsequent books and anthologies have a similar gender-specific orientation, including her advice books on housekeeping and cooking, two novels of domestic life, an anthology of literature for brides, and editions of the letters of Lady Mary Wortley Montagu and of Madame de Sévigné.[31]

Hale's transformation in her book publications to a woman-centered Victorian ideology is best demonstrated by her most ambitious—and most explicitly gendered—book, **Woman's Record; or, Sketches of All Distinguished Women from 'The Beginning' till**

A.D. 1850, first issued in 1853. Dividing history into four eras, this nine-hundred-page work presents biographical essays on more than sixteen hundred women, ranging from Sappho and Cleopatra to Emma Willard and Hale herself. As Nina Baym has observed, **Woman's Record** reconceived history with women at its center.[32] In the sketches of the many writers featured, Hale often included samples of their work, giving **Woman's Record** some of the miscellaneous qualities of a magazine. Hale's commitment to this woman-centered book continued well past its initial publication. She continued her biographical researches and issued revised and expanded editions of the work in 1855 and 1870. . . .

Notes

[13] For a brief discussion of the novel's treatment of such traits as connected with the republic's prosperity, see Nina Baym, *Feminism and American Literary History Essays* (Mew Brunswick, N J: Rutgers University Press, 1992) 168-71.

[14] Sarah Josepha Hale, *Northwood: A Tale of New England,* 2 vols. (Boston: Bowles and Dearborn, 1827), 1: 23, 6, 129.

[15] In this section I have relied on Jacob Blanck, *Bibliography of American Literature;* (New Haven: Yale University Press, 1955-91) and Isabelle Webb Entrikin, *Sarah Josepha Hale and Godey's Lady's Book* (Lancaster, Penn.: Lancaster Press, 1946).

[16] Hale and subsequent scholars have exaggerated the popular and critical success of *Northwood* and its impact on Hale's being offered the editorship of the *Ladies' Magazine.* The only known source indicating actual sales figures—the 28 April 1827 issue of the *Boston Spectator*—did report that *Northwood* was outselling comparable works published in Boston during the past several years, but it gave neither information about sales outside Boston nor any exact figures. Furthermore, the timing of this announcement—it appeared during the same month as the novel's publication—suggests that rather than providing information about actual sales, the *Spectator* announcement may have been intended as an advertisement for Hale, one of the magazine's frequent contributors.

Information about the critical success of *Northwood* has also been exaggerated, as the novel received limited and somewhat mixed reviews. The *Boston Lyceum,* for instance, commended *Northwood*'s "many beauties of an unusual kind" and predicted "deserved popularity," but it also examined its "faults," specifically the need for "more boldness in the development of intellectual capacity, more vividness in descriptive scenery, and more actual skill and power exerted in laying open the inmost recesses of the human heart"

(*Boston Lyceum,* 15 April 1827, 219). The only truly positive reviews of the novel, moreover, can hardly be considered disinterested critical evaluations. One appeared in the *United States Review and Literary Gazette,* a magazine published by the same company that issued Hale's novel. Another appeared in 1833, six years after the novel's publication. By this time Hale had already achieved considerable fame as both an editor and an author. This late review therefore represents an attempt to add authority to Hale's already established literary reputation rather than an examination of a beginning writer's abilities (*American Monthly Review,* Sept. 1833, 239).

Hale was indeed offered the editing position at the *Ladies' Magazine* shortly after the novel's publication, but she probably received that offer not because of the novel's success but because friends of her husband came to her aid. According to Isabelle Webb Entrikin, the magazine's publisher was probably associated with Hale's husband's Masonic order, which had also published her first volume of poetry (*Sarah Josepha Hale* 17). This claim is substantiated by Elizabeth Oakes Smith's recollection that the Masons had "rallied to Mrs. Hale's assistance" and started the magazine themselves in order to make her editor. See Smith, *Selections from the Autobiography of Elizabeth Oakes Smith,* ed. Mary Alice Wyman (Lewiston, Maine: Lewiston, 1924), 97.

[17] Like many nineteenth-century periodicals, Hale's *Ladies' Magazine* used several different titles, including *The Ladies' Magazine, The Ladies' Magazine and Literary Gazette,* and *American Ladies' Magazine.* Like most studies, this one will refer to the periodical by the title *Ladies' Magazine,* regardless of the title on a particular issue under consideration. The abbreviation *LM* will be used within parenthetical citations.

[18] For overviews of early American magazines for women, see Lawrence Martin, "The Genesis of *Godey's Lady's Book," New England Quarterly* 1 (1928): 41-70; and Bertha Monica Stearns, "Before *Godey's*" (New York: Knopf, 1977) 248-55.

[19] Douglas, *The Feminization of American Culture American Literature* 2 (1930): 85.

[20] On appeals to moral criticism, see Nina Baym, *Novels, Readers, and Reviewers: Responses to Fiction in Antebellum America* (Ithaca, N.Y.: Cornell University Press, 1984), 173-95.

[21] Fashion plates continued as regular features through 1833, though often with Hale's denouncement of the interest of American women in foreign fashions. During the last three years of the publication of the *Ladies' Magazine,* however, no fashion drawings appeared, despite their increased frequency in other magazines. Entrikin reports that Hale dropped the engravings and fashion plates after becoming part owner of the magazine (*Sarah Josepha Hale,* 53).

[22] An unsigned essay titled "Education," published in the *Ladies' Magazine,* assumed that "females" had "an equality of intellect" and then argued for the importance of mothers' educating their sons. Women may obtain an "influence in society, that will be paramount to authority . . . if they are careful to train their young sons to industry, and teach them knowledge, and inspire them with the spirit of enterprize and the love of excellence" (*LM,* Sept. 1828, 422-23).

[23] Hale's motives in accepting Godey's offer are not certain, but the *Ladies' Magazine* apparently faced financial difficulties. Several appeals to delinquent subscribers appeared in 1836, and in the announcement of her new position, Hale said that more than one thousand dollars was due the *Ladies' Magazine* (*LM,* July 1836, 424; Nov. 1836, 664). Hale may also have accepted the new position because Godey agreed to let her remain in Boston, since her youngest son attended Harvard. She did not move to Philadelphia until 1841, when her son graduated.

The *Lady's Book* also used the titles *Godey's Lady's Book and Ladies' American Magazine, Godey's Magazine and Lady's Book, Godey's Lady's Book and Magazine,* and *Godey's Magazine.*

[24] At various times other people were listed as editors, though their duties varied considerably. From 1842 until 1846, for example, Morton McMichael (later mayor of Philadelphia) was identified as one of the editors. His role, like Louis Godey's, is probably best understood as that of a publisher.

[25] In one column, for instance, Godey wrote: "Mrs. Hale is not the fashion editor. How often will it be necessary for us to repeat this? Address Fashion Editor, care of L. A. Godey" (*GLB,* April 1859, 378).

[26] Hale boasted: "Our writers in this department are among the most accomplished in the country. Mrs. Sedgwick, Mrs. Embury, Mrs. Gilman, Mrs. Smith, Miss Leslie, Mrs. Lee Hentz, Mrs. Stephens, Miss Gooch, Mrs. Woodhull, and many others will grace our 'Conversaziónes.'" She also promised essays by Emma Willard and her sister, Almira Phelps (*GLB,* Jan. 1837, 4-5).

[27] For a brief but good overview of *Sketches of American Character* and *Traits of American Life,* see Baym, *Feminism and American Literary History* 171-72.

[28] Sarah Josepha Hale, *Sketches of American Character* (Boston: Putnam and Hunt, 1829), 8.

[29] For a good overview of Hale's contributions to children's literature, see M. Sarah Smedman, "Sarah Josepha Hale," in *American Writers for Children Before 1900,* ed. Glenn E. Estes, Dictionary of Literary Biography, no. 42 (Detroit: Gale Research, 1985), 207-17.

[30] Hale, *Ladies' Wreath* 4.

[31] Hale's advice books on housekeeping and cooking include *The Good Housekeeper; or, The Way to Live Well and to Be Well While We Live* (1839), *The Ladies' New Book of Cookery: A Practical System* (1852), *The New Household Receipt-Book* (1853), which was expanded as *Mrs. Hale's Receipts for the Million* (1857), and *Manners; or, Happy Homes and Good Society All the Year Round* (1867). *Keeping House and Housekeeping* (1845) and *Boarding Out: A Tale of Domestic Life* (1846) are both novels of domestic life. Hale edited *The White Veil: A Bridal Gift* in 1854. *The Letters of Madame de Sévigné, to Her Daughter and Friends* and *The Letters of Lady Mary Wortley Montagu* were both published in 1856. For a complete bibliography of Hale's work, see Entrikin, *Sarah Josepha Hale* 137-55; and Blanck, *Bibliography of American Literature.*

[32] On Hale's *Woman's Record,* see Baym, "Onward Christian Women: Sarah J. Hale's History of the World," *new England Quarterly* 63 (1990): 249-70. Portions of that essay appear in Baym, *Feminism and American Literary History.*

Patricia Okker (essay date 1995)

SOURCE: "The Professionalization of Authorship" in *Our Sister Editors: Sarah J. Hale and the Tradition of Nineteenth-Century American Women Editors,* University of Georgia Press, 1995, pp. 84-109.

[In the following excerpt, Okker examines Hale's views on writing, especially writing by women.]

Although Hale did contribute to the successful careers of writers like [Edgar Allan] Poe, [Lydia] Sigourney, and [Harriet Beecher] Stowe, she did not encourage all writers. In fact, she often used her editorial pages to discuss the difficulties associated with professional literary careers. While clearly discouraging to some would-be writers, Hale's editorials about authorship may have helped writers like Poe and Stowe even more than her publication of their works, for in these editorials Hale repeatedly rejected the idea that anyone could become an author. Like any other occupation that required training, talent, and hard work, authorship, according to Hale, deserved professional respect.

Hale's editorial support for professional authorship is evident in her many descriptions of a continuum of writers, ranging from the amateur to the professional. She made clear distinctions between "anonymous or voluntary contributors" and "regularly engaged and paid writers" [*Godey's Lady's Book* (hereafter GLB)] April 1840, 190), and she accepted the idea that the two groups deserved different treatment. Although she advocated adequate compensation, Hale did not generally pay beginning writers, and she explained that commissioned work would receive her first consideration. Writers who submitted material on a "voluntary" basis should expect longer delays (*GLB,* Dec. 1840, 282). In another editorial, Hale offered three categories of writers whose work she had refused. The first class, identified as *"Promising,"* demonstrated "literary talent," and Hale recommended "persevering study." Those in the second category, "the *mediocre,*" exhibited no such promise, though Hale conceded the posibility of eventual success. For the unfortunate writers in the final category, *"Hopeless,"* Hale offered no prospects of public acclaim and urged them to write only for their own benefit (*GLB,* June 1841, 282).

Implicit in these categories is Hale's notion that along the continuum of writers is the authorial apprentice. Clearly, for Hale, neither talent nor ambition alone could guarantee literary success. Even those with "literary talent" had to dedicate themselves to "persevering study," and as Hale explained in another editorial, many "persons mistake a desire, for the ability to perform" (*GLB,* March 1852, 229). Hale's interest in a writer's apprenticeship also emerged in the instructions she repeatedly offered to would-be contributors. In one essay, she admonished correspondents for not writing "as they would speak," and she suggested that they abandon their ideas of needing "a lofty theme, and long words and pompous descriptions" [*Ladies' Magazine,* hereafter *LM*] Feb. 1829, 92). Similar notions of an apprenticeship appear in the published announcements Hale made regarding submissions. Although she kindly omitted the authors' names, Hale published titles of rejected manuscripts, along with brief explanations—"dull" or "boring" or "imperfect versification," for example. At times, those rationales were rather severe. She rejected one manuscript titled "My Life" on the grounds that it was "a very useless one, as described" (*GLB,* June 1857, 562). However harsh such a practice may seem today, beginning writers appear to have accepted Hale's practice as part of their training. Frances Hodgson Burnett, whose first published story appeared in the *Lady's Book,* apparently read the announcements of rejected manuscripts in hope of improving her writing.[29]

Throughout her descriptions of the authorial apprentice, Hale presented herself as the master writer responsible for instructing apprentices and maintaining professional standards. As an editor, Hale had the authority to command that arduous preparation. Significantly, when guiding younger writers in the process of becoming professional authors, Hale repeatedly abandoned the sisterly editorial voice she used with readers and invoked the persona of a protecting but strict parent. Like the parent who knows that what a child wants is sometimes not best, Hale once explained that "contributors sometimes offer their first fruit. They should thank us for declining it." Similarly, Hale once rejected a story with the explanation that "the author must not be discouraged. She can write better" (*GLB,* March 1865, 280; Feb. 1841, 96). Hale's persona as the master writer parallels the kind of apprenticeship she envisioned as the basis of mother-daughter relationships. While these mothers trained daughters to become housewives and mothers, Hale taught younger writers to become professional authors.[30]

Even in some of its fiction, the *Lady's Book* presented editors as responsible for maintaining professional standards. One of several humorous depictions of the editorial process, the 1860 story "Scene in 'Our' Sanctum; or, A Peep Behind the Curtain," signed only by "One Who Has 'Been Thar,'" emphasizes the abundance of unpublishable material submitted to magazine editors. Unable to face the submissions alone, two men read aloud to each other in order to divide the work and to allow one the pleasure of smoking. As the editors read, they interject their own aggravations and beg each other to read more rapidly. One poem defines hope as "hopeful, ever hoping," which is later rhymed with "never moping"; two others are titled "What the Trees Said?" and "Written on a Daisy When Confined by Sickness." A similar story, titled "How We Filled the Columns," featured rejected manuscripts such as "Lines on a Drowning Newfoundland Dog" and "The Ensanguined Wedding Ring and Bloody Lock of Hair" (*GLB,* Aug. 1860, 139-44; March 1865, 232-37). Although these two narratives achieve their humor at the expense of inexperienced writers, the effect of the story is similar to the stance taken in Hale's editorial columns. Writing is portrayed as an arduous task, requiring talent and experience, and the editor has the responsibility to maintain professional standards of authorship.

A similar vision of authorship is evident in Hale's use of the term *scribblings.* In contrast to Nathaniel Hawthorne, who used the word to complain about the financially successful writers of the day, Hale used *scribblings* to refer to unpublishable, amateur writings. In one editorial she explained that she would accept only "carefully prepared articles—not 'scribblings'" (*GLB,* April 1865, 373). Although Hawthorne clearly wished to enjoy commercial success himself, his and Hale's uses of the term *scribbling* imply a significantly different understanding of authorship, specifically in regard to its economics. Hawthorne's insistence that he would be "ashamed" of himself if his works proved as popular as the women's "trash" suggests that he believed that writers paid well for their work were

somehow inferior.[31] In contrast to Hawthorne's financially successful "scribbling" writers, Hale's scribblers were amateurs who worked quickly and easily; professional writers, in contrast, earned their salaries, not because they pandered to their audiences but because they had talent *and* worked hard. Thus, however much Hawthorne wished to earn his living by writing, his association of payment with lack of true artistry is based on an eighteenth-century model of the leisured gentleman author. Hale, on the other hand, envisioned a truly professional model of authorship.

Although she was most concerned with distinguishing amateur and professional writers, even professional writers had to submit to Hale as the authority responsible for maintaining standards. Hale claimed to reject a model of reviewing based on finding fault, but she repeatedly voiced her objections to published writings, though never with the kind of savage tone she associated with male critics. In virtually every essay on Cooper, for instance, Hale focused on style, faulting his *Notions of the Americans,* for example, for its "affectation" and "artificial manner of detailing unimportant events, and of describing common scenery" (*LM,* Sept. 1828, 431). In her review of *The Bravo,* Hale summarized her overall opinion of Cooper's technical abilities: "We do not pretend greatly to admire the style of Mr. Cooper. His dialogue is frequently encumbered with unnecessary words, and there seems to be an incongruity in the solemn manner of expression, which he so pertinaciously puts into the mouths of all his characters, the ignorant as well as the learned" (*LM,* Jan. 1832, 45). Cooper was by no means the only professional writer who earned Hale's reproofs. Although Hale praised Herman Melville's *Moby-Dick* as a "perfect literary whale" (*GLB,* Feb. 1852, 166), *Pierre* so frustrated her that she wrote her review in a brutal parody of Melville's style.[32]

That Hale criticized writers as popular as Cooper and those like Melville, whose talents she praised highly elsewhere, demonstrates once again her belief in the difficulty of authorship. Even when faulting writers, Hale strengthened their position as professionals: her criticisms reminded readers that writers who achieved success especially deserved support and respect. Regardless of her treatment of individual writers, Hale urged readers to remember the rarity of literary success and to think of the author as a professional, who, like the physician or minister, had dedicated his or her life to acquiring the necessary skills.

Hale's response to women writers deserves particular attention, because she is sometimes quoted as limiting women's authorial opportunities, and indeed her periodical essays did at times question women's literary ambitions. In an essay in the *Ladies' Magazine* published in 1829, for example, Hale declared that she had "no wish to tinge all her sex *blue* . . . to turn our country into a great literary factory, and set all our young ladies to spinning their brains," and in an 1852 essay about women writers, Hale argued that "a good pair of stockings, or a well-made petticoat, is a much better thing than a feeble attempt at literature" (*LM,* Jan. 1829, 3; *GLB,* March 1852, 229). Similarly, both Hale's editorial columns and the fiction of the *Lady's Book* tended to denounce writers, especially women, who pursued authorship for fame or wealth.

These published concerns notwithstanding, nothing in Hale's own career suggests that she had any misgivings about women pursuing professional authorship. Unlike those women writers Mary Kelley has described as showing ambivalence about publicity, Hale frequently promoted herself before the public as a professional writer and editor. She published many autobiographical sketches and exhibited considerable interest in furthering her reputation. Hale's sense of herself as a professional author is further demonstrated by her response to a personal letter requesting a complete edition of her works in 1855. In her reply Hale explained that no such edition existed "as yet," but she described how her books might be purchased, and she classified her "large number of books" by which were "most important" and "most popular." Hale evidently continued to hope for a collected edition of her works. She collected her manuscripts, letters, and papers throughout her life, and her will appointed her children as literary executors.[33] Similarly, Hale's correspondence with her book publishers reveals that she was comfortable and capable in handling the business aspects of her profession. In her letters to Harper and Brothers regarding the publication of **Woman's Record,** for example, Hale skillfully clarified responsibilities, offered suggestions about the size of the book and its promotion, negotiated her payment, and proposed other projects. She even chastised the publisher for delaying her book: "It will become obsolete. One or two of the ladies, ranked with the *living* when I completed my task, are now *dead.*"[34]

Although Hale did sometimes discourage other women from becoming authors, generally her responses to women writers were consistent with her own professional identity. Indeed, Hale's prudence was based not on any ambivalence about the propriety of literary women but on her recognition of the obstacles facing all professional writers. In warning women about these difficulties, Hale again presented authorship as a profession. Writing, she maintained, was not for the "feeble" but for the talented. . . .

. . . . .

Hale's support of professional women writers is also evident in her use of the term *genius.* Like most nineteenth-century reviewers, she used *genius* to indicate the highest level of literary achievement, but unlike many of her contemporaries, she was likely to use the term equally for men and women. As Nina Baym has observed in her study of nineteenth-century reviewers of novels, *genius* and *woman* were often perceived as incompatible expressions. While reviewers enthusiastically endorsed signs of genius in men, they often treated similar traits in women uneasily. As Baym explains, women writers were praised for how well they expressed womanhood in general rather than for their individual voices or visions. Whereas individuality was admired among male writers, the primary standard for greatness among women writers was representativeness.[36]

Hale, in contrast, frequently described women writers as geniuses, and she associated female genius with boldness and originality—qualities other reviewers often found problematic in women. In **Woman's Record** Hale characterized Charlotte Brontë as an "original genius" and praised *Shirley* for its "original and striking thought" and its "free, bold spirit, that charms by its spontaneous vigor." Similarly, although Hale objected to Rochester's characterization in *Jane Eyre,* as did many reviewers, she acknowledged the novel's "vigour, animation, originality, an arrest that never flags." Hale also celebrated risk-taking in women writers, another trait generally acclaimed only in men. In a sketch of Sara Jane Lippincott (**"Grace Greenwood"**), for example, Hale glorified the bold pursuit of literary excellence. An "inferior genius," Hale explained, "would have been satisfied with the honours won," and a "fearful mind would have hesitated to risk, by any effort to widen her sway, a failure."[37]

Essays in the *Ladies' Magazine* and the *Lady's Book* also demonstrate that Hale did not consider genius and women mutually exclusive. One early essay in the *Ladies' Magazine* described "originality of thought" as "the polar star of our female writers" (*LM,* Sept. 1830, 407). Even essays about literary men associated women with genius. An unsigned 1833 essay, titled "True Genius Always at Home" defined the literary "man of genius," using domestic rhetoric associated with women. According to this essay, the man of genius "constructs a domain of his own; and no man is so truly at home as in his own abode. He draws around him a hallowed circle, and in it he moves, and lives, and breathes. The scenes are his own, the atmosphere is his own, every thing within it is his own—immortally his own. Others may wander there, and gaze and admire, but they must still acknowledge that it is his. He only, as its rightful possessor, can stand within it with the proud consciousness that he is *at home*" (*LM,* Feb. 1833, 53-54). Given the association of women with domesticity throughout the *Ladies' Magazine,* the use of the metaphor *at home* here to define the male genius demonstrates that genius is not an exclusively masculine trait. Quite the contrary—this essay implicitly creates a feminine definition of genius.

Although *genius* and *feminine* were compatible terms in Hale's view, she did employ her understanding of an essential sexual difference to differentiate between male and female genius. In one editorial in 1857, Hale specifically refuted the idea that "genius has no sex." According to Hale, men's and women's writings demonstrate distinct differences, with women's writing exhibiting a tenderness and morality impossible in men's. Significantly, Hale documented this female writing even among writers whom she did not associate with a Christian aesthetic. Writing of George Sand, for instance, whom Hale depicted as lacking appropriate Christian influence, she insisted that "the superior moral sense of the woman is clearly discerned." Likewise, Hale explained that the "woman's nature" of Madame de Staël was "as clearly defined in her writings as it could have been in the form of her hand, or in the tone of her voice" (*GLB*, Feb. 1857, 177). Although Hale claimed that both men's and women's writings were "delightful," she did imply a hierarchy, with women's writing achieving the higher status:

> Is not moral power better than mechanical invention? Is not the love, which purifies the heart and makes the sanctity of home, stronger even than the "red right arm of war"?
>
> Why should women wish to be or to do or to write like men? Is not the feminine genius the most angel-like? (*GLB*, Feb. 1857, 178)

The notion of a separate "feminine genius" was, of course, hardly unusual among nineteenth-century critics, but Hale's description of that genius as "stronger" than men's does differ significantly from the assertions of most of her counterparts, who generally regarded women's genius as inferior to men's.

While Hale's celebration of feminine genius challenged contemporary cultural definitions, in other ways her understanding of female authorship corresponded with limited expectations of women's ability. Specifically, Hale expected great women writers to be models not only of authorship but also of domesticity. Like many other nineteenth-century reviewers, Hale exhibited considerable interest in women's—but not men's—private lives, and in her essays on women writers, Hale shifted from biography to literary text with no sense of disjunction. Furthermore, when describing the function of biographies, Hale insisted that personal details should take precedence over women's public accomplishments: "The private histories of eminent persons are always sought after with eagerness; and were this passion for biographical literature, rightly fostered and directed, it would have a most powerful influence in promoting the intellectual and moral improvement of women. But to do this, greatness, in its worldly sense . . . must not be the object of eulogy; or rather, the domestic virtues must possess a prominance [*sic*] in the pictures which

are held up for the admiration and consequent imitation of women" (*LM*, Sept. 1829, 393). As Baym explains, such practices were common among nineteenth-century reviewers, and biographical information and essays about women writers' private lives were frequent features in magazines.[38]

Although Hale's biographical essays frequently exhibited admiration of women like Lydia Sigourney, who demonstrated that there was "no incompatibility between literary pursuits and domestic duties" (*GLB*, Oct. 1865, 358), the focus on a woman's private life clearly restricted women writers. Women's literary successes were praiseworthy only when combined with domestic achievements. Male authors, in contrast, had no such requirements and were judged solely on the basis of their writings. Much of the fiction in the *Lady's Book* suggests the difficulty—and even the impossibility—of combining these accomplishments. An unsigned story, for example, titled "Why I Am Not an Authoress," tells of Nellie, a young writer, working on her first novel. At first Nellie abstains from all domestic and social obligations in order to pursue her writing: she refuses party invitations, neglects her clothes and hair, and wears permanent ink stains on her hands, earning her the nickname Miss Fingerblotter. When her family finally convinces her to attend a ball however, Nellie's life is transformed. She falls in love, agrees to marry, and eventually abandons her writing because her husband has advised her to "relinquish public fame" for a "happy domestic life." Neither Nellie nor her husband considers the possibility that she could be both a writer and a wife (*GLB*, April 1857, 314).

As clear as Nellie's choices are, the writer's position about Nellie's choice between marriage and writing is far from certain, since the story itself undercuts the supposed opposition of domestic and literary goals. Although the narrator has supposedly denounced writing, her story—told in the first person—is published in the *Lady's Book*. By mentioning her marriage, the narrator indicates that the writing took place after her wedding and her supposed renunciation of literature. Although the story was probably written by someone other than Hale, in many ways it embodies Hale's ambivalence about women writers and domesticity. On the one hand, Hale generally warned women not to pursue literature single-mindedly, insisting that they always fulfill their domestic duties. On the other hand, she did encourage women to move beyond their domestic spheres. She published the work of women writers, paid them generously, and welcomed them to the commercial world of authorship.

A similar ambivalence emerges within Hale's expectation that women writers should be moral as well as domestic. Although she sometimes praised books by men without considering the books' morality—including Poe's *Tales of the Grotesque and Arabesque,*

Melville's *Moby-Dick,* and Thoreau's *Cape Cod*—she rarely gave the same treatment to books by women.[39] Indeed, when defining the goals of female authorship and genius in **Woman's Record,** Hale emphasized what she called "the moral effect of mental power." She explained, "The genius which causes or creates the greatest amount of good to humanity should take the highest rank."[40] Similarly, in an essay memorializing Lydia Sigourney's "poetic genius" in the *Lady's Book,* Hale declared that "piety is essential to the genius of a woman" (*GLB,* Oct. 1865, 358).

Hale's position here on the moral integrity of women writers coincides with her general theory of sexual difference. According to Hale's **Woman's Record,** all women—including those who write—should focus on moral instruction. Hale praised Charlotte Brontë primarily, then, not for her literary technique but for being "an instructress"—"the noblest pursuit of woman"—and Alice Carey, she asserted, was a "guiding angel." Conversely, women writers who neglected their duties as society's moral guardians troubled Hale, regardless of whether or not they were geniuses. When describing George Sand, for instance, Hale acknowledged her "genius of an order capable of soaring to the most exalted heights," yet she regretted that Sand lacked the "saving influences of moral and Christian training." Disapproving of Sand's interest in politics, which Hale viewed as corrupting, she wished that Sand's "genius should teach truth, and inspire hearts to love the good." If Sand applied herself in this way, Hale insisted, she could expect "a mightier effect on her country than any plan of social reform political expediency could devise."[41] Hale's treatment of the woman author, then, matches her portrait of all women: they should provide moral instruction.

Undoubtedly, Hale's association of women writers with morality and domesticity was restrictive. Her belief that some women writers had transgressed the bounds of proper femininity demonstrates her limited notion of female authorship. But scholars have been too quick to dismiss Hale's theory of authorship. Writers and critics have long prescribed limits to literature's aims, and religion and morality have been quite common criteria for determining literary worth. However limited, Hale's association of morality and literature implies a radical rereading of authorship. Although she was particularly concerned with women writers' morality, Hale expected all great writers—regardless of sex—to fulfill her moral standards. When describing William Cullen Bryant as "one of the brightest lights of American genius," Hale focused on the "truth of moral sentiment" in his poetry (*LM,* April 1832, 185). Given Hale's theory of sexual difference, which posited women as society's moral force, her concern for moral truth in literature elevated the status of women writers. According to Hale, the best writers had the greatest positive effect on readers. Since women were society's natural teachers and moral leaders, she concluded, women were more likely to achieve literary greatness than men.

Such a conclusion might explain why Hale continually discussed the gender of writers who were women, but did not do so for men. Whereas many nineteenth-century reviewers belittled the literary accomplishments of women, Hale's position assumed that women's moral superiority gave them—not men—the greatest potential for literary excellence.[42] To be a great writer, a woman must only be true to her natural abilities. A man, on the other hand, must aspire to womanhood. In contrast to earlier ideas of the author as a scholarly gentleman, therefore, Hale advocated a feminized model of authorship.

Hale's ideas of feminized and professional authors were directly related. Unlike writers like Hawthorne, who could secure government appointments when their writing provided insufficient income, women writers had few, if any, options for paid labor. As Hale well knew, if women were to write, they would have to be paid; and if they were paid, they would write. The professionalization and feminization of authorship, in other words, were mutually dependent strategies.

Hale's contributions to the professionalization of authorship challenge some basic assumptions of American literary historians about the role of women's magazines. Hardly on the fringes of the literary world—as is so frequently assumed—the *Ladies' Magazine* and the *Lady's Book* played leading roles in the construction of literary professionalism and helped establish the careers of many of the nation's writers, both men and women. Authorship, considered by some periodicals of the time as little more than a hobby, became in the pages of Hale's magazines a profession, requiring years of study, a difficult apprenticeship, and enormous talent. In addition, Hale redefined authorship as a pursuit appropriate for women, in contradistinction to the male-identified notions of the author, such as the eighteenth-century ideal of the scholarly gentleman. In creating the idea of a professional woman author, Hale changed the way society imagined all writers.

Notes

[29] Constance Buel Burnett, *Happily Ever After: A Portrait of Frances Hodgson Burnett* (New York: Vanguard Press, n.d.), 69-71.

[30] For a historical account of similar relations among nineteenth-century mothers and daughters in the United States, see Carroll Smith-Rosenberg, "The Female World of Love and Ritual: Relations Between Women in Nineteenth-Century America," *Signs* 1 (1975): 16.

[31] Nathaniel Hawthorne, *The Letters, 1853-1856,* ed. Thomas Woodson, James A. Rubino, L. Neal Smith,

and Norman Holmes Pearson, vol. 17 of *The Cente-nary Edition of the Works of Nathaniel Hawthorne* (Columbus: Ohio State University Press, 1987), 304.

[32] For a sense of Hale's parody of *Pierre,* consider its concluding sentence: "We have listened to its outbreathing of sweet-swarming sounds, and their melodious, mournful, wonderful, and unintelligible melodiousness has 'dropped like pendulous, glittering icicles,' with soft-ringing silveriness, upon our never-to-be-delighted-sufficiently organs of hearing; and, in the insignificant significancies of that deftly-stealing and wonderfully-serpenting melodiousness, we have found an infinite, unbounded, inexpressible mysteri-ousness of nothingness" (*GLB,* Oct. 1852, 390).

[33] Mary Kelley, *Private Woman, Public Stage: Liter-ary Domesticity in Nineteenth-Century America* (New York: Oxford University Press, 1984). letter from Sarah Josepha Hale to Kennedy Furlong, 17 Feb. 1855, Yale Collection of American Literature, Beinecke Rare Book and Manuscript Library, Yale University, New Haven, Conn.; Isabelle Webb Entrikin, *Sarah Josepha Hale and "Godey's Lady's Book"* (Lancaster, Pa.: Lancaster Press, 1946) 125.

[34] Letter from Sarah Josepha Hale to Harpers, 24 July 1850, Pierpont Morgan Library, New York, MA 1950. For more on relationships between women writers and publishers, see Susan Coultrap-McQuin, *Doing Liter-ary Business: American Women Writers in the Nine-teenth Century* (Chapel Hill: University of North Caro-lina Press, 1990). . . .

[36] Nina Baym, *Novels, Readers, and Reviewers: Re-sponses to Fiction in Antebellum America* (Ithaca, N.Y.: Cornell University Press, 1984) 249-58.

[37] Hale, *Woman's Record* 597-98, 624.

[38] Baym, *Novels, Readers, and Reviewers,* 254.

[39] In her review of *Tales of the Grotesque and Ara-besque,* Hale portrayed Poe as "a writer of rare and various abilities" with a "mind of unusual grasp—a vigorous power of analysis, and an acuteness of per-ception" (*GLB,* Jan. 1840, 46). Hale admired Thoreau's *Cape Cod* for treating the "barren subject" with "most undreamed-of interest," and she explained that "the roar of the ocean becomes a grand anthem in his ears" (*GLB,* June 1865, 556).

[40] Hale, *Woman's Record,* 719.

[41] Ibid. 597, 615, 624.

[42] For a general discussion of belittling behaviors, see Joanna Russ, *How to Suppress Women's Writing* (Aus-tin: University of Texas Press, 1985).

Susan M. Griffin (essay date 1997)

SOURCE: "'The Dark Stranger': Sensationalism and Anti-Catholicism in Sarah Josepha Hale's *Traits of American Life*," *Legacy,* Vol. 14, No. 1, 1997, pp. 13-24.

[*In the following excerpt, Griffin focuses on the Prot-estant-Catholic conflict in Hale's story "The Catholic Convert."*]

In **"The Romance of Travelling,"** one of the sketches collected in Sarah Josepha Hale's 1835 ***Traits of American Life,*** Hale focuses on Lake Sunapee, New Hampshire, as a typical American landscape, which "gives to the heart a sensation like that of suddenly meeting the smiling face of a friend" (195). Hale fol-lows the landscape tradition of focussing on the reflec-tive and imaginative qualities that water lends to land-scape (195; Novak 40-41). Conventional, too, is Hale's discovery of a ruined habitation in the landscape, a site that marks time's passing and signals historical depth. Yet the "remembrance connected with the lake" and its ruin which provides the material for Hale's story is hardly a conventionally poetic one. For Lake Sunapee was once, Hale tells her audience, the source of a whirlwind that devastated a local farming family. The parents escaped unharmed, but their home became the ruin and their infant, Mary, disappeared—only her gown was recovered. "Whether her little form was reduced to atoms by the grinding storm, or thrown by the wind into the lake, or carried into the wilderness, is a secret the last trumpet only can reveal," intones Hale (207). As if this grisly speculation were not enough, Hale ends the story by encouraging her readers to journey from the scene of devastation to the Ohio River, where they will find the resettled farmer, who will explain that he has relocated because he "could not bear to eat the fish of the lake, for fear they might have been fattening on the flesh of his child" (208)!

The shining surface of Lake Sunapee that so resembles a smiling familiar friend contains and conceals a nar-rative of horrors. Hale's writing, usually characterized as "early realism" or "domestic fiction," participates in what nineteenth-century readers would come to recog-nize as the sensational: the interpenetration of the fa-miliar and the shocking. Indeed, the sensational was repeatedly attacked precisely because it blurred bound-aries, because it showed a middleclass respectability infected by crime and sin. David S. Reynolds, in *Be-neath the American Renaissance,* describes in detail the influence that such popular literature had on the canonical authors of the period. In both earlier studies of dime novels and more recent explorations of the work of writers like Lippard and Thompson, such popular fiction is defined as antithetical (indeed, inimi-cal) to domestic fiction written by women. The cel-ebration of these works' subversive excesses, both in their depiction of violence and sexuality (and violent sexuality) and in their stylistic outrageousness, is underscored by contrast to what is assumed to be the constricted realm and tone of domestic fiction.

Yet Hale's actual fictional practice is decidedly less generically pure than such critical distinctions might lead us to expect. Such eclecticism is hinted at in Lucy M. Freibert and Barbara A. White's designation of Hale's 1827 **Northwood** as mixing "the typical moralism and melodrama of the period with description of daily life in New England" (183). In this essay, I focus on an especially provocative instance of a contemporary sensational plot at work in Hale's domestic national literature. **"The Catholic Convert,"** the second piece in **Traits of American Life,** is, I argue, Hale's version of the lurid stories of escaped nuns so popular in 1830s America. Hale's rendering of this anti-Catholic plot is significant because it provides a concrete example of how a popular rhetoric and plot can traverse a variety of discourses, eroding strict separation between "high" literature and "low" popular fiction, as well as between male sensationalism and female domesticity.[1]

The significance of **"The Catholic Convert"** is political as well. While feminist scholars have long discussed the variety of ways in which Protestantism informed and fostered American women's culture (e.g., Cott, Douglas, Sklar, Tompkins), only very recently has that culture's relation to and role in the virulent anti-Catholicism of the period begun to be explored (Baym, *American Women Writers;* Franchot; Hedrick). In *Roads to Rome,* Jenny Franchot argues that antebellum anti-Catholicism provided American Protestantism with a means of bolstering its own identity as well as a medium in which to explore the tensions and contradictions implicit in that identity. Hale employs the escaped nun's story to exactly these ends: she critiques both the Catholicism and the newly debased Protestantism that threaten America. Hale's narrative offers rescue and redemption not only to the young woman seduced by Catholicism, but also to her "audience," a Protestant couple led astray by the selfishness and materialism that pervade post-revolutionary America. In **"The Catholic Convert,"** Hale sets a contemporary version of an ancient tale in the American landscape in order to lead her readership, through feeling, to remembrance of lost values.[2]

What I am calling escaped nuns' narratives were "autobiographical" accounts of Protestant females' sufferings that proliferated in the 1830s. George Bourne's fictional *Lorette* (1833), as well as the (purportedly) nonfictional Rebecca Reed's *Six Months in a Convent* (1835) and Maria Monk's *Awful Disclosures of the Hotel Dieu Nunnery in Montreal* (1836), were enormously popular and inspired a host of imitators.[3] *Lorette* is listed as one of Frank Luther Mott's "Better

Sellers"; *Six Months in a Convent* sold ten thousand copies in the first week and an estimated two hundred thousand within a month; *Awful Disclosures* sold twenty thousand copies within a few weeks and three hundred thousand by 1860 (Mott, Billington). Escaped nuns' narratives circulated in a variety of venues, from "factual" accounts published in Protestant newspapers to dime novels. While some book versions were published locally, others were issued by mainstream publishers like Van Nostrand and Dwight, D. Appleton, and Harper and Brothers. These books thrilled their Protestant readership with horrific stories of the physical and mental torture endured by women imprisoned in Roman Catholic convents. Of course, such narratives had been traditional in the literature of anti-Catholicism at least since the Reformation. The eighteenth-century Gothic novel, with its lascivious monks and ghostly veiled nuns, drew heavily on that tradition (Tarr).

The escaped nuns' narratives that resurface in antebellum America all follow a general pattern. The protagonist is usually a young Protestant girl who has been lured into convent life. Often a priest (usually a Jesuit) has obtained power over the protagonist through the confessional, eliciting her secrets, invading her privacy, violating her innocence, perverting her emotions, and sapping her independence and will. Typical, too, are kidnappings in which the protagonist is bundled into a carriage in the dead of night and taken secretly to an unknown destination. Once in the convent, she is allowed no communication with her family, friends, or lovers; all letters, for example, are intercepted or destroyed. Indeed, if those who love her manage to track the young woman down, the Mother Superior of the convent denies that she is present, sometimes claiming that she has died. Life in the convent is, at best, deadening and disillusioning; at worst, it combines sadistic "penances" with sexual violation (i.e., convents turn out to be "priests' brothels"). Daring clandestine escape offers the only hope of release.

As a reader and writer of Protestant millennial history—what Nina Baym has called "History from the Divine Point of View"—Hale knew well the chronicle of Catholicism's crimes (*American Women Writers* 46-66). Further, Hale, who claimed that Ann Radcliffe's *The Mysteries of Udolpho* was the first novel she read (and that at age seven), was certainly familiar with the Gothic tradition on which escaped nuns' narratives drew. And we do know of Hale's reaction to at least one antebellum story about an escaped nun, a reaction which offers an explanatory context for her own rendering of the plot in **"The Catholic Convert."** In the September 1834 issue of the *American Ladies' Magazine,* Hale expressed her outrage at the burning of the Ursuline convent at Charlestown, Massachusetts. The convent had been attacked by a mob on the night of 11 August 1834. As the nuns and their students fled into the night, their female sanctuary was ransacked and burned to the ground. The crowd had been incited to this action at least in part because of a false story which had circulated in the *Mercantile Journal* and elsewhere about a nun (Elizabeth Harrison/Sister Mary John) who had escaped only to be reimprisoned in the convent.[4]

Hale dismisses the story of Harrison's escape and recapture as a recycled Gothic plot: "This Monk Lewis story was mostly a fiction" (422). Instead, Hale tells a different narrative of female victimhood, focussing on the "community of helpless women attacked" by male violence (418). This community was, in fact, primarily a *Protestant* one—only one-eighth of the Charlestown convent students were Catholics (Franchot 138). While professing that "we certainly should not select a Catholic seminary as the place of education for our own daughters," Hale nonetheless defends the Protestant parents' decision to educate their daughters with the Ursulines: "Of all the protestant young ladies, and there have been several hundred educated at the Ursuline Convent since its foundation, *not a single individual has embraced the Catholic faith!*" (425).

In the November 1834 issue of *American Ladies' Magazine,* Hale returns to the subject, this time in order to defend herself against the Protestant press who had read her comments as pro-Catholic. Hale offers evidence of her staunch opposition to Rome: "The prevalence of popery would be, in our opinion, the greatest moral calamity—excepting the prevalence of *infidelity!*—which could befal our nation" (519). Regarding the popular theory that the Pope and the Austrian government were funding Jesuits to infiltrate America and found convents and colleges such "as will enable these European tyrants through their partisan emissaries here, to overthrow and destroy our civil and religious liberties," Hale says, "it probably is true" (519). Nonetheless, she argues that these schemes are the work of "priests and the despots of the old world," not of lay Catholics (519). Hale again mocks the escaped nun story and reiterates her arguments against persecution. The bulk of the essay, however, takes the Charlestown controversy as an occasion for introducing one of Hale's favorite subjects: female education (Hoffman 49). The chains and veils that concern her are mental ones: "The catholic religion does not allow the free exercise of mind—the nuns are shrouded in the veil of bigotry. . . . [I]t is not within the compass of their design to make woman an intellectual and rational companion of man" (521). In short, convent schools cannot produce *American wives.* Why, then, are more and more Protestant females being educated in convent schools? Because there are so few Protestant schools. Explaining, in the words of her title, "How to Prevent the Increase of Convents," Hale argues that Americans must offer superior and cheaper Protestant education for girls and women.

Hale continues with the topic in the December 1834 "Convents Are Increasing." Here, she turns to the Protestant mission that Ray Allen Billington, in his chapter on American nativism between 1835 and 1840, calls "Saving the West from the Pope." Arguing that "the Great West is the arena where the struggle between the Protestant and Catholic principles is mainly to be carried on," Hale warns that, without adequate funding for Protestant female education, the men of the West, themselves well educated in institutions like Lyman Beecher's Lane Seminary, will be condemned to marry convent-educated women (561).[5] The Protestant missionary work of such men will be all for nought, Hale insists, if they are not accompanied by educated female missionaries: "What avails it to send out Missionaries to heathen lands to preach to the men the religion of the Cross, while the women are training their sons in the creed of Juggernaut?" (563).[6] A single male convert is just that, but convert a female, and you convert an entire family. Hale's implication is that the missionary crisis abroad mirrors the problem of the wild, unsettled region at home. Unless American women are offered an educational alternative, "convents will increase, and Catholicism become permanently rooted in our country" (561, 564).

Franchot demonstrates how "the attack on convents in Jacksonian and antebellum America intricately voiced Protestant perplexities over the ongoing construction of the 'cult of domesticity'" (120). Hale's voice contributes to that intricacy in these three articles. The image of the convent provides a structure for discussion, not only of Catholicism's role in and threat to contemporary Protestant America, but woman's privileged place in the nation's making and preservation. Rather than accepting the nativist story of Elizabeth Harrison's escape, Hale takes the Charlestown incident as an opportunity to tell a quite different story about why American women are in convents and about what must be done to rescue them.

Shortly after these three articles appeared, Hale collected and published ***Traits of American Life.*** But the escaped nun's story that she includes, **"The Catholic Convert,"** was, in fact, originally published in the August and September 1830 issues of *Ladies' Magazines* as **"The Unknown."** It is the only piece that gets a completely new title when it is republished in *Traits.*[7] Predating, in its original form, the popular narratives by Bourne, Monk, Reed, and others, **"The Catholic Convert"** signals, with its new title, a focus on the Protestant-Catholic competition for souls that was dominating the popular imagination in 1835. What Hale's title leaves ambiguous, of course, is which way the conversion runs: Is this a story of a convert to or from Catholicism? The ambivalence is significant, since, in her version of the escaped nun's narrative, Hale deliberately turns some of Protestantism's favorite attacks on Rome back onto American Protestants themselves.

The story, set in Brattleborough, Vermont, opens with an insistence on the typicality of two of its characters:

> Mr. Theophilus Redfield, and his wife Susanna, were . . . in their own sphere, a pattern couple: prudent, pious, and prosperous, gathering the maxims that guided their temporal course from the economies of Franklin, and their summary of religious faith from the Westminster Catechism. (51)

In both their typicality and their role as the audience for the internal narrative that Hale will introduce, Theophilus and Susanna Redfield are figures for Hale's readership. Describing the Redfields as guided by traditional American and Protestant precepts, Hale goes on to question immediately the adequacy of any such set of rules. She asserts that the young should study instead "the works of Nature and the Book of Revelation," and that they should reason from their own sensory and emotional experiences, from what "their own hearts have felt" (52). Accepting a religious theory "on trust," as the Redfields' post-revolutionary generation of Americans has come to do, actually means absolving one's self from individual responsibility and conscience (52).

Hale's critical description of American Protestantism is, in fact, a standard Protestant characterization of *Catholic* religious practices: deferring to a set of rules dictated by a priest, then turning to that same priest for absolution, the Catholic abdicates his or her own primary and singular relationship with God. Hale turns this critique against her pious Protestant characters, censuring the way in which they seek refuge in the letter of the law in order to justify their fundamentally unchristian economic behavior: "[W]hile they kept the Sabbath day with pharisaical strictness, the other six days were their own," days in which their lives are guided solely by the selfish standard of "pecuniary profit" (53, 52). Class and economics are central topics throughout *Traits of American Life.* Hale's focus here on the Redfields' selfishness reflects the growing anxiety in antebellum America about the shift from self-sacrificing, communitarian republicanism to self-aggrandizing, market-based individualism.[8] In **"The Catholic Convert,"** Hale frames this political problem in religious terms. The Redfields' lives and practices are guided by pragmatic, material considerations. As neighbors, church members, and citizens, they live in a realm of (economic) fact, where spirituality and sentiment hold no sway.

Having delineated the deficiencies in these typical Americans, Hale offers a remedy, albeit an indirect one. What will remake the Redfields into true Americans is a story. "Did you ever, reader mine, visit Brattleborough . . . ?" Hale asks, explaining that this site, like most of "our young country," lacks "the fallen column, the ivied tower and the desolate city" (54-55).

The Redfields completely disregard their Brattleborough farm's "beautiful situation and scenery," regarding it merely "as being worth so much cash" (54). Nonetheless, the "strange circumstance" Hale is about to narrate has taught even the Redfields to see Brattleborough as "romantic"—clearly they are meant to set the "reader mine" an instructive example (55).

Hale's efforts to "story" the American landscape here are repeated throughout *Traits*,[9] because, as she argues in **"The Romance of Travelling,"** "the perpetuity of the Union" hangs on such literary work (187). Landscape's educative role as a tool of political unification rests on its ability to evoke association, an ability that depends, in turn, on the stories told about it. The political efficacy of a literary landscape is made explicit in an 1845 *Godey's* column in which Hale proposes that the nation's sectional conflict can be overcome by American women writing to their children who had removed to the territories. Those letters, Hale instructs, should dwell on the shared landscape of the past, evoking "the feelings that humanize the heart and . . . [impart] the love of country to the patriot" (qtd. in Tonkovich 158). As Nicole Tonkovich explains, "In Hale's formulation, these local memories would function quite literally as *loci communae,* common places, performing the same function as did . . . [a] rhetorical mnemonic device" (159). Americans must come to recall the landscape's history as their own, and such memory traces are fashioned through reading.

In **"The Catholic Convert,"** the story that will transform the Redfields" (and the reader's) feeling towards the landscape commences via the entrance of the gothic. A late night knock at the Redfields' door reveals "a tall man, a stranger, habited in black, with a black handkerchief drawn up nearly to his temples, his hat pulled over his forehead" (56). This mysterious stranger, who refuses to reveal his name, offers the Redfields a large sum of money if they will accept a young woman and a boy as boarders for a year. There is one condition: the Redfields must ask the boarders no questions, must not seek to discover their identities or origins. The couple agree, offering to regularize the agreement with a receipt and a written contract. However, "the dark stranger" refuses: "[S]hould I take a bond, you might, in the way of trade, consider it fair to take every advantage possible. But now, when I treat you with the confidence of a Christian, you will not fail in doing as you would be done by" (58, 62). Echoing her opening critique of the Redfields, Hale distinguishes between a business arrangement whereby both parties pursue their own self-interests and a relationship that rests on mutual expectations of "Christian" behavior.

Fittingly enough, given this sensational beginning, the young woman, Mary, turns out to be a runaway nun of sorts. The shape of Mary's early life, formed by parental neglect, is one that will become familiar to readers of anti-Catholic narratives in the 1830s, 1840s, and 1850s. Although both of her parents were Protestants, at her mother's death, Mary's grief-stricken father (Mr. Marshall, the dark stranger) committed her to the care of a Catholic woman, thinking "a creed was of very little consequence" (85). Years later, he reawakens to his paternal duties and attempts to reclaim Mary and recreate a family home. But he is too late. Mary has been seduced into Catholicism. Using the intimacy of the confessional, a stealthy Jesuit priest has so entrammeled and perverted her mind and soul that she thinks it is a sin to love her "heretic" father; Mary "trembled and wept with horror and grief, whenever any parental tenderness . . . had called forth a return of [her] affectionate confidence" (86). Invoking the sensational language of sadism and torture, Hale declares that such "religious bigotry and fanaticism . . . binds the soul in chains, which rust and canker, till a moral paralysis ensues, and all the natural and innocent feelings of the heart are turned to vile and cruel purposes" (86). As in her "How to" article, Hale here participates selectively in the rhetoric of popular anti-Catholic literature in which, as Franchot notes, "captivity structured nativist perceptions not only of papal machinations but also of Catholic dogma itself" (109).

Having penetrated the family circle, the Jesuit steals into the family home: "[N]otwithstanding all my vigilance, I could not prevent her confessor from seeing her and advising her; and he used his power over her to frighten and intimidate, till she resolved to enter a convent," Mary's father complains (87). Faced with what Franchot calls "the age's new experience of damnation: the broken parental heart" (116),[10] Mr. Marshall can thwart Mary's clandestine nighttime escape to the convent only by fleeing with her to Brattleborough. Whisked away in the dead of night to a secret destination, Mary is separated by her father from the man who holds sway over her mind, heart, and body. The two fathers' actions are pointedly parallel: if Mr. Marshall carries Mary off to a secluded spot where the holy father cannot see or even communicate with her, he is merely countering the Jesuit plot that Hale's Protestant readers suspect—"knowing," as they do, that all Catholic priests use the confessional to obtain intimacy with and control over young women, that the next step is imprisonment in a convent, and that Jesuits are particularly expert in such matters.

Mary is initially described in a way that a nineteenth-century audience would read as "nun" and that illustrates Protestant ambivalence about sisterhoods.[11] Heavily veiled when she arrives, she confines herself to her room at first, creating her own convent cell within the Redfields' domestic space. When she does reveal herself, Mary's unearthly beauty marks her as lacking the attributes necessary to Protestant womanhood: "[W]hen her eyelids droop, it seems as if she

was at prayer, and she looks so angel-like that it made me [Mrs. Redfield] feel a little afraid to gaze upon her" (65); she has "the pale unanimated beauty of a statue, rather than the loveliness of youth, health, and innocent happiness" (73); she prefers "the deepest solitude" (73) to the company even of family, and appears at first to care for her brother out of duty rather than love.

Colleen McDannell has traced in detail the differences between Protestant and Catholic domestic religion in nineteenth-century America. McDannell offers nuanced and specific support for the work of previous scholars (Baym, Cott, Douglas, Ryan, Sklar) who describe the way Protestantism increasingly located itself in domestic moral instruction. This "child-centered, mother-directed, and individual" moral pedagogy was iconized in the image of the mother reading the Bible to the child circled in her embrace (152, 132). In contrast, McDannell shows, "social and economic conditions . . . kept Catholics from developing a middle-class domestic piety until almost the close of the century. Traditional Catholicism, with its preference for celibate life, church-centered rituals, and private piety worked against the establishment of family religion" (152). These differences were pilloried by Protestant propagandists, who typically depicted Catholic dwellings as unhomelike and Catholic women as unwomanly: "With a drunken Irish father, wild children, and a mother working in the mills, the Irish immigrant family was contrasted to the 'proper' Protestant family" (154).

Hale's criticism in *Traits* is directed less at the "slovenly" Irish and more at the anti-domesticity she finds in the Catholic religion's celebration of celibacy and emotional asceticism. She will make her charge against Catholicism explicit later in *Woman's Record:* "The Roman Catholic church degraded women, when it degraded marriage by making the celibacy of the priests a condition of greater holiness than married life" (152).[12] For Hale, domestic sentiment is a model for and source of religious feeling. The perversity of the Catholic Church is that it takes advantage of the religiosity generated by human love in order to confine men and women to lives where such love is forbidden. The holy Protestant image of mother and child absorbed in what Richard Brodhead has identified as "disciplinary intimacy" or "discipline through love" was deliberately and explicitly constructed through contrast with images of archaic, patriarchal, external physical authority: the schoolmaster wielding a rod, the slaveowner brandishing a whip, the Irish father waving a fist, and, I would add, the Jesuit exercising a despotic, arbitrary authority, backed by the inquisitorial instruments of torture secreted in convents (Brodhead 13-47). But in **"The Catholic Convert,"** Hale argues that, for a true woman, even what appears to be an archaic religion of external rules is actually a matter of feeling. Mary became a Catholic, not because a priest forced her into frightened compliance, but because the substitute mother she loved was Catholic.[13] Perversion comes about when the scheming Jesuit father not only teaches her that family love is sin, but also condemns her to a life in which she will never be a mother, will never recreate mother love in her children.

Hale's retelling of world history in *Woman's Record* represents Catholic women's rescue from the convent by Gutenberg and Luther, by the printing press and the Reformation. "It was by reading the Word of God that the nine nuns of Nimptsch discerned the contrast between the Christian life, and the daily routine of the cloister. They left their superstitions and returned to the duties God imposes on the sex," a return exemplified by the case of Catharine Bora, who married Martin Luther and became a mother (*Woman's Record* 152). Similarly, Mary is rescued from the convent (as it were), not by her father's direct combat with the priest, nor the Redfields' substitute parenting, nor through theological arguments, but by the male who initiates her into Bible reading and marriage.[14] Mary's first step towards normal Protestant femaleness comes from mothering her brother, a task which draws her out of her solitary room and into intimacy with the family. The second, and decisive, step comes with her love for Mr. Watson, the young Protestant minister who teaches her to study Nature, the Bible, and, eventually, their mutual love as the true sources of religious feeling. The relationship's turning point comes when, during a long walk in the countryside, Watson gives Mary her first Bible:

A deep glow overspread his face as he put the sacred volume into her hand. . . .

"[I]f there be a sin, let it rest on my head" [cried Watson].

"O, no! no!" said Mary quickly. "If it is sin, the Saviour will surely forgive it—and I have so longed to read the Bible"—She paused and blushed—and after a few more entreaties from Watson, consented to keep the volume. (75-76).

Clearly, this is a seduction scene. However, instead of a scheming, "celibate" priest perverting the young girl in the closed, secret space of the confessional, Hale represents the Protestant minister and maiden alike as awakening to a new life of holy conjugal feeling as they explore the American landscape. If the Catholic Mary resembles a cloistered, celibate nun, removed from human emotions, the Protestant Mary, at play in Nature, is a healthy young woman eligible for love and marriage.

The treasure buried in the Brattleborough landscape turns out to be a romantic narrative of a rescue into domesticity through reading:[15] "Mary, the sweet nun, returned to the south, the happy wife of the Rev. Alexander Watson" (97). Husband and wife will go as missionaries to convert the South from its twin apostasies of Romanism and separatism. Mary's rescue is the Republic's—and it is also the Redfields'. At the close of the story, Hale focusses on Mrs. Redfield, the figure for the woman reader who is Hale's primary concern. Mary's romantic narrative softens and refines the older woman, making her kinder and more contented. Telling and retelling "the strange story," Mrs. Redfield becomes "quite a lady" (97). Remembering, Mrs. Redfield reshapes herself from a money-hungry, garrulous gossip into the Victorian middle-class ideal.

Notoriously unclassifiable as to her feminism, Hale also proves eclectic as to the style and genre of her writing.[16] **"The Catholic Convert"** is typical of *Traits of American Life* in that it participates in American history writing, the nativist landscape tradition, the New World revision of the Gothic, the literatures of religious and political controversy—and it does so by means of the sensational. Hale's authorial pattern suggests that recognizing the range and diversity *within* women's writing is a step towards exploring women writers' part in shaping traditions and genres other than the domestic. For instance, I have read **"The Catholic Convert"** within the context of anti-Catholic convent literature, but, given the early date of **"The Unknown,"** one might well reverse the procedure and look for reactions to and revisions of Hale's story in the more notorious later versions of escaped nuns' narratives. Certainly, to choose another obvious example, we can find in Hale's Mr. Marshall (a character itself drawn from the Gothic) a general precursor to Twain's mysterious strangers, and can recognize as well a quite specific set of resonances between **"The Unknown"/ "The Catholic Convert"** and "The Man Who Corrupted Hadleyburg": the unknown man who appears late at night offering wealth to the upstanding, honest couple; the community whose goodness is an untested matter of precept rather than a felt reality; the contrast between a group of self-aggrandizing individuals and a real community bound by charity. After a century of critical celebration of Twain's flight from the feminine, his famous "dark side" may turn out to be linked to the *Ladies'*.[17]

"The Catholic Convert" ends with a vision of marital happiness, of a unified Republic, of a middle-class household refined by female gentility; it ends, that is, as domestic fiction. Yet that vision rests on its author's and audience's knowledge of sensational and anti-Catholic characters and plots. Franchot shows how the enduringly popular *Foxe's Book of Martyrs* "mythologized Catholicism into a virtual demon of antidomesticity" (128). Hale summons and then exorcises that demon's nineteenth-century literary manifestations: the nun, the Jesuit, the convent, and the confessional. The masked intruder returns as the Protestant father; the Jesuit is relegated to the past; the nun turns out to have been only a virgin, waiting to become a bride, yet *Traits of American Life* has its origins nonetheless in a dark stranger, **"The Unknown."**

Notes

My thanks to Tamar Heller for her useful reading of an earlier version of this essay, as well as to the two *Legacy* readers for helpful suggestions.

[1] While David S. Reynolds disputes the power and pervasiveness of domestic fiction, he retains the opposition, which dates back at least to Leslie A. Fiedler. Recent republication of sensation fiction by nineteenth-century American women writers like Louisa May Alcott has drawn that opposition into question, as has the critical work of Christopher Looby and G. M. Goshgarian. While they do not explicitly discuss sensation fiction, Lucy M. Freibert and Barbara A. White, and Nina Baym in *American Women Writers,* insist on the generic diversity of American women's writing. In Britain, as Elizabeth Helsinger, Robin Lauterbach Sheets, and William Veeder demonstrate, sensation novels were primarily written by, for, and about women (123). They astutely suggest in an aside that "America's most shocking fiction may in fact be women's *religious* novels" (123).

[2] For an analysis of Hale's construction of her *Godey's* readership as "conversational partners" (167), see Tonkovich.

[3] On escaped nun's tales, see Franchot, Griffin, and Reynolds, *Faith in Fiction.*

[4] For a fuller account of the Charlestown incident and the events surrounding it, see Billington and Franchot. Part of the context for Harrison's story was Reed's narrative, which was not published until after the burning, but apparently was in circulation before it.

[5] Hale would later support the efforts of Catherine Beecher (Lyman's daughter) to educate young women, serving as a member of her American Woman's Educational Association (Sklar 224).

[6] On Hale's support for female missionaries, see Baym, "Onward Christian Women."

[7] Hale also makes some minor revisions, including changing the last name of the father in the story from M'Leod to Marshall.

[8] On this transformation, see Forgie, Haltunnen. Gregory Clark and S. Michael Halloran's volume charts the rhetorical changes that accompany this ideological shift.

[9] This is a project that Hale shares with the writers and painters of the Hudson River schools. While there is a substantial scholarship on canonical authors' engagement with the work of storying the American landscape, it is symptomatic of the gender divide that still obtains in American studies that little attention has been paid to women writers' share in this task. On male writers' and painters' work, see, for example, Callow, Ferguson, Nevius, Novak, Ringe. See Baym, *American Women Writers,* for a discussion of how "topographical" poems written by women historicized local sites (67-91). See Brodhead for connections between travel literature, local-color writing, and women writers in the second half of the nineteenth century.

[10] Franchot also delineates the Jesuit as an "alternatively constructed masculine power" who rivals and threatens the Protestant father (108).

[11] On the depiction of nuns in nineteenth-century paintings, see Casteras. For nineteenth-century attitudes towards sisterhoods, see Franchot and Vicinus.

[12] On *Woman's Record* as Protestant women's history, see also Baym, "Onward Christian Women," and "Sarah Hale, Political Writer," *Feminism* (167-82).

[13] Mary's father's plan for wooing her away from Catholicism rests on his recognition of religion's emotional basis: "Her creed was that of feeling; she had been educated a Catholic; and it requires something more powerful than arguments or advice to overcome the prepossessions of our childhood. I knew, in short, that her feeling must, by some means, become interested for Protestants; that she must become attached to individuals of this religion'" (90).

[14] As a female ruled by heart, Mrs. Redfield does recognize that her husband's clumsy attempts to convert Mary by reason (i.e., by reading from Revelations about the "scarlet-coloured beast" [71]) will not avail. "She did not think a girl so young as Mary would be much influenced by the reasonableness of a proposition; she must be led by gentle persuasions, and by those tender appeals that would move her feelings" (71). Mrs. Redfield therefore invites Mr. Watson, the young minister, to board with them.

[15] For another story in *Traits* that follows a similar pattern, see **"The Silver Mine,"** in which the narrator bemoans the fact that "not a single fairy ring has been discovered, or any tradition preserved, that the gay elves ever set foot in our land" (99) and sets about remedying that situation by telling a "marvellous story" of a dream about a man in black who mysteriously directs a deacon in Newport, New Hampshire, to a silver mine, hidden beneath a blasted tree. Typical of this volume's focus on middle-class domesticity is the outcome: although, after a perilous search, the deacon does find

the treasure, he returns home empty-handed, explaining to his wife that he has realized "how vain was gold and silver; and I felt that should my children be corrupted by the riches I there sought, how terrible would be my guilt, and the accusations of my conscience! I thought I had enough—I had health and strength, and, with the blessing of God, I could support you and our children" (110).

[16] See Baym's "Sarah Hale, Political Writer," *Feminism* (167-82) for a summary of the disagreements over Hale's stance.

[17] Twain was certainly familiar with some of Hale's work. In a 26 October 1853 letter to his brothers, he describes a dam by referring to an engraving in *Godey's* (*Letters* 21). For two recent studies that explore Twain's use of the feminine and the sentimental, see Stoneley and Camfield.

Works Cited

Baym, Nina. *American Women Writers and the Work of History, 1790-1860.* New Brunswick: Rutgers UP, 1995.

———. *Feminism and American Literary History.* New Brunswick: Rutgers UP, 1992.

———. "Onward Christian Women: Sarah J. Hale's History of the World." *New England Quarterly* 63 (1990): 249-70.

———. *Woman's Fiction: A Guide to Novels by and about Women in America, 1820-1870.* Ithaca: Cornell UP, 1978.

Billington, Ray Allen. *The Protestant Crusade, 1800-1860: A Study of the Origins of American Nativism.* New York: Macmillan, 1938.

Bourne, George. *Lorette. The History of Louise, Daughter of a Canadian Nun, Exhibiting the Interior of Female Convents.* 1833. 2nd ed. New York: Small, 1834.

Brodhead, Richard. *Cultures of Letters: Scenes of Reading and Writing in Nineteenth-Century America.* Chicago: U of Chicago P, 1993.

Callow, James T. *Kindred Spirits: Knickerbocker Writers and American Artists, 1807-1855.* Chapel Hill: U of North Carolina P, 1967.

Camfield, Gregg. *Sentimental Twain: Samuel Clemens in the Maze of Moral Philosophy.* Philadelphia: U of Pennsylvania P, 1994.

Casteras, Susan P. "Virgin Vows: The Early Victorian Artists' Portrayal of Nuns and Novices." *Victorian Studies* 24 (1981-82): 157-84.

Clark, Gregory, and S. Michael Hallorn, eds. *Oratorical Culture in Nineteenth-Century America: Transformations in the Theory and Practice of Rhetoric.* Carbondale: Southern Illinois UP, 1993.

Cott, Nancy. *The Bonds of Womanhood: "Woman's Sphere" in New England, 1780-1835.* New Haven: Yale UP, 1977.

Douglas, Ann. *The Feminization of American Culture.* New York: Knopf, 1977.

Ferguson, Robert A. "William Cullen Bryant: The Creative Context of the Poet." *New England Quarterly* 53 (1980): 31-63.

Fielder, Leslie A. *Love and Death in the American Novel.* New York: Criterion, 1960.

Forgie, George B. *Patricide in the House Divided: A Psychological Interpretation of Lincoln and His Age.* New York: Norton, 1979.

Franchot, Jenny. *Roads to Rome: The Antebellum Protestant Encounter with Catholicism.* Berkeley: U of California P, 1994.

Freibert, Lucy M., and Barbara A. White, eds. *Hidden Hands: An Anthology of American Women Writers, 1790-1870.* New Brunswick: Rutgers UP, 1985.

Goshgarian, G. M. *To Kiss the Chastening Rod: Domestic Fiction and Sexual Ideology in the American Renaissance.* Ithaca: Cornell UP, 1992.

Griffin, Susan Mary. "Awful Disclosures: Female Evidence in the Escaped Nun's Tale." *PMLA* 111 (1996): 93-107.

Hale, Sarah Josepha. "Convents are Increasing." *American Ladies' Magazine* 7 (Dec. 1834): 560-64.

———. "How to Prevent the Increase of Convents." *American Ladies' Magazine* 7 (Nov. 1834): 517-21.

———. *Traits of American Life.* Philadelphia: Carey, 1835.

———. "The Unknown." *Ladies' Magazine* 3 (Aug.-Sept. 1830): 338-53, 385-93.

———. "The Ursuline Convent." *American Ladies' Magazine* 7 (Sept. 1834): 418-26.

———. *Woman's Record; or, Sketches of All Distinguished Women from the Creation to A.D. 1854. Arranged in four eras. With selections from female writers of every age.* 2nd ed. New York: Harper, 1855.

Haltunnen, Karen. *Confidence Men and Painted Women: A Study of Middle-Class Culture in America, 1830-1870.* New Haven: Yale UP, 1982.

Hedrick, Joan D. *Harriet Beecher Stowe: A Life.* New York: Oxford UP, 1994.

Helsinger, Elizabeth, Robin Lauterbach Sheets, and William Veeder. *The Woman Question: Society and Literature in Britain and America, 1837-1883.* Vol. 3. Chicago: U of Chicago P, 1989. 3 vols. 1989.

Hoffman, Nicole Tonkovich. "*Legacy* Profile: Sarah Josepha Hale, 1788-1874." *Legacy* 7.2 (1990): 47-55.

Looby, Christopher. "George Thompson's 'Romance of the Real': Transgression and Taboo in American Sensation Fiction." *American Literature* 65 (1994): 651-72.

McDannell, Colleen. *The Christian Home in Victorian America, 1840-1900.* Bloomington: Indiana UP, 1986.

Monk, Maria. *Awful Disclosures of the Hotel Dieu Nunnery of Montreal, Revised, with an Appendix.* 1836. New York: Arno, 1977.

Mott, Frank Luther. *Golden Multitudes: The Story of Best Sellers in the United States.* New York: Macmillan, 1947.

Nevius, Blake. *Cooper's Landscapes: An Essay on the Picturesque Vision.* Berkeley: U of California P, 1976.

Novak, Barbara. *Nature and Culture: American Landscape and Painting, 1825-1875.* New York: Oxford UP, 1980.

Reed, Rebecca Theresa. *Six Months in a Convent, or, The Narrative of Rebecca Theresa Reed, Who was Under the Influence of the Roman Catholics about Two Years, and an Inmate of the Ursuline Convent on Mount Benedict, Charlestown, Mass., Nearly Six Months, in the Years 1831-1832 With Some Preliminary Suggestions by the Committee of Publication.* 1835. New York: Arno, 1977.

Reynolds, David S. *Beneath the American Renaissance: The Subversive Imagination in the Age of Emerson and Melville.* Cambridge: Harvard UP, 1988.

———. *Faith in Fiction: The Emergence of Religious Literature in America.* Cambridge: Harvard UP, 1981.

Ringe, Donald A. *The Pictorial Mode: Space and Time in the Art of Bryant, Irving, and Cooper.* Lexington: UP of Kentucky, 1971.

Ryan, Mary P. *Cradle of the Middle Class: The Family in Oneida County, New York, 1790-1895.* New York: Cambridge UP, 1981.

Sklar, Kathryn Kish. *Catherine Beecher: A Study in American Domesticity.* New York: Norton, 1976.

Stoneley, Peter. *Mark Twain and the Feminine Aesthetic.* Cambridge: Cambridge UP, 1992.

Tarr, Mary Muriel. *Catholicism in Gothic Fiction.* New York: Garland, 1979.

Tompkins, Jane. *Sensational Designs: The Cultural Work of American Fiction, 1790-1860.* New York: Oxford UP, 1985.

Tonkovich, Nicole. "Rhetorical Power in the Victorian Parlor: *Godey's Lady's Book* and the Gendering of Nineteenth-Century Rhetoric." *Oratorical Culture in Nineteenth-Century America: Transformations in the Theory and Practice of Rhetoric.* Ed. Gregory Clark and S. Michael Halloran. Carbondale: Southern Illinois UP, 1993. 158-83.

Twain, Mark. *Mark Twain's Letters.* Ed. Edgar Marquess Branch, Michael B. Frank, and Kenneth M. Sanderson. Vol. 1. Berkeley: U of California P, 1988. 4 vols. to date. 1988—.

Vicinus, Martha. "Church Communities: Sisterhoods and Deaconnesses' Houses." *Independent Women: Work and Community for Single Women, 1850-1920.* Chicago: U of Chicago P, 1985. 46-84.

FURTHER READING

Bibliography

Blanck, Jacob. "Sarah Josepha Buell Hale, 1788-1879." In *Bibliography of American Literature*, Vol. 3, 319-40. New Haven: Yale University Press, 1959.

 Contains a detailed list of Hale's writings.

Biographies

Hoffman, Nicole Tonkovich. "Sarah Josepha Hale (1788-1874 [*sic*])." *Legacy* 7, No. 2 (1990): 47-55.

 Brief survey of Hale's life and works. Includes bibliography.

Martin, Lawrence. "The Genesis of *Godey's Lady's Book*." *New England Quarterly* 1 (1928): 41-70.

 A discussion of Hale's aims and activities as an editor.

Rogers, Sherbrooke. *Sarah Josepha Hale: A New England Pioneer, 1788-1879.* Grantham, N.H.: Tompson & Rutter, 1985.

 An overview of Hale's life, focusing primarily on her work as an editor and her campaigns for various causes.

Tonkovich, Nicole. *Domesticity with a Difference: The Nonfiction of Catharine Beecher, Sarah J. Hale, Fanny Fern, and Margaret Fuller*. Jackson: University Press of Mississippi, 1997.

A comparative study which includes biographical information on Hale as well as an analysis of her views on the role of women.

Criticism

Leverenz, David. *Manhood and the American Renaissance*. Ithaca, NY: Cornell University Press, 1989.

Contains a section on Hale's editorship of *Godey's Lady's Book*, asserting that she pursued a "duplicitous" strategy of appealing to the authority of men while condemning them as brutes.

Additional coverage of Hale's life and career is contained in the following sources published by The Gale Group: *Dictionary of Literary Biography*, **Vols. 1, 42, and 73.**

Nineteenth-Century
Literature Criticism

Cumulative Indexes
Volumes 1-75

How to Use This Index

The main references

Calvino, Italo
1923–1985 .... CLC **5, 8, 11, 22, 33, 39,**
73; SSC 3

list all author entries in the following Gale Literary Criticism series:

BLC = *Black Literature Criticism*
CLC = *Contemporary Literary Criticism*
CLR = *Children's Literature Review*
CMLC = *Classical and Medieval Literature Criticism*
DA = *DISCovering Authors*
DAB = *DISCovering Authors: British*
DAC = *DISCovering Authors: Canadian*
DAM = *DISCovering Authors: Modules*
 DRAM: *Dramatists Module;* *MST*: *Most-Studied Authors Module;*
 MULT: *Multicultural Authors Module;* *NOV*: *Novelists Module;*
 POET: *Poets Module;* *POP*: *Popular Fiction and Genre Authors Module*
DC = *Drama Criticism*
HLC = *Hispanic Literature Criticism*
LC = *Literature Criticism from 1400 to 1800*
NCLC = *Nineteenth-Century Literature Criticism*
PC = *Poetry Criticism*
SSC = *Short Story Criticism*
TCLC = *Twentieth-Century Literary Criticism*
WLC = *World Literature Criticism, 1500 to the Present*

The cross-references

See also CANR 23; CA 85-88;
 obituary CA116

list all author entries in the following Gale biographical and literary sources:

AAYA = *Authors & Artists for Young Adults*
AITN = *Authors in the News*
BEST = *Bestsellers*
BW = *Black Writers*
CA = *Contemporary Authors*
CAAS = *Contemporary Authors Autobiography Series*
CABS = *Contemporary Authors Bibliographical Series*
CANR = *Contemporary Authors New Revision Series*
CAP = *Contemporary Authors Permanent Series*
CDALB = *Concise Dictionary of American Literary Biography*
CDBLB = *Concise Dictionary of British Literary Biography*
DLB = *Dictionary of Literary Biography*
DLBD = *Dictionary of Literary Biography Documentary Series*
DLBY = *Dictionary of Literary Biography Yearbook*
HW = *Hispanic Writers*
JRDA = *Junior DISCovering Authors*
MAICYA = *Major Authors and Illustrators for Children and Young Adults*
MTCW = *Major 20th-Century Writers*
NNAL = *Native North American Literature*
SAAS = *Something about the Author Autobiography Series*
SATA = *Something about the Author*
YABC = *Yesterday's Authors of Books for Children*

Literary Criticism Series
Cumulative Author Index

20/1631
See Upward, Allen

A/C Cross
See Lawrence, T(homas) E(dward)

Abasiyanik, Sait Faik 1906-1954
See Sait Faik
See also CA 123

Abbey, Edward 1927-1989   CLC 36, 59
See also CA 45-48; 128; CANR 2, 41

Abbott, Lee K(ittredge) 1947-   CLC 48
See also CA 124; CANR 51; DLB 130

Abe, Kobo 1924-1993CLC 8, 22, 53, 81; DAM
NOV
See also CA 65-68; 140; CANR 24, 60; DLB
182; MTCW 1

Abelard, Peter c. 1079-c. 1142   CMLC 11
See also DLB 115, 208

Abell, Kjeld 1901-1961   CLC 15
See also CA 111

Abish, Walter 1931-   CLC 22
See also CA 101; CANR 37; DLB 130

Abrahams, Peter (Henry) 1919-   CLC 4
See also BW 1; CA 57-60; CANR 26; DLB 117;
MTCW 1

Abrams, M(eyer) H(oward) 1912-   CLC 24
See also CA 57-60; CANR 13, 33; DLB 67

Abse, Dannie 1923- CLC 7, 29; DAB; DAM
POET
See also CA 53-56; CAAS 1; CANR 4, 46, 74;
DLB 27

Achebe, (Albert) Chinua(lumogu) 1930-C L C
1, 3, 5, 7, 11, 26, 51, 75; BLC 1; DA; DAB;
DAC; DAM MST, MULT, NOV; WLC
See also AAYA 15; BW 2; CA 1-4R; CANR 6,
26, 47, 73; CLR 20; DLB 117; MAICYA;
MTCW 1; SATA 40; SATA-Brief 38

Acker, Kathy 1948-1997   CLC 45, 111
See also CA 117; 122; 162; CANR 55

Ackroyd, Peter 1949-   CLC 34, 52
See also CA 123; 127; CANR 51, 74; DLB 155;
INT 127

Acorn, Milton 1923-   CLC 15; DAC
See also CA 103; DLB 53; INT 103

Adamov, Arthur 1908-1970 CLC 4, 25; DAM
DRAM
See also CA 17-18; 25-28R; CAP 2; MTCW 1

Adams, Alice (Boyd) 1926-CLC 6, 13, 46; SSC
24
See also CA 81-84; CANR 26, 53, 75; DLBY
86; INT CANR-26; MTCW 1

Adams, Andy 1859-1935   TCLC 56
See also YABC 1

Adams, Brooks 1848-1927   TCLC 80
See also CA 123; DLB 47

Adams, Douglas (Noel) 1952-   CLC 27, 60;
DAM POP
See also AAYA 4; BEST 89:3; CA 106; CANR
34, 64; DLBY 83; JRDA

Adams, Francis 1862-1893   NCLC 33

Adams, Henry (Brooks) 1838-1918 TCLC 4,
52; DA; DAB; DAC; DAM MST
See also CA 104; 133; DLB 12, 47, 189

Adams, Richard (George) 1920-CLC 4, 5, 18;
DAM NOV
See also AAYA 16; AITN 1, 2; CA 49-52;
CANR 3, 35; CLR 20; JRDA; MAICYA;
MTCW 1; SATA 7, 69

Adamson, Joy(-Friederike Victoria) 1910-1980
CLC 17
See also CA 69-72; 93-96; CANR 22; MTCW
1; SATA 11; SATA-Obit 22

Adcock, Fleur 1934-   CLC 41
See also CA 25-28R; CAAS 23; CANR 11, 34,
69; DLB 40

Addams, Charles (Samuel) 1912-1988CLC 30
See also CA 61-64; 126; CANR 12

Addams, Jane 1860-1945   TCLC 76

Addison, Joseph 1672-1719   LC 18
See also CDBLB 1660-1789; DLB 101

Adler, Alfred (F.) 1870-1937   TCLC 61
See also CA 119; 159

Adler, C(arole) S(chwerdtfeger) 1932-CLC 35
See also AAYA 4; CA 89-92; CANR 19, 40;
JRDA; MAICYA; SAAS 15; SATA 26, 63,
102

Adler, Renata 1938-   CLC 8, 31
See also CA 49-52; CANR 5, 22, 52; MTCW 1

Ady, Endre 1877-1919   TCLC 11
See also CA 107

A.E. 1867-1935   TCLC 3, 10
See also Russell, George William

Aeschylus 525B.C.-456B.C.   CMLC 11; DA;
DAB; DAC; DAM DRAM, MST; DC 8;
WLCS
See also DLB 176

Aesop 620(?)B.C.-564(?)B.C.   CMLC 24
See also CLR 14; MAICYA; SATA 64

Affable Hawk
See MacCarthy, Sir(Charles Otto) Desmond

Africa, Ben
See Bosman, Herman Charles

Afton, Effie
See Harper, Frances Ellen Watkins

Agapida, Fray Antonio
See Irving, Washington

Agee, James (Rufus) 1909-1955 TCLC 1, 19;
DAM NOV
See also AITN 1; CA 108; 148; CDALB 1941-
1968; DLB 2, 26, 152

Aghill, Gordon
See Silverberg, Robert

Agnon, S(hmuel) Y(osef Halevi) 1888-1970
CLC 4, 8, 14; SSC 30
See also CA 17-18; 25-28R; CANR 60; CAP 2;
MTCW 1

Agrippa von Nettesheim, Henry Cornelius
1486-1535   LC 27

Aherne, Owen
See Cassill, R(onald) V(erlin)

Ai 1947-   CLC 4, 14, 69
See also CA 85-88; CAAS 13; CANR 70; DLB
120

Aickman, Robert (Fordyce) 1914-1981 C L C
57

See also CA 5-8R; CANR 3, 72

Aiken, Conrad (Potter) 1889-1973CLC 1, 3, 5,
10, 52; DAM NOV, POET; SSC 9
See also CA 5-8R; 45-48; CANR 4, 60; CDALB
1929-1941; DLB 9, 45, 102; MTCW 1; SATA
3, 30

Aiken, Joan (Delano) 1924-   CLC 35
See also AAYA 1, 25; CA 9-12R; CANR 4, 23,
34, 64; CLR 1, 19; DLB 161; JRDA;
MAICYA; MTCW 1; SAAS 1; SATA 2, 30,
73

Ainsworth, William Harrison 1805-1882
NCLC 13
See also DLB 21; SATA 24

Aitmatov, Chingiz (Torekulovich) 1928- C L C
71
See also CA 103; CANR 38; MTCW 1; SATA
56

Akers, Floyd
See Baum, L(yman) Frank

Akhmadulina, Bella Akhatovna 1937-   C L C
53; DAM POET
See also CA 65-68

Akhmatova, Anna 1888-1966CLC 11, 25, 64;
DAM POET; PC 2
See also CA 19-20; 25-28R; CANR 35; CAP 1;
MTCW 1

Aksakov, Sergei Timofeyvich 1791-1859
NCLC 2
See also DLB 198

Aksenov, Vassily
See Aksyonov, Vassily (Pavlovich)

Akst, Daniel 1956-   CLC 109
See also CA 161

Aksyonov, Vassily (Pavlovich) 1932- CLC 22,
37, 101
See also CA 53-56; CANR 12, 48

Akutagawa, Ryunosuke 1892-1927 TCLC 16
See also CA 117; 154

Alain 1868-1951   TCLC 41
See also CA 163

Alain-Fournier   TCLC 6
See also Fournier, Henri Alban
See also DLB 65

Alarcon, Pedro Antonio de 1833-1891NCLC 1

Alas (y Urena), Leopoldo (Enrique Garcia)
1852-1901   TCLC 29
See also CA 113; 131; HW

Albee, Edward (Franklin III) 1928-CLC 1, 2,
3, 5, 9, 11, 13, 25, 53, 86, 113; DA; DAB;
DAC; DAM DRAM, MST; WLC
See also AITN 1; CA 5-8R; CABS 3; CANR 8,
54, 74; CDALB 1941-1968; DLB 7; INT
CANR-8; MTCW 1

Alberti, Rafael 1902-   CLC 7
See also CA 85-88; DLB 108

Albert the Great 1200(?)-1280   CMLC 16
See also DLB 115

Alcala-Galiano, Juan Valera y
See Valera y Alcala-Galiano, Juan

Alcott, Amos Bronson 1799-1888   NCLC 1
See also DLB 1

Alcott, Louisa May 1832-1888 NCLC 6, 58;
DA; DAB; DAC; DAM MST, NOV; SSC
27; WLC
See also AAYA 20; CDALB 1865-1917; CLR
1, 38; DLB 1, 42, 79; DLBD 14; JRDA;
MAICYA; SATA 100; YABC 1

Aldanov, M. A.
See Aldanov, Mark (Alexandrovich)

Aldanov, Mark (Alexandrovich) 1886(?)-1957
TCLC 23
See also CA 118

Aldington, Richard 1892-1962 CLC 49
See also CA 85-88; CANR 45; DLB 20, 36, 100,
149

Aldiss, Brian W(ilson) 1925- CLC 5, 14, 40;
DAM NOV
See also CA 5-8R; CAAS 2; CANR 5, 28, 64;
DLB 14; MTCW 1; SATA 34

Alegria, Claribel 1924-CLC 75; DAM MULT
See also CA 131; CAAS 15; CANR 66; DLB
145; HW

Alegria, Fernando 1918- CLC 57
See also CA 9-12R; CANR 5, 32, 72; HW

Aleichem, Sholom TCLC 1, 35; SSC 33
See also Rabinovitch, Sholem

Aleixandre, Vicente 1898-1984 CLC 9, 36;
DAM POET; PC 15
See also CA 85-88; 114; CANR 26; DLB 108;
HW; MTCW 1

Alepoudelis, Odysseus
See Elytis, Odysseus

Aleshkovsky, Joseph 1929-
See Aleshkovsky, Yuz
See also CA 121; 128

Aleshkovsky, Yuz CLC 44
See also Aleshkovsky, Joseph

Alexander, Lloyd (Chudley) 1924- CLC 35
See also AAYA 1, 27; CA 1-4R; CANR 1, 24,
38, 55; CLR 1, 5, 48; DLB 52; JRDA;
MAICYA; MTCW 1; SAAS 19; SATA 3, 49,
81

Alexander, Samuel 1859-1938 TCLC 77

Alexie, Sherman (Joseph, Jr.) 1966- CLC 96;
DAM MULT
See also CA 138; CANR 65; DLB 175, 206;
NNAL

Alfau, Felipe 1902- CLC 66
See also CA 137

Alger, Horatio, Jr. 1832-1899 NCLC 8
See also DLB 42; SATA 16

Algren, Nelson 1909-1981CLC 4, 10, 33; SSC
33
See also CA 13-16R; 103; CANR 20, 61;
CDALB 1941-1968; DLB 9; DLBY 81, 82;
MTCW 1

Ali, Ahmed 1910- CLC 69
See also CA 25-28R; CANR 15, 34

Alighieri, Dante
See Dante

Allan, John B.
See Westlake, Donald E(dwin)

Allan, Sidney
See Hartmann, Sadakichi

Allan, Sydney
See Hartmann, Sadakichi

Allen, Edward 1948- CLC 59

Allen, Fred 1894-1956 TCLC 87

Allen, Paula Gunn 1939- CLC 84; DAM
MULT
See also CA 112; 143; CANR 63; DLB 175;
NNAL

Allen, Roland
See Ayckbourn, Alan

Allen, Sarah A.
See Hopkins, Pauline Elizabeth

Allen, Sidney H.
See Hartmann, Sadakichi

Allen, Woody 1935- CLC 16, 52; DAM POP
See also AAYA 10; CA 33-36R; CANR 27, 38,
63; DLB 44; MTCW 1

Allende, Isabel 1942- CLC 39, 57, 97; DAM
MULT, NOV; HLC; WLCS
See also AAYA 18; CA 125; 130; CANR 51,
74; DLB 145; HW; INT 130; MTCW 1

Alleyn, Ellen
See Rossetti, Christina (Georgina)

Allingham, Margery (Louise) 1904-1966CLC
19
See also CA 5-8R; 25-28R; CANR 4, 58; DLB
77; MTCW 1

Allingham, William 1824-1889 NCLC 25
See also DLB 35

Allison, Dorothy E. 1949- CLC 78
See also CA 140; CANR 66

Allston, Washington 1779-1843 NCLC 2
See also DLB 1

Almedingen, E. M. CLC 12
See also Almedingen, Martha Edith von
See also SATA 3

Almedingen, Martha Edith von 1898-1971
See Almedingen, E. M.
See also CA 1-4R; CANR 1

Almodovar, Pedro 1949(?)- CLC 114
See also CA 133; CANR 72

Almqvist, Carl Jonas Love 1793-1866 NCLC
42

Alonso, Damaso 1898-1990 CLC 14
See also CA 110; 131; 130; CANR 72; DLB
108; HW

Alov
See Gogol, Nikolai (Vasilyevich)

Alta 1942- CLC 19
See also CA 57-60

Alter, Robert B(ernard) 1935- CLC 34
See also CA 49-52; CANR 1, 47

Alther, Lisa 1944- CLC 7, 41
See also CA 65-68; CAAS 30; CANR 12, 30,
51; MTCW 1

Althusser, L.
See Althusser, Louis

Althusser, Louis 1918-1990 CLC 106
See also CA 131; 132

Altman, Robert 1925- CLC 16, 116
See also CA 73-76; CANR 43

Alvarez, A(lfred) 1929- CLC 5, 13
See also CA 1-4R; CANR 3, 33, 63; DLB 14,
40

Alvarez, Alejandro Rodriguez 1903-1965
See Casona, Alejandro
See also CA 131; 93-96; HW

Alvarez, Julia 1950- CLC 93
See also AAYA 25; CA 147; CANR 69

Alvaro, Corrado 1896-1956 TCLC 60
See also CA 163

Amado, Jorge 1912- CLC 13, 40, 106; DAM
MULT, NOV; HLC
See also CA 77-80; CANR 35, 74; DLB 113;
MTCW 1

Ambler, Eric 1909-1998 CLC 4, 6, 9
See also CA 9-12R; 171; CANR 7, 38, 74; DLB
77; MTCW 1

Amichai, Yehuda 1924- CLC 9, 22, 57, 116
See also CA 85-88; CANR 46, 60; MTCW 1

Amichai, Yehudah
See Amichai, Yehuda

Amiel, Henri Frederic 1821-1881 NCLC 4

Amis, Kingsley (William) 1922-1995CLC 1, 2,
3, 5, 8, 13, 40, 44; DA; DAB; DAC; DAM
MST, NOV
See also AITN 2; CA 9-12R; 150; CANR 8, 28,
54; CDBLB 1945-1960; DLB 15, 27, 100,
139; DLBY 96; INT CANR-8; MTCW 1

Amis, Martin (Louis) 1949- CLC 4, 9, 38, 62,
101
See also BEST 90:3; CA 65-68; CANR 8, 27,
54, 73; DLB 14, 194; INT CANR-27

Ammons, A(rchie) R(andolph) 1926-CLC 2, 3,
5, 8, 9, 25, 57, 108; DAM POET; PC 16
See also AITN 1; CA 9-12R; CANR 6, 36, 51,
73; DLB 5, 165; MTCW 1

Amo, Tauraatua i
See Adams, Henry (Brooks)

Amory, Thomas 1691(?)-1788 LC 48

Anand, Mulk Raj 1905- CLC 23, 93; DAM
NOV
See also CA 65-68; CANR 32, 64; MTCW 1

Anatol
See Schnitzler, Arthur

Anaximander c. 610B.C.-c. 546B.C.CMLC 22

Anaya, Rudolfo A(lfonso) 1937- CLC 23;
DAM MULT, NOV; HLC
See also AAYA 20; CA 45-48; CAAS 4; CANR
1, 32, 51; DLB 82, 206; HW 1; MTCW 1

Andersen, Hans Christian 1805-1875NCLC 7;
DA; DAB; DAC; DAM MST, POP; SSC
6; WLC
See also CLR 6; MAICYA; SATA 100; YABC
1

Anderson, C. Farley
See Mencken, H(enry) L(ouis); Nathan, George
Jean

Anderson, Jessica (Margaret) Queale 1916-
CLC 37
See also CA 9-12R; CANR 4, 62

Anderson, Jon (Victor) 1940- CLC 9; DAM
POET
See also CA 25-28R; CANR 20

Anderson, Lindsay (Gordon) 1923-1994CLC
20
See also CA 125; 128; 146

Anderson, Maxwell 1888-1959TCLC 2; DAM
DRAM
See also CA 105; 152; DLB 7

Anderson, Poul (William) 1926- CLC 15
See also AAYA 5; CA 1-4R; CAAS 2; CANR
2, 15, 34, 64; DLB 8; INT CANR-15; MTCW
1; SATA 90; SATA-Brief 39

Anderson, Robert (Woodruff) 1917-CLC 23;
DAM DRAM
See also AITN 1; CA 21-24R; CANR 32; DLB
7

Anderson, Sherwood 1876-1941 TCLC 1, 10,
24; DA; DAB; DAC; DAM MST, NOV;
SSC 1; WLC
See also CA 104; 121; CANR 61; CDALB
1917-1929; DLB 4, 9, 86; DLBD 1; MTCW
1

Andier, Pierre
See Desnos, Robert

Andouard
See Giraudoux, (Hippolyte) Jean

Andrade, Carlos Drummond de CLC 18
See also Drummond de Andrade, Carlos

Andrade, Mario de 1893-1945 TCLC 43

Andreae, Johann V(alentin) 1586-1654LC 32
See also DLB 164

Andreas-Salome, Lou 1861-1937 TCLC 56
See also DLB 66

Andress, Lesley

See Sanders, Lawrence

Andrewes, Lancelot 1555-1626　　　**LC 5**
See also DLB 151, 172

Andrews, Cicily Fairfield
See West, Rebecca

Andrews, Elton V.
See Pohl, Frederik

Andreyev, Leonid (Nikolaevich) 1871-1919
TCLC 3
See also CA 104

Andric, Ivo 1892-1975　　　　　**CLC 8**
See also CA 81-84; 57-60; CANR 43, 60; DLB
147; MTCW 1

Androvar
See Prado (Calvo), Pedro

Angelique, Pierre
See Bataille, Georges

Angell, Roger 1920-　　　　　**CLC 26**
See also CA 57-60; CANR 13, 44, 70; DLB 171,
185

Angelou, Maya 1928-**CLC 12, 35, 64, 77; BLC
1; DA; DAB; DAC; DAM MST, MULT,
POET, POP; WLCS**
See also AAYA 7, 20; BW 2; CA 65-68; CANR
19, 42, 65; CLR 53; DLB 38; MTCW 1;
SATA 49

Anna Comnena 1083-1153　　　**CMLC 25**

Annensky, Innokenty (Fyodorovich) 1856-1909
TCLC 14
See also CA 110; 155

Annunzio, Gabriele d'
See D'Annunzio, Gabriele

Anodos
See Coleridge, Mary E(lizabeth)

Anon, Charles Robert
See Pessoa, Fernando (Antonio Nogueira)

Anouilh, Jean (Marie Lucien Pierre) 1910-1987
**CLC 1, 3, 8, 13, 40, 50; DAM DRAM; DC
8**
See also CA 17-20R; 123; CANR 32; MTCW 1

Anthony, Florence
See Ai

Anthony, John
See Ciardi, John (Anthony)

Anthony, Peter
See Shaffer, Anthony (Joshua); Shaffer, Peter
(Levin)

Anthony, Piers 1934-　　**CLC 35; DAM POP**
See also AAYA 11; CA 21-24R; CANR 28, 56,
73; DLB 8; MTCW 1; SAAS 22; SATA 84

Anthony, Susan B(rownell) 1916-1991 **TCLC
84**
See also CA 89-92; 134

Antoine, Marc
See Proust, (Valentin-Louis-George-Eugene-)
Marcel

Antoninus, Brother
See Everson, William (Oliver)

Antonioni, Michelangelo 1912-　　**CLC 20**
See also CA 73-76; CANR 45

Antschel, Paul 1920-1970
See Celan, Paul
See also CA 85-88; CANR 33, 61; MTCW 1

Anwar, Chairil 1922-1949　　　**TCLC 22**
See also CA 121

Apess, William 1798-1839(?)**NCLC 73; DAM
MULT**
See also DLB 175; NNAL

Apollinaire, Guillaume 1880-1918**TCLC 3, 8,
51; DAM POET; PC 7**
See also Kostrowitzki, Wilhelm Apollinaris de
See also CA 152

Appelfeld, Aharon 1932-　　　**CLC 23, 47**

See also CA 112; 133

Apple, Max (Isaac) 1941-　　　**CLC 9, 33**
See also CA 81-84; CANR 19, 54; DLB 130

Appleman, Philip (Dean) 1926-　　**CLC 51**
See also CA 13-16R; CAAS 18; CANR 6, 29,
56

Appleton, Lawrence
See Lovecraft, H(oward) P(hillips)

Apteryx
See Eliot, T(homas) S(tearns)

Apuleius, (Lucius Madaurensis) 125(?)-175(?)
CMLC 1

Aquin, Hubert 1929-1977　　　**CLC 15**
See also CA 105; DLB 53

Aragon, Louis 1897-1982　　**CLC 3, 22; DAM
NOV, POET**
See also CA 69-72; 108; CANR 28, 71; DLB
72; MTCW 1

Arany, Janos 1817-1882　　　**NCLC 34**

Aranyos, Kakay
See Mikszath, Kalman

Arbuthnot, John 1667-1735　　　**LC 1**
See also DLB 101

Archer, Herbert Winslow
See Mencken, H(enry) L(ouis)

Archer, Jeffrey (Howard) 1940-　　**CLC 28;
DAM POP**
See also AAYA 16; BEST 89:3; CA 77-80;
CANR 22, 52; INT CANR-22

Archer, Jules 1915-　　　　**CLC 12**
See also CA 9-12R; CANR 6, 69; SAAS 5;
SATA 4, 85

Archer, Lee
See Ellison, Harlan (Jay)

Arden, John 1930-**CLC 6, 13, 15; DAM DRAM**
See also CA 13-16R; CAAS 4; CANR 31, 65,
67; DLB 13; MTCW 1

Arenas, Reinaldo 1943-1990　**CLC 41; DAM
MULT; HLC**
See also CA 124; 128; 133; CANR 73; DLB
145; HW

Arendt, Hannah 1906-1975　　**CLC 66, 98**
See also CA 17-20R; 61-64; CANR 26, 60;
MTCW 1

Aretino, Pietro 1492-1556　　　**LC 12**

Arghezi, Tudor 1880-1967　　　**CLC 80**
See also Theodorescu, Ion N.
See also CA 167

Arguedas, Jose Maria 1911-1969 **CLC 10, 18**
See also CA 89-92; CANR 73; DLB 113; HW

Argueta, Manlio 1936-　　　　**CLC 31**
See also CA 131; CANR 73; DLB 145; HW

Ariosto, Ludovico 1474-1533　　　**LC 6**

Aristides
See Epstein, Joseph

Aristophanes 450B.C.-385B.C.**CMLC 4; DA;
DAB; DAC; DAM DRAM, MST; DC 2;
WLCS**
See also DLB 176

Aristotle 384B.C.-322B.C.　　　**CMLC 31; DA;
DAB; DAC; DAM MST; WLCS**
See also DLB 176

Arlt, Roberto (Godofredo Christophersen)
1900-1942**TCLC 29; DAM MULT; HLC**
See also CA 123; 131; CANR 67; HW

Armah, Ayi Kwei 1939-　**CLC 5, 33; BLC 1;
DAM MULT, POET**
See also BW 1; CA 61-64; CANR 21, 64; DLB
117; MTCW 1

Armatrading, Joan 1950-　　　**CLC 17**
See also CA 114

Arnette, Robert
See Silverberg, Robert

**Arnim, Achim von (Ludwig Joachim von
Arnim)** 1781-1831　　**NCLC 5; SSC 29**
See also DLB 90

Arnim, Bettina von 1785-1859　　**NCLC 38**
See also DLB 90

Arnold, Matthew 1822-1888**NCLC 6, 29; DA;
DAB; DAC; DAM MST, POET; PC 5;
WLC**
See also CDBLB 1832-1890; DLB 32, 57

Arnold, Thomas 1795-1842　　　**NCLC 18**
See also DLB 55

Arnow, Harriette (Louisa) Simpson 1908-1986
CLC 2, 7, 18
See also CA 9-12R; 118; CANR 14; DLB 6;
MTCW 1; SATA 42; SATA-Obit 47

Arouet, Francois-Marie
See Voltaire

Arp, Hans
See Arp, Jean

Arp, Jean 1887-1966　　　　**CLC 5**
See also CA 81-84; 25-28R; CANR 42

Arrabal
See Arrabal, Fernando

Arrabal, Fernando 1932-　　**CLC 2, 9, 18, 58**
See also CA 9-12R; CANR 15

Arrick, Fran　　　　　　　　**CLC 30**
See also Gaberman, Judie Angell

Artaud, Antonin (Marie Joseph) 1896-1948
TCLC 3, 36; DAM DRAM
See also CA 104; 149

Arthur, Ruth M(abel) 1905-1979　　**CLC 12**
See also CA 9-12R; 85-88; CANR 4; SATA 7,
26

Artsybashev, Mikhail (Petrovich) 1878-1927
TCLC 31
See also CA 170

Arundel, Honor (Morfydd) 1919-1973**CLC 17**
See also CA 21-22; 41-44R; CAP 2; CLR 35;
SATA 4; SATA-Obit 24

Arzner, Dorothy 1897-1979　　　**CLC 98**

Asch, Sholem 1880-1957　　　**TCLC 3**
See also CA 105

Ash, Shalom
See Asch, Sholem

Ashbery, John (Lawrence) 1927-**CLC 2, 3, 4,
6, 9, 13, 15, 25, 41, 77; DAM POET**
See also CA 5-8R; CANR 9, 37, 66; DLB 5,
165; DLBY 81; INT CANR-9; MTCW 1

Ashdown, Clifford
See Freeman, R(ichard) Austin

Ashe, Gordon
See Creasey, John

Ashton-Warner, Sylvia (Constance) 1908-1984
CLC 19
See also CA 69-72; 112; CANR 29; MTCW 1

Asimov, Isaac 1920-1992 **CLC 1, 3, 9, 19, 26,
76, 92; DAM POP**
See also AAYA 13; BEST 90:2; CA 1-4R; 137;
CANR 2, 19, 36, 60; CLR 12; DLB 8; DLBY
92; INT CANR-19; JRDA; MAICYA;
MTCW 1; SATA 1, 26, 74

Assis, Joaquim Maria Machado de
See Machado de Assis, Joaquim Maria

Astley, Thea (Beatrice May) 1925-　　**CLC 41**
See also CA 65-68; CANR 11, 43

Aston, James
See White, T(erence) H(anbury)

Asturias, Miguel Angel 1899-1974 **CLC 3, 8,
13; DAM MULT, NOV; HLC**
See also CA 25-28; 49-52; CANR 32; CAP 2;
DLB 113; HW; MTCW 1

Atares, Carlos Saura
See Saura (Atares), Carlos

Atheling, William
See Pound, Ezra (Weston Loomis)

Atheling, William, Jr.
See Blish, James (Benjamin)

Atherton, Gertrude (Franklin Horn) 1857-1948
TCLC 2
See also CA 104; 155; DLB 9, 78, 186

Atherton, Lucius
See Masters, Edgar Lee

Atkins, Jack
See Harris, Mark

Atkinson, Kate **CLC 99**
See also CA 166

Attaway, William (Alexander) 1911-1986**CLC
92; BLC 1; DAM MULT**
See also BW 2; CA 143; DLB 76

Atticus
See Fleming, Ian (Lancaster); Wilson, (Thomas)
Woodrow

Atwood, Margaret (Eleanor) 1939-**CLC 2, 3,
4, 8, 13, 15, 25, 44, 84; DA; DAB; DAC;
DAM MST, NOV, POET; PC 8; SSC 2;
WLC**
See also AAYA 12; BEST 89:2; CA 49-52;
CANR 3, 24, 33, 59; DLB 53; INT CANR-
24; MTCW 1; SATA 50

Aubigny, Pierre d'
See Mencken, H(enry) L(ouis)

Aubin, Penelope 1685-1731(?) **LC 9**
See also DLB 39

Auchincloss, Louis (Stanton) 1917-**CLC 4, 6,
9, 18, 45; DAM NOV; SSC 22**
See also CA 1-4R; CANR 6, 29, 55; DLB 2;
DLBY 80; INT CANR-29; MTCW 1

Auden, W(ystan) H(ugh) 1907-1973**CLC 1, 2,
3, 4, 6, 9, 11, 14, 43; DA; DAB; DAC; DAM
DRAM, MST, POET; PC 1; WLC**
See also AAYA 18; CA 9-12R; 45-48; CANR
5, 61; CDBLB 1914-1945; DLB 10, 20;
MTCW 1

Audiberti, Jacques 1900-1965 **CLC 38; DAM
DRAM**
See also CA 25-28R

Audubon, John James 1785-1851 **NCLC 47**

Auel, Jean M(arie) 1936-**CLC 31, 107; DAM
POP**
See also AAYA 7; BEST 90:4; CA 103; CANR
21, 64; INT CANR-21; SATA 91

Auerbach, Erich 1892-1957 **TCLC 43**
See also CA 118; 155

Augier, Emile 1820-1889 **NCLC 31**
See also DLB 192

August, John
See De Voto, Bernard (Augustine)

Augustine, St. 354-430 **CMLC 6; DAB**

Aurelius
See Bourne, Randolph S(illiman)

Aurobindo, Sri
See Ghose, Aurabinda

Austen, Jane 1775-1817 **NCLC 1, 13, 19, 33,
51; DA; DAB; DAC; DAM MST, NOV;
WLC**
See also AAYA 19; CDBLB 1789-1832; DLB
116

Auster, Paul 1947- **CLC 47**
See also CA 69-72; CANR 23, 52, 75

Austin, Frank
See Faust, Frederick (Schiller)

Austin, Mary (Hunter) 1868-1934 **TCLC 25**
See also CA 109; DLB 9, 78, 206

Autran Dourado, Waldomiro
See Dourado, (Waldomiro Freitas) Autran

Averroes 1126-1198 **CMLC 7**

See also DLB 115

Avicenna 980-1037 **CMLC 16**
See also DLB 115

Avison, Margaret 1918- **CLC 2, 4, 97; DAC;
DAM POET**
See also CA 17-20R; DLB 53; MTCW 1

Axton, David
See Koontz, Dean R(ay)

Ayckbourn, Alan 1939- **CLC 5, 8, 18, 33, 74;
DAB; DAM DRAM**
See also CA 21-24R; CANR 31, 59; DLB 13;
MTCW 1

Aydy, Catherine
See Tennant, Emma (Christina)

Ayme, Marcel (Andre) 1902-1967 **CLC 11**
See also CA 89-92; CANR 67; CLR 25; DLB
72; SATA 91

Ayrton, Michael 1921-1975 **CLC 7**
See also CA 5-8R; 61-64; CANR 9, 21

Azorin **CLC 11**
See also Martinez Ruiz, Jose

Azuela, Mariano 1873-1952 **TCLC 3; DAM
MULT; HLC**
See also CA 104; 131; HW; MTCW 1

Baastad, Babbis Friis
See Friis-Baastad, Babbis Ellinor

Bab
See Gilbert, W(illiam) S(chwenck)

Babbis, Eleanor
See Friis-Baastad, Babbis Ellinor

Babel, Isaac
See Babel, Isaak (Emmanuilovich)

Babel, Isaak (Emmanuilovich) 1894-1941(?)
TCLC 2, 13; SSC 16
See also CA 104; 155

Babits, Mihaly 1883-1941 **TCLC 14**
See also CA 114

Babur 1483-1530 **LC 18**

Bacchelli, Riccardo 1891-1985 **CLC 19**
See also CA 29-32R; 117

Bach, Richard (David) 1936- **CLC 14; DAM
NOV, POP**
See also AITN 1; BEST 89:2; CA 9-12R; CANR
18; MTCW 1; SATA 13

Bachman, Richard
See King, Stephen (Edwin)

Bachmann, Ingeborg 1926-1973 **CLC 69**
See also CA 93-96; 45-48; CANR 69; DLB 85

Bacon, Francis 1561-1626 **LC 18, 32**
See also CDBLB Before 1660; DLB 151

Bacon, Roger 1214(?)-1292 **CMLC 14**
See also DLB 115

Bacovia, George **TCLC 24**
See also Vasiliu, Gheorghe

Badanes, Jerome 1937- **CLC 59**

Bagehot, Walter 1826-1877 **NCLC 10**
See also DLB 55

Bagnold, Enid 1889-1981 **CLC 25; DAM
DRAM**
See also CA 5-8R; 103; CANR 5, 40; DLB 13,
160, 191; MAICYA; SATA 1, 25

Bagritsky, Eduard 1895-1934 **TCLC 60**

Bagrjana, Elisaveta
See Belcheva, Elisaveta

Bagryana, Elisaveta **CLC 10**
See also Belcheva, Elisaveta
See also DLB 147

Bailey, Paul 1937- **CLC 45**
See also CA 21-24R; CANR 16, 62; DLB 14

Baillie, Joanna 1762-1851 **NCLC 71**
See also DLB 93

Bainbridge, Beryl (Margaret) 1933-**CLC 4, 5,
8, 10, 14, 18, 22, 62; DAM NOV**

See also CA 21-24R; CANR 24, 55, 75; DLB
14; MTCW 1

Baker, Elliott 1922- **CLC 8**
See also CA 45-48; CANR 2, 63

Baker, Jean H. **TCLC 3, 10**
See also Russell, George William

Baker, Nicholson 1957- **CLC 61; DAM POP**
See also CA 135; CANR 63

Baker, Ray Stannard 1870-1946 **TCLC 47**
See also CA 118

Baker, Russell (Wayne) 1925- **CLC 31**
See also BEST 89:4; CA 57-60; CANR 11, 41,
59; MTCW 1

Bakhtin, M.
See Bakhtin, Mikhail Mikhailovich

Bakhtin, M. M.
See Bakhtin, Mikhail Mikhailovich

Bakhtin, Mikhail
See Bakhtin, Mikhail Mikhailovich

Bakhtin, Mikhail Mikhailovich 1895-1975
CLC 83
See also CA 128; 113

Bakshi, Ralph 1938(?)- **CLC 26**
See also CA 112; 138

Bakunin, Mikhail (Alexandrovich) 1814-1876
NCLC 25, 58

Baldwin, James (Arthur) 1924-1987**CLC 1, 2,
3, 4, 5, 8, 13, 15, 17, 42, 50, 67, 90; BLC 1;
DA; DAB; DAC; DAM MST, MULT, NOV,
POP; DC 1; SSC 10, 33; WLC**
See also AAYA 4; BW 1; CA 1-4R; 124; CABS
1; CANR 3, 24; CDALB 1941-1968; DLB
2, 7, 33; DLBY 87; MTCW 1; SATA 9;
SATA-Obit 54

Ballard, J(ames) G(raham) 1930-**CLC 3, 6, 14,
36; DAM NOV, POP; SSC 1**
See also AAYA 3; CA 5-8R; CANR 15, 39, 65;
DLB 14, 207; MTCW 1; SATA 93

Balmont, Konstantin (Dmitriyevich) 1867-1943
TCLC 11
See also CA 109; 155

Baltausis, Vincas
See Mikszath, Kalman

Balzac, Honore de 1799-1850**NCLC 5, 35, 53;
DA; DAB; DAC; DAM MST, NOV; SSC
5; WLC**
See also DLB 119

Bambara, Toni Cade 1939-1995 **CLC 19, 88;
BLC 1; DA; DAC; DAM MST, MULT;
WLCS**
See also AAYA 5; BW 2; CA 29-32R; 150;
CANR 24, 49; DLB 38; MTCW 1

Bamdad, A.
See Shamlu, Ahmad

Banat, D. R.
See Bradbury, Ray (Douglas)

Bancroft, Laura
See Baum, L(yman) Frank

Banim, John 1798-1842 **NCLC 13**
See also DLB 116, 158, 159

Banim, Michael 1796-1874 **NCLC 13**
See also DLB 158, 159

Banjo, The
See Paterson, A(ndrew) B(arton)

Banks, Iain
See Banks, Iain M(enzies)

Banks, Iain M(enzies) 1954- **CLC 34**
See also CA 123; 128; CANR 61; DLB 194;
INT 128

Banks, Lynne Reid **CLC 23**
See also Reid Banks, Lynne
See also AAYA 6

Banks, Russell 1940- **CLC 37, 72**

See also CA 65-68; CAAS 15; CANR 19, 52, 73; DLB 130
Banville, John 1945-   **CLC 46**
See also CA 117; 128; DLB 14; INT 128
Banville, Theodore (Faullain) de 1832-1891
NCLC 9
Baraka, Amiri 1934-CLC 1, 2, 3, 5, 10, 14, 33, 115; BLC 1; DA; DAC; DAM MST, MULT, POET, POP; DC 6; PC 4; WLCS
See also Jones, LeRoi
See also BW 2; CA 21-24R; CABS 3; CANR 27, 38, 61; CDALB 1941-1968; DLB 5, 7, 16, 38; DLBD 8; MTCW 1
Barbauld, Anna Laetitia 1743-1825NCLC 50
See also DLB 107, 109, 142, 158
Barbellion, W. N. P.   **TCLC 24**
See also Cummings, Bruce F(rederick)
Barbera, Jack (Vincent) 1945-   **CLC 44**
See also CA 110; CANR 45
Barbey d'Aurevilly, Jules Amedee 1808-1889
NCLC 1; SSC 17
See also DLB 119
Barbusse, Henri 1873-1935   **TCLC 5**
See also CA 105; 154; DLB 65
Barclay, Bill
See Moorcock, Michael (John)
Barclay, William Ewert
See Moorcock, Michael (John)
Barea, Arturo 1897-1957   **TCLC 14**
See also CA 111
Barfoot, Joan 1946-   **CLC 18**
See also CA 105
Baring, Maurice 1874-1945   **TCLC 8**
See also CA 105; 168; DLB 34
Baring-Gould, Sabine 1834-1924   **TCLC 88**
See also DLB 156, 190
Barker, Clive 1952-   **CLC 52; DAM POP**
See also AAYA 10; BEST 90:3; CA 121; 129; CANR 71; INT 129; MTCW 1
Barker, George Granville 1913-1991 **CLC 8, 48; DAM POET**
See also CA 9-12R; 135; CANR 7, 38; DLB 20; MTCW 1
Barker, Harley Granville
See Granville-Barker, Harley
See also DLB 10
Barker, Howard 1946-   **CLC 37**
See also CA 102; DLB 13
Barker, Jane 1652-1732   **LC 42**
Barker, Pat(ricia) 1943-   **CLC 32, 94**
See also CA 117; 122; CANR 50; INT 122
Barlach, Ernst 1870-1938   **TCLC 84**
See also DLB 56, 118
Barlow, Joel 1754-1812   **NCLC 23**
See also DLB 37
Barnard, Mary (Ethel) 1909-   **CLC 48**
See also CA 21-22; CAP 2
Barnes, Djuna 1892-1982CLC 3, 4, 8, 11, 29; SSC 3
See also CA 9-12R; 107; CANR 16, 55; DLB 4, 9, 45; MTCW 1
Barnes, Julian (Patrick) 1946- CLC 42; DAB
See also CA 102; CANR 19, 54; DLB 194; DLBY 93
Barnes, Peter 1931-   **CLC 5, 56**
See also CA 65-68; CAAS 12; CANR 33, 34, 64; DLB 13; MTCW 1
Barnes, William 1801-1886   **NCLC 75**
See also DLB 32
Baroja (y Nessi), Pio 1872-1956TCLC 8; HLC
See also CA 104
Baron, David
See Pinter, Harold

Baron Corvo
See Rolfe, Frederick (William Serafino Austin Lewis Mary)
Barondess, Sue K(aufman) 1926-1977 **CLC 8**
See also Kaufman, Sue
See also CA 1-4R; 69-72; CANR 1
Baron de Teive
See Pessoa, Fernando (Antonio Nogueira)
Baroness Von S.
See Zangwill, Israel
Barres, (Auguste-) Maurice 1862-1923TCLC 47
See also CA 164; DLB 123
Barreto, Afonso Henrique de Lima
See Lima Barreto, Afonso Henrique de
Barrett, (Roger) Syd 1946-   **CLC 35**
Barrett, William (Christopher) 1913-1992
CLC 27
See also CA 13-16R; 139; CANR 11, 67; INT CANR-11
Barrie, J(ames) M(atthew) 1860-1937 T C L C 2; DAB; DAM DRAM
See also CA 104; 136; CDBLB 1890-1914; CLR 16; DLB 10, 141, 156; MAICYA; SATA 100; YABC 1
Barrington, Michael
See Moorcock, Michael (John)
Barrol, Grady
See Bograd, Larry
Barry, Mike
See Malzberg, Barry N(athaniel)
Barry, Philip 1896-1949   **TCLC 11**
See also CA 109; DLB 7
Bart, Andre Schwarz
See Schwarz-Bart, Andre
Barth, John (Simmons) 1930-CLC 1, 2, 3, 5, 7, 9, 10, 14, 27, 51, 89; DAM NOV; SSC 10
See also AITN 1, 2; CA 1-4R; CABS 1; CANR 5, 23, 49, 64; DLB 2; MTCW 1
Barthelme, Donald 1931-1989CLC 1, 2, 3, 5, 6, 8, 13, 23, 46, 59, 115; DAM NOV; SSC 2
See also CA 21-24R; 129; CANR 20, 58; DLB 2; DLBY 80, 89; MTCW 1; SATA 7; SATA-Obit 62
Barthelme, Frederick 1943-   **CLC 36, 117**
See also CA 114; 122; DLBY 85; INT 122
Barthes, Roland (Gerard) 1915-1980CLC 24, 83
See also CA 130; 97-100; CANR 66; MTCW 1
Barzun, Jacques (Martin) 1907-   **CLC 51**
See also CA 61-64; CANR 22
Bashevis, Isaac
See Singer, Isaac Bashevis
Bashkirtseff, Marie 1859-1884   **NCLC 27**
Basho
See Matsuo Basho
Bass, Kingsley B., Jr.
See Bullins, Ed
Bass, Rick 1958-   **CLC 79**
See also CA 126; CANR 53
Bassani, Giorgio 1916-   **CLC 9**
See also CA 65-68; CANR 33; DLB 128, 177; MTCW 1
Bastos, Augusto (Antonio) Roa
See Roa Bastos, Augusto (Antonio)
Bataille, Georges 1897-1962   **CLC 29**
See also CA 101; 89-92
Bates, H(erbert) E(rnest) 1905-1974CLC 46; DAB; DAM POP; SSC 10
See also CA 93-96; 45-48; CANR 34; DLB 162, 191; MTCW 1
Bauchart
See Camus, Albert

Baudelaire, Charles 1821-1867 NCLC 6, 29, 55; DA; DAB; DAC; DAM MST, POET; PC 1; SSC 18; WLC
Baudrillard, Jean 1929-   **CLC 60**
Baum, L(yman) Frank 1856-1919   **TCLC 7**
See also CA 108; 133; CLR 15; DLB 22; JRDA; MAICYA; MTCW 1; SATA 18, 100
Baum, Louis F.
See Baum, L(yman) Frank
Baumbach, Jonathan 1933-   **CLC 6, 23**
See also CA 13-16R; CAAS 5; CANR 12, 66; DLBY 80; INT CANR-12; MTCW 1
Bausch, Richard (Carl) 1945-   **CLC 51**
See also CA 101; CAAS 14; CANR 43, 61; DLB 130
Baxter, Charles (Morley) 1947- CLC 45, 78; DAM POP
See also CA 57-60; CANR 40, 64; DLB 130
Baxter, George Owen
See Faust, Frederick (Schiller)
Baxter, James K(eir) 1926-1972   **CLC 14**
See also CA 77-80
Baxter, John
See Hunt, E(verette) Howard, (Jr.)
Bayer, Sylvia
See Glassco, John
Baynton, Barbara 1857-1929   **TCLC 57**
Beagle, Peter S(oyer) 1939-   **CLC 7, 104**
See also CA 9-12R; CANR 4, 51, 73; DLBY 80; INT CANR-4; SATA 60
Bean, Normal
See Burroughs, Edgar Rice
Beard, Charles A(ustin) 1874-1948 TCLC 15
See also CA 115; DLB 17; SATA 18
Beardsley, Aubrey 1872-1898   **NCLC 6**
Beattie, Ann 1947-CLC 8, 13, 18, 40, 63; DAM NOV, POP; SSC 11
See also BEST 90:2; CA 81-84; CANR 53, 73; DLBY 82; MTCW 1
Beattie, James 1735-1803   **NCLC 25**
See also DLB 109
Beauchamp, Kathleen Mansfield 1888-1923
See Mansfield, Katherine
See also CA 104; 134; DA; DAC; DAM MST
Beaumarchais, Pierre-Augustin Caron de 1732-1799   **DC 4**
See also DAM DRAM
Beaumont, Francis 1584(?)-1616LC 33; DC 6
See also CDBLB Before 1660; DLB 58, 121
Beauvoir, Simone (Lucie Ernestine Marie Bertrand) de 1908-1986CLC 1, 2, 4, 8, 14, 31, 44, 50, 71; DA; DAB; DAC; DAM MST, NOV; WLC
See also CA 9-12R; 118; CANR 28, 61; DLB 72; DLBY 86; MTCW 1
Becker, Carl (Lotus) 1873-1945   **TCLC 63**
See also CA 157; DLB 17
Becker, Jurek 1937-1997   **CLC 7, 19**
See also CA 85-88; 157; CANR 60; DLB 75
Becker, Walter 1950-   **CLC 26**
Beckett, Samuel (Barclay) 1906-1989 CLC 1, 2, 3, 4, 6, 9, 10, 11, 14, 18, 29, 57, 59, 83; DA; DAB; DAC; DAM DRAM, MST, NOV; SSC 16; WLC
See also CA 5-8R; 130; CANR 33, 61; CDBLB 1945-1960; DLB 13, 15; DLBY 90; MTCW 1
Beckford, William 1760-1844   **NCLC 16**
See also DLB 39
Beckman, Gunnel 1910-   **CLC 26**
See also CA 33-36R; CANR 15; CLR 25; MAICYA; SAAS 9; SATA 6
Becque, Henri 1837-1899   **NCLC 3**

See also DLB 192

Beddoes, Thomas Lovell 1803-1849 **NCLC 3**
See also DLB 96

Bede c. 673-735 **CMLC 20**
See also DLB 146

Bedford, Donald F.
See Fearing, Kenneth (Flexner)

Beecher, Catharine Esther 1800-1878 **NCLC 30**
See also DLB 1

Beecher, John 1904-1980 **CLC 6**
See also AITN 1; CA 5-8R; 105; CANR 8

Beer, Johann 1655-1700 **LC 5**
See also DLB 168

Beer, Patricia 1924- **CLC 58**
See also CA 61-64; CANR 13, 46; DLB 40

Beerbohm, Max
See Beerbohm, (Henry) Max(imilian)

Beerbohm, (Henry) Max(imilian) 1872-1956 **TCLC 1, 24**
See also CA 104; 154; DLB 34, 100

Beer-Hofmann, Richard 1866-1945 **TCLC 60**
See also CA 160; DLB 81

Begiebing, Robert J(ohn) 1946- **CLC 70**
See also CA 122; CANR 40

Behan, Brendan 1923-1964 **CLC 1, 8, 11, 15, 79; DAM DRAM**
See also CA 73-76; CANR 33; CDBLB 1945-1960; DLB 13; MTCW 1

Behn, Aphra 1640(?)-1689 **LC 1, 30, 42; DA; DAB; DAC; DAM DRAM, MST, NOV, POET; DC 4; PC 13; WLC**
See also DLB 39, 80, 131

Behrman, S(amuel) N(athaniel) 1893-1973 **CLC 40**
See also CA 13-16; 45-48; CAP 1; DLB 7, 44

Belasco, David 1853-1931 **TCLC 3**
See also CA 104; 168; DLB 7

Belcheva, Elisaveta 1893- **CLC 10**
See also Bagryana, Elisaveta

Beldone, Phil "Cheech"
See Ellison, Harlan (Jay)

Beleno
See Azuela, Mariano

Belinski, Vissarion Grigoryevich 1811-1848 **NCLC 5**
See also DLB 198

Belitt, Ben 1911- **CLC 22**
See also CA 13-16R; CAAS 4; CANR 7; DLB 5

Bell, Gertrude (Margaret Lowthian) 1868-1926 **TCLC 67**
See also CA 167; DLB 174

Bell, J. Freeman
See Zangwill, Israel

Bell, James Madison 1826-1902 **TCLC 43; BLC 1; DAM MULT**
See also BW 1; CA 122; 124; DLB 50

Bell, Madison Smartt 1957- **CLC 41, 102**
See also CA 111; CANR 28, 54, 73

Bell, Marvin (Hartley) 1937- **CLC 8, 31; DAM POET**
See also CA 21-24R; CAAS 14; CANR 59; DLB 5; MTCW 1

Bell, W. L. D.
See Mencken, H(enry) L(ouis)

Bellamy, Atwood C.
See Mencken, H(enry) L(ouis)

Bellamy, Edward 1850-1898 **NCLC 4**
See also DLB 12

Bellin, Edward J.
See Kuttner, Henry

Belloc, (Joseph) Hilaire (Pierre Sebastien Rene Swanton) 1870-1953 **TCLC 7, 18; DAM POET; PC 24**
See also CA 106; 152; DLB 19, 100, 141, 174; YABC 1

Belloc, Joseph Peter Rene Hilaire
See Belloc, (Joseph) Hilaire (Pierre Sebastien Rene Swanton)

Belloc, Joseph Pierre Hilaire
See Belloc, (Joseph) Hilaire (Pierre Sebastien Rene Swanton)

Belloc, M. A.
See Lowndes, Marie Adelaide (Belloc)

Bellow, Saul 1915- **CLC 1, 2, 3, 6, 8, 10, 13, 15, 25, 33, 34, 63, 79; DA; DAB; DAC; DAM MST, NOV, POP; SSC 14; WLC**
See also AITN 2; BEST 89:3; CA 5-8R; CABS 1; CANR 29, 53; CDALB 1941-1968; DLB 2, 28; DLBD 3; DLBY 82; MTCW 1

Belser, Reimond Karel Maria de 1929-
See Ruyslinck, Ward
See also CA 152

Bely, Andrey **TCLC 7; PC 11**
See also Bugayev, Boris Nikolayevich

Belyi, Andrei
See Bugayev, Boris Nikolayevich

Benary, Margot
See Benary-Isbert, Margot

Benary-Isbert, Margot 1889-1979 **CLC 12**
See also CA 5-8R; 89-92; CANR 4, 72; CLR 12; MAICYA; SATA 2; SATA-Obit 21

Benavente (y Martinez), Jacinto 1866-1954 **TCLC 3; DAM DRAM, MULT**
See also CA 106; 131; HW; MTCW 1

Benchley, Peter (Bradford) 1940- **CLC 4, 8; DAM NOV, POP**
See also AAYA 14; AITN 2; CA 17-20R; CANR 12, 35, 66; MTCW 1; SATA 3, 89

Benchley, Robert (Charles) 1889-1945 **TCLC 1, 55**
See also CA 105; 153; DLB 11

Benda, Julien 1867-1956 **TCLC 60**
See also CA 120; 154

Benedict, Ruth (Fulton) 1887-1948 **TCLC 60**
See also CA 158

Benedict, Saint c. 480-c. 547 **CMLC 29**

Benedikt, Michael 1935- **CLC 4, 14**
See also CA 13-16R; CANR 7; DLB 5

Benet, Juan 1927- **CLC 28**
See also CA 143

Benet, Stephen Vincent 1898-1943 **TCLC 7; DAM POET; SSC 10**
See also CA 104; 152; DLB 4, 48, 102; DLBY 97; YABC 1

Benet, William Rose 1886-1950 **TCLC 28; DAM POET**
See also CA 118; 152; DLB 45

Benford, Gregory (Albert) 1941- **CLC 52**
See also CA 69-72; CAAS 27; CANR 12, 24, 49; DLBY 82

Bengtsson, Frans (Gunnar) 1894-1954 **TCLC 48**
See also CA 170

Benjamin, David
See Slavitt, David R(ytman)

Benjamin, Lois
See Gould, Lois

Benjamin, Walter 1892-1940 **TCLC 39**
See also CA 164

Benn, Gottfried 1886-1956 **TCLC 3**
See also CA 106; 153; DLB 56

Bennett, Alan 1934- **CLC 45, 77; DAB; DAM MST**
See also CA 103; CANR 35, 55; MTCW 1

Bennett, (Enoch) Arnold 1867-1931 **TCLC 5, 20**
See also CA 106; 155; CDBLB 1890-1914; DLB 10, 34, 98, 135

Bennett, Elizabeth
See Mitchell, Margaret (Munnerlyn)

Bennett, George Harold 1930-
See Bennett, Hal
See also BW 1; CA 97-100

Bennett, Hal **CLC 5**
See also Bennett, George Harold
See also DLB 33

Bennett, Jay 1912- **CLC 35**
See also AAYA 10; CA 69-72; CANR 11, 42; JRDA; SAAS 4; SATA 41, 87; SATA-Brief 27

Bennett, Louise (Simone) 1919- **CLC 28; BLC 1; DAM MULT**
See also BW 2; CA 151; DLB 117

Benson, E(dward) F(rederic) 1867-1940 **TCLC 27**
See also CA 114; 157; DLB 135, 153

Benson, Jackson J. 1930- **CLC 34**
See also CA 25-28R; DLB 111

Benson, Sally 1900-1972 **CLC 17**
See also CA 19-20; 37-40R; CAP 1; SATA 1, 35; SATA-Obit 27

Benson, Stella 1892-1933 **TCLC 17**
See also CA 117; 155; DLB 36, 162

Bentham, Jeremy 1748-1832 **NCLC 38**
See also DLB 107, 158

Bentley, E(dmund) C(lerihew) 1875-1956 **TCLC 12**
See also CA 108; DLB 70

Bentley, Eric (Russell) 1916- **CLC 24**
See also CA 5-8R; CANR 6, 67; INT CANR-6

Beranger, Pierre Jean de 1780-1857 **NCLC 34**

Berdyaev, Nicolas
See Berdyaev, Nikolai (Aleksandrovich)

Berdyaev, Nikolai (Aleksandrovich) 1874-1948 **TCLC 67**
See also CA 120; 157

Berdyayev, Nikolai (Aleksandrovich)
See Berdyaev, Nikolai (Aleksandrovich)

Berendt, John (Lawrence) 1939- **CLC 86**
See also CA 146; CANR 75

Beresford, J(ohn) D(avys) 1873-1947 **TCLC 81**
See also CA 112; 155; DLB 162, 178, 197

Bergelson, David 1884-1952 **TCLC 81**

Berger, Colonel
See Malraux, (Georges-)Andre

Berger, John (Peter) 1926- **CLC 2, 19**
See also CA 81-84; CANR 51; DLB 14, 207

Berger, Melvin H. 1927- **CLC 12**
See also CA 5-8R; CANR 4; CLR 32; SAAS 2; SATA 5, 88

Berger, Thomas (Louis) 1924- **CLC 3, 5, 8, 11, 18, 38; DAM NOV**
See also CA 1-4R; CANR 5, 28, 51; DLB 2; DLBY 80; INT CANR-28; MTCW 1

Bergman, (Ernst) Ingmar 1918- **CLC 16, 72**
See also CA 81-84; CANR 33, 70

Bergson, Henri(-Louis) 1859-1941 **TCLC 32**
See also CA 164

Bergstein, Eleanor 1938- **CLC 4**
See also CA 53-56; CANR 5

Berkoff, Steven 1937- **CLC 56**
See also CA 104; CANR 72

Bermant, Chaim (Icyk) 1929- **CLC 40**
See also CA 57-60; CANR 6, 31, 57

Bern, Victoria
See Fisher, M(ary) F(rances) K(ennedy)

Bernanos, (Paul Louis) Georges 1888-1948
    TCLC 3
    See also CA 104; 130; DLB 72
Bernard, April 1956-   **CLC 59**
    See also CA 131
Berne, Victoria
    See Fisher, M(ary) F(rances) K(ennedy)
Bernhard, Thomas 1931-1989 **CLC 3, 32, 61**
    See also CA 85-88; 127; CANR 32, 57; DLB
    85, 124; MTCW 1
Bernhardt, Sarah (Henriette Rosine) 1844-1923
    TCLC 75
    See also CA 157
Berriault, Gina 1926- **CLC 54, 109; SSC 30**
    See also CA 116; 129; CANR 66; DLB 130
Berrigan, Daniel 1921-   **CLC 4**
    See also CA 33-36R; CAAS 1; CANR 11, 43;
    DLB 5
Berrigan, Edmund Joseph Michael, Jr. 1934-
    1983
    See Berrigan, Ted
    See also CA 61-64; 110; CANR 14
Berrigan, Ted   **CLC 37**
    See also Berrigan, Edmund Joseph Michael, Jr.
    See also DLB 5, 169
Berry, Charles Edward Anderson 1931-
    See Berry, Chuck
    See also CA 115
Berry, Chuck   **CLC 17**
    See also Berry, Charles Edward Anderson
Berry, Jonas
    See Ashbery, John (Lawrence)
Berry, Wendell (Erdman) 1934- **CLC 4, 6, 8,**
    27, 46; DAM POET
    See also AITN 1; CA 73-76; CANR 50, 73; DLB
    5, 6
Berryman, John 1914-1972 **CLC 1, 2, 3, 4, 6, 8,**
    10, 13, 25, 62; DAM POET
    See also CA 13-16; 33-36R; CABS 2; CANR
    35; CAP 1; CDALB 1941-1968; DLB 48;
    MTCW 1
Bertolucci, Bernardo 1940-   **CLC 16**
    See also CA 106
Berton, Pierre (Francis Demarigny) 1920-
    CLC 104
    See also CA 1-4R; CANR 2, 56; DLB 68; SATA
    99
Bertrand, Aloysius 1807-1841   **NCLC 31**
Bertran de Born c. 1140-1215   **CMLC 5**
Besant, Annie (Wood) 1847-1933   **TCLC 9**
    See also CA 105
Bessie, Alvah 1904-1985   **CLC 23**
    See also CA 5-8R; 116; CANR 2; DLB 26
Bethlen, T. D.
    See Silverberg, Robert
Beti, Mongo   **CLC 27; BLC 1; DAM MULT**
    See also Biyidi, Alexandre
Betjeman, John 1906-1984 **CLC 2, 6, 10, 34,**
    43; DAB; DAM MST, POET
    See also CA 9-12R; 112; CANR 33, 56; CDBLB
    1945-1960; DLB 20; DLBY 84; MTCW 1
Bettelheim, Bruno 1903-1990   **CLC 79**
    See also CA 81-84; 131; CANR 23, 61; MTCW
    1
Betti, Ugo 1892-1953   **TCLC 5**
    See also CA 104; 155
Betts, Doris (Waugh) 1932-   **CLC 3, 6, 28**
    See also CA 13-16R; CANR 9, 66; DLBY 82;
    INT CANR-9
Bevan, Alistair
    See Roberts, Keith (John Kingston)
Bey, Pilaff
    See Douglas, (George) Norman

Bialik, Chaim Nachman 1873-1934 **TCLC 25**
    See also CA 170
Bickerstaff, Isaac
    See Swift, Jonathan
Bidart, Frank 1939-   **CLC 33**
    See also CA 140
Bienek, Horst 1930-   **CLC 7, 11**
    See also CA 73-76; DLB 75
Bierce, Ambrose (Gwinett) 1842-1914(?)
    TCLC 1, 7, 44; DA; DAC; DAM MST; SSC
    9; WLC
    See also CA 104; 139; CDALB 1865-1917;
    DLB 11, 12, 23, 71, 74, 186
Biggers, Earl Derr 1884-1933   **TCLC 65**
    See also CA 108; 153
Billings, Josh
    See Shaw, Henry Wheeler
Billington, (Lady) Rachel (Mary) 1942- **C L C**
    43
    See also AITN 2; CA 33-36R; CANR 44
Binyon, T(imothy) J(ohn) 1936-   **CLC 34**
    See also CA 111; CANR 28
Bioy Casares, Adolfo 1914-1984**CLC 4, 8, 13,**
    88; DAM MULT; HLC; SSC 17
    See also CA 29-32R; CANR 19, 43, 66; DLB
    113; HW; MTCW 1
Bird, Cordwainer
    See Ellison, Harlan (Jay)
Bird, Robert Montgomery 1806-1854**NCLC 1**
    See also DLB 202
Birkerts, Sven 1951-   **CLC 116**
    See also CA 128; 133; CAAS 29; INT 133
Birney, (Alfred) Earle 1904-1995**CLC 1, 4, 6,**
    11; DAC; DAM MST, POET
    See also CA 1-4R; CANR 5, 20; DLB 88;
    MTCW 1
Biruni, al 973-1048(?)   **CMLC 28**
Bishop, Elizabeth 1911-1979 **CLC 1, 4, 9, 13,**
    15, 32; DA; DAC; DAM MST, POET; PC
    3
    See also CA 5-8R; 89-92; CABS 2; CANR 26,
    61; CDALB 1968-1988; DLB 5, 169;
    MTCW 1; SATA-Obit 24
Bishop, John 1935-   **CLC 10**
    See also CA 105
Bissett, Bill 1939-   **CLC 18; PC 14**
    See also CA 69-72; CAAS 19; CANR 15; DLB
    53; MTCW 1
Bitov, Andrei (Georgievich) 1937-   **CLC 57**
    See also CA 142
Biyidi, Alexandre 1932-
    See Beti, Mongo
    See also BW 1; CA 114; 124; MTCW 1
Bjarme, Brynjolf
    See Ibsen, Henrik (Johan)
Bjoernson, Bjoernstjerne (Martinius) 1832-
    1910   **TCLC 7, 37**
    See also CA 104
Black, Robert
    See Holdstock, Robert P.
Blackburn, Paul 1926-1971   **CLC 9, 43**
    See also CA 81-84; 33-36R; CANR 34; DLB
    16; DLBY 81
Black Elk 1863-1950 **TCLC 33; DAM MULT**
    See also CA 144; NNAL
Black Hobart
    See Sanders, (James) Ed(ward)
Blacklin, Malcolm
    See Chambers, Aidan
Blackmore, R(ichard) D(oddridge) 1825-1900
    TCLC 27
    See also CA 120; DLB 18
Blackmur, R(ichard) P(almer) 1904-1965

CLC 2, 24
    See also CA 11-12; 25-28R; CANR 71; CAP 1;
    DLB 63
Black Tarantula
    See Acker, Kathy
Blackwood, Algernon (Henry) 1869-1951
    TCLC 5
    See also CA 105; 150; DLB 153, 156, 178
Blackwood, Caroline 1931-1996**CLC 6, 9, 100**
    See also CA 85-88; 151; CANR 32, 61, 65; DLB
    14, 207; MTCW 1
Blade, Alexander
    See Hamilton, Edmond; Silverberg, Robert
Blaga, Lucian 1895-1961   **CLC 75**
    See also CA 157
Blair, Eric (Arthur) 1903-1950
    See Orwell, George
    See also CA 104; 132; DA; DAB; DAC; DAM
    MST, NOV; MTCW 1; SATA 29
Blair, Hugh 1718-1800   **NCLC 75**
Blais, Marie-Claire 1939-**CLC 2, 4, 6, 13, 22;**
    DAC; DAM MST
    See also CA 21-24R; CAAS 4; CANR 38, 75;
    DLB 53; MTCW 1
Blaise, Clark 1940-   **CLC 29**
    See also AITN 2; CA 53-56; CAAS 3; CANR
    5, 66; DLB 53
Blake, Fairley
    See De Voto, Bernard (Augustine)
Blake, Nicholas
    See Day Lewis, C(ecil)
    See also DLB 77
Blake, William 1757-1827 **NCLC 13, 37, 57;**
    DA; DAB; DAC; DAM MST, POET; PC
    12; WLC
    See also CDBLB 1789-1832; CLR 52; DLB 93,
    163; MAICYA; SATA 30
Blasco Ibanez, Vicente 1867-1928 **TCLC 12;**
    DAM NOV
    See also CA 110; 131; HW; MTCW 1
Blatty, William Peter 1928-**CLC 2; DAM POP**
    See also CA 5-8R; CANR 9
Bleeck, Oliver
    See Thomas, Ross (Elmore)
Blessing, Lee 1949-   **CLC 54**
Blish, James (Benjamin) 1921-1975 **CLC 14**
    See also CA 1-4R; 57-60; CANR 3; DLB 8;
    MTCW 1; SATA 66
Bliss, Reginald
    See Wells, H(erbert) G(eorge)
Blixen, Karen (Christentze Dinesen) 1885-1962
    See Dinesen, Isak
    See also CA 25-28; CANR 22, 50; CAP 2;
    MTCW 1; SATA 44
Bloch, Robert (Albert) 1917-1994   **CLC 33**
    See also CA 5-8R; 146; CAAS 20; CANR 5;
    DLB 44; INT CANR-5; SATA 12; SATA-Obit
    82
Blok, Alexander (Alexandrovich) 1880-1921
    TCLC 5; PC 21
    See also CA 104
Blom, Jan
    See Breytenbach, Breyten
Bloom, Harold 1930-   **CLC 24, 103**
    See also CA 13-16R; CANR 39, 75; DLB 67
Bloomfield, Aurelius
    See Bourne, Randolph S(illiman)
Blount, Roy (Alton), Jr. 1941-   **CLC 38**
    See also CA 53-56; CANR 10, 28, 61; INT
    CANR-28; MTCW 1
Bloy, Leon 1846-1917   **TCLC 22**
    See also CA 121; DLB 123
Blume, Judy (Sussman) 1938-   **CLC 12, 30;**

DAM NOV, POP
See also AAYA 3, 26; CA 29-32R; CANR 13, 37, 66; CLR 2, 15; DLB 52; JRDA; MAICYA; MTCW 1; SATA 2, 31, 79

Blunden, Edmund (Charles) 1896-1974 **C L C 2, 56**
See also CA 17-18; 45-48; CANR 54; CAP 2; DLB 20, 100, 155; MTCW 1

Bly, Robert (Elwood) 1926- **CLC 1, 2, 5, 10, 15, 38; DAM POET**
See also CA 5-8R; CANR 41, 73; DLB 5; MTCW 1

Boas, Franz 1858-1942   **TCLC 56**
See also CA 115

Bobette
See Simenon, Georges (Jacques Christian)

Boccaccio, Giovanni 1313-1375   **CMLC 13; SSC 10**

Bochco, Steven 1943-   **CLC 35**
See also AAYA 11; CA 124; 138

Bodel, Jean 1167(?)-1210   **CMLC 28**

Bodenheim, Maxwell 1892-1954   **TCLC 44**
See also CA 110; DLB 9, 45

Bodker, Cecil 1927-   **CLC 21**
See also CA 73-76; CANR 13, 44; CLR 23; MAICYA; SATA 14

Boell, Heinrich (Theodor) 1917-1985 **CLC 2, 3, 6, 9, 11, 15, 27, 32, 72; DA; DAB; DAC; DAM MST, NOV; SSC 23; WLC**
See also CA 21-24R; 116; CANR 24; DLB 69; DLBY 85; MTCW 1

Boerne, Alfred
See Doeblin, Alfred

Boethius 480(?)-524(?)   **CMLC 15**
See also DLB 115

Bogan, Louise 1897-1970 **CLC 4, 39, 46, 93; DAM POET; PC 12**
See also CA 73-76; 25-28R; CANR 33; DLB 45, 169; MTCW 1

Bogarde, Dirk   **CLC 19**
See also Van Den Bogarde, Derek Jules Gaspard Ulric Niven
See also DLB 14

Bogosian, Eric 1953-   **CLC 45**
See also CA 138

Bograd, Larry 1953-   **CLC 35**
See also CA 93-96; CANR 57; SAAS 21; SATA 33, 89

Boiardo, Matteo Maria 1441-1494   **LC 6**

Boileau-Despreaux, Nicolas 1636-1711 **LC 3**

Bojer, Johan 1872-1959   **TCLC 64**

Boland, Eavan (Aisling) 1944- **CLC 40, 67, 113; DAM POET**
See also CA 143; CANR 61; DLB 40

Boll, Heinrich
See Boell, Heinrich (Theodor)

Bolt, Lee
See Faust, Frederick (Schiller)

Bolt, Robert (Oxton) 1924-1995 **CLC 14; DAM DRAM**
See also CA 17-20R; 147; CANR 35, 67; DLB 13; MTCW 1

Bombet, Louis-Alexandre-Cesar
See Stendhal

Bomkauf
See Kaufman, Bob (Garnell)

Bonaventura   **NCLC 35**
See also DLB 90

Bond, Edward 1934- **CLC 4, 6, 13, 23; DAM DRAM**
See also CA 25-28R; CANR 38, 67; DLB 13; MTCW 1

Bonham, Frank 1914-1989   **CLC 12**

See also AAYA 1; CA 9-12R; CANR 4, 36; JRDA; MAICYA; SAAS 3; SATA 1, 49; SATA-Obit 62

Bonnefoy, Yves 1923-   **CLC 9, 15, 58; DAM MST, POET**
See also CA 85-88; CANR 33, 75; MTCW 1

Bontemps, Arna(ud Wendell) 1902-1973 **C L C 1, 18; BLC 1; DAM MULT, NOV, POET**
See also BW 1; CA 1-4R; 41-44R; CANR 4, 35; CLR 6; DLB 48, 51; JRDA; MAICYA; MTCW 1; SATA 2, 44; SATA-Obit 24

Booth, Martin 1944-   **CLC 13**
See also CA 93-96; CAAS 2

Booth, Philip 1925-   **CLC 23**
See also CA 5-8R; CANR 5; DLBY 82

Booth, Wayne C(layson) 1921-   **CLC 24**
See also CA 1-4R; CAAS 5; CANR 3, 43; DLB 67

Borchert, Wolfgang 1921-1947   **TCLC 5**
See also CA 104; DLB 69, 124

Borel, Petrus 1809-1859   **NCLC 41**

Borges, Jorge Luis 1899-1986 **CLC 1, 2, 3, 4, 6, 8, 9, 10, 13, 19, 44, 48, 83; DA; DAB; DAC; DAM MST, MULT; HLC; PC 22; SSC 4; WLC**
See also AAYA 26; CA 21-24R; CANR 19, 33, 75; DLB 113; DLBY 86; HW; MTCW 1

Borowski, Tadeusz 1922-1951   **TCLC 9**
See also CA 106; 154

Borrow, George (Henry) 1803-1881 **NCLC 9**
See also DLB 21, 55, 166

Bosman, Herman Charles 1905-1951 **T C L C 49**
See also Malan, Herman
See also CA 160

Bosschere, Jean de 1878(?)-1953 **TCLC 19**
See also CA 115

Boswell, James 1740-1795 **LC 4; DA; DAB; DAC; DAM MST; WLC**
See also CDBLB 1660-1789; DLB 104, 142

Bottoms, David 1949-   **CLC 53**
See also CA 105; CANR 22; DLB 120; DLBY 83

Boucicault, Dion 1820-1890   **NCLC 41**

Boucolon, Maryse 1937(?)-
See Conde, Maryse
See also CA 110; CANR 30, 53

Bourget, Paul (Charles Joseph) 1852-1935 **TCLC 12**
See also CA 107; DLB 123

Bourjaily, Vance (Nye) 1922-   **CLC 8, 62**
See also CA 1-4R; CAAS 1; CANR 2, 72; DLB 2, 143

Bourne, Randolph S(illiman) 1886-1918 **TCLC 16**
See also CA 117; 155; DLB 63

Bova, Ben(jamin William) 1932- **CLC 45**
See also AAYA 16; CA 5-8R; CAAS 18; CANR 11, 56; CLR 3; DLBY 81; INT CANR-11; MAICYA; MTCW 1; SATA 6, 68

Bowen, Elizabeth (Dorothea Cole) 1899-1973 **CLC 1, 3, 6, 11, 15, 22; DAM NOV; SSC 3, 28**
See also CA 17-18; 41-44R; CANR 35; CAP 2; CDBLB 1945-1960; DLB 15, 162; MTCW 1

Bowering, George 1935-   **CLC 15, 47**
See also CA 21-24R; CAAS 16; CANR 10; DLB 53

Bowering, Marilyn R(uthe) 1949- **CLC 32**
See also CA 101; CANR 49

Bowers, Edgar 1924-   **CLC 9**
See also CA 5-8R; CANR 24; DLB 5

Bowie, David   **CLC 17**
See also Jones, David Robert

Bowles, Jane (Sydney) 1917-1973 **CLC 3, 68**
See also CA 19-20; 41-44R; CAP 2

Bowles, Paul (Frederick) 1910- **CLC 1, 2, 19, 53; SSC 3**
See also CA 1-4R; CAAS 1; CANR 1, 19, 50, 75; DLB 5, 6; MTCW 1

Box, Edgar
See Vidal, Gore

Boyd, Nancy
See Millay, Edna St. Vincent

Boyd, William 1952-   **CLC 28, 53, 70**
See also CA 114; 120; CANR 51, 71

Boyle, Kay 1902-1992 **CLC 1, 5, 19, 58; SSC 5**
See also CA 13-16R; 140; CAAS 1; CANR 29, 61; DLB 4, 9, 48, 86; DLBY 93; MTCW 1

Boyle, Mark
See Kienzle, William X(avier)

Boyle, Patrick 1905-1982   **CLC 19**
See also CA 127

Boyle, T. C. 1948-
See Boyle, T(homas) Coraghessan

Boyle, T(homas) Coraghessan 1948- **CLC 36, 55, 90; DAM POP; SSC 16**
See also BEST 90:4; CA 120; CANR 44; DLBY 86

Boz
See Dickens, Charles (John Huffam)

Brackenridge, Hugh Henry 1748-1816 **N C L C 7**
See also DLB 11, 37

Bradbury, Edward P.
See Moorcock, Michael (John)

Bradbury, Malcolm (Stanley) 1932- **CLC 32, 61; DAM NOV**
See also CA 1-4R; CANR 1, 33; DLB 14, 207; MTCW 1

Bradbury, Ray (Douglas) 1920- **CLC 1, 3, 10, 15, 42, 98; DA; DAB; DAC; DAM MST, NOV, POP; SSC 29; WLC**
See also AAYA 15; AITN 1, 2; CA 1-4R; CANR 2, 30, 75; CDALB 1968-1988; DLB 2, 8; MTCW 1; SATA 11, 64

Bradford, Gamaliel 1863-1932   **TCLC 36**
See also CA 160; DLB 17

Bradley, David (Henry, Jr.) 1950- **CLC 23; BLC 1; DAM MULT**
See also BW 1; CA 104; CANR 26; DLB 33

Bradley, John Ed(mund, Jr.) 1958- **CLC 55**
See also CA 139

Bradley, Marion Zimmer 1930- **CLC 30; DAM POP**
See also AAYA 9; CA 57-60; CAAS 10; CANR 7, 31, 51, 75; DLB 8; MTCW 1; SATA 90

Bradstreet, Anne 1612(?)-1672 **LC 4, 30; DA; DAC; DAM MST, POET; PC 10**
See also CDALB 1640-1865; DLB 24

Brady, Joan 1939-   **CLC 86**
See also CA 141

Bragg, Melvyn 1939-   **CLC 10**
See also BEST 89:3; CA 57-60; CANR 10, 48; DLB 14

Brahe, Tycho 1546-1601   **LC 45**

Braine, John (Gerard) 1922-1986 **CLC 1, 3, 41**
See also CA 1-4R; 120; CANR 1, 33; CDBLB 1945-1960; DLB 15; DLBY 86; MTCW 1

Bramah, Ernest 1868-1942   **TCLC 72**
See also CA 156; DLB 70

Brammer, William 1930(?)-1978   **CLC 31**
See also CA 77-80

Brancati, Vitaliano 1907-1954   **TCLC 12**
See also CA 109

Brancato, Robin F(idler) 1936- **CLC 35**
See also AAYA 9; CA 69-72; CANR 11, 45;
CLR 32; JRDA; SAAS 9; SATA 97
Brand, Max
See Faust, Frederick (Schiller)
Brand, Millen 1906-1980 **CLC 7**
See also CA 21-24R; 97-100; CANR 72
Branden, Barbara **CLC 44**
See also CA 148
Brandes, Georg (Morris Cohen) 1842-1927
TCLC 10
See also CA 105
Brandys, Kazimierz 1916- **CLC 62**
Branley, Franklyn M(ansfield) 1915-**CLC 21**
See also CA 33-36R; CANR 14, 39; CLR 13;
MAICYA; SAAS 16; SATA 4, 68
Brathwaite, Edward Kamau 1930- **CLC 11;
BLCS; DAM POET**
See also BW 2; CA 25-28R; CANR 11, 26, 47;
DLB 125
Brautigan, Richard (Gary) 1935-1984**CLC 1,
3, 5, 9, 12, 34, 42; DAM NOV**
See also CA 53-56; 113; CANR 34; DLB 2, 5,
206; DLBY 80, 84; MTCW 1; SATA 56
Brave Bird, Mary 1953-
See Crow Dog, Mary (Ellen)
See also NNAL
Braverman, Kate 1950- **CLC 67**
See also CA 89-92
Brecht, (Eugen) Bertolt (Friedrich) 1898-1956
**TCLC 1, 6, 13, 35; DA; DAB; DAC; DAM
DRAM, MST; DC 3; WLC**
See also CA 104; 133; CANR 62; DLB 56, 124;
MTCW 1
Brecht, Eugen Berthold Friedrich
See Brecht, (Eugen) Bertolt (Friedrich)
Bremer, Fredrika 1801-1865 **NCLC 11**
Brennan, Christopher John 1870-1932**T C L C
17**
See also CA 117
Brennan, Maeve 1917-1993 **CLC 5**
See also CA 81-84; CANR 72
Brent, Linda
See Jacobs, Harriet A(nn)
Brentano, Clemens (Maria) 1778-1842**N C L C
1**
See also DLB 90
Brent of Bin Bin
See Franklin, (Stella Maria Sarah) Miles
(Lampe)
Brenton, Howard 1942- **CLC 31**
See also CA 69-72; CANR 33, 67; DLB 13;
MTCW 1
Breslin, James 1930-1996
See Breslin, Jimmy
See also CA 73-76; CANR 31, 75; DAM NOV;
MTCW 1
Breslin, Jimmy **CLC 4, 43**
See also Breslin, James
See also AITN 1; DLB 185
Bresson, Robert 1901- **CLC 16**
See also CA 110; CANR 49
Breton, Andre 1896-1966**CLC 2, 9, 15, 54; PC
15**
See also CA 19-20; 25-28R; CANR 40, 60; CAP
2; DLB 65; MTCW 1
Breytenbach, Breyten 1939(?)- **CLC 23, 37;
DAM POET**
See also CA 113; 129; CANR 61
Bridgers, Sue Ellen 1942- **CLC 26**
See also AAYA 8; CA 65-68; CANR 11, 36;
CLR 18; DLB 52; JRDA; MAICYA; SAAS
1; SATA 22, 90

Bridges, Robert (Seymour) 1844-1930 **T C L C
1; DAM POET**
See also CA 104; 152; CDBLB 1890-1914;
DLB 19, 98
Bridie, James **TCLC 3**
See Mavor, Osborne Henry
See also DLB 10
Brin, David 1950- **CLC 34**
See also AAYA 21; CA 102; CANR 24, 70; INT
CANR-24; SATA 65
Brink, Andre (Philippus) 1935- **CLC 18, 36,
106**
See also CA 104; CANR 39, 62; INT 103;
MTCW 1
Brinsmead, H(esba) F(ay) 1922- **CLC 21**
See also CA 21-24R; CANR 10; CLR 47;
MAICYA; SAAS 5; SATA 18, 78
Brittain, Vera (Mary) 1893(?)-1970 **CLC 23**
See also CA 13-16; 25-28R; CANR 58; CAP 1;
DLB 191; MTCW 1
Broch, Hermann 1886-1951 **TCLC 20**
See also CA 117; DLB 85, 124
Brock, Rose
See Hansen, Joseph
Brodkey, Harold (Roy) 1930-1996 **CLC 56**
See also CA 111; 151; CANR 71; DLB 130
Brodskii, Iosif
See Brodsky, Joseph
Brodsky, Iosif Alexandrovich 1940-1996
See Brodsky, Joseph
See also AITN 1; CA 41-44R; 151; CANR 37;
DAM POET; MTCW 1
Brodsky, Joseph 1940-1996 **CLC 4, 6, 13, 36,
100; PC 9**
See also Brodskii, Iosif; Brodsky, Iosif
Alexandrovich
Brodsky, Michael (Mark) 1948- **CLC 19**
See also CA 102; CANR 18, 41, 58
Bromell, Henry 1947- **CLC 5**
See also CA 53-56; CANR 9
Bromfield, Louis (Brucker) 1896-1956**T C L C
11**
See also CA 107; 155; DLB 4, 9, 86
Broner, E(sther) M(asserman) 1930- **CLC 19**
See also CA 17-20R; CANR 8, 25, 72; DLB 28
Bronk, William 1918- **CLC 10**
See also CA 89-92; CANR 23; DLB 165
Bronstein, Lev Davidovich
See Trotsky, Leon
Bronte, Anne 1820-1849 **NCLC 71**
See also DLB 21, 199
Bronte, Charlotte 1816-1855 **NCLC 3, 8, 33,
58; DA; DAB; DAC; DAM MST, NOV;
WLC**
See also AAYA 17; CDBLB 1832-1890; DLB
21, 159, 199
Bronte, Emily (Jane) 1818-1848**NCLC 16, 35;
DA; DAB; DAC; DAM MST, NOV, POET;
PC 8; WLC**
See also AAYA 17; CDBLB 1832-1890; DLB
21, 32, 199
Brooke, Frances 1724-1789 **LC 6, 48**
See also DLB 39, 99
Brooke, Henry 1703(?)-1783 **LC 1**
See also DLB 39
Brooke, Rupert (Chawner) 1887-1915 **T C L C
2, 7; DA; DAB; DAC; DAM MST, POET;
PC 24; WLC**
See also CA 104; 132; CANR 61; CDBLB
1914-1945; DLB 19; MTCW 1
Brooke-Haven, P.
See Wodehouse, P(elham) G(renville)
Brooke-Rose, Christine 1926(?)- **CLC 40**

See also CA 13-16R; CANR 58; DLB 14
Brookner, Anita 1928- **CLC 32, 34, 51; DAB;
DAM POP**
See also CA 114; 120; CANR 37, 56; DLB 194;
DLBY 87; MTCW 1
Brooks, Cleanth 1906-1994 **CLC 24, 86, 110**
See also CA 17-20R; 145; CANR 33, 35; DLB
63; DLBY 94; INT CANR-35; MTCW 1
Brooks, George
See Baum, L(yman) Frank
Brooks, Gwendolyn 1917- **CLC 1, 2, 4, 5, 15,
49; BLC 1; DA; DAC; DAM MST, MULT,
POET; PC 7; WLC**
See also AAYA 20; AITN 1; BW 2; CA 1-4R;
CANR 1, 27, 52, 75; CDALB 1941-1968;
CLR 27; DLB 5, 76, 165; MTCW 1; SATA 6
Brooks, Mel **CLC 12**
See Kaminsky, Melvin
See also AAYA 13; DLB 26
Brooks, Peter 1938- **CLC 34**
See also CA 45-48; CANR 1
Brooks, Van Wyck 1886-1963 **CLC 29**
See also CA 1-4R; CANR 6; DLB 45, 63, 103
Brophy, Brigid (Antonia) 1929-1995 **CLC 6,
11, 29, 105**
See also CA 5-8R; 149; CAAS 4; CANR 25,
53; DLB 14; MTCW 1
Brosman, Catharine Savage 1934- **CLC 9**
See also CA 61-64; CANR 21, 46
Brossard, Nicole 1943- **CLC 115**
See also CA 122; CAAS 16; DLB 53
Brother Antoninus
See Everson, William (Oliver)
The Brothers Quay
See Quay, Stephen; Quay, Timothy
Broughton, T(homas) Alan 1936- **CLC 19**
See also CA 45-48; CANR 2, 23, 48
Broumas, Olga 1949- **CLC 10, 73**
See also CA 85-88; CANR 20, 69
Brown, Alan 1950- **CLC 99**
See also CA 156
Brown, Charles Brockden 1771-1810 **N C L C
22, 74**
See also CDALB 1640-1865; DLB 37, 59, 73
Brown, Christy 1932-1981 **CLC 63**
See also CA 105; 104; CANR 72; DLB 14
Brown, Claude 1937- **CLC 30; BLC 1; DAM
MULT**
See also AAYA 7; BW 1; CA 73-76
Brown, Dee (Alexander) 1908- **CLC 18, 47;
DAM POP**
See also CA 13-16R; CAAS 6; CANR 11, 45,
60; DLBY 80; MTCW 1; SATA 5
Brown, George
See Wertmueller, Lina
Brown, George Douglas 1869-1902 **TCLC 28**
See also CA 162
Brown, George Mackay 1921-1996**CLC 5, 48,
100**
See also CA 21-24R; 151; CAAS 6; CANR 12,
37, 67; DLB 14, 27, 139; MTCW 1; SATA
35
Brown, (William) Larry 1951- **CLC 73**
See also CA 130; 134; INT 133
Brown, Moses
See Barrett, William (Christopher)
Brown, Rita Mae 1944-**CLC 18, 43, 79; DAM
NOV, POP**
See also CA 45-48; CANR 2, 11, 35, 62; INT
CANR-11; MTCW 1
Brown, Roderick (Langmere) Haig-
See Haig-Brown, Roderick (Langmere)
Brown, Rosellen 1939- **CLC 32**

See also CA 77-80; CAAS 10; CANR 14, 44

Brown, Sterling Allen 1901-1989 **CLC 1, 23, 59; BLC 1; DAM MULT, POET**
See also BW 1; CA 85-88; 127; CANR 26, 74; DLB 48, 51, 63; MTCW 1

Brown, Will
See Ainsworth, William Harrison

Brown, William Wells 1813-1884 **NCLC 2; BLC 1; DAM MULT; DC 1**
See also DLB 3, 50

Browne, (Clyde) Jackson 1948(?)- **CLC 21**
See also CA 120

Browning, Elizabeth Barrett 1806-1861 **NCLC 1, 16, 61, 66; DA; DAB; DAC; DAM MST, POET; PC 6; WLC**
See also CDBLB 1832-1890; DLB 32, 199

Browning, Robert 1812-1889 **NCLC 19; DA; DAB; DAC; DAM MST, POET; PC 2; WLCS**
See also CDBLB 1832-1890; DLB 32, 163; YABC 1

Browning, Tod 1882-1962 **CLC 16**
See also CA 141; 117

Brownson, Orestes Augustus 1803-1876 **NCLC 50**
See also DLB 1, 59, 73

Bruccoli, Matthew J(oseph) 1931- **CLC 34**
See also CA 9-12R; CANR 7; DLB 103

Bruce, Lenny **CLC 21**
See also Schneider, Leonard Alfred

Bruin, John
See Brutus, Dennis

Brulard, Henri
See Stendhal

Brulls, Christian
See Simenon, Georges (Jacques Christian)

Brunner, John (Kilian Houston) 1934-1995 **CLC 8, 10; DAM POP**
See also CA 1-4R; 149; CAAS 8; CANR 2, 37; MTCW 1

Bruno, Giordano 1548-1600 **LC 27**

Brutus, Dennis 1924- **CLC 43; BLC 1; DAM MULT, POET; PC 24**
See also BW 2; CA 49-52; CAAS 14; CANR 2, 27, 42; DLB 117

Bryan, C(ourtlandt) D(ixon) B(arnes) 1936- **CLC 29**
See also CA 73-76; CANR 13, 68; DLB 185; INT CANR-13

Bryan, Michael
See Moore, Brian

Bryant, William Cullen 1794-1878 **NCLC 6, 46; DA; DAB; DAC; DAM MST, POET; PC 20**
See also CDALB 1640-1865; DLB 3, 43, 59, 189

Bryusov, Valery Yakovlevich 1873-1924 **TCLC 10**
See also CA 107; 155

Buchan, John 1875-1940 **TCLC 41; DAB; DAM POP**
See also CA 108; 145; DLB 34, 70, 156; YABC 2

Buchanan, George 1506-1582 **LC 4**
See also DLB 152

Buchheim, Lothar-Guenther 1918- **CLC 6**
See also CA 85-88

Buchner, (Karl) Georg 1813-1837 **NCLC 26**

Buchwald, Art(hur) 1925- **CLC 33**
See also AITN 1; CA 5-8R; CANR 21, 67; MTCW 1; SATA 10

Buck, Pearl S(ydenstricker) 1892-1973 **CLC 7, 11, 18; DA; DAB; DAC; DAM MST, NOV**

See also AITN 1; CA 1-4R; 41-44R; CANR 1, 34; DLB 9, 102; MTCW 1; SATA 1, 25

Buckler, Ernest 1908-1984 **CLC 13; DAC; DAM MST**
See also CA 11-12; 114; CAP 1; DLB 68; SATA 47

Buckley, Vincent (Thomas) 1925-1988 **CLC 57**
See also CA 101

Buckley, William F(rank), Jr. 1925- **CLC 7, 18, 37; DAM POP**
See also AITN 1; CA 1-4R; CANR 1, 24, 53; DLB 137; DLBY 80; INT CANR-24; MTCW 1

Buechner, (Carl) Frederick 1926- **CLC 2, 4, 6, 9; DAM NOV**
See also CA 13-16R; CANR 11, 39, 64; DLBY 80; INT CANR-11; MTCW 1

Buell, John (Edward) 1927- **CLC 10**
See also CA 1-4R; CANR 71; DLB 53

Buero Vallejo, Antonio 1916- **CLC 15, 46**
See also CA 106; CANR 24, 49, 75; HW; MTCW 1

Bufalino, Gesualdo 1920(?)- **CLC 74**
See also DLB 196

Bugayev, Boris Nikolayevich 1880-1934 **TCLC 7; PC 11**
See also Bely, Andrey
See also CA 104; 165

Bukowski, Charles 1920-1994 **CLC 2, 5, 9, 41, 82, 108; DAM NOV, POET; PC 18**
See also CA 17-20R; 144; CANR 40, 62; DLB 5, 130, 169; MTCW 1

Bulgakov, Mikhail (Afanas'evich) 1891-1940 **TCLC 2, 16; DAM DRAM, NOV; SSC 18**
See also CA 105; 152

Bulgya, Alexander Alexandrovich 1901-1956 **TCLC 53**
See also Fadeyev, Alexander
See also CA 117

Bullins, Ed 1935- **CLC 1, 5, 7; BLC 1; DAM DRAM, MULT; DC 6**
See also BW 2; CA 49-52; CAAS 16; CANR 24, 46, 73; DLB 7, 38; MTCW 1

Bulwer-Lytton, Edward (George Earle Lytton) 1803-1873 **NCLC 1, 45**
See also DLB 21

Bunin, Ivan Alexeyevich 1870-1953 **TCLC 6; SSC 5**
See also CA 104

Bunting, Basil 1900-1985 **CLC 10, 39, 47; DAM POET**
See also CA 53-56; 115; CANR 7; DLB 20

Bunuel, Luis 1900-1983 **CLC 16, 80; DAM MULT; HLC**
See also CA 101; 110; CANR 32; HW

Bunyan, John 1628-1688 **LC 4; DA; DAB; DAC; DAM MST; WLC**
See also CDBLB 1660-1789; DLB 39

Burckhardt, Jacob (Christoph) 1818-1897 **NCLC 49**

Burford, Eleanor
See Hibbert, Eleanor Alice Burford

Burgess, Anthony **CLC 1, 2, 4, 5, 8, 10, 13, 15, 22, 40, 62, 81, 94; DAB**
See also Wilson, John (Anthony) Burgess
See also AAYA 25; AITN 1; CDBLB 1960 to Present; DLB 14, 194

Burke, Edmund 1729(?)-1797 **LC 7, 36; DA; DAB; DAC; DAM MST; WLC**
See also DLB 104

Burke, Kenneth (Duva) 1897-1993 **CLC 2, 24**
See also CA 5-8R; 143; CANR 39, 74; DLB 45, 63; MTCW 1

Burke, Leda
See Garnett, David

Burke, Ralph
See Silverberg, Robert

Burke, Thomas 1886-1945 **TCLC 63**
See also CA 113; 155; DLB 197

Burney, Fanny 1752-1840 **NCLC 12, 54**
See also DLB 39

Burns, Robert 1759-1796 **LC 3, 29, 40; DA; DAB; DAC; DAM MST, POET; PC 6; WLC**
See also CDBLB 1789-1832; DLB 109

Burns, Tex
See L'Amour, Louis (Dearborn)

Burnshaw, Stanley 1906- **CLC 3, 13, 44**
See also CA 9-12R; DLB 48; DLBY 97

Burr, Anne 1937- **CLC 6**
See also CA 25-28R

Burroughs, Edgar Rice 1875-1950 **TCLC 2, 32; DAM NOV**
See also AAYA 11; CA 104; 132; DLB 8; MTCW 1; SATA 41

Burroughs, William S(eward) 1914-1997 **CLC 1, 2, 5, 15, 22, 42, 75, 109; DA; DAB; DAC; DAM MST, NOV, POP; WLC**
See also AITN 2; CA 9-12R; 160; CANR 20, 52; DLB 2, 8, 16, 152; DLBY 81, 97; MTCW 1

Burton, Richard F. 1821-1890 **NCLC 42**
See also DLB 55, 184

Busch, Frederick 1941- **CLC 7, 10, 18, 47**
See also CA 33-36R; CAAS 1; CANR 45, 73; DLB 6

Bush, Ronald 1946- **CLC 34**
See also CA 136

Bustos, F(rancisco)
See Borges, Jorge Luis

Bustos Domecq, H(onorio)
See Bioy Casares, Adolfo; Borges, Jorge Luis

Butler, Octavia E(stelle) 1947- **CLC 38; BLCS; DAM MULT**
See also AAYA 18; BW 2; CA 73-76; CANR 12, 24, 38, 73; DLB 33; MTCW 1; SATA 84

Butler, Robert Olen (Jr.) 1945- **CLC 81; DAM POP**
See also CA 112; CANR 66; DLB 173; INT 112

Butler, Samuel 1612-1680 **LC 16, 43**
See also DLB 101, 126

Butler, Samuel 1835-1902 **TCLC 1, 33; DA; DAB; DAC; DAM MST, NOV; WLC**
See also CA 143; CDBLB 1890-1914; DLB 18, 57, 174

Butler, Walter C.
See Faust, Frederick (Schiller)

Butor, Michel (Marie Francois) 1926- **CLC 1, 3, 8, 11, 15**
See also CA 9-12R; CANR 33, 66; DLB 83; MTCW 1

Butts, Mary 1892(?)-1937 **TCLC 77**
See also CA 148

Buzo, Alexander (John) 1944- **CLC 61**
See also CA 97-100; CANR 17, 39, 69

Buzzati, Dino 1906-1972 **CLC 36**
See also CA 160; 33-36R; DLB 177

Byars, Betsy (Cromer) 1928- **CLC 35**
See also AAYA 19; CA 33-36R; CANR 18, 36, 57; CLR 1, 16; DLB 52; INT CANR-18; JRDA; MAICYA; MTCW 1; SAAS 1; SATA 4, 46, 80

Byatt, A(ntonia) S(usan Drabble) 1936- **CLC 19, 65; DAM NOV, POP**
See also CA 13-16R; CANR 13, 33, 50, 75; DLB 14, 194; MTCW 1

Byrne, David 1952-   CLC 26
See also CA 127
Byrne, John Keyes 1926-
See Leonard, Hugh
See also CA 102; INT 102
Byron, George Gordon (Noel) 1788-1824
NCLC 2, 12; DA; DAB; DAC; DAM MST,
POET; PC 16; WLC
See also CDBLB 1789-1832; DLB 96, 110
Byron, Robert 1905-1941   TCLC 67
See also CA 160; DLB 195
C. 3. 3.
See Wilde, Oscar (Fingal O'Flahertie Wills)
Caballero, Fernan 1796-1877   NCLC 10
Cabell, Branch
See Cabell, James Branch
Cabell, James Branch 1879-1958   TCLC 6
See also CA 105; 152; DLB 9, 78
Cable, George Washington 1844-1925 T C L C
4; SSC 4
See also CA 104; 155; DLB 12, 74; DLBD 13
Cabral de Melo Neto, Joao 1920-   CLC 76;
DAM MULT
See also CA 151
Cabrera Infante, G(uillermo) 1929-CLC 5, 25,
45; DAM MULT; HLC
See also CA 85-88; CANR 29, 65; DLB 113;
HW; MTCW 1
Cade, Toni
See Bambara, Toni Cade
Cadmus and Harmonia
See Buchan, John
Caedmon fl. 658-680   CMLC 7
See also DLB 146
Caeiro, Alberto
See Pessoa, Fernando (Antonio Nogueira)
Cage, John (Milton, Jr.) 1912-1992 CLC 41
See also CA 13-16R; 169; CANR 9; DLB 193;
INT CANR-9
Cahan, Abraham 1860-1951   TCLC 71
See also CA 108; 154; DLB 9, 25, 28
Cain, G.
See Cabrera Infante, G(uillermo)
Cain, Guillermo
See Cabrera Infante, G(uillermo)
Cain, James M(allahan) 1892-1977CLC 3, 11,
28
See also AITN 1; CA 17-20R; 73-76; CANR 8,
34, 61; MTCW 1
Caine, Mark
See Raphael, Frederic (Michael)
Calasso, Roberto 1941-   CLC 81
See also CA 143
Calderon de la Barca, Pedro 1600-1681 L C
23; DC 3
Caldwell, Erskine (Preston) 1903-1987CLC 1,
8, 14, 50, 60; DAM NOV; SSC 19
See also AITN 1; CA 1-4R; 121; CAAS 1;
CANR 2, 33; DLB 9, 86; MTCW 1
Caldwell, (Janet Miriam) Taylor (Holland)
1900-1985CLC 2, 28, 39; DAM NOV, POP
See also CA 5-8R; 116; CANR 5; DLBD 17
Calhoun, John Caldwell 1782-1850NCLC 15
See also DLB 3
Calisher, Hortense 1911-CLC 2, 4, 8, 38; DAM
NOV; SSC 15
See also CA 1-4R; CANR 1, 22, 67; DLB 2;
INT CANR-22; MTCW 1
Callaghan, Morley Edward 1903-1990CLC 3,
14, 41, 65; DAC; DAM MST
See also CA 9-12R; 132; CANR 33, 73; DLB
68; MTCW 1
Callimachus c. 305B.C.-c. 240B.C. CMLC 18

See also DLB 176
Calvin, John 1509-1564   LC 37
Calvino, Italo 1923-1985CLC 5, 8, 11, 22, 33,
39, 73; DAM NOV; SSC 3
See also CA 85-88; 116; CANR 23, 61; DLB
196; MTCW 1
Cameron, Carey 1952-   CLC 59
See also CA 135
Cameron, Peter 1959-   CLC 44
See also CA 125; CANR 50
Campana, Dino 1885-1932   TCLC 20
See also CA 117; DLB 114
Campanella, Tommaso 1568-1639   LC 32
Campbell, John W(ood, Jr.) 1910-1971 C L C
32
See also CA 21-22; 29-32R; CANR 34; CAP 2;
DLB 8; MTCW 1
Campbell, Joseph 1904-1987   CLC 69
See also AAYA 3; BEST 89:2; CA 1-4R; 124;
CANR 3, 28, 61; MTCW 1
Campbell, Maria 1940-   CLC 85; DAC
See also CA 102; CANR 54; NNAL
Campbell, (John) Ramsey 1946-CLC 42; SSC
19
See also CA 57-60; CANR 7; INT CANR-7
Campbell, (Ignatius) Roy (Dunnachie) 1901-
1957   TCLC 5
See also CA 104; 155; DLB 20
Campbell, Thomas 1777-1844   NCLC 19
See also DLB 93; 144
Campbell, Wilfred   TCLC 9
See also Campbell, William
Campbell, William 1858(?)-1918
See Campbell, Wilfred
See also CA 106; DLB 92
Campion, Jane   CLC 95
See also CA 138
Campos, Alvaro de
See Pessoa, Fernando (Antonio Nogueira)
Camus, Albert 1913-1960CLC 1, 2, 4, 9, 11, 14,
32, 63, 69; DA; DAB; DAC; DAM DRAM,
MST, NOV; DC 2; SSC 9; WLC
See also CA 89-92; DLB 72; MTCW 1
Canby, Vincent 1924-   CLC 13
See also CA 81-84
Cancale
See Desnos, Robert
Canetti, Elias 1905-1994CLC 3, 14, 25, 75, 86
See also CA 21-24R; 146; CANR 23, 61; DLB
85, 124; MTCW 1
Canfield, Dorothea F.
See Fisher, Dorothy (Frances) Canfield
Canfield, Dorothea Frances
See Fisher, Dorothy (Frances) Canfield
Canfield, Dorothy
See Fisher, Dorothy (Frances) Canfield
Canin, Ethan 1960-   CLC 55
See also CA 131; 135
Cannon, Curt
See Hunter, Evan
Cao, Lan 1961-   CLC 109
See also CA 165
Cape, Judith
See Page, P(atricia) K(athleen)
Capek, Karel 1890-1938   TCLC 6, 37; DA;
DAB; DAC; DAM DRAM, MST, NOV; DC
1; WLC
See also CA 104; 140
Capote, Truman 1924-1984CLC 1, 3, 8, 13, 19,
34, 38, 58; DA; DAB; DAC; DAM MST,
NOV, POP; SSC 2; WLC
See also CA 5-8R; 113; CANR 18, 62; CDALB
1941-1968; DLB 2, 185; DLBY 80, 84;

MTCW 1; SATA 91
Capra, Frank 1897-1991   CLC 16
See also CA 61-64; 135
Caputo, Philip 1941-   CLC 32
See also CA 73-76; CANR 40
Caragiale, Ion Luca 1852-1912   TCLC 76
See also CA 157
Card, Orson Scott 1951-CLC 44, 47, 50; DAM
POP
See also AAYA 11; CA 102; CANR 27, 47, 73;
INT CANR-27; MTCW 1; SATA 83
Cardenal, Ernesto 1925-   CLC 31; DAM
MULT, POET; HLC; PC 22
See also CA 49-52; CANR 2, 32, 66; HW;
MTCW 1
Cardozo, Benjamin N(athan) 1870-1938
TCLC 65
See also CA 117; 164
Carducci, Giosue (Alessandro Giuseppe) 1835-
1907   TCLC 32
See also CA 163
Carew, Thomas 1595(?)-1640   LC 13
See also DLB 126
Carey, Ernestine Gilbreth 1908-   CLC 17
See also CA 5-8R; CANR 71; SATA 2
Carey, Peter 1943-   CLC 40, 55, 96
See also CA 123; 127; CANR 53; INT 127;
MTCW 1; SATA 94
Carleton, William 1794-1869   NCLC 3
See also DLB 159
Carlisle, Henry (Coffin) 1926-   CLC 33
See also CA 13-16R; CANR 15
Carlsen, Chris
See Holdstock, Robert P.
Carlson, Ron(ald F.) 1947-   CLC 54
See also CA 105; CANR 27
Carlyle, Thomas 1795-1881   NCLC 70; DA;
DAB; DAC; DAM MST
See also CDBLB 1789-1832; DLB 55; 144
Carman, (William) Bliss 1861-1929 TCLC 7;
DAC
See also CA 104; 152; DLB 92
Carnegie, Dale 1888-1955   TCLC 53
Carossa, Hans 1878-1956   TCLC 48
See also CA 170; DLB 66
Carpenter, Don(ald Richard) 1931-1995C L C
41
See also CA 45-48; 149; CANR 1, 71
Carpenter, Edward 1844-1929   TCLC 88
See also CA 163
Carpentier (y Valmont), Alejo 1904-1980CLC
8, 11, 38, 110; DAM MULT; HLC
See also CA 65-68; 97-100; CANR 11, 70; DLB
113; HW
Carr, Caleb 1955(?)-   CLC 86
See also CA 147; CANR 73
Carr, Emily 1871-1945   TCLC 32
See also CA 159; DLB 68
Carr, John Dickson 1906-1977   CLC 3
See also Fairbairn, Roger
See also CA 49-52; 69-72; CANR 3, 33, 60;
MTCW 1
Carr, Philippa
See Hibbert, Eleanor Alice Burford
Carr, Virginia Spencer 1929-   CLC 34
See also CA 61-64; DLB 111
Carrere, Emmanuel 1957-   CLC 89
Carrier, Roch 1937-CLC 13, 78; DAC; DAM
MST
See also CA 130; CANR 61; DLB 53
Carroll, James P. 1943(?)-   CLC 38
See also CA 81-84; CANR 73
Carroll, Jim 1951-   CLC 35

See also AAYA 17; CA 45-48; CANR 42

Carroll, Lewis   **NCLC 2, 53; PC 18; WLC**
See also Dodgson, Charles Lutwidge
See also CDBLB 1832-1890; CLR 2, 18; DLB
18, 163, 178; JRDA

Carroll, Paul Vincent 1900-1968   **CLC 10**
See also CA 9-12R; 25-28R; DLB 10

Carruth, Hayden 1921- **CLC 4, 7, 10, 18, 84;**
PC 10
See also CA 9-12R; CANR 4, 38, 59; DLB 5,
165; INT CANR-4; MTCW 1; SATA 47

Carson, Rachel Louise 1907-1964   **CLC 71;**
DAM POP
See also CA 77-80; CANR 35; MTCW 1; SATA
23

Carter, Angela (Olive) 1940-1992 **CLC 5, 41,**
76; SSC 13
See also CA 53-56; 136; CANR 12, 36, 61; DLB
14, 207; MTCW 1; SATA 66; SATA-Obit 70

Carter, Nick
See Smith, Martin Cruz

Carver, Raymond 1938-1988 **CLC 22, 36, 53,**
55; DAM NOV; SSC 8
See also CA 33-36R; 126; CANR 17, 34, 61;
DLB 130; DLBY 84, 88; MTCW 1

Cary, Elizabeth, Lady Falkland 1585-1639
LC 30

Cary, (Arthur) Joyce (Lunel) 1888-1957
TCLC 1, 29
See also CA 104; 164; CDBLB 1914-1945;
DLB 15, 100

Casanova de Seingalt, Giovanni Jacopo 1725-
1798   **LC 13**

Casares, Adolfo Bioy
See Bioy Casares, Adolfo

Casely-Hayford, J(oseph) E(phraim) 1866-1930
TCLC 24; BLC 1; DAM MULT
See also BW 2; CA 123; 152

Casey, John (Dudley) 1939-   **CLC 59**
See also BEST 90:2; CA 69-72; CANR 23

Casey, Michael 1947-   **CLC 2**
See also CA 65-68; DLB 5

Casey, Patrick
See Thurman, Wallace (Henry)

Casey, Warren (Peter) 1935-1988   **CLC 12**
See also CA 101; 127; INT 101

Casona, Alejandro   **CLC 49**
See also Alvarez, Alejandro Rodriguez

Cassavetes, John 1929-1989   **CLC 20**
See also CA 85-88; 127

Cassian, Nina 1924-   **PC 17**

Cassill, R(onald) V(erlin) 1919- **CLC 4, 23**
See also CA 9-12R; CAAS 1; CANR 7, 45; DLB
6

Cassirer, Ernst 1874-1945   **TCLC 61**
See also CA 157

Cassity, (Allen) Turner 1929- **CLC 6, 42**
See also CA 17-20R; CAAS 8; CANR 11; DLB
105

Castaneda, Carlos 1931(?)-   **CLC 12**
See also CA 25-28R; CANR 32, 66; HW;
MTCW 1

Castedo, Elena 1937-   **CLC 65**
See also CA 132

Castedo-Ellerman, Elena
See Castedo, Elena

Castellanos, Rosario 1925-1974**CLC 66; DAM**
MULT; HLC
See also CA 131; 53-56; CANR 58; DLB 113;
HW

Castelvetro, Lodovico 1505-1571   **LC 12**

Castiglione, Baldassare 1478-1529   **LC 12**

Castle, Robert

See Hamilton, Edmond

Castro, Guillen de 1569-1631   **LC 19**

Castro, Rosalia de 1837-1885 **NCLC 3; DAM**
MULT

Cather, Willa
See Cather, Willa Sibert

Cather, Willa Sibert 1873-1947 **TCLC 1, 11,**
31; DA; DAB; DAC; DAM MST, NOV;
SSC 2; WLC
See also AAYA 24; CA 104; 128; CDALB 1865-
1917; DLB 9, 54, 78; DLBD 1; MTCW 1;
SATA 30

Catherine, Saint 1347-1380   **CMLC 27**

Cato, Marcus Porcius 234B.C.-149B.C.
CMLC 21

Catton, (Charles) Bruce 1899-1978 **CLC 35**
See also AITN 1; CA 5-8R; 81-84; CANR 7,
74; DLB 17; SATA 2; SATA-Obit 24

Catullus c. 84B.C.-c. 54B.C.   **CMLC 18**

Cauldwell, Frank
See King, Francis (Henry)

Caunitz, William J. 1933-1996   **CLC 34**
See also BEST 89:3; CA 125; 130; 152; CANR
73; INT 130

Causley, Charles (Stanley) 1917-   **CLC 7**
See also CA 9-12R; CANR 5, 35; CLR 30; DLB
27; MTCW 1; SATA 3, 66

Caute, (John) David 1936-   **CLC 29; DAM**
NOV
See also CA 1-4R; CAAS 4; CANR 1, 33, 64;
DLB 14

Cavafy, C(onstantine) P(eter) 1863-1933
TCLC 2, 7; DAM POET
See also Kavafis, Konstantinos Petrou
See also CA 148

Cavallo, Evelyn
See Spark, Muriel (Sarah)

Cavanna, Betty   **CLC 12**
See also Harrison, Elizabeth Cavanna
See also JRDA; MAICYA; SAAS 4; SATA 1,
30

Cavendish, Margaret Lucas 1623-1673**LC 30**
See also DLB 131

Caxton, William 1421(?)-1491(?)   **LC 17**
See also DLB 170

Cayer, D. M.
See Duffy, Maureen

Cayrol, Jean 1911-   **CLC 11**
See also CA 89-92; DLB 83

Cela, Camilo Jose 1916-**CLC 4, 13, 59; DAM**
MULT; HLC
See also BEST 90:2; CA 21-24R; CAAS 10;
CANR 21, 32; DLBY 89; HW; MTCW 1

Celan, Paul   **CLC 10, 19, 53, 82; PC 10**
See also Antschel, Paul
See also DLB 69

Celine, Louis-Ferdinand CLC 1, 3, 4, 7, 9, 15,
47
See also Destouches, Louis-Ferdinand
See also DLB 72

Cellini, Benvenuto 1500-1571   **LC 7**

Cendrars, Blaise 1887-1961   **CLC 18, 106**
See also Sauser-Hall, Frederic

Cernuda (y Bidon), Luis 1902-1963 **CLC 54;**
DAM POET
See also CA 131; 89-92; DLB 134; HW

Cervantes (Saavedra), Miguel de 1547-1616
LC 6, 23; DA; DAB; DAC; DAM MST,
NOV; SSC 12; WLC

Cesaire, Aime (Fernand) 1913- **CLC 19, 32,**
112; BLC 1; DAM MULT, POET; PC 25
See also BW 2; CA 65-68; CANR 24, 43;
MTCW 1

Chabon, Michael 1963-   **CLC 55**
See also CA 139; CANR 57

Chabrol, Claude 1930-   **CLC 16**
See also CA 110

Challans, Mary 1905-1983
See Renault, Mary
See also CA 81-84; 111; CANR 74; SATA 23;
SATA-Obit 36

Challis, George
See Faust, Frederick (Schiller)

Chambers, Aidan 1934-   **CLC 35**
See also AAYA 27; CA 25-28R; CANR 12, 31,
58; JRDA; MAICYA; SAAS 12; SATA 1, 69

Chambers, James 1948-
See Cliff, Jimmy
See also CA 124

Chambers, Jessie
See Lawrence, D(avid) H(erbert Richards)

Chambers, Robert W(illiam) 1865-1933
TCLC 41
See also CA 165; DLB 202

Chandler, Raymond (Thornton) 1888-1959
TCLC 1, 7; SSC 23
See also AAYA 25; CA 104; 129; CANR 60;
CDALB 1929-1941; DLBD 6; MTCW 1

Chang, Eileen 1920-1995   **SSC 28**
See also CA 166

Chang, Jung 1952-   **CLC 71**
See also CA 142

Chang Ai-Ling
See Chang, Eileen

Channing, William Ellery 1780-1842 **NCLC**
17
See also DLB 1, 59

Chaplin, Charles Spencer 1889-1977**CLC 16**
See also Chaplin, Charlie
See also CA 81-84; 73-76

Chaplin, Charlie
See Chaplin, Charles Spencer
See also DLB 44

Chapman, George 1559(?)-1634**LC 22; DAM**
DRAM
See also DLB 62, 121

Chapman, Graham 1941-1989   **CLC 21**
See also Monty Python
See also CA 116; 129; CANR 35

Chapman, John Jay 1862-1933   **TCLC 7**
See also CA 104

Chapman, Lee
See Bradley, Marion Zimmer

Chapman, Walker
See Silverberg, Robert

Chappell, Fred (Davis) 1936-   **CLC 40, 78**
See also CA 5-8R; CAAS 4; CANR 8, 33, 67;
DLB 6, 105

Char, Rene(-Emile) 1907-1988**CLC 9, 11, 14,**
55; DAM POET
See also CA 13-16R; 124; CANR 32; MTCW 1

Charby, Jay
See Ellison, Harlan (Jay)

Chardin, Pierre Teilhard de
See Teilhard de Chardin, (Marie Joseph) Pierre

Charles I 1600-1649   **LC 13**

Charriere, Isabelle de 1740-1805   **NCLC 66**

Charyn, Jerome 1937-   **CLC 5, 8, 18**
See also CA 5-8R; CAAS 1; CANR 7, 61;
DLBY 83; MTCW 1

Chase, Mary (Coyle) 1907-1981   **DC 1**
See also CA 77-80; 105; SATA 17; SATA-Obit
29

Chase, Mary Ellen 1887-1973   **CLC 2**
See also CA 13-16; 41-44R; CAP 1; SATA 10

Chase, Nicholas

See Hyde, Anthony
Chateaubriand, Francois Rene de 1768-1848
NCLC 3
See also DLB 119
Chatterje, Sarat Chandra 1876-1936(?)
See Chatterji, Saratchandra
See also CA 109
Chatterji, Bankim Chandra 1838-1894**NCLC 19**
Chatterji, Saratchandra **TCLC 13**
See Chatterje, Sarat Chandra
Chatterton, Thomas 1752-1770 **LC 3; DAM POET**
See also DLB 109
Chatwin, (Charles) Bruce 1940-1989**CLC 28, 57, 59; DAM POP**
See also AAYA 4; BEST 90:1; CA 85-88; 127; DLB 194, 204
Chaucer, Daniel
See Ford, Ford Madox
Chaucer, Geoffrey 1340(?)-1400 **LC 17; DA; DAB; DAC; DAM MST, POET; PC 19; WLCS**
See also CDBLB Before 1660; DLB 146
Chaviaras, Strates 1935-
See Haviaras, Stratis
See also CA 105
Chayefsky, Paddy **CLC 23**
See also Chayefsky, Sidney
See also DLB 7, 44; DLBY 81
Chayefsky, Sidney 1923-1981
See Chayefsky, Paddy
See also CA 9-12R; 104; CANR 18; DAM DRAM
Chedid, Andree 1920- **CLC 47**
See also CA 145
Cheever, John 1912-1982 **CLC 3, 7, 8, 11, 15, 25, 64; DA; DAB; DAC; DAM MST, NOV, POP; SSC 1; WLC**
See also CA 5-8R; 106; CABS 1; CANR 5, 27; CDALB 1941-1968; DLB 2, 102; DLBY 80, 82; INT CANR-5; MTCW 1
Cheever, Susan 1943- **CLC 18, 48**
See also CA 103; CANR 27, 51; DLBY 82; INT CANR-27
Chekhonte, Antosha
See Chekhov, Anton (Pavlovich)
Chekhov, Anton (Pavlovich) 1860-1904**TCLC 3, 10, 31, 55; DA; DAB; DAC; DAM DRAM, MST; DC 9; SSC 2, 28; WLC**
See also CA 104; 124; SATA 90
Chernyshevsky, Nikolay Gavrilovich 1828-1889 **NCLC 1**
Cherry, Carolyn Janice 1942-
See Cherryh, C. J.
See also CA 65-68; CANR 10
Cherryh, C. J. **CLC 35**
See also Cherry, Carolyn Janice
See also AAYA 24; DLBY 80; SATA 93
Chesnutt, Charles W(addell) 1858-1932
TCLC 5, 39; BLC 1; DAM MULT; SSC 7
See also BW 1; CA 106; 125; DLB 12, 50, 78; MTCW 1
Chester, Alfred 1929(?)-1971 **CLC 49**
See also CA 33-36R; DLB 130
Chesterton, G(ilbert) K(eith) 1874-1936
TCLC 1, 6, 64; DAM NOV, POET; SSC 1
See also CA 104; 132; CANR 73; CDBLB 1914-1945; DLB 10, 19, 34, 70, 98, 149, 178; MTCW 1; SATA 27
Chiang, Pin-chin 1904-1986
See Ding Ling
See also CA 118

Ch'ien Chung-shu 1910- **CLC 22**
See also CA 130; CANR 73; MTCW 1
Child, L. Maria
See Child, Lydia Maria
Child, Lydia Maria 1802-1880 **NCLC 6, 73**
See also DLB 1, 74; SATA 67
Child, Mrs.
See Child, Lydia Maria
Child, Philip 1898-1978 **CLC 19, 68**
See also CA 13-14; CAP 1; SATA 47
Childers, (Robert) Erskine 1870-1922 **TCLC 65**
See also CA 113; 153; DLB 70
Childress, Alice 1920-1994**CLC 12, 15, 86, 96; BLC 1; DAM DRAM, MULT, NOV; DC 4**
See also AAYA 8; BW 2; CA 45-48; 146; CANR 3, 27, 50, 74; CLR 14; DLB 7, 38; JRDA; MAICYA; MTCW 1; SATA 7, 48, 81
Chin, Frank (Chew, Jr.) 1940- **DC 7**
See also CA 33-36R; CANR 71; DAM MULT; DLB 206
Chislett, (Margaret) Anne 1943- **CLC 34**
See also CA 151
Chitty, Thomas Willes 1926- **CLC 11**
See also Hinde, Thomas
See also CA 5-8R
Chivers, Thomas Holley 1809-1858**NCLC 49**
See also DLB 3
Chomette, Rene Lucien 1898-1981
See Clair, Rene
See also CA 103
Chopin, Kate **TCLC 5, 14; DA; DAB; SSC 8; WLCS**
See also Chopin, Katherine
See also CDALB 1865-1917; DLB 12, 78
Chopin, Katherine 1851-1904
See Chopin, Kate
See also CA 104; 122; DAC; DAM MST, NOV
Chretien de Troyes c. 12th cent. - **CMLC 10**
See also DLB 208
Christie
See Ichikawa, Kon
Christie, Agatha (Mary Clarissa) 1890-1976
CLC 1, 6, 8, 12, 39, 48, 110; DAB; DAC; DAM NOV
See also AAYA 9; AITN 1, 2; CA 17-20R; 61-64; CANR 10, 37; CDBLB 1914-1945; DLB 13, 77; MTCW 1; SATA 36
Christie, (Ann) Philippa
See Pearce, Philippa
See also CA 5-8R; CANR 4
Christine de Pizan 1365(?)-1431(?) **LC 9**
See also DLB 208
Chubb, Elmer
See Masters, Edgar Lee
Chulkov, Mikhail Dmitrievich 1743-1792**LC 2**
See also DLB 150
Churchill, Caryl 1938- **CLC 31, 55; DC 5**
See also CA 102; CANR 22, 46; DLB 13; MTCW 1
Churchill, Charles 1731-1764 **LC 3**
See also DLB 109
Chute, Carolyn 1947- **CLC 39**
See also CA 123
Ciardi, John (Anthony) 1916-1986 **CLC 10, 40, 44; DAM POET**
See also CA 5-8R; 118; CAAS 2; CANR 5, 33; CLR 19; DLB 5; DLBY 86; INT CANR-5; MAICYA; MTCW 1; SAAS 26; SATA 1, 65; SATA-Obit 46
Cicero, Marcus Tullius 106B.C.-43B.C.
CMLC 3
Cimino, Michael 1943- **CLC 16**

See also CA 105
Cioran, E(mil) M. 1911-1995 **CLC 64**
See also CA 25-28R; 149
Cisneros, Sandra 1954-**CLC 69; DAM MULT; HLC; SSC 32**
See also AAYA 9; CA 131; CANR 64; DLB 122, 152; HW
Cixous, Helene 1937- **CLC 92**
See also CA 126; CANR 55; DLB 83; MTCW 1
Clair, Rene **CLC 20**
See also Chomette, Rene Lucien
Clampitt, Amy 1920-1994 **CLC 32; PC 19**
See also CA 110; 146; CANR 29; DLB 105
Clancy, Thomas L., Jr. 1947-
See Clancy, Tom
See also CA 125; 131; CANR 62; INT 131; MTCW 1
Clancy, Tom **CLC 45, 112; DAM NOV, POP**
See also Clancy, Thomas L., Jr.
See also AAYA 9; BEST 89:1, 90:1
Clare, John 1793-1864 **NCLC 9; DAB; DAM POET; PC 23**
See also DLB 55, 96
Clarin
See Alas (y Urena), Leopoldo (Enrique Garcia)
Clark, Al C.
See Goines, Donald
Clark, (Robert) Brian 1932- **CLC 29**
See also CA 41-44R; CANR 67
Clark, Curt
See Westlake, Donald E(dwin)
Clark, Eleanor 1913-1996 **CLC 5, 19**
See also CA 9-12R; 151; CANR 41; DLB 6
Clark, J. P.
See Clark, John Pepper
See also DLB 117
Clark, John Pepper 1935- **CLC 38; BLC 1; DAM DRAM, MULT; DC 5**
See also Clark, J. P.
See also BW 1; CA 65-68; CANR 16, 72
Clark, M. R.
See Clark, Mavis Thorpe
Clark, Mavis Thorpe 1909- **CLC 12**
See also CA 57-60; CANR 8, 37; CLR 30; MAICYA; SAAS 5; SATA 8, 74
Clark, Walter Van Tilburg 1909-1971**CLC 28**
See also CA 9-12R; 33-36R; CANR 63; DLB 9, 206; SATA 8
Clark Bekederemo, J(ohnson) P(epper)
See Clark, John Pepper
Clarke, Arthur C(harles) 1917-**CLC 1, 4, 13, 18, 35; DAM POP; SSC 3**
See also AAYA 4; CA 1-4R; CANR 2, 28, 55, 74; JRDA; MAICYA; MTCW 1; SATA 13, 70
Clarke, Austin 1896-1974 **CLC 6, 9; DAM POET**
See also CA 29-32; 49-52; CAP 2; DLB 10, 20
Clarke, Austin C(hesterfield) 1934-**CLC 8, 53; BLC 1; DAC; DAM MULT**
See also BW 1; CA 25-28R; CAAS 16; CANR 14, 32, 68; DLB 53, 125
Clarke, Gillian 1937- **CLC 61**
See also CA 106; DLB 40
Clarke, Marcus (Andrew Hislop) 1846-1881 **NCLC 19**
Clarke, Shirley 1925- **CLC 16**
Clash, The
See Headon, (Nicky) Topper; Jones, Mick; Simonon, Paul; Strummer, Joe
Claudel, Paul (Louis Charles Marie) 1868-1955 **TCLC 2, 10**

See also CA 104; 165; DLB 192

Claudius, Matthias 1740-1815   **NCLC 75**
See also DLB 97

Clavell, James (duMaresq) 1925-1994**CLC 6, 25, 87; DAM NOV, POP**
See also CA 25-28R; 146; CANR 26, 48; MTCW 1

Cleaver, (Leroy) Eldridge 1935-1998**CLC 30; BLC 1; DAM MULT**
See also BW 1; CA 21-24R; 167; CANR 16, 75

Cleese, John (Marwood) 1939-   **CLC 21**
See also Monty Python
See also CA 112; 116; CANR 35; MTCW 1

Cleishbotham, Jebediah
See Scott, Walter

Cleland, John 1710-1789   **LC 2, 48**
See also DLB 39

Clemens, Samuel Langhorne 1835-1910
See Twain, Mark
See also CA 104; 135; CDALB 1865-1917; DA; DAB; DAC; DAM MST, NOV; DLB 11, 12, 23, 64, 74, 186, 189; JRDA; MAICYA; SATA 100; YABC 2

Cleophil
See Congreve, William

Clerihew, E.
See Bentley, E(dmund) C(lerihew)

Clerk, N. W.
See Lewis, C(live) S(taples)

Cliff, Jimmy   **CLC 21**
See also Chambers, James

Clifton, (Thelma) Lucille 1936- **CLC 19, 66; BLC 1; DAM MULT, POET; PC 17**
See also BW 2; CA 49-52; CANR 2, 24, 42; CLR 5; DLB 5, 41; MAICYA; MTCW 1; SATA 20, 69

Clinton, Dirk
See Silverberg, Robert

Clough, Arthur Hugh 1819-1861   **NCLC 27**
See also DLB 32

Clutha, Janet Paterson Frame 1924-
See Frame, Janet
See also CA 1-4R; CANR 2, 36; MTCW 1

Clyne, Terence
See Blatty, William Peter

Cobalt, Martin
See Mayne, William (James Carter)

Cobb, Irvin S. 1876-1944   **TCLC 77**
See also DLB 11, 25, 86

Cobbett, William 1763-1835   **NCLC 49**
See also DLB 43, 107, 158

Coburn, D(onald) L(ee) 1938-   **CLC 10**
See also CA 89-92

Cocteau, Jean (Maurice Eugene Clement) 1889-1963**CLC 1, 8, 15, 16, 43; DA; DAB; DAC; DAM DRAM, MST, NOV; WLC**
See also CA 25-28; CANR 40; CAP 2; DLB 65; MTCW 1

Codrescu, Andrei 1946-**CLC 46; DAM POET**
See also CA 33-36R; CAAS 19; CANR 13, 34, 53

Coe, Max
See Bourne, Randolph S(illiman)

Coe, Tucker
See Westlake, Donald E(dwin)

Coen, Ethan 1958-   **CLC 108**
See also CA 126

Coen, Joel 1955-   **CLC 108**
See also CA 126

The Coen Brothers
See Coen, Ethan; Coen, Joel

Coetzee, J(ohn) M(ichael) 1940- **CLC 23, 33, 66, 117; DAM NOV**

See also CA 77-80; CANR 41, 54, 74; MTCW 1

Coffey, Brian
See Koontz, Dean R(ay)

Cohan, George M(ichael) 1878-1942**TCLC 60**
See also CA 157

Cohen, Arthur A(llen) 1928-1986   **CLC 7, 31**
See also CA 1-4R; 120; CANR 1, 17, 42; DLB 28

Cohen, Leonard (Norman) 1934- **CLC 3, 38; DAC; DAM MST**
See also CA 21-24R; CANR 14, 69; DLB 53; MTCW 1

Cohen, Matt 1942-   **CLC 19; DAC**
See also CA 61-64; CAAS 18; CANR 40; DLB 53

Cohen-Solal, Annie 19(?)-   **CLC 50**

Colegate, Isabel 1931-   **CLC 36**
See also CA 17-20R; CANR 8, 22, 74; DLB 14; INT CANR-22; MTCW 1

Coleman, Emmett
See Reed, Ishmael

Coleridge, M. E.
See Coleridge, Mary E(lizabeth)

Coleridge, Mary E(lizabeth) 1861-1907**TCLC 73**
See also CA 116; 166; DLB 19, 98

Coleridge, Samuel Taylor 1772-1834**NCLC 9, 54; DA; DAB; DAC; DAM MST, POET; PC 11; WLC**
See also CDBLB 1789-1832; DLB 93, 107

Coleridge, Sara 1802-1852   **NCLC 31**
See also DLB 199

Coles, Don 1928-   **CLC 46**
See also CA 115; CANR 38

Coles, Robert (Martin) 1929-   **CLC 108**
See also CA 45-48; CANR 3, 32, 66, 70; INT CANR-32; SATA 23

Colette, (Sidonie-Gabrielle) 1873-1954**TCLC 1, 5, 16; DAM NOV; SSC 10**
See also CA 104; 131; DLB 65; MTCW 1

Collett, (Jacobine) Camilla (Wergeland) 1813-1895   **NCLC 22**

Collier, Christopher 1930-   **CLC 30**
See also AAYA 13; CA 33-36R; CANR 13, 33; JRDA; MAICYA; SATA 16, 70

Collier, James L(incoln) 1928-**CLC 30; DAM POP**
See also AAYA 13; CA 9-12R; CANR 4, 33, 60; CLR 3; JRDA; MAICYA; SAAS 21; SATA 8, 70

Collier, Jeremy 1650-1726   **LC 6**

Collier, John 1901-1980   **SSC 19**
See also CA 65-68; 97-100; CANR 10; DLB 77

Collingwood, R(obin) G(eorge) 1889(?)-1943 **TCLC 67**
See also CA 117; 155

Collins, Hunt
See Hunter, Evan

Collins, Linda 1931-   **CLC 44**
See also CA 125

Collins, (William) Wilkie 1824-1889**NCLC 1, 18**
See also CDBLB 1832-1890; DLB 18, 70, 159

Collins, William 1721-1759   **LC 4, 40; DAM POET**
See also DLB 109

Collodi, Carlo 1826-1890   **NCLC 54**
See also Lorenzini, Carlo
See also CLR 5

Colman, George 1732-1794
See Glassco, John

Colt, Winchester Remington
See Hubbard, L(afayette) Ron(ald)

Colter, Cyrus 1910-   **CLC 58**
See also BW 1; CA 65-68; CANR 10, 66; DLB 33

Colton, James
See Hansen, Joseph

Colum, Padraic 1881-1972   **CLC 28**
See also CA 73-76; 33-36R; CANR 35; CLR 36; MAICYA; MTCW 1; SATA 15

Colvin, James
See Moorcock, Michael (John)

Colwin, Laurie (E.) 1944-1992**CLC 5, 13, 23, 84**
See also CA 89-92; 139; CANR 20, 46; DLBY 80; MTCW 1

Comfort, Alex(ander) 1920-**CLC 7; DAM POP**
See also CA 1-4R; CANR 1, 45

Comfort, Montgomery
See Campbell, (John) Ramsey

Compton-Burnett, I(vy) 1884(?)-1969**CLC 1, 3, 10, 15, 34; DAM NOV**
See also CA 1-4R; 25-28R; CANR 4; DLB 36; MTCW 1

Comstock, Anthony 1844-1915   **TCLC 13**
See also CA 110; 169

Comte, Auguste 1798-1857   **NCLC 54**

Conan Doyle, Arthur
See Doyle, Arthur Conan

Conde, Maryse 1937-   **CLC 52, 92; BLCS; DAM MULT**
See also Boucolon, Maryse
See also BW 2

Condillac, Etienne Bonnot de 1714-1780 **LC 26**

Condon, Richard (Thomas) 1915-1996**CLC 4, 6, 8, 10, 45, 100; DAM NOV**
See also BEST 90:3; CA 1-4R; 151; CAAS 1; CANR 2, 23; INT CANR-23; MTCW 1

Confucius 551B.C.-479B.C.   **CMLC 19; DA; DAB; DAC; DAM MST; WLCS**

Congreve, William 1670-1729 **LC 5, 21; DA; DAB; DAC; DAM DRAM, MST, POET; DC 2; WLC**
See also CDBLB 1660-1789; DLB 39, 84

Connell, Evan S(helby), Jr. 1924-**CLC 4, 6, 45; DAM NOV**
See also AAYA 7; CA 1-4R; CAAS 2; CANR 2, 39; DLB 2; DLBY 81; MTCW 1

Connelly, Marc(us Cook) 1890-1980   **CLC 7**
See also CA 85-88; 102; CANR 30; DLB 7; DLBY 80; SATA-Obit 25

Connor, Ralph   **TCLC 31**
See also Gordon, Charles William
See also DLB 92

Conrad, Joseph 1857-1924**TCLC 1, 6, 13, 25, 43, 57; DA; DAB; DAC; DAM MST, NOV; SSC 9; WLC**
See also AAYA 26; CA 104; 131; CANR 60; CDBLB 1890-1914; DLB 10, 34, 98, 156; MTCW 1; SATA 27

Conrad, Robert Arnold
See Hart, Moss

Conroy, Pat
See Conroy, (Donald) Pat(rick)

Conroy, (Donald) Pat(rick) 1945-**CLC 30, 74; DAM NOV, POP**
See also AAYA 8; AITN 1; CA 85-88; CANR 24, 53; DLB 6; MTCW 1

Constant (de Rebecque), (Henri) Benjamin 1767-1830   **NCLC 6**
See also DLB 119

Conybeare, Charles Augustus

See Eliot, T(homas) S(tearns)
Cook, Michael 1933-   **CLC 58**
See also CA 93-96; CANR 68; DLB 53
Cook, Robin 1940-   **CLC 14; DAM POP**
See also BEST 90:2; CA 108; 111; CANR 41;
INT 111
Cook, Roy
See Silverberg, Robert
Cooke, Elizabeth 1948-   **CLC 55**
See also CA 129
Cooke, John Esten 1830-1886   **NCLC 5**
See also DLB 3
Cooke, John Estes
See Baum, L(yman) Frank
Cooke, M. E.
See Creasey, John
Cooke, Margaret
See Creasey, John
Cook-Lynn, Elizabeth 1930- **CLC 93; DAM
MULT**
See also CA 133; DLB 175; NNAL
Cooney, Ray   **CLC 62**
Cooper, Douglas 1960-   **CLC 86**
Cooper, Henry St. John
See Creasey, John
Cooper, J(oan) California   **CLC 56; DAM
MULT**
See also AAYA 12; BW 1; CA 125; CANR 55
Cooper, James Fenimore 1789-1851 **NCLC 1,
27, 54**
See also AAYA 22; CDALB 1640-1865; DLB
3; SATA 19
Coover, Robert (Lowell) 1932- **CLC 3, 7, 15,
32, 46, 87; DAM NOV; SSC 15**
See also CA 45-48; CANR 3, 37, 58; DLB 2;
DLBY 81; MTCW 1
Copeland, Stewart (Armstrong) 1952- **CLC 26**
Copernicus, Nicolaus 1473-1543   **LC 45**
Coppard, A(lfred) E(dgar) 1878-1957 **T C L C
5; SSC 21**
See also CA 114; 167; DLB 162; YABC 1
Coppee, Francois 1842-1908   **TCLC 25**
See also CA 170
Coppola, Francis Ford 1939-   **CLC 16**
See also CA 77-80; CANR 40; DLB 44
Corbiere, Tristan 1845-1875   **NCLC 43**
Corcoran, Barbara 1911-   **CLC 17**
See also AAYA 14; CA 21-24R; CAAS 2;
CANR 11, 28, 48; CLR 50; DLB 52; JRDA;
SAAS 20; SATA 3, 77
Cordelier, Maurice
See Giraudoux, (Hippolyte) Jean
Corelli, Marie 1855-1924   **TCLC 51**
See also Mackay, Mary
See also DLB 34, 156
Corman, Cid 1924-   **CLC 9**
See also Corman, Sidney
See also CAAS 2; DLB 5, 193
Corman, Sidney 1924-
See Corman, Cid
See also CA 85-88; CANR 44; DAM POET
Cormier, Robert (Edmund) 1925- **CLC 12, 30;
DA; DAB; DAC; DAM MST, NOV**
See also AAYA 3, 19; CA 1-4R; CANR 5, 23;
CDALB 1968-1988; CLR 12, 55; DLB 52;
INT CANR-23; JRDA; MAICYA; MTCW 1;
SATA 10, 45, 83
Corn, Alfred (DeWitt III) 1943-   **CLC 33**
See also CA 104; CAAS 25; CANR 44; DLB
120; DLBY 80
Corneille, Pierre 1606-1684   **LC 28; DAB;
DAM MST**
Cornwell, David (John Moore) 1931- **CLC 9,
15; DAM POP**
See also le Carre, John
See also CA 5-8R; CANR 13, 33, 59; MTCW 1
Corso, (Nunzio) Gregory 1930-   **CLC 1, 11**
See also CA 5-8R; CANR 41; DLB 5, 16;
MTCW 1
Cortazar, Julio 1914-1984 **CLC 2, 3, 5, 10, 13,
15, 33, 34, 92; DAM MULT, NOV; HLC;
SSC 7**
See also CA 21-24R; CANR 12, 32; DLB 113;
HW; MTCW 1
CORTES, HERNAN 1484-1547   **LC 31**
Corvinus, Jakob
See Raabe, Wilhelm (Karl)
Corwin, Cecil
See Kornbluth, C(yril) M.
Cosic, Dobrica 1921-   **CLC 14**
See also CA 122; 138; DLB 181
Costain, Thomas B(ertram) 1885-1965 **C L C
30**
See also CA 5-8R; 25-28R; DLB 9
Costantini, Humberto 1924(?)-1987   **CLC 49**
See also CA 131; 122; HW
Costello, Elvis 1955-   **CLC 21**
Cotes, Cecil V.
See Duncan, Sara Jeannette
Cotter, Joseph Seamon Sr. 1861-1949 **T C L C
28; BLC 1; DAM MULT**
See also BW 1; CA 124; DLB 50
Couch, Arthur Thomas Quiller
See Quiller-Couch, Sir Arthur (Thomas)
Coulton, James
See Hansen, Joseph
Couperus, Louis (Marie Anne) 1863-1923
TCLC 15
See also CA 115
Coupland, Douglas 1961- **CLC 85; DAC; DAM
POP**
See also CA 142; CANR 57
Court, Wesli
See Turco, Lewis (Putnam)
Courtenay, Bryce 1933-   **CLC 59**
See also CA 138
Courtney, Robert
See Ellison, Harlan (Jay)
Cousteau, Jacques-Yves 1910-1997   **CLC 30**
See also CA 65-68; 159; CANR 15, 67; MTCW
1; SATA 38, 98
Coventry, Francis 1725-1754   **LC 46**
Cowan, Peter (Walkinshaw) 1914-   **SSC 28**
See also CA 21-24R; CANR 9, 25, 50
Coward, Noel (Peirce) 1899-1973 **CLC 1, 9, 29,
51; DAM DRAM**
See also AITN 1; CA 17-18; 41-44R; CANR
35; CAP 2; CDBLB 1914-1945; DLB 10;
MTCW 1
Cowley, Abraham 1618-1667   **LC 43**
See also DLB 131, 151
Cowley, Malcolm 1898-1989   **CLC 39**
See also CA 5-8R; 128; CANR 3, 55; DLB 4,
48; DLBY 81, 89; MTCW 1
Cowper, William 1731-1800   **NCLC 8; DAM
POET**
See also DLB 104, 109
Cox, William Trevor 1928-   **CLC 9, 14, 71;
DAM NOV**
See also Trevor, William
See also CA 9-12R; CANR 4, 37, 55; DLB 14;
INT CANR-37; MTCW 1
Coyne, P. J.
See Masters, Hilary
Cozzens, James Gould 1903-1978 **CLC 1, 4, 11,
92**
See also CA 9-12R; 81-84; CANR 19; CDALB
1941-1968; DLB 9; DLBD 2; DLBY 84, 97;
MTCW 1
Crabbe, George 1754-1832   **NCLC 26**
See also DLB 93
Craddock, Charles Egbert
See Murfree, Mary Noailles
Craig, A. A.
See Anderson, Poul (William)
Craik, Dinah Maria (Mulock) 1826-1887
NCLC 38
See also DLB 35, 163; MAICYA; SATA 34
Cram, Ralph Adams 1863-1942   **TCLC 45**
See also CA 160
Crane, (Harold) Hart 1899-1932 **TCLC 2, 5,
80; DA; DAB; DAC; DAM MST, POET;
PC 3; WLC**
See also CA 104; 127; CDALB 1917-1929;
DLB 4, 48; MTCW 1
Crane, R(onald) S(almon) 1886-1967 **CLC 27**
See also CA 85-88; DLB 63
Crane, Stephen (Townley) 1871-1900 **T C L C
11, 17, 32; DA; DAB; DAC; DAM MST,
NOV, POET; SSC 7; WLC**
See also AAYA 21; CA 109; 140; CDALB 1865-
1917; DLB 12, 54, 78; YABC 2
Cranshaw, Stanley
See Fisher, Dorothy (Frances) Canfield
Crase, Douglas 1944-   **CLC 58**
See also CA 106
Crashaw, Richard 1612(?)-1649   **LC 24**
See also DLB 126
Craven, Margaret 1901-1980   **CLC 17; DAC**
See also CA 103
Crawford, F(rancis) Marion 1854-1909 **TCLC
10**
See also CA 107; 168; DLB 71
Crawford, Isabella Valancy 1850-1887 **N C L C
12**
See also DLB 92
Crayon, Geoffrey
See Irving, Washington
Creasey, John 1908-1973   **CLC 11**
See also CA 5-8R; 41-44R; CANR 8, 59; DLB
77; MTCW 1
Crebillon, Claude Prosper Jolyot de (fils) 1707-
1777   **LC 1, 28**
Credo
See Creasey, John
Credo, Alvaro J. de
See Prado (Calvo), Pedro
Creeley, Robert (White) 1926- **CLC 1, 2, 4, 8,
11, 15, 36, 78; DAM POET**
See also CA 1-4R; CAAS 10; CANR 23, 43;
DLB 5, 16, 169; DLBD 17; MTCW 1
Crews, Harry (Eugene) 1935-   **CLC 6, 23, 49**
See also AITN 1; CA 25-28R; CANR 20, 57;
DLB 6, 143, 185; MTCW 1
Crichton, (John) Michael 1942- **CLC 2, 6, 54,
90; DAM NOV, POP**
See also AAYA 10; AITN 2; CA 25-28R; CANR
13, 40, 54; DLBY 81; INT CANR-13; JRDA;
MTCW 1; SATA 9, 88
Crispin, Edmund   **CLC 22**
See also Montgomery, (Robert) Bruce
See also DLB 87
Cristofer, Michael 1945(?)-   **CLC 28; DAM
DRAM**
See also CA 110; 152; DLB 7
Croce, Benedetto 1866-1952   **TCLC 37**
See also CA 120; 155
Crockett, David 1786-1836   **NCLC 8**
See also DLB 3, 11

Crockett, Davy
See Crockett, David
Crofts, Freeman Wills 1879-1957   **TCLC 55**
See also CA 115; DLB 77
Croker, John Wilson 1780-1857   **NCLC 10**
See also DLB 110
Crommelynck, Fernand 1885-1970   **CLC 75**
See also CA 89-92
Cromwell, Oliver 1599-1658   **LC 43**
Cronin, A(rchibald) J(oseph) 1896-1981**C L C**
32
See also CA 1-4R; 102; CANR 5; DLB 191;
SATA 47; SATA-Obit 25
Cross, Amanda
See Heilbrun, Carolyn G(old)
Crothers, Rachel 1878(?)-1958   **TCLC 19**
See also CA 113; DLB 7
Croves, Hal
See Traven, B.
Crow Dog, Mary (Ellen) (?)-   **CLC 93**
See also Brave Bird, Mary
See also CA 154
Crowfield, Christopher
See Stowe, Harriet (Elizabeth) Beecher
Crowley, Aleister   **TCLC 7**
See also Crowley, Edward Alexander
Crowley, Edward Alexander 1875-1947
See Crowley, Aleister
See also CA 104
Crowley, John 1942-   **CLC 57**
See also CA 61-64; CANR 43; DLBY 82; SATA
65
Crud
See Crumb, R(obert)
Crumarums
See Crumb, R(obert)
Crumb, R(obert) 1943-   **CLC 17**
See also CA 106
Crumbum
See Crumb, R(obert)
Crumski
See Crumb, R(obert)
Crum the Bum
See Crumb, R(obert)
Crunk
See Crumb, R(obert)
Crustt
See Crumb, R(obert)
Cryer, Gretchen (Kiger) 1935-   **CLC 21**
See also CA 114; 123
Csath, Geza 1887-1919   **TCLC 13**
See also CA 111
Cudlip, David 1933-   **CLC 34**
Cullen, Countee 1903-1946**TCLC 4, 37; BLC**
1; DA; DAC; DAM MST, MULT, POET;
PC 20; WLCS
See also BW 1; CA 108; 124; CDALB 1917-
1929; DLB 4, 48, 51; MTCW 1; SATA 18
Cum, R.
See Crumb, R(obert)
Cummings, Bruce F(rederick) 1889-1919
See Barbellion, W. N. P.
See also CA 123
Cummings, E(dward) E(stlin) 1894-1962**CLC**
1, 3, 8, 12, 15, 68; DA; DAB; DAC; DAM
MST, POET; PC 5; WLC
See also CA 73-76; CANR 31; CDALB 1929-
1941; DLB 4, 48; MTCW 1
Cunha, Euclides (Rodrigues Pimenta) da 1866-
1909   **TCLC 24**
See also CA 123
Cunningham, E. V.
See Fast, Howard (Melvin)

Cunningham, J(ames) V(incent) 1911-1985
CLC 3, 31
See also CA 1-4R; 115; CANR 1, 72; DLB 5
Cunningham, Julia (Woolfolk) 1916- **CLC 12**
See also CA 9-12R; CANR 4, 19, 36; JRDA;
MAICYA; SAAS 2; SATA 1, 26
Cunningham, Michael 1952-   **CLC 34**
See also CA 136
Cunninghame Graham, R(obert) B(ontine)
1852-1936   **TCLC 19**
See also Graham, R(obert) B(ontine)
Cunninghame
See also CA 119; DLB 98
Currie, Ellen 19(?)-   **CLC 44**
Curtin, Philip
See Lowndes, Marie Adelaide (Belloc)
Curtis, Price
See Ellison, Harlan (Jay)
Cutrate, Joe
See Spiegelman, Art
Cynewulf c. 770-c. 840   **CMLC 23**
Czaczkes, Shmuel Yosef
See Agnon, S(hmuel) Y(osef Halevi)
Dabrowska, Maria (Szumska) 1889-1965**CLC**
15
See also CA 106
Dabydeen, David 1955-   **CLC 34**
See also BW 1; CA 125; CANR 56
Dacey, Philip 1939-   **CLC 51**
See also CA 37-40R; CAAS 17; CANR 14, 32,
64; DLB 105
Dagerman, Stig (Halvard) 1923-1954 **T C L C**
17
See also CA 117; 155
Dahl, Roald 1916-1990**CLC 1, 6, 18, 79; DAB;**
DAC; DAM MST, NOV, POP
See also AAYA 15; CA 1-4R; 133; CANR 6,
32, 37, 62; CLR 1, 7, 41; DLB 139; JRDA;
MAICYA; MTCW 1; SATA 1, 26, 73; SATA-
Obit 65
Dahlberg, Edward 1900-1977   **CLC 1, 7, 14**
See also CA 9-12R; 69-72; CANR 31, 62; DLB
48; MTCW 1
Daitch, Susan 1954-   **CLC 103**
See also CA 161
Dale, Colin   **TCLC 18**
See also Lawrence, T(homas) E(dward)
Dale, George E.
See Asimov, Isaac
Daly, Elizabeth 1878-1967   **CLC 52**
See also CA 23-24; 25-28R; CANR 60; CAP 2
Daly, Maureen 1921-   **CLC 17**
See also AAYA 5; CANR 37; JRDA; MAICYA;
SAAS 1; SATA 2
Damas, Leon-Gontran 1912-1978   **CLC 84**
See also BW 1; CA 125; 73-76
Dana, Richard Henry Sr. 1787-1879**NCLC 53**
Daniel, Samuel 1562(?)-1619   **LC 24**
See also DLB 62
Daniels, Brett
See Adler, Renata
Dannay, Frederic 1905-1982   **CLC 11; DAM**
POP
See also Queen, Ellery
See also CA 1-4R; 107; CANR 1, 39; DLB 137;
MTCW 1
D'Annunzio, Gabriele 1863-1938**TCLC 6, 40**
See also CA 104; 155
Danois, N. le
See Gourmont, Remy (-Marie-Charles) de
Dante 1265-1321   **CMLC 3, 18; DA; DAB;**
DAC; DAM MST, POET; PC 21; WLCS
d'Antibes, Germain

See Simenon, Georges (Jacques Christian)
Danticat, Edwidge 1969-   **CLC 94**
See also CA 152; CANR 73
Danvers, Dennis 1947-   **CLC 70**
Danziger, Paula 1944-   **CLC 21**
See also AAYA 4; CA 112; 115; CANR 37; CLR
20; JRDA; MAICYA; SATA 36, 63, 102;
SATA-Brief 30
Da Ponte, Lorenzo 1749-1838   **NCLC 50**
Dario, Ruben 1867-1916   **TCLC 4; DAM**
MULT; HLC; PC 15
See also CA 131; HW; MTCW 1
Darley, George 1795-1846   **NCLC 2**
See also DLB 96
Darrow, Clarence (Seward) 1857-1938**T C L C**
81
See also CA 164
Darwin, Charles 1809-1882   **NCLC 57**
See also DLB 57, 166
Daryush, Elizabeth 1887-1977   **CLC 6, 19**
See also CA 49-52; CANR 3; DLB 20
Dasgupta, Surendranath 1887-1952**TCLC 81**
See also CA 157
Dashwood, Edmee Elizabeth Monica de la Pas-
ture 1890-1943
See Delafield, E. M.
See also CA 119; 154
Daudet, (Louis Marie) Alphonse 1840-1897
NCLC 1
See also DLB 123
Daumal, Rene 1908-1944   **TCLC 14**
See also CA 114
Davenant, William 1606-1668   **LC 13**
See also DLB 58, 126
Davenport, Guy (Mattison, Jr.) 1927-**CLC 6,**
14, 38; SSC 16
See also CA 33-36R; CANR 23, 73; DLB 130
Davidson, Avram 1923-1993
See Queen, Ellery
See also CA 101; 171; CANR 26; DLB 8
Davidson, Donald (Grady) 1893-1968**CLC 2,**
13, 19
See also CA 5-8R; 25-28R; CANR 4; DLB 45
Davidson, Hugh
See Hamilton, Edmond
Davidson, John 1857-1909   **TCLC 24**
See also CA 118; DLB 19
Davidson, Sara 1943-   **CLC 9**
See also CA 81-84; CANR 44, 68; DLB 185
Davie, Donald (Alfred) 1922-1995 **CLC 5, 8,**
10, 31
See also CA 1-4R; 149; CAAS 3; CANR 1, 44;
DLB 27; MTCW 1
Davies, Ray(mond Douglas) 1944-   **CLC 21**
See also CA 116; 146
Davies, Rhys 1901-1978   **CLC 23**
See also CA 9-12R; 81-84; CANR 4; DLB 139,
191
Davies, (William) Robertson 1913-1995 **C L C**
2, 7, 13, 25, 42, 75, 91; DA; DAB; DAC;
DAM MST, NOV, POP; WLC
See also BEST 89:2; CA 33-36R; 150; CANR
17, 42; DLB 68; INT CANR-17; MTCW 1
Davies, W(illiam) H(enry) 1871-1940**TCLC 5**
See also CA 104; DLB 19, 174
Davies, Walter C.
See Kornbluth, C(yril) M.
Davis, Angela (Yvonne) 1944- **CLC 77; DAM**
MULT
See also BW 2; CA 57-60; CANR 10
Davis, B. Lynch
See Bioy Casares, Adolfo; Borges, Jorge Luis
Davis, Harold Lenoir 1894-1960   **CLC 49**

See also CA 89-92; DLB 9, 206

Davis, Rebecca (Blaine) Harding 1831-1910
TCLC 6
See also CA 104; DLB 74

Davis, Richard Harding 1864-1916 **TCLC 24**
See also CA 114; DLB 12, 23, 78, 79, 189;
DLBD 13

Davison, Frank Dalby 1893-1970 **CLC 15**
See also CA 116

Davison, Lawrence H.
See Lawrence, D(avid) H(erbert Richards)

Davison, Peter (Hubert) 1928- **CLC 28**
See also CA 9-12R; CAAS 4; CANR 3, 43; DLB
5

Davys, Mary 1674-1732 **LC 1, 46**
See also DLB 39

Dawson, Fielding 1930- **CLC 6**
See also CA 85-88; DLB 130

Dawson, Peter
See Faust, Frederick (Schiller)

Day, Clarence (Shepard, Jr.) 1874-1935
TCLC 25
See also CA 108; DLB 11

Day, Thomas 1748-1789 **LC 1**
See also DLB 39; YABC 1

Day Lewis, C(ecil) 1904-1972 **CLC 1, 6, 10;
DAM POET; PC 11**
See also Blake, Nicholas
See also CA 13-16; 33-36R; CANR 34; CAP 1;
DLB 15, 20; MTCW 1

Dazai Osamu 1909-1948 **TCLC 11**
See also Tsushima, Shuji
See also CA 164; DLB 182

de Andrade, Carlos Drummond
See Drummond de Andrade, Carlos

Deane, Norman
See Creasey, John

**de Beauvoir, Simone (Lucie Ernestine Marie
Bertrand)**
See Beauvoir, Simone (Lucie Ernestine Marie
Bertrand) de

de Beer, P.
See Bosman, Herman Charles

de Brissac, Malcolm
See Dickinson, Peter (Malcolm)

de Chardin, Pierre Teilhard
See Teilhard de Chardin, (Marie Joseph) Pierre

Dee, John 1527-1608 **LC 20**

Deer, Sandra 1940- **CLC 45**

De Ferrari, Gabriella 1941- **CLC 65**
See also CA 146

Defoe, Daniel 1660(?)-1731 **LC 1, 42; DA;
DAB; DAC; DAM MST, NOV; WLC**
See also AAYA 27; CDBLB 1660-1789; DLB
39, 95, 101; JRDA; MAICYA; SATA 22

de Gourmont, Remy(-Marie-Charles)
See Gourmont, Remy (-Marie-Charles) de

de Hartog, Jan 1914- **CLC 19**
See also CA 1-4R; CANR 1

de Hostos, E. M.
See Hostos (y Bonilla), Eugenio Maria de

de Hostos, Eugenio M.
See Hostos (y Bonilla), Eugenio Maria de

Deighton, Len **CLC 4, 7, 22, 46**
See also Deighton, Leonard Cyril
See also AAYA 6; BEST 89:2; CDBLB 1960 to
Present; DLB 87

Deighton, Leonard Cyril 1929-
See Deighton, Len
See also CA 9-12R; CANR 19, 33, 68; DAM
NOV, POP; MTCW 1

Dekker, Thomas 1572(?)-1632 **LC 22; DAM
DRAM**

See also CDBLB Before 1660; DLB 62, 172

Delafield, E. M. 1890-1943 **TCLC 61**
See also Dashwood, Edmee Elizabeth Monica
de la Pasture
See also DLB 34

de la Mare, Walter (John) 1873-1956 **TCLC 4,
53; DAB; DAC; DAM MST, POET; SSC
14; WLC**
See also CA 163; CDBLB 1914-1945; CLR 23;
DLB 162; SATA 16

Delaney, Franey
See O'Hara, John (Henry)

Delaney, Shelagh 1939- **CLC 29; DAM DRAM**
See also CA 17-20R; CANR 30, 67; CDBLB
1960 to Present; DLB 13; MTCW 1

Delany, Mary (Granville Pendarves) 1700-1788
LC 12

Delany, Samuel R(ay, Jr.) 1942- **CLC 8, 14, 38;
BLC 1; DAM MULT**
See also AAYA 24; BW 2; CA 81-84; CANR
27, 43; DLB 8, 33; MTCW 1

De La Ramee, (Marie) Louise 1839-1908
See Ouida
See also SATA 20

de la Roche, Mazo 1879-1961 **CLC 14**
See also CA 85-88; CANR 30; DLB 68; SATA
64

De La Salle, Innocent
See Hartmann, Sadakichi

Delbanco, Nicholas (Franklin) 1942- **CLC 6,
13**
See also CA 17-20R; CAAS 2; CANR 29, 55;
DLB 6

del Castillo, Michel 1933- **CLC 38**
See also CA 109

Deledda, Grazia (Cosima) 1875(?)-1936
TCLC 23
See also CA 123

Delibes, Miguel **CLC 8, 18**
See also Delibes Setien, Miguel

Delibes Setien, Miguel 1920-
See Delibes, Miguel
See also CA 45-48; CANR 1, 32; HW; MTCW
1

DeLillo, Don 1936- **CLC 8, 10, 13, 27, 39, 54,
76; DAM NOV, POP**
See also BEST 89:1; CA 81-84; CANR 21; DLB
6, 173; MTCW 1

de Lisser, H. G.
See De Lisser, H(erbert) G(eorge)
See also DLB 117

De Lisser, H(erbert) G(eorge) 1878-1944
TCLC 12
See also de Lisser, H. G.
See also BW 2; CA 109; 152

Deloney, Thomas 1560(?)-1600 **LC 41**
See also DLB 167

Deloria, Vine (Victor), Jr. 1933- **CLC 21;
DAM MULT**
See also CA 53-56; CANR 5, 20, 48; DLB 175;
MTCW 1; NNAL; SATA 21

Del Vecchio, John M(ichael) 1947- **CLC 29**
See also CA 110; DLBD 9

de Man, Paul (Adolph Michel) 1919-1983
CLC 55
See also CA 128; 111; CANR 61; DLB 67;
MTCW 1

De Marinis, Rick 1934- **CLC 54**
See also CA 57-60; CAAS 24; CANR 9, 25, 50

Dembry, R. Emmet
See Murfree, Mary Noailles

Demby, William 1922- **CLC 53; BLC 1; DAM
MULT**

See also BW 1; CA 81-84; DLB 33

de Menton, Francisco
See Chin, Frank (Chew, Jr.)

Demijohn, Thom
See Disch, Thomas M(ichael)

de Montherlant, Henry (Milon)
See Montherlant, Henry (Milon) de

Demosthenes 384B.C.-322B.C. **CMLC 13**
See also DLB 176

de Natale, Francine
See Malzberg, Barry N(athaniel)

Denby, Edwin (Orr) 1903-1983 **CLC 48**
See also CA 138; 110

Denis, Julio
See Cortazar, Julio

Denmark, Harrison
See Zelazny, Roger (Joseph)

Dennis, John 1658-1734 **LC 11**
See also DLB 101

Dennis, Nigel (Forbes) 1912-1989 **CLC 8**
See also CA 25-28R; 129; DLB 13, 15; MTCW
1

Dent, Lester 1904(?)-1959 **TCLC 72**
See also CA 112; 161

De Palma, Brian (Russell) 1940- **CLC 20**
See also CA 109

De Quincey, Thomas 1785-1859 **NCLC 4**
See also CDBLB 1789-1832; DLB 110; 144

Deren, Eleanora 1908(?)-1961
See Deren, Maya
See also CA 111

Deren, Maya 1917-1961 **CLC 16, 102**
See also Deren, Eleanora

Derleth, August (William) 1909-1971 **CLC 31**
See also CA 1-4R; 29-32R; CANR 4; DLB 9;
DLBD 17; SATA 5

Der Nister 1884-1950 **TCLC 56**

de Routisie, Albert
See Aragon, Louis

Derrida, Jacques 1930- **CLC 24, 87**
See also CA 124; 127

Derry Down Derry
See Lear, Edward

Dersonnes, Jacques
See Simenon, Georges (Jacques Christian)

Desai, Anita 1937- **CLC 19, 37, 97; DAB; DAM
NOV**
See also CA 81-84; CANR 33, 53; MTCW 1;
SATA 63

de Saint-Luc, Jean
See Glassco, John

de Saint Roman, Arnaud
See Aragon, Louis

Descartes, Rene 1596-1650 **LC 20, 35**

De Sica, Vittorio 1901(?)-1974 **CLC 20**
See also CA 117

Desnos, Robert 1900-1945 **TCLC 22**
See also CA 121; 151

Destouches, Louis-Ferdinand 1894-1961 **CLC
9, 15**
See also Celine, Louis-Ferdinand
See also CA 85-88; CANR 28; MTCW 1

de Tolignac, Gaston
See Griffith, D(avid Lewelyn) W(ark)

Deutsch, Babette 1895-1982 **CLC 18**
See also CA 1-4R; 108; CANR 4; DLB 45;
SATA 1; SATA-Obit 33

Devenant, William 1606-1649 **LC 13**

Devkota, Laxmiprasad 1909-1959 **TCLC 23**
See also CA 123

De Voto, Bernard (Augustine) 1897-1955
TCLC 29
See also CA 113; 160; DLB 9

De Vries, Peter 1910-1993 **CLC 1, 2, 3, 7, 10, 28, 46; DAM NOV**
See also CA 17-20R; 142; CANR 41; DLB 6; DLBY 82; MTCW 1
Dexter, John
See Bradley, Marion Zimmer
Dexter, Martin
See Faust, Frederick (Schiller)
Dexter, Pete 1943- **CLC 34, 55; DAM POP**
See also BEST 89:2; CA 127; 131; INT 131; MTCW 1
Diamano, Silmang
See Senghor, Leopold Sedar
Diamond, Neil 1941- **CLC 30**
See also CA 108
Diaz del Castillo, Bernal 1496-1584 **LC 31**
di Bassetto, Corno
See Shaw, George Bernard
Dick, Philip K(indred) 1928-1982 **CLC 10, 30, 72; DAM NOV, POP**
See also AAYA 24; CA 49-52; 106; CANR 2, 16; DLB 8; MTCW 1
Dickens, Charles (John Huffam) 1812-1870 **NCLC 3, 8, 18, 26, 37, 50; DA; DAB; DAC; DAM MST, NOV; SSC 17; WLC**
See also AAYA 23; CDBLB 1832-1890; DLB 21, 55, 70, 159, 166; JRDA; MAICYA; SATA 15
Dickey, James (Lafayette) 1923-1997 **CLC 1, 2, 4, 7, 10, 15, 47, 109; DAM NOV, POET, POP**
See also AITN 1, 2; CA 9-12R; 156; CABS 2; CANR 10, 48, 61; CDALB 1968-1988; DLB 5, 193; DLBD 7; DLBY 82, 93, 96, 97; INT CANR-10; MTCW 1
Dickey, William 1928-1994 **CLC 3, 28**
See also CA 9-12R; 145; CANR 24; DLB 5
Dickinson, Charles 1951- **CLC 49**
See also CA 128
Dickinson, Emily (Elizabeth) 1830-1886 **NCLC 21; DA; DAB; DAC; DAM MST, POET; PC 1; WLC**
See also AAYA 22; CDALB 1865-1917; DLB 1; SATA 29
Dickinson, Peter (Malcolm) 1927- **CLC 12, 35**
See also AAYA 9; CA 41-44R; CANR 31, 58; CLR 29; DLB 87, 161; JRDA; MAICYA; SATA 5, 62, 95
Dickson, Carr
See Carr, John Dickson
Dickson, Carter
See Carr, John Dickson
Diderot, Denis 1713-1784 **LC 26**
Didion, Joan 1934- **CLC 1, 3, 8, 14, 32; DAM NOV**
See also AITN 1; CA 5-8R; CANR 14, 52; CDALB 1968-1988; DLB 2, 173, 185; DLBY 81, 86; MTCW 1
Dietrich, Robert
See Hunt, E(verette) Howard, (Jr.)
Difusa, Pati
See Almodovar, Pedro
Dillard, Annie 1945- **CLC 9, 60, 115; DAM NOV**
See also AAYA 6; CA 49-52; CANR 3, 43, 62; DLBY 80; MTCW 1; SATA 10
Dillard, R(ichard) H(enry) W(ilde) 1937- **CLC 5**
See also CA 21-24R; CAAS 7; CANR 10; DLB 5
Dillon, Eilis 1920-1994 **CLC 17**
See also CA 9-12R; 147; CAAS 3; CANR 4, 38; CLR 26; MAICYA; SATA 2, 74; SATA-Obit 83

Dimont, Penelope
See Mortimer, Penelope (Ruth)
Dinesen, Isak **CLC 10, 29, 95; SSC 7**
See also Blixen, Karen (Christentze Dinesen)
Ding Ling **CLC 68**
See also Chiang, Pin-chin
Diphusa, Patty
See Almodovar, Pedro
Disch, Thomas M(ichael) 1940- **CLC 7, 36**
See also AAYA 17; CA 21-24R; CAAS 4; CANR 17, 36, 54; CLR 18; DLB 8; MAICYA; MTCW 1; SAAS 15; SATA 92
Disch, Tom
See Disch, Thomas M(ichael)
d'Isly, Georges
See Simenon, Georges (Jacques Christian)
Disraeli, Benjamin 1804-1881 **NCLC 2, 39**
See also DLB 21, 55
Ditcum, Steve
See Crumb, R(obert)
Dixon, Paige
See Corcoran, Barbara
Dixon, Stephen 1936- **CLC 52; SSC 16**
See also CA 89-92; CANR 17, 40, 54; DLB 130
Doak, Annie
See Dillard, Annie
Dobell, Sydney Thompson 1824-1874 **NCLC 43**
See also DLB 32
Doblin, Alfred **TCLC 13**
See also Doeblin, Alfred
Dobrolyubov, Nikolai Alexandrovich 1836-1861 **NCLC 5**
Dobson, Austin 1840-1921 **TCLC 79**
See also DLB 35; 144
Dobyns, Stephen 1941- **CLC 37**
See also CA 45-48; CANR 2, 18
Doctorow, E(dgar) L(aurence) 1931- **CLC 6, 11, 15, 18, 37, 44, 65, 113; DAM NOV, POP**
See also AAYA 22; AITN 2; BEST 89:3; CA 45-48; CANR 2, 33, 51; CDALB 1968-1988; DLB 2, 28, 173; DLBY 80; MTCW 1
Dodgson, Charles Lutwidge 1832-1898
See Carroll, Lewis
See also CLR 2; DA; DAB; DAC; DAM MST, NOV, POET; MAICYA; SATA 100; YABC 2
Dodson, Owen (Vincent) 1914-1983 **CLC 79; BLC 1; DAM MULT**
See also BW 1; CA 65-68; 110; CANR 24; DLB 76
Doeblin, Alfred 1878-1957 **TCLC 13**
See also Doblin, Alfred
See also CA 110; 141; DLB 66
Doerr, Harriet 1910- **CLC 34**
See also CA 117; 122; CANR 47; INT 122
Domecq, H(onorio) Bustos
See Bioy Casares, Adolfo; Borges, Jorge Luis
Domini, Rey
See Lorde, Audre (Geraldine)
Dominique
See Proust, (Valentin-Louis-George-Eugene-) Marcel
Don, A
See Stephen, SirLeslie
Donaldson, Stephen R. 1947- **CLC 46; DAM POP**
See also CA 89-92; CANR 13, 55; INT CANR-13
Donleavy, J(ames) P(atrick) 1926- **CLC 1, 4, 6, 10, 45**
See also AITN 2; CA 9-12R; CANR 24, 49, 62; DLB 6, 173; INT CANR-24; MTCW 1

Donne, John 1572-1631 **LC 10, 24; DA; DAB; DAC; DAM MST, POET; PC 1; WLC**
See also CDBLB Before 1660; DLB 121, 151
Donnell, David 1939(?)- **CLC 34**
Donoghue, P. S.
See Hunt, E(verette) Howard, (Jr.)
Donoso (Yanez), Jose 1924-1996 **CLC 4, 8, 11, 32, 99; DAM MULT; HLC**
See also CA 81-84; 155; CANR 32, 73; DLB 113; HW; MTCW 1
Donovan, John 1928-1992 **CLC 35**
See also AAYA 20; CA 97-100; 137; CLR 3; MAICYA; SATA 72; SATA-Brief 29
Don Roberto
See Cunninghame Graham, R(obert) B(ontine)
Doolittle, Hilda 1886-1961 **CLC 3, 8, 14, 31, 34, 73; DA; DAC; DAM MST, POET; PC 5; WLC**
See also H. D.
See also CA 97-100; CANR 35; DLB 4, 45; MTCW 1
Dorfman, Ariel 1942- **CLC 48, 77; DAM MULT; HLC**
See also CA 124; 130; CANR 67, 70; HW; INT 130
Dorn, Edward (Merton) 1929- **CLC 10, 18**
See also CA 93-96; CANR 42; DLB 5; INT 93-96
Dorris, Michael (Anthony) 1945-1997 **CLC 109; DAM MULT, NOV**
See also AAYA 20; BEST 90:1; CA 102; 157; CANR 19, 46, 75; DLB 175; NNAL; SATA 75; SATA-Obit 94
Dorris, Michael A.
See Dorris, Michael (Anthony)
Dorsan, Luc
See Simenon, Georges (Jacques Christian)
Dorsange, Jean
See Simenon, Georges (Jacques Christian)
Dos Passos, John (Roderigo) 1896-1970 **CLC 1, 4, 8, 11, 15, 25, 34, 82; DA; DAB; DAC; DAM MST, NOV; WLC**
See also CA 1-4R; 29-32R; CANR 3; CDALB 1929-1941; DLB 4, 9; DLBD 1, 15; DLBY 96; MTCW 1
Dossage, Jean
See Simenon, Georges (Jacques Christian)
Dostoevsky, Fedor Mikhailovich 1821-1881 **NCLC 2, 7, 21, 33, 43; DA; DAB; DAC; DAM MST, NOV; SSC 2, 33; WLC**
Doughty, Charles M(ontagu) 1843-1926 **TCLC 27**
See also CA 115; DLB 19, 57, 174
Douglas, Ellen **CLC 73**
See also Haxton, Josephine Ayres; Williamson, Ellen Douglas
Douglas, Gavin 1475(?)-1522 **LC 20**
See also DLB 132
Douglas, George
See Brown, George Douglas
Douglas, Keith (Castellain) 1920-1944 **TCLC 40**
See also CA 160; DLB 27
Douglas, Leonard
See Bradbury, Ray (Douglas)
Douglas, Michael
See Crichton, (John) Michael
Douglas, (George) Norman 1868-1952 **TCLC 68**
See also CA 119; 157; DLB 34, 195
Douglas, William
See Brown, George Douglas
Douglass, Frederick 1817(?)-1895 **NCLC 7, 55;**

BLC 1; DA; DAC; DAM MST, MULT; WLC
See also CDALB 1640-1865; DLB 1, 43, 50, 79; SATA 29

Dourado, (Waldomiro Freitas) Autran 1926-
CLC 23, 60
See also CA 25-28R; CANR 34

Dourado, Waldomiro Autran
See Dourado, (Waldomiro Freitas) Autran

Dove, Rita (Frances) 1952-**CLC 50, 81; BLCS; DAM MULT, POET; PC 6**
See also BW 2; CA 109; CAAS 19; CANR 27, 42, 68; DLB 120

Doveglion
See Villa, Jose Garcia

Dowell, Coleman 1925-1985 **CLC 60**
See also CA 25-28R; 117; CANR 10; DLB 130

Dowson, Ernest (Christopher) 1867-1900
TCLC 4
See also CA 105; 150; DLB 19, 135

Doyle, A. Conan
See Doyle, Arthur Conan

Doyle, Arthur Conan 1859-1930**TCLC 7; DA; DAB; DAC; DAM MST, NOV; SSC 12; WLC**
See also AAYA 14; CA 104; 122; CDBLB 1890-1914; DLB 18, 70, 156, 178; MTCW 1; SATA 24

Doyle, Conan
See Doyle, Arthur Conan

Doyle, John
See Graves, Robert (von Ranke)

Doyle, Roddy 1958(?)- **CLC 81**
See also AAYA 14; CA 143; CANR 73; DLB 194

Doyle, Sir A. Conan
See Doyle, Arthur Conan

Doyle, Sir Arthur Conan
See Doyle, Arthur Conan

Dr. A
See Asimov, Isaac; Silverstein, Alvin

Drabble, Margaret 1939-**CLC 2, 3, 5, 8, 10, 22, 53; DAB; DAC; DAM MST, NOV, POP**
See also CA 13-16R; CANR 18, 35, 63; CDBLB 1960 to Present; DLB 14, 155; MTCW 1; SATA 48

Drapier, M. B.
See Swift, Jonathan

Drayham, James
See Mencken, H(enry) L(ouis)

Drayton, Michael 1563-1631 **LC 8; DAM POET**
See also DLB 121

Dreadstone, Carl
See Campbell, (John) Ramsey

Dreiser, Theodore (Herman Albert) 1871-1945
TCLC 10, 18, 35, 83; DA; DAC; DAM MST, NOV; SSC 30; WLC
See also CA 106; 132; CDALB 1865-1917; DLB 9, 12, 102, 137; DLBD 1; MTCW 1

Drexler, Rosalyn 1926- **CLC 2, 6**
See also CA 81-84; CANR 68

Dreyer, Carl Theodor 1889-1968 **CLC 16**
See also CA 116

Drieu la Rochelle, Pierre(-Eugene) 1893-1945
TCLC 21
See also CA 117; DLB 72

Drinkwater, John 1882-1937 **TCLC 57**
See also CA 109; 149; DLB 10, 19, 149

Drop Shot
See Cable, George Washington

Droste-Hulshoff, Annette Freiin von 1797-1848
NCLC 3

See also DLB 133

Drummond, Walter
See Silverberg, Robert

Drummond, William Henry 1854-1907**TCLC 25**
See also CA 160; DLB 92

Drummond de Andrade, Carlos 1902-1987
CLC 18
See also Andrade, Carlos Drummond de
See also CA 132; 123

Drury, Allen (Stuart) 1918-1998 **CLC 37**
See also CA 57-60; 170; CANR 18, 52; INT CANR-18

Dryden, John 1631-1700**LC 3, 21; DA; DAB; DAC; DAM DRAM, MST, POET; DC 3; PC 25; WLC**
See also CDBLB 1660-1789; DLB 80, 101, 131

Duberman, Martin (Bauml) 1930- **CLC 8**
See also CA 1-4R; CANR 2, 63

Dubie, Norman (Evans) 1945- **CLC 36**
See also CA 69-72; CANR 12; DLB 120

Du Bois, W(illiam) E(dward) B(urghardt) 1868-1963 **CLC 1, 2, 13, 64, 96; BLC 1; DA; DAC; DAM MST, MULT, NOV; WLC**
See also BW 1; CA 85-88; CANR 34; CDALB 1865-1917; DLB 47, 50, 91; MTCW 1; SATA 42

Dubus, Andre 1936- **CLC 13, 36, 97; SSC 15**
See also CA 21-24R; CANR 17; DLB 130; INT CANR-17

Duca Minimo
See D'Annunzio, Gabriele

Ducharme, Rejean 1941- **CLC 74**
See also CA 165; DLB 60

Duclos, Charles Pinot 1704-1772 **LC 1**

Dudek, Louis 1918- **CLC 11, 19**
See also CA 45-48; CAAS 14; CANR 1; DLB 88

Duerrenmatt, Friedrich 1921-1990 **CLC 1, 4, 8, 11, 15, 43, 102; DAM DRAM**
See also CA 17-20R; CANR 33; DLB 69, 124; MTCW 1

Duffy, Bruce (?)- **CLC 50**

Duffy, Maureen 1933- **CLC 37**
See also CA 25-28R; CANR 33, 68; DLB 14; MTCW 1

Dugan, Alan 1923- **CLC 2, 6**
See also CA 81-84; DLB 5

du Gard, Roger Martin
See Martin du Gard, Roger

Duhamel, Georges 1884-1966 **CLC 8**
See also CA 81-84; 25-28R; CANR 35; DLB 65; MTCW 1

Dujardin, Edouard (Emile Louis) 1861-1949
TCLC 13
See also CA 109; DLB 123

Dulles, John Foster 1888-1959 **TCLC 72**
See also CA 115; 149

Dumas, Alexandre (pere)
See Dumas, Alexandre (Davy de la Pailleterie)

Dumas, Alexandre (Davy de la Pailleterie) 1802-1870 **NCLC 11; DA; DAB; DAC; DAM MST, NOV; WLC**
See also DLB 119, 192; SATA 18

Dumas, Alexandre (fils) 1824-1895**NCLC 71; DC 1**
See also AAYA 22; DLB 192

Dumas, Claudine
See Malzberg, Barry N(athaniel)

Dumas, Henry L. 1934-1968 **CLC 6, 62**
See also BW 1; CA 85-88; DLB 41

du Maurier, Daphne 1907-1989**CLC 6, 11, 59; DAB; DAC; DAM MST, POP; SSC 18**

See also CA 5-8R; 128; CANR 6, 55; DLB 191; MTCW 1; SATA 27; SATA-Obit 60

Dunbar, Paul Laurence 1872-1906 **TCLC 2, 12; BLC 1; DA; DAC; DAM MST, MULT, POET; PC 5; SSC 8; WLC**
See also BW 1; CA 104; 124; CDALB 1865-1917; DLB 50, 54, 78; SATA 34

Dunbar, William 1460(?)-1530(?) **LC 20**
See also DLB 132, 146

Duncan, Dora Angela
See Duncan, Isadora

Duncan, Isadora 1877(?)-1927 **TCLC 68**
See also CA 118; 149

Duncan, Lois 1934- **CLC 26**
See also AAYA 4; CA 1-4R; CANR 2, 23, 36; CLR 29; JRDA; MAICYA; SAAS 2; SATA 1, 36, 75

Duncan, Robert (Edward) 1919-1988**CLC 1, 2, 4, 7, 15, 41, 55; DAM POET; PC 2**
See also CA 9-12R; 124; CANR 28, 62; DLB 5, 16, 193; MTCW 1

Duncan, Sara Jeannette 1861-1922 **TCLC 60**
See also CA 157; DLB 92

Dunlap, William 1766-1839 **NCLC 2**
See also DLB 30, 37, 59

Dunn, Douglas (Eaglesham) 1942- **CLC 6, 40**
See also CA 45-48; CANR 2, 33; DLB 40; MTCW 1

Dunn, Katherine (Karen) 1945- **CLC 71**
See also CA 33-36R; CANR 72

Dunn, Stephen 1939- **CLC 36**
See also CA 33-36R; CANR 12, 48, 53; DLB 105

Dunne, Finley Peter 1867-1936 **TCLC 28**
See also CA 108; DLB 11, 23

Dunne, John Gregory 1932- **CLC 28**
See also CA 25-28R; CANR 14, 50; DLBY 80

Dunsany, Edward John Moreton Drax Plunkett 1878-1957
See Dunsany, Lord
See also CA 104; 148; DLB 10

Dunsany, Lord **TCLC 2, 59**
See also Dunsany, Edward John Moreton Drax Plunkett
See also DLB 77, 153, 156

du Perry, Jean
See Simenon, Georges (Jacques Christian)

Durang, Christopher (Ferdinand) 1949-**CLC 27, 38**
See also CA 105; CANR 50

Duras, Marguerite 1914-1996**CLC 3, 6, 11, 20, 34, 40, 68, 100**
See also CA 25-28R; 151; CANR 50; DLB 83; MTCW 1

Durban, (Rosa) Pam 1947- **CLC 39**
See also CA 123

Durcan, Paul 1944-**CLC 43, 70; DAM POET**
See also CA 134

Durkheim, Emile 1858-1917 **TCLC 55**

Durrell, Lawrence (George) 1912-1990 **CLC 1, 4, 6, 8, 13, 27, 41; DAM NOV**
See also CA 9-12R; 132; CANR 40; CDBLB 1945-1960; DLB 15, 27, 204; DLBY 90; MTCW 1

Durrenmatt, Friedrich
See Duerrenmatt, Friedrich

Dutt, Toru 1856-1877 **NCLC 29**

Dwight, Timothy 1752-1817 **NCLC 13**
See also DLB 37

Dworkin, Andrea 1946- **CLC 43**
See also CA 77-80; CAAS 21; CANR 16, 39; INT CANR-16; MTCW 1

Dwyer, Deanna

See Koontz, Dean R(ay)

Dwyer, K. R.
See Koontz, Dean R(ay)

Dwyer, Thomas A. 1923-   **CLC 114**
See also CA 115

Dye, Richard
See De Voto, Bernard (Augustine)

Dylan, Bob 1941-   **CLC 3, 4, 6, 12, 77**
See also CA 41-44R; DLB 16

Eagleton, Terence (Francis) 1943-
See Eagleton, Terry
See also CA 57-60; CANR 7, 23, 68; MTCW 1

Eagleton, Terry   **CLC 63**
See also Eagleton, Terence (Francis)

Early, Jack
See Scoppettone, Sandra

East, Michael
See West, Morris L(anglo)

Eastaway, Edward
See Thomas, (Philip) Edward

Eastlake, William (Derry) 1917-1997 **CLC 8**
See also CA 5-8R; 158; CAAS 1; CANR 5, 63;
DLB 6, 206; INT CANR-5

Eastman, Charles A(lexander) 1858-1939
TCLC 55; DAM MULT
See also DLB 175; NNAL; YABC 1

Eberhart, Richard (Ghormley) 1904- **CLC 3, 11, 19, 56; DAM POET**
See also CA 1-4R; CANR 2; CDALB 1941-
1968; DLB 48; MTCW 1

Eberstadt, Fernanda 1960-   **CLC 39**
See also CA 136; CANR 69

Echegaray (y Eizaguirre), Jose (Maria Waldo)
1832-1916   **TCLC 4**
See also CA 104; CANR 32; HW; MTCW 1

Echeverria, (Jose) Esteban (Antonino) 1805-
1851   **NCLC 18**

Echo
See Proust, (Valentin-Louis-George-Eugene-)
Marcel

Eckert, Allan W. 1931-   **CLC 17**
See also AAYA 18; CA 13-16R; CANR 14, 45;
INT CANR-14; SAAS 21; SATA 29, 91;
SATA-Brief 27

Eckhart, Meister 1260(?)-1328(?)   **CMLC 9**
See also DLB 115

Eckmar, F. R.
See de Hartog, Jan

Eco, Umberto 1932- **CLC 28, 60; DAM NOV, POP**
See also BEST 90:1; CA 77-80; CANR 12, 33,
55; DLB 196; MTCW 1

Eddison, E(ric) R(ucker) 1882-1945 **TCLC 15**
See also CA 109; 156

Eddy, Mary (Morse) Baker 1821-1910 **T C L C 71**
See also CA 113

Edel, (Joseph) Leon 1907-1997   **CLC 29, 34**
See also CA 1-4R; 161; CANR 1, 22; DLB 103;
INT CANR-22

Eden, Emily 1797-1869   **NCLC 10**

Edgar, David 1948-   **CLC 42; DAM DRAM**
See also CA 57-60; CANR 12, 61; DLB 13;
MTCW 1

Edgerton, Clyde (Carlyle) 1944-   **CLC 39**
See also AAYA 17; CA 118; 134; CANR 64;
INT 134

Edgeworth, Maria 1768-1849   **NCLC 1, 51**
See also DLB 116, 159, 163; SATA 21

Edmonds, Paul
See Kuttner, Henry

Edmonds, Walter D(umaux) 1903-1998 **C L C 35**

See also CA 5-8R; CANR 2; DLB 9; MAICYA;
SAAS 4; SATA 1, 27; SATA-Obit 99

Edmondson, Wallace
See Ellison, Harlan (Jay)

Edson, Russell   **CLC 13**
See also CA 33-36R

Edwards, Bronwen Elizabeth
See Rose, Wendy

Edwards, G(erald) B(asil) 1899-1976 **CLC 25**
See also CA 110

Edwards, Gus 1939-   **CLC 43**
See also CA 108; INT 108

Edwards, Jonathan 1703-1758   **LC 7; DA; DAC; DAM MST**
See also DLB 24

Efron, Marina Ivanovna Tsvetaeva
See Tsvetaeva (Efron), Marina (Ivanovna)

Ehle, John (Marsden, Jr.) 1925-   **CLC 27**
See also CA 9-12R

Ehrenbourg, Ilya (Grigoryevich)
See Ehrenburg, Ilya (Grigoryevich)

Ehrenburg, Ilya (Grigoryevich) 1891-1967
CLC 18, 34, 62
See also CA 102; 25-28R

Ehrenburg, Ilyo (Grigoryevich)
See Ehrenburg, Ilya (Grigoryevich)

Ehrenreich, Barbara 1941-   **CLC 110**
See also BEST 90:4; CA 73-76; CANR 16, 37,
62; MTCW 1

Eich, Guenter 1907-1972   **CLC 15**
See also CA 111; 93-96; DLB 69, 124

Eichendorff, Joseph Freiherr von 1788-1857
NCLC 8
See also DLB 90

Eigner, Larry   **CLC 9**
See also Eigner, Laurence (Joel)
See also CAAS 23; DLB 5

Eigner, Laurence (Joel) 1927-1996
See Eigner, Larry
See also CA 9-12R; 151; CANR 6; DLB 193

Einstein, Albert 1879-1955   **TCLC 65**
See also CA 121; 133; MTCW 1

Eiseley, Loren Corey 1907-1977   **CLC 7**
See also AAYA 5; CA 1-4R; 73-76; CANR 6;
DLBD 17

Eisenstadt, Jill 1963-   **CLC 50**
See also CA 140

Eisenstein, Sergei (Mikhailovich) 1898-1948
TCLC 57
See also CA 114; 149

Eisner, Simon
See Kornbluth, C(yril) M.

Ekeloef, (Bengt) Gunnar 1907-1968 **CLC 27; DAM POET; PC 23**
See also CA 123; 25-28R

Ekelof, (Bengt) Gunnar
See Ekeloef, (Bengt) Gunnar

Ekelund, Vilhelm 1880-1949   **TCLC 75**

Ekwensi, C. O. D.
See Ekwensi, Cyprian (Odiatu Duaka)

Ekwensi, Cyprian (Odiatu Duaka) 1921- **CLC 4; BLC 1; DAM MULT**
See also BW 2; CA 29-32R; CANR 18, 42, 74;
DLB 117; MTCW 1; SATA 66

Elaine   **TCLC 18**
See also Leverson, Ada

El Crummo
See Crumb, R(obert)

Elder, Lonne III 1931-1996   **DC 8**
See also BLC 1; BW 1; CA 81-84; 152; CANR
25; DAM MULT; DLB 7, 38, 44

Elia
See Lamb, Charles

Eliade, Mircea 1907-1986   **CLC 19**
See also CA 65-68; 119; CANR 30, 62; MTCW
1

Eliot, A. D.
See Jewett, (Theodora) Sarah Orne

Eliot, Alice
See Jewett, (Theodora) Sarah Orne

Eliot, Dan
See Silverberg, Robert

Eliot, George 1819-1880 **NCLC 4, 13, 23, 41, 49; DA; DAB; DAC; DAM MST, NOV; PC 20; WLC**
See also CDBLB 1832-1890; DLB 21, 35, 55

Eliot, John 1604-1690   **LC 5**
See also DLB 24

Eliot, T(homas) S(tearns) 1888-1965 **CLC 1, 2, 3, 6, 9, 10, 13, 15, 24, 34, 41, 55, 57, 113; DA; DAB; DAC; DAM DRAM, MST, POET; PC 5; WLC**
See also CA 5-8R; 25-28R; CANR 41; CDALB
1929-1941; DLB 7, 10, 45, 63; DLBY 88;
MTCW 1

Elizabeth 1866-1941   **TCLC 41**

Elkin, Stanley L(awrence) 1930-1995 **CLC 4, 6, 9, 14, 27, 51, 91; DAM NOV, POP; SSC 12**
See also CA 9-12R; 148; CANR 8, 46; DLB 2,
28; DLBY 80; INT CANR-8; MTCW 1

Elledge, Scott   **CLC 34**

Elliot, Don
See Silverberg, Robert

Elliott, Don
See Silverberg, Robert

Elliott, George P(aul) 1918-1980   **CLC 2**
See also CA 1-4R; 97-100; CANR 2

Elliott, Janice 1931-   **CLC 47**
See also CA 13-16R; CANR 8, 29; DLB 14

Elliott, Sumner Locke 1917-1991   **CLC 38**
See also CA 5-8R; 134; CANR 2, 21

Elliott, William
See Bradbury, Ray (Douglas)

Ellis, A. E.   **CLC 7**

Ellis, Alice Thomas   **CLC 40**
See also Haycraft, Anna
See also DLB 194

Ellis, Bret Easton 1964- **CLC 39, 71, 117; DAM POP**
See also AAYA 2; CA 118; 123; CANR 51, 74;
INT 123

Ellis, (Henry) Havelock 1859-1939 **TCLC 14**
See also CA 109; 169; DLB 190

Ellis, Landon
See Ellison, Harlan (Jay)

Ellis, Trey 1962-   **CLC 55**
See also CA 146

Ellison, Harlan (Jay) 1934-   **CLC 1, 13, 42; DAM POP; SSC 14**
See also CA 5-8R; CANR 5, 46; DLB 8; INT
CANR-5; MTCW 1

Ellison, Ralph (Waldo) 1914-1994 **CLC 1, 3, 11, 54, 86, 114; BLC 1; DA; DAB; DAC; DAM MST, MULT, NOV; SSC 26; WLC**
See also AAYA 19; BW 1; CA 9-12R; 145;
CANR 24, 53; CDALB 1941-1968; DLB 2,
76; DLBY 94; MTCW 1

Ellmann, Lucy (Elizabeth) 1956-   **CLC 61**
See also CA 128

Ellmann, Richard (David) 1918-1987 **CLC 50**
See also BEST 89:2; CA 1-4R; 122; CANR 2,
28, 61; DLB 103; DLBY 87; MTCW 1

Elman, Richard (Martin) 1934-1997 **CLC 19**
See also CA 17-20R; 163; CAAS 3; CANR 47

Elron

See Hubbard, L(afayette) Ron(ald)

Eluard, Paul   **TCLC 7, 41**
See also Grindel, Eugene

Elyot, Sir Thomas 1490(?)-1546   **LC 11**

Elytis, Odysseus 1911-1996 **CLC 15, 49, 100;
   DAM POET; PC 21**
See also CA 102; 151; MTCW 1

Emecheta, (Florence Onye) Buchi 1944-**C L C
   14, 48; BLC 2; DAM MULT**
See also BW 2; CA 81-84; CANR 27; DLB 117;
   MTCW 1; SATA 66

Emerson, Mary Moody 1774-1863 **NCLC 66**

Emerson, Ralph Waldo 1803-1882 **NCLC 1,
   38; DA; DAB; DAC; DAM MST, POET;
   PC 18; WLC**
See also CDALB 1640-1865; DLB 1, 59, 73

Eminescu, Mihail 1850-1889   **NCLC 33**

Empson, William 1906-1984**CLC 3, 8, 19, 33,
   34**
See also CA 17-20R; 112; CANR 31, 61; DLB
   20; MTCW 1

Enchi, Fumiko (Ueda) 1905-1986   **CLC 31**
See also CA 129; 121

Ende, Michael (Andreas Helmuth) 1929-1995
   CLC 31
See also CA 118; 124; 149; CANR 36; CLR
   14; DLB 75; MAICYA; SATA 61; SATA-
   Brief 42; SATA-Obit 86

Endo, Shusaku 1923-1996 **CLC 7, 14, 19, 54,
   99; DAM NOV**
See also CA 29-32R; 153; CANR 21, 54; DLB
   182; MTCW 1

Engel, Marian 1933-1985   **CLC 36**
See also CA 25-28R; CANR 12; DLB 53; INT
   CANR-12

Engelhardt, Frederick
See Hubbard, L(afayette) Ron(ald)

Enright, D(ennis) J(oseph) 1920-**CLC 4, 8, 31**
See also CA 1-4R; CANR 1, 42; DLB 27; SATA
   25

Enzensberger, Hans Magnus 1929- **CLC 43**
See also CA 116; 119

Ephron, Nora 1941-   **CLC 17, 31**
See also AITN 2; CA 65-68; CANR 12, 39

Epicurus 341B.C.-270B.C.   **CMLC 21**
See also DLB 176

Epsilon
See Betjeman, John

Epstein, Daniel Mark 1948-   **CLC 7**
See also CA 49-52; CANR 2, 53

Epstein, Jacob 1956-   **CLC 19**
See also CA 114

Epstein, Joseph 1937-   **CLC 39**
See also CA 112; 119; CANR 50, 65

Epstein, Leslie 1938-   **CLC 27**
See also CA 73-76; CAAS 12; CANR 23, 69

Equiano, Olaudah 1745(?)-1797 **LC 16; BLC
   2; DAM MULT**
See also DLB 37, 50

ER   **TCLC 33**
See also CA 160; DLB 85

Erasmus, Desiderius 1469(?)-1536   **LC 16**

Erdman, Paul E(mil) 1932-   **CLC 25**
See also AITN 1; CA 61-64; CANR 13, 43

Erdrich, Louise 1954-   **CLC 39, 54; DAM
   MULT, NOV, POP**
See also AAYA 10; BEST 89:1; CA 114; CANR
   41, 62; DLB 152, 175, 206; MTCW 1;
   NNAL; SATA 94

Erenburg, Ilya (Grigoryevich)
See Ehrenburg, Ilya (Grigoryevich)

Erickson, Stephen Michael 1950-
See Erickson, Steve

See also CA 129

Erickson, Steve 1950-   **CLC 64**
See also Erickson, Stephen Michael
See also CANR 60, 68

Ericson, Walter
See Fast, Howard (Melvin)

Eriksson, Buntel
See Bergman, (Ernst) Ingmar

Ernaux, Annie 1940-   **CLC 88**
See also CA 147

Erskine, John 1879-1951   **TCLC 84**
See also CA 112; 159; DLB 9, 102

Eschenbach, Wolfram von
See Wolfram von Eschenbach

Eseki, Bruno
See Mphahlele, Ezekiel

Esenin, Sergei (Alexandrovich) 1895-1925
   TCLC 4
See also CA 104

Eshleman, Clayton 1935-   **CLC 7**
See also CA 33-36R; CAAS 6; DLB 5

Espriella, Don Manuel Alvarez
See Southey, Robert

Espriu, Salvador 1913-1985   **CLC 9**
See also CA 154; 115; DLB 134

Espronceda, Jose de 1808-1842   **NCLC 39**

Esse, James
See Stephens, James

Esterbrook, Tom
See Hubbard, L(afayette) Ron(ald)

Estleman, Loren D. 1952-**CLC 48; DAM NOV,
   POP**
See also AAYA 27; CA 85-88; CANR 27, 74;
   INT CANR-27; MTCW 1

Euclid 306B.C.-283B.C.   **CMLC 25**

Eugenides, Jeffrey 1960(?)-   **CLC 81**
See also CA 144

Euripides c. 485B.C.-406B.C.**CMLC 23; DA;
   DAB; DAC; DAM DRAM, MST; DC 4;
   WLCS**
See also DLB 176

Evan, Evin
See Faust, Frederick (Schiller)

Evans, Caradoc 1878-1945   **TCLC 85**

Evans, Evan
See Faust, Frederick (Schiller)

Evans, Marian
See Eliot, George

Evans, Mary Ann
See Eliot, George

Evarts, Esther
See Benson, Sally

Everett, Percival L. 1956-   **CLC 57**
See also BW 2; CA 129

Everson, R(onald) G(ilmour) 1903- **CLC 27**
See also CA 17-20R; DLB 88

Everson, William (Oliver) 1912-1994 **CLC 1,
   5, 14**
See also CA 9-12R; 145; CANR 20; DLB 5,
   16; MTCW 1

Evtushenko, Evgenii Aleksandrovich
See Yevtushenko, Yevgeny (Alexandrovich)

Ewart, Gavin (Buchanan) 1916-1995**CLC 13,
   46**
See also CA 89-92; 150; CANR 17, 46; DLB
   40; MTCW 1

Ewers, Hanns Heinz 1871-1943   **TCLC 12**
See also CA 109; 149

Ewing, Frederick R.
See Sturgeon, Theodore (Hamilton)

Exley, Frederick (Earl) 1929-1992 **CLC 6, 11**
See also AITN 2; CA 81-84; 138; DLB 143;
   DLBY 81

Eynhardt, Guillermo
See Quiroga, Horacio (Sylvestre)

Ezekiel, Nissim 1924-   **CLC 61**
See also CA 61-64

Ezekiel, Tish O'Dowd 1943-   **CLC 34**
See also CA 129

Fadeyev, A.
See Bulgya, Alexander Alexandrovich

Fadeyev, Alexander   **TCLC 53**
See also Bulgya, Alexander Alexandrovich

Fagen, Donald 1948-   **CLC 26**

Fainzilberg, Ilya Arnoldovich 1897-1937
See Ilf, Ilya
See also CA 120; 165

Fair, Ronald L. 1932-   **CLC 18**
See also BW 1; CA 69-72; CANR 25; DLB 33

Fairbairn, Roger
See Carr, John Dickson

Fairbairns, Zoe (Ann) 1948-   **CLC 32**
See also CA 103; CANR 21

Falco, Gian
See Papini, Giovanni

Falconer, James
See Kirkup, James

Falconer, Kenneth
See Kornbluth, C(yril) M.

Falkland, Samuel
See Heijermans, Herman

Fallaci, Oriana 1930-   **CLC 11, 110**
See also CA 77-80; CANR 15, 58; MTCW 1

Faludy, George 1913-   **CLC 42**
See also CA 21-24R

Faludy, Gyoergy
See Faludy, George

Fanon, Frantz 1925-1961   **CLC 74; BLC 2;
   DAM MULT**
See also BW 1; CA 116; 89-92

Fanshawe, Ann 1625-1680   **LC 11**

Fante, John (Thomas) 1911-1983   **CLC 60**
See also CA 69-72; 109; CANR 23; DLB 130;
   DLBY 83

Farah, Nuruddin 1945-**CLC 53; BLC 2; DAM
   MULT**
See also BW 2; CA 106; DLB 125

Fargue, Leon-Paul 1876(?)-1947   **TCLC 11**
See also CA 109

Farigoule, Louis
See Romains, Jules

Farina, Richard 1936(?)-1966   **CLC 9**
See also CA 81-84; 25-28R

Farley, Walter (Lorimer) 1915-1989 **CLC 17**
See also CA 17-20R; CANR 8, 29; DLB 22;
   JRDA; MAICYA; SATA 2, 43

Farmer, Philip Jose 1918-   **CLC 1, 19**
See also CA 1-4R; CANR 4, 35; DLB 8; MTCW
   1; SATA 93

Farquhar, George 1677-1707   **LC 21; DAM
   DRAM**
See also DLB 84

Farrell, J(ames) G(ordon) 1935-1979 **CLC 6**
See also CA 73-76; 89-92; CANR 36; DLB 14;
   MTCW 1

Farrell, James T(homas) 1904-1979**CLC 1, 4,
   8, 11, 66; SSC 28**
See also CA 5-8R; 89-92; CANR 9, 61; DLB 4,
   9, 86; DLBD 2; MTCW 1

Farren, Richard J.
See Betjeman, John

Farren, Richard M.
See Betjeman, John

Fassbinder, Rainer Werner 1946-1982**CLC 20**
See also CA 93-96; 106; CANR 31

Fast, Howard (Melvin) 1914- **CLC 23; DAM**

NOV
See also AAYA 16; CA 1-4R; CAAS 18; CANR 1, 33, 54, 75; DLB 9; INT CANR-33; SATA 7

Faulcon, Robert
See Holdstock, Robert P.

Faulkner, William (Cuthbert) 1897-1962**CLC 1, 3, 6, 8, 9, 11, 14, 18, 28, 52, 68; DA; DAB; DAC; DAM MST, NOV; SSC 1; WLC**
See also AAYA 7; CA 81-84; CANR 33; CDALB 1929-1941; DLB 9, 11, 44, 102; DLBD 2; DLBY 86, 97; MTCW 1

Fauset, Jessie Redmon 1884(?)-1961**CLC 19, 54; BLC 2; DAM MULT**
See also BW 1; CA 109; DLB 51

Faust, Frederick (Schiller) 1892-1944(?) **TCLC 49; DAM POP**
See also CA 108; 152

Faust, Irvin 1924-   **CLC 8**
See also CA 33-36R; CANR 28, 67; DLB 2, 28; DLBY 80

Fawkes, Guy
See Benchley, Robert (Charles)

Fearing, Kenneth (Flexner) 1902-1961 **CLC 51**
See also CA 93-96; CANR 59; DLB 9

Fecamps, Elise
See Creasey, John

Federman, Raymond 1928-   **CLC 6, 47**
See also CA 17-20R; CAAS 8; CANR 10, 43; DLBY 80

Federspiel, J(uerg) F. 1931-   **CLC 42**
See also CA 146

Feiffer, Jules (Ralph) 1929-   **CLC 2, 8, 64; DAM DRAM**
See also AAYA 3; CA 17-20R; CANR 30, 59; DLB 7, 44; INT CANR-30; MTCW 1; SATA 8, 61

Feige, Hermann Albert Otto Maximilian
See Traven, B.

Feinberg, David B. 1956-1994   **CLC 59**
See also CA 135; 147

Feinstein, Elaine 1930-   **CLC 36**
See also CA 69-72; CAAS 1; CANR 31, 68; DLB 14, 40; MTCW 1

Feldman, Irving (Mordecai) 1928-   **CLC 7**
See also CA 1-4R; CANR 1; DLB 169

Felix-Tchicaya, Gerald
See Tchicaya, Gerald Felix

Fellini, Federico 1920-1993   **CLC 16, 85**
See also CA 65-68; 143; CANR 33

Felsen, Henry Gregor 1916-   **CLC 17**
See also CA 1-4R; CANR 1; SAAS 2; SATA 1

Fenno, Jack
See Calisher, Hortense

Fenton, James Martin 1949-   **CLC 32**
See also CA 102; DLB 40

Ferber, Edna 1887-1968   **CLC 18, 93**
See also AITN 1; CA 5-8R; 25-28R; CANR 68; DLB 9, 28, 86; MTCW 1; SATA 7

Ferguson, Helen
See Kavan, Anna

Ferguson, Samuel 1810-1886   **NCLC 33**
See also DLB 32

Fergusson, Robert 1750-1774   **LC 29**
See also DLB 109

Ferling, Lawrence
See Ferlinghetti, Lawrence (Monsanto)

Ferlinghetti, Lawrence (Monsanto) 1919(?)- **CLC 2, 6, 10, 27, 111; DAM POET; PC 1**
See also CA 5-8R; CANR 3, 41, 73; CDALB 1941-1968; DLB 5, 16; MTCW 1

Fernandez, Vicente Garcia Huidobro

See Huidobro Fernandez, Vicente Garcia

Ferrer, Gabriel (Francisco Victor) Miro
See Miro (Ferrer), Gabriel (Francisco Victor)

Ferrier, Susan (Edmonstone) 1782-1854 **NCLC 8**
See also DLB 116

Ferrigno, Robert 1948(?)-   **CLC 65**
See also CA 140

Ferron, Jacques 1921-1985   **CLC 94; DAC**
See also CA 117; 129; DLB 60

Feuchtwanger, Lion 1884-1958   **TCLC 3**
See also CA 104; DLB 66

Feuillet, Octave 1821-1890   **NCLC 45**
See also DLB 192

Feydeau, Georges (Leon Jules Marie) 1862-1921   **TCLC 22; DAM DRAM**
See also CA 113; 152; DLB 192

Fichte, Johann Gottlieb 1762-1814 **NCLC 62**
See also DLB 90

Ficino, Marsilio 1433-1499   **LC 12**

Fiedeler, Hans
See Doeblin, Alfred

Fiedler, Leslie A(aron) 1917-   **CLC 4, 13, 24**
See also CA 9-12R; CANR 7, 63; DLB 28, 67; MTCW 1

Field, Andrew 1938-   **CLC 44**
See also CA 97-100; CANR 25

Field, Eugene 1850-1895   **NCLC 3**
See also DLB 23, 42, 140; DLBD 13; MAICYA; SATA 16

Field, Gans T.
See Wellman, Manly Wade

Field, Michael 1915-1971   **TCLC 43**
See also CA 29-32R

Field, Peter
See Hobson, Laura Z(ametkin)

Fielding, Henry 1707-1754   **LC 1, 46; DA; DAB; DAC; DAM DRAM, MST, NOV; WLC**
See also CDBLB 1660-1789; DLB 39, 84, 101

Fielding, Sarah 1710-1768   **LC 1, 44**
See also DLB 39

Fields, W. C. 1880-1946   **TCLC 80**
See also DLB 44

Fierstein, Harvey (Forbes) 1954-   **CLC 33; DAM DRAM, POP**
See also CA 123; 129

Figes, Eva 1932-   **CLC 31**
See also CA 53-56; CANR 4, 44; DLB 14

Finch, Anne 1661-1720   **LC 3; PC 21**
See also DLB 95

Finch, Robert (Duer Claydon) 1900- **CLC 18**
See also CA 57-60; CANR 9, 24, 49; DLB 88

Findley, Timothy 1930-   **CLC 27, 102; DAC; DAM MST**
See also CA 25-28R; CANR 12, 42, 69; DLB 53

Fink, William
See Mencken, H(enry) L(ouis)

Firbank, Louis 1942-
See Reed, Lou
See also CA 117

Firbank, (Arthur Annesley) Ronald 1886-1926 **TCLC 1**
See also CA 104; DLB 36

Fisher, Dorothy (Frances) Canfield 1879-1958 **TCLC 87**
See also CA 114; 136; DLB 9, 102; MAICYA; YABC 1

Fisher, M(ary) F(rances) K(ennedy) 1908-1992 **CLC 76, 87**
See also CA 77-80; 138; CANR 44

Fisher, Roy 1930-   **CLC 25**

See also CA 81-84; CAAS 10; CANR 16; DLB 40

Fisher, Rudolph 1897-1934**TCLC 11; BLC 2; DAM MULT; SSC 25**
See also BW 1; CA 107; 124; DLB 51, 102

Fisher, Vardis (Alvero) 1895-1968   **CLC 7**
See also CA 5-8R; 25-28R; CANR 68; DLB 9, 206

Fiske, Tarleton
See Bloch, Robert (Albert)

Fitch, Clarke
See Sinclair, Upton (Beall)

Fitch, John IV
See Cormier, Robert (Edmund)

Fitzgerald, Captain Hugh
See Baum, L(yman) Frank

FitzGerald, Edward 1809-1883   **NCLC 9**
See also DLB 32

Fitzgerald, F(rancis) Scott (Key) 1896-1940 **TCLC 1, 6, 14, 28, 55; DA; DAB; DAC; DAM MST, NOV; SSC 6, 31; WLC**
See also AAYA 24; AITN 1; CA 110; 123; CDALB 1917-1929; DLB 4, 9, 86; DLBD 1, 15, 16; DLBY 81, 96; MTCW 1

Fitzgerald, Penelope 1916-   **CLC 19, 51, 61**
See also CA 85-88; CAAS 10; CANR 56; DLB 14, 194

Fitzgerald, Robert (Stuart) 1910-1985**CLC 39**
See also CA 1-4R; 114; CANR 1; DLBY 80

FitzGerald, Robert D(avid) 1902-1987**CLC 19**
See also CA 17-20R

Fitzgerald, Zelda (Sayre) 1900-1948**TCLC 52**
See also CA 117; 126; DLBY 84

Flanagan, Thomas (James Bonner) 1923-   **CLC 25, 52**
See also CA 108; CANR 55; DLBY 80; INT 108; MTCW 1

Flaubert, Gustave 1821-1880**NCLC 2, 10, 19, 62, 66; DA; DAB; DAC; DAM MST, NOV; SSC 11; WLC**
See also DLB 119

Flecker, Herman Elroy
See Flecker, (Herman) James Elroy

Flecker, (Herman) James Elroy 1884-1915 **TCLC 43**
See also CA 109; 150; DLB 10, 19

Fleming, Ian (Lancaster) 1908-1964 **CLC 3, 30; DAM POP**
See also AAYA 26; CA 5-8R; CANR 59; CDBLB 1945-1960; DLB 87, 201; MTCW 1; SATA 9

Fleming, Thomas (James) 1927-   **CLC 37**
See also CA 5-8R; CANR 10; INT CANR-10; SATA 8

Fletcher, John 1579-1625   **LC 33; DC 6**
See also CDBLB Before 1660; DLB 58

Fletcher, John Gould 1886-1950   **TCLC 35**
See also CA 107; 167; DLB 4, 45

Fleur, Paul
See Pohl, Frederik

Flooglebuckle, Al
See Spiegelman, Art

Flying Officer X
See Bates, H(erbert) E(rnest)

Fo, Dario 1926- **CLC 32, 109; DAM DRAM; DC 10**
See also CA 116; 128; CANR 68; DLBY 97; MTCW 1

Fogarty, Jonathan Titulescu Esq.
See Farrell, James T(homas)

Folke, Will
See Bloch, Robert (Albert)

Follett, Ken(neth Martin) 1949-   **CLC 18;**

DAM NOV, POP
See also AAYA 6; BEST 89:4; CA 81-84; CANR 13, 33, 54; DLB 87; DLBY 81; INT CANR-33; MTCW 1

Fontane, Theodor 1819-1898 **NCLC 26**
See also DLB 129

Foote, Horton 1916- **CLC 51, 91; DAM DRAM**
See also CA 73-76; CANR 34, 51; DLB 26; INT CANR-34

Foote, Shelby 1916- **CLC 75; DAM NOV, POP**
See also CA 5-8R; CANR 3, 45, 74; DLB 2, 17

Forbes, Esther 1891-1967 **CLC 12**
See also AAYA 17; CA 13-14; 25-28R; CAP 1; CLR 27; DLB 22; JRDA; MAICYA; SATA 2, 100

Forche, Carolyn (Louise) 1950- **CLC 25, 83, 86; DAM POET; PC 10**
See also CA 109; 117; CANR 50, 74; DLB 5, 193; INT 117

Ford, Elbur
See Hibbert, Eleanor Alice Burford

Ford, Ford Madox 1873-1939 **TCLC 1, 15, 39, 57; DAM NOV**
See also CA 104; 132; CANR 74; CDBLB 1914-1945; DLB 162; MTCW 1

Ford, Henry 1863-1947 **TCLC 73**
See also CA 115; 148

Ford, John 1586-(?) **DC 8**
See also CDBLB Before 1660; DAM DRAM; DLB 58

Ford, John 1895-1973 **CLC 16**
See also CA 45-48

Ford, Richard 1944- **CLC 46, 99**
See also CA 69-72; CANR 11, 47

Ford, Webster
See Masters, Edgar Lee

Foreman, Richard 1937- **CLC 50**
See also CA 65-68; CANR 32, 63

Forester, C(ecil) S(cott) 1899-1966 **CLC 35**
See also CA 73-76; 25-28R; DLB 191; SATA 13

Forez
See Mauriac, Francois (Charles)

Forman, James Douglas 1932- **CLC 21**
See also AAYA 17; CA 9-12R; CANR 4, 19, 42; JRDA; MAICYA; SATA 8, 70

Fornes, Maria Irene 1930- **CLC 39, 61; DC 10**
See also CA 25-28R; CANR 28; DLB 7; HW; INT CANR-28; MTCW 1

Forrest, Leon (Richard) 1937-1997 **CLC 4; BLCS**
See also BW 2; CA 89-92; 162; CAAS 7; CANR 25, 52; DLB 33

Forster, E(dward) M(organ) 1879-1970 **CLC 1, 2, 3, 4, 9, 10, 13, 15, 22, 45, 77; DA; DAB; DAC; DAM MST, NOV; SSC 27; WLC**
See also AAYA 2; CA 13-14; 25-28R; CANR 45; CAP 1; CDBLB 1914-1945; DLB 34, 98, 162, 178, 195; DLBD 10; MTCW 1; SATA 57

Forster, John 1812-1876 **NCLC 11**
See also DLB 144, 184

Forsyth, Frederick 1938- **CLC 2, 5, 36; DAM NOV, POP**
See also BEST 89:4; CA 85-88; CANR 38, 62; DLB 87; MTCW 1

Forten, Charlotte L. **TCLC 16; BLC 2**
See also Grimke, Charlotte L(ottie) Forten
See also DLB 50

Foscolo, Ugo 1778-1827 **NCLC 8**

Fosse, Bob **CLC 20**
See also Fosse, Robert Louis

Fosse, Robert Louis 1927-1987

See Fosse, Bob
See also CA 110; 123

Foster, Stephen Collins 1826-1864 **NCLC 26**

Foucault, Michel 1926-1984 **CLC 31, 34, 69**
See also CA 105; 113; CANR 34; MTCW 1

Fouque, Friedrich (Heinrich Karl) de la Motte 1777-1843 **NCLC 2**
See also DLB 90

Fourier, Charles 1772-1837 **NCLC 51**

Fournier, Henri Alban 1886-1914
See Alain-Fournier
See also CA 104

Fournier, Pierre 1916- **CLC 11**
See also Gascar, Pierre
See also CA 89-92; CANR 16, 40

Fowles, John (Philip) 1926- **CLC 1, 2, 3, 4, 6, 9, 10, 15, 33, 87; DAB; DAC; DAM MST; SSC 33**
See also CA 5-8R; CANR 25, 71; CDBLB 1960 to Present; DLB 14, 139, 207; MTCW 1; SATA 22

Fox, Paula 1923- **CLC 2, 8**
See also AAYA 3; CA 73-76; CANR 20, 36, 62; CLR 1, 44; DLB 52; JRDA; MAICYA; MTCW 1; SATA 17, 60

Fox, William Price (Jr.) 1926- **CLC 22**
See also CA 17-20R; CAAS 19; CANR 11; DLB 2; DLBY 81

Foxe, John 1516(?)-1587 **LC 14**
See also DLB 132

Frame, Janet 1924- **CLC 2, 3, 6, 22, 66, 96; SSC 29**
See also Clutha, Janet Paterson Frame

France, Anatole **TCLC 9**
See also Thibault, Jacques Anatole Francois
See also DLB 123

Francis, Claude 19(?)- **CLC 50**

Francis, Dick 1920- **CLC 2, 22, 42, 102; DAM POP**
See also AAYA 5, 21; BEST 89:3; CA 5-8R; CANR 9, 42, 68; CDBLB 1960 to Present; DLB 87; INT CANR-9; MTCW 1

Francis, Robert (Churchill) 1901-1987 **CLC 15**
See also CA 1-4R; 123; CANR 1

Frank, Anne(lies Marie) 1929-1945 **TCLC 17; DA; DAB; DAC; DAM MST; WLC**
See also AAYA 12; CA 113; 133; CANR 68; MTCW 1; SATA 87; SATA-Brief 42

Frank, Bruno 1887-1945 **TCLC 81**
See also DLB 118

Frank, Elizabeth 1945- **CLC 39**
See also CA 121; 126; INT 126

Frankl, Viktor E(mil) 1905-1997 **CLC 93**
See also CA 65-68; 161

Franklin, Benjamin
See Hasek, Jaroslav (Matej Frantisek)

Franklin, Benjamin 1706-1790 **LC 25; DA; DAB; DAC; DAM MST; WLCS**
See also CDALB 1640-1865; DLB 24, 43, 73

Franklin, (Stella Maria Sarah) Miles (Lampe) 1879-1954 **TCLC 7**
See also CA 104; 164

Fraser, (Lady) Antonia (Pakenham) 1932- **CLC 32, 107**
See also CA 85-88; CANR 44, 65; MTCW 1; SATA-Brief 32

Fraser, George MacDonald 1925- **CLC 7**
See also CA 45-48; CANR 2, 48, 74

Fraser, Sylvia 1935- **CLC 64**
See also CA 45-48; CANR 1, 16, 60

Frayn, Michael 1933- **CLC 3, 7, 31, 47; DAM DRAM, NOV**

See also CA 5-8R; CANR 30, 69; DLB 13, 14, 194; MTCW 1

Fraze, Candida (Merrill) 1945- **CLC 50**
See also CA 126

Frazer, J(ames) G(eorge) 1854-1941 **TCLC 32**
See also CA 118

Frazer, Robert Caine
See Creasey, John

Frazer, Sir James George
See Frazer, J(ames) G(eorge)

Frazier, Charles 1950- **CLC 109**
See also CA 161

Frazier, Ian 1951- **CLC 46**
See also CA 130; CANR 54

Frederic, Harold 1856-1898 **NCLC 10**
See also DLB 12, 23; DLBD 13

Frederick, John
See Faust, Frederick (Schiller)

Frederick the Great 1712-1786 **LC 14**

Fredro, Aleksander 1793-1876 **NCLC 8**

Freeling, Nicolas 1927- **CLC 38**
See also CA 49-52; CAAS 12; CANR 1, 17, 50; DLB 87

Freeman, Douglas Southall 1886-1953 **TCLC 11**
See also CA 109; DLB 17; DLBD 17

Freeman, Judith 1946- **CLC 55**
See also CA 148

Freeman, Mary Eleanor Wilkins 1852-1930 **TCLC 9; SSC 1**
See also CA 106; DLB 12, 78

Freeman, R(ichard) Austin 1862-1943 **TCLC 21**
See also CA 113; DLB 70

French, Albert 1943- **CLC 86**
See also CA 167

French, Marilyn 1929- **CLC 10, 18, 60; DAM DRAM, NOV, POP**
See also CA 69-72; CANR 3, 31; INT CANR-31; MTCW 1

French, Paul
See Asimov, Isaac

Freneau, Philip Morin 1752-1832 **NCLC 1**
See also DLB 37, 43

Freud, Sigmund 1856-1939 **TCLC 52**
See also CA 115; 133; CANR 69; MTCW 1

Friedan, Betty (Naomi) 1921- **CLC 74**
See also CA 65-68; CANR 18, 45, 74; MTCW 1

Friedlander, Saul 1932- **CLC 90**
See also CA 117; 130; CANR 72

Friedman, B(ernard) H(arper) 1926- **CLC 7**
See also CA 1-4R; CANR 3, 48

Friedman, Bruce Jay 1930- **CLC 3, 5, 56**
See also CA 9-12R; CANR 25, 52; DLB 2, 28; INT CANR-25

Friel, Brian 1929- **CLC 5, 42, 59, 115; DC 8**
See also CA 21-24R; CANR 33, 69; DLB 13; MTCW 1

Friis-Baastad, Babbis Ellinor 1921-1970 **CLC 12**
See also CA 17-20R; 134; SATA 7

Frisch, Max (Rudolf) 1911-1991 **CLC 3, 9, 14, 18, 32, 44; DAM DRAM, NOV**
See also CA 85-88; 134; CANR 32, 74; DLB 69, 124; MTCW 1

Fromentin, Eugene (Samuel Auguste) 1820-1876 **NCLC 10**
See also DLB 123

Frost, Frederick
See Faust, Frederick (Schiller)

Frost, Robert (Lee) 1874-1963 **CLC 1, 3, 4, 9, 10, 13, 15, 26, 34, 44; DA; DAB; DAC;**

DAM MST, POET; PC 1; WLC
See also AAYA 21; CA 89-92; CANR 33;
CDALB 1917-1929; DLB 54; DLBD 7;
MTCW 1; SATA 14

Froude, James Anthony 1818-1894 **NCLC 43**
See also DLB 18, 57, 144

Froy, Herald
See Waterhouse, Keith (Spencer)

Fry, Christopher 1907- **CLC 2, 10, 14; DAM DRAM**
See also CA 17-20R; CAAS 23; CANR 9, 30, 74; DLB 13; MTCW 1; SATA 66

Frye, (Herman) Northrop 1912-1991 **CLC 24, 70**
See also CA 5-8R; 133; CANR 8, 37; DLB 67, 68; MTCW 1

Fuchs, Daniel 1909-1993 **CLC 8, 22**
See also CA 81-84; 142; CAAS 5; CANR 40; DLB 9, 26, 28; DLBY 93

Fuchs, Daniel 1934- **CLC 34**
See also CA 37-40R; CANR 14, 48

Fuentes, Carlos 1928- **CLC 3, 8, 10, 13, 22, 41, 60, 113; DA; DAB; DAC; DAM MST, MULT, NOV; HLC; SSC 24; WLC**
See also AAYA 4; AITN 2; CA 69-72; CANR 10, 32, 68; DLB 113; HW; MTCW 1

Fuentes, Gregorio Lopez y
See Lopez y Fuentes, Gregorio

Fugard, (Harold) Athol 1932- **CLC 5, 9, 14, 25, 40, 80; DAM DRAM; DC 3**
See also AAYA 17; CA 85-88; CANR 32, 54; MTCW 1

Fugard, Sheila 1932- **CLC 48**
See also CA 125

Fuller, Charles (H., Jr.) 1939- **CLC 25; BLC 2; DAM DRAM, MULT; DC 1**
See also BW 2; CA 108; 112; DLB 38; INT 112; MTCW 1

Fuller, John (Leopold) 1937- **CLC 62**
See also CA 21-24R; CANR 9, 44; DLB 40

Fuller, Margaret **NCLC 5, 50**
See also Ossoli, Sarah Margaret (Fuller marchesa d')

Fuller, Roy (Broadbent) 1912-1991 **CLC 4, 28**
See also CA 5-8R; 135; CAAS 10; CANR 53; DLB 15, 20; SATA 87

Fulton, Alice 1952- **CLC 52**
See also CA 116; CANR 57; DLB 193

Furphy, Joseph 1843-1912 **TCLC 25**
See also CA 163

Fussell, Paul 1924- **CLC 74**
See also BEST 90:1; CA 17-20R; CANR 8, 21, 35, 69; INT CANR-21; MTCW 1

Futabatei, Shimei 1864-1909 **TCLC 44**
See also CA 162; DLB 180

Futrelle, Jacques 1875-1912 **TCLC 19**
See also CA 113; 155

Gaboriau, Emile 1835-1873 **NCLC 14**

Gadda, Carlo Emilio 1893-1973 **CLC 11**
See also CA 89-92; DLB 177

Gaddis, William 1922- **CLC 1, 3, 6, 8, 10, 19, 43, 86**
See also CA 17-20R; CANR 21, 48; DLB 2; MTCW 1

Gage, Walter
See Inge, William (Motter)

Gaines, Ernest J(ames) 1933- **CLC 3, 11, 18, 86; BLC 2; DAM MULT**
See also AAYA 18; AITN 1; BW 2; CA 9-12R; CANR 6, 24, 42, 75; CDALB 1968-1988; DLB 2, 33, 152; DLBY 80; MTCW 1; SATA 86

Gaitskill, Mary 1954- **CLC 69**

See also CA 128; CANR 61

Galdos, Benito Perez
See Perez Galdos, Benito

Gale, Zona 1874-1938 **TCLC 7; DAM DRAM**
See also CA 105; 153; DLB 9, 78

Galeano, Eduardo (Hughes) 1940- **CLC 72**
See also CA 29-32R; CANR 13, 32; HW

Galiano, Juan Valera y Alcala
See Valera y Alcala-Galiano, Juan

Galilei, Galileo 1546-1642 **LC 45**

Gallagher, Tess 1943- **CLC 18, 63; DAM POET; PC 9**
See also CA 106; DLB 120

Gallant, Mavis 1922- **CLC 7, 18, 38; DAC; DAM MST; SSC 5**
See also CA 69-72; CANR 29, 69; DLB 53; MTCW 1

Gallant, Roy A(rthur) 1924- **CLC 17**
See also CA 5-8R; CANR 4, 29, 54; CLR 30; MAICYA; SATA 4, 68

Gallico, Paul (William) 1897-1976 **CLC 2**
See also AITN 1; CA 5-8R; 69-72; CANR 23; DLB 9, 171; MAICYA; SATA 13

Gallo, Max Louis 1932- **CLC 95**
See also CA 85-88

Gallois, Lucien
See Desnos, Robert

Gallup, Ralph
See Whitemore, Hugh (John)

Galsworthy, John 1867-1933 **TCLC 1, 45; DA; DAB; DAC; DAM DRAM, MST, NOV; SSC 22; WLC**
See also CA 104; 141; CANR 75; CDBLB 1890-1914; DLB 10, 34, 98, 162; DLBD 16

Galt, John 1779-1839 **NCLC 1**
See also DLB 99, 116, 159

Galvin, James 1951- **CLC 38**
See also CA 108; CANR 26

Gamboa, Federico 1864-1939 **TCLC 36**
See also CA 167

Gandhi, M. K.
See Gandhi, Mohandas Karamchand

Gandhi, Mahatma
See Gandhi, Mohandas Karamchand

Gandhi, Mohandas Karamchand 1869-1948 **TCLC 59; DAM MULT**
See also CA 121; 132; MTCW 1

Gann, Ernest Kellogg 1910-1991 **CLC 23**
See also AITN 1; CA 1-4R; 136; CANR 1

Garcia, Cristina 1958- **CLC 76**
See also CA 141; CANR 73

Garcia Lorca, Federico 1898-1936 **TCLC 1, 7, 49; DA; DAB; DAC; DAM DRAM, MST, MULT, POET; DC 2; HLC; PC 3; WLC**
See also CA 104; 131; DLB 108; HW; MTCW 1

Garcia Marquez, Gabriel (Jose) 1928- **CLC 2, 3, 8, 10, 15, 27, 47, 55, 68; DA; DAB; DAC; DAM MST, MULT, NOV, POP; HLC; SSC 8; WLC**
See also AAYA 3; BEST 89:1, 90:4; CA 33-36R; CANR 10, 28, 50, 75; DLB 113; HW; MTCW 1

Gard, Janice
See Latham, Jean Lee

Gard, Roger Martin du
See Martin du Gard, Roger

Gardam, Jane 1928- **CLC 43**
See also CA 49-52; CANR 2, 18, 33, 54; CLR 12; DLB 14, 161; MAICYA; MTCW 1; SAAS 9; SATA 39, 76; SATA-Brief 28

Gardner, Herb(ert) 1934- **CLC 44**
See also CA 149

Gardner, John (Champlin), Jr. 1933-1982 **CLC 2, 3, 5, 7, 8, 10, 18, 28, 34; DAM NOV, POP; SSC 7**
See also AITN 1; CA 65-68; 107; CANR 33, 73; DLB 2; DLBY 82; MTCW 1; SATA 40; SATA-Obit 31

Gardner, John (Edmund) 1926- **CLC 30; DAM POP**
See also CA 103; CANR 15, 69; MTCW 1

Gardner, Miriam
See Bradley, Marion Zimmer

Gardner, Noel
See Kuttner, Henry

Gardons, S. S.
See Snodgrass, W(illiam) D(e Witt)

Garfield, Leon 1921-1996 **CLC 12**
See also AAYA 8; CA 17-20R; 152; CANR 38, 41; CLR 21; DLB 161; JRDA; MAICYA; SATA 1, 32, 76; SATA-Obit 90

Garland, (Hannibal) Hamlin 1860-1940 **TCLC 3; SSC 18**
See also CA 104; DLB 12, 71, 78, 186

Garneau, (Hector de) Saint-Denys 1912-1943 **TCLC 13**
See also CA 111; DLB 88

Garner, Alan 1934- **CLC 17; DAB; DAM POP**
See also AAYA 18; CA 73-76; CANR 15, 64; CLR 20; DLB 161; MAICYA; MTCW 1; SATA 18, 69

Garner, Hugh 1913-1979 **CLC 13**
See also CA 69-72; CANR 31; DLB 68

Garnett, David 1892-1981 **CLC 3**
See also CA 5-8R; 103; CANR 17; DLB 34

Garos, Stephanie
See Katz, Steve

Garrett, George (Palmer) 1929- **CLC 3, 11, 51; SSC 30**
See also CA 1-4R; CAAS 5; CANR 1, 42, 67; DLB 2, 5, 130, 152; DLBY 83

Garrick, David 1717-1779 **LC 15; DAM DRAM**
See also DLB 84

Garrigue, Jean 1914-1972 **CLC 2, 8**
See also CA 5-8R; 37-40R; CANR 20

Garrison, Frederick
See Sinclair, Upton (Beall)

Garth, Will
See Hamilton, Edmond; Kuttner, Henry

Garvey, Marcus (Moziah, Jr.) 1887-1940 **TCLC 41; BLC 2; DAM MULT**
See also BW 1; CA 120; 124

Gary, Romain **CLC 25**
See also Kacew, Romain
See also DLB 83

Gascar, Pierre **CLC 11**
See also Fournier, Pierre

Gascoyne, David (Emery) 1916- **CLC 45**
See also CA 65-68; CANR 10, 28, 54; DLB 20; MTCW 1

Gaskell, Elizabeth Cleghorn 1810-1865 **NCLC 70; DAB; DAM MST; SSC 25**
See also CDBLB 1832-1890; DLB 21, 144, 159

Gass, William H(oward) 1924- **CLC 1, 2, 8, 11, 15, 39; SSC 12**
See also CA 17-20R; CANR 30, 71; DLB 2; MTCW 1

Gasset, Jose Ortega y
See Ortega y Gasset, Jose

Gates, Henry Louis, Jr. 1950- **CLC 65; BLCS; DAM MULT**
See also BW 2; CA 109; CANR 25, 53, 75; DLB 67

Gautier, Theophile 1811-1872 **NCLC 1, 59;**

DAM POET; PC 18; SSC 20
See also DLB 119

Gawsworth, John
See Bates, H(erbert) E(rnest)

Gay, Oliver
See Gogarty, Oliver St. John

Gaye, Marvin (Penze) 1939-1984   **CLC 26**
See also CA 112

Gebler, Carlo (Ernest) 1954-   **CLC 39**
See also CA 119; 133

Gee, Maggie (Mary) 1948-   **CLC 57**
See also CA 130; DLB 207

Gee, Maurice (Gough) 1931-   **CLC 29**
See also CA 97-100; CANR 67; SATA 46, 101

Gelbart, Larry (Simon) 1923-   **CLC 21, 61**
See also CA 73-76; CANR 45

Gelber, Jack 1932-   **CLC 1, 6, 14, 79**
See also CA 1-4R; CANR 2; DLB 7

Gellhorn, Martha (Ellis) 1908-1998 **CLC 14, 60**
See also CA 77-80; 164; CANR 44; DLBY 82

Genet, Jean 1910-1986 **CLC 1, 2, 5, 10, 14, 44, 46; DAM DRAM**
See also CA 13-16R; CANR 18; DLB 72; DLBY 86; MTCW 1

Gent, Peter 1942-   **CLC 29**
See also AITN 1; CA 89-92; DLBY 82

Gentlewoman in New England, A
See Bradstreet, Anne

Gentlewoman in Those Parts, A
See Bradstreet, Anne

George, Jean Craighead 1919-   **CLC 35**
See also AAYA 8; CA 5-8R; CANR 25; CLR 1; DLB 52; JRDA; MAICYA; SATA 2, 68

George, Stefan (Anton) 1868-1933 **TCLC 2, 14**
See also CA 104

Georges, Georges Martin
See Simenon, Georges (Jacques Christian)

Gerhardi, William Alexander
See Gerhardie, William Alexander

Gerhardie, William Alexander 1895-1977 **CLC 5**
See also CA 25-28R; 73-76; CANR 18; DLB 36

Gerstler, Amy 1956-   **CLC 70**
See also CA 146

Gertler, T.   **CLC 34**
See also CA 116; 121; INT 121

Ghalib   **NCLC 39**
See also Ghalib, Hsadullah Khan

Ghalib, Hsadullah Khan 1797-1869
See Ghalib
See also DAM POET

Ghelderode, Michel de 1898-1962 **CLC 6, 11; DAM DRAM**
See also CA 85-88; CANR 40

Ghiselin, Brewster 1903-   **CLC 23**
See also CA 13-16R; CAAS 10; CANR 13

Ghose, Aurabinda 1872-1950   **TCLC 63**
See also CA 163

Ghose, Zulfikar 1935-   **CLC 42**
See also CA 65-68; CANR 67

Ghosh, Amitav 1956-   **CLC 44**
See also CA 147

Giacosa, Giuseppe 1847-1906   **TCLC 7**
See also CA 104

Gibb, Lee
See Waterhouse, Keith (Spencer)

Gibbon, Lewis Grassic   **TCLC 4**
See also Mitchell, James Leslie

Gibbons, Kaye 1960- **CLC 50, 88; DAM POP**
See also CA 151; CANR 75

Gibran, Kahlil 1883-1931   **TCLC 1, 9; DAM**

POET, POP; PC 9
See also CA 104; 150

Gibran, Khalil
See Gibran, Kahlil

Gibson, William 1914-   **CLC 23; DA; DAB; DAC; DAM DRAM, MST**
See also CA 9-12R; CANR 9, 42, 75; DLB 7; SATA 66

Gibson, William (Ford) 1948-   **CLC 39, 63; DAM POP**
See also AAYA 12; CA 126; 133; CANR 52

Gide, Andre (Paul Guillaume) 1869-1951 **TCLC 5, 12, 36; DA; DAB; DAC; DAM MST, NOV; SSC 13; WLC**
See also CA 104; 124; DLB 65; MTCW 1

Gifford, Barry (Colby) 1946-   **CLC 34**
See also CA 65-68; CANR 9, 30, 40

Gilbert, Frank
See De Voto, Bernard (Augustine)

Gilbert, W(illiam) S(chwenck) 1836-1911 **TCLC 3; DAM DRAM, POET**
See also CA 104; SATA 36

Gilbreth, Frank B., Jr. 1911-   **CLC 17**
See also CA 9-12R; SATA 2

Gilchrist, Ellen 1935- **CLC 34, 48; DAM POP; SSC 14**
See also CA 113; 116; CANR 41, 61; DLB 130; MTCW 1

Giles, Molly 1942-   **CLC 39**
See also CA 126

Gill, Eric 1882-1940   **TCLC 85**

Gill, Patrick
See Creasey, John

Gilliam, Terry (Vance) 1940-   **CLC 21**
See also Monty Python
See also AAYA 19; CA 108; 113; CANR 35; INT 113

Gillian, Jerry
See Gilliam, Terry (Vance)

Gilliatt, Penelope (Ann Douglass) 1932-1993 **CLC 2, 10, 13, 53**
See also AITN 2; CA 13-16R; 141; CANR 49; DLB 14

Gilman, Charlotte (Anna) Perkins (Stetson) 1860-1935   **TCLC 9, 37; SSC 13**
See also CA 106; 150

Gilmour, David 1949-   **CLC 35**
See also CA 138, 147

Gilpin, William 1724-1804   **NCLC 30**

Gilray, J. D.
See Mencken, H(enry) L(ouis)

Gilroy, Frank D(aniel) 1925-   **CLC 2**
See also CA 81-84; CANR 32, 64; DLB 7

Gilstrap, John 1957(?)-   **CLC 99**
See also CA 160

Ginsberg, Allen 1926-1997 **CLC 1, 2, 3, 4, 6, 13, 36, 69, 109; DA; DAB; DAC; DAM MST, POET; PC 4; WLC**
See also AITN 1; CA 1-4R; 157; CANR 2, 41, 63; CDALB 1941-1968; DLB 5, 16, 169; MTCW 1

Ginzburg, Natalia 1916-1991 **CLC 5, 11, 54, 70**
See also CA 85-88; 135; CANR 33; DLB 177; MTCW 1

Giono, Jean 1895-1970   **CLC 4, 11**
See also CA 45-48; 29-32R; CANR 2, 35; DLB 72; MTCW 1

Giovanni, Nikki 1943- **CLC 2, 4, 19, 64, 117; BLC 2; DA; DAB; DAC; DAM MST, MULT, POET; PC 19; WLCS**
See also AAYA 22; AITN 1; BW 2; CA 29-32R; CAAS 6; CANR 18, 41, 60; CLR 6; DLB 5, 41; INT CANR-18; MAICYA; MTCW 1;

SATA 24

Giovene, Andrea 1904-   **CLC 7**
See also CA 85-88

Gippius, Zinaida (Nikolayevna) 1869-1945
See Hippius, Zinaida
See also CA 106

Giraudoux, (Hippolyte) Jean 1882-1944 **TCLC 2, 7; DAM DRAM**
See also CA 104; DLB 65

Gironella, Jose Maria 1917-   **CLC 11**
See also CA 101

Gissing, George (Robert) 1857-1903 **TCLC 3, 24, 47**
See also CA 105; 167; DLB 18, 135, 184

Giurlani, Aldo
See Palazzeschi, Aldo

Gladkov, Fyodor (Vasilyevich) 1883-1958 **TCLC 27**
See also CA 170

Glanville, Brian (Lester) 1931-   **CLC 6**
See also CA 5-8R; CAAS 9; CANR 3, 70; DLB 15, 139; SATA 42

Glasgow, Ellen (Anderson Gholson) 1873-1945 **TCLC 2, 7**
See also CA 104; 164; DLB 9, 12

Glaspell, Susan 1882(?)-1948 **TCLC 55; DC 10**
See also CA 110; 154; DLB 7, 9, 78; YABC 2

Glassco, John 1909-1981   **CLC 9**
See also CA 13-16R; 102; CANR 15; DLB 68

Glasscock, Amnesia
See Steinbeck, John (Ernst)

Glasser, Ronald J. 1940(?)-   **CLC 37**

Glassman, Joyce
See Johnson, Joyce

Glendinning, Victoria 1937-   **CLC 50**
See also CA 120; 127; CANR 59; DLB 155

Glissant, Edouard 1928- **CLC 10, 68; DAM MULT**
See also CA 153

Gloag, Julian 1930-   **CLC 40**
See also AITN 1; CA 65-68; CANR 10, 70

Glowacki, Aleksander
See Prus, Boleslaw

Gluck, Louise (Elisabeth) 1943- **CLC 7, 22, 44, 81; DAM POET; PC 16**
See also CA 33-36R; CANR 40, 69; DLB 5

Glyn, Elinor 1864-1943   **TCLC 72**
See also DLB 153

Gobineau, Joseph Arthur (Comte) de 1816-1882   **NCLC 17**
See also DLB 123

Godard, Jean-Luc 1930-   **CLC 20**
See also CA 93-96

Godden, (Margaret) Rumer 1907-   **CLC 53**
See also AAYA 6; CA 5-8R; CANR 4, 27, 36, 55; CLR 20; DLB 161; MAICYA; SAAS 12; SATA 3, 36

Godoy Alcayaga, Lucila 1889-1957
See Mistral, Gabriela
See also BW 2; CA 104; 131; DAM MULT; HW; MTCW 1

Godwin, Gail (Kathleen) 1937- **CLC 5, 8, 22, 31, 69; DAM POP**
See also CA 29-32R; CANR 15, 43, 69; DLB 6; INT CANR-15; MTCW 1

Godwin, William 1756-1836   **NCLC 14**
See also CDBLB 1789-1832; DLB 39, 104, 142, 158, 163

Goebbels, Josef
See Goebbels, (Paul) Joseph

Goebbels, (Paul) Joseph 1897-1945 **TCLC 68**
See also CA 115; 148

Goebbels, Joseph Paul

See Goebbels, (Paul) Joseph

Goethe, Johann Wolfgang von 1749-1832
**NCLC 4, 22, 34; DA; DAB; DAC; DAM
DRAM, MST, POET; PC 5; WLC**
See also DLB 94

Gogarty, Oliver St. John 1878-1957**TCLC 15**
See also CA 109; 150; DLB 15, 19

Gogol, Nikolai (Vasilyevich) 1809-1852**NCLC
5, 15, 31; DA; DAB; DAC; DAM DRAM,
MST; DC 1; SSC 4, 29; WLC**
See also DLB 198

Goines, Donald 1937(?)-1974**CLC 80; BLC 2;
DAM MULT, POP**
See also AITN 1; BW 1; CA 124; 114; DLB 33

Gold, Herbert 1924- **CLC 4, 7, 14, 42**
See also CA 9-12R; CANR 17, 45; DLB 2;
DLBY 81

Goldbarth, Albert 1948- **CLC 5, 38**
See also CA 53-56; CANR 6, 40; DLB 120

Goldberg, Anatol 1910-1982 **CLC 34**
See also CA 131; 117

Goldemberg, Isaac 1945- **CLC 52**
See also CA 69-72; CAAS 12; CANR 11, 32;
HW

Golding, William (Gerald) 1911-1993**CLC 1,
2, 3, 8, 10, 17, 27, 58, 81; DA; DAB; DAC;
DAM MST, NOV; WLC**
See also AAYA 5; CA 5-8R; 141; CANR 13,
33, 54; CDBLB 1945-1960; DLB 15, 100;
MTCW 1

Goldman, Emma 1869-1940 **TCLC 13**
See also CA 110; 150

Goldman, Francisco 1954- **CLC 76**
See also CA 162

Goldman, William (W.) 1931- **CLC 1, 48**
See also CA 9-12R; CANR 29, 69; DLB 44

Goldmann, Lucien 1913-1970 **CLC 24**
See also CA 25-28; CAP 2

Goldoni, Carlo 1707-1793**LC 4; DAM DRAM**

Goldsberry, Steven 1949- **CLC 34**
See also CA 131

Goldsmith, Oliver 1728-1774 **LC 2, 48; DA;
DAB; DAC; DAM DRAM, MST, NOV,
POET; DC 8; WLC**
See also CDBLB 1660-1789; DLB 39, 89, 104,
109, 142; SATA 26

Goldsmith, Peter
See Priestley, J(ohn) B(oynton)

Gombrowicz, Witold 1904-1969**CLC 4, 7, 11,
49; DAM DRAM**
See also CA 19-20; 25-28R; CAP 2

Gomez de la Serna, Ramon 1888-1963**CLC 9**
See also CA 153; 116; HW

Goncharov, Ivan Alexandrovich 1812-1891
NCLC 1, 63

Goncourt, Edmond (Louis Antoine Huot) de
1822-1896 **NCLC 7**
See also DLB 123

Goncourt, Jules (Alfred Huot) de 1830-1870
NCLC 7
See also DLB 123

Gontier, Fernande 19(?)- **CLC 50**

Gonzalez Martinez, Enrique 1871-1952
TCLC 72
See also CA 166; HW

Goodman, Paul 1911-1972 **CLC 1, 2, 4, 7**
See also CA 19-20; 37-40R; CANR 34; CAP 2;
DLB 130; MTCW 1

Gordimer, Nadine 1923-**CLC 3, 5, 7, 10, 18, 33,
51, 70; DA; DAB; DAC; DAM MST, NOV;
SSC 17; WLCS**
See also CA 5-8R; CANR 3, 28, 56; INT CANR-
28; MTCW 1

Gordon, Adam Lindsay 1833-1870 **NCLC 21**

Gordon, Caroline 1895-1981**CLC 6, 13, 29, 83;
SSC 15**
See also CA 11-12; 103; CANR 36; CAP 1;
DLB 4, 9, 102; DLBD 17; DLBY 81; MTCW
1

Gordon, Charles William 1860-1937
See Connor, Ralph
See also CA 109

Gordon, Mary (Catherine) 1949- **CLC 13, 22**
See also CA 102; CANR 44; DLB 6; DLBY
81; INT 102; MTCW 1

Gordon, N. J.
See Bosman, Herman Charles

Gordon, Sol 1923- **CLC 26**
See also CA 53-56; CANR 4; SATA 11

Gordone, Charles 1925-1995**CLC 1, 4; DAM
DRAM; DC 8**
See also BW 1; CA 93-96; 150; CANR 55; DLB
7; INT 93-96; MTCW 1

Gore, Catherine 1800-1861 **NCLC 65**
See also DLB 116

Gorenko, Anna Andreevna
See Akhmatova, Anna

Gorky, Maxim 1868-1936**TCLC 8; DAB; SSC
28; WLC**
See also Peshkov, Alexei Maximovich

Goryan, Sirak
See Saroyan, William

Gosse, Edmund (William) 1849-1928**TCLC 28**
See also CA 117; DLB 57, 144, 184

Gotlieb, Phyllis Fay (Bloom) 1926- **CLC 18**
See also CA 13-16R; CANR 7; DLB 88

Gottesman, S. D.
See Kornbluth, C(yril) M.; Pohl, Frederik

Gottfried von Strassburg fl. c. 1210- **CMLC
10**
See also DLB 138

Gould, Lois **CLC 4, 10**
See also CA 77-80; CANR 29; MTCW 1

Gourmont, Remy (-Marie-Charles) de 1858-
1915 **TCLC 17**
See also CA 109; 150

Govier, Katherine 1948- **CLC 51**
See also CA 101; CANR 18, 40

Goyen, (Charles) William 1915-1983**CLC 5, 8,
14, 40**
See also AITN 2; CA 5-8R; 110; CANR 6, 71;
DLB 2; DLBY 83; INT CANR-6

Goytisolo, Juan 1931- **CLC 5, 10, 23; DAM
MULT; HLC**
See also CA 85-88; CANR 32, 61; HW; MTCW
1

Gozzano, Guido 1883-1916 **PC 10**
See also CA 154; DLB 114

Gozzi, (Conte) Carlo 1720-1806 **NCLC 23**

Grabbe, Christian Dietrich 1801-1836**NCLC
2**
See also DLB 133

Grace, Patricia 1937- **CLC 56**

Gracian y Morales, Baltasar 1601-1658**LC 15**

Gracq, Julien **CLC 11, 48**
See also Poirier, Louis
See also DLB 83

Grade, Chaim 1910-1982 **CLC 10**
See also CA 93-96; 107

Graduate of Oxford, A
See Ruskin, John

Grafton, Garth
See Duncan, Sara Jeannette

Graham, John
See Phillips, David Graham

Graham, Jorie 1951- **CLC 48**

See also CA 111; CANR 63; DLB 120

Graham, R(obert) B(ontine) Cunninghame
See Cunninghame Graham, R(obert) B(ontine)
See also DLB 98, 135, 174

Graham, Robert
See Haldeman, Joe (William)

Graham, Tom
See Lewis, (Harry) Sinclair

Graham, W(illiam) S(ydney) 1918-1986 **CLC
29**
See also CA 73-76; 118; DLB 20

Graham, Winston (Mawdsley) 1910- **CLC 23**
See also CA 49-52; CANR 2, 22, 45, 66; DLB
77

Grahame, Kenneth 1859-1932**TCLC 64; DAB**
See also CA 108; 136; CLR 5; DLB 34, 141,
178; MAICYA; SATA 100; YABC 1

Granovsky, Timofei Nikolaevich 1813-1855
NCLC 75
See also DLB 198

Grant, Skeeter
See Spiegelman, Art

Granville-Barker, Harley 1877-1946**TCLC 2;
DAM DRAM**
See also Barker, Harley Granville
See also CA 104

Grass, Guenter (Wilhelm) 1927-**CLC 1, 2, 4, 6,
11, 15, 22, 32, 49, 88; DA; DAB; DAC;
DAM MST, NOV; WLC**
See also CA 13-16R; CANR 20, 75; DLB 75,
124; MTCW 1

Gratton, Thomas
See Hulme, T(homas) E(rnest)

Grau, Shirley Ann 1929- **CLC 4, 9; SSC 15**
See also CA 89-92; CANR 22, 69; DLB 2; INT
CANR-22; MTCW 1

Gravel, Fern
See Hall, James Norman

Graver, Elizabeth 1964- **CLC 70**
See also CA 135; CANR 71

Graves, Richard Perceval 1945- **CLC 44**
See also CA 65-68; CANR 9, 26, 51

Graves, Robert (von Ranke) 1895-1985 **CLC
1, 2, 6, 11, 39, 44, 45; DAB; DAC; DAM
MST, POET; PC 6**
See also CA 5-8R; 117; CANR 5, 36; CDBLB
1914-1945; DLB 20, 100, 191; DLBD 18;
DLBY 85; MTCW 1; SATA 45

Graves, Valerie
See Bradley, Marion Zimmer

Gray, Alasdair (James) 1934- **CLC 41**
See also CA 126; CANR 47, 69; DLB 194; INT
126; MTCW 1

Gray, Amlin 1946- **CLC 29**
See also CA 138

Gray, Francine du Plessix 1930- **CLC 22;
DAM NOV**
See also BEST 90:3; CA 61-64; CAAS 2;
CANR 11, 33, 75; INT CANR-11; MTCW 1

Gray, John (Henry) 1866-1934 **TCLC 19**
See also CA 119; 162

Gray, Simon (James Holliday) 1936- **CLC 9,
14, 36**
See also AITN 1; CA 21-24R; CAAS 3; CANR
32, 69; DLB 13; MTCW 1

Gray, Spalding 1941-**CLC 49, 112; DAM POP;
DC 7**
See also CA 128; CANR 74

Gray, Thomas 1716-1771**LC 4, 40; DA; DAB;
DAC; DAM MST; PC 2; WLC**
See also CDBLB 1660-1789; DLB 109

Grayson, David
See Baker, Ray Stannard

Grayson, Richard (A.) 1951-   **CLC 38**
    See also CA 85-88; CANR 14, 31, 57
Greeley, Andrew M(oran) 1928-   **CLC 28;**
    DAM POP
    See also CA 5-8R; CAAS 7; CANR 7, 43, 69;
    MTCW 1
Green, Anna Katharine 1846-1935 **TCLC 63**
    See also CA 112; 159; DLB 202
Green, Brian
    See Card, Orson Scott
Green, Hannah
    See Greenberg, Joanne (Goldenberg)
Green, Hannah 1927(?)-1996   **CLC 3**
    See also CA 73-76; CANR 59
Green, Henry 1905-1973   **CLC 2, 13, 97**
    See also Yorke, Henry Vincent
    See also DLB 15
Green, Julian (Hartridge) 1900-1998
    See Green, Julien
    See also CA 21-24R; 169; CANR 33; DLB 4,
    72; MTCW 1
Green, Julien   **CLC 3, 11, 77**
    See also Green, Julian (Hartridge)
Green, Paul (Eliot) 1894-1981 **CLC 25; DAM**
    DRAM
    See also AITN 1; CA 5-8R; 103; CANR 3; DLB
    7, 9; DLBY 81
Greenberg, Ivan 1908-1973
    See Rahv, Philip
    See also CA 85-88
Greenberg, Joanne (Goldenberg) 1932- **C L C**
    7, 30
    See also AAYA 12; CA 5-8R; CANR 14, 32,
    69; SATA 25
Greenberg, Richard 1959(?)-   **CLC 57**
    See also CA 138
Greene, Bette 1934-   **CLC 30**
    See also AAYA 7; CA 53-56; CANR 4; CLR 2;
    JRDA; MAICYA; SAAS 16; SATA 8, 102
Greene, Gael   **CLC 8**
    See also CA 13-16R; CANR 10
Greene, Graham (Henry) 1904-1991 **CLC 1, 3,**
    6, 9, 14, 18, 27, 37, 70, 72; DA; DAB; DAC;
    DAM MST, NOV; SSC 29; WLC
    See also AITN 2; CA 13-16R; 133; CANR 35,
    61; CDBLB 1945-1960; DLB 13, 15, 77,
    100, 162, 201, 204; DLBY 91; MTCW 1;
    SATA 20
Greene, Robert 1558-1592   **LC 41**
    See also DLB 62, 167
Greer, Richard
    See Silverberg, Robert
Gregor, Arthur 1923-   **CLC 9**
    See also CA 25-28R; CAAS 10; CANR 11;
    SATA 36
Gregor, Lee
    See Pohl, Frederik
Gregory, Isabella Augusta (Persse) 1852-1932
    TCLC 1
    See also CA 104; DLB 10
Gregory, J. Dennis
    See Williams, John A(lfred)
Grendon, Stephen
    See Derleth, August (William)
Grenville, Kate 1950-   **CLC 61**
    See also CA 118; CANR 53
Grenville, Pelham
    See Wodehouse, P(elham) G(renville)
Greve, Felix Paul (Berthold Friedrich) 1879-
    1948
    See Grove, Frederick Philip
    See also CA 104; 141; DAC; DAM MST
Grey, Zane 1872-1939   **TCLC 6; DAM POP**

See also CA 104; 132; DLB 9; MTCW 1
Grieg, (Johan) Nordahl (Brun) 1902-1943
    TCLC 10
    See also CA 107
Grieve, C(hristopher) M(urray) 1892-1978
    CLC 11, 19; DAM POET
    See also MacDiarmid, Hugh; Pteleon
    See also CA 5-8R; 85-88; CANR 33; MTCW 1
Griffin, Gerald 1803-1840   **NCLC 7**
    See also DLB 159
Griffin, John Howard 1920-1980   **CLC 68**
    See also AITN 1; CA 1-4R; 101; CANR 2
Griffin, Peter 1942-   **CLC 39**
    See also CA 136
Griffith, D(avid Lewelyn) W(ark) 1875(?)-1948
    TCLC 68
    See also CA 119; 150
Griffith, Lawrence
    See Griffith, D(avid Lewelyn) W(ark)
Griffiths, Trevor 1935-   **CLC 13, 52**
    See also CA 97-100; CANR 45; DLB 13
Griggs, Sutton Elbert 1872-1930(?) **TCLC 77**
    See also CA 123; DLB 50
Grigson, Geoffrey (Edward Harvey) 1905-1985
    CLC 7, 39
    See also CA 25-28R; 118; CANR 20, 33; DLB
    27; MTCW 1
Grillparzer, Franz 1791-1872   **NCLC 1**
    See also DLB 133
Grimble, Reverend Charles James
    See Eliot, T(homas) S(tearns)
Grimke, Charlotte L(ottie) Forten 1837(?)-1914
    See Forten, Charlotte L.
    See also BW 1; CA 117; 124; DAM MULT,
    POET
Grimm, Jacob Ludwig Karl 1785-1863 **NCLC**
    3
    See also DLB 90; MAICYA; SATA 22
Grimm, Wilhelm Karl 1786-1859   **NCLC 3**
    See also DLB 90; MAICYA; SATA 22
Grimmelshausen, Johann Jakob Christoffel von
    1621-1676   **LC 6**
    See also DLB 168
Grindel, Eugene 1895-1952
    See Eluard, Paul
    See also CA 104
Grisham, John 1955-   **CLC 84; DAM POP**
    See also AAYA 14; CA 138; CANR 47, 69
Grossman, David 1954-   **CLC 67**
    See also CA 138
Grossman, Vasily (Semenovich) 1905-1964
    CLC 41
    See also CA 124; 130; MTCW 1
Grove, Frederick Philip   **TCLC 4**
    See also Greve, Felix Paul (Berthold Friedrich)
    See also DLB 92
Grubb
    See Crumb, R(obert)
Grumbach, Doris (Isaac) 1918- **CLC 13, 22, 64**
    See also CA 5-8R; CAAS 2; CANR 9, 42, 70;
    INT CANR-9
Grundtvig, Nicolai Frederik Severin 1783-1872
    NCLC 1
Grunge
    See Crumb, R(obert)
Grunwald, Lisa 1959-   **CLC 44**
    See also CA 120
Guare, John 1938-   **CLC 8, 14, 29, 67; DAM**
    DRAM
    See also CA 73-76; CANR 21, 69; DLB 7;
    MTCW 1
Gudjonsson, Halldor Kiljan 1902-1998
    See Laxness, Halldor

See also CA 103; 164
Guenter, Erich
    See Eich, Guenter
Guest, Barbara 1920-   **CLC 34**
    See also CA 25-28R; CANR 11, 44; DLB 5,
    193
Guest, Judith (Ann) 1936- **CLC 8, 30; DAM**
    NOV, POP
    See also AAYA 7; CA 77-80; CANR 15, 75;
    INT CANR-15; MTCW 1
Guevara, Che   **CLC 87; HLC**
    See also Guevara (Serna), Ernesto
Guevara (Serna), Ernesto 1928-1967
    See Guevara, Che
    See also CA 127; 111; CANR 56; DAM MULT;
    HW
Guild, Nicholas M. 1944-   **CLC 33**
    See also CA 93-96
Guillemin, Jacques
    See Sartre, Jean-Paul
Guillen, Jorge 1893-1984   **CLC 11; DAM**
    MULT, POET
    See also CA 89-92; 112; DLB 108; HW
Guillen, Nicolas (Cristobal) 1902-1989 **C L C**
    48, 79; BLC 2; DAM MST, MULT, POET;
    HLC; PC 23
    See also BW 2; CA 116; 125; 129; HW
Guillevic, (Eugene) 1907-   **CLC 33**
    See also CA 93-96
Guillois
    See Desnos, Robert
Guillois, Valentin
    See Desnos, Robert
Guiney, Louise Imogen 1861-1920 **TCLC 41**
    See also CA 160; DLB 54
Guiraldes, Ricardo (Guillermo) 1886-1927
    TCLC 39
    See also CA 131; HW; MTCW 1
Gumilev, Nikolai (Stepanovich) 1886-1921
    TCLC 60
    See also CA 165
Gunesekera, Romesh 1954-   **CLC 91**
    See also CA 159
Gunn, Bill   **CLC 5**
    See also Gunn, William Harrison
    See also DLB 38
Gunn, Thom(son William) 1929- **CLC 3, 6, 18,**
    32, 81; DAM POET
    See also CA 17-20R; CANR 9, 33; CDBLB
    1960 to Present; DLB 27; INT CANR-33;
    MTCW 1
Gunn, William Harrison 1934(?)-1989
    See Gunn, Bill
    See also AITN 1; BW 1; CA 13-16R; 128;
    CANR 12, 25
Gunnars, Kristjana 1948-   **CLC 69**
    See also CA 113; DLB 60
Gurdjieff, G(eorgei) I(vanovich) 1877(?)-1949
    TCLC 71
    See also CA 157
Gurganus, Allan 1947- **CLC 70; DAM POP**
    See also BEST 90:1; CA 135
Gurney, A(lbert) R(amsdell), Jr. 1930- **C L C**
    32, 50, 54; DAM DRAM
    See also CA 77-80; CANR 32, 64
Gurney, Ivor (Bertie) 1890-1937   **TCLC 33**
    See also CA 167
Gurney, Peter
    See Gurney, A(lbert) R(amsdell), Jr.
Guro, Elena 1877-1913   **TCLC 56**
Gustafson, James M(oody) 1925-   **CLC 100**
    See also CA 25-28R; CANR 37
Gustafson, Ralph (Barker) 1909-   **CLC 36**

See also CA 21-24R; CANR 8, 45; DLB 88

Gut, Gom
See Simenon, Georges (Jacques Christian)

Guterson, David 1956-   **CLC 91**
See also CA 132; CANR 73

Guthrie, A(lfred) B(ertram), Jr. 1901-1991
CLC 23
See also CA 57-60; 134; CANR 24; DLB 6;
SATA 62; SATA-Obit 67

Guthrie, Isobel
See Grieve, C(hristopher) M(urray)

Guthrie, Woodrow Wilson 1912-1967
See Guthrie, Woody
See also CA 113; 93-96

Guthrie, Woody   **CLC 35**
See also Guthrie, Woodrow Wilson

Guy, Rosa (Cuthbert) 1928-   **CLC 26**
See also AAYA 4; BW 2; CA 17-20R; CANR
14, 34; CLR 13; DLB 33; JRDA; MAICYA;
SATA 14, 62

Gwendolyn
See Bennett, (Enoch) Arnold

H. D.   **CLC 3, 8, 14, 31, 34, 73; PC 5**
See also Doolittle, Hilda

H. de V.
See Buchan, John

Haavikko, Paavo Juhani 1931-   **CLC 18, 34**
See also CA 106

Habbema, Koos
See Heijermans, Herman

Habermas, Juergen 1929-   **CLC 104**
See also CA 109

Habermas, Jurgen
See Habermas, Juergen

Hacker, Marilyn 1942- **CLC 5, 9, 23, 72, 91;
DAM POET**
See also CA 77-80; CANR 68; DLB 120

Haeckel, Ernst Heinrich (Philipp August) 1834-
1919   **TCLC 83**
See also CA 157

Haggard, H(enry) Rider 1856-1925 **TCLC 11**
See also CA 108; 148; DLB 70, 156, 174, 178;
SATA 16

Hagiosy, L.
See Larbaud, Valery (Nicolas)

Hagiwara Sakutaro 1886-1942 **TCLC 60; PC
18**

Haig, Fenil
See Ford, Ford Madox

Haig-Brown, Roderick (Langmere) 1908-1976
CLC 21
See also CA 5-8R; 69-72; CANR 4, 38; CLR
31; DLB 88; MAICYA; SATA 12

Hailey, Arthur 1920- **CLC 5; DAM NOV, POP**
See also AITN 2; BEST 90:3; CA 1-4R; CANR
2, 36, 75; DLB 88; DLBY 82; MTCW 1

Hailey, Elizabeth Forsythe 1938-   **CLC 40**
See also CA 93-96; CAAS 1; CANR 15, 48;
INT CANR-15

Haines, John (Meade) 1924-   **CLC 58**
See also CA 17-20R; CANR 13, 34; DLB 5

Hakluyt, Richard 1552-1616   **LC 31**

Haldeman, Joe (William) 1943-   **CLC 61**
See also CA 53-56; CAAS 25; CANR 6, 70,
72; DLB 8; INT CANR-6

Hale, Sarah Josepha (Buell) 1788-1879 **NCLC
75**
See also DLB 1, 42, 73

Haley, Alex(ander Murray Palmer) 1921-1992
**CLC 8, 12, 76; BLC 2; DA; DAB; DAC;
DAM MST, MULT, POP**
See also AAYA 26; BW 2; CA 77-80; 136;
CANR 61; DLB 38; MTCW 1

Haliburton, Thomas Chandler 1796-1865
NCLC 15
See also DLB 11, 99

Hall, Donald (Andrew, Jr.) 1928- **CLC 1, 13,
37, 59; DAM POET**
See also CA 5-8R; CAAS 7; CANR 2, 44, 64;
DLB 5; SATA 23, 97

Hall, Frederic Sauser
See Sauser-Hall, Frederic

Hall, James
See Kuttner, Henry

Hall, James Norman 1887-1951   **TCLC 23**
See also CA 123; SATA 21

Hall, Radclyffe
See Hall, (Marguerite) Radclyffe

Hall, (Marguerite) Radclyffe 1886-1943
TCLC 12
See also CA 110; 150; DLB 191

Hall, Rodney 1935-   **CLC 51**
See also CA 109; CANR 69

Halleck, Fitz-Greene 1790-1867   **NCLC 47**
See also DLB 3

Halliday, Michael
See Creasey, John

Halpern, Daniel 1945-   **CLC 14**
See also CA 33-36R

Hamburger, Michael (Peter Leopold) 1924-
CLC 5, 14
See also CA 5-8R; CAAS 4; CANR 2, 47; DLB
27

Hamill, Pete 1935-   **CLC 10**
See also CA 25-28R; CANR 18, 71

Hamilton, Alexander 1755(?)-1804 **NCLC 49**
See also DLB 37

Hamilton, Clive
See Lewis, C(live) S(taples)

Hamilton, Edmond 1904-1977   **CLC 1**
See also CA 1-4R; CANR 3; DLB 8

Hamilton, Eugene (Jacob) Lee
See Lee-Hamilton, Eugene (Jacob)

Hamilton, Franklin
See Silverberg, Robert

Hamilton, Gail
See Corcoran, Barbara

Hamilton, Mollie
See Kaye, M(ary) M(argaret)

Hamilton, (Anthony Walter) Patrick 1904-1962
CLC 51
See also CA 113; DLB 10

Hamilton, Virginia 1936- **CLC 26; DAM
MULT**
See also AAYA 2, 21; BW 2; CA 25-28R;
CANR 20, 37, 73; CLR 1, 11, 40; DLB 33,
52; INT CANR-20; JRDA; MAICYA;
MTCW 1; SATA 4, 56, 79

Hammett, (Samuel) Dashiell 1894-1961 **C L C
3, 5, 10, 19, 47; SSC 17**
See also AITN 1; CA 81-84; CANR 42; CDALB
1929-1941; DLBD 6; DLBY 96; MTCW 1

Hammon, Jupiter 1711(?)-1800(?) **NCLC 5;
BLC 2; DAM MULT, POET; PC 16**
See also DLB 31, 50

Hammond, Keith
See Kuttner, Henry

Hamner, Earl (Henry), Jr. 1923-   **CLC 12**
See also AITN 2; CA 73-76; DLB 6

Hampton, Christopher (James) 1946- **CLC 4**
See also CA 25-28R; DLB 13; MTCW 1

Hamsun, Knut   **TCLC 2, 14, 49**
See also Pedersen, Knut

Handke, Peter 1942- **CLC 5, 8, 10, 15, 38; DAM
DRAM, NOV**
See also CA 77-80; CANR 33, 75; DLB 85, 124;

MTCW 1

Hanley, James 1901-1985   **CLC 3, 5, 8, 13**
See also CA 73-76; 117; CANR 36; DLB 191;
MTCW 1

Hannah, Barry 1942-   **CLC 23, 38, 90**
See also CA 108; 110; CANR 43, 68; DLB 6;
INT 110; MTCW 1

Hannon, Ezra
See Hunter, Evan

Hansberry, Lorraine (Vivian) 1930-1965 **CLC
17, 62; BLC 2; DA; DAB; DAC; DAM
DRAM, MST, MULT; DC 2**
See also AAYA 25; BW 1; CA 109; 25-28R;
CABS 3; CANR 58; CDALB 1941-1968;
DLB 7, 38; MTCW 1

Hansen, Joseph 1923-   **CLC 38**
See also CA 29-32R; CAAS 17; CANR 16, 44,
66; INT CANR-16

Hansen, Martin A(lfred) 1909-1955 **TCLC 32**
See also CA 167

Hanson, Kenneth O(stlin) 1922-   **CLC 13**
See also CA 53-56; CANR 7

Hardwick, Elizabeth (Bruce) 1916- **CLC 13;
DAM NOV**
See also CA 5-8R; CANR 3, 32, 70; DLB 6;
MTCW 1

Hardy, Thomas 1840-1928 **TCLC 4, 10, 18, 32,
48, 53, 72; DA; DAB; DAC; DAM MST,
NOV, POET; PC 8; SSC 2; WLC**
See also CA 104; 123; CDBLB 1890-1914;
DLB 18, 19, 135; MTCW 1

Hare, David 1947-   **CLC 29, 58**
See also CA 97-100; CANR 39; DLB 13;
MTCW 1

Harewood, John
See Van Druten, John (William)

Harford, Henry
See Hudson, W(illiam) H(enry)

Hargrave, Leonie
See Disch, Thomas M(ichael)

Harjo, Joy 1951-   **CLC 83; DAM MULT**
See also CA 114; CANR 35, 67; DLB 120, 175;
NNAL

Harlan, Louis R(udolph) 1922-   **CLC 34**
See also CA 21-24R; CANR 25, 55

Harling, Robert 1951(?)-   **CLC 53**
See also CA 147

Harmon, William (Ruth) 1938-   **CLC 38**
See also CA 33-36R; CANR 14, 32, 35; SATA
65

Harper, F. E. W.
See Harper, Frances Ellen Watkins

Harper, Frances E. W.
See Harper, Frances Ellen Watkins

Harper, Frances E. Watkins
See Harper, Frances Ellen Watkins

Harper, Frances Ellen
See Harper, Frances Ellen Watkins

Harper, Frances Ellen Watkins 1825-1911
**TCLC 14; BLC 2; DAM MULT, POET;
PC 21**
See also BW 1; CA 111; 125; DLB 50

Harper, Michael S(teven) 1938-   **CLC 7, 22**
See also BW 1; CA 33-36R; CANR 24; DLB
41

Harper, Mrs. F. E. W.
See Harper, Frances Ellen Watkins

Harris, Christie (Lucy) Irwin 1907- **CLC 12**
See also CA 5-8R; CANR 6; CLR 47; DLB 88;
JRDA; MAICYA; SAAS 10; SATA 6, 74

Harris, Frank 1856-1931   **TCLC 24**
See also CA 109; 150; DLB 156, 197

Harris, George Washington 1814-1869 **NCLC**

23
See also DLB 3, 11

Harris, Joel Chandler 1848-1908   **TCLC 2; SSC 19**
See also CA 104; 137; CLR 49; DLB 11, 23, 42, 78, 91; MAICYA; SATA 100; YABC 1

Harris, John (Wyndham Parkes Lucas) Beynon 1903-1969
See Wyndham, John
See also CA 102; 89-92

Harris, MacDonald   **CLC 9**
See also Heiney, Donald (William)

Harris, Mark 1922-   **CLC 19**
See also CA 5-8R; CAAS 3; CANR 2, 55; DLB 2; DLBY 80

Harris, (Theodore) Wilson 1921-   **CLC 25**
See also BW 2; CA 65-68; CAAS 16; CANR 11, 27, 69; DLB 117; MTCW 1

Harrison, Elizabeth Cavanna 1909-
See Cavanna, Betty
See also CA 9-12R; CANR 6, 27

Harrison, Harry (Max) 1925-   **CLC 42**
See also CA 1-4R; CANR 5, 21; DLB 8; SATA 4

Harrison, James (Thomas) 1937- **CLC 6, 14, 33, 66; SSC 19**
See also CA 13-16R; CANR 8, 51; DLBY 82; INT CANR-8

Harrison, Jim
See Harrison, James (Thomas)

Harrison, Kathryn 1961-   **CLC 70**
See also CA 144; CANR 68

Harrison, Tony 1937-   **CLC 43**
See also CA 65-68; CANR 44; DLB 40; MTCW 1

Harriss, Will(ard Irvin) 1922-   **CLC 34**
See also CA 111

Harson, Sley
See Ellison, Harlan (Jay)

Hart, Ellis
See Ellison, Harlan (Jay)

Hart, Josephine 1942(?)-**CLC 70; DAM POP**
See also CA 138; CANR 70

Hart, Moss 1904-1961 **CLC 66; DAM DRAM**
See also CA 109; 89-92; DLB 7

Harte, (Francis) Bret(t) 1836(?)-1902**TCLC 1, 25; DA; DAC; DAM MST; SSC 8; WLC**
See also CA 104; 140; CDALB 1865-1917; DLB 12, 64, 74, 79, 186; SATA 26

Hartley, L(eslie) P(oles) 1895-1972**CLC 2, 22**
See also CA 45-48; 37-40R; CANR 33; DLB 15, 139; MTCW 1

Hartman, Geoffrey H. 1929-   **CLC 27**
See also CA 117; 125; DLB 67

Hartmann, Sadakichi 1867-1944   **TCLC 73**
See also CA 157; DLB 54

Hartmann von Aue c. 1160-c. 1205**CMLC 15**
See also DLB 138

Hartmann von Aue 1170-1210   **CMLC 15**

Haruf, Kent 1943-   **CLC 34**
See also CA 149

Harwood, Ronald 1934-   **CLC 32; DAM DRAM, MST**
See also CA 1-4R; CANR 4, 55; DLB 13

Hasegawa Tatsunosuke
See Futabatei, Shimei

Hasek, Jaroslav (Matej Frantisek) 1883-1923 **TCLC 4**
See also CA 104; 129; MTCW 1

Hass, Robert 1941-   **CLC 18, 39, 99; PC 16**
See also CA 111; CANR 30, 50, 71; DLB 105, 206; SATA 94

Hastings, Hudson

See Kuttner, Henry

Hastings, Selina   **CLC 44**

Hathorne, John 1641-1717   **LC 38**

Hatteras, Amelia
See Mencken, H(enry) L(ouis)

Hatteras, Owen   **TCLC 18**
See also Mencken, H(enry) L(ouis); Nathan, George Jean

Hauptmann, Gerhart (Johann Robert) 1862-1946   **TCLC 4; DAM DRAM**
See also CA 104; 153; DLB 66, 118

Havel, Vaclav 1936- **CLC 25, 58, 65; DAM DRAM; DC 6**
See also CA 104; CANR 36, 63; MTCW 1

Haviaras, Stratis   **CLC 33**
See also Chaviaras, Strates

Hawes, Stephen 1475(?)-1523(?)   **LC 17**
See also DLB 132

Hawkes, John (Clendennin Burne, Jr.) 1925-1998   **CLC 1, 2, 3, 4, 7, 9, 14, 15, 27, 49**
See also CA 1-4R; 167; CANR 2, 47, 64; DLB 2, 7; DLBY 80; MTCW 1

Hawking, S. W.
See Hawking, Stephen W(illiam)

Hawking, Stephen W(illiam) 1942- **CLC 63, 105**
See also AAYA 13; BEST 89:1; CA 126; 129; CANR 48

Hawkins, Anthony Hope
See Hope, Anthony

Hawthorne, Julian 1846-1934   **TCLC 25**
See also CA 165

Hawthorne, Nathaniel 1804-1864 **NCLC 39; DA; DAB; DAC; DAM MST, NOV; SSC 3, 29; WLC**
See also AAYA 18; CDALB 1640-1865; DLB 1, 74; YABC 2

Haxton, Josephine Ayres 1921-
See Douglas, Ellen
See also CA 115; CANR 41

Hayaseca y Eizaguirre, Jorge
See Echegaray (y Eizaguirre), Jose (Maria Waldo)

Hayashi, Fumiko 1904-1951   **TCLC 27**
See also CA 161; DLB 180

Haycraft, Anna
See Ellis, Alice Thomas
See also CA 122

Hayden, Robert E(arl) 1913-1980 **CLC 5, 9, 14, 37; BLC 2; DA; DAC; DAM MST, MULT, POET; PC 6**
See also BW 1; CA 69-72; 97-100; CABS 2; CANR 24, 75; CDALB 1941-1968; DLB 5, 76; MTCW 1; SATA 19; SATA-Obit 26

Hayford, J(oseph) E(phraim) Casely
See Casely-Hayford, J(oseph) E(phraim)

Hayman, Ronald 1932-   **CLC 44**
See also CA 25-28R; CANR 18, 50; DLB 155

Haywood, Eliza 1693(?)-1756   **LC 44**
See also DLB 39

Haywood, Eliza (Fowler) 1693(?)-1756 **LC 1, 44**

Hazlitt, William 1778-1830   **NCLC 29**
See also DLB 110, 158

Hazzard, Shirley 1931-   **CLC 18**
See also CA 9-12R; CANR 4, 70; DLBY 82; MTCW 1

Head, Bessie 1937-1986 **CLC 25, 67; BLC 2; DAM MULT**
See also BW 2; CA 29-32R; 119; CANR 25; DLB 117; MTCW 1

Headon, (Nicky) Topper 1956(?)-   **CLC 30**

Heaney, Seamus (Justin) 1939- **CLC 5, 7, 14,**

25, 37, 74, 91; DAB; DAM POET; PC 18; WLCS
See also CA 85-88; CANR 25, 48, 75; CDBLB 1960 to Present; DLB 40; DLBY 95; MTCW 1

Hearn, (Patricio) Lafcadio (Tessima Carlos) 1850-1904   **TCLC 9**
See also CA 105; 166; DLB 12, 78, 189

Hearne, Vicki 1946-   **CLC 56**
See also CA 139

Hearon, Shelby 1931-   **CLC 63**
See also AITN 2; CA 25-28R; CANR 18, 48

Heat-Moon, William Least   **CLC 29**
See also Trogdon, William (Lewis)
See also AAYA 9

Hebbel, Friedrich 1813-1863**NCLC 43; DAM DRAM**
See also DLB 129

Hebert, Anne 1916-**CLC 4, 13, 29; DAC; DAM MST, POET**
See also CA 85-88; CANR 69; DLB 68; MTCW 1

Hecht, Anthony (Evan) 1923- **CLC 8, 13, 19; DAM POET**
See also CA 9-12R; CANR 6; DLB 5, 169

Hecht, Ben 1894-1964   **CLC 8**
See also CA 85-88; DLB 7, 9, 25, 26, 28, 86

Hedayat, Sadeq 1903-1951   **TCLC 21**
See also CA 120

Hegel, Georg Wilhelm Friedrich 1770-1831 **NCLC 46**
See also DLB 90

Heidegger, Martin 1889-1976   **CLC 24**
See also CA 81-84; 65-68; CANR 34; MTCW 1

Heidenstam, (Carl Gustaf) Verner von 1859-1940   **TCLC 5**
See also CA 104

Heifner, Jack 1946-   **CLC 11**
See also CA 105; CANR 47

Heijermans, Herman 1864-1924   **TCLC 24**
See also CA 123

Heilbrun, Carolyn G(old) 1926-   **CLC 25**
See also CA 45-48; CANR 1, 28, 58

Heine, Heinrich 1797-1856**NCLC 4, 54; PC 25**
See also DLB 90

Heinemann, Larry (Curtiss) 1944-   **CLC 50**
See also CA 110; CAAS 21; CANR 31; DLBD 9; INT CANR-31

Heiney, Donald (William) 1921-1993
See Harris, MacDonald
See also CA 1-4R; 142; CANR 3, 58

Heinlein, Robert A(nson) 1907-1988**CLC 1, 3, 8, 14, 26, 55; DAM POP**
See also AAYA 17; CA 1-4R; 125; CANR 1, 20, 53; DLB 8; JRDA; MAICYA; MTCW 1; SATA 9, 69; SATA-Obit 56

Helforth, John
See Doolittle, Hilda

Hellenhofferu, Vojtech Kapristian z
See Hasek, Jaroslav (Matej Frantisek)

Heller, Joseph 1923-**CLC 1, 3, 5, 8, 11, 36, 63; DA; DAB; DAC; DAM MST, NOV, POP; WLC**
See also AAYA 24; AITN 1; CA 5-8R; CABS 1; CANR 8, 42, 66; DLB 2, 28; DLBY 80; INT CANR-8; MTCW 1

Hellman, Lillian (Florence) 1906-1984**CLC 2, 4, 8, 14, 18, 34, 44, 52; DAM DRAM; DC 1**
See also AITN 1, 2; CA 13-16R; 112; CANR 33; DLB 7; DLBY 84; MTCW 1

Helprin, Mark 1947-**CLC 7, 10, 22, 32; DAM NOV, POP**

See also CA 81-84; CANR 47, 64; DLBY 85; MTCW 1

Helvetius, Claude-Adrien 1715-1771 **LC 26**

Helyar, Jane Penelope Josephine 1933-
See Poole, Josephine
See also CA 21-24R; CANR 10, 26; SATA 82

Hemans, Felicia 1793-1835 **NCLC 71**
See also DLB 96

Hemingway, Ernest (Miller) 1899-1961 **C L C 1, 3, 6, 8, 10, 13, 19, 30, 34, 39, 41, 44, 50, 61, 80; DA; DAB; DAC; DAM MST, NOV; SSC 1, 25; WLC**
See also AAYA 19; CA 77-80; CANR 34; CDALB 1917-1929; DLB 4, 9, 102; DLBD 1, 15, 16; DLBY 81, 87, 96; MTCW 1

Hempel, Amy 1951- **CLC 39**
See also CA 118; 137; CANR 70

Henderson, F. C.
See Mencken, H(enry) L(ouis)

Henderson, Sylvia
See Ashton-Warner, Sylvia (Constance)

Henderson, Zenna (Chlarson) 1917-1983 **S S C 29**
See also CA 1-4R; 133; CANR 1; DLB 8; SATA 5

Henley, Beth **CLC 23; DC 6**
See also Henley, Elizabeth Becker
See also CABS 3; DLBY 86

Henley, Elizabeth Becker 1952-
See Henley, Beth
See also CA 107; CANR 32, 73; DAM DRAM, MST; MTCW 1

Henley, William Ernest 1849-1903 **TCLC 8**
See also CA 105; DLB 19

Hennissart, Martha
See Lathen, Emma
See also CA 85-88; CANR 64

Henry, O. **TCLC 1, 19; SSC 5; WLC**
See also Porter, William Sydney

Henry, Patrick 1736-1799 **LC 25**

Henryson, Robert 1430(?)-1506(?) **LC 20**
See also DLB 146

Henry VIII 1491-1547 **LC 10**

Henschke, Alfred
See Klabund

Hentoff, Nat(han Irving) 1925- **CLC 26**
See also AAYA 4; CA 1-4R; CAAS 6; CANR 5, 25; CLR 1, 52; INT CANR-25; JRDA; MAICYA; SATA 42, 69; SATA-Brief 27

Heppenstall, (John) Rayner 1911-1981 **C L C 10**
See also CA 1-4R; 103; CANR 29

Heraclitus c. 540B.C.-c. 450B.C. **CMLC 22**
See also DLB 176

Herbert, Frank (Patrick) 1920-1986 **CLC 12, 23, 35, 44, 85; DAM POP**
See also AAYA 21; CA 53-56; 118; CANR 5, 43; DLB 8; INT CANR-5; MTCW 1; SATA 9, 37; SATA-Obit 47

Herbert, George 1593-1633 **LC 24; DAB; DAM POET; PC 4**
See also CDBLB Before 1660; DLB 126

Herbert, Zbigniew 1924-1998 **CLC 9, 43; DAM POET**
See also CA 89-92; 169; CANR 36, 74; MTCW 1

Herbst, Josephine (Frey) 1897-1969 **CLC 34**
See also CA 5-8R; 25-28R; DLB 9

Hergesheimer, Joseph 1880-1954 **TCLC 11**
See also CA 109; DLB 102, 9

Herlihy, James Leo 1927-1993 **CLC 6**
See also CA 1-4R; 143; CANR 2

Hermogenes fl. c. 175- **CMLC 6**

Hernandez, Jose 1834-1886 **NCLC 17**

Herodotus c. 484B.C.-429B.C. **CMLC 17**
See also DLB 176

Herrick, Robert 1591-1674 **LC 13; DA; DAB; DAC; DAM MST, POP; PC 9**
See also DLB 126

Herring, Guilles
See Somerville, Edith

Herriot, James 1916-1995 **CLC 12; DAM POP**
See also Wight, James Alfred
See also AAYA 1; CA 148; CANR 40; SATA 86

Herrmann, Dorothy 1941- **CLC 44**
See also CA 107

Herrmann, Taffy
See Herrmann, Dorothy

Hersey, John (Richard) 1914-1993 **CLC 1, 2, 7, 9, 40, 81, 97; DAM POP**
See also CA 17-20R; 140; CANR 33; DLB 6, 185; MTCW 1; SATA 25; SATA-Obit 76

Herzen, Aleksandr Ivanovich 1812-1870 **NCLC 10, 61**

Herzl, Theodor 1860-1904 **TCLC 36**
See also CA 168

Herzog, Werner 1942- **CLC 16**
See also CA 89-92

Hesiod c. 8th cent. B.C.- **CMLC 5**
See also DLB 176

Hesse, Hermann 1877-1962 **CLC 1, 2, 3, 6, 11, 17, 25, 69; DA; DAB; DAC; DAM MST, NOV; SSC 9; WLC**
See also CA 17-18; CAP 2; DLB 66; MTCW 1; SATA 50

Hewes, Cady
See De Voto, Bernard (Augustine)

Heyen, William 1940- **CLC 13, 18**
See also CA 33-36R; CAAS 9; DLB 5

Heyerdahl, Thor 1914- **CLC 26**
See also CA 5-8R; CANR 5, 22, 66, 73; MTCW 1; SATA 2, 52

Heym, Georg (Theodor Franz Arthur) 1887-1912 **TCLC 9**
See also CA 106

Heym, Stefan 1913- **CLC 41**
See also CA 9-12R; CANR 4; DLB 69

Heyse, Paul (Johann Ludwig von) 1830-1914 **TCLC 8**
See also CA 104; DLB 129

Heyward, (Edwin) DuBose 1885-1940 **T C L C 59**
See also CA 108; 157; DLB 7, 9, 45; SATA 21

Hibbert, Eleanor Alice Burford 1906-1993 **CLC 7; DAM POP**
See also BEST 90:4; CA 17-20R; 140; CANR 9, 28, 59; SATA 2; SATA-Obit 74

Hichens, Robert (Smythe) 1864-1950 **T C L C 64**
See also CA 162; DLB 153

Higgins, George V(incent) 1939- **CLC 4, 7, 10, 18**
See also CA 77-80; CAAS 5; CANR 17, 51; DLB 2; DLBY 81; INT CANR-17; MTCW 1

Higginson, Thomas Wentworth 1823-1911 **TCLC 36**
See also CA 162; DLB 1, 64

Highet, Helen
See MacInnes, Helen (Clark)

Highsmith, (Mary) Patricia 1921-1995 **CLC 2, 4, 14, 42, 102; DAM NOV, POP**
See also CA 1-4R; 147; CANR 1, 20, 48, 62; MTCW 1

Highwater, Jamake (Mamake) 1942(?)- **C L C 12**
See also AAYA 7; CA 65-68; CAAS 7; CANR 10, 34; CLR 17; DLB 52; DLBY 85; JRDA; MAICYA; SATA 32, 69; SATA-Brief 30

Highway, Tomson 1951- **CLC 92; DAC; DAM MULT**
See also CA 151; CANR 75; NNAL

Higuchi, Ichiyo 1872-1896 **NCLC 49**

Hijuelos, Oscar 1951- **CLC 65; DAM MULT, POP; HLC**
See also AAYA 25; BEST 90:1; CA 123; CANR 50, 75; DLB 145; HW

Hikmet, Nazim 1902(?)-1963 **CLC 40**
See also CA 141; 93-96

Hildegard von Bingen 1098-1179 **CMLC 20**
See also DLB 148

Hildesheimer, Wolfgang 1916-1991 **CLC 49**
See also CA 101; 135; DLB 69, 124

Hill, Geoffrey (William) 1932- **CLC 5, 8, 18, 45; DAM POET**
See also CA 81-84; CANR 21; CDBLB 1960 to Present; DLB 40; MTCW 1

Hill, George Roy 1921- **CLC 26**
See also CA 110; 122

Hill, John
See Koontz, Dean R(ay)

Hill, Susan (Elizabeth) 1942- **CLC 4, 113; DAB; DAM MST, NOV**
See also CA 33-36R; CANR 29, 69; DLB 14, 139; MTCW 1

Hillerman, Tony 1925- **CLC 62; DAM POP**
See also AAYA 6; BEST 89:1; CA 29-32R; CANR 21, 42, 65; DLB 206; SATA 6

Hillesum, Etty 1914-1943 **TCLC 49**
See also CA 137

Hilliard, Noel (Harvey) 1929- **CLC 15**
See also CA 9-12R; CANR 7, 69

Hillis, Rick 1956- **CLC 66**
See also CA 134

Hilton, James 1900-1954 **TCLC 21**
See also CA 108; 169; DLB 34, 77; SATA 34

Himes, Chester (Bomar) 1909-1984 **CLC 2, 4, 7, 18, 58, 108; BLC 2; DAM MULT**
See also BW 2; CA 25-28R; 114; CANR 22; DLB 2, 76, 143; MTCW 1

Hinde, Thomas **CLC 6, 11**
See also Chitty, Thomas Willes

Hindin, Nathan
See Bloch, Robert (Albert)

Hine, (William) Daryl 1936- **CLC 15**
See also CA 1-4R; CAAS 15; CANR 1, 20; DLB 60

Hinkson, Katharine Tynan
See Tynan, Katharine

Hinton, S(usan) E(loise) 1950- **CLC 30, 111; DA; DAB; DAC; DAM MST, NOV**
See also AAYA 2; CA 81-84; CANR 32, 62; CLR 3, 23; JRDA; MAICYA; MTCW 1; SATA 19, 58

Hippius, Zinaida **TCLC 9**
See also Gippius, Zinaida (Nikolayevna)

Hiraoka, Kimitake 1925-1970
See Mishima, Yukio
See also CA 97-100; 29-32R; DAM DRAM; MTCW 1

Hirsch, E(ric) D(onald), Jr. 1928- **CLC 79**
See also CA 25-28R; CANR 27, 51; DLB 67; INT CANR-27; MTCW 1

Hirsch, Edward 1950- **CLC 31, 50**
See also CA 104; CANR 20, 42; DLB 120

Hitchcock, Alfred (Joseph) 1899-1980 **CLC 16**
See also AAYA 22; CA 159; 97-100; SATA 27; SATA-Obit 24

Hitler, Adolf 1889-1945 **TCLC 53**
See also CA 117; 147

Hoagland, Edward 1932- **CLC 28**
See also CA 1-4R; CANR 2, 31, 57; DLB 6;
SATA 51

Hoban, Russell (Conwell) 1925- **CLC 7, 25;
DAM NOV**
See also CA 5-8R; CANR 23, 37, 66; CLR 3;
DLB 52; MAICYA; MTCW 1; SATA 1, 40,
78

Hobbes, Thomas 1588-1679 **LC 36**
See also DLB 151

Hobbs, Perry
See Blackmur, R(ichard) P(almer)

Hobson, Laura Z(ametkin) 1900-1986 **CLC 7,
25**
See also CA 17-20R; 118; CANR 55; DLB 28;
SATA 52

Hochhuth, Rolf 1931- **CLC 4, 11, 18; DAM
DRAM**
See also CA 5-8R; CANR 33, 75; DLB 124;
MTCW 1

Hochman, Sandra 1936- **CLC 3, 8**
See also CA 5-8R; DLB 5

Hochwaelder, Fritz 1911-1986 **CLC 36; DAM
DRAM**
See also CA 29-32R; 120; CANR 42; MTCW 1

Hochwalder, Fritz
See Hochwaelder, Fritz

Hocking, Mary (Eunice) 1921- **CLC 13**
See also CA 101; CANR 18, 40

Hodgins, Jack 1938- **CLC 23**
See also CA 93-96; DLB 60

Hodgson, William Hope 1877(?)-1918 **TCLC
13**
See also CA 111; 164; DLB 70, 153, 156, 178

Hoeg, Peter 1957- **CLC 95**
See also CA 151; CANR 75

Hoffman, Alice 1952- **CLC 51; DAM NOV**
See also CA 77-80; CANR 34, 66; MTCW 1

Hoffman, Daniel (Gerard) 1923- **CLC 6, 13, 23**
See also CA 1-4R; CANR 4; DLB 5

Hoffman, Stanley 1944- **CLC 5**
See also CA 77-80

Hoffman, William M(oses) 1939- **CLC 40**
See also CA 57-60; CANR 11, 71

Hoffmann, E(rnst) T(heodor) A(madeus) 1776-
1822 **NCLC 2; SSC 13**
See also DLB 90; SATA 27

Hofmann, Gert 1931- **CLC 54**
See also CA 128

Hofmannsthal, Hugo von 1874-1929 **TCLC 11;
DAM DRAM; DC 4**
See also CA 106; 153; DLB 81, 118

Hogan, Linda 1947- **CLC 73; DAM MULT**
See also CA 120; CANR 45, 73; DLB 175;
NNAL

Hogarth, Charles
See Creasey, John

Hogarth, Emmett
See Polonsky, Abraham (Lincoln)

Hogg, James 1770-1835 **NCLC 4**
See also DLB 93, 116, 159

Holbach, Paul Henri Thiry Baron 1723-1789
LC 14

Holberg, Ludvig 1684-1754 **LC 6**

Holden, Ursula 1921- **CLC 18**
See also CA 101; CAAS 8; CANR 22

Holderlin, (Johann Christian) Friedrich 1770-
1843 **NCLC 16; PC 4**

Holdstock, Robert
See Holdstock, Robert P.

Holdstock, Robert P. 1948- **CLC 39**

See also CA 131

Holland, Isabelle 1920- **CLC 21**
See also AAYA 11; CA 21-24R; CANR 10, 25,
47; JRDA; MAICYA; SATA 8, 70

Holland, Marcus
See Caldwell, (Janet Miriam) Taylor (Holland)

Hollander, John 1929- **CLC 2, 5, 8, 14**
See also CA 1-4R; CANR 1, 52; DLB 5; SATA
13

Hollander, Paul
See Silverberg, Robert

Holleran, Andrew 1943(?)- **CLC 38**
See also CA 144

Hollinghurst, Alan 1954- **CLC 55, 91**
See also CA 114; DLB 207

Hollis, Jim
See Summers, Hollis (Spurgeon, Jr.)

Holly, Buddy 1936-1959 **TCLC 65**

Holmes, Gordon
See Shiel, M(atthew) P(hipps)

Holmes, John
See Souster, (Holmes) Raymond

Holmes, John Clellon 1926-1988 **CLC 56**
See also CA 9-12R; 125; CANR 4; DLB 16

Holmes, Oliver Wendell, Jr. 1841-1935 **TCLC
77**
See also CA 114

Holmes, Oliver Wendell 1809-1894 **NCLC 14**
See also CDALB 1640-1865; DLB 1, 189;
SATA 34

Holmes, Raymond
See Souster, (Holmes) Raymond

Holt, Victoria
See Hibbert, Eleanor Alice Burford

Holub, Miroslav 1923-1998 **CLC 4**
See also CA 21-24R; 169; CANR 10

Homer c. 8th cent. B.C.- **CMLC 1, 16; DA;
DAB; DAC; DAM MST, POET; PC 23;
WLCS**
See also DLB 176

Hongo, Garrett Kaoru 1951- **PC 23**
See also CA 133; CAAS 22; DLB 120

Honig, Edwin 1919- **CLC 33**
See also CA 5-8R; CAAS 8; CANR 4, 45; DLB
5

Hood, Hugh (John Blagdon) 1928- **CLC 15, 28**
See also CA 49-52; CAAS 17; CANR 1, 33;
DLB 53

Hood, Thomas 1799-1845 **NCLC 16**
See also DLB 96

Hooker, (Peter) Jeremy 1941- **CLC 43**
See also CA 77-80; CANR 22; DLB 40

hooks, bell **CLC 94; BLCS**
See also Watkins, Gloria

Hope, A(lec) D(erwent) 1907- **CLC 3, 51**
See also CA 21-24R; CANR 33, 74; MTCW 1

Hope, Anthony 1863-1933 **TCLC 83**
See also CA 157; DLB 153, 156

Hope, Brian
See Creasey, John

Hope, Christopher (David Tully) 1944- **CLC
52**
See also CA 106; CANR 47; SATA 62

Hopkins, Gerard Manley 1844-1889 **NCLC
17; DA; DAB; DAC; DAM MST, POET;
PC 15; WLC**
See also CDBLB 1890-1914; DLB 35, 57

Hopkins, John (Richard) 1931-1998 **CLC 4**
See also CA 85-88; 169

Hopkins, Pauline Elizabeth 1859-1930 **TCLC
28; BLC 2; DAM MULT**
See also BW 2; CA 141; DLB 50

Hopkinson, Francis 1737-1791 **LC 25**

See also DLB 31

Hopley-Woolrich, Cornell George 1903-1968
See Woolrich, Cornell
See also CA 13-14; CANR 58; CAP 1

Horatio
See Proust, (Valentin-Louis-George-Eugene-)
Marcel

Horgan, Paul (George Vincent O'Shaughnessy)
1903-1995 **CLC 9, 53; DAM NOV**
See also CA 13-16R; 147; CANR 9, 35; DLB
102; DLBY 85; INT CANR-9; MTCW 1;
SATA 13; SATA-Obit 84

Horn, Peter
See Kuttner, Henry

Hornem, Horace Esq.
See Byron, George Gordon (Noel)

Horney, Karen (Clementine Theodore
Danielsen) 1885-1952 **TCLC 71**
See also CA 114; 165

Hornung, E(rnest) W(illiam) 1866-1921
TCLC 59
See also CA 108; 160; DLB 70

Horovitz, Israel (Arthur) 1939- **CLC 56; DAM
DRAM**
See also CA 33-36R; CANR 46, 59; DLB 7

Horvath, Odon von
See Horvath, Oedoen von
See also DLB 85, 124

Horvath, Oedoen von 1901-1938 **TCLC 45**
See also Horvath, Odon von
See also CA 118

Horwitz, Julius 1920-1986 **CLC 14**
See also CA 9-12R; 119; CANR 12

Hospital, Janette Turner 1942- **CLC 42**
See also CA 108; CANR 48

Hostos, E. M. de
See Hostos (y Bonilla), Eugenio Maria de

Hostos, Eugenio M. de
See Hostos (y Bonilla), Eugenio Maria de

Hostos, Eugenio Maria
See Hostos (y Bonilla), Eugenio Maria de

Hostos (y Bonilla), Eugenio Maria de 1839-1903
TCLC 24
See also CA 123; 131; HW

Houdini
See Lovecraft, H(oward) P(hillips)

Hougan, Carolyn 1943- **CLC 34**
See also CA 139

Household, Geoffrey (Edward West) 1900-1988
CLC 11
See also CA 77-80; 126; CANR 58; DLB 87;
SATA 14; SATA-Obit 59

Housman, A(lfred) E(dward) 1859-1936
**TCLC 1, 10; DA; DAB; DAC; DAM MST,
POET; PC 2; WLCS**
See also CA 104; 125; DLB 19; MTCW 1

Housman, Laurence 1865-1959 **TCLC 7**
See also CA 106; 155; DLB 10; SATA 25

Howard, Elizabeth Jane 1923- **CLC 7, 29**
See also CA 5-8R; CANR 8, 62

Howard, Maureen 1930- **CLC 5, 14, 46**
See also CA 53-56; CANR 31, 75; DLBY 83;
INT CANR-31; MTCW 1

Howard, Richard 1929- **CLC 7, 10, 47**
See also AITN 1; CA 85-88; CANR 25; DLB 5;
INT CANR-25

Howard, Robert E(rvin) 1906-1936 **TCLC 8**
See also CA 105; 157

Howard, Warren F.
See Pohl, Frederik

Howe, Fanny (Quincy) 1940- **CLC 47**
See also CA 117; CAAS 27; CANR 70; SATA-
Brief 52

Howe, Irving 1920-1993   **CLC 85**
    See also CA 9-12R; 141; CANR 21, 50; DLB
    67; MTCW 1
Howe, Julia Ward 1819-1910   **TCLC 21**
    See also CA 117; DLB 1, 189
Howe, Susan 1937-   **CLC 72**
    See also CA 160; DLB 120
Howe, Tina 1937-   **CLC 48**
    See also CA 109
Howell, James 1594(?)-1666   **LC 13**
    See also DLB 151
Howells, W. D.
    See Howells, William Dean
Howells, William D.
    See Howells, William Dean
Howells, William Dean 1837-1920 **TCLC 7, 17, 41**
    See also CA 104; 134; CDALB 1865-1917;
    DLB 12, 64, 74, 79, 189
Howes, Barbara 1914-1996   **CLC 15**
    See also CA 9-12R; 151; CAAS 3; CANR 53;
    SATA 5
Hrabal, Bohumil 1914-1997   **CLC 13, 67**
    See also CA 106; 156; CAAS 12; CANR 57
Hroswitha of Gandersheim c. 935-c. 1002
    CMLC 29
    See also DLB 148
Hsun, Lu
    See Lu Hsun
Hubbard, L(afayette) Ron(ald) 1911-1986
    CLC 43; DAM POP
    See also CA 77-80; 118; CANR 52
Huch, Ricarda (Octavia) 1864-1947 **TCLC 13**
    See also CA 111; DLB 66
Huddle, David 1942-   **CLC 49**
    See also CA 57-60; CAAS 20; DLB 130
Hudson, Jeffrey
    See Crichton, (John) Michael
Hudson, W(illiam) H(enry) 1841-1922 **TCLC 29**
    See also CA 115; DLB 98, 153, 174; SATA 35
Hueffer, Ford Madox
    See Ford, Ford Madox
Hughart, Barry 1934-   **CLC 39**
    See also CA 137
Hughes, Colin
    See Creasey, John
Hughes, David (John) 1930-   **CLC 48**
    See also CA 116; 129; DLB 14
Hughes, Edward James
    See Hughes, Ted
    See also DAM MST, POET
Hughes, (James) Langston 1902-1967 **CLC 1, 5, 10, 15, 35, 44, 108; BLC 2; DA; DAB; DAC; DAM DRAM, MST, MULT, POET; DC 3; PC 1; SSC 6; WLC**
    See also AAYA 12; BW 1; CA 1-4R; 25-28R;
    CANR 1, 34; CDALB 1929-1941; CLR 17;
    DLB 4, 7, 48, 51, 86; JRDA; MAICYA;
    MTCW 1; SATA 4, 33
Hughes, Richard (Arthur Warren) 1900-1976
    CLC 1, 11; DAM NOV
    See also CA 5-8R; 65-68; CANR 4; DLB 15,
    161; MTCW 1; SATA 8; SATA-Obit 25
Hughes, Ted 1930-1998   **CLC 2, 4, 9, 14, 37; DAB; DAC; PC 7**
    See also Hughes, Edward James
    See also CA 1-4R; 171; CANR 1, 33, 66; CLR
    3; DLB 40, 161; MAICYA; MTCW 1; SATA
    49; SATA-Brief 27
Hugo, Richard F(ranklin) 1923-1982 **CLC 6, 18, 32; DAM POET**
    See also CA 49-52; 108; CANR 3; DLB 5, 206

Hugo, Victor (Marie) 1802-1885 **NCLC 3, 10, 21; DA; DAB; DAC; DAM DRAM, MST, NOV, POET; PC 17; WLC**
    See also DLB 119, 192; SATA 47
Huidobro, Vicente
    See Huidobro Fernandez, Vicente Garcia
Huidobro Fernandez, Vicente Garcia 1893-1948   **TCLC 31**
    See also CA 131; HW
Hulme, Keri 1947-   **CLC 39**
    See also CA 125; CANR 69; INT 125
Hulme, T(homas) E(rnest) 1883-1917 **TCLC 21**
    See also CA 117; DLB 19
Hume, David 1711-1776   **LC 7**
    See also DLB 104
Humphrey, William 1924-1997   **CLC 45**
    See also CA 77-80; 160; CANR 68; DLB 6
Humphreys, Emyr Owen 1919-   **CLC 47**
    See also CA 5-8R; CANR 3, 24; DLB 15
Humphreys, Josephine 1945-   **CLC 34, 57**
    See also CA 121; 127; INT 127
Huneker, James Gibbons 1857-1921 **TCLC 65**
    See also DLB 71
Hungerford, Pixie
    See Brinsmead, H(esba) F(ay)
Hunt, E(verette) Howard, (Jr.) 1918- **CLC 3**
    See also AITN 1; CA 45-48; CANR 2, 47
Hunt, Kyle
    See Creasey, John
Hunt, (James Henry) Leigh 1784-1859 **NCLC 1, 70; DAM POET**
    See also DLB 96, 110, 144
Hunt, Marsha 1946-   **CLC 70**
    See also BW 2; CA 143
Hunt, Violet 1866(?)-1942   **TCLC 53**
    See also DLB 162, 197
Hunter, E. Waldo
    See Sturgeon, Theodore (Hamilton)
Hunter, Evan 1926-   **CLC 11, 31; DAM POP**
    See also CA 5-8R; CANR 5, 38, 62; DLBY 82;
    INT CANR-5; MTCW 1; SATA 25
Hunter, Kristin (Eggleston) 1931-   **CLC 35**
    See also AITN 1; BW 1; CA 13-16R; CANR
    13; CLR 3; DLB 33; INT CANR-13;
    MAICYA; SAAS 10; SATA 12
Hunter, Mollie 1922-   **CLC 21**
    See also McIlwraith, Maureen Mollie Hunter
    See also AAYA 13; CANR 37; CLR 25; DLB
    161; JRDA; MAICYA; SAAS 7; SATA 54
Hunter, Robert (?)-1734   **LC 7**
Hurston, Zora Neale 1903-1960 **CLC 7, 30, 61; BLC 2; DA; DAC; DAM MST, MULT, NOV; SSC 4; WLCS**
    See also AAYA 15; BW 1; CA 85-88; CANR
    61; DLB 51, 86; MTCW 1
Huston, John (Marcellus) 1906-1987 **CLC 20**
    See also CA 73-76; 123; CANR 34; DLB 26
Hustvedt, Siri 1955-   **CLC 76**
    See also CA 137
Hutten, Ulrich von 1488-1523   **LC 16**
    See also DLB 179
Huxley, Aldous (Leonard) 1894-1963 **CLC 1, 3, 4, 5, 8, 11, 18, 35, 79; DA; DAB; DAC; DAM MST, NOV; WLC**
    See also AAYA 11; CA 85-88; CANR 44;
    CDBLB 1914-1945; DLB 36, 100, 162, 195;
    MTCW 1; SATA 63
Huxley, T(homas) H(enry) 1825-1895 **NCLC 67**
    See also DLB 57
Huysmans, Joris-Karl 1848-1907 **TCLC 7, 69**
    See also CA 104; 165; DLB 123

Hwang, David Henry 1957-   **CLC 55; DAM DRAM; DC 4**
    See also CA 127; 132; INT 132
Hyde, Anthony 1946-   **CLC 42**
    See also CA 136
Hyde, Margaret O(ldroyd) 1917-   **CLC 21**
    See also CA 1-4R; CANR 1, 36; CLR 23; JRDA;
    MAICYA; SAAS 8; SATA 1, 42, 76
Hynes, James 1956(?)-   **CLC 65**
    See also CA 164
Ian, Janis 1951-   **CLC 21**
    See also CA 105
Ibanez, Vicente Blasco
    See Blasco Ibanez, Vicente
Ibarguengoitia, Jorge 1928-1983   **CLC 37**
    See also CA 124; 113; HW
Ibsen, Henrik (Johan) 1828-1906 **TCLC 2, 8, 16, 37, 52; DA; DAB; DAC; DAM DRAM, MST; DC 2; WLC**
    See also CA 104; 141
Ibuse, Masuji 1898-1993   **CLC 22**
    See also CA 127; 141; DLB 180
Ichikawa, Kon 1915-   **CLC 20**
    See also CA 121
Idle, Eric 1943-   **CLC 21**
    See also Monty Python
    See also CA 116; CANR 35
Ignatow, David 1914-1997 **CLC 4, 7, 14, 40**
    See also CA 9-12R; 162; CAAS 3; CANR 31,
    57; DLB 5
Ihimaera, Witi 1944-   **CLC 46**
    See also CA 77-80
Ilf, Ilya   **TCLC 21**
    See also Fainzilberg, Ilya Arnoldovich
Illyes, Gyula 1902-1983   **PC 16**
    See also CA 114; 109
Immermann, Karl (Lebrecht) 1796-1840
    NCLC 4, 49
    See also DLB 133
Ince, Thomas H. 1882-1924   **TCLC 89**
    See also DLB 88
Inchbald, Elizabeth 1753-1821   **NCLC 62**
    See also DLB 39, 89
Inclan, Ramon (Maria) del Valle
    See Valle-Inclan, Ramon (Maria) del
Infante, G(uillermo) Cabrera
    See Cabrera Infante, G(uillermo)
Ingalls, Rachel (Holmes) 1940-   **CLC 42**
    See also CA 123; 127
Ingamells, Reginald Charles
    See Ingamells, Rex
Ingamells, Rex 1913-1955   **TCLC 35**
    See also CA 167
Inge, William (Motter) 1913-1973 **CLC 1, 8, 19; DAM DRAM**
    See also CA 9-12R; CDALB 1941-1968; DLB
    7; MTCW 1
Ingelow, Jean 1820-1897   **NCLC 39**
    See also DLB 35, 163; SATA 33
Ingram, Willis J.
    See Harris, Mark
Innaurato, Albert (F.) 1948(?)-   **CLC 21, 60**
    See also CA 115; 122; INT 122
Innes, Michael
    See Stewart, J(ohn) I(nnes) M(ackintosh)
Innis, Harold Adams 1894-1952   **TCLC 77**
    See also DLB 88
Ionesco, Eugene 1909-1994 **CLC 1, 4, 6, 9, 11, 15, 41, 86; DA; DAB; DAC; DAM DRAM, MST; WLC**
    See also CA 9-12R; 144; CANR 55; MTCW 1;
    SATA 7; SATA-Obit 79
Iqbal, Muhammad 1873-1938   **TCLC 28**
Ireland, Patrick

See O'Doherty, Brian
Iron, Ralph
   See Schreiner, Olive (Emilie Albertina)
Irving, John (Winslow) 1942-CLC **13, 23, 38, 112; DAM NOV, POP**
   See also AAYA 8; BEST 89:3; CA 25-28R; CANR 28, 73; DLB 6; DLBY 82; MTCW 1
Irving, Washington 1783-1859 **NCLC 2, 19; DA; DAB; DAC; DAM MST; SSC 2; WLC**
   See also CDALB 1640-1865; DLB 3, 11, 30, 59, 73, 74, 186; YABC 2
Irwin, P. K.
   See Page, P(atricia) K(athleen)
Isaacs, Jorge Ricardo 1837-1895 **NCLC 70**
Isaacs, Susan 1943-   **CLC 32; DAM POP**
   See also BEST 89:1; CA 89-92; CANR 20, 41, 65; INT CANR-20; MTCW 1
Isherwood, Christopher (William Bradshaw) 1904-1986   **CLC 1, 9, 11, 14, 44; DAM DRAM, NOV**
   See also CA 13-16R; 117; CANR 35; DLB 15, 195; DLBY 86; MTCW 1
Ishiguro, Kazuo 1954-   **CLC 27, 56, 59, 110; DAM NOV**
   See also BEST 90:2; CA 120; CANR 49; DLB 194; MTCW 1
Ishikawa, Hakuhin
   See Ishikawa, Takuboku
Ishikawa, Takuboku 1886(?)-1912 **TCLC 15; DAM POET; PC 10**
   See also CA 113; 153
Iskander, Fazil 1929-   **CLC 47**
   See also CA 102
Isler, Alan (David) 1934-   **CLC 91**
   See also CA 156
Ivan IV 1530-1584   **LC 17**
Ivanov, Vyacheslav Ivanovich 1866-1949 **TCLC 33**
   See also CA 122
Ivask, Ivar Vidrik 1927-1992   **CLC 14**
   See also CA 37-40R; 139; CANR 24
Ives, Morgan
   See Bradley, Marion Zimmer
J. R. S.
   See Gogarty, Oliver St. John
Jabran, Kahlil
   See Gibran, Kahlil
Jabran, Khalil
   See Gibran, Kahlil
Jackson, Daniel
   See Wingrove, David (John)
Jackson, Jesse 1908-1983   **CLC 12**
   See also BW 1; CA 25-28R; 109; CANR 27; CLR 28; MAICYA; SATA 2, 29; SATA-Obit 48
Jackson, Laura (Riding) 1901-1991
   See Riding, Laura
   See also CA 65-68; 135; CANR 28; DLB 48
Jackson, Sam
   See Trumbo, Dalton
Jackson, Sara
   See Wingrove, David (John)
Jackson, Shirley 1919-1965   **CLC 11, 60, 87; DA; DAC; DAM MST; SSC 9; WLC**
   See also AAYA 9; CA 1-4R; 25-28R; CANR 4, 52; CDALB 1941-1968; DLB 6; SATA 2
Jacob, (Cyprien-)Max 1876-1944   **TCLC 6**
   See also CA 104
Jacobs, Harriet A(nn) 1813(?)-1897NCLC **67**
Jacobs, Jim 1942-   **CLC 12**
   See also CA 97-100; INT 97-100
Jacobs, W(illiam) W(ymark) 1863-1943 **TCLC 22**

See also CA 121; 167; DLB 135
Jacobsen, Jens Peter 1847-1885   **NCLC 34**
Jacobsen, Josephine 1908-   **CLC 48, 102**
   See also CA 33-36R; CAAS 18; CANR 23, 48
Jacobson, Dan 1929-   **CLC 4, 14**
   See also CA 1-4R; CANR 2, 25, 66; DLB 14, 207; MTCW 1
Jacqueline
   See Carpentier (y Valmont), Alejo
Jagger, Mick 1944-   **CLC 17**
Jahiz, al- c. 780-c. 869   **CMLC 25**
Jakes, John (William) 1932- **CLC 29; DAM NOV, POP**
   See also BEST 89:4; CA 57-60; CANR 10, 43, 66; DLBY 83; INT CANR-10; MTCW 1; SATA 62
James, Andrew
   See Kirkup, James
James, C(yril) L(ionel) R(obert) 1901-1989 **CLC 33; BLCS**
   See also BW 2; CA 117; 125; 128; CANR 62; DLB 125; MTCW 1
James, Daniel (Lewis) 1911-1988
   See Santiago, Danny
   See also CA 125
James, Dynely
   See Mayne, William (James Carter)
James, Henry Sr. 1811-1882   **NCLC 53**
James, Henry 1843-1916 **TCLC 2, 11, 24, 40, 47, 64; DA; DAB; DAC; DAM MST, NOV; SSC 8, 32; WLC**
   See also CA 104; 132; CDALB 1865-1917; DLB 12, 71, 74, 189; DLBD 13; MTCW 1
James, M. R.
   See James, Montague (Rhodes)
   See also DLB 156
James, Montague (Rhodes) 1862-1936 **T C L C 6; SSC 16**
   See also CA 104; DLB 201
James, P. D. 1920-   **CLC 18, 46**
   See also White, Phyllis Dorothy James
   See also BEST 90:2; CDBLB 1960 to Present; DLB 87; DLBD 17
James, Philip
   See Moorcock, Michael (John)
James, William 1842-1910   **TCLC 15, 32**
   See also CA 109
James I 1394-1437   **LC 20**
Jameson, Anna 1794-1860   **NCLC 43**
   See also DLB 99, 166
Jami, Nur al-Din 'Abd al-Rahman 1414-1492 **LC 9**
Jammes, Francis 1868-1938   **TCLC 75**
Jandl, Ernst 1925-   **CLC 34**
Janowitz, Tama 1957- **CLC 43; DAM POP**
   See also CA 106; CANR 52
Japrisot, Sebastien 1931-   **CLC 90**
Jarrell, Randall 1914-1965CLC **1, 2, 6, 9, 13, 49; DAM POET**
   See also CA 5-8R; 25-28R; CABS 2; CANR 6, 34; CDALB 1941-1968; CLR 6; DLB 48, 52; MAICYA; MTCW 1; SATA 7
Jarry, Alfred 1873-1907 **TCLC 2, 14; DAM DRAM; SSC 20**
   See also CA 104; 153; DLB 192
Jarvis, E. K.
   See Bloch, Robert (Albert); Ellison, Harlan (Jay); Silverberg, Robert
Jeake, Samuel, Jr.
   See Aiken, Conrad (Potter)
Jean Paul 1763-1825   **NCLC 7**
Jefferies, (John) Richard 1848-1887NCLC **47**
   See also DLB 98, 141; SATA 16

Jeffers, (John) Robinson 1887-1962CLC **2, 3, 11, 15, 54; DA; DAC; DAM MST, POET; PC 17; WLC**
   See also CA 85-88; CANR 35; CDALB 1917-1929; DLB 45; MTCW 1
Jefferson, Janet
   See Mencken, H(enry) L(ouis)
Jefferson, Thomas 1743-1826   **NCLC 11**
   See also CDALB 1640-1865; DLB 31
Jeffrey, Francis 1773-1850   **NCLC 33**
   See also DLB 107
Jelakowitch, Ivan
   See Heijermans, Herman
Jellicoe, (Patricia) Ann 1927-   **CLC 27**
   See also CA 85-88; DLB 13
Jen, Gish   **CLC 70**
   See also Jen, Lillian
Jen, Lillian 1956(?)-
   See Jen, Gish
   See also CA 135
Jenkins, (John) Robin 1912-   **CLC 52**
   See also CA 1-4R; CANR 1; DLB 14
Jennings, Elizabeth (Joan) 1926- **CLC 5, 14**
   See also CA 61-64; CAAS 5; CANR 8, 39, 66; DLB 27; MTCW 1; SATA 66
Jennings, Waylon 1937-   **CLC 21**
Jensen, Johannes V. 1873-1950   **TCLC 41**
   See also CA 170
Jensen, Laura (Linnea) 1948-   **CLC 37**
   See also CA 103
Jerome, Jerome K(lapka) 1859-1927TCLC **23**
   See also CA 119; DLB 10, 34, 135
Jerrold, Douglas William 1803-1857NCLC **2**
   See also DLB 158, 159
Jewett, (Theodora) Sarah Orne 1849-1909 **TCLC 1, 22; SSC 6**
   See also CA 108; 127; CANR 71; DLB 12, 74; SATA 15
Jewsbury, Geraldine (Endsor) 1812-1880 **NCLC 22**
   See also DLB 21
Jhabvala, Ruth Prawer 1927-CLC **4, 8, 29, 94; DAB; DAM NOV**
   See also CA 1-4R; CANR 2, 29, 51, 74; DLB 139, 194; INT CANR-29; MTCW 1
Jibran, Kahlil
   See Gibran, Kahlil
Jibran, Khalil
   See Gibran, Kahlil
Jiles, Paulette 1943-   **CLC 13, 58**
   See also CA 101; CANR 70
Jimenez (Mantecon), Juan Ramon 1881-1958 **TCLC 4; DAM MULT, POET; HLC; PC 7**
   See also CA 104; 131; CANR 74; DLB 134; HW; MTCW 1
Jimenez, Ramon
   See Jimenez (Mantecon), Juan Ramon
Jimenez Mantecon, Juan
   See Jimenez (Mantecon), Juan Ramon
Jin, Ha 1956-   **CLC 109**
   See also CA 152
Joel, Billy   **CLC 26**
   See also Joel, William Martin
Joel, William Martin 1949-
   See Joel, Billy
   See also CA 108
John, Saint 7th cent.   **CMLC 27**
John of the Cross, St. 1542-1591   **LC 18**
Johnson, B(ryan) S(tanley William) 1933-1973 **CLC 6, 9**
   See also CA 9-12R; 53-56; CANR 9; DLB 14, 40

Johnson, Benj. F. of Boo
See Riley, James Whitcomb
Johnson, Benjamin F. of Boo
See Riley, James Whitcomb
Johnson, Charles (Richard) 1948-CLC 7, 51,
65; BLC 2; DAM MULT
See also BW 2; CA 116; CAAS 18; CANR 42,
66; DLB 33
Johnson, Denis 1949-   CLC 52
See also CA 117; 121; CANR 71; DLB 120
Johnson, Diane 1934-   CLC 5, 13, 48
See also CA 41-44R; CANR 17, 40, 62; DLBY
80; INT CANR-17; MTCW 1
Johnson, Eyvind (Olof Verner) 1900-1976
CLC 14
See also CA 73-76; 69-72; CANR 34
Johnson, J. R.
See James, C(yril) L(ionel) R(obert)
Johnson, James Weldon 1871-1938 TCLC 3,
19; BLC 2; DAM MULT, POET; PC 24
See also BW 1; CA 104; 125; CDALB 1917-
1929; CLR 32; DLB 51; MTCW 1; SATA 31
Johnson, Joyce 1935-   CLC 58
See also CA 125; 129
Johnson, Lionel (Pigot) 1867-1902 TCLC 19
See also CA 117; DLB 19
Johnson, Marguerite (Annie)
See Angelou, Maya
Johnson, Mel
See Malzberg, Barry N(athaniel)
Johnson, Pamela Hansford 1912-1981CLC 1,
7, 27
See also CA 1-4R; 104; CANR 2, 28; DLB 15;
MTCW 1
Johnson, Robert 1911(?)-1938   TCLC 69
Johnson, Samuel 1709-1784LC 15; DA; DAB;
DAC; DAM MST; WLC
See also CDBLB 1660-1789; DLB 39, 95, 104,
142
Johnson, Uwe 1934-1984   CLC 5, 10, 15, 40
See also CA 1-4R; 112; CANR 1, 39; DLB 75;
MTCW 1
Johnston, George (Benson) 1913-   CLC 51
See also CA 1-4R; CANR 5, 20; DLB 88
Johnston, Jennifer 1930-   CLC 7
See also CA 85-88; DLB 14
Jolley, (Monica) Elizabeth 1923-CLC 46; SSC
19
See also CA 127; CAAS 13; CANR 59
Jones, Arthur Llewellyn 1863-1947
See Machen, Arthur
See also CA 104
Jones, D(ouglas) G(ordon) 1929-   CLC 10
See also CA 29-32R; CANR 13; DLB 53
Jones, David (Michael) 1895-1974CLC 2, 4, 7,
13, 42
See also CA 9-12R; 53-56; CANR 28; CDBLB
1945-1960; DLB 20, 100; MTCW 1
Jones, David Robert 1947-
See Bowie, David
See also CA 103
Jones, Diana Wynne 1934-   CLC 26
See also AAYA 12; CA 49-52; CANR 4, 26,
56; CLR 23; DLB 161; JRDA; MAICYA;
SAAS 7; SATA 9, 70
Jones, Edward P. 1950-   CLC 76
See also BW 2; CA 142
Jones, Gayl 1949-   CLC 6, 9; BLC 2; DAM
MULT
See also BW 2; CA 77-80; CANR 27, 66; DLB
33; MTCW 1
Jones, James 1921-1977   CLC 1, 3, 10, 39
See also AITN 1, 2; CA 1-4R; 69-72; CANR 6;

DLB 2, 143; DLBD 17; MTCW 1
Jones, John J.
See Lovecraft, H(oward) P(hillips)
Jones, LeRoi   CLC 1, 2, 3, 5, 10, 14
See also Baraka, Amiri
Jones, Louis B. 1953-   CLC 65
See also CA 141; CANR 73
Jones, Madison (Percy, Jr.) 1925-   CLC 4
See also CA 13-16R; CAAS 11; CANR 7, 54;
DLB 152
Jones, Mervyn 1922-   CLC 10, 52
See also CA 45-48; CAAS 5; CANR 1; MTCW
1
Jones, Mick 1956(?)-   CLC 30
Jones, Nettie (Pearl) 1941-   CLC 34
See also BW 2; CA 137; CAAS 20
Jones, Preston 1936-1979   CLC 10
See also CA 73-76; 89-92; DLB 7
Jones, Robert F(rancis) 1934-   CLC 7
See also CA 49-52; CANR 2, 61
Jones, Rod 1953-   CLC 50
See also CA 128
Jones, Terence Graham Parry 1942- CLC 21
See also Jones, Terry; Monty Python
See also CA 112; 116; CANR 35; INT 116
Jones, Terry
See Jones, Terence Graham Parry
See also SATA 67; SATA-Brief 51
Jones, Thom 1945(?)-   CLC 81
See also CA 157
Jong, Erica 1942-   CLC 4, 6, 8, 18, 83; DAM
NOV, POP
See also AITN 1; BEST 90:2; CA 73-76; CANR
26, 52, 75; DLB 2, 5, 28, 152; INT CANR-
26; MTCW 1
Jonson, Ben(jamin) 1572(?)-1637   LC 6, 33;
DA; DAB; DAC; DAM DRAM, MST,
POET; DC 4; PC 17; WLC
See also CDBLB Before 1660; DLB 62, 121
Jordan, June 1936-CLC 5, 11, 23, 114; BLCS;
DAM MULT, POET
See also AAYA 2; BW 2; CA 33-36R; CANR
25, 70; CLR 10; DLB 38; MAICYA; MTCW
1; SATA 4
Jordan, Neil (Patrick) 1950-   CLC 110
See also CA 124; 130; CANR 54; INT 130
Jordan, Pat(rick M.) 1941-   CLC 37
See also CA 33-36R
Jorgensen, Ivar
See Ellison, Harlan (Jay)
Jorgenson, Ivar
See Silverberg, Robert
Josephus, Flavius c. 37-100   CMLC 13
Josipovici, Gabriel 1940-   CLC 6, 43
See also CA 37-40R; CAAS 8; CANR 47; DLB
14
Joubert, Joseph 1754-1824   NCLC 9
Jouve, Pierre Jean 1887-1976   CLC 47
See also CA 65-68
Jovine, Francesco 1902-1950   TCLC 79
Joyce, James (Augustine Aloysius) 1882-1941
TCLC 3, 8, 16, 35, 52; DA; DAB; DAC;
DAM MST, NOV, POET; PC 22; SSC 3,
26; WLC
See also CA 104; 126; CDBLB 1914-1945;
DLB 10, 19, 36, 162; MTCW 1
Jozsef, Attila 1905-1937   TCLC 22
See also CA 116
Juana Ines de la Cruz 1651(?)-1695LC 5; PC
24
Judd, Cyril
See Kornbluth, C(yril) M.; Pohl, Frederik
Julian of Norwich 1342(?)-1416(?)   LC 6

See also DLB 146
Junger, Sebastian 1962-   CLC 109
See also CA 165
Juniper, Alex
See Hospital, Janette Turner
Junius
See Luxemburg, Rosa
Just, Ward (Swift) 1935-   CLC 4, 27
See also CA 25-28R; CANR 32; INT CANR-
32
Justice, Donald (Rodney) 1925-   CLC 6, 19,
102; DAM POET
See also CA 5-8R; CANR 26, 54, 74; DLBY
83; INT CANR-26
Juvenal   CMLC 8
See also Juvenalis, Decimus Junius
Juvenalis, Decimus Junius 55(?)-c. 127(?)
See Juvenal
Juvenis
See Bourne, Randolph S(illiman)
Kacew, Romain 1914-1980
See Gary, Romain
See also CA 108; 102
Kadare, Ismail 1936-   CLC 52
See also CA 161
Kadohata, Cynthia   CLC 59
See also CA 140
Kafka, Franz 1883-1924TCLC 2, 6, 13, 29, 47,
53; DA; DAB; DAC; DAM MST, NOV;
SSC 5, 29; WLC
See also CA 105; 126; DLB 81; MTCW 1
Kahanovitsch, Pinkhes
See Der Nister
Kahn, Roger 1927-   CLC 30
See also CA 25-28R; CANR 44, 69; DLB 171;
SATA 37
Kain, Saul
See Sassoon, Siegfried (Lorraine)
Kaiser, Georg 1878-1945   TCLC 9
See also CA 106; DLB 124
Kaletski, Alexander 1946-   CLC 39
See also CA 118; 143
Kalidasa fl. c. 400-   CMLC 9; PC 22
Kallman, Chester (Simon) 1921-1975 CLC 2
See also CA 45-48; 53-56; CANR 3
Kaminsky, Melvin 1926-
See Brooks, Mel
See also CA 65-68; CANR 16
Kaminsky, Stuart M(elvin) 1934-   CLC 59
See also CA 73-76; CANR 29, 53
Kane, Francis
See Robbins, Harold
Kane, Paul
See Simon, Paul (Frederick)
Kane, Wilson
See Bloch, Robert (Albert)
Kanin, Garson 1912-   CLC 22
See also AITN 1; CA 5-8R; CANR 7; DLB 7
Kaniuk, Yoram 1930-   CLC 19
See also CA 134
Kant, Immanuel 1724-1804   NCLC 27, 67
See also DLB 94
Kantor, MacKinlay 1904-1977   CLC 7
See also CA 61-64; 73-76; CANR 60, 63; DLB
9, 102
Kaplan, David Michael 1946-   CLC 50
Kaplan, James 1951-   CLC 59
See also CA 135
Karageorge, Michael
See Anderson, Poul (William)
Karamzin, Nikolai Mikhailovich 1766-1826
NCLC 3
See also DLB 150

Karapanou, Margarita 1946-   CLC 13
See also CA 101

Karinthy, Frigyes 1887-1938   TCLC 47
See also CA 170

Karl, Frederick R(obert) 1927-   CLC 34
See also CA 5-8R; CANR 3, 44

Kastel, Warren
See Silverberg, Robert

Kataev, Evgeny Petrovich 1903-1942
See Petrov, Evgeny
See also CA 120

Kataphusin
See Ruskin, John

Katz, Steve 1935-   CLC 47
See also CA 25-28R; CAAS 14, 64; CANR 12;
DLBY 83

Kauffman, Janet 1945-   CLC 42
See also CA 117; CANR 43; DLBY 86

Kaufman, Bob (Garnell) 1925-1986 CLC 49
See also BW 1; CA 41-44R; 118; CANR 22;
DLB 16, 41

Kaufman, George S. 1889-1961CLC 38; DAM
DRAM
See also CA 108; 93-96; DLB 7; INT 108

Kaufman, Sue   CLC 3, 8
See also Barondess, Sue K(aufman)

Kavafis, Konstantinos Petrou 1863-1933
See Cavafy, C(onstantine) P(eter)
See also CA 104

Kavan, Anna 1901-1968   CLC 5, 13, 82
See also CA 5-8R; CANR 6, 57; MTCW 1

Kavanagh, Dan
See Barnes, Julian (Patrick)

Kavanagh, Patrick (Joseph) 1904-1967 C L C
22
See also CA 123; 25-28R; DLB 15, 20; MTCW
1

Kawabata, Yasunari 1899-1972 CLC 2, 5, 9,
18, 107; DAM MULT; SSC 17
See also CA 93-96; 33-36R; DLB 180

Kaye, M(ary) M(argaret) 1909-   CLC 28
See also CA 89-92; CANR 24, 60; MTCW 1;
SATA 62

Kaye, Mollie
See Kaye, M(ary) M(argaret)

Kaye-Smith, Sheila 1887-1956   TCLC 20
See also CA 118; DLB 36

Kaymor, Patrice Maguilene
See Senghor, Leopold Sedar

Kazan, Elia 1909-   CLC 6, 16, 63
See also CA 21-24R; CANR 32

Kazantzakis, Nikos 1883(?)-1957 TCLC 2, 5,
33
See also CA 105; 132; MTCW 1

Kazin, Alfred 1915-   CLC 34, 38
See also CA 1-4R; CAAS 7; CANR 1, 45; DLB
67

Keane, Mary Nesta (Skrine) 1904-1996
See Keane, Molly
See also CA 108; 114; 151

Keane, Molly   CLC 31
See also Keane, Mary Nesta (Skrine)
See also INT 114

Keates, Jonathan 1946(?)-   CLC 34
See also CA 163

Keaton, Buster 1895-1966   CLC 20

Keats, John 1795-1821NCLC 8, 73; DA; DAB;
DAC; DAM MST, POET; PC 1; WLC
See also CDBLB 1789-1832; DLB 96, 110

Keene, Donald 1922-   CLC 34
See also CA 1-4R; CANR 5

Keillor, Garrison   CLC 40, 115
See also Keillor, Gary (Edward)

See also AAYA 2; BEST 89:3; DLBY 87; SATA
58

Keillor, Gary (Edward) 1942-
See Keillor, Garrison
See also CA 111; 117; CANR 36, 59; DAM
POP; MTCW 1

Keith, Michael
See Hubbard, L(afayette) Ron(ald)

Keller, Gottfried 1819-1890 NCLC 2; SSC 26
See also DLB 129

Keller, Nora Okja   CLC 109

Kellerman, Jonathan 1949-   CLC 44; DAM
POP
See also BEST 90:1; CA 106; CANR 29, 51;
INT CANR-29

Kelley, William Melvin 1937-   CLC 22
See also BW 1; CA 77-80; CANR 27; DLB 33

Kellogg, Marjorie 1922-   CLC 2
See also CA 81-84

Kellow, Kathleen
See Hibbert, Eleanor Alice Burford

Kelly, M(ilton) T(erry) 1947-   CLC 55
See also CA 97-100; CAAS 22; CANR 19, 43

Kelman, James 1946-   CLC 58, 86
See also CA 148; DLB 194

Kemal, Yashar 1923-   CLC 14, 29
See also CA 89-92; CANR 44

Kemble, Fanny 1809-1893   NCLC 18
See also DLB 32

Kemelman, Harry 1908-1996   CLC 2
See also AITN 1; CA 9-12R; 155; CANR 6, 71;
DLB 28

Kempe, Margery 1373(?)-1440(?)   LC 6
See also DLB 146

Kempis, Thomas a 1380-1471   LC 11

Kendall, Henry 1839-1882   NCLC 12

Keneally, Thomas (Michael) 1935- CLC 5, 8,
10, 14, 19, 27, 43, 117; DAM NOV
See also CA 85-88; CANR 10, 50, 74; MTCW
1

Kennedy, Adrienne (Lita) 1931-CLC 66; BLC
2; DAM MULT; DC 5
See also BW 2; CA 103; CAAS 20; CABS 3;
CANR 26, 53; DLB 38

Kennedy, John Pendleton 1795-1870NCLC 2
See also DLB 3

Kennedy, Joseph Charles 1929-
See Kennedy, X. J.
See also CA 1-4R; CANR 4, 30, 40; SATA 14,
86

Kennedy, William 1928-   CLC 6, 28, 34, 53;
DAM NOV
See also AAYA 1; CA 85-88; CANR 14, 31;
DLB 143; DLBY 85; INT CANR-31; MTCW
1; SATA 57

Kennedy, X. J.   CLC 8, 42
See also Kennedy, Joseph Charles
See also CAAS 9; CLR 27; DLB 5; SAAS 22

Kenny, Maurice (Francis) 1929-   CLC 87;
DAM MULT
See also CA 144; CAAS 22; DLB 175; NNAL

Kent, Kelvin
See Kuttner, Henry

Kenton, Maxwell
See Southern, Terry

Kenyon, Robert O.
See Kuttner, Henry

Kepler, Johannes 1571-1630   LC 45

Kerouac, Jack   CLC 1, 2, 3, 5, 14, 29, 61
See also Kerouac, Jean-Louis Lebris de
See also AAYA 25; CDALB 1941-1968; DLB
2, 16; DLBD 3; DLBY 95

Kerouac, Jean-Louis Lebris de 1922-1969

See Kerouac, Jack
See also AITN 1; CA 5-8R; 25-28R; CANR 26,
54; DA; DAB; DAC; DAM MST, NOV,
POET, POP; MTCW 1; WLC

Kerr, Jean 1923-   CLC 22
See also CA 5-8R; CANR 7; INT CANR-7

Kerr, M. E.   CLC 12, 35
See also Meaker, Marijane (Agnes)
See also AAYA 2, 23; CLR 29; SAAS 1

Kerr, Robert   CLC 55

Kerrigan, (Thomas) Anthony 1918-CLC 4, 6
See also CA 49-52; CAAS 11; CANR 4

Kerry, Lois
See Duncan, Lois

Kesey, Ken (Elton) 1935- CLC 1, 3, 6, 11, 46,
64; DA; DAB; DAC; DAM MST, NOV,
POP; WLC
See also AAYA 25; CA 1-4R; CANR 22, 38,
66; CDALB 1968-1988; DLB 2, 16, 206;
MTCW 1; SATA 66

Kesselring, Joseph (Otto) 1902-1967CLC 45;
DAM DRAM, MST
See also CA 150

Kessler, Jascha (Frederick) 1929-   CLC 4
See also CA 17-20R; CANR 8, 48

Kettelkamp, Larry (Dale) 1933-   CLC 12
See also CA 29-32R; CANR 16; SAAS 3; SATA
2

Key, Ellen 1849-1926   TCLC 65

Keyber, Conny
See Fielding, Henry

Keyes, Daniel 1927-CLC 80; DA; DAC; DAM
MST, NOV
See also AAYA 23; CA 17-20R; CANR 10, 26,
54, 74; SATA 37

Keynes, John Maynard 1883-1946 TCLC 64
See also CA 114; 162, 163; DLBD 10

Khanshendel, Chiron
See Rose, Wendy

Khayyam, Omar 1048-1131 CMLC 11; DAM
POET; PC 8

Kherdian, David 1931-   CLC 6, 9
See also CA 21-24R; CAAS 2; CANR 39; CLR
24; JRDA; MAICYA; SATA 16, 74

Khlebnikov, Velimir   TCLC 20
See also Khlebnikov, Viktor Vladimirovich

Khlebnikov, Viktor Vladimirovich 1885-1922
See Khlebnikov, Velimir
See also CA 117

Khodasevich, Vladislav (Felitsianovich) 1886-
1939   TCLC 15
See also CA 115

Kielland, Alexander Lange 1849-1906 T C L C
5
See also CA 104

Kiely, Benedict 1919-   CLC 23, 43
See also CA 1-4R; CANR 2; DLB 15

Kienzle, William X(avier) 1928-   CLC 25;
DAM POP
See also CA 93-96; CAAS 1; CANR 9, 31, 59;
INT CANR-31; MTCW 1

Kierkegaard, Soren 1813-1855   NCLC 34

Killens, John Oliver 1916-1987   CLC 10
See also BW 2; CA 77-80; 123; CAAS 2; CANR
26; DLB 33

Killigrew, Anne 1660-1685   LC 4
See also DLB 131

Kim
See Simenon, Georges (Jacques Christian)

Kincaid, Jamaica 1949- CLC 43, 68; BLC 2;
DAM MULT, NOV
See also AAYA 13; BW 2; CA 125; CANR 47,
59; DLB 157

King, Francis (Henry) 1923-**CLC 8, 53; DAM NOV**
See also CA 1-4R; CANR 1, 33; DLB 15, 139; MTCW 1

King, Kennedy
See Brown, George Douglas

King, Martin Luther, Jr. 1929-1968 **CLC 83; BLC 2; DA; DAB; DAC; DAM MST, MULT; WLCS**
See also BW 2; CA 25-28; CANR 27, 44; CAP 2; MTCW 1; SATA 14

King, Stephen (Edwin) 1947-**CLC 12, 26, 37, 61, 113; DAM NOV, POP; SSC 17**
See also AAYA 1, 17; BEST 90:1; CA 61-64; CANR 1, 30, 52; DLB 143; DLBY 80; JRDA; MTCW 1; SATA 9, 55

King, Steve
See King, Stephen (Edwin)

King, Thomas 1943- **CLC 89; DAC; DAM MULT**
See also CA 144; DLB 175; NNAL; SATA 96

Kingman, Lee **CLC 17**
See also Natti, (Mary) Lee
See also SAAS 3; SATA 1, 67

Kingsley, Charles 1819-1875 **NCLC 35**
See also DLB 21, 32, 163, 190; YABC 2

Kingsley, Sidney 1906-1995 **CLC 44**
See also CA 85-88; 147; DLB 7

Kingsolver, Barbara 1955-**CLC 55, 81; DAM POP**
See also AAYA 15; CA 129; 134; CANR 60; DLB 206; INT 134

Kingston, Maxine (Ting Ting) Hong 1940-**CLC 12, 19, 58; DAM MULT, NOV; WLCS**
See also AAYA 8; CA 69-72; CANR 13, 38, 74; DLB 173; DLBY 80; INT CANR-13; MTCW 1; SATA 53

Kinnell, Galway 1927- **CLC 1, 2, 3, 5, 13, 29**
See also CA 9-12R; CANR 10, 34, 66; DLB 5; DLBY 87; INT CANR-34; MTCW 1

Kinsella, Thomas 1928- **CLC 4, 19**
See also CA 17-20R; CANR 15; DLB 27; MTCW 1

Kinsella, W(illiam) P(atrick) 1935- **CLC 27, 43; DAC; DAM NOV, POP**
See also AAYA 7; CA 97-100; CAAS 7; CANR 21, 35, 66, 75; INT CANR-21; MTCW 1

Kipling, (Joseph) Rudyard 1865-1936 **TCLC 8, 17; DA; DAB; DAC; DAM MST, POET; PC 3; SSC 5; WLC**
See also CA 105; 120; CANR 33; CDBLB 1890-1914; CLR 39; DLB 19, 34, 141, 156; MAICYA; MTCW 1; SATA 100; YABC 2

Kirkup, James 1918- **CLC 1**
See also CA 1-4R; CAAS 4; CANR 2; DLB 27; SATA 12

Kirkwood, James 1930(?)-1989 **CLC 9**
See also AITN 2; CA 1-4R; 128; CANR 6, 40

Kirshner, Sidney
See Kingsley, Sidney

Kis, Danilo 1935-1989 **CLC 57**
See also CA 109; 118; 129; CANR 61; DLB 181; MTCW 1

Kivi, Aleksis 1834-1872 **NCLC 30**

Kizer, Carolyn (Ashley) 1925-**CLC 15, 39, 80; DAM POET**
See also CA 65-68; CAAS 5; CANR 24, 70; DLB 5, 169

Klabund 1890-1928 **TCLC 44**
See also CA 162; DLB 66

Klappert, Peter 1942- **CLC 57**
See also CA 33-36R; DLB 5

Klein, A(braham) M(oses) 1909-1972**CLC 19; DAB; DAC; DAM MST**
See also CA 101; 37-40R; DLB 68

Klein, Norma 1938-1989 **CLC 30**
See also AAYA 2; CA 41-44R; 128; CANR 15, 37; CLR 2, 19; INT CANR-15; JRDA; MAICYA; SAAS 1; SATA 7, 57

Klein, T(heodore) E(ibon) D(onald) 1947-**CLC 34**
See also CA 119; CANR 44, 75

Kleist, Heinrich von 1777-1811 **NCLC 2, 37; DAM DRAM; SSC 22**
See also DLB 90

Klima, Ivan 1931- **CLC 56; DAM NOV**
See also CA 25-28R; CANR 17, 50

Klimentov, Andrei Platonovich 1899-1951
See Platonov, Andrei
See also CA 108

Klinger, Friedrich Maximilian von 1752-1831 **NCLC 1**
See also DLB 94

Klingsor the Magician
See Hartmann, Sadakichi

Klopstock, Friedrich Gottlieb 1724-1803 **NCLC 11**
See also DLB 97

Knapp, Caroline 1959- **CLC 99**
See also CA 154

Knebel, Fletcher 1911-1993 **CLC 14**
See also AITN 1; CA 1-4R; 140; CAAS 3; CANR 1, 36; SATA 36; SATA-Obit 75

Knickerbocker, Diedrich
See Irving, Washington

Knight, Etheridge 1931-1991**CLC 40; BLC 2; DAM POET; PC 14**
See also BW 1; CA 21-24R; 133; CANR 23; DLB 41

Knight, Sarah Kemble 1666-1727 **LC 7**
See also DLB 24, 200

Knister, Raymond 1899-1932 **TCLC 56**
See also DLB 68

Knowles, John 1926- **CLC 1, 4, 10, 26; DA; DAC; DAM MST, NOV**
See also AAYA 10; CA 17-20R; CANR 40, 74; CDALB 1968-1988; DLB 6; MTCW 1; SATA 8, 89

Knox, Calvin M.
See Silverberg, Robert

Knox, John c. 1505-1572 **LC 37**
See also DLB 132

Knye, Cassandra
See Disch, Thomas M(ichael)

Koch, C(hristopher) J(ohn) 1932- **CLC 42**
See also CA 127

Koch, Christopher
See Koch, C(hristopher) J(ohn)

Koch, Kenneth 1925- **CLC 5, 8, 44; DAM POET**
See also CA 1-4R; CANR 6, 36, 57; DLB 5; INT CANR-36; SATA 65

Kochanowski, Jan 1530-1584 **LC 10**

Kock, Charles Paul de 1794-1871 **NCLC 16**

Koda Shigeyuki 1867-1947
See Rohan, Koda
See also CA 121

Koestler, Arthur 1905-1983**CLC 1, 3, 6, 8, 15, 33**
See also CA 1-4R; 109; CANR 1, 33; CDBLB 1945-1960; DLBY 83; MTCW 1

Kogawa, Joy Nozomi 1935- **CLC 78; DAC; DAM MST, MULT**
See also CA 101; CANR 19, 62; SATA 99

Kohout, Pavel 1928- **CLC 13**

See also CA 45-48; CANR 3

Koizumi, Yakumo
See Hearn, (Patricio) Lafcadio (Tessima Carlos)

Kolmar, Gertrud 1894-1943 **TCLC 40**
See also CA 167

Komunyakaa, Yusef 1947-**CLC 86, 94; BLCS**
See also CA 147; DLB 120

Konrad, George
See Konrad, Gyoergy

Konrad, Gyoergy 1933- **CLC 4, 10, 73**
See also CA 85-88

Konwicki, Tadeusz 1926- **CLC 8, 28, 54, 117**
See also CA 101; CAAS 9; CANR 39, 59; MTCW 1

Koontz, Dean R(ay) 1945- **CLC 78; DAM NOV, POP**
See also AAYA 9; BEST 89:3, 90:2; CA 108; CANR 19, 36, 52; MTCW 1; SATA 92

Kopernik, Mikolaj
See Copernicus, Nicolaus

Kopit, Arthur (Lee) 1937-**CLC 1, 18, 33; DAM DRAM**
See also AITN 1; CA 81-84; CABS 3; DLB 7; MTCW 1

Kops, Bernard 1926- **CLC 4**
See also CA 5-8R; DLB 13

Kornbluth, C(yril) M. 1923-1958 **TCLC 8**
See also CA 105; 160; DLB 8

Korolenko, V. G.
See Korolenko, Vladimir Galaktionovich

Korolenko, Vladimir
See Korolenko, Vladimir Galaktionovich

Korolenko, Vladimir G.
See Korolenko, Vladimir Galaktionovich

Korolenko, Vladimir Galaktionovich 1853-1921 **TCLC 22**
See also CA 121

Korzybski, Alfred (Habdank Skarbek) 1879-1950 **TCLC 61**
See also CA 123; 160

Kosinski, Jerzy (Nikodem) 1933-1991**CLC 1, 2, 3, 6, 10, 15, 53, 70; DAM NOV**
See also CA 17-20R; 134; CANR 9, 46; DLB 2; DLBY 82; MTCW 1

Kostelanetz, Richard (Cory) 1940- **CLC 28**
See also CA 13-16R; CAAS 8; CANR 38

Kostrowitzki, Wilhelm Apollinaris de 1880-1918
See Apollinaire, Guillaume
See also CA 104

Kotlowitz, Robert 1924- **CLC 4**
See also CA 33-36R; CANR 36

Kotzebue, August (Friedrich Ferdinand) von 1761-1819 **NCLC 25**
See also DLB 94

Kotzwinkle, William 1938- **CLC 5, 14, 35**
See also CA 45-48; CANR 3, 44; CLR 6; DLB 173; MAICYA; SATA 24, 70

Kowna, Stancy
See Szymborska, Wislawa

Kozol, Jonathan 1936- **CLC 17**
See also CA 61-64; CANR 16, 45

Kozoll, Michael 1940(?)- **CLC 35**

Kramer, Kathryn 19(?)- **CLC 34**

Kramer, Larry 1935-**CLC 42; DAM POP; DC 8**
See also CA 124; 126; CANR 60

Krasicki, Ignacy 1735-1801 **NCLC 8**

Krasinski, Zygmunt 1812-1859 **NCLC 4**

Kraus, Karl 1874-1936 **TCLC 5**
See also CA 104; DLB 118

Kreve (Mickevicius), Vincas 1882-1954**TCLC 27**

See also CA 170

Kristeva, Julia 1941-   **CLC 77**
See also CA 154

Kristofferson, Kris 1936-   **CLC 26**
See also CA 104

Krizanc, John 1956-   **CLC 57**

Krleza, Miroslav 1893-1981   **CLC 8, 114**
See also CA 97-100; 105; CANR 50; DLB 147

Kroetsch, Robert 1927- **CLC 5, 23, 57; DAC; DAM POET**
See also CA 17-20R; CANR 8, 38; DLB 53; MTCW 1

Kroetz, Franz
See Kroetz, Franz Xaver

Kroetz, Franz Xaver 1946-   **CLC 41**
See also CA 130

Kroker, Arthur (W.) 1945-   **CLC 77**
See also CA 161

Kropotkin, Peter (Aleksieevich) 1842-1921 **TCLC 36**
See also CA 119

Krotkov, Yuri 1917-   **CLC 19**
See also CA 102

Krumb
See Crumb, R(obert)

Krumgold, Joseph (Quincy) 1908-1980 **C L C 12**
See also CA 9-12R; 101; CANR 7; MAICYA; SATA 1, 48; SATA-Obit 23

Krumwitz
See Crumb, R(obert)

Krutch, Joseph Wood 1893-1970   **CLC 24**
See also CA 1-4R; 25-28R; CANR 4; DLB 63, 206

Krutzch, Gus
See Eliot, T(homas) S(tearns)

Krylov, Ivan Andreevich 1768(?)-1844 **N C L C 1**
See also DLB 150

Kubin, Alfred (Leopold Isidor) 1877-1959 **TCLC 23**
See also CA 112; 149; DLB 81

Kubrick, Stanley 1928-   **CLC 16**
See also CA 81-84; CANR 33; DLB 26

Kumin, Maxine (Winokur) 1925- **CLC 5, 13, 28; DAM POET; PC 15**
See also AITN 2; CA 1-4R; CAAS 8; CANR 1, 21, 69; DLB 5; MTCW 1; SATA 12

Kundera, Milan 1929- **CLC 4, 9, 19, 32, 68, 115; DAM NOV; SSC 24**
See also AAYA 2; CA 85-88; CANR 19, 52, 74; MTCW 1

Kunene, Mazisi (Raymond) 1930- **CLC 85**
See also BW 1; CA 125; DLB 117

Kunitz, Stanley (Jasspon) 1905- **CLC 6, 11, 14; PC 19**
See also CA 41-44R; CANR 26, 57; DLB 48; INT CANR-26; MTCW 1

Kunze, Reiner 1933-   **CLC 10**
See also CA 93-96; DLB 75

Kuprin, Aleksandr Ivanovich 1870-1938 **TCLC 5**
See also CA 104

Kureishi, Hanif 1954(?)-   **CLC 64**
See also CA 139; DLB 194

Kurosawa, Akira 1910-1998 **CLC 16; DAM MULT**
See also AAYA 11; CA 101; 170; CANR 46

Kushner, Tony 1957(?)- **CLC 81; DAM DRAM; DC 10**
See also CA 144; CANR 74

Kuttner, Henry 1915-1958   **TCLC 10**
See also Vance, Jack

See also CA 107; 157; DLB 8

Kuzma, Greg 1944-   **CLC 7**
See also CA 33-36R; CANR 70

Kuzmin, Mikhail 1872(?)-1936   **TCLC 40**
See also CA 170

Kyd, Thomas 1558-1594 **LC 22; DAM DRAM; DC 3**
See also DLB 62

Kyprianos, Iossif
See Samarakis, Antonis

La Bruyere, Jean de 1645-1696   **LC 17**

Lacan, Jacques (Marie Emile) 1901-1981 **CLC 75**
See also CA 121; 104

Laclos, Pierre Ambroise Francois Choderlos de 1741-1803   **NCLC 4**

La Colere, Francois
See Aragon, Louis

Lacolere, Francois
See Aragon, Louis

La Deshabilleuse
See Simenon, Georges (Jacques Christian)

Lady Gregory
See Gregory, Isabella Augusta (Persse)

Lady of Quality, A
See Bagnold, Enid

La Fayette, Marie (Madelaine Pioche de la Vergne Comtes 1634-1693   **LC 2**

Lafayette, Rene
See Hubbard, L(afayette) Ron(ald)

Laforgue, Jules 1860-1887 **NCLC 5, 53; PC 14; SSC 20**

Lagerkvist, Paer (Fabian) 1891-1974 **CLC 7, 10, 13, 54; DAM DRAM, NOV**
See also Lagerkvist, Par
See also CA 85-88; 49-52; MTCW 1

Lagerkvist, Par   **SSC 12**
See also Lagerkvist, Paer (Fabian)

Lagerloef, Selma (Ottiliana Lovisa) 1858-1940 **TCLC 4, 36**
See also Lagerlof, Selma (Ottiliana Lovisa)
See also CA 108; SATA 15

Lagerlof, Selma (Ottiliana Lovisa)
See Lagerloef, Selma (Ottiliana Lovisa)
See also CLR 7; SATA 15

La Guma, (Justin) Alex(ander) 1925-1985 **CLC 19; BLCS; DAM NOV**
See also BW 1; CA 49-52; 118; CANR 25; DLB 117; MTCW 1

Laidlaw, A. K.
See Grieve, C(hristopher) M(urray)

Lainez, Manuel Mujica
See Mujica Lainez, Manuel
See also HW

Laing, R(onald) D(avid) 1927-1989 **CLC 95**
See also CA 107; 129; CANR 34; MTCW 1

Lamartine, Alphonse (Marie Louis Prat) de 1790-1869 **NCLC 11; DAM POET; PC 16**

Lamb, Charles 1775-1834 **NCLC 10; DA; DAB; DAC; DAM MST; WLC**
See also CDBLB 1789-1832; DLB 93, 107, 163; SATA 17

Lamb, Lady Caroline 1785-1828 **NCLC 38**
See also DLB 116

Lamming, George (William) 1927- **CLC 2, 4, 66; BLC 2; DAM MULT**
See also BW 2; CA 85-88; CANR 26; DLB 125; MTCW 1

L'Amour, Louis (Dearborn) 1908-1988 **C L C 25, 55; DAM NOV, POP**
See also AAYA 16; AITN 2; BEST 89:2; CA 1-4R; 125; CANR 3, 25, 40; DLB 207; DLBY 80; MTCW 1

Lampedusa, Giuseppe (Tomasi) di 1896-1957 **TCLC 13**
See also Tomasi di Lampedusa, Giuseppe
See also CA 164; DLB 177

Lampman, Archibald 1861-1899 **NCLC 25**
See also DLB 92

Lancaster, Bruce 1896-1963   **CLC 36**
See also CA 9-10; CANR 70; CAP 1; SATA 9

Lanchester, John   **CLC 99**

Landau, Mark Alexandrovich
See Aldanov, Mark (Alexandrovich)

Landau-Aldanov, Mark Alexandrovich
See Aldanov, Mark (Alexandrovich)

Landis, Jerry
See Simon, Paul (Frederick)

Landis, John 1950-   **CLC 26**
See also CA 112; 122

Landolfi, Tommaso 1908-1979   **CLC 11, 49**
See also CA 127; 117; DLB 177

Landon, Letitia Elizabeth 1802-1838 **N C L C 15**
See also DLB 96

Landor, Walter Savage 1775-1864 **NCLC 14**
See also DLB 93, 107

Landwirth, Heinz 1927-
See Lind, Jakov
See also CA 9-12R; CANR 7

Lane, Patrick 1939- **CLC 25; DAM POET**
See also CA 97-100; CANR 54; DLB 53; INT 97-100

Lang, Andrew 1844-1912   **TCLC 16**
See also CA 114; 137; DLB 98, 141, 184; MAICYA; SATA 16

Lang, Fritz 1890-1976   **CLC 20, 103**
See also CA 77-80; 69-72; CANR 30

Lange, John
See Crichton, (John) Michael

Langer, Elinor 1939-   **CLC 34**
See also CA 121

Langland, William 1330(?)-1400(?) **LC 19; DA; DAB; DAC; DAM MST, POET**
See also DLB 146

Langstaff, Launcelot
See Irving, Washington

Lanier, Sidney 1842-1881 **NCLC 6; DAM POET**
See also DLB 64; DLBD 13; MAICYA; SATA 18

Lanyer, Aemilia 1569-1645   **LC 10, 30**
See also DLB 121

Lao-Tzu
See Lao Tzu

Lao Tzu fl. 6th cent. B.C.-   **CMLC 7**

Lapine, James (Elliot) 1949-   **CLC 39**
See also CA 123; 130; CANR 54; INT 130

Larbaud, Valery (Nicolas) 1881-1957 **TCLC 9**
See also CA 106; 152

Lardner, Ring
See Lardner, Ring(gold) W(ilmer)

Lardner, Ring W., Jr.
See Lardner, Ring(gold) W(ilmer)

Lardner, Ring(gold) W(ilmer) 1885-1933 **TCLC 2, 14; SSC 32**
See also CA 104; 131; CDALB 1917-1929; DLB 11, 25, 86; DLBD 16; MTCW 1

Laredo, Betty
See Codrescu, Andrei

Larkin, Maia
See Wojciechowska, Maia (Teresa)

Larkin, Philip (Arthur) 1922-1985 **CLC 3, 5, 8, 9, 13, 18, 33, 39, 64; DAB; DAM MST, POET; PC 21**
See also CA 5-8R; 117; CANR 24, 62; CDBLB

1960 to Present; DLB 27; MTCW 1

Larra (y Sanchez de Castro), Mariano Jose de 1809-1837 **NCLC 17**

Larsen, Eric 1941- **CLC 55**
See also CA 132

Larsen, Nella 1891-1964 **CLC 37; BLC 2; DAM MULT**
See also BW 1; CA 125; DLB 51

Larson, Charles R(aymond) 1938- **CLC 31**
See also CA 53-56; CANR 4

Larson, Jonathan 1961-1996 **CLC 99**
See also CA 156

Las Casas, Bartolome de 1474-1566 **LC 31**

Lasch, Christopher 1932-1994 **CLC 102**
See also CA 73-76; 144; CANR 25; MTCW 1

Lasker-Schueler, Else 1869-1945 **TCLC 57**
See also DLB 66, 124

Laski, Harold 1893-1950 **TCLC 79**

Latham, Jean Lee 1902-1995 **CLC 12**
See also AITN 1; CA 5-8R; CANR 7; CLR 50; MAICYA; SATA 2, 68

Latham, Mavis
See Clark, Mavis Thorpe

Lathen, Emma **CLC 2**
See also Hennissart, Martha; Latsis, Mary J(ane)

Lathrop, Francis
See Leiber, Fritz (Reuter, Jr.)

Latsis, Mary J(ane) 1927(?)-1997
See Lathen, Emma
See also CA 85-88; 162

Lattimore, Richmond (Alexander) 1906-1984 **CLC 3**
See also CA 1-4R; 112; CANR 1

Laughlin, James 1914-1997 **CLC 49**
See also CA 21-24R; 162; CAAS 22; CANR 9, 47; DLB 48; DLBY 96, 97

Laurence, (Jean) Margaret (Wemyss) 1926-1987 **CLC 3, 6, 13, 50, 62; DAC; DAM MST; SSC 7**
See also CA 5-8R; 121; CANR 33; DLB 53; MTCW 1; SATA-Obit 50

Laurent, Antoine 1952- **CLC 50**

Lauscher, Hermann
See Hesse, Hermann

Lautreamont, Comte de 1846-1870 **NCLC 12; SSC 14**

Laverty, Donald
See Blish, James (Benjamin)

Lavin, Mary 1912-1996 **CLC 4, 18, 99; SSC 4**
See also CA 9-12R; 151; CANR 33; DLB 15; MTCW 1

Lavond, Paul Dennis
See Kornbluth, C(yril) M.; Pohl, Frederik

Lawler, Raymond Evenor 1922- **CLC 58**
See also CA 103

Lawrence, D(avid) H(erbert Richards) 1885-1930 **TCLC 2, 9, 16, 33, 48, 61; DA; DAB; DAC; DAM MST, NOV, POET; SSC 4, 19; WLC**
See also CA 104; 121; CDBLB 1914-1945; DLB 10, 19, 36, 98, 162, 195; MTCW 1

Lawrence, T(homas) E(dward) 1888-1935 **TCLC 18**
See also Dale, Colin
See also CA 115; 167; DLB 195

Lawrence of Arabia
See Lawrence, T(homas) E(dward)

Lawson, Henry (Archibald Hertzberg) 1867-1922 **TCLC 27; SSC 18**
See also CA 120

Lawton, Dennis
See Faust, Frederick (Schiller)

Laxness, Halldor **CLC 25**
See also Gudjonsson, Halldor Kiljan

Layamon fl. c. 1200- **CMLC 10**
See also DLB 146

Laye, Camara 1928-1980 **CLC 4, 38; BLC 2; DAM MULT**
See also BW 1; CA 85-88; 97-100; CANR 25; MTCW 1

Layton, Irving (Peter) 1912- **CLC 2, 15; DAC; DAM MST, POET**
See also CA 1-4R; CANR 2, 33, 43, 66; DLB 88; MTCW 1

Lazarus, Emma 1849-1887 **NCLC 8**

Lazarus, Felix
See Cable, George Washington

Lazarus, Henry
See Slavitt, David R(ytman)

Lea, Joan
See Neufeld, John (Arthur)

Leacock, Stephen (Butler) 1869-1944 **TCLC 2; DAC; DAM MST**
See also CA 104; 141; DLB 92

Lear, Edward 1812-1888 **NCLC 3**
See also CLR 1; DLB 32, 163, 166; MAICYA; SATA 18, 100

Lear, Norman (Milton) 1922- **CLC 12**
See also CA 73-76

Leautaud, Paul 1872-1956 **TCLC 83**
See also DLB 65

Leavis, F(rank) R(aymond) 1895-1978 **CLC 24**
See also CA 21-24R; 77-80; CANR 44; MTCW 1

Leavitt, David 1961- **CLC 34; DAM POP**
See also CA 116; 122; CANR 50, 62; DLB 130; INT 122

Leblanc, Maurice (Marie Emile) 1864-1941 **TCLC 49**
See also CA 110

Lebowitz, Fran(ces Ann) 1951(?)- **CLC 11, 36**
See also CA 81-84; CANR 14, 60, 70; INT CANR-14; MTCW 1

Lebrecht, Peter
See Tieck, (Johann) Ludwig

le Carre, John **CLC 3, 5, 9, 15, 28**
See also Cornwell, David (John Moore)
See also BEST 89:4; CDBLB 1960 to Present; DLB 87

Le Clezio, J(ean) M(arie) G(ustave) 1940- **CLC 31**
See also CA 116; 128; DLB 83

Leconte de Lisle, Charles-Marie-Rene 1818-1894 **NCLC 29**

Le Coq, Monsieur
See Simenon, Georges (Jacques Christian)

Leduc, Violette 1907-1972 **CLC 22**
See also CA 13-14; 33-36R; CANR 69; CAP 1

Ledwidge, Francis 1887(?)-1917 **TCLC 23**
See also CA 123; DLB 20

Lee, Andrea 1953- **CLC 36; BLC 2; DAM MULT**
See also BW 1; CA 125

Lee, Andrew
See Auchincloss, Louis (Stanton)

Lee, Chang-rae 1965- **CLC 91**
See also CA 148

Lee, Don L. **CLC 2**
See also Madhubuti, Haki R.

Lee, George W(ashington) 1894-1976 **CLC 52; BLC 2; DAM MULT**
See also BW 1; CA 125; DLB 51

Lee, (Nelle) Harper 1926- **CLC 12, 60; DA; DAB; DAC; DAM MST, NOV; WLC**
See also AAYA 13; CA 13-16R; CANR 51; CDALB 1941-1968; DLB 6; MTCW 1; SATA 11

Lee, Helen Elaine 1959(?)- **CLC 86**
See also CA 148

Lee, Julian
See Latham, Jean Lee

Lee, Larry
See Lee, Lawrence

Lee, Laurie 1914-1997 **CLC 90; DAB; DAM POP**
See also CA 77-80; 158; CANR 33, 73; DLB 27; MTCW 1

Lee, Lawrence 1941-1990 **CLC 34**
See also CA 131; CANR 43

Lee, Li-Young 1957- **PC 24**
See also CA 153; DLB 165

Lee, Manfred B(ennington) 1905-1971 **CLC 11**
See also Queen, Ellery
See also CA 1-4R; 29-32R; CANR 2; DLB 137

Lee, Shelton Jackson 1957(?)- **CLC 105; BLCS; DAM MULT**
See also Lee, Spike
See also BW 2; CA 125; CANR 42

Lee, Spike
See Lee, Shelton Jackson
See also AAYA 4

Lee, Stan 1922- **CLC 17**
See also AAYA 5; CA 108; 111; INT 111

Lee, Tanith 1947- **CLC 46**
See also AAYA 15; CA 37-40R; CANR 53; SATA 8, 88

Lee, Vernon **TCLC 5; SSC 33**
See also Paget, Violet
See also DLB 57, 153, 156, 174, 178

Lee, William
See Burroughs, William S(eward)

Lee, Willy
See Burroughs, William S(eward)

Lee-Hamilton, Eugene (Jacob) 1845-1907 **TCLC 22**
See also CA 117

Leet, Judith 1935- **CLC 11**

Le Fanu, Joseph Sheridan 1814-1873 **NCLC 9, 58; DAM POP; SSC 14**
See also DLB 21, 70, 159, 178

Leffland, Ella 1931- **CLC 19**
See also CA 29-32R; CANR 35; DLBY 84; INT CANR-35; SATA 65

Leger, Alexis
See Leger, (Marie-Rene Auguste) Alexis Saint-Leger

Leger, (Marie-Rene Auguste) Alexis Saint-Leger 1887-1975 **CLC 4, 11, 46; DAM POET; PC 23**
See also CA 13-16R; 61-64; CANR 43; MTCW 1

Leger, Saintleger
See Leger, (Marie-Rene Auguste) Alexis Saint-Leger

Le Guin, Ursula K(roeber) 1929- **CLC 8, 13, 22, 45, 71; DAB; DAC; DAM MST, POP; SSC 12**
See also AAYA 9, 27; AITN 1; CA 21-24R; CANR 9, 32, 52, 74; CDALB 1968-1988; CLR 3, 28; DLB 8, 52; INT CANR-32; JRDA; MAICYA; MTCW 1; SATA 4, 52, 99

Lehmann, Rosamond (Nina) 1901-1990 **CLC 5**
See also CA 77-80; 131; CANR 8, 73; DLB 15

Leiber, Fritz (Reuter, Jr.) 1910-1992 **CLC 25**
See also CA 45-48; 139; CANR 2, 40; DLB 8; MTCW 1; SATA 45; SATA-Obit 73

Leibniz, Gottfried Wilhelm von 1646-1716 **LC 35**
See also DLB 168

Leimbach, Martha 1963-
See Leimbach, Marti
See also CA 130
Leimbach, Marti   **CLC 65**
See also Leimbach, Martha
Leino, Eino   **TCLC 24**
See also Loennbohm, Armas Eino Leopold
Leiris, Michel (Julien) 1901-1990   **CLC 61**
See also CA 119; 128; 132
Leithauser, Brad 1953-   **CLC 27**
See also CA 107; CANR 27; DLB 120
Lelchuk, Alan 1938-   **CLC 5**
See also CA 45-48; CAAS 20; CANR 1, 70
Lem, Stanislaw 1921-   **CLC 8, 15, 40**
See also CA 105; CAAS 1; CANR 32; MTCW
1
Lemann, Nancy 1956-   **CLC 39**
See also CA 118; 136
Lemonnier, (Antoine Louis) Camille 1844-1913
TCLC 22
See also CA 121
Lenau, Nikolaus 1802-1850   **NCLC 16**
L'Engle, Madeleine (Camp Franklin) 1918-
CLC 12; DAM POP
See also AAYA 1; AITN 2; CA 1-4R; CANR 3,
21, 39, 66; CLR 1, 14; DLB 52; JRDA;
MAICYA; MTCW 1; SAAS 15; SATA 1, 27,
75
Lengyel, Jozsef 1896-1975   **CLC 7**
See also CA 85-88; 57-60; CANR 71
Lenin 1870-1924
See Lenin, V. I.
See also CA 121; 168
Lenin, V. I.   **TCLC 67**
See also Lenin
Lennon, John (Ono) 1940-1980   **CLC 12, 35**
See also CA 102
Lennox, Charlotte Ramsay 1729(?)-1804
NCLC 23
See also DLB 39
Lentricchia, Frank (Jr.) 1940-   **CLC 34**
See also CA 25-28R; CANR 19
Lenz, Siegfried 1926-   **CLC 27; SSC 33**
See also CA 89-92; DLB 75
Leonard, Elmore (John, Jr.) 1925-**CLC 28, 34,
71; DAM POP**
See also AAYA 22; AITN 1; BEST 89:1, 90:4;
CA 81-84; CANR 12, 28, 53; DLB 173; INT
CANR-28; MTCW 1
Leonard, Hugh   **CLC 19**
See also Byrne, John Keyes
See also DLB 13
Leonov, Leonid (Maximovich) 1899-1994
CLC 92; DAM NOV
See also CA 129; CANR 74; MTCW 1
Leopardi, (Conte) Giacomo 1798-1837**NCLC
22**
Le Reveler
See Artaud, Antonin (Marie Joseph)
Lerman, Eleanor 1952-   **CLC 9**
See also CA 85-88; CANR 69
Lerman, Rhoda 1936-   **CLC 56**
See also CA 49-52; CANR 70
Lermontov, Mikhail Yuryevich 1814-1841
NCLC 47; PC 18
See also DLB 205
Leroux, Gaston 1868-1927   **TCLC 25**
See also CA 108; 136; CANR 69; SATA 65
Lesage, Alain-Rene 1668-1747   **LC 2, 28**
Leskov, Nikolai (Semyonovich) 1831-1895
NCLC 25
Lessing, Doris (May) 1919-**CLC 1, 2, 3, 6, 10,
15, 22, 40, 94; DA; DAB; DAC; DAM MST,**

NOV; SSC 6; WLCS
See also CA 9-12R; CAAS 14; CANR 33, 54;
CDBLB 1960 to Present; DLB 15, 139;
DLBY 85; MTCW 1
Lessing, Gotthold Ephraim 1729-1781 **LC 8**
See also DLB 97
Lester, Richard 1932-   **CLC 20**
Lever, Charles (James) 1806-1872 **NCLC 23**
See also DLB 21
Leverson, Ada 1865(?)-1936(?)   **TCLC 18**
See also Elaine
See also CA 117; DLB 153
Levertov, Denise 1923-1997**CLC 1, 2, 3, 5, 8,
15, 28, 66; DAM POET; PC 11**
See also CA 1-4R; 163; CAAS 19; CANR 3,
29, 50; DLB 5, 165; INT CANR-29; MTCW
1
Levi, Jonathan   **CLC 76**
Levi, Peter (Chad Tigar) 1931-   **CLC 41**
See also CA 5-8R; CANR 34; DLB 40
Levi, Primo 1919-1987   **CLC 37, 50; SSC 12**
See also CA 13-16R; 122; CANR 12, 33, 61,
70; DLB 177; MTCW 1
Levin, Ira 1929-   **CLC 3, 6; DAM POP**
See also CA 21-24R; CANR 17, 44, 74; MTCW
1; SATA 66
Levin, Meyer 1905-1981   **CLC 7; DAM POP**
See also AITN 1; CA 9-12R; 104; CANR 15;
DLB 9, 28; DLBY 81; SATA 21; SATA-Obit
27
Levine, Norman 1924-   **CLC 54**
See also CA 73-76; CAAS 23; CANR 14, 70;
DLB 88
Levine, Philip 1928-   **CLC 2, 4, 5, 9, 14, 33;
DAM POET; PC 22**
See also CA 9-12R; CANR 9, 37, 52; DLB 5
Levinson, Deirdre 1931-   **CLC 49**
See also CA 73-76; CANR 70
Levi-Strauss, Claude 1908-   **CLC 38**
See also CA 1-4R; CANR 6, 32, 57; MTCW 1
Levitin, Sonia (Wolff) 1934-   **CLC 17**
See also AAYA 13; CA 29-32R; CANR 14, 32;
CLR 53; JRDA; MAICYA; SAAS 2; SATA
4, 68
Levon, O. U.
See Kesey, Ken (Elton)
Levy, Amy 1861-1889   **NCLC 59**
See also DLB 156
Lewes, George Henry 1817-1878   **NCLC 25**
See also DLB 55, 144
Lewis, Alun 1915-1944   **TCLC 3**
See also CA 104; DLB 20, 162
Lewis, C. Day
See Day Lewis, C(ecil)
Lewis, C(live) S(taples) 1898-1963**CLC 1, 3, 6,
14, 27; DA; DAB; DAC; DAM MST, NOV,
POP; WLC**
See also AAYA 3; CA 81-84; CANR 33, 71;
CDBLB 1945-1960; CLR 3, 27; DLB 15,
100, 160; JRDA; MAICYA; MTCW 1; SATA
13, 100
Lewis, Janet 1899-   **CLC 41**
See also Winters, Janet Lewis
See also CA 9-12R; CANR 29, 63; CAP 1;
DLBY 87
Lewis, Matthew Gregory 1775-1818**NCLC 11,
62**
See also DLB 39, 158, 178
Lewis, (Harry) Sinclair 1885-1951 **TCLC 4,
13, 23, 39; DA; DAB; DAC; DAM MST,
NOV; WLC**
See also CA 104; 133; CDALB 1917-1929;
DLB 9, 102; DLBD 1; MTCW 1

Lewis, (Percy) Wyndham 1882(?)-1957**TCLC
2, 9**
See also CA 104; 157; DLB 15
Lewisohn, Ludwig 1883-1955   **TCLC 19**
See also CA 107; DLB 4, 9, 28, 102
Lewton, Val 1904-1951   **TCLC 76**
Leyner, Mark 1956-   **CLC 92**
See also CA 110; CANR 28, 53
Lezama Lima, Jose 1910-1976**CLC 4, 10, 101;
DAM MULT**
See also CA 77-80; CANR 71; DLB 113; HW
L'Heureux, John (Clarke) 1934-   **CLC 52**
See also CA 13-16R; CANR 23, 45
Liddell, C. H.
See Kuttner, Henry
Lie, Jonas (Lauritz Idemil) 1833-1908(?)
TCLC 5
See also CA 115
Lieber, Joel 1937-1971   **CLC 6**
See also CA 73-76; 29-32R
Lieber, Stanley Martin
See Lee, Stan
Lieberman, Laurence (James) 1935- **CLC 4,
36**
See also CA 17-20R; CANR 8, 36
Lieh Tzu fl. 7th cent. B.C.-5th cent. B.C.
CMLC 27
Lieksman, Anders
See Haavikko, Paavo Juhani
Li Fei-kan 1904-
See Pa Chin
See also CA 105
Lifton, Robert Jay 1926-   **CLC 67**
See also CA 17-20R; CANR 27; INT CANR-
27; SATA 66
Lightfoot, Gordon 1938-   **CLC 26**
See also CA 109
Lightman, Alan P(aige) 1948-   **CLC 81**
See also CA 141; CANR 63
Ligotti, Thomas (Robert) 1953-**CLC 44; SSC
16**
See also CA 123; CANR 49
Li Ho 791-817   **PC 13**
Liliencron, (Friedrich Adolf Axel) Detlev von
1844-1909   **TCLC 18**
See also CA 117
Lilly, William 1602-1681   **LC 27**
Lima, Jose Lezama
See Lezama Lima, Jose
Lima Barreto, Afonso Henrique de 1881-1922
TCLC 23
See also CA 117
Limonov, Edward 1944-   **CLC 67**
See also CA 137
Lin, Frank
See Atherton, Gertrude (Franklin Horn)
Lincoln, Abraham 1809-1865   **NCLC 18**
Lind, Jakov   **CLC 1, 2, 4, 27, 82**
See also Landwirth, Heinz
See also CAAS 4
Lindbergh, Anne (Spencer) Morrow 1906-
CLC 82; DAM NOV
See also CA 17-20R; CANR 16, 73; MTCW 1;
SATA 33
Lindsay, David 1878-1945   **TCLC 15**
See also CA 113
Lindsay, (Nicholas) Vachel 1879-1931 **TCLC
17; DA; DAC; DAM MST, POET; PC 23;
WLC**
See also CA 114; 135; CDALB 1865-1917;
DLB 54; SATA 40
Linke-Poot
See Doeblin, Alfred

Linney, Romulus 1930-   CLC 51
  See also CA 1-4R; CANR 40, 44
Linton, Eliza Lynn 1822-1898   NCLC 41
  See also DLB 18
Li Po 701-763   CMLC 2
Lipsius, Justus 1547-1606   LC 16
Lipsyte, Robert (Michael) 1938-CLC 21; DA;
  DAC; DAM MST, NOV
  See also AAYA 7; CA 17-20R; CANR 8, 57;
  CLR 23; JRDA; MAICYA; SATA 5, 68
Lish, Gordon (Jay) 1934-   CLC 45; SSC 18
  See also CA 113; 117; DLB 130; INT 117
Lispector, Clarice 1925(?)-1977   CLC 43
  See also CA 139; 116; CANR 71; DLB 113
Littell, Robert 1935(?)-   CLC 42
  See also CA 109; 112; CANR 64
Little, Malcolm 1925-1965
  See Malcolm X
  See also BW 1; CA 125; 111; DA; DAB; DAC;
  DAM MST, MULT; MTCW 1
Littlewit, Humphrey Gent.
  See Lovecraft, H(oward) P(hillips)
Litwos
  See Sienkiewicz, Henryk (Adam Alexander
  Pius)
Liu, E 1857-1909   TCLC 15
  See also CA 115
Lively, Penelope (Margaret) 1933-   CLC 32,
  50; DAM NOV
  See also CA 41-44R; CANR 29, 67; CLR 7;
  DLB 14, 161, 207; JRDA; MAICYA; MTCW
  1; SATA 7, 60, 101
Livesay, Dorothy (Kathleen) 1909-CLC 4, 15,
  79; DAC; DAM MST, POET
  See also AITN 2; CA 25-28R; CAAS 8; CANR
  36, 67; DLB 68; MTCW 1
Livy c. 59B.C.-c. 17   CMLC 11
Lizardi, Jose Joaquin Fernandez de 1776-1827
  NCLC 30
Llewellyn, Richard
  See Llewellyn Lloyd, Richard Dafydd Vivian
  See also DLB 15
Llewellyn Lloyd, Richard Dafydd Vivian 1906-
  1983   CLC 7, 80
  See also Llewellyn, Richard
  See also CA 53-56; 111; CANR 7, 71; SATA
  11; SATA-Obit 37
Llosa, (Jorge) Mario (Pedro) Vargas
  See Vargas Llosa, (Jorge) Mario (Pedro)
Lloyd, Manda
  See Mander, (Mary) Jane
Lloyd Webber, Andrew 1948-
  See Webber, Andrew Lloyd
  See also AAYA 1; CA 116; 149; DAM DRAM;
  SATA 56
Llull, Ramon c. 1235-c. 1316   CMLC 12
Lobb, Ebenezer
  See Upward, Allen
Locke, Alain (Le Roy) 1886-1954 TCLC 43;
  BLCS
  See also BW 1; CA 106; 124; DLB 51
Locke, John 1632-1704   LC 7, 35
  See also DLB 101
Locke-Elliott, Sumner
  See Elliott, Sumner Locke
Lockhart, John Gibson 1794-1854   NCLC 6
  See also DLB 110, 116, 144
Lodge, David (John) 1935-CLC 36; DAM POP
  See also BEST 90:1; CA 17-20R; CANR 19,
  53; DLB 14, 194; INT CANR-19; MTCW 1
Lodge, Thomas 1558-1625   LC 41
Lodge, Thomas 1558-1625   LC 41
  See also DLB 172

Loennbohm, Armas Eino Leopold 1878-1926
  See Leino, Eino
  See also CA 123
Loewinsohn, Ron(ald William) 1937-CLC 52
  See also CA 25-28R; CANR 71
Logan, Jake
  See Smith, Martin Cruz
Logan, John (Burton) 1923-1987   CLC 5
  See also CA 77-80; 124; CANR 45; DLB 5
Lo Kuan-chung 1330(?)-1400(?)   LC 12
Lombard, Nap
  See Johnson, Pamela Hansford
London, Jack   TCLC 9, 15, 39; SSC 4; WLC
  See also London, John Griffith
  See also AAYA 13; AITN 2; CDALB 1865-
  1917; DLB 8, 12, 78; SATA 18
London, John Griffith 1876-1916
  See London, Jack
  See also CA 110; 119; CANR 73; DA; DAB;
  DAC; DAM MST, NOV; JRDA; MAICYA;
  MTCW 1
Long, Emmett
  See Leonard, Elmore (John, Jr.)
Longbaugh, Harry
  See Goldman, William (W.)
Longfellow, Henry Wadsworth 1807-1882
  NCLC 2, 45; DA; DAB; DAC; DAM MST,
  POET; WLCS
  See also CDALB 1640-1865; DLB 1, 59; SATA
  19
Longinus c. 1st cent. -   CMLC 27
  See also DLB 176
Longley, Michael 1939-   CLC 29
  See also CA 102; DLB 40
Longus fl. c. 2nd cent. -   CMLC 7
Longway, A. Hugh
  See Lang, Andrew
Lonnrot, Elias 1802-1884   NCLC 53
Lopate, Phillip 1943-   CLC 29
  See also CA 97-100; DLBY 80; INT 97-100
Lopez Portillo (y Pacheco), Jose 1920-CLC 46
  See also CA 129; HW
Lopez y Fuentes, Gregorio 1897(?)-1966C L C
  32
  See also CA 131; HW
Lorca, Federico Garcia
  See Garcia Lorca, Federico
Lord, Bette Bao 1938-   CLC 23
  See also BEST 90:3; CA 107; CANR 41; INT
  107; SATA 58
Lord Auch
  See Bataille, Georges
Lord Byron
  See Byron, George Gordon (Noel)
Lorde, Audre (Geraldine) 1934-1992CLC 18,
  71; BLC 2; DAM MULT, POET; PC 12
  See also BW 1; CA 25-28R; 142; CANR 16,
  26, 46; DLB 41; MTCW 1
Lord Houghton
  See Milnes, Richard Monckton
Lord Jeffrey
  See Jeffrey, Francis
Lorenzini, Carlo 1826-1890
  See Collodi, Carlo
  See also MAICYA; SATA 29, 100
Lorenzo, Heberto Padilla
  See Padilla (Lorenzo), Heberto
Loris
  See Hofmannsthal, Hugo von
Loti, Pierre   TCLC 11
  See also Viaud, (Louis Marie) Julien
  See also DLB 123
Louie, David Wong 1954-   CLC 70

See also CA 139
Louis, Father M.
  See Merton, Thomas
Lovecraft, H(oward) P(hillips) 1890-1937
  TCLC 4, 22; DAM POP; SSC 3
  See also AAYA 14; CA 104; 133; MTCW 1
Lovelace, Earl 1935-   CLC 51
  See also BW 2; CA 77-80; CANR 41, 72; DLB
  125; MTCW 1
Lovelace, Richard 1618-1657   LC 24
  See also DLB 131
Lowell, Amy 1874-1925   TCLC 1, 8; DAM
  POET; PC 13
  See also CA 104; 151; DLB 54, 140
Lowell, James Russell 1819-1891   NCLC 2
  See also CDALB 1640-1865; DLB 1, 11, 64,
  79, 189
Lowell, Robert (Traill Spence, Jr.) 1917-1977
  CLC 1, 2, 3, 4, 5, 8, 9, 11, 15, 37; DA; DAB;
  DAC; DAM MST, NOV; PC 3; WLC
  See also CA 9-12R; 73-76; CABS 2; CANR 26,
  60; DLB 5, 169; MTCW 1
Lowndes, Marie Adelaide (Belloc) 1868-1947
  TCLC 12
  See also CA 107; DLB 70
Lowry, (Clarence) Malcolm 1909-1957T C L C
  6, 40; SSC 31
  See also CA 105; 131; CANR 62; CDBLB
  1945-1960; DLB 15; MTCW 1
Lowry, Mina Gertrude 1882-1966
  See Loy, Mina
  See also CA 113
Loxsmith, John
  See Brunner, John (Kilian Houston)
Loy, Mina   CLC 28; DAM POET; PC 16
  See also Lowry, Mina Gertrude
  See also DLB 4, 54
Loyson-Bridet
  See Schwob, Marcel (Mayer Andre)
Lucas, Craig 1951-   CLC 64
  See also CA 137; CANR 71
Lucas, E(dward) V(errall) 1868-1938 T C L C
  73
  See also DLB 98, 149, 153; SATA 20
Lucas, George 1944-   CLC 16
  See also AAYA 1, 23; CA 77-80; CANR 30;
  SATA 56
Lucas, Hans
  See Godard, Jean-Luc
Lucas, Victoria
  See Plath, Sylvia
Lucian c. 120-c. 180   CMLC 32
  See also DLB 176
Ludlam, Charles 1943-1987   CLC 46, 50
  See also CA 85-88; 122; CANR 72
Ludlum, Robert 1927-CLC 22, 43; DAM NOV,
  POP
  See also AAYA 10; BEST 89:1, 90:3; CA 33-
  36R; CANR 25, 41, 68; DLBY 82; MTCW
  1
Ludwig, Ken   CLC 60
Ludwig, Otto 1813-1865   NCLC 4
  See also DLB 129
Lugones, Leopoldo 1874-1938   TCLC 15
  See also CA 116; 131; HW
Lu Hsun 1881-1936   TCLC 3; SSC 20
  See also Shu-Jen, Chou
Lukacs, George   CLC 24
  See also Lukacs, Gyorgy (Szegeny von)
Lukacs, Gyorgy (Szegeny von) 1885-1971
  See Lukacs, George
  See also CA 101; 29-32R; CANR 62
Luke, Peter (Ambrose Cyprian) 1919-1995

CLC 38
See also CA 81-84; 147; CANR 72; DLB 13
Lunar, Dennis
See Mungo, Raymond
Lurie, Alison 1926-   **CLC 4, 5, 18, 39**
See also CA 1-4R; CANR 2, 17, 50; DLB 2;
MTCW 1; SATA 46
Lustig, Arnost 1926-   **CLC 56**
See also AAYA 3; CA 69-72; CANR 47; SATA
56
Luther, Martin 1483-1546   **LC 9, 37**
See also DLB 179
Luxemburg, Rosa 1870(?)-1919   **TCLC 63**
See also CA 118
Luzi, Mario 1914-   **CLC 13**
See also CA 61-64; CANR 9, 70; DLB 128
Lyly, John 1554(?)-1606 LC 41; **DAM DRAM;
DC 7**
See also DLB 62, 167
L'Ymagier
See Gourmont, Remy (-Marie-Charles) de
Lynch, B. Suarez
See Bioy Casares, Adolfo; Borges, Jorge Luis
Lynch, David (K.) 1946-   **CLC 66**
See also CA 124; 129
Lynch, James
See Andreyev, Leonid (Nikolaevich)
Lynch Davis, B.
See Bioy Casares, Adolfo; Borges, Jorge Luis
Lyndsay, Sir David 1490-1555   **LC 20**
Lynn, Kenneth S(chuyler) 1923-   **CLC 50**
See also CA 1-4R; CANR 3, 27, 65
Lynx
See West, Rebecca
Lyons, Marcus
See Blish, James (Benjamin)
Lyre, Pinchbeck
See Sassoon, Siegfried (Lorraine)
Lytle, Andrew (Nelson) 1902-1995   **CLC 22**
See also CA 9-12R; 150; CANR 70; DLB 6;
DLBY 95
Lyttelton, George 1709-1773   **LC 10**
Maas, Peter 1929-   **CLC 29**
See also CA 93-96; INT 93-96
Macaulay, Rose 1881-1958   **TCLC 7, 44**
See also CA 104; DLB 36
Macaulay, Thomas Babington 1800-1859
NCLC 42
See also CDBLB 1832-1890; DLB 32, 55
MacBeth, George (Mann) 1932-1992 CLC 2, 5,
9
See also CA 25-28R; 136; CANR 61, 66; DLB
40; MTCW 1; SATA 4; SATA-Obit 70
MacCaig, Norman (Alexander) 1910-CLC 36;
DAB; DAM POET
See also CA 9-12R; CANR 3, 34; DLB 27
MacCarthy, Sir(Charles Otto) Desmond 1877-
1952   **TCLC 36**
See also CA 167
MacDiarmid, Hugh CLC 2, 4, 11, 19, 63; PC 9
See also Grieve, C(hristopher) M(urray)
See also CDBLB 1945-1960; DLB 20
MacDonald, Anson
See Heinlein, Robert A(nson)
Macdonald, Cynthia 1928-   **CLC 13, 19**
See also CA 49-52; CANR 4, 44; DLB 105
MacDonald, George 1824-1905   **TCLC 9**
See also CA 106; 137; DLB 18, 163, 178;
MAICYA; SATA 33, 100
Macdonald, John
See Millar, Kenneth
MacDonald, John D(ann) 1916-1986 **CLC 3,
27, 44; DAM NOV, POP**

See also CA 1-4R; 121; CANR 1, 19, 60; DLB
8; DLBY 86; MTCW 1
Macdonald, John Ross
See Millar, Kenneth
Macdonald, Ross   **CLC 1, 2, 3, 14, 34, 41**
See Millar, Kenneth
See also DLBD 6
MacDougal, John
See Blish, James (Benjamin)
MacEwen, Gwendolyn (Margaret) 1941-1987
CLC 13, 55
See also CA 9-12R; 124; CANR 7, 22; DLB
53; SATA 50; SATA-Obit 55
Macha, Karel Hynek 1810-1846   **NCLC 46**
Machado (y Ruiz), Antonio 1875-1939 TCLC
3
See also CA 104; DLB 108
Machado de Assis, Joaquim Maria 1839-1908
TCLC 10; BLC 2; SSC 24
See also CA 107; 153
Machen, Arthur   **TCLC 4; SSC 20**
See also Jones, Arthur Llewellyn
See also DLB 36, 156, 178
Machiavelli, Niccolo 1469-1527 LC 8, 36; **DA;
DAB; DAC; DAM MST; WLCS**
MacInnes, Colin 1914-1976   **CLC 4, 23**
See also CA 69-72; 65-68; CANR 21; DLB 14;
MTCW 1
MacInnes, Helen (Clark) 1907-1985 CLC 27,
39; DAM POP
See also CA 1-4R; 117; CANR 1, 28, 58; DLB
87; MTCW 1; SATA 22; SATA-Obit 44
Mackay, Mary 1855-1924
See Corelli, Marie
See also CA 118
Mackenzie, Compton (Edward Montague)
1883-1972   **CLC 18**
See also CA 21-22; 37-40R; CAP 2; DLB 34,
100
Mackenzie, Henry 1745-1831   **NCLC 41**
See also DLB 39
Mackintosh, Elizabeth 1896(?)-1952
See Tey, Josephine
See also CA 110
MacLaren, James
See Grieve, C(hristopher) M(urray)
Mac Laverty, Bernard 1942-   **CLC 31**
See also CA 116; 118; CANR 43; INT 118
MacLean, Alistair (Stuart) 1922(?)-1987 CLC
3, 13, 50, 63; DAM POP
See also CA 57-60; 121; CANR 28, 61; MTCW
1; SATA 23; SATA-Obit 50
Maclean, Norman (Fitzroy) 1902-1990 **CLC
78; DAM POP; SSC 13**
See also CA 102; 132; CANR 49; DLB 206
MacLeish, Archibald 1892-1982 CLC 3, 8, 14,
68; DAM POET
See also CA 9-12R; 106; CANR 33, 63; DLB
4, 7, 45; DLBY 82; MTCW 1
MacLennan, (John) Hugh 1907-1990 **CLC 2,
14, 92; DAC; DAM MST**
See also CA 5-8R; 142; CANR 33; DLB 68;
MTCW 1
MacLeod, Alistair 1936-CLC 56; **DAC; DAM
MST**
See also CA 123; DLB 60
Macleod, Fiona
See Sharp, William
MacNeice, (Frederick) Louis 1907-1963 C L C
1, 4, 10, 53; DAB; DAM POET
See also CA 85-88; CANR 61; DLB 10, 20;
MTCW 1
MacNeill, Dand

See Fraser, George MacDonald
Macpherson, James 1736-1796   **LC 29**
See also Ossian
See also DLB 109
Macpherson, (Jean) Jay 1931-   **CLC 14**
See also CA 5-8R; DLB 53
MacShane, Frank 1927-   **CLC 39**
See also CA 9-12R; CANR 3, 33; DLB 111
Macumber, Mari
See Sandoz, Mari(e Susette)
Madach, Imre 1823-1864   **NCLC 19**
Madden, (Jerry) David 1933-   **CLC 5, 15**
See also CA 1-4R; CAAS 3; CANR 4, 45; DLB
6; MTCW 1
Maddern, Al(an)
See Ellison, Harlan (Jay)
Madhubuti, Haki R. 1942-CLC 6, 73; BLC 2;
DAM MULT, POET; PC 5
See also Lee, Don L.
See also BW 2; CA 73-76; CANR 24, 51, 73;
DLB 5, 41; DLBD 8
Maepenn, Hugh
See Kuttner, Henry
Maepenn, K. H.
See Kuttner, Henry
Maeterlinck, Maurice 1862-1949   **TCLC 3;
DAM DRAM**
See also CA 104; 136; DLB 192; SATA 66
Maginn, William 1794-1842   **NCLC 8**
See also DLB 110, 159
Mahapatra, Jayanta 1928-   **CLC 33; DAM
MULT**
See also CA 73-76; CAAS 9; CANR 15, 33, 66
Mahfouz, Naguib (Abdel Aziz Al-Sabilgi)
1911(?)-
See Mahfuz, Najib
See also BEST 89:2; CA 128; CANR 55; DAM
NOV; MTCW 1
Mahfuz, Najib   **CLC 52, 55**
See also Mahfouz, Naguib (Abdel Aziz Al-
Sabilgi)
See also DLBY 88
Mahon, Derek 1941-   **CLC 27**
See also CA 113; 128; DLB 40
Mailer, Norman 1923-CLC 1, 2, 3, 4, 5, 8, 11,
**14, 28, 39, 74, 111; DA; DAB; DAC; DAM
MST, NOV, POP**
See also AITN 2; CA 9-12R; CABS 1; CANR
28, 74; CDALB 1968-1988; DLB 2, 16, 28,
185; DLBD 3; DLBY 80, 83; MTCW 1
Maillet, Antonine 1929-   **CLC 54; DAC**
See also CA 115; 120; CANR 46, 74; DLB 60;
INT 120
Mais, Roger 1905-1955   **TCLC 8**
See also BW 1; CA 105; 124; DLB 125; MTCW
1
Maistre, Joseph de 1753-1821   **NCLC 37**
Maitland, Frederic 1850-1906   **TCLC 65**
Maitland, Sara (Louise) 1950-   **CLC 49**
See also CA 69-72; CANR 13, 59
Major, Clarence 1936-CLC 3, 19, 48; BLC 2;
DAM MULT
See also BW 2; CA 21-24R; CAAS 6; CANR
13, 25, 53; DLB 33
Major, Kevin (Gerald) 1949-   **CLC 26; DAC**
See also AAYA 16; CA 97-100; CANR 21, 38;
CLR 11; DLB 60; INT CANR-21; JRDA;
MAICYA; SATA 32, 82
Maki, James
See Ozu, Yasujiro
Malabaila, Damiano
See Levi, Primo
Malamud, Bernard 1914-1986 CLC 1, 2, 3, 5,

8, 9, 11, 18, 27, 44, 78, 85; DA; DAB; DAC; DAM MST, NOV, POP; SSC 15; WLC
See also AAYA 16; CA 5-8R; 118; CABS 1; CANR 28, 62; CDALB 1941-1968; DLB 2, 28, 152; DLBY 80, 86; MTCW 1

Malan, Herman
See Bosman, Herman Charles; Bosman, Herman Charles

Malaparte, Curzio 1898-1957   **TCLC 52**

Malcolm, Dan
See Silverberg, Robert

Malcolm X   **CLC 82, 117; BLC 2; WLCS**
See also Little, Malcolm

Malherbe, Francois de 1555-1628   **LC 5**

Mallarme, Stephane 1842-1898 **NCLC 4, 41; DAM POET; PC 4**

Mallet-Joris, Francoise 1930-   **CLC 11**
See also CA 65-68; CANR 17; DLB 83

Malley, Ern
See McAuley, James Phillip

Mallowan, Agatha Christie
See Christie, Agatha (Mary Clarissa)

Maloff, Saul 1922-   **CLC 5**
See also CA 33-36R

Malone, Louis
See MacNeice, (Frederick) Louis

Malone, Michael (Christopher) 1942-**CLC 43**
See also CA 77-80; CANR 14, 32, 57

Malory, (Sir) Thomas 1410(?)-1471(?)**LC 11; DA; DAB; DAC; DAM MST; WLCS**
See also CDBLB Before 1660; DLB 146; SATA 59; SATA-Brief 33

Malouf, (George Joseph) David 1934-**CLC 28, 86**
See also CA 124; CANR 50

Malraux, (Georges-)Andre 1901-1976**CLC 1, 4, 9, 13, 15, 57; DAM NOV**
See also CA 21-22; 69-72; CANR 34, 58; CAP 2; DLB 72; MTCW 1

Malzberg, Barry N(athaniel) 1939-   **CLC 7**
See also CA 61-64; CAAS 4; CANR 16; DLB 8

Mamet, David (Alan) 1947-**CLC 9, 15, 34, 46, 91; DAM DRAM; DC 4**
See also AAYA 3; CA 81-84; CABS 3; CANR 15, 41, 67, 72; DLB 7; MTCW 1

Mamoulian, Rouben (Zachary) 1897-1987 **CLC 16**
See also CA 25-28R; 124

Mandelstam, Osip (Emilievich) 1891(?)-1938(?) **TCLC 2, 6; PC 14**
See also CA 104; 150

Mander, (Mary) Jane 1877-1949   **TCLC 31**
See also CA 162

Mandeville, John fl. 1350-   **CMLC 19**
See also DLB 146

Mandiargues, Andre Pieyre de   **CLC 41**
See also Pieyre de Mandiargues, Andre
See also DLB 83

Mandrake, Ethel Belle
See Thurman, Wallace (Henry)

Mangan, James Clarence 1803-1849**NCLC 27**

Maniere, J.-E.
See Giraudoux, (Hippolyte) Jean

Mankiewicz, Herman (Jacob) 1897-1953 **TCLC 85**
See also CA 120; 169; DLB 26

Manley, (Mary) Delariviere 1672(?)-1724 **L C 1, 42**
See also DLB 39, 80

Mann, Abel
See Creasey, John

Mann, Emily 1952-   **DC 7**
See also CA 130; CANR 55

Mann, (Luiz) Heinrich 1871-1950   **TCLC 9**
See also CA 106; 164; DLB 66

Mann, (Paul) Thomas 1875-1955 **TCLC 2, 8, 14, 21, 35, 44, 60; DA; DAB; DAC; DAM MST, NOV; SSC 5; WLC**
See also CA 104; 128; DLB 66; MTCW 1

Mannheim, Karl 1893-1947   **TCLC 65**

Manning, David
See Faust, Frederick (Schiller)

Manning, Frederic 1887(?)-1935   **TCLC 25**
See also CA 124

Manning, Olivia 1915-1980   **CLC 5, 19**
See also CA 5-8R; 101; CANR 29; MTCW 1

Mano, D. Keith 1942-   **CLC 2, 10**
See also CA 25-28R; CAAS 6; CANR 26, 57; DLB 6

Mansfield, KatherineTCLC 2, 8, 39; DAB; SSC 9, 23; WLC
See also Beauchamp, Kathleen Mansfield
See also DLB 162

Manso, Peter 1940-   **CLC 39**
See also CA 29-32R; CANR 44

Mantecon, Juan Jimenez
See Jimenez (Mantecon), Juan Ramon

Manton, Peter
See Creasey, John

Man Without a Spleen, A
See Chekhov, Anton (Pavlovich)

Manzoni, Alessandro 1785-1873   **NCLC 29**

Map, Walter 1140-1209   **CMLC 32**

Mapu, Abraham (ben Jekutiel) 1808-1867 **NCLC 18**

Mara, Sally
See Queneau, Raymond

Marat, Jean Paul 1743-1793   **LC 10**

Marcel, Gabriel Honore 1889-1973   **CLC 15**
See also CA 102; 45-48; MTCW 1

Marchbanks, Samuel
See Davies, (William) Robertson

Marchi, Giacomo
See Bassani, Giorgio

Margulies, Donald   **CLC 76**

Marie de France c. 12th cent. -   **CMLC 8; PC 22**
See also DLB 208

Marie de l'Incarnation 1599-1672   **LC 10**

Marier, Captain Victor
See Griffith, D(avid Lewelyn) W(ark)

Mariner, Scott
See Pohl, Frederik

Marinetti, Filippo Tommaso 1876-1944**TCLC 10**
See also CA 107; DLB 114

Marivaux, Pierre Carlet de Chamblain de 1688-1763   **LC 4; DC 7**

Markandaya, Kamala   **CLC 8, 38**
See also Taylor, Kamala (Purnaiya)

Markfield, Wallace 1926-   **CLC 8**
See also CA 69-72; CAAS 3; DLB 2, 28

Markham, Edwin 1852-1940   **TCLC 47**
See also CA 160; DLB 54, 186

Markham, Robert
See Amis, Kingsley (William)

Marks, J
See Highwater, Jamake (Mamake)

Marks-Highwater, J
See Highwater, Jamake (Mamake)

Markson, David M(errill) 1927-   **CLC 67**
See also CA 49-52; CANR 1

Marley, Bob   **CLC 17**
See also Marley, Robert Nesta

Marley, Robert Nesta 1945-1981
See Marley, Bob

See also CA 107; 103

Marlowe, Christopher 1564-1593 **LC 22, 47; DA; DAB; DAC; DAM DRAM, MST; DC 1; WLC**
See also CDBLB Before 1660; DLB 62

Marlowe, Stephen 1928-
See Queen, Ellery
See also CA 13-16R; CANR 6, 55

Marmontel, Jean-Francois 1723-1799   **LC 2**

Marquand, John P(hillips) 1893-1960**CLC 2, 10**
See also CA 85-88; CANR 73; DLB 9, 102

Marques, Rene 1919-1979   **CLC 96; DAM MULT; HLC**
See also CA 97-100; 85-88; DLB 113; HW

Marquez, Gabriel (Jose) Garcia
See Garcia Marquez, Gabriel (Jose)

Marquis, Don(ald Robert Perry) 1878-1937 **TCLC 7**
See also CA 104; 166; DLB 11, 25

Marric, J. J.
See Creasey, John

Marryat, Frederick 1792-1848   **NCLC 3**
See also DLB 21, 163

Marsden, James
See Creasey, John

Marsh, (Edith) Ngaio 1899-1982 **CLC 7, 53; DAM POP**
See also CA 9-12R; CANR 6, 58; DLB 77; MTCW 1

Marshall, Garry 1934-   **CLC 17**
See also AAYA 3; CA 111; SATA 60

Marshall, Paule 1929-   **CLC 27, 72; BLC 3; DAM MULT; SSC 3**
See also BW 2; CA 77-80; CANR 25, 73; DLB 157; MTCW 1

Marshallik
See Zangwill, Israel

Marsten, Richard
See Hunter, Evan

Marston, John 1576-1634**LC 33; DAM DRAM**
See also DLB 58, 172

Martha, Henry
See Harris, Mark

Marti, Jose 1853-1895**NCLC 63; DAM MULT; HLC**

Martial c. 40-c. 104   **PC 10**

Martin, Ken
See Hubbard, L(afayette) Ron(ald)

Martin, Richard
See Creasey, John

Martin, Steve 1945-   **CLC 30**
See also CA 97-100; CANR 30; MTCW 1

Martin, Valerie 1948-   **CLC 89**
See also BEST 90:2; CA 85-88; CANR 49

Martin, Violet Florence 1862-1915 **TCLC 51**

Martin, Webber
See Silverberg, Robert

Martindale, Patrick Victor
See White, Patrick (Victor Martindale)

Martin du Gard, Roger 1881-1958 **TCLC 24**
See also CA 118; DLB 65

Martineau, Harriet 1802-1876   **NCLC 26**
See also DLB 21, 55, 159, 163, 166, 190; YABC 2

Martines, Julia
See O'Faolain, Julia

Martinez, Enrique Gonzalez
See Gonzalez Martinez, Enrique

Martinez, Jacinto Benavente y
See Benavente (y Martinez), Jacinto

Martinez Ruiz, Jose 1873-1967
See Azorin; Ruiz, Jose Martinez

See also CA 93-96; HW

Martinez Sierra, Gregorio 1881-1947**TCLC 6**
See also CA 115

Martinez Sierra, Maria (de la O'LeJarraga)
1874-1974 **TCLC 6**
See also CA 115

Martinsen, Martin
See Follett, Ken(neth Martin)

Martinson, Harry (Edmund) 1904-1978 **C L C
14**
See also CA 77-80; CANR 34

Marut, Ret
See Traven, B.

Marut, Robert
See Traven, B.

Marvell, Andrew 1621-1678 **LC 4, 43; DA;
DAB; DAC; DAM MST, POET; PC 10;
WLC**
See also CDBLB 1660-1789; DLB 131

Marx, Karl (Heinrich) 1818-1883 **NCLC 17**
See also DLB 129

Masaoka Shiki **TCLC 18**
See also Masaoka Tsunenori

Masaoka Tsunenori 1867-1902
See Masaoka Shiki
See also CA 117

Masefield, John (Edward) 1878-1967**CLC 11,
47; DAM POET**
See also CA 19-20; 25-28R; CANR 33; CAP 2;
CDBLB 1890-1914; DLB 10, 19, 153, 160;
MTCW 1; SATA 19

Maso, Carole 19(?)- **CLC 44**
See also CA 170

Mason, Bobbie Ann 1940-**CLC 28, 43, 82; SSC
4**
See also AAYA 5; CA 53-56; CANR 11, 31,
58; DLB 173; DLBY 87; INT CANR-31;
MTCW 1

Mason, Ernst
See Pohl, Frederik

Mason, Lee W.
See Malzberg, Barry N(athaniel)

Mason, Nick 1945- **CLC 35**

Mason, Tally
See Derleth, August (William)

Mass, William
See Gibson, William

Master Lao
See Lao Tzu

Masters, Edgar Lee 1868-1950 **TCLC 2, 25;
DA; DAC; DAM MST, POET; PC 1;
WLCS**
See also CA 104; 133; CDALB 1865-1917;
DLB 54; MTCW 1

Masters, Hilary 1928- **CLC 48**
See also CA 25-28R; CANR 13, 47

Mastrosimone, William 19(?)- **CLC 36**

Mathe, Albert
See Camus, Albert

Mather, Cotton 1663-1728 **LC 38**
See also CDALB 1640-1865; DLB 24, 30, 140

Mather, Increase 1639-1723 **LC 38**
See also DLB 24

Matheson, Richard Burton 1926- **CLC 37**
See also CA 97-100; DLB 8, 44; INT 97-100

Mathews, Harry 1930- **CLC 6, 52**
See also CA 21-24R; CAAS 6; CANR 18, 40

Mathews, John Joseph 1894-1979 **CLC 84;
DAM MULT**
See also CA 19-20; 142; CANR 45; CAP 2;
DLB 175; NNAL

Mathias, Roland (Glyn) 1915- **CLC 45**
See also CA 97-100; CANR 19, 41; DLB 27

Matsuo Basho 1644-1694 **PC 3**
See also DAM POET

Mattheson, Rodney
See Creasey, John

Matthews, Greg 1949- **CLC 45**
See also CA 135

Matthews, William (Procter, III) 1942-1997
CLC 40
See also CA 29-32R; 162; CAAS 18; CANR
12, 57; DLB 5

Matthias, John (Edward) 1941- **CLC 9**
See also CA 33-36R; CANR 56

Matthiessen, Peter 1927-**CLC 5, 7, 11, 32, 64;
DAM NOV**
See also AAYA 6; BEST 90:4; CA 9-12R;
CANR 21, 50, 73; DLB 6, 173; MTCW 1;
SATA 27

Maturin, Charles Robert 1780(?)-1824**N C L C
6**
See also DLB 178

Matute (Ausejo), Ana Maria 1925- **CLC 11**
See also CA 89-92; MTCW 1

Maugham, W. S.
See Maugham, W(illiam) Somerset

Maugham, W(illiam) Somerset 1874-1965
**CLC 1, 11, 15, 67, 93; DA; DAB; DAC;
DAM DRAM, MST, NOV; SSC 8; WLC**
See also CA 5-8R; 25-28R; CANR 40; CDBLB
1914-1945; DLB 10, 36, 77, 100, 162, 195;
MTCW 1; SATA 54

Maugham, William Somerset
See Maugham, W(illiam) Somerset

Maupassant, (Henri Rene Albert) Guy de 1850-
1893**NCLC 1, 42; DA; DAB; DAC; DAM
MST; SSC 1; WLC**
See also DLB 123

Maupin, Armistead 1944-**CLC 95; DAM POP**
See also CA 125; 130; CANR 58; INT 130

Maurhut, Richard
See Traven, B.

Mauriac, Claude 1914-1996 **CLC 9**
See also CA 89-92; 152; DLB 83

Mauriac, Francois (Charles) 1885-1970 **C L C
4, 9, 56; SSC 24**
See also CA 25-28; CAP 2; DLB 65; MTCW 1

Mavor, Osborne Henry 1888-1951
See Bridie, James
See also CA 104

Maxwell, William (Keepers, Jr.) 1908-**CLC 19**
See also CA 93-96; CANR 54; DLBY 80; INT
93-96

May, Elaine 1932- **CLC 16**
See also CA 124; 142; DLB 44

Mayakovski, Vladimir (Vladimirovich) 1893-
1930 **TCLC 4, 18**
See also CA 104; 158

Mayhew, Henry 1812-1887 **NCLC 31**
See also DLB 18, 55, 190

Mayle, Peter 1939(?)- **CLC 89**
See also CA 139; CANR 64

Maynard, Joyce 1953- **CLC 23**
See also CA 111; 129; CANR 64

Mayne, William (James Carter) 1928-**CLC 12**
See also AAYA 20; CA 9-12R; CANR 37; CLR
25; JRDA; MAICYA; SAAS 11; SATA 6, 68

Mayo, Jim
See L'Amour, Louis (Dearborn)

Maysles, Albert 1926- **CLC 16**
See also CA 29-32R

Maysles, David 1932- **CLC 16**

Mazer, Norma Fox 1931- **CLC 26**
See also AAYA 5; CA 69-72; CANR 12, 32,
66; CLR 23; JRDA; MAICYA; SAAS 1;

SATA 24, 67

Mazzini, Guiseppe 1805-1872 **NCLC 34**

McAuley, James Phillip 1917-1976 **CLC 45**
See also CA 97-100

McBain, Ed
See Hunter, Evan

McBrien, William Augustine 1930- **CLC 44**
See also CA 107

McCaffrey, Anne (Inez) 1926-**CLC 17; DAM
NOV, POP**
See also AAYA 6; AITN 2; BEST 89:2; CA 25-
28R; CANR 15, 35, 55; CLR 49; DLB 8;
JRDA; MAICYA; MTCW 1; SAAS 11; SATA
8, 70

McCall, Nathan 1955(?)- **CLC 86**
See also CA 146

McCann, Arthur
See Campbell, John W(ood, Jr.)

McCann, Edson
See Pohl, Frederik

McCarthy, Charles, Jr. 1933-
See McCarthy, Cormac
See also CANR 42, 69; DAM POP

McCarthy, Cormac 1933- **CLC 4, 57, 59, 101**
See also McCarthy, Charles, Jr.
See also DLB 6, 143

McCarthy, Mary (Therese) 1912-1989**CLC 1,
3, 5, 14, 24, 39, 59; SSC 24**
See also CA 5-8R; 129; CANR 16, 50, 64; DLB
2; DLBY 81; INT CANR-16; MTCW 1

McCartney, (James) Paul 1942- **CLC 12, 35**
See also CA 146

McCauley, Stephen (D.) 1955- **CLC 50**
See also CA 141

McClure, Michael (Thomas) 1932-**CLC 6, 10**
See also CA 21-24R; CANR 17, 46; DLB 16

McCorkle, Jill (Collins) 1958- **CLC 51**
See also CA 121; DLBY 87

McCourt, Frank 1930- **CLC 109**
See also CA 157

McCourt, James 1941- **CLC 5**
See also CA 57-60

McCoy, Horace (Stanley) 1897-1955**TCLC 28**
See also CA 108; 155; DLB 9

McCrae, John 1872-1918 **TCLC 12**
See also CA 109; DLB 92

McCreigh, James
See Pohl, Frederik

McCullers, (Lula) Carson (Smith) 1917-1967
**CLC 1, 4, 10, 12, 48, 100; DA; DAB; DAC;
DAM MST, NOV; SSC 9, 24; WLC**
See also AAYA 21; CA 5-8R; 25-28R; CABS
1, 3; CANR 18; CDALB 1941-1968; DLB
2, 7, 173; MTCW 1; SATA 27

McCulloch, John Tyler
See Burroughs, Edgar Rice

McCullough, Colleen 1938(?)- **CLC 27, 107;
DAM NOV, POP**
See also CA 81-84; CANR 17, 46, 67; MTCW
1

McDermott, Alice 1953- **CLC 90**
See also CA 109; CANR 40

McElroy, Joseph 1930- **CLC 5, 47**
See also CA 17-20R

McEwan, Ian (Russell) 1948- **CLC 13, 66;
DAM NOV**
See also BEST 90:4; CA 61-64; CANR 14, 41,
69; DLB 14, 194; MTCW 1

McFadden, David 1940- **CLC 48**
See also CA 104; DLB 60; INT 104

McFarland, Dennis 1950- **CLC 65**
See also CA 165

McGahern, John 1934- **CLC 5, 9, 48; SSC 17**

See also CA 17-20R; CANR 29, 68; DLB 14;
MTCW 1

McGinley, Patrick (Anthony) 1937- **CLC 41**
See also CA 120; 127; CANR 56; INT 127

McGinley, Phyllis 1905-1978 **CLC 14**
See also CA 9-12R; 77-80; CANR 19; DLB 11,
48; SATA 2, 44; SATA-Obit 24

McGinniss, Joe 1942- **CLC 32**
See also AITN 2; BEST 89:2; CA 25-28R;
CANR 26, 70; DLB 185; INT CANR-26

McGivern, Maureen Daly
See Daly, Maureen

McGrath, Patrick 1950- **CLC 55**
See also CA 136; CANR 65

McGrath, Thomas (Matthew) 1916-1990CLC
28, 59; DAM POET
See also CA 9-12R; 132; CANR 6, 33; MTCW
1; SATA 41; SATA-Obit 66

McGuane, Thomas (Francis III) 1939-CLC 3,
7, 18, 45
See also AITN 2; CA 49-52; CANR 5, 24, 49;
DLB 2; DLBY 80; INT CANR-24; MTCW
1

McGuckian, Medbh 1950- **CLC 48; DAM
POET**
See also CA 143; DLB 40

McHale, Tom 1942(?)-1982 **CLC 3, 5**
See also AITN 1; CA 77-80; 106

McIlvanney, William 1936- **CLC 42**
See also CA 25-28R; CANR 61; DLB 14, 207

McIlwraith, Maureen Mollie Hunter
See Hunter, Mollie
See also SATA 2

McInerney, Jay 1955-CLC 34, 112; DAM POP
See also AAYA 18; CA 116; 123; CANR 45,
68; INT 123

McIntyre, Vonda N(eel) 1948- **CLC 18**
See also CA 81-84; CANR 17, 34, 69; MTCW
1

McKay, ClaudeTCLC 7, 41; BLC 3; DAB; PC
2
See also McKay, Festus Claudius
See also DLB 4, 45, 51, 117

McKay, Festus Claudius 1889-1948
See McKay, Claude
See also BW 1; CA 104; 124; CANR 73; DA;
DAC; DAM MST, MULT, NOV, POET;
MTCW 1; WLC

McKuen, Rod 1933- **CLC 1, 3**
See also AITN 1; CA 41-44R; CANR 40

McLoughlin, R. B.
See Mencken, H(enry) L(ouis)

McLuhan, (Herbert) Marshall 1911-1980
CLC 37, 83
See also CA 9-12R; 102; CANR 12, 34, 61;
DLB 88; INT CANR-12; MTCW 1

McMillan, Terry (L.) 1951- CLC 50, 61, 112;
BLCS; DAM MULT, NOV, POP
See also AAYA 21; BW 2; CA 140; CANR 60

McMurtry, Larry (Jeff) 1936-CLC 2, 3, 7, 11,
27, 44; DAM NOV, POP
See also AAYA 15; AITN 2; BEST 89:2; CA 5-
8R; CANR 19, 43, 64; CDALB 1968-1988;
DLB 2, 143; DLBY 80, 87; MTCW 1

McNally, T. M. 1961- **CLC 82**

McNally, Terrence 1939- **CLC 4, 7, 41, 91;
DAM DRAM**
See also CA 45-48; CANR 2, 56; DLB 7

McNamer, Deirdre 1950- **CLC 70**

McNeile, Herman Cyril 1888-1937
See Sapper
See also DLB 77

McNickle, (William) D'Arcy 1904-1977 C L C
89; DAM MULT
See also CA 9-12R; 85-88; CANR 5, 45; DLB
175; NNAL; SATA-Obit 22

McPhee, John (Angus) 1931-   **CLC 36**
See also BEST 90:1; CA 65-68; CANR 20, 46,
64, 69; DLB 185; MTCW 1

McPherson, James Alan 1943- CLC 19, 77;
BLCS
See also BW 1; CA 25-28R; CAAS 17; CANR
24, 74; DLB 38; MTCW 1

McPherson, William (Alexander) 1933- C L C
34
See also CA 69-72; CANR 28; INT CANR-28

Mead, George Herbert 1873-1958 **TCLC 89**

Mead, Margaret 1901-1978 **CLC 37**
See also AITN 1; CA 1-4R; 81-84; CANR 4;
MTCW 1; SATA-Obit 20

Meaker, Marijane (Agnes) 1927-
See Kerr, M. E.
See also CA 107; CANR 37, 63; INT 107;
JRDA; MAICYA; MTCW 1; SATA 20, 61,
99

Medoff, Mark (Howard) 1940- **CLC 6, 23;
DAM DRAM**
See also AITN 1; CA 53-56; CANR 5; DLB 7;
INT CANR-5

Medvedev, P. N.
See Bakhtin, Mikhail Mikhailovich

Meged, Aharon
See Megged, Aharon

Meged, Aron
See Megged, Aharon

Megged, Aharon 1920- **CLC 9**
See also CA 49-52; CAAS 13; CANR 1

Mehta, Ved (Parkash) 1934- **CLC 37**
See also CA 1-4R; CANR 2, 23, 69; MTCW 1

Melanter
See Blackmore, R(ichard) D(oddridge)

Melies, Georges 1861-1938 **TCLC 81**

Melikow, Loris
See Hofmannsthal, Hugo von

Melmoth, Sebastian
See Wilde, Oscar (Fingal O'Flahertie Wills)

Meltzer, Milton 1915- **CLC 26**
See also AAYA 8; CA 13-16R; CANR 38; CLR
13; DLB 61; JRDA; MAICYA; SAAS 1;
SATA 1, 50, 80

Melville, Herman 1819-1891NCLC 3, 12, 29,
45, 49; DA; DAB; DAC; DAM MST, NOV;
SSC 1, 17; WLC
See also AAYA 25; CDALB 1640-1865; DLB
3, 74; SATA 59

Menander c. 342B.C.-c. 292B.C. **CMLC 9;
DAM DRAM; DC 3**
See also DLB 176

Mencken, H(enry) L(ouis) 1880-1956 T C L C
13
See also CA 105; 125; CDALB 1917-1929;
DLB 11, 29, 63, 137; MTCW 1

Mendelsohn, Jane 1965(?)- **CLC 99**
See also CA 154

Mercer, David 1928-1980CLC 5; DAM DRAM
See also CA 9-12R; 102; CANR 23; DLB 13;
MTCW 1

Merchant, Paul
See Ellison, Harlan (Jay)

Meredith, George 1828-1909 **TCLC 17, 43;
DAM POET**
See also CA 117; 153; CDBLB 1832-1890;
DLB 18, 35, 57, 159

Meredith, William (Morris) 1919-CLC 4, 13,
22, 55; DAM POET
See also CA 9-12R; CAAS 14; CANR 6, 40;

DLB 5

Merezhkovsky, Dmitry Sergeyevich 1865-1941
TCLC 29
See also CA 169

Merimee, Prosper 1803-1870NCLC 6, 65; SSC
7
See also DLB 119, 192

Merkin, Daphne 1954- **CLC 44**
See also CA 123

Merlin, Arthur
See Blish, James (Benjamin)

Merrill, James (Ingram) 1926-1995CLC 2, 3,
6, 8, 13, 18, 34, 91; DAM POET
See also CA 13-16R; 147; CANR 10, 49, 63;
DLB 5, 165; DLBY 85; INT CANR-10;
MTCW 1

Merriman, Alex
See Silverberg, Robert

Merriman, Brian 1747-1805 **NCLC 70**

Merritt, E. B.
See Waddington, Miriam

Merton, Thomas 1915-1968 CLC 1, 3, 11, 34,
83; PC 10
See also CA 5-8R; 25-28R; CANR 22, 53; DLB
48; DLBY 81; MTCW 1

Merwin, W(illiam) S(tanley) 1927- CLC 1, 2,
3, 5, 8, 13, 18, 45, 88; DAM POET
See also CA 13-16R; CANR 15, 51; DLB 5,
169; INT CANR-15; MTCW 1

Metcalf, John 1938- **CLC 37**
See also CA 113; DLB 60

Metcalf, Suzanne
See Baum, L(yman) Frank

Mew, Charlotte (Mary) 1870-1928 **TCLC 8**
See also CA 105; DLB 19, 135

Mewshaw, Michael 1943- **CLC 9**
See also CA 53-56; CANR 7, 47; DLBY 80

Meyer, June
See Jordan, June

Meyer, Lynn
See Slavitt, David R(ytman)

Meyer-Meyrink, Gustav 1868-1932
See Meyrink, Gustav
See also CA 117

Meyers, Jeffrey 1939- **CLC 39**
See also CA 73-76; CANR 54; DLB 111

Meynell, Alice (Christina Gertrude Thompson)
1847-1922 **TCLC 6**
See also CA 104; DLB 19, 98

Meyrink, Gustav **TCLC 21**
See also Meyer-Meyrink, Gustav
See also DLB 81

Michaels, Leonard 1933- CLC 6, 25; SSC 16
See also CA 61-64; CANR 21, 62; DLB 130;
MTCW 1

Michaux, Henri 1899-1984 **CLC 8, 19**
See also CA 85-88; 114

Micheaux, Oscar 1884-1951 **TCLC 76**
See also DLB 50

Michelangelo 1475-1564 **LC 12**

Michelet, Jules 1798-1874 **NCLC 31**

Michels, Robert 1876-1936 **TCLC 88**

Michener, James A(lbert) 1907(?)-1997 C L C
1, 5, 11, 29, 60, 109; DAM NOV, POP
See also AAYA 27; AITN 1; BEST 90:1; CA 5-
8R; 161; CANR 21, 45, 68; DLB 6; MTCW
1

Mickiewicz, Adam 1798-1855 **NCLC 3**

Middleton, Christopher 1926- **CLC 13**
See also CA 13-16R; CANR 29, 54; DLB 40

Middleton, Richard (Barham) 1882-1911
TCLC 56
See also DLB 156

Middleton, Stanley 1919- **CLC 7, 38**
See also CA 25-28R; CAAS 23; CANR 21, 46;
DLB 14
Middleton, Thomas 1580-1627 **LC 33; DAM DRAM, MST; DC 5**
See also DLB 58
Migueis, Jose Rodrigues 1901- **CLC 10**
Mikszath, Kalman 1847-1910 **TCLC 31**
See also CA 170
Miles, Jack **CLC 100**
Miles, Josephine (Louise) 1911-1985**CLC 1, 2, 14, 34, 39; DAM POET**
See also CA 1-4R; 116; CANR 2, 55; DLB 48
Militant
See Sandburg, Carl (August)
Mill, John Stuart 1806-1873 **NCLC 11, 58**
See also CDBLB 1832-1890; DLB 55, 190
Millar, Kenneth 1915-1983 **CLC 14; DAM POP**
See also Macdonald, Ross
See also CA 9-12R; 110; CANR 16, 63; DLB 2; DLBD 6; DLBY 83; MTCW 1
Millay, E. Vincent
See Millay, Edna St. Vincent
Millay, Edna St. Vincent 1892-1950 **TCLC 4, 49; DA; DAB; DAC; DAM MST, POET; PC 6; WLCS**
See also CA 104; 130; CDALB 1917-1929; DLB 45; MTCW 1
Miller, Arthur 1915-**CLC 1, 2, 6, 10, 15, 26, 47, 78; DA; DAB; DAC; DAM DRAM, MST; DC 1; WLC**
See also AAYA 15; AITN 1; CA 1-4R; CABS 3; CANR 2, 30, 54; CDALB 1941-1968; DLB 7; MTCW 1
Miller, Henry (Valentine) 1891-1980**CLC 1, 2, 4, 9, 14, 43, 84; DA; DAB; DAC; DAM MST, NOV; WLC**
See also CA 9-12R; 97-100; CANR 33, 64; CDALB 1929-1941; DLB 4, 9; DLBY 80; MTCW 1
Miller, Jason 1939(?)- **CLC 2**
See also AITN 1; CA 73-76; DLB 7
Miller, Sue 1943- **CLC 44; DAM POP**
See also BEST 90:3; CA 139; CANR 59; DLB 143
Miller, Walter M(ichael, Jr.) 1923-**CLC 4, 30**
See also CA 85-88; DLB 8
Millett, Kate 1934- **CLC 67**
See also AITN 1; CA 73-76; CANR 32, 53; MTCW 1
Millhauser, Steven (Lewis) 1943-**CLC 21, 54, 109**
See also CA 110; 111; CANR 63; DLB 2; INT 111
Millin, Sarah Gertrude 1889-1968 **CLC 49**
See also CA 102; 93-96
Milne, A(lan) A(lexander) 1882-1956**TCLC 6, 88; DAB; DAC; DAM MST**
See also CA 104; 133; CLR 1, 26; DLB 10, 77, 100, 160; MAICYA; MTCW 1; SATA 100; YABC 1
Milner, Ron(ald) 1938-**CLC 56; BLC 3; DAM MULT**
See also AITN 1; BW 1; CA 73-76; CANR 24; DLB 38; MTCW 1
Milnes, Richard Monckton 1809-1885 **NCLC 61**
See also DLB 32, 184
Milosz, Czeslaw 1911- **CLC 5, 11, 22, 31, 56, 82; DAM MST, POET; PC 8; WLCS**
See also CA 81-84; CANR 23, 51; MTCW 1
Milton, John 1608-1674 **LC 9, 43; DA; DAB;**

DAC; DAM MST, POET; PC 19; WLC
See also CDBLB 1660-1789; DLB 131, 151
Min, Anchee 1957- **CLC 86**
See also CA 146
Minehaha, Cornelius
See Wedekind, (Benjamin) Frank(lin)
Miner, Valerie 1947- **CLC 40**
See also CA 97-100; CANR 59
Minimo, Duca
See D'Annunzio, Gabriele
Minot, Susan 1956- **CLC 44**
See also CA 134
Minus, Ed 1938- **CLC 39**
Miranda, Javier
See Bioy Casares, Adolfo
Mirbeau, Octave 1848-1917 **TCLC 55**
See also DLB 123, 192
Miro (Ferrer), Gabriel (Francisco Victor) 1879-1930 **TCLC 5**
See also CA 104
Mishima, Yukio 1925-1970**CLC 2, 4, 6, 9, 27; DC 1; SSC 4**
See also Hiraoka, Kimitake
See also DLB 182
Mistral, Frederic 1830-1914 **TCLC 51**
See also CA 122
Mistral, Gabriela **TCLC 2; HLC**
See also Godoy Alcayaga, Lucila
Mistry, Rohinton 1952- **CLC 71; DAC**
See also CA 141
Mitchell, Clyde
See Ellison, Harlan (Jay); Silverberg, Robert
Mitchell, James Leslie 1901-1935
See Gibbon, Lewis Grassic
See also CA 104; DLB 15
Mitchell, Joni 1943- **CLC 12**
See also CA 112
Mitchell, Joseph (Quincy) 1908-1996**CLC 98**
See also CA 77-80; 152; CANR 69; DLB 185; DLBY 96
Mitchell, Margaret (Munnerlyn) 1900-1949 **TCLC 11; DAM NOV, POP**
See also AAYA 23; CA 109; 125; CANR 55; DLB 9; MTCW 1
Mitchell, Peggy
See Mitchell, Margaret (Munnerlyn)
Mitchell, S(ilas) Weir 1829-1914 **TCLC 36**
See also CA 165; DLB 202
Mitchell, W(illiam) O(rmond) 1914-1998**CLC 25; DAC; DAM MST**
See also CA 77-80; 165; CANR 15, 43; DLB 88
Mitchell, William 1879-1936 **TCLC 81**
Mitford, Mary Russell 1787-1855 **NCLC 4**
See also DLB 110, 116
Mitford, Nancy 1904-1973 **CLC 44**
See also CA 9-12R; DLB 191
Miyamoto, Yuriko 1899-1951 **TCLC 37**
See also CA 170; DLB 180
Miyazawa, Kenji 1896-1933 **TCLC 76**
See also CA 157
Mizoguchi, Kenji 1898-1956 **TCLC 72**
See also CA 167
Mo, Timothy (Peter) 1950(?)- **CLC 46**
See also CA 117; DLB 194; MTCW 1
Modarressi, Taghi (M.) 1931- **CLC 44**
See also CA 121; 134; INT 134
Modiano, Patrick (Jean) 1945- **CLC 18**
See also CA 85-88; CANR 17, 40; DLB 83
Moerck, Paal
See Roelvaag, O(le) E(dvart)
Mofolo, Thomas (Mokopu) 1875(?)-1948
TCLC 22; BLC 3; DAM MULT

See also CA 121; 153
Mohr, Nicholasa 1938-**CLC 12; DAM MULT; HLC**
See also AAYA 8; CA 49-52; CANR 1, 32, 64; CLR 22; DLB 145; HW; JRDA; SAAS 8; SATA 8, 97
Mojtabai, A(nn) G(race) 1938- **CLC 5, 9, 15, 29**
See also CA 85-88
Moliere 1622-1673**LC 10, 28; DA; DAB; DAC; DAM DRAM, MST; WLC**
Molin, Charles
See Mayne, William (James Carter)
Molnar, Ferenc 1878-1952 **TCLC 20; DAM DRAM**
See also CA 109; 153
Momaday, N(avarre) Scott 1934- **CLC 2, 19, 85, 95; DA; DAB; DAC; DAM MST, MULT, NOV, POP; PC 25; WLCS**
See also AAYA 11; CA 25-28R; CANR 14, 34, 68; DLB 143, 175; INT CANR-14; MTCW 1; NNAL; SATA 48; SATA-Brief 30
Monette, Paul 1945-1995 **CLC 82**
See also CA 139; 147
Monroe, Harriet 1860-1936 **TCLC 12**
See also CA 109; DLB 54, 91
Monroe, Lyle
See Heinlein, Robert A(nson)
Montagu, Elizabeth 1720-1800 **NCLC 7**
Montagu, Mary (Pierrepont) Wortley 1689-1762 **LC 9; PC 16**
See also DLB 95, 101
Montagu, W. H.
See Coleridge, Samuel Taylor
Montague, John (Patrick) 1929- **CLC 13, 46**
See also CA 9-12R; CANR 9, 69; DLB 40; MTCW 1
Montaigne, Michel (Eyquem) de 1533-1592
LC 8; DA; DAB; DAC; DAM MST; WLC
Montale, Eugenio 1896-1981**CLC 7, 9, 18; PC 13**
See also CA 17-20R; 104; CANR 30; DLB 114; MTCW 1
Montesquieu, Charles-Louis de Secondat 1689-1755 **LC 7**
Montgomery, (Robert) Bruce 1921-1978
See Crispin, Edmund
See also CA 104
Montgomery, L(ucy) M(aud) 1874-1942
TCLC 51; DAC; DAM MST
See also AAYA 12; CA 108; 137; CLR 8; DLB 92; DLBD 14; JRDA; MAICYA; SATA 100; YABC 1
Montgomery, Marion H., Jr. 1925- **CLC 7**
See also AITN 1; CA 1-4R; CANR 3, 48; DLB 6
Montgomery, Max
See Davenport, Guy (Mattison, Jr.)
Montherlant, Henry (Milon) de 1896-1972
CLC 8, 19; DAM DRAM
See also CA 85-88; 37-40R; DLB 72; MTCW 1
Monty Python
See Chapman, Graham; Cleese, John (Marwood); Gilliam, Terry (Vance); Idle, Eric; Jones, Terence Graham Parry; Palin, Michael (Edward)
See also AAYA 7
Moodie, Susanna (Strickland) 1803-1885
NCLC 14
See also DLB 99
Mooney, Edward 1951-
See Mooney, Ted

Author Index

See also CA 130
Mooney, Ted   **CLC 25**
  See also Mooney, Edward
Moorcock, Michael (John) 1939-**CLC 5, 27, 58**
  See also AAYA 26; CA 45-48; CAAS 5; CANR
  2, 17, 38, 64; DLB 14; MTCW 1; SATA 93
Moore, Brian 1921- **CLC 1, 3, 5, 7, 8, 19, 32,**
  90; DAB; DAC; DAM MST
  See also CA 1-4R; CANR 1, 25, 42, 63; MTCW
  1
Moore, Edward
  See Muir, Edwin
Moore, G. E. 1873-1958   **TCLC 89**
Moore, George Augustus 1852-1933**TCLC 7;**
  SSC 19
  See also CA 104; DLB 10, 18, 57, 135
Moore, Lorrie   **CLC 39, 45, 68**
  See also Moore, Marie Lorena
Moore, Marianne (Craig) 1887-1972**CLC 1, 2,**
  4, 8, 10, 13, 19, 47; DA; DAB; DAC; DAM
  MST, POET; PC 4; WLCS
  See also CA 1-4R; 33-36R; CANR 3, 61;
  CDALB 1929-1941; DLB 45; DLBD 7;
  MTCW 1; SATA 20
Moore, Marie Lorena 1957-
  See Moore, Lorrie
  See also CA 116; CANR 39
Moore, Thomas 1779-1852   **NCLC 6**
  See also DLB 96, 144
Morand, Paul 1888-1976   **CLC 41; SSC 22**
  See also CA 69-72; DLB 65
Morante, Elsa 1918-1985   **CLC 8, 47**
  See also CA 85-88; 117; CANR 35; DLB 177;
  MTCW 1
Moravia, Alberto 1907-1990**CLC 2, 7, 11, 27,**
  46; SSC 26
  See also Pincherle, Alberto
  See also DLB 177
More, Hannah 1745-1833   **NCLC 27**
  See also DLB 107, 109, 116, 158
More, Henry 1614-1687   **LC 9**
  See also DLB 126
More, Sir Thomas 1478-1535   **LC 10, 32**
Moreas, Jean   **TCLC 18**
  See also Papadiamantopoulos, Johannes
Morgan, Berry 1919-   **CLC 6**
  See also CA 49-52; DLB 6
Morgan, Claire
  See Highsmith, (Mary) Patricia
Morgan, Edwin (George) 1920-   **CLC 31**
  See also CA 5-8R; CANR 3, 43; DLB 27
Morgan, (George) Frederick 1922- **CLC 23**
  See also CA 17-20R; CANR 21
Morgan, Harriet
  See Mencken, H(enry) L(ouis)
Morgan, Jane
  See Cooper, James Fenimore
Morgan, Janet 1945-   **CLC 39**
  See also CA 65-68
Morgan, Lady 1776(?)-1859   **NCLC 29**
  See also DLB 116, 158
Morgan, Robin (Evonne) 1941-   **CLC 2**
  See also CA 69-72; CANR 29, 68; MTCW 1;
  SATA 80
Morgan, Scott
  See Kuttner, Henry
Morgan, Seth 1949(?)-1990   **CLC 65**
  See also CA 132
Morgenstern, Christian 1871-1914 **TCLC 8**
  See also CA 105
Morgenstern, S.
  See Goldman, William (W.)
Moricz, Zsigmond 1879-1942   **TCLC 33**

See also CA 165
Morike, Eduard (Friedrich) 1804-1875**NCLC**
  10
  See also DLB 133
Moritz, Karl Philipp 1756-1793   **LC 2**
  See also DLB 94
Morland, Peter Henry
  See Faust, Frederick (Schiller)
Morley, Christopher (Darlington) 1890-1957
  TCLC 87
  See also CA 112; DLB 9
Morren, Theophil
  See Hofmannsthal, Hugo von
Morris, Bill 1952-   **CLC 76**
Morris, Julian
  See West, Morris L(anglo)
Morris, Steveland Judkins 1950(?)-
  See Wonder, Stevie
  See also CA 111
Morris, William 1834-1896   **NCLC 4**
  See also CDBLB 1832-1890; DLB 18, 35, 57,
  156, 178, 184
Morris, Wright 1910-1998**CLC 1, 3, 7, 18, 37**
  See also CA 9-12R; 167; CANR 21; DLB 2,
  206; DLBY 81; MTCW 1
Morrison, Arthur 1863-1945   **TCLC 72**
  See also CA 120; 157; DLB 70, 135, 197
Morrison, Chloe Anthony Wofford
  See Morrison, Toni
Morrison, James Douglas 1943-1971
  See Morrison, Jim
  See also CA 73-76; CANR 40
Morrison, Jim   **CLC 17**
  See also Morrison, James Douglas
Morrison, Toni 1931-**CLC 4, 10, 22, 55, 81, 87;**
  BLC 3; DA; DAB; DAC; DAM MST,
  MULT, NOV, POP
  See also AAYA 1, 22; BW 2; CA 29-32R;
  CANR 27, 42, 67; CDALB 1968-1988; DLB
  6, 33, 143; DLBY 81; MTCW 1; SATA 57
Morrison, Van 1945-   **CLC 21**
  See also CA 116; 168
Morrissy, Mary 1958-   **CLC 99**
Mortimer, John (Clifford) 1923- **CLC 28, 43;**
  DAM DRAM, POP
  See also CA 13-16R; CANR 21, 69; CDBLB
  1960 to Present; DLB 13; INT CANR-21;
  MTCW 1
Mortimer, Penelope (Ruth) 1918-   **CLC 5**
  See also CA 57-60; CANR 45
Morton, Anthony
  See Creasey, John
Mosca, Gaetano 1858-1941   **TCLC 75**
Mosher, Howard Frank 1943-   **CLC 62**
  See also CA 139; CANR 65
Mosley, Nicholas 1923-   **CLC 43, 70**
  See also CA 69-72; CANR 41, 60; DLB 14, 207
Mosley, Walter 1952- **CLC 97; BLCS; DAM**
  MULT, POP
  See also AAYA 17; BW 2; CA 142; CANR 57
Moss, Howard 1922-1987 **CLC 7, 14, 45, 50;**
  DAM POET
  See also CA 1-4R; 123; CANR 1, 44; DLB 5
Mossgiel, Rab
  See Burns, Robert
Motion, Andrew (Peter) 1952-   **CLC 47**
  See also CA 146; DLB 40
Motley, Willard (Francis) 1909-1965 **CLC 18**
  See also BW 1; CA 117; 106; DLB 76, 143
Motoori, Norinaga 1730-1801   **NCLC 45**
Mott, Michael (Charles Alston) 1930-**CLC 15,**
  34
  See also CA 5-8R; CAAS 7; CANR 7, 29

Mountain Wolf Woman 1884-1960   **CLC 92**
  See also CA 144; NNAL
Moure, Erin 1955-   **CLC 88**
  See also CA 113; DLB 60
Mowat, Farley (McGill) 1921-**CLC 26; DAC;**
  DAM MST
  See also AAYA 1; CA 1-4R; CANR 4, 24, 42,
  68; CLR 20; DLB 68; INT CANR-24; JRDA;
  MAICYA; MTCW 1; SATA 3, 55
Mowatt, Anna Cora 1819-1870   **NCLC 74**
Moyers, Bill 1934-   **CLC 74**
  See also AITN 2; CA 61-64; CANR 31, 52
Mphahlele, Es'kia
  See Mphahlele, Ezekiel
  See also DLB 125
Mphahlele, Ezekiel 1919-1983 **CLC 25; BLC**
  3; DAM MULT
  See also Mphahlele, Es'kia
  See also BW 2; CA 81-84; CANR 26
Mqhayi, S(amuel) E(dward) K(rune Loliwe)
  1875-1945**TCLC 25; BLC 3; DAM MULT**
  See also CA 153
Mrozek, Slawomir 1930-   **CLC 3, 13**
  See also CA 13-16R; CAAS 10; CANR 29;
  MTCW 1
Mrs. Belloc-Lowndes
  See Lowndes, Marie Adelaide (Belloc)
Mtwa, Percy (?)-   **CLC 47**
Mueller, Lisel 1924-   **CLC 13, 51**
  See also CA 93-96; DLB 105
Muir, Edwin 1887-1959   **TCLC 2, 87**
  See also CA 104; DLB 20, 100, 191
Muir, John 1838-1914   **TCLC 28**
  See also CA 165; DLB 186
Mujica Lainez, Manuel 1910-1984   **CLC 31**
  See also Lainez, Manuel Mujica
  See also CA 81-84; 112; CANR 32; HW
Mukherjee, Bharati 1940-**CLC 53, 115; DAM**
  NOV
  See also BEST 89:2; CA 107; CANR 45, 72;
  DLB 60; MTCW 1
Muldoon, Paul 1951-**CLC 32, 72; DAM POET**
  See also CA 113; 129; CANR 52; DLB 40; INT
  129
Mulisch, Harry 1927-   **CLC 42**
  See also CA 9-12R; CANR 6, 26, 56
Mull, Martin 1943-   **CLC 17**
  See also CA 105
Muller, Wilhelm   **NCLC 73**
Mulock, Dinah Maria
  See Craik, Dinah Maria (Mulock)
Munford, Robert 1737(?)-1783   **LC 5**
  See also DLB 31
Mungo, Raymond 1946-   **CLC 72**
  See also CA 49-52; CANR 2
Munro, Alice 1931-   **CLC 6, 10, 19, 50, 95;**
  DAC; DAM MST, NOV; SSC 3; WLCS
  See also AITN 2; CA 33-36R; CANR 33, 53,
  75; DLB 53; MTCW 1; SATA 29
Munro, H(ector) H(ugh) 1870-1916
  See Saki
  See also CA 104; 130; CDBLB 1890-1914; DA;
  DAB; DAC; DAM MST, NOV; DLB 34, 162;
  MTCW 1; WLC
Murdoch, (Jean) Iris 1919-**CLC 1, 2, 3, 4, 6, 8,**
  11, 15, 22, 31, 51; DAB; DAC; DAM MST,
  NOV
  See also CA 13-16R; CANR 8, 43, 68; CDBLB
  1960 to Present; DLB 14, 194; INT CANR-
  8; MTCW 1
Murfree, Mary Noailles 1850-1922 **SSC 22**
  See also CA 122; DLB 12, 74
Murnau, Friedrich Wilhelm

See Plumpe, Friedrich Wilhelm
Murphy, Richard 1927- **CLC 41**
See also CA 29-32R; DLB 40
Murphy, Sylvia 1937- **CLC 34**
See also CA 121
Murphy, Thomas (Bernard) 1935- **CLC 51**
See also CA 101
Murray, Albert L. 1916- **CLC 73**
See also BW 2; CA 49-52; CANR 26, 52; DLB 38
Murray, Judith Sargent 1751-1820 **NCLC 63**
See also DLB 37, 200
Murray, Les(lie) A(llan) 1938-**CLC 40; DAM POET**
See also CA 21-24R; CANR 11, 27, 56
Murry, J. Middleton
See Murry, John Middleton
Murry, John Middleton 1889-1957 **TCLC 16**
See also CA 118; DLB 149
Musgrave, Susan 1951- **CLC 13, 54**
See also CA 69-72; CANR 45
Musil, Robert (Edler von) 1880-1942 **TCLC 12, 68; SSC 18**
See also CA 109; CANR 55; DLB 81, 124
Muske, Carol 1945- **CLC 90**
See also Muske-Dukes, Carol (Anne)
Muske-Dukes, Carol (Anne) 1945-
See Muske, Carol
See also CA 65-68; CANR 32, 70
Musset, (Louis Charles) Alfred de 1810-1857 **NCLC 7**
See also DLB 192
My Brother's Brother
See Chekhov, Anton (Pavlovich)
Myers, L(eopold) H(amilton) 1881-1944 **TCLC 59**
See also CA 157; DLB 15
Myers, Walter Dean 1937- **CLC 35; BLC 3; DAM MULT, NOV**
See also AAYA 4, 23; BW 2; CA 33-36R; CANR 20, 42, 67; CLR 4, 16, 35; DLB 33; INT CANR-20; JRDA; MAICYA; SAAS 2; SATA 41, 71; SATA-Brief 27
Myers, Walter M.
See Myers, Walter Dean
Myles, Symon
See Follett, Ken(neth Martin)
Nabokov, Vladimir (Vladimirovich) 1899-1977 **CLC 1, 2, 3, 6, 8, 11, 15, 23, 44, 46, 64; DA; DAB; DAC; DAM MST, NOV; SSC 11; WLC**
See also CA 5-8R; 69-72; CANR 20; CDALB 1941-1968; DLB 2; DLBD 3; DLBY 80, 91; MTCW 1
Nagai Kafu 1879-1959 **TCLC 51**
See also Nagai Sokichi
See also DLB 180
Nagai Sokichi 1879-1959
See Nagai Kafu
See also CA 117
Nagy, Laszlo 1925-1978 **CLC 7**
See also CA 129; 112
Naidu, Sarojini 1879-1943 **TCLC 80**
Naipaul, Shiva(dhar Srinivasa) 1945-1985 **CLC 32, 39; DAM NOV**
See also CA 110; 112; 116; CANR 33; DLB 157; DLBY 85; MTCW 1
Naipaul, V(idiadhar) S(urajprasad) 1932- **CLC 4, 7, 9, 13, 18, 37, 105; DAB; DAC; DAM MST, NOV**
See also CA 1-4R; CANR 1, 33, 51; CDBLB 1960 to Present; DLB 125, 204, 206; DLBY 85; MTCW 1

Nakos, Lilika 1899(?)- **CLC 29**
Narayan, R(asipuram) K(rishnaswami) 1906- **CLC 7, 28, 47; DAM NOV; SSC 25**
See also CA 81-84; CANR 33, 61; MTCW 1; SATA 62
Nash, (Frediric) Ogden 1902-1971 **CLC 23; DAM POET; PC 21**
See also CA 13-14; 29-32R; CANR 34, 61; CAP 1; DLB 11; MAICYA; MTCW 1; SATA 2, 46
Nashe, Thomas 1567-1601(?) **LC 41**
See also DLB 167
Nashe, Thomas 1567-1601 **LC 41**
Nathan, Daniel
See Dannay, Frederic
Nathan, George Jean 1882-1958 **TCLC 18**
See also Hatteras, Owen
See also CA 114; 169; DLB 137
Natsume, Kinnosuke 1867-1916
See Natsume, Soseki
See also CA 104
Natsume, Soseki 1867-1916 **TCLC 2, 10**
See also Natsume, Kinnosuke
See also DLB 180
Natti, (Mary) Lee 1919-
See Kingman, Lee
See also CA 5-8R; CANR 2
Naylor, Gloria 1950-**CLC 28, 52; BLC 3; DA; DAC; DAM MST, MULT, NOV, POP; WLCS**
See also AAYA 6; BW 2; CA 107; CANR 27, 51, 74; DLB 173; MTCW 1
Neihardt, John Gneisenau 1881-1973**CLC 32**
See also CA 13-14; CANR 65; CAP 1; DLB 9, 54
Nekrasov, Nikolai Alekseevich 1821-1878 **NCLC 11**
Nelligan, Emile 1879-1941 **TCLC 14**
See also CA 114; DLB 92
Nelson, Willie 1933- **CLC 17**
See also CA 107
Nemerov, Howard (Stanley) 1920-1991**CLC 2, 6, 9, 36; DAM POET; PC 24**
See also CA 1-4R; 134; CABS 2; CANR 1, 27, 53; DLB 5, 6; DLBY 83; INT CANR-27; MTCW 1
Neruda, Pablo 1904-1973**CLC 1, 2, 5, 7, 9, 28, 62; DA; DAB; DAC; DAM MST, MULT, POET; HLC; PC 4; WLC**
See also CA 19-20; 45-48; CAP 2; HW; MTCW 1
Nerval, Gerard de 1808-1855**NCLC 1, 67; PC 13; SSC 18**
Nervo, (Jose) Amado (Ruiz de) 1870-1919 **TCLC 11**
See also CA 109; 131; HW
Nessi, Pio Baroja y
See Baroja (y Nessi), Pio
Nestroy, Johann 1801-1862 **NCLC 42**
See also DLB 133
Netterville, Luke
See O'Grady, Standish (James)
Neufeld, John (Arthur) 1938- **CLC 17**
See also AAYA 11; CA 25-28R; CANR 11, 37, 56; CLR 52; MAICYA; SAAS 3; SATA 6, 81
Neville, Emily Cheney 1919- **CLC 12**
See also CA 5-8R; CANR 3, 37; JRDA; MAICYA; SAAS 2; SATA 1
Newbound, Bernard Slade 1930-
See Slade, Bernard
See also CA 81-84; CANR 49; DAM DRAM
Newby, P(ercy) H(oward) 1918-1997 **CLC 2,**

13; DAM NOV
See also CA 5-8R; 161; CANR 32, 67; DLB 15; MTCW 1
Newlove, Donald 1928- **CLC 6**
See also CA 29-32R; CANR 25
Newlove, John (Herbert) 1938- **CLC 14**
See also CA 21-24R; CANR 9, 25
Newman, Charles 1938- **CLC 2, 8**
See also CA 21-24R
Newman, Edwin (Harold) 1919- **CLC 14**
See also AITN 1; CA 69-72; CANR 5
Newman, John Henry 1801-1890 **NCLC 38**
See also DLB 18, 32, 55
Newton, (Sir)Isaac 1642-1727 **LC 35**
Newton, Suzanne 1936- **CLC 35**
See also CA 41-44R; CANR 14; JRDA; SATA 5, 77
Nexo, Martin Andersen 1869-1954 **TCLC 43**
Nezval, Vitezslav 1900-1958 **TCLC 44**
See also CA 123
Ng, Fae Myenne 1957(?)- **CLC 81**
See also CA 146
Ngema, Mbongeni 1955- **CLC 57**
See also BW 2; CA 143
Ngugi, James T(hiong'o) **CLC 3, 7, 13**
See also Ngugi wa Thiong'o
Ngugi wa Thiong'o 1938- **CLC 36; BLC 3; DAM MULT, NOV**
See also Ngugi, James T(hiong'o)
See also BW 2; CA 81-84; CANR 27, 58; DLB 125; MTCW 1
Nichol, B(arrie) P(hillip) 1944-1988 **CLC 18**
See also CA 53-56; DLB 53; SATA 66
Nichols, John (Treadwell) 1940- **CLC 38**
See also CA 9-12R; CAAS 2; CANR 6, 70; DLBY 82
Nichols, Leigh
See Koontz, Dean R(ay)
Nichols, Peter (Richard) 1927- **CLC 5, 36, 65**
See also CA 104; CANR 33; DLB 13; MTCW 1
Nicolas, F. R. E.
See Freeling, Nicolas
Niedecker, Lorine 1903-1970 **CLC 10, 42; DAM POET**
See also CA 25-28; CAP 2; DLB 48
Nietzsche, Friedrich (Wilhelm) 1844-1900 **TCLC 10, 18, 55**
See also CA 107; 121; DLB 129
Nievo, Ippolito 1831-1861 **NCLC 22**
Nightingale, Anne Redmon 1943-
See Redmon, Anne
See also CA 103
Nightingale, Florence 1820-1910 **TCLC 85**
See also DLB 166
Nik. T. O.
See Annensky, Innokenty (Fyodorovich)
Nin, Anais 1903-1977 **CLC 1, 4, 8, 11, 14, 60; DAM NOV, POP; SSC 10**
See also AITN 2; CA 13-16R; 69-72; CANR 22, 53; DLB 2, 4, 152; MTCW 1
Nishida, Kitaro 1870-1945 **TCLC 83**
Nishiwaki, Junzaburo 1894-1982 **PC 15**
See also CA 107
Nissenson, Hugh 1933- **CLC 4, 9**
See also CA 17-20R; CANR 27; DLB 28
Niven, Larry **CLC 8**
See also Niven, Laurence Van Cott
See also AAYA 27; DLB 8
Niven, Laurence Van Cott 1938-
See Niven, Larry
See also CA 21-24R; CAAS 12; CANR 14, 44, 66; DAM POP; MTCW 1; SATA 95

Nixon, Agnes Eckhardt 1927- CLC 21
See also CA 110
Nizan, Paul 1905-1940 TCLC 40
See also CA 161; DLB 72
Nkosi, Lewis 1936- CLC 45; BLC 3; DAM
MULT
See also BW 1; CA 65-68; CANR 27; DLB 157
Nodier, (Jean) Charles (Emmanuel) 1780-1844
NCLC 19
See also DLB 119
Noguchi, Yone 1875-1947 TCLC 80
Nolan, Christopher 1965- CLC 58
See also CA 111
Noon, Jeff 1957- CLC 91
See also CA 148
Norden, Charles
See Durrell, Lawrence (George)
Nordhoff, Charles (Bernard) 1887-1947
TCLC 23
See also CA 108; DLB 9; SATA 23
Norfolk, Lawrence 1963- CLC 76
See also CA 144
Norman, Marsha 1947-CLC 28; DAM DRAM;
DC 8
See also CA 105; CABS 3; CANR 41; DLBY
84
Normyx
See Douglas, (George) Norman
Norris, Frank 1870-1902 SSC 28
See also Norris, (Benjamin) Frank(lin, Jr.)
See also CDALB 1865-1917; DLB 12, 71, 186
Norris, (Benjamin) Frank(lin, Jr.) 1870-1902
TCLC 24
See also Norris, Frank
See also CA 110; 160
Norris, Leslie 1921- CLC 14
See also CA 11-12; CANR 14; CAP 1; DLB 27
North, Andrew
See Norton, Andre
North, Anthony
See Koontz, Dean R(ay)
North, Captain George
See Stevenson, Robert Louis (Balfour)
North, Milou
See Erdrich, Louise
Northrup, B. A.
See Hubbard, L(afayette) Ron(ald)
North Staffs
See Hulme, T(homas) E(rnest)
Norton, Alice Mary
See Norton, Andre
See also MAICYA; SATA 1, 43
Norton, Andre 1912- CLC 12
See also Norton, Alice Mary
See also AAYA 14; CA 1-4R; CANR 68; CLR
50; DLB 8, 52; JRDA; MTCW 1; SATA 91
Norton, Caroline 1808-1877 NCLC 47
See also DLB 21, 159, 199
Norway, Nevil Shute 1899-1960
See Shute, Nevil
See also CA 102; 93-96
Norwid, Cyprian Kamil 1821-1883 NCLC 17
Nosille, Nabrah
See Ellison, Harlan (Jay)
Nossack, Hans Erich 1901-1978 CLC 6
See also CA 93-96; 85-88; DLB 69
Nostradamus 1503-1566 LC 27
Nosu, Chuji
See Ozu, Yasujiro
Notenburg, Eleanora (Genrikhovna) von
See Guro, Elena
Nova, Craig 1945- CLC 7, 31
See also CA 45-48; CANR 2, 53

Novak, Joseph
See Kosinski, Jerzy (Nikodem)
Novalis 1772-1801 NCLC 13
See also DLB 90
Novis, Emile
See Weil, Simone (Adolphine)
Nowlan, Alden (Albert) 1933-1983 CLC 15;
DAC; DAM MST
See also CA 9-12R; CANR 5; DLB 53
Noyes, Alfred 1880-1958 TCLC 7
See also CA 104; DLB 20
Nunn, Kem CLC 34
See also CA 159
Nye, Robert 1939- CLC 13, 42; DAM NOV
See also CA 33-36R; CANR 29, 67; DLB 14;
MTCW 1; SATA 6
Nyro, Laura 1947- CLC 17
Oates, Joyce Carol 1938-CLC 1, 2, 3, 6, 9, 11,
15, 19, 33, 52, 108; DA; DAB; DAC; DAM
MST, NOV, POP; SSC 6; WLC
See also AAYA 15; AITN 1; BEST 89:2; CA 5-
8R; CANR 25, 45, 74; CDALB 1968-1988;
DLB 2, 5, 130; DLBY 81; INT CANR-25;
MTCW 1
O'Brien, Darcy 1939-1998 CLC 11
See also CA 21-24R; 167; CANR 8, 59
O'Brien, E. G.
See Clarke, Arthur C(harles)
O'Brien, Edna 1936- CLC 3, 5, 8, 13, 36, 65,
116; DAM NOV; SSC 10
See also CA 1-4R; CANR 6, 41, 65; CDBLB
1960 to Present; DLB 14; MTCW 1
O'Brien, Fitz-James 1828-1862 NCLC 21
See also DLB 74
O'Brien, Flann CLC 1, 4, 5, 7, 10, 47
See O Nuallain, Brian
O'Brien, Richard 1942- CLC 17
See also CA 124
O'Brien, (William) Tim(othy) 1946- CLC 7,
19, 40, 103; DAM POP
See also AAYA 16; CA 85-88; CANR 40, 58;
DLB 152; DLBD 9; DLBY 80
Obstfelder, Sigbjoern 1866-1900 TCLC 23
See also CA 123
O'Casey, Sean 1880-1964 CLC 1, 5, 9, 11, 15,
88; DAB; DAC; DAM DRAM, MST;
WLCS
See also CA 89-92; CANR 62; CDBLB 1914-
1945; DLB 10; MTCW 1
O'Cathasaigh, Sean
See O'Casey, Sean
Ochs, Phil 1940-1976 CLC 17
See also CA 65-68
O'Connor, Edwin (Greene) 1918-1968CLC 14
See also CA 93-96; 25-28R
O'Connor, (Mary) Flannery 1925-1964 C L C
1, 2, 3, 6, 10, 13, 15, 21, 66, 104; DA; DAB;
DAC; DAM MST, NOV; SSC 1, 23; WLC
See also AAYA 7; CA 1-4R; CANR 3, 41;
CDALB 1941-1968; DLB 2, 152; DLBD 12;
DLBY 80; MTCW 1
O'Connor, Frank CLC 23; SSC 5
See also O'Donovan, Michael John
See also DLB 162
O'Dell, Scott 1898-1989 CLC 30
See also AAYA 3; CA 61-64; 129; CANR 12,
30; CLR 1, 16; DLB 52; JRDA; MAICYA;
SATA 12, 60
Odets, Clifford 1906-1963CLC 2, 28, 98; DAM
DRAM; DC 6
See also CA 85-88; CANR 62; DLB 7, 26;
MTCW 1
O'Doherty, Brian 1934- CLC 76

See also CA 105
O'Donnell, K. M.
See Malzberg, Barry N(athaniel)
O'Donnell, Lawrence
See Kuttner, Henry
O'Donovan, Michael John 1903-1966CLC 14
See also O'Connor, Frank
See also CA 93-96
Oe, Kenzaburo 1935- CLC 10, 36, 86; DAM
NOV; SSC 20
See also CA 97-100; CANR 36, 50, 74; DLB
182; DLBY 94; MTCW 1
O'Faolain, Julia 1932- CLC 6, 19, 47, 108
See also CA 81-84; CAAS 2; CANR 12, 61;
DLB 14; MTCW 1
O'Faolain, Sean 1900-1991 CLC 1, 7, 14, 32,
70; SSC 13
See also CA 61-64; 134; CANR 12, 66; DLB
15, 162; MTCW 1
O'Flaherty, Liam 1896-1984CLC 5, 34; SSC 6
See also CA 101; 113; CANR 35; DLB 36, 162;
DLBY 84; MTCW 1
Ogilvy, Gavin
See Barrie, J(ames) M(atthew)
O'Grady, Standish (James) 1846-1928 T C L C
5
See also CA 104; 157
O'Grady, Timothy 1951- CLC 59
See also CA 138
O'Hara, Frank 1926-1966 CLC 2, 5, 13, 78;
DAM POET
See also CA 9-12R; 25-28R; CANR 33; DLB
5, 16, 193; MTCW 1
O'Hara, John (Henry) 1905-1970CLC 1, 2, 3,
6, 11, 42; DAM NOV; SSC 15
See also CA 5-8R; 25-28R; CANR 31, 60;
CDALB 1929-1941; DLB 9, 86; DLBD 2;
MTCW 1
O Hehir, Diana 1922- CLC 41
See also CA 93-96
Okigbo, Christopher (Ifenayichukwu) 1932-
1967 CLC 25, 84; BLC 3; DAM MULT,
POET; PC 7
See also BW 1; CA 77-80; CANR 74; DLB 125;
MTCW 1
Okri, Ben 1959- CLC 87
See also BW 2; CA 130; 138; CANR 65; DLB
157; INT 138
Olds, Sharon 1942- CLC 32, 39, 85; DAM
POET; PC 22
See also CA 101; CANR 18, 41, 66; DLB 120
Oldstyle, Jonathan
See Irving, Washington
Olesha, Yuri (Karlovich) 1899-1960 CLC 8
See also CA 85-88
Oliphant, Laurence 1829(?)-1888 NCLC 47
See also DLB 18, 166
Oliphant, Margaret (Oliphant Wilson) 1828-
1897 NCLC 11, 61; SSC 25
See also DLB 18, 159, 190
Oliver, Mary 1935- CLC 19, 34, 98
See also CA 21-24R; CANR 9, 43; DLB 5, 193
Olivier, Laurence (Kerr) 1907-1989 CLC 20
See also CA 111; 150; 129
Olsen, Tillie 1912-CLC 4, 13, 114; DA; DAB;
DAC; DAM MST; SSC 11
See also CA 1-4R; CANR 1, 43, 74; DLB 28,
206; DLBY 80; MTCW 1
Olson, Charles (John) 1910-1970CLC 1, 2, 5,
6, 9, 11, 29; DAM POET; PC 19
See also CA 13-16; 25-28R; CABS 2; CANR
35, 61; CAP 1; DLB 5, 16, 193; MTCW 1
Olson, Toby 1937- CLC 28

See also CA 65-68; CANR 9, 31
Olyesha, Yuri
See Olesha, Yuri (Karlovich)
Ondaatje, (Philip) Michael 1943-**CLC 14, 29, 51, 76; DAB; DAC; DAM MST**
See also CA 77-80; CANR 42, 74; DLB 60
Oneal, Elizabeth 1934-
See Oneal, Zibby
See also CA 106; CANR 28; MAICYA; SATA 30, 82
Oneal, Zibby   **CLC 30**
See also Oneal, Elizabeth
See also AAYA 5; CLR 13; JRDA
O'Neill, Eugene (Gladstone) 1888-1953**TCLC 1, 6, 27, 49; DA; DAB; DAC; DAM DRAM, MST; WLC**
See also AITN 1; CA 110; 132; CDALB 1929-1941; DLB 7; MTCW 1
Onetti, Juan Carlos 1909-1994   **CLC 7, 10; DAM MULT, NOV; SSC 23**
See also CA 85-88; 145; CANR 32, 63; DLB 113; HW; MTCW 1
O Nuallain, Brian 1911-1966
See O'Brien, Flann
See also CA 21-22; 25-28R; CAP 2
Ophuls, Max 1902-1957   **TCLC 79**
See also CA 113
Opie, Amelia 1769-1853   **NCLC 65**
See also DLB 116, 159
Oppen, George 1908-1984   **CLC 7, 13, 34**
See also CA 13-16R; 113; CANR 8; DLB 5, 165
Oppenheim, E(dward) Phillips 1866-1946
TCLC 45
See also CA 111; DLB 70
Opuls, Max
See Ophuls, Max
Origen c. 185-c. 254   **CMLC 19**
Orlovitz, Gil 1918-1973   **CLC 22**
See also CA 77-80; 45-48; DLB 2, 5
Orris
See Ingelow, Jean
Ortega y Gasset, Jose 1883-1955   **TCLC 9; DAM MULT; HLC**
See also CA 106; 130; HW; MTCW 1
Ortese, Anna Maria 1914-   **CLC 89**
See also DLB 177
Ortiz, Simon J(oseph) 1941- **CLC 45; DAM MULT, POET; PC 17**
See also CA 134; CANR 69; DLB 120, 175; NNAL
Orton, Joe   **CLC 4, 13, 43; DC 3**
See also Orton, John Kingsley
See also CDBLB 1960 to Present; DLB 13
Orton, John Kingsley 1933-1967
See Orton, Joe
See also CA 85-88; CANR 35, 66; DAM DRAM; MTCW 1
Orwell, George **TCLC 2, 6, 15, 31, 51; DAB; WLC**
See also Blair, Eric (Arthur)
See also CDBLB 1945-1960; DLB 15, 98, 195
Osborne, David
See Silverberg, Robert
Osborne, George
See Silverberg, Robert
Osborne, John (James) 1929-1994**CLC 1, 2, 5, 11, 45; DA; DAB; DAC; DAM DRAM, MST; WLC**
See also CA 13-16R; 147; CANR 21, 56; CDBLB 1945-1960; DLB 13; MTCW 1
Osborne, Lawrence 1958-   **CLC 50**
Oshima, Nagisa 1932-   **CLC 20**

See also CA 116; 121
Oskison, John Milton 1874-1947 **TCLC 35; DAM MULT**
See also CA 144; DLB 175; NNAL
Ossian c. 3rd cent. -   **CMLC 28**
See also Macpherson, James
Ossoli, Sarah Margaret (Fuller marchesa d') 1810-1850
See Fuller, Margaret
See also SATA 25
Ostrovsky, Alexander 1823-1886**NCLC 30, 57**
Otero, Blas de 1916-1979   **CLC 11**
See also CA 89-92; DLB 134
Otto, Rudolf 1869-1937   **TCLC 85**
Otto, Whitney 1955-   **CLC 70**
See also CA 140
Ouida   **TCLC 43**
See also De La Ramee, (Marie) Louise
See also DLB 18, 156
Ousmane, Sembene 1923-   **CLC 66; BLC 3**
See also BW 1; CA 117; 125; MTCW 1
Ovid 43B.C.-18(?)**CMLC 7; DAM POET; PC 2**
Owen, Hugh
See Faust, Frederick (Schiller)
Owen, Wilfred (Edward Salter) 1893-1918
TCLC 5, 27; DA; DAB; DAC; DAM MST, POET; PC 19; WLC
See also CA 104; 141; CDBLB 1914-1945; DLB 20
Owens, Rochelle 1936-   **CLC 8**
See also CA 17-20R; CAAS 2; CANR 39
Oz, Amos 1939-**CLC 5, 8, 11, 27, 33, 54; DAM NOV**
See also CA 53-56; CANR 27, 47, 65; MTCW 1
Ozick, Cynthia 1928- **CLC 3, 7, 28, 62; DAM NOV, POP; SSC 15**
See also BEST 90:1; CA 17-20R; CANR 23, 58; DLB 28, 152; DLBY 82; INT CANR-23; MTCW 1
Ozu, Yasujiro 1903-1963   **CLC 16**
See also CA 112
Pacheco, C.
See Pessoa, Fernando (Antonio Nogueira)
Pa Chin   **CLC 18**
See also Li Fei-kan
Pack, Robert 1929-   **CLC 13**
See also CA 1-4R; CANR 3, 44; DLB 5
Padgett, Lewis
See Kuttner, Henry
Padilla (Lorenzo), Heberto 1932-   **CLC 38**
See also AITN 1; CA 123; 131; HW
Page, Jimmy 1944-   **CLC 12**
Page, Louise 1955-   **CLC 40**
See also CA 140
Page, P(atricia) K(athleen) 1916- **CLC 7, 18; DAC; DAM MST; PC 12**
See also CA 53-56; CANR 4, 22, 65; DLB 68; MTCW 1
Page, Thomas Nelson 1853-1922   **SSC 23**
See also CA 118; DLB 12, 78; DLBD 13
Pagels, Elaine Hiesey 1943-   **CLC 104**
See also CA 45-48; CANR 2, 24, 51
Paget, Violet 1856-1935
See Lee, Vernon
See also CA 104; 166
Paget-Lowe, Henry
See Lovecraft, H(oward) P(hillips)
Paglia, Camille (Anna) 1947-   **CLC 68**
See also CA 140; CANR 72
Paige, Richard
See Koontz, Dean R(ay)

Paine, Thomas 1737-1809   **NCLC 62**
See also CDALB 1640-1865; DLB 31, 43, 73, 158
Pakenham, Antonia
See Fraser, (Lady) Antonia (Pakenham)
Palamas, Kostes 1859-1943   **TCLC 5**
See also CA 105
Palazzeschi, Aldo 1885-1974   **CLC 11**
See also CA 89-92; 53-56; DLB 114
Paley, Grace 1922- **CLC 4, 6, 37; DAM POP; SSC 8**
See also CA 25-28R; CANR 13, 46, 74; DLB 28; INT CANR-13; MTCW 1
Palin, Michael (Edward) 1943-   **CLC 21**
See also Monty Python
See also CA 107; CANR 35; SATA 67
Palliser, Charles 1947-   **CLC 65**
See also CA 136
Palma, Ricardo 1833-1919   **TCLC 29**
See also CA 168
Pancake, Breece Dexter 1952-1979
See Pancake, Breece D'J
See also CA 123; 109
Pancake, Breece D'J   **CLC 29**
See also Pancake, Breece Dexter
See also DLB 130
Panko, Rudy
See Gogol, Nikolai (Vasilyevich)
Papadiamantis, Alexandros 1851-1911**TCLC 29**
See also CA 168
Papadiamantopoulos, Johannes 1856-1910
See Moreas, Jean
See also CA 117
Papini, Giovanni 1881-1956   **TCLC 22**
See also CA 121
Paracelsus 1493-1541   **LC 14**
See also DLB 179
Parasol, Peter
See Stevens, Wallace
Pardo Bazan, Emilia 1851-1921   **SSC 30**
Pareto, Vilfredo 1848-1923   **TCLC 69**
Parfenie, Maria
See Codrescu, Andrei
Parini, Jay (Lee) 1948-   **CLC 54**
See also CA 97-100; CAAS 16; CANR 32
Park, Jordan
See Kornbluth, C(yril) M.; Pohl, Frederik
Park, Robert E(zra) 1864-1944   **TCLC 73**
See also CA 122; 165
Parker, Bert
See Ellison, Harlan (Jay)
Parker, Dorothy (Rothschild) 1893-1967**CLC 15, 68; DAM POET; SSC 2**
See also CA 19-20; 25-28R; CAP 2; DLB 11, 45, 86; MTCW 1
Parker, Robert B(rown) 1932-**CLC 27; DAM NOV, POP**
See also BEST 89:4; CA 49-52; CANR 1, 26, 52; INT CANR-26; MTCW 1
Parkin, Frank 1940-   **CLC 43**
See also CA 147
Parkman, Francis, Jr. 1823-1893   **NCLC 12**
See also DLB 1, 30, 186
Parks, Gordon (Alexander Buchanan) 1912-
CLC 1, 16; BLC 3; DAM MULT
See also AITN 2; BW 2; CA 41-44R; CANR 26, 66; DLB 33; SATA 8
Parmenides c. 515B.C.-c. 450B.C. **CMLC 22**
See also DLB 176
Parnell, Thomas 1679-1718   **LC 3**
See also DLB 94
Parra, Nicanor 1914-   **CLC 2, 102; DAM**

MULT; HLC
See also CA 85-88; CANR 32; HW; MTCW 1

Parrish, Mary Frances
See Fisher, M(ary) F(rances) K(ennedy)

Parson
See Coleridge, Samuel Taylor

Parson Lot
See Kingsley, Charles

Partridge, Anthony
See Oppenheim, E(dward) Phillips

Pascal, Blaise 1623-1662   **LC 35**

Pascoli, Giovanni 1855-1912   **TCLC 45**
See also CA 170

Pasolini, Pier Paolo 1922-1975   **CLC 20, 37, 106; PC 17**
See also CA 93-96; 61-64; CANR 63; DLB 128, 177; MTCW 1

Pasquini
See Silone, Ignazio

Pastan, Linda (Olenik) 1932- **CLC 27; DAM POET**
See also CA 61-64; CANR 18, 40, 61; DLB 5

Pasternak, Boris (Leonidovich) 1890-1960   **CLC 7, 10, 18, 63; DA; DAB; DAC; DAM MST, NOV, POET; PC 6; SSC 31; WLC**
See also CA 127; 116; MTCW 1

Patchen, Kenneth 1911-1972   **CLC 1, 2, 18; DAM POET**
See also CA 1-4R; 33-36R; CANR 3, 35; DLB 16, 48; MTCW 1

Pater, Walter (Horatio) 1839-1894   **NCLC 7**
See also CDBLB 1832-1890; DLB 57, 156

Paterson, A(ndrew) B(arton) 1864-1941   **TCLC 32**
See also CA 155; SATA 97

Paterson, Katherine (Womeldorf) 1932- **C L C 12, 30**
See also AAYA 1; CA 21-24R; CANR 28, 59; CLR 7, 50; DLB 52; JRDA; MAICYA; MTCW 1; SATA 13, 53, 92

Patmore, Coventry Kersey Dighton 1823-1896   **NCLC 9**
See also DLB 35, 98

Paton, Alan (Stewart) 1903-1988 **CLC 4, 10, 25, 55, 106; DA; DAB; DAC; DAM MST, NOV; WLC**
See also AAYA 26; CA 13-16; 125; CANR 22; CAP 1; DLBD 17; MTCW 1; SATA 11; SATA-Obit 56

Paton Walsh, Gillian 1937-
See Walsh, Jill Paton
See also CANR 38; JRDA; MAICYA; SAAS 3; SATA 4, 72

Patton, George S. 1885-1945   **TCLC 79**

Paulding, James Kirke 1778-1860   **NCLC 2**
See also DLB 3, 59, 74

Paulin, Thomas Neilson 1949-
See Paulin, Tom
See also CA 123; 128

Paulin, Tom   **CLC 37**
See also Paulin, Thomas Neilson
See also DLB 40

Paustovsky, Konstantin (Georgievich) 1892-1968   **CLC 40**
See also CA 93-96; 25-28R

Pavese, Cesare 1908-1950   **TCLC 3; PC 13; SSC 19**
See also CA 104; 169; DLB 128, 177

Pavic, Milorad 1929-   **CLC 60**
See also CA 136; DLB 181

Payne, Alan
See Jakes, John (William)

Paz, Gil

See Lugones, Leopoldo

Paz, Octavio 1914-1998**CLC 3, 4, 6, 10, 19, 51, 65; DA; DAB; DAC; DAM MST, MULT, POET; HLC; PC 1; WLC**
See also CA 73-76; 165; CANR 32, 65; DLBY 90; HW; MTCW 1

p'Bitek, Okot 1931-1982   **CLC 96; BLC 3; DAM MULT**
See also BW 2; CA 124; 107; DLB 125; MTCW 1

Peacock, Molly 1947-   **CLC 60**
See also CA 103; CAAS 21; CANR 52; DLB 120

Peacock, Thomas Love 1785-1866 **NCLC 22**
See also DLB 96, 116

Peake, Mervyn 1911-1968   **CLC 7, 54**
See also CA 5-8R; 25-28R; CANR 3; DLB 15, 160; MTCW 1; SATA 23

Pearce, Philippa   **CLC 21**
See also Christie, (Ann) Philippa
See also CLR 9; DLB 161; MAICYA; SATA 1, 67

Pearl, Eric
See Elman, Richard (Martin)

Pearson, T(homas) R(eid) 1956-   **CLC 39**
See also CA 120; 130; INT 130

Peck, Dale 1967-   **CLC 81**
See also CA 146; CANR 72

Peck, John 1941-   **CLC 3**
See also CA 49-52; CANR 3

Peck, Richard (Wayne) 1934-   **CLC 21**
See also AAYA 1, 24; CA 85-88; CANR 19, 38; CLR 15; INT CANR-19; JRDA; MAICYA; SAAS 2; SATA 18, 55, 97

Peck, Robert Newton 1928-   **CLC 17; DA; DAC; DAM MST**
See also AAYA 3; CA 81-84; CANR 31, 63; CLR 45; JRDA; MAICYA; SAAS 1; SATA 21, 62

Peckinpah, (David) Sam(uel) 1925-1984 **C L C 20**
See also CA 109; 114

Pedersen, Knut 1859-1952
See Hamsun, Knut
See also CA 104; 119; CANR 63; MTCW 1

Peeslake, Gaffer
See Durrell, Lawrence (George)

Peguy, Charles Pierre 1873-1914   **TCLC 10**
See also CA 107

Peirce, Charles Sanders 1839-1914 **TCLC 81**

Pena, Ramon del Valle y
See Valle-Inclan, Ramon (Maria) del

Pendennis, Arthur Esquir
See Thackeray, William Makepeace

Penn, William 1644-1718   **LC 25**
See also DLB 24

PEPECE
See Prado (Calvo), Pedro

Pepys, Samuel 1633-1703 **LC 11; DA; DAB; DAC; DAM MST; WLC**
See also CDBLB 1660-1789; DLB 101

Percy, Walker 1916-1990**CLC 2, 3, 6, 8, 14, 18, 47, 65; DAM NOV, POP**
See also CA 1-4R; 131; CANR 1, 23, 64; DLB 2; DLBY 80, 90; MTCW 1

Percy, William Alexander 1885-1942**TCLC 84**
See also CA 163

Perec, Georges 1936-1982   **CLC 56, 116**
See also CA 141; DLB 83

Pereda (y Sanchez de Porrua), Jose Maria de 1833-1906   **TCLC 16**
See also CA 117

Pereda y Porrua, Jose Maria de

See Pereda (y Sanchez de Porrua), Jose Maria de

Peregoy, George Weems
See Mencken, H(enry) L(ouis)

Perelman, S(idney) J(oseph) 1904-1979 **C L C 3, 5, 9, 15, 23, 44, 49; DAM DRAM; SSC 32**
See also AITN 1, 2; CA 73-76; 89-92; CANR 18; DLB 11, 44; MTCW 1

Peret, Benjamin 1899-1959   **TCLC 20**
See also CA 117

Peretz, Isaac Loeb 1851(?)-1915   **TCLC 16; SSC 26**
See also CA 109

Peretz, Yitzkhok Leibush
See Peretz, Isaac Loeb

Perez Galdos, Benito 1843-1920   **TCLC 27**
See also CA 125; 153; HW

Perrault, Charles 1628-1703   **LC 2**
See also MAICYA; SATA 25

Perry, Brighton
See Sherwood, Robert E(mmet)

Perse, St.-John
See Leger, (Marie-Rene Auguste) Alexis Saint-Leger

Perutz, Leo 1882-1957   **TCLC 60**
See also DLB 81

Peseenz, Tulio F.
See Lopez y Fuentes, Gregorio

Pesetsky, Bette 1932-   **CLC 28**
See also CA 133; DLB 130

Peshkov, Alexei Maximovich 1868-1936
See Gorky, Maxim
See also CA 105; 141; DA; DAC; DAM DRAM, MST, NOV

Pessoa, Fernando (Antonio Nogueira) 1898-1935   **TCLC 27; HLC; PC 20**
See also CA 125

Peterkin, Julia Mood 1880-1961   **CLC 31**
See also CA 102; DLB 9

Peters, Joan K(aren) 1945-   **CLC 39**
See also CA 158

Peters, Robert L(ouis) 1924-   **CLC 7**
See also CA 13-16R; CAAS 8; DLB 105

Petofi, Sandor 1823-1849   **NCLC 21**

Petrakis, Harry Mark 1923-   **CLC 3**
See also CA 9-12R; CANR 4, 30

Petrarch 1304-1374 **CMLC 20; DAM POET; PC 8**

Petrov, Evgeny   **TCLC 21**
See also Kataev, Evgeny Petrovich

Petry, Ann (Lane) 1908-1997   **CLC 1, 7, 18**
See also BW 1; CA 5-8R; 157; CAAS 6; CANR 4, 46; CLR 12; DLB 76; JRDA; MAICYA; MTCW 1; SATA 5; SATA-Obit 94

Petursson, Halligrimur 1614-1674   **LC 8**

Peychinovich
See Vazov, Ivan (Minchov)

Phaedrus 18(?)B.C.-55(?)   **CMLC 25**

Philips, Katherine 1632-1664   **LC 30**
See also DLB 131

Philipson, Morris H. 1926-   **CLC 53**
See also CA 1-4R; CANR 4

Phillips, Caryl 1958- **CLC 96; BLCS; DAM MULT**
See also BW 2; CA 141; CANR 63; DLB 157

Phillips, David Graham 1867-1911 **TCLC 44**
See also CA 108; DLB 9, 12

Phillips, Jack
See Sandburg, Carl (August)

Phillips, Jayne Anne 1952-**CLC 15, 33; SSC 16**
See also CA 101; CANR 24, 50; DLBY 80; INT CANR-24; MTCW 1

Phillips, Richard
See Dick, Philip K(indred)
Phillips, Robert (Schaeffer) 1938- **CLC 28**
See also CA 17-20R; CAAS 13; CANR 8; DLB 105
Phillips, Ward
See Lovecraft, H(oward) P(hillips)
Piccolo, Lucio 1901-1969 **CLC 13**
See also CA 97-100; DLB 114
Pickthall, Marjorie L(owry) C(hristie) 1883-1922 **TCLC 21**
See also CA 107; DLB 92
Pico della Mirandola, Giovanni 1463-1494 **LC 15**
Piercy, Marge 1936- **CLC 3, 6, 14, 18, 27, 62**
See also CA 21-24R; CAAS 1; CANR 13, 43, 66; DLB 120; MTCW 1
Piers, Robert
See Anthony, Piers
Pieyre de Mandiargues, Andre 1909-1991
See Mandiargues, Andre Pieyre de
See also CA 103; 136; CANR 22
Pilnyak, Boris **TCLC 23**
See also Vogau, Boris Andreyevich
Pincherle, Alberto 1907-1990 **CLC 11, 18; DAM NOV**
See Moravia, Alberto
See also CA 25-28R; 132; CANR 33, 63; MTCW 1
Pinckney, Darryl 1953- **CLC 76**
See also BW 2; CA 143
Pindar 518B.C.-446B.C. **CMLC 12; PC 19**
See also DLB 176
Pineda, Cecile 1942- **CLC 39**
See also CA 118
Pinero, Arthur Wing 1855-1934 **TCLC 32; DAM DRAM**
See also CA 110; 153; DLB 10
Pinero, Miguel (Antonio Gomez) 1946-1988 **CLC 4, 55**
See also CA 61-64; 125; CANR 29; HW
Pinget, Robert 1919-1997 **CLC 7, 13, 37**
See also CA 85-88; 160; DLB 83
Pink Floyd
See Barrett, (Roger) Syd; Gilmour, David; Mason, Nick; Waters, Roger; Wright, Rick
Pinkney, Edward 1802-1828 **NCLC 31**
Pinkwater, Daniel Manus 1941- **CLC 35**
See also Pinkwater, Manus
See also AAYA 1; CA 29-32R; CANR 12, 38; CLR 4; JRDA; MAICYA; SAAS 3; SATA 46, 76
Pinkwater, Manus
See Pinkwater, Daniel Manus
See also SATA 8
Pinsky, Robert 1940- **CLC 9, 19, 38, 94; DAM POET**
See also CA 29-32R; CAAS 4; CANR 58; DLBY 82
Pinta, Harold
See Pinter, Harold
Pinter, Harold 1930- **CLC 1, 3, 6, 9, 11, 15, 27, 58, 73; DA; DAB; DAC; DAM DRAM, MST; WLC**
See also CA 5-8R; CANR 33, 65; CDBLB 1960 to Present; DLB 13; MTCW 1
Piozzi, Hester Lynch (Thrale) 1741-1821 **NCLC 57**
See also DLB 104, 142
Pirandello, Luigi 1867-1936 **TCLC 4, 29; DA; DAB; DAC; DAM DRAM, MST; DC 5; SSC 22; WLC**
See also CA 104; 153

Pirsig, Robert M(aynard) 1928- **CLC 4, 6, 73; DAM POP**
See also CA 53-56; CANR 42, 74; MTCW 1; SATA 39
Pisarev, Dmitry Ivanovich 1840-1868 **NCLC 25**
Pix, Mary (Griffith) 1666-1709 **LC 8**
See also DLB 80
Pixerecourt, (Rene Charles) Guilbert de 1773-1844 **NCLC 39**
See also DLB 192
Plaatje, Sol(omon) T(shekisho) 1876-1932 **TCLC 73; BLCS**
See also BW 2; CA 141
Plaidy, Jean
See Hibbert, Eleanor Alice Burford
Planche, James Robinson 1796-1880 **NCLC 42**
Plant, Robert 1948- **CLC 12**
Plante, David (Robert) 1940- **CLC 7, 23, 38; DAM NOV**
See also CA 37-40R; CANR 12, 36, 58; DLBY 83; INT CANR-12; MTCW 1
Plath, Sylvia 1932-1963 **CLC 1, 2, 3, 5, 9, 11, 14, 17, 50, 51, 62, 111; DA; DAB; DAC; DAM MST, POET; PC 1; WLC**
See also AAYA 13; CA 19-20; CANR 34; CAP 2; CDALB 1941-1968; DLB 5, 6, 152; MTCW 1; SATA 96
Plato 428(?)B.C.-348(?)B.C. **CMLC 8; DA; DAB; DAC; DAM MST; WLCS**
See also DLB 176
Platonov, Andrei **TCLC 14**
See also Klimentov, Andrei Platonovich
Platt, Kin 1911- **CLC 26**
See also AAYA 11; CA 17-20R; CANR 11; JRDA; SAAS 17; SATA 21, 86
Plautus c. 251B.C.-184B.C. **CMLC 24; DC 6**
Plick et Plock
See Simenon, Georges (Jacques Christian)
Plimpton, George (Ames) 1927- **CLC 36**
See also AITN 1; CA 21-24R; CANR 32, 70; DLB 185; MTCW 1; SATA 10
Pliny the Elder c. 23-79 **CMLC 23**
Plomer, William Charles Franklin 1903-1973 **CLC 4, 8**
See also CA 21-22; CANR 34; CAP 2; DLB 20, 162, 191; MTCW 1; SATA 24
Plowman, Piers
See Kavanagh, Patrick (Joseph)
Plum, J.
See Wodehouse, P(elham) G(renville)
Plumly, Stanley (Ross) 1939- **CLC 33**
See also CA 108; 110; DLB 5, 193; INT 110
Plumpe, Friedrich Wilhelm 1888-1931 **TCLC 53**
See also CA 112
Po Chu-i 772-846 **CMLC 24**
Poe, Edgar Allan 1809-1849 **NCLC 1, 16, 55; DA; DAB; DAC; DAM MST, POET; PC 1; SSC 1, 22; WLC**
See also AAYA 14; CDALB 1640-1865; DLB 3, 59, 73, 74; SATA 23
Poet of Titchfield Street, The
See Pound, Ezra (Weston Loomis)
Pohl, Frederik 1919- **CLC 18; SSC 25**
See also AAYA 24; CA 61-64; CAAS 1; CANR 11, 37; DLB 8; INT CANR-11; MTCW 1; SATA 24
Poirier, Louis 1910-
See Gracq, Julien
See also CA 122; 126
Poitier, Sidney 1927- **CLC 26**
See also BW 1; CA 117

Polanski, Roman 1933- **CLC 16**
See also CA 77-80
Poliakoff, Stephen 1952- **CLC 38**
See also CA 106; DLB 13
Police, The
See Copeland, Stewart (Armstrong); Summers, Andrew James; Sumner, Gordon Matthew
Polidori, John William 1795-1821 **NCLC 51**
See also DLB 116
Pollitt, Katha 1949- **CLC 28**
See also CA 120; 122; CANR 66; MTCW 1
Pollock, (Mary) Sharon 1936- **CLC 50; DAC; DAM DRAM, MST**
See also CA 141; DLB 60
Polo, Marco 1254-1324 **CMLC 15**
Polonsky, Abraham (Lincoln) 1910- **CLC 92**
See also CA 104; DLB 26; INT 104
Polybius c. 200B.C.-c. 118B.C. **CMLC 17**
See also DLB 176
Pomerance, Bernard 1940- **CLC 13; DAM DRAM**
See also CA 101; CANR 49
Ponge, Francis (Jean Gaston Alfred) 1899-1988 **CLC 6, 18; DAM POET**
See also CA 85-88; 126; CANR 40
Pontoppidan, Henrik 1857-1943 **TCLC 29**
See also CA 170
Poole, Josephine **CLC 17**
See also Helyar, Jane Penelope Josephine
See also SAAS 2; SATA 5
Popa, Vasko 1922-1991 **CLC 19**
See also CA 112; 148; DLB 181
Pope, Alexander 1688-1744 **LC 3; DA; DAB; DAC; DAM MST, POET; WLC**
See also CDBLB 1660-1789; DLB 95, 101
Porter, Connie (Rose) 1959(?)- **CLC 70**
See also BW 2; CA 142; SATA 81
Porter, Gene(va Grace) Stratton 1863(?)-1924 **TCLC 21**
See also CA 112
Porter, Katherine Anne 1890-1980 **CLC 1, 3, 7, 10, 13, 15, 27, 101; DA; DAB; DAC; DAM MST, NOV; SSC 4, 31**
See also AITN 2; CA 1-4R; 101; CANR 1, 65; DLB 4, 9, 102; DLBD 12; DLBY 80; MTCW 1; SATA 39; SATA-Obit 23
Porter, Peter (Neville Frederick) 1929- **CLC 5, 13, 33**
See also CA 85-88; DLB 40
Porter, William Sydney 1862-1910
See Henry, O.
See also CA 104; 131; CDALB 1865-1917; DA; DAB; DAC; DAM MST; DLB 12, 78, 79; MTCW 1; YABC 2
Portillo (y Pacheco), Jose Lopez
See Lopez Portillo (y Pacheco), Jose
Post, Melville Davisson 1869-1930 **TCLC 39**
See also CA 110
Potok, Chaim 1929- **CLC 2, 7, 14, 26, 112; DAM NOV**
See also AAYA 15; AITN 1, 2; CA 17-20R; CANR 19, 35, 64; DLB 28, 152; INT CANR-19; MTCW 1; SATA 33
Potter, (Helen) Beatrix 1866-1943
See Webb, (Martha) Beatrice (Potter)
See also MAICYA
Potter, Dennis (Christopher George) 1935-1994 **CLC 58, 86**
See also CA 107; 145; CANR 33, 61; MTCW 1
Pound, Ezra (Weston Loomis) 1885-1972 **CLC 1, 2, 3, 4, 5, 7, 10, 13, 18, 34, 48, 50, 112; DA; DAB; DAC; DAM MST, POET; PC 4; WLC**

See also CA 5-8R; 37-40R; CANR 40; CDALB
1917-1929; DLB 4, 45, 63; DLBD 15;
MTCW 1

Povod, Reinaldo 1959-1994   **CLC 44**
See also CA 136; 146

Powell, Adam Clayton, Jr. 1908-1972**CLC 89;
BLC 3; DAM MULT**
See also BW 1; CA 102; 33-36R

Powell, Anthony (Dymoke) 1905-**CLC 1, 3, 7,
9, 10, 31**
See also CA 1-4R; CANR 1, 32, 62; CDBLB
1945-1960; DLB 15; MTCW 1

Powell, Dawn 1897-1965   **CLC 66**
See also CA 5-8R; DLBY 97

Powell, Padgett 1952-   **CLC 34**
See also CA 126; CANR 63

Power, Susan 1961-   **CLC 91**

Powers, J(ames) F(arl) 1917-**CLC 1, 4, 8, 57;
SSC 4**
See also CA 1-4R; CANR 2, 61; DLB 130;
MTCW 1

Powers, John J(ames) 1945-
See Powers, John R.
See also CA 69-72

Powers, John R.   **CLC 66**
See also Powers, John J(ames)

Powers, Richard (S.) 1957-   **CLC 93**
See also CA 148

Pownall, David 1938-   **CLC 10**
See also CA 89-92; CAAS 18; CANR 49; DLB
14

Powys, John Cowper 1872-1963**CLC 7, 9, 15,
46**
See also CA 85-88; DLB 15; MTCW 1

Powys, T(heodore) F(rancis) 1875-1953
TCLC 9
See also CA 106; DLB 36, 162

Prado (Calvo), Pedro 1886-1952   **TCLC 75**
See also CA 131; HW

Prager, Emily 1952-   **CLC 56**

Pratt, E(dwin) J(ohn) 1883(?)-1964 **CLC 19;
DAC; DAM POET**
See also CA 141; 93-96; DLB 92

Premchand   **TCLC 21**
See also Srivastava, Dhanpat Rai

Preussler, Otfried 1923-   **CLC 17**
See also CA 77-80; SATA 24

Prevert, Jacques (Henri Marie) 1900-1977
CLC 15
See also CA 77-80; 69-72; CANR 29, 61;
MTCW 1; SATA-Obit 30

Prevost, Abbe (Antoine Francois) 1697-1763
LC 1

Price, (Edward) Reynolds 1933-**CLC 3, 6, 13,
43, 50, 63; DAM NOV; SSC 22**
See also CA 1-4R; CANR 1, 37, 57; DLB 2;
INT CANR-37

Price, Richard 1949-   **CLC 6, 12**
See also CA 49-52; CANR 3; DLBY 81

Prichard, Katharine Susannah 1883-1969
CLC 46
See also CA 11-12; CANR 33; CAP 1; MTCW
1; SATA 66

Priestley, J(ohn) B(oynton) 1894-1984**CLC 2,
5, 9, 34; DAM DRAM, NOV**
See also CA 9-12R; 113; CANR 33; CDBLB
1914-1945; DLB 10, 34, 77, 100, 139; DLBY
84; MTCW 1

Prince 1958(?)-   **CLC 35**

Prince, F(rank) T(empleton) 1912-   **CLC 22**
See also CA 101; CANR 43; DLB 20

Prince Kropotkin
See Kropotkin, Peter (Aleksieevich)

Prior, Matthew 1664-1721   **LC 4**
See also DLB 95

Prishvin, Mikhail 1873-1954   **TCLC 75**

Pritchard, William H(arrison) 1932- **CLC 34**
See also CA 65-68; CANR 23; DLB 111

Pritchett, V(ictor) S(awdon) 1900-1997 **C L C
5, 13, 15, 41; DAM NOV; SSC 14**
See also CA 61-64; 157; CANR 31, 63; DLB
15, 139; MTCW 1

Private 19022
See Manning, Frederic

Probst, Mark 1925-   **CLC 59**
See also CA 130

Prokosch, Frederic 1908-1989   **CLC 4, 48**
See also CA 73-76; 128; DLB 48

Propertius, Sextus 50(?)B.C.-15(?)B.C.**CMLC
32**

Prophet, The
See Dreiser, Theodore (Herman Albert)

Prose, Francine 1947-   **CLC 45**
See also CA 109; 112; CANR 46; SATA 101

Proudhon
See Cunha, Euclides (Rodrigues Pimenta) da

Proulx, Annie
See Proulx, E(dna) Annie

Proulx, E(dna) Annie 1935-   **CLC 81; DAM
POP**
See also CA 145; CANR 65

**Proust, (Valentin-Louis-George-Eugene-)
Marcel** 1871-1922 **TCLC 7, 13, 33; DA;
DAB; DAC; DAM MST, NOV; WLC**
See also CA 104; 120; DLB 65; MTCW 1

Prowler, Harley
See Masters, Edgar Lee

Prus, Boleslaw 1845-1912   **TCLC 48**

Pryor, Richard (Franklin Lenox Thomas) 1940-
CLC 26
See also CA 122

Przybyszewski, Stanislaw 1868-1927**TCLC 36**
See also CA 160; DLB 66

Pteleon
See Grieve, C(hristopher) M(urray)
See also DAM POET

Puckett, Lute
See Masters, Edgar Lee

Puig, Manuel 1932-1990**CLC 3, 5, 10, 28, 65;
DAM MULT; HLC**
See also CA 45-48; CANR 2, 32, 63; DLB 113;
HW; MTCW 1

Pulitzer, Joseph 1847-1911   **TCLC 76**
See also CA 114; DLB 23

Purdy, A(lfred) W(ellington) 1918- **CLC 3, 6,
14, 50; DAC; DAM MST, POET**
See also CA 81-84; CAAS 17; CANR 42, 66;
DLB 88

Purdy, James (Amos) 1923- **CLC 2, 4, 10, 28,
52**
See also CA 33-36R; CAAS 1; CANR 19, 51;
DLB 2; INT CANR-19; MTCW 1

Pure, Simon
See Swinnerton, Frank Arthur

Pushkin, Alexander (Sergeyevich) 1799-1837
**NCLC 3, 27; DA; DAB; DAC; DAM
DRAM, MST, POET; PC 10; SSC 27;
WLC**
See also DLB 205; SATA 61

P'u Sung-ling 1640-1715   **LC 3; SSC 31**

Putnam, Arthur Lee
See Alger, Horatio, Jr.

Puzo, Mario 1920-**CLC 1, 2, 6, 36, 107; DAM
NOV, POP**
See also CA 65-68; CANR 4, 42, 65; DLB 6;
MTCW 1

Pygge, Edward
See Barnes, Julian (Patrick)

Pyle, Ernest Taylor 1900-1945
See Pyle, Ernie
See also CA 115; 160

Pyle, Ernie 1900-1945   **TCLC 75**
See also Pyle, Ernest Taylor
See also DLB 29

Pyle, Howard 1853-1911   **TCLC 81**
See also CA 109; 137; CLR 22; DLB 42, 188;
DLBD 13; MAICYA; SATA 16, 100

Pym, Barbara (Mary Crampton) 1913-1980
CLC 13, 19, 37, 111
See also CA 13-14; 97-100; CANR 13, 34; CAP
1; DLB 14, 207; DLBY 87; MTCW 1

Pynchon, Thomas (Ruggles, Jr.) 1937-**CLC 2,
3, 6, 9, 11, 18, 33, 62, 72; DA; DAB; DAC;
DAM MST, NOV, POP; SSC 14; WLC**
See also BEST 90:2; CA 17-20R; CANR 22,
46, 73; DLB 2, 173; MTCW 1

Pythagoras c. 570B.C.-c. 500B.C.   **CMLC 22**
See also DLB 176

Q
See Quiller-Couch, SirArthur (Thomas)

Qian Zhongshu
See Ch'ien Chung-shu

Qroll
See Dagerman, Stig (Halvard)

Quarrington, Paul (Lewis) 1953-   **CLC 65**
See also CA 129; CANR 62

Quasimodo, Salvatore 1901-1968   **CLC 10**
See also CA 13-16; 25-28R; CAP 1; DLB 114;
MTCW 1

Quay, Stephen 1947-   **CLC 95**

Quay, Timothy 1947-   **CLC 95**

Queen, Ellery   **CLC 3, 11**
See also Dannay, Frederic; Davidson, Avram;
Lee, Manfred B(ennington); Marlowe,
Stephen; Sturgeon, Theodore (Hamilton);
Vance, John Holbrook

Queen, Ellery, Jr.
See Dannay, Frederic; Lee, Manfred
B(ennington)

Queneau, Raymond 1903-1976 **CLC 2, 5, 10,
42**
See also CA 77-80; 69-72; CANR 32; DLB 72;
MTCW 1

Quevedo, Francisco de 1580-1645   **LC 23**

Quiller-Couch, SirArthur (Thomas) 1863-1944
TCLC 53
See also CA 118; 166; DLB 135, 153, 190

Quin, Ann (Marie) 1936-1973   **CLC 6**
See also CA 9-12R; 45-48; DLB 14

Quinn, Martin
See Smith, Martin Cruz

Quinn, Peter 1947-   **CLC 91**

Quinn, Simon
See Smith, Martin Cruz

Quiroga, Horacio (Sylvestre) 1878-1937
TCLC 20; DAM MULT; HLC
See also CA 117; 131; HW; MTCW 1

Quoirez, Francoise 1935-   **CLC 9**
See also Sagan, Francoise
See also CA 49-52; CANR 6, 39, 73; MTCW 1

Raabe, Wilhelm (Karl) 1831-1910 **TCLC 45**
See also CA 167; DLB 129

Rabe, David (William) 1940-   **CLC 4, 8, 33;
DAM DRAM**
See also CA 85-88; CABS 3; CANR 59; DLB 7

Rabelais, Francois 1483-1553**LC 5; DA; DAB;
DAC; DAM MST; WLC**

Rabinovitch, Sholem 1859-1916
See Aleichem, Sholom

See also CA 104
Rachilde 1860-1953   **TCLC 67**
See also DLB 123, 192
Racine, Jean 1639-1699 **LC 28; DAB; DAM MST**
Radcliffe, Ann (Ward) 1764-1823**NCLC 6, 55**
See also DLB 39, 178
Radiguet, Raymond 1903-1923   **TCLC 29**
See also CA 162; DLB 65
Radnoti, Miklos 1909-1944   **TCLC 16**
See also CA 118
Rado, James 1939-   **CLC 17**
See also CA 105
Radvanyi, Netty 1900-1983
See Seghers, Anna
See also CA 85-88; 110
Rae, Ben
See Griffiths, Trevor
Raeburn, John (Hay) 1941-   **CLC 34**
See also CA 57-60
Ragni, Gerome 1942-1991   **CLC 17**
See also CA 105; 134
Rahv, Philip 1908-1973   **CLC 24**
See also Greenberg, Ivan
See also DLB 137
Raimund, Ferdinand Jakob 1790-1836**NCLC 69**
See also DLB 90
Raine, Craig 1944-   **CLC 32, 103**
See also CA 108; CANR 29, 51; DLB 40
Raine, Kathleen (Jessie) 1908-   **CLC 7, 45**
See also CA 85-88; CANR 46; DLB 20; MTCW 1
Rainis, Janis 1865-1929   **TCLC 29**
See also CA 170
Rakosi, Carl 1903-   **CLC 47**
See also Rawley, Callman
See also CAAS 5; DLB 193
Raleigh, Richard
See Lovecraft, H(oward) P(hillips)
Raleigh, Sir Walter 1554(?)-1618   **LC 31, 39**
See also CDBLB Before 1660; DLB 172
Rallentando, H. P.
See Sayers, Dorothy L(eigh)
Ramal, Walter
See de la Mare, Walter (John)
Ramana Maharshi 1879-1950   **TCLC 84**
Ramon, Juan
See Jimenez (Mantecon), Juan Ramon
Ramos, Graciliano 1892-1953   **TCLC 32**
See also CA 167
Rampersad, Arnold 1941-   **CLC 44**
See also BW 2; CA 127; 133; DLB 111; INT 133
Rampling, Anne
See Rice, Anne
Ramsay, Allan 1684(?)-1758   **LC 29**
See also DLB 95
Ramuz, Charles-Ferdinand 1878-1947**TCLC 33**
See also CA 165
Rand, Ayn 1905-1982 **CLC 3, 30, 44, 79; DA; DAC; DAM MST, NOV, POP; WLC**
See also AAYA 10; CA 13-16R; 105; CANR 27, 73; MTCW 1
Randall, Dudley (Felker) 1914-**CLC 1; BLC 3; DAM MULT**
See also BW 1; CA 25-28R; CANR 23; DLB 41
Randall, Robert
See Silverberg, Robert
Ranger, Ken
See Creasey, John

Ransom, John Crowe 1888-1974 **CLC 2, 4, 5, 11, 24; DAM POET**
See also CA 5-8R; 49-52; CANR 6, 34; DLB 45, 63; MTCW 1
Rao, Raja 1909-   **CLC 25, 56; DAM NOV**
See also CA 73-76; CANR 51; MTCW 1
Raphael, Frederic (Michael) 1931-**CLC 2, 14**
See also CA 1-4R; CANR 1; DLB 14
Ratcliffe, James P.
See Mencken, H(enry) L(ouis)
Rathbone, Julian 1935-   **CLC 41**
See also CA 101; CANR 34, 73
Rattigan, Terence (Mervyn) 1911-1977**CLC 7; DAM DRAM**
See also CA 85-88; 73-76; CDBLB 1945-1960; DLB 13; MTCW 1
Ratushinskaya, Irina 1954-   **CLC 54**
See also CA 129; CANR 68
Raven, Simon (Arthur Noel) 1927-   **CLC 14**
See also CA 81-84
Ravenna, Michael
See Welty, Eudora
Rawley, Callman 1903-
See Rakosi, Carl
See also CA 21-24R; CANR 12, 32
Rawlings, Marjorie Kinnan 1896-1953**TCLC 4**
See also AAYA 20; CA 104; 137; CANR 74; DLB 9, 22, 102; DLBD 17; JRDA; MAICYA; SATA 100; YABC 1
Ray, Satyajit 1921-1992   **CLC 16, 76; DAM MULT**
See also CA 114; 137
Read, Herbert Edward 1893-1968   **CLC 4**
See also CA 85-88; 25-28R; DLB 20, 149
Read, Piers Paul 1941-   **CLC 4, 10, 25**
See also CA 21-24R; CANR 38; DLB 14; SATA 21
Reade, Charles 1814-1884   **NCLC 2, 74**
See also DLB 21
Reade, Hamish
See Gray, Simon (James Holliday)
Reading, Peter 1946-   **CLC 47**
See also CA 103; CANR 46; DLB 40
Reaney, James 1926-   **CLC 13; DAC; DAM MST**
See also CA 41-44R; CAAS 15; CANR 42; DLB 68; SATA 43
Rebreanu, Liviu 1885-1944   **TCLC 28**
See also CA 165
Rechy, John (Francisco) 1934- **CLC 1, 7, 14, 18, 107; DAM MULT; HLC**
See also CA 5-8R; CAAS 4; CANR 6, 32, 64; DLB 122; DLBY 82; HW; INT CANR-6
Redcam, Tom 1870-1933   **TCLC 25**
Reddin, Keith   **CLC 67**
Redgrove, Peter (William) 1932- **CLC 6, 41**
See also CA 1-4R; CANR 3, 39; DLB 40
Redmon, Anne   **CLC 22**
See also Nightingale, Anne Redmon
See also DLBY 86
Reed, Eliot
See Ambler, Eric
Reed, Ishmael 1938-**CLC 2, 3, 5, 6, 13, 32, 60; BLC 3; DAM MULT**
See also BW 2; CA 21-24R; CANR 25, 48, 74; DLB 2, 5, 33, 169; DLBD 8; MTCW 1
Reed, John (Silas) 1887-1920   **TCLC 9**
See also CA 106
Reed, Lou   **CLC 21**
See also Firbank, Louis
Reeve, Clara 1729-1807   **NCLC 19**
See also DLB 39

Reich, Wilhelm 1897-1957   **TCLC 57**
Reid, Christopher (John) 1949-   **CLC 33**
See also CA 140; DLB 40
Reid, Desmond
See Moorcock, Michael (John)
Reid Banks, Lynne 1929-
See Banks, Lynne Reid
See also CA 1-4R; CANR 6, 22, 38; CLR 24; JRDA; MAICYA; SATA 22, 75
Reilly, William K.
See Creasey, John
Reiner, Max
See Caldwell, (Janet Miriam) Taylor (Holland)
Reis, Ricardo
See Pessoa, Fernando (Antonio Nogueira)
Remarque, Erich Maria 1898-1970 **CLC 21; DA; DAB; DAC; DAM MST, NOV**
See also AAYA 27; CA 77-80; 29-32R; DLB 56; MTCW 1
Remington, Frederic 1861-1909   **TCLC 89**
See also CA 108; 169; DLB 12, 186, 188; SATA 41
Remizov, A.
See Remizov, Aleksei (Mikhailovich)
Remizov, A. M.
See Remizov, Aleksei (Mikhailovich)
Remizov, Aleksei (Mikhailovich) 1877-1957 **TCLC 27**
See also CA 125; 133
Renan, Joseph Ernest 1823-1892   **NCLC 26**
Renard, Jules 1864-1910   **TCLC 17**
See also CA 117
Renault, Mary   **CLC 3, 11, 17**
See also Challans, Mary
See also DLBY 83
Rendell, Ruth (Barbara) 1930- **CLC 28, 48; DAM POP**
See also Vine, Barbara
See also CA 109; CANR 32, 52, 74; DLB 87; INT CANR-32; MTCW 1
Renoir, Jean 1894-1979   **CLC 20**
See also CA 129; 85-88
Resnais, Alain 1922-   **CLC 16**
Reverdy, Pierre 1889-1960   **CLC 53**
See also CA 97-100; 89-92
Rexroth, Kenneth 1905-1982 **CLC 1, 2, 6, 11, 22, 49, 112; DAM POET; PC 20**
See also CA 5-8R; 107; CANR 14, 34, 63; CDALB 1941-1968; DLB 16, 48, 165; DLBY 82; INT CANR-14; MTCW 1
Reyes, Alfonso 1889-1959   **TCLC 33**
See also CA 131; HW
Reyes y Basoalto, Ricardo Eliecer Neftali
See Neruda, Pablo
Reymont, Wladyslaw (Stanislaw) 1868(?)-1925 **TCLC 5**
See also CA 104
Reynolds, Jonathan 1942-   **CLC 6, 38**
See also CA 65-68; CANR 28
Reynolds, Joshua 1723-1792   **LC 15**
See also DLB 104
Reynolds, Michael Shane 1937-   **CLC 44**
See also CA 65-68; CANR 9
Reznikoff, Charles 1894-1976   **CLC 9**
See also CA 33-36; 61-64; CAP 2; DLB 28, 45
Rezzori (d'Arezzo), Gregor von 1914-1998 **CLC 25**
See also CA 122; 136; 167
Rhine, Richard
See Silverstein, Alvin
Rhodes, Eugene Manlove 1869-1934**TCLC 53**
Rhodius, Apollonius c. 3rd cent. B.C.- **CMLC 28**

See also DLB 176

R'hoone
See Balzac, Honore de

Rhys, Jean 1890(?)-1979 **CLC 2, 4, 6, 14, 19, 51; DAM NOV; SSC 21**
See also CA 25-28R; 85-88; CANR 35, 62; CDBLB 1945-1960; DLB 36, 117, 162; MTCW 1

Ribeiro, Darcy 1922-1997 **CLC 34**
See also CA 33-36R; 156

Ribeiro, Joao Ubaldo (Osorio Pimentel) 1941- **CLC 10, 67**
See also CA 81-84

Ribman, Ronald (Burt) 1932- **CLC 7**
See also CA 21-24R; CANR 46

Ricci, Nino 1959- **CLC 70**
See also CA 137

Rice, Anne 1941- **CLC 41; DAM POP**
See also AAYA 9; BEST 89:2; CA 65-68; CANR 12, 36, 53, 74

Rice, Elmer (Leopold) 1892-1967 **CLC 7, 49; DAM DRAM**
See also CA 21-22; 25-28R; CAP 2; DLB 4, 7; MTCW 1

Rice, Tim(othy Miles Bindon) 1944- **CLC 21**
See also CA 103; CANR 46

Rich, Adrienne (Cecile) 1929- **CLC 3, 6, 7, 11, 18, 36, 73, 76; DAM POET; PC 5**
See also CA 9-12R; CANR 20, 53, 74; DLB 5, 67; MTCW 1

Rich, Barbara
See Graves, Robert (von Ranke)

Rich, Robert
See Trumbo, Dalton

Richard, Keith **CLC 17**
See also Richards, Keith

Richards, David Adams 1950- **CLC 59; DAC**
See also CA 93-96; CANR 60; DLB 53

Richards, I(vor) A(rmstrong) 1893-1979 **CLC 14, 24**
See also CA 41-44R; 89-92; CANR 34, 74; DLB 27

Richards, Keith 1943-
See Richard, Keith
See also CA 107

Richardson, Anne
See Roiphe, Anne (Richardson)

Richardson, Dorothy Miller 1873-1957 **TCLC 3**
See also CA 104; DLB 36

Richardson, Ethel Florence (Lindesay) 1870-1946
See Richardson, Henry Handel
See also CA 105

Richardson, Henry Handel **TCLC 4**
See also Richardson, Ethel Florence (Lindesay)
See also DLB 197

Richardson, John 1796-1852 **NCLC 55; DAC**
See also DLB 99

Richardson, Samuel 1689-1761 **LC 1, 44; DA; DAB; DAC; DAM MST, NOV; WLC**
See also CDBLB 1660-1789; DLB 39

Richler, Mordecai 1931- **CLC 3, 5, 9, 13, 18, 46, 70; DAC; DAM MST, NOV**
See also AITN 1; CA 65-68; CANR 31, 62; CLR 17; DLB 53; MAICYA; MTCW 1; SATA 44, 98; SATA-Brief 27

Richter, Conrad (Michael) 1890-1968 **CLC 30**
See also AAYA 21; CA 5-8R; 25-28R; CANR 23; DLB 9; MTCW 1; SATA 3

Ricostranza, Tom
See Ellis, Trey

Riddell, Charlotte 1832-1906 **TCLC 40**

See also CA 165; DLB 156

Riding, Laura **CLC 3, 7**
See also Jackson, Laura (Riding)

Riefenstahl, Berta Helene Amalia 1902-
See Riefenstahl, Leni
See also CA 108

Riefenstahl, Leni **CLC 16**
See also Riefenstahl, Berta Helene Amalia

Riffe, Ernest
See Bergman, (Ernst) Ingmar

Riggs, (Rolla) Lynn 1899-1954 **TCLC 56; DAM MULT**
See also CA 144; DLB 175; NNAL

Riis, Jacob A(ugust) 1849-1914 **TCLC 80**
See also CA 113; 168; DLB 23

Riley, James Whitcomb 1849-1916 **TCLC 51; DAM POET**
See also CA 118; 137; MAICYA; SATA 17

Riley, Tex
See Creasey, John

Rilke, Rainer Maria 1875-1926 **TCLC 1, 6, 19; DAM POET; PC 2**
See also CA 104; 132; CANR 62; DLB 81; MTCW 1

Rimbaud, (Jean Nicolas) Arthur 1854-1891 **NCLC 4, 35; DA; DAB; DAC; DAM MST, POET; PC 3; WLC**

Rinehart, Mary Roberts 1876-1958 **TCLC 52**
See also CA 108; 166

Ringmaster, The
See Mencken, H(enry) L(ouis)

Ringwood, Gwen(dolyn Margaret) Pharis 1910-1984 **CLC 48**
See also CA 148; 112; DLB 88

Rio, Michel 19(?)- **CLC 43**

Ritsos, Giannes
See Ritsos, Yannis

Ritsos, Yannis 1909-1990 **CLC 6, 13, 31**
See also CA 77-80; 133; CANR 39, 61; MTCW 1

Ritter, Erika 1948(?)- **CLC 52**

Rivera, Jose Eustasio 1889-1928 **TCLC 35**
See also CA 162; HW

Rivers, Conrad Kent 1933-1968 **CLC 1**
See also BW 1; CA 85-88; DLB 41

Rivers, Elfrida
See Bradley, Marion Zimmer

Riverside, John
See Heinlein, Robert A(nson)

Rizal, Jose 1861-1896 **NCLC 27**

Roa Bastos, Augusto (Antonio) 1917- **CLC 45; DAM MULT; HLC**
See also CA 131; DLB 113; HW

Robbe-Grillet, Alain 1922- **CLC 1, 2, 4, 6, 8, 10, 14, 43**
See also CA 9-12R; CANR 33, 65; DLB 83; MTCW 1

Robbins, Harold 1916-1997 **CLC 5; DAM NOV**
See also CA 73-76; 162; CANR 26, 54; MTCW 1

Robbins, Thomas Eugene 1936-
See Robbins, Tom
See also CA 81-84; CANR 29, 59; DAM NOV, POP; MTCW 1

Robbins, Tom **CLC 9, 32, 64**
See also Robbins, Thomas Eugene
See also BEST 90:3; DLBY 80

Robbins, Trina 1938- **CLC 21**
See also CA 128

Roberts, Charles G(eorge) D(ouglas) 1860-1943 **TCLC 8**
See also CA 105; CLR 33; DLB 92; SATA 88;

SATA-Brief 29

Roberts, Elizabeth Madox 1886-1941 **TCLC 68**
See also CA 111; 166; DLB 9, 54, 102; SATA 33; SATA-Brief 27

Roberts, Kate 1891-1985 **CLC 15**
See also CA 107; 116

Roberts, Keith (John Kingston) 1935- **CLC 14**
See also CA 25-28R; CANR 46

Roberts, Kenneth (Lewis) 1885-1957 **TCLC 23**
See also CA 109; DLB 9

Roberts, Michele (B.) 1949- **CLC 48**
See also CA 115; CANR 58

Robertson, Ellis
See Ellison, Harlan (Jay); Silverberg, Robert

Robertson, Thomas William 1829-1871 **NCLC 35; DAM DRAM**

Robeson, Kenneth
See Dent, Lester

Robinson, Edwin Arlington 1869-1935 **TCLC 5; DA; DAC; DAM MST, POET; PC 1**
See also CA 104; 133; CDALB 1865-1917; DLB 54; MTCW 1

Robinson, Henry Crabb 1775-1867 **NCLC 15**
See also DLB 107

Robinson, Jill 1936- **CLC 10**
See also CA 102; INT 102

Robinson, Kim Stanley 1952- **CLC 34**
See also AAYA 26; CA 126

Robinson, Lloyd
See Silverberg, Robert

Robinson, Marilynne 1944- **CLC 25**
See also CA 116; DLB 206

Robinson, Smokey **CLC 21**
See also Robinson, William, Jr.

Robinson, William, Jr. 1940-
See Robinson, Smokey
See also CA 116

Robison, Mary 1949- **CLC 42, 98**
See also CA 113; 116; DLB 130; INT 116

Rod, Edouard 1857-1910 **TCLC 52**

Roddenberry, Eugene Wesley 1921-1991
See Roddenberry, Gene
See also CA 110; 135; CANR 37; SATA 45; SATA-Obit 69

Roddenberry, Gene **CLC 17**
See also Roddenberry, Eugene Wesley
See also AAYA 5; SATA-Obit 69

Rodgers, Mary 1931- **CLC 12**
See also CA 49-52; CANR 8, 55; CLR 20; INT CANR-8; JRDA; MAICYA; SATA 8

Rodgers, W(illiam) R(obert) 1909-1969 **CLC 7**
See also CA 85-88; DLB 20

Rodman, Eric
See Silverberg, Robert

Rodman, Howard 1920(?)-1985 **CLC 65**
See also CA 118

Rodman, Maia
See Wojciechowska, Maia (Teresa)

Rodriguez, Claudio 1934- **CLC 10**
See also DLB 134

Roelvaag, O(le) E(dvart) 1876-1931 **TCLC 17**
See also CA 117; 171; DLB 9

Roethke, Theodore (Huebner) 1908-1963 **CLC 1, 3, 8, 11, 19, 46, 101; DAM POET; PC 15**
See also CA 81-84; CABS 2; CDALB 1941-1968; DLB 5, 206; MTCW 1

Rogers, Samuel 1763-1855 **NCLC 69**
See also DLB 93

Rogers, Thomas Hunton 1927- **CLC 57**
See also CA 89-92; INT 89-92

Rogers, Will(iam Penn Adair) 1879-1935 **TCLC 8, 71; DAM MULT**

See also CA 105; 144; DLB 11; NNAL
Rogin, Gilbert 1929- **CLC 18**
See also CA 65-68; CANR 15
Rohan, Koda **TCLC 22**
See also Koda Shigeyuki
Rohlfs, Anna Katharine Green
See Green, Anna Katharine
Rohmer, Eric **CLC 16**
See also Scherer, Jean-Marie Maurice
Rohmer, Sax **TCLC 28**
See also Ward, Arthur Henry Sarsfield
See also DLB 70
Roiphe, Anne (Richardson) 1935- **CLC 3, 9**
See also CA 89-92; CANR 45, 73; DLBY 80;
INT 89-92
Rojas, Fernando de 1465-1541 **LC 23**
Rolfe, Frederick (William Serafino Austin Lewis Mary) 1860-1913 **TCLC 12**
See also CA 107; DLB 34, 156
Rolland, Romain 1866-1944 **TCLC 23**
See also CA 118; DLB 65
Rolle, Richard c. 1300-c. 1349 **CMLC 21**
See also DLB 146
Rolvaag, O(le) E(dvart)
See Roelvaag, O(le) E(dvart)
Romain Arnaud, Saint
See Aragon, Louis
Romains, Jules 1885-1972 **CLC 7**
See also CA 85-88; CANR 34; DLB 65; MTCW 1
Romero, Jose Ruben 1890-1952 **TCLC 14**
See also CA 114; 131; HW
Ronsard, Pierre de 1524-1585 **LC 6; PC 11**
Rooke, Leon 1934- **CLC 25, 34; DAM POP**
See also CA 25-28R; CANR 23, 53
Roosevelt, Theodore 1858-1919 **TCLC 69**
See also CA 115; 170; DLB 47, 186
Roper, William 1498-1578 **LC 10**
Roquelaure, A. N.
See Rice, Anne
Rosa, Joao Guimaraes 1908-1967 **CLC 23**
See also CA 89-92; DLB 113
Rose, Wendy 1948- **CLC 85; DAM MULT; PC 13**
See also CA 53-56; CANR 5, 51; DLB 175;
NNAL; SATA 12
Rosen, R. D.
See Rosen, Richard (Dean)
Rosen, Richard (Dean) 1949- **CLC 39**
See also CA 77-80; CANR 62; INT CANR-30
Rosenberg, Isaac 1890-1918 **TCLC 12**
See also CA 107; DLB 20
Rosenblatt, Joe **CLC 15**
See also Rosenblatt, Joseph
Rosenblatt, Joseph 1933-
See Rosenblatt, Joe
See also CA 89-92; INT 89-92
Rosenfeld, Samuel
See Tzara, Tristan
Rosenstock, Sami
See Tzara, Tristan
Rosenstock, Samuel
See Tzara, Tristan
Rosenthal, M(acha) L(ouis) 1917-1996 **CLC 28**
See also CA 1-4R; 152; CAAS 6; CANR 4, 51;
DLB 5; SATA 59
Ross, Barnaby
See Dannay, Frederic
Ross, Bernard L.
See Follett, Ken(neth Martin)
Ross, J. H.
See Lawrence, T(homas) E(dward)

Ross, John Hume
See Lawrence, T(homas) E(dward)
Ross, Martin
See Martin, Violet Florence
See also DLB 135
Ross, (James) Sinclair 1908- **CLC 13; DAC; DAM MST; SSC 24**
See also CA 73-76; DLB 88
Rossetti, Christina (Georgina) 1830-1894
NCLC 2, 50, 66; DA; DAB; DAC; DAM MST, POET; PC 7; WLC
See also DLB 35, 163; MAICYA; SATA 20
Rossetti, Dante Gabriel 1828-1882 **NCLC 4; DA; DAB; DAC; DAM MST, POET; WLC**
See also CDBLB 1832-1890; DLB 35
Rossner, Judith (Perelman) 1935- **CLC 6, 9, 29**
See also AITN 2; BEST 90:3; CA 17-20R;
CANR 18, 51, 73; DLB 6; INT CANR-18;
MTCW 1
Rostand, Edmond (Eugene Alexis) 1868-1918
TCLC 6, 37; DA; DAB; DAC; DAM DRAM, MST; DC 10
See also CA 104; 126; DLB 192; MTCW 1
Roth, Henry 1906-1995 **CLC 2, 6, 11, 104**
See also CA 11-12; 149; CANR 38, 63; CAP 1;
DLB 28; MTCW 1
Roth, Philip (Milton) 1933- **CLC 1, 2, 3, 4, 6, 9, 15, 22, 31, 47, 66, 86; DA; DAB; DAC; DAM MST, NOV, POP; SSC 26; WLC**
See also BEST 90:3; CA 1-4R; CANR 1, 22,
36, 55; CDALB 1968-1988; DLB 2, 28, 173;
DLBY 82; MTCW 1
Rothenberg, Jerome 1931- **CLC 6, 57**
See also CA 45-48; CANR 1; DLB 5, 193
Roumain, Jacques (Jean Baptiste) 1907-1944
TCLC 19; BLC 3; DAM MULT
See also BW 1; CA 117; 125
Rourke, Constance (Mayfield) 1885-1941
TCLC 12
See also CA 107; YABC 1
Rousseau, Jean-Baptiste 1671-1741 **LC 9**
Rousseau, Jean-Jacques 1712-1778 **LC 14, 36; DA; DAB; DAC; DAM MST; WLC**
Roussel, Raymond 1877-1933 **TCLC 20**
See also CA 117
Rovit, Earl (Herbert) 1927- **CLC 7**
See also CA 5-8R; CANR 12
Rowe, Elizabeth Singer 1674-1737 **LC 44**
See also DLB 39, 95
Rowe, Nicholas 1674-1718 **LC 8**
See also DLB 84
Rowley, Ames Dorrance
See Lovecraft, H(oward) P(hillips)
Rowson, Susanna Haswell 1762(?)-1824
NCLC 5, 69
See also DLB 37, 200
Roy, Arundhati 1960(?)- **CLC 109**
See also CA 163; DLBY 97
Roy, Gabrielle 1909-1983 **CLC 10, 14; DAB; DAC; DAM MST**
See also CA 53-56; 110; CANR 5, 61; DLB 68;
MTCW 1
Royko, Mike 1932-1997 **CLC 109**
See also CA 89-92; 157; CANR 26
Rozewicz, Tadeusz 1921- **CLC 9, 23; DAM POET**
See also CA 108; CANR 36, 66; MTCW 1
Ruark, Gibbons 1941- **CLC 3**
See also CA 33-36R; CAAS 23; CANR 14, 31,
57; DLB 120
Rubens, Bernice (Ruth) 1923- **CLC 19, 31**
See also CA 25-28R; CANR 33, 65; DLB 14,
207; MTCW 1

Rubin, Harold
See Robbins, Harold
Rudkin, (James) David 1936- **CLC 14**
See also CA 89-92; DLB 13
Rudnik, Raphael 1933- **CLC 7**
See also CA 29-32R
Ruffian, M.
See Hasek, Jaroslav (Matej Frantisek)
Ruiz, Jose Martinez **CLC 11**
See also Martinez Ruiz, Jose
Rukeyser, Muriel 1913-1980 **CLC 6, 10, 15, 27; DAM POET; PC 12**
See also CA 5-8R; 93-96; CANR 26, 60; DLB
48; MTCW 1; SATA-Obit 22
Rule, Jane (Vance) 1931- **CLC 27**
See also CA 25-28R; CAAS 18; CANR 12; DLB 60
Rulfo, Juan 1918-1986 **CLC 8, 80; DAM MULT; HLC; SSC 25**
See also CA 85-88; 118; CANR 26; DLB 113;
HW; MTCW 1
Rumi, Jalal al-Din 1297-1373 **CMLC 20**
Runeberg, Johan 1804-1877 **NCLC 41**
Runyon, (Alfred) Damon 1884(?)-1946 **TCLC 10**
See also CA 107; 165; DLB 11, 86, 171
Rush, Norman 1933- **CLC 44**
See also CA 121; 126; INT 126
Rushdie, (Ahmed) Salman 1947- **CLC 23, 31, 55, 100; DAB; DAC; DAM MST, NOV, POP; WLCS**
See also BEST 89:3; CA 108; 111; CANR 33,
56; DLB 194; INT 111; MTCW 1
Rushforth, Peter (Scott) 1945- **CLC 19**
See also CA 101
Ruskin, John 1819-1900 **TCLC 63**
See also CA 114; 129; CDBLB 1832-1890;
DLB 55, 163, 190; SATA 24
Russ, Joanna 1937- **CLC 15**
See also CANR 11, 31, 65; DLB 8; MTCW 1
Russell, George William 1867-1935
See Baker, Jean H.
See also CA 104; 153; CDBLB 1890-1914;
DAM POET
Russell, (Henry) Ken(neth Alfred) 1927- **CLC 16**
See also CA 105
Russell, William Martin 1947- **CLC 60**
See also CA 164
Rutherford, Mark **TCLC 25**
See also White, William Hale
See also DLB 18
Ruyslinck, Ward 1929- **CLC 14**
See also Belser, Reimond Karel Maria de
Ryan, Cornelius (John) 1920-1974 **CLC 7**
See also CA 69-72; 53-56; CANR 38
Ryan, Michael 1946- **CLC 65**
See also CA 49-52; DLBY 82
Ryan, Tim
See Dent, Lester
Rybakov, Anatoli (Naumovich) 1911- **CLC 23, 53**
See also CA 126; 135; SATA 79
Ryder, Jonathan
See Ludlum, Robert
Ryga, George 1932-1987 **CLC 14; DAC; DAM MST**
See also CA 101; 124; CANR 43; DLB 60
S. H.
See Hartmann, Sadakichi
S. S.
See Sassoon, Siegfried (Lorraine)
Saba, Umberto 1883-1957 **TCLC 33**

See also CA 144; DLB 114
Sabatini, Rafael 1875-1950 **TCLC 47**
See also CA 162
Sabato, Ernesto (R.) 1911-**CLC 10, 23; DAM MULT; HLC**
See also CA 97-100; CANR 32, 65; DLB 145; HW; MTCW 1
Sa-Carniero, Mario de 1890-1916 **TCLC 83**
Sacastru, Martin
See Bioy Casares, Adolfo
Sacher-Masoch, Leopold von 1836(?)-1895 **NCLC 31**
Sachs, Marilyn (Stickle) 1927- **CLC 35**
See also AAYA 2; CA 17-20R; CANR 13, 47; CLR 2; JRDA; MAICYA; SAAS 2; SATA 3, 68
Sachs, Nelly 1891-1970 **CLC 14, 98**
See also CA 17-18; 25-28R; CAP 2
Sackler, Howard (Oliver) 1929-1982 **CLC 14**
See also CA 61-64; 108; CANR 30; DLB 7
Sacks, Oliver (Wolf) 1933- **CLC 67**
See also CA 53-56; CANR 28, 50; INT CANR-28; MTCW 1
Sadakichi
See Hartmann, Sadakichi
Sade, Donatien Alphonse Francois, Comte de 1740-1814 **NCLC 47**
Sadoff, Ira 1945- **CLC 9**
See also CA 53-56; CANR 5, 21; DLB 120
Saetone
See Camus, Albert
Safire, William 1929- **CLC 10**
See also CA 17-20R; CANR 31, 54
Sagan, Carl (Edward) 1934-1996**CLC 30, 112**
See also AAYA 2; CA 25-28R; 155; CANR 11, 36, 74; MTCW 1; SATA 58; SATA-Obit 94
Sagan, Francoise **CLC 3, 6, 9, 17, 36**
See also Quoirez, Francoise
See also DLB 83
Sahgal, Nayantara (Pandit) 1927- **CLC 41**
See also CA 9-12R; CANR 11
Saint, H(arry) F. 1941- **CLC 50**
See also CA 127
St. Aubin de Teran, Lisa 1953-
See Teran, Lisa St. Aubin de
See also CA 118; 126; INT 126
Saint Birgitta of Sweden c. 1303-1373**C M L C 24**
Sainte-Beuve, Charles Augustin 1804-1869 **NCLC 5**
Saint-Exupery, Antoine (Jean Baptiste Marie Roger) de 1900-1944 **TCLC 2, 56; DAM NOV; WLC**
See also CA 108; 132; CLR 10; DLB 72; MAICYA; MTCW 1; SATA 20
St. John, David
See Hunt, E(verette) Howard, (Jr.)
Saint-John Perse
See Leger, (Marie-Rene Auguste) Alexis Saint-Leger
Saintsbury, George (Edward Bateman) 1845-1933 **TCLC 31**
See also CA 160; DLB 57, 149
Sait Faik **TCLC 23**
See also Abasiyanik, Sait Faik
Saki **TCLC 3; SSC 12**
See also Munro, H(ector) H(ugh)
Sala, George Augustus **NCLC 46**
Salama, Hannu 1936- **CLC 18**
Salamanca, J(ack) R(ichard) 1922-**CLC 4, 15**
See also CA 25-28R
Sale, J. Kirkpatrick
See Sale, Kirkpatrick

Sale, Kirkpatrick 1937- **CLC 68**
See also CA 13-16R; CANR 10
Salinas, Luis Omar 1937- **CLC 90; DAM MULT; HLC**
See also CA 131; DLB 82; HW
Salinas (y Serrano), Pedro 1891(?)-1951 **TCLC 17**
See also CA 117; DLB 134
Salinger, J(erome) D(avid) 1919-**CLC 1, 3, 8, 12, 55, 56; DA; DAB; DAC; DAM MST, NOV, POP; SSC 2, 28; WLC**
See also AAYA 2; CA 5-8R; CANR 39; CDALB 1941-1968; CLR 18; DLB 2, 102, 173; MAICYA; MTCW 1; SATA 67
Salisbury, John
See Caute, (John) David
Salter, James 1925- **CLC 7, 52, 59**
See also CA 73-76; DLB 130
Saltus, Edgar (Everton) 1855-1921 **TCLC 8**
See also CA 105; DLB 202
Saltykov, Mikhail Evgrafovich 1826-1889 **NCLC 16**
Samarakis, Antonis 1919- **CLC 5**
See also CA 25-28R; CAAS 16; CANR 36
Sanchez, Florencio 1875-1910 **TCLC 37**
See also CA 153; HW
Sanchez, Luis Rafael 1936- **CLC 23**
See also CA 128; DLB 145; HW
Sanchez, Sonia 1934- **CLC 5, 116; BLC 3; DAM MULT; PC 9**
See also BW 2; CA 33-36R; CANR 24, 49, 74; CLR 18; DLB 41; DLBD 8; MAICYA; MTCW 1; SATA 22
Sand, George 1804-1876**NCLC 2, 42, 57; DA; DAB; DAC; DAM MST, NOV; WLC**
See also DLB 119, 192
Sandburg, Carl (August) 1878-1967**CLC 1, 4, 10, 15, 35; DA; DAB; DAC; DAM MST, POET; PC 2; WLC**
See also AAYA 24; CA 5-8R; 25-28R; CANR 35; CDALB 1865-1917; DLB 17, 54; MAICYA; MTCW 1; SATA 8
Sandburg, Charles
See Sandburg, Carl (August)
Sandburg, Charles A.
See Sandburg, Carl (August)
Sanders, (James) Ed(ward) 1939- **CLC 53**
See also CA 13-16R; CAAS 21; CANR 13, 44; DLB 16
Sanders, Lawrence 1920-1998**CLC 41; DAM POP**
See also BEST 89:4; CA 81-84; 165; CANR 33, 62; MTCW 1
Sanders, Noah
See Blount, Roy (Alton), Jr.
Sanders, Winston P.
See Anderson, Poul (William)
Sandoz, Mari(e Susette) 1896-1966 **CLC 28**
See also CA 1-4R; 25-28R; CANR 17, 64; DLB 9; MTCW 1; SATA 5
Saner, Reg(inald Anthony) 1931- **CLC 9**
See also CA 65-68
Sankara 788-820 **CMLC 32**
Sannazaro, Jacopo 1456(?)-1530 **LC 8**
Sansom, William 1912-1976 **CLC 2, 6; DAM NOV; SSC 21**
See also CA 5-8R; 65-68; CANR 42; DLB 139; MTCW 1
Santayana, George 1863-1952 **TCLC 40**
See also CA 115; DLB 54, 71; DLBD 13
Santiago, Danny **CLC 33**
See also James, Daniel (Lewis)
See also DLB 122

Santmyer, Helen Hoover 1895-1986 **CLC 33**
See also CA 1-4R; 118; CANR 15, 33; DLBY 84; MTCW 1
Santoka, Taneda 1882-1940 **TCLC 72**
Santos, Bienvenido N(uqui) 1911-1996 **C L C 22; DAM MULT**
See also CA 101; 151; CANR 19, 46
Sapper **TCLC 44**
See also McNeile, Herman Cyril
Sapphire
See Sapphire, Brenda
Sapphire, Brenda 1950- **CLC 99**
Sappho fl. 6th cent. B.C.- **CMLC 3; DAM POET; PC 5**
See also DLB 176
Sarduy, Severo 1937-1993 **CLC 6, 97**
See also CA 89-92; 142; CANR 58; DLB 113; HW
Sargeson, Frank 1903-1982 **CLC 31**
See also CA 25-28R; 106; CANR 38
Sarmiento, Felix Ruben Garcia
See Dario, Ruben
Saro-Wiwa, Ken(ule Beeson) 1941-1995**C L C 114**
See also BW 2; CA 142; 150; CANR 60; DLB 157
Saroyan, William 1908-1981**CLC 1, 8, 10, 29, 34, 56; DA; DAB; DAC; DAM DRAM, MST, NOV; SSC 21; WLC**
See also CA 5-8R; 103; CANR 30; DLB 7, 9, 86; DLBY 81; MTCW 1; SATA 23; SATA-Obit 24
Sarraute, Nathalie 1900-**CLC 1, 2, 4, 8, 10, 31, 80**
See also CA 9-12R; CANR 23, 66; DLB 83; MTCW 1
Sarton, (Eleanor) May 1912-1995 **CLC 4, 14, 49, 91; DAM POET**
See also CA 1-4R; 149; CANR 1, 34, 55; DLB 48; DLBY 81; INT CANR-34; MTCW 1; SATA 36; SATA-Obit 86
Sartre, Jean-Paul 1905-1980**CLC 1, 4, 7, 9, 13, 18, 24, 44, 50, 52; DA; DAB; DAC; DAM DRAM, MST, NOV; DC 3; SSC 32; WLC**
See also CA 9-12R; 97-100; CANR 21; DLB 72; MTCW 1
Sassoon, Siegfried (Lorraine) 1886-1967**C L C 36; DAB; DAM MST, NOV, POET; PC 12**
See also CA 104; 25-28R; CANR 36; DLB 20, 191; DLBD 18; MTCW 1
Satterfield, Charles
See Pohl, Frederik
Saul, John (W. III) 1942-**CLC 46; DAM NOV, POP**
See also AAYA 10; BEST 90:4; CA 81-84; CANR 16, 40; SATA 98
Saunders, Caleb
See Heinlein, Robert A(nson)
Saura (Atares), Carlos 1932- **CLC 20**
See also CA 114; 131; HW
Sauser-Hall, Frederic 1887-1961 **CLC 18**
See also Cendrars, Blaise
See also CA 102; 93-96; CANR 36, 62; MTCW 1
Saussure, Ferdinand de 1857-1913 **TCLC 49**
Savage, Catharine
See Brosman, Catharine Savage
Savage, Thomas 1915- **CLC 40**
See also CA 126; 132; CAAS 15; INT 132
Savan, Glenn 19(?)- **CLC 50**
Sayers, Dorothy L(eigh) 1893-1957 **TCLC 2, 15; DAM POP**
See also CA 104; 119; CANR 60; CDBLB 1914-

1945; DLB 10, 36, 77, 100; MTCW 1

Sayers, Valerie 1952-   **CLC 50**
See also CA 134; CANR 61

Sayles, John (Thomas) 1950- **CLC 7, 10, 14**
See also CA 57-60; CANR 41; DLB 44

Scammell, Michael 1935-   **CLC 34**
See also CA 156

Scannell, Vernon 1922-   **CLC 49**
See also CA 5-8R; CANR 8, 24, 57; DLB 27;
SATA 59

Scarlett, Susan
See Streatfeild, (Mary) Noel

Scarron
See Mikszath, Kalman

Schaeffer, Susan Fromberg 1941- **CLC 6, 11,
22**
See also CA 49-52; CANR 18, 65; DLB 28;
MTCW 1; SATA 22

Schary, Jill
See Robinson, Jill

Schell, Jonathan 1943-   **CLC 35**
See also CA 73-76; CANR 12

Schelling, Friedrich Wilhelm Joseph von 1775-
1854   **NCLC 30**
See also DLB 90

Schendel, Arthur van 1874-1946   **TCLC 56**

Scherer, Jean-Marie Maurice 1920-
See Rohmer, Eric
See also CA 110

Schevill, James (Erwin) 1920-   **CLC 7**
See also CA 5-8R; CAAS 12

Schiller, Friedrich 1759-1805 **NCLC 39, 69;
DAM DRAM**
See also DLB 94

Schisgal, Murray (Joseph) 1926-   **CLC 6**
See also CA 21-24R; CANR 48

Schlee, Ann 1934-   **CLC 35**
See also CA 101; CANR 29; SATA 44; SATA-
Brief 36

Schlegel, August Wilhelm von 1767-1845
NCLC 15
See also DLB 94

Schlegel, Friedrich 1772-1829   **NCLC 45**
See also DLB 90

Schlegel, Johann Elias (von) 1719(?)-1749**LC
5**

Schlesinger, Arthur M(eier), Jr. 1917-**CLC 84**
See also AITN 1; CA 1-4R; CANR 1, 28, 58;
DLB 17; INT CANR-28; MTCW 1; SATA
61

Schmidt, Arno (Otto) 1914-1979   **CLC 56**
See also CA 128; 109; DLB 69

Schmitz, Aron Hector 1861-1928
See Svevo, Italo
See also CA 104; 122; MTCW 1

Schnackenberg, Gjertrud 1953-   **CLC 40**
See also CA 116; DLB 120

Schneider, Leonard Alfred 1925-1966
See Bruce, Lenny
See also CA 89-92

Schnitzler, Arthur 1862-1931**TCLC 4; SSC 15**
See also CA 104; DLB 81, 118

Schoenberg, Arnold 1874-1951   **TCLC 75**
See also CA 109

Schonberg, Arnold
See Schoenberg, Arnold

Schopenhauer, Arthur 1788-1860   **NCLC 51**
See also DLB 90

Schor, Sandra (M.) 1932(?)-1990   **CLC 65**
See also CA 132

Schorer, Mark 1908-1977   **CLC 9**
See also CA 5-8R; 73-76; CANR 7; DLB 103

Schrader, Paul (Joseph) 1946-   **CLC 26**

See also CA 37-40R; CANR 41; DLB 44

Schreiner, Olive (Emilie Albertina) 1855-1920
TCLC 9
See also CA 105; 154; DLB 18, 156, 190

Schulberg, Budd (Wilson) 1914-   **CLC 7, 48**
See also CA 25-28R; CANR 19; DLB 6, 26,
28; DLBY 81

Schulz, Bruno 1892-1942**TCLC 5, 51; SSC 13**
See also CA 115; 123

Schulz, Charles M(onroe) 1922-   **CLC 12**
See also CA 9-12R; CANR 6; INT CANR-6;
SATA 10

Schumacher, E(rnst) F(riedrich) 1911-1977
CLC 80
See also CA 81-84; 73-76; CANR 34

Schuyler, James Marcus 1923-1991**CLC 5, 23;
DAM POET**
See also CA 101; 134; DLB 5, 169; INT 101

Schwartz, Delmore (David) 1913-1966**CLC 2,
4, 10, 45, 87; PC 8**
See also CA 17-18; 25-28R; CANR 35; CAP 2;
DLB 28, 48; MTCW 1

Schwartz, Ernst
See Ozu, Yasujiro

Schwartz, John Burnham 1965-   **CLC 59**
See also CA 132

Schwartz, Lynne Sharon 1939-   **CLC 31**
See also CA 103; CANR 44

Schwartz, Muriel A.
See Eliot, T(homas) S(tearns)

Schwarz-Bart, Andre 1928-   **CLC 2, 4**
See also CA 89-92

Schwarz-Bart, Simone 1938- **CLC 7; BLCS**
See also BW 2; CA 97-100

Schwob, Marcel (Mayer Andre) 1867-1905
TCLC 20
See also CA 117; 168; DLB 123

Sciascia, Leonardo 1921-1989 **CLC 8, 9, 41**
See also CA 85-88; 130; CANR 35; DLB 177;
MTCW 1

Scoppettone, Sandra 1936-   **CLC 26**
See also AAYA 11; CA 5-8R; CANR 41, 73;
SATA 9, 92

Scorsese, Martin 1942-   **CLC 20, 89**
See also CA 110; 114; CANR 46

Scotland, Jay
See Jakes, John (William)

Scott, Duncan Campbell 1862-1947 **TCLC 6;
DAC**
See also CA 104; 153; DLB 92

Scott, Evelyn 1893-1963   **CLC 43**
See also CA 104; 112; CANR 64; DLB 9, 48

Scott, F(rancis) R(eginald) 1899-1985**CLC 22**
See also CA 101; 114; DLB 88; INT 101

Scott, Frank
See Scott, F(rancis) R(eginald)

Scott, Joanna 1960-   **CLC 50**
See also CA 126; CANR 53

Scott, Paul (Mark) 1920-1978   **CLC 9, 60**
See also CA 81-84; 77-80; CANR 33; DLB 14,
207; MTCW 1

Scott, Sarah 1723-1795   **LC 44**
See also DLB 39

Scott, Walter 1771-1832 **NCLC 15, 69; DA;
DAB; DAC; DAM MST, NOV, POET; PC
13; SSC 32; WLC**
See also AAYA 22; CDBLB 1789-1832; DLB
93, 107, 116, 144, 159; YABC 2

Scribe, (Augustin) Eugene 1791-1861 **NCLC
16; DAM DRAM; DC 5**
See also DLB 192

Scrum, R.
See Crumb, R(obert)

Scudery, Madeleine de 1607-1701   **LC 2**

Scum
See Crumb, R(obert)

Scumbag, Little Bobby
See Crumb, R(obert)

Seabrook, John
See Hubbard, L(afayette) Ron(ald)

Sealy, I. Allan 1951-   **CLC 55**

Search, Alexander
See Pessoa, Fernando (Antonio Nogueira)

Sebastian, Lee
See Silverberg, Robert

Sebastian Owl
See Thompson, Hunter S(tockton)

Sebestyen, Ouida 1924-   **CLC 30**
See also AAYA 8; CA 107; CANR 40; CLR 17;
JRDA; MAICYA; SAAS 10; SATA 39

Secundus, H. Scriblerus
See Fielding, Henry

Sedges, John
See Buck, Pearl S(ydenstricker)

Sedgwick, Catharine Maria 1789-1867**NCLC
19**
See also DLB 1, 74

Seelye, John (Douglas) 1931-   **CLC 7**
See also CA 97-100; CANR 70; INT 97-100

Seferiades, Giorgos Stylianou 1900-1971
See Seferis, George
See also CA 5-8R; 33-36R; CANR 5, 36;
MTCW 1

Seferis, George   **CLC 5, 11**
See also Seferiades, Giorgos Stylianou

Segal, Erich (Wolf) 1937- **CLC 3, 10; DAM
POP**
See also BEST 89:1; CA 25-28R; CANR 20,
36, 65; DLBY 86; INT CANR-20; MTCW 1

Seger, Bob 1945-   **CLC 35**

Seghers, Anna   **CLC 7**
See also Radvanyi, Netty
See also DLB 69

Seidel, Frederick (Lewis) 1936-   **CLC 18**
See also CA 13-16R; CANR 8; DLBY 84

Seifert, Jaroslav 1901-1986 **CLC 34, 44, 93**
See also CA 127; MTCW 1

Sei Shonagon c. 966-1017(?)   **CMLC 6**

Sejour, Victor 1817-1874   **DC 10**
See also DLB 50

Sejour Marcou et Ferrand, Juan Victor
See Sejour, Victor

Selby, Hubert, Jr. 1928-**CLC 1, 2, 4, 8; SSC 20**
See also CA 13-16R; CANR 33; DLB 2

Selzer, Richard 1928-   **CLC 74**
See also CA 65-68; CANR 14

Sembene, Ousmane
See Ousmane, Sembene

Senancour, Etienne Pivert de 1770-1846
NCLC 16
See also DLB 119

Sender, Ramon (Jose) 1902-1982**CLC 8; DAM
MULT; HLC**
See also CA 5-8R; 105; CANR 8; HW; MTCW
1

Seneca, Lucius Annaeus 4B.C.-65 **CMLC 6;
DAM DRAM; DC 5**

Senghor, Leopold Sedar 1906- **CLC 54; BLC
3; DAM MULT, POET; PC 25**
See also BW 2; CA 116; 125; CANR 47, 74;
MTCW 1

Serling, (Edward) Rod(man) 1924-1975 **CLC
30**
See also AAYA 14; AITN 1; CA 162; 57-60;
DLB 26

Serna, Ramon Gomez de la

See Gomez de la Serna, Ramon

Serpieres
See Guillevic, (Eugene)

Service, Robert
See Service, Robert W(illiam)
See also DAB; DLB 92

Service, Robert W(illiam) 1874(?)-1958**TCLC
15; DA; DAC; DAM MST, POET; WLC**
See also Service, Robert
See also CA 115; 140; SATA 20

Seth, Vikram 1952-**CLC 43, 90; DAM MULT**
See also CA 121; 127; CANR 50, 74; DLB 120;
INT 127

Seton, Cynthia Propper 1926-1982   **CLC 27**
See also CA 5-8R; 108; CANR 7

Seton, Ernest (Evan) Thompson 1860-1946
TCLC 31
See also CA 109; DLB 92; DLBD 13; JRDA;
SATA 18

Seton-Thompson, Ernest
See Seton, Ernest (Evan) Thompson

Settle, Mary Lee 1918-   **CLC 19, 61**
See also CA 89-92; CAAS 1; CANR 44; DLB
6; INT 89-92

Seuphor, Michel
See Arp, Jean

**Sevigne, Marie (de Rabutin-Chantal) Marquise
de** 1626-1696   **LC 11**

Sewall, Samuel 1652-1730   **LC 38**
See also DLB 24

Sexton, Anne (Harvey) 1928-1974**CLC 2, 4, 6,
8, 10, 15, 53; DA; DAB; DAC; DAM MST,
POET; PC 2; WLC**
See also CA 1-4R; 53-56; CABS 2; CANR 3,
36; CDALB 1941-1968; DLB 5, 169;
MTCW 1; SATA 10

Shaara, Michael (Joseph, Jr.) 1929-1988**CLC
15; DAM POP**
See also AITN 1; CA 102; 125; CANR 52;
DLBY 83

Shackleton, C. C.
See Aldiss, Brian W(ilson)

Shacochis, Bob   **CLC 39**
See also Shacochis, Robert G.

Shacochis, Robert G. 1951-
See Shacochis, Bob
See also CA 119; 124; INT 124

Shaffer, Anthony (Joshua) 1926-   **CLC 19;
DAM DRAM**
See also CA 110; 116; DLB 13

Shaffer, Peter (Levin) 1926-**CLC 5, 14, 18, 37,
60; DAB; DAM DRAM, MST; DC 7**
See also CA 25-28R; CANR 25, 47, 74; CDBLB
1960 to Present; DLB 13; MTCW 1

Shakey, Bernard
See Young, Neil

Shalamov, Varlam (Tikhonovich) 1907(?)-1982
CLC 18
See also CA 129; 105

Shamlu, Ahmad 1925-   **CLC 10**

Shammas, Anton 1951-   **CLC 55**

Shange, Ntozake 1948-**CLC 8, 25, 38, 74; BLC
3; DAM DRAM, MULT; DC 3**
See also AAYA 9; BW 2; CA 85-88; CABS 3;
CANR 27, 48, 74; DLB 38; MTCW 1

Shanley, John Patrick 1950-   **CLC 75**
See also CA 128; 133

Shapcott, Thomas W(illiam) 1935-   **CLC 38**
See also CA 69-72; CANR 49

Shapiro, Jane   **CLC 76**

Shapiro, Karl (Jay) 1913-**CLC 4, 8, 15, 53; PC
25**
See also CA 1-4R; CAAS 6; CANR 1, 36, 66;

DLB 48; MTCW 1

Sharp, William 1855-1905   **TCLC 39**
See also CA 160; DLB 156

Sharpe, Thomas Ridley 1928-
See Sharpe, Tom
See also CA 114; 122; INT 122

Sharpe, Tom   **CLC 36**
See also Sharpe, Thomas Ridley
See also DLB 14

Shaw, Bernard   **TCLC 45**
See also Shaw, George Bernard
See also BW 1

Shaw, G. Bernard
See Shaw, George Bernard

Shaw, George Bernard 1856-1950**TCLC 3, 9,
21; DA; DAB; DAC; DAM DRAM, MST;
WLC**
See also Shaw, Bernard
See also CA 104; 128; CDBLB 1914-1945;
DLB 10, 57, 190; MTCW 1

Shaw, Henry Wheeler 1818-1885   **NCLC 15**
See also DLB 11

Shaw, Irwin 1913-1984 **CLC 7, 23, 34; DAM
DRAM, POP**
See also AITN 1; CA 13-16R; 112; CANR 21;
CDALB 1941-1968; DLB 6, 102; DLBY 84;
MTCW 1

Shaw, Robert 1927-1978   **CLC 5**
See also AITN 1; CA 1-4R; 81-84; CANR 4;
DLB 13, 14

Shaw, T. E.
See Lawrence, T(homas) E(dward)

Shawn, Wallace 1943-   **CLC 41**
See also CA 112

Shea, Lisa 1953-   **CLC 86**
See also CA 147

Sheed, Wilfrid (John Joseph) 1930-**CLC 2, 4,
10, 53**
See also CA 65-68; CANR 30, 66; DLB 6;
MTCW 1

Sheldon, Alice Hastings Bradley 1915(?)-1987
See Tiptree, James, Jr.
See also CA 108; 122; CANR 34; INT 108;
MTCW 1

Sheldon, John
See Bloch, Robert (Albert)

Shelley, Mary Wollstonecraft (Godwin) 1797-
1851**NCLC 14, 59; DA; DAB; DAC; DAM
MST, NOV; WLC**
See also AAYA 20; CDBLB 1789-1832; DLB
110, 116, 159, 178; SATA 29

Shelley, Percy Bysshe 1792-1822   **NCLC 18;
DA; DAB; DAC; DAM MST, POET; PC
14; WLC**
See also CDBLB 1789-1832; DLB 96, 110, 158

Shepard, Jim 1956-   **CLC 36**
See also CA 137; CANR 59; SATA 90

Shepard, Lucius 1947-   **CLC 34**
See also CA 128; 141

Shepard, Sam 1943- **CLC 4, 6, 17, 34, 41, 44;
DAM DRAM; DC 5**
See also AAYA 1; CA 69-72; CABS 3; CANR
22; DLB 7; MTCW 1

Shepherd, Michael
See Ludlum, Robert

Sherburne, Zoa (Morin) 1912-   **CLC 30**
See also AAYA 13; CA 1-4R; CANR 3, 37;
MAICYA; SAAS 18; SATA 3

Sheridan, Frances 1724-1766   **LC 7**
See also DLB 39, 84

Sheridan, Richard Brinsley 1751-1816**NCLC
5; DA; DAB; DAC; DAM DRAM, MST;
DC 1; WLC**

See also CDBLB 1660-1789; DLB 89

Sherman, Jonathan Marc   **CLC 55**

Sherman, Martin 1941(?)-   **CLC 19**
See also CA 116; 123

Sherwin, Judith Johnson 1936-   **CLC 7, 15**
See also CA 25-28R; CANR 34

Sherwood, Frances 1940-   **CLC 81**
See also CA 146

Sherwood, Robert E(mmet) 1896-1955**TCLC
3; DAM DRAM**
See also CA 104; 153; DLB 7, 26

Shestov, Lev 1866-1938   **TCLC 56**

Shevchenko, Taras 1814-1861   **NCLC 54**

Shiel, M(atthew) P(hipps) 1865-1947**TCLC 8**
See also Holmes, Gordon
See also CA 106; 160; DLB 153

Shields, Carol 1935-   **CLC 91, 113; DAC**
See also CA 81-84; CANR 51, 74

Shields, David 1956-   **CLC 97**
See also CA 124; CANR 48

Shiga, Naoya 1883-1971   **CLC 33; SSC 23**
See also CA 101; 33-36R; DLB 180

Shikibu, Murasaki c. 978-c. 1014   **CMLC 1**

Shilts, Randy 1951-1994   **CLC 85**
See also AAYA 19; CA 115; 127; 144; CANR
45; INT 127

Shimazaki, Haruki 1872-1943
See Shimazaki Toson
See also CA 105; 134

Shimazaki Toson 1872-1943   **TCLC 5**
See also Shimazaki, Haruki
See also DLB 180

Sholokhov, Mikhail (Aleksandrovich) 1905-
1984   **CLC 7, 15**
See also CA 101; 112; MTCW 1; SATA-Obit
36

Shone, Patric
See Hanley, James

Shreve, Susan Richards 1939-   **CLC 23**
See also CA 49-52; CAAS 5; CANR 5, 38, 69;
MAICYA; SATA 46, 95; SATA-Brief 41

Shue, Larry 1946-1985**CLC 52; DAM DRAM**
See also CA 145; 117

Shu-Jen, Chou 1881-1936
See Lu Hsun
See also CA 104

Shulman, Alix Kates 1932-   **CLC 2, 10**
See also CA 29-32R; CANR 43; SATA 7

Shuster, Joe 1914-   **CLC 21**

Shute, Nevil   **CLC 30**
See also Norway, Nevil Shute

Shuttle, Penelope (Diane) 1947-   **CLC 7**
See also CA 93-96; CANR 39; DLB 14, 40

Sidney, Mary 1561-1621   **LC 19, 39**

Sidney, Sir Philip 1554-1586 **LC 19, 39; DA;
DAB; DAC; DAM MST, POET**
See also CDBLB Before 1660; DLB 167

Siegel, Jerome 1914-1996   **CLC 21**
See also CA 116; 169; 151

Siegel, Jerry
See Siegel, Jerome

Sienkiewicz, Henryk (Adam Alexander Pius)
1846-1916   **TCLC 3**
See also CA 104; 134

Sierra, Gregorio Martinez
See Martinez Sierra, Gregorio

Sierra, Maria (de la O'LeJarraga) Martinez
See Martinez Sierra, Maria (de la O'LeJarraga)

Sigal, Clancy 1926-   **CLC 7**
See also CA 1-4R

Sigourney, Lydia Howard (Huntley) 1791-1865
NCLC 21
See also DLB 1, 42, 73

Siguenza y Gongora, Carlos de 1645-1700 **L C 8**

Sigurjonsson, Johann 1880-1919　**TCLC 27**
See also CA 170

Sikelianos, Angelos 1884-1951　**TCLC 39**

Silkin, Jon 1930-　　　　**CLC 2, 6, 43**
See also CA 5-8R; CAAS 5; DLB 27

Silko, Leslie (Marmon) 1948-**CLC 23, 74, 114; DA; DAC; DAM MST, MULT, POP; WLCS**
See also AAYA 14; CA 115; 122; CANR 45, 65; DLB 143, 175; NNAL

Sillanpaa, Frans Eemil 1888-1964　**CLC 19**
See also CA 129; 93-96; MTCW 1

Sillitoe, Alan 1928-　**CLC 1, 3, 6, 10, 19, 57**
See also AITN 1; CA 9-12R; CAAS 2; CANR 8, 26, 55; CDBLB 1960 to Present; DLB 14, 139; MTCW 1; SATA 61

Silone, Ignazio 1900-1978　　　　**CLC 4**
See also CA 25-28; 81-84; CANR 34; CAP 2; MTCW 1

Silver, Joan Micklin 1935-　　　**CLC 20**
See also CA 114; 121; INT 121

Silver, Nicholas
See Faust, Frederick (Schiller)

Silverberg, Robert 1935- **CLC 7; DAM POP**
See also AAYA 24; CA 1-4R; CAAS 3; CANR 1, 20, 36; DLB 8; INT CANR-20; MAICYA; MTCW 1; SATA 13, 91

Silverstein, Alvin 1933-　　　　**CLC 17**
See also CA 49-52; CANR 2; CLR 25; JRDA; MAICYA; SATA 8, 69

Silverstein, Virginia B(arbara Opshelor) 1937-
CLC 17
See also CA 49-52; CANR 2; CLR 25; JRDA; MAICYA; SATA 8, 69

Sim, Georges
See Simenon, Georges (Jacques Christian)

Simak, Clifford D(onald) 1904-1988**CLC 1, 55**
See also CA 1-4R; 125; CANR 1, 35; DLB 8; MTCW 1; SATA-Obit 56

Simenon, Georges (Jacques Christian) 1903-1989　**CLC 1, 2, 3, 8, 18, 47; DAM POP**
See also CA 85-88; 129; CANR 35; DLB 72; DLBY 89; MTCW 1

Simic, Charles 1938-　　**CLC 6, 9, 22, 49, 68; DAM POET**
See also CA 29-32R; CAAS 4; CANR 12, 33, 52, 61; DLB 105

Simmel, Georg 1858-1918　　　　**TCLC 64**
See also CA 157

Simmons, Charles (Paul) 1924-　　**CLC 57**
See also CA 89-92; INT 89-92

Simmons, Dan 1948-　**CLC 44; DAM POP**
See also AAYA 16; CA 138; CANR 53

Simmons, James (Stewart Alexander) 1933-
CLC 43
See also CA 105; CAAS 21; DLB 40

Simms, William Gilmore 1806-1870 **NCLC 3**
See also DLB 3, 30, 59, 73

Simon, Carly 1945-　　　　　　**CLC 26**
See also CA 105

Simon, Claude 1913-1984　**CLC 4, 9, 15, 39; DAM NOV**
See also CA 89-92; CANR 33; DLB 83; MTCW 1

Simon, (Marvin) Neil 1927-**CLC 6, 11, 31, 39, 70; DAM DRAM**
See also AITN 1; CA 21-24R; CANR 26, 54; DLB 7; MTCW 1

Simon, Paul (Frederick) 1941(?)-　**CLC 17**
See also CA 116; 153

Simonon, Paul 1956(?)-　　　　**CLC 30**

Simpson, Harriette
See Arnow, Harriette (Louisa) Simpson

Simpson, Louis (Aston Marantz) 1923-**CLC 4, 7, 9, 32; DAM POET**
See also CA 1-4R; CAAS 4, CANR 1, 61; DLB 5; MTCW 1

Simpson, Mona (Elizabeth) 1957-　**CLC 44**
See also CA 122; 135; CANR 68

Simpson, N(orman) F(rederick) 1919-**CLC 29**
See also CA 13-16R; DLB 13

Sinclair, Andrew (Annandale) 1935-　**CLC 2, 14**
See also CA 9-12R; CAAS 5; CANR 14, 38; DLB 14; MTCW 1

Sinclair, Emil
See Hesse, Hermann

Sinclair, Iain 1943-　　　　　　**CLC 76**
See also CA 132

Sinclair, Iain MacGregor
See Sinclair, Iain

Sinclair, Irene
See Griffith, D(avid Lewelyn) W(ark)

Sinclair, Mary Amelia St. Clair 1865(?)-1946
See Sinclair, May
See also CA 104

Sinclair, May 1863-1946　　　**TCLC 3, 11**
See also Sinclair, Mary Amelia St. Clair
See also CA 166; DLB 36, 135

Sinclair, Roy
See Griffith, D(avid Lewelyn) W(ark)

Sinclair, Upton (Beall) 1878-1968 **CLC 1, 11, 15, 63; DA; DAB; DAC; DAM MST, NOV; WLC**
See also CA 5-8R; 25-28R; CANR 7; CDALB 1929-1941; DLB 9; INT CANR-7; MTCW 1; SATA 9

Singer, Isaac
See Singer, Isaac Bashevis

Singer, Isaac Bashevis 1904-1991**CLC 1, 3, 6, 9, 11, 15, 23, 38, 69, 111; DA; DAB; DAC; DAM MST, NOV; SSC 3; WLC**
See also AITN 1, 2; CA 1-4R; 134; CANR 1, 39; CDALB 1941-1968; CLR 1; DLB 6, 28, 52; DLBY 91; JRDA; MAICYA; MTCW 1; SATA 3, 27; SATA-Obit 68

Singer, Israel Joshua 1893-1944　　**TCLC 33**
See also CA 169

Singh, Khushwant 1915-　　　　**CLC 11**
See also CA 9-12R; CAAS 9; CANR 6

Singleton, Ann
See Benedict, Ruth (Fulton)

Sinjohn, John
See Galsworthy, John

Sinyavsky, Andrei (Donatevich) 1925-1997
CLC 8
See also CA 85-88; 159

Sirin, V.
See Nabokov, Vladimir (Vladimirovich)

Sissman, L(ouis) E(dward) 1928-1976**CLC 9, 18**
See also CA 21-24R; 65-68; CANR 13; DLB 5

Sisson, C(harles) H(ubert) 1914-　　**CLC 8**
See also CA 1-4R; CAAS 3; CANR 3, 48; DLB 27

Sitwell, Dame Edith 1887-1964 **CLC 2, 9, 67; DAM POET; PC 3**
See also CA 9-12R; CANR 35; CDBLB 1945-1960; DLB 20; MTCW 1

Siwaarmill, H. P.
See Sharp, William

Sjoewall, Maj 1935-　　　　　　**CLC 7**
See also CA 65-68; CANR 73

Sjowall, Maj
See Sjoewall, Maj

Skelton, John 1463-1529　　　　**PC 25**

Skelton, Robin 1925-1997　　　**CLC 13**
See also AITN 2; CA 5-8R; 160; CAAS 5; CANR 28; DLB 27, 53

Skolimowski, Jerzy 1938-　　　**CLC 20**
See also CA 128

Skram, Amalie (Bertha) 1847-1905 **TCLC 25**
See also CA 165

Skvorecky, Josef (Vaclav) 1924- **CLC 15, 39, 69; DAC; DAM NOV**
See also CA 61-64; CAAS 1; CANR 10, 34, 63; MTCW 1

Slade, Bernard　　　　　　　**CLC 11, 46**
See also Newbound, Bernard Slade
See also CAAS 9; DLB 53

Slaughter, Carolyn 1946-　　　**CLC 56**
See also CA 85-88

Slaughter, Frank G(ill) 1908-　　**CLC 29**
See also AITN 2; CA 5-8R; CANR 5; INT CANR-5

Slavitt, David R(ytman) 1935-　**CLC 5, 14**
See also CA 21-24R; CAAS 3; CANR 41; DLB 5, 6

Slesinger, Tess 1905-1945　　　**TCLC 10**
See also CA 107; DLB 102

Slessor, Kenneth 1901-1971　　　**CLC 14**
See also CA 102; 89-92

Slowacki, Juliusz 1809-1849　　**NCLC 15**

Smart, Christopher 1722-1771　**LC 3; DAM POET; PC 13**
See also DLB 109

Smart, Elizabeth 1913-1986　　　**CLC 54**
See also CA 81-84; 118; DLB 88

Smiley, Jane (Graves) 1949-**CLC 53, 76; DAM POP**
See also CA 104; CANR 30, 50, 74; INT CANR-30

Smith, A(rthur) J(ames) M(arshall) 1902-1980
CLC 15; DAC
See also CA 1-4R; 102; CANR 4; DLB 88

Smith, Adam 1723-1790　　　　　**LC 36**
See also DLB 104

Smith, Alexander 1829-1867　　**NCLC 59**
See also DLB 32, 55

Smith, Anna Deavere 1950-　　　**CLC 86**
See also CA 133

Smith, Betty (Wehner) 1896-1972　**CLC 19**
See also CA 5-8R; 33-36R; DLBY 82; SATA 6

Smith, Charlotte (Turner) 1749-1806 **N C L C 23**
See also DLB 39, 109

Smith, Clark Ashton 1893-1961　　**CLC 43**
See also CA 143

Smith, Dave　　　　　　　　**CLC 22, 42**
See also Smith, David (Jeddie)
See also CAAS 7; DLB 5

Smith, David (Jeddie) 1942-
See Smith, Dave
See also CA 49-52; CANR 1, 59; DAM POET

Smith, Florence Margaret 1902-1971
See Smith, Stevie
See also CA 17-18; 29-32R; CANR 35; CAP 2; DAM POET; MTCW 1

Smith, Iain Crichton 1928-1998　　**CLC 64**
See also CA 21-24R; 171; DLB 40, 139

Smith, John 1580(?)-1631　　　　　**LC 9**
See also DLB 24, 30

Smith, Johnston
See Crane, Stephen (Townley)

Smith, Joseph, Jr. 1805-1844　　**NCLC 53**

Smith, Lee 1944-　　　　　　**CLC 25, 73**
See also CA 114; 119; CANR 46; DLB 143;

DLBY 83; INT 119

Smith, Martin
See Smith, Martin Cruz

Smith, Martin Cruz 1942-   **CLC 25; DAM MULT, POP**
See also BEST 89:4; CA 85-88; CANR 6, 23, 43, 65; INT CANR-23; NNAL

Smith, Mary-Ann Tirone 1944-   **CLC 39**
See also CA 118; 136

Smith, Patti 1946-   **CLC 12**
See also CA 93-96; CANR 63

Smith, Pauline (Urmson) 1882-1959 **TCLC 25**

Smith, Rosamond
See Oates, Joyce Carol

Smith, Sheila Kaye
See Kaye-Smith, Sheila

Smith, Stevie   **CLC 3, 8, 25, 44; PC 12**
See also Smith, Florence Margaret
See also DLB 20

Smith, Wilbur (Addison) 1933-   **CLC 33**
See also CA 13-16R; CANR 7, 46, 66; MTCW 1

Smith, William Jay 1918-   **CLC 6**
See also CA 5-8R; CANR 44; DLB 5; MAICYA; SAAS 22; SATA 2, 68

Smith, Woodrow Wilson
See Kuttner, Henry

Smolenskin, Peretz 1842-1885   **NCLC 30**

Smollett, Tobias (George) 1721-1771 **LC 2, 46**
See also CDBLB 1660-1789; DLB 39, 104

Snodgrass, W(illiam) D(e Witt) 1926- **CLC 2, 6, 10, 18, 68; DAM POET**
See also CA 1-4R; CANR 6, 36, 65; DLB 5; MTCW 1

Snow, C(harles) P(ercy) 1905-1980 **CLC 1, 4, 6, 9, 13, 19; DAM NOV**
See also CA 5-8R; 101; CANR 28; CDBLB 1945-1960; DLB 15, 77; DLBD 17; MTCW 1

Snow, Frances Compton
See Adams, Henry (Brooks)

Snyder, Gary (Sherman) 1930- **CLC 1, 2, 5, 9, 32; DAM POET; PC 21**
See also CA 17-20R; CANR 30, 60; DLB 5, 16, 165

Snyder, Zilpha Keatley 1927-   **CLC 17**
See also AAYA 15; CA 9-12R; CANR 38; CLR 31; JRDA; MAICYA; SAAS 2; SATA 1, 28, 75

Soares, Bernardo
See Pessoa, Fernando (Antonio Nogueira)

Sobh, A.
See Shamlu, Ahmad

Sobol, Joshua   **CLC 60**

Socrates 469B.C.-399B.C.   **CMLC 27**

Soderberg, Hjalmar 1869-1941   **TCLC 39**

Sodergran, Edith (Irene)
See Soedergran, Edith (Irene)

Soedergran, Edith (Irene) 1892-1923 **T C L C 31**

Softly, Edgar
See Lovecraft, H(oward) P(hillips)

Softly, Edward
See Lovecraft, H(oward) P(hillips)

Sokolov, Raymond 1941-   **CLC 7**
See also CA 85-88

Solo, Jay
See Ellison, Harlan (Jay)

Sologub, Fyodor   **TCLC 9**
See also Teternikov, Fyodor Kuzmich

Solomons, Ikey Esquir
See Thackeray, William Makepeace

Solomos, Dionysios 1798-1857   **NCLC 15**

Solwoska, Mara
See French, Marilyn

Solzhenitsyn, Aleksandr I(sayevich) 1918- **CLC 1, 2, 4, 7, 9, 10, 18, 26, 34, 78; DA; DAB; DAC; DAM MST, NOV; SSC 32; WLC**
See also AITN 1; CA 69-72; CANR 40, 65; MTCW 1

Somers, Jane
See Lessing, Doris (May)

Somerville, Edith 1858-1949   **TCLC 51**
See also DLB 135

Somerville & Ross
See Martin, Violet Florence; Somerville, Edith

Sommer, Scott 1951-   **CLC 25**
See also CA 106

Sondheim, Stephen (Joshua) 1930- **CLC 30, 39; DAM DRAM**
See also AAYA 11; CA 103; CANR 47, 68

Song, Cathy 1955-   **PC 21**
See also CA 154; DLB 169

Sontag, Susan 1933- **CLC 1, 2, 10, 13, 31, 105; DAM POP**
See also CA 17-20R; CANR 25, 51, 74; DLB 2, 67; MTCW 1

Sophocles 496(?)B.C.-406(?)B.C.   **CMLC 2; DA; DAB; DAC; DAM DRAM, MST; DC 1; WLCS**
See also DLB 176

Sordello 1189-1269   **CMLC 15**

Sorel, Julia
See Drexler, Rosalyn

Sorrentino, Gilbert 1929- **CLC 3, 7, 14, 22, 40**
See also CA 77-80; CANR 14, 33; DLB 5, 173; DLBY 80; INT CANR-14

Soto, Gary 1952-   **CLC 32, 80; DAM MULT; HLC**
See also AAYA 10; CA 119; 125; CANR 50, 74; CLR 38; DLB 82; HW; INT 125; JRDA; SATA 80

Soupault, Philippe 1897-1990   **CLC 68**
See also CA 116; 147; 131

Souster, (Holmes) Raymond 1921- **CLC 5, 14; DAC; DAM POET**
See also CA 13-16R; CAAS 14; CANR 13, 29, 53; DLB 88; SATA 63

Southern, Terry 1924(?)-1995   **CLC 7**
See also CA 1-4R; 150; CANR 1, 55; DLB 2

Southey, Robert 1774-1843   **NCLC 8**
See also DLB 93, 107, 142; SATA 54

Southworth, Emma Dorothy Eliza Nevitte 1819-1899   **NCLC 26**

Souza, Ernest
See Scott, Evelyn

Soyinka, Wole 1934- **CLC 3, 5, 14, 36, 44; BLC 3; DA; DAB; DAC; DAM DRAM, MST, MULT; DC 2; WLC**
See also BW 2; CA 13-16R; CANR 27, 39; DLB 125; MTCW 1

Spackman, W(illiam) M(ode) 1905-1990 **C L C 46**
See also CA 81-84; 132

Spacks, Barry (Bernard) 1931-   **CLC 14**
See also CA 154; CANR 33; DLB 105

Spanidou, Irini 1946-   **CLC 44**

Spark, Muriel (Sarah) 1918- **CLC 2, 3, 5, 8, 13, 18, 40, 94; DAB; DAC; DAM MST, NOV; SSC 10**
See also CA 5-8R; CANR 12, 36; CDBLB 1945-1960; DLB 15, 139; INT CANR-12; MTCW 1

Spaulding, Douglas
See Bradbury, Ray (Douglas)

Spaulding, Leonard
See Bradbury, Ray (Douglas)

Spence, J. A. D.
See Eliot, T(homas) S(tearns)

Spencer, Elizabeth 1921-   **CLC 22**
See also CA 13-16R; CANR 32, 65; DLB 6; MTCW 1; SATA 14

Spencer, Leonard G.
See Silverberg, Robert

Spencer, Scott 1945-   **CLC 30**
See also CA 113; CANR 51; DLBY 86

Spender, Stephen (Harold) 1909-1995 **CLC 1, 2, 5, 10, 41, 91; DAM POET**
See also CA 9-12R; 149; CANR 31, 54; CDBLB 1945-1960; DLB 20; MTCW 1

Spengler, Oswald (Arnold Gottfried) 1880-1936 **TCLC 25**
See also CA 118

Spenser, Edmund 1552(?)-1599 **LC 5, 39; DA; DAB; DAC; DAM MST, POET; PC 8; WLC**
See also CDBLB Before 1660; DLB 167

Spicer, Jack 1925-1965 **CLC 8, 18, 72; DAM POET**
See also CA 85-88; DLB 5, 16, 193

Spiegelman, Art 1948-   **CLC 76**
See also AAYA 10; CA 125; CANR 41, 55, 74

Spielberg, Peter 1929-   **CLC 6**
See also CA 5-8R; CANR 4, 48; DLBY 81

Spielberg, Steven 1947-   **CLC 20**
See also AAYA 8, 24; CA 77-80; CANR 32; SATA 32

Spillane, Frank Morrison 1918-
See Spillane, Mickey
See also CA 25-28R; CANR 28, 63; MTCW 1; SATA 66

Spillane, Mickey   **CLC 3, 13**
See Spillane, Frank Morrison

Spinoza, Benedictus de 1632-1677   **LC 9**

Spinrad, Norman (Richard) 1940-   **CLC 46**
See also CA 37-40R; CAAS 19; CANR 20; DLB 8; INT CANR-20

Spitteler, Carl (Friedrich Georg) 1845-1924 **TCLC 12**
See also CA 109; DLB 129

Spivack, Kathleen (Romola Drucker) 1938- **CLC 6**
See also CA 49-52

Spoto, Donald 1941-   **CLC 39**
See also CA 65-68; CANR 11, 57

Springsteen, Bruce (F.) 1949-   **CLC 17**
See also CA 111

Spurling, Hilary 1940-   **CLC 34**
See also CA 104; CANR 25, 52

Spyker, John Howland
See Elman, Richard (Martin)

Squires, (James) Radcliffe 1917-1993 **CLC 51**
See also CA 1-4R; 140; CANR 6, 21

Srivastava, Dhanpat Rai 1880(?)-1936
See Premchand
See also CA 118

Stacy, Donald
See Pohl, Frederik

Stael, Germaine de 1766-1817
See Stael-Holstein, Anne Louise Germaine Necker Baronn
See also DLB 119

Stael-Holstein, Anne Louise Germaine Necker Baronn 1766-1817   **NCLC 3**
See also Stael, Germaine de
See also DLB 192

Stafford, Jean 1915-1979 **CLC 4, 7, 19, 68; SSC 26**

See also CA 1-4R; 85-88; CANR 3, 65; DLB 2, 173; MTCW 1; SATA-Obit 22

Stafford, William (Edgar) 1914-1993 **CLC 4, 7, 29; DAM POET**
See also CA 5-8R; 142; CAAS 3; CANR 5, 22; DLB 5, 206; INT CANR-22

Stagnelius, Eric Johan 1793-1823 **NCLC 61**

Staines, Trevor
See Brunner, John (Kilian Houston)

Stairs, Gordon
See Austin, Mary (Hunter)

Stannard, Martin 1947- **CLC 44**
See also CA 142; DLB 155

Stanton, Elizabeth Cady 1815-1902 **TCLC 73**
See also CA 171; DLB 79

Stanton, Maura 1946- **CLC 9**
See also CA 89-92; CANR 15; DLB 120

Stanton, Schuyler
See Baum, L(yman) Frank

Stapledon, (William) Olaf 1886-1950 **T C L C 22**
See also CA 111; 162; DLB 15

Starbuck, George (Edwin) 1931-1996 **CLC 53; DAM POET**
See also CA 21-24R; 153; CANR 23

Stark, Richard
See Westlake, Donald E(dwin)

Staunton, Schuyler
See Baum, L(yman) Frank

Stead, Christina (Ellen) 1902-1983 **CLC 2, 5, 8, 32, 80**
See also CA 13-16R; 109; CANR 33, 40; MTCW 1

Stead, William Thomas 1849-1912 **TCLC 48**
See also CA 167

Steele, Richard 1672-1729 **LC 18**
See also CDBLB 1660-1789; DLB 84, 101

Steele, Timothy (Reid) 1948- **CLC 45**
See also CA 93-96; CANR 16, 50; DLB 120

Steffens, (Joseph) Lincoln 1866-1936 **T C L C 20**
See also CA 117

Stegner, Wallace (Earle) 1909-1993 **CLC 9, 49, 81; DAM NOV; SSC 27**
See also AITN 1; BEST 90:3; CA 1-4R; 141; CAAS 9; CANR 1, 21, 46; DLB 9, 206; DLBY 93; MTCW 1

Stein, Gertrude 1874-1946 **TCLC 1, 6, 28, 48; DA; DAB; DAC; DAM MST, NOV, POET; PC 18; WLC**
See also CA 104; 132; CDALB 1917-1929; DLB 4, 54, 86; DLBD 15; MTCW 1

Steinbeck, John (Ernst) 1902-1968 **CLC 1, 5, 9, 13, 21, 34, 45, 75; DA; DAB; DAC; DAM DRAM, MST, NOV; SSC 11; WLC**
See also AAYA 12; CA 1-4R; 25-28R; CANR 1, 35; CDALB 1929-1941; DLB 7, 9; DLBD 2; MTCW 1; SATA 9

Steinem, Gloria 1934- **CLC 63**
See also CA 53-56; CANR 28, 51; MTCW 1

Steiner, George 1929- **CLC 24; DAM NOV**
See also CA 73-76; CANR 31, 67; DLB 67; MTCW 1; SATA 62

Steiner, K. Leslie
See Delany, Samuel R(ay, Jr.)

Steiner, Rudolf 1861-1925 **TCLC 13**
See also CA 107

Stendhal 1783-1842 **NCLC 23, 46; DA; DAB; DAC; DAM MST, NOV; SSC 27; WLC**
See also DLB 119

Stephen, Adeline Virginia
See Woolf, (Adeline) Virginia

Stephen, Sir Leslie 1832-1904 **TCLC 23**

See also CA 123; DLB 57, 144, 190

Stephen, Sir Leslie
See Stephen, Sir Leslie

Stephen, Virginia
See Woolf, (Adeline) Virginia

Stephens, James 1882(?)-1950 **TCLC 4**
See also CA 104; DLB 19, 153, 162

Stephens, Reed
See Donaldson, Stephen R.

Steptoe, Lydia
See Barnes, Djuna

Sterchi, Beat 1949- **CLC 65**

Sterling, Brett
See Bradbury, Ray (Douglas); Hamilton, Edmond

Sterling, Bruce 1954- **CLC 72**
See also CA 119; CANR 44

Sterling, George 1869-1926 **TCLC 20**
See also CA 117; 165; DLB 54

Stern, Gerald 1925- **CLC 40, 100**
See also CA 81-84; CANR 28; DLB 105

Stern, Richard (Gustave) 1928- **CLC 4, 39**
See also CA 1-4R; CANR 1, 25, 52; DLBY 87; INT CANR-25

Sternberg, Josef von 1894-1969 **CLC 20**
See also CA 81-84

Sterne, Laurence 1713-1768 **LC 2, 48; DA; DAB; DAC; DAM MST, NOV; WLC**
See also CDBLB 1660-1789; DLB 39

Sternheim, (William Adolf) Carl 1878-1942 **TCLC 8**
See also CA 105; DLB 56, 118

Stevens, Mark 1951- **CLC 34**
See also CA 122

Stevens, Wallace 1879-1955 **TCLC 3, 12, 45; DA; DAB; DAC; DAM MST, POET; PC 6; WLC**
See also CA 104; 124; CDALB 1929-1941; DLB 54; MTCW 1

Stevenson, Anne (Katharine) 1933- **CLC 7, 33**
See also CA 17-20R; CAAS 9; CANR 9, 33; DLB 40; MTCW 1

Stevenson, Robert Louis (Balfour) 1850-1894 **NCLC 5, 14, 63; DA; DAB; DAC; DAM MST, NOV; SSC 11; WLC**
See also AAYA 24; CDBLB 1890-1914; CLR 10, 11; DLB 18, 57, 141, 156, 174; DLBD 13; JRDA; MAICYA; SATA 100; YABC 2

Stewart, J(ohn) I(nnes) M(ackintosh) 1906-1994 **CLC 7, 14, 32**
See also CA 85-88; 147; CAAS 3; CANR 47; MTCW 1

Stewart, Mary (Florence Elinor) 1916- **CLC 7, 35, 117; DAB**
See also CA 1-4R; CANR 1, 59; SATA 12

Stewart, Mary Rainbow
See Stewart, Mary (Florence Elinor)

Stifle, June
See Campbell, Maria

Stifter, Adalbert 1805-1868 **NCLC 41; SSC 28**
See also DLB 133

Still, James 1906- **CLC 49**
See also CA 65-68; CAAS 17; CANR 10, 26; DLB 9; SATA 29

Sting 1951-
See Sumner, Gordon Matthew
See also CA 167

Stirling, Arthur
See Sinclair, Upton (Beall)

Stitt, Milan 1941- **CLC 29**
See also CA 69-72

Stockton, Francis Richard 1834-1902
See Stockton, Frank R.

See also CA 108; 137; MAICYA; SATA 44

Stockton, Frank R. **TCLC 47**
See also Stockton, Francis Richard
See also DLB 42, 74; DLBD 13; SATA-Brief 32

Stoddard, Charles
See Kuttner, Henry

Stoker, Abraham 1847-1912
See Stoker, Bram
See also CA 105; 150; DA; DAC; DAM MST, NOV; SATA 29

Stoker, Bram 1847-1912 **TCLC 8; DAB; WLC**
See also Stoker, Abraham
See also AAYA 23; CDBLB 1890-1914; DLB 36, 70, 178

Stolz, Mary (Slattery) 1920- **CLC 12**
See also AAYA 8; AITN 1; CA 5-8R; CANR 13, 41; JRDA; MAICYA; SAAS 3; SATA 10, 71

Stone, Irving 1903-1989 **CLC 7; DAM POP**
See also AITN 1; CA 1-4R; 129; CAAS 3; CANR 1, 23; INT CANR-23; MTCW 1; SATA 3; SATA-Obit 64

Stone, Oliver (William) 1946- **CLC 73**
See also AAYA 15; CA 110; CANR 55

Stone, Robert (Anthony) 1937- **CLC 5, 23, 42**
See also CA 85-88; CANR 23, 66; DLB 152; INT CANR-23; MTCW 1

Stone, Zachary
See Follett, Ken(neth Martin)

Stoppard, Tom 1937- **CLC 1, 3, 4, 5, 8, 15, 29, 34, 63, 91; DA; DAB; DAC; DAM DRAM, MST; DC 6; WLC**
See also CA 81-84; CANR 39, 67; CDBLB 1960 to Present; DLB 13; DLBY 85; MTCW 1

Storey, David (Malcolm) 1933- **CLC 2, 4, 5, 8; DAM DRAM**
See also CA 81-84; CANR 36; DLB 13, 14, 207; MTCW 1

Storm, Hyemeyohsts 1935- **CLC 3; DAM MULT**
See also CA 81-84; CANR 45; NNAL

Storm, Theodor 1817-1888 **SSC 27**

Storm, (Hans) Theodor (Woldsen) 1817-1888 **NCLC 1; SSC 27**
See also DLB 129

Storni, Alfonsina 1892-1938 **TCLC 5; DAM MULT; HLC**
See also CA 104; 131; HW

Stoughton, William 1631-1701 **LC 38**
See also DLB 24

Stout, Rex (Todhunter) 1886-1975 **CLC 3**
See also AITN 2; CA 61-64; CANR 71

Stow, (Julian) Randolph 1935- **CLC 23, 48**
See also CA 13-16R; CANR 33; MTCW 1

Stowe, Harriet (Elizabeth) Beecher 1811-1896 **NCLC 3, 50; DA; DAB; DAC; DAM MST, NOV; WLC**
See also CDALB 1865-1917; DLB 1, 12, 42, 74, 189; JRDA; MAICYA; YABC 1

Strachey, (Giles) Lytton 1880-1932 **TCLC 12**
See also CA 110; DLB 149; DLBD 10

Strand, Mark 1934- **CLC 6, 18, 41, 71; DAM POET**
See also CA 21-24R; CANR 40, 65; DLB 5; SATA 41

Straub, Peter (Francis) 1943- **CLC 28, 107; DAM POP**
See also BEST 89:1; CA 85-88; CANR 28, 65; DLBY 84; MTCW 1

Strauss, Botho 1944- **CLC 22**
See also CA 157; DLB 124

Streatfeild, (Mary) Noel 1895(?)-1986 CLC 21
  See also CA 81-84; 120; CANR 31; CLR 17;
    DLB 160; MAICYA; SATA 20; SATA-Obit
    48
Stribling, T(homas) S(igismund) 1881-1965
  CLC 23
  See also CA 107; DLB 9
Strindberg, (Johan) August 1849-1912 TCLC
  1, 8, 21, 47; DA; DAB; DAC; DAM DRAM,
  MST; WLC
  See also CA 104; 135
Stringer, Arthur 1874-1950   TCLC 37
  See also CA 161; DLB 92
Stringer, David
  See Roberts, Keith (John Kingston)
Stroheim, Erich von 1885-1957   TCLC 71
Strugatskii, Arkadii (Natanovich) 1925-1991
  CLC 27
  See also CA 106; 135
Strugatskii, Boris (Natanovich) 1933- CLC 27
  See also CA 106
Strummer, Joe 1953(?)-   CLC 30
Stuart, Don A.
  See Campbell, John W(ood, Jr.)
Stuart, Ian
  See MacLean, Alistair (Stuart)
Stuart, Jesse (Hilton) 1906-1984 CLC 1, 8, 11,
  14, 34; SSC 31
  See also CA 5-8R; 112; CANR 31; DLB 9, 48,
    102; DLBY 84; SATA 2; SATA-Obit 36
Sturgeon, Theodore (Hamilton) 1918-1985
  CLC 22, 39
  See also Queen, Ellery
  See also CA 81-84; 116; CANR 32; DLB 8;
    DLBY 85; MTCW 1
Sturges, Preston 1898-1959   TCLC 48
  See also CA 114; 149; DLB 26
Styron, William 1925- CLC 1, 3, 5, 11, 15, 60;
  DAM NOV, POP; SSC 25
  See also BEST 90:4; CA 5-8R; CANR 6, 33,
    74; CDALB 1968-1988; DLB 2, 143; DLBY
    80; INT CANR-6; MTCW 1
Su, Chien 1884-1918
  See Su Man-shu
  See also CA 123
Suarez Lynch, B.
  See Bioy Casares, Adolfo; Borges, Jorge Luis
Suckow, Ruth 1892-1960   SSC 18
  See also CA 113; DLB 9, 102
Sudermann, Hermann 1857-1928   TCLC 15
  See also CA 107; DLB 118
Sue, Eugene 1804-1857   NCLC 1
  See also DLB 119
Sueskind, Patrick 1949-   CLC 44
  See also Suskind, Patrick
Sukenick, Ronald 1932-   CLC 3, 4, 6, 48
  See also CA 25-28R; CAAS 8; CANR 32; DLB
    173; DLBY 81
Suknaski, Andrew 1942-   CLC 19
  See also CA 101; DLB 53
Sullivan, Vernon
  See Vian, Boris
Sully Prudhomme 1839-1907   TCLC 31
Su Man-shu   TCLC 24
  See also Su, Chien
Summerforest, Ivy B.
  See Kirkup, James
Summers, Andrew James 1942-   CLC 26
Summers, Andy
  See Summers, Andrew James
Summers, Hollis (Spurgeon, Jr.) 1916- CLC 10
  See also CA 5-8R; CANR 3; DLB 6
Summers, (Alphonsus Joseph-Mary Augustus)

Montague 1880-1948   TCLC 16
  See also CA 118; 163
Sumner, Gordon Matthew   CLC 26
  See also Sting
Surtees, Robert Smith 1803-1864   NCLC 14
  See also DLB 21
Susann, Jacqueline 1921-1974   CLC 3
  See also AITN 1; CA 65-68; 53-56; MTCW 1
Su Shih 1036-1101   CMLC 15
Suskind, Patrick
  See Sueskind, Patrick
  See also CA 145
Sutcliff, Rosemary 1920-1992 CLC 26; DAB;
  DAC; DAM MST, POP
  See also AAYA 10; CA 5-8R; 139; CANR 37;
    CLR 1, 37; JRDA; MAICYA; SATA 6, 44,
    78; SATA-Obit 73
Sutro, Alfred 1863-1933   TCLC 6
  See also CA 105; DLB 10
Sutton, Henry
  See Slavitt, David R(ytman)
Svevo, Italo 1861-1928 TCLC 2, 35; SSC 25
  See also Schmitz, Aron Hector
Swados, Elizabeth (A.) 1951-   CLC 12
  See also CA 97-100; CANR 49; INT 97-100
Swados, Harvey 1920-1972   CLC 5
  See also CA 5-8R; 37-40R; CANR 6; DLB 2
Swan, Gladys 1934-   CLC 69
  See also CA 101; CANR 17, 39
Swarthout, Glendon (Fred) 1918-1992 CLC 35
  See also CA 1-4R; 139; CANR 1, 47; SATA 26
Sweet, Sarah C.
  See Jewett, (Theodora) Sarah Orne
Swenson, May 1919-1989 CLC 4, 14, 61, 106;
  DA; DAB; DAC; DAM MST, POET; PC
  14
  See also CA 5-8R; 130; CANR 36, 61; DLB 5;
    MTCW 1; SATA 15
Swift, Augustus
  See Lovecraft, H(oward) P(hillips)
Swift, Graham (Colin) 1949-   CLC 41, 88
  See also CA 117; 122; CANR 46, 71; DLB 194
Swift, Jonathan 1667-1745   LC 1, 42; DA;
  DAB; DAC; DAM MST, NOV, POET; PC
  9; WLC
  See also CDBLB 1660-1789; CLR 53; DLB 39,
    95, 101; SATA 19
Swinburne, Algernon Charles 1837-1909
  TCLC 8, 36; DA; DAB; DAC; DAM MST,
  POET; PC 24; WLC
  See also CA 105; 140; CDBLB 1832-1890;
    DLB 35, 57
Swinfen, Ann   CLC 34
Swinnerton, Frank Arthur 1884-1982 CLC 31
  See also CA 108; DLB 34
Swithen, John
  See King, Stephen (Edwin)
Sylvia
  See Ashton-Warner, Sylvia (Constance)
Symmes, Robert Edward
  See Duncan, Robert (Edward)
Symonds, John Addington 1840-1893 NCLC
  34
  See also DLB 57, 144
Symons, Arthur 1865-1945   TCLC 11
  See also CA 107; DLB 19, 57, 149
Symons, Julian (Gustave) 1912-1994 CLC 2,
  14, 32
  See also CA 49-52; 147; CAAS 3; CANR 3,
    33, 59; DLB 87, 155; DLBY 92; MTCW 1
Synge, (Edmund) J(ohn) M(illington) 1871-
  1909   TCLC 6, 37; DAM DRAM; DC 2
  See also CA 104; 141; CDBLB 1890-1914;

DLB 10, 19
Syruc, J.
  See Milosz, Czeslaw
Szirtes, George 1948-   CLC 46
  See also CA 109; CANR 27, 61
Szymborska, Wislawa 1923-   CLC 99
  See also CA 154; DLBY 96
T. O., Nik
  See Annensky, Innokenty (Fyodorovich)
Tabori, George 1914-   CLC 19
  See also CA 49-52; CANR 4, 69
Tagore, Rabindranath 1861-1941 TCLC 3, 53;
  DAM DRAM, POET; PC 8
  See also CA 104; 120; MTCW 1
Taine, Hippolyte Adolphe 1828-1893 NCLC
  15
Talese, Gay 1932-   CLC 37
  See also AITN 1; CA 1-4R; CANR 9, 58; DLB
    185; INT CANR-9; MTCW 1
Tallent, Elizabeth (Ann) 1954-   CLC 45
  See also CA 117; CANR 72; DLB 130
Tally, Ted 1952-   CLC 42
  See also CA 120; 124; INT 124
Talvik, Heiti 1904-1947   TCLC 87
Tamayo y Baus, Manuel 1829-1898 NCLC 1
Tammsaare, A(nton) H(ansen) 1878-1940
  TCLC 27
  See also CA 164
Tam'si, Tchicaya U
  See Tchicaya, Gerald Felix
Tan, Amy (Ruth) 1952- CLC 59; DAM MULT,
  NOV, POP
  See also AAYA 9; BEST 89:3; CA 136; CANR
    54; DLB 173; SATA 75
Tandem, Felix
  See Spitteler, Carl (Friedrich Georg)
Tanizaki, Jun'ichiro 1886-1965 CLC 8, 14, 28;
  SSC 21
  See also CA 93-96; 25-28R; DLB 180
Tanner, William
  See Amis, Kingsley (William)
Tao Lao
  See Storni, Alfonsina
Tarassoff, Lev
  See Troyat, Henri
Tarbell, Ida M(inerva) 1857-1944   TCLC 40
  See also CA 122; DLB 47
Tarkington, (Newton) Booth 1869-1946 TCLC
  9
  See also CA 110; 143; DLB 9, 102; SATA 17
Tarkovsky, Andrei (Arsenyevich) 1932-1986
  CLC 75
  See also CA 127
Tartt, Donna 1964(?)-   CLC 76
  See also CA 142
Tasso, Torquato 1544-1595   LC 5
Tate, (John Orley) Allen 1899-1979 CLC 2, 4,
  6, 9, 11, 14, 24
  See also CA 5-8R; 85-88; CANR 32; DLB 4,
    45, 63; DLBD 17; MTCW 1
Tate, Ellalice
  See Hibbert, Eleanor Alice Burford
Tate, James (Vincent) 1943-   CLC 2, 6, 25
  See also CA 21-24R; CANR 29, 57; DLB 5,
    169
Tavel, Ronald 1940-   CLC 6
  See also CA 21-24R; CANR 33
Taylor, C(ecil) P(hilip) 1929-1981   CLC 27
  See also CA 25-28R; 105; CANR 47
Taylor, Edward 1642(?)-1729   LC 11; DA;
  DAB; DAC; DAM MST, POET
  See also DLB 24
Taylor, Eleanor Ross 1920-   CLC 5

See also CA 81-84; CANR 70

Taylor, Elizabeth 1912-1975　　**CLC 2, 4, 29**
See also CA 13-16R; CANR 9, 70; DLB 139;
MTCW 1; SATA 13

Taylor, Frederick Winslow 1856-1915 **T C L C 76**

Taylor, Henry (Splawn) 1942-　　**CLC 44**
See also CA 33-36R; CAAS 7; CANR 31; DLB 5

Taylor, Kamala (Purnaiya) 1924-
See Markandaya, Kamala
See also CA 77-80

Taylor, Mildred D.　　**CLC 21**
See also AAYA 10; BW 1; CA 85-88; CANR
25; CLR 9; DLB 52; JRDA; MAICYA; SAAS
5; SATA 15, 70

Taylor, Peter (Hillsman) 1917-1994**CLC 1, 4, 18, 37, 44, 50, 71; SSC 10**
See also CA 13-16R; 147; CANR 9, 50; DLBY
81, 94; INT CANR-9; MTCW 1

Taylor, Robert Lewis 1912-1998　　**CLC 14**
See also CA 1-4R; 170; CANR 3, 64; SATA 10

Tchekhov, Anton
See Chekhov, Anton (Pavlovich)

Tchicaya, Gerald Felix 1931-1988　**CLC 101**
See also CA 129; 125

Tchicaya U Tam'si
See Tchicaya, Gerald Felix

Teasdale, Sara 1884-1933　　**TCLC 4**
See also CA 104; 163; DLB 45; SATA 32

Tegner, Esaias 1782-1846　　**NCLC 2**

Teilhard de Chardin, (Marie Joseph) Pierre
1881-1955　　**TCLC 9**
See also CA 105

Temple, Ann
See Mortimer, Penelope (Ruth)

Tennant, Emma (Christina) 1937-**CLC 13, 52**
See also CA 65-68; CAAS 9; CANR 10, 38,
59; DLB 14

Tenneshaw, S. M.
See Silverberg, Robert

Tennyson, Alfred 1809-1892　　**NCLC 30, 65;
DA; DAB; DAC; DAM MST, POET; PC 6; WLC**
See also CDBLB 1832-1890; DLB 32

Teran, Lisa St. Aubin de　　**CLC 36**
See also St. Aubin de Teran, Lisa

Terence 195(?)B.C.-159B.C. **CMLC 14; DC 7**

Teresa de Jesus, St. 1515-1582　　**LC 18**

Terkel, Louis 1912-
See Terkel, Studs
See also CA 57-60; CANR 18, 45, 67; MTCW 1

Terkel, Studs　　**CLC 38**
See also Terkel, Louis
See also AITN 1

Terry, C. V.
See Slaughter, Frank G(ill)

Terry, Megan 1932-　　**CLC 19**
See also CA 77-80; CABS 3; CANR 43; DLB 7

Tertullian c. 155-c. 245　　**CMLC 29**

Tertz, Abram
See Sinyavsky, Andrei (Donatevich)

Tesich, Steve 1943(?)-1996　　**CLC 40, 69**
See also CA 105; 152; DLBY 83

Tesla, Nikola 1856-1943　　**TCLC 88**

Teternikov, Fyodor Kuzmich 1863-1927
See Sologub, Fyodor
See also CA 104

Tevis, Walter 1928-1984　　**CLC 42**
See also CA 113

Tey, Josephine　　**TCLC 14**
See also Mackintosh, Elizabeth

See also DLB 77

Thackeray, William Makepeace 1811-1863
**NCLC 5, 14, 22, 43; DA; DAB; DAC; DAM
MST, NOV; WLC**
See also CDBLB 1832-1890; DLB 21, 55, 159,
163; SATA 23

Thakura, Ravindranatha
See Tagore, Rabindranath

Tharoor, Shashi 1956-　　**CLC 70**
See also CA 141

Thelwell, Michael Miles 1939-　　**CLC 22**
See also BW 2; CA 101

Theobald, Lewis, Jr.
See Lovecraft, H(oward) P(hillips)

Theodorescu, Ion N. 1880-1967
See Arghezi, Tudor
See also CA 116

Theriault, Yves 1915-1983　　**CLC 79; DAC;
DAM MST**
See also CA 102; DLB 88

Theroux, Alexander (Louis) 1939- **CLC 2, 25**
See also CA 85-88; CANR 20, 63

Theroux, Paul (Edward) 1941- **CLC 5, 8, 11,
15, 28, 46; DAM POP**
See also BEST 89:4; CA 33-36R; CANR 20,
45, 74; DLB 2; MTCW 1; SATA 44

Thesen, Sharon 1946-　　**CLC 56**
See also CA 163

Thevenin, Denis
See Duhamel, Georges

Thibault, Jacques Anatole Francois 1844-1924
See France, Anatole
See also CA 106; 127; DAM NOV; MTCW 1

Thiele, Colin (Milton) 1920-　　**CLC 17**
See also CA 29-32R; CANR 12, 28, 53; CLR
27; MAICYA; SAAS 2; SATA 14, 72

Thomas, Audrey (Callahan) 1935-**CLC 7, 13,
37, 107; SSC 20**
See also AITN 2; CA 21-24R; CAAS 19; CANR
36, 58; DLB 60; MTCW 1

Thomas, D(onald) M(ichael) 1935-　**CLC 13,
22, 31**
See also CA 61-64; CAAS 11; CANR 17, 45,
75; CDBLB 1960 to Present; DLB 40, 207;
INT CANR-17; MTCW 1

Thomas, Dylan (Marlais) 1914-1953**TCLC 1,
8, 45; DA; DAB; DAC; DAM DRAM,
MST, POET; PC 2; SSC 3; WLC**
See also CA 104; 120; CANR 65; CDBLB
1945-1960; DLB 13, 20, 139; MTCW 1;
SATA 60

Thomas, (Philip) Edward 1878-1917　**T C L C
10; DAM POET**
See also CA 106; 153; DLB 19

Thomas, Joyce Carol 1938-　　**CLC 35**
See also AAYA 12; BW 2; CA 113; 116; CANR
48; CLR 19; DLB 33; INT 116; JRDA;
MAICYA; MTCW 1; SAAS 7; SATA 40, 78

Thomas, Lewis 1913-1993　　**CLC 35**
See also CA 85-88; 143; CANR 38, 60; MTCW 1

Thomas, M. Carey 1857-1935　　**TCLC 89**

Thomas, Paul
See Mann, (Paul) Thomas

Thomas, Piri 1928-　　**CLC 17**
See also CA 73-76; HW

Thomas, R(onald) S(tuart) 1913- **CLC 6, 13,
48; DAB; DAM POET**
See also CA 89-92; CAAS 4; CANR 30;
CDBLB 1960 to Present; DLB 27; MTCW 1

Thomas, Ross (Elmore) 1926-1995　**CLC 39**
See also CA 33-36R; 150; CANR 22, 63

Thompson, Francis Clegg

See Mencken, H(enry) L(ouis)

Thompson, Francis Joseph 1859-1907**TCLC 4**
See also CA 104; CDBLB 1890-1914; DLB 19

Thompson, Hunter S(tockton) 1939- **CLC 9,
17, 40, 104; DAM POP**
See also BEST 89:1; CA 17-20R; CANR 23,
46, 74; DLB 185; MTCW 1

Thompson, James Myers
See Thompson, Jim (Myers)

Thompson, Jim (Myers) 1906-1977(?)**CLC 69**
See also CA 140

Thompson, Judith　　**CLC 39**

Thomson, James 1700-1748　　**LC 16, 29, 40;
DAM POET**
See also DLB 95

Thomson, James 1834-1882 **NCLC 18; DAM
POET**
See also DLB 35

Thoreau, Henry David 1817-1862**NCLC 7, 21,
61; DA; DAB; DAC; DAM MST; WLC**
See also CDALB 1640-1865; DLB 1

Thornton, Hall
See Silverberg, Robert

Thucydides c. 455B.C.-399B.C.　　**CMLC 17**
See also DLB 176

Thurber, James (Grover) 1894-1961　**CLC 5,
11, 25; DA; DAB; DAC; DAM DRAM,
MST, NOV; SSC 1**
See also CA 73-76; CANR 17, 39; CDALB
1929-1941; DLB 4, 11, 22, 102; MAICYA;
MTCW 1; SATA 13

Thurman, Wallace (Henry) 1902-1934**T C L C
6; BLC 3; DAM MULT**
See also BW 1; CA 104; 124; DLB 51

Ticheburn, Cheviot
See Ainsworth, William Harrison

Tieck, (Johann) Ludwig 1773-1853 **NCLC 5,
46; SSC 31**
See also DLB 90

Tiger, Derry
See Ellison, Harlan (Jay)

Tilghman, Christopher 1948(?)-　　**CLC 65**
See also CA 159

Tillinghast, Richard (Williford) 1940-**CLC 29**
See also CA 29-32R; CAAS 23; CANR 26, 51

Timrod, Henry 1828-1867　　**NCLC 25**
See also DLB 3

Tindall, Gillian (Elizabeth) 1938-　　**CLC 7**
See also CA 21-24R; CANR 11, 65

Tiptree, James, Jr.　　**CLC 48, 50**
See also Sheldon, Alice Hastings Bradley
See also DLB 8

Titmarsh, Michael Angelo
See Thackeray, William Makepeace

**Tocqueville, Alexis (Charles Henri Maurice
Clerel, Comte) de** 1805-1859**NCLC 7, 63**

Tolkien, J(ohn) R(onald) R(euel) 1892-1973
**CLC 1, 2, 3, 8, 12, 38; DA; DAB; DAC;
DAM MST, NOV, POP; WLC**
See also AAYA 10; AITN 1; CA 17-18; 45-48;
CANR 36; CAP 2; CDBLB 1914-1945; DLB
15, 160; JRDA; MAICYA; MTCW 1; SATA
2, 32, 100; SATA-Obit 24

Toller, Ernst 1893-1939　　**TCLC 10**
See also CA 107; DLB 124

Tolson, M. B.
See Tolson, Melvin B(eaunorus)

Tolson, Melvin B(eaunorus) 1898(?)-1966
CLC 36, 105; BLC 3; DAM MULT, POET
See also BW 1; CA 124; 89-92; DLB 48, 76

Tolstoi, Aleksei Nikolaevich
See Tolstoy, Alexey Nikolaevich

Tolstoy, Alexey Nikolaevich 1882-1945**T C L C**

18
See also CA 107; 158
Tolstoy, Count Leo
See Tolstoy, Leo (Nikolaevich)
Tolstoy, Leo (Nikolaevich) 1828-1910TCLC 4,
11, 17, 28, 44, 79; DA; DAB; DAC; DAM
MST, NOV; SSC 9, 30; WLC
See also CA 104; 123; SATA 26
Tomasi di Lampedusa, Giuseppe 1896-1957
See Lampedusa, Giuseppe (Tomasi) di
See also CA 111
Tomlin, Lily   CLC 17
See also Tomlin, Mary Jean
Tomlin, Mary Jean 1939(?)-
See Tomlin, Lily
See also CA 117
Tomlinson, (Alfred) Charles 1927-CLC 2, 4, 6,
13, 45; DAM POET; PC 17
See also CA 5-8R; CANR 33; DLB 40
Tomlinson, H(enry) M(ajor) 1873-1958TCLC
71
See also CA 118; 161; DLB 36, 100, 195
Tonson, Jacob
See Bennett, (Enoch) Arnold
Toole, John Kennedy 1937-1969   CLC 19, 64
See also CA 104; DLBY 81
Toomer, Jean 1894-1967CLC 1, 4, 13, 22; BLC
3; DAM MULT; PC 7; SSC 1; WLCS
See also BW 1; CA 85-88; CDALB 1917-1929;
DLB 45, 51; MTCW 1
Torley, Luke
See Blish, James (Benjamin)
Tornimparte, Alessandra
See Ginzburg, Natalia
Torre, Raoul della
See Mencken, H(enry) L(ouis)
Torrey, E(dwin) Fuller 1937-   CLC 34
See also CA 119; CANR 71
Torsvan, Ben Traven
See Traven, B.
Torsvan, Benno Traven
See Traven, B.
Torsvan, Berick Traven
See Traven, B.
Torsvan, Berwick Traven
See Traven, B.
Torsvan, Bruno Traven
See Traven, B.
Torsvan, Traven
See Traven, B.
Tournier, Michel (Edouard) 1924-CLC 6, 23,
36, 95
See also CA 49-52; CANR 3, 36, 74; DLB 83;
MTCW 1; SATA 23
Tournimparte, Alessandra
See Ginzburg, Natalia
Towers, Ivar
See Kornbluth, C(yril) M.
Towne, Robert (Burton) 1936(?)-   CLC 87
See also CA 108; DLB 44
Townsend, Sue   CLC 61
See also Townsend, Susan Elaine
See also SATA 55, 93; SATA-Brief 48
Townsend, Susan Elaine 1946-
See Townsend, Sue
See also CA 119; 127; CANR 65; DAB; DAC;
DAM MST
Townshend, Peter (Dennis Blandford) 1945-
CLC 17, 42
See also CA 107
Tozzi, Federigo 1883-1920   TCLC 31
See also CA 160
Traill, Catharine Parr 1802-1899   NCLC 31

See also DLB 99
Trakl, Georg 1887-1914   TCLC 5; PC 20
See also CA 104; 165
Transtroemer, Tomas (Goesta) 1931-CLC 52,
65; DAM POET
See also CA 117; 129; CAAS 17
Transtromer, Tomas Gosta
See Transtroemer, Tomas (Goesta)
Traven, B. (?)-1969   CLC 8, 11
See also CA 19-20; 25-28R; CAP 2; DLB 9,
56; MTCW 1
Treitel, Jonathan 1959-   CLC 70
Tremain, Rose 1943-   CLC 42
See also CA 97-100; CANR 44; DLB 14
Tremblay, Michel 1942- CLC 29, 102; DAC;
DAM MST
See also CA 116; 128; DLB 60; MTCW 1
Trevanian   CLC 29
See also Whitaker, Rod(ney)
Trevor, Glen
See Hilton, James
Trevor, William 1928-CLC 7, 9, 14, 25, 71, 116;
SSC 21
See also Cox, William Trevor
See also DLB 14, 139
Trifonov, Yuri (Valentinovich) 1925-1981
CLC 45
See also CA 126; 103; MTCW 1
Trilling, Lionel 1905-1975   CLC 9, 11, 24
See also CA 9-12R; 61-64; CANR 10; DLB 28,
63; INT CANR-10; MTCW 1
Trimball, W. H.
See Mencken, H(enry) L(ouis)
Tristan
See Gomez de la Serna, Ramon
Tristram
See Housman, A(lfred) E(dward)
Trogdon, William (Lewis) 1939-
See Heat-Moon, William Least
See also CA 115; 119; CANR 47; INT 119
Trollope, Anthony 1815-1882NCLC 6, 33; DA;
DAB; DAC; DAM MST, NOV; SSC 28;
WLC
See also CDBLB 1832-1890; DLB 21, 57, 159;
SATA 22
Trollope, Frances 1779-1863   NCLC 30
See also DLB 21, 166
Trotsky, Leon 1879-1940   TCLC 22
See also CA 118; 167
Trotter (Cockburn), Catharine 1679-1749L C
8
See also DLB 84
Trout, Kilgore
See Farmer, Philip Jose
Trow, George W. S. 1943-   CLC 52
See also CA 126
Troyat, Henri 1911-   CLC 23
See also CA 45-48; CANR 2, 33, 67; MTCW 1
Trudeau, G(arretson) B(eekman) 1948-
See Trudeau, Garry B.
See also CA 81-84; CANR 31; SATA 35
Trudeau, Garry B.   CLC 12
See also Trudeau, G(arretson) B(eekman)
See also AAYA 10; AITN 2
Truffaut, Francois 1932-1984   CLC 20, 101
See also CA 81-84; 113; CANR 34
Trumbo, Dalton 1905-1976   CLC 19
See also CA 21-24R; 69-72; CANR 10; DLB
26
Trumbull, John 1750-1831   NCLC 30
See also DLB 31
Trundlett, Helen B.
See Eliot, T(homas) S(tearns)

Tryon, Thomas 1926-1991   CLC 3, 11; DAM
POP
See also AITN 1; CA 29-32R; 135; CANR 32;
MTCW 1
Tryon, Tom
See Tryon, Thomas
Ts'ao Hsueh-ch'in 1715(?)-1763   LC 1
Tsushima, Shuji 1909-1948
See Dazai Osamu
See also CA 107
Tsvetaeva (Efron), Marina (Ivanovna) 1892-
1941   TCLC 7, 35; PC 14
See also CA 104; 128; CANR 73; MTCW 1
Tuck, Lily 1938-   CLC 70
See also CA 139
Tu Fu 712-770   PC 9
See also DAM MULT
Tunis, John R(oberts) 1889-1975   CLC 12
See also CA 61-64; CANR 62; DLB 22, 171;
JRDA; MAICYA; SATA 37; SATA-Brief 30
Tuohy, Frank   CLC 37
See also Tuohy, John Francis
See also DLB 14, 139
Tuohy, John Francis 1925-
See Tuohy, Frank
See also CA 5-8R; CANR 3, 47
Turco, Lewis (Putnam) 1934-   CLC 11, 63
See also CA 13-16R; CAAS 22; CANR 24, 51;
DLBY 84
Turgenev, Ivan 1818-1883   NCLC 21; DA;
DAB; DAC; DAM MST, NOV; DC 7; SSC
7; WLC
Turgot, Anne-Robert-Jacques 1727-1781 L C
26
Turner, Frederick 1943-   CLC 48
See also CA 73-76; CAAS 10; CANR 12, 30,
56; DLB 40
Tutu, Desmond M(pilo) 1931-CLC 80; BLC 3;
DAM MULT
See also BW 1; CA 125; CANR 67
Tutuola, Amos 1920-1997CLC 5, 14, 29; BLC
3; DAM MULT
See also BW 2; CA 9-12R; 159; CANR 27, 66;
DLB 125; MTCW 1
Twain, MarkTCLC 6, 12, 19, 36, 48, 59; SSC 6,
26; WLC
See also Clemens, Samuel Langhorne
See also AAYA 20; DLB 11, 12, 23, 64, 74
Tyler, Anne 1941- CLC 7, 11, 18, 28, 44, 59,
103; DAM NOV, POP
See also AAYA 18; BEST 89:1; CA 9-12R;
CANR 11, 33, 53; DLB 6, 143; DLBY 82;
MTCW 1; SATA 7, 90
Tyler, Royall 1757-1826   NCLC 3
See also DLB 37
Tynan, Katharine 1861-1931   TCLC 3
See also CA 104; 167; DLB 153
Tyutchev, Fyodor 1803-1873   NCLC 34
Tzara, Tristan 1896-1963   CLC 47; DAM
POET
See also CA 153; 89-92
Uhry, Alfred 1936-   CLC 55; DAM DRAM,
POP
See also CA 127; 133; INT 133
Ulf, Haerved
See Strindberg, (Johan) August
Ulf, Harved
See Strindberg, (Johan) August
Ulibarri, Sabine R(eyes) 1919-CLC 83; DAM
MULT
See also CA 131; DLB 82; HW
Unamuno (y Jugo), Miguel de 1864-1936
TCLC 2, 9; DAM MULT, NOV; HLC; SSC

11
See also CA 104; 131; DLB 108; HW; MTCW 1

Undercliffe, Errol
See Campbell, (John) Ramsey
Underwood, Miles
See Glassco, John
Undset, Sigrid 1882-1949TCLC 3; DA; DAB; DAC; DAM MST, NOV; WLC
See also CA 104; 129; MTCW 1
Ungaretti, Giuseppe 1888-1970CLC 7, 11, 15
See also CA 19-20; 25-28R; CAP 2; DLB 114
Unger, Douglas 1952-   CLC 34
See also CA 130
Unsworth, Barry (Forster) 1930-   CLC 76
See also CA 25-28R; CANR 30, 54; DLB 194
Updike, John (Hoyer) 1932-CLC 1, 2, 3, 5, 7, 9, 13, 15, 23, 34, 43, 70; DA; DAB; DAC; DAM MST, NOV, POET, POP; SSC 13, 27; WLC
See also CA 1-4R; CABS 1; CANR 4, 33, 51; CDALB 1968-1988; DLB 2, 5, 143; DLBD 3; DLBY 80, 82, 97; MTCW 1
Upshaw, Margaret Mitchell
See Mitchell, Margaret (Munnerlyn)
Upton, Mark
See Sanders, Lawrence
Upward, Allen 1863-1926   TCLC 85
See also CA 117; DLB 36
Urdang, Constance (Henriette) 1922-CLC 47
See also CA 21-24R; CANR 9, 24
Uriel, Henry
See Faust, Frederick (Schiller)
Uris, Leon (Marcus) 1924- CLC 7, 32; DAM NOV, POP
See also AITN 1, 2; BEST 89:2; CA 1-4R; CANR 1, 40, 65; MTCW 1; SATA 49
Urmuz
See Codrescu, Andrei
Urquhart, Jane 1949-   CLC 90; DAC
See also CA 113; CANR 32, 68
Ustinov, Peter (Alexander) 1921-   CLC 1
See also AITN 1; CA 13-16R; CANR 25, 51; DLB 13
U Tam'si, Gerald Felix Tchicaya
See Tchicaya, Gerald Felix
U Tam'si, Tchicaya
See Tchicaya, Gerald Felix
Vachss, Andrew (Henry) 1942-   CLC 106
See also CA 118; CANR 44
Vachss, Andrew H.
See Vachss, Andrew (Henry)
Vaculik, Ludvik 1926-   CLC 7
See also CA 53-56; CANR 72
Vaihinger, Hans 1852-1933   TCLC 71
See also CA 116; 166
Valdez, Luis (Miguel) 1940- CLC 84; DAM MULT; DC 10; HLC
See also CA 101; CANR 32; DLB 122; HW
Valenzuela, Luisa 1938- CLC 31, 104; DAM MULT; SSC 14
See also CA 101; CANR 32, 65; DLB 113; HW
Valera y Alcala-Galiano, Juan 1824-1905
TCLC 10
See also CA 106
Valery, (Ambroise) Paul (Toussaint Jules) 1871-1945   TCLC 4, 15; DAM POET; PC 9
See also CA 104; 122; MTCW 1
Valle-Inclan, Ramon (Maria) del 1866-1936
TCLC 5; DAM MULT; HLC
See also CA 106; 153; DLB 134
Vallejo, Antonio Buero
See Buero Vallejo, Antonio

Vallejo, Cesar (Abraham) 1892-1938TCLC 3, 56; DAM MULT; HLC
See also CA 105; 153; HW
Valles, Jules 1832-1885   NCLC 71
See also DLB 123
Vallette, Marguerite Eymery
See Rachilde
Valle Y Pena, Ramon del
See Valle-Inclan, Ramon (Maria) del
Van Ash, Cay 1918-   CLC 34
Vanbrugh, Sir John 1664-1726 LC 21; DAM DRAM
See also DLB 80
Van Campen, Karl
See Campbell, John W(ood, Jr.)
Vance, Gerald
See Silverberg, Robert
Vance, Jack   CLC 35
See also Kuttner, Henry; Vance, John Holbrook
See also DLB 8
Vance, John Holbrook 1916-
See Queen, Ellery; Vance, Jack
See also CA 29-32R; CANR 17, 65; MTCW 1
Van Den Bogarde, Derek Jules Gaspard Ulric Niven 1921-
See Bogarde, Dirk
See also CA 77-80
Vandenburgh, Jane   CLC 59
See also CA 168
Vanderhaeghe, Guy 1951-   CLC 41
See also CA 113; CANR 72
van der Post, Laurens (Jan) 1906-1996CLC 5
See also CA 5-8R; 155; CANR 35; DLB 204
van de Wetering, Janwillem 1931-   CLC 47
See also CA 49-52; CANR 4, 62
Van Dine, S. S.   TCLC 23
See also Wright, Willard Huntington
Van Doren, Carl (Clinton) 1885-1950 TCLC 18
See also CA 111; 168
Van Doren, Mark 1894-1972   CLC 6, 10
See also CA 1-4R; 37-40R; CANR 3; DLB 45; MTCW 1
Van Druten, John (William) 1901-1957TCLC 2
See also CA 104; 161; DLB 10
Van Duyn, Mona (Jane) 1921- CLC 3, 7, 63, 116; DAM POET
See also CA 9-12R; CANR 7, 38, 60; DLB 5
Van Dyne, Edith
See Baum, L(yman) Frank
van Itallie, Jean-Claude 1936-   CLC 3
See also CA 45-48; CAAS 2; CANR 1, 48; DLB 7
van Ostaijen, Paul 1896-1928   TCLC 33
See also CA 163
Van Peebles, Melvin 1932- CLC 2, 20; DAM MULT
See also BW 2; CA 85-88; CANR 27, 67
Vansittart, Peter 1920-   CLC 42
See also CA 1-4R; CANR 3, 49
Van Vechten, Carl 1880-1964   CLC 33
See also CA 89-92; DLB 4, 9, 51
Van Vogt, A(lfred) E(lton) 1912-   CLC 1
See also CA 21-24R; CANR 28; DLB 8; SATA 14
Varda, Agnes 1928-   CLC 16
See also CA 116; 122
Vargas Llosa, (Jorge) Mario (Pedro) 1936-
CLC 3, 6, 9, 10, 15, 31, 42, 85; DA; DAB; DAC; DAM MST, MULT, NOV; HLC
See also CA 73-76; CANR 18, 32, 42, 67; DLB 145; HW; MTCW 1

Vasiliu, Gheorghe 1881-1957
See Bacovia, George
See also CA 123
Vassa, Gustavus
See Equiano, Olaudah
Vassilikos, Vassilis 1933-   CLC 4, 8
See also CA 81-84; CANR 75
Vaughan, Henry 1621-1695   LC 27
See also DLB 131
Vaughn, Stephanie   CLC 62
Vazov, Ivan (Minchov) 1850-1921 TCLC 25
See also CA 121; 167; DLB 147
Veblen, Thorstein B(unde) 1857-1929 TCLC 31
See also CA 115; 165
Vega, Lope de 1562-1635   LC 23
Venison, Alfred
See Pound, Ezra (Weston Loomis)
Verdi, Marie de
See Mencken, H(enry) L(ouis)
Verdu, Matilde
See Cela, Camilo Jose
Verga, Giovanni (Carmelo) 1840-1922TCLC 3; SSC 21
See also CA 104; 123
Vergil 70B.C.-19B.C.   CMLC 9; DA; DAB; DAC; DAM MST, POET; PC 12; WLCS
Verhaeren, Emile (Adolphe Gustave) 1855-1916
TCLC 12
See also CA 109
Verlaine, Paul (Marie) 1844-1896NCLC 2, 51; DAM POET; PC 2
Verne, Jules (Gabriel) 1828-1905TCLC 6, 52
See also AAYA 16; CA 110; 131; DLB 123; JRDA; MAICYA; SATA 21
Very, Jones 1813-1880   NCLC 9
See also DLB 1
Vesaas, Tarjei 1897-1970   CLC 48
See also CA 29-32R
Vialis, Gaston
See Simenon, Georges (Jacques Christian)
Vian, Boris 1920-1959   TCLC 9
See also CA 106; 164; DLB 72
Viaud, (Louis Marie) Julien 1850-1923
See Loti, Pierre
See also CA 107
Vicar, Henry
See Felsen, Henry Gregor
Vicker, Angus
See Felsen, Henry Gregor
Vidal, Gore 1925-CLC 2, 4, 6, 8, 10, 22, 33, 72; DAM NOV, POP
See also AITN 1; BEST 90:2; CA 5-8R; CANR 13, 45, 65; DLB 6, 152; INT CANR-13; MTCW 1
Viereck, Peter (Robert Edwin) 1916- CLC 4
See also CA 1-4R; CANR 1, 47; DLB 5
Vigny, Alfred (Victor) de 1797-1863NCLC 7; DAM POET
See also DLB 119, 192
Vilakazi, Benedict Wallet 1906-1947TCLC 37
See also CA 168
Villa, Jose Garcia 1904-1997   PC 22
See also CA 25-28R; CANR 12
Villaurrutia, Xavier 1903-1950   TCLC 80
See also HW
Villiers de l'Isle Adam, Jean Marie Mathias Philippe Auguste, Comte de 1838-1889
NCLC 3; SSC 14
See also DLB 123
Villon, Francois 1431-1463(?)   PC 13
See also DLB 208
Vinci, Leonardo da 1452-1519   LC 12

Vine, Barbara **CLC 50**
See also Rendell, Ruth (Barbara)
See also BEST 90:4
Vinge, Joan (Carol) D(ennison) 1948-**CLC 30;**
SSC 24
See also CA 93-96; CANR 72; SATA 36
Violis, G.
See Simenon, Georges (Jacques Christian)
Virgil
See Vergil
Visconti, Luchino 1906-1976 **CLC 16**
See also CA 81-84; 65-68; CANR 39
Vittorini, Elio 1908-1966 **CLC 6, 9, 14**
See also CA 133; 25-28R
Vivekananda, Swami 1863-1902 **TCLC 88**
Vizenor, Gerald Robert 1934-**CLC 103; DAM**
MULT
See also CA 13-16R; CAAS 22; CANR 5, 21,
44, 67; DLB 175; NNAL
Vizinczey, Stephen 1933- **CLC 40**
See also CA 128; INT 128
Vliet, R(ussell) G(ordon) 1929-1984 **CLC 22**
See also CA 37-40R; 112; CANR 18
Vogau, Boris Andreyevich 1894-1937(?)
See Pilnyak, Boris
See also CA 123
Vogel, Paula A(nne) 1951- **CLC 76**
See also CA 108
Voigt, Cynthia 1942- **CLC 30**
See also AAYA 3; CA 106; CANR 18, 37, 40;
CLR 13, 48; INT CANR-18; JRDA;
MAICYA; SATA 48, 79; SATA-Brief 33
Voigt, Ellen Bryant 1943- **CLC 54**
See also CA 69-72; CANR 11, 29, 55; DLB 120
Voinovich, Vladimir (Nikolaevich) 1932-**C L C**
10, 49
See also CA 81-84; CAAS 12; CANR 33, 67;
MTCW 1
Vollmann, William T. 1959- **CLC 89; DAM**
NOV, POP
See also CA 134; CANR 67
Voloshinov, V. N.
See Bakhtin, Mikhail Mikhailovich
Voltaire 1694-1778 **LC 14; DA; DAB; DAC;**
DAM DRAM, MST; SSC 12; WLC
von Aschendrof, BaronIgnatz
See Ford, Ford Madox
von Daeniken, Erich 1935- **CLC 30**
See also AITN 1; CA 37-40R; CANR 17, 44
von Daniken, Erich
See von Daeniken, Erich
von Heidenstam, (Carl Gustaf) Verner
See Heidenstam, (Carl Gustaf) Verner von
von Heyse, Paul (Johann Ludwig)
See Heyse, Paul (Johann Ludwig von)
von Hofmannsthal, Hugo
See Hofmannsthal, Hugo von
von Horvath, Odon
See Horvath, Oedoen von
von Horvath, Oedoen
See Horvath, Oedoen von
von Liliencron, (Friedrich Adolf Axel) Detlev
See Liliencron, (Friedrich Adolf Axel) Detlev
von
Vonnegut, Kurt, Jr. 1922-**CLC 1, 2, 3, 4, 5, 8,**
12, 22, 40, 60, 111; DA; DAB; DAC; DAM
MST, NOV, POP; SSC 8; WLC
See also AAYA 6; AITN 1; BEST 90:4; CA 1-
4R; CANR 1, 25, 49, 75; CDALB 1968-
1988; DLB 2, 8, 152; DLBD 3; DLBY 80;
MTCW 1
Von Rachen, Kurt
See Hubbard, L(afayette) Ron(ald)

von Rezzori (d'Arezzo), Gregor
See Rezzori (d'Arezzo), Gregor voh
von Sternberg, Josef
See Sternberg, Josef von
Vorster, Gordon 1924- **CLC 34**
See also CA 133
Vosce, Trudie
See Ozick, Cynthia
Voznesensky, Andrei (Andreievich) 1933-
CLC 1, 15, 57; DAM POET
See also CA 89-92; CANR 37; MTCW 1
Waddington, Miriam 1917- **CLC 28**
See also CA 21-24R; CANR 12, 30; DLB 68
Wagman, Fredrica 1937- **CLC 7**
See also CA 97-100; INT 97-100
Wagner, Linda W.
See Wagner-Martin, Linda (C.)
Wagner, Linda Welshimer
See Wagner-Martin, Linda (C.)
Wagner, Richard 1813-1883 **NCLC 9**
See also DLB 129
Wagner-Martin, Linda (C.) 1936- **CLC 50**
See also CA 159
Wagoner, David (Russell) 1926- **CLC 3, 5, 15**
See also CA 1-4R; CAAS 3; CANR 2, 71; DLB
5; SATA 14
Wah, Fred(erick James) 1939- **CLC 44**
See also CA 107; 141; DLB 60
Wahloo, Per 1926-1975 **CLC 7**
See also CA 61-64; CANR 73
Wahloo, Peter
See Wahloo, Per
Wain, John (Barrington) 1925-1994 **CLC 2,**
11, 15, 46
See also CA 5-8R; 145; CAAS 4; CANR 23,
54; CDBLB 1960 to Present; DLB 15, 27,
139, 155; MTCW 1
Wajda, Andrzej 1926- **CLC 16**
See also CA 102
Wakefield, Dan 1932- **CLC 7**
See also CA 21-24R; CAAS 7
Wakoski, Diane 1937- **CLC 2, 4, 7, 9, 11, 40;**
DAM POET; PC 15
See also CA 13-16R; CAAS 1; CANR 9, 60;
DLB 5; INT CANR-9
Wakoski-Sherbell, Diane
See Wakoski, Diane
Walcott, Derek (Alton) 1930-**CLC 2, 4, 9, 14,**
25, 42, 67, 76; BLC 3; DAB; DAC; DAM
MST, MULT, POET; DC 7
See also BW 2; CA 89-92; CANR 26, 47, 75;
DLB 117; DLBY 81; MTCW 1
Waldman, Anne (Lesley) 1945- **CLC 7**
See also CA 37-40R; CAAS 17; CANR 34, 69;
DLB 16
Waldo, E. Hunter
See Sturgeon, Theodore (Hamilton)
Waldo, Edward Hamilton
See Sturgeon, Theodore (Hamilton)
Walker, Alice (Malsenior) 1944- **CLC 5, 6, 9,**
19, 27, 46, 58, 103; BLC 3; DA; DAB;
DAC; DAM MST, MULT, NOV, POET,
POP; SSC 5; WLCS
See also AAYA 3; BEST 89:4; BW 2; CA 37-
40R; CANR 9, 27, 49, 66; CDALB 1968-
1988; DLB 6, 33, 143; INT CANR-27;
MTCW 1; SATA 31
Walker, David Harry 1911-1992 **CLC 14**
See also CA 1-4R; 137; CANR 1; SATA 8;
SATA-Obit 71
Walker, Edward Joseph 1934-
See Walker, Ted
See also CA 21-24R; CANR 12, 28, 53

Walker, George F. 1947- **CLC 44, 61; DAB;**
DAC; DAM MST
See also CA 103; CANR 21, 43, 59; DLB 60
Walker, Joseph A. 1935- **CLC 19; DAM**
DRAM, MST
See also BW 1; CA 89-92; CANR 26; DLB 38
Walker, Margaret (Abigail) 1915- **CLC 1, 6;**
BLC; DAM MULT; PC 20
See also BW 2; CA 73-76; CANR 26, 54; DLB
76, 152; MTCW 1
Walker, Ted **CLC 13**
See also Walker, Edward Joseph
See also DLB 40
Wallace, David Foster 1962- **CLC 50, 114**
See also CA 132; CANR 59
Wallace, Dexter
See Masters, Edgar Lee
Wallace, (Richard Horatio) Edgar 1875-1932
TCLC 57
See also CA 115; DLB 70
Wallace, Irving 1916-1990 **CLC 7, 13; DAM**
NOV, POP
See also AITN 1; CA 1-4R; 132; CAAS 1;
CANR 1, 27; INT CANR-27; MTCW 1
Wallant, Edward Lewis 1926-1962**CLC 5, 10**
See also CA 1-4R; CANR 22; DLB 2, 28, 143;
MTCW 1
Walley, Byron
See Card, Orson Scott
Walpole, Horace 1717-1797 **LC 2**
See also DLB 39, 104
Walpole, Hugh (Seymour) 1884-1941**TCLC 5**
See also CA 104; 165; DLB 34
Walser, Martin 1927- **CLC 27**
See also CA 57-60; CANR 8, 46; DLB 75, 124
Walser, Robert 1878-1956 **TCLC 18; SSC 20**
See also CA 118; 165; DLB 66
Walsh, Jill Paton **CLC 35**
See also Paton Walsh, Gillian
See also AAYA 11; CLR 2; DLB 161; SAAS 3
Walter, Villiam Christian
See Andersen, Hans Christian
Wambaugh, Joseph (Aloysius, Jr.) 1937-**C L C**
3, 18; DAM NOV, POP
See also AITN 1; BEST 89:3; CA 33-36R;
CANR 42, 65; DLB 6; DLBY 83; MTCW 1
Wang Wei 699(?)-761(?) **PC 18**
Ward, Arthur Henry Sarsfield 1883-1959
See Rohmer, Sax
See also CA 108
Ward, Douglas Turner 1930- **CLC 19**
See also BW 1; CA 81-84; CANR 27; DLB 7,
38
Ward, Mary Augusta
See Ward, Mrs. Humphry
Ward, Mrs. Humphry 1851-1920 **TCLC 55**
See also DLB 18
Ward, Peter
See Faust, Frederick (Schiller)
Warhol, Andy 1928(?)-1987 **CLC 20**
See also AAYA 12; BEST 89:4; CA 89-92; 121;
CANR 34
Warner, Francis (Robert le Plastrier) 1937-
CLC 14
See also CA 53-56; CANR 11
Warner, Marina 1946- **CLC 59**
See also CA 65-68; CANR 21, 55; DLB 194
Warner, Rex (Ernest) 1905-1986 **CLC 45**
See also CA 89-92; 119; DLB 15
Warner, Susan (Bogert) 1819-1885 **NCLC 31**
See also DLB 3, 42
Warner, Sylvia (Constance) Ashton
See Ashton-Warner, Sylvia (Constance)

Warner, Sylvia Townsend 1893-1978 CLC 7,
19; SSC 23
See also CA 61-64; 77-80; CANR 16, 60; DLB
34, 139; MTCW 1
Warren, Mercy Otis 1728-1814 NCLC 13
See also DLB 31, 200
Warren, Robert Penn 1905-1989 CLC 1, 4, 6,
8, 10, 13, 18, 39, 53, 59; DA; DAB; DAC;
DAM MST, NOV, POET; SSC 4; WLC
See also AITN 1; CA 13-16R; 129; CANR 10,
47; CDALB 1968-1988; DLB 2, 48, 152;
DLBY 80, 89; INT CANR-10; MTCW 1;
SATA 46; SATA-Obit 63
Warshofsky, Isaac
See Singer, Isaac Bashevis
Warton, Thomas 1728-1790 LC 15; DAM
POET
See also DLB 104, 109
Waruk, Kona
See Harris, (Theodore) Wilson
Warung, Price 1855-1911 TCLC 45
Warwick, Jarvis
See Garner, Hugh
Washington, Alex
See Harris, Mark
Washington, Booker T(aliaferro) 1856-1915
TCLC 10; BLC 3; DAM MULT
See also BW 1; CA 114; 125; SATA 28
Washington, George 1732-1799 LC 25
See also DLB 31
Wassermann, (Karl) Jakob 1873-1934 T C L C
6
See also CA 104; DLB 66
Wasserstein, Wendy 1950- CLC 32, 59, 90;
DAM DRAM; DC 4
See also CA 121; 129; CABS 3; CANR 53; INT
129; SATA 94, 75
Waterhouse, Keith (Spencer) 1929- CLC 47
See also CA 5-8R; CANR 38, 67; DLB 13, 15;
MTCW 1
Waters, Frank (Joseph) 1902-1995 CLC 88
See also CA 5-8R; 149; CAAS 13; CANR 3,
18, 63; DLBY 86
Waters, Roger 1944- CLC 35
Watkins, Frances Ellen
See Harper, Frances Ellen Watkins
Watkins, Gerrold
See Malzberg, Barry N(athaniel)
Watkins, Gloria 1955(?)-
See hooks, bell
See also BW 2; CA 143
Watkins, Paul 1964- CLC 55
See also CA 132; CANR 62
Watkins, Vernon Phillips 1906-1967 CLC 43
See also CA 9-10; 25-28R; CAP 1; DLB 20
Watson, Irving S.
See Mencken, H(enry) L(ouis)
Watson, John H.
See Farmer, Philip Jose
Watson, Richard F.
See Silverberg, Robert
Waugh, Auberon (Alexander) 1939- CLC 7
See also CA 45-48; CANR 6, 22; DLB 14, 194
Waugh, Evelyn (Arthur St. John) 1903-1966
CLC 1, 3, 8, 13, 19, 27, 44, 107; DA; DAB;
DAC; DAM MST, NOV, POP; WLC
See also CA 85-88; 25-28R; CANR 22; CDBLB
1914-1945; DLB 15, 162, 195; MTCW 1
Waugh, Harriet 1944- CLC 6
See also CA 85-88; CANR 22
Ways, C. R.
See Blount, Roy (Alton), Jr.
Waystaff, Simon

See Swift, Jonathan
Webb, (Martha) Beatrice (Potter) 1858-1943
TCLC 22
See also Potter, (Helen) Beatrix
See also CA 117; DLB 190
Webb, Charles (Richard) 1939- CLC 7
See also CA 25-28R
Webb, James H(enry), Jr. 1946- CLC 22
See also CA 81-84
Webb, Mary (Gladys Meredith) 1881-1927
TCLC 24
See also CA 123; DLB 34
Webb, Mrs. Sidney
See Webb, (Martha) Beatrice (Potter)
Webb, Phyllis 1927- CLC 18
See also CA 104; CANR 23; DLB 53
Webb, Sidney (James) 1859-1947 TCLC 22
See also CA 117; 163; DLB 190
Webber, Andrew Lloyd CLC 21
See also Lloyd Webber, Andrew
Weber, Lenora Mattingly 1895-1971 CLC 12
See also CA 19-20; 29-32R; CAP 1; SATA 2;
SATA-Obit 26
Weber, Max 1864-1920 TCLC 69
See also CA 109
Webster, John 1579(?)-1634(?) LC 33; DA;
DAB; DAC; DAM DRAM, MST; DC 2;
WLC
See also CDBLB Before 1660; DLB 58
Webster, Noah 1758-1843 NCLC 30
Wedekind, (Benjamin) Frank(lin) 1864-1918
TCLC 7; DAM DRAM
See also CA 104; 153; DLB 118
Weidman, Jerome 1913-1998 CLC 7
See also AITN 2; CA 1-4R; 171; CANR 1; DLB
28
Weil, Simone (Adolphine) 1909-1943 TCLC 23
See also CA 117; 159
Weininger, Otto 1880-1903 TCLC 84
Weinstein, Nathan
See West, Nathanael
Weinstein, Nathan von Wallenstein
See West, Nathanael
Weir, Peter (Lindsay) 1944- CLC 20
See also CA 113; 123
Weiss, Peter (Ulrich) 1916-1982 CLC 3, 15, 51;
DAM DRAM
See also CA 45-48; 106; CANR 3; DLB 69, 124
Weiss, Theodore (Russell) 1916- CLC 3, 8, 14
See also CA 9-12R; CAAS 2; CANR 46; DLB
5
Welch, (Maurice) Denton 1915-1948 TCLC 22
See also CA 121; 148
Welch, James 1940- CLC 6, 14, 52; DAM
MULT, POP
See also CA 85-88; CANR 42, 66; DLB 175;
NNAL
Weldon, Fay 1931- CLC 6, 9, 11, 19, 36, 59;
DAM POP
See also CA 21-24R; CANR 16, 46, 63; CDBLB
1960 to Present; DLB 14, 194; INT CANR-
16; MTCW 1
Wellek, Rene 1903-1995 CLC 28
See also CA 5-8R; 150; CAAS 7; CANR 8; DLB
63; INT CANR-8
Weller, Michael 1942- CLC 10, 53
See also CA 85-88
Weller, Paul 1958- CLC 26
Wellershoff, Dieter 1925- CLC 46
See also CA 89-92; CANR 16, 37
Welles, (George) Orson 1915-1985 CLC 20, 80
See also CA 93-96; 117
Wellman, John McDowell 1945-

See Wellman, Mac
See also CA 166
Wellman, Mac 1945- CLC 65
See also Wellman, John McDowell; Wellman,
John McDowell
Wellman, Manly Wade 1903-1986 CLC 49
See also CA 1-4R; 118; CANR 6, 16, 44; SATA
6; SATA-Obit 47
Wells, Carolyn 1869(?)-1942 TCLC 35
See also CA 113; DLB 11
Wells, H(erbert) G(eorge) 1866-1946 TCLC 6,
12, 19; DA; DAB; DAC; DAM MST, NOV;
SSC 6; WLC
See also AAYA 18; CA 110; 121; CDBLB 1914-
1945; DLB 34, 70, 156, 178; MTCW 1;
SATA 20
Wells, Rosemary 1943- CLC 12
See also AAYA 13; CA 85-88; CANR 48; CLR
16; MAICYA; SAAS 1; SATA 18, 69
Welty, Eudora 1909- CLC 1, 2, 5, 14, 22, 33,
105; DA; DAB; DAC; DAM MST, NOV;
SSC 1, 27; WLC
See also CA 9-12R; CABS 1; CANR 32, 65;
CDALB 1941-1968; DLB 2, 102, 143;
DLBD 12; DLBY 87; MTCW 1
Wen I-to 1899-1946 TCLC 28
Wentworth, Robert
See Hamilton, Edmond
Werfel, Franz (Viktor) 1890-1945 TCLC 8
See also CA 104; 161; DLB 81, 124
Wergeland, Henrik Arnold 1808-1845 N C L C
5
Wersba, Barbara 1932- CLC 30
See also AAYA 2; CA 29-32R; CANR 16, 38;
CLR 3; DLB 52; JRDA; MAICYA; SAAS 2;
SATA 1, 58
Wertmueller, Lina 1928- CLC 16
See also CA 97-100; CANR 39
Wescott, Glenway 1901-1987 CLC 13
See also CA 13-16R; 121; CANR 23, 70; DLB
4, 9, 102
Wesker, Arnold 1932- CLC 3, 5, 42; DAB;
DAM DRAM
See also CA 1-4R; CAAS 7; CANR 1, 33;
CDBLB 1960 to Present; DLB 13; MTCW 1
Wesley, Richard (Errol) 1945- CLC 7
See also BW 1; CA 57-60; CANR 27; DLB 38
Wessel, Johan Herman 1742-1785 LC 7
West, Anthony (Panther) 1914-1987 CLC 50
See also CA 45-48; 124; CANR 3, 19; DLB 15
West, C. P.
See Wodehouse, P(elham) G(renville)
West, (Mary) Jessamyn 1902-1984 CLC 7, 17
See also CA 9-12R; 112; CANR 27; DLB 6;
DLBY 84; MTCW 1; SATA-Obit 37
West, Morris L(anglo) 1916- CLC 6, 33
See also CA 5-8R; CANR 24, 49, 64; MTCW 1
West, Nathanael 1903-1940 TCLC 1, 14, 44;
SSC 16
See also CA 104; 125; CDALB 1929-1941;
DLB 4, 9, 28; MTCW 1
West, Owen
See Koontz, Dean R(ay)
West, Paul 1930- CLC 7, 14, 96
See also CA 13-16R; CAAS 7; CANR 22, 53;
DLB 14; INT CANR-22
West, Rebecca 1892-1983 CLC 7, 9, 31, 50
See also CA 5-8R; 109; CANR 19; DLB 36;
DLBY 83; MTCW 1
Westall, Robert (Atkinson) 1929-1993 CLC 17
See also AAYA 12; CA 69-72; 141; CANR 18,
68; CLR 13; JRDA; MAICYA; SAAS 2;
SATA 23, 69; SATA-Obit 75

Westermarck, Edward 1862-1939 **TCLC 87**

Westlake, Donald E(dwin) 1933- **CLC 7, 33; DAM POP**
See also CA 17-20R; CAAS 13; CANR 16, 44, 65; INT CANR-16

Westmacott, Mary
See Christie, Agatha (Mary Clarissa)

Weston, Allen
See Norton, Andre

Wetcheek, J. L.
See Feuchtwanger, Lion

Wetering, Janwillem van de
See van de Wetering, Janwillem

Wetherald, Agnes Ethelwyn 1857-1940 **TCLC 81**
See also DLB 99

Wetherell, Elizabeth
See Warner, Susan (Bogert)

Whale, James 1889-1957 **TCLC 63**

Whalen, Philip 1923- **CLC 6, 29**
See also CA 9-12R; CANR 5, 39; DLB 16

Wharton, Edith (Newbold Jones) 1862-1937 **TCLC 3, 9, 27, 53; DA; DAB; DAC; DAM MST, NOV; SSC 6; WLC**
See also AAYA 25; CA 104; 132; CDALB 1865-1917; DLB 4, 9, 12, 78, 189; DLBD 13; MTCW 1

Wharton, James
See Mencken, H(enry) L(ouis)

Wharton, William (a pseudonym) CLC 18, 37
See also CA 93-96; DLBY 80; INT 93-96

Wheatley (Peters), Phillis 1754(?)-1784 **LC 3; BLC 3; DA; DAC; DAM MST, MULT, POET; PC 3; WLC**
See also CDALB 1640-1865; DLB 31, 50

Wheelock, John Hall 1886-1978 **CLC 14**
See also CA 13-16R; 77-80; CANR 14; DLB 45

White, E(lwyn) B(rooks) 1899-1985 **CLC 10, 34, 39; DAM POP**
See also AITN 2; CA 13-16R; 116; CANR 16, 37; CLR 1, 21; DLB 11, 22; MAICYA; MTCW 1; SATA 2, 29, 100; SATA-Obit 44

White, Edmund (Valentine III) 1940- **CLC 27, 110; DAM POP**
See also AAYA 7; CA 45-48; CANR 3, 19, 36, 62; MTCW 1

White, Patrick (Victor Martindale) 1912-1990 **CLC 3, 4, 5, 7, 9, 18, 65, 69**
See also CA 81-84; 132; CANR 43; MTCW 1

White, Phyllis Dorothy James 1920-
See James, P. D.
See also CA 21-24R; CANR 17, 43, 65; DAM POP; MTCW 1

White, T(erence) H(anbury) 1906-1964 **CLC 30**
See also AAYA 22; CA 73-76; CANR 37; DLB 160; JRDA; MAICYA; SATA 12

White, Terence de Vere 1912-1994 **CLC 49**
See also CA 49-52; 145; CANR 3

White, Walter F(rancis) 1893-1955 **TCLC 15**
See also White, Walter
See also BW 1; CA 115; 124; DLB 51

White, William Hale 1831-1913
See Rutherford, Mark
See also CA 121

Whitehead, E(dward) A(nthony) 1933- **CLC 5**
See also CA 65-68; CANR 58

Whitemore, Hugh (John) 1936- **CLC 37**
See also CA 132; INT 132

Whitman, Sarah Helen (Power) 1803-1878 **NCLC 19**
See also DLB 1

Whitman, Walt(er) 1819-1892 **NCLC 4, 31; DA; DAB; DAC; DAM MST, POET; PC 3; WLC**
See also CDALB 1640-1865; DLB 3, 64; SATA 20

Whitney, Phyllis A(yame) 1903- **CLC 42; DAM POP**
See also AITN 2; BEST 90:3; CA 1-4R; CANR 3, 25, 38, 60; JRDA; MAICYA; SATA 1, 30

Whittemore, (Edward) Reed (Jr.) 1919- **CLC 4**
See also CA 9-12R; CAAS 8; CANR 4; DLB 5

Whittier, John Greenleaf 1807-1892 **NCLC 8, 59**
See also DLB 1

Whittlebot, Hernia
See Coward, Noel (Peirce)

Wicker, Thomas Grey 1926-
See Wicker, Tom
See also CA 65-68; CANR 21, 46

Wicker, Tom **CLC 7**
See also Wicker, Thomas Grey

Wideman, John Edgar 1941- **CLC 5, 34, 36, 67; BLC 3; DAM MULT**
See also BW 2; CA 85-88; CANR 14, 42, 67; DLB 33, 143

Wiebe, Rudy (Henry) 1934- **CLC 6, 11, 14; DAC; DAM MST**
See also CA 37-40R; CANR 42, 67; DLB 60

Wieland, Christoph Martin 1733-1813 **NCLC 17**
See also DLB 97

Wiene, Robert 1881-1938 **TCLC 56**

Wieners, John 1934- **CLC 7**
See also CA 13-16R; DLB 16

Wiesel, Elie(zer) 1928- **CLC 3, 5, 11, 37; DA; DAB; DAC; DAM MST, NOV; WLCS**
See also AAYA 7; AITN 1; CA 5-8R; CAAS 4; CANR 8, 40, 65; DLB 83; DLBY 87; INT CANR-8; MTCW 1; SATA 56

Wiggins, Marianne 1947- **CLC 57**
See also BEST 89:3; CA 130; CANR 60

Wight, James Alfred 1916-1995
See Herriot, James
See also CA 77-80; SATA 55; SATA-Brief 44

Wilbur, Richard (Purdy) 1921- **CLC 3, 6, 9, 14, 53, 110; DA; DAB; DAC; DAM MST, POET**
See also CA 1-4R; CABS 2; CANR 2, 29; DLB 5, 169; INT CANR-29; MTCW 1; SATA 9

Wild, Peter 1940- **CLC 14**
See also CA 37-40R; DLB 5

Wilde, Oscar (Fingal O'Flahertie Wills) 1854(?)-1900 **TCLC 1, 8, 23, 41; DA; DAB; DAC; DAM DRAM, MST, NOV; SSC 11; WLC**
See also CA 104; 119; CDBLB 1890-1914; DLB 10, 19, 34, 57, 141, 156, 190; SATA 24

Wilder, Billy **CLC 20**
See also Wilder, Samuel
See also DLB 26

Wilder, Samuel 1906-
See Wilder, Billy
See also CA 89-92

Wilder, Thornton (Niven) 1897-1975 **CLC 1, 5, 6, 10, 15, 35, 82; DA; DAB; DAC; DAM DRAM, MST, NOV; DC 1; WLC**
See also AITN 2; CA 13-16R; 61-64; CANR 40; DLB 4, 7, 9; DLBY 97; MTCW 1

Wilding, Michael 1942- **CLC 73**
See also CA 104; CANR 24, 49

Wiley, Richard 1944- **CLC 44**
See also CA 121; 129; CANR 71

Wilhelm, Kate **CLC 7**

See also Wilhelm, Katie Gertrude
See also AAYA 20; CAAS 5; DLB 8; INT CANR-17

Wilhelm, Katie Gertrude 1928-
See Wilhelm, Kate
See also CA 37-40R; CANR 17, 36, 60; MTCW 1

Wilkins, Mary
See Freeman, Mary Eleanor Wilkins

Willard, Nancy 1936- **CLC 7, 37**
See also CA 89-92; CANR 10, 39, 68; CLR 5; DLB 5, 52; MAICYA; MTCW 1; SATA 37, 71; SATA-Brief 30

William of Ockham 1285-1347 **CMLC 32**

Williams, Ben Ames 1889-1953 **TCLC 89**
See also DLB 102

Williams, C(harles) K(enneth) 1936- **CLC 33, 56; DAM POET**
See also CA 37-40R; CAAS 26; CANR 57; DLB 5

Williams, Charles
See Collier, James L(incoln)

Williams, Charles (Walter Stansby) 1886-1945 **TCLC 1, 11**
See also CA 104; 163; DLB 100, 153

Williams, (George) Emlyn 1905-1987 **CLC 15; DAM DRAM**
See also CA 104; 123; CANR 36; DLB 10, 77; MTCW 1

Williams, Hank 1923-1953 **TCLC 81**

Williams, Hugo 1942- **CLC 42**
See also CA 17-20R; CANR 45; DLB 40

Williams, J. Walker
See Wodehouse, P(elham) G(renville)

Williams, John A(lfred) 1925- **CLC 5, 13; BLC 3; DAM MULT**
See also BW 2; CA 53-56; CAAS 3; CANR 6, 26, 51; DLB 2, 33; INT CANR-6

Williams, Jonathan (Chamberlain) 1929- **CLC 13**
See also CA 9-12R; CAAS 12; CANR 8; DLB 5

Williams, Joy 1944- **CLC 31**
See also CA 41-44R; CANR 22, 48

Williams, Norman 1952- **CLC 39**
See also CA 118

Williams, Sherley Anne 1944- **CLC 89; BLC 3; DAM MULT, POET**
See also BW 2; CA 73-76; CANR 25; DLB 41; INT CANR-25; SATA 78

Williams, Shirley
See Williams, Sherley Anne

Williams, Tennessee 1911-1983 **CLC 1, 2, 5, 7, 8, 11, 15, 19, 30, 39, 45, 71, 111; DA; DAB; DAC; DAM DRAM, MST; DC 4; WLC**
See also AITN 1, 2; CA 5-8R; 108; CABS 3; CANR 31; CDALB 1941-1968; DLB 7; DLBD 4; DLBY 83; MTCW 1

Williams, Thomas (Alonzo) 1926-1990 **CLC 14**
See also CA 1-4R; 132; CANR 2

Williams, William C.
See Williams, William Carlos

Williams, William Carlos 1883-1963 **CLC 1, 2, 5, 9, 13, 22, 42, 67; DA; DAB; DAC; DAM MST, POET; PC 7; SSC 31**
See also CA 89-92; CANR 34; CDALB 1917-1929; DLB 4, 16, 54, 86; MTCW 1

Williamson, David (Keith) 1942- **CLC 56**
See also CA 103; CANR 41

Williamson, Ellen Douglas 1905-1984
See Douglas, Ellen
See also CA 17-20R; 114; CANR 39

Williamson, Jack **CLC 29**

See also Williamson, John Stewart
See also CAAS 8; DLB 8
Williamson, John Stewart 1908-
See also Williamson, Jack
See also CA 17-20R; CANR 23, 70
Willie, Frederick
See Lovecraft, H(oward) P(hillips)
Willingham, Calder (Baynard, Jr.) 1922-1995
CLC 5, 51
See also CA 5-8R; 147; CANR 3; DLB 2, 44;
MTCW 1
Willis, Charles
See Clarke, Arthur C(harles)
Willy
See Colette, (Sidonie-Gabrielle)
Willy, Colette
See Colette, (Sidonie-Gabrielle)
Wilson, A(ndrew) N(orman) 1950- **CLC 33**
See also CA 112; 122; DLB 14, 155, 194
Wilson, Angus (Frank Johnstone) 1913-1991
CLC 2, 3, 5, 25, 34; SSC 21
See also CA 5-8R; 134; CANR 21; DLB 15,
139, 155; MTCW 1
Wilson, August 1945-**CLC 39, 50, 63; BLC 3;**
DA; DAB; DAC; DAM DRAM, MST,
MULT; DC 2; WLCS
See also AAYA 16; BW 2; CA 115; 122; CANR
42, 54; MTCW 1
Wilson, Brian 1942- **CLC 12**
Wilson, Colin 1931- **CLC 3, 14**
See also CA 1-4R; CAAS 5; CANR 1, 22, 33;
DLB 14, 194; MTCW 1
Wilson, Dirk
See Pohl, Frederik
Wilson, Edmund 1895-1972**CLC 1, 2, 3, 8, 24**
See also CA 1-4R; 37-40R; CANR 1, 46; DLB
63; MTCW 1
Wilson, Ethel Davis (Bryant) 1888(?)-1980
CLC 13; DAC; DAM POET
See also CA 102; DLB 68; MTCW 1
Wilson, John 1785-1854 **NCLC 5**
Wilson, John (Anthony) Burgess 1917-1993
See Burgess, Anthony
See also CA 1-4R; 143; CANR 2, 46; DAC;
DAM NOV; MTCW 1
Wilson, Lanford 1937- **CLC 7, 14, 36; DAM**
DRAM
See also CA 17-20R; CABS 3; CANR 45; DLB
7
Wilson, Robert M. 1944- **CLC 7, 9**
See also CA 49-52; CANR 2, 41; MTCW 1
Wilson, Robert McLiam 1964- **CLC 59**
See also CA 132
Wilson, Sloan 1920- **CLC 32**
See also CA 1-4R; CANR 1, 44
Wilson, Snoo 1948- **CLC 33**
See also CA 69-72
Wilson, William S(mith) 1932- **CLC 49**
See also CA 81-84
Wilson, (Thomas) Woodrow 1856-1924**TCLC**
79
See also CA 166; DLB 47
Winchilsea, Anne (Kingsmill) Finch Counte
1661-1720
See Finch, Anne
Windham, Basil
See Wodehouse, P(elham) G(renville)
Wingrove, David (John) 1954- **CLC 68**
See also CA 133
Wintergreen, Jane
See Duncan, Sara Jeannette
Winters, Janet Lewis **CLC 41**
See also Lewis, Janet

See also DLBY 87
Winters, (Arthur) Yvor 1900-1968 **CLC 4, 8,**
32
See also CA 11-12; 25-28R; CAP 1; DLB 48;
MTCW 1
Winterson, Jeanette 1959-**CLC 64; DAM POP**
See also CA 136; CANR 58; DLB 207
Winthrop, John 1588-1649 **LC 31**
See also DLB 24, 30
Wiseman, Frederick 1930- **CLC 20**
See also CA 159
Wister, Owen 1860-1938 **TCLC 21**
See also CA 108; 162; DLB 9, 78, 186; SATA
62
Witkacy
See Witkiewicz, Stanislaw Ignacy
Witkiewicz, Stanislaw Ignacy 1885-1939
TCLC 8
See also CA 105; 162
Wittgenstein, Ludwig (Josef Johann) 1889-1951
TCLC 59
See also CA 113; 164
Wittig, Monique 1935(?)- **CLC 22**
See also CA 116; 135; DLB 83
Wittlin, Jozef 1896-1976 **CLC 25**
See also CA 49-52; 65-68; CANR 3
Wodehouse, P(elham) G(renville) 1881-1975
CLC 1, 2, 5, 10, 22; DAB; DAC; DAM
NOV; SSC 2
See also AITN 2; CA 45-48; 57-60; CANR 3,
33; CDBLB 1914-1945; DLB 34, 162;
MTCW 1; SATA 22
Woiwode, L.
See Woiwode, Larry (Alfred)
Woiwode, Larry (Alfred) 1941- **CLC 6, 10**
See also CA 73-76; CANR 16; DLB 6; INT
CANR-16
Wojciechowska, Maia (Teresa) 1927-**CLC 26**
See also AAYA 8; CA 9-12R; CANR 4, 41; CLR
1; JRDA; MAICYA; SAAS 1; SATA 1, 28,
83
Wolf, Christa 1929- **CLC 14, 29, 58**
See also CA 85-88; CANR 45; DLB 75; MTCW
1
Wolfe, Gene (Rodman) 1931- **CLC 25; DAM**
POP
See also CA 57-60; CAAS 9; CANR 6, 32, 60;
DLB 8
Wolfe, George C. 1954- **CLC 49; BLCS**
See also CA 149
Wolfe, Thomas (Clayton) 1900-1938**TCLC 4,**
13, 29, 61; DA; DAB; DAC; DAM MST,
NOV; SSC 33; WLC
See also CA 104; 132; CDALB 1929-1941;
DLB 9, 102; DLBD 2, 16; DLBY 85, 97;
MTCW 1
Wolfe, Thomas Kennerly, Jr. 1930-
See Wolfe, Tom
See also CA 13-16R; CANR 9, 33, 70; DAM
POP; DLB 185; INT CANR-9; MTCW 1
Wolfe, Tom **CLC 1, 2, 9, 15, 35, 51**
See also Wolfe, Thomas Kennerly, Jr.
See also AAYA 8; AITN 2; BEST 89:1; DLB
152
Wolff, Geoffrey (Ansell) 1937- **CLC 41**
See also CA 29-32R; CANR 29, 43
Wolff, Sonia
See Levitin, Sonia (Wolff)
Wolff, Tobias (Jonathan Ansell) 1945- **C L C**
39, 64
See also AAYA 16; BEST 90:2; CA 114; 117;
CAAS 22; CANR 54; DLB 130; INT 117
Wolfram von Eschenbach c. 1170-c. 1220

CMLC 5
See also DLB 138
Wolitzer, Hilma 1930- **CLC 17**
See also CA 65-68; CANR 18, 40; INT CANR-
18; SATA 31
Wollstonecraft, Mary 1759-1797 **LC 5**
See also CDBLB 1789-1832; DLB 39, 104, 158
Wonder, Stevie **CLC 12**
See also Morris, Steveland Judkins
Wong, Jade Snow 1922- **CLC 17**
See also CA 109
Woodberry, George Edward 1855-1930
TCLC 73
See also CA 165; DLB 71, 103
Woodcott, Keith
See Brunner, John (Kilian Houston)
Woodruff, Robert W.
See Mencken, H(enry) L(ouis)
Woolf, (Adeline) Virginia 1882-1941**TCLC 1,**
5, 20, 43, 56; DA; DAB; DAC; DAM MST,
NOV; SSC 7; WLC
See also CA 104; 130; CANR 64; CDBLB
1914-1945; DLB 36, 100, 162; DLBD 10;
MTCW 1
Woolf, Virginia Adeline
See Woolf, (Adeline) Virginia
Woollcott, Alexander (Humphreys) 1887-1943
TCLC 5
See also CA 105; 161; DLB 29
Woolrich, Cornell 1903-1968 **CLC 77**
See also Hopley-Woolrich, Cornell George
Wordsworth, Dorothy 1771-1855 **NCLC 25**
See also DLB 107
Wordsworth, William 1770-1850 **NCLC 12,**
38; DA; DAB; DAC; DAM MST, POET;
PC 4; WLC
See also CDBLB 1789-1832; DLB 93, 107
Wouk, Herman 1915-**CLC 1, 9, 38; DAM NOV,**
POP
See also CA 5-8R; CANR 6, 33, 67; DLBY 82;
INT CANR-6; MTCW 1
Wright, Charles (Penzel, Jr.) 1935-**CLC 6, 13,**
28
See also CA 29-32R; CAAS 7; CANR 23, 36,
62; DLB 165; DLBY 82; MTCW 1
Wright, Charles Stevenson 1932- **CLC 49;**
BLC 3; DAM MULT, POET
See also BW 1; CA 9-12R; CANR 26; DLB 33
Wright, Frances 1795-1852 **NCLC 74**
See also DLB 73
Wright, Jack R.
See Harris, Mark
Wright, James (Arlington) 1927-1980**CLC 3,**
5, 10, 28; DAM POET
See also AITN 2; CA 49-52; 97-100; CANR 4,
34, 64; DLB 5, 169; MTCW 1
Wright, Judith (Arandell) 1915- **CLC 11, 53;**
PC 14
See also CA 13-16R; CANR 31; MTCW 1;
SATA 14
Wright, L(aurali) R. 1939- **CLC 44**
See also CA 138
Wright, Richard (Nathaniel) 1908-1960 **C L C**
1, 3, 4, 9, 14, 21, 48, 74; BLC 3; DA; DAB;
DAC; DAM MST, MULT, NOV; SSC 2;
WLC
See also AAYA 5; BW 1; CA 108; CANR 64;
CDALB 1929-1941; DLB 76, 102; DLBD
2; MTCW 1
Wright, Richard B(ruce) 1937- **CLC 6**
See also CA 85-88; DLB 53
Wright, Rick 1945- **CLC 35**
Wright, Rowland

See Wells, Carolyn
Wright, Stephen 1946-   **CLC 33**
Wright, Willard Huntington 1888-1939
   See Van Dine, S. S.
   See also CA 115; DLBD 16
Wright, William 1930-   **CLC 44**
   See also CA 53-56; CANR 7, 23
Wroth, LadyMary 1587-1653(?)   **LC 30**
   See also DLB 121
Wu Ch'eng-en 1500(?)-1582(?)   **LC 7**
Wu Ching-tzu 1701-1754   **LC 2**
Wurlitzer, Rudolph 1938(?)-   **CLC 2, 4, 15**
   See also CA 85-88; DLB 173
Wycherley, William 1641-1715**LC 8, 21; DAM
   DRAM**
   See also CDBLB 1660-1789; DLB 80
Wylie, Elinor (Morton Hoyt) 1885-1928
   TCLC 8; PC 23
   See also CA 105; 162; DLB 9, 45
Wylie, Philip (Gordon) 1902-1971   **CLC 43**
   See also CA 21-22; 33-36R; CAP 2; DLB 9
Wyndham, John   **CLC 19**
   See also Harris, John (Wyndham Parkes Lucas)
   Beynon
Wyss, Johann David Von 1743-1818**NCLC 10**
   See also JRDA; MAICYA; SATA 29; SATA-
   Brief 27
Xenophon c. 430B.C.-c. 354B.C.   **CMLC 17**
   See also DLB 176
Yakumo Koizumi
   See Hearn, (Patricio) Lafcadio (Tessima Carlos)
Yanez, Jose Donoso
   See Donoso (Yanez), Jose
Yanovsky, Basile S.
   See Yanovsky, V(assily) S(emenovich)
Yanovsky, V(assily) S(emenovich) 1906-1989
   CLC 2, 18
   See also CA 97-100; 129
Yates, Richard 1926-1992   **CLC 7, 8, 23**
   See also CA 5-8R; 139; CANR 10, 43; DLB 2;
   DLBY 81, 92; INT CANR-10
Yeats, W. B.
   See Yeats, William Butler
Yeats, William Butler 1865-1939**TCLC 1, 11,
   18, 31; DA; DAB; DAC; DAM DRAM,
   MST, POET; PC 20; WLC**
   See also CA 104; 127; CANR 45; CDBLB
   1890-1914; DLB 10, 19, 98, 156; MTCW 1
Yehoshua, A(braham) B. 1936-   **CLC 13, 31**
   See also CA 33-36R; CANR 43
Yep, Laurence Michael 1948-   **CLC 35**
   See also AAYA 5; CA 49-52; CANR 1, 46; CLR
   3, 17, 54; DLB 52; JRDA; MAICYA; SATA
   7, 69
Yerby, Frank G(arvin) 1916-1991   **CLC 1, 7,
   22; BLC 3; DAM MULT**
   See also BW 1; CA 9-12R; 136; CANR 16, 52;
   DLB 76; INT CANR-16; MTCW 1
Yesenin, Sergei Alexandrovich
   See Esenin, Sergei (Alexandrovich)
Yevtushenko, Yevgeny (Alexandrovich) 1933-
   CLC 1, 3, 13, 26, 51; DAM POET
   See also CA 81-84; CANR 33, 54; MTCW 1
Yezierska, Anzia 1885(?)-1970   **CLC 46**
   See also CA 126; 89-92; DLB 28; MTCW 1
Yglesias, Helen 1915-   **CLC 7, 22**
   See also CA 37-40R; CAAS 20; CANR 15, 65;
   INT CANR-15; MTCW 1
Yokomitsu Riichi 1898-1947   **TCLC 47**
   See also CA 170
Yonge, Charlotte (Mary) 1823-1901**TCLC 48**
   See also CA 109; 163; DLB 18, 163; SATA 17
York, Jeremy

See Creasey, John
York, Simon
   See Heinlein, Robert A(nson)
Yorke, Henry Vincent 1905-1974   **CLC 13**
   See also Green, Henry
   See also CA 85-88; 49-52
Yosano Akiko 1878-1942   **TCLC 59; PC 11**
   See also CA 161
Yoshimoto, Banana   **CLC 84**
   See also Yoshimoto, Mahoko
Yoshimoto, Mahoko 1964-
   See Yoshimoto, Banana
   See also CA 144
Young, Al(bert James) 1939-**CLC 19; BLC 3;
   DAM MULT**
   See also BW 2; CA 29-32R; CANR 26, 65; DLB
   33
Young, Andrew (John) 1885-1971   **CLC 5**
   See also CA 5-8R; CANR 7, 29
Young, Collier
   See Bloch, Robert (Albert)
Young, Edward 1683-1765   **LC 3, 40**
   See also DLB 95
Young, Marguerite (Vivian) 1909-1995 **C L C
   82**
   See also CA 13-16; 150; CAP 1
Young, Neil 1945-   **CLC 17**
   See also CA 110
Young Bear, Ray A. 1950-   **CLC 94; DAM
   MULT**
   See also CA 146; DLB 175; NNAL
Yourcenar, Marguerite 1903-1987**CLC 19, 38,
   50, 87; DAM NOV**
   See also CA 69-72; CANR 23, 60; DLB 72;
   DLBY 88; MTCW 1
Yurick, Sol 1925-   **CLC 6**
   See also CA 13-16R; CANR 25
Zabolotsky, Nikolai Alekseevich 1903-1958
   TCLC 52
   See also CA 116; 164
Zamiatin, Yevgenii
   See Zamyatin, Evgeny Ivanovich
Zamora, Bernice (B. Ortiz) 1938-   **CLC 89;
   DAM MULT; HLC**
   See also CA 151; DLB 82; HW
Zamyatin, Evgeny Ivanovich 1884-1937
   TCLC 8, 37
   See also CA 105; 166
Zangwill, Israel 1864-1926   **TCLC 16**
   See also CA 109; 167; DLB 10, 135, 197
Zappa, Francis Vincent, Jr. 1940-1993
   See Zappa, Frank
   See also CA 108; 143; CANR 57
Zappa, Frank   **CLC 17**
   See also Zappa, Francis Vincent, Jr.
Zaturenska, Marya 1902-1982   **CLC 6, 11**
   See also CA 13-16R; 105; CANR 22
Zeami 1363-1443   **DC 7**
Zelazny, Roger (Joseph) 1937-1995 **CLC 21**
   See also AAYA 7; CA 21-24R; 148; CANR 26,
   60; DLB 8; MTCW 1; SATA 57; SATA-Brief
   39
Zhdanov, Andrei Alexandrovich 1896-1948
   TCLC 18
   See also CA 117; 167
Zhukovsky, Vasily (Andreevich) 1783-1852
   NCLC 35
   See also DLB 205
Ziegenhagen, Eric   **CLC 55**
Zimmer, Jill Schary
   See Robinson, Jill
Zimmerman, Robert
   See Dylan, Bob

Zindel, Paul 1936-**CLC 6, 26; DA; DAB; DAC;
   DAM DRAM, MST, NOV; DC 5**
   See also AAYA 2; CA 73-76; CANR 31, 65;
   CLR 3, 45; DLB 7, 52; JRDA; MAICYA;
   MTCW 1; SATA 16, 58, 102
Zinov'Ev, A. A.
   See Zinoviev, Alexander (Aleksandrovich)
Zinoviev, Alexander (Aleksandrovich) 1922-
   CLC 19
   See also CA 116; 133; CAAS 10
Zoilus
   See Lovecraft, H(oward) P(hillips)
Zola, Emile (Edouard Charles Antoine) 1840-
   1902**TCLC 1, 6, 21, 41; DA; DAB; DAC;
   DAM MST, NOV; WLC**
   See also CA 104; 138; DLB 123
Zoline, Pamela 1941-   **CLC 62**
   See also CA 161
Zorrilla y Moral, Jose 1817-1893   **NCLC 6**
Zoshchenko, Mikhail (Mikhailovich) 1895-1958
   TCLC 15; SSC 15
   See also CA 115; 160
Zuckmayer, Carl 1896-1977   **CLC 18**
   See also CA 69-72; DLB 56, 124
Zuk, Georges
   See Skelton, Robin
Zukofsky, Louis 1904-1978**CLC 1, 2, 4, 7, 11,
   18; DAM POET; PC 11**
   See also CA 9-12R; 77-80; CANR 39; DLB 5,
   165; MTCW 1
Zweig, Paul 1935-1984   **CLC 34, 42**
   See also CA 85-88; 113
Zweig, Stefan 1881-1942   **TCLC 17**
   See also CA 112; 170; DLB 81, 118
Zwingli, Huldreich 1484-1531   **LC 37**
   See also DLB 179

Literary Criticism Series
Cumulative Topic Index

This index lists all topic entries in Gale's *Classical and Medieval Literature Criticism, Contemporary Literary Criticism, Literature Criticism from 1400 to 1800, Nineteenth-Century Literature Criticism,* and *Twentieth-Century Literary Criticism.*

Age of Johnson LC 15: 1-87
Johnson*s London, 3-15
aesthetics of neoclassicism, 15-36
"age of prose and reason," 36-45
clubmen and bluestockings, 45-56
printing technology, 56-62
periodicals: "a map of busy life," 62-74
transition, 74-86

Age of Spenser LC 39: 1-70
Overviews, 2-21
Literary Style, 22-34
Poets and the Crown, 34-70

AIDS in Literature CLC 81: 365-416

Alcohol and Literature TCLC 70: 1-58
overview, 2-8
fiction, 8-48
poetry and drama, 48-58

American Abolitionism NCLC 44: 1-73
overviews, 2-26
abolitionist ideals, 26-46
the literature of abolitionism, 46-72

American Black Humor Fiction TCLC 54: 1-85
characteristics of black humor, 2-13
origins and development, 13-38
black humor distinguished from related literary trends, 38-60
black humor and society, 60-75
black humor reconsidered, 75-83

American Civil War in Literature NCLC 32: 1-109
overviews, 2-20
regional perspectives, 20-54
fiction popular during the war, 54-79
the historical novel, 79-108

American Frontier in Literature NCLC 28: 1-103
definitions, 2-12
development, 12-17
nonfiction writing about the frontier, 17-30
frontier fiction, 30-45
frontier protagonists, 45-66
portrayals of Native Americans, 66-86
feminist readings, 86-98
twentieth-century reaction against frontier literature, 98-100

American Humor Writing NCLC 52: 1-59
overviews, 2-12
the Old Southwest, 12-42
broader impacts, 42-5
women humorists, 45-58

American Mercury, The TCLC 74: 1-80

American Popular Song, Golden Age of TCLC 42: 1-49
background and major figures, 2-34
the lyrics of popular songs, 34-47

American Proletarian Literature TCLC 54: 86-175
overviews, 87-95
American proletarian literature and the American Communist Party, 95-111
ideology and literary merit, 111-7
novels, 117-36
Gastonia, 136-48
drama, 148-54
journalism, 154-9
proletarian literature in the United States, 159-74

American Romanticism NCLC 44: 74-138
overviews, 74-84
sociopolitical influences, 84-104
Romanticism and the American frontier, 104-15
thematic concerns, 115-37

American Western Literature TCLC 46: 1-100
definition and development of American Western literature, 2-7
characteristics of the Western novel, 8-23
Westerns as history and fiction, 23-34
critical reception of American Western literature, 34-41
the Western hero, 41-73
women in Western fiction, 73-91
later Western fiction, 91-9

Art and Literature TCLC 54: 176-248
overviews, 176-93
definitions, 193-219
influence of visual arts on literature, 219-31
spatial form in literature, 231-47

Arthurian Literature CMLC 10: 1-127
historical context and literary beginnings, 2-27
development of the legend through Malory, 27-64
development of the legend from Malory to the Victorian Age, 65-81
themes and motifs, 81-95
principal characters, 95-125

Arthurian Revival NCLC 36: 1-77
overviews, 2-12
Tennyson and his influence, 12-43
other leading figures, 43-73
the Arthurian legend in the visual arts, 73-6

Australian Literature TCLC 50: 1-94
origins and development, 2-21
characteristics of Australian literature, 21-33
historical and critical perspectives, 33-41
poetry, 41-58
fiction, 58-76
drama, 76-82
Aboriginal literature, 82-91

Beat Generation, Literature of the TCLC 42: 50-102
overviews, 51-9
the Beat generation as a social phenomenon, 59-62

development, 62-5
Beat literature, 66-96
influence, 97-100

The Bell Curve Controversy CLC 91:
281-330

Bildungsroman in Nineteenth-Century
Literature NCLC 20: 92-168
surveys, 93-113
in Germany, 113-40
in England, 140-56
female *Bildungsroman,* 156-67

Bloomsbury Group TCLC 34: 1-73
history and major figures, 2-13
definitions, 13-7
influences, 17-27
thought, 27-40
prose, 40-52
and literary criticism, 52-4
political ideals, 54-61
response to, 61-71

The Blues in Literature TCLC 82: 1-71

Bly, Robert, *Iron John: A Book about Men
and Men*s Work* CLC 70: 414-62

The Book of J CLC 65: 289-311
Buddhism and Literature TCLC 70: 59-
164
eastern literature, 60-113
western literature, 113-63

Businessman in American Literature
TCLC 26: 1-48
portrayal of the businessman, 1-32
themes and techniques in business
fiction, 32-47

**Catholicism in Nineteenth-Century
American Literature** NCLC 64: 1-58
overviews, 3-14
polemical literature, 14-46
Catholicism in literature, 47-57

Celtic Mythology CMLC 26: 1-111
overviews, 2-22
Celtic myth as literature and history, 22-
48
Celtic religion: Druids and divinities,
48-80
Fionn MacCuhaill and the Fenian cycle,
80-111

Celtic Twilight
See **Irish Literary Renaissance**

Chartist Movement and Literature, The

NCLC 60: 1-84
overview: nineteenth-century working-
class fiction, 2-19
Chartist fiction and poetry, 19-73
the Chartist press, 73-84

**Children*s Literature,
Nineteenth-Century** NCLC 52: 60-135
overviews, 61-72
moral tales, 72-89
fairy tales and fantasy, 90-119
making men/making women, 119-34

Civic Critics, Russian NCLC 20: 402-46
principal figures and background, 402-9
and Russian Nihilism, 410-6
aesthetic and critical views, 416-45

The Cockney School NCLC 68: 1-64
overview, 2-7
Blackwood's Magazine and the
contemporary critical response, 7-24
the political and social import of the
Cockneys and their critics, 24-63

**Colonial America: The Intellectual
Background** LC 25: 1-98
overviews, 2-17
philosophy and politics, 17-31
early religious influences in Colonial
America, 31-60
consequences of the Revolution, 60-78
religious influences in
post-revolutionary America, 78-87
colonial literary genres, 87-97

**Colonialism in Victorian English Litera-
ture** NCLC 56: 1-77
overviews, 2-34
colonialism and gender, 34-51
monsters and the occult, 51-76

**Columbus, Christopher, Books on the
Quincentennial of His Arrival in the New
World** CLC 70: 329-60

Comic Books TCLC 66: 1-139
historical and critical perspectives, 2-48
superheroes, 48-67
underground comix, 67-88
comic books and society, 88-122
adult comics and graphic novels, 122-36

Connecticut Wits NCLC 48: 1-95
general overviews, 2-40
major works, 40-76
intellectual context, 76-95

Crime in Literature TCLC 54: 249-307
evolution of the criminal figure in

literature, 250-61
crime and society, 261-77
literary perspectives on crime and
punishment, 277-88
writings by criminals, 288-306

**Czechoslovakian Literature of the
Twentieth Century** TCLC 42: 103-96
through World War II, 104-35
de-Stalinization, the Prague Spring, and
contemporary literature, 135-72
Slovak literature, 172-85
Czech science fiction, 185-93

Dadaism TCLC 46: 101-71
background and major figures, 102-16
definitions, 116-26
manifestos and commentary by
Dadaists, 126-40
theater and film, 140-58
nature and characteristics of Dadaist
writing, 158-70

Darwinism and Literature NCLC 32:
110-206
background, 110-31
direct responses to Darwin, 131-71
collateral effects of Darwinism, 171-205

**Death in Nineteenth-Century British
Literature** NCLC 68: 65-142
overviews, 66-92
responses to death, 92-102
feminist perspectives, 103-17
striving for immortality, 117-41

Death in Literature TCLC 78:1-183
fiction, 2-115
poetry, 115-46
drama, 146-81

de Man, Paul, Wartime Journalism of
CLC 55: 382-424

Detective Fiction, Nineteenth-Century
NCLC 36: 78-148
origins of the genre, 79-100
history of nineteenth-century detective
fiction, 101-33
significance of nineteenth-century
detective fiction, 133-46

Detective Fiction, Twentieth-Century
TCLC 38: 1-96
genesis and history of the detective
story, 3-22
defining detective fiction, 22-32
evolution and varieties, 32-77
the appeal of detective fiction, 77-90

Disease and Literature TCLC 66: 140-283
　overviews, 141-65
　disease in nineteenth-century literature,
　　165-81
　tuberculosis and literature, 181-94
　women and disease in literature,
　　194-221
　plague literature, 221-53
　AIDS in literature, 253-82

**The Double in Nineteenth-Century
Literature** NCLC 40: 1-95
　genesis and development of the theme,
　　2-15
　the double and Romanticism, 16-27
　sociological views, 27-52
　psychological interpretations, 52-87
　philosophical considerations, 87-95

Dramatic Realism NCLC 44: 139-202
　overviews, 140-50
　origins and definitions, 150-66
　impact and influence, 166-93
　realist drama and tragedy, 193-201

Drugs and Literature TCLC 78: 184-282
　overviews, 185-201
　pre-twentieth-century literature, 201-42
　twentieth-century literature, 242-82

Eastern Mythology CMLC 26: 112-92
　heroes and kings, 113-51
　cross-cultural perspective, 151-69
　relations to history and society, 169-92

**Electronic "Books": Hypertext and
Hyperfiction** CLC 86: 367-404
　books vs. CD-ROMS, 367-76
　hypertext and hyperfiction, 376-95
　implications for publishing, libraries,
　　and the public, 395-403

Eliot, T. S., Centenary of Birth CLC 55:
345-75

Elizabethan Drama LC 22: 140-240
　origins and influences, 142-67
　characteristics and conventions, 167-83
　theatrical production, 184-200
　histories, 200-12
　comedy, 213-20
　tragedy, 220-30

Elizabethan Prose Fiction LC 41: 1-70
　overviews, 1-15
　origins and influences, 15-43
　style and structure, 43-69

The Encyclopedists LC 26: 172-253
　overviews, 173-210

　intellectual background, 210-32
　views on esthetics, 232-41
　views on women, 241-52

English Caroline Literature LC 13:
221-307
　background, 222-41
　evolution and varieties, 241-62
　the Cavalier mode, 262-75
　court and society, 275-91
　politics and religion, 291-306

English Decadent Literature of the 1890s
NCLC 28: 104-200
　fin de siècle: the Decadent period,
　　105-19
　definitions, 120-37
　major figures: "the tragic generation,"
　　137-50
　French literature and English literary
　　Decadence, 150-7
　themes, 157-61
　poetry, 161-82
　periodicals, 182-96

English Essay, Rise of the LC 18: 238-308
　definitions and origins, 236-54
　influence on the essay, 254-69
　historical background, 269-78
　the essay in the seventeenth century,
　　279-93
　the essay in the eighteenth century,
　　293-307

English Mystery Cycle Dramas LC 34:
1-88
　overviews, 1-27
　the nature of dramatic performances,
　　27-42
　the medieval worldview and the mystery
　　cycles, 43-67
　the doctrine of repentance and the
　　mystery cycles, 67-76
　the fall from grace in the mystery cycles,
　　76-88

English Revolution, Literature of the LC
43: 1-58
　overviews, 2-24
　pamphlets of the English Revolution,
　　24-38
　political Sermons of the English
　　Revolution, 38-48
　poetry of the English Revolution, 48-57

English Romantic Hellenism NCLC 68:
143-250
　overviews, 144-69
　historical development of English
　　Romantic Hellenism, 169-91

　influence of Greek mythology on the
　　Romantics, 191-229
　influence of Greek literature, art, and
　　culture on the Romantics, 229-50

English Romantic Poetry NCLC 28:
201-327
　overviews and reputation, 202-37
　major subjects and themes, 237-67
　forms of Romantic poetry, 267-78
　politics, society, and Romantic poetry,
　　278-99
　philosophy, religion, and Romantic
　　poetry, 299-324

Espionage Literature TCLC 50: 95-159
　overviews, 96-113
　espionage fiction/formula fiction,
　　113-26
　spies in fact and fiction, 126-38
　the female spy, 138-44
　social and psychological perspectives,
　　144-58

European Romanticism NCLC 36:
149-284
　definitions, 149-77
　origins of the movement, 177-82
　Romantic theory, 182-200
　themes and techniques, 200-23
　Romanticism in Germany, 223-39
　Romanticism in France, 240-61
　Romanticism in Italy, 261-4
　Romanticism in Spain, 264-8
　impact and legacy, 268-82

Existentialism and Literature TCLC 42:
197-268
　overviews and definitions, 198-209
　history and influences, 209-19
　Existentialism critiqued and defended,
　　220-35
　philosophical and religious perspectives,
　　235-41
　Existentialist fiction and drama, 241-67

Familiar Essay NCLC 48: 96-211
　definitions and origins, 97-130
　overview of the genre, 130-43
　elements of form and style, 143-59
　elements of content, 159-73
　the Cockneys: Hazlitt, Lamb, and Hunt,
　　173-91
　status of the genre, 191-210

The Faust Legend LC 47: 1-117

Fear in Literature TCLC 74: 81-258
　overviews, 81
　pre-twentieth-century literature, 123
　twentieth-century literature, 182

Feminism in the 1990s: Commentary on Works by Naomi Wolf, Susan Faludi, and Camille Paglia CLC 76: 377-415

Feminist Criticism in 1990 CLC 65: 312-60

Fifteenth-Century English Literature LC 17: 248-334
background, 249-72
poetry, 272-315
drama, 315-23
prose, 323-33

Film and Literature TCLC 38: 97-226
overviews, 97-119
film and theater, 119-34
film and the novel, 134-45
the art of the screenplay, 145-66
genre literature/genre film, 167-79
the writer and the film industry, 179-90
authors on film adaptations of their works, 190-200
fiction into film: comparative essays, 200-23

French Drama in the Age of Louis XIV LC 28: 94-185
overview, 95-127
tragedy, 127-46
comedy, 146-66
tragicomedy, 166-84

French Enlightenment LC 14: 81-145
the question of definition, 82-9
Le siècle des lumières, 89-94
women and the salons, 94-105
censorship, 105-15
the philosophy of reason, 115-31
influence and legacy, 131-44

French Realism NCLC 52: 136-216
origins and definitions, 137-70
issues and influence, 170-98
realism and representation, 198-215

French Revolution and English Literature NCLC 40: 96-195
history and theory, 96-123
romantic poetry, 123-50
the novel, 150-81
drama, 181-92
children*s literature, 192-5

Futurism, Italian TCLC 42: 269-354
principles and formative influences, 271-9
manifestos, 279-88
literature, 288-303
theater, 303-19

art, 320-30
music, 330-6
architecture, 336-9
and politics, 339-46
reputation and significance, 346-51

Gaelic Revival
See **Irish Literary Renaissance**

Gates, Henry Louis, Jr., and African-American Literary Criticism CLC 65: 361-405

Gay and Lesbian Literature CLC 76: 416-39

German Exile Literature TCLC 30: 1-58
the writer and the Nazi state, 1-10
definition of, 10-4
life in exile, 14-32
surveys, 32-50
Austrian literature in exile, 50-2
German publishing in the United States, 52-7

German Expressionism TCLC 34: 74-160
history and major figures, 76-85
aesthetic theories, 85-109
drama, 109-26
poetry, 126-38
film, 138-42
painting, 142-7
music, 147-53
and politics, 153-8

Glasnost **and Contemporary Soviet Literature** CLC 59: 355-97

Gothic Novel NCLC 28: 328-402
development and major works, 328-34
definitions, 334-50
themes and techniques, 350-78
in America, 378-85
in Scotland, 385-91
influence and legacy, 391-400

Graphic Narratives CLC 86: 405-32
history and overviews, 406-21
the "Classics Illustrated" series, 421-2
reviews of recent works, 422-32

Greek Historiography CMLC 17: 1-49

Greek Mythology CMLC-26 193-320
overviews, 194-209
origins and development of Greek mythology, 209-29
cosmogonies and divinities in Greek mythology, 229-54
heroes and heroines in Greek mythol-

ogy, 254-80
women in Greek mythology, 280-320

Harlem Renaissance TCLC 26: 49-125
principal issues and figures, 50-67
the literature and its audience, 67-74
theme and technique in poetry, fiction, and drama, 74-115
and American society, 115-21
achievement and influence, 121-2

Havel, Václav, Playwright and President CLC 65: 406-63

Historical Fiction, Nineteenth-Century NCLC 48: 212-307
definitions and characteristics, 213-36
Victorian historical fiction, 236-65
American historical fiction, 265-88
realism in historical fiction, 288-306

Holocaust and the Atomic Bomb: Fifty Years Later CLC 91: 331-82
the Holocaust remembered, 333-52
Anne Frank revisited, 352-62
the atomic bomb and American memory, 362-81

Holocaust Denial Literature TCLC 58: 1-110
overviews, 1-30
Robert Faurisson and Noam Chomsky, 30-52
Holocaust denial literature in America, 52-71
library access to Holocaust denial literature, 72-5
the authenticity of Anne Frank*s diary, 76-90
David Irving and the "normalization" of Hitler, 90-109

Holocaust, Literature of the TCLC 42: 355-450
historical overview, 357-61
critical overview, 361-70
diaries and memoirs, 370-95
novels and short stories, 395-425
poetry, 425-41
drama, 441-8

Homosexuality in Nineteenth-Century Literature NCLC 56: 78-182
defining homosexuality, 80-111
Greek love, 111-44
trial and danger, 144-81

Hungarian Literature of the Twentieth Century TCLC 26: 126-88
surveys of, 126-47

Nyugat and early twentieth-century literature, 147-56
mid-century literature, 156-68
and politics, 168-78
since the 1956 revolt, 178-87

Hysteria in Nineteenth-Century Literature NCLC 64: 59-184
the history of hysteria, 60-75
the gender of hysteria, 75-103
hysteria and women's narratives, 103-57
hysteria in nineteenth-century poetry, 157-83

Imagism TCLC 74: 259-454
history and development, 260
major figures, 288
sources and influences, 352
Imagism and other movements, 397
influence and legacy, 431

Indian Literature in English TCLC 54: 308-406
overview, 309-13
origins and major figures, 313-25
the Indo-English novel, 325-55
Indo-English poetry, 355-67
Indo-English drama, 367-72
critical perspectives on Indo-English literature, 372-80
modern Indo-English literature, 380-9
Indo-English authors on their work, 389-404

Industrial Revolution in Literature, The NCLC 56: 183-273
historical and cultural perspectives, 184-201
contemporary reactions to the machine, 201-21
themes and symbols in literature, 221-73

The Irish Famine as Represented in Nineteenth-Century Literature NCLC 64: 185-261
overviews, 187-98
historical background, 198-212
famine novels, 212-34
famine poetry, 234-44
famine letters and eye-witness accounts, 245-61

Irish Literary Renaissance TCLC 46: 172-287
overview, 173-83
development and major figures, 184-202
influence of Irish folklore and mythology, 202-22
Irish poetry, 222-34
Irish drama and the Abbey Theatre, 234-56
Irish fiction, 256-86

Irish Nationalism and Literature NCLC 44: 203-73
the Celtic element in literature, 203-19
anti-Irish sentiment and the Celtic response, 219-34
literary ideals in Ireland, 234-45
literary expressions, 245-73

Italian Futurism
See **Futurism, Italian**

Italian Humanism LC 12: 205-77
origins and early development, 206-18
revival of classical letters, 218-23
humanism and other philosophies, 224-39
humanisms and humanists, 239-46
the plastic arts, 246-57
achievement and significance, 258-76

Italian Romanticism NCLC 60: 85-145
origins and overviews, 86-101
Italian Romantic theory, 101-25
the language of Romanticism, 125-45

Jacobean Drama LC 33: 1-37
the Jacobean worldview: an era of transition, 2-14
the moral vision of Jacobean drama, 14-22
Jacobean tragedy, 22-3
the Jacobean masque, 23-36

Jewish-American Fiction TCLC 62: 1-181
overviews, 2-24
major figures, 24-48
Jewish writers and American life, 48-78
Jewish characters in American fiction, 78-108
themes in Jewish-American fiction, 108-43
Jewish-American women writers, 143-59
the Holocaust and Jewish-American fiction, 159-81

Knickerbocker Group, The NCLC 56: 274-341
overviews, 276-314
Knickerbocker periodicals, 314-26
writers and artists, 326-40

Lake Poets, The NCLC 52: 217-304
characteristics of the Lake Poets and their works, 218-27
literary influences and collaborations, 227-66

defining and developing Romantic ideals, 266-84
embracing Conservatism, 284-303

Larkin, Philip, Controversy CLC 81: 417-64

Latin American Literature, Twentieth-Century TCLC 58: 111-98
historical and critical perspectives, 112-36
the novel, 136-45
the short story, 145-9
drama, 149-60
poetry, 160-7
the writer and society, 167-86
Native Americans in Latin American literature, 186-97

Madness in Twentieth-Century Literature TCLC 50: 160-225
overviews, 161-71
madness and the creative process, 171-86
suicide, 186-91
madness in American literature, 191-207
madness in German literature, 207-13
madness and feminist artists, 213-24

Memoirs of Trauma CLC 109: 419-466
overview, 420
criticism, 429

Metaphysical Poets LC 24: 356-439
early definitions, 358-67
surveys and overviews, 367-92
cultural and social influences, 392-406
stylistic and thematic variations, 407-38

Modern Essay, The TCLC 58: 199-273
overview, 200-7
the essay in the early twentieth century, 207-19
characteristics of the modern essay, 219-32
modern essayists, 232-45
the essay as a literary genre, 245-73

Modern Japanese Literature TCLC 66: 284-389
poetry, 285-305
drama, 305-29
fiction, 329-61
western influences, 361-87

Modernism TCLC 70: 165-275
definitions, 166-184
Modernism and earlier influences, 184-200
stylistic and thematic traits, 200-229

poetry and drama, 229-242
redefining Modernism, 242-275

**Muckraking Movement in American
Journalism** TCLC 34: 161-242
   development, principles, and major
      figures, 162-70
   publications, 170-9
   social and political ideas, 179-86
   targets, 186-208
   fiction, 208-19
   decline, 219-29
   impact and accomplishments, 229-40

**Multiculturalism in Literature and
Education** CLC 70: 361-413

Music and Modern Literature TCLC 62:
182-329
   overviews, 182-211
   musical form/literary form, 211-32
   music in literature, 232-50
   the influence of music on literature,
      250-73
   literature and popular music, 273-303
   jazz and poetry, 303-28

Native American Literature CLC 76:
440-76

Natural School, Russian NCLC 24: 205-40
   history and characteristics, 205-25
   contemporary criticism, 225-40

Naturalism NCLC 36: 285-382
   definitions and theories, 286-305
   critical debates on Naturalism, 305-16
   Naturalism in theater, 316-32
   European Naturalism, 332-61
   American Naturalism, 361-72
   the legacy of Naturalism, 372-81

Negritude TCLC 50: 226-361
   origins and evolution, 227-56
   definitions, 256-91
   Negritude in literature, 291-343
   Negritude reconsidered, 343-58

New Criticism TCLC 34: 243-318
   development and ideas, 244-70
   debate and defense, 270-99
   influence and legacy, 299-315

The New World in Renaissance Literature
LC 31: 1-51
   overview, 1-18
   utopia vs. terror, 18-31
   explorers and Native Americans, 31-51

New York Intellectuals and *Partisan*

Review TCLC 30: 117-98
   development and major figures, 118-28
   influence of Judaism, 128-39
   Partisan Review, 139-57
   literary philosophy and practice, 157-75
   political philosophy, 175-87
   achievement and significance, 187-97

The New Yorker TCLC 58: 274-357
   overviews, 274-95
   major figures, 295-304
   New Yorker style, 304-33
   fiction, journalism, and humor at *The
      New Yorker,* 333-48
   the new *New Yorker,* 348-56

Newgate Novel NCLC 24: 166-204
   development of Newgate literature,
      166-73
   Newgate Calendar, 173-7
   Newgate fiction, 177-95
   Newgate drama, 195-204

**Nigerian Literature of the Twentieth
Century** TCLC 30: 199-265
   surveys of, 199-227
   English language and African life,
      227-45
   politics and the Nigerian writer, 245-54
   Nigerian writers and society, 255-62

**Nineteenth-Century Native American
Autobiography** NCLC 64: 262-389
   overview, 263-8
   problems of authorship, 268-81
   the evolution of Native American
      autobiography, 281-304
   political issues, 304-15
   gender and autobiography, 316-62
   autobiographical works during the turn
      of the century, 362-88

Norse Mythology CMLC-26: 321-85
   history and mythological tradition, 322-
      44
   Eddic poetry, 344-74
   Norse mythology and other traditions,
      374-85

Northern Humanism LC 16: 281-356
   background, 282-305
   precursor of the Reformation, 305-14
   the Brethren of the Common Life, the
      Devotio Moderna, and education,
      314-40
   the impact of printing, 340-56

Novel of Manners, The NCLC 56: 342-96
   social and political order, 343-53
   domestic order, 353-73

depictions of gender, 373-83
the American novel of manners, 383-95

**Nuclear Literature: Writings and
Criticism in the Nuclear Age** TCLC 46:
288-390
   overviews, 290-301
   fiction, 301-35
   poetry, 335-8
   nuclear war in Russo-Japanese litera-
      ture, 338-55
   nuclear war and women writers, 355-67
   the nuclear referent and literary
      criticism, 367-88

Occultism in Modern Literature TCLC 50:
362-406
   influence of occultism on literature,
      363-72
   occultism, literature, and society, 372-87
   fiction, 387-96
   drama, 396-405

**Opium and the Nineteenth-Century
Literary Imagination** NCLC 20: 250-301
   original sources, 250-62
   historical background, 262-71
   and literary society, 271-9
   and literary creativity, 279-300

The Oxford Movement NCLC 72: 1-197
   overviews, 2-24
   background, 24-59
   and education, 59-69
   religious responses, 69-128
   literary aspects, 128-178
   political implications, 178-196

The Parnassian Movement NCLC 72:
198-241
   overviews, 199-231
   and epic form, 231-38
   and positivism, 238-41

Periodicals, Nineteenth-Century British
NCLC 24: 100-65
   overviews, 100-30
   in the Romantic Age, 130-41
   in the Victorian era, 142-54
   and the reviewer, 154-64

Plath, Sylvia, and the Nature of Biography
CLC 86: 433-62
   the nature of biography, 433-52
   reviews of *The Silent Woman,* 452-61

**Political Theory from the 15th to the 18th
Century** LC 36: 1-55
   Overview, 1-26
   Natural Law, 26-42

Empiricism, 42-55

Polish Romanticism NCLC 52: 305-71
overviews, 306-26
major figures, 326-40
Polish Romantic drama, 340-62
influences, 362-71

Popular Literature TCLC 70: 279-382
overviews, 280-324
"formula" fiction, 324-336
readers of popular literature, 336-351
evolution of popular literature, 351-382

The Portrayal of Jews in Nineteenth-Century English Literature NCLC 72: 242-368
overviews, 244-77
Anglo-Jewish novels, 277-303
depictions by non-Jewish writers, 303-44
Hebraism versus Hellenism, 344-67

Pre-Raphaelite Movement NCLC 20: 302-401
overview, 302-4
genesis, 304-12
Germ and *Oxford and Cambridge Magazine,* 312-20
Robert Buchanan and the "Fleshly School of Poetry," 320-31
satires and parodies, 331-4
surveys, 334-51
aesthetics, 351-75
sister arts of poetry and painting, 375-94
influence, 394-9

Preromanticism LC 40: 1-56
overviews, 2-14
defining the period, 14-23
new directions in poetry and prose, 23-45
the focus on the self, 45-56

Presocratic Philosophy CMLC 22: 1-56
overviews, 3-24
the Ionians and the Pythagoreans, 25-35
Heraclitus, the Eleatics, and the Atomists, 36-47
the Sophists, 47-55

Protestant Reformation, Literature of the LC 37: 1-83
overviews, 1-49
humanism and scholasticism, 49-69
the reformation and literature, 69-82

Psychoanalysis and Literature TCLC 38: 227-338
overviews, 227-46

Freud on literature, 246-51
psychoanalytic views of the literary process, 251-61
psychoanalytic theories of response to literature, 261-88
psychoanalysis and literary criticism, 288-312
psychoanalysis as literature/literature as psychoanalysis, 313-34

Rap Music CLC 76: 477-50

Renaissance Natural Philosophy LC 27: 201-87
cosmology, 201-28
astrology, 228-54
magic, 254-86

Restoration Drama LC 21: 184-275
general overviews, 185-230
Jeremy Collier stage controversy, 230-9
other critical interpretations, 240-75

Revising the Literary Canon CLC 81: 465-509

Robin Hood, Legend of LC 19: 205-58
origins and development of the Robin Hood legend, 206-20
representations of Robin Hood, 220-44
Robin Hood as hero, 244-56

Rushdie, Salman, *Satanic Verses* Controversy CLC 55 214-63; 59: 404-56

Russian Nihilism NCLC 28: 403-47
definitions and overviews, 404-17
women and Nihilism, 417-27
literature as reform: the Civic Critics, 427-33
Nihilism and the Russian novel: Turgenev and Dostoevsky, 433-47

Russian Thaw TCLC 26: 189-247
literary history of the period, 190-206
theoretical debate of socialist realism, 206-11
Novy Mir, 211-7
Literary Moscow, 217-24
Pasternak, *Zhivago,* and the Nobel Prize, 224-7
poetry of liberation, 228-31
Brodsky trial and the end of the Thaw, 231-6
achievement and influence, 236-46

Salem Witch Trials LC-38: 1-145
overviews, 2-30
historical background, 30-65
judicial background, 65-78

the search for causes, 78-115
the role of women in the trials, 115-44

Salinger, J. D., Controversy Surrounding *In Search of J. D. Salinger* CLC 55: 325-44

Science Fiction, Nineteenth-Century NCLC 24: 241-306
background, 242-50
definitions of the genre, 251-6
representative works and writers, 256-75
themes and conventions, 276-305

Scottish Chaucerians LC 20: 363-412

Scottish Poetry, Eighteenth-Century LC 29: 95-167
overviews, 96-114
the Scottish Augustans, 114-28
the Scots Vernacular Revival, 132-63
Scottish poetry after Burns, 163-6

Sea in Literature, The TCLC 82: 72-191
drama, 73-79
poetry, 79-119
fiction, 119-191

Sentimental Novel, The NCLC 60: 146-245
overviews, 147-58
the politics of domestic fiction, 158-79
a literature of resistance and repression, 179-212
the reception of sentimental fiction, 213-44

Sex and Literature TCLC 82: 192-434
overviews, 193-216
drama, 216-263
poetry, 263-287
fiction, 287-431

Sherlock Holmes Centenary TCLC 26: 248-310
Doyle*s life and the composition of the Holmes stories, 248-59
life and character of Holmes, 259-78
method, 278-9
Holmes and the Victorian world, 279-92
Sherlockian scholarship, 292-301
Doyle and the development of the detective story, 301-7
Holmes*s continuing popularity, 307-9

Slave Narratives, American NCLC 20: 1-91
background, 2-9

Topic Index

overviews, 9-24
contemporary responses, 24-7
language, theme, and technique, 27-70
historical authenticity, 70-5
antecedents, 75-83
role in development of Black American
    literature, 83-8

Spanish Civil War Literature TCLC 26:
311-85
    topics in, 312-33
    British and American literature, 333-59
    French literature, 359-62
    Spanish literature, 362-73
    German literature, 373-5
    political idealism and war literature,
        375-83

Spanish Golden Age Literature LC 23:
262-332
    overviews, 263-81
    verse drama, 281-304
    prose fiction, 304-19
    lyric poetry, 319-31

Spasmodic School of Poetry NCLC 24:
307-52
    history and major figures, 307-21
    the Spasmodics on poetry, 321-7
    Firmilian and critical disfavor, 327-39
    theme and technique, 339-47
    influence, 347-51

Steinbeck, John, Fiftieth Anniversary of
The Grapes of Wrath CLC 59: 311-54

Sturm und Drang NCLC 40: 196-276
    definitions, 197-238
    poetry and poetics, 238-58
    drama, 258-75

**Supernatural Fiction in the Nineteenth
Century** NCLC 32: 207-87
    major figures and influences, 208-35
    the Victorian ghost story, 236-54
    the influence of science and occultism,
        254-66
    supernatural fiction and society, 266-86

Supernatural Fiction, Modern TCLC 30:
59-116
    evolution and varieties, 60-74
    "decline" of the ghost story, 74-86
    as a literary genre, 86-92
    technique, 92-101
    nature and appeal, 101-15

Surrealism TCLC 30: 334-406
    history and formative influences, 335-43
    manifestos, 343-54

philosophic, aesthetic, and political
    principles, 354-75
poetry, 375-81
novel, 381-6
drama, 386-92
film, 392-8
painting and sculpture, 398-403
achievement, 403-5

Symbolism, Russian TCLC 30: 266-333
    doctrines and major figures, 267-92
    theories, 293-8
    and French Symbolism, 298-310
    themes in poetry, 310-4
    theater, 314-20
    and the fine arts, 320-32

Symbolist Movement, French NCLC 20:
169-249
    background and characteristics, 170-86
    principles, 186-91
    attacked and defended, 191-7
    influences and predecessors, 197-211
    and Decadence, 211-6
    theater, 216-26
    prose, 226-33
    decline and influence, 233-47

Television and Literature TCLC 78: 283-
426
    television and literacy, 283-98
    reading vs. watching, 298-341
    adaptations, 341-62
    literary genres and television, 362-90
    television genres and literature, 390-410
    children's literature/children's televi-
        sion, 410-25

Theater of the Absurd TCLC 38: 339-415
    "The Theater of the Absurd," 340-7
    major plays and playwrights, 347-58
    and the concept of the absurd, 358-86
    theatrical techniques, 386-94
    predecessors of, 394-402
    influence of, 402-13

Tin Pan Alley
See **American Popular Song, Golden Age
of**

Transcendentalism, American NCLC 24:
1-99
    overviews, 3-23
    contemporary documents, 23-41
    theological aspects of, 42-52
    and social issues, 52-74
    literature of, 74-96

Travel Writing in the Nineteenth Century
NCLC 44: 274-392

the European grand tour, 275-303
the Orient, 303-47
North America, 347-91

Travel Writing in the Twentieth Century
TCLC 30: 407-56
    conventions and traditions, 407-27
    and fiction writing, 427-43
    comparative essays on travel writers,
        443-54

True-Crime Literature CLC 99: 333-433
    history and analysis, 334-407
    reviews of true-crime publications, 407-
        23
    writing instruction, 424-29
    author profiles, 429-33

Ulysses **and the Process of Textual
Reconstruction** TCLC 26: 386-416
    evaluations of the new *Ulysses,* 386-94
    editorial principles and procedures,
        394-401
    theoretical issues, 401-16

Utopian Literature, Nineteenth-Century
NCLC 24: 353-473
    definitions, 354-74
    overviews, 374-88
    theory, 388-408
    communities, 409-26
    fiction, 426-53
    women and fiction, 454-71

Utopian Literature, Renaissance LC-32:
1-63
    overviews, 2-25
    classical background, 25-33
    utopia and the social contract, 33-9
    origins in mythology, 39-48
    utopia and the Renaissance country
        house, 48-52
    influence of millenarianism, 52-62

Vampire in Literature TCLC 46: 391-454
    origins and evolution, 392-412
    social and psychological perspectives,
        413-44
    vampire fiction and science fiction,
        445-53

Victorian Autobiography NCLC 40:
277-363
    development and major characteristics,
        278-88
    themes and techniques, 289-313
    the autobiographical tendency in
        Victorian prose and poetry, 313-47
    Victorian women*s autobiographies,
        347-62

Victorian Fantasy Literature NCLC 60: 246-384
overviews, 247-91
major figures, 292-366
women in Victorian fantasy literature, 366-83

Victorian Hellenism NCLC 68: 251-376
overviews, 252-78
the meanings of Hellenism, 278-335
the literary influence, 335-75

Victorian Novel NCLC 32: 288-454
development and major characteristics, 290-310
themes and techniques, 310-58
social criticism in the Victorian novel, 359-97
urban and rural life in the Victorian novel, 397-406
women in the Victorian novel, 406-25
Mudie*s Circulating Library, 425-34
the late-Victorian novel, 434-51

Vietnam War in Literature and Film CLC 91: 383-437
overview, 384-8
prose, 388-412
film and drama, 412-24
poetry, 424-35

Vorticism TCLC 62: 330-426
Wyndham Lewis and Vorticism, 330-8
characteristics and principles of Vorticism, 338-65
Lewis and Pound, 365-82
Vorticist writing, 382-416
Vorticist painting, 416-26

Women's Diaries, Nineteenth-Century NCLC 48: 308-54
overview, 308-13
diary as history, 314-25
sociology of diaries, 325-34
diaries as psychological scholarship, 334-43
diary as autobiography, 343-8
diary as literature, 348-53

Women Writers, Seventeenth-Century LC 30: 2-58
overview, 2-15
women and education, 15-9
women and autobiography, 19-31
women's diaries, 31-9
early feminists, 39-58

World War I Literature TCLC 34: 392-486
overview, 393-403

English, 403-27
German, 427-50
American, 450-66
French, 466-74
and modern history, 474-82

Yellow Journalism NCLC 36: 383-456
overviews, 384-96
major figures, 396-413

Young Playwrights Festival
1988—CLC 55: 376-81
1989—CLC 59: 398-403
1990—CLC 65: 444-8

Topic Index

NCLC Cumulative Nationality Index

AMERICAN
Alcott, Amos Bronson **1**
Alcott, Louisa May **6, 58**
Alger, Horatio **8**
Allston, Washington **2**
Apess, William **73**
Audubon, John James **47**
Barlow, Joel **23**
Beecher, Catharine Esther **30**
Bellamy, Edward **4**
Bird, Robert Montgomery **1**
Brackenridge, Hugh Henry **7**
Brentano, Clemens (Maria) **1**
Brown, Charles Brockden **22, 74**
Brown, William Wells **2**
Brownson, Orestes **50**
Bryant, William Cullen **6, 46**
Calhoun, John Caldwell **15**
Channing, William Ellery **17**
Child, Lydia Maria **6, 73**
Chivers, Thomas Holley **49**
Cooke, John Esten **5**
Cooper, James Fenimore **1, 27, 54**
Crockett, David **8**
Dana, Richard Henry, Sr. **53**
Dickinson, Emily (Elizabeth) **21**
Douglass, Frederick **7, 55**
Dunlap, William **2**
Dwight, Timothy **13**
Emerson, Mary Moody **66**
Emerson, Ralph Waldo **1, 38**
Field, Eugene **3**
Foster, Stephen Collins **26**
Frederic, Harold **10**
Freneau, Philip Morin **1**
Fuller, Margaret **5, 50**
Hale, Sarah Josepha **75**
Halleck, Fitz-Greene **47**

Hamilton, Alexander **49**
Hammon, Jupiter **5**
Harris, George Washington **23**
Hawthorne, Nathaniel **2, 10, 17, 23, 39**
Holmes, Oliver Wendell **14**
Irving, Washington **2, 19**
Jacobs, Harriet **67**
James, Henry, Sr. **53**
Jefferson, Thomas **11**
Kennedy, John Pendleton **2**
Lanier, Sidney **6**
Lazarus, Emma **8**
Lincoln, Abraham **18**
Longfellow, Henry Wadsworth **2, 45**
Lowell, James Russell **2**
Melville, Herman **3, 12, 29, 45, 49**
Mowatt, Anna Cora **74**
Murray, Judith Sargent **63**
Parkman, Francis **12**
Paulding, James Kirke **2**
Pinkney, Edward **31**
Poe, Edgar Allan **1, 16, 55**
Rowson, Susanna Haswell **5, 69**
Sand, George **57**
Sedgwick, Catharine Maria **19**
Shaw, Henry Wheeler **15**
Sheridan, Richard Brinsley **5**
Signourney, Lydia Howard (Huntley) **21**
Simms, William Gilmore **3**
Smith, Joseph, Jr. **53**
Southworth, Emma Dorothy Eliza Nevitte **26**
Stowe, Harriet (Elizabeth) Beecher **3, 50**
Thoreau, Henry David **7, 21**
Timrod, Henry **25**
Trumbull, John **30**
Tyler, Royall **3**
Very, Jones **9**
Warner, Susan (Bogert) **31**

Warren, Mercy Otis **13**
Webster, Noah **30**
Whitman, Sarah Helen (Power) **19**
Whitman, Walt(er) **4, 31**
Whittier, John Greenleaf **8**

ARGENTINIAN
Echeverria, (Jose) Esteban (Antonino) **18**
Hernandez, Jose **17**

AUSTRALIAN
Adams, Francis **33**
Clarke, Marcus (Andrew Hislop) **19**
Gordon, Adam Lindsay **21**
Kendall, Henry **12**

AUSTRIAN
Grillparzer, Franz **1**
Lenau, Nikolaus **16**
Nestroy, Johann **42**
Raimund, Ferdinand Jakob **69**
Sacher-Masoch, Leopold von **31**
Stifter, Adalbert **41**

CANADIAN
Crawford, Isabella Valancy **12**
Haliburton, Thomas Chandler **15**
Lampman, Archibald **25**
Moodie, Susanna (Strickland) **14**
Richardson, John **55**
Traill, Catharine Parr **31**

COLUMBIAN
Isaacs, Jorge Ricardo **70**

CUBAN
Martí, José **63**

CZECH
Macha, Karel Hynek **46**

DANISH
Andersen; Hans Christian **7**
Grundtvig. Nicolai Frederik Severin **1**
Jacobsen, Jens Peter **34**
Kierkegaard, Soren **34**

ENGLISH
Ainsworth, William Harrison **13**
Arnold, Matthew **6, 29**
Arnold, Thomas **18**
Austen, Jane **1, 13, 19, 33, 51**
Bagehot, Walter **10**
Barbauld, Anna Laetitia **50**
Barnes, William **75**
Beardsley, Aubrey **6**
Beckford, William **16**
Beddoes, Thomas Lovell **3**
Bentham, Jeremy **38**
Blake, William **13, 37, 57**
Borrow, George (Henry) **9**
Bronte, Anne **4, 71**
Bronte, Charlotte **3, 8, 33, 58**
Bronte, (Jane) Emily **16, 35**
Browning, Elizabeth Barrett **1, 16, 66**
Browning, Robert **19**
Bulwer-Lytton, Edward (George Earle Lytton) **1, 45**
Burney, Fanny **12, 54**
Burton, Richard F. **42**
Byron, George Gordon (Noel) **2, 12**
Carlyle, Thomas **22**
Carroll, Lewis **2, 53**
Clare, John **9**
Clough, Arthur Hugh **27**
Cobbett, William **49**
Coleridge, Samuel Taylor **9, 54**
Coleridge, Sara **31**
Collins, (William) Wilkie **1, 18**
Cowper, William **8**
Crabbe, George **26**
Craik, Dinah Maria (Mulock) **38**
Darwin, Charles **57**
De Quincey, Thomas **4**
Dickens, Charles (John Huffam) **3, 8, 18, 26, 37, 50**
Disraeli, Benjamin **2, 39**
Dobell, Sydney Thompson **43**
Eden, Emily **10**
Eliot, George **4, 13, 23, 41, 49**
FitzGerald, Edward **9**
Forster, John **11**
Froude, James Anthony **43**
Gaskell, Elizabeth Cleghorn **5, 70**
Gilpin, William **30**
Godwin, William **14**
Gore, Catherine **65**
Hazlitt, William **29**
Hemans, Felicia **29, 71**
Hood, Thomas **16**
Hopkins, Gerard Manley **17**
Hunt (James Henry) Leigh **1, 70**
Huxley, T. H. **67**
Inchbald, Elizabeth **62**
Ingelow, Jean **39**
Jefferies, (John) Richard **47**
Jerrold, Douglas William **2**
Jewsbury, Geraldine (Endsor) **22**
Keats, John **8, 73**
Kemble, Fanny **18**
Kingsley, Charles **35**

Lamb, Charles **10**
Lamb, Lady Caroline **38**
Landon, Letitia Elizabeth **15**
Landor, Walter Savage **14**
Lear, Edward **3**
Lennox, Charlotte Ramsay **23**
Lewes, George Henry **25**
Lewis, Matthew Gregory **11, 62**
Linton, Eliza Lynn **41**
Macaulay, Thomas Babington **42**
Marryat, Frederick **3**
Martineau, Harriet **26**
Mayhew, Henry **31**
Mill, John Stuart **11, 58**
Mitford, Mary Russell **4**
Montagu, Elizabeth **7**
More, Hannah **27**
Morris, William **4**
Newman, John Henry **38**
Norton, Caroline **47**
Oliphant, Laurence **47**
Opie, Amelia **65**
Paine, Thomas **62**
Pater, Walter (Horatio) **7**
Patmore, Coventry **9**
Peacock, Thomas Love **22**
Piozzi, Hester **57**
Planche, James Robinson **42**
Polidori, John Willam **51**
Radcliffe, Ann (Ward) **6, 55**
Reade, Charles **2, 74**
Reeve, Clara **19**
Robertson, Thomas William **35**
Robinson, Henry Crabb **15**
Rogers, Samuel **69**
Rossetti, Christina (Georgina) **2, 50, 66**
Rossetti, Dante Gabriel **4**
Sala, George Augustus **46**
Shelley, Mary Wollstonecraft (Godwin) **14**
Shelley, Percy Bysshe **18**
Smith, Charlotte (Turner) **23**
Southey, Robert **8**
Surtees, Robert Smith **14**
Symonds, John Addington **34**
Tennyson, Alfred **30, 65**
Thackeray, William Makepeace **5, 14, 22, 43**
Trollope, Anthony **6, 33**
Trollope, Frances **30**
Wordsworth, Dorothy **25**
Wordsworth, William **12, 38**

FILIPINO
Rizal, Jose **27**

FINNISH
Kivi, Aleksis **30**
Lonnrot, Elias **53**
Runeberg, Johan **41**

FRENCH
Augier, Emile **31**
Balzac, Honore de **5, 35, 53**
Banville, Theodore (Faullain) de **9**
Barbey d'Aurevilly, Jules Amedee **1**
Baudelaire, Charles **6, 29, 55**
Becque, Henri **3**
Beranger, Pierre Jean de **34**
Bertrand, Aloysius **31**
Borel, Petrus **41**
Chateaubriand, Francois Rene de **3**
Comte, Auguste **54**
Constant (de Rebecque), (Henri) Benjamin **6**
Corbiere, Tristan **43**

Daudet, (Louis Marie) Alphonse **1**
Dumas, Alexandre **9**
Dumas, Alexandre (Davy de la Pailleterie) **11, 71**
Feuillet, Octave **45**
Flaubert, Gustave **2, 10, 19, 62, 66**
Fourier, Charles **51**
Fromentin, Eugene (Samuel Auguste) **10**
Gaboriau, Emile **14**
Gautier, Theophile **1**
Gobineau, Joseph Arthur (Comte) de **17**
Goncourt, Edmond (Louis Antoine Huot) de **7**
Goncourt, Jules (Alfred Huot) de **7**
Hugo, Victor (Marie) **3, 10, 21**
Joubert, Joseph **9**
Kock, Charles Paul de **16**
Laclos, Pierre Ambroise Francois Choderlos de **4**
Laforgue, Jules **5, 53**
Lamartine, Alphonse (Marie Louis Prat) de **11**
Lautreamont, Comte de **12**
Leconte de Lisle, Charles-Marie-Rene **29**
Maistre, Joseph de **37**
Mallarme, Stephane **4, 41**
Maupassant, (Henri Rene Albert) Guy de **1, 42**
Merimee, Prosper **6, 65**
Michelet, Jules **31**
Musset, (Louis Charles) Alfred de **7**
Nerval, Gerard de **1, 67**
Nodier, (Jean) Charles (Emmanuel) **19**
Pixerecourt, Guilbert de **39**
Renan, Joseph Ernest **26**
Rimbaud, (Jean Nicolas) Arthur **4, 35**
Sade, Donatien Alphonse Francois **3**
Sainte-Beuve, Charles Augustin **5**
Sand, George **2, 42, 57**
Scribe, (Augustin) Eugene **16**
Senancour, Etienne Pivert de **16**
Stael-Holstein, Anne Louise Germaine Necker **3**
Stendhal **23, 46**
Sue, Eugene **1**
Taine, Hippolyte Adolphe **15**
Tocqueville, Alexis (Charles Henri Maurice Clerel) **7, 63**
Valles, Jules **71**
Verlaine, Paul (Marie) **2, 51**
Vigny, Alfred (Victor) de **7**
Villiers de l'Isle Adam, Jean Marie Mathias Philippe Auguste **3**

GERMAN
Amim, Achim von (Ludwig Joachim von Amim) **5**
Amim, Bettina von **38**
Bonaventura **35**
Buchner, (Karl) Georg **26**
Claudius, Matthias **75**
Droste-Hulshoff, Annette Freiin von **3**
Eichendorff, Joseph Freiherr von **8**
Fichte, Johann Gottlieb **62**
Fontane, Theodor **26**
Fouque, Friedrich (Heinrich Karl) de la Motte **2**
Goethe, Johann Wolfgang von **4, 22, 34**
Grabbe, Christian Dietrich **2**
Grimm, Jacob Ludwig Karl **3**
Grimm, Wilhelm Karl **3**
Hebbel, Friedrich **43**
Hegel, Georg Wilhelm Friedrich **46**
Heine, Heinrich **4, 54**
Hoffmann, E(rnst) T(heodor) A(madeus) **2**
Holderlin, (Johann Christian) Friedrich **16**
Immerman, Karl (Lebrecht) **4, 49**
Jean Paul **7**
Kant, Immanuel **27, 67**
Kleist, Heinrich von **2, 37**

Klinger, Friedrich Maximilian von 1
Klopstock, Friedrich Gottlieb 11
Kotzebue, August (Friedrich Ferdinand) von 25
Ludwig, Otto 4
Marx, Karl (Heinrich) 17
Morike, Eduard (Friedrich) 10
Müller, Wilhelm 73
Novalis 13
Schelling, Friedrich Wilhelm Joseph von 30
Schiller, Friedrich 39, 69
Schlegel, August Wilhelm von 15
Schlegel, Friedrich 45
Schopenhauer, Arthur 51
Storm, (Hans) Theodor (Woldsen) 1
Tieck, (Johann) Ludwig 5, 46
Wagner, Richard 9
Wieland, Christoph Martin 17

GREEK
Solomos, Dionysios 15

HUNGARIAN
Arany, Janos 34
Madach, Imre 19
Petofi, Sandor 21

INDIAN
Chatterji, Bankim Chandra 19
Dutt, Toru 29
Ghalib 39

IRISH
Allingham, William 25
Banim, John 13
Banim, Michael 13
Boucicault, Dion 41
Carleton, William 3
Croker, John Wilson 10
Darley, George 2
Edgeworth, Maria 1, 51
Ferguson, Samuel 33
Griffin, Gerald 7
Jameson, Anna 43
Le Fanu, Joseph Sheridan 9, 58
Lever, Charles (James) 23
Maginn, William 8
Mangan, James Clarence 27
Maturin, Charles Robert 6
Merriman, Brian 70
Moore, Thomas 6
Morgan, Lady 29
O'Brien, Fitz-James 21

ITALIAN
Collodi, Carlo (Carlo Lorenzini) 54
Da Ponte, Lorenzo 50
Foscolo, Ugo 8
Gozzi, (Conte) Carlo 23
Leopardi, (Conte) Giacomo 22
Manzoni, Alessandro 29
Mazzini, Guiseppe 34
Nievo, Ippolito 22

JAPANESE
Higuchi Ichiyo 49
Motoori, Norinaga 45

LITHUANIAN
Mapu, Abraham (ben Jekutiel) 18

MEXICAN
Lizardi, Jose Joaquin Fernandez de 30

NORWEGIAN
Collett, (Jacobine) Camilla (Wergeland) 22
Wergeland, Henrik Arnold 5

POLISH
Fredro, Aleksander 8
Krasicki, Ignacy 8
Krasinski, Zygmunt 4
Mickiewicz, Adam 3
Norwid, Cyprian Kamil 17
Slowacki, Juliusz 15

ROMANIAN
Eminescu, Mihail 33

RUSSIAN
Aksakov, Sergei Timofeyvich 2
Bakunin, Mikhail (Alexandrovich) 25, 58
Bashkirtseff, Marie 27
Belinski, Vissarion Grigoryevich 5
Chernyshevsky, Nikolay Gavrilovich 1
Dobrolyubov, Nikolai Alexandrovich 5
Dostoevsky, Fedor Mikhailovich 2, 7, 21, 33, 43
Gogol, Nikolai (Vasilyevich) 5, 15, 31
Goncharov, Ivan Alexandrovich 1, 63
Granovskii, Timofei Nikolaevich 75
Herzen, Aleksandr Ivanovich 10
Karamzin, Nikolai Mikhailovich 3
Krylov, Ivan Andreevich 1
Lermontov, Mikhail Yuryevich 5
Leskov, Nikolai (Semyonovich) 25

Nekrasov, Nikolai Alekseevich 11
Ostrovsky, Alexander 30, 57
Pisarev, Dmitry Ivanovich 25
Pushkin, Alexander (Sergeyevich) 3, 27
Saltykov, Mikhail Evgrafovich 16
Smolenskin, Peretz 30
Turgenev, Ivan 21
Tyutchev, Fyodor 34
Zhukovsky, Vasily 35

SCOTTISH
Baillie, Joanna 2, 71
Beattie, James 25
Blair, Hugh 75
Campbell, Thomas 19
Carlyle, Thomas 22, 70
Ferrier, Susan (Edmonstone) 8
Galt, John 1
Hogg, James 4
Jeffrey, Francis 33
Lockhart, John Gibson 6
Mackenzie, Henry 41
Oliphant, Margaret (Oliphant Wilson) 11
Scott, Walter 15, 69
Stevenson, Robert Louis (Balfour) 5, 14, 63
Thomson, James, 18
Wilson, John 5
Wright, Frances 74

SPANISH
Alarcon, Pedro Antonio de 1
Caballero, Fernan 10
Castro, Rosalia de 3
Espronceda, Jose de 39
Larra (y Sanchez de Castro), Mariano Jose de 17
Tamayo y Baus, Manuel 1
Zorrilla y Moral, Jose 6

SWEDISH
Almqvist, Carl Jonas Love 42
Bremer, Fredrika 11
Tegner, Esaias 2

SWISS
Amiel, Henri Frederic 4
Burckhardt, Jacob 49
Charriere, Isabelle de 66
Keller, Gottfried 2
Wyss, Johann David Von 10

UKRAINIAN
Taras Shevchenko 54

Nationality Index

NCLC-75 Title Index

"Abenlied" (Claudius) **75**:190

"Address" (Barnes) **75**:43

"Als er sein Weib und's Kind an Ihrer Brust Schlafend Fand" (Claudius) **75**:192

"An Meinen Sohn Johannes 1799" (Claudius) **75**:210

Antwort an Andres auf seinen letzten Brief (Claudius) **75**:193

"Eine asiatische Vorlesung" (Claudius) **75**:211, 214-15

Asmus, omnia sua secum portans oder Sämtlich Werke des Wandsbecker Boten (Claudius) **75**:183, 192

Auch ein Beitrag über die neue Politik (Claudius) **75**:194

"Das Bauernlied" (Claudius) **75**:190

Bauernlieder (Claudius) **75**:190

"The Beam in Grenley Church" (Barnes) **75**:75

"The Best Man in the Vield" (Barnes) **75**:77

Der Besuch in St. Hiob zu** (Claudius) **75**:190

"Das Betrübte Madchen" (Claudius) **75**:191

"The Bird's Nest" (Hale) **75**:284-85, 289

"A Bit O' Sly Coorten" (Barnes) **75**:78, 82, 93

"Black and White" (Barnes) **75**:98

"Blackmwore Maidens" (Barnes) **75**:4, 101

Boarding Out; or, Domestic Life (Hale) **75**:341

"Boarding Schools" (Hale) **75**:345

"Bob the Fiddler" (Barnes) **75**:77, 81

"Brief über den Durchgang der Venus" (Claudius) **75**:201-03

"Ein Brief, von C. an D." (Claudius) **75**:202

"Briefe an Andres" (Claudius) **75**:210-12, 216-18

"A Brisk Wind" (Barnes) **75**:37, 97

"The Broken Heart" (Barnes) **75**:7

"Burncombe Hollow" (Barnes) **75**:15

"The Bwoate" (Barnes) **75**:58, 90

"The Catholic Convert" (Hale) **75**:357-61

"Character and Intelligence of the Britons" (Barnes) **75**:64

"Christmas Hymm" (Hale) **75**:284

"The Clote" (Barnes) **75**:23

"Clouds" (Barnes) **75**:94

"Coach" (Barnes) **75**:8

"The Cock" (Barnes) **75**:54

Collected Works (Claudius) **75**:207, 210-11, 215, 218, 220

"The Common A-Took In" (Barnes) **75**:43, 48, 57, 93, 101

The Compassionate Beneficence of the Deity (Blair) **75**:116

"The Conversazióne" (Hale) **75**:347-8

"The Cost of Improvement" (Barnes) **75**:103

A Critical Dissertation on the Poems of Ossian (Blair) **75**:115, 117-18, 125-26, 136

"Culver Dell and the Squire" (Barnes) **75**:57, 104

"Dedikation" (Claudius) **75**:207

"Ein defekter locus communis" (Claudius) **75**:213

Dictionary of Poetical Quotations (Hale) **75**:284, 341

"Dobbin Dead" (Barnes) **75**:35

"Don't Ceäre" (Barnes) **75**:9

"Dorset Folk and Dorset" (Barnes) **75**:57

Early England and the Saxon-English (Barnes) **75**:40, 103

"Easter Zunday" (Barnes) **75**:77

"Eclogues" (Barnes) **75**:95

"Editor's Table" (Hale) **75**:317

Einfältiger Hausvater-Bericht uber die christlich Religion (Claudius) **75**:193, 210, 214-16, 220

"Ellen Brine ov Allenburn" (Barnes) **75**:8, 46

"Ellen Dare o'Lindenore" (Barnes) **75**:58

"Englyn" (Barnes) **75**:54

" Er schuf sie ein Männlein und Fräulein" (Claudius) **75**:192

Ernst und Kurzweil, von meinem Vetter an mich (Claudius) **75**:197

"Erwin and Linda" (Barnes) **75**:76

"Evenen in the Village" (Barnes) **75**:83, 88-9, 95

"Evenen Twilight" (Barnes) **75**:95

"Fall Time" (Barnes) **75**:32

"Farmer's Sons" (Barnes) **75**:101

"The Farmer's Woldest Da'ter" (Barnes) **75**:6, 101

"Father Come Hwome" (Barnes) **75**:101

"Fatherhood" (Barnes) **75**:7

"Feäir Ellen Dare" (Barnes) **75**:58

"Fellowship" (Barnes) **75**:109

"Fiddler Bob" (Barnes)
See "Bob the Fiddler"

Flora's Interpreter; or, The American Book of Flowers and Sentiments (Hale) **75**:349

"Frau Rebekka mit den Kindern, an einem Maimorgen" (Claudius) **75**:190

"The Geäte A-Vallen To" (Barnes) **75**:14, 64, 97, 99

"Geburt und Wiedergeburt" (Claudius) **75**:210, 214, 216

Gespräche, die Freiheit betreffend (Claudius) **75**:194

"A Ghost" (Barnes) **75**:75

"The Girt Woak Tree That's in the Dell" (Barnes) **75**:36, 108

"Girt Wold House o'Mossy Stwone" (Barnes) **75**:6, 103

"Giulia" (Barnes) **75**:30

"The Gold Pen-A Poem, Inscribed to the Gentleman Who Presented the Gift" (Hale) 75:284

"Good Measter Collins" (Barnes) 75:73

"Good Night" (Barnes) 75:33

"Grace Greenwood" (Hale) 75:353

A Grammar and Glossary of the Dorset Dialect (Barnes) 75:27, 40, 53, 65, 79

"Grammer A-Crippled" (Barnes) 75:48, 67

"Grammer's Shoes" (Barnes) 75:77

"Green" (Barnes) 75:46, 68

"Grief an' Gladness" (Barnes) 75:32

"Gruffmoody Grim" (Barnes) 75:79

"Guy Faux's Night" (Barnes) 75:77

"Gwain Down the Steps vor Water" (Barnes) 75:6

"Gwain to Brookwell" (Barnes) 75:4

"Hallowed Pleäces" (Barnes) 75:7, 59

"The Happy Daes When I Wer Young" (Barnes) 75:22, 56

"Happy Sundays for Children" (Hale) 75:282

"Harvest Hwome" (Barnes) 75:78

"Hay-Carren" (Barnes) 75:77

"Hay-Meaken" (Barnes) 75:77

"The Headstwone" (Barnes) 75:8

"The Heare" (Barnes) 75:35

"Herrenston" (Barnes) 75:104-05

"Hill or Dell" (Barnes) 75:87

"Hope A-Left Behind" (Barnes) 75:7

Humilis Domus: Some Thoughts on the Abodes, Life and Social Conditions of the Poor, Especially in Dorsetshire (Barnes) 75:57-8, 102, 106

Hwomely Rhymes. A Second Collection of Poems in the Dorset Dialect (Barnes) 75:18, 40, 69, 79

"The Hwomestead a-Vell Into Hand" (Barnes) 75:102

"Hymn to Charity" (Hale) 75:343

"I and the Dog" (Barnes) 75:36

"I Got Two Vields" (Barnes) 75:101

"I Saw A Boy" (Barnes) 75:70

"If Ever I See" (Hale) 75:279, 286

Impetus philosophicus (Claudius) 75:190

"In Ev'ry Dream Thy Lovely Features Rise" (Barnes) 75:70

"In Our Abode in Arby Wood" (Barnes) 75:54

"In Tenderness To Me Whom Thou Didst Spurn" (Barnes) 75:70

"In the Spring" (Barnes) 75:21

"In the Stillness o'Night" (Barnes) 75:71

"It Snows" (Hale) 75:279, 283, 285, 293

"The Ivy" (Barnes) 75:8

"Jeäne" (Barnes) 75:6, 7, 30, 71

"Jenny Away from Home" (Barnes) 75:58

"Jessie Lee" (Barnes) 75:58, 89-90

"John Bloom in Lon'on" (Barnes) 75:101

"Joy Passing By" (Barnes) 75:59

"Keepen Up O' Christmas" (Barnes) 75:77

Keeping House and Housekeeping (Hale) 75:341

"Knowlwood" (Barnes) 75:58

"Eine Korrespondent mit mir selbst" (Claudius) 75:209

"Korrespondenz zwischen mir und meinem Vetter, die Bibelübersetzungen betreffend" (Claudius) 75:209-10

"Kriegslied" (Claudius) 75:183, 194

The Ladies' Wreath (Hale) 75:337, 341, 349

"The Lane" (Barnes)
See "The Leane"

"Leady-Day an' Ridden House" (Barnes) 75:77, 81, 83

"The Leady's Tower" (Barnes) 75:72-3

"The Leane" (Barnes) 75:15-16, 55, 68, 101, 104

"Leaves" (Barnes) 75:15

Lectures on Rhetoric and Belles Lettres (Blair) 75:115-19, 123, 127, 131, 133, 136-37, 141-44, 146-47, 149-50, 157, 160, 164-65, 177

"The Lew O' the Rick" (Barnes) 75:79

Liberia, or Mr. Peyton's Experiments (Hale) 75:317, 321, 326, 328, 330-1, 339-341

"Die Liebe" (Claudius) 75:193

Life North and South: Showing the True Character of Both (Hale) 75:315, 339

"The Lilac" (Barnes) 75:38

"Linden Lea" (Barnes) 75:33

"The Little Lost Sister" (Barnes) 75:58

"The Lloyds" (Hale) 75:298

"A Lot o' Maidens A-Runnèn the Vields" (Barnes) 75:67

"The 'Lotments" ("Rusticus gaudens") (Barnes) 75:18, 43-4, 93, 101, 104

"The Lottery Ticket" (Hale) 75:298

"The Love Child" (Barnes) 75:7, 57

"The Maid o' Newton" (Barnes) 75:58, 89

"The Maid Vor My Bride" (Barnes) 75:71

Manners; or, Happy Homes and Good Society All the Year Round (Hale) 75:283

"Married Peäir's Love Walk" (Barnes) 75:7

"Mary and Her Little Lamb" (Hale)
See "Mary"s Lamb"

"Mary Had a Little Lamb" (Hale)
See "Mary"s Lamb"

"Mary"s Lamb" (Hale) 75:279, 284-94, 323, 349

"Mary's Little Lamb" (Hale)
See "Mary"s Lamb"

"May" (Barnes) 75:6

"The May-Tree" (Barnes) 75:32

"Meäry Wedded" (Barnes) 75:58, 71

"Melhill Feast" (Barnes) 75:20, 26, 30, 68, 94

"The Milk-maid o' the Farm" (Barnes) 75:58, 77

"Minden House" (Barnes) 75:78

Morgengespräch zwischen A. und dem Kandidaten Bertram (Claudius) 75:197, 210-11, 217

"The Morning Moon" (Barnes) 75:72

"The Motherless Child" (Barnes) 75:58

"The Mother's Dream" (Barnes) 75:17

"My Country" (Hale) 75:286

"My Darling Julia" (Barnes)
See "My Dearest Julia"

"My Dearest Julia" (Barnes) 75:72-3

My Little Song Book (Hale)
See *School Song Book*

"My Love is Good" (Barnes) 75:6, 8, 58

"My Love's Guardian Angel" (Barnes) 75:17, 21

"My Orcha'd in Linden Lea" (Barnes) 75:20, 29, 46, 60, 69, 87-8, 96, 101

Nachricht von meiner Aidienz beim Kaiser von Japan (Claudius) 75:183, 194

Neue Erfindung (Claudius) 75:193

"The New Poor Laws" ("Rusticus Res Politicas Animadvertens") (Barnes) 75:43-4, 101, 103

Northwood: A Tale of New England (Hale) 75:280, 295, 301, 311-15, 317-19, 321,326, 328-30, 336-37, 339, 341, 343-44, 349, 357

"Not Sing at Night" (Barnes) 75:22

Notes on Ancient Britain and the Britons (Barnes) 75:40, 46, 107

"The Old Bardic Poetry" (Barnes) 75:46, 53-4

"On Gentleness" (Blair) 75:154

"On Sensibility" (Blair) 75:155

"Open Vields" (Barnes) 75:101

Ormond Grosvenor (Hale) 75:320

Orra: A Lapland Tale (Barnes) 75:14-15, 18, 22, 26, 69-70, 92

"Our Be'th Place" (Barnes) 75:59

"Our Father in Heaven" (Hale) 75:279, 286

"Our Father's Works" (Barnes) 75:79

"Our Granite Hills" (Hale) 75:284

An Outline of English Speech-Craft (Barnes) 75:27, 40, 65

An Outline of Rede-Craft (Barnes) 75:27, 40

Parentation uber Anselmo (Claudius) 75:191

"The Parrock" (Barnes) 75:70

"Passe-Temps" (Claudius) 75:212, 218

Paul Erdmanns Fest (Claudius) 75:182-83, 186-87

"Pentridge by the River" (Barnes) 75:59

Philological Grammar (Barnes) 75:19, 26, 40, 64-5

"Plorata Veris Lachrymis" (Barnes) 75:72

Poems for Our Children (Hale) 75:284-86, 288-89, 341, 349

Poems of Rural Life in Common English (Barnes) 75:18, 40, 69

Poems of Rural Life in the Dorset Dialect (Barnes) 75:18, 40, 52-3, 67-81, 83, 85, 92

Poems of Rural Life in the Dorset Dialect; Third Collection (Barnes) 75:18, 40, 69

Poems Partly of Rural Life in National English (Barnes) 75:15, 40, 69, 85

Poetical Pieces (Barnes) 75:14, 69

"Polly Be-en Upzides Wi' Tom" (Barnes) 75:78

"The Poor Scholar" (Hale) 75:298

"Praise o' Do'set" (Barnes) 75:8, 101, 108

"Prayer" (Hale) 75:284, 285

Predigt eines Laienbruders zu Neujahr 1814 (Claudius) 75:213, 215, 218

"The Railroad" (Barnes) 75:73

"Readen ov a Headstone" (Barnes) 75:8

"The Rest" (Barnes) 75:69

"Riddles: Anne and Joey A-Ta'ken" (Barnes) 75:78

"Rings" (Barnes) 75:46

"Rivers Don't Gi'e Out" (Barnes) 75:88

"The Romance of Travelling" (Hale) 75:356, 359

"The Rooks" (Barnes) 75:34, 40

"Rustic Childhood" (Barnes) 75:15, 85

"Rusticus Dolens; or, Inclosures of Common" (Barnes)
See "The Common A-Took In"

"Rusticus Emigrans or Over Sea to Settle" (Barnes) 75:43-4, 101

"Rusticus gaudens" (Barnes)
See "The 'Lotments"

"Rusticus Res Politicas Animadvertens" (Barnes)
See "The New Poor Laws"

"Ruth, A Short Drama From the Bible" (Barnes) 75:70, 73-4

"Sabbath Lays" (Barnes) **75**:70, 74

Sämtliche Werke (Claudius) **75**:182-84, 201

School Song Book (Hale) **75**:286, 349

"Der Schwarze in der Zuckerplantage" (Claudius) **75**:183

Se Gefylsta (Barnes) **75**:40

"Season Tokens" (Barnes) **75**:70

Select Poems of Rural Life in the Dorset Dialect (Barnes) **75**:40

Select Poems of William Barnes (Barnes) **75**:10, 23, 40, 95

Selected Poems of William Barnes (Barnes) **75**:40, 52, 54

A Selection from Unpublished Poems (Barnes) **75**:18, 40

Sermons of Blair (Blair) **75**:116, 123, 129-32

"The Settle an' the Girt Wood Vire" (Barnes) **75**:70, 77, 82

"Shaftesbury Feäir" (Barnes) **75**:67, 98

"Shrodon Feäir" (Barnes) **75**:77

"The Shy Man" (Barnes) **75**:8-9

"The Silver Mine" (Hale) **75**:297, 362

Sketches of American Character (Hale) **75**:296, 319, 349

"The Sky A-Clearèn" (Barnes) **75**:17

"The Slantèn Light o' Fall" (Barnes) **75**:7

"Sleep Did Come Wi' The Dew" (Barnes) **75**:101

"Some Thoughts on the Abodes, Life and Social Conditions of the Poor, especially in Dorsetshire" (Barnes) **75**:102

"Song of Songs" (Barnes) **75**:99

Songs For Children (Hale) **75**:286

"Sound o' Water" (Barnes) **75**:88

"Spring" (Barnes) **75**:34

"The Springs" (Hale) **75**:300

Steht Homer z. Ex. unterm Spruch des Aristoteles & Compagnie? (Claudius) **75**:196

"The String Token" (Barnes) **75**:36

"The Stwonen Porch" (Barnes) **75**:103

"Täglich zu singen" (Claudius) **75**:190

Tändeleien und Erzählungen (Claudius) **75**:191-92

"Thatchen O' the Rick" (Barnes) **75**:77

"The Thorns in the Geate" (Barnes) **75**:73

"Thoughts on Beauty and Art" (Barnes) **75**:28, 55, 65-6

"Thoughts Suggested at the Bazaar at Kingston House" (Barnes) **75**:42

"The Thunder Storm" (Hale) **75**:286

"The Times" (Barnes) **75**:23, 43-4, 96, 101, 105, 108-09

"Times o' Year" (Barnes) **75**:20, 26, 68

Tiw: or, a View on the Roots and Stems of the English as a Teutonic Tongue (Barnes) **75**:26-7, 40, 65

"To Julia" (Barnes) **75**:70

"To the Hon Mrs Norton, the Poetess, on Meeting Her at Frampton House" (Barnes) **75**:85

Traits of American Life (Hale) **75**:296, 319, 349, 356-62

"Trees Be Company" (Barnes) **75**:36

"Troubles of the Day" (Barnes) **75**:20

"The Turn of the Day" (Barnes) **75**:33

"The Turnstile" (Barnes) **75**:8

"Tweil" (Barnes) **75**:7, 79

Twenty Poems in Common English (Barnes) **75**:40

"Two Farms in Woone" (Barnes) **75**:43-4, 93, 101

"Two Trees Were We" (Barnes) **75**:70

Über das Genie (Claudius) **75**:195-96, 205, 209-10, 212-14, 219

"Über den Ausdruck: 'Stilles Verdienst'" (Claudius) **75**:211

"Über die Unsterblichkeit der Seele" (Claudius) **75**:210, 216

"Über ein Sprichwort" (Claudius) **75**:213

"Übungen im Stil" (Claudius) **75**:210, 218

"Uncle and Aunt" (Barnes) **75**:13, 48

"Uncle Out O' Debt and' Out O' Danger" (Barnes) **75**:70

"The Unioners" (Barnes)
See "The Times"

"The Unknown" (Hale) **75**:358, 361-2

Valet an meine Leser (Claudius) **75**:198, 214-16

"The Veairies" (Barnes) **75**:75

"Vellen O' the Tree" (Barnes) **75**:76, 95

Verflucht sei der Acker um deinetwellen (Claudius) **75**:191

"Ein Versuch in Versen" (Claudius) **75**:193

"Vields By Watervalls" (Barnes) **75**:31

Views of Labour and Gold (Barnes) **75**:23, 40, 51-2, 60, 66, 102, 107

"The Voices that Be Gone" (Barnes) **75**:59

"Vom Gewissen: In Briefen an Andres" (Claudius) **75**:218

"Vom Vaterunser" (Claudius) **75**:217

"Von Projekten und Projektmachern" (Claudius) **75**:203

"The Waggon A-Stooded" (Barnes) **75**:78

"Walter Wilson" (Hale) **75**:298

Wandsbeck, eine Art von Romanze (Claudius) **75**:196

Der Wandsbecker Bote (Claudius) **75**:192, 195, 201

"The Water Crowfoot" (Barnes) **75**:22, 28, 37

"The Water Crowvoot" (Barnes)
See "The Water Crowfoot"

"Wedding and Funeral" (Hale) **75**:296

"The Weepen Leady" (Barnes) **75**:76

"Went Hwome" (Barnes) **75**:53

"What Dick and I Did" (Barnes) **75**:78

"White an' Blue" (Barnes) **75**:17, 22, 46

"The White Road up Athirt the Hill" (Barnes) **75**:87

"Whitsuntide an' Club Walken" (Barnes) **75**:95

"The Wife A-Lost" (Barnes) **75**:7, 73

"The Wife A-Prais'd" (Barnes) **75**:73

"A Winter in the Country" (Hale) **75**:298

"Winter Joys" (Hale) **75**:294

"A Winter Night" (Barnes) **75**:15, 97

"A Witch" (Barnes) **75**:75

"Withstanders" (Barnes) **75**:9

"Woak Hill" (Barnes) **75**:8, 13, 46, 48

"Woak Wer Good Enough Woonce" (Barnes) **75**:69, 82

"A Wold Friend" (Barnes) **75**:9

"The Wold Waggon" (Barnes) **75**:82-3

"The Wold Wall" (Barnes) **75**:20, 26, 67-8

"Woman the Poet of Nature" (Hale) **75**:324-25

Woman's Record; or, Sketches of All Distinguished Women, from "The Beginning" Till A.D. 1850. (Hale) **75**:280, 283, 303-05, 307-09, 317, 335-42, 349, 353, 355, 360-61

"The Woody Hollow" (Barnes) **75**:95

"Woone smile mwore" (Barnes) **75**:7

Works of Shakespeare (Blair) **75**:129-30, 132

"The Year Clock" (Barnes) **75**:32

"The Zilver-Weed" (Barnes) **75**:38

"Zitten Out the Wold Year" (Barnes) **75**:77

"A Zong" (Barnes) **75**:71

"Zummer" (Barnes) **75**:6

"Zummer an' Winter" (Barnes) **75**:9 32

"Zummer Stream" (Barnes) **75**:22, 59

"Zummer Thoughts in Winter Time" (Barnes) **75**:22, 32

"Zunsheen in the Winter" (Barnes) **75**:32

ISBN 0-7876-2877-8

90000